A guide to the dictiona

headword

bash *verb*
1 to hit hard or wildly: *The boys bashed each other. | He bashed the ball.*

change of part of speech

bash *noun*
2 a try or attempt: *Give it a bash.*

phrase or sentence to show how the word is used

Word Use: definition 2 is more suited to everyday language

bat[1] *noun*
1 the stick used to hit the ball in games like cricket and baseball **2 off your own bat** on your own, without help or advice

words that are spelt the same but have different histories

a common phrase using the headword

Word Building: **bat** *verb* (**batted, batting**) **batsman** *noun* **batter** *noun*

bat[2] *noun*
a mouse-like winged mammal which is active at night

part of speech

baulk (rhymes with *fork*) *verb*
to stop and refuse to do something: *The horse baulked at the jump. | to baulk at making a speech*

billabong *noun*
a waterhole which used to be part of a river

how to say the word

word history — where the word comes from

Word History: from an Aboriginal language called Wiradhuri

burglary (say *ber-glə-ree*) *noun*
the crime of breaking into a building to steal things

Word Building: the plural is **burglaries** □ **burglar** *noun* **burgle** *verb*

bushwhacker *noun*
someone who lives in the bush

Word Use: another word is **bushie** □ both these words are more suited to everyday language

word building — other members of the headword's family

word use — telling you something interesting or confusing about the word

buy *verb*
1 to get by paying money for **2** to accept: *I don't buy that idea.*

Word Use: be careful – this sounds like **by** and **bye**
Word Building: other forms are **I bought, I have bought, I am buying** □ **buy** *noun* something bought: *a good buy*

equal spellings — showing you that the word can be spelt either way

civilised or **civilized** *adjective*
1 highly developed: *The Chinese have been a civilised race for thousands of years.*
2 polite and controlled: *They expected him to be angry but he wrote a very civilised letter.*

THE MACQUARIE JUNIOR DICTIONARY

Second Edition

This book/dictionary belongs to:
Michelle

THE MACQUARIE JUNIOR DICTIONARY

Second Edition

General Editor
David Blair

The Jacaranda Press

This edition published 1992 by
THE JACARANDA PRESS
33 Park Road, Milton, Qld 4064

Offices also in Sydney and Melbourne

Reprinted in Singapore 1993, 1994, 1995, 1996

First edition 1985

Typeset in 9/9 pt Plantin

National Library of Australia
Cataloguing-in-Publication data

The Macquarie junior dictionary.

2nd ed.
ISBN 0 7016 3026 4.

1. English language — Dictionaries, Juvenile.
I. Blair, David, 1942– .

423

The illustration on the cover is the Macquarie University crest.

Contents

Editorial staff

First Edition

General Editor — David Blair, MA (Syd)
Lecturer in Linguistics
Macquarie University

Executive Editor — Susan Butler

Senior Editor — Linsay Knight

Editors — Jessie Terry
Alison Moore
Pat Kreuiter

Writers — Ann Atkinson
Helen Bateman
Leah Bloomfield
Alison Clark
Maureen Colman

Computer Coordinator — Pat Kreuiter

Computer Programmers — Robert Mannell
William E. Smith

Editorial Assistants — Marjorie Atkinson
Kristine Burnet
Jenny Cant
Klay Lamprell
Maureen Leslie
Anne Teong

Second Edition

General Editor — David Blair, MA (Syd)
Lecturer in Linguistics
Macquarie University

Publisher — Richard Tardif

Executive Editor — Ann Atkinson

Senior Editor — Linsay Knight

Proof Editor — Alison Moore

Editorial Assistant — Kristine Burnet

Editorial Committee, The Macquarie Dictionary — Editor in Chief: Arthur Delbridge, AO, MA (Lond), BA, DipEd (Syd), HonDLitt (Macq)

John Bernard, BSc, BA, PhD, DipEd (Syd)

David Blair, MA (Syd)

Pamela Peters, BA (Melb), MA (Syd)

Susan Butler, BA (Syd)

Richard Tardif, BA (Syd), MGenStud (NSW)

Preface to the Second Edition

The Second Edition of the *Macquarie Junior Dictionary* is designed for children to use in the later years of primary school, although some will be ready for it sooner and many will find it useful to take to secondary school with them.

We have written the entries in a style which is clear and simple, free of the abbreviations and codes which dictionaries for adults find so necessary. This means that there are fewer distractions from the main business of dictionary entries, which is to provide simple guidance to the meanings of words. It also means that the dictionary is ideally suited for teaching children what dictionaries *do*: the major functions of dictionaries are all present in the *Macquarie Junior*, but in an explicit and readable form.

The *Macquarie Junior* is part of a graded set of dictionaries. Each one introduces the elements of dictionary style that are appropriate for the children they are designed for. Even before school, many children will have enjoyed a gentle introduction to dictionaries with *My Macquarie Picture Dictionary. My First Macquarie*, encountered by many at the start of their primary schooling, brings in such things as multiple senses of words and examples of words in use. After the *Junior* has taken them on to secondary schooling, the *Macquarie Student Dictionary* and the *Pocket Macquarie* progressively lead the students to more difficult words and more adult formats. Other materials, such as the *Macquarie Theme Dictionary* (Big Book) and the similarly graded *Macquarie* thesauruses, are part of this set of reference materials which is designed to grow with the needs of your children. Exciting additions to this set are the *Macquarie Young Writers Book* and the *Macquarie Student Writers Guide*. These guides provide the extra tips for writers that cannot be covered in a dictionary because of lack of space. All are intended to enable natural progression towards adult-style dictionaries and thesauruses, having provided a sound model of how such books work and what information they are likely to contain.

Dictionaries are used most often for two reasons: one is to discover the meaning of a word, and the other is to check the spelling. We have attempted in this Second Edition to balance these requirements. We have given priority to hard words at the expense of those easy ones that no-one ever bothers to look up, while recognising that it may be either the meaning or the spelling that makes a word difficult. Some of the easy ones we have included are there as examples of parts of speech that were not included in the First Edition: prepositions and conjunctions. We may also include a word in order to give advice about confusing homonyms that it has, or because it has irregular forms that need explaining.

Guidance as to pronunciation is given when the spelling doesn't clearly show how the word should be said. Definitions are numbered, and are usually given in order of their commonness. Phrases or short sentences are given to illustrate their use, where this seems useful.

At the end of the definitions, extra information is often given under the three headings **Word Use**, **Word Building** and **Word History**.

The **Word Use** field contains information about any alternative spellings of the word that are not mentioned at the top of its entry, about its level of usage, and about its synonyms and antonyms. This field is where the student is warned against confusing the word with others that are similar in form or meaning. It also gives information about sets of words such as the names of male, female and young animals.

The **Word Building** field contains information about the inflections of the word. Plurals of nouns are given when they are not simply formed by adding *-s*. Parts of verbs are given if they are irregular, or end in *-y*, or double the consonants before the inflection. The comparative and superlative forms of adjectives and adverbs are given if they are not merely the result of adding *-er*, *-est*, *more* or *most*. For all these inflections, help is given in any case where young readers may be in doubt, even if the formation is in fact a regular one. The **Word Building** field also contains other words that can be derived easily from the headword, usually by adding a suffix. Often these words are given a brief definition or an example of use. Prefixes have been added as headwords in the Second Edition, to show how words are formed.

The **Word History** field, new to this Second Edition, gives a simple origin, or etymology, for selected words. No attempt is made to trace the word through all its stages, but the earliest known language of origin is given without codes or abbreviations. Every word of Aboriginal origin has been given a word history to show which of Australia's many Aboriginal languages the word came from. We hope that teachers in particular will find the **Word History** section useful, and that students will gain a better understanding of the changing nature of our language.

David Blair

How to Use the Dictionary

Where can I find the word?

The words in the dictionary appear in alphabetical order, so the one you are looking up (the **headword**) is easy to find.

Get as close as you can to it by following the letters you're sure about and then check several words until you find the one you're after.

If you still can't find the word, it may be that it begins with a letter that you don't sound when you say the word, or one that is said differently to normal. You can check this by looking up the section called **'If at first you don't succeed . . .'** on page 601.

Headwords which are spelt in the same way, but have different histories are entered separately and have small numbers after them to show this difference, such as **bat**[1] and **bat**[2].

How do I say it?

It is sometimes quite hard to work out how to say a word. In these cases, a pronunciation guide is given, using one of three methods:

bicentenary (say *buy-sən-teen-ə-ree*)

It's easy to follow this system, but if you're in any doubt, turn to the inside cover of the dictionary, and you will find a guide.

bream (sounds like *brim*) *noun*

This is used when the headword sounds just like another, simpler word.

baulk (rhymes with *fork*) *verb*

If you know how to say **fork**, it's easy to work out how to say **baulk**, which rhymes with it.

What is the part of speech?

This appears after the headword or pronunciation guide. The word could, for example, be a verb such as **decide**, a noun such as **kangaroo**, an adjective such as **funny**, an adverb such as **gingerly**, or an interjection such as **hello**.

bash *verb*
1 to hit hard or wildly: *The boys bashed each other. / He bashed the ball.*
bash *noun*
2 a try or attempt: *Give it a bash.*

As you can see, if there is a change in the part of speech, in this case from verb to noun, the headword is listed again.

What does it mean?

The **definition** follows the part of speech and tells you what the word means. If it has more than one meaning, the definitions are numbered, with the most commonly used meaning coming first.

Sometimes, a helpful phrase or sentence follows the definition, showing you how to use the word. If there are two, they are separated by a slash (/).

baulk (rhymes with *fork*) *verb*
to stop and refuse to do something: *The horse baulked at the jump. / to baulk at making a speech*

A **secondary headword** is a phrase containing the headword, but with a special meaning. It appears in **bold** letters, followed by a definition.

bat[1] *noun*
1 the stick used to hit the ball in games like cricket and baseball **2 off your own bat** on your own, without help or advice

What else should I know about the word?

The **Word Use** box gives you extra information about the word. Here are some examples:

llama (rhymes with *farmer*) *noun*

Word Use: be careful – this sounds like **lama**

bushwhacker *noun*

Word Use: another word is **bushie** □ both these words are more suited to everyday language

'Both these words are more suited to everyday language' means that you are more likely to use or hear the words when talking with your friends than on formal occasions or in written language.

common noun *noun*

Word Use: compare this with a **proper noun**

Are there other words related to the headword or other forms of the word?

In the **Word Building** box you will find words that are in the same family as the headword. They are given with their part of speech and sometimes a short definition or a phrase to show how the word is used. If the word is sometimes found in different forms that are spelt in an irregular way these are also listed in brackets. Here are some examples:

bat[1] *noun*

Word Building: **bat** *verb* (**batted**, **batting**) **batsman** *noun* **batter** *noun*

publish *verb*

Word Building: **publisher** *noun* a person or company that publishes books

You will also find information about other forms of the word. For example:

bicentenary (say *buy-sən-<u>teen</u>-ə-ree*) *noun*

Word Building: the plural is **bicentenaries**

bite *verb*

Word Building: other verb forms are **I bit, I have bitten, I am biting**

bleary *adjective*

Word Building: other forms are **blearier, bleariest**

Where does the word come from?

The **Word History** box gives you information about the origin of the word. The words we use every day come from all sorts of places. Some come from languages other than English; some come from the names of people or places; and some were made up by writers or inventors.

baboon *noun*

Word History: from a French word meaning a 'stupid person'

boomerang *noun*

Word History: from an Aboriginal language called Dharuk

abacus (say *ab-ə-kəs*) *noun*
a frame with rods through it which hold beads used for counting

Word Building: the plural is **abaci**

abalone (say *ab-ə-loh-nee*) *noun*
a type of shellfish that is good to eat

abandon[1] *verb*
1 to leave and not mean to come back: *The man abandoned his car.* **2** to give up: *to abandon hope / to abandon the cricket match because of rain*

Word Building: **abandonment** *noun*

abandon[2] *noun*
freedom from worry or care: *When the war was over people danced with abandon.*

abattoir (say *ab-ə-twah*) *noun*
a building or place where animals are killed for food: *The abattoir has closed down.*

Word Building: the plural form **abattoirs** is often used

abbey *noun*
a building or group of buildings where monks or nuns live

Word Use: similar words are **monastery** or **convent**
Word Building: **abbess** *noun* a nun in charge of a convent **abbot** *noun* a monk in charge of a monastery

abbreviate *verb*
to make shorter by leaving out some letters: *We abbreviate "Mister" to "Mr".*

Word Use: the short form of this is **abbrev.** or **abbr.**
Word Building: **abbreviation** *noun*

abdicate *verb*
to give up a position, especially the throne: *King Edward VIII abdicated in 1936.*

Word Building: **abdication** *noun*

abdomen (say *ab-də-mən*) *noun*
1 the main part of the body that contains the stomach and other organs **2** the last section of the body of an insect or spider

Word Use: a similar word for definition 1 is **belly**
Word Building: **abdominal** *adjective*

abduct *verb*
to kidnap or carry away by force

Word Building: **abduction** *noun* **abductor** *noun*

abhor (say *əb-haw*) *verb*
to think of with disgust and hate: *I abhor cruelty to animals.*

Word Use: a similar word is **loathe**
Word Building: other forms are **I abhorred, I have abhorred, I am abhorring** □ **abhorrent** *adjective* hateful **abhorrence** *noun* loathing **abhorrently** *adverb*

abide *verb*
1 to stay: *Abide with me.* **2** to put up with: *I can't abide rude people.* **3 abide by** to accept or act according to: *to abide by the rules*

Word Building: other forms are **I abode** or **abided, I have abode** or **abided, I am abiding** □ **abiding** *adjective* **abode** *noun*

ability *noun*
1 the power to do or act: *The baby has the ability to crawl now.* **2** skill: *She has great ability in music.*

Word Use: a similar word for definition 2 is **talent**
Word Building: the plural is **abilities**

ablaze *adjective*
1 on fire **2** shining brightly: *The house was ablaze with lights.*

able *adjective*
1 having enough power, skill, or time: *Is he able to come to the party?* **2** skilled: *an able pianist*

Word Building: **ably** *adverb*

abnormal *adjective*
unusual: *The heat is abnormal for this time of the year.*

Word Use: the opposite of this is **normal**
Word Building: **abnormality** *noun* (**abnormalities**) **abnormally** *adverb*

abode *noun*
1 the place where you live
abode *verb*
2 *the past form of the verb* **abide**

Word Use: this is an old-fashioned word for **house**

abolish *verb*
to put an end to: *to abolish slavery*

Word Building: **abolition** *noun*

abominable *adjective*
hateful or disgusting: *Slavery was an abominable practice.*

Word Building: **abominate** *verb* **abomination** *noun* **abominably** *adverb*

aboriginal *adjective*
1 having to do with the earliest inhabitants of a country **2 Aboriginal** having to do with Australian Aborigines

Aborigine *noun*
one of the race of people who have lived in Australia from earliest known times

Word History: from a Latin word meaning "from the beginning"

abortion *noun*
the removal of a baby from its mother's womb before it has grown enough to live on its own

Word Building: **abort** *verb* **abortionist** *noun*

abound *verb*
1 to exist in great numbers: *Fish abound in this river.* **2 abound with** to be filled with: *This river abounds with fish.*

Word Building: **abounding** *adjective*

about *preposition*
1 concerning or having to do with: *a book about pirates* **2** close to: *a boy about your age* **3** in various directions around: *to wander about the place* **4 about to** going to do something very soon: *about to leave*
about *adverb*
5 near: *about 100 kilometres | about half an hour* **6** nearly or almost: *I'm about ready.* **7** nearby: *He's somewhere about.*

Word Use: definition 6 is more suited to everyday language

above *adverb*
1 in or to a higher place: *the sky above*
above *preposition*
2 higher than: *flying above the clouds | the class above mine* **3 above all** most important of all

Word Use: a similar word for definition 1 is **overhead** □ the opposite of this is **below**

abrasion *noun*
a wound or sore that is caused by a scrape: *an abrasion on the knee*

abrasive *adjective*
used for rubbing or grinding: *an abrasive powder for kitchen cleaning*

Word Building: **abrasive** *noun*

abreast *adverb*
1 side by side: *They walked four abreast along the lane.* **2** keeping up with or not behind the latest developments: *I try to keep abreast of the latest fashions. | They are abreast with the latest developments in AIDS research.*

Word Use: definition 2 is followed by *of* or *with*

abridge *verb*
to shorten by leaving some parts out: *We had to abridge your story to make it fit in the school magazine.*

Word Building: **abridged** *adjective* **abridgement** *noun*

abroad *adverb*
out of your own country: *to go abroad*

abrupt *adjective*
1 sudden or without warning: *an abrupt end to a story* **2** rude and quick-tempered: *He made an abrupt remark.*

Word Use: a similar word for definition 2 is **brusque**
Word Building: **abruptly** *adverb* **abruptness** *noun*
Word History: from a Latin word meaning "broken off"

abscess (say *ab*-*ses*) *noun*
an infected swelling in part of the body: *an abscess under his tooth*

abscissa (say *ab*-*sis*-*ə*) *noun*
the horizontal distance on a graph

abscond *verb*
to run away secretly: *The treasurer absconded with the funds.*

Word Building: **absconder** *noun*

abseil (rhymes with *fail*) *verb*
to lower yourself down a cliff, using ropes

absent *adjective*
1 away or not present: *Kylie is absent from school today.* **2** missing or not found: *His usual smile was absent from his face.*

Word Building: **absentee** *noun* someone who is away **absence** *noun* **absent** *verb* **absenteeism** *noun* **absently** *adverb*

absent-minded *adjective*
forgetful or vague

Word Building: **absent-mindedly** *adverb*

absolute *adjective*
complete or perfect: *He told the absolute truth.*

Word Building: **absolutely** *adverb*

absorb *verb*
to soak up or drink in: *This sponge will absorb the spilt milk.* | *The student absorbed all the facts.*

Word Building: **absorbing** *adjective* very interesting: *an absorbing book* **absorbent** *adjective* **absorption** *noun*

abstain *verb*
to keep yourself from doing something: *I wish people would abstain from smoking.*

Word Use: compare this with **refrain**
Word Building: **abstention** *noun* an act of abstaining **abstinence** *noun* the habit of abstaining **abstinent** *adjective*

abstract *adjective*
1 having to do with ideas rather than things: *My composition was about horses, but Jill wrote an abstract one about love.*
2 hard to understand: *abstract arguments*

Word Use: the opposite of this is **concrete**
Word Building: **abstraction** *noun* **abstractly** *adverb*

abstracted *adjective*
lost in thought: *My mother has an abstracted look on her face.*

Word Use: a word with a similar meaning is **preoccupied**

abstract noun *noun*
a word which refers to something that our five senses (touch, sight, hearing, smell, and taste) can't pick up: *"Fear", "love", "size", and "beauty" are all abstract nouns.*

Word Use: the opposite of this is **concrete noun**

abstruse *adjective*
hard to understand: *abstruse answers*

Word Building: **abstrusely** *adverb* **abstruseness** *noun*
Word History: from a Latin word meaning "concealed"

absurd *adjective*
1 foolish or without common sense: *an absurd question* **2** very funny: *an absurd clown*

Word Use: a similar word for definition 1 is **ridiculous** □ a similar word for definition 2 is **comical**
Word Building: **absurdity** *noun* **absurdly** *adverb*

abundant *adjective*
plentiful or more than enough: *The canteen has an abundant supply of sausage rolls.*

Word Building: **abundance** *noun* **abundantly** *adverb*

abuse (rhymes with *shoes*) *verb*
1 to speak nastily to **2** to use wrongly: *Don't abuse your pencil by chewing it.*
abuse (rhymes with *goose*) *noun*
3 insults or hurtful language **4** wrong use

Word Building: **abusive** *adjective* **abusively** *adverb* **abusiveness** *noun*

abysmal *adjective*
so bad that it could not be worse: *an abysmal exam result*

Word Use: **abysmally** *adverb*

abyss (rhymes with *kiss*) *noun*
a hole or space that is too deep to measure

Word History: from a Greek word meaning "without a bottom"

acacia (say *ə*-*kay*-*shə*) *noun*
a small tree that grows in warm areas of the world, and has small, ball-shaped yellow flowers

Word Use: it is also called **wattle**

academic *adjective*
1 belonging to a college or university: *academic studies* **2** full of theory instead of common sense: *an academic argument*

Word Building: **academic** *noun* **academically** *adverb*

academy *noun*
a school or society for learning

Word Building: the plural is **academies**

accede (say *ək-seed*) *verb*
to agree or consent: *I accede to your wishes.*

accelerate (say *ək-sel-ə-rayt*) *verb*
to move faster or speed up

Word Building: **acceleration** *noun*

accelerator (say *ək-sel-ə-ray-tə*) *noun*
a pedal in a car, which the driver presses to make the car go faster

accent (say *ak-sent*) *noun*
1 your own way of speaking: *I have an Australian accent.* **2** a stress or stronger tone given to part of a word or a musical note, to make it different from the rest **3** a mark showing a stress or emphasis

Word Building: **accent** *verb* **accentual** *adjective*

accentuate (say *ək-sen-chooh-ayt*) *verb*
to give importance to: *The brown eye shadow accentuates your eyes.*

Word Building: **accentuation** *noun*

accept (say *ək-sept*) *verb*
to take or receive willingly: *I accept your invitation.*

Word Building: **acceptable** *adjective* **acceptance** *noun* **accepted** *adjective*

access (say *ak-ses*) *noun*
1 the right of coming to: *We have access to our headmaster.* **2** a way of getting to: *This street gives easy access to the highway.*

access *verb*
3 to find in a computer: *to access information*

Word Building: **accessible** *adjective* **accessibility** *noun*

accessory (say *ək-ses-ə-ree*) *noun*
1 something added but not necessary: *My red handbag is an accessory that matches my red dress.* **2** someone who helps carry out a crime: *The person who hid the thief was charged with being an accessory to the crime.*

Word Building: the plural is **accessories**

accident (say *ak-sə-dənt*) *noun*
1 an unwanted or unlucky happening: *We had a bad accident in our car.* **2** something that happens by chance: *We met the boys by accident.*

Word Building: **accidental** *adjective:* an accidental meeting **accidentally** *adverb*

acclaim *verb*
to praise with sounds of approval: *The singer was acclaimed with shouts and clapping.*

Word Use: another word with a similar meaning is **applaud**
Word Building: **acclamation** *noun*

acclimatise or **acclimatize** *verb*
to get used to new conditions: *He acclimatised slowly to living in the bush.*

Word Building: **acclimatisation** *noun*

accommodate *verb*
1 to have space for: *This motel accommodates 200 people.* **2** to change or adapt: *to accommodate themselves to a new plan*

Word Building: **accommodation** *noun*

accompany *verb*
1 to go or be with: *to accompany a friend* **2** to play or sing with: *My mother accompanies me on the piano while I play the violin.*

Word Building: other forms are **I accompanied, I have accompanied, I am accompanying** □ **accompaniment** *noun* a part written to play with a tune

accomplice (say *ə-kum-pləs*) *noun*
someone who shares in a crime: *The robber's accomplice drove the getaway car.*

accomplish (say *ə-kum-plish*) *verb*
to carry out successfully

Word Use: similar words are **perform** and **finish**
Word Building: **accomplished** *adjective* highly skilled: *an accomplished violinist* **accomplishment** *noun*

accord *noun*
agreement or harmony: *The brothers are in accord with each other.*

Word Building: **accordance** *noun* **accordant** *adjective* **according** *adverb* **accordingly** *adverb*

accordion *noun*
a musical instrument that is squeezed to produce sound, and which you play using buttons or keys

Word Building: **accordionist** *noun* an accordion player

accost *verb*
to come up and speak to, usually in an unpleasant way: *The bully accosted me in the playground today.*

Word History: from a Latin word meaning "put side by side"

account *noun*
1 a sum of money in a bank or building society which you can add to or take away from **2** a record of money paid out and received by a person or business **3** a list of particular happenings: *I'll give you an account of my day at school.* **4** importance or value: *things of no account* **5** judgment or consideration: *I will take that into account.*
account *verb*
6 account for to explain: *That accounts for his disappearance.*

accountant *noun*
someone whose job is to examine and record all the money that is earned and spent in a business

Word Building: **accountancy** *noun* the work of an accountant **accounting** *noun*

accumulate *verb*
to collect or pile up: *He accumulated a large collection of stamps.* | *Don't let papers accumulate on your desk.*

Word Building: **accumulation** *noun* **accumulator** *noun* **accumulative** *adjective*

accurate *adjective*
correct or exact: *an accurate copy*

Word Building: **accuracy** *noun* **accurately** *adverb*

accuse *verb*
to blame openly for doing something wrong: *He accused his friend of cheating.*

Word Building: **accused** *noun* someone charged with a crime: *The Judge let the accused go free.* **accusation** *noun* **accusatory** *adjective* **accuser** *noun*

accustomed *adjective*
1 usual: *The library opened at the accustomed time.* **2 accustomed to** in the habit of: *She is accustomed to working hard.*

Word Building: **accustom** *verb: to accustom yourself to the heat*

ace *noun*
1 a playing card with a single spot: *the ace of spades* **2** a serve in tennis which the other player cannot touch with their racquet **3** an expert: *an ace at dancing* | *a flying ace from World War I*

Word Building: **ace** *adjective* excellent: *an ace party*

acetylene (say *ə-set-ə-leen*) *noun*
a gas which, when combined with oxygen, burns with a very hot flame and is used in welding

Word Use: acetylene is used in an **oxyacetylene burner**

ache (rhymes with *cake*) *noun*
a dull continuous pain: *a stomach ache*

Word Building: **ache** *verb: My leg is aching.*

achieve *verb*
to gain or bring about by effort: *to achieve an ambition*

Word Building: **achievement** *noun* **achiever** *noun*

acid *noun*
1 a chemical substance which can eat away metals
acid *adjective*
2 sour: *Lemons have an acid taste.* | *an acid remark*

Word Building: **acidic** *adjective* **acidity** *noun*

acknowledge *verb*
1 to admit to be real or true: *He acknowledged that he was to blame.*
2 to show that you have received: *to acknowledge a signal* | *to acknowledge an invitation*

Word Building: **acknowledgment** *noun*

acne (say *ak-nee*) *noun*
a rash with a lot of pimples, especially on your face

acorn *noun*
a nut with a cup-shaped bottom part, which grows on an oak tree

acoustics (say *ə-kooh-stiks*) *noun*
1 the science or study of sound **2** the properties of a building which affect the quality of the sounds produced in it: *The concert hall has good acoustics.*

Word Building: **acoustic** *adjective* **acoustically** *adverb*

acquaint *verb*
to tell, inform or make familiar: *You should acquaint the police with anything you know about a crime.*

Word Building: **acquainted** *adjective*

acquaintance *noun*
1 knowledge: *acquaintance with the facts*
2 a person you know: *He is an acquaintance, but I wouldn't call him a friend.*

acquire *verb*
to get or obtain: *She has acquired a new bike.*

Word Building: **acquisitive** *adjective* eager to collect things **acquisition** *noun*

acquit *verb*
1 to declare innocent: *They were acquitted by the jury.* **2 acquit yourself** perform: *He acquitted himself well in the exam.*

Word Use: the opposite of definition 1 is **convict**
Word Building: other forms are **I acquitted, I have acquitted, I am acquitting** □ **acquittal** *noun*

acre (rhymes with *baker*) *noun*
a large area of land in the old measurement system, that is equal to almost half a hectare

acrid *adjective*
having a bitter or unpleasant taste or smell

Word Use: a similar word is **pungent**

acrobat *noun*
someone who performs daring gymnastic tricks: *The acrobat at the circus walked the tightrope.*

Word Building: **acrobatic** *adjective* **acrobatics** *noun*
Word History: from a Greek word meaning "walking on tiptoe"

acronym (say *ak-rə-nim*) *noun*
a word made from the first letters of other words: *"ANZAC" is an acronym from "Australian and New Zealand Army Corps".*

acrostic (say *ə-kros-tik*) *noun*
a series of words or lines, often of a poem, in which the first or last letters form a word, a phrase, the alphabet, or anything like this

acrylic (say *ə-kril-ik*) *noun*
a synthetic material used for clothing

Word Building: **acrylic** *adjective: an acrylic jumper*

act *noun*
1 something done or performed: *an act of bravery* **2** a law or order: *an act of Parliament* **3** one of the main divisions of a stage play: *A ghost appeared in the third act of the play.* **4** a single performance in a concert: *a singing act*

act *verb*
5 to do something: *He acted quickly when danger was near.* **6** to do someone's duties when they are unable to: *to act as headmistress while she is away* **7** to play the part of: *to act Peter Pan in the school play* **8** to behave as: *to act the fool*

Word Building: **acting** *noun* **actor** *noun* **actress** *noun*

action *noun*
1 an act or deed: *a brave action*
2 the state of being active: *The nurses went into action when the ambulance arrived.*
3 a way of moving: *the action of a horse*

activate *verb*
to make active or set in motion: *He activated the machine by pulling a lever.*

Word Building: **activation** *noun*

active *adjective*
1 taking part or doing things: *She is active on the Committee.* **2** continuously busy: *He leads an active life.* **3** able to move quickly: *an active puppy* **4** having to do with a verb which has the doer of the action as its subject, as "punished" in *His father punished him.*

Word Use: compare definition 4 with **passive**

activist *noun*
someone who works very hard for something they believe in: *John's uncle was an activist in the peace movement.*

activity *noun*
a thing you do, often energetically: *The main activity for the day was swimming.*

Word Building: the plural is **activities**

actor *noun*
someone who acts the part of a character in a play: *The actor who played the killer was frightening.*

actress *noun*
a girl or woman who acts in a play

Word Building: the plural is **actresses**

actual *adjective*
real or existing

Word Building: **actually** *adverb*

acumen (say *ak-yə-mən*) *noun*
good judgment: *His business acumen helped him to make money.*

acupuncture (say *ak-yə-punk-chə*) *noun*
a Chinese type of medicine which treats illness or pain by sticking needles into certain parts of the body

Word Building: **acupuncturist** *noun*

acute *adjective*
1 very sudden and severe: *an acute attack of asthma* **2** clever: *an acute remark* **3** having less than 90°: *an acute angle*

Word Building: **acutely** *adverb* **acuteness** *noun*
Word History: from a Latin word meaning "sharpened"

AD
short for anno domini, *Latin words meaning* "in the year of our Lord": *Man first walked on the moon in AD 1969.*

Word Use: our calendar dates events from the year of Christ's birth; years after this are called **AD** and years before this are **BC**

adage (say *ad-ij*) *noun*
a wise saying: *"More haste less speed" is a common adage.*

Word Use: a similar word is **proverb**

adagio (say *ə-dah-zhee-oh*) *adverb*
played or sung slowly and calmly

Word Use: an instruction in music

adamant (say *ad-ə-mənt*) *adjective*
staying firm in what you decide: *She was adamant that she would not go.*

adapt *verb*
1 to change or adjust: *We adapted the design of our model aeroplane so that it flew better.* **2 adapt to** become used to: *She found it hard to adapt to a new school.*

Word Building: **adaptor** *noun* an extra part which changes a machine or tool to a different use **adaptability** *noun* **adaptable** *adjective* **adaptation** *noun*

add *verb*
1 to join so as to increase: *to add another bead to the necklace* **2** to find the sum of: *to add up all the numbers* **3 add to** to increase or make bigger: *to add to his surprise*

adder *noun*
a small venomous snake

addict (say *ad-ikt*) *noun*
someone who can't do without something, especially drugs: *a coffee addict*

Word Building: **addiction** *noun* **addictive** *adjective*
Word History: from a Latin word meaning "devoted"

addition *noun*
1 something added which increases the size or number of things: *A new bathroom is the latest addition to our house.* **2** the act of adding numbers together

Word Building: **additional** *adjective* **additionally** *adverb*

additive *noun*
something which is added, especially a chemical added to food to keep it fresh

address *noun*
1 the details of the place where you live
2 a formal speech: *to give an address at a meeting*

address *verb*
3 to write the receiver's name, street and town on: *I addressed the letter wrongly.*
4 to speak to: *The politician addressed the meeting.*

Word Building: the plural form of the noun is **addresses**

adenoids *plural noun*
soft growth at the back of the nose which sometimes blocks it and has to be removed

adept *adjective*
skilful: *She was adept at ball games.*

Word Building: **adeptness** *noun*

adequate *adjective*
suitable or enough: *That light jacket isn't adequate for this cold weather.*

Word Building: **adequacy** *noun* **adequately** *adverb*

adhere *verb*
to stick firmly: *The grass seeds adhered to our socks.* | *They adhered strictly to the rules.*

Word Building: **adherent** *noun* someone who follows or supports a person or idea **adherence** *noun*

adhesive *noun*
a substance which sticks things together

Word Building: **adhesive** *adjective* sticky **adhesion** *noun*

adjacent (say *ə-jay-sənt*) *adjective*
lying near or close: *Our block of land was adjacent to the railway line.*

adjective *noun*
a word which describes a noun, such as "tall" in *a tall building*

Word Use: the abbreviation is **adj.**
Word Building: **adjectival** *adjective* **adjectivally** *adverb*

adjourn (say *ə-jern*) *verb*
1 to put off: *We will adjourn the meeting till tomorrow.* **2** to move: *Shall we adjourn to the living room?*

Word Building: **adjournment** *noun*

adjudicate (say *ə-jooh-də-kayt*) *verb*
to act as judge: *The headmaster adjudicated in our debate.*

Word Building: **adjudication** *noun* **adjudicator** *noun*

adjust *verb*
to cause to fit or work properly: *I adjusted my belt. / I adjusted the tuning on the TV.*

Word Building: **adjustable** *adjective* **adjustment** *noun*

administer *verb*
1 to run or have charge of: *A solicitor administered his inheritance.* **2** to give: *The vet administered a big dose of medicine to the sick horse.*

Word Use: another form of this word is **administrate**

administration *noun*
the people that run a business or government: *If you don't like the rules, complain to the administration.*

Word Building: **administrative** *adjective* **administrator** *noun*

admiral *noun*
the highest ranking officer in the Navy

Word Building: **admiralty** *noun* the office or duty of an admiral

admire *verb*
to think very highly of

Word Building: **admirable** *adjective* excellent **admirably** *adverb* **admiration** *noun* **admirer** *noun*

admit *verb*
1 to let in: *Only admit one car at a time.* **2** to agree to the truth of: *He admitted his guilt.*

Word Use: for definition 2 you usually only admit something bad □ a similar word is **confess**
Word Building: other forms are **I admitted, I have admitted, I am admitting** □ **admittance** *noun: No admittance after the performance has started.* **admission** *noun*

admonish *verb*
to warn or caution: *We admonished the boys not to be noisy.*

Word Building: **admonition** *noun* **admonitory** *adjective*

adolescence (say *ad-ə-les-əns*) *noun*
the time between being a child and being grown-up

Word Building: **adolescent** *noun* a teenager **adolescent** *adjective*

adopt *verb*
to take as your own: *They adopted the baby.*

Word Use: compare this with **foster**
Word Building: **adoptive** *adjective* related by adoption **adoption** *noun*

adore *verb*
to feel very strong love for: *The children adored their puppy.*

Word Building: **adorable** *adjective* **adoring** *adjective* **adoration** *noun*

adorn *verb*
to make more beautiful or pleasant: *Flowers adorned her hair.*

Word Use: similar words are **decorate** and **embellish**
Word Building: **adorningly** *adverb* **adornment** *noun*

adrenalin (say *ə-dren-ə-lən*) *noun*
a chemical which your body sends into your blood when you are feeling anxious or stressed, or when you are involved in strenuous activity. It makes your heart beat faster and it increases your blood pressure and the amount of sugar in your blood.

Word Use: another spelling is **adrenaline** □ this word is related to the word **adrenal** which is based on the Latin word for the kidneys; the **adrenal glands,** which make adrenalin, are found near the top of the kidneys

adult *adjective*
1 grown-up or mature: *This film is only suitable for an adult audience.*
adult *noun*
2 someone who is fully grown

Word Building: **adulthood** *noun*

adulterate *verb*
to spoil by adding something inferior: *to adulterate food*

Word Building: **adulteration** *noun*

adultery *noun*
a sexual relationship in which at least one of the two people is married to someone else

Word Building: **adulterer** *noun* **adulterous** *adjective*

advance *verb*
1 to move or bring forwards: *He advanced his chess piece across the board. | She advanced to the front of the room.*
2 to improve or develop: *The new students are advancing rapidly in learning English.*
advance *noun*
3 progress or movement forwards
4 a loan: *an advance of $10* **5 in advance a** in front or before: *in advance of other pupils* **b** ahead of time: *They paid the rent in advance.*

Word Building: **advanced** *adjective* **advancement** *noun*

advantage *noun*
something that puts you ahead of others: *Her strong arms gave her an advantage in swimming.*

Word Building: **advantageous** *adjective* **advantageously** *adverb*

adventure *noun*
an exciting experience

Word Building: **adventurer** *noun* **adventurous** *adjective* **adventurously** *adverb*

adverb *noun*
a word which tells you something extra about a verb, adjective or another adverb, such as "beautifully" in *singing beautifully*

Word Use: the short form of this is **adv.**
Word Building: **adverbial** *adjective*

adversary (say *ad-vəs-ree*) *noun*
someone you compete against or fight with

Word Building: the plural is **adversaries** □ **adverse** *adjective* hostile **adversity** *noun* misfortune

advertise (say *ad-və-tuyz*) *verb*
to praise or draw attention to, especially in order to sell: *We advertised our car in the newspapers.*

Word Building: **advertiser** *noun* **advertising** *noun*

advertisement (say *əd-vert-əs-mənt*) *noun*
a notice telling you about an event that is coming, or about something lost or for sale

advice (say *əd-vuys*) *noun*
an opinion someone gives you to help you decide what to do: *George gave me advice about the best way to fix my bike.*

advisable *adjective*
sensible: *It's advisable not to take the steep, dangerous track.*

Word Building: **advisability** *noun*

advise (say *əd-vuyz*) *verb*
to tell what you think should be done: *We advised them not to go to the desert in summer.*

advocate (say *ad-və-kət*) *noun*
1 someone who speaks in favour of a person or cause: *the criminal's advocate | an advocate of peace*
advocate (say *ad-və-kayt*) *verb*
2 to speak in favour of: *We advocate peace rather than war.*

aeon (say *ee-ən*) *noun*
a long period of time: *aeons ago when dinosaurs lived*

Word Use: another spelling is **eon**
Word History: from a Greek word meaning "a lifetime" or "an age"

aerial *noun*
1 a wire or rod that you put up to receive radio or television signals
aerial *adjective*
2 living in or reaching into the air: *The plant has aerial roots.*

aero- *prefix*
a word part meaning **1** air: *aerobics* **2** gas: *aerosol* **3** aeroplane: *aerodrome*

aerobics *plural noun*
exercises done to improve your heart and lungs

aerodrome *noun*
a landing field for aeroplanes which is smaller than an airport but which has hangars and other buildings

aeronautics *noun*
the science of flight

Word Building: **aeronautical** *adjective*
Word History: from a Latin word meaning "sailing in the air"

aeroplane *noun*
a winged machine which is driven through the air by its propellers or jet engines

aerosol (say *air-rə-sol*) *noun*
a container for keeping liquids, such as paint or household cleaner, under pressure so that you can spray them

aesthetics or **esthetics** (say *əs-thet-iks*) *noun*
the study of beauty, especially in art

Word Building: **aesthete** *noun* **aesthetic** *adjective*

affable *adjective*
friendly and approachable: *The affable old man told the children stories of his travels.*

Word Building: **affability** *noun* **affably** *adverb*

affair *noun*
1 an event or matter: *Tell us about the whole affair.* **2** a sexual relationship between two people

affect[1] *verb*
to cause a change in: *His sad story affected our mood. / The heat affected the milk and turned it bad.*

Word Use: don't confuse this word with **effect,** which is usually a noun, but which can be a verb meaning "to produce, or bring about"
Word Building: **affected** *adjective* moved or touched: *I am always very affected when I hear beautiful music.*

affect[2] *verb*
to pretend or make a show of: *He affected not to know what we were talking about, though we knew he really did.*

Word Building: **affected** *adjective* artificial: *The actress's voice was very affected.*

affectation *noun*
an exaggerated sort of behaviour: *Her parents thought her way of talking was an affectation.*

affection *noun*
warm feelings of love

Word Building: **affectionate** *adjective* **affectionately** *adverb*

affiliate *verb*
to join or become connected: *Our business will affiliate with a larger company.*

Word Building: **affiliate** *noun* **affiliation** *noun*
Word History: from a Latin word meaning "adopt as a son"

affinity *noun*
a natural liking or sense of closeness: *She felt an affinity for the girl her own age.*

Word Building: the plural is **affinities**

affirm *verb*
to declare definitely: *The minister affirmed his support for the poor.*

Word Building: **affirmation** *noun* agreement

affirmative *adjective*
agreeing: *an affirmative reply*

Word Use: the opposite is **negative**
Word Building: **affirmatively** *adverb*

afflict *verb*
to trouble greatly or cause pain: *He was afflicted with sickness.*

Word Building: **affliction** *noun*

affluent (say *af-looh-ənt*) *adjective*
wealthy or rich: *an affluent country*

Word Building: **affluence** *noun*

afford *verb*
to have enough money to pay for: *They couldn't afford a new car.*

affront *noun*
something that hurts your pride or your feelings: *His rudeness was an affront to the visitors.*

Word Building: **affronted** *adjective* offended **affront** *verb*

afraid *adjective*
1 frightened or feeling fear **2** feeling sorry or regretful: *I'm afraid I can't come.*

afresh *adverb*
again: *After each interruption she started the book afresh.*

aft (rhymes with *raft*) *adverb*
at or towards the back of a ship: *He went aft to his cabin.*

Word Use: the opposite of this is **fore**

aftermath *noun*
conditions which follow a disaster: *the aftermath of the fire*

afternoon *noun*
the time from midday till evening

agate (rhymes with *maggot*) *noun*
a type of hard stone which is often marked with stripes or swirls of colour

age *noun*
1 the length of time that someone or something has existed: *Joe is thirteen years of age.* **2** a period of historical time: *the Middle Ages* **3** a stage of human life: *old age*

age *verb*
4 to grow old or look older: *Our grandmother has aged since her illness.*

Word Building: other verb forms are **I aged, I have aged, I am ageing** or **aging** □ **aged** *adjective* very old

agency (say *ay-jən-see*) *noun*
an organisation which helps or acts for people: *You can go to an employment agency if you need help finding a job.*

Word Building: the plural is **agencies**

agenda (say *ə-jen-də*) *noun*
the list or plan of what has to be done or talked about, especially at a meeting: *There were three items for discussion on the agenda.*

agent (say *ay-jənt*) *noun*
1 someone who acts or organises things for you: *a travel agent* **2** something used for a special purpose: *a cleaning agent*

aggravate (say *ag-rə-vayt*) *verb*
1 to make worse: *Tiredness aggravated his bad temper.* **2** to annoy: *Don't aggravate the teacher by shuffling your feet.*

Word Building: **aggravation** *noun*

aggregate (say *ag-rə-gət*) *noun*
the total or sum of single things: *the aggregate of all your marks in the test*

Word Building: **aggregation** *noun* **aggregately** *adverb* **aggregative** *adjective*

aggressive *adjective*
likely to attack: *an aggressive guard dog*

Word Building: **aggression** *noun* **aggressively** *adverb* **aggressiveness** *noun* **aggressor** *noun*

aggrieved *adjective*
feeling hurt or wronged: *She was aggrieved that no-one asked her to join the party.*

aghast (rhymes with *mast*) *adjective*
shocked and frightened: *They were aghast at the unexpected result of their plan.*

agile (say *aj-uyl*) *adjective*
lively and active: *an agile gymnast*

Word Building: **agilely** *adverb* **agility** *noun*

agitate *verb*
1 to disturb or shake about: *to agitate the water* **2** to try to get public support: *to agitate for a change of government*

Word Building: **agitatedly** *adverb* **agitation** *noun* **agitator** *noun*

agnostic (say *ag-nos-tik*) *noun*
someone who believes that you can't know anything about God

Word Use: you should compare this word with **atheist**
Word Building: **agnostic** *adjective* **agnosticism** *noun*

agog *adjective*
excited and eager: *Santa's sleigh arrived and the children were all agog.*

Word History: from French words meaning "in a merry mood"

agony *noun*
great pain or suffering

Word Building: the plural is **agonies** □ **agonise** *verb*

agrarian (say *ə-grair-ree-ən*) *adjective*
having to do with the land or farming: *an agrarian way of life*

agree *verb*
1 to say yes: *I agreed to share my toffees.* **2** to have the same opinion **3** to arrange: *We agreed to meet after lunch.* **4 agree with a** to suit: *The food doesn't agree with me.* **b** to think like

agreeable *adjective*
1 pleasant or likeable: *agreeable weather* **2** willing to agree: *We will go now if you are agreeable.*

Word Building: **agreeableness** *noun* **agreeably** *adverb*

agreement *noun*
1 the same way of thinking: *John and I are in agreement about that film.* **2** arrangement: *They came to an agreement about sharing the bike.*

Word Use: a word with a similar meaning to definition 2 is **pact**

agriculture *noun*
farming: *Much of Australia's wealth comes from agriculture.*

Word Building: **agricultural** *adjective* **agriculturalist** *noun* **agriculturally** *adverb*

aid *noun*
1 help or support **2 first aid** emergency help to someone

Word Building: **aid** *verb*

AIDS (say *aydz*) *noun*
a disease caused by a virus called HIV which breaks down the body's natural defences, causing very bad infections, skin tumours and death

Word History: an acronym made by joining the first letters of *acquired immune deficiency syndrome*

ailing *adjective*
not well, or sickly: *an ailing child*

Word Building: **ailment** *noun* an illness **ail** *verb*

aim *verb*
1 to direct or point: *to aim that remark at him* | *to aim a gun carefully before firing* **2** to try very hard: *We aim to succeed.*

aim *noun*
3 a purpose or target: *Our aim was to win the race.* **4 take aim** to point a weapon

Word Building: **aimless** *adjective* without purpose **aimlessly** *adverb*

air *noun*
1 the mixture of gases which surrounds the earth and which we breathe
2 appearance: *She has an air of success.*
3 a tune or melody

air *verb*
4 to let air into: *Open the window to air the room.* **5** to make known to people: *The meeting was a chance for her to air her views.*

Word Building: **airing** *noun: to give clothes an airing* **airless** *adjective* stuffy

aircraft *noun*
any machine that can fly, such as an aeroplane or helicopter

air force *noun*
the part of a country's armed forces which uses planes for attack and defence

airline *noun*
a company which provides a regular plane service for passengers and goods

Word Building: **airliner** *noun* a large passenger aircraft

airport *noun*
a large area where planes land and take off, usually with buildings for staff, passengers, and planes

air-pressure *noun*
1 the pressure caused by the weight of the atmosphere at a particular place on the earth **2** the pressure of air, usually inside a tyre

Word Use: other names for definition 1 are **atmospheric pressure** and **barometric pressure** □ you measure the pressure in definition 1 with a barometer

airtight *adjective*
tightly closed so that air can't get in or out: *an airtight jar*

airy *adjective*
1 having air moving through it: *an airy room* **2** careless or light-hearted: *He went off with an airy wave of his hand.*

Word Building: other forms are **airier, airiest** □ **airily** *adverb* **airiness** *noun*

aisle (rhymes with *pile*) *noun*
a clear path between seats in a church or hall

ajar *adverb*
partly open: *Leave the door ajar.*

akimbo *adverb*
with your hands on your hips and your elbows pointing out: *to stand with arms akimbo*

akin *adjective*
related or alike: *Emus are akin to ostriches.*

alacrity (say *ə-lak-rə-tee*) *noun*
cheerful willingness: *Jane went to do the messages with alacrity.*

alarm *noun*
1 a warning sound or signal **2** sudden fear caused by discovering that you're in danger: *The smell of smoke filled me with alarm.*

alarm *verb*
3 to frighten: *The sudden shout alarmed him.*

Word Building: **alarming** *adjective* **alarmist** *noun*
Word History: from Italian words meaning "to arms"

albatross *noun*
a very large seabird that can fly long distances

Word Building: the plural is **albatrosses**

albino (say *al-bee-noh*) *noun*
a human or an animal with pale skin, white hair and pink eyes

Word Building: the plural is **albinos** □ **albino** *adjective*

album *noun*
1 a book with blank pages used for keeping things like photographs and stamps
2 a long-playing record

alcohol *noun*
a colourless liquid which is found in some drinks and which makes you drunk if you have too much

alcoholic *noun*
someone who continually drinks too much alcohol

Word Building: **alcoholic** *adjective*

alcoholism *noun*
a disease caused by drinking too much alcohol for a long time

alcove *noun*
a small space or recess set off the main part, especially in a room

alderman *noun*
a man or woman elected to a local council: *He complained to the alderman about the holes in the footpaths.*

Word Building: the plural is **aldermen**

ale *noun*
beer not flavoured with hops

alert *adjective*
watchful and quick to react: *The guards are alert to any danger.*

Word Building: **alert** *verb* **alertness** *noun*

algae (say *al-jee*) *plural noun*
seaweed or pondweed

Word Building: the singular form is **alga**

algebra *noun*
the branch of maths which uses letters to stand for numbers

Word Building: **algebraic** *adjective* **algebraically** *adverb*

algorism *noun*
a sum in arithmetic

algorithm *noun*
a step-by-step method for doing a sum

alias (say *ay-lee-əs*) *noun*
1 a false name: *The criminal is said to be living under an alias in South America.*
alias *adverb*
2 also called: *Superman, alias Clark Kent*

Word Building: the plural is **aliases**
Word History: from a Latin word meaning "at another time or place"

alibi (say *al-ə-buy*) *noun*
a defence by someone that they were somewhere else when a crime was committed

alien (say *ay-lee-ən*) *noun*
1 someone who is not a citizen of the country in which they are living
2 a foreigner: *aliens from outer space*

Word Building: **alien** *adjective*
Word History: from a Latin word meaning "belonging to another"

alienate *verb*
to make unfriendly: *The Prime Minister alienated his supporters.*

Word Building: **alienation** *noun*

alight[1] *verb*
1 to get down: *to alight from a horse / to alight from a train* **2** to settle or stay after coming down: *a bird alights on a branch*

Word Building: other forms are **I alighted, I have alighted, I am alighting**

alight[2] *adjective*
burning or lighted up: *The fire is alight at last.*

align (rhymes with *fine*) *verb*
to bring into line: *to align the pictures on the wall*

Word Building: **alignment** *noun*

alike *adverb*
1 in the same manner: *She treats all pupils alike.*
alike *adjective*
2 similar: *Their clothes are alike.*

alimentary canal (say *al-ə-ment-ree*) *noun*
the passage in an animal's body which extends from the mouth to the anus and which is used for digesting food

Word Use: another name for this is **alimentary tract**

alkali (say *al-kə-luy*) *noun*
a chemical that reduces the effect of acid

Word Building: **alkaline** *adjective*
Word History: from an Arabic word for the ashes of certain beach plants

allay (say *ə-lay*) *verb*
to make less or relieve: *to allay suspicion / to allay the pain*

allege (say *ə-lej*) *verb*
to declare without proof: *Kim alleged that Mandy broke the window.*

Word Building: **allegation** *noun* **allegedly** *adverb*

allegiance (say *ə-lee-jəns*) *noun*
loyalty or faithfulness: *They swore allegiance to the queen.*

allegory (say *al-ə-gree*) *noun*
a story which seems simple but has an extra underlying meaning

Word Building: the plural is **allegories** □ **allegorical** *adjective*

allegro *adverb*
played or sung at a fast speed

Word Use: an instruction in music

allergy (say *al-ə-jee*) *noun*
an unusual sensitivity to things that are normally harmless, like pollen, dust and certain foods: *I sneezed in the pet shop because of my allergy to cats.*

Word Building: the plural is **allergies** □ **allergen** *noun* something which causes an allergic reaction **allergic** *adjective*

alleviate (say *ə-lee-vee-ayt*) *verb*
to make easier to bear: *The aspirin has alleviated the pain.*

Word Building: **alleviation** *noun*

alley *noun*
1 a narrow lane between buildings
2 a long narrow enclosure with a smooth wooden floor for games like tenpin bowling

Word Building: the plural is **alleys**

alliance (say *ə-luy-əns*) *noun*
an agreement to work together: *Australia has a military alliance with the United States. / The local people are in alliance to prevent the building of a freeway.*

alligator *noun*
an animal like a crocodile, but with a broader snout, found mainly in America

Word History: from a Latin word meaning "lizard"

alliteration *noun*
the repeated use of the same letter or sound to start two or more words in a group, as in "Around the rugged rocks the ragged rascal ran"

Word Building: **alliterative** *adjective*

allocate *verb*
to set apart for a special purpose: *to allocate some of your pocket money for sweets*

Word Building: **allocation** *noun*

allot *verb*
1 to hand out or distribute: *to allot equal shares* **2** to set apart: *to allot money for the new park*

Word Use: a similar word for definition 2 is **allocate**
Word Building: other forms are **I allotted, I have allotted, I am allotting** □ **allotment** *noun*

allow *verb*
1 to give permission to or for: *Will your parents allow you to come?* **2** to set aside: *to allow space for a margin*

Word Building: **allowed** *adjective* permitted

allowance *noun*
1 money given for a special purpose: *a travelling allowance* **2 make allowance for** to take into account: *Please make allowance for my broken arm.*

alloy *noun*
a metal made by mixing different metals together: *Bronze is an alloy of copper and tin.*

all right *adjective*
1 safe: *I'm all right now.* **2** adequate or good enough to accept: *Your answer is all right, but it could have been more interesting.*

all right *adverb*
3 correctly or to an acceptable standard: *She did her homework all right.*

Word Use: another spelling for definition 3 is **alright**

allude *verb*
to refer casually: *She alluded to his late arrival.*

Word Building: **allusion** *noun* passing mention of something **allusive** *adjective* **allusively** *adverb*
Word History: from a Latin word meaning "play with"

allure *noun*
temptation or attraction: *the allure of the toy shop*

Word Building: **allure** *verb* **alluring** *adjective*

alluvial *adjective*
made of sand or mud which has been washed down by a river: *alluvial soil*

ally (say *al-uy*) *noun*
1 a country which has signed an agreement to help another country: *an ally in times of war* **2** a friend or supporter

ally (say *ə-luy*) *verb*
3 to join together to help one another

Word Building: the plural form of the noun is **allies** □ other verb forms are **they allied, they have allied, they are allying** □ **alliance** *noun*

almanac (say *awl-mə-nak*) *noun*
a calendar which gives information about the sun, moon, tides, weather or other special information

Word Use: an old-fashioned spelling is **almanack**

almighty *adjective*
1 very powerful: *an almighty king* **2** very great: *to be in almighty trouble* **3 the Almighty** God

almond (say *ah-mənd*) *noun*
an oval-shaped, cream-coloured nut with a sweet taste

alms (sounds like *arms*) *plural noun*
money and other gifts given to poor people

Word Use: a similar word is **charity**

alone *adjective*
1 by yourself: *to live alone* **2** only: *She alone knows the real story.*

Word Building: **aloneness** *noun*

aloof (rhymes with *roof*) *adjective*
1 withdrawn and proud: *She seems aloof and unfriendly, but she's really only shy.*
aloof *adverb*
2 at a distance apart: *to stand aloof from the crowd*

aloud *adverb*
1 in a normal speaking voice: *to read aloud* **2** loudly: *to cry aloud with pain*

alp *noun*
1 a high mountain **2 alps** a high mountain range, usually covered with snow, such as the Australian Alps or the Swiss Alps

Word Building: **alpine** *adjective* having to do with a cold mountainous place: *alpine flowers*

alphabet *noun*
all the letters of a language arranged in their usual order

Word Building: **alphabetical** *adjective* **alphabetically** *adverb* **alphabetisation** *noun* **alphabetise** *verb*
Word History: from Greek words for the letters "A" and "B"

Alsatian (say *al-say-shən*) *noun*
a large, strong, wolf-like dog, often trained as a guard dog and used by the police

Word Use: another name is **German shepherd**

altar *noun*
a table which is used for religious ceremonies in a church or temple

Word Use: be careful – this sounds like **alter**

alter *verb*
to change: *Your appearance alters as you grow up. / She has altered her hairstyle again.*

Word Use: be careful – this sounds like **altar**
Word Building: **alteration** *noun*

altercation *noun*
an angry disagreement or dispute

alternate (say *awl-tə-nayt*) *verb*
1 to follow one another in turn: *Day and night alternate with each other.*

alternate (say *awl-ter-nət*) *adjective*
2 every second one of a series: *They visit their grandmother on alternate weekends.*

Word Use: be careful – don't confuse definition 2 with **alternative**

alternative (say *awl-ter-nə-tiv*) *noun*
1 one of two or more choices: *to provide orange juice as an alternative to milk / a list of alternatives*
alternative *adjective*
2 giving a choice between one thing and another: *the alternative route to Brisbane*

Word Use: be careful – don't confuse definition 2 with **alternate**

although (say *awl-dhoh*) *conjunction*
even though: *I'm still tired although I had an early night.*

altimeter (say *al-tə-meet-ə*) *noun*
the instrument in a plane which measures altitude or height

altitude *noun*
height above sea level: *to fly at a high altitude*

alto (say *al-toh*) *noun*
1 the range of musical notes which can be sung by a female singer with a low voice: *She sings alto in the choir.* **2** a woman with a low singing voice

Word Use: another word is **contralto** □ **alto** range is higher than **bass, baritone** and **tenor** but lower than **soprano**
Word Building: **alto** *adjective: He plays the alto saxophone.*
Word History: from a Latin word for "high"

altogether *adverb*
1 completely or totally: *to be altogether correct* **2** in total: *That costs $10 altogether.* **3** on the whole: *Altogether, I'm glad its over.*

aluminium (say *al-yə-min-ee-əm*) *noun*
a lightweight silver-grey metal which is used to make drink cans and cooking utensils and can be rolled into thin sheets of silver foil

always *adverb*
1 all the time: *She is always here.* **2** every time: *She always wears purple lipstick.*

a.m.
short for ante meridiem, *Latin words meaning* "before noon": *I get up at 6 a.m.*

amalgamate (say *ə-mal-gə-mayt*) *verb*
to mix together or combine: *to amalgamate two classes / The classes amalgamated when the teacher was away.*

Word Building: **amalgamation** *noun*

amateur (say *am-ə-tə*) *noun*
1 an athlete who does not earn money from playing sport **2** someone who does something for enjoyment and not to earn money from it **3** someone who does a job unskilfully: *This fence must have been built by an amateur.*

Word Use: the opposite of this is **professional**
Word Building: **amateurish** *adjective* **amateur** *adjective*
Word History: from a Latin word for "lover"

amaze *verb*
to surprise and astonish: *Peter's friends were amazed when he won the race.*

Word Building: **amazement** *noun* **amazing** *adjective*

amazon (say *am-ə-zən*) *noun*
a tall powerful woman

Word Building: **amazonian** *adjective*

ambassador *noun*
1 the chief official who is sent by a government to represent it in a foreign country **2** someone, such as a famous singer or sports star, who brings credit to their own country while visiting another

amber *noun*
1 a hard yellow-brown substance which can be polished as a gem stone **2** the yellowish-brown colour used as the warning light of a traffic signal

ambergris (say *am-bə-grees*) *noun*
a waxy substance taken from the intestines of the sperm whale, used in making perfume

Word History: from French words meaning "grey amber"

ambi- *prefix*
a word part meaning both *or* on both sides: *ambidextrous*

Word History: this prefix comes from Latin

ambidextrous *adjective*
able to use both hands equally well

Word Building: **ambidexterity** *noun*

ambiguous (say *am-big-yooh-əs*) *adjective*
with more than one meaning: *to give an ambiguous reply*

Word Building: **ambiguity** *noun* (**ambiguities**) **ambiguously** *adverb*

ambition *noun*
1 strong desire for something in the future, especially money or fame: *to be poor but filled with ambition* **2** the object that is desired: *His ambition is to win the race.*

Word Building: **ambitious** *adjective* **ambitiously** *adverb*

ambivalent (say *am-biv-ə-lənt*) *adjective*
having opposite and conflicting feelings towards someone or something: *Although I enjoy parties I am ambivalent about going to one without my best friend.*

Word Building: **ambivalence** *noun* **ambivalently** *adverb*

amble *verb*
to walk at a relaxed or comfortable pace

Word Building: **ambling** *adjective*

ambulance *noun*
a vehicle which is specially equipped to carry sick or injured people and which is driven by experts in First Aid

ambush *verb*
1 to attack after lying in wait in a hidden place
ambush *noun*
2 a sudden attack from a hidden place

amenable *adjective*
agreeable and cooperative: *amenable to the idea of a picnic*

Word Building: **amenably** *adverb*

amend *verb*
1 to alter: *to amend a law* **2** to improve or correct: *to amend bad behaviour*

Word Building: **amendment** *noun*

amends *plural noun*
in the phrase **make amends** to make up for wrong or injury done: *to make amends for hurting someone*

amenity *noun*
anything which makes a place more comfortable and pleasant: *a motel with such amenities as hot showers, laundry, swimming pool and restaurant*

Word Building: the plural is **amenities**

amethyst (say *am-ə-thəst*) *noun*
a purple-coloured precious stone

Word History: from a Greek word meaning "a remedy for drunkenness"

amiable (say *aym-ee-ə-bəl*) *adjective*
friendly and good-natured: *an amiable conversation*

Word Building: **amiability** *noun* **amiably** *adverb*

ammonia *noun*
a strong-smelling gas, often dissolved in water to make a liquid which may be used for cleaning

ammunition *noun*
powder or bullets used in firing guns or other weapons

amnesia *noun*
loss of memory: *He suffered from amnesia after he hit his head in the accident.*

amnesty *noun*
a pardon given to everyone, usually for crimes against a government

amoeba (say *ə-mee-bə*) *noun*
a one-celled animal which can only be seen with a microscope

Word Building: the plural is **amoebae** (say *ə-mee-bee*) or **amoebas** □ **amoebic** *adjective*
Word History: from a Greek word meaning "change"

amorous *adjective*
feeling or showing love, especially of a sexual kind: *an amorous boy* / *an amorous smile*

Word Building: **amorously** *adverb* **amorousness** *noun*

amount *noun*
1 quantity or extent: *Is there a large or small amount of food left?* **2** total of two or more things: *What is the amount of the bill?*
amount *verb*
3 amount to to add up to or be equal to: *The cost of her shopping trip amounted to $20.* / *Her advice didn't amount to much in the end.*

ampersand *noun*
the sign "&" which is used to mean "and" as in *Cobb & Co.*

amphi- *prefix*
a word part meaning **1** of both kinds: *amphibian* **2** around: *amphitheatre*

Word History: this prefix comes from Greek

amphibian *noun*
an animal that begins life in the water and lives on land as an adult, such as a frog

Word Building: **amphibious** *adjective* able to live or move both on land and in water

amphitheatre *noun*
a round building with an open area in the centre and rows of seats rising around it: *The ancient Romans watched plays in amphitheatres.*

ample *adjective*
1 more than enough in size or amount: *There was ample space for us all to fit in.*
2 large or well filled out: *She has an ample figure.*

Word Use: a similar word to definition 1 is **abundant**
Word Building: **ampleness** *noun* **amply** *adverb*

amplify *verb*
1 to make louder: *The microphone will amplify my speech.* **2** to enlarge or expand by adding details: *Please amplify your story so that I can understand what happened.*

Word Building: other forms are **I amplified, I have amplified, I am amplifying** □ **amplification** *noun*

amputate *verb*
to cut off in a medical operation: *The doctor amputated his injured leg.*

Word Building: **amputee** *noun* someone who has had a limb amputated **amputation** *noun*

amuse *verb*
1 to entertain so that the time passes pleasantly: *Linda amused herself reading.*
2 to make laugh or smile: *His jokes amused them.*

Word Building: **amusedly** *adverb* **amusingly** *adverb*

amusement *noun*
1 the feeling of being amused
2 something which amuses, such as a concert or a merry-go-round

anaemia or **anemia** (say *ə-neem-ee-ə*) *noun*
a lack of red blood cells or red colouring in the blood, making someone look pale and weak

Word Building: **anaemic** *adjective* pale and sickly

anaesthetic or **anesthetic** (say *an-əs-thet-ik*) *noun*
a drug that makes you unable to feel pain: *He was given an anaesthetic before the operation.*

Word Building: **anaesthetise** *verb* to make unable to feel pain **anaesthetist** *noun* the doctor who gives an anaesthetic **anaesthesia** *noun*

anagram *noun*
a word made by changing the order of the letters in another word: *"Caned" is an anagram of "dance".*

analgesic (say *an-əl-jee-zik*) *noun*
a medicine that removes or lessens pain

Word Building: **analgesia** *noun* the inability to feel pain **analgesic** *adjective* causing the removal of pain

analog *adjective*
showing measurement by use of a display or pointer that keeps on changing, such as the needle on a car speedometer: *an analog watch*

Word Use: compare this with definition 2 of **digital**

analogy *noun*
a likeness between two or more things which makes you compare them: *Teachers sometimes draw an analogy between the heart and a pump.*

Word Building: the plural is **analogies** □ **analogous** *adjective* similar **analogously** *adverb*

analyse *verb*
1 to examine in detail in order to find out the meaning: *to analyse behaviour / to analyse a story* **2** to separate into parts: *The scientist analysed the strange liquid.*

Word Building: **analyst** *noun* **analytical** *adjective* **analytically** *adverb*

analysis (say *ə-nal-ə-səs*) *noun*
1 the act of analysing **2** separation into parts

Word Use: compare definition 2 with **synthesis**

anarchy (say *an-ə-kee*) *noun*
1 a society where there is no government or law **2** any situation where there is no control or rules: *There was anarchy in the classroom when the teacher was not there.*

Word Building: **anarchism** *noun* **anarchist** *noun*
Word History: from a Greek word meaning "lack of a ruler"

anatomy *noun*
1 the structure of an animal or plant: *Bones are an important part of the human anatomy.* **2** the study or science of the structure of animals and plants

Word Building: **anatomical** *adjective* **anatomist** *noun*

ancestor *noun*
someone related to you who lived long ago: *What country did your ancestors come from?*

Word Use: the study of who your ancestors were is called **genealogy**
Word Building: **ancestral** *adjective* **ancestrally** *adverb* **ancestry** *noun*

anchor (rhymes with *banker*) *noun*
a heavy object chained to a boat and dropped into the water to stop it from floating away

Word Building: **anchor** *verb* **anchorage** *noun*

anchovy (say *an-chə-vee*) *noun*
a small fish with a very salty taste, often made into a paste for eating

Word Building: the plural is **anchovies**

ancient (say *ayn-shənt*) *adjective*
1 happening or living long ago: *ancient history / the ancient Romans* **2** very old: *an ancient man*

andante (say *an-dan-tay*) *adverb*
played or sung fairly slowly and evenly

Word Use: an instruction in music
Word History: from an Italian word meaning "walking"

anecdote (say *an-ək-doht*) *noun*
a short story that tells about a funny or interesting person or event: *I can tell you a lot of anecdotes about our holiday.*

Word Building: **anecdotal** *adjective*

anemone (say *ə-nem-ə-nee*) *noun*
1 a small flower, usually red, blue or white **2** an animal that lives in the sea and catches food with its tentacles

Word Use: another name for definition 2 is **sea-anemone**
Word History: from a Greek word meaning "windflower"

angel *noun*
1 one of God's messengers or attendants, usually pictured to look like humans with wings **2** someone who is very kind, good or beautiful

Word Building: **angelic** *adjective* **angelically** *adverb*

anger *noun*
1 a strong feeling of annoyance caused by thinking that something wrong has been done to you

anger *verb*
2 to make angry: *Jack's rudeness angered him.*

Word Use: a similar but less common word for definition 1 is **wrath**

angle[1] *noun*
1 the pointed shape made when two straight lines or surfaces meet each other: *The streets met at a sharp angle.* **2** point of view: *a new angle on the problem*
angle[1] *verb*
3 to bend, move or place at an angle: *He angled the ball away from the fielder.* **4** to put a bias or slant on: *He angled the question to suit himself.*

angle[2] *verb*
to fish with a hook and line

Word Building: **angler** *noun*

angry *adjective*
feeling or showing anger: *an angry man / an angry look*

Word Use: you are angry *with* or *at* a person, but you are angry *about* or *at* a thing or something that has happened
Word Building: other forms are **angrier, angriest** □ **angrily** *adverb*

anguish *noun*
very great pain, sorrow or worry: *She suffered anguish over her daughter's disappearance.*

Word Building: **anguish** *verb*

angular *adjective*
having a pointed or sharp shape like an angle: *His face had angular features.*

Word Building: **angularity** *noun*

animal *noun*
1 a living thing that is not a plant and can feel and move about **2** any animal except a human being: *Many people keep animals as pets.* **3** someone who is rough and badly-behaved

animate (say *<u>an</u>-ə-mayt*) *verb*
1 to make lively and energetic: *The thought of going to the beach animated her.* **2** to make move as if alive: *to animate cartoons*
animate (say *<u>an</u>-ə-mət*) *adjective*
3 alive: *animate creatures*

Word Building: **animated** *adjective* **animation** *noun*

animosity *noun*
a strong feeling of dislike or unfriendliness: *She looked at her enemy with animosity.*

aniseed *noun*
a strong-smelling seed which is used in cooking and medicines

ankle *noun*
the part of the body which joins the foot to the leg

anklet *noun*
an ornament worn around the ankle

annals (say *<u>an</u>-əlz*) *plural noun*
historical records that are kept year by year

Word Building: **annalist** *noun*

annex *verb*
to obtain and join to what is already owned: *The farmer annexed the neighbouring land.*

Word Building: **annexation** *noun*

annexe *noun*
a building added on to a larger building

annihilate (say *ə-<u>nuy</u>-ə-layt*) *verb*
to destroy or defeat completely: *They annihilated the enemy's army.*

Word Building: **annihilation** *noun*

anniversary *noun*
a yearly celebration of something which took place in an earlier year: *our fifth wedding anniversary*

Word Building: the plural is **anniversaries**

announce *verb*
to tell or make known in public: *Felicity announced that she was leaving school.*

Word Building: **announcement** *noun*

announcer *noun*
someone on radio or television who talks about or introduces a program

annoy *verb*
to irritate or make cranky: *Very loud music annoys me.*

Word Building: **annoyance** *noun*

annual *adjective*
1 happening once a year: *Our school sports day is an annual event.*
annual *noun*
2 a plant that lives for one season or year **3** a book or magazine published once a year

Word Building: **annually** *adverb*

anoint *verb*
to put ointment or oil on: *The priest anointed the dying man.*

Word Building: **anointment** *noun*

anonymous (say *ə-non-ə-məs*) *adjective*
having no name given: *The book was written by an anonymous author.*

Word Building: **anonymity** *noun* **anonymously** *adverb*

answer *noun*
1 a reply or response **2** a solution to a problem
answer *verb*
3 to respond or reply: *She answered with a nod.* **4** to reply to: *Hurry up and answer the question.* **5 answer back** to make a rude or cheeky reply

answerable *adjective*
1 responsible: *I am answerable for my child's safety.* **2** able to be solved or answered

ant *noun*
a small insect that usually lives in a large family group or community called a colony

antagonise or **antagonize**
(say *an-tag-ə-nuyz*) *verb*
to make angry or make an enemy of: *The bully antagonised the children by spoiling their game.*

Word Building: **antagonist** *noun* an enemy or opponent **antagonism** *noun* **antagonistic** *adjective*

antarctic (say *ant-ahk-tik*) *adjective*
1 having to do with the area near the South Pole
antarctic *noun*
2 the Antarctic the area near the South Pole

Word Use: another name for definition 2 is **Antarctica**
Word History: from a Greek word meaning "opposite the north"

ante- *prefix*
a word part meaning before in space or time: *antecedent*

Word History: this prefix comes from Latin

anteater *noun*
an animal with a long sticky tongue that feeds on ants or termites

Word Use: different varieties are called **echidnas** or **numbats**

antecedent (say *ant-ə-seed-ənt*) *noun*
anything that goes before another

antelope *noun*
a slight swift animal which has horns, chews its cud and is related to cattle, sheep and goats

antenna *noun*
1 a sense organ or feeler found on the head of insects or crabs **2** a radio or television aerial

Word Building: the plural for definition 1 is **antennae** □ the plural for definition 2 is **antennas**

anthem *noun*
1 a ceremonial song for an organisation or country: *"Advance Australia Fair" is Australia's national anthem.* **2** a hymn with words taken from the Bible

anthology *noun*
a collection of poems, plays or short stories by various authors or from various books

Word Building: the plural is **anthologies** □ **anthologist** *noun*
Word History: from a Greek word meaning "a gathering of flowers"

anthropology *noun*
the scientific study of the beginnings and growth of mankind

Word Building: **anthropologist** *noun*

anti- *prefix*
a word part meaning **1** against: *antibiotic* **2** opposed to: *anticlockwise*

Word Use: another spelling is **ant-**
Word History: this prefix comes from Greek

antibiotic *noun*
a drug capable of killing bacteria and other germs

Word Building: **antibiotic** *adjective*

anticipate *verb*
1 to know or realise in advance what is going to happen or what to expect: *to anticipate the disaster | to anticipate the excitement of Christmas* **2** to think of or mention before the proper time: *To anticipate your objection, I think you're being too cautious.*

Word Building: **anticipation** *noun* **anticipatory** *adjective*

anticlockwise *adjective*
going round in the opposite direction to the hands on a clock face

Word Use: the opposite of this is **clockwise**

antics *plural noun*
strange actions or movements of the body

antidote *noun*
something to stop the bad effects caused by a disease or a poison: *The doctor gave Kate the antidote for the spider bite.*

antipathy (say *an-tip-ə-thee*) *noun*
a feeling of strong dislike: *The dog had a strong antipathy to strangers.*

Word Building: **antipathetic** *adjective*

antipodes (say *an-tip-ə-deez*) *plural noun*
1 places directly opposite each other on the earth **2 the Antipodes** Australia as the antipodes of Britain

Word Building: **antipodean** *adjective*

antiquated (say *an-tə-kway-təd*) *adjective*
old-fashioned or out of date: *an antiquated textbook*

Word Building: **antiquary** *noun* an expert on ancient things **antiquarian** *adjective*

antique (say *an-teek*) *noun*
an object of art or piece of furniture which was made long ago: *I collect antiques.*

Word Building: **antique** *adjective* dating from earlier times
Word History: from a Latin word meaning "old"

antiquity (say *an-tik-wə-tee*) *noun*
1 ancient times or the early stages of history **2** great age: *a family of great antiquity*

Word Building: the plural is **antiquities**

antiseptic *noun*
a chemical used to kill germs that produce disease

Word Building: **antiseptic** *adjective*

antithesis (say *an-tith-ə-səs*) *noun*
1 the direct opposite: *Andrew was the antithesis of a good student.* **2** a contrast between two opposites: *the antithesis between light and dark*

Word Building: the plural is **antitheses**

antivenene (say *an-tee-və-neen*) *noun*
an injection to fight the venom from a spider or snake bite

antler *noun*
a long, hard, branch-like horn on the head of a male deer and other similar animals

antonym (say *ant-ə-nim*) *noun*
a word which has an opposite meaning to another word: *"Fast" is the antonym of "slow".*

anus *noun*
the opening in someone's bottom where waste material from the bowel comes out

Word Building: **anal** *adjective*

anvil *noun*
a heavy iron block with a smooth surface on which hot metals are hammered and shaped before they go cold and hard

anxiety (say *ang-zuy-ə-tee*) *noun*
1 worry or uneasy feelings: *A mother feels anxiety if her child becomes lost.*
2 eagerness: *His anxiety to do well made him try harder.*

Word Building: the plural is **anxieties**

anxious (say *ang-shəs*) *adjective*
1 full of anxiety or worry: *She was very anxious about her sick dog.* **2** eager: *He was anxious to please his father.*

Word Building: **anxiously** *adverb*

Anzac *noun*
1 the name given to a member of the Australian and New Zealand Army Corps during World War I: *The Anzacs fought their first battle at Gallipoli.* **2** a soldier from Australia or New Zealand

Word History: an acronym made by joining the first letters of the words *Australian* and *New Zealand Army Corps*

aorta (say *ay-aw-tə*) *noun*
the main artery carrying blood from the left side of the heart to nearly all parts of the body

Word Building: **aortic** *adjective*

apart *adverb*
1 to pieces: *He took the calculator apart to see how it worked.* **2** separated or not together: *You must keep these animals apart.*

Word Building: **apart** *adjective*

apartheid (say *ə-pah-tayt*) *noun*
a policy of the separation of races in a country according to their differences in colour: *Because of apartheid in South Africa white people do not mix with coloured people.*

apartment *noun*
1 a single room or set of rooms, among others in a building **2** a home unit

apathy (say *ap-ə-thee*) *noun*
no feeling for, or interest in things other people find interesting or exciting: *He was sunk in apathy after his father's death.*

Word Building: **apathetic** *adjective* **apathetically** *adverb*

ape *noun*
1 a large monkey without a tail
ape *verb*
2 to imitate or copy: *The child aped the strange way the clown was walking.*

aperture (say *ap-ə-chə*) *noun*
a hole, crack or other opening, especially the opening in a camera that limits the amount of light it lets in

apex *noun*
the peak, summit or highest point: *Every mountain has an apex.*

Word Building: the plural is **apexes** or **apices**

aphid (say *ay-fəd*) *noun*
a small insect which sucks the sap from plants

Word Use: it is also called **aphis**
Word Building: the plural is **aphides**

apiary *noun*
a place where beehives are kept

Word Building: the plural is **apiaries** □ **apiarist** *noun*

aplomb (say *ə-plom*) *noun*
the ability to handle difficult or unusual situations: *The boy introduced the guest speaker with aplomb.*

apocalypse (say *ə-pok-ə-lips*) *noun*
the discovery or revealing of some great event, such as the end of the world

Word Building: **apocalyptic** *adjective*

apologise or **apologize** *verb*
to say you are sorry: *She apologised for being late.*

Word Building: **apologetic** *adjective* full of regret **apology** *noun* (**apologies**)

apostle (say *ə-pos-əl*) *noun*
1 one of the followers of Christ chosen by him to spread his teachings **2** someone who strongly supports a new idea: *an apostle of change in education*

Word Building: **apostolic** *adjective* having to do with an apostle, or with the pope
Word History: from a Greek word meaning "someone sent away"

apostrophe (say *ə-pos-trə-fee*) *noun*
1 a sign (') used to show a letter has been left out, as in *They're here.* **2** a sign (') used with *s* to show something is owned, as in *Tom's hat* and *the lions' manes*

appal *verb*
to make very fearful: *The thought of nuclear war appals me.*

Word Building: other forms are **it appalled, it has appalled, it is appalling**
Word History: from a French word meaning "become or make pale"

apparatus (say *ap-ə-rah-təs*) *noun*
a collection of tools or machines used for a particular purpose: *the apparatus used by firemen*

Word Use: a similar word is **equipment**
Word Building: the plural is **apparatus** or **apparatuses**

apparel *noun*
your outer clothing

Word Use: a similar but old-fashioned word is **raiment**

apparent *adjective*
1 able to be seen or understood: *My spelling error was apparent when I checked in the dictionary.* **2** seeming, not necessarily real: *the apparent motion of the sun*

Word Building: **apparently** *adverb*

apparition *noun*
something that appears in an unusual way: *A ghostly apparition in the empty house frightened me.*

Word Use: a similar word is **spectre**

appeal *noun*
1 a call or request for something needed: *The school made an appeal for money for a new library.* **2** the ability to attract or interest: *Sport has an appeal for most people.*
appeal *verb*
3 to make an appeal: *The referee appealed for fair play.*

appear *verb*
1 to come into view: *The sun appeared over the horizon.* **2** to seem or have a certain look: *The boy appears to be sick.*

Word Building: **appearance** *noun*

appease *verb*
1 to make peaceful, quiet or happy: *He appeased the angry customer.* **2** to satisfy: *to appease hunger*

Word Use: a similar word for definition 1 is **placate**
Word Building: **appeasement** *noun*

appendicitis (say *ə-pen-də-suy-təs*) *noun*
a painful inflammation of the appendix

appendix *noun*
1 a section added to the main part of a book to give extra information **2** a small

tube-like piece of flesh joined to the bowel in the right side of the abdomen

Word Building: the plural is **appendixes** or **appendices**

appetising or **appetizing** *adjective*
looking or smelling good to eat: *the appetising smell of roast lamb*

Word Building: **appetiser** *noun* food or drink that makes you feel like eating more

appetite *noun*
the wish for food or drink: *Exercise gives you a good appetite.*

applaud *verb*
to praise or express approval, especially by clapping your hands or calling out: *The audience applauded the actors in the play.*

Word Building: **applause** *noun*

apple *noun*
a crisp round fruit with thin red or green skin

appliance *noun*
a tool which has a motor worked by electricity: *My mother has some useful kitchen appliances.*

applicable (say *ə-plik-ə-bəl*) *adjective*
suitable or able to be used: *a rule only applicable to children*

Word Building: **applicability** *noun* **applicably** *adverb*

applicant *noun*
someone who asks or requests: *an applicant for a job*

Word Use: a similar word is **candidate**

application *noun*
1 a request: *to make an application for a job* **2** something put or laid on: *an application of paint*

apply (rhymes with *fly*) *verb*
1 to ask: *to apply for a job* **2** to put on: *to apply make-up* **3** to put to use: *to apply rules*

Word Building: other forms are **I applied, I have applied, I am applying** □ **applied** *adjective* put to practical use: *applied science* **applier** *noun*

appoint *verb*
to choose for special duties: *The headmaster appointed the school captain.*

Word Use: a similar word is **select**
Word Building: **appointee** *noun*

appointment *noun*
1 the arrangement of a special time: *an appointment to see the dentist*
2 the placing of someone in a special position: *the appointment of a new school captain* **3** the job or special position to which someone is appointed

appraise *verb*
to judge the value of: *The judges appraised the paintings in the competition.*

Word Building: **appraisal** *noun*

appreciable (say *ə-preesh-əb-əl*) *adjective*
1 able to be seen or noticed: *There has been an appreciable increase in the number of people who do not smoke.* **2** fairly large: *We have travelled an appreciable distance.*

Word Use: a similar word for definition 1 is **noticeable**
Word Building: **appreciably** *adverb*

appreciate *verb*
to think highly of: *I appreciate your help.*

Word Use: a similar word is **value**
Word Building: **appreciation** *noun* **appreciative** *adjective*

apprehend *verb*
to take into keeping: *The police apprehended the thieves.*

apprehension *noun*
fear that something might happen: *I went to the headmaster in apprehension.*

Word Building: **apprehensive** *adjective*

apprentice *noun*
someone who is learning a trade

Word Building: **apprenticeship** *noun*

approach *verb*
1 to come near to: *to approach your house* **2** to come to with a request or an idea: *I approached the headmaster for permission to leave.*

approachable *adjective*
friendly and easy to talk to: *My teacher is very approachable.*

appropriate (say *ə-proh-pree-ət*) *adjective*
1 suitable for a particular use: *appropriate clothes for wet weather*

appropriate (say *ə-proh-pree-ayt*) *verb*
2 to take for your own use: *She appropriated Tom's desk.*

Word Building: **appropriately** *adverb* **appropriateness** *noun* **appropriation** *noun*

approval *noun*
agreement or permission: *The teacher needed the headmaster's approval before sending the class home.*

approve *verb*
1 to agree to: *My father approved my plan.* **2 approve of** to consider good or satisfactory: *to approve of your attitude*

approximate *adjective*
nearly right: *Tell me the approximate number of children in the class.*

Word Building: **approximately** *adverb* **approximation** *noun*

apricot *noun*
a small, round, yellow fruit with soft juicy flesh and one large seed inside

April (say *ayp-rəl*) *noun*
the fourth month of the year, with 30 days

Word Use: the abbreviation is **Ap** or **Apr**

apron *noun*
a piece of clothing worn in front to protect the clothes underneath it

Word History: from a Latin word meaning "napkin" or "cloth"

apt *adjective*
1 likely or inclined: *Our baby is apt to cry when mother leaves the room.* **2** suitable or appropriate: *an apt remark* **3** quick to learn: *an apt pupil*

Word Building: **aptly** *adverb* **aptness** *noun*

aptitude *noun*
the ability to learn quickly: *an aptitude for music*

Word Use: a similar word is **talent**

aqualung *noun*
a cylinder of air strapped to the back of a diver, with a tube that takes air to the mouth or nose

aquamarine *noun*
a greenish-blue stone used in jewellery

Word History: from Latin words meaning "sea water"

aquarium (say *ə-kwair-ree-əm*) *noun*
a glass tank in which fish and water plants are kept

Word Building: the plural is **aquariums** or **aquaria**

aquatic (say *ə-kwot-ik*) *adjective*
1 living or growing in water **2** done in or on water: *aquatic sports*

aqueduct (say *ak-wə-dukt*) *noun*
a bridge built for carrying a water pipe or channel across a valley

aquiline *adjective*
curved or hooked like an eagle's beak: *an aquiline nose*

arable *adjective*
suitable for growing crops: *arable land*

Word History: from a Latin word meaning "that can be ploughed"

arbitrary *adjective*
based on your own feelings and ideas rather than on rules or reasons: *an arbitrary decision*

Word Building: **arbitrarily** *adverb* **arbitrariness** *noun*

arbitration *noun*
the settling of a disagreement by someone chosen to do so

Word Building: **arbitrate** *verb* **arbitrator** *noun*

arboreal (say *ah-baw-ree-əl*) *adjective*
having to do with, or living in trees: *Monkeys are arboreal animals.*

arbour or **arbor** *noun*
a shady place formed by trees and shrubs

arc *noun*
a curved line

Word History: from a Latin word meaning a "bow"

arcade *noun*
a covered passage with shops on either side

arch *noun*
1 a curved structure which helps support a bridge or building or forms the top of a doorway

arch *verb*
2 to curve or make into a curved shape: *A horse arches its neck.*

Word Building: the plural of the noun is **arches** □ other verb forms are **it arches, it arched, it has arched, it is arching**

archaeology or **archeology**
(say *ah-kee-ol-ə-jee*) *noun*
the study of the people and customs of ancient times made by digging up and describing the remains of buried cities

Word Building: **archaeologist** *noun* **archaeological** *adjective*

archaic (say *ah-<u>kay</u>-ik*) *adjective*
so old-fashioned that it is not used any more: *an archaic word*

Word Building: **archaism** *noun*

archangel (say *<u>ahk</u>-ayn-jəl*) *noun*
one of the chief angels

archbishop *noun*
a head bishop

archer *noun*
someone who shoots with a bow and arrows

Word Building: **archery** *noun*

archipelago (say *ah-kə-<u>pel</u>-ə-goh*) *noun*
1 a large body of water with many islands **2** a group of islands in a sea

Word Building: the plural is **archipelagos** or **archipelagoes**
Word History: from an Italian word meaning the "chief sea"

architect (say *<u>ah</u>-kə-tekt*) *noun*
someone whose job is to plan new buildings and make sure they are built correctly

Word History: from a Greek word meaning the "chief builder"

architecture *noun*
the art or science of drawing up plans for buildings

Word Building: **architectural** *adjective*

architrave (say *<u>ah</u>-kə-trayv*) *noun*
the frame around a doorway or window

archives (say *<u>ah</u>-kuyvz*) *plural noun*
a collection of historical documents about a family, business or country: *The archives are kept in the library.*

Word Building: **archival** *adjective* **archivist** *noun*

arctic *adjective*
1 having to do with the area near the North Pole **2** very cold
arctic *noun*
3 the Arctic the area near the North Pole

Word History: from a Greek word meaning "of the bear" (constellation of stars) or "northern"

ardent *adjective*
enthusiastic or full of feeling: *an ardent admirer of poetry | ardent promises of lasting love*

Word Building: **ardency** *noun* **ardently** *adverb*

ardour or **ardor** (rhymes with *harder*) *noun*
1 a very strong feeling: *the ardour of love for your country* **2** eagerness or enthusiasm: *Rain does not dampen his ardour for bushwalking.*

arduous *adjective*
needing a lot of hard work: *Climbing mountains is an arduous sport.*

Word Use: a similar word is **strenuous**

area *noun*
1 a particular part: *a suburban area | an area of the body* **2** the size of a flat or curved surface: *The area of this hall is 100 square metres.*

arena *noun*
an enclosed space for sports events

Word History: from a Latin word meaning "sand" or "sandy place"

arguable *adjective*
1 able to be proved by argument: *He put forward an arguable case for having classroom monitors.* **2** doubtful

Word Building: **arguably** *adverb*

argue *verb*
to quarrel or disagree: *James argued with Lisa about which film to see.*

Word Building: other forms are **I argued, I have argued, I am arguing**

argument *noun*
1 a quarrel or disagreement **2** a reason: *a good argument for doing exercises*

argumentative *adjective*
liking to argue or quarrelsome: *an argumentative person*

aria (say *<u>ah</u>-ree-ə*) *noun*
a song sung by one person in an opera

arid *adjective*
dry and hot: *an arid desert*

Word Building: **aridity** *noun*

arise *verb*
1 to appear or come into being: *The question of new school colours may arise.*
2 to rise or move upwards: *He told them to arise and follow him.*

Word Building: other forms are **I arose, I have arisen, I am arising**

aristocracy (say *a-rə-<u>stok</u>-rə-see*) *noun*
the people of highest rank

Word Use: a similar word is **nobility**

aristocrat (say *a-rə-stə-krat*) *noun*
someone who belongs to the nobility of a country, such as a duke or an earl

Word Building: **aristocratic** *adjective* **aristocratically** *adverb*

arithmetic *noun*
calculation with numbers

Word Building: **arithmetical** *adjective* **arithmetician** *noun*

ark *noun*
the large covered boat built by Noah to escape from the Flood

arm[1] *noun*
1 the part of your body from shoulder to hand **2** the part of a chair on which your arm rests

arm[2] *verb*
to supply weapons to

Word Building: **armed** *adjective: the armed forces*

armada (say *ah-mah-də*) *noun*
a large number of warships

armadillo (say *ah-mə-dil-oh*) *noun*
a South American burrowing animal with a covering of bony plates

Word Building: the plural is **armadillos**

armament *noun*
the weapons on an aeroplane or warship

armistice (say *ahm-ə-stəs*) *noun*
an agreement between countries at war to stop fighting and talk about peace

Word Use: a similar word is **truce**

armour or **armor** *noun*
1 metal or leather covering that knights used to wear when fighting **2** the protective plates on warships and planes

Word Building: **armoured** *adjective: an armoured car*

armoury or **armory** *noun*
a place for storing weapons

Word Building: the plural is **armouries**

armpit *noun*
the hollow part under your arm at the shoulder

arms *plural noun*
weapons: *The soldiers were given arms to fight with.*

army *noun*
1 the part of a country's armed forces which is trained to fight on land **2** a large number: *An army of workers cleaned up after the fire.*

Word Building: the plural is **armies**

aroma *noun*
a pleasant smell: *the aroma of coffee*

Word Use: a similar word is **fragrance,** used mostly of flowers and perfumes
Word Building: **aromatic** *adjective*
Word History: from a Greek word meaning "spice" or "sweet herb"

arouse *verb*
1 to bring into being: *to arouse doubts*
2 to wake from sleep

Word Building: **arousal** *noun*

arpeggio (say *ah-pej-ee-oh*) *noun*
a musical chord played by sounding its notes one after the other

Word Building: the plural is **arpeggios**
Word History: from an Italian word meaning "play on the harp"

arrange *verb*
1 to put in order: *to arrange books on a shelf* **2** to plan: *to arrange a party*

Word Use: a similar word is **organise**
Word Building: **arrangement** *noun*

array *verb*
1 to put into position: *The soldiers were arrayed for battle.*
array *noun*
2 a group of things on show: *an excellent array of children's art*

arrest *verb*
1 to take prisoner: *The policeman arrested the thief.* **2** to stop: *The sandbags arrested the flood waters.*
arrest *noun*
3 capture by police: *under arrest*

arrive *verb*
1 to reach the end of a journey
2 to come: *The moment has arrived.*

Word Building: **arrival** *noun*
Word History: from a Latin word meaning "come to shore"

arrogant (say *a-rə-gənt*) *adjective*
showing that you think you are very important

Word Use: a similar word is **haughty**
Word Building: **arrogance** *noun* **arrogantly** *adverb*

arrow *noun*
1 a thin, pointed piece of wood shot from a bow **2** a sign used to point the way to go

arrowroot *noun*
a white floury substance used in cooking

arsenal *noun*
a store of weapons and ammunition

arsenic *noun*
a poisonous chemical substance

arson *noun*
the deliberate burning of a building or other valuable property

Word Building: **arsonist** *noun*

art *noun*
1 the production and expression of what is beautiful, especially by painting, drawing or sculpture **2** the beautiful things people make: *Our city has a building where works of art are kept.* **3** a skill: *There is an art in making good furniture.*

artefact (say *ah-tə-fakt*) *noun*
a useful thing made by someone

Word Use: another spelling is **artifact**

artery *noun*
a blood vessel which takes blood from the heart to other parts of the body

Word Building: the plural is **arteries** □ **arterial** *adjective*

artesian bore (say *ah-tee-zhən*) *noun*
a well sunk through a layer of rock holding water, in which pressure keeps the water rising to the surface and pumping is not needed

Word Use: another name is **artesian well**

arthritis (say *ah-thruy-təs*) *noun*
a disease that causes swelling and pain in the joints of the body

Word Building: **arthritic** *adjective*

artichoke *noun*
a thick round flower which grows on a thistle-like plant and is used as a vegetable

article *noun*
1 a particular thing: *an article of clothing*
2 a piece of writing about a particular subject in a newspaper or magazine
3 a word, such as "a", "an" and "the", which comes before a noun to show that it relates to one particular person or thing

Word Use: a similar word for definitions 1 and 2 is **item**

articulate (say *ah-tik-yə-layt*) *verb*
1 to speak clearly: *He articulated every word so that everyone could hear.*

articulate (say *ah-tik-yə-lət*) *adjective*
2 able to put your ideas clearly into words

Word Use: a similar word for definition 2 is **fluent**
Word Building: **articulately** *adverb* **articulation** *noun*

articulated *adjective*
having joints or divisions: *A semi-trailer is an articulated truck.*

artificial *adjective*
made by human beings

Word Use: the opposite of this is **natural**
Word Building: **artificiality** *noun* **artificially** *adverb*

artillery *noun*
1 large guns on wheels **2** the part of an army that uses these guns

artisan *noun*
a skilled worker who makes things

artist *noun*
1 someone who creates beautiful things, such as a painter or sculptor
2 a performer or entertainer

Word Building: **artistic** *noun* able to create beautiful things **artistically** *adverb* **artistry** *noun*

arvo *noun*
a short form of **afternoon**

Word Use: this word is more suited to everyday language

asbestos *noun*
a grey substance which is mined, and was once used to make fireproof materials

ascend *verb*
to climb or go upwards: *I ascended the ladder.* | *Smoke ascended from the chimney.*

Word Use: the opposite is **descend**
Word Building: **ascension** *noun* an upward movement. Christ's rising from earth to heaven is called the **Ascension**. **ascent** *noun*

ascertain (say *as-ə-tayn*) *verb*
to find out or determine: *to ascertain the truth*

Word Building: **ascertainable** *adjective* **ascertainment** *noun*

ascetic (say *ə-set-ik*) *noun*
someone who, for religious reasons, lives simply without many of the usual comforts of life

Word Building: **ascetically** *adverb* **asceticism** *noun*
Word History: from a Greek word meaning "monk" or "hermit"

ash[1] *noun*
1 the powder left after something has been burnt: *cigarette ash | The ashes are in the fireplace.* **2 ashes** what is left after a human body has been cremated

Word Building: **ashy** *adjective* (**ashier, ashiest**)

ash[2] *noun*
a tree from which we get a valuable hard timber

ashamed *adjective*
1 feeling shame or sorrow: *After I hit her I felt ashamed.* **2** unwilling because you're afraid of being laughed at: *ashamed to put your hand up*

Word Building: **ashamedly** *adverb*

aside *adverb*
1 on or to one side: *to turn aside*
aside *noun*
2 words spoken quietly so that only some people present can hear: *"Curses! Foiled again", said the villain in an aside to the audience.*

ask *verb*
1 to enquire: *I will ask the way.* **2** to put a question to: *I will ask him.* **3** to invite: *I will ask her to the party.*

askance (say ə-skans) *adverb*
showing distrust: *He looked askance at my offer.*

askew (rhymes with *few*) *adverb*
out of position: *He knocked my hat askew.*

Word Use: a similar word is **awry**

asleep *adverb*
1 in or into a state of sleep: *I fell asleep.*
asleep *adjective*
2 sleeping: *He is asleep.* **3** numb: *My foot is asleep.*

asp *noun*
a small venomous snake found in Egypt

asparagus *noun*
a plant with long green shoots, used as a vegetable

aspect *noun*
1 the way a thing appears: *the burnt aspect of the land after the bushfire | to think about every aspect of a problem* **2** the direction a building faces: *a northern aspect*

asperity *noun*
roughness or harshness of manner: *He looked at me with some asperity.*

aspersion *noun*
a harmful remark: *He cast aspersions on my character.*

asphalt (say *ash-felt*) *noun*
a black sticky substance like tar, mixed with crushed rock and used for making roads

aspic *noun*
a jelly used to set fish, meat or vegetables in a mould

aspire *verb*
to aim eagerly: *to aspire to be school captain*

Word Building: **aspirant** *noun* **aspiration** *noun*

aspirin *noun*
a drug used to stop pain

ass *noun*
a long-eared animal in the same family as the horse

Word Use: another word for this animal is **donkey**
Word Building: the plural is **asses**

assassin (say ə-sas-ən) *noun*
someone who murders a well-known person such as a politician

Word Building: **assassinate** *verb* **assassination** *noun*

assault *noun*
an attack: *to make an assault on the fort*

Word Building: **assault** *verb*

assemble *verb*
1 to bring or put together: *to assemble a machine* **2** to come together: *We assembled in the playground.*

assembly *noun*
1 a number of people gathered together for a special purpose **2** the putting together of something that is in parts: *a factory for the assembly of motor cars*

Word Building: the plural is **assemblies**

assent *verb*
to agree: *to assent to her suggestion*

Word Building: **assent** *noun*

assert *verb*
to state or declare strongly: *to assert your innocence*

Word Building: **assertion** *noun* a strong positive statement **assertiveness** *noun* the quality of expressing yourself strongly **assertive** *adjective*

assess *verb*
to work out the value of: *to assess your work*

Word Building: **assessment** *noun* **assessor** *noun*

asset *noun*
1 something you own: *A house is a valuable asset.* **2** anything of value: *Good health is an asset.*

assignment *noun*
a particular task: *Our assignment was to write a composition.*

Word Building: **assign** *verb*

assimilate *verb*
to take in and make part of yourself: *I assimilated the information.*

Word Building: **assimilation** *noun*

assist *verb*
to help: *She assisted me with my homework.*

Word Building: **assistant** *noun* **assistance** *noun*

associate (say *ə-soh-see-ayt*) *verb*
1 to connect in your mind: *I associate the beach with holidays.* **2** to spend time with or to work with: *I associate with people who enjoy the same hobbies.*

associate (say *ə-soh-see-ət*) *noun*
3 a partner or someone who shares your interests: *She is my associate in business.*

Word Use: a similar word for definition 3 is **colleague**

association *noun*
1 a group of people interested in the same thing: *an association of stamp collectors*
2 the connection of ideas in your mind: *the association of sleep with bed*

assonance *noun*
the repetition of the same vowel sound in words close together, as in "fly high"

Word Building: **assonant** *adjective*

assortment *noun*
a collection of things of various kinds: *an assortment of lollies*

Word Building: **assorted** *adjective*

assume *verb*
1 to believe without proof: *Don't assume that he'll come – ask him!* **2** to agree to carry out: *to assume the duties of school captain*

Word Building: **assumption** *noun*

assurance *noun*
1 a promise or guarantee: *to give an assurance of continuing support*
2 confidence or faith in your own ability: *to do something with assurance*

assure *verb*
1 to tell with certainty: *He assured us he would come.* **2** to make sure or certain: *Hard work assures success.*

asterisk (say *as-tə-risk*) *noun*
a star shape (*) used in printing or writing to show something has been written at the bottom of a page

Word History: from a Greek word meaning a "star"

astern *adverb*
behind or at the back of

Word Use: this word is only used of ships or boats

asteroid *noun*
one of the hundreds of tiny planets lying between Mars and Jupiter

Word History: from a Greek word meaning "like a star"

asthma (say *as-mə*) *noun*
a breathing disorder which causes wheezing, coughing and a feeling of tightness in the chest

Word Building: **asthmatic** *noun* **asthmatic** *adjective*

astonish *verb*
to amaze or surprise greatly

Word Building: **astonishment** *noun* **astonishing** *adjective*

astray *adverb*
away from the proper path: *to go astray*

astride *adverb*
with the legs on either side of: *He stood astride the low fence.*

astringent (say *ə-strin-jənt*) *noun*
1 a liquid put on the skin to tighten it and cause it to tingle

astringent *adjective*
2 tightening and refreshing the skin: *an astringent after-shave lotion* **3** harsh or bitter: *astringent remarks about their behaviour*

Word Building: **astringency** *noun*

astrology *noun*
the study of the possible effects of the stars and planets on our lives

Word Use: don't confuse it with **astronomy**
Word Building: **astrologer** *noun* **astrological** *adjective*

astronaut *noun*
someone specially trained to travel in a spaceship

Word Building: **astronautics** *noun* the science of flight in space

astronomical *adjective*
1 having to do with astronomy **2** very large: *The patient got an astronomical bill from the hospital.*

astronomy *noun*
the scientific study of the sun, moon, stars and planets

Word Use: don't confuse it with **astrology**
Word Building: **astronomer** *noun*

astute *adjective*
having clear and quick understanding: *an astute business executive*

Word Use: a similar word is **shrewd,** which refers especially to money and practical matters
Word Building: **astuteness** *noun*

asunder *adverb*
in or into pieces: *to tear asunder*

Word Use: the word is a bit old-fashioned now and is used mostly in books

asylum (say *ə-suy-ləm*) *noun*
1 protection or safety: *political asylum in another country* **2** a shelter that offers safety or care

Word Use: a similar word is **sanctuary**

atheist (say *ay-thee-əst*) *noun*
someone who believes that there is no God

Word Use: you should compare this word with **agnostic**
Word Building: **atheism** *noun* **atheistic** *adjective*

athlete (say *ath-leet*) *noun*
someone who trains in sports such as running, jumping, or throwing

Word Building: **athletic** *adjective* **athletics** *noun*

atlas *noun*
a book of maps

atmosphere *noun*
1 the air that surrounds the earth
2 a feeling or mood: *an unpleasant atmosphere in the room after a quarrel*

Word Building: **atmospheric** *adjective*

atoll *noun*
a coral island with a salt water lake in the middle

atom *noun*
the smallest part that an element can be divided into and still keep its special qualities or take part in a chemical reaction

Word History: from a Greek word meaning "not able to be divided"

atomic *adjective*
1 having to do with atoms **2** driven by atomic energy: *an atomic submarine*
3 using atomic weapons: *atomic warfare*

atomic bomb *noun*
a bomb which explodes with great force because of the energy released from the splitting of atoms

atomic energy *noun*
the energy or power which is obtained by causing changes within atoms

atonal (say *ay-tohn-əl*) *adjective*
not in any musical key: *The composer wrote a piece of atonal music for the school orchestra.*

atone *verb*
to make up or show you are sorry: *I atoned for my laziness by helping with the housework.*

Word Building: **atonement** *noun*

atrocious (say *ə-troh-shəs*) *adjective*
1 terribly wicked or cruel: *an atrocious crime* **2** very bad or lacking in taste: *atrocious taste in clothes*

Word Building: **atrociousness** *noun*

atrocity (say *ə-tros-ə-tee*) *noun*
a terribly wicked or cruel act

Word Building: the plural is **atrocities**

atrophy (say *at-rə-fee*) *verb*
to lose strength or size: *Muscles atrophy if they aren't used.*

Word Building: other forms are **it atrophied, it has atrophied, it is atrophying**

attach *verb*
1 to fasten or join: *Attach the label to the suitcase.* **2 be attached to** to like or love: *She is very attached to her old suitcase.*

attack *verb*
1 to begin to use force or weapons: *The army attacked at dawn.* **2** to use force or weapons against: *to attack the enemy*

3 to go to work on strongly: *to attack a difficult task*

Word Building: **attack** *noun*

attain *verb*
to reach or achieve by trying hard: *He attained a high pass in English.*

Word Building: **attainable** *adjective* **attainment** *noun*

attempt *verb*
1 to try: *to attempt to swim* **2** to try to do: *to attempt a course of study*
attempt *noun*
3 an effort or try: *I said I would make an attempt to climb the mountain.*

attend *verb*
1 to be present at **2** to look after: *The nurse attended the patient.* **3** to pay attention or take notice: *to attend to your teacher*

Word Building: **attendance** *noun*

attendant *noun*
someone who helps or looks after someone else: *a cloakroom attendant*

attention *noun*
1 the act of fixing your mind on something: *This job needs all your attention.* **2** a position in which you stand straight and still: *The soldiers stood at attention.*

Word Building: **attentive** *adjective* observant or paying attention

attic *noun*
a room or a space directly under the roof of a building: *We store junk in the attic.*

attire *verb*
to dress, particularly for a special occasion: *to attire yourself in your best clothes*

Word Building: **attire** *noun*

attitude *noun*
1 a way of holding your body: *He stood in a threatening attitude.* **2** the way you think or behave: *Ben has a helpful attitude to small children.*

attorney (say *ə-ter-nee*) *noun*
a person, usually a solicitor, appointed by someone to do business for them

Word Building: the plural is **attorneys**

attract *verb*
to pull or draw: *A magnet attracts steel pins. / His smile attracts people.*

Word Building: **attraction** *noun*

attractive *adjective*
1 pleasing: *an attractive idea* **2** pleasing to look at: *an attractive man*

attribute (say *ə-trib-yooht*) *verb*
1 to think of as belonging or due: *The crop failure may be attributed to the drought.*
attribute (say *at-rə-byooht*) *noun*
2 something thought of as belonging: *Wisdom is one of her attributes.*

Word Building: **attribution** *noun* **attributive** *adjective*

atypical (say *ay-tip-ik-əl*) *adjective*
not typical, or different from usual: *Anna's grumpiness is atypical of her usual pleasant nature.*

auburn *adjective*
reddish-brown: *auburn hair*

auction *noun*
1 a public sale at which things are sold to the person who offers the most money
auction *verb*
2 to sell by auction: *They decided to auction the cottage.*

Word Building: **auctioneer** *noun* someone whose job is to sell things by auction

audacious *adjective*
bold or daring: *an audacious reply to the teacher / an audacious attempt on Mount Everest*

Word Building: **audacity** *noun*

audible *adjective*
able to be heard: *His voice was barely audible over the noise of the stereo.*

Word Building: **audibility** *noun*

audience *noun*
1 a group of people listening or watching **2** an interview with someone important: *an audience with the Queen*

audit *noun*
an inspection and checking of business accounts, usually once a year

Word Building: **audit** *verb* **auditor** *noun*

audition *noun*
1 a test given to see how suitable an actor or performer is for a particular job: *Elsa is having an audition for a part in the new play.*
audition *verb*
2 to test by giving an audition to: *The bandmaster auditioned two new trumpet players.* **3** to give a trial performance: *They auditioned for the choir.*

Word Use: an audition for a part in a film is called a **film test**
Word History: from a Latin word meaning "a hearing"

auditorium *noun*
a hall or other large space for meetings or concerts

auditory *adjective*
having to do with hearing or the ears: *an auditory signal*

augment *verb*
to make larger: *He works at night to augment his income.*

Word Building: **augmentation** *noun*

august (say *aw-gust*) *adjective*
causing you to feel awe and respect: *the august atmosphere of Canberra's War Memorial*

August (say *aw-gəst*) *noun*
the eighth month of the year, with 31 days

Word Use: the abbreviation is **Aug**
Word History: named after the first Roman emperor, *Augustus* Caesar

aunt *noun*
1 the sister of your father or mother
2 your uncle's wife

aura *noun*
a special character or atmosphere: *The garden has an aura of peace.*

aural *adjective*
having to do with hearing or listening: *The first part of the music exam was an aural test.*

aurora (say *ə-raw-rə*) *noun*
a natural display of moving lights in the sky

auspicious *adjective*
favourable or showing signs of success: *an auspicious occasion*

Aussie (say *oz-ee*) *noun*
an Australian

Word Use: this word is more suited to everyday language
Word Building: **Aussie** *adjective*

austere (say *ost-ear*) *adjective*
1 severely simple: *The nuns live in austere surroundings.* **2** stern or grim: *The doctor had an austere manner.*

Word Building: **austerity** *noun*

authentic *adjective*
genuine or real: *an authentic diamond*

Word Building: **authenticate** *verb* to prove to be genuine **authenticity** *noun*

author *noun*
1 someone who writes a book, article or poem **2** the creator of anything: *Wellington was the author of Napoleon's downfall.*

Word Building: **authorship** *noun*

authorise or **authorize** *verb*
1 to give legal power to: *He authorised the deputy to decide the question.* **2** to approve officially: *The grant for the new library has been authorised.*

Word Building: **authorisation** *noun*

authoritarian *adjective*
acting without considering people's freedom: *an authoritarian government*

Word Building: **authoritarianism** *noun*

authority *noun*
1 the right to decide or judge: *The courts have authority over people who come before them.* **2** a right that gives power: *The police have authority to control traffic.*
3 a reliable source of information: *She is an authority on gardening.*

Word Building: the plural is **authorities** □ **authoritative** *adjective* having or giving authority

autistic *adjective*
suffering from an illness of the mind in which you live in your own imagination and are not very aware of other people

Word Building: **autism** *noun*

auto- *prefix*
a word part meaning self: *autobiography*

Word History: this prefix comes from Greek

autobiography *noun*
your own life story written by yourself

Word Building: the plural is **autobiographies** □ **autobiographical** *adjective*

autocracy (say *aw-tok-rə-see*) *noun*
1 unlimited rule by one person over others **2** a country ruled by someone with unlimited power

Word Building: the plural is **autocracies** □ **autocrat** *noun* **autocratic** *adjective*

autograph *noun*
someone's own handwriting, especially their signature

Word Building: **autograph** *verb*

automatic *adjective*
1 working or going by itself: *an automatic washing machine* **2** like a machine: *Their reaction to the bell was automatic.*
automatic *noun*
3 a car with a gear change that works by itself

Word Building: **automatically** *adverb*

automation (say *aw-tə-may-shən*) *noun*
the use of machines instead of people to do jobs in factories

automaton (say *aw-tom-ə-tən*) *noun*
a robot or someone who acts like a robot

Word Building: the plural is **automata**

automobile *noun*
an American word for **car**

autonomous (say *aw-ton-ə-məs*) *adjective*
self-governing: *Papua New Guinea is now an autonomous nation.*

Word Use: a similar word is **independent**

autopsy *noun*
the examination of a dead body to discover the cause of death

Word Use: it can also be called a **post-mortem**
Word Building: the plural is **autopsies**
Word History: from a Greek word meaning "seeing with your own eyes"

autumn *noun*
the season of the year following summer, when the leaves change colour and fall from some trees

Word Building: **autumnal** *adjective*

auxiliary *adjective*
1 aiding or helping: *an auxiliary verb*
2 kept in case it is needed or in reserve: *an auxiliary engine*

Word Building: **auxiliary** *noun* (**auxiliaries**)

available *adjective*
ready, or able to be used: *There are three tennis courts available. / Peter is available to help.*

Word Building: **availability** *noun*

avalanche *noun*
a large mass of ice and snow sliding or falling suddenly down a mountain slope

avarice (say *av-ə-rəs*) *noun*
greediness for money

Word Building: **avaricious** *adjective*

avenge *verb*
to get revenge for: *"I will avenge my father's murder!" cried the knight as he drew his sword.*

Word Building: **avenger** *noun*

avenue *noun*
a street or road, especially one lined with trees

average *noun*
1 the result of dividing the sum of two or more quantities by the number of quantities: *The average of 1, 2 and 3 is 2.*
2 an ordinary amount, kind, quality or rate: *Her ability is well above the average.*
average *verb*
3 to do or have an average: *to average twelve kilometres a week on your bike / to average four meals a day*

averse *adjective*
opposed or not willing: *averse to work*

aversion *noun*
1 a strong dislike: *I have an aversion to spinach.* **2** a person or thing disliked: *Smoking is my pet aversion.*

avert *verb*
1 to turn away: *She averted her eyes.*
2 to prevent: *to avert danger*

aviary *noun*
a large cage or enclosure where birds are kept

Word Building: the plural is **aviaries**
Word History: from the Latin word for "bird"

aviation *noun*
the science or act of flying in a plane: *Amy Johnson was a pioneer of aviation.*

Word Building: **aviator** *noun* pilot

avid *adjective*
keen or eager: *an avid swimmer*

Word Building: **avidity** *noun* **avidly** *adverb*

avocado *noun*
a green pear-shaped fruit used in salads

Word Building: the plural is **avocados**

avoid *verb*
to keep away from: *to avoid danger / to avoid a boring film*

Word Building: **avoidable** *adjective* **avoidance** *noun*
Word History: from a French word meaning "empty out"

await *verb*
1 to wait for: *I await your commands.*
2 to be ready for: *Supper awaits you.*

awake *verb*
1 to wake up: *When I awoke the sun was shining.* **2** to excite or stir up: *to awake his interest*

Word Building: other forms are **I awoke, I have awoken, I am awaking**

awaken *verb*
to wake up or alert: *A kookaburra awakened the campers. / Frank awakened them to their danger.*

awakening *noun*
1 a waking up from sleep **2** a renewing of interest: *an awakening among the people in the cause of peace*

award *verb*
1 to give for merit or achievement: *to award prizes*
award *noun*
2 something won by merit or achievement: *an award for bravery* **3** a ruling about wages and conditions of work given by an industrial court: *the metal industry award*

aware *adjective*
having a feeling or knowledge: *He was aware of a stealthy step behind him.*

Word Building: **awareness** *noun*

awe *noun*
a feeling of great respect mixed with fear: *The convicts were in awe of the overseer's whip.*

Word Building: **awe** *verb*

awesome *adjective*
filling you with feelings of respect and fear: *an awesome height above the valley*

awful *adjective*
very bad or unpleasant: *an awful mess*

Word Use: this word used to mean the same as **awesome** but it was overused and lost much of its force □ compare **fantastic**

awkward *adjective*
1 clumsy: *an awkward girl who is always bumping into things* **2** inconvenient: *an awkward room to furnish / an awkward time*

Word Building: **awkwardness** *noun*

awning *noun*
a covering to give shelter from the weather: *a shop awning*

awry (rhymes with *fly*) *adverb*
1 turned to one side: *to wear your hat awry / to look awry* **2** wrong or amiss: *Our plans went awry.*

Word Use: sometimes for definition 1 you can use the word **askew**

axe *noun*
1 a tool with a blade for chopping
2 have an axe to grind to have private or selfish reasons for doing things
3 the axe a a cutting down or reduction of spending **b** the sack or dismissal from a job

Word Use: definition 3 is more suited to everyday language
Word Building: **axe** *verb*

axiom *noun*
something that is obviously true

Word Building: **axiomatic** *adjective*

axis *noun*
1 an imaginary line which something revolves around: *The earth rotates on its axis once every 24 hours.* **2** a central line that divides something exactly in half: *an axis of symmetry*

Word Building: the plural is **axes** (say *ak-seez*)

axle *noun*
the rod in the middle of a wheel on which the wheel turns

axolotl (say *aks-ə-lot-l*) *noun*
an amphibian with a long tail and short legs, found in Mexican lakes: *We kept our axolotl in the tank with our goldfish.*

ayatollah (say *uy-ə-tol-ə*) *noun*
the name given to a Muslim religious leader in Iran

azalea (say *ə-zayl-yə*) *noun*
a shrub with attractive flowers that bloom in spring

azure (say *ay-zhə*) *adjective*
pale blue or sky-blue

babble *verb*
to speak quickly and unclearly: *The shy boy babbled his answer.*

Word Building: **babble** *noun* **babbler** *noun*

baboon *noun*
a large monkey with a mouth like a dog and a short tail, found in Africa and Arabia

Word History: from a French word meaning a "stupid person"

baby *noun*
1 a very young child or animal
baby *adjective*
2 like or suitable for a baby: *a baby face* | *baby clothes*
baby *verb*
3 to treat like a baby: *to baby the child*

Word Building: the plural form of the noun is **babies** □ other verb forms are **I babied, I have babied, I am babying** □ **babyish** *adjective*

bachelor *noun*
a man who isn't married

back *noun*
1 the part of something that is farthest from the front: *the back of the room* **2** the rear part of your body, from your neck to the bottom of your spine **3** a defending player in football and other games
back *verb*
4 to reverse: *Dad backed the car into the garage.* **5** to support: *They backed their local team.* **6** to bet on: *Back a horse in the next race.*
back *adverb*
7 at or to the rear: to step back **8** in reply or in return: *to write back* | *to pay back* **9** in or towards an earlier time or place: *to go back to your home*

Word Building: **backer** *noun* someone who gives money to support a business, film, play, and so on **back** *adjective*

backbone *noun*
1 the spine of your body or the similar set of bones in some animals **2** courage to stand up for what you believe

backfire *verb*
1 to make a loud explosive sound because petrol was burnt too early: *The car's engine backfired.* **2** to have a very different effect from what you intended: *Our plan backfired.*

Word Building: **backfire** *noun*

backgammon *noun*
a board game in which two people take turns to move pieces after throwing dice

background *noun*
1 the back part of a view or scene: *in the background of the picture* **2** the events and conditions that lead up to and explain something: *the background of today's disaster* **3** your social position, experience and education **4 in the background** out of sight, or not noticed

backing *noun*
1 support of any kind, such as a piece of material placed behind another to strengthen it or money made available to help a project **2** musical background for a singer

backlog *noun*
a piling up of things that need to be done or looked at: *There is a backlog of letters to be answered.*

backstroke *noun*
a stroke in swimming in which you lie on your back and move your arms backwards in turn

backup *noun*
1 support or help: *We will give your plan a lot of backup.* **2** something kept in reserve, to be used when it is needed: *We will keep the extra food as a backup in case we run out.* **3** a second copy of a computer file, disk, or tape, to be used if the original becomes damaged, lost, or destroyed

Word Use: another spelling is **back-up**
Word Building: **back up** *verb* to make a copy as a backup **backup** *adjective*

backward *adjective*
1 turned or moving towards the back: *a backward look* / *a backward step* **2** behind the others in growth, or ability to learn: *a backward reader*

Word Building: **backward** *adverb* **backwards** *adjective* **backwards** *adverb*

backwater *noun*
1 a pool of still, stale water that is joined to a river but not reached by its current **2** a place where nothing seems to happen

backyard *noun*
the enclosed area behind a house

Word Building: **backyard** *adjective*

bacon *noun*
the salted meat from the back and sides of a pig

bacteria *plural noun*
microscopic living bodies that can cause disease and decay

Word Building: **bacterial** *adjective*
Word History: from a Greek word meaning "a little stick"

bad *adjective*
1 not good in behaviour **2** serious or severe: *a bad accident* / *a bad mistake* **3** sick or unhealthy: *I was sick but I'm not bad now.* **4** rotten or decayed: *bad meat*

Word Building: **worse** and **worst** describe greater degrees of badness □ **badness** *noun* **badly** *adverb*

badge *noun*
a disc or label that you wear on your clothes to show people what you're a member or supporter of

badger *noun*
1 a burrowing mammal found in Europe and America, which has a white mark on its head

badger *verb*
2 to pester or annoy: *He badgered his parents with questions.*

badminton *noun*
a game in which two players hit a feathered shuttlecock over a high net

Word History: named after Badminton, a village in England, where the game was first played

baffle *verb*
to confuse or puzzle: *The unusual question baffled me.*

Word Building: **bafflement** *noun* **baffling** *adjective* **bafflingly** *adverb*

bag *noun*
1 a container for holding or carrying things: *a bag of cement* / *a shopping bag* **2 bags** plenty or a lot: *She's got bags of money.*

Word Use: definition 2 is more suited to everyday language
Word Building: **bag** *verb* (**bagged, bagging**)

bagel (say <u>bay</u>-gəl) *noun*
a small hard roll, in the shape of a ring and made of dough

Word History: this word comes from Yiddish

baggage *noun*
the suitcases and boxes which belong to a traveller: *I left my baggage with a porter.*

Word Use: a similar word is **luggage**

bagpipes *plural noun*
a musical instrument you play by blowing into a bag with pipes attached

bail[1] *noun*
money which must be paid so that someone who is charged with a crime can go free until they are tried in court

Word Building: **bail** *verb*

bail[2] *noun*
one of the two small pieces of wood that rest on top of cricket stumps

bail[3] *verb*
another spelling for **bale**[2]

bait *noun*
1 food used on a hook, or in a trap, to catch fish or animals **2** food with poison in it, used to kill or drug animals

bait *verb*
3 to use bait **4** to tease in order to upset or annoy

bake *verb*
1 to cook in an oven **2** to make hard by heating: *to bake pots in a kiln*

baker *noun*
someone whose job is to bake bread and cakes

Word Building: **bakery** *noun* the place where bread and cakes are baked

baker's dozen *noun*
thirteen

baklava (say *bə-klah-və, bak-lə-və*) *noun*
a cake made from thin pastry, nuts and honey, first made in Greece, Turkey, and so on

balaclava (say *bal-ə-klah-və*) *noun*
a knitted cap that pulls down over your head and under your chin: *Your grey balaclava looks like a helmet.*

Word History: named after Balaclava, a seaport on the Black Sea, where soldiers first wore these caps in the Crimean War which lasted from 1853 to 1856

balance *verb*
1 to make or keep steady: *I can't balance on my new skates. | He balanced a stick on his nose.* **2** to be equal, especially in weight: *Do these scales balance?*
balance *noun*
3 steadiness: *balance of judgment | I can't keep my balance.* **4** the difference between the total of the money paid into, and the money taken out of, an account **5** an instrument for weighing, often a swaying bar with containers hanging at the ends

Word Use: a similar word for definition 5 is **scales**

balcony *noun*
1 an upstairs veranda that often has a roof and railings **2** the highest floor of seats in a theatre

Word Building: the plural is **balconies**

bald *adjective*
1 without hair: *a bald head | a bald man*
2 plain and to the point: *a bald statement*

Word Building: **balding** *adjective* **baldness** *noun*

bale[1] *noun*
a large amount of goods to be stored or transported, such as wool, hay or straw, tied up tightly with cords or wire

bale[2] *verb*
1 to empty a boat with a bucket or can: *They baled furiously after each wave hit them.* **2 bale out** to jump from a plane with a parachute: *When the engine failed he baled out.*

Word Use: another spelling is **bail**

baleful *adjective*
full of hate: *The bull watched him with a baleful expression before charging.*

Word Building: **balefully** *adverb* **balefulness** *noun*

ball[1] *noun*
1 a round or egg-shaped thing which you can bounce, or which you can kick, catch or hit in games **2** something which is shaped like a ball: *a ball of string | a ball of wool*

ball[2] *noun*
a very grand or formal dance: *My parents wore their best evening clothes to the ball.*

ballad *noun*
a simple poem with short verses, which tells a story and is often turned into a song

ballast *noun*
heavy material carried by a ship to keep it steady, or by a balloon to control its height

ballerina (say *bal-ə-ree-nə*) *noun*
a girl or woman ballet-dancer

ballet (say *bal-ay*) *noun*
a formal sort of dancing, performed by a group, who act out a story, using graceful and controlled movements

Word History: from an Italian word meaning a "little ball"

ballistics *noun*
the study of the movement of missiles, bullets, or other objects fired from a gun

Word Building: **ballistic** *adjective*

balloon *noun*
1 a small rubber bag which is filled with air or gas and used as a toy **2** a large bag filled with hot air or other light gas, which may have a basket for passengers and can rise and float in the air
balloon *verb*
3 to swell out: *The sail ballooned in the wind.*

Word Building: **balloonist** *noun* someone who travels by balloon
Word History: from an Italian word meaning "ball"

ballot *noun*
1 a ticket or paper you must fill in to record your vote: *They counted our ballots to see who had won the election.* **2** a secret way of voting

Word Use: another word for definition 2 is **secret ballot**
Word Building: **ballot** *verb* (**balloted, balloting**)

ballpoint pen *noun*
a pen whose point is a small ball which rolls around

Word Use: another name is **ballpoint**

balm (rhymes with *farm*) *noun*
1 a sweet-smelling ointment or oil which heals or makes something less painful
2 something soothing: *The good news was balm to the anxious parents.*

balmy *adjective*
fine or pleasant: *In the balmy spring weather they were often outdoors.*

Word Building: other forms are **balmier, balmiest**

balsa (say *bawl-sə*) *noun*
the very light wood of the balsa tree, often used to make rafts

balsam (say *bawl-səm*) *noun*
1 a sweet-smelling gum that comes from some trees **2** a kind of garden plant with red, pink or white flowers

balustrade (say *bal-ə-strayd*) *noun*
a rail with a row of short pillars holding it up, usually part of a balcony or staircase

Word Building: **baluster** *noun* one of the short pillars in the row

bamboo *noun*
a woody, tree-like plant whose hollow stem is used for building and making light furniture

bamboozle *verb*
to confuse or deceive: *He bamboozled them with conjuring tricks.*

Word Use: a similar word is **baffle**

ban *verb*
to bar or forbid: *Our teacher banned yo-yos from the classroom.*

Word Building: other forms are **I banned, I have banned, I am banning**

banal (say *bə-nahl*) *adjective*
ordinary and unoriginal: *The TV film was so banal that we turned it off.*

Word Building: **banality** *noun*

banana *noun*
a long curved fruit with a yellow skin

band[1] *noun*
1 a group of people acting together: *a band of outlaws* **2** a group of musicians: *a rock band* | *a brass band*

Word Building: **band** *verb* to join in a group

band[2] *noun*
1 a strip of material for tying, binding or decorating: *a hat band* | *a rubber band*
2 a narrow strip that contrasts with its surroundings: *a band of red paint*

Word Use: a similar word for definition 2 is **stripe**
Word Building: **banded** *adjective* striped

bandage *noun*
a strip of cotton or elastic material used to bind up a wound

Word Building: **bandage** *verb*

bandanna (say *ban-dan-ə*) *noun*
a bright scarf: *The cowboy wore a red bandanna around his neck.*

Word Use: another spelling is **bandana**
Word History: from a Hindustani word for a form of dyeing in which the cloth is tied to stop some parts from receiving the dye

bandicoot *noun*
a rat-like Australian marsupial which feeds at night on insects, worms and plant roots

Word History: from a Telugu word (a language spoken in south-eastern India) for the pig-rat of India and Sri Lanka

bandit *noun*
an armed robber

bandy *verb*
1 to exchange: *The rivals bandied insults, then punches.*
bandy *adjective*
2 having legs bending outwards at the knees: *The old jockey has bandy legs from so much riding.* **3 bandy-legged** having crooked legs

Word Building: other verb forms are **I bandied, I have bandied, I am bandying**

bane *noun*
someone or something that ruins or destroys: *The school bully is the bane of my life.*

Word Building: **baneful** *adjective* **banefully** *adverb* **banefulness** *noun*

bang *noun*
1 a sudden loud noise: *the loud bang of a firecracker*

bang *verb*
2 to hit or shut noisily: *They banged the cymbals together. | The door banged.*

bangle *noun*
a band worn as an ornament round your wrist or ankle

banish *verb*
to send away as a punishment: *The evil magician was banished from his country forever.*

Word Building: **banishment** *noun*

banister *noun*
the rail that runs along a stairway: *She slid down the banister.*

Word Use: another spelling is **bannister**

banjo *noun*
a musical instrument with a round body which you play by plucking or strumming its strings

Word Building: the plural is **banjos** □ **banjoist** *noun*

bank[1] *noun*
1 a pile or mass: *a bank of earth | a huge cloud bank* **2** the land beside a river or stream

bank[1] *verb*
3 to make into a pile or mass: *to bank up the snow* **4** to tip or slope sideways: *The aeroplane banked steeply, then straightened out.*

bank[2] *noun*
1 a place where you can keep your money and take it out again when you wish

bank[2] *verb*
2 to place in a bank **3 bank on** to rely on: *I'm banking on you to help.* **4 bank up** to gather or accumulate: *The line of cars banked up.*

bankbook *noun*
a book given by a savings bank to customers as a record of how much money they have

Word Use: another word for this is **passbook**

bankrupt *adjective*
1 unable to pay money you owe to other people: *He became bankrupt when his business failed.*

bankrupt *noun*
2 someone who is unable to pay their debts

Word Building: **bankrupt** *verb* to make bankrupt **bankruptcy** *noun*

banksia *noun*
an Australian shrub or tree with leathery, notched leaves and tiny yellow flowers massed together in spikes

Word History: named after the naturalist Joseph *Banks*

banner *noun*
a flag which sometimes has a message or slogan on it: *The marchers carried a big banner which said "Peace".*

banquet *noun*
a large formal dinner for many guests: *At the jubilee banquet there was good food but too many speeches.*

Word Use: a similar word is **feast**
Word Building: **banquet** *verb* (**banqueted, banqueting**)

bantam *noun*
a small breed of domestic fowl

Word History: named after *Bantam*, a village in western Java, where these fowls are said to have come from

banter *noun*
playful teasing: *Their banter never led to a fight.*

Word Building: **banter** *verb*

baptism *noun*
a Christian ceremony in which someone is sprinkled with, or put under, water to show that they are accepted as a member of the church

Word Use: a similar word is **christening**
Word Building: **baptise** *verb* **baptismal** *adjective*

bar *noun*
1 a long plank or piece of metal or other hard material, often used as a barrier: *the top bar of the fence* **2** the counter in a hotel where drinks are served **3 a** one of the upright lines drawn across the stave in written music, to separate the groups of beats **b** the part between two of these lines

bar *verb*
4 to stop or prevent: *Guards barred them from entering.*

Word Use: another name for definition 3a is **bar-line** □ a similar word for definition 4 is **ban**
Word Building: other verb forms are **I barred, I have barred, I am barring**

barb *noun*
1 the sharp point that sticks out backwards on a fish-hook, arrowhead or fence wire **2** a hurtful remark

Word Building: **barbed** *adjective: barbed wire*

barbarian (say *bah-bair-ree-ən*) *noun*
someone with bad manners and not much education

Word Building: **barbarian** *adjective: The invading barbarian tribes destroyed the town's statues.* **barbarism** *noun* **barbarity** *noun*
Word History: first used by the ancient Greeks and Romans to describe a person belonging to an uncivilised country

barbaric (say *bah-ba-rik*) *adjective*
wild, savage or cruel: *barbaric acts of torture*

Word Building: **barbarous** *adjective* crude or rough in manners or style **barbarically** *adverb* **barbarously** *adverb*

barbecue *noun*
1 a fireplace or metal frame for cooking meat over an open fire **2** an outdoor meal or party where the food is cooked on a barbecue

Word Use: other spellings are **barbeque** and **bar-b-q**, but many people say these shouldn't be used in your best writing □ short forms are **barbie** and **barby**
Word Building: **barbecue** *verb*

barber *noun*
someone whose job is to cut men's hair and to shave or trim their beards

barbiturate (say *bah-bit-chə-rət*) *noun*
a drug used to ease pain or to calm and soothe someone, and which you can get addicted to

bar code *noun*
a printed code with a series of vertical bars that identify all goods being sold in a shop, which a computerised cash register can scan

Word Building: **bar coding** *noun*

bard *noun*
a poet or singer

Word Use: this is an old-fashioned word
Word Building: **bardic** *adjective*

bare *adjective*
1 uncovered or naked: *bare walls / bare knees* **2** plain or simple: *the bare truth*

Word Building: **barely** *adverb* just, or no more than **bareness** *noun*

bargain *noun*
1 something bought cheaply: *The shoes were a bargain at half price.* **2** an agreement or arrangement to buy or sell something

Word Building: **bargain** *verb* to argue for a better price **bargainer** *noun*

barge *noun*
1 a flat-bottomed boat that carries cargo
barge *verb*
2 to make way by pushing or shoving: *He barged through the crowd.*

baritone *noun*
1 the range of musical notes which can be sung by a male singer with a fairly deep voice: *He sings baritone in the choir.*
2 a man with a fairly deep singing voice

Word Use: **baritone** range is higher than a **bass** but lower than **soprano, alto** and **tenor**
Word Building: **baritone** *adjective*

barium (say *bair-ree-əm*) *noun*
a substance which shows up on X-ray when it is swallowed

bark[1] *verb*
to make the noise of a dog

Word Building: **bark** *noun*

bark[2] *noun*
1 the outer covering of a tree
bark[2] *verb*
2 to scrape or graze: *She barked her elbow on the edge of the table.*

barley *noun*
a grain used as food, and in making beer and whisky

bar mitzvah (say *bah mits-və*) *noun*
the Jewish ceremony and feast held when a boy reaches his thirteenth birthday and is old enough to take on religious responsibilities

Word History: from a Hebrew word meaning "son of the commandment"

barn *noun*
a shed to store hay or shelter animals

barnacle *noun*
a shellfish which clings to the bottoms of ships and other underwater objects

barometer *noun*
an instrument that measures air pressure, used to help work out what height you're at and what changes in the weather can be expected: *The barometer is falling, which means we shall have bad weather.*

Word Use: when you use a barometer to see what height you're at it is called an **altimeter**
Word Building: **barometric** *adjective*

baron *noun*
a nobleman: *The baron left his castle to fight for the king.*

Word Building: **baroness** *noun* **baronial** *adjective*

barrack *verb*
to shout encouragement: *We barracked for our favourite team.*

Word Building: **barracker** *noun*

barracks *plural noun*
the buildings where soldiers live

barrage (say *ba-rahzh*) *noun*
an overwhelming attack, especially of gunfire: *a barrage of questions | a barrage of bullets*

Word Building: **barrage** *verb*

barrel *noun*
1 a large container made of vertical strips of wood held together with iron hoops
2 the metal tube of a gun

barren *adjective*
unable to produce children or crops: *a barren woman | barren land*

barricade *noun*
a barrier or wall, especially one built in a hurry: *a barricade to stop traffic | The street-fighters hid behind a barricade of rubble.*

Word Building: **barricade** *verb* to block or defend with a barricade

barrier *noun*
anything which bars or blocks the way: *a road barrier | a trade barrier*

barrister *noun*
a lawyer whose main work is in the higher courts, where important cases are heard

Word Use: compare this with **solicitor**

barrow *noun*
1 a street seller's cart **2** a wheelbarrow

barter *verb*
to trade by swapping food and other goods instead of using money

base[1] *noun*
1 the bottom part of anything, which gives support: *the base of a statue* **2** the centre of operations: *Report back to base when you finish your mission.* **3** the starting point for a counting system in maths, such as ten in the decimal system **4** one of the four fixed positions in baseball which the players run to

Word Building: **base** *verb* rest or fix: *to base an argument on facts*

base[2] *adjective*
mean or selfish: *a base trick*

Word Use: this is a slightly old-fashioned word
Word Building: **basely** *adverb* **baseness** *noun*

baseball *noun*
1 a game played by two teams with a bat and a ball, on a field with four bases which the batter must pass to score a run **2** the ball used in this game

basement *noun*
a room or area of a building below the ground floor

bash *verb*
1 to hit hard or wildly: *The boys bashed each other. | He bashed the ball.*
bash *noun*
2 a try or attempt: *Give it a bash.*

Word Use: definition 2 is more suited to everyday language

bashful *adjective*
very modest or shy: *She felt bashful about making a speech.*

Word Building: **bashfully** *adverb* **bashfulness** *noun*

basic *adjective*
main or most important: *The basic ingredient for toffee is sugar.*

Word Building: **basically** *adverb*

basil *noun*
a herb used in cooking and salads

Word History: from a Greek word meaning "royal"

basin *noun*
1 a sink or container that holds water for washing **2** a bowl for mixing or cooking **3** an area of water surrounded by land: *a river basin* **4** land drained by a river

basis *noun*
1 a foundation or support that forms the base of something: *The basis of the story was an incident that really took place.*
2 the main part or ingredient

Word Building: the plural is **bases** (say *bay-seez*)

bask (rhymes with *ask*) *verb*
to lie in or enjoy warmth: *to bask in the sun*

basket *noun*
a woven container for storing or carrying: *a clothes basket* | *a shopping basket*

basketball *noun*
1 a game played by two teams who try to score points by shooting a ball through a hoop or basket at the top of the other team's goal post **2** the ball used in this game

bass (sounds like *base*) *noun*
1 the range of musical notes which can be sung by a male singer with a deep voice: *He sings bass in the choir.* **2** a man with a deep singing voice

Word Use: **bass** range is lower than a **soprano**, **alto**, **tenor** and **baritone**
Word Building: **bass** *adjective*

basset *noun*
a long-bodied dog with short legs and long ears, used for hunting foxes and badgers

Word Use: also called a **basset hound**

bassinette *noun*
the basket in which a very young baby sleeps

Word Use: another spelling is **bassinet**

bassoon (say *bə-soohn*) *noun*
a bass woodwind instrument

Word Building: **bassoonist** *noun*

bastard *noun*
1 someone whose parents were not married when he or she was born
2 a person, especially someone who is very unpleasant

Word Use: using definition 2 is not polite and might offend people

bastion (say *bas-tee-ən*) *noun*
1 a fortified place **2** a strong supporter: *He is a bastion of the old way of life.*

Word History: from an Italian word meaning "build"

bat[1] *noun*
1 the stick used to hit the ball in games like cricket and baseball **2 off your own bat** on your own, without help or advice

Word Building: **bat** *verb* (**batted**, **batting**) **batsman** *noun* **batter** *noun*

bat[2] *noun*
a mouse-like winged mammal which is active at night

batch *noun*
a number of things made at the same time or grouped together: *a batch of biscuits* | *this year's batch of students*

Word Building: the plural is **batches**

bath *noun*
1 a container for washing yourself in, which is large enough for you to sit or lie in **2** the water used in the bath

Word Building: **bath** *verb: to bath the baby*

bathe *verb*
1 to wash clean: *Bathe your sore eye in salty water.* **2** to swim: *We bathed in the creek.*

Word Building: **bather** *noun* swimmer
bathers *plural noun* a swimsuit

batik *noun*
1 a way of dyeing cloth in which the parts not to be coloured are covered with wax
2 cloth dyed in this way

Word History: from a Malay word meaning "painted"

baton *noun*
1 a thin stick used by the conductor of an orchestra to beat time **2** a short stick, especially one handed by one runner to the next in a relay race

battalion *noun*
an army unit of three or more smaller groups of soldiers known as companies

batten *noun*
a light strip of wood, used to strengthen or support something

batter[1] *verb*
to beat or hit hard or often: *to batter on the door*

Word Building: **battery** *noun* the act of beating **battering** *noun*

batter[2] *noun*
a mixture of flour, eggs and milk or water beaten together for use in cooking

battery *noun*
1 a group of electric cells connected together to make or store electricity: *a torch battery* | *a car battery* **2** a group of guns or machines to be used together
3 a large number of cages in which chickens and other animals are kept

Word Building: the plural is **batteries**

battle *noun*
a large-scale or serious fight: *a battle between armies | a battle to save the old building*

Word Building: **embattled** *adjective* caught in a battle **battle** *verb* **battler** *noun*

battlement *noun*
a wall with openings for shooting through: *The archers shot their arrows from the battlement.*

battleship *noun*
a heavily armed warship

bauble (say *baw-bəl*) *noun*
a cheap bright ornament: *to hang baubles on the Christmas tree*

Word History: from a Latin word meaning "pretty"

baulk (rhymes with *fork*) *verb*
to stop and refuse to do something: *The horse baulked at the jump. | to baulk at making a speech*

bauxite (say *bawk-suyt*) *noun*
the rock that you crush to get aluminium

bawdy *adjective*
containing rough talk and jokes about sex: *a bawdy story*

Word Use: other forms are **bawdier, bawdiest**
Word Building: **bawdily** *adverb* **bawdiness** *noun*

bawl *verb*
1 to cry noisily: *He bawled when the ball hit him.* **2** to shout out loudly: *to bawl from across the playground* **3 bawl out** to scold harshly: *to bawl someone out for lying*

Word Building: **bawl** *noun*

bay[1] *noun*
a sheltered part of a sea or lake, formed by a curve in its shore

bay[2] *verb*
1 to howl like a dog: *to bay at the moon*
bay[2] *noun*
2 the deep long bark of a hunting dog
3 at bay a forced to stand and face an enemy: *The kangaroo stood at bay.*
b away or at a distance: *I kept my sad thoughts at bay by working hard.*

bay[3] *noun*
a space, section or area: *a bomb bay | a parking bay*

bay[4] *adjective*
reddish-brown: *a bay horse*

bayonet *noun*
a blade for stabbing which can be joined to the end of a rifle

Word Building: **bayonet** *verb* (**bayoneted, bayoneting**) to stab with a bayonet
Word History: named after *Bayonne* in France, where these weapons were first made

bazaar (say *bə-zah*) *noun*
1 a market with stalls selling many different kinds of goods **2** a sale to raise money for charity

BC
short for "before Christ": *Julius Caesar invaded Britain in 55 BC.*

Word Use: our calendar dates events from the year of Christ's birth; years before this are called **BC** and years after this are **AD**

beach *noun*
1 the sandy or pebbly land at the edge of a sea, lake or river
beach *verb*
2 to drive or pull onto the beach from the water: *We beached the boat when we reached the shore.*

beacon *noun*
a signal which shows the way or warns of danger: *We lit a fire on the hill to serve as a beacon for the fishermen.*

bead *noun*
1 a small ball with a hole through the middle, which can be threaded on a string **2** a drop of liquid: *beads of sweat* **3 beads** a necklace

Word Building: **beady** *adjective* (**beadier, beadiest**): *beady little eyes*

beagle *noun*
a small hunting dog with short legs and long ears

beak *noun*
the hard, horny part of a bird's mouth

Word Use: a similar word is **bill**
Word Building: **beaked** *adjective*

beaker *noun*
1 a large cup or mug **2** a glass container with a pouring lip shaped like a beak, used in laboratories

beam *noun*
1 a long strong piece of wood, concrete or metal often used as a support: *beams supporting the floor | a balancing beam for gymnastics* **2** the widest part of a ship: *ten metres across the beam* **3** a ray of light: *the beam of a search light | a sunbeam* **4 off**

beam wrong: *The answer was completely off beam.*

beam *verb*
5 to send out rays of light **6** to smile happily: *She beamed when she heard the good news.*

Word Use: definition 4 is more suited to everyday language

bean *noun*
1 a plant with smooth seeds growing in a long pod **2** the seed or pod of a bean plant which can be eaten fresh or dried **3 full of beans** full of energy: *The children are full of beans now the holidays have started.* **4 spill the beans** to let out a secret

Word Use: definitions 3 and 4 are more suited to everyday language

beanbag *noun*
1 a large cushion that you can sit on, filled with pellets **2** a small cloth bag filled with beans and thrown in catching games

bear[1] *verb*
1 to hold up or carry: *a branch strong enough to bear your weight | The swimmer was borne along on the tide.* **2** to put up with or tolerate: *I can't bear pain. | I can't bear people who tell tales.* **3** to produce or give birth to: *This tree bears oranges. | She bore three children.* **4** to have or show: *The sisters bear no resemblance to each other. | to bear signs of damage* **5 bear out** to prove right: *The facts bear me out.* **6 bear up** to keep cheerful in times of trouble

Word Use: the word **born** as in *She was born in 1980* also came from this verb
Word Building: other forms are **I bore, I have borne, I am bearing** □ **bearer** *noun* someone who brings or carries something: *the bearer of good news* **bearable** *adjective* **bearably** *adverb*

bear[2] *noun*
a large heavy mammal with short rough fur and a very short tail

beard *noun*
1 the hair that grows on a man's chin and face **2** a beardlike tuft, such as that on a goat's jaw, below a bird's beak and growing on wheat

beard *verb*
3 to defy or oppose: *to beard the lion in his den*

Word Building: **bearded** *adjective*

bearing *noun*
1 the way you stand or behave: *a king of noble bearing* **2** a supporting part of a machine **3 bearing on** connection or relevance to: *This information has no bearing on the problem.* **4 bearings** direction or position: *We lost our bearings in the dark.*

Word Use: a similar word for definition 1 is **carriage**

beast *noun*
1 a four-footed animal **2** a rough, cruel person, especially someone you dislike

Word Building: **beastly** *adjective* horrible or nasty **beastliness** *noun*

beat *verb*
1 to hit again and again: *to beat a drum | to beat someone severely | The rain beat on the window.* **2** to make any movement over and over again: *My heart beat loudly. | A bird was beating its wings.* **3** to stir thoroughly: *to beat cream* **4** to defeat: *She beat him in the race.* **5 beat it** to leave: *We'd better beat it before someone comes.* **6 beat up** to attack and hurt: *The school bully beat him up.*

beat *noun*
7 a sound made over and over again: *the beat of a drum* **8** regular rhythm in music: *The conductor kept the beat while the orchestra played.* **9** a path or route which someone usually takes: *A policeman walks a beat.*

Word Use: definition 5 is more suited to everyday language
Word Building: other verb forms are **I beat, I have beaten, I am beating** □ **beating** *noun: to give someone a beating* **beater** *noun*

beaut *adjective*
very good and enjoyable: *a beaut party*

Word Use: this word is more suited to everyday language

beautician *noun*
someone who works in a beauty salon

beautiful *adjective*
pleasing and enjoyable to look at, touch, smell, taste or hear: *beautiful music | a beautiful face*

Word Building: **beautifully** *adverb*

beauty *noun*
1 the quality of being beautiful: *a garden famous for its beauty* **2** a beautiful person or thing: *My new bike is a beauty.*

3 advantage: *The beauty of this machine is that it runs on batteries.*

Word Building: the plural is **beauties** □ **beauteous** *adjective* **beautify** *verb* (**beautified, beautifying**)

beaver *noun*
a brown furry animal of North America, with sharp teeth, webbed back feet and a wide flat tail, which builds dams in streams

beckon *verb*
to signal by waving your hand, or nodding your head: *He beckoned them to follow.*

become *verb*
1 to come to be: *to become hungry* **2** to suit or look good on: *That dress becomes you.* **3 become of** happen to: *What will become of me?*

Word Building: other forms are **I became, I have become, I am becoming**

becoming *adjective*
1 proper or suitable: *behaviour which is becoming to a ten year old* **2** flattering or making you look attractive: *a becoming dress*

Word Building: **becomingly** *adverb*

bed *noun*
1 a place to sleep, especially a piece of furniture with a mattress, pillow and covers **2** a plot of earth in a garden: *a flower bed* **3** the ground under a sea or river: *a river bed* **4** a base or foundation **5** a layer of rock

Word Building: **bed** *verb* (**bedded, bedding**) **bedding** *noun* the things you make your bed with, especially sheets and blankets

bedlam *noun*
a scene of great noise and confusion: *There was bedlam in the room when the teacher was away.*

bedouin (say *bed-ooh-ən*) *noun*
a wandering Arab who lives in the deserts of North Africa or the Middle East

Word Use: another spelling is **Bedouin**

bedraggled (say *bə-drag-əld*) *adjective*
wet, dirty and hanging limply: *long bedraggled hair*

bedridden *adjective*
forced to stay in bed: *I was bedridden with the flu.*

bedrock *noun*
1 the solid, unbroken rock under the top layers of soil **2** the bottom level of anything: *The team's spirits hit bedrock when they lost another match.*

bee *noun*
1 a stinging insect with four wings, which collects nectar and pollen from flowers to make into honey **2** a small group of people gathered together for some type of work: *a sewing bee* **3** a contest: *a spelling bee*

Word Use: the place where bees live is called a **beehive** or **hive,** and a group of bees together is called a **swarm**

beech *noun*
a tree with smooth grey bark and triangular nuts, whose hard wood is useful for making furniture

beef *noun*
the meat from a cow or bull: *roast beef for dinner*

Word Building: **beefy** *adjective* (**beefier, beefiest**) solid and with plenty of muscles

beeline *noun*
a direct line, like the course bees take when returning to the hive: *The children made a beeline for the food.*

beer *noun*
an alcoholic drink made from malt and flavoured with hops

beet *noun*
a plant with a root that is good to eat and from which sugar can be made

beetle *noun*
a large insect with two pairs of wings, one of which is hard and protects the delicate flying wings underneath

Word History: from an Old English word meaning "biter"

beetroot *noun*
the red root of the beet plant which is eaten as a vegetable

befall *verb*
to happen to: *Whatever befalls us, we will be together.*

Word Building: other forms are **it befell, it has befallen**

befriend *verb*
to aid or be friendly towards: *to befriend a stray kitten*

befuddled *adjective*
confused or muddled: *We felt befuddled by so many people talking at once.*

beg *verb*
to ask humbly: *I beg you to forgive me. / to beg for money to buy food*

Word Building: other forms are **I begged, I have begged, I am begging**

beggar *noun*
1 someone who lives by begging **2** someone you feel sorry for: *You poor beggar.*

Word Use: definition 2 is more suited to everyday language
Word Building: **beggarly** *adjective* very poor **beggar** *verb*

begin *verb*
to start or commence: *Please begin work now. / How did the trouble begin?*

Word Building: other forms are **I began, I have begun, I am beginning** □ **beginning** *noun* the time or place when something begins

beginner *noun*
someone who is just learning something

begrudge *verb*
1 to envy: *They begrudged him his good luck.* **2** to be unwilling to give: *They begrudged paying for bad service.*

beguile (say *bə-guyl*) *verb*
to charm or enchant: *The children were beguiled by the witch's magic.*

Word Building: **beguiling** *adjective* charming

behalf *noun*
in the phrase **on behalf of** on the side of or for: *to speak on behalf of my friend*

behave *verb*
1 to act: *to behave like a child* **2 behave yourself** to act properly or in an acceptable way: *to behave yourself in school*

Word Building: **behaviour** *noun* the way you behave

behead *verb*
to cut off the head of: *They beheaded many people during the French Revolution.*

beige (say *bayzh*) *adjective*
very light brown

being *noun*
1 something which lives: *beings from outer space / a human being* **2** existence or life: *to come into being*

belated *adjective*
late: *I forgot her birthday so I sent a belated birthday card.*

Word Use: this word is never used of people, only of things
Word Building: **belatedly** *adverb* **belatedness** *noun*

belch *verb*
1 to pass wind noisily from your stomach through your mouth: *Fizzy drink makes me belch.* **2** to throw out violently: *The volcano belched out lava.*

belch *noun*
3 the rumbling noise you make when belching

Word Use: a similar word for definitions 1 and 3 is **burp**
Word Building: the plural form of the noun is **belches**

belfry (say *bel-free*) *noun*
a tower with a bell hanging in it: *the belfry of the local church*

Word Building: the plural is **belfries**

belief *noun*
1 something that you believe and accept as true: *It is my belief that children should enjoy school.* **2** trust or faith: *belief in God*

believe *verb*
1 to trust or have confidence in: *I can't believe that story.* **2** to think: *I believe they will be late.* **3 believe in** to accept as real or true: *Do you believe in fairies?* **4 make believe** to pretend: *Let's make believe we're creatures from outer space.*

Word Building: **believer** *noun* someone who believes, especially in God **believable** *adjective* **believably** *adverb*

belittle *verb*
to make seem unimportant: *She hurt their feelings when she belittled their work.*

bell *noun*
1 a hollow metal cup with a clapper hanging inside which can hit the side of the cup and make a ringing sound **2** the ringing sound of a bell **3** something which makes the sound of a bell

bellbird *noun*
a small bird that has a clear ringing call like the sound of a bell and lives in bushy areas along the east coast of Australia

belligerent (say *be-lij-ə-rənt*) *adjective*
1 angry and aggressive: *We were surprised by her belligerent behaviour.* **2** involved in a war: *a belligerent country*

Word Building: **belligerence** *noun* **belligerently** *adverb*

bellow (rhymes with *yellow*) *verb*
to roar or cry loudly: *to bellow an answer | The bull bellowed with anger.*

Word Building: **bellow** *noun* **bellowing** *noun*

bellows *plural noun*
an instrument for pumping air: *We pumped the bellows to make the fire burn brightly.*

belly *noun*
1 the front part of the body containing the stomach and intestines: *to hit someone in the belly* **2** the inside of anything: *the belly of a ship*

Word Use: a similar word for definition 1 is **abdomen**
Word Building: the plural is **bellies**

belongings *plural noun*
things that you own: *Our belongings are stored in a warehouse.*

Word Use: a similar word is **possessions**

beloved (say *bə-luv-əd, -luvd*) *adjective*
1 much loved: *a beloved friend*
beloved *noun*
2 someone you love very much: *to kiss your beloved*

below *adverb*
1 beneath: *to grow below the sea | to live in the flat below*
below *preposition*
2 lower than: *below the knee | below the usual cost*

Word Use: the opposite of this is **above**

belt *noun*
1 a strip of strong material, often worn around your waist or hips **2** a large strip of land where a particular thing is grown: *the wheat belt | a belt of trees*
belt *verb*
3 to fasten with a belt **4** to beat or hit very hard: *to belt someone as a punishment* **5 belt out** to sing very loudly **6 belt up** **a** to be quiet: *Why don't you belt up?* **b** to fasten a safety belt

Word Use: definitions 5 and 6 are more suited to everyday language
Word Building: **belting** *noun* a beating

bemused (say *bə-myoohzd*) *adjective*
1 muddled or confused **2** lost in thought: *a bemused look on her face*

bench *noun*
1 a seat long enough for several people: *a park bench* **2** a strong work-table: *a carpenter's bench* **3** a seat for members of parliament or judges in court: *the opposition benches | The prisoner stood before the bench.*

Word Building: the plural is **benches**

bend *verb*
1 to turn or curve in a particular direction: *to bend a piece of wire | The road bends to the left.* **2** to stoop: *to bend over to pick up something* **3 bend over backwards** to try as hard as you can: *I bent over backwards to get you a ticket to the concert.*
bend *noun*
4 a curve or change in direction: *a bend in the road*

Word Building: other verb forms are **I bent, I have bent, I am bending**

bene- *prefix*
a word part meaning well: *benediction*

Word History: this prefix comes from Latin

beneath *adverb*
1 below: *It's buried beneath the rubble.*
beneath *preposition*
2 under or below: *The skin beneath her makeup was deathly white.*

benediction (say *ben-ə-dik-shən*) *noun*
the blessing at the end of a church service

benefactor *noun*
someone who gives help or money to those who need it

Word Building: **beneficence** *noun* **beneficent** *adjective*

beneficial *adjective*
helpful: *beneficial advice | the beneficial effect of a good night's sleep*

Word Building: **beneficially** *adverb*

beneficiary (say *ben-ə-fish-ə-ree*) *noun*
someone who receives assistance, especially money left in a will

Word Building: the plural is **beneficiaries**

benefit *noun*
1 anything that is good for you: *the benefits of education* **2** a concert to raise money for charity
benefit *verb*
3 to be good for: *A holiday will benefit you greatly.*

Word Building: other verb forms are **I benefited, I have benefited, I am benefiting**

benevolent *adjective*
wanting to help other people: *The Red Cross is a benevolent organisation.*

Word Building: **benevolence** *noun* **benevolently** *adverb*

benign (rhymes with *mine*) *adjective*
1 kind and gentle: *a benign smile* **2** not harmful to the body: *The lump taken out of her neck by the doctor was benign.*

Word Use: the opposite of this is **malignant**
Word Building: **benignity** *noun* **benignly** *adverb*

bent *adjective*
1 crooked or curved: *a bent hairpin*
2 bent on determined or set on: *bent on playing football*
bent *noun*
3 a liking or preference: *a bent for painting*

bequeath *verb*
to hand down or pass on to someone who comes after you: *to bequeath money in a will*

Word Building: **bequest** *noun* money left by someone in a will

bereaved *adjective*
sad because of someone's death: *The bereaved husband wept at his wife's funeral.*

Word Building: **bereavement** *noun* the loss of someone dear to you **bereave** *verb*

beret (say *be-ray*) *noun*
a soft round cap

Word History: from a Latin word meaning "cloak"

berry *noun*
a small fruit, often brightly coloured

Word Use: be careful – this sounds like **bury**
Word Building: the plural is **berries**

berserk (say *bə-zerk*) *adjective*
uncontrollably crazy and wild: *The dogs went berserk when they were untied.*

berth *noun*
1 a place to sleep on a boat or train: *Our cabin has four berths.* **2** a place where a ship can tie up
berth *verb*
3 to tie up at a dock: *The ship berthed at 7 o'clock.*

beseech *verb*
to ask anxiously: *Help me, I beseech you!*

Word Building: other forms are **I besought** or **I beseeched, I have besought** or **I have beseeched, I am beseeching**

besiege *verb*
1 to crowd round and surround: *The enemy troops besieged the town for three weeks.* **2** to set upon or attack: *The speaker was besieged with questions.*

best *adjective*
1 finest or highest quality **2** favourite: *my best friend*
best *adverb*
3 most successfully: *She swims best.*
4 most: *I like him best.*
best *noun*
5 your nicest clothes: *to put on your best for the party*

Word Building: for other forms of the adjective see **good** □ for other forms of the adverb see **well**

best man *noun*
the chief attendant or helper of the bridegroom at a wedding

bestow (rhymes with *show*) *verb*
to give as a gift or reward: *The queen bestowed a medal on the soldier for bravery.*

Word Building: **bestowal** *noun*

bet *noun*
1 a promise that you will give money or something like that to someone who differs from you, if that person is right and you are wrong: *Ann made a bet that she was taller than Kate.* **2** the money or thing that you promised: *She lost her bet.*
bet *verb*
3 to risk as part of a bet: *I bet you ten cents I can jump this fence.* **4** to make a bet

Word Building: other forms are **I bet** or **I betted, I have bet** or **I have betted, I am betting**

betray *verb*
1 to be unfaithful or disloyal to: *The spy betrayed his country by selling important secrets to the enemy.* **2** show or reveal: *His face betrayed his anger. | to betray a secret*

Word Building: **betrayal** *noun* **betrayer** *noun*

betroth (rhymes with *clothe*) *verb*
to promise to marry

Word Building: **betrothal** *noun* **betrothed** *noun* **betrothed** *adjective*

better *adjective*
1 of higher quality, or of more value: *This furniture is made of better wood than that.*
2 larger, or greater: *It took him the better part of his life to build his house.*

3 improved in health: *I hope you are feeling better today.*

better *adverb*
4 in an improved or more suitable manner: *She behaved better today.*

better *verb*
5 to improve: *He bettered his score in the first round by ten points.*

beverage *noun*
a drink of any kind

beware *verb*
to be careful : *If you go in, beware of the dog.*

Word Use: this verb is usually followed by *of*

bewilder *verb*
to confuse or puzzle: *The maze completely bewildered him.*

Word Use: a similar word is **perplex**
Word Building: **bewilderment** *noun*

bewitch *verb*
1 to put under a magic spell **2** to charm: *The little girl bewitched the audience with her delightful appearance.*

bi- *prefix*
a word part meaning **1** two: *bicycle* **2** twice: *bigamy* **3** doubly: *binoculars*

Word History: this prefix comes from Latin

bias (say *buy-əs*) *noun*
1 a strong opinion which often stops you from seeing the other side of an argument: *The teacher's bias towards football was obvious.* **2** a slanting line or direction

Word Building: **bias** *verb* (**biased, biasing**) **biased** *adjective*

bib *noun*
1 a small cloth tied under a baby's chin to protect its clothes at mealtime **2** the part of an apron or pair of overalls above the waist

Word History: from a Latin word meaning "drink"

Bible *noun*
the sacred book of the Christian religion, consisting of the Old and New Testaments

Word Building: **biblical** *adjective*
Word History: from a Greek word meaning "book"

biblio- *prefix*
a word part meaning book: *bibliography*

Word History: this prefix comes from Greek

bibliography (say *bib-lee-og-rə-fee*) *noun*
1 a list of all the books read or used by a writer when writing a book or essay
2 a list of everything written by a particular writer, or about a particular subject: *a bibliography of Australian wildlife*

Word Building: the plural is **bibliographies** □ **bibliographer** *noun* **bibliographic** *adjective* **bibliographical** *adjective*

bicentenary (say *buy-sən-teen-ə-ree*) *noun*
a 200th anniversary: *Australia had its bicentenary in 1988.*

Word Building: the plural is **bicentenaries** □ **bicentennial** *adjective*

biceps (say *buy-seps*) *noun*
a large muscle at the top of your arm or the back of your thigh that helps you to bend your elbow or knee

Word History: from a Latin word meaning "two-headed", as this muscle is joined at the top in two places

bicker *verb*
to squabble or argue about little things

bicycle *noun*
a two-wheeled machine for riding on, which you steer by handlebars and drive by pushing pedals

Word Use: the shortened form is **bike** which is more suited to everyday language
Word Building: **bicyclist** *noun*

bid *verb*
1 to order or command: *The queen bids her people to do as she wishes.* **2** to say or tell: *The teacher bids her class good morning every day.* **3** to offer or make an offer to buy at an auction: *She bid $200 for the table. / He bid for the chair.*

bid *noun*
4 the amount offered for something, especially at an auction **5** an attempt to achieve a goal or purpose

Word Building: other verb forms for definitions 1 and 2 are **I bade** (sounds like *bad*), **I have bidden, I am bidding** □ other verb forms for definition 3 are **I bid, I have bidden, I am bidding** □ **bidder** *noun* **bidding** *noun*

biennial (say *buy-en-ee-əl*) *adjective*
1 happening every two years **2** living for two years: *Onions and parsnips are biennial plants.*

Word Building: **biennial** *noun* **biennially** *adverb*

bier (sounds like *beer*) *noun*
a stand on which a dead body, or the coffin holding it, rests before it is buried

bifocals *plural noun*
a pair of glasses with lenses which have two parts, one for seeing things far away and one for seeing things close to you

Word Building: **bifocal** *adjective*

big *adjective*
1 large in size or amount: *A giraffe is a big animal.* **2** elder: *her big brother*
3 important: *big business*

Word Building: other forms are **bigger, biggest**

bigamy (say *big-ə-mee*) *noun*
the crime of marrying someone while you are still married to someone else

Word Building: **bigamist** *noun* **bigamous** *adjective*

bight (sounds like *bite*) *noun*
a bend or curve in the shore of the sea

Word Use: be careful – this sounds like **bite** and **byte**

bigot (say *big-ət*) *noun*
someone who is convinced that his opinion is right and who gets irritated by people who disagree

Word Building: **bigoted** *adjective* **bigotry** *noun*

bike *noun*
a bicycle or motorcycle

Word Use: this word is more suited to everyday language

bikini (say *bə-kee-nee*) *noun*
a two-piece swimming costume for women

Word History: named after Bikini Atoll in the northern Pacific Ocean, where the United States tested nuclear bombs from 1946 to 1958

bilateral *adjective*
of or affecting two sides: *The two countries came to a bilateral agreement about trade.*

bile *noun*
a bitter yellowish liquid which is produced by the liver and which helps you digest food

bilingual (say *buy-ling-gwəl*) *adjective*
able to speak two languages

Word Building: **bilingualism** *noun* **bilingually** *adverb*

bilious (say *bil-yəs*) *adjective*
1 having, or caused by, too much bile: *a bilious attack* **2** feeling sick in the stomach

Word Building: **biliousness** *noun*

bill[1] *noun*
1 a written statement telling you how much money you owe for something
2 a poster or advertisement on display
3 a plan for a new law to be presented to Parliament

Word Building: **bill** *verb*

bill[2] *noun*
a bird's beak

billabong *noun*
a waterhole which used to be part of a river

Word History: from an Aboriginal language called Wiradhuri

billet *noun*
a place for someone to live for a while: *The soldier was given a billet in the captain's own home.*

Word Building: **billet** *verb* (**billeted, billeting**): *We billeted a student from Japan in our home.*

billiards (say *bil-yədz*) *noun*
a game played by two or more people on a special table, with hard balls hit by a long stick called a cue

billow *noun*
1 a large wave: *the billows of the ocean*
billow *verb*
2 to swirl or rise like billows: *Smoke billowed from the chimney.*

Word Building: **billowy** *adjective*

billy *noun*
a tin container with a lid, used for boiling water

Word Building: the plural is **billies**

billycart *noun*
a four-wheeled cart which has a box for a seat and which you steer by ropes attached to its front axle

billy-goat *noun*
a male goat

Word Use: the female is a **nanny-goat;** the young is a **kid**

bin *noun*
a box or container used to store things: *Put the empty packet in the garbage bin.*

binary (say *buy-nə-ree*) *adjective*
1 made up of two parts or things **2** using the numbers 0 and 1: *binary code*

bind (rhymes with *find*) *verb*
1 to tie up or fasten: *The girls bind their hair with ribbons.* **2** to cover or bandage: *to bind up her arm* **3** to fasten with a cover: *to bind a book*

bind *noun*
4 a nuisance or a bore: *Doing the dishes is a bind.*

Word Use: definition 4 is more suited to everyday language
Word Building: other forms are **I bound, I have bound, I am binding** □ **binder** *noun* **binding** *noun*

bindi-eye *noun*
a small spiky weed

Word Use: it is also called a **bindy**
Word History: from Aboriginal languages called Kamilaroi and Yuwaalaraay

binge *noun*
a period of too much eating, drinking or spending money

Word Use: this word is more suited to everyday language

bingo *noun*
a gambling game in which you cross numbers, called in any order, off a card

Word Use: other names for this are **housie-housie** and **lotto**

binoculars (say *bə-nok-yəl-əz*) *plural noun*
double magnifying glasses for both eyes, used for making distant objects seem nearer

Word Building: **binocular** *adjective* using two eyes

bio- *prefix*
a word part meaning life *or* living things: *biology*

Word History: this prefix comes from Greek

biodegradable *adjective*
able to be broken down by the action of very small living things like bacteria: *Most detergents are biodegradable.*

biography *noun*
the story of a person's life, written by someone else

Word Use: compare this with **autobiography**
Word Building: the plural is **biographies** □ **biographer** *noun* **biographical** *adjective*

biology *noun*
the science or study of all living things

Word Building: **biological** *adjective* **biologist** *noun*

bionic (say *buy-on-ik*) *adjective*
having parts of your body replaced by electronic equipment so as to give you superhuman strength

biopsy *noun*
the removal of a small section of someone's body to check if it is diseased

Word Building: the plural is **biopsies**

birch *noun*
a tree of cold countries, with slender branches and smooth bark

Word Building: the plural is **birches**

bird *noun*
1 a two-legged creature which lays eggs and has wings and feathers **2** a person: *He's a funny old bird.* **3** a girl

Word Use: definitions 2 and 3 are more suited to everyday language

birth *noun*
1 the act of being born **2** any beginning: *the birth of a nation.*

birthday *noun*
1 the day on which someone is born
2 the annual celebration of the day of someone's birth: *It is my eleventh birthday today.*

biscuit (say *bis-kət*) *noun*
a small thin cake which has been baked until it is crisp

Word History: from Latin words meaning "cooked twice"

bisect *verb*
to cut or divide into two parts or two equal parts

Word Building: **bisector** *noun* a line that bisects an angle **bisection** *noun*

bisexual *noun*
1 an animal, human or plant which has both male and female sex organs
2 someone who is sexually attracted to both males and females

bishop *noun*
1 a church minister of high rank, in charge of a whole district **2** a chess piece which can only move diagonally

Word Use: **episcopal** is a word meaning "having to do with a bishop"
Word Building: **bishopric** *noun* the district the bishop is in charge of

bison (say *<u>buy</u>-sən*) *noun*
a large American buffalo with high shoulders and shaggy hair

Word Building: the plural is also **bison**

bistro (say *<u>bis</u>-troh*) *noun*
a small restaurant or wine bar

bit[1] *noun*
1 a metal bar placed in a horse's mouth and attached to the reins, used to help control it **2** the part of some tools which is used for cutting and making holes

bit[2] *noun*
a small piece or amount of something

bit[3] *noun*
a single basic unit of information, used in connection with computers

bitch *noun*
1 a female dog, fox or wolf **2** an unpleasant or bad-tempered woman

bitch *verb*
3 to complain: *He was bitching about his teacher.*

Word Use: for definition 1 the male animal is **dog** □ the use of this word as in definition 2 will offend people □ definition 3 is more suited to everyday language
Word Building: the plural form of the noun is **bitches** □ **bitchiness** *noun* **bitchy** *adjective*

bite *verb*
1 to grab or cut or take a piece out with your teeth: *He bit the apple.* **2** to hurt or sting: *The mosquitoes are biting tonight.* **3** to take the bait: *The fish were biting well yesterday.*

bite *noun*
4 a wound made by biting **5** a snack or small amount of food: *I'll just have a bite to eat at the restaurant.* **6** the act of biting: *The baby had one or two bites of the biscuit.*

Word Use: be careful – this sounds like **bight** and **byte**
Word Building: other forms are **I bit, I have bitten, I am biting**

bitter *adjective*
1 having a sharp unpleasant taste **2** hard to accept or bear: *He felt a bitter sorrow when his mother died.* **3** very cold: *a bitter wind.*

Word Building: **bitterly** *adverb* **bitterness** *noun*

bitumen (say *<u>bit</u>-chə-mən*) *noun*
1 a sticky black mixture, like tar or asphalt, used to make roads **2** a tarred road: *You must ride your bike on the bitumen, not on the footpath.*

bivouac (say *<u>biv</u>-ə-wak*) *noun*
1 a camp set up for a short time: *The soldiers went on a bivouac in the bush for the weekend.*

bivouac *verb*
2 to camp out: *The cadets bivouacked for a week at the end of each term.*

Word Building: other verb forms are **we bivouacked, we have bivouacked, we are bivouacking**

bizarre (say *bə-<u>zah</u>*) *adjective*
very strange or unusual

blab *verb*
1 to talk too much: *My friend blabbed for hours.* **2** to tell or reveal without thinking

Word Building: other forms are **I blabbed, I have blabbed, I am blabbing** □ **blabbermouth** *noun* someone who blabs

black *adjective*
1 completely dark, or without colour and brightness: *a black night | a black dress* **2** having dark-coloured skin **3** sad or gloomy: *It was a black day for the children when their dog died.* **4** angry: *He gave me a black look.* **5** evil or wicked: *Murder is a black deed.* **6** without milk or cream: *I have my coffee black.*

black *noun*
7 someone who has dark-coloured skin

Word Building: **blacken** *verb*

blackberry *noun*
a prickly plant which grows in tangled bushes, or its small, sweet, black or purple fruit

Word Building: the plural is **blackberries**

blackboard *noun*
a smooth dark board that you use for writing or drawing on with chalk

blackcurrant *noun*
a small black fruit which grows on a garden shrub

blackguard (say *<u>blag</u>-ahd*) *noun*
someone who is dishonourable

blackhead *noun*
a small, black-tipped pimple, usually on your face

blackmail *noun*
the act of demanding money from someone by threatening to reveal secrets about them

Word Building: **blackmail** *verb* **blackmailer** *noun*

blackout *noun*
1 an electrical power failure **2** a loss of memory, consciousness or sight which lasts for a short time

blacksmith *noun*
someone who makes or repairs things made of iron

bladder *noun*
1 a bag of skin inside your body which stores urine until it is passed out **2** any bag that gets bigger if you fill it with air or liquid, like the rubber bag inside a football

blade *noun*
1 the flat cutting part of a knife, sword or dagger **2** the leaf of a plant: *a blade of grass* **3** the thin flat part of something, like an oar or a bone

blame *noun*
1 the responsibility for a mistake: *He shares the blame for the accident.*
blame *verb*
2 to place blame on

Word Building: **blameless** *adjective* **blameworthy** *adjective*

blanch *verb*
1 to make or become white or pale: *The man blanched with fear.* **2** to put in boiling water for a short time, and then in cold, in order to remove the skins or to kill germs before freezing: *to blanch nuts, vegetables, or fruit*

bland *adjective*
1 pleasant or polite but often without real feeling: *a bland smile* **2** smooth and mild: *bland food*

Word Building: **blandly** *adverb* **blandness** *noun*

blank *adjective*
1 not written or printed on: *a blank piece of paper* **2** showing no understanding or interest: *He had a blank look on his face.*
blank *noun*
3 an empty space left for someone to fill in: *Just fill in the blanks on this form please.*
4 a gun cartridge which has powder inside it but no bullet: *The army uses blanks for its practice shooting.*

Word Building: **blankly** *adverb* **blankness** *noun*
Word History: from a French word meaning "white"

blanket *noun*
1 a large piece of soft woollen or cotton material, used as a bed covering **2** any layer or covering that hides something: *There was a blanket of snow covering the ground.*

blare (rhymes with *hair*) *verb*
to make a loud harsh sound: *The car horns blared.*

Word Building: **blare** *noun: the blare of traffic*

blasé (say *blah-zay*) *adjective*
not caring about and bored by the enjoyments and pleasures of life

Word Use: the accent over the "e" is a clue that this word was originally French

blaspheme (say *blas-feem*) *verb*
to speak without respect about God or sacred things

Word Building: **blasphemer** *noun* **blasphemy** *noun* (**blasphemies**)

blast *noun*
1 a sudden strong gust of wind or air
2 the shrill sound of a whistle or horn
3 an explosion **4** a severe criticism: *The teacher gave him a blast for being late.*
blast *verb*
5 to set off explosives **6** to criticise: *Her mother blasted her for being so naughty.*

Word Use: definitions 4 and 6 are more suited to everyday language

blatant (say *blay-tənt*) *adjective*
very obvious: *a blatant lie*

Word Building: **blatancy** *noun* **blatantly** *adverb*
Word History: made up by the English poet Edmund Spenser and based on a Latin word meaning "babble"

blaze[1] *noun*
1 a bright flame or fire **2** a gleam or glow of brightness: *a sudden blaze of sunlight* **3** a bright or sparkling display: *The garden was a blaze of colour.*
4 sudden fury: *a blaze of temper*
blaze[1] *verb*
5 to burn brightly: *The fire blazed in the fireplace.* **6** to shine or glow like a flame: *The oval blazed with lights during the match.*

blaze[2] *noun*
1 a mark made on a tree to point out a path **2** a white patch on the face of a horse or cow
blaze[2] *verb*
3 to mark a path with blazes: *The scouts blazed a trail through the bush.*

blazer *noun*
a jacket, sometimes with a crest sewn on the pocket

bleach *verb*
1 to make white, pale or colourless: *My mother bleached the stains out of my dress.*
bleach *noun*
2 a chemical used for bleaching

bleak *adjective*
1 cold and harsh: *A bleak winter wind was blowing.* **2** empty and dreary: *A prisoner in gaol has a bleak life.*

bleary *adjective*
dimmed from tears or tiredness: *bleary eyes*

Word Building: other forms are **blearier, bleariest** □ **blearily** *adverb* **bleariness** *noun*

bleat *verb*
1 to make the cry of a sheep or goat
2 to complain

Word Building: **bleat** *noun*

bleed *verb*
1 to lose blood **2** to draw or drain blood, liquid or air from: *to bleed the brakes of a car*

Word Building: other forms are **I bled, I have bled, I am bleeding**

blemish *verb*
to spoil with a spot or stain

Word Use: a similar word is **mar**
Word Building: **blemish** *noun* (**blemishes**)

blend *verb*
to mix or combine: *He blended the flour and water. / The flour and water blended well.*

Word Building: **blend** *noun*

blender *noun*
an electric appliance which chops and mixes food

bless *verb*
to make sacred: *The bishop blessed the church.*

Word Building: **blessings** *plural noun* good things given by God **blessed** *adjective* **blessedly** *adverb* **blessedness** *noun*

blight *noun*
1 a plant disease: *tomato blight*
2 something that damages or destroys

Word Building: **blight** *verb*

blind *adjective*
1 not able to see **2** unwilling to understand or be fair: *He was blind with anger.*
blind *verb*
3 to make unable to see
blind *noun*
4 a window cover which keeps out light
5 a cover for hiding the truth

Word Building: **blindly** *adverb* **blindness** *noun*

blindfold *verb*
to cover the eyes of, to prevent from seeing: *His captors blindfolded him.*

Word Building: **blindfold** *noun* a cover for the eyes

blink *verb*
to shut and open the eyes quickly and often: *I blinked in the bright sunlight.*

Word Building: **blink** *noun*

bliss *noun*
great happiness

Word Building: **blissful** *adjective* **blissfully** *adverb*

blister *noun*
1 a small watery swelling on your skin
blister *verb*
2 to cause blisters on: *The hot sun blistered my bare shoulders.* **3** to get blisters: *My bare shoulders blistered at the beach.*

Word Building: **blistering** *adjective: blistering heat* **blistery** *adjective*
Word History: from a French word meaning "clod" or "lump"

blithe *adjective*
happy or cheerful

Word Building: **blithely** *adverb*

blitz *noun*
a sudden attack: *a blitz on a city in wartime / a blitz on drivers who drink*

Word Building: **blitz** *verb*

blizzard *noun*
a snowstorm with strong winds

bloat *verb*
to make bigger or cause to swell, especially with air or water

bloc *noun*
a group of countries sharing the same political ideas: *the communist bloc*

Word Use: be careful – this sounds like **block**

block *noun*
1 a solid piece of hard material: *a child's building block* **2** a piece of land on which a house is built **3** a group of buildings or houses surrounded by streets
block *verb*
4 to be in the way of: *The accident blocked the traffic.*

Word Use: a similar word for definition 4 is **obstruct** □ be careful – this sounds like **bloc**
Word Building: **blockage** *noun*

blockade *noun*
the closing of a port by enemy ships or soldiers to stop supplies going in or out

Word Use: a similar word is **siege**
Word Building: **blockade** *verb*

blockbuster *noun*
1 a heavy powerful bomb dropped during World War II, espcially on fortifications **2** anything large and exciting: *The new James Bond movie is an absolute blockbuster.*

Word Use: definition 2 is more suited to everyday language

bloke *noun*
a man

Word Use: this word is more suited to everyday language

blond *adjective*
having light-coloured hair and skin

Word Building: **blonde** *noun* a woman with light-coloured hair **blond** *noun*
Word History: from a Latin word meaning "yellow"

blood *noun*
1 the fluid that flows through the arteries and veins of your body **2 in cold blood** calmly and without feeling

bloodbath *noun*
the cruel killing of a large number of people

Word Use: a similar word is **massacre**

bloodcurdling *adjective*
very frightening and horrible: *a bloodcurdling tale of evil and murder*

bloodhound *noun*
a large dog with a good sense of smell, used for hunting animals or finding lost people

bloodshot *adjective*
showing streaks of blood: *bloodshot eyes*

bloodthirsty *adjective*
wanting to kill: *The bloodthirsty pirates took no prisoners.*

Word Use: a similar word is **murderous**

bloody *adjective*
1 with blood on it **2** causing loss of life: *a bloody battle* **3** very great: *a bloody pest | a bloody miracle*

Word Use: the use of this word as in definition 3 might offend people
Word Building: other forms are **bloodier**, **bloodiest**

bloom *verb*
to produce flowers: *The rose bush blooms in summer.*

Word Building: **bloom** *noun* a flower **blooming** *adjective*

bloomers *plural noun*
loose underpants, worn by women

Word History: named after a Mrs Amelia Bloomer, a magazine publisher of New York, who helped make these pants popular in about 1850

blossom *noun*
1 the flower of a fruit tree
blossom *verb*
2 to produce flowers **3** to develop: *He blossomed into a fine athlete.*

blot *noun*
1 a spot of ink on paper **2** a stain: *a blot on your reputation*
blot *verb*
3 to dry or soak up: *to blot the ink* **4 blot out** to take away: *to blot out a bad memory*

Word Building: other verb forms are **I blotted, I have blotted, I am blotting**

blotch *noun*
a large unevenly shaped mark

Word Use: the plural is **blotches**
Word Building: **blotchy** *adjective*

blouse (say *blowz*) *noun*
a loosely fitting shirt usually gathered, or tucked in, at the waist

blow[1] *noun*
1 a hard stroke with the hand or something held in it **2** a sudden shock: *a blow to your pride*

blow[2] *verb*
1 to be in motion: *The winds blow.* **2** to be moved by the wind: *Dust blew down the street.* **3** to produce a current of air, with bellows or your mouth: *Blow on the fire.* **4** to make a noise by blowing into: *Blow the whistle.* **5** to burn out or burst: *The light bulb has blown. / The tyre blew.* **6** to put out with a puff of air: *Blow out the candle.* **7 blow up a** to force air into: *to blow up a balloon* **b** to destroy with explosives: *to blow up a bridge*

blow[2] *noun*
8 a storm with strong wind

Word Building: other verb forms are **it blew, it has blown, it is blowing**

blowfly *noun*
a fly which lays eggs on meat and rubbish

Word Building: the plural is **blowflies**

blubber *noun*
1 the fat of a whale or similar sea animal

blubber *verb*
2 to cry noisily

bludge *verb*
to avoid doing what you should: *While others worked, he bludged.*

Word Building: **bludger** *noun*

bludgeon (say <u>bluj</u>-ən) *noun*
a short heavy piece of wood used as a weapon

Word Building: **bludgeon** *verb* to hit with a bludgeon

blue *adjective*
1 having the colour of a clear sky **2** sad and depressed: *I'm feeling blue.* **3 true blue** loyal

blue *noun*
4 the colour blue **5** a mistake

Word Use: definitions 2 and 5 are more suited to everyday language
Word Building: other forms of the adjective are **bluer, bluest**

bluebottle *noun*
1 a small blue sea animal with long tentacles which can sting you **2** a large blue and green fly

blueprint *noun*
1 a copy of a building plan printed in white on blue paper **2** any detailed plan which can be copied at a later time

blues *plural noun*
1 feelings of sadness: *to have the blues* **2** a type of song, with sad words and a slow melody, first sung by black Americans

Word Use: definition 1 is more suited to everyday language
Word History: short for *blue devils*

blue-tongue *noun*
a large Australian lizard with a broad blue tongue

bluff[1] *noun*
a wide steep cliff

bluff[2] *verb*
1 to trick by showing you aren't afraid: *She bluffed her way past the guard, whistling as she went.* **2** to pretend you aren't afraid hoping you will get your own way: *Don't take any notice of him, he's only bluffing.*

bluff[2] *noun*
3 a pretence of having no fear: *It was a big bluff.*

blunder *noun*
1 a silly mistake

blunder *verb*
2 to make a silly mistake **3** to move or act clumsily: *I blundered into the cupboard.*

blunt *adjective*
1 not sharp: *a blunt knife* **2** plain or direct: *a blunt refusal*

Word Use: a similar word for definition 2 is **straightforward**
Word Building: **blunt** *verb* **bluntly** *adverb* **bluntness** *noun*

blur *verb*
1 to make unclear or confused: *Tears blurred my sight.*

blur *noun*
2 something that is unclear or confused: *We drove so fast the countryside was a blur.*

Word Building: other verb forms are **it blurred, it has blurred, it is blurring** □ **blurry** *adjective* (**blurrier, blurriest**)

blurb *noun*
information about a book or record, often printed on its cover

Word History: made up by the American humorist and illustrator, Gelett Burgess, who lived from 1866 to 1951

blush *verb*
to become red in the face when you're embarrassed or ashamed

Word Building: **blush** *noun* (**blushes**)

bluster *verb*
1 to speak or act in a noisy or violent way: *He blustered when he was criticised.* **2** to force by blustering: *He blustered his way through.*

Word Building: **blustery** *adjective* loud and violent: *a blustery wind*

BMX *noun*
a strongly-built bicycle, good for riding in rough areas

Word History: short for *Bicycle Motocross*, with the *cross* changed to *X* and pronounced as the letter "x"

boa constrictor *noun*
a snake which winds round its victim to crush and kill it

boar *noun*
a male pig

Word Use: the female is a **sow;** the young is a **piglet**

board *noun*
1 a flat piece of wood, cut into long thin pieces: *a floor board* **2** a thin flat piece of wood or other material made for a special purpose: *a chess board* | *an ironing-board* | *a noticeboard* **3** a group of people who are in charge of a business or organisation: *the board of the club*
board *verb*
4 to get on: *to board a ship or bus* **5** to pay for the use of a room, or for a room and meals: *I board at the hotel.*

boarder *noun*
1 a pupil who lives at a school **2** someone who pays for meals and a room to sleep in: *Mrs Smith takes in boarders.*

boast *verb*
1 to speak with too much pride: *She boasted about her son's ability.*
boast *noun*
2 something which is spoken of with pride

Word Building: **boaster** *noun* **boastful** *adjective* **boastfully** *adverb* **boastfulness** *noun*

boat *noun*
1 a small uncovered vessel for carrying people or things over water **2 in the same boat** in the same unpleasant situation

Word Building: **boating** *noun* travelling in boats: *Boating is my favourite sport.*

boater *noun*
a straw hat with a hard flat brim

boat people *plural noun*
people who escape from South-East Asian countries in boats

Word Use: people who are forced to leave their own country are **refugees**

bob[1] *noun*
1 a short quick movement: *a bob of the head*
bob[1] *verb*
2 to make a short quick movement up and down: *The float bobbed in the water.*
3 bob up to come into sight suddenly: *He bobbed up from behind the tree.*

Word Building: other verb forms are **I bobbed, I have bobbed, I am bobbing**

bob[2] *noun*
1 a short haircut for women and children
bob[2] *verb*
2 to cut short: *He bobbed the horse's tail.*

Word Building: other verb forms are **I bobbed, I have bobbed, I am bobbing**

bobbin *noun*
a small reel on which thread is wound for use in a sewing machine or in spinning

bodice (say *bod*-əs) *noun*
the part of a woman's dress above the waist

body *noun*
1 the whole physical structure of a person or animal **2** the physical part of a person or animal without the head, arms or legs **3** a dead person or animal **4** the main part: *the body of a car* | *the body of the speech* **5** a group of people or things: *a body of friends*

Word Use: a similar word for definition 2 is **trunk** □ a similar word for definition 3 is **corpse**
Word Building: the plural is **bodies** □ **bodily** *adjective*

bog *noun*
1 an area of muddy ground
bog *verb*
2 to make or become stuck: *The mud bogged the car.* | *The car was bogged in the mud.*

Word Building: other verb forms are **it bogged, it has bogged, it is bogging** □ **boggy** *adjective* (**boggier, boggiest**)

bogey (say *boh*-gee) *noun*
a swimming hole

Word Use: another spelling is **bogie**
Word History: from an Aboriginal language called Dharuk

boggle *verb*
to show fear or surprise

Word Building: other forms are **I boggled, I have boggled, I am boggling**

bogie (say *boh-gee*) *noun*
1 a small trolley used by workmen on a railway line **2** a set of wheels supporting a railway engine or carriage

bogong *noun*
a large Australian moth sometimes used as food

Word Use: another spelling is **bugong**
Word History: from a word meaning "high plains" in an Aboriginal language called Ngarigo

bogus (say *boh-gəs*) *adjective*
not real or true: *The bogus doctor was arrested by the police.*

Word Use: a similar word is **sham**

bogy (say *boh-gee*) *noun*
anything that frightens or worries you

Word Building: the plural is **bogies**

boil[1] *verb*
1 to cause to become so hot that bubbles form and steam comes off: *I boiled water for tea.* **2** to become as hot as that: *The water boiled.* **3** to hold, or be in, a boiling liquid: *The kettle is boiling.* | *The peas are boiling.* **4** to cook by boiling: *I boiled the potatoes.*

boil[2] *noun*
an infected swollen sore under your skin

boiler *noun*
1 a container with a lid used for boiling things **2** a closed container in which steam is produced to drive engines

boilersuit *noun*
overalls with sleeves, used when doing hard dirty work

boisterous *adjective*
rough and noisy

Word Building: **boisterously** *adverb* **boisterousness** *noun*

bold *adjective*
1 without fear **2** having no shame or modesty **3** rude **4** easy to see: *bold handwriting*

Word Building: **boldly** *adverb* **boldness** *noun* **embolden** *verb*

bolster (say *bohl-stə*) *noun*
1 a long round pillow **2** a support: *a bolster to your courage*

bolster *verb*
3 to help make strong: *Success bolstered his shattered pride.*

bolt *noun*
1 a sliding bar which fastens a door or gate **2** a thick metal pin which holds pieces of wood or metal together **3 a bolt of lightning** a flash in the sky, with thunder

bolt *verb*
4 to fasten with a bolt **5** to run away because you are afraid: *They bolted when they saw the police.*

Word Use: another word for definition 3 is **thunderbolt**

bomb *noun*
1 a container filled with an explosive and used as a weapon **2** an old car

bomb *verb*
3 to attack with bombs

Word Use: definition 2 is more suited to everyday language
Word Building: **bomber** *noun*

bombast *noun*
words or remarks that sound important but are often not sincere: *His speech was full of bombast.*

Word Building: **bombastic** *adjective* **bombastically** *adverb*
Word History: from a Latin word meaning "silkworm" or "silk"

bombshell *noun*
1 a bomb **2** something which causes surprise and shock

bond *noun*
1 something that joins or holds together: *a bond of friendship* **2** a promise or agreement: *to sign a bond to work for the government*

bond *verb*
3 to join or hold together: *to bond with glue*

bondage *noun*
the state of being controlled by someone or something

Word Use: a similar word is **slavery**

bone *noun*
1 one of the separate pieces of hard tissue that form a skeleton: *a hip bone* **2 have a bone to pick** to have something to argue about

bone *verb*
3 to take out the bones of: *to bone a fish*

Word Building: **bony** *adjective* (**bonier, boniest**)

bonfire *noun*
a large outdoor fire

bongo *noun*
one of a pair of small drums, which you play by beating with your fingers

Word Building: the plural is **bongos** or **bongoes**

bonnet *noun*
1 a close-fitting hat, tied under the chin: *a baby's bonnet* **2** any other hood or protective covering, such as the metal cover over the engine of a car

bonsai (say *bon-suy*) *noun*
1 the art of keeping trees and shrubs very small by cutting their roots and branches **2** a tree or shrub grown this way

Word History: from the Japanese word for "pot" added to the Japanese word meaning "to plant"

bonus *noun*
extra money paid to a worker as a reward for good work

bonzer *adjective*
excellent or pleasing: *a bonzer picnic*

Word Use: another spelling is **bonza** □ this is more suited to everyday language, although it sounds old-fashioned to many people

boobook *noun*
a small brownish owl with a white-spotted back and wings, found in Australia and New Zealand

book *noun*
1 a number of pages bound together inside a cover, for writing in or for reading
book *verb*
2 to reserve or buy early: *They booked seats on the train.* | *to book theatre tickets* **3** to record or take the name of: *A policeman booked Joe for speeding.*

Word Building: **booking** *noun*

bookish *adjective*
eager to read or study: *The athletic girls teased Jane for being bookish.*

bookkeeping *noun*
the job of keeping records of all the money earned and spent in a business

Word Building: **bookkeeper** *noun*

bookmaker *noun*
someone who takes the bets of other people, especially at a racecourse

Word Building: **bookmaking** *noun*

bookworm *noun*
someone who loves reading

boom[1] *verb*
1 to make a deep echoing noise: *His voice boomed in the cave.* **2** to suddenly do very well: *During the gold rush business was booming.*

Word Building: **boom** *noun*

boom[2] *noun*
1 a long pole, used to keep the bottom of a sail straight **2** a movable arm that holds a microphone or floodlight above the actors in a television or film studio

boomer *noun*
a large male kangaroo

boomerang *noun*
a curved stick used as a weapon by the Aborigines, which sometimes returns when you throw it

Word History: from an Aboriginal language called Dharuk

boon *noun*
a help or advantage: *The car is a boon now that I live so far from the city.*

boor (say *baw*) *noun*
someone who is rude or inconsiderate

Word Building: **boorish** *adjective* **boorishly** *adverb*
Word History: from the Dutch word meaning "peasant"

boost *verb*
to lift or increase: *to boost the child onto his shoulders* | *The teacher's praise boosted the nervous boy's confidence.*

Word Building: **boost** *noun* an upward push **booster** *noun* something which gives an increase

boot[1] *noun*
1 a shoe which covers part of the leg **2** a separate space for baggage at the back of a car

boot[2] *verb*
to start up a computer by loading its memory system

Word Use: you can also use **boot up**

booth *noun*
a small closed-in place usually made just big enough for one person: *a telephone booth* | *a ticket booth*

bootleg *adjective*
made illegally: *The old man went to gaol for making bootleg whisky.*

booty *noun*
anything taken or won, especially in times of war: *The pirates shared their booty of gold.*

booze *noun*
alcoholic drink: *They bought some booze for the party.*

Word Use: this word is more suited to everyday language
Word Building: **booze** *verb: to booze at the pub* **boozer** *noun* **boozy** *adjective*

border *noun*
1 the edge or side of anything: *to sew a pattern around the border* **2** a boundary line that separates one country or state from another

Word Building: **border** *verb*

borderline *adjective*
near the edge or boundary: *a borderline pass in the exam*

bore[1] *verb*
1 to make a round hole: *to bore through wood*

bore[1] *noun*
2 a deep hole drilled to reach an underground water supply

bore[2] *verb*
to tire or weary: *She bores me with her complaints.*

Word Building: **bore** *noun* a dull person **boredom** *noun* **boring** *adjective*

bore[3] *verb*
a form of **bear**[1]

borer *noun*
an insect that bores into wood

Word Use: a similar word is **termite**

born *verb*
a form of **bear**[1]

boronia (say *bə-roh-nee-ə*) *noun*
an Australian shrub with small pink or brown flowers

Word History: named after the Italian botanist, Francesco *Borone*, who lived from 1769 to 1794

borrow *verb*
to take or get on the understanding that you have to return it: *I borrow three library books every week.*

Word Building: **borrower** *noun*

bosom (say *booz-əm*) *noun*
someone's chest or breast, especially a woman's

boss *noun*
someone who employs and directs people, or controls a business

Word Building: **boss** *verb* to order around **bossy** *adjective* (**bossier, bossiest**) acting like a boss

botany *noun*
the study of plants

Word Building: **botanist** *noun* someone who studies plants **botanical** *adjective*

botch *verb*
to spoil or bungle: *He botched the cake by taking it out of the oven too soon.*

Word Building: **botch** *noun*

bother *verb*
1 to annoy or pester: *The flies bothered them so much they couldn't concentrate.* **2** to worry or confuse: *The maths problem bothered him.*

Word Building: **bothersome** *adjective*

bottle *noun*
a glass container used for holding liquids: *milk bottles*

Word Building: **bottle** *verb* to put in a bottle

bottlebrush *noun*
an Australian plant with red or pink brush-like flowers

bottleneck *noun*
a place where progress becomes slow, especially the narrow part of a road where traffic cannot flow freely

bougainvillea (say *boh-gən-vil-ee-ə*) *noun*
a tropical plant with brilliantly coloured leaves, widely grown in parts of Australia

Word History: named after Louis Antoine de Bougainville, a French scientist and explorer of the Pacific region, who lived from 1729 to 1811

bough (rhymes with *cow*) *noun*
one of the larger main branches of a tree

boulder (rhymes with *colder*) *noun*
a large smooth rock

boulevard (say *booh-lə-vahd*) *noun*
a wide avenue or city street lined with trees

bounce *verb*
1 to strike against and return: *The ball bounced on the pavement.* **2** to throw

against and cause to return: *He bounced the ball along the footpath.* **3** to be returned unpaid: *His cheque bounced.*

Word Use: definition 3 is more suited to everyday language
Word Building: **bouncing** *adjective* big, strong and healthy **bounce**

bound[1] *adjective*
1 tied up: *The prisoner held out his bound hands.* **2** fastened within a cover: *a book nicely bound* **3** sure: *If you don't put the bike away, it's bound to be stolen.* **4** having a duty, or under an obligation: *Once you've promised you're really bound to help.*

bound[2] *verb*
to move with big steps or leaps: *to bound over a fence | to bound after a ball*

Word Building: **bound** *noun* a leap

boundary *noun*
1 a dividing line or limit: *the boundary between states | He rode around the farm's boundary.* **2** a hit in cricket which sends the ball beyond the boundary of the field

Word Building: the plural is **boundaries**

bountiful *adjective*
plentiful or generous: *The rains produced a bountiful harvest.*

Word Building: **bountifully** *adverb*

bounty *noun*
1 generosity **2** a reward given for a special purpose: *There was a bounty for the killing of wild pigs which were causing damage.*

Word Building: the plural is **bounties**

bouquet (say *booh-kay, boh-*) *noun*
a bunch of flowers

Word Use: the "t" is silent because this came from French

bout *noun*
1 a contest: *a wrestling bout* **2** a period or spell: *a bout of hard work | a bout of flu*

boutique (say *booh-teek*) *noun*
a small shop, especially one that sells expensive or fashionable clothes

Word Use: the pronunciation is unusual because this word came from French

bovine (say *boh-vuyn*) *adjective*
having to do with the family of cud-chewing animals that includes cows, bulls and oxen

bow[1] (rhymes with *cow*) *verb*
to bend or stoop down: *The men bowed and the women curtsied to the queen.*

Word Building: **bow** *noun*

bow[2] (rhymes with *so*) *noun*
1 a piece of wood bent by a string stretched between its ends, which is used to shoot arrows **2** a knot, made up of two loops and two ends **3** the special stick used to play stringed instruments like the violin

bow[3] (rhymes with *cow*) *noun*
the front end of a boat

bowel *noun*
the long tube in your body which carries food from the stomach out of the body

Word Use: the plural **bowels** is often used □ another word for this is **intestine**
Word History: from a Latin word meaning "sausage"

bower *noun*
a leafy shelter

bowerbird *noun*
an Australian bird which makes a bower-like shelter where it keeps special objects and courts its mate

bowl[1] *noun*
1 a deep round dish used for holding food or liquid **2** something shaped like a bowl: *the bowl of a pipe*

bowl[2] *verb*
1 to throw or roll: *to bowl a hoop along the ground* **2** to throw a cricket ball with a straight arm towards the batsman **3** to get out by bowling: *He bowled the opening batsman with his first ball.*

Word Building: **bowl** *noun* a heavy weighted ball used in the game of bowls **bowler** *noun*

bowler *noun*
a hard felt hat with a rounded top and a narrow brim

bowls *noun*
a game in which heavy balls are rolled across a lawn

box[1] *noun*
1 a wooden or cardboard container with a lid **2** a small room or raised stand: *a box at the theatre | a witness box* **3 the box** a television set

Word Use: definition 3 is more suited to everyday language
Word Building: the plural is **boxes**

box[2] *verb*
to hit with your hand or fist

Word Building: **boxer** *noun* someone who fights with his fists **boxing** *noun*

box office *noun*
the place in a theatre where tickets are sold

boy *noun*
a male child

Word Use: another word that sounds the same is **buoy**
Word Building: **boyhood** *noun* **boyish** *adjective* **boyishly** *adverb*

boycott *verb*
1 to refuse to go to: *to boycott a meeting* **2** to stop buying or using: *to boycott the new soap powder*

Word History: named after Captain Charles C Boycott, 1832 to 1897, an Irish land agent who was ignored by his tenants when he refused to lower rents in hard times

bra *noun*
underwear which supports the breasts

Word History: a shortened form of **brassiere**

brace *noun*
1 something which holds parts together or in place **2 braces a** wires placed on your teeth to help straighten them **b** straps worn over your shoulders for holding up your trousers

Word Building: **brace** *verb* to steady

bracelet *noun*
a chain or band worn around your wrist

Word History: from a Latin word meaning "arm"

bracken *noun*
a fern which is often found in the wetter parts of Australia

brackets *plural noun*
either of the two sets of signs ( ) or [ ] used to enclose words which interrupt a sentence but add information to it, as in *John (the butcher's son) brought meat for our barbecue.*

brackish *adjective*
slightly salty: *The cattle wouldn't drink the brackish water.*

brag *verb*
to boast

Word Building: other forms are **I bragged, I have bragged, I am bragging** □ **braggart** *noun* someone who is always boasting

braid *verb*
1 to weave or plait

braid *noun*
2 a plait: *She wore her hair in one long braid.* **3** a woven trimming: *The officer's uniform was edged with braid.*

braille (rhymes with *rail*) *noun*
a system of printing using raised dots which blind people can read by touch

Word History: named after its inventor, Louis Braille, 1809 to 1852

brain *noun*
1 the soft greyish mass of nerve cells inside your skull, which controls feeling, thinking and movement **2** understanding or intelligence: *He has a good brain.* **3** a very clever or well-informed person: *She's a real brain.*

Word Use: definition 2 is often plural as in *He has brains.* □ **cerebral** is a word meaning "having to do with the brain"
Word Building: **brainy** *adjective* (**brainier, brainiest**) clever

brainstorm *noun*
a sudden brilliant idea

braise *verb*
to fry quickly in a pan, then stew gently in a covered pot

brake *noun*
something which slows or stops a machine

Word Building: **brake** *verb* to slow or stop

bramble *noun*
any thorny bush growing wild

Word Building: **brambly** *adjective*

bran *noun*
the outer shell of wheat or rye, sometimes used in breakfast cereal

branch *noun*
1 the limb of a tree or shrub **2** a part or section which divides from the main part: *the branch of a river* **3** part of a large organisation: *the local branch of my bank*

branch *verb*
4 to divide or separate **5 branch out** to develop in a new direction

Word Building: the plural form of the noun is **branches**

brand *noun*
1 the mark or label on something which shows where it comes from or who makes it **2** the particular kind or make of something: *my favourite brand of jam*

Word Building: **brand** *verb* to mark with a brand

brandish *verb*
to shake or wave: *The soldiers brandished their swords.*

brandy *noun*
a strong alcoholic drink made from wine

Word Building: the plural is **brandies**

brash *adjective*
bold or over-confident: *The brash youth offended everyone with his bragging.*

Word Building: **brashly** *adverb*

brass *noun*
1 a yellowish metal mixed from copper and zinc **2** the group name for the trumpet and horn family of musical instruments: *The conductor brought in the strings, the woodwinds and then the brass.*

Word Building: **brass** *adjective: brass instruments* **brassy** *adjective* **braze** *verb* **brazen** *adjective*

brassiere (say *braz-ee-ə*) *noun*
underwear which supports the breasts

Word Use: this is the full form of **bra**

brat *noun*
a child: *She told the woman to quieten her brats.*

Word Use: this word is usually used in an unfriendly way

bravado (say *brə-vah-doh*) *noun*
bravery and confidence which is often pretended: *He was full of bravado until the time came for him to perform.*

brave *adjective*
full of courage

Word Building: **brave** *verb* **bravely** *adverb* **bravery** *noun*
Word History: from a Spanish word meaning "vicious" (first used about bulls)

brawl *noun*
a noisy quarrel or fight

Word Building: **brawl** *verb*

brawn *noun*
1 well-developed muscles or muscular strength: *to be all brawn and no brains*
2 cooked meat, pressed in a mould and set in its own jelly, used with salads and in sandwiches

Word Building: **brawny** *adjective* (**brawnier, brawniest**) strong and muscly

bray *noun*
the loud harsh noise a donkey makes

Word Building: **bray** *verb*

brazen *adjective*
1 made of brass **2** cheeky or rude: *brazen behaviour*

Word Use: a word with a similar meaning to definition 2 is **insolent**

brazier *noun*
a metal container for holding burning fuel and used for heating or cooking

breach *noun*
1 a failure to keep or observe: *a breach of promise | a breach of the law* **2** a gap or opening: *a breach in the line of defence*

Word Building: the plural is **breaches** □ **breach** *verb*

bread (say *bred*) *noun*
1 a food made by baking flour and water, usually with yeast to make it rise: *a loaf of bread* **2** a general word for food: *to earn our daily bread* **3** money

Word Use: definition 3 is more suited to everyday language

breadth *noun*
the distance from one side to the other

Word Use: a similar word is **width**

breadwinner *noun*
someone who earns the money to keep a family

break *verb*
1 to divide into pieces violently **2** to fail to keep: *to break a promise* **3** to crack a bone of: *to break a leg* **4** to do better than: *to break a record in running* **5** to interrupt: *to break the silence* **6** to make known: *to break the news* **7** to change in tone: *His voice broke.* **8** to begin racing before the starting signal has been given: *Two swimmers broke.* **9 break down a** to collapse **b** to overcome **c** to stop working properly **10 break up a** to separate or finish: *to break up a marriage* **b** to finish a school term for the holidays **c** to explode into laughter

break *noun*
11 a gap: *a break in the fence* **12** an attempt to escape: *a break for freedom* **13** a short rest: *They took a break from work.*

Word Use: definition 10c is more suited to everyday language
Word Building: other verb forms are **I broke, I have broken, I am breaking** □ **breakable** *adjective* **breakage** *noun*

breakdown *noun*
1 a collapse or failure: *a nervous breakdown* **2** separation into simple parts: *the breakdown of soil* **3** an analysis: *a breakdown of all our accounts*

breakfast *noun*
the first meal of the day

Word Building: **breakfast** *verb* to have breakfast

breakneck *adjective*
dangerous: *to drive at a breakneck speed*

breakthrough *noun*
any important new development which allows for further progress to take place: *a breakthrough in finding a cure for cancer*

bream (sounds like *brim*) *noun*
an Australian saltwater fish which is good for eating

breast *noun*
1 *an old-fashioned word for* **chest** **2** one of the two parts of a woman's body that produce milk

breast stroke *noun*
a way of swimming in which your arms move outwards and back from your chest and your legs kick in a frog-like manner

breath *noun*
1 the air taken into your lungs and let out again: *short of breath* **2** an act of breathing once: *Take a deep breath.* **3** a light current: *A breath of air cooled the stuffy room.*

Word Building: **breathy** *adjective* **breathless** *adjective*

breathalyser *noun*
a machine used to measure the amount of alcohol in someone's breath

breathe *verb*
1 to draw in and give out air: *We breathe without thinking.* **2** to speak softly **3** to live or exist: *Everything that breathed was destroyed in the flood.*

Word Building: **breather** *noun* a pause for rest

breathtaking *adjective*
causing excitement or pleasure: *a breathtaking adventure | breathtaking beauty*

breech *noun*
the barrel of a gun

breeches (rhymes with *stitches*) *plural noun*
trousers covering the hips and thighs: *riding breeches*

breed *verb*
1 to produce young: *Rats were breeding in the garbage.* **2** to produce, by keeping the parents for the purpose: *He breeds prize bulls.* **3** to cause: *Dirt breeds disease.*
breed *noun*
4 a type or kind: *a breed of sheep*

Word Building: other verb forms are **I bred, I have bred, I am breeding** □ **breeder** *noun* someone who breeds animals

breeding *noun*
1 the mating and rearing of animals
2 good manners which are the result of training

breeze *noun*
a light wind or movement of air

Word Building: **breezy** *adjective* (**breezier, breeziest**) **breezily** *adverb* **breeziness** *noun*

brethren (say bredh-rən) *plural noun*
brothers

Word Use: this is an old-fashioned word

brevity (say brev-ə-tee) *noun*
shortness or briefness: *The brevity of his speech surprised us.*

brew *verb*
1 to make or prepare: *Let's brew a pot of tea. | to brew a stronger beer* **2** to cause or bring about: *to brew trouble* **3** to be forming or gathering: *Trouble is brewing.*

Word Building: **brewery** *noun* (**breweries**) a place where beer is made **brew** *noun* **brewer** *noun*

briar (rhymes with *fire*) *noun*
a prickly bush

bribe *noun*
money or a gift given to someone if they promise to do something they shouldn't for you

Word Building: **bribe** *verb: He tried to bribe the policeman to let him go.* **bribery** *noun*

brick *noun*
1 a small hard block of baked clay, used for building **2** something shaped like a brick: *a brick of ice-cream*

Word Building: **bricklayer** *noun* someone who builds with bricks

bride *noun*
a woman who is going to be married or who has just been married

Word Building: **bridal** *adjective* having to do with a bride or a wedding

bridegroom *noun*
a man who is going to be married or who has just been married

bridesmaid *noun*
an unmarried woman who helps a bride on her wedding day

bridge[1] *noun*
1 a structure built over a river, road or railway line, to provide a way of getting from one side to the other **2** a raised platform above the deck of a ship for the captain or other senior officers **3** the upper part of your nose

bridge[1] *verb*
4 to make a bridge over: *When the government bridged the river, ferries were no longer needed.*

bridge[2] *noun*
a card game for two pairs of players

bridle *noun*
1 the leather straps, bit and reins fitted around a horse's head and used to control it

bridle *verb*
2 to put a bridle on **3** to curb or restrain: *Bridle your temper.*

brief *adjective*
1 short: *a brief visit* / *a brief speech* / *a brief skirt*

brief *noun*
2 an outline of information or instructions on a subject, especially for use by a barrister conducting a legal case

Word Building: **brevity** *noun* **briefness** *noun* **briefly** *adverb*

briefcase *noun*
a flat rectangular case for carrying books and papers

briefs *plural noun*
close-fitting underpants without legs

brigade *noun*
1 a large group of soldiers **2** a group of people trained for a special purpose: *a fire brigade*

Word Building: **brigadier** *noun* an army officer in charge of a brigade

brigalow *noun*
a type of acacia that grows in Queensland and northern New South Wales, and which has strong heavy wood used by the Aborigines for carving

Word History: from an Aboriginal language called Kamilaroi

brigand (say *brig-ənd*) *noun*
one of a gang of robbers who live in mountain or forest areas

bright *adjective*
1 shining or giving a strong light: *a bright silver coin* / *a bright lamp* **2** clever: *a bright pupil* **3** cheerful and happy: *Sad people need bright company.*

Word Building: **brighten** *verb* **brightly** *adverb* **brightness** *noun*

brilliant *adjective*
1 shining brightly **2** extraordinarily clever: *a brilliant plan* / *a brilliant pianist*

Word Building: **brilliance** *noun* **brilliantly** *adverb*

brim *noun*
1 the top edge or rim of something hollow: *He filled the glass to the brim.* **2** the outer edge of a hat

Word History: from an Old English word meaning "sea"

brindled *adjective*
grey or brownish-yellow with darker streaks or spots

brine *noun*
strongly salted water, often used in preserving some foods

Word Building: **briny** *adjective: the briny sea*

bring *verb*
1 to carry: *I will bring the book.* **2** to cause to come: *The drought brought suffering to everyone.*

Word Building: other forms are **I brought, I have brought, I am bringing**

brink *noun*
the edge of a steep or dangerous place or time: *the brink of a cliff* / *on the brink of war*

brisk *adjective*
fast and lively: *a brisk walk* / *a brisk breeze*

Word Building: **briskly** *adverb* **briskness** *noun*

bristle *noun*
1 a short stiff hair or hairlike material: *pigs bristles | the bristles of a brush*
bristle *verb*
2 to raise the bristles: *The dog bristled when it saw the burglar.* **3** to show anger: *He bristled at the idea.*

Word Building: **bristly** *adjective: a bristly beard*

brittle *adjective*
likely to break easily: *brittle shells*

Word Building: **brittleness** *noun*

broach *verb*
to ask about for the first time: *I broached the subject of buying a dictionary.*

broad *adjective*
1 very wide: *a broad river | broad knowledge* **2** widely spread or complete: *broad daylight* **3** not detailed: *the broad outline of the story* **4** having a strong accent: *He speaks broad Australian.*

Word Building: **broaden** *verb* **broadly** *adverb*

broadcast *verb*
1 to send by radio: *to broadcast a program* **2** to send radio messages or programs: *They are broadcasting now.*

Word Building: other forms are **I broadcast, I have broadcast, I am broadcasting** □ **broadcast** *noun* **broadcaster** *noun*

broad-minded *adjective*
able to accept other people's ideas and ways

Word Use: a similar word is **tolerant**
Word Building: **broad-mindedly** *adverb* **broad-mindedness** *noun*

broadside *noun*
the firing of all the guns on one side of a ship

brocade (say *brə-kayd*) *noun*
cloth woven with a raised pattern on it

Word Building: **brocaded** *adjective*

broccoli (say *brok-ə-lee*) *noun*
a green vegetable similar to a cauliflower

brochure (say *broh-shə*) *noun*
a small book with a paper cover, containing information or advertisements

Word Use: a word with a similar meaning is **pamphlet**
Word History: from a French word meaning "stitch"

brogue[1] (say *brohg*) *noun*
a broad accent, especially an Irish one

brogue[2] (say *brohg*) *noun*
a strongly made, comfortable shoe

broke *adjective*
having no money

Word Use: this word is more suited to everyday language □ this word comes from the verb **break**

broken *adjective*
1 separated into pieces: *a broken plate* **2** not working because of the breaking of one of the parts: *a broken watch | a broken arm* **3** not kept or obeyed: *a broken promise | broken rules* **4** imperfectly spoken: *He spoke broken English.*

Word Use: this word comes from the verb **break**

broker *noun*
someone who buys or sells things for someone else: *a stockbroker or wool broker*

Word Building: **brokerage** *noun*

brolga *noun*
a large silvery-grey bird with long legs, which dances

Word Use: this used to be better known as **native companion**
Word History: from an Aboriginal language called Kamilaroi

bronchitis (say *brong-kuy-təs*) *noun*
an illness in which the lining of the air passages in the chest becomes red and sore

brontosaurus (say *bron-tə-saw-rəs*) *noun*
a giant lizard-like animal that died out millions of years ago

Word Use: a brontosaurus is a type of **dinosaur**
Word History: from a Greek word for "thunder" added to a Greek word for "lizard"

bronze *noun*
1 a brown-coloured metal mixed from copper and tin
bronze *adjective*
2 of the colour of bronze

brooch (rhymes with *coach*) *noun*
an ornament made to be fastened to your clothes with a pin

Word Building: the plural is **brooches**

brood *noun*
1 a number of young animals, especially birds, hatched at the same time

brood *verb*
2 to sit on eggs to hatch them **3 brood on** to worry about: *She brooded on her failure.*

Word Building: **broody** *adjective: a broody hen*

brook (rhymes with *book*) *noun*
a small stream

Word Use: Australians usually call this a **creek**

broom *noun*
a brush with a long handle, used for sweeping

broth *noun*
a thin soup of fish, meat or vegetables

brothel *noun*
a house where prostitutes work

brother *noun*
1 a male relative who has the same parents as you **2** a fellow worker or colleague: *They are brothers in the fight against crime.* **3** a male member of certain church organisations

Word Building: **brotherhood** *noun* **brotherly** *adjective*

brother-in-law *noun*
1 the brother of your husband or your wife **2** the husband of your sister **3** the husband of the sister of your wife or husband

Word Building: the plural is **brothers-in-law**

brow (rhymes with *now*) *noun*
1 the bony ridge over your eye **2** the hair growing on that ridge **3** the edge or top of a steep place: *the brow of a hill*

Word Use: another word for definition 1 is **forehead** □ another word for definition 2 is **eyebrow**

browbeat *verb*
to bully

Word Building: other forms are **he browbeat, he has browbeaten, he is browbeating**

brownie *noun*
1 a brown fairy believed to secretly do your housework at night **2** a thick brown biscuit

browse *verb*
1 to feed or graze: *The cattle browsed in the clover.* **2** to glance casually through a book or at the goods in a shop

Word Building: **browse** *noun* **browser** *noun*

bruise *verb*
1 to cause a discoloured mark on the body: *The punch bruised my arm.* **2** to develop such a bruised mark: *I bruise easily.*

Word Building: **bruiser** *noun* someone who is strong and tough **bruise** *noun*

brumby *noun*
a wild horse living freely in the bush

Word Building: the plural is **brumbies**
Word History: perhaps from an Aboriginal language, or perhaps named after Lieutenant Brumby, a horse-breeder who let some horses run wild in the early 1800s

brunch *noun*
a meal in midmorning instead of breakfast and lunch

Word Use: this word is called a **blended** or **portmanteau word**
Word Building: the plural is **brunches**
Word History: made by joining the first two letters of *br(eakfast)* to the last four letters of *(l)unch*

brunette *noun*
a woman or girl with dark hair

brunt *noun*
the main shock or force: *to bear the brunt of an attack*

brush[1] *noun*
1 an instrument made of hair or bristles set in a handle: *a paint brush | a hair brush* **2** an act of brushing: *Give my coat a brush.* **3** an argument: *I had a brush with him over using my paints.*
brush[1] *verb*
4 to use a brush on: *Brush your hair every day.* **5** to touch lightly: *She brushed me as she passed.* **6 brush aside** to ignore: *He brushed my arguments aside.*

Word Building: the plural of the noun is **brushes**

brush[2] *noun*
a thick growth of bushes

brusque (say *brusk, broosk*) *adjective*
quick to say something and not very polite: *His brusque manner upsets people.*

Word Building: **brusquely** *adverb* **brusqueness** *noun*

brussels sprout *noun*
a green vegetable like a tiny cabbage

brutal *adjective*
savagely cruel: *a brutal blow*

Word Building: **brutality** *noun* **brutally** *adverb*

brute *noun*
1 an animal or beast **2** a cruel person

bubble *noun*
1 a small ball of air or gas rising through liquid **2** a small ball of air in a fine coating of liquid: *to blow bubbles*

Word Building: **bubble** *verb* to send up bubbles **bubbly** *adjective*

bubblegum *noun*
chewing gum which can be blown into bubbles

bubbler *noun*
a small fountain which sends up a short stream of drinking water

buccaneer *noun*
a pirate

buck[1] *noun*
a male deer, rabbit or hare

Word Use: the female animal is called a **doe**

buck[2] *verb*
1 to jump with arched back and stiff legs: *The young horse bucked the first time he was saddled.* **2** to throw by bucking: *The horse bucked his rider off.*

bucket *noun*
a round open container with a flat bottom and a handle

Word Building: **bucketful** *noun*

buckle *noun*
1 a clasp for fastening a belt or strap **2** a bend or bulge in a sheet of hard material
buckle *verb*
3 to fasten with a buckle **4** to cause to bend or bulge: *The heat buckled the record.* **5** to bend or bulge: *The heat caused the record to buckle.*

bucktooth *noun*
a tooth in your upper jaw that sticks out

Word Building: the plural is **buckteeth** □ **bucktoothed** *adjective*

bucolic (say *byooh-kol-ik*) *adjective*
having to do with farming or the country: *living in bucolic isolation*

Word Use: a word with a similar meaning is **rustic**

bud *noun*
1 a flower or leaf before it has fully opened **2** a small shoot on the stem of a plant which will grow into a leaf or flower

Word Building: **bud** *verb* (**budded, budding**) to produce buds

Buddhism (say *bood-iz-əm*) *noun*
a world religion, founded by the teacher Buddha who lived in India about the sixth century BC

Word Building: **Buddhist** *noun* a follower of Buddhism **Buddhist** *adjective: a Buddhist temple*
Word History: named after *Buddha,* a Sanskrit name meaning "wise" or "enlightened"

buddy *noun*
a friend or mate: *my best buddy*

Word Use: this is more suited to everyday language
Word Building: the plural is **buddies**

budge *verb*
to move: *I won't budge until you return. | I can't budge that heavy table.*

Word Use: this is usually used with the word *not*

budgerigar (say *buj-ə-ree-gah*) *noun*
a small yellow and green parakeet found in inland parts of Australia, but also kept in cages and bred in other colours

Word Use: the shortened form is **budgie**
Word History: probably from an Aboriginal language called Kamilaroi

budget *noun*
1 a plan showing what money you will earn and how you will spend it
budget *verb*
2 to make such a plan
budget *adjective*
3 not costing much: *budget clothes*

Word Building: other verb forms are **I budgeted, I have budgeted, I am budgeting**

buff *adjective*
1 light yellow
buff *noun*
2 an expert: *a film buff*

buffalo *noun*
a kind of ox sometimes used for pulling heavy loads, especially in India, now found roaming wild in northern Australia

Word Building: the plural is **buffalos** or **buffaloes**

buffer *noun*
something that softens a blow, especially one of the two springs at each end of a railway carriage to take the shock of a collision

buffet[1] (say *buf-ət*) *verb*
to strike, shake or knock about: *The big waves buffeted the boat.*

Word Building: other forms are **it buffeted, it has buffeted, it is buffeting** □ **buffet** *noun* a blow or a slap

buffet[2] (say <u>*buf*</u>*-ay*) *noun*
1 a table or counter holding food **2** a low cupboard for holding cups and plates
buffet[2] *adjective*
3 set out on a table from which you serve yourself: *a buffet dinner*

Word Use: this word came from French

buffoon *noun*
someone who acts the fool

Word Building: **buffoonery** *noun* **buffoonish** *adjective*

bug *noun*
1 any tiny insect **2** an illness caused by an infection **3** something that is going wrong: *There's a bug in my computer program.* **4** a hidden microphone
bug *verb*
5 to hide a microphone in: *The spy bugged the room.* **6** to annoy: *Your silliness bugs me.*

Word Use: this word is more suited to everyday language
Word Building: other verb forms are **I bugged, I have bugged, I am bugging**

bugbear *noun*
something that worries or annoys you: *Exams are my bugbear.*

buggy *noun*
a light carriage with two wheels, pulled by one horse

Word Building: the plural is **buggies**

bugle (say <u>*byooh*</u>*-gəl*) *noun*
a wind instrument, used in the army to sound signals

Word Building: **bugler** *noun*
Word History: from a Latin word meaning "ox"

build *verb*
1 to make by joining parts together: *to build a house / to build a model aeroplane*
2 build up to increase or make stronger
build *noun*
3 the shape of someone's body: *a heavy build*

Word Building: other verb forms are **I built, I have built, I am building** □ **builder** *noun*

building *noun*
something built for people to live or work in, such as a house or office block

bulb *noun*
1 the rounded root-like stem of certain plants, such as the onion **2** anything with a shape like that: *an electric light bulb*

Word Building: **bulbous** *adjective*

bulge *noun*
a round part that swells out

Word Building: **bulge** *verb*

bulk *noun*
1 the size of something including its length, width and depth: *a ship's bulk*
2 the main part: *The bulk of the work has been done.*

Word Building: **bulky** *adjective* (**bulkier, bulkiest**) **bulkiness** *noun*

bull *noun*
1 a male of the cattle family **2** a male elephant, whale or seal

Word Use: the female of definition 1 is a **cow**; the young of definition 1 is a **calf**

bull ant *noun*
a large ant which can give a painful bite

Word Use: another name is **bulldog ant**

bulldog *noun*
a type of dog with a large head and a small strong body

bulldozer *noun*
a powerful tractor with a blade in front, used to move trees and rocks and to level land

Word Building: **bulldoze** *verb*

bullet *noun*
a small piece of metal shot from a small gun

bulletin *noun*
a short written or spoken news report: *the latest bulletin on the floods*

bullfight *noun*
an entertainment in which a man fights with, and usually kills, a bull

Word Building: **bullfighter** *noun* **bullfighting** *noun*

bullion (say <u>*bool*</u>*-yən*) *noun*
bars of gold or silver

bullock *noun*
a bull that has had its sex organs removed

Word Use: a word with a similar meaning is **steer**
Word Building: **bullocky** *noun* the driver of a bullock team

bullroarer *noun*
a thin piece of wood on a string, which is whirled in the air to make a roaring noise, used by the Aborigines in their religious ceremonies

Word Use: the Aboriginal name for this is **churinga**

bullseye *noun*
1 the central spot on a target **2** a round hard sweet

bully *noun*
someone who hurts, frightens or orders about smaller or weaker people

Word Building: the plural is **bullies** □ **bully** *verb* (**bullied, bullying**) to behave as a bully towards

bulrush *noun*
a kind of tall rush which grows in wet places, such as on the banks of rivers, and which is used to make mats, and so on

Word Building: another spelling is **bull-rush**

bumblebee *noun*
a large hairy kind of bee

bump *verb*
1 to knock against: *I bumped the table*
2 to hit: *I bumped my head on the tree.*
3 bump into to meet by chance
4 bump off to kill

bump *noun*
5 a light hit or knock **6** a small raised area: *a bump on the head / a bump on the road*

Word Use: definition 4 is more suited to everyday language
Word Building: **bumpy** *adjective* (**bumpier, bumpiest**)

bumper bar *noun*
the bar across the front or back of a car which protects it in a collision

Word Use: a short form of this is **bumper**

bumpkin *noun*
someone who is awkward and clumsy

Word Use: this word is insulting
Word History: from a Dutch word meaning "little barrel"

bumptious (say *bump-shəs*) *adjective*
showing your importance in a way that offends people: *a bumptious young man*

Word Building: **bumptiously** *adverb* **bumptiousness** *noun*

bun *noun*
1 a kind of round bread roll which can be plain or sweetened **2** hair arranged at the back of your head in the shape of a bun

bunch *noun*
a group of things joined or gathered together: *a bunch of grapes / a bunch of roses*

Word Use: the plural is **bunches**
Word Building: **bunch** *verb* to gather together

bundle *noun*
1 a group of things loosely held together: *a bundle of sticks*

bundle *verb*
2 to put together loosely: *I bundled the books into my bag.* **3** to send away quickly: *I bundled them out of the room.*

bung *noun*
1 a stopper for the hole in a wine cask

bung *verb*
2 to close with a bung, or to block with any obstruction: *The drain is bunged up.*
3 to throw or toss: *Bung it over here, Bruce!*

Word Use: definition 3 is more suited to everyday language

bungalow *noun*
a house with only one storey

bungle *verb*
to do badly: *He bungled the job.*

Word Building: **bungle** *noun* something badly done **bungler** *noun*

bunion (rhymes with *onion*) *noun*
a swelling of a joint on the foot, especially on the big toe

bunk *noun*
1 a bed built like a shelf, in a ship's cabin **2** one of a pair of beds built one above the other

bunker[1] *noun*
1 a large container for fuel **2** a sandy hollow on a golf course

bunker[2] *noun*
an underground air-raid shelter

bunkum *noun*
insincere or foolish talk

bunting *noun*
brightly coloured cloth used to make flags for decoration

bunyip *noun*
an imaginary creature of Aboriginal legend, said to live in swamps and billabongs

Word History: from an Aboriginal language called Wemba

buoy (say *boy*) *noun*
1 a float anchored in the water, which marks channels and hidden rocks **2** a ring used to help people stay afloat

Word Use: a similar word for definition 2 is **lifebuoy** □ be careful – this sounds like **boy**
Word Building: **buoy** *verb*

buoyant (say *boy-ənt*) *adjective*
1 able to float: *This rubber ring will keep you buoyant.* **2** light-hearted and cheerful

Word Building: **buoyancy** *noun* **buoyantly** *adverb*

burden *noun*
1 a load: *to carry a heavy burden* **2** a difficult job that you don't really want to do: *The children found looking after the animals a burden.*

Word Building: **burden** *verb* to load: *I won't burden you with my problems.* **burdensome** *adjective*

bureau (say *byooh-roh*) *noun*
1 a writing-desk with drawers **2** a government office where people can get information: *a tourist bureau*

Word Use: definition 2 sometimes has a capital: *the Weather Bureau*
Word Building: the plural is **bureaus** or **bureaux**

bureaucracy (say *byooh-rok-rə-see*) *noun*
1 unnecessary rules about the way things have to be done in government offices
2 the bureaucracy the people who make these rules

Word Building: the plural is **bureaucracies** □ **bureaucrat** *noun* a member of the bureaucracy **bureaucratic** *adjective* **bureaucratically** *adverb*

burglary (say *ber-glə-ree*) *noun*
the crime of breaking into a building to steal things

Word Building: the plural is **burglaries** □ **burglar** *noun* **burgle** *verb*

burgundy *noun*
1 a type of wine **2** a rich dark red colour

Word History: from *Burgundy*, the region in south-eastern France where this wine comes from

burial (say *be-ree-əl*) *noun*
the act of putting a dead person into a grave: *We all went to the cemetery for our grandfather's burial.*

Word Use: do not confuse this with **funeral**
Word Building: **bury** *verb* (**buried, burying**)

burlesque (say *ber-lesk*) *noun*
a play or a book which makes people laugh by making fun of serious matters

burly *adjective*
big and solidly built: *a burly fellow*

Word Building: other forms are **burlier, burliest**

burn *verb*
1 to set or be on fire: *to burn the wood / The wood is burning.* **2** to give out heat and light: *This sand burns. / The lights burn all night.* **3** to turn black or red by heat or fire: *Put on a sunhat in case your face burns. / to burn the toast* **4** to hurt by heat or fire: *to burn your fingers in the flame*
5 to feel strongly: *to burn with anger*
6 burn off to clear land by setting fire to the trees

burn *noun*
7 a sore made by something hot: *She had a bad burn from the iron.*

Word Building: other verb forms are **I burnt** or **I burned, I have burnt** or **I have burned, I am burning**

burner *noun*
the part of a stove or lamp where the flame comes out

burning *adjective*
very interesting and important: *a burning question*

burnish *verb*
to make bright and shiny by polishing: *to burnish the copper pot*

Word Building: **burnished** *adjective: Her hair shone like burnished gold.*

burp *verb*
1 to noisily pass wind from your stomach through your mouth: *Drinking lemonade makes me burp.* **2** to help to burp, especially by patting on the back: *to burp the baby after its feed*

Word Use: **belch** is a more old-fashioned word for this
Word Building: **burp** *noun*

burr *noun*
the prickly case around some seeds, such as a chestnut seed

burrow *noun*
1 a hole in the ground dug by an animal, to live and shelter in: *The wombat was hiding in its burrow.*
burrow *verb*
2 to dig a burrow **3** to search with a digging movement: *She burrowed in her bag.*

bursary *noun*
money given to a student to help pay for school fees, textbooks, uniforms and other expenses

Word Building: the plural is **bursaries** □ **bursar** *noun* the person in charge of money at a school or college

burst *verb*
1 to split or break open: *The sausages burst when we cooked them.* | *to burst a balloon* **2** to rush suddenly: *The children burst into the room.* **3** to be full or overflowing: *The shopping basket was bursting with goodies.* **4** to express your feelings suddenly: *to burst out laughing*
burst *noun*
5 a sudden effort, or action: *a burst of speed* | *a burst of clapping*

Word Building: other forms are **it burst, it has burst, it is bursting**

bury (rhymes with *very*) *verb*
1 to put in the ground and cover with earth: *Dogs bury their bones.* **2** to cover over completely: *Her books were buried under a pile of clothing.* **3 bury yourself** to occupy yourself completely so that you don't notice anything else: *to bury yourself in a book*

Word Use: be careful – this sounds like **berry**
Word Building: other forms are **I buried, I have buried, I am burying** □ **burial** *noun*

bus *noun*
a long vehicle with many seats, for carrying passengers: *to catch the bus to school*

Word Building: the plural is **buses**
Word History: a shortened form of **omnibus**

bush *noun*
1 a plant like a small tree with many branches coming out from the trunk near the ground: *a rose bush* **2** a tree-covered area of land **3 the bush** the Australian country as opposed to the city: *Our cousins live in the bush.* **4 beat about the bush** to take a long time coming to the point in a conversation

Word Building: the plural is **bushes** □ **bushy** *adjective* thick or dense like a bush: *a fox's bushy tail*

bush band *noun*
a group of musicians who perform Australian folk music, using instruments such as the accordion and guitar

bushcraft *noun*
knowledge of how to live in and travel through rough bush country

bushed *adjective*
1 very tired: *We are bushed after a hard day's work.* **2** lost or confused: *I was completely bushed when I couldn't find her house.*

bushel *noun*
an old-fashioned measure of large quantities of goods such as grain or fruit

bushfire *noun*
a fire in the bush or forest

bushman *noun*
someone who lives in the bush and knows how to survive there

Word Building: **bushmanship** *noun*

bushranger *noun*
someone who hid in the bush and lived by robbing travellers: *Ned Kelly was a famous Australian bushranger.*

Word Building: **bushranging** *noun*

bushwalking *noun*
walking through the bush for exercise or pleasure

Word Building: **bushwalk** *verb*
bushwalker *noun*

bushwhacker *noun*
someone who lives in the bush

Word Use: another word is **bushie** □ both these words are more suited to everyday language

business (say *biz*-nəs) *noun*
1 the work someone does to earn a living **2** buying and selling goods to make a profit: *to be in business* **3** a matter which someone has a right to know about: *My exam mark is none of your business.* **4 mean business** to be serious: *Those guard dogs look as if they mean business.*

Word Building: the plural is **businesses** □ **businesslike** *adjective* practical and well-organised **businessman** *noun* **businesswoman** *noun*

busker *noun*
a musician who performs in the street hoping to get donations of money from people passing by

Word Building: **busk** *verb*

bust[1] *noun*
1 a woman's breasts or chest **2** a sculpture of someone's head and shoulders

bust[2] *verb*
1 to break or burst: *to bust a balloon* **2** to arrest: *He was busted for selling drugs.* **3 bust in** to rush in suddenly **4 bust up** to quarrel and separate: *I have busted up with my boyfriend.* **5 go bust** to lose all your money: *His business has gone bust.*

Word Use: this word is more suited to everyday language
Word Building: **busted** *adjective* broken

bustard (sounds like *busted*) *noun*
a large heavy bird which can run fast and lives in the grassy plains of Australia

Word History: from a Latin word meaning "slow bird"

bustle[1] *verb*
to move or act busily: *She bustled about tidying the house.*

bustle[2] *noun*
a pad or wire frame worn in the olden days to puff out the back of a woman's skirt

busy *adjective*
1 fully occupied: *I can't come now as I am busy doing my homework.* **2** full of activity: *Saturday morning is a busy time at the shops.* **3** already in use: *The telephone was busy.*

busy *verb*
4 to make or keep busy: *I shall busy myself tidying up my room.*

Word Use: another word for definition 3 is **engaged**
Word Building: other adjective forms are **busier, busiest** □ other verb forms are **I busied, I have busied, I am busying** □ **busily** *adverb* **busyness** *noun*

busybody *noun*
somebody who interferes in other people's business

Word Building: the plural is **busybodies**

butcher *noun*
1 someone who prepares and cuts up meat to sell **2** a cruel and violent murderer

butcher *verb*
3 to kill violently: *The murderer butchered his victims.* **4** to make a terrible mess of: *That new hairdresser butchered my hair.*

Word Building: **butchery** *noun*

butcherbird *noun*
a black and grey Australian bird which hangs its dead prey on branches

butler *noun*
the head male servant in a large house

Word History: from a French word meaning "bottle"

butt[1] *noun*
1 the thick blunt end of a weapon or tool: *the butt of a rifle* **2** an end which is not used up: *a cigarette butt*

butt[2] *noun*
1 someone who is a target: *He is always the butt of their jokes.* **2** a wall of earth which stops bullets or arrows fired at targets in front of it

butt[3] *verb*
to push with the head or horns: *The goat butted me.*

Word Building: **butt** *noun*

butter *noun*
soft yellow spread made from cream

Word Building: **butter** *verb* to spread butter on **buttery** *adjective*

butterfly *noun*
an insect with large wings which are often brightly coloured

Word Building: the plural is **butterflies**

butterfly stroke *noun*
a stroke in swimming in which both your arms are lifted together from the water and thrown forward

buttermilk *noun*
a sour liquid left after butter has been made from cream

butterscotch *noun*
a kind of toffee or flavouring

buttock *noun*
either of the two rounded parts of the body at the base of your back

button *noun*
1 a small, usually round, object sewn onto clothing to join two parts together **2** anything shaped like a button, such as a small knob you press to ring a bell

Word Building: **button** *verb* (**buttoned, buttoning**): *I buttoned my cardigan.*

buttonhole *noun*
1 a slit in a garment through which buttons are passed to fasten it **2** a flower worn in a buttonhole on the lapel of a coat

buttress *noun*
a support for a wall or building

Word Building: the plural is **buttresses** □ **buttress** *verb*

buxom (say <u>*buks*</u>*-əm*) *adjective*
plump and attractive: *She's a buxom lass.*

buy *verb*
1 to get by paying money for **2** to accept: *I don't buy that idea.*

Word Use: be careful – this sounds like **by** and **bye**
Word Building: other forms are **I bought, I have bought, I am buying** □ **buy** *noun* something bought: *a good buy*

buyer *noun*
1 someone who buys: *We have a buyer for our old car.* **2** someone whose job is to buy stock for a store: *He is the chief buyer for a supermarket.*

buzz *noun*
1 a low, humming sound: *the buzz of bees / a buzz of conversation*
buzz *verb*
2 to make a buzzing noise **3 buzz off** to go or leave

Word Use: definition 3 is more suited to everyday language
Word Building: **buzzer** *noun*
Word History: this imitates the sound that bees make

buzzard *noun*
a large bird belonging to the hawk family

by *preposition*
1 near to: *I live by the school.* **2** using as a way: *to come in by the main gate / to travel by train*

by *adverb*
3 near: *I live close by.* **4** past something nearby: *The car sped by.*

Word Use: be careful – this sounds like **buy** and **bye**

by- *prefix*
a word part meaning **1** secondary: *by-product* **2** out of the way: *byway* **3** near: *bystander*

Word Use: another spelling is **bye-**

bye *noun*
a run in cricket made from a ball not hit by the batsman

Word Use: be careful – this sounds like **buy** and **by**

by-election *noun*
an extra election held to fill the seat of a member of parliament who has died or retired

bypass *noun*
a road built around a town or a busy traffic area

Word Building: **bypass** *verb* to use or make a bypass

by-product *noun*
something produced in addition to the main product: *Asphalt is a by-product of making petrol.*

bystander *noun*
someone who happens to be present at, but takes no part in, what is occurring

byte *noun*
a unit of information stored by a computer

Word Use: be careful – this sounds like **bight** and **bite**

byway *noun*
a road not used very often

cab *noun*
1 a taxi **2** the covered part of a truck where the driver sits

cabanossi (say *kab-ə-nos-ee*) *noun*
a thin beef sausage with seasoning, which you buy already cooked

cabaret (say *kab-ə-ray*) *noun*
a musical or comedy show performed at a restaurant or club

cabbage *noun*
a kind of vegetable with large green leaves

cabbage tree *noun*
a tall palm with large leaves and with buds that you can eat, found growing along the coast of eastern Australia

Word Use: another name is **cabbage tree palm** □ in the early days of the colony people made wide-brimmed hats from the leaves of this palm

cabin *noun*
1 a small house or hut **2** a room in a ship where passengers sleep **3** the space inside a plane where the crew and passengers sit

cabinet *noun*
1 a piece of furniture with shelves and drawers **2** the group of leading people in a government

Word Use: definition 2 is often spelt with a capital letter

cable *noun*
1 thick strong rope, chain or several wires twisted together **2** a bundle of wires that carry electricity **3** a telegram sent to another country

cache (sounds like *cash*) *noun*
1 a hiding place for storing things **2** the things that are hidden in a cache

cackle *verb*
to laugh or talk with the kind of noisy sound that a hen makes after laying an egg

Word Building: **cackle** *noun*

cacophony (say *kə-kof-ə-nee*) *noun*
a loud unmusical sound: *The dogs started a cacophony of barking.*

Word Building: **cacophonous** *adjective*

cactus *noun*
a spiky plant which stores water in its thick skin and grows in hot dry places

Word Building: the plural is either **cacti** or **cactuses**

cadaver (say *kə-dav-ə*) *noun*
a dead body, particularly of a human being

Word Use: a similar word is **corpse**

caddie *noun*
someone who is paid to carry a golfer's playing clubs and find the ball

Word Use: another spelling is **caddy**

caddy *noun*
a small box or tin in which tea is kept

Word Building: the plural is **caddies**

cadence (say *kay-dəns*) *noun*
1 the rising and falling of sounds, especially in the sound of your voice when reading poetry **2** a group of musical notes or chords which show the end of a section or piece of music

cadet *noun*
someone who is being trained in a job or an organisation, like the army or a school military group

Word Building: **cadetship** *noun*

cafe (say kaf-ay) *noun*
a restaurant where coffee and small meals are served

Word Use: the "e" is pronounced because this comes from the French word *café* which means "coffee"

cafeteria *noun*
a cheap self-service restaurant

Word History: from an American Spanish word for a coffee shop

caffeine (say kaf-een) *noun*
a stimulating drug found in coffee and tea which stops you falling asleep

cage *noun*
1 an enclosure made of wires or bars, in which animals or birds are kept
2 anything that is like a prison

Word Building: **cage** *verb: The prisoner was caged in his cell.*

cagey *adjective*
careful not to tell very much: *He became very cagey when the police questioned him.*

Word Use: a similar word is **secretive**
Word Building: other forms are **cagier**, **cagiest** □ **cagily** *adverb* **caginess** *noun*

cajole (say kə-johl) *verb*
to persuade by praising or making promises

Word Use: a similar word is **coax**
Word Building: **cajolery** *noun*

cake *noun*
1 a sweet food, usually made with butter or margarine, flour, sugar, eggs and a flavouring, which is baked in an oven
2 a small mass of something with a definite shape: *a fish cake* | *a cake of soap*
cake *verb*
3 to cover with a thick crust of something: *She caked her face with make-up.*

calamari (say kal-ə-mah-ree) *noun*
squid when it is cooked

Word Use: compare "cow" and **beef**, "deer" and **venison**
Word History: from the Italian name for this food

calamity *noun*
a terrible happening or disaster

Word Building: the plural is **calamities** □ **calamitous** *adjective* **calamitously** *adverb*

calcium (say kal-see-əm) *noun*
a soft silver-white metal that is found in limestone and chalk, and in teeth and bones

calculate *verb*
1 to work out using mathematics: *He got out his ruler and calculated the area of the square.* **2** to work out by thinking about: *She calculated that it was worth taking the risk.*

Word Building: **calculated** *adjective* done deliberately or with careful planning: *a calculated insult* **calculation** *noun*

calculating *adjective*
very careful and shrewd: *a calculating look*

calculator *noun*
a small electronic machine that can be used to do sums

calendar *noun*
a chart that shows the days and weeks of each month of the year

Word History: from a Latin word meaning "account book"

calf[1] (say kahf) *noun*
a young cow, whale, elephant or seal

Word Building: the plural is **calves**

calf[2] (say kahf) *noun*
the back part of your leg, below the knee

Word Building: the plural is **calves**

calibre (say kal-ə-bə) *noun*
1 the measurement across something round, like a bullet or the barrel of a gun **2** the ability or character of a person: *You can't rely on a person of that calibre.*

Word Building: **calibrate** *verb* to measure the calibre of, or to adjust **calibration** *noun*

calico *noun*
a rough cotton cloth, usually whitish in colour

Word History: named after *Calicut*, a city on the coast of India where this cloth was first made

call *verb*
1 to cry out in a loud voice **2** to order to happen: *The headmistress called a staff meeting.* **3** to read out aloud: *The teacher called the roll.* **4** to shout out to **5** to ask or order to come: *We'd better call a doctor.* **6** to telephone: *Please call me tonight.* **7** to give a name to: *His parents called him Peter.* **8** to give a description to: *She called me a cheat.* **9 call at** to make a short stop at: *Maria called at the shop on her way home.* **10 call for** to need or be suitable for: *His success calls for a party.* **11 call off** to cancel or

postpone: *They called off the sports carnival because of rain.* **12 call on** to make a short visit to: *Why don't we call on Jim?*

call *noun*
13 a shout or cry **14** a short visit **15** a telephone conversation: *a long-distance call*

Word Building: **caller** *noun*

calligraphy (say *kə-lig-rə-fee*) *noun*
the art of doing beautiful handwriting

Word Building: **calligrapher** *noun* **calligraphic** *adjective*

calling *noun*
someone's job, profession or trade

calliper *noun*
a metal splint used as a support for an injured leg or arm

callous *adjective*
showing no concern for another person's feelings: *She gave a callous answer to his call for help.*

Word Use: a similar word is **insensitive**
Word Building: **callousness** *noun*

callus *noun*
a hard thick part of your skin caused by something rubbing against it: *I've got a callus on my thumb from the handle of my tennis racquet.*

calm *adjective*
1 still, with no rough movements: *a calm sea* **2** not windy: *a calm day* **3** not getting excited or upset: *He always stays calm when there is trouble.*

Word Building: **calm** *verb: to calm someone's fears* **calm** *noun* **calmness** *noun* **calmly** *adverb*

calorie *noun*
a measurement of heat or the energy value of food: *That cake is full of calories.*

Word Use: this measurement is now being replaced by **kilojoule**

camel *noun*
an animal with a humped back, used to carry people and loads across the desert

cameo (say *kam-ee-oh*) *noun*
1 a piece of jewellery made from a stone or shell which has been carved so that the design stands out from its background **2** a small but interesting part in a film or play

camera *noun*
a machine which takes photographs

camouflage (say *kam-ə-flahzh*) *noun*
a kind of disguise, either natural or man-made, that makes something hard to see against its surroundings: *The colour of that insect gives it a good camouflage.*

Word Building: **camouflage** *verb*

camp[1] *noun*
1 a group of tents, caravans or shelters for outdoor living **2** a place for these kinds of shelters

camp[1] *verb*
3 to live for a while in a tent: *We camped in the bush during our holidays.*

Word Building: **camper** *noun*

camp[2] *adjective*
1 in an exaggerated or amusing style: *The new play is very camp.* | *a camp hairstyle* **2** homosexual

campaign (say *kam-payn*) *noun*
1 a series of planned attacks by an army, in a particular area or for a particular purpose: *How many soldiers fought in that campaign?* **2** any planned series of actions with a particular purpose: *They started a campaign to change the school uniform.*

Word Building: **campaign** *verb* **campaigner** *noun*

campervan *noun*
a motor van with a cabin for the driver at the front and a kitchen, beds, and so on, at the back

Word Use: the short form of this is **camper** □ compare this with a **caravan**

campus *noun*
the grounds of a university or college

Word History: from a Latin word meaning "field"

can[1] *noun*
a tin container for food and drink: *a can of oil* | *a can of apples*

Word Building: **can** *verb* (**canned, canning**) to put in a can **canned** *adjective*

can[2] *verb*
1 to be able to: *You can lift that box.* **2** to have permission to: *Can I speak to you a moment?*

Word Use: this verb is a helping verb, always used with another one in the form **I can** or **I could** □ some people say you should always use **may** not **can** for definition 2

canal (say *kə-nal*) *noun*
a man-made waterway for ships or barges

canary *noun*
a small yellow bird that sings sweetly and is often kept as a pet

Word Building: the plural is **canaries**
Word History: named after the *Canary* Islands where these birds were first seen

canasta *noun*
a card game played by two to six people

cancel *verb*
1 to call off: *to cancel a picnic* **2** to cross out by drawing lines through: *He cancelled my name on the list of competitors.*

Word Building: other forms are **I cancelled, I have cancelled, I am cancelling** □ **cancellation** *noun*

cancer *noun*
the harmful growth of a group of cells in someone's body, which destroys the nearby cells and can spread throughout the whole body, often causing death

Word Building: **cancerous** *adjective*

candelabrum (say *kan-də-lah-brəm*) *noun*
an ornamental holder for a number of candles

Word Building: the plural is **candelabra**

candid *adjective*
1 honest and sincere: *He gave a candid answer to the judge's question.* **2** taken without people knowing: *candid photos*

Word Building: **candidly** *adverb* **candidness** *noun*

candidate *noun*
1 someone sitting for an examination
2 someone who is applying for a job, an award or a place in parliament

Word Building: **candidacy** *noun* **candidature** *noun*
Word History: from a Latin word meaning "dressed in white", after the white togas that Roman candidates wore when they were standing for office

candle *noun*
a piece of wax containing a wick which is burnt to give light

candour or **candor** (rhymes with *panda*) *noun*
honesty and sincerity: *He answered with complete candour.*

candy *noun*
a sweet made of boiled sugar

Word Building: the plural is **candies** □ **candied** *adjective* cooked in sugar **candy** *verb* (**candied, candying**)

cane *noun*
1 the thin woody stem of bamboo, sugarcane and other similar plants
cane *verb*
2 to beat with a cane

cane toad *noun*
a toad brought into Queensland to get rid of cane beetles and which is now a pest

canine (say *kay-nuyn*) *adjective*
1 having to do with dogs
canine *noun*
2 any animal belonging to the dog family: *Foxes and wolves are canines.* **3** the pointed tooth on each side of your upper and lower jaws

canister *noun*
a small container, often made of metal: *a tea canister*

cannabis (say *kan-ə-bəs*) *noun*
another name for **marijuana**

cannibal *noun*
someone who eats human flesh

Word Building: **cannabalise** *verb* **cannabalism** *noun*

cannon *noun*
a large gun on wheels

cannot *verb*
a form of **can not**

canoe (say *kə-nooh*) *noun*
a light narrow boat that you move by using paddles

Word Building: **canoe** *verb* (**canoed, canoeing**) **canoeist** *noun*

canon[1] *noun*
1 a law or rule **2** a set of church laws
3 a piece of music in which the same tune is played or sung by two or more parts overlapping each other

canon[2] *noun*
a clergyman connected with a cathedral

canopy (say *kan-ə-pee*) *noun*
an ornamental or protective covering: *a bed canopy | a canopy of trees*

Word Building: the plural is **canopies** □ **canopied** *adjective*
Word History: from a Greek word meaning "mosquito net"

can't *verb*
a short form of **cannot**

cantankerous *adjective*
bad-tempered and quarrelsome: *a cantankerous neighbour*

Word Building: **cantankerously** *adverb* **cantankerousness** *noun*

canteen *noun*
1 a cafeteria or a counter where food is sold in a factory, office or school **2** a box holding cutlery **3** a small container for carrying drinking water

canter *noun*
the movement of a horse which is a little slower than a gallop

Word Building: **canter** *verb*

cantor *noun*
a Jewish church leader who sings during the religious service

canvas *noun*
1 heavy cotton cloth used for sails, tents and other similar articles **2** a piece of this used for painting on: *an artist's canvas*

canvass *verb*
to ask for votes or support from: *The candidate canvassed the voters in his electorate.*

Word Building: **canvasser** *noun*

canyon *noun*
a deep valley with steep sides

cap *noun*
1 a soft close-fitting hat with a peak to shade the face **2** membership of a particular sports team: *He got his cap in the rowing team.* **3** a lid or top **4** a small explosive used in toy guns to make a loud bang

cap *verb*
5 to put a cap or top on **6** to improve upon: *He capped his previous record in the high jump.*

Word Building: other verb forms are **I capped, I have capped, I am capping**

capable *adjective*
1 having ability or skill: *He is a capable cook.* **2 capable of a** able to: *He is capable of running a kilometre.* **b** likely to do: *He is capable of murder.*

Word Building: **capability** *noun* **capably** *adverb*

capacity *noun*
1 quantity or amount which can be held or contained: *This jug's capacity is one litre.* **2** mental ability: *a pupil's capacity to learn a language* **3** the position or standing of someone: *I am arresting you in my capacity as a policeman.*

Word Building: the plural is **capacities**

cape[1] *noun*
a loose cloak which is fastened at your neck and hangs over your shoulders

cape[2] *noun*
a piece of land jutting out into the sea

caper *verb*
to jump or dance about

Word Building: **caper** *noun*

capillary (say *kə-pil-ə-ree*) *noun*
one of the smallest blood vessels in your body

Word Building: the plural is **capillaries** □ **capillary** *adjective*

capital *noun*
1 the main city of a state or country: *Canberra is the capital of Australia.* **2** a large letter: *People's names start with a capital.* **3** the amount of money owned by a business or person **4** any form of wealth used to produce more wealth

capital *adjective*
5 chief or main: *a capital city* **6 capital punishment** punishment by death

Word Building: **capitalise** *verb* **capitalisation** *noun*

capitalism *noun*
the economic system under which industries are owned privately and not by the government

Word Use: compare this with **communism**
Word Building: **capitalist** *noun*

capitulate (say *kə-pit-chə-layt*) *verb*
to give in or surrender: *The enemy capitulated.*

Word Building: **capitulation** *noun*

cappuccino (say *kap-ə-cheen-oh*) *noun*
coffee with frothy milk added, made with a special machine

Word History: from an Italian word meaning "hood"

caprice (say *kə-prees*) *noun*
a sudden change of mind without an apparent reason

Word Use: a word with a similar meaning is **whim**
Word Building: **capricious** *adjective* **capriciousness** *noun*

capsicum (say *kap-sə-kəm*) *noun*
a type of pepper plant and its green or red fruit, which is used in salads or to flavour food

Word History: from a Latin word meaning "box"

capsize *verb*
to turn over: *The boat capsized.* | *The large waves capsized the boat.*

capsule *noun*
1 a small case or covering, like the one that holds a dose of powdered medicine **2** the part of a spaceship which holds the crew or instruments

captain *noun*
1 someone who is in charge of a ship or aeroplane **2** someone who commands a group of soldiers **3** a leader: *captain of the basketball team*

Word Building: **captaincy** *noun*

caption *noun*
a heading for a newspaper article or a title for a picture or cartoon

Word Building: **caption** *verb*

captivate *verb*
to charm and delight: *She captivated the audience with her singing.*

Word Building: **captivation** *noun*

captive *noun*
someone who has been taken prisoner

Word Building: **captive** *adjective* **captivity** *noun*

capture *verb*
to take by force

Word Building: **captor** *noun* someone who captures **capture** *noun*

car *noun*
1 a vehicle driven by its own engine, for carrying passengers along roads **2** a railway carriage or wagon

Word Use: the full name of definition 1 is **motor car**

carafe (say *kə-rahf*) *noun*
a glass bottle used for serving water, wine or fruit juice at a meal table

caramel *noun*
1 a type of sweet, or a colouring or flavouring made from burnt sugar **2** a caramel colour

caramel *adjective*
3 light brown

carat *noun*
1 a unit of weight for measuring gems, equal to 200 milligrams **2** a measure of the purity of gold: *Pure gold is 24 carats.*

caravan *noun*
1 a covered van that can be pulled by a car, and in which you can live, especially when you are on holidays **2** a group of people travelling together, especially across a desert

Word Use: compare definition 1 with a **campervan**

caraway *noun*
a herb with small seeds which are used in cooking

carbine *noun*
a rifle with a short barrel

carbohydrate *noun*
a chemical compound, such as sugar or starch, which is present in all living things

carbon *noun*
a common element found in all living things as well as in such substances as diamonds, graphite and coal

carbon dioxide *noun*
a colourless gas which has no smell and does not burn, used in industry as dry ice and in fizzy drinks

carbon monoxide *noun*
a colourless, poisonous gas which has no smell

carbon paper *noun*
paper that is coated with carbon, used between sheets of writing or typing paper to make copies

carbuncle *noun*
a painful pus-filled swelling, like a large boil

carburettor (say *kah-byə-ret-ə*) *noun*
the part of an engine in which fuel and air are mixed together to form an explosive gas

carcass (say *kah-kəs*) *noun*
the dead body of an animal

Word Use: another spelling is **carcase**

card[1] *noun*
1 a piece of stiff paper or cardboard, usually small and oblong-shaped: *a birthday card* | *a business card* **2** one of a set of cards used for playing games such as rummy or bridge **3 on the cards** likely to happen

card[2] *noun*
a type of comb, used to get the knots out of wool or cotton before it is spun

Word Building: **card** *verb*

cardboard *noun*
a thick stiff sort of paper

cardi- *prefix*
a word part meaning heart: *cardiac*

Word Use: another spelling is **cardio-**
Word History: this prefix comes from Greek

cardiac *adjective*
having to do with the heart: *a cardiac disease*

cardigan *noun*
a knitted jacket with buttons down the front

Word History: named after the 7th Earl of Cardigan, 1797 to 1868

cardinal *adjective*
1 chief or of first importance: *a cardinal point to remember*

cardinal *noun*
2 a high-ranking priest in the Roman Catholic Church

Word Use: a similar word for definition 1 is **fundamental**

cardinal number *noun*
a term used in maths for a number such as "1", "2", "3" and so on, which tells you how many things are in a given set but not the order in which they appear

Word Use: compare this with **ordinal number**

care *noun*
1 worry or anxiety: *She was worn out by care.* **2** thoughtful attention: *Do your work with care.* **3** protection or charge: *under the care of a doctor* **4 care of** at the address of: *You can write to him care of his mother.*

care *verb*
5 to worry: *I care about the future.*
6 care for **a** to like or love **b** to look after: *We must help care for the sick.*

Word Building: **carefree** *adjective* without care **carer** *noun*

career *noun*
1 the job or profession in which you earn your living: *a business career | a career in law*

career *verb*
2 to move rapidly and wildly: *The car's brakes failed and it careered down the hill.*

careful *adjective*
1 taking care to avoid risks: *a careful driver* **2** putting time and effort into your work

Word Use: another word for definition 1 is **cautious** □ another word for definition 2 is **thorough**
Word Building: **carefully** *adverb* **carefulness** *noun*

careless *adjective*
1 done without paying enough attention: *careless work* **2** done or said without thinking: *A careless remark can be hurtful.*

Word Building: **carelessly** *adverb* **carelessness** *noun*

caress (say *kə-res*) *noun*
an action which shows affection, such as a gentle touch, a hug or a kiss

Word Building: **caress** *verb* to touch with affection
Word History: from a Latin word meaning "dear"

caret (say *ka-rət*) *noun*
a mark (‸) you make in writing or printing to show where something has to be added

caretaker *noun*
someone who looks after a building

cargo *noun*
the goods carried on a ship

Word Building: the plural is **cargoes**

caricature (say *ka-ri-kə-choo-ə*) *noun*
a picture or description of someone or something which makes fun of their unusual features

Word Building: **caricaturist** *noun* someone who draws caricatures **caricature** *verb*

carillon (say *kə-ril-yən*) *noun*
a set of bells hung in a tower and used to play tunes

Word Building: **carillonist** *noun* someone who plays these bells

carnage *noun*
the killing of many people: *the carnage of war*

Word Use: a word with a similar meaning is **massacre**

carnal *adjective*
having to do with the body

carnation *noun*
a garden plant with red, pink, or white flowers

carnival *noun*
1 a period of time during which sporting events are held: *an athletics carnival / a surfing carnival* **2** a time of processions and public merry-making, usually for a special occasion: *The city is holding a New Year Carnival in the main street.*

Word Use: a similar word for definition 2 is **festival**

carnivore *noun*
an animal that eats meat: *Cats and dogs are carnivores.*

Word Use: compare with **herbivore, insectivore** and **omnivore**
Word Building: **carnivorous** *adjective*

carob (say *ka-rəb*) *noun*
a tree which bears a long pod with seeds in a sweet pulp

carol *noun*
a joyful song, especially a Christmas song or hymn

Word Building: **carol** *verb* (**carolled, carolling**) **caroller** *noun*

carousel (say *ka-rə-sel*) *noun*
1 a merry-go-round **2** the continuously moving belt from which travellers get their bags at the end of a journey by ship, aeroplane or bus

carp *noun*
a large freshwater fish that is good to eat

Word Building: the plural is also **carp**

carpenter *noun*
someone who makes things out of wood and puts up wooden parts of a building

Word Building: **carpentry** *noun* woodwork

carpet *noun*
a thick, woven floor covering

Word Building: **carpet** *verb* (**carpeted, carpeting**) to cover with a carpet

carriage *noun*
1 one of the passenger-carrying cars on a train **2** a vehicle on wheels for carrying people, pulled by a horse or horses **3** the way you hold your head and body when you walk or stand

Word Use: other words for definition 3 are **bearing** and **deportment**

carrion *noun*
the rotting flesh of dead animals

carrot *noun*
an orange-coloured root vegetable

carry *verb*
1 to take from one place to another: *to carry something in your pocket / to carry cargo by ship* **2** to take or bring: *sounds carried by the wind / electricity carried by cables* **3** to walk, stand or behave: *She carries herself well.* **4 carry away** to excite: *She was carried away by the beautiful music.* **5 carry on a** to conduct: *to carry on a business* **b** to continue: *Carry on with what you were doing.* **6 carry out** to complete: *to carry out a plan*

Word Building: other forms are **I carried, I have carried, I am carrying** □ **carrier** *noun* someone or something that carries

cart *noun*
a small vehicle, sometimes pulled by a horse, used for carrying a load

Word Building: **cart** *verb* **carter** *noun*

cartilage *noun*
a firm, elastic substance forming part of your bone structure

carton *noun*
a cardboard box often used for packaging food: *a milk carton / a carton of tinned fish*

cartoon *noun*
1 a funny drawing **2** a film made of many slightly different drawings which give the effect of movement when put through a projector

Word Building: **cartoonist** *noun*
Word History: from a Latin word meaning "paper"

cartridge *noun*
1 a case which holds the explosive powder, and often also the bullet, for a rifle or other gun **2** a container, especially for the recording tape for a computer or tape-recorder, or for the ink for some types of pen

cartwheel *noun*
1 the large wooden wheel of a cart
2 a sideways somersault with legs and arms outstretched

carve *verb*
1 to shape by cutting: *He carved a doll from a piece of wood.* **2** to cut up or cut into slices: *to carve a turkey / to carve a leg of lamb*

Word Building: **carved** *adjective* **carver** *noun* **carving** *noun*

cascade *noun*
1 a waterfall over steep rocks
cascade *verb*
2 to fall like a cascade: *The ferns cascaded over the cliff.*

case[1] *noun*
1 an example: *a case of forgetfulness | a case of measles* **2** a list of facts or reasons: *This is our case for a new library.* **3** a charge against someone in a court of law **4** the form of a noun or pronoun which shows its relation to other words in a sentence

Word Use: for definition 4 the three cases are **subjective, objective** and **possessive**

case[2] *noun*
1 a container: *a pencil case | a case of apples* **2** a suitcase: *My case is packed with my holiday clothes.*

casement *noun*
a hinged window which opens like a door

cash *noun*
1 money in notes or coins, rather than cheques: *Have you any cash in your pocket?* **2** money available straight away: *Will you pay cash or charge it?*

Word Use: for definition 2 compare **credit**
Word Building: **cash** *verb* to give or get cash for

cashew *noun*
a small curved nut that you can eat

cashier *noun*
someone who is in charge of the money in a shop or bank

cashmere *noun*
fine wool obtained from the Kashmir goats of India, often used to make clothes

casino (say *kə-see-noh*) *noun*
a building or large room where gambling games are played

Word Building: the plural is **casinos**
Word History: from a Latin word meaning "cottage"

cask *noun*
a barrel for holding wine and other liquids

casket *noun*
a small chest or box

cassata (say *kə-sah-tə*) *noun*
an Italian iced dessert, like gelato, made with chopped nuts or mixed dried fruit, and so on

cassava (say *kə-sah-və*) *noun*
a family of tropical plants whose roots are used for food

casserole *noun*
1 a covered baking dish **2** the food, usually a mixture of meat and vegetables, cooked in it

cassette *noun*
1 the plastic container holding the recording tape used in videos and tape-recorders
cassette *adjective*
2 designed for playing cassettes: *a cassette recorder*

cassock *noun*
a long garment worn by members of the clergy

cassowary (say *kas-ə-wə-ree*) *noun*
a large three-toed bird found in Australasia, which is smaller than an ostrich and cannot fly

Word Building: the plural is **cassowaries**

cast *verb*
1 to throw out or fling: *to cast a fishing line | to cast a stone* **2** to cause to fall: *The sun cast a shadow over the field.* **3** to throw off or shed: *A snake casts its old skin.* **4** to select for a play: *They cast him as the dragon.* **5** to form in a mould: *The decorative iron railings were cast in 1900.*
cast *noun*
6 all the actors in a play **7** a mould of plaster around a broken limb **8** a permanent squint: *He has a cast in his eye.*

Word Building: other forms are **he cast, he has cast, he is casting**

castanets *plural noun*
a pair of shell-shaped pieces of ivory or wood which you hold in the palm of your hand and strike together in time to music and dancing

Word History: from a Latin word meaning "chestnut"

castaway *noun*
someone who has been ship-wrecked

caste *noun*
1 one of the social groups or divisions into which Hindus are born **2** any strictly followed system of social divisions

castigate *verb*
to criticise or punish severely

Word Building: **castigation** *noun* **castigator** *noun*

castle *noun*
1 a large strongly-built fort, used as a home by princes or nobles in the olden

days **2** a piece in chess, shaped like a castle

Word Use: another name for definition 2 is **rook**

castor *noun*
1 a small wheel attached to the bottom of a bed or under the legs of some tables and chairs to make them easier to move
2 a bottle with holes in the top, for holding sugar or salt

castor oil *noun*
a sticky oil pressed from the seeds of a plant and used as a medicine

castrate *verb*
to remove the testicles from: *to castrate the bull*

Word Building: **castration** *noun*

casual *adjective*
1 happening by chance: *a casual meeting*
2 without thinking: *a casual remark*
3 informal: *I wear casual clothes on holidays.* **4** employed occasionally: *a casual worker*

Word Building: **casual** *noun* a worker employed occasionally **casually** *adverb*

casualty *noun*
someone hurt or killed in an accident or war

Word Building: the plural is **casualties**

casuarina (say *kazh-yə-ree-nə*) *noun*
a type of Australian tree or shrub with leaves which are like the needles of a pine tree and cones with a rather flat top

Word Use: another name is **she-oak**

cat *noun*
1 a small furry animal often kept as a pet **2** a member of the cat family, which includes lions, tigers and other similar animals **3** a spiteful girl or woman

Word Use: a similar word for definition 2 is **feline**
Word Building: **catty** *adjective* (**cattier, cattiest**) spiteful

catacomb (say *kat-ə-kohm, -koohm*) *noun*
a series of underground tunnels and caves or rooms, once used as burial places

catalogue (say *kat-ə-log*) *noun*
a list, usually in alphabetical order, of names, books or articles on sale or display and some information about them: *a catalogue of artists | a library catalogue | a sales catalogue*

Word Building: **catalogue** *verb* **cataloguer** *noun*

catalyst (say *kat-ə-ləst*) *noun*
someone or something that causes a change or a reaction

Word Building: **catalyse** *verb* **catalysis** *noun* **catalytic** *adjective*

catamaran *noun*
a boat with two hulls

Word Use: the shortened form is **cat**
Word History: from a Tamil word meaning "tied tree" or "wood"

catapult *noun*
1 a Y-shaped stick with a length of elastic joined to the prongs, used for shooting stones at things **2** a device for launching planes from the deck of a ship

Word Use: other names for definition 1 are **shanghai, sling** and **slingshot**
Word Building: **catapult** *verb* to throw or be thrown, as if from a catapult

cataract *noun*
1 a large waterfall **2** a disease of the eye causing loss of sight

catastrophe (say *kə-tas-trə-fee*) *noun*
a sudden disaster

Word Building: **catastrophic** *adjective* **catastrophically** *adverb*

catch *verb*
1 to capture, especially after a chase **2** to take in the hands: *to catch a ball* **3** to be in time for: *to catch a bus* **4** to get or contract: *to catch a cold* **5** to surprise or come upon suddenly: *I caught him stealing.* **6 catch on a** to become popular **b** to understand **7 catch up** to reach or become level: *He caught up with the rest of the class. | I ran and caught up to the leaders.*

Word Building: other forms are **I caught, I have caught, I am catching** □ **catchy** *adjective* easy to remember **catch** *noun*

catechism (say *kat-ə-kiz-əm*) *noun*
a book of questions and answers meant to help you learn about your religion

Word Building: **catechise** *verb* **catechist** *noun*

category *noun*
a group or division of people or things

Word Building: the plural is **categories** □ **categorical** *adjective* clear and plain, with no doubt **categorically** *adverb* **categorise** *verb*

cater *verb*
to supply food and drink: *My mother is catering for my party.*

Word Building: **caterer** *noun* a supplier, especially of food

caterpillar *noun*
the worm-like grub or larva of a moth or butterfly

caterwaul (say *kat-ə-wawl*) *verb*
to cry or howl like quarrelling cats

cathedral *noun*
the main church in a district which acts as a bishop's headquarters

cattle *noun*
farm animals such as cows, bulls and oxen: *The cattle are grazing in the far paddock.*

catwalk *noun*
a long narrow platform on which models walk to display clothes

caucus (say *kaw-kəs*) *noun*
a meeting of the members of parliament belonging to a particular political party

Word History: from an American Indian word meaning "adviser"

cauldron (say *kawl-drən*) *noun*
a large rounded kettle or boiler with a lid and handles

cauliflower *noun*
a vegetable with a large round head of white flowers

cause *noun*
1 someone or something which brings about an effect or result: *His joke was the cause of all the laughter.* **2** something that you believe in: *Peace is a cause worth working for.*

cause *verb*
3 to bring about: *to cause trouble*

Word Building: **causal** *adjective* **causally** *adverb* **causation** *noun*

causeway *noun*
a raised road or path across low or wet ground

caustic (say *kos-tik*) *adjective*
1 capable of burning or eating away living cells: *caustic soda* **2** critical or sarcastic: *a caustic remark*

Word Building: **caustically** *adverb*

cauterise or **cauterize** (say *kaw-tə-ruyz*) *verb*
to burn with a hot instrument, especially to kill germs: *to cauterise a wound*

Word Building: **cauterisation** *noun*

caution *noun*
1 great care when there is danger: *Use caution in crossing city streets.* **2** a warning

Word Building: **caution** *verb* to warn **cautionary** *adjective* **cautious** *adjective* **cautiously** *adverb*

cavalcade *noun*
a procession of people on horseback or in horse-drawn carriages

cavalier (say *kav-ə-lear*) *noun*
1 a soldier or knight on horseback

cavalier *adjective*
2 not caring about important things: *He had a cavalier attitude to his work.*

cavalry *noun*
a group of soldiers on horses

cave *noun*
1 a hollow place in a hillside

cave *verb*
2 to explore caves **3** to fall or sink: *The ground caved in under their feet.*

cavern (say *kav-ən*) *noun*
a large cave

Word Building: **cavernous** *adjective* **cavernously** *adverb*

caviar (say *kav-ee-ah*) *noun*
the salted eggs of sturgeon and other large fish

cavity *noun*
an empty space or hollow: *a cavity in a wall | a cavity in a tooth*

Word Building: the plural of this is **cavities**

cavort (say *kə-vawt*) *verb*
to dance or jump about

CD *noun*
a short form of **compact disc**

cease *verb*
to stop: *The noise ceased. | We will cease work now.*

Word Building: **cessation** *noun* a pause or stopping **ceaseless** *adjective* without stopping **ceaselessly** *adverb*

cedar (rhymes with *reader*) *noun*
a type of tree, whose wood is often used to make furniture

cede (sounds like *seed*) *verb*
to give away by making a solemn written promise: *to cede land*

ceiling *noun*
1 the inside lining that covers the top of a room **2** the top limit that something can reach: *We should put a ceiling on the price of bread.*

celebrate *verb*
1 to honour with ceremonies and festivities: *Christians celebrate the birth of Jesus at Christmas.* **2** to perform solemnly: *to celebrate mass* **3** to have a party: *When exams are over, we're going to celebrate.*

Word Use: definition 3 is more suited to everyday language
Word Building: **celebrant** *noun* **celebrated** *adjective* famous **celebration** *noun*

celebrity (say *sə-leb-rə-tee*) *noun*
a famous or well-known person

Word Use: a similar word is **personality**
Word Building: the plural is **celebrities**

celery *noun*
a vegetable with long green stalks that are good to eat

celestial *adjective*
having to do with heaven

celibacy (say *sel-ə-bə-see*) *noun*
the condition of being unmarried and refraining from sexual intercourse: *Roman Catholic priests live under vows of celibacy.*

Word Building: **celibate** *adjective*

cell *noun*
1 a small room in a prison or a convent **2** the tiny basic parts of all living matter: *plant cells | blood cells | nerve cells* **3** part of an electric battery

Word Building: **cellular** *adjective* having many small holes or cells

cellar *noun*
1 an underground room **2** a supply of wines

cello (say *chel-oh*) *noun*
an instrument shaped like a large violin, which has four strings and is held upright on the floor between the knees of the player

Word Use: the **cello** sounds lower than the **violin** and **viola** and higher than the **double bass**
Word Building: **cellist** *noun*
Word History: this is short for **violoncello**

cellulose (say *sel-yə-lohs*) *noun*
important material that forms the cell walls of plants and is found in wood, cotton, hemp and paper

Celsius *adjective*
relating to a scale of temperature in which 0° is the melting point of ice and 100° is the boiling point of water

Word History: named after A Celsius, 1701 to 1744, who was a Swedish astronomer

cement *noun*
1 a mixture of clay and limestone, used for making concrete **2** a type of glue

Word Building: **cement** *verb*

cemetery *noun*
a burial ground or graveyard

Word Building: the plural is **cemeteries**

cenotaph (say *sen-ə-tahf*) *noun*
a public memorial to those killed in war

censor *noun*
someone who is specially chosen to decide what books, films or news reports are to be made available to the public

Word Building: **censorious** *adjective* critical and fault-finding **censor** *verb*

censorship *noun*
the act or practice of censoring

censure (say *sen-shə*) *verb*
to find fault with, or condemn: *The manager censured the clerk for being late so often.*

Word Building: **censure** *noun*

census *noun*
an official counting of all the people who live in a place or country

cent *noun*
a coin worth a hundredth of a dollar

centaur (say *sen-taw*) *noun*
a creature of Greek legend, said to be half man and half horse

centenary (say *sen-teen-ə-ree*) *noun*
a 100th anniversary

Word Building: the plural is **centenaries** □ **centenarian** *noun* someone who is 100 years old **centennial** *adjective*

centi- *prefix*
a word part showing a hundredth part of a given unit: centimetre

Word Use: another spelling is **cent-**
Word History: this prefix comes from Latin

Centigrade *adjective*
an old-fashioned word for **Celsius**

centimetre *noun*
a hundredth of a metre

centipede *noun*
a small insect-like creature with a long thin body and many pairs of legs

centre *noun*
1 the middle point of an area: *the centre of a circle* **2** a place for a particular activity: *a shopping centre*
centre *verb*
3 to bring or come to a centre: *She centred her mind on the job. / Attention centred on the winner.*

Word Building: **central** *adjective* **centralise** *verb* **centrally** *adverb*

centrefold *noun*
the double page in the middle of a magazine, usually having a large photograph for pinning up on a wall

centri- *prefix*
a word part meaning centre: *centrifugal*

Word Use: other spellings are **centr-** and **centro-**
Word History: this prefix comes from Latin and Greek

centrifugal (say *sen-trif-yə-gəl*) *adjective*
moving outwards from the centre: *centrifugal force*

centurion *noun*
the leader of one hundred men in the Roman army

century *noun*
1 a period of 100 years **2** any group of 100: *He scored a century in the cricket match.*

Word Building: the plural is **centuries**

ceramic (say *sə-ram-ik*) *adjective*
1 made of clay: *a ceramic pot*
ceramic *noun*
2 ceramics the craft of making things out of clay: *Ceramics is taught at the art school.* **3** the things made: *We sell ceramics in our craft shop.*

cereal *noun*
1 a grain plant, such as wheat, maize or rice **2** a food made from grain, especially a breakfast food

Word Use: be careful – this sounds like **serial**

cerebral (say *se-rə-brəl*) *adjective*
having to do with the brain

ceremony *noun*
the solemn actions performed on an important occasion: *a wedding ceremony / the opening ceremony for the new school*

Word Building: the plural is **ceremonies** □ **ceremonial** *adjective* belonging to or used for a ceremony **ceremonious** *adjective* elaborately polite: *a ceremonious welcome*

cerise (say *sə-rees*) *adjective*
cherry red

certain *adjective*
1 confident or having no doubt: *She was certain that she had seen him.* **2** sure: *It is certain to happen.* **3** definite or particular, but not named: *a certain person*

Word Building: **certainly** *adverb* **certainty** *noun*

certificate *noun*
a written paper stating certain facts: *a certificate of health / a birth certificate*

certify *verb*
to state in writing or declare as fact

Word Building: other forms are **I certified, I have certified, I am certifying** □ **certification** *noun* **certifier** *noun*

cervix *noun*
the entrance to the womb

Word Building: the plural is **cervixes** or **cervices** (say *suh-vuy-seez*) □ **cervical** *adjective*

chafe *verb*
1 to wear down or make sore by rubbing: *This saddle chafes my horse.* **2** to become impatient: *She chafed at the delay.*

chaff *noun*
1 the husks or dry outer coverings of grain: *to separate the wheat from the chaff*
2 straw cut up small and used for animal feed

chagrin (say *shag-rən*) *noun*
a feeling of anger and disappointment: *She found to her chagrin that they had already left.*

chain *noun*
1 a series of metal rings joined together
2 a series of connected things: *a mountain chain / a chain of events* **3** a number of shops, hotels or theatres that belong to one owner

Word Building: **chain** *verb* to fasten with a chain

chainsaw *noun*
a saw which has teeth on a revolving chain driven by a motor

chair *noun*
1 a seat with a back and often with arms
chair *verb*
2 to act as a chairperson: *to chair a meeting*

chairperson *noun*
someone who controls a meeting

Word Building: **chairman** *noun* **chairwoman** *noun*

chalet (say *shal-ay*) *noun*
a mountain cottage, sometimes used as a holiday house

chalice *noun*
a cup for wine in Christian religious services

chalk *noun*
1 soft white limestone **2** a stick of this for drawing or writing on blackboards

Word Building: **chalkiness** *noun* **chalky** *adjective*

challenge *verb*
1 to invite to take part or compete in a test of skill or strength: *to challenge someone to fight* **2** to make demands on: *This job will challenge your abilities.*

Word Building: **challenge** *noun* **challenger** *noun*

chamber *noun*
1 a room, often a private room: *in my lady's chamber* **2 chambers** rooms of barristers and judges

Word Use: definition 1 is old-fashioned

chamber music *noun*
music for a small group of players, suitable for playing in a room rather than in a large concert hall

chameleon (say *kə-mee-lee-ən*) *noun*
a lizard that can change its skin colour to blend into its surroundings

Word History: from a Greek word meaning a "ground lion"

chamois (say *sham-ee*) *noun*
a soft cloth for polishing

Word Use: other spellings are **chammy** and **shammy**

champagne (say *sham-payn*) *noun*
a bubbly white wine

Word History: named after *Champagne*, the region in France where this wine is made

champion *noun*
1 someone or something that holds first place in a sport or contest **2** someone who fights for a cause: *She is a champion of women's rights.*

Word Building: **championship** *noun*

chance *noun*
1 the absence of any known reason for something happening: *They met by chance.* **2** risk: *to take a chance* **3** opportunity: *Now is your chance to tell him.*

chandelier (say *shan-də-lear*) *noun*
a branched holder for a number of lights, hanging from the ceiling

change *verb*
1 to alter or make different: *You must change your habits.* **2** to become different: *She has changed since her illness.* **3** to exchange, especially for something else **4** to give or get smaller money for: *to change a $10 note* **5** to change your clothes: *It is time you changed for the party.*

change *noun*
6 something different from before: *a change in the weather* **7** the money you get back when what you've bought costs less than the amount you handed over **8** coins of small value: *I need change for the bus.*

Word Building: **changeability** *noun* **changeable** *adjective* **changeably** *adverb* **changeless** *adjective*

channel *noun*
1 a waterway: *a stormwater channel* **2** a passage which ships use to travel between two seas **3** a frequency band for radio or television **4** a way of communicating: *He approached the Minister through the usual channels.*

Word Building: **channel** *verb* (**channelled, channelling**)

chant *noun*
1 a simple tune, often repeating one note, for church singing **2** words repeated in a sing-song way

Word Building: **chant** *verb*

chaos (say *kay-os*) *noun*
total disorder

Word Building: **chaotic** *adjective* **chaotically** *adverb*

chap *noun*
a man or boy

Word Use: this word is more suited to everyday language

chapel *noun*
a small church or part of a large one

chaperone (say *shap-ə-rohn*) *verb*
to accompany in order to ensure respectable behaviour: *The teacher will chaperone the children at the school dance.*

Word Building: chaperone *noun* an older person who is responsible for younger, less experienced people

chaplain *noun*
a clergyman who works in a school, hospital or the armed forces

Word Building: chaplaincy *noun* the office or job of a chaplain

chapped *adjective*
cracked and made rough: *She has chapped hands from the wind.*

chapter *noun*
one of the main divisions of a book, usually with a number and a title

char *verb*
1 to burn to charcoal **2** to scorch or burn slightly

Word Building: other forms are **it charred, it has charred, it is charring**

character *noun*
1 someone in a story or play **2** the special things about you that make you different from someone else **3** an odd or interesting person: *He's quite a character.* **4** honesty, or high moral standards: *a person of character* **5** a mark, letter or other symbol, used in writing and printing

Word Building: characterise *verb* to be typical of or describe the character of **characterisation** *noun*

characteristic *adjective*
1 typical or showing the special qualities: *That boasting is characteristic of him.*
characteristic *noun*
2 a special feature: *Large loops are a characteristic of her handwriting.*

Word Building: characteristically *adverb*

charade (say *shə-rahd*) *noun*
1 charades a game in which half the players have to guess a word acted out by the others in a series of short plays
2 any silly pretence which obviously isn't working: *The government should stop this charade, and get on with running the country.*

charcoal *noun*
partly burnt wood used as a fuel or in sticks for drawing

charge *verb*
1 to blame or accuse: *The police charged her with speeding.* **2** to write down as a debt: *Charge it to my account.* **3** to ask as the price: *They charge a dollar each for mangoes.* **4** to supply with electrical energy: *to charge a battery* **5** to attack by rushing violently
charge *noun*
6 an accusation or blame **7** cost or price **8** an amount of explosive to be let off all at once **9 in charge** in control: *Betty is in charge of the tickets.*

Word Building: charger *noun* a war-horse

chariot *noun*
a two-wheeled carriage used in ancient times

Word Building: charioteer *noun* the driver of a chariot

charisma (say *kə-riz-mə*) *noun*
the power to attract and influence people: *A successful leader should have charisma.*

Word Building: charismatic *adjective*
Word History: from a Greek word meaning "gift"

charity *noun*
1 the giving of help or money to people who need it **2** an organisation for providing help: *Several charities have put up shelters for the homeless.*

Word Building: the plural is **charities** □ **charitable** *adjective* **charitableness** *noun* **charitably** *adverb*

charlatan (say *shah-lə-tən*) *noun*
someone who claims to have knowledge or skill that they don't really have: *He was treated by a charlatan and now his rash is worse than ever.*

Word Use: a similar word is **quack**
Word History: from an Italian word meaning "chatter"

charm *noun*
1 the power of pleasing and attracting: *The new assistant has a great deal of charm.* **2** a magic spell **3** an ornament or trinket supposed to bring good luck

Word Building: charm *verb* **charmer** *noun* **charming** *adjective* **charmingly** *adverb*

chart *noun*
1 a map, especially of the sea **2** a printed sheet giving information, often as a table or with pictures **3 charts** an up-to-date list of the best-selling popular records

Word Building: chart *verb: to chart unknown seas*

charter *noun*
1 a document giving certain legal rights: *The settlers were given a land charter.*
charter *verb*
2 to hire: *They chartered a boat for their holiday.*

chase *verb*
1 to follow quickly in order to catch or overtake
chase *noun*
2 a hunt or pursuit **3** a large area of land set aside for plants and animals

chasm (say kaz-əm) *noun*
a deep gap or opening in the ground

chassis (say shaz-ee) *noun*
the frame, wheels and sometimes the machinery of a car or truck, designed to support its body

Word Building: the plural is also **chassis** (say shaz-eez)

chaste *adjective*
1 pure and without sexual experience
2 decent and clean: *chaste language*

Word Building: **chastity** *noun: The knights of old took vows of chastity.* **chastely** *adverb*

chastise *verb*
to punish or scold: *His father chastised him for breaking the window.*

Word Building: **chastisement** *noun*

chat *verb*
to talk in a friendly way: *The sisters chatted about their recent holidays.*

Word Building: other forms are **I chatted, I have chatted, I am chatting** □ **chat** *noun* **chattily** *adverb* **chattiness** *noun* **chatty** *adjective*

chatter *verb*
1 to talk quickly, often without making sense **2** to make a rapid clicking noise: *Her teeth were chattering with the cold.*

Word Building: **chatterbox** *noun* someone who talks a lot **chatter** *noun*

chauffeur (say shoh-fə, shoh-fer) *noun*
someone whose job is to drive you in your own car: *The chauffeur drives the judge to the court every day.*

chauvinism (say shoh-və-niz-əm) *noun*
unthinking support of any cause or group: *male chauvinism*

Word Building: **chauvinist** *noun* **chauvinistic** *adjective* **chauvinistically** *adverb*

cheap *adjective*
1 of a low price: *You can buy cheap fruit at the market.* **2** of poor quality: *Those shirts are made of cheap material.*

Word Building: **cheapen** *verb* **cheaply** *adverb* **cheapness** *noun*

cheat *verb*
1 to be dishonest: *to cheat in an exam / to cheat at cards* **2** to take from by tricking: *to cheat someone out of $10*

Word Building: **cheat** *noun* someone who cheats **cheater** *noun*

check *verb*
1 to stop or prevent: *The fallen tree across the road checked their progress.* **2** to find out the correctness of: *Please check the names on this list.*
check *noun*
3 something that stops or holds back: *The accident was a check to her career.* **4** a test for correctness **5** a pattern of squares **6** in chess, the position of the king when it is threatened with a direct attack

Word Building: **checked** *adjective*

checkmate *noun*
in chess, the act of trapping your opponent's king so ending the game

Word Building: **checkmate** *verb*

checkup *noun*
a test to make sure that all is in order, especially your health: *She went to the doctor for her yearly checkup.*

cheddar *noun*
a fairly hard yellow cheese

Word History: named after *Cheddar*, a town in Somerset in England, famous for its cheese

cheek *noun*
1 either side of your face, below your eyes **2** boldness or lack of respect: *He had the cheek to tell me to mind my own business.*

cheeky *adjective*
impudent or lacking respect: *Her cheeky behaviour annoyed the teacher.*

Word Building: other forms are **cheekier, cheekiest** □ **cheekily** *adverb* **cheekiness** *noun*

cheer *noun*
1 a shout of encouragement or approval
cheer *verb*
2 to greet with shouts of approval: *They cheered the winner.* **3 cheer up** to make or become happier: *The news of his arrival*

cheered us up. | *We cheered up when we heard the news.*

Word Building: **cheery** *adjective* (**cheerier, cheeriest**) **cheerful** *adjective* **cheerfully** *adverb* **cheerily** *adverb*

cheese *noun*
a food made from milk curds

Word Building: **cheesy** *adjective* **cheesiness** *noun*

cheetah *noun*
a leopard-like animal that belongs to the cat family and is the fastest animal on earth

chef (say *shef*) *noun*
a cook, especially the head cook in a restaurant

chemical *adjective*
1 of or about chemistry

chemical *noun*
2 a substance obtained by or used in chemistry

Word Building: **chemically** *adverb*

chemist *noun*
1 a scientist who studies and does research in chemistry **2** someone who has studied drugs and medicines and keeps a shop selling them

Word Use: another word for definition 2 is **pharmacist**

chemistry *noun*
the science of what substances are made of and the ways they react with each other

cheque (say *chek*) *noun*
a written order asking a bank to pay a certain amount of money to a particular person

Word Building: **chequebook** *noun* a book of printed forms for cheques

chequered *adjective*
1 marked with squares **2** marked by changes in good or bad luck: *a chequered career*

Word Building: **chequer** *noun* a pattern of squares

cherish *verb*
to look after tenderly: *He cherishes his pet rabbit.*

Word History: from a French word meaning "dear"

cherry *noun*
1 a small juicy fruit with a stone in the middle, varying in colour from pink to black

cherry *adjective*
2 bright red

Word Building: the plural form of the noun is **cherries**

cherub *noun*
1 an angel, pictured as a child with wings **2** a child with a chubby face

Word Building: the plural for definition 1 is **cherubim** and for definition 2 is **cherubs** □ **cherubic** *adjective* round and innocent-looking: *a cherubic face*

chess *noun*
a game played by two people, each with sixteen pieces, on a chequered board

Word Building: **chessman** *noun* one of the pieces used in the game

chest *noun*
1 the front part of your body from your neck to your waist **2** a box, usually large and strong with a hinged lid

chestnut *noun*
1 a European tree or its hard brown nuts

chestnut *adjective*
2 reddish-brown

chew *verb*
to bite and crush with your teeth

Word Building: **chewy** *adjective*

chic (say *sheek*) *adjective*
attractive and stylish: *Your new dress is very chic.*

Word History: from a French word, which is why it sounds like this

chick *noun*
a young chicken or other bird

chicken *noun*
1 a young hen or rooster, or its meat: *roast chicken for dinner* **2** a coward: *He's too much of a chicken to climb that tree.*

chicken *verb*
3 chicken out to back out because you are scared

Word Use: definitions 2 and 3 are more suited to everyday language
Word Building: **chicken** *adjective* cowardly

chickenpox *noun*
a disease, common in children, causing fever and itchy blisters

chide *verb*
to scold or find fault with: *She chided me for not tidying my room.*

Word Building: other forms are **I chided** or **chid, I have chid** or **I have chidden, I am chiding** □ **chidingly** *adverb*

chief *noun*
1 the head person or boss in a group
chief *adjective*
2 most important or main: *My chief problem is with spelling.*

Word Building: **chiefly** *adverb*

chieftain (say *cheef-tən*) *noun*
the leader of a tribe

chiffon (say *shə-fon*) *noun*
light see-through material made of silk or nylon

chilblain *noun*
a red swelling on your fingers or toes caused by the cold

child *noun*
1 a boy or girl **2** a son or daughter

Word Building: the plural is **children** □ **childhood** *noun* the time spent as a child **childproof** *adjective* made so that children can't use or damage it

childish *adjective*
1 silly or stupid: *childish behaviour* **2** of or like a child

Word Building: **childishly** *adverb* **childishness** *noun*

chill *noun*
1 coldness: *There's a chill in the air.*
2 a cold, shivery feeling, often the first stage of a cold: *Take off your wet clothes before you catch a chill.*
chill *verb*
3 to make or become cold

Word Building: **chill** *adjective: a chill wind* **chilly** *adjective* (**chillier, chilliest**) **chilliness** *noun*

chilli *noun*
a type of small capsicum which tastes hot

chime *noun*
1 a ringing, musical sound: *the chime of the church bells* **2 chimes** a set of metal tubes or bells which make musical sounds when rung

Word Building: **chime** *verb*
Word History: from a Latin word meaning "cymbal"

chimney *noun*
a long tube running from a fireplace to the roof of a building, which draws smoke away from a fire

Word Building: the plural is **chimneys**

chimpanzee *noun*
a small African ape which is very intelligent and can easily be trained to perform tricks

Word Use: the short form is **chimp**

chin *noun*
the part of your face below your mouth

china (rhymes with *miner*) *noun*
plates, cups and bowls made from porcelain clay: *We use the best china when guests come for dinner.*

Word Use: a similar word is **crockery**
Word Building: **china** *adjective* made of porcelain
Word History: named after the country of China where delicate crockery was first made

chintz *noun*
shiny brightly-patterned cotton material, used to make curtains and furniture coverings

Word Building: the plural is **chintzes** □ **chintzy** *adjective* shiny and cheap-looking

chip *noun*
1 a small piece chopped or split off something larger: *a chip of wood / potato chips* **2** a gap where a small piece has broken off: *This plate has a chip in it.*
3 a tiny square which contains electronic circuits, used in a computer, watch or electronic game: *a silicon chip*
chip *verb*
4 to cut or break off in small pieces
5 chip in **a** to contribute money or help: *We all chipped in to buy her birthday present.* **b** to interrupt: *It's rude to chip in while others are talking.*

Word Use: definition 5 is more suited to everyday language
Word Building: other verb forms are **I chipped, I have chipped, I am chipping**

chipmunk *noun*
a type of small striped squirrel that lives in the forests of North America and Asia

chiropractor (say *kuy-rə-prak-tə*) *noun*
someone trained to treat back pain and other types of illness by massaging and adjusting the spine.

Word Building: **chiropractic** *noun* the method of treating disease used by chiropractors

chirp *verb*
to make a short high sound like a bird or insect

Word Use: another form of the word is **chirrup**
Word Building: **chirp** *noun*

chirpy *adjective*
lively and cheerful

Word Building: other forms are **chirpier, chirpiest** □ **chirpily** *adverb*

chisel *noun*
1 a cutting tool with a sharp end, used to shape wood and stone

chisel *verb*
2 to cut with or use a chisel **3** to cheat or trick: *He chiselled me out of my savings.*

Word Use: definition 3 is more suited to everyday language
Word Building: other verb forms are **I chiselled, I have chiselled, I am chiselling** □ **chiseller** *noun* a cheat or swindler

chivalry (say *<u>shiv</u>-əl-ree*) *noun*
1 polite behaviour, especially of a gentleman towards a lady **2** the qualities of courtesy and bravery which were valued amongst medieval knights

Word Building: **chivalrous** *adjective* **chivalrously** *adverb* **chivalrousness** *noun*

chive *noun*
a small grass-like herb which tastes like onion and is used in cooking

chlorine (say *<u>klaw</u>-reen*) *noun*
a poisonous greenish-yellow gas with a strong irritating smell, which is dissolved in water and used to bleach clothes or to disinfect swimming pools

Word Building: **chlorinate** *verb:* to disinfect with chlorine **chlorination** *noun*

chlorophyll (say *<u>klo</u>-rə-fil*) *noun*
the green colouring in leaves and plants, which traps the energy of sunlight and is sometimes used as a dye

chock *noun*
a block of wood wedged under something to stop it moving: *Put a chock under the door to stop it closing.*

Word Building: **chock** *verb: to chock open the door*

chocolate *noun*
1 a sweet food or drink made from the seeds of a small, tropical American tree

chocolate *adjective*
2 made with or from chocolate **3** dark brown

Word History: from a Nahuatl word (spoken by the Aztecs and others) meaning "bitter water"

choice *noun*
1 the act of choosing or selecting **2** the thing chosen: *The blue one is my choice.* **3** a number of things from which you can choose: *a wide choice of colours*

choice *adjective*
4 excellent or worthy of being chosen: *a choice apple*

choir (say *<u>kwuy</u>-ə*) *noun*
an organised group of people who sing together, especially in a church

Word Use: a similar word is **chorus**

choke *verb*
1 to suffocate or stop breathing: *This tight collar is choking me. / He choked on a fishbone.* **2** to clog up or congest: *Mud and leaves are choking the drain.*

choke *noun*
3 a device used when starting an engine, which controls the amount of air that is mixed with the petrol

Word Building: **choker** *noun* a tight necklace or band around the neck

choko *noun*
a green pear-shaped vegetable with a prickly skin, which grows on a vine

cholera (say *<u>kol</u>-ə-rə*) *noun*
an infectious tropical disease which can kill you

cholesterol (say *ke-<u>les</u>-tə-rol*) *noun*
a substance found in your liver, blood, brain, or in other places, such as the yolk of eggs. It is thought that if a person has too much in their bloodstream they have a greater risk of getting heart disease.

choose *verb*
1 to pick out or select: *Choose a number between one and ten. / Don't rush me while I'm choosing.* **2** to decide or prefer: *She chose not to go to the party.*

Word Building: other forms are **I chose, I have chosen, I am choosing** □ **choosy** *adjective* hard to please

chop *verb*
1 to cut by hitting with quick heavy blows: *to chop wood with an axe*

chop *noun*
2 a quick cutting stroke **3** a slice of meat with bone in it: *lamb chops* **4 get the chop a** to be killed **b** to be dismissed from work

Word Use: definition 4 is more suited to everyday language
Word Building: other verb forms are **I chopped, I have chopped, I am chopping**

chopper *noun*
1 someone or something that chops, especially a butcher's cleaver **2** *an everyday word for* **helicopter**

choppy *adjective*
forming short broken waves: *a choppy sea*

Word Building: other forms are **choppier, choppiest**

chopsticks *plural noun*
a pair of thin smooth sticks, used in Asia instead of a knife and fork to pick up food

chord (say *kawd*) *noun*
three or more musical notes played together: *to play chords on a guitar*

Word Use: be careful – this sounds like **cord**

chore (say *chaw*) *noun*
a boring or unpleasant job

choreography (say *ko-ree-og-rə-fee*) *noun*
the art of designing ballets and dances

Word Building: **choreograph** *verb* **choreographer** *noun*

chorister (say *ko-ris-tə*) *noun*
someone who sings in a choir

chortle *verb*
to chuckle loudly with amusement

Word Use: this is called a **blended** or **portmanteau word**
Word History: made up by Lewis Carroll in *Through the Looking-Glass* in 1871; a blend of **chuckle** and **snort**

chorus (say *kaw-rəs*) *noun*
1 the part of a song that is repeated after each verse **2** a piece of music for several people to sing together **3** a group of people or a choir singing together

Word Use: a similar word for definition 1 is **refrain**
Word Building: **choral** *adjective* sung by a choir or chorus **chorus** *verb* to sing or say together

christen (say *kris-ən*) *verb*
1 to give a name to, especially at baptism: *We christened the baby Peter William. / We christened the new boat Mary-Belle.* **2** to use for the first time: *Have you christened your new bike yet?*

Word Building: **christening** *noun* the ceremony of baptism

Christianity *noun*
a world religion based on the teachings of Jesus Christ

Word Building: **Christian** *noun* a follower of the teachings of Jesus Christ **Christian** *adjective: the Christian faith*
Word History: named after Jesus *Christ*, from a Hebrew name meaning "anointed"

Christian name *noun*
your first or given name: *His Christian names are Robert James and his surname is Bell.*

Word Use: people who are not Christians prefer to say "first name" or "given name"

Christmas *noun*
a church festival of the birth of Jesus Christ, celebrated on 25 December

chromatic *adjective*
1 relating to a musical scale that moves by small steps, using all of the twelve semitones **2** having to do with colour

Word Building: **chromatically** *adverb*

chrome *noun*
a hard, shiny, silver-coloured metal used to cover other metals to protect them and to stop rust

Word Building: **chrome-plated** *adjective* covered in chrome
Word History: this is short for **chromium**

chromosome (say *kroh-mə-sohm*) *noun*
a tiny threadlike body found in the central part of all living cells, which carries the characteristics of the organism: *A human cell has 23 pairs of chromosomes.*

chronic *adjective*
1 constant or continuing for a long time: *She has chronic asthma.* **2** very bad: *a chronic shortage of bread*

Word Use: definition 2 is more suited to everyday language
Word Building: **chronically** *adverb*

chronicle *noun*
a record or history of events: *the chronicles of ancient Rome*

Word Building: **chronicle** *verb* to record events **chronicler** *noun*

chronological *adjective*
arranged in order according to when it happened: *I wrote down the most important events in my life in chronological order.*

Word Building: **chronology** *noun* a record of past events in order of time **chronologically** *adverb*

chrysalis (say *kris-ə-ləs*) *noun*
the form that a butterfly or moth takes when changing from a grub to an adult insect, inside a hard-shelled cocoon

Word Building: the plural is either **chrysalises** or **chrysalids**

chrysanthemum (say *krə-santh-ə-məm*) *noun*
a tall plant with big white or brightly-coloured flowers, often given as a present on Mother's Day

chubby *adjective*
plump and round: *a chubby baby*

Word Building: other forms are **chubbier, chubbiest** □ **chubbiness** *noun*

chuck *verb*
1 to throw or fling: *to chuck the ball over the fence* **2** to vomit **3 chuck it in** to give up without finishing: *I'm bored with playing football so I'll chuck it in.*

Word Use: this word is more suited to everyday language
Word Building: **chuck** *noun* a toss or throw

chuckle *verb*
to laugh softly

Word Building: **chuckle** *noun*

chunk *noun*
a thick piece or lump: *a chunk of fresh bread*

Word Building: **chunky** *adjective* (**chunkier, chunkiest**) thick or bulky **chunkiness** *noun*

church *noun*
1 a building where Christians gather to worship **2** the worship of God in a church **3 Church** an organisation of Christians who share the same religious beliefs: *the Catholic Church | the Anglican Church*

churn *noun*
1 a large metal container for milk
2 a machine for making butter from cream or milk

churn *verb*
3 to shake or stir in order to make into butter: *to churn cream* **4** to move about violently: *Her stomach churned with excitement.*

chute (sounds like *shoot*) *noun*
a sloping channel or passage for sending or carrying things to a lower level: *a laundry chute*

chutney *noun*
a spicy jam-like food made from fruit, sugar and vinegar

cicada (say *sə-kah-də*) *noun*
a large flying insect which is found in trees in the summer and which makes a very loud shrill sound in hot weather

cider (say *suy-də*) *noun*
a drink, sometimes containing alcohol, made from apples

Word History: from a Hebrew word meaning "strong drink"

cigar (say *sə-gah*) *noun*
tobacco leaves rolled tightly together for smoking

cigarette *noun*
a roll of shredded tobacco, for smoking, inside a cylinder of very thin paper

cinder *noun*
a burnt and blackened piece of wood or coal

cine- *prefix*
a word part meaning motion: *cinema*

Word History: this prefix comes from Greek

cinema *noun*
a theatre where films are shown

Word Use: you can also say **the pictures**
Word History: a shortened form of **cinematograph**

cinnamon (say *sin-ə-mən*) *noun*
a yellowish or reddish-brown spice made from the inner bark of certain trees and used in cooking

cipher (say *suy-fə*) *noun*
secret writing or a code: *The message was sent in cipher so the enemy could not understand it.*

Word Use: another spelling is **cypher**
Word Building: **cipher** *verb* to write in code

circle *noun*
1 a perfectly round shape **2** anything that has the shape of a circle or part of a circle: *Sit in a circle to listen to the story.*
3 a group of people who do things together: *a sewing circle* **4** the upper

section of seats in a theatre or cinema: *the dress circle*

circle *verb*
5 to move around in a circle: *The plane circled the airport. / The plane circled three times before landing.*

Word Building: **circular** *adjective* round or shaped like a circle **circular** *noun* a letter or notice sent to a number of people **circularity** *noun* **encircle** *verb*

circuit (say *ser-kət*) *noun*
1 a circular path or roundabout journey: *The visitors made a circuit of the school.* **2** a circular racing track **3** an arrangement of wires joined so as to carry an electric current: *a closed circuit*

Word Building: **circuitous** (say *sə-kyooh-ə-təs*) *adjective: a circuitous route home*

circulate *verb*
1 to move in a circle or circuit: *Blood circulates through your body.* **2** to pass from place to place or person to person: *The news circulated quickly. / We circulated a petition.*

circulation *noun*
1 continuous circular movement: *the circulation of blood through the body* **2** the number of copies of a newspaper or magazine sent out: *The local paper has a circulation of 20 000.*

circum- *prefix*
this word part has to do with movement all around or on all sides: circumference

Word History: this prefix comes from Latin

circumcise *verb*
to cut away the skin around the end of the penis of: *to circumcise a baby boy*

Word Building: **circumcision** *noun*

circumference *noun*
the distance around something, especially around a circle or circular object: *You can measure the circumference of a tree trunk with a tape measure.*

Word Use: a similar word is **perimeter**

circumnavigate *verb*
to sail round: *to circumnavigate the earth*

Word Building: **circumnavigation** *noun*

circumspect *adjective*
cautious and watchful

Word Building: **circumspection** *noun*

circumstance *noun*
1 a condition which influences a person or an event **2 circumstances** financial position: *They used to be rich, but now their circumstances have changed.*

circus *noun*
1 a travelling show with performing animals, clowns, jugglers and acrobats
2 an open area with seats on all sides, used for chariot races and other sports in ancient Rome

Word History: from a Greek word meaning "ring"

cirrus (say *si-rəs*) *noun*
high feathery cloud

cistern (say *sis-tən*) *noun*
a tank for holding water, such as the one above a toilet

citadel *noun*
a fort or strongly defended place, built to protect or control a city

cite *verb*
to mention or refer to: *The soldier was cited for bravery in the official dispatch. / The teacher cited three examples to explain the meaning of the word.*

Word Building: **citation** *noun* a mention

citizen *noun*
1 a member of a nation who has certain rights and duties: *All Australian citizens over the age of eighteen must vote in the election.* **2** someone who lives in a particular place: *a citizen of Adelaide*

Word Use: compare definition 1 with **alien**
Word Building: **citizenship** *noun*

citrus *noun*
a small evergreen tree such as the lemon, orange, lime, grapefruit or mandarin

Word Building: **citrus** *adjective: citrus fruit*

city *noun*
1 a large or important town **2** the people who live in a city: *The whole city turned out to watch the parade.*

Word Building: the plural is **cities**

civic *adjective*
of or concerning a city or citizens: *The council buildings are in the civic centre. / It is your civic duty to put litter in the bins provided.*

civil *adjective*
1 having to do with the government: *civil affairs* **2** having to do with citizens or the people: *civil liberties* **3** polite or courteous: *His way of asking was so civil that we did what he wanted.*

Word Building: **civility** *noun* **civilly** *adverb*

civilian *adjective*
having to do with ordinary life: *The soldier left the army and entered civilian life as a bus driver.*

Word Building: **civilian** *noun*

civilisation or **civilization** *noun*
the highly developed life of a particular people, including their science, art and writing: *The ancient Greeks brought civilisation to the tribes they ruled.* | *Chinese civilisation*

Word Building: **civilise** *verb*

civilised or **civilized** *adjective*
1 highly developed: *The Chinese have been a civilised race for thousands of years.* **2** polite and controlled: *They expected him to be angry but he wrote a very civilised letter.*

civil war *noun*
a war between people living in the same country

claim *verb*
1 to ask for, as if it's your right: *He claims his share of the money.* **2** to say definitely: *She claims that her story is true.*
claim *noun*
3 a demand: *The children make too many claims on her.* **4** the right to something: *After all your hard work you have a claim to some holidays.* **5** something claimed, such as a piece of land for mining

Word Building: **claimable** *adjective* **claimer** *noun*

clairvoyant (say *klair-voy-ənt*) *adjective*
claiming to be able to see into the future

Word Building: **clairvoyance** *noun* **clairvoyant** *noun*

clam *noun*
a large shellfish whose two shells are hinged and can be tightly closed

clamber *verb*
to climb up with difficulty: *He clambered onto the roof.*

clammy *adjective*
cold, damp and sticky

Word Building: other forms are **clammier, clammiest** □ **clamminess** *noun*

clamour or **clamor** (say *klam-ə*) *noun*
the loud noise of many voices: *an angry clamour*

Word Building: **clamour** *verb* to make a loud noise or ask noisily **clamorous** *adjective*

clamp *noun*
1 a tool which holds things tightly together
clamp *verb*
2 to hold tightly: *He clamped his teeth together in anger.* **3** to press down: *The lid was clamped onto the box then locked.*

clan *noun*
a group of related families who share a common ancestor

Word Building: **clannish** *adjective* very close, like the members of a clan

clandestine (say *klan-des-tən*) *adjective*
secret and unlawful: *The freedom fighters held clandestine meetings away from the town.*

Word Building: **clandestinely** *adverb*

clang *verb*
to ring loudly

Word Building: **clangour** *noun* a loud metallic sound **clangorous** *adjective*

clap *verb*
1 to hit your hands together noisily, especially in applause **2** to show approval or enjoyment of, by clapping: *We clapped our favourite actor.* **3** to shut away immediately: *The recaptured prisoner was clapped into gaol.*
clap *noun*
4 a loud sudden noise: *There was a clap of thunder.* **5** a sign of approval, by clapping: *They've done well – let's give them a clap.*

Word Building: other verb forms are **I clapped, I have clapped, I am clapping** □ **clapper** *noun* something that claps, especially the tongue of a bell

clarify *verb*
to make clear: *to clarify butter* | *to clarify the answer to the problem*

Word Building: other forms are **I clarified, I have clarified, I am clarifying** □ **clarification** *noun*

clarinet *noun*
a musical instrument belonging to the woodwind family which makes a deeper sound than the flute

Word Building: **clarinettist** *noun* a clarinet player
Word History: from a French word meaning "little clarion" (an old-fashioned high trumpet)

clarity *noun*
clearness: *You could see the riverbed because of the clarity of the water. / The clarity of her arguments convinced us she was right.*

clash *verb*
1 to make a loud harsh noise **2** to disagree or differ: *Their opinions clashed.* **3** to happen at the same time: *Their favourite television shows clashed.*

Word Building: **clash** *noun*

clasp *noun*
1 something which fastens things together **2** a firm hold

Word Building: **clasp** *verb* to hold tightly

class *noun*
1 a group of people or things which are alike in some way **2** a group of pupils who are taught together **3** someone's place in society, judged by their possessions or their family: *the middle class* **4** the level of comfort in travel: *In the plane's first class, dinner is served.*

Word Building: the plural is **classes** □ **class** *verb* to put in a group

classic *adjective*
1 of high quality: *That vintage car is a classic model in perfect condition.* **2** typical: *The actress had a classic case of nerves.*
classic *noun*
3 someone or something known to be excellent: *"Gone With The Wind" is now considered a film classic.* **4 classics** the writings and language of ancient Greece and Rome

classical *adjective*
1 classic **2** traditional: *They listened to Mozart and Beethoven and other classical music.*

Word Building: **classically** *adverb*

classified ad *noun*
a short advertisement in a newspaper, usually advertising a job or something for sale

classify *verb*
to group according to quality or likeness: *When we had classified the apples the good ones were packed and the bad ones thrown out.*

Word Building: other forms are **I classified, I have classified, I am classifying** □ **classifiable** *adjective* **classification** *noun* **classified** *adjective*

clatter *verb*
to rattle loudly

Word Building: **clatter** *noun* disturbance

clause (say *klawz*) *noun*
a group of words which contains a subject and a verb, which may be a part of a sentence or a whole sentence, such as *after the boy arrived* and *She heard the news.*

claustrophobia (say *klos-trə-foh-bee-ə*) *noun*
the fear of being shut in a small place

Word Building: **claustrophobic** *adjective*

claves *plural noun*
a simple musical instrument which consists of two wooden sticks which are hit together

clavichord (say *klav-ə-kawd*) *noun*
an early type of piano, whose strings are softly struck with metal blades

claw *noun*
1 the sharp curved nail on the foot of an animal or bird **2** the sharp pincers of crabs and lobsters
claw *verb*
3 to scratch or seize with nails or claws

clay *noun*
a dense earth which holds water and is used in making pottery and bricks

Word Building: **clayey** *adjective*

clean *adjective*
1 without dirt or stains **2** fair: *It was a clean fight.* **3** without a mark: *She started a clean page.* **4** with a smooth edge: *It was a clean cut that would heal easily.*
clean *verb*
5 to remove dirt from: *She cleaned herself in the shower.*

Word Building: **cleaner** *noun* **cleanliness** *noun* **cleanly** *adverb* **cleanness** *noun*

cleanse (say *klenz*) *verb*
to make clean or pure: *to cleanse the skin*

Word Building: **cleanser** *noun*

clear *adjective*
1 light or bright: *It was a clear sunny day.* **2** transparent: *clear glass.* **3** easily understood: *The children need clear*

examples. **4** without doubt: *a clear win.* **5** open or free from obstacles: *a clear road*

clear *verb*
6 to become light or bright: *After a cloudy morning the sky cleared.* **7** to free from blockage: *He cleared the gutters on the roof.* **8** to free from blame: *The jury's verdict cleared her of guilt.* **9 clear up** to make easier to understand: *Can you clear up this point for me?*

Word Building: **clear** *adverb: to get clear away* **clearly** *adverb* **clearness** *noun*

clearance *noun*
1 the space between two things: *The truck had a clearance of ten centimetres under the bridge.* **2** permission to go ahead with something: *They needed a clearance from the council to build their home of mud bricks.*

clearing *noun*
a piece of cleared land in the middle of bush or forest

clearway *noun*
a busy street or highway on which cars may park only in case of emergency

cleat *noun*
a wedge-shaped piece of wood or metal which a climber drives into a steep mountain side to make a foothold

cleavage *noun*
a division or split

cleaver *noun*
a chopper with a long blade, used by butchers for cutting meat

clef *noun*
a symbol placed on a line of music that shows the height or pitch of the notes: *treble clef*

Word History: from a Latin word meaning "key"

cleft *noun*
a narrow opening or split

clench *verb*
to close or press tightly: *to clench your teeth in pain | to clench your fist in anger*

clergy *noun*
the priests and ministers of the Christian church

Word Building: **clergyman** *noun* someone who belongs to the clergy **clerical** *adjective: a clerical collar* **cleric** *noun*

clerk (rhymes with *bark*) *noun*
someone who works in an office, keeping records and accounts and sorting letters and papers

Word Building: **clerical** *adjective* having to do with office workers and clerks

clever *adjective*
1 good at thinking quickly **2** able or skilful: *He's clever with his hands.*

Word Building: **cleverly** *adverb* **cleverness** *noun*

cliché (say *klee-shay*) *noun*
a saying which has become stale or dull because it has been used too often, such as *as old as the hills*

Word Use: there is an accent over the "e" because this was originally a French word
Word Building: **clichéed** *adjective*

click *noun*
a slight sharp sound

Word Building: **click** *verb* **clicker** *noun*

client *noun*
a customer, especially of a lawyer or someone in a similar profession

cliff *noun*
a steep rocky slope

climate *noun*
the usual weather of a particular place

Word Building: **climatic** *adjective* having to do with weather **climatically** *adverb*

climax *noun*
the highest or most important and exciting point of anything: *The climax of the show was a fireworks display at night.*

Word Building: **climactic** *adjective* **climactically** *adverb*

climb *verb*
1 to move or rise upwards: *She climbed the ladder. | The aeroplane climbs slowly into the sky.* **2** to slope upwards: *The mountain climbs to a sharp peak.*

Word Building: **climb** *noun* **climber** *noun*

clinch *verb*
1 to settle once and for all: *The two men clinched the sale by signing the papers.*

clinch *noun*
2 a close hold in boxing, which slows your opponent's punches

Word Building: **clincher** *noun*

cling *verb*
to hold tightly: *The child was clinging to his mother.*

Word Building: other forms are **I clung, I have clung, I am clinging** □ **clingy** *adjective*

clinic *noun*
a medical centre where you can go to see a doctor or have special treatment, such as an X-ray

Word Building: **clinical** *adjective* **clinically** *adverb*

clip[1] *verb*
1 to cut off or shorten with scissors or shears: *The shearer clipped the sheep's wool. / Dad clipped the ends of his moustache.* **2** to punch a hole in: *The bus conductor clipped our tickets.* **3** to give a sharp hit: *He clipped the man on the jaw.*
clip[1] *noun*
4 a trimming: *Please give my hair a clip.* **5** a short section of a film: *The actors saw clips of the film as it was being made.*

Word Building: other verb forms are **I clipped, I have clipped, I am clipping** □ **clipped** *adjective* **clipping** *noun*

clip[2] *noun*
something which holds things in place: *My bag is open because the clip keeps coming undone.*

Word Building: **clip** *verb* to fasten

clipper *noun*
1 a cutting tool, especially for your hair or nails **2** a fast sailing ship

Word Use: definition 1 is often plural **clippers**

clique (rhymes with *meek*) *noun*
a small close group of people who keep themselves apart from others

Word Building: **cliquey** *adjective* **cliquish** *adjective* **cliquish** *adverb*
Word History: from a French word meaning "people hired to applaud in a theatre"

cloak *noun*
1 a sleeveless coat or cape which does up at your neck
cloak *verb*
2 to hide or keep hidden: *to cloak your feelings*

clock *noun*
something which measures and tells you the time

Word Building: **clock** *verb* to time

clockwise *adjective*
going around in the same direction as the hands on a clock face

Word Use: the opposite is **anticlockwise**

clockwork *noun*
1 the workings of a clock or a wind-up toy **2 like clockwork** smoothly and without interruption: *Our travel plans went like clockwork.*

clod *noun*
1 a lump, especially of earth **2** a dull or stupid person

Word Building: **cloddish** *adjective* dull or stupid

clog *verb*
1 to block or become blocked: *Leaves clogged the gutter.*
clog *noun*
2 a heavy wooden shoe

Word Building: other verb forms are **it clogged, it has clogged, it is clogging**

cloister (say *kloy-stə*) *noun*
1 a covered path by the side of a building such as a church **2** a place where nuns or priests live quietly, away from the rest of the world

Word Building: **cloister** *verb* to seclude or confine, as in a cloister

clone *noun*
the offspring of a plant or animal which is exactly the same as its parent and has been formed not by the joining of male and female cells but from one of its parent's own cells

Word Building: **clone** *verb*
Word History: from a Greek word meaning "slip" or "twig"

close (say *klohz*) *verb*
1 to block off: *Heavy snow closed the road.* **2** to shut: *The door closed in the wind. / She closed the window.* **3** to refuse entry to: *Police closed the sports ground.* **4** to end: *After two hours the meeting finally closed. / He closed his show with a song.*
close (say *klohs*) *adjective*
5 narrow or tight: *The shoes are a close fit.* **6** hard to breathe: *The air in the hot room was too close and someone fainted.* **7** near each other: *The children are close in age. / They felt very close after all they had been through.* **8** thorough: *This book needs close study.*

Word Building: **close** *noun* conclusion **close** *adverb* **closed** *adjective* **closely** *adverb* **closeness** *noun*

closet (say <u>kloz</u>-*ət*) *noun*
1 a cupboard or small room where things are stored **2** a toilet

clot *noun*
1 a solid lump: *a blood clot* **2** a fool
clot *verb*
3 to thicken or form into clots: *The blood from his cut began to clot and dry up.*

Word Use: definition 2 is more suited to everyday language
Word Building: other verb forms are **it clotted, it has clotted, it is clotting**

cloth *noun*
a piece of material or fabric: *Her skirt was made of woollen cloth. / He wiped the milk up with a cloth.*

clothe (say *klohdh*) *verb*
to provide with clothes: *to clothe the needy children*

Word Building: **clothing** *noun*

clothes (say *klohdhz*) *plural noun*
the things you wear

cloud *noun*
1 a white or grey mass of water vapour, ice, smoke or dust that floats in the air **2** anything which looks or acts like a cloud: *a cloud of steam / a cloud of sandflies*
cloud *verb*
3 to darken or become darker: *Anger clouded her face. / The mirror clouded with steam.*

Word Building: **cloudiness** *noun* **cloudily** *adverb* **cloudy** *adjective*

clout *noun*
1 a hit with the hand: *He gave the boy a clout on the shoulder.* **2** power or influence: *You need some clout to get a good job like that.*

Word Building: **clout** *verb* to hit

clove *noun*
the dried flower bud of a tropical tree, used as a spice

clover *noun*
a plant with leaves divided into three parts and a white flower, often used as food for cattle

clown *noun*
someone in a circus, often dressed up with a white face, a red nose and silly clothes, who makes people laugh

Word Use: a similar word is **jester**
Word Building: **clown** *verb* to act the fool **clowning** *noun* **clownish** *adjective*

club *noun*
1 a heavy stick, used as a weapon **2** a stick used to hit the ball in games like golf **3** a group of people who share a particular interest or hobby: *We started a chess club at school.* **4** a place run by a group, which offers entertainment and cheap food and drink to those who belong **5** the clover-shaped black sign on some playing cards
club *verb*
6 to beat with a club **7 club in** to join together: *Everyone in the office clubbed in to buy her a card.*

Word Building: other verb forms are **I clubbed, I have clubbed, I am clubbing**

cluck *verb*
to make the sound a hen makes when calling her chicks

Word Building: **clucky** *adjective* feeling a strong desire to have children

clue *noun*
something which helps to explain a puzzle or mystery: *a clue in a detective story*

Word Building: **clueless** *adjective* stupid **cluey** *adjective*

clump *noun*
a group of things growing together, such as trees or grasses

Word Building: **clump** *verb*

clumsy *adjective*
1 awkward in the way you move about **2** without skill: *a clumsy workman*

Word Building: other forms are **clumsier, clumsiest** □ **clumsily** *adverb* **clumsiness** *noun*

cluster *noun*
a number of things growing or placed close together: *a cluster of grapes / a cluster of stars*

Word Building: **cluster** *verb* to gather in close groups

clutch *verb*
1 to seize or hold tightly: *The baby clutched the kitten.* **2 clutch at** to try to seize: *He clutched at the rope.*
clutch *noun*
3 a tight hold **4** part of a machine which is used in changing gears **5 clutches** power: *Now the witch had Ivan in her clutches.*

clutter *verb*
to make untidy: *Papers clutter the dining room table.*

Word Building: **clutter** *noun*

co- *prefix*
a word part meaning **1** with: *cohesion* **2** at the same time: *coincidence*

Word History: this prefix comes from Latin

coach *noun*
1 a closed carriage pulled by horses **2** a tourist bus **3** a railway carriage **4** someone who trains athletes

Word Building: **coach** *verb* to train

coagulate (say *koh-ag-yə-layt*) *verb*
to change from a liquid into a thick lump, such as a clot

Word Building: **coagulation** *noun*

coal *noun*
a black or dark brown rock, formed from the remains of ancient trees, used as fuel

coalesce (say *koh-ə-les*) *verb*
to grow or join together: *The many small groups coalesced into one strong party.*

Word Building: **coalescence** *noun* **coalescent** *adjective*

coalition (say *koh-ə-lish-ən*) *noun*
the joining together of two or more groups, at least for a while: *a coalition of political parties*

Word Building: **coalitionist** *noun*

coarse (say *kaws*) *adjective*
1 thick or rough: *coarse material | coarse sand* **2** rude or offensive: *coarse jokes | coarse manners*

Word Use: be careful – this sounds like **course**
Word Building: **coarsely** *adverb* **coarsen** *verb* **coarseness** *noun*

coast *noun*
1 the seashore or the land beside the sea
coast *verb*
2 to go downhill in a car or on a bike without using power

Word Building: **coastal** *adjective*
Word History: from a Latin word meaning "rib" or "side"

coastguard *noun*
someone whose job is to patrol the coast of a country, helping ships in danger and looking out for smugglers or illegal fishing boats

coat *noun*
1 a piece of clothing with sleeves, that you wear over other clothes **2** the fur or wool of an animal **3** a layer: *The house needs a coat of paint.*

Word Building: **coat** *verb* to cover

coating *noun*
a covering: *a coating of batter | a coating of flour*

coat of arms *noun*
the special design, often with a motto, belonging to a noble family or nation: *The knight had his coat of arms painted on his tunic and his shield.*

coax (say *kohks*) *verb*
to persuade gently and patiently: *She coaxed the sick child to eat.*

Word Building: **coaxer** *noun* **coaxingly** *adverb*

cob *noun*
1 a stocky horse with short legs **2** a male swan **3** the head on which corn seeds grow: *a cob of corn*

cobalt (say *koh-bawlt*) *noun*
a silver-white metal which gives a blue colouring to pottery

Word History: from a German word for "goblin"

cobble *noun*
a rounded paving stone

Word Building: **cobble** *verb* to mend: *to cobble shoes*

cobbler *noun*
someone who mends shoes

Word Use: this is an old-fashioned word

cobra *noun*
a venomous snake which can spread out the skin of its neck like a hood

cobweb *noun*
1 the fine thread spun by a spider to catch insects **2** something very light or fine

Word Building: **cobwebby** *adjective*

cocaine (say *koh-kayn*) *noun*
a bitter drug which is made from the leaves of a South American shrub

cock *noun*
1 a rooster or male bird **2** the hammer of a gun

cockatoo *noun*
a crested parrot

cockeyed (say kok-uyd) *adjective*
1 crooked: *Your tie is cockeyed.* **2** foolish or absurd: *a cockeyed plan* **3** having a squinting eye

cockle *noun*
1 a shellfish found in Europe, that is good to eat **2 cockles** deep feelings: *Their kindness warms the cockles of your heart.*

cockpit *noun*
1 the front end of a plane where the pilots sit **2** the driver's seat in a racing car

cockroach *noun*
an insect which lives in the dark warm places where food is stored and comes out at night

cocktail *noun*
1 an alcoholic drink made of a spirit mixed with wine, fruit juice, and so on, often chilled and sweetened **2** fruit or tomato juice taken before a meal to stimulate the appetite

Word Building: **cocktail** *adjective* small enough to be eaten in your fingers: *cocktail sausages*

cocky[1] *adjective*
too confident or smart: *The new boys on the job are cocky, until they find out how hard it is.*

Word Use: this word is more suited to everyday language □ another more formal word with a similar meaning is **cocksure**
Word Building: other forms are **cockier**, **cockiest** □ **cockily** *adverb* **cockiness** *noun*

cocky[2] *noun*
1 a cockatoo **2** a farmer, especially of a small farm

Word Building: the plural is **cockies**

cocoa (say koh-koh) *noun*
1 the crushed and powdered seeds of a tropical tree **2** a drink made from the brown powder which is also used to make chocolate

coconut *noun*
the large hard nut of the coconut palm, which is lined with white flesh and contains a clear milk

cocoon (say kə-koohn) *noun*
the covering which grubs such as the silkworm spin around themselves before their next stage of growth

Word Building: **cocoon** *verb* to cover or protect
Word History: from a French word meaning "shell"

cod *noun*
a kind of large fish

coda (say koh-də) *noun*
the part which finishes a piece of music

coddle *verb*
1 to look after very well: *His mother coddled him after he was sick.* **2** to cook in water very slowly: *to coddle eggs*

code *noun*
1 a set of rules or laws: *a legal code / a code of honour* **2** a secret language, or a system such as the dots and dashes used in telegraphing messages

Word Building: **code** or **encode** *verb* to put in a code **codify** *verb* (**codified**, **codifying**) **decode** *verb*

coeducation *noun*
the joint teaching of boys and girls, in the same school or classroom

Word Building: **coeducational** *adjective*

coerce (say koh-ers) *verb*
to force: *The shopkeeper was coerced at gunpoint to open the till.*

Word Building: **coercion** *noun* **coercive** *adjective*

coffee *noun*
1 a drink made from the roasted and ground beans of a tropical shrub **2** the brown powder you use to make this drink

coffin *noun*
the wooden box in which a dead body is buried or cremated

cog *noun*
1 one of the toothlike bits sticking out of a wheel which connects it with another wheel **2** one of many unimportant people in an organisation

cogitate (say koj-ə-tayt) *verb*
to think hard

Word Building: **cogitation** *noun* **cogitative** *adjective*

cognac (say kon-yak) *noun*
a high quality brandy

Word History: named after the French town called *Cognac* where this drink was first made

coherent (say koh-hear-rənt) *adjective*
1 sticking together firmly: *coherent surfaces* **2** agreeing or well thought out: *a coherent argument*

Word Use: the opposite of definition 2 is **incoherent**
Word Building: **cohere** *verb* **coherence** *noun* **coherently** *adverb*

cohesion (say *koh-hee-zhən*) *noun*
the state of sticking together or being connected

Word Building: **cohesive** *adjective*

coil *verb*
1 to wind into loops: *to coil ropes* **2** to form into loops: *The snake coiled itself and struck.*

Word Building: **coil** *noun* a loop or spiral

coin *noun*
1 a metal piece of money
coin *verb*
2 to make coins **3** to invent: *to coin a word*

Word Building: **coinage** *noun* metal coins
Word History: from a Latin word meaning "wedge"

coincide (say *koh-ən-suyd*) *verb*
1 to happen together by chance **2** to agree: *Our opinions coincide on this point.*

coincidence (say *koh-in-sə-dəns*) *noun*
the surprising fact of things happening together by chance: *It was just a coincidence that we were on the same ship to Italy.*

Word Building: **coincidental** *adjective* **coincidentally** *adverb*

coke *noun*
a solid fuel made from heating coal

colander (say *kol-ən-də*) *noun*
a bowl with many small holes, which is used in the kitchen for draining off liquid

Word Use: another form of the word is **cullender**

cold *adjective*
1 having or feeling a lack of warmth: *It's a cold day.* | *My hands are cold.*
2 unfriendly: *Our neighbours were cold at first.*
cold *noun*
3 the absence of heat **4** a viral illness which usually comes with a blocked or a runny nose

Word Building: **coldly** *adverb* **coldness** *noun*

cold-blooded *adjective*
1 without feelings of pity: *a cold-blooded murder* **2** having a blood temperature which changes as the temperature of the surrounding air or water changes: *Reptiles and fish are cold-blooded animals.*

Word Use: the opposite of definition 2 is **warm-blooded**
Word Building: **cold-bloodedly** *adverb* **cold-bloodedness** *noun*

coleslaw *noun*
a salad made with sliced raw cabbage

colic (say *kol-ik*) *noun*
a sharp pain in your stomach

Word Building: **colicky** *adjective*

collaborate *verb*
1 to work together: *They collaborated on the project.* **2** to work together with an enemy inside your own country: *He collaborated with the invaders.*

Word Building: **collaboration** *noun* **collaborative** *adjective* **collaborator** *noun*

collage (say *kə-lahzh*) *noun*
a picture made from pieces of paper, cloth or other materials, pasted onto paper or board

collapse *verb*
1 to fall down or fall apart suddenly: *The old man collapsed in the street.* | *The whole building collapsed when the wall gave way.*
2 to be made so that parts can be folded flat together: *This chair collapses.*

Word Building: **collapse** *noun* **collapsible** *adjective*

collar *noun*
1 the part of a piece of clothing that is worn around your neck **2** a leather band put around an animal's neck
collar *verb*
3 to seize by the collar or neck: *The policeman collared the escaping criminal.*

Word Use: definition 3 is more suited to everyday language

collarbone *noun*
one of the two thin bones that go from the front of your neck to either shoulder

collate (say *kə-layt*) *verb*
to gather together in proper order: *I must collate the pages of my story.*

Word Building: **collation** *noun* **collator** *noun*

colleague (say *kol-eeg*) *noun*
someone you work with, usually in the same job

collect *verb*
1 to gather together or assemble: *Please collect all the rubbish from the floor. | A crowd collected around the smashed car.*
2 to gather and keep examples of: *She collects stamps as a hobby.* **3** to gather money: *We are collecting for the poor.*
4 to call for and take away: *Please collect the parcel at the post office.*

Word Building: **collected** *adjective* self-controlled **collectedly** *adverb* **collection** *noun* **collector** *noun*

collective *adjective*
1 having to do with a group of people taken as a whole: *It will be done more quickly if we make a collective effort.*

collective *noun*
2 a group of people who share what they own and who work together for the good of them all

Word Building: **collectively** *adverb*

collective noun *noun*
a noun that is singular in its form but which stands for a group of individual objects or people: *"Family", "jury" and "clergy" are all collective nouns.*

college *noun*
1 a place for learning, rather like a university, that you can go to after you finish high school **2** a place within a university where students live **3** a large private school

collide *verb*
to crash together: *The cars collided.*

Word Building: **collision** *noun*

collie *noun*
a kind of dog with long thick hair and a bushy tail, often used in other countries to guard sheep

colliery *noun*
a coalmine with all its buildings and equipment

Word Building: the plural is **collieries** □ **collier** *noun* a coalminer

colloquial (say *kə-loh-kwee-əl*) *adjective*
suitable for everyday language: *"Arvo" is a colloquial way of saying "afternoon".*

Word Building: **colloquialism** *noun* **colloquially** *adverb*

cologne (say *kə-lohn*) *noun*
a kind of perfume

Word Use: other names are **eau de Cologne** or **Cologne water**
Word History: named after the German city of *Cologne* where the perfume has been made since 1709

colon (say *koh-lən*) *noun*
a punctuation mark (:) which is used to separate the main part of a sentence from a list of examples, as in *I want you to bring the following things: a pencil, a rubber, and a piece of paper.*

colonel (say *ker-nəl*) *noun*
a senior officer in the army

colonise or **colonize** *verb*
to start a colony in: *England colonised Australia.*

Word Building: **colonisation** *noun* **colonist** *noun*

colony (say *kol-ə-nee*) *noun*
1 a group of people who leave their home and form a settlement in a new land ruled by the parent country **2** the land settled in this way: *The early settlements in Australia were colonies of Britain.*
3 a group of animals or plants of the same kind that live close together

Word Building: the plural is **colonies** □ **colonial** *noun* someone who lives in a colony **colonial** *adjective*

colossal *adjective*
1 very great in size **2** splendid or marvellous: *That film was colossal.*

Word Use: definition 2 is more suited to everyday language
Word Building: **colossally** *adverb*

colour or **color** *noun*
1 the look that something has which is caused by the way light is reflected by it: *The main colours are red, orange, yellow, green, blue, indigo and violet.* **2** the colour of someone's skin **3** something used to give colour, such as paint or dye
4 details that make something interesting: *That story has a lot of colour.*

colour or **color** *verb*
5 to put colour on to **6** to go red in the face **7** to influence or change: *His jealousy coloured the way he told the story.*

Word Building: **colourful** *adjective* **colourfully** *adverb* **colouring** *noun* **colourless** *adjective*

colour-blindness or **color-blindness** *noun*
a fault in someone's eyesight that stops them from being able to tell the difference

between some colours, such as red and green

Word Building: **colour-blind** *adjective*

coloured or **colored** *adjective*
1 having colour **2** belonging to a group of people that do not have white skin

colt *noun*
a male horse that is younger than four years old

Word Building: **coltish** *adjective*

column (say kol-əm) *noun*
1 a long upright support or pillar
2 anything with a similar shape to a column: *a column of smoke | The children formed two columns.* **3** an upright row of numbers or of print going down a page
4 a piece of writing on a particular subject that appears regularly in a newspaper or magazine: *I like reading the fashion column.*

Word Building: **columnist** *noun* someone who writes a newspaper or magazine column
columnar *adjective*

coma *noun*
a very long, deep, unnatural sleep caused by sickness or an injury

Word Building: **comatose** *adjective*

comb *noun*
1 a piece of plastic or metal with a set of thin pointed teeth, that is used to tidy or hold back hair **2** a comb-shaped part on the head of a hen, rooster or turkey
comb *verb*
3 to tidy with a comb **4** to search carefully: *They combed the room for the missing purse.*

combat *verb*
1 to fight against: *He must combat his liking for sweets. | The army was trained to combat an air attack.*
combat *noun*
2 a fight or struggle

Word Building: **combatant** *noun*
combatant *adjective*

combine *verb*
to mix or join together: *You combine flour and water to make paste. | The two schools decided to combine.*

Word Building: **combination** *noun*

combustion *noun*
the process of catching alight or burning

Word Building: **combustible** *adjective* able to burn

come *verb*
1 to move towards a person or place: *Please come here.* **2** to arrive or happen: *Christmas comes in December. | I hope my turn will come soon.* **3** to appear: *The light comes and goes.* **4** to reach or extend: *I want the dress to come below my knees.*
5 come across to meet or find: *I came across her at the shops.* **6 come from** to live in or be born into: *I come from Australia. | I come from an Italian family.*
7 come over to happen to or have an effect on: *What has come over her to make her so quiet?* **8 come to** to add up to or equal: *What does the bill come to?*
9 come up with to suggest or produce: *Nicole came up with a very good idea.*

Word Building: other forms are **I came, I have come, I am coming**

comedian *noun*
someone who performs and writes comedy shows

Word Building: **comedienne** *noun* a female comedian

comedy *noun*
1 a play, film, story or other entertainment that is funny or makes you feel happy
2 any funny event or series of events

Word Building: the plural is **comedies**
Word History: from a Greek word for "amusement" added to a Greek word for "singer"

comet *noun*
an object in space that moves around the sun and has a bright central part surrounded by a misty part that finishes in the shape of a tail

Word History: from a Greek word meaning "long-haired"

comfort (say kum-fət) *verb*
1 to cheer or make feel less sad or worried: *He comforted the baby by cuddling her.*
comfort *noun*
2 a feeling of being less sad or worried
3 someone or something that comforts: *My mother is a comfort to me.* **4** pleasant enjoyment with no troubles or needs: *They live a life of comfort.*

Word Building: **comforter** *noun*
comforting *adjective* **comfortingly** *adverb*

comfortable *adjective*
1 giving comfort: *a comfortable armchair | a comfortable way of life* **2** feeling comfort in your body or mind: *I am quite*

comfortable sitting here. / I am comfortable about those problems now.

Word Building: **comfortably** *adverb*

comic *adjective*
1 having to do with comedy: *He is a comic actor.* 2 funny or amusing: *She had a comic look on her face.*

comic *noun*
3 a magazine containing a series of drawings that tell a funny story or an adventure story 4 a comic actor or person

comical *adjective*
funny or amusing: *She put on a comical voice to make us laugh.*

comma *noun*
a punctuation mark (,) that is used to show small breaks in a sentence

command *verb*
1 to order or direct, usually with the right to be obeyed: *The teacher commanded silence. / He commanded her to come immediately.* 2 to be in charge of: *He commanded the army during the battle.* 3 to deserve and get: *Her position commands respect.*

command *noun*
4 an order: *He gave the command to stop.* 5 power to give orders or be in charge: *Who is in command of these men?*

Word Building: **commandeer** *verb* to take or seize officially **commander** *noun* **commandant** *noun*

commandment *noun*
1 a command or order 2 a holy command or rule, such as one of the Ten Commandments that the Bible says God gave to Moses

commando *noun*
someone who belongs to a small fighting force that is specially trained to make quick attacks inside enemy areas

Word Building: the plural is **commandos** or **commandoes**

commemorate *verb*
to keep alive or honour the memory of: *This stone commemorates the opening of the school. / Anzac Day commemorates the men who fought at Gallipoli.*

Word Building: **commemoration** *noun* **commemorative** *adjective*

commence *verb*
to begin or start: *Commence work now.*

Word Building: **commencement** *noun*

commend *verb*
1 to suggest as being suitable for trust, a reward, or a job: *She commended her friend as a babysitter. / He was commended for a medal after the war.* 2 to praise: *I commend you for your good work.*

Word Use: a similar word to definition 1 is **recommend**
Word Building: **commendable** *adjective* deserving praise **commendation** *noun* **commendatory** *adjective*

comment *noun*
a short note or remark that gives an opinion or explanation

Word Building: **comment** *verb*

commentary *noun*
a series of written or spoken comments: *He is listening to the sports commentary on the radio.*

Word Building: the plural is **commentaries** □ **commentate** *verb* **commentator** *noun*

commerce *noun*
the buying and selling of goods carried on between different countries or between different parts of the same country

Word Use: a similar word is **trade**

commercial (say *kə-<u>mer</u>-shəl*) *adjective*
1 having to do with commerce: *Australia established a commercial relationship with China.* 2 likely to be sold in great numbers: *We need products that are commercial.* 3 aimed at making money rather than keeping to standards of high quality: *That is a very commercial film.* 4 relying on money from advertising: *a commercial TV station*

commercial *noun*
5 an advertisement on radio or television

Word Building: **commercialise** *verb* **commercialism** *noun*

commiserate *verb*
to share someone's sorrow or disappointment: *He commiserated with her when she failed the exam.*

Word Use: a similar word is **sympathise**
Word Building: **commiseration** *noun*

commission *noun*
1 an order, direction or particular duty, given by someone who is in charge 2 a written paper giving someone a particular duty or rank in the army or navy 3 a group of people who have been given particular official duties: *A commission was set up to investigate traffic accidents.* 4 use or service: *Is your car out*

of commission today? **5** a sum of money given to an employee, such as a sales representative, for each successful effort: *He received 10% commission on each car he sold.*

commission *verb*
6 to give a duty or task to: *The teacher commissioned her to hand out the books each day.*

Word Use: definition 3 is often spelt with a capital letter, as in *a Royal Commission*

commissioner *noun*
1 someone who is a member of an official commission **2** someone who is in charge of a government department

Word Use: definition 2 is often spelt with a capital letter, as in *the Commissioner for Taxation*

commit *verb*
1 to give into someone's charge or trust: *I am committing these important papers to you.* **2** to put into a particular form in order to keep: *She committed the poem to memory.* **3** to hand over for punishment: *The judge committed him to prison.* **4** to do or perform: *He committed a crime.*
5 commit yourself to bind yourself by making a promise: *Don't commit yourself before you are sure you like the job.*

Word Building: other forms are **I committed, I have committed, I am committing** □ **commitment** *noun* **committed** *adjective* **committal** *noun*

committee *noun*
a group of people selected from a larger group to discuss or make decisions about a particular subject: *A committee was chosen to run the school magazine.*

commodity *noun*
something useful, especially something that is bought and sold: *This shop has a wide range of stoves, refrigerators and other household commodities.*

Word Building: the plural is **commodities**

commodore *noun*
1 a senior captain in the navy **2** the president of a boat club

common *adjective*
1 shared by two or more people: *common property / common action* **2** general or shared by all: *common knowledge* **3** found or happening often: *a common flower / a common event* **4** impolite or vulgar
5 ordinary or not having any special rank: *the common people*

Word Building: **commonly** *adverb*

commoner *noun*
an ordinary person, who is not one of the ruling class in a society

common noun *noun*
a noun which can be used for any one of a class of things and which does not have a capital letter: *"Robert" is not a common noun, but "boy" is.*

Word Use: compare this with a **proper noun**

commonsense *noun*
the ability to behave sensibly and make sensible decisions

commonwealth *noun*
1 all the people of a country or state
2 Commonwealth a country that is made up of several states, in which there is one government for the whole country as well as a government for each of the states: *the Commonwealth of Australia* **3** a group of people or countries united by a common interest

commotion *noun*
a wild or noisy disturbance: *There was great commotion in the classroom when the teacher went out.*

communal *adjective*
shared by several people: *The flats have their own bathrooms but a communal laundry.*

commune[1] (say *kə-myoohn*) *verb*
to talk together so that each person understands the other's thoughts or feelings

commune[2] (say *kom-yoohn*) *noun*
a group of people who live together, sharing their property and work, and following their own rules and standards

Word Use: a similar word is **collective**

communicate *verb*
1 to pass on or make known to someone: *We will communicate the news to her.*
2 to share thoughts or feelings: *They communicate well with each other.*

Word Building: **communicative** *adjective* **communicator** *noun*

communication *noun*
1 the passing on or sharing of thoughts, ideas or information **2** something that is communicated, such as a piece of news
3 communications ways of passing on information, such as by telephone, radio or television

communion *noun*
1 the sharing of thoughts, feelings or interests: *I enjoy the communion of my friends.* **2 Communion** a Christian ceremony in which bread and wine are blessed and eaten as the body and blood of Christ or as symbols of them

Word Use: definition 2 is also called **Holy Communion**

communiqué (say *kə-myoohn-ə-kay*) *noun*
an official news report

communism *noun*
1 a way of living in which all property is owned equally by all the people in a society **2** a way of organising a country, in which there is only one political party and all trade and business is run by the government

Word Use: compare this with **capitalism**
Word Building: **communist** *noun*

community *noun*
a large or small group of people who live near each other and share common interests

Word Building: the plural is **communities**

commute *verb*
1 to travel regularly between home and work: *I commute by bus.* **2** to change and make less punishing: *The judge commuted his death sentence to life imprisonment.*

Word Building: **commuter** *noun* someone who travels a long way to work by public transport
Word History: from a Latin word meaning "change wholly"

compact (say *kom-pakt*) *adjective*
1 fitted or packed closely together

compact (say *kom-pakt*) *verb*
2 to join or pack closely together

Word Building: **compactly** *adverb* **compactness** *noun*

compact disc *noun*
a disc, about 12 cm across, for storing information which can be read by a laser beam and then sent to a hi-fi system, a computer monitor or a television

Word Use: the short form is **CD**

companion *noun*
1 someone who goes out with or travels with another: *Are you taking a companion to the party?* **2** someone or something that matches or goes with another: *I wish I could find the companion to this sock.*

Word Building: **companionable** *adjective* friendly **companionship** *noun*

company (say *kum-pə-nee*) *noun*
1 a group of people brought together for a purpose, such as to run a business organisation: *a company that makes fridges | a theatrical company* **2** guests: *We've got company tonight.* **3** a group of soldiers forming part of an army

Word Building: the plural is **companies**

comparative *adjective*
1 having to do with comparison **2** judged by comparison: *They live in comparative poverty.* **3** having to do with the form of an adjective or adverb which expresses a greater degree: *"Smoother" is the comparative form of "smooth" and "more easily" is the comparative form of "easily".*

Word Use: a similar word for definition 2 is **relative** □ compare definition 3 with **superlative**
Word Building: **comparatively** *adverb: They are comparatively poor.*

compare *verb*
1 to show to be similar: *You can compare the heart to a pump.* **2** to look for the similarities and differences of: *He compared his new bike with John's.* **3** to be as good as: *Australian beaches compare with any in the world.*

Word Building: **comparable** *adjective* **comparison** *noun*

compartment *noun*
a separate space, room or section: *a compartment in a railway carriage*

compass (say *kum-pəs*) *noun*
1 an instrument with a magnetic needle pointing to north which is used to find direction **2** extent or range: *a wide compass of knowledge | the compass of a singer's voice* **3 compasses** an instrument for measuring and drawing circles, which has two legs hinged together

Word Building: **compass** *verb*
Word History: from a Latin word meaning "single step"

compassion *noun*
a feeling of sorrow or pity for someone

Word Use: a similar word is **sympathy**
Word Building: **compassionate** *adjective* **compassionately** *adverb*

compatible *adjective*
1 able to agree or exist side by side: *a compatible married couple | compatible ideas* **2** able to be used together: *The two computers are compatible with each other.*

Word Building: **compatibility** *noun* **compatibly** *adverb*

compatriot (say *kom-pat-ree-ət*) *noun*
someone from your own country: *I met a lot of my compatriots while I was in Greece.*

compel *verb*
1 to force to do something: *They can compel you to attend school.* **2** to bring about as if by force: *His angry look compelled an immediate answer.*

Word Building: other forms are **I compelled, I have compelled, I am compelling** □ **compelling** *adjective* holding your attention forcefully

compensate *verb*
1 to make up to: *We will compensate you for your expenses.* **2 compensate for** to make up for: *Nothing can compensate for his loss.*

Word Use: a similar word to definition 1 is **recompense**
Word Building: **compensation** *noun* **compensator** *noun* **compensatory** *adjective*

compere (say *kom-pair*) *noun*
someone who introduces the acts in a show

Word Building: **compere** *verb*

compete *verb*
to set yourself against one or more people to gain or win something: *The shops lowered their prices to compete for customers.*

Word Building: **competitor** *noun* someone who competes

competent *adjective*
able or skilful: *He is a competent rider.*

Word Building: **competence** *noun* **competency** *noun*

competition *noun*
1 a test or situation in which people compete against each other **2** a feeling or act of competing: *There is a lot of competition between the top runners.* **3** the people against whom someone competes: *What's the competition like?*

Word Use: a similar word for definition 2 is **rivalry**

competitive *adjective*
1 having to do with or decided by competition: *a competitive exam* **2** liking competition: *a competitive person*

Word Building: **competitively** *adverb*

compile *verb*
to collect and put together into one list, account or book

Word Building: **compilation** *noun* **compiler** *noun*

complacent *adjective*
pleased or satisfied with yourself

Word Building: **complacence** *noun* **complacency** *noun* **complacently** *adverb*

complain *verb*
1 to find fault **2** to tell about your illnesses, troubles or pains: *She is always complaining.*

Word Building: **complainer** *noun* **complaining** *adjective* **complainingly** *adverb*

complaint *noun*
1 an expression of dissatisfaction, blame or pain: *He made a complaint about the poor service in the shop.* **2** a sickness or illness

complement (say *kom-plə-mənt*) *noun*
1 something which completes or makes perfect: *The flute was a perfect complement to the sound of the guitar.* **2** the number that is required: *The hockey team now has its full complement of players.*

Word Use: be careful – this sounds like **compliment**
Word Building: **complement** *verb* to complete **complementary** *adjective*

complete *adjective*
1 having all its parts: *a complete set of coloured pencils* **2** finished: *My piano practice is complete.* **3** total or absolute: *Your bedroom is a complete mess.*
complete *verb*
4 to finish: *She completed her homework.* **5** to make whole or entire: *to complete a set of tools*

Word Building: **completely** *adverb* **completeness** *noun* **completion** *noun*

complex *adjective*
1 made up of parts connected with each other **2** difficult to understand or explain: *Maths is too complex for me.*
complex *noun*
3 a group of buildings or shops: *a shopping complex*

Word Building: the plural is **complexes** □ **complexity** *noun*

complexion *noun*
1 the colour and appearance of your skin, especially of your face **2** aspect or character: *The new evidence puts a different complexion on the murder case.*

compliant (say *kəm-pluy-ənt*) *adjective*
agreeable or willing to do what is asked or required

Word Building: **compliance** *noun*

complicate *verb*
to make harder to understand or deal with: *Too many directions can complicate a map.*

Word Building: **complicated** *adjective* **complication** *noun*
Word History: from a Latin word meaning "folded together"

complicity *noun*
the state of being a partner or taking part: *complicity in crime*

compliment (say *kom-plə-mənt*) *noun*
1 words or actions expressing praise and admiration: *She paid him a compliment about his new jumper.*
compliment (say *kom-plə-ment*) *verb*
2 to pay a compliment to

Word Use: be careful – this sounds like **complement**

complimentary *adjective*
1 praising, or expressing a compliment **2** free or without cost: *He gave them complimentary tickets to the show.*

comply *verb*
to act in agreement with a request, wish, command or rule

Word Building: other forms are **I complied, I have complied, I am complying**

component *noun*
a part of a whole: *The picture tube is an important component of a television set.*

Word Building: **component** *adjective: a component ingredient*

compose *verb*
1 to make by putting parts together **2** to make up or form: *Smog is composed of smoke and fog.* **3** to write music or poetry **4 compose yourself** to make your mind and body quiet and calm

Word Building: **composed** *adjective* **composedly** *adverb* **composer** *noun*

composite (say *kom-pə-zət*) *noun*
something made up of different parts

Word Building: **composite** *adjective: a composite picture*

composition *noun*
1 the putting together of parts to make a whole **2** the way in which parts are combined, or make-up: *What is the composition of smog?* **3** something that has been composed, such as a piece of music **4** a short essay, written as a school exercise

compost *noun*
a mixture of rotting materials, like old vegetable peelings, leaves and manure, used as a fertiliser for the garden

composure (say *kəm-poh-zhə*) *noun*
calmness of mind, or self-control

compound[1] (say *kom-pownd*) *adjective*
1 made up of two or more parts: *"Bedroom" is a compound word.*
compound[1] (say *kom-pownd*) *noun*
2 a mixture **3** a chemical substance made by joining two or more chemicals: *When hydrogen and oxygen are joined together, they form a compound called water.*
compound[1] (say *kəm-pownd*) *verb*
4 to mix or combine **5** to add to, or increase

compound[2] (say *kom-pownd*) *noun*
a closed-off area with buildings where people can stay or be kept: *a prison compound*

comprehend *verb*
1 to understand the meaning of: *I can't comprehend the story.* **2** to take in or include: *The new National Park comprehends all the old reserves.*

Word Building: **comprehensive** *adjective* including a great deal **comprehendingly** *adverb* **comprehensible** *adjective*
Word History: from a Latin word meaning "seize"

comprehension *noun*
1 the ability to understand or the act of understanding: *Computers are beyond my comprehension.* **2** a school exercise in reading and understanding, usually tested by a set of short questions

compress (say *kəm-pres*) *verb*
1 to press together, or force into less space: *Wool is compressed into bales ready for transportation.*

compress (say *<u>kom</u>-pres*) *noun*
2 a soft pad of cloth applied to an injury and held in place with a bandage

Word Building: **compression** *noun* **compressor** *noun*

comprise *verb*
to include or be composed of: *This school comprises an infants section and a primary section.*

compromise (say *<u>kom</u>-prə-muyz*) *noun*
1 the settlement of an argument by both sides agreeing to give way a bit: *Our compromise is to take turns on the bike.* **2** something midway between two other things: *Jogging is a compromise between walking and running.*

compromise *verb*
3 to lay open to suspicion or bad comments from others: *You will compromise yourself as class captain if you talk like that.*

compulsion *noun*
the use of force or pressure

compulsory *adjective*
forced or required: *Attendance at school is compulsory for all children.*

Word Building: **compulsorily** *adverb* **compulsoriness** *noun*

compute *verb*
to calculate or to work out using maths: *to compute the distance of the moon from the earth*

Word Building: **computation** *noun*

computer *noun*
an electronic machine which does mathematical calculations very quickly, and which stores and gives out information, according to a set of stored instructions called a program

Word Building: **computerise** *verb*

computer terminal *noun*
a machine linked up to a computer and used for receiving or giving information

comrade (say *<u>kom</u>-rayd, <u>kom</u>-rəd*) *noun*
a close friend or mate

Word Building: **comradeship** *noun*
Word History: from a Latin word meaning "chamber" or "room"

con *noun*
a trick or swindle

Word Use: this word is more suited to everyday language
Word Building: **con** *adjective: a con man | a con game* **con** *verb* (**conned, conning**)
Word History: this is a shortened form of **confidence trick**

concave *adjective*
hollow and curved like the inside of a circle: *A saucer is slightly concave.*

Word Use: the opposite of this is **convex**

conceal *verb*
1 to hide or keep from sight: *He concealed the knife in his coat pocket.* **2** to keep secret: *She concealed her real reason for coming.*

Word Building: **concealment** *noun*

concede *verb*
1 to admit as true or certain: *Everyone concedes that the earth is round.* **2** to allow someone to have or do something: *He conceded us the right to choose our own team.*

Word Building: **concession** *noun* something given or conceded

conceit *noun*
pride in yourself and your own importance or ability

Word Building: **conceited** *adjective* **conceitedly** *adverb* **conceitedness** *noun*

conceive *verb*
1 to think of: *to conceive a plan* **2** to become pregnant

Word Building: **conceivable** *adjective* **conceivably** *adverb*

concentrate *verb*
1 to focus or direct towards one point: *She concentrated the light on his face.* **2** to direct your attention to one subject: *to concentrate on watching the ball* **3** to make stronger or purer: *Some detergents have been concentrated by removing some of the water from them.*

concentrate *noun*
4 a substance that has been concentrated

Word Building: **concentration** *noun*

concentration camp *noun*
a prison camp for prisoners of war or enemies of a country

concentric *adjective*
having the same centre: *When you drop a stone into water, the ripples form concentric circles.*

concept *noun*
general idea or understanding of something: *My concept of computer programming is very vague.*

Word Building: **conceptualise** *verb* to form an idea of **conceptual** *adjective* **conceptually** *adverb*

conception *noun*
1 an idea or thought: *Her conception of how the house should look was different to his.*
2 the beginning of pregnancy, or the act of conceiving a child

concern *verb*
1 to be of interest or importance: *This problem concerns us all.* **2** to be anxious or troubled: *I am concerned about your cough.*

concern *noun*
3 a matter of interest or importance: *It's no concern of mine.* **4** worry or anxiety: *The father's concern for his child's safety was obvious.*

Word Building: **concerned** *adjective* interested **concerning** *preposition*

concert *noun*
1 a public musical performance by one or more musicians or other performers
2 agreement in a plan or action: *The children acted in concert to recover the stolen money.*

Word Building: **concerted** *adjective* arranged by agreement

concertina *noun*
1 a small musical instrument like an accordion

concertina *verb*
2 to fold up or collapse like a concertina

Word Building: other verb forms are **it concertinaed, it has concertinaed, it is concertinaing**

concerto (say *kən-cher-toh, kən-sher-toh*) *noun*
a piece of music for one or more solo instruments, such as a piano or violin, and an orchestra

Word Building: the plural is **concertos** or **concerti**

conciliate *verb*
to make friendly or calm

Word Use: a similar word is **reconcile**
Word Building: **conciliation** *noun* the way of working out arguments, especially between trade unionists and employers **conciliator** *noun* **conciliatory** *adverb*

concise *adjective*
expressing a lot in a few words: *a concise account of what happened*

Word Building: **concisely** *adverb* **conciseness** *noun* **concision** *noun*
Word History: from a Latin word meaning "cut up" or "cut off"

conclude *verb*
1 to finish or bring to an end: *After a short speech, she concluded. / The teacher concluded her lesson with two examples.*
2 to arrange or settle: *The two businessmen concluded an agreement.* **3** to decide by working out: *After reading the whole book she concluded the real reason for the murder.*

Word Building: **conclusive** *adjective* convincing, or decisive **conclusion** *noun* **conclusively** *adverb*

concoct *verb*
1 to make up or invent: *He concocted a story to cover up for his absence.* **2** to make up by combining parts, or to prepare: *She concocted a quick, easy meal.*

Word Building: **concoction** *noun*
Word History: from a Latin word meaning "cooked together" or "digested"

concrete *noun*
1 a mixture of cement, sand, water and gravel, which hardens as it dries and is used in building

concrete *adjective*
2 made of this mixture: *a concrete floor.*
3 real or existing as an actual thing, not just an idea: *A wedding ring is a concrete object, but the feeling of love is not.*

Word Use: the opposite of definition 3 is **abstract**
Word Building: **concrete** *verb*

concrete noun *noun*
a word which refers to something that our five senses (touch, sight, hearing, smell and taste) can pick up: *"Boat", "sun" and "dog" are all concrete nouns.*

Word Use: the opposite of this is **abstract noun**

concubine (say *kong-kyooh-buyn*) *noun*
a man's second or other wife, in a country where a man can be married to more than one woman at a time

concur *verb*
to agree: *I concur with that decision.*

Word Building: other forms are **I concurred, I have concurred, I am concurring** □ **concurrent** *adjective* occurring together: *concurrent events* **concurrence** *noun* **concurrently** *adverb*

concussion *noun*
1 a shock, or violent shaking caused by a blow or collision **2** an injury or jarring of the brain or spine caused by a blow or fall

Word Building: **concuss** *verb*

condemn (say *kən-dem*) *verb*
1 to express strong disapproval of: *He condemned the child's bad behaviour.* **2** to judge someone to be guilty or sentence them to punishment: *The murderer was condemned to death.* **3** to decide something is no longer fit for use: *The old building was condemned by council.*

Word Building: **condemnation** *noun* **condemnatory** *adjective*

condensation *noun*
the changing of a gas to a liquid or solid: *When steam hits something cold, condensation occurs.* **2** something that has been condensed: *This book is a condensation of a much larger novel.*

condense *verb*
1 to make thicker or reduce the volume of: *to condense milk* **2** to change from a gas to a liquid or solid: *to condense steam to get water* **3** to say or write something in fewer words: *He condensed his story into just a few pages.*

Word Building: **condenser** *noun*

condescend *verb*
1 to agree, even though it's below your social level: *The queen condescended to have a meal with her servants.* **2** to act as if you are in a higher social position than others

Word Building: **condescending** *adjective* **condescendingly** *adverb* **condescension** *noun*

condition *noun*
1 the state of someone or something: *The runner was in top condition before the race. / The car was rusty and in very poor condition.* **2** anything that is required before another thing can be done: *Having a licence is a condition of driving a car.*

condition *verb*
3 to put in a fit state: *Long-distance runners condition themselves for their races by training.* **4** to influence or affect: *What we are taught by our parents and teachers conditions the way we live.*

conditional *adjective*
depending on something else: *They made a conditional agreement to go to the beach only if the weather was good.*

Word Building: **conditionality** *noun* **conditionally** *adverb*

condolences *plural noun*
the expressions of sympathy you make to someone when a relative or friend of theirs has just died: *Please accept my condolences on the death of your husband.*

Word Building: **condolence** *noun: letters of condolence* **condolatory** *adjective* **condole** *verb* **condolingly** *adverb*

condone *verb*
to pardon, excuse or overlook: *His mother condoned his boldness because she thought he might be sick.*

conduct (say *kon-dukt*) *noun*
1 someone's behaviour or way of acting: *Her conduct was very rude all evening.*

conduct (say *kən-dukt*) *verb*
2 to behave: *He conducted himself well today.* **3** to manage or carry on: *The politician conducted a well-planned campaign.* **4** to direct or lead an orchestra or choir **5** to lead: *The mayor conducted us on a tour of the city.* **6** to be a channel for electricity, heat or sound: *The air conducts sound waves to our ears.*

Word Building: **conduction** *noun* **conductive** *adjective* **conductivity** *noun*

conductor *noun*
1 a guide or a leader **2** someone who collects fares on a tram, train or bus **3** something that easily conducts heat, electricity or sound: *Copper is a good conductor of heat.*

cone *noun*
1 a solid shape with a flat round bottom, whose sides meet at the top in a point **2** anything shaped like this: *an ice-cream cone* **3** the cone-like fruit of pine and fir trees

Word Building: **conic** *adjective* **conical** *adjective* **conically** *adverb*

confectionery *noun*
lollies, candies or sweets

Word Building: **confection** *noun* **confectioner** *noun*

confederacy *noun*
a group of people or countries joined together for a common purpose or reason

Word Building: the plural is **confederacies** □ **confederate** *noun* an ally or supporter **confederate** *adjective* **confederation** *noun*

confer *verb*
1 to give as a gift, favour or honour: *The queen conferred a medal for bravery on the boy.* **2** to talk together: *We conferred for some time about the situation.*

Word Building: other forms are **I conferred, I have conferred, I am conferring**

conference *noun*
a meeting arranged to discuss something special

confess *verb*
1 to admit or own up: *I confess that I broke the cup. / The prisoner confessed.* **2** to tell your mistakes or sins, especially to a priest

Word Building: **confession** *noun* **confessional** *noun* **confessor** *noun*

confetti *noun*
small bits of coloured paper, thrown at weddings or carnivals

confide *verb*
to trust or tell, as a secret: *She confided in her best friend. / He confided all his secrets to his brother.*

Word Building: **confidant** *noun* someone you confide in

confidence *noun*
1 trust or faith in someone **2** a belief in yourself and what you can do: *She played the tournament with plenty of confidence.* **3** a secret: *He told me his confidences after school.*

confident *adjective*
having a strong belief or feeling certain: *I am confident that he will arrive soon.*

Word Building: **confidently** *adverb*

confidential *adjective*
1 secret or not public: *The policeman wrote out a confidential report.* **2** trusted with secrets or private matters: *The director of the company had a confidential secretary.*

Word Building: **confidentiality** *noun* **confidentially** *adverb*

confine (say *kən-fuyn*) *verb*
1 to restrict or keep within limits: *I confine myself to one chocolate a day.* **2** to shut or keep in: *He was confined to prison for three months.*

Word Building: **confinement** *noun*

confirm *verb*
1 to make certain or sure: *He confirmed our table booking at the restaurant.* **2** to strengthen or make firm: *What you have told me confirms what I already thought.* **3** to admit as a member of a church in a special ceremony

Word Building: **confirmed** *adjective* firmly settled in a habit or condition **confirmable** *adjective* **confirmation** *noun*

confiscate *verb*
to take and keep: *The teacher confiscated my comic.*

Word Building: **confiscation** *noun*
Word History: from a Latin word meaning "put away in a chest"

conflict *(say kən-flikt)* *verb*
1 to disagree or clash: *Our ideas conflict because we are too different.*

conflict (say *kon-flikt*) *noun*
2 a fight or disagreement: *a conflict between nations*

conform *verb*
1 to act according to rules or laws **2** to be like or similar to: *Her hairstyle conforms to the latest fashion trend.*

Word Building: **conformist** *noun* **conformity** *noun*

confound *verb*
to surprise or puzzle: *He confounded the experts by solving the problem.*

confront *verb*
1 to meet face to face: *He turned the corner and was confronted by his mother.* **2** to face boldly or bravely: *She confronted her problem without hesitation.*

Word Building: **confrontation** *noun*

confuse *verb*
1 to mix up or puzzle: *The teacher's instructions have confused me.* **2** to be unable to tell the difference between: *I always confuse one type of car with another.*

Word Use: a similar word is **perplex**
Word Building: **confused** *adjective* **confusing** *adjective* **confusingly** *adverb* **confusion** *noun*

congeal *verb*
to thicken or become solid: *Cooking fat or dripping congeals as it cools.*

congenial *adjective*
pleasant or agreeable: *a more congenial job / congenial friends*

Word Building: **congeniality** *noun* **congenially** *adverb*

congenital *adjective*
existing or being there when you are born: *congenital heart disease*

Word Building: **congenitally** *adverb*

congest *verb*
to fill too much or to become overcrowded: *Cars are congesting the road.*

Word Building: **congestion** *noun*

congratulate *verb*
to praise and show pleasure to: *They congratulated her on her victory.*

Word Building: **congratulation** *noun* **congratulatory** *adjective*

congregate *verb*
to gather together: *The people congregated on the river bank.*

Word Building: **congregation** *noun* a group of people gathered together, especially in a church

congress *noun*
a meeting of people to discuss ideas of interest to them all: *A congress of health workers was held here last week.*

Word Use: a similar word is **conference**

conifer *noun*
an evergreen tree which grows cones, like the pine or fir

Word Building: **coniferous** *adjective*

conjunction *noun*
1 a combination or joining together: *the conjunction of two rivers* **2** a word, such as "and" or "because", used to join parts of a sentence

conjure (say *kun-jə*) *verb*
to do magic tricks

Word Building: **conjurer** *noun*

connect *verb*
1 to join or unite: *Connect this wire to the end of that rod. | These wires should connect somewhere.* **2 be connected with** to have to do or be associated with: *Are you connected with the church?*

Word Building: **connection** *noun* **connective** *adjective*

connoisseur (say *kon-ə-ser*) *noun*
someone who has a special interest or knowledge of a particular subject: *a connoisseur of stained glass | a connoisseur of wine*

Word History: from a Latin word meaning "come to know"

conquer *verb*
to overcome by force: *The Germans conquered the French in World War II.*

Word Building: **conqueror** *noun* **conquest** *noun*

conscience (say *kon-shəns*) *noun*
the ability to see the difference between right and wrong in what you do

conscientious (say *kon-shee-en-shəs*) *adjective*
1 careful and particular: *a conscientious worker* **2** doing or controlled by what you believe to be right: *a conscientious objector to war*

Word Building: **conscientiously** *adverb* **conscientiousness** *noun*

conscious (say *kon-shəs*) *adjective*
1 aware or having knowledge: *I was not conscious of the bell.* **2** aware of what is happening around you: *The injured man was still conscious.*

Word Building: **consciously** *adverb* **consciousness** *noun*

conscript (say *kən-skript*) *verb*
1 to force to join the army, navy or air force

conscript (*kon-skript*) *noun*
2 someone who has been conscripted

Word Building: **conscription** *noun*

consecrate *verb*
1 to declare holy: *The bishop consecrated the new church.* **2** to devote: *They consecrated themselves to God.*

Word Building: **consecration** *noun*

consecutive *adjective*
following one after another: *The instructions were given in consecutive order.*

Word Building: **consecutively** *adverb*

consensus *noun*
a general agreement

consent *verb*
1 to agree: *They consented to go with him.*

consent *noun*
2 agreement: *They met by common consent.*

consequence *noun*
1 an outcome or result: *This mess is the consequence of your foolishness.*
2 importance or value: *a matter of no consequence*

Word Building: **consequent** *adjective* **consequential** *adjective* **consequently** *adverb*

conservation *noun*
the protection of nature or of historic buildings, and the careful use of natural things

Word Building: **conservationist** *noun*

conservative *adjective*
1 careful or moderate: *a conservative opinion | conservative dress* **2** opposed to new ideas and sudden change of any kind: *a conservative political party*

Word Building: **conservatism** *noun* **conservative** *noun* **conservatively** *adverb*

conservatorium *noun*
a school where you can learn music

conservatory *noun*
a room or building made of glass, where plants are displayed

Word Building: the plural is **conservatories**

conserve (say *kən-<u>serv</u>*) *verb*
1 to keep from being lost or wasted: *to conserve petrol*

conserve (say *<u>kon</u>-serv*) *noun*
2 a type of jam

consider *verb*
1 to think about: *I will consider the problem.* **2** to think or believe: *I consider him to be the fastest swimmer.*

considerable *adjective*
large or important enough to think about

Word Building: **considerably** *adverb*

considerate *adjective*
thoughtful of other people's needs and feelings

Word Building: **considerately** *adverb*

consideration *noun*
1 careful thought: *I will give the problem my consideration.* **2** something taken, or that should be taken, into account **3** thoughtfulness for others

consist *verb*
to be made up: *The book consists of two parts.*

consistency *noun*
1 agreement or harmony: *There is a consistency about his story which is convincing.* **2** an amount of thickness: *Mix the ingredients until they are the consistency of cream.*

consistent *adjective*
1 agreeing: *The message is consistent with what we heard before.* **2** acting or thinking in the same way throughout: *He is always consistent in applying the rules.*

Word Building: **consistently** *adverb*

console[1] (say *kən-<u>sohl</u>*) *verb*
to comfort or cheer up: *He tried to console her for the loss of the kitten.*

Word Building: **consolable** *adjective* **consolation** *noun* **consolingly** *adverb*

console[2] (say *<u>kon</u>-sohl*) *noun*
a control panel, especially of a computer

consonant *noun*
1 a speech sound made by blocking the flow of your breath by the tongue or lips **2** any letter of the alphabet, except *a, e, i, o* or *u*

Word Use: compare this with **vowel**
Word History: from a Latin word meaning "sounding together"

consort (say *<u>kon</u>-sawt*) *noun*
the husband of a ruling queen or the wife of a king

conspicuous *adjective*
noticeable or standing out: *She was conspicuous in her red jumper.*

conspire *verb*
to plan secretly together: *The men conspired to hijack a plane.*

Word Building: **conspiracy** *noun* (**conspiracies**) **conspirator** *noun* **conspiratorial** *adjective*

constable (say *<u>kun</u>-stə-bəl*) *noun*
a police officer of the lowest rank

Word History: from Latin words meaning "count of the stable" or "master of the horse"

constant *adjective*
1 going on without stopping: *Her success has been a constant source of pleasure.*
2 faithful: *He has been constant in looking after his mother.*

Word Building: **constancy** *noun* **constantly** *adverb*
Word History: from a Latin word meaning "standing firm"

constellation *noun*
a group of stars

consternation *noun*
shock or fear causing you to feel confused: *We were thrown into consternation at the news of his disappearance.*

constipation *noun*
the unpleasant condition of not being able to empty your bowels regularly or easily

Word Building: **constipate** *verb* **constipated** *adjective*

constituency *noun*
another word for **electorate**

Word Building: the plural is **constituencies** □ **constituent** *noun*

constitute *verb*
to make up or form: *His absence constitutes only part of the problem.*

constitution *noun*
1 the health or condition of your body: *Jim has a strong constitution.* **2** a set of basic rules: *the Australian constitution | the constitution of the rowing club*

Word Building: **constitutional** *adjective* **constitutionally** *adverb*

constraint *noun*
1 something that restricts or controls the way you behave or what you can do at certain times: *There is a constraint on doctors not to advertise for patients.*
2 control or the keeping back of your natural feelings and impulses: *During hard times we don't spend much money and we act with constraint.*

Word Building: **constrain** *verb* to compel, or restrain **constrained** *adjective*

constrict *verb*
to make tighter or narrower: *a drug to constrict the blood vessels*

Word Use: the opposite of this is **dilate**
Word Building: **constriction** *noun*

construct *verb*
to build: *to construct a house | to construct a theory*

Word Building: **construction** *noun*

constructive *adjective*
helpful or useful: *to make constructive suggestions*

consul *noun*
an official sent by a government to represent it in a foreign country

Word Building: **consular** *adjective* **consulate** *noun* **consulship** *noun*

consult *verb*
to seek advice from: *to consult a doctor | to consult a dictionary*

Word Building: **consultant** *noun* **consultation** *noun*

consume *verb*
1 to eat: *to consume a meat pie* **2** to use up or destroy: *They consumed the stock of paper. | The building was consumed by fire.*

consumer *noun*
someone who uses goods and services: *Advertising is designed to make consumers buy more.*

Word Use: the opposite of this is **producer**

consumption *noun*
1 eating or using up **2** *an old-fashioned word for* **tuberculosis**

contact *noun*
1 a meeting or touching: *to make contact with someone* **2** the moving part of a switch that completes and breaks an electrical circuit **3** a useful person to meet: *a business contact*

Word Building: **contact** *verb: to contact an old friend*

contact lenses *plural noun*
lenses to improve your sight and which fit closely over the iris or coloured part of your eye

contagious *adjective*
catching or easily spread from one person to another: *Chicken pox is a contagious disease. | Happiness is contagious.*

Word Building: **contagion** *noun* **contagiously** *adverb*

contain *verb*
to have inside itself: *This jug contains milk. | This book contains instructions.*

container *noun*
1 anything that contains or can contain
2 a very large crate for carrying goods on ships or trucks

contaminate *verb*
to make dirty or impure: *This meat has been contaminated by flies.*

Word Building: **contamination** *noun*

contemplate *verb*
to look at or consider thoughtfully: *He contemplated the letter for several minutes. | She is contemplating going to Melbourne.*

Word Building: **contemplative** *adjective* **comtemplation** *noun*

contemporary *adjective*
1 existing at the same time: *Francis Greenway was contemporary with Governor Macquarie.* **2** modern or existing now: *The room was decorated in contemporary style.*

Word Building: **contemporary** *noun* (**contemporaries**) **contemporaneous** *adjective*

contempt *noun*
the feeling that someone or something is mean and disgraceful: *They felt contempt for the person who had robbed the blind woman.*

Word Use: a similar word is **scorn**

contemptible *adjective*
deserving contempt: *Tripping up the other runner was a contemptible action.*

Word Building: **contemptibly** *adverb*

contemptuous *adjective*
showing contempt: *She was contemptuous of Lisa's clumsy attempts to dance.*

Word Use: a similar word is **supercilious**
Word Building: **contemptuously** *adverb*

contend *verb*
1 to fight or struggle: *She had to contend with illness.* **2** to say firmly: *He contends that he is only having a look.*

Word Building: **contender** *noun* **contention** *noun*

content (say *kən-tent*) *adjective*
1 pleased or satisfied: *He is content with what he has.*
content *verb*
2 to please or satisfy: *She contented herself with a quick snack.*

Word Building: **contentedly** *adverb* **contentment** *noun*

contents (say *kon-tents*) *plural noun*
whatever is inside or contained in: *the contents of a bottle* | *The contents of a book are often listed in an index.*

contest (say *kon-test*) *noun*
1 a competition
contest (say *kən-test*) *verb*
2 to struggle for: *They contested the leadership.*

Word Building: **contestant** *noun*

context *noun*
the surrounding circumstances or words: *It was unfair to take his remarks about his brother out of context.*

continent *noun*
1 one of the main land masses of the world: *Australia is one of the seven continents.* **2 the Continent** the mainland of Europe, separate from the British Isles

Word Building: **continental** *adjective*
Word History: from a Latin word meaning "holding together"

continual *adjective*
happening often: *He got into trouble for his continual lateness.*

Word Use: don't confuse this word with **continuous**
Word Building: **continually** *adverb*

continue *verb*
1 to keep on: *They continued to walk in the rain.* **2** to go on after being interrupted: *We will continue tomorrow.* **3** to go on with: *to continue a story* | *to continue a journey tomorrow*

Word Building: **continuation** *noun* **continuity** *noun*

continuous *adjective*
1 going on without stopping: *the continuous sound of his breathing* **2** having to do with the form of a verb which shows that something is continuing, such as "am running" in *I am running*

Word Use: don't confuse this word with **continual**
Word Building: **continuously** *adverb* **continuousness** *noun*
Word History: from a Latin word meaning "hanging together"

contort *verb*
to twist out of shape

Word Building: **contortion** *noun* **contortionist** *noun*

contour *noun*
1 the shape or outline: *the contour of the land* **2** a line on a map joining points of equal height

contra- *prefix*
a word part meaning against, opposite, *or* opposing: *contradict*

Word History: this prefix comes from Latin

contraband *noun*
goods imported or exported illegally

contraception *noun*
the prevention of pregnancy

Word Use: another name for this is **birth control**
Word Building: **contraceptive** *adjective* **contraceptive** *noun*

contract (say *kon-trakt*) *noun*
1 an agreement, especially a legal one: *They signed the contract for building the house.*

contract (say *kən-trakt*) *verb*
2 to become smaller: *Metal contracts when it is cooled.* **3** to make an agreement

Word Building: **contractual** *adjective* belonging to a contract **contraction** *noun*

contradict *verb*
1 to deny or say the opposite of: *Whatever he says, you contradict him.* **2** to be the direct opposite of: *This experiment contradicts the results we got before.*

Word Building: **contradiction** *noun* **contradictory** *adjective*

contralto *noun*
1 the lowest range of musical notes which can be sung by a female singer
2 a woman who sings contralto

Word Use: another name is **alto** □ **contralto** range is higher than a **tenor, baritone** or **bass** but lower than a **soprano**

contraption *noun*
a complicated gadget or piece of machinery: *Sam has invented a contraption for exercising his pet mice.*

Word Use: a similar word is **device**

contrary *adjective*
1 opposed or different: *My opinion is contrary to yours.*
contrary *noun*
2 the opposite: *You say he is right, but I can prove the contrary.* **3 on the contrary** in opposition to what has been said: *On the contrary, you are wrong.*

Word Building: **contrarily** *adverb*

contrast (say *kən-trahst*) *verb*
1 to compare in order to show differences: *Contrast last year's result with this year's.* **2** to show a difference in comparison: *The red flowers of the grevillea contrast with its green leaves.*
contrast (say *kon-trahst*) *noun*
3 a marked difference: *a colour contrast | a contrast in attitude*

contribute (say *kən-trib-yooht*) *verb*
1 to donate or pay a share: *to contribute to a fund* **2** to give to, or write for, a magazine or newspaper: *I have contributed a story to the school magazine.*

Word Building: **contribution** *noun* **contributor** *noun* **contributory** *adjective*

contrite (say *kən-truyt, kon-truyt*) *adjective*
feeling sorry or sad that you have done something wrong: *She looked so contrite that I had to forgive her.*

Word Building: **contritely** *adverb* **contrition** *noun*

contrive *verb*
to invent or plan cleverly: *He contrived to be absent at the time.*

Word Building: **contrivance** *noun*

control *verb*
1 to be in charge of or direct: *Miss Bond controls the library.* **2** to adjust as necessary: *This tap controls the flow of water.* **3** to keep in check: *to control your temper*
control *noun*
4 command or check: *Keep your dog under control.*

Word Building: other verb forms are **I controlled, I have controlled, I am controlling** □ **controllable** *adjective* **controller** *noun*

controversy (say *kon-trə-ver-see, kən-trov-ə-see*) *noun*
an argument or difference of opinion: *The position of the new airport is a matter of controversy.*

Word Building: the plural is **controversies** □ **controversial** *adjective: a controversial issue*

conundrum (say *kə-nun-drəm*) *noun*
a riddle or puzzle

convalesce (say *kon-və-les*) *verb*
to grow stronger after an illness: *He is convalescing at home after a long stay in hospital.*

Word Building: **convalescence** *noun* **convalescent** *adjective* **convalescent** *noun*

convection *noun*
the spreading of heat by the movement of heated air or water

Word Building: **convector** *noun*

convene *verb*
to call or gather together: *to convene a meeting | to convene for a quick talk about tactics*

Word Building: **convener** *noun*

convenient *adjective*
suited to your needs: *a convenient house | a convenient time*

Word Building: **convenience** *noun* **conveniently** *adverb*

convent *noun*
1 a group of buildings where nuns live
2 a school run by nuns

convention *noun*
1 a large meeting: *A science convention was held at the university.* **2** a rule, often unwritten, which everyone accepts: *There are certain conventions about the use of the tennis courts.*

Word Building: **conventional** *adjective* **conventionalism** *noun* **conventionally** *adverb*

converge *verb*
to join up or meet at a particular place: *The roads converge at the roundabout. / The families will converge by the river for a picnic.*

Word Building: **convergence** *noun* **convergent** *adjective*

conversation *noun*
talk among people: *We had an interesting conversation about a new film.*

Word Building: **conversational** *adjective* **conversationalist** *noun*

converse[1] (say *kən-vers*) *verb*
to have a talk: *We conversed about music.*

converse[2] (say *kon-vers*) *adjective*
1 turned about or opposite: *to go in a converse direction*
converse[2] *noun*
2 the opposite: *He says it is possible but the converse is true.*

Word Building: **conversely** *adverb*

convert (say *kən-vert*) *verb*
1 to change completely: *Cinderella's fairy godmother converted her rags into a ball gown.* **2** to change the belief of: *His friends converted him from rugby to soccer.*
convert (say *kon-vert*) *noun*
3 someone who has changed their religion or other beliefs

Word Building: **convertible** *adjective* able to be changed **conversion** *noun*

convex *adjective*
curved or bulging outwards: *a convex mirror*

Word Use: the opposite is **concave**
Word Building: **convexity** *noun*

convey (say *kən-vay*) *verb*
to carry: *The bus conveyed us to town. / His words conveyed a message of sympathy.*

Word Building: **conveyance** *noun* a car or other vehicle **conveyable** *adjective* **conveyer** or **conveyor** *noun*
Word History: from a Latin word meaning "way" or "journey"

convict (say *kən-vikt*) *verb*
1 to find guilty of a crime, especially after a legal trial
convict (say *kon-vikt*) *noun*
2 someone who has been found guilty of a crime: *English convicts used to be sent to Australia to serve their sentences.*

conviction *noun*
1 the occasion of being found guilty: *As it was his first conviction he was let off with a warning.* **2** strong belief: *He spoke with a voice filled with conviction.*

convince *verb*
to make feel sure, or persuade: *We finally convinced him that he was wrong.*

Word Building: **convincing** *adjective* **convincingly** *adverb*

convoy *noun*
a number of ships or vehicles travelling together, sometimes for protection: *The ocean liner set sail with a convoy of small boats.*

Word Building: **convoy** *verb* to travel with as an escort

cook *verb*
1 to heat until ready for eating
cook *noun*
2 someone who cooks or prepares food

Word Building: **cookery** *noun* the art of cooking

cool *adjective*
1 not too cold: *a cool morning* **2** **a** calm or unexcited: *She remained cool.*
b unfriendly: *to be cool towards someone you distrust* **3** attractive or fashionable: *It's not cool to wear those wide trousers.*
cool *verb*
4 to become or make cool

Word Use: definition 3 is more suited to everyday language
Word Building: **cool** *noun: in the cool of the evening* **coolly** *adverb* **coolness** *noun*

coolamon (say *kooh-lə-mon*) *noun*
a wooden dish used by the Aborigines

Word History: from an Aboriginal language called Kamilaroi

coolibah (say *kooh-lə-bah*) *noun*
a gum tree found in inland Australia which has short twisted branches

Word Use: another spelling is **coolabah**
Word History: from an Aboriginal language called Yuwaaliyaay

coop *noun*
1 a small cage for hens
coop *verb*
2 coop up to keep in a small place: *We were all cooped up in one room.*

cooperate (say *koh-op-ə-rayt*) *verb*
1 to work together: *The two city councils cooperated to build a new pool.* **2** to be helpful: *When we complained about the noise they cooperated by turning down the volume.*

Word Building: **cooperative** *adjective* helpful **cooperation** *noun*

coordinate (say *koh-awd-ən-ayt*) *verb*
1 to combine or put together: *It's hard to coordinate the different things I want to do.* **2** to match or go well together: *The colours of your coat and blouse do not coordinate.* **3** to move together smoothly: *When he dances he can't coordinate his feet.*

Word Building: **coordinate** *noun* **coordination** *noun* **coordinator** *noun*

cop *noun*
1 a member of the police force
cop *verb*
2 to get: *He copped a punch on the nose.* **3 cop it** to get into trouble **4 cop this!** look at this!

Word Use: this word is more suited to everyday language
Word Building: other forms are **I copped, I have copped, I am copping**

cope *verb*
to manage or get on: *How are you coping in your new job?*

copper *noun*
1 a fairly soft reddish-brown metal **2** a large container made of copper for boiling dirty clothes

Word Building: **copper** *adjective*

copulate *verb*
to have sexual intercourse

Word Building: **copulation** *noun*

copy *noun*
1 something which is made the same as something else: *The secretary took my letter and made two copies.* **2** a single example of the same book or magazine
copy *verb*
3 to do or make the same as: *Copy me until you've learned the steps.* | *to copy a set of numbers*

Word Building: the plural form of the noun is **copies** □ other verb forms are **I copied, I have copied, I am copying** □ **copier** *noun* a machine for making photocopies

copyright law *noun*
the law which says who may use or copy someone's books, music, films or computer programs

coral *noun*
the hard colourful shapes formed from the skeletons of small sea animals

cord *noun*
1 a strong string, not as thick as rope
2 wire, which is protected by cloth or plastic, used to connect electrical goods to a power point **3** a ribbed material, such as corduroy: *He was wearing a jacket of cord.*

Word Use: another name for definition 2 is **flex** □ be careful – this sounds like **chord**
Word History: from a Greek word meaning "gut"

cordial *adjective*
1 warmly friendly: *a cordial welcome*
cordial *noun*
2 a fruit-flavoured syrup that you mix with water to make a drink

Word Building: **cordiality** *noun* **cordially** *adverb*

corduroy *noun*
a cotton material with a pattern of ridges

core *noun*
the inner or middle part, especially of fruit

Word Use: be careful – this sounds like **corps**
Word Building: **core** *verb* to remove the core

corgi (say *kaw-gee*) *noun*
a dog with short legs and a thick body

Word Building: the plural is **corgis**

corkscrew *noun*
a sharp metal spiral with a handle, for pulling corks out of bottles

corn[1] *noun*
1 a grain plant that you eat as a vegetable or grind to make flour
corn[1] *verb*
2 to preserve by salting: *to corn beef*

corn[2] *noun*
a hard painful lump on your toes or other parts of your feet

corner *noun*
1 the place where two straight edges meet: *a street corner* | *the corner of a room* | *the*

corners of a table **2** a place or region: *The travellers come from all the corners of the earth.*

corner *verb*
3 to trap: *The dog cornered the cat in a narrow lane.* **4** to turn a corner, especially at speed: *This car corners well.*

Word Building: **corner** *adjective: a corner shop*

cornet *noun*
a wind instrument like the trumpet, but smaller

cornflour *noun*
the fine flour made from rice or maize which is used in cooking, especially to thicken sauces

coronation *noun*
the crowning of a king or queen

coroner *noun*
the official who is in charge of a court inquiry into the cause of sudden or unexplained deaths

coronet *noun*
a small crown

corporal[1] *adjective*
physical or having to do with your body: *corporal punishment*

corporal[2] *noun*
a junior officer in the army

corporation *noun*
a business or other united group of people: *The children's parents formed a corporation to run their own school.*

corps (say *kaw*) *noun*
1 a unit of soldiers **2** a group of people in the same job: *the press corps*

Word Use: be careful – this sounds like **core**

corpse *noun*
a dead body, especially of a human being

Word Use: a similar word is **cadaver**

correct *verb*
1 to remove or point out the mistakes of

correct *adjective*
2 free from mistakes **3** acceptable or proper: *correct behaviour*

Word Building: **correction** *noun* **corrective** *adjective* **correctly** *adverb* **correctness** *noun*

correspond *verb*
1 to match or be similar: *Those figures almost correspond.* **2** to write letters: *We used to correspond every week.*

Word Building: **corresponding** *adjective* **correspondingly** *adverb*

correspondence *noun*
1 letters **2** similarity: *Is there any correspondence between the two accounts of what happened?*

correspondent (say *ko-rə-spon-dənt*) *noun*
1 someone who writes letters **2** a reporter paid to send in articles and news reports from a distant place

corridor *noun*
a connecting passage in a building

corroboree (say *kə-rob-ə-ree*) *noun*
an Aboriginal gathering with dancing and singing

Word History: from an Aboriginal language called Dharuk

corrode (say *kə-rohd*) *verb*
to gradually eat away: *Rust had corroded the old car.*

Word Building: **corrosion** *noun* **corrosive** *adjective*

corrugated (say *ko-rə-gayt-əd*) *adjective*
ridged or bumpy: *The roof was made of corrugated iron.*

Word Building: **corrugate** *verb* to wrinkle **corrugation** *noun*

corrupt *adjective*
1 dishonest or able to be bribed

corrupt *verb*
2 to make dishonest, especially by bribery **3** to change from good to bad: *to corrupt the language*

Word Building: **corruptible** *adjective* **corruption** *noun* **corruptly** *adverb*

corset *noun*
underwear which gives shape or firm support to the body

Word Building: **corsetry** *noun*

cosmetic *adjective*
meant to improve the look of your skin and hair: *the cosmetic effect of lipstick*

Word Building: **cosmetic** *noun* a beauty aid **cosmetically** *adverb*

cosmic *adjective*
having to do with the universe: *cosmic laws*

Word Building: **cosmically** *adverb*
Word History: from a Greek word meaning "of the world"

cosmonaut *noun*
another name for **astronaut**

cosmopolitan (say *koz-mə-pol-ət-ən*) *adjective*
1 having people or customs from many parts of the world: *a cosmopolitan city*
2 feeling at home in many parts of the world: *a cosmopolitan outlook*

cosmos (say *koz-mos*) *noun*
the universe

cost *noun*
1 the price to be paid for something **2** a loss or expense: *The battle was won at the cost of many lives.*

Word Building: **cost** *verb: It cost him his life.*

costly *adjective*
expensive or costing a great deal

Word Building: **costliness** *noun*

costume *noun*
a set of clothes, especially for dressing up or for a particular purpose: *The actors had very simple costumes.* | *a swimming costume*

cosy *adjective*
1 close and friendly: *There was a cosy atmosphere in the room.*
cosy *noun*
2 a knitted cover for keeping a teapot warm

Word Building: other adjective forms are **cosier, cosiest** □ **cosily** *adverb* **cosiness** *noun*

cot *noun*
a child's bed with raised sides

cottage *noun*
a small one-storey house

cottage cheese *noun*
a cheese made from curdled skimmed milk

cotton *noun*
1 a light material made from the soft white hairs covering the seeds of the cotton plant **2** a thread used for sewing

cottonwool *noun*
cotton in a soft and fluffy state used especially for cleaning your skin and dressing wounds

couch *noun*
1 a seat like an long armchair for two or more people **2** a padded bed without sides, often used in a doctor's surgery
couch *verb*
3 to put into words: *The message is couched in very difficult language.*

Word Building: the plural of the noun is **couches**

cough (rhymes with *off*) *noun*
the noisy blast of air from your lungs which you get in some illnesses, or when something is stuck in your throat

Word Building: **cough** *verb*

could (say *kood*) *verb*
past tense of **can**[2]

council *noun*
1 a group of people that meets regularly to discuss or decide certain things **2** the government of a small area such as a city or its suburbs: *She was elected to the shire council.*

Word Building: **councillor** *noun* a member of a council

counsel *noun*
1 advice **2** a lawyer who is paid to give advice to someone in a court case

Word Building: **counsel** *verb* (**counselled, counselling**) to advise **counsellor** *noun* an adviser, especially a psychologist

count[1] *verb*
1 to add up: *He counted the trucks as they passed.* **2** to name the numbers: *She had to count up to ten slowly.* **3** to include: *That makes five of us, counting Jim.*
4 to matter: *What you want doesn't count in prison.* **5 count on** to depend on: *The boss is counting on us being on time.*

Word Building: **count** *noun*

count[2] *noun*
a European noble

Word Building: **countess** *noun*
Word History: from a Latin word meaning "companion"

countenance *noun*
your face or its expression: *a happy countenance*

counter[1] *noun*
1 a long shelf or bar where goods are sold or food is eaten **2** something used for keeping count, especially in a game

counter[2] *adverb*
1 in the opposite direction
counter[2] *verb*
2 to move against: *He countered their plan with strong arguments.*

Word Building: **counter** *adjective* opposed

counterfeit (say *kown-tə-feet*) *adjective*
made to imitate or look like, especially to deceive: *counterfeit money*

Word Building: **counterfeit** *noun* an imitation **counterfeit** *verb* **counterfeiter** *noun*

counterpart *noun*
one of two people or things which matches or looks like the other

country *noun*
1 an area of land separated from other areas: *Europe is divided into different countries.* **2** the land where someone is born **3** the undeveloped land beyond the towns and cities

Word Building: the plural is **countries** □ **countrified** *adjective* looking like a country area

county *noun*
a large area within a state, bigger than a shire

Word Building: the plural is **counties**

coup (rhymes with *boo*) *noun*
a sudden effective move: *The generals have been in power since the army coup.*

Word Use: the "p" in **coup** is silent because this is a French word

couple (rhymes with *supple*) *noun*
1 two people, especially if married: *the couple next door* **2** any two things: *a couple of apples*

couple *verb*
3 to join or link together: *The carriages had to be coupled before the train could leave.*

Word Building: **coupling** *noun*

couplet (say *kup-lət*) *noun*
a pair of lines of poetry which rhyme

coupon (say *kooh-pon*) *noun*
1 a ticket or card which you can exchange for goods or money **2** a form which must be filled in to order goods, or enter a competition

courage (say *ku-rij*) *noun*
the strength to do or face something you find frightening: *She hasn't the courage to learn to drive.*

Word Building: **courageous** *adjective* brave **courageously** *adverb*

courier (say *koo-ree-ə*) *noun*
1 someone who carries messages or parcels for others **2** someone who looks after a group of tourists and their travel arrangements

Word History: from a Latin word meaning "run"

course (rhymes with *horse*) *noun*
1 one stage of a meal: *We had meat and potatoes for the main course.* **2** a series, especially of lessons: *I'm doing a course of exercises.* **3** the ground or water on which a race takes place **4** movement or progress: *the ship's course* | *in the course of the year* **5 of course** certainly: *Of course you will come.*

Word Use: be careful – this sounds like **coarse**
Word Building: **course** *verb* to race

court (rhymes with *short*) *noun*
1 the hard ground where games such as tennis and basketball are played **2** the palace of a king or queen and the people who live or work there **3** the place where legal cases and trials are heard **4** a courtyard or space enclosed by walls

court *verb*
5 to try to win love or favour: *The prince courted the beautiful princess.*

Word Building: **courtier** *noun* someone who serves the king or queen at court **courtly** *adjective: courtly manners* **courtship**

courteous (say *ker-tee-əs*) *adjective*
well-mannered or polite: *a courteous boy* | *a courteous reply*

Word Building: **courteously** *adverb*

courtesy (say *ker-tə-see*) *noun*
1 politeness and good manners
2 permission: *The poems are printed by courtesy of the author.*

court martial *noun*
a court of officers which tries anyone in the armed forces who breaks the military law

Word Building: the plural can be **court martials** or **courts martial** □ **court-martial** *verb* (**court-martialled, court-martialling**)

courtyard *noun*
an area enclosed by walls or buildings

cousin (say *kuz-ən*) *noun*
a son or daughter of your uncle or aunt

cove *noun*
a small bay or inlet

covenant *noun*
a solemn promise: *The rainbow is said to be God's covenant never again to flood the earth.*

cover *verb*
1 to hide: *She covered her face with her hands.* 2 to lie over or be spread over: *A quilt covered the bed.* 3 to protect: *to be covered by insurance* 4 to include: *This list covers everything we need.* 5 to be enough to pay for: *Ten dollars should cover expenses.* 6 to get news of: *Three reporters were covering the fire.* 7 to travel over: *We covered a long distance today.*

cover *noun*
8 something which covers: *a book cover* 9 shelter: *The rabbit ran for cover into its burrow.*

Word Building: **coverage** *noun: the TV coverage of the football match* **covering** *noun: a light covering of snow*

covet (say *kuv-ət*) *verb*
to want very much to have: *John covets that car of yours.*

Word Building: **covetous** *adjective* greedy **covetously** *adverb* **covetousness** *noun*

cow *noun*
the female of cattle and of some other large animals, such as the whale

coward *noun*
someone who acts badly or weakly out of fear

Word Building: **cowardice** *noun* **cowardly** *adverb*

cower *verb*
to draw away in fear: *The puppy was cowering under a table.*

coxswain (say *kok-sən*) *noun*
the person who steers a boat, especially in rowing

Word Use: the short form is **cox**

coy *adjective*
shy, or pretending to be shy

Word Building: **coyly** *adverb* **coyness** *noun*

coyote (say *koy-oh-tee*) *noun*
a North American wild dog which howls at night

crab *noun*
a hard-shelled sea animal with eight legs around a flattish body and a large pair of pincers

crack *verb*
1 to split, often with a sharp noise: *The glass jug cracked.* 2 to flick with a loud noise: *The stockman cracked his whip.* 3 to give up: *At first he would not confess but finally he cracked.* 4 to break into: *The robbers cracked the safe.* 5 to find the answer to: *to crack a code* 6 to tell: *to crack a joke*

crack *noun*
7 a sudden sharp noise 8 the line of a split: *Cracks appeared but the bowl didn't break.* 9 a hard blow: *He gave himself a crack with the hammer.*

Word Building: **crack** *adjective* first-rate **cracked** *adjective*

cracker *noun*
1 a thin, crisp, unsweetened biscuit 2 a firework 3 a twisted roll of paper with a surprise inside, which explodes when you pull it

Word Use: another name for definition 3 is **bonbon**

crackle *verb*
to make a crunching sound: *The dry leaves crackled underfoot.*

Word Building: **crackle** *noun*

cradle *noun*
1 a baby's small bed, usually on rockers 2 a frame which supports or protects: *The window cleaners were in a cradle halfway up a building.* 3 a box on rockers used to separate gold dust from sand and dirt

cradle *verb*
4 to hold or rock, as if in a cradle

craft *noun*
1 skilfulness 2 cunning 3 a job or trade needing special skill with your hands 4 a boat or an aircraft

Word Use: for definition 4 the plural is **craft**
Word Building: **craft** *verb* to make individually **craftsman** *noun* **craftsmanship** *noun*

crafty *adjective*
clever in a tricky or cunning way

Word Building: other forms are **craftier, craftiest** □ **craftily** *adverb* **craftiness** *noun*

crag *noun*
a steep rock sticking up from a cliff or mountain

Word Building: **craggy** *adjective* (**craggier, craggiest**)

cram *verb*
1 to stuff tightly: *Sue crammed the papers under her bed.* 2 to fill very full, especially with food

Word Building: other forms are **I crammed, I have crammed, I am cramming**

cramp *noun*
a sudden painful tightening of a muscle in your body: *a stomach cramp*

crane *noun*
1 a large bird with long legs, neck and bill, which feeds in shallow water **2** a machine with a long moving arm, which can lift and move heavy weights around

crane *verb*
3 to stretch in order to see: *to crane your neck*

crank *noun*
1 a bar for winding or levering: *He used the crank to jack up his car.* **2** an odd person

cranky *adjective*
bad-tempered or irritable

Word Building: other forms are **crankier, crankiest** □ **crankily** *adverb* **crankiness** *noun*

cranny *noun*
a narrow opening, especially in rock

Word Building: the plural is **crannies**

crash *verb*
1 to run into or hit noisily: *The car crashed into the tree.* **2** to fall and smash: *The aeroplane crashed.*

crash *noun*
3 the noise of breaking or hitting **4** an accident or collision

Word Building: the plural form of the noun is **crashes**

crate *noun*
a large wooden box

crater *noun*
1 the cup-shaped opening at the top of a volcano **2** a round hole in the ground, like one made by a meteorite or a bomb

Word History: from the Greek word for a bowl for mixing wine and water

cravat (say *krə-vat*) *noun*
a man's scarf, loosely tied at the throat

crave *verb*
to want desperately: *The thirsty man craved a drink. / I crave one favour.*

Word Building: **craving** *noun*

crawl *verb*
1 to go slowly, especially on hands and knees **2** to flatter or be nice to someone to gain an advantage: *He is crawling to the teacher so that he'll be chosen for the team.*

crawl *noun*
3 a crawling movement **4** a fast style of swimming in which your head and the front of your body are kept flat to the water, with legs kicking and your arms used in turn

Word Use: other names for definition 4 are **freestyle** or **Australian crawl**
Word Building: **crawler** *noun*

crayfish *noun*
a hard-shelled freshwater animal which looks like a small lobster

Word Use: another name for it is **yabby**
Word Building: the plural can be either **crayfish** or **crayfishes**

crayon *noun*
a greasy chalk used for drawing and colouring

craze *verb*
1 to madden: *The wind crazed the horses.*

craze *noun*
2 a short-lived fashion: *a craze for yoyos*

crazy *adjective*
1 mad or insane **2** odd or irregular: *crazy paving*

Word Building: other forms are **crazier, craziest** □ **crazily** *adverb* **craziness** *noun*

creak *verb*
to make a squeaking noise: *The floor boards creaked.*

Word Building: **creaky** *adjective*

cream *noun*
1 the rich top of milk **2** anything which is thick and smooth: *face cream* **3** the top or best part: *Only the cream of athletes go to the Olympic Games.*

cream *adjective*
4 having a yellowish white colour

Word Building: **creaminess** *noun* **creamy** *adjective*

crease *noun*
a sharp line or fold, especially in material or paper

Word Building: **crease** *verb* to fold or wrinkle **creased** *adjective*

create (say *kree-ayt*) *verb*
1 to make or invent **2** to make into: *He was created a knight.*

Word Building: **creative** *adjective* good at making or inventing things **creatively** *adverb* **creativity** *noun* **creator** *noun*

creation (say *kree-ay-shən*) *noun*
1 something which has been made or invented **2** the act of creating

creature (say *kree-chə*) *noun*
any living thing: *Noah took two of every creature onto his ark.*

creche (say *kraysh, kresh*) *noun*
a nursery for babies and young children

Word History: from a German word meaning "crib"

credit *noun*
1 trust or belief: *I don't put much credit in his promise to pay.* **2** praise or approval: *Give her credit for trying.* **3** the amount someone is allowed to spend or borrow: *How much credit do I have?* **4** money paid into an account **5 on credit** with agreement to pay later

credit *verb*
6 to believe: *Hal was so surprised he couldn't credit what he heard.* **7** to enter on the credit side of an account

Word Use: for definition 5 compare **cash** □ someone you owe money to is your **creditor** and someone who owes you money is your **debtor** □ compare definitions 4 and 7 with **debit**
Word Building: other verb forms are **I credited, I have credited, I am crediting** □ **creditable** *adjective* something which brings praise **creditably** *adverb*

creed *noun*
a statement of belief

creek *noun*
a small stream

creep *verb*
1 to go very slowly and quietly: *She crept out of the house so as not to wake anyone.* **2** to crawl along the ground

creep *noun*
3 an unpleasant person: *He's a real creep.* **4 the creeps** a feeling of fear or disgust

Word Use: definitions 3 and 4 are more suited to everyday language
Word Building: other verb forms are **I crept, I have crept, I am creeping** □ **creepy** *adjective* frightening or unpleasant **creepiness** *noun*

creeper *noun*
a plant which climbs walls or grows along the ground

cremate *verb*
to burn to ashes: *The dead man had asked for his body to be cremated.*

Word Building: **crematorium** *noun* the place where bodies are burned **cremation** *noun*

crepe (rhymes with *grape*) *noun*
1 a light crinkled material made of cotton or silk **2** a finely wrinkled paper **3** a thin pancake

crescendo (say *krə-shen-doh*) *adverb*
increasingly loud or forceful

Word Use: an instruction in music

crescent (say *krez-ənt*) *noun*
1 the curved shape of the moon when it is still new **2** anything with a similar shape, especially a curved street

Word Use: when definition 2 is the name of a street, you spell it with a capital letter and its abbreviation is **Cres**

cress *noun*
a fast-growing herb whose leaves are used in salads

crest *noun*
1 the feathers or growth on the top of the heads of some birds **2** the very top of anything: *on the crest of success* **3** part of a coat of arms which is used as a badge: *Their blazer pockets were embroidered with the school crest.*

Word Building: **crest** *verb* to reach the top of **crested** *adjective*

crestfallen *adjective*
disappointed or sad: *He looks quite crestfallen at missing the train.*

crevasse (say *krə-vas*) *noun*
a deep crack in a glacier or river of ice

crevice (say *krev-əs*) *noun*
a crack forming an opening: *a crevice in a rock*

crew *noun*
the group of people who work on a ship or aeroplane

Word Building: **crew** *verb: to crew a boat*

crib *noun*
1 a baby's cot **2** a box or rack used to hold food for cattle and horses

cricket[1] *noun*
a leaping insect, similar to a grasshopper, which makes a loud noise by rubbing its wings on its abdomen

Word History: from a French word that imitates the sound these insects make

cricket[2] *noun*
a team game played with ball, bat and wickets

Word Building: **cricketer** *noun*
Word History: from a French word meaning "stick"

crime *noun*
1 an act which breaks the law **2** the breaking of laws: *Crime is a serious problem in most cities.*

criminal *adjective*
having to do with crime: *criminal activities*

Word Building: **criminal** *noun* someone who is guilty of a crime **criminally** *adverb*

crimp *verb*
to make curly: *to crimp hair*

crimson *adjective*
deep, purplish-red

Word Building: **crimson** *verb* to become crimson, often when you blush **crimson** *noun*

cringe *verb*
to bend or bow down in fear

Word Use: a similar word is **cower**

crinkle *verb*
to wrinkle or crease: *His face crinkled with laughter.*

Word Building: **crinkle** *noun* **crinkly** *adjective*

cripple *noun*
1 someone who has lost the use of one or more limbs
cripple *verb*
2 to damage or make lame

crisis *noun*
1 a time of danger or trouble **2** a turning point, especially in the course of an illness

Word Building: the plural is **crises** (say *kruy-seez*)

crisp *adjective*
1 hard, dry and easily broken: *crisp biscuits* **2** cool, dry and fresh: *crisp air* **3** clean and neat: *a crisp uniform*
crisp *noun*
4 a thin slice of fried potato eaten cold

Word Building: **crispy** *adjective* (**crispier**, **crispiest**) **crispness** *noun*

criterion (say *kruyt-ear-ree-ən*) *noun*
a standard or rule for testing something

Word Building: the plural is **criteria**

critic *noun*
1 someone who is a judge of quality or excellence: *The newspaper's literary critic praised the author's latest novel.* **2** someone who finds fault

critical *adjective*
1 likely to find fault **2** having to do with a crisis: *He kept calm at the critical moment.*

Word Building: **critically** *adverb: critically ill*

criticise or **criticize** (say *krit-ə-suyz*) *verb*
to find fault with: *to criticise someone's manners*

Word Building: **criticism** *noun*

croak *verb*
to make a low hoarse sound: *The frogs croaked in the pond.*

Word Building: **croaky** *adjective*

crockery *noun*
cups, plates, dishes and similar articles made of china or pottery

Word Use: a similar word is **china**

crocodile *noun*
a large lizard-like reptile found living in the waters of tropical countries

Word History: from a Greek word meaning "lizard"

crook[1] *noun*
1 a bent or curved part: *the crook of your elbow* **2** a stick with a bend or curve at one end: *a shepherd's crook* **3** a dishonest person

Word Use: definition 3 is more suited to everyday language
Word Building: **crook** *verb* to bend or curve: *to crook your finger*

crook[2] *adjective*
1 sick: *I feel crook.* **2** unpleasant: *Scrubbing floors is a crook job.*

Word Use: this word is more suited to everyday language

crooked (say *krook-əd*) *adjective*
1 bent: *a crooked stick* **2** dishonest

Word Use: definition 2 is more suited to everyday language

croon *verb*
to sing in a soft or sentimental way

Word Building: **crooner** *noun*

crop *noun*
1 products grown in the ground: *a good wheat crop* | *a crop of apples* **2** a short whip used by horse riders
crop *verb*
3 to cut short: *to crop a horse's tail*
4 crop up to come as a surprise: *a problem cropped up*

Word Building: other verb forms are **I cropped, I have cropped, I am cropping**

croquet (say *kroh-kay*) *noun*
a game played by hitting wooden balls with mallets through metal arches set in a lawn

cross *noun*
1 anything in the shape made by two lines going through each other such as "+" or "×" **2** the result of mixing breeds of animals or plants: *My dog is a cross between a terrier and a beagle.*
cross *verb*
3 to draw a line across: *to cross a cheque*
4 to form a cross with: *cross your fingers*
5 to pass in the way of: *He crossed my path.* **6** to go from one side of to another: *The bridge crosses the river.*
7 cross out to draw a line through
cross *adjective*
8 lying or passing across: *a cross wind*
9 annoyed: *My aunt was cross with me.*

Word Building: **crossly** *adverb* **crossness** *noun*

cross-examine *verb*
to question in order to check the truth of something already stated

Word Building: **cross-examination** *noun* **cross-examiner** *noun*

crossing *noun*
1 a moving across: *The first crossing of the Blue Mountains by white men took place in 1813.* **2** a place where a road, river or railway line can be crossed

crotchet (say *krot-chət*) *noun*
a musical note equal to the time of one beat

crotchety *adjective*
bad-tempered or irritable

crouch *verb*
to bend your knees and lean forward: *I crouched behind the shrub to hide myself.*

Word Building: **crouch** *noun*

croupier (say *krooh-pee-ə*) *noun*
someone who takes and pays out the money at a gambling table

crow[1] *noun*
a black shiny bird with a rough-sounding call

crow[2] *verb*
1 to make the sound of a rooster **2** to boast

Word Building: other forms for definition 1 are **it crew, it has crowed, it is crowing**

crowbar *noun*
an iron bar used as a lever or to break hard ground

crowd *noun*
1 a large number of people or things gathered closely together
crowd *verb*
2 to gather in large numbers: *Children crowded around the clown.* **3** to squeeze or push: *They crowded into the room.*

Word Building: **crowded** *adjective*

crown *noun*
1 an ornament made of gold and jewels worn on the head of a king or queen
2 the top or highest part: *the crown of your head*
crown *verb*
3 to put a crown on: *The Archbishop crowned the new king.* **4** to honour or reward: *Success crowned his efforts.*

crucial (say *krooh-shəl*) *adjective*
of greatest importance: *a crucial decision*

crucifix (say *krooh-sə-fiks*) *noun*
a cross with the figure of Jesus on it

Word History: from a Latin word meaning "fixed to a cross"

crucify (say *krooh-sə-fuy*) *verb*
to put to death by nailing to a cross

Word Building: **crucifixion** *noun*

crude *adjective*
1 in a natural state: *crude oil* **2** rude and not in good taste: *a crude joke* **3** not carefully done: *a crude drawing*

Word Building: **crudely** *adverb* **crudeness** *noun* **crudity** *noun*

cruel *adjective*
liking or likely to cause pain: *a cruel person* | *a cruel remark*

Word Building: **cruelly** *adverb* **cruelty** *noun*

cruet (say *krooh-ət*) *noun*
a set of small containers for salt, pepper and mustard

cruise *verb*
1 to sail from place to place: *The battleship cruised in enemy waters.* **2** to travel at a moderate speed

Word Building: **cruise** *noun: a holiday cruise* **cruiser** *noun*

crumb *noun*
1 a small piece of bread, cake or other dry food

crumb *verb*
2 to break into crumbs **3** to coat with crumbs: *to crumb steak*

crumble *verb*
to break into small pieces: *I crumbled the cake. / The wall was crumbling with age.*

Word Building: **crumbly** *adjective*

crumpet *noun*
a kind of flat cake, eaten toasted and buttered

crumple *verb*
1 to crush into wrinkles: *I crumpled the paper in my hands.* **2** to break down or collapse: *Her face crumpled into tears. / The building crumpled after the blast.*

crunch *verb*
to crush or grind noisily

crusade *noun*
a strong movement of support: *a crusade to save the park*

Word Building: **crusade** *verb* **crusader** *noun*

crush *verb*
1 to press together between hard surfaces **2** to break into small pieces: *to crush rocks* **3** to defeat totally: *to crush a rebellion*

crush *noun*
4 a strong liking which often doesn't last long: *to have a crush on a film star*

crust *noun*
1 the outside surface of bread or a piece of it **2** any hard outer surface

Word Building: **crusty** *adjective* (**crustier, crustiest**)

crustacean (say *krus-<u>tay</u>-shən*) *noun*
a type of animal, such as a crab or crayfish, with a hard shell instead of a skeleton, and which usually lives in water

crutch *noun*
a stick which fits under the arm to help an injured person walk

cry *verb*
1 to shed tears **2** to shout: *We cried for help.*

cry *noun*
3 a fit of weeping **4** a shout: *A great cry went up.*

Word Building: other verb forms are **I cried, I have cried, I am crying** □ the plural of the noun is **cries**

crypt (say *kript*) *noun*
an underground room under a church, often used as a burial place

Word History: from a Greek word meaning "hidden"

cryptic (say *<u>krip</u>-tik*) *adjective*
mysterious, or difficult to understand: *a cryptic message*

Word Building: **cryptically** *adverb*

crystal *noun*
1 a clear mineral which looks like ice **2** a single grain or piece of this **3** clear sparkling glass

Word Building: **crystal** *adjective: a crystal bowl* **crystalline** *adjective*

crystallise or **crystallize** *verb*
1 to form into crystals **2** to coat with sugar

Word Building: **crystallisation** *noun*

cub *noun*
the young of certain animals such as the lion and bear

cubbyhouse *noun*
a child's playhouse

cube *noun*
1 a solid shape with six equal square sides **2** the result of multiplying a number by itself twice: *The cube of 3 is 3 × 3 × 3, or 27.*

Word Building: **cubic** *adjective*

cube root *noun*
the number which, when multiplied by itself twice, gives the cube: *The cube root of 27 is 3.*

cubicle *noun*
a partly enclosed small space: *a toilet cubicle*

cuckoo (say *<u>koo</u>-kooh*) *noun*
a bird which is known for its habit of laying its eggs in the nests of other birds

cucumber *noun*
a long thin vegetable which is used in salads

cud *noun*
food which cattle and some other animals return from their first stomach to chew a second time

cuddle *verb*
to hug gently

Word Building: **cuddle** *noun* **cuddly** *adjective*

cudgel *noun*
a short thick stick used as a weapon

Word Building: **cudgel** *verb* (**cudgelled, cudgelling**)

cue[1] *noun*
anything said or done as a signal for what follows, especially in a play: *The ringing of a bell was the maid's cue to enter.*

Word Building: **cue** *verb* (**cued, cueing**)

cue[2] *noun*
a long stick used to hit the ball in billiards and other similar games

Word Building: **cue** *verb* (**cued, cueing**)

cuff[1] *noun*
1 a band or fold at the wrist of a sleeve
2 a part turned up at the end of a trouser leg

cuff[2] *verb*
to hit with your open hand

cuisenaire rods (say *kweez-ə-nair*) *plural noun*
coloured wooden blocks of different lengths, used in teaching numbers to children

cul-de-sac *noun*
a short street which is closed at one end

cull *verb*
to pick out or choose the best from: *to cull ideas or information*

Word Building: **cull** *noun*

culminate *verb*
to reach the highest point: *His efforts culminated in success.*

Word Building: **culmination** *noun*

culottes *plural noun*
trousers which are cut wide to look like a skirt

culprit *noun*
someone who has done something wrong: *After he broke the shop window the culprit ran away.*

cult *noun*
1 a religion **2** a strong, almost religious devotion to a person or thing: *the cult of jogging*

cultivate *verb*
1 to dig the soil for planting and growing: *He cultivates wheat on his farm.* **2** to develop or improve: *to cultivate the mind*

Word Use: a similar word for definition 1 is **till**
Word Building: **cultivated** *adjective* **cultivation** *noun* **cultivator** *noun*

culture *noun*
skills, arts, beliefs and customs passed on from one generation to another: *the culture of Japan*

Word Building: **cultural** *adjective: cultural achievements*

cumbersome *adjective*
awkward to handle: *a cumbersome parcel*

cumquat (say *kum-kwot*) *noun*
a fruit like a small mandarin but much sourer

Word Use: another spelling is **kumquat**
Word History: from a Chinese word meaning "gold orange"

cumulus (say *kyooh-myə-ləs*) *noun*
a cloud, usually white, which is flat at the bottom and has round heaps at the top

Word Building: the plural is **cumuli**

cuneiform (say *kyooh-nə-fawm*) *adjective*
1 wedge-shaped

cuneiform *noun*
2 characters used in writing in ancient Persia and some nearby countries

cunning *noun*
skill used in a clever plan, or in tricking other people

Word Building: **cunning** *adjective* **cunningly** *adverb*

cup *noun*
1 a small container with a handle on the side used for drinking **2** an ornamental bowl, usually of silver or gold, given as a prize

cup *verb*
3 to form into the shape of a cup: *to cup your hands*

Word Building: other verb forms are **I cupped, I have cupped, I am cupping**

cupboard (say *kub-əd*) *noun*
a piece of furniture or a built-in space with doors, used for storing things

curate (say *kyooh-rət*) *noun*
a clergyman who helps a rector or vicar

Word Building: **curacy** *noun* the position of a curate

curator (say *kyooh-ray-tə*) *noun*
someone who looks after a museum, art gallery or similar kind of collection

curb *verb*
to control or hold back: *Curb your temper.*

Word Building: **curb** *noun*

curd *noun*
a jelly-like substance formed in milk which has been treated with an acid, eaten fresh or used to make cheese

curdle *verb*
to form into curd: *I curdled the custard by accidentally letting it boil. / The milk curdled on the hot day.*

cure *noun*
1 a medicine or treatment which gets rid of an illness or disability
cure *verb*
2 to bring back to good health **3** to treat so as to preserve or finish properly: *to cure meat / to cure concrete*

Word Building: **curable** *adjective* **curative** *adjective*

curfew *noun*
an order which says people are not allowed to be out on the streets after a certain time at night

curious *adjective*
1 wanting to learn: *to be curious about butterflies* **2** interesting because strange or new: *a curious custom*

Word Building: **curiosity** *noun* **curiously** *adverb*

curl *noun*
1 a small ring of hair **2** a curved or twisted shape: *There were curls of chocolate on the cake.*

Word Building: **curl** *verb: The vine curled round the tree.* **curly** *adjective* (**curlier, curliest**)

curlew (say *ker-lyooh*) *noun*
a type of long-legged shore-bird

currant *noun*
a small, dried, seedless grape

Word Use: be careful – this word sounds like **current**

currawong *noun*
a large black-and-white or greyish Australian bird with a large pointed bill and a loud ringing call

Word History: probably from an Aboriginal language called Yagara

currency *noun*
money in current use in a country

current *adjective*
1 belonging to the present: *current problems*
current *noun*
2 a flow or movement: *a strong current in the river / a current of air from a fan / a current of electricity*

Word Use: be careful – this word sounds like **currant**

curriculum (say *kə-rik-yə-ləm*) *noun*
a set of courses of study: *the school curriculum*

Word Building: the plural is **curriculums** or **curricula**

curry[1] *noun*
a spicy sauce or dish of meat and vegetables which tastes hot

Word Building: the plural is **curries** □ **curry** *verb* (**curried, currying**) to prepare with this sauce

curry[2] *verb*
to rub with a brush or comb to clean: *to curry a horse*

Word Building: other forms are **I curried, I have curried, I am currying**

curse *noun*
1 a wish that evil will happen to someone: *to put a curse on someone* **2** a swear word or blasphemy: *to utter a curse*

Word Building: **curse** *verb* **cursed** *adjective*

cursor *noun*
1 the sliding part of a measuring tool **2** a moving dot or line on a computer video screen showing where the next words will appear

curt *adjective*
rudely brief in speech or manner: *He gave me a curt nod.*

Word Building: **curtly** *adverb* **curtness** *noun*

curtail *verb*
to cut short: *We had to curtail our holiday.*

Word Building: **curtailment** *noun*

curtain *noun*
a piece of material hanging from a rod over a window or across the front of a stage

Word Building: **curtain** *verb*

curtsy *noun*
a respectful bow made by a woman bending her knees with one foot in front of the other

Word Building: the plural is **curtsies** □ **curtsy** *verb* (**curtsied, curtsying**)

curve *noun*
a bending line or shape with no angles: *a curve in a road | the curves of the letter "s"*

Word Building: **curvature** *noun* **curve** *verb* **curvy** *adjective*

cuscus *noun*
a small furry animal like a possum, which has a long tail and lives in New Guinea and northern Queensland

cushion *noun*
1 a soft pad used to sit on, or lean against, especially on a chair
cushion *verb*
2 to place on a cushion **3** to lessen the force or effect of: *Thick bushes cushioned his fall.*

custard *noun*
a food made of milk, eggs and sugar and eaten as a dessert

custody *noun*
1 keeping or care: *The family jewels are in safe custody at the bank.* **2** imprisonment: *The policeman took the suspect into custody.*

Word Building: **custodial** *adjective* **custodian** *noun*

custom *noun*
1 habit or usual practice **2 customs** a tax paid on goods brought into the country

customary *adjective*
usual or according to custom

Word Building: **customarily** *adverb*

custom-built *adjective*
made in the way you ordered

customer *noun*
someone who buys goods from other people

cut *verb*
1 to make an opening in with something sharp: *to cut your finger* **2** to separate or make shorter with something sharp: *to cut a string* **3** to cross: *One line cut another at right angles. | The river rose and cut the road.* **4** to lower: *to cut prices* **5** to be able to cut: *This knife cuts well.* **6 cut off** to stop: *He cut me off before I finished speaking.*
cut *noun*
7 the result of cutting or a piece cut off: *a cut on your leg | a cut of meat* **8** a reduction or lowering: *a cut in the price*

Word Building: other verb forms are **I cut, I have cut, I am cutting**

cute (say *kyooht*) *adjective*
very pretty or sweet: *a cute child | a cute party dress*

Word Use: this word is more suited to everyday language
Word Building: **cutely** *adverb* **cuteness** *noun*

cuticle *noun*
the skin around the edges of a finger nail or toe nail

cutlass *noun*
a short, heavy, slightly curved sword

cutlery *noun*
the knives, forks and spoons used for eating

cutlet *noun*
a small cut of meat, usually lamb or veal, that contains a rib

cyanide *noun*
a very poisonous salt

cycle *noun*
1 a series of events happening in a regular repeating order: *the cycle of the seasons*
2 a bicycle

Word Building: **cycle** *verb* to ride a bicycle **cyclic** *adjective* occurring in cycles **cyclist** *noun*
Word History: from a Greek word meaning "ring" or "circle"

cyclone *noun*
a tropical storm with strong winds

Word Building: **cyclonic** *adjective*
Word History: from a Greek word meaning "moving in a circle"

cygnet (say *sig-nət*) *noun*
a young swan

cylinder *noun*
1 a tube-shaped object, either hollow or solid, with perfectly circular ends **2** the part of an engine in which the piston moves

Word Building: **cylindrical** *adjective* shaped like a cylinder

cymbal *noun*
one of a pair of curved brass plates which are struck together to make a sharp, musical, ringing sound

Word Building: **cymbalist** *noun*

cynic *noun*
someone who does not believe in the goodness of people or events and is often scornful of them

Word Building: **cynical** *adjective* **cynicism** *noun*

cypress *noun*
an evergreen cone-bearing tree with dark overlapping leaves

cyst (say *sist*) *noun*
a small growth that appears in your body or under your skin, often containing liquid

Word Building: **cystic** *adjective*

czar (say *zah*) *noun*
the emperor of Russia in former times

Word Use: another spelling is **tsar**

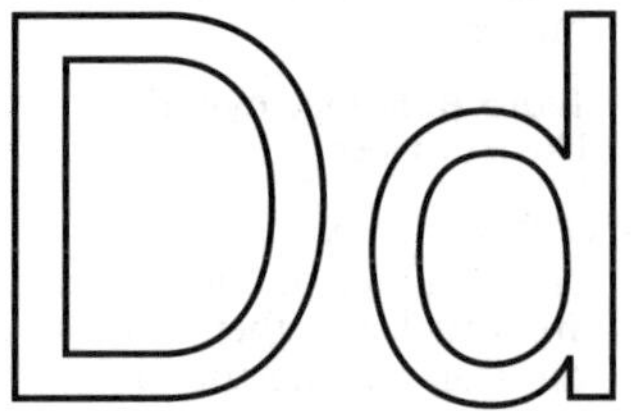

dab *verb*
1 to put on gently: *She dabbed a little perfume behind her ears.*
dab *noun*
2 a small amount: *a dab of lipstick*

Word Building: other verb forms are **I dabbed, I have dabbed, I am dabbing**

dabble *verb*
1 to splash in water: *to dabble your toes*
2 dabble in to do as a hobby: *to dabble in painting*

Word Building: **dabbler** *noun*

dachshund (say *daks-ənd*) *noun*
a small dog with a long body and very short legs

Word History: from the German words for "badger" and "dog"

daddy-long-legs *noun*
a small spider with long, very thin legs

Word Use: the plural form is the same as the singular

daffodil (say *daf-ə-dil*) *noun*
a plant which has yellow bell-shaped flowers in spring

daft (say *dahft*) *adjective*
foolish or slightly mad

Word Building: **daftly** *adverb* **daftness** *noun*

dagger *noun*
a weapon with a short pointed blade for stabbing

daily *adjective*
done or happening every day: *our daily chores*

Word Building: **daily** *adverb*

dainty *adjective*
small and delicate: *to take dainty steps*

Word Building: other forms are **daintier, daintiest** □ **daintily** *adverb* **daintiness** *noun*

dairy *noun*
1 the place on a farm where cows are milked **2** a cool place where milk and cream are stored and made into butter and cheese

Word Use: don't confuse the spelling with **diary**
Word Building: the plural is **dairies** □ **dairy** *adjective: dairy products*

dais (say *day-əs*) *noun*
a raised platform at the end of a hall, for a speaker's desk and microphone

daisy *noun*
a common plant which has white or brightly-coloured flowers with many petals surrounding a yellow centre

Word Building: the plural is **daisies**
Word History: from an Old English word meaning "day's eye"

dam[1] *noun*
1 a lot of water held back by a strong wall built across a river **2** the wall itself **3** a waterhole dug out of the ground on a farm

Word Building: **dam** *verb* (**dammed, damming**) to hold back: *They dammed the river to provide water for the town.*

dam[2] *noun*
a horse's mother

damage (say *dam-ij*) *verb*
1 to harm or injure
damage *noun*
2 harm or injury **3 damages** money that a court says you should get to make

up for an injury or loss: *The court awarded her damages of a million dollars.*

Word Building: **damageable** *adjective*

dame *noun*
1 Dame the title used to address a woman of high rank: *Dame of the Order of Australia* **2** a woman: *There were no dames at the party.*

Word Use: definition 2 is mostly used in America by men in everyday language and may offend some women

damn (rhymes with *ham*) *verb*
1 to wish extreme suffering and misery upon: *to damn him for his evil deeds*
damn *interjection*
2 an expression of anger or annoyance, as in *"Damn! I've missed the last train."*

Word Use: definition 1 used to mean that God would punish the person damned □ the use of definition 2 may offend some people
Word Building: **damnation** *noun* everlasting punishment in hell

damned (say *damd*) *adjective*
1 condemned to punishment in hell: *a damned soul* **2** very great: *She's a damned nuisance.*
damned *adverb*
3 very or extremely: *She's damned late.*

Word Use: definitions 2 and 3 are used by some people in everyday language to express strong feeling

damp *adjective*
slightly wet or moist

Word Building: **damp** or **dampen** *verb* to moisten **damp** *noun* **damply** *adverb* **dampness** *noun*

damper *noun*
bread made from flour and water mixed to make a dough and baked in the coals of an open fire

dance *noun*
1 a series of rhythmical steps, usually performed in time to music **2** a party for dancing: *A new band played at the dance on Saturday.*

Word Building: **dance** *verb: to dance a waltz* **dancer** *noun*

dandelion (say *dan-dee-luy-ən*) *noun*
a wild plant with bright yellow flowers which form light downy balls when they go to seed

Word History: from French words meaning "lion's tooth" (the leaves look like teeth)

dandruff *noun*
small white flakes of dead skin from your scalp

danger *noun*
1 a possible cause of harm or injury: *A careless driver is a danger on the road.*
2 a situation in which harm or injury may happen: *When the volcano erupted the people were in great danger.*

Word Building: **dangerous** *adjective: a dangerous weapon* **endangered** *adjective* put in danger: *an endangered species* **dangerously** *adverb* **dangerousness** *noun*

dangle *verb*
to hang so as to swing to and fro

dank *adjective*
unpleasantly damp or moist: *a dank cave*

Word Building: **dankly** *adverb* **dankness** *noun*

dapper *adjective*
neat and smart

dapple *verb*
to mark with spots or patches: *Sunlight dappled the leaves.*

Word Building: **dappled** *adjective*

dare (rhymes with *pair*) *verb*
1 to be bold or courageous enough: *The teacher was so angry that nobody dared to speak.* **2** to challenge: *I dare you to jump off the roof.*
dare *noun*
3 a challenge to do something risky

Word Building: other forms are **I dared** or **I durst, I have dared, I am daring** □ **daring** *adjective* bold and adventurous **daringly** *adverb*

daredevil *noun*
someone who is very daring or reckless

dark *adjective*
1 with very little or no light: *the dark cave* **2** more like black than white: *a dark colour* **3** angry-looking or gloomy: *He gave us a dark look.*
dark *noun*
4 absence of light: *My little brother is afraid of the dark.* **5** night: *Please come home before dark.*

Word Building: **darken** *verb* to make or become dark **darkly** *adverb* **darkness** *noun*

darkroom *noun*
a room which is sealed so that no light can get in, used for developing and printing film

darling *noun*
someone who is loved very much: *Our new baby is a darling.*

Word Building: **darling** *adjective*

darn *verb*
to mend with crossing rows of stitches: *to darn a hole in my socks*

Word Building: **darn** *noun* a darned patch in clothing

dart *noun*
1 a small metal arrow which is thrown by hand, usually as part of a game or sport
dart *verb*
2 to move suddenly or quickly

dash *verb*
1 to rush or move quickly: *to dash across the road* **2** to throw or smash violently: *to dash a cup to the floor* **3** to spoil or ruin: *to dash someone's hopes* **4 dash off** to write or make quickly: *to dash off a letter*
dash *noun*
5 a sudden or speedy rush **6** a small amount: *a dash of salt* **7** a horizontal line (—) used as punctuation to show a break in a sentence

Word Building: the plural of the noun is **dashes**

dashboard *noun*
the panel in a car or plane which is in front of the driver's seat and has instruments for measuring things like speed, the distance you have travelled and the temperature of the engine

Word Use: a shortened form is **dash**

dashing *adjective*
smartly dressed and high-spirited: *a dashing young man*

Word Building: **dashingly** *adverb*

data (rhymes with *later* or *starter*) *plural noun*
facts or information: *to gather data for a report on schools in Australia*

Word Use: the singular form is **datum** □ you can use either a singular or plural verb with **data:** *Your data is incorrect. / Your data are incorrect.*

database *noun*
a collection of data stored in a computer

date[1] *noun*
1 the day or year of something happening, or a statement of it in numbers: *What's the date of Easter next year? / Today's date is the 29th.* **2** the period of time to which something belongs: *This old coin is valuable because of its early date.* **3** an appointment made for a particular time or someone with whom you have an appointment: *a date with the dentist / Do you have a date for the dance on Saturday?* **4 out of date** old-fashioned: *The dress I bought last year is already out of date.*
date[1] *verb*
5 to mark with a date: *to date a letter* **6** to belong to a particular time: *This vase dates from 50 BC.* **7** to go out with your girlfriend or boyfriend

Word Use: definition 7 is more suited to everyday language
Word Building: **dated** *adjective* old-fashioned
Word History: from Latin words meaning "things given"

date[2] *noun*
the small brown fruit that grows on the date palm tree, which tastes very sweet and is often dried for eating

daub (say *dawb*) *verb*
to cover or coat, especially with something soft or sticky like paint or mud: *to daub a canvas with paint*

Word Building: **daub** *noun* sticky clay or mud: *a hut made of wattle and daub*

daughter (say *daw-tə*) *noun*
someone's female child: *My parents have two daughters.*

daughter-in-law *noun*
the wife of your son

Word Building: the plural is **daughters-in-law**

daunt (say *dawnt*) *verb*
to discourage or make frightened: *We're not daunted by the rain.*

Word Building: **daunting** *adjective*
Word History: from a Latin word meaning "tame" or "subdue"

dawdle *verb*
to waste time by being slow: *to dawdle on your way home*

Word Building: **dawdler** *noun*

dawn *noun*
1 the time of day when it begins to get light **2** the beginning of anything: *the dawn of civilisation*
dawn *verb*
3 to begin: *A new day has dawned.*
4 dawn on to begin to be understood by: *It finally dawned on him that he needs to practise.*

day *noun*
1 the time between sunrise and sunset when the sky is light **2** the 24 hour period between midnight of one day and the following midnight: *There are seven days in a week.* **3** the time when you are actively doing things: *Have you had a good day?* **4** a particular time or period: *There was no television in my grandmother's day.*

Word Use: definition 4 can also be used in the plural form as in *the olden days*

daydream *verb*
to dreamily imagine pleasant things: *I often daydream about horses.*

Word Building: **daydream** *noun* **daydreamer** *noun*

daylight saving *noun*
a system of putting the clock forward by one or more hours during the summer months so as to add more hours of daylight to the time that most people are awake: *6 o'clock in standard time becomes 7 o'clock in daylight saving.*

Word Use: another name is **summertime**

daze *verb*
to stun, confuse or bewilder: *dazed by a knock on the head | dazed by success*

Word Building: **daze** *noun: to be in a daze* **dazedly** *adverb*

dazzle *verb*
1 to make blind by a sudden intense brightness **2** to amaze or surprise: *The children dazzled the audience with their display of gymnastics.*

Word Building: **dazzling** *adjective*

deacon (say *dee-kən*) *noun*
someone who assists a priest and has certain duties in the Christian Church

Word Building: **deaconess** *noun*

dead *adjective*
1 no longer alive or useful: *dead leaves | a dead match* **2** numb or unable to feel anything: *to be dead to pain after an anaesthetic* **3** very tired or exhausted: *She felt dead after chopping wood all day.* **4** complete or absolute: *dead silence*

dead *adverb*
5 completely or absolutely: *You're dead right. | He stopped dead.*

deaden *verb*
to weaken or dull: *Carpet deadens the sound of footsteps.*

deadline *noun*
the latest time for finishing something: *The deadline for your project is next Friday.*

deadlock *noun*
the point which people reach in an argument when neither side will give way

deadly *adjective*
likely to cause death: *a deadly poison*

Word Building: other forms are **deadlier, deadliest** □ **deadliness** *noun* **deadly** *adverb*

deaf (say *def*) *adjective*
1 not able to hear well **2 turn a deaf ear** to refuse to listen

Word Building: **deafen** *verb* to make deaf **deafening** *adjective* **deafeningly** *adverb* **deafness** *noun*

deal *verb*
1 to give out or hand out: *to deal the cards* **2** to do business or trade: *to deal with a biscuit company | to deal in rare books* **3 deal with a** to be about: *This book deals with Australian explorers.* **b** to take action against: *The teacher will deal with the children who broke the window.* **c** to treat or behave towards: *Our teacher always deals fairly with us.*

deal *noun*
4 quantity or amount: *a great deal of noise* **5** an arrangement or agreement: *We made a deal not to fight any more.*

Word Building: other verb forms are **I dealt, I have dealt, I am dealing** □ **dealings** *plural noun* business or connections between people

dealer *noun*
1 someone who buys and sells things: *a car dealer* **2** the player who gives out the cards in a card game

dean *noun*
the head priest in charge of a cathedral

Word History: from a Latin word meaning "chief of ten"

dear *adjective*
1 greatly loved: *a dear friend* **2** costing too much **3 Dear** respected: *Dear Sir or Madam*

Word Building: **dear** *noun* someone you love **dearly** *adverb*

death *noun*
1 the end of life: *A car accident caused his death.* **2** the end or destruction of anything: *the death of our hopes of winning a gold medal* **3 sick to death of** bored and annoyed with

Word Building: **deathly** *adverb* like or as in death: *deathly pale*

debate *noun*
1 an organised discussion: *a debate in Parliament* **2** an organised contest in which two teams of speakers put forward opposite views on a chosen subject

Word Building: **debatable** *adjective* open to question or discussion **debate** *verb* to argue or discuss **debater** *noun*

debit *noun*
1 a record of the money that is taken out of an account, such as your bank account
debit *verb*
2 to charge with a debt: *The central computer will debit your account for this purchase.*

Word Use: compare this with **credit** (definitions 4 and 7)

debonair (say *deb-ə-nair*) *adjective*
cheerful and with pleasant manners

debris (say *deb-ree, də-bree*) *noun*
the rubbish left when something is broken or destroyed

Word Use: the "s" is silent because this word comes from French

debt (rhymes with *met*) *noun*
1 anything that you owe someone else
2 bad debt a debt that will not be paid: *The shopkeeper was owed $1000 in bad debts.*

Word Use: someone who owes you money is your **debtor** and someone you owe money to is your **creditor**
Word Building: **indebted** *adjective*

deca- *prefix*
a word part expressing ten times a given unit: decade, decagon, decahedron

Word Use: other spellings are **dec-**, **dek-**, or **deka-**
Word History: this prefix comes from Greek

decade (say *dek-ayd*) *noun*
a period of time lasting ten years

Word History: from a Greek word meaning "a group of ten"

decaffeinated (say *dee-kaf-ə-nayt-əd*) *adjective*
with the drug caffeine taken out: *decaffeinated coffee*

decagon (say *dek-ə-gon*) *noun*
a flat shape with ten straight sides

Word Building: **decagonal** *adjective*

decahedron (say *dek-ə-heed-rən*) *noun*
a solid shape with ten flat faces

Word Building: the plural is **decahedrons** or **decahedra**

decanter (say *də-kan-tə*) *noun*
a container, often with a spout, for serving wine, water or juice at the table

Word Building: **decant** *verb* to pour gently from one container into another

decapitate *verb*
to cut off the head of

Word Building: **decapitation** *noun*

decathlon (say *də-kath-lən*) *noun*
a contest in which athletes compete for the highest score in ten different events

decay (say *də-kay*) *verb*
to rot or go bad

Word Building: **decay** *noun*

decease (say *də-sees*) *noun*
death: *After his wife's decease Bob stayed home to care for the children.*

Word Building: **deceased** *adjective* dead **deceased** *noun: The will of the deceased was read.*

deceive *verb*
to trick or mislead: *She deceived us by saying she'd found the money when she'd really stolen it.*

Word Building: **deceit** *noun* **deceitful** *adjective* **deceitfully** *adverb* **deceitfulness** *noun*

December *noun*
the twelfth month of the year, with 31 days

Word Use: the abbreviation is **Dec**
Word History: the Latin name for the tenth month of the early Roman year

decent (say *dee-sənt*) *adjective*
1 respectable or proper: *decent behaviour* **2** reasonable or good enough: *to earn a decent wage* **3** kind and helpful: *It was decent of you to give me a lift home.*

Word Building: **decency** *noun* **decently** *adverb*

deception *noun*
a trick or something that deceives

Word Building: **deceptive** *adjective* **deceptively** *adverb*

deci- *prefix*
a word part expressing $\frac{1}{10}$ of a given unit: decimal

decibel (say *des-ə-bel*) *noun*
a measure of loudness used to show how much louder one sound is than another

decide *verb*
1 to make up your mind: *I couldn't work out whether to go or not, but I've decided now.* **2** to judge or settle: *We will ask the teacher to decide the argument.*

Word Building: **decision** *noun*

decided *adjective*
1 definite and obvious: *a decided difference between my writing and yours* **2** having firmly made up your mind: *I tried to persuade him but he was quite decided.*

Word Building: **decidedly** *adverb* definitely

deciduous (say *də-sid-yooh-əs*) *adjective*
losing their leaves every year: *They have a nice mix of deciduous trees and evergreens in their garden.*

Word Use: compare with **evergreen**
Word History: from a Latin word meaning "falling down"

decimal *adjective*
1 based on tenths or on the number ten: *decimal currency*
decimal *noun*
2 a decimal fraction or number

Word Building: **decimate** *verb* to destroy every tenth one or a great number: *The soldiers decimated the enemy in a fierce battle.*
decimalise *verb* **decimally** *adverb*

decimal fraction *noun*
a fraction in which the bottom number is 10, 100, 1 000, 10 000, and so on, usually written with just the top number and a dot in front of it, as $0.4 = \frac{4}{10}$, $0.04 = \frac{4}{100}$

decimal number *noun*
a number consisting of a whole number and a decimal fraction, separated by a dot, such as *4.23*

decimal point *noun*
the dot in a decimal fraction

decipher (say *də-suy-fə*) *verb*
to solve or find the meaning of: *to decipher a code*

Word Use: compare with **cipher**
Word Building: **decipherable** *adjective* able to be understood or read **indecipherable** *adjective* not able to be understood or read

decision *noun*
1 the act of making up your mind: *a difficult decision* **2** an opinion or judgment: *The judge's decision is final.*
3 firmness and certainty in all you think and do: *a man of decision*

Word Building: **decisive** *adjective: a decisive victory*

deck *noun*
1 the floor of a ship or bus **2** an open, raised platform or veranda, usually made of wood **3 on deck** on duty or ready for action
deck *verb*
4 to decorate or dress: *to deck the Christmas tree with tinsel*

Word History: from a Dutch word meaning "cover"

declare (say *də-klair*) *verb*
1 to announce or make known officially: *The government declared war.* **2** to close a cricket innings before all ten wickets have fallen

Word Building: **declaration** *noun* an announcement

decline *verb*
1 to refuse politely: *to decline an invitation / I asked him to the party but he declined.*
2 to become worse or less: *His health has declined. / School attendance declines in wet weather.*

Word Building: **decline** *noun*

decode *verb*
to translate from code into the original language or form: *to decode a message*

Word Building: **decoder** *noun*

decompose *verb*
to rot or break up: *Leaves decomposed under the forest trees.*

Word Building: **decomposition** *noun*

decorate *verb*
1 to make bright and pretty by adding something like paint, wallpaper or streamers: *to decorate a room / to decorate the Christmas tree* **2** to honour with a medal or badge: *to be decorated for bravery*

Word Building: **decor** *noun* the way a room is decorated or furnished **decoration** *noun* **decorative** *adjective* **decoratively** *adverb* **decorator** *noun*

decorum (say *də-kaw-rəm*) *noun*
proper behaviour, speech or dress: *to act with decorum at school assembly*

Word Building: **decorous** *adjective*

decoy (say *dee-koy*) *noun*
something or someone that tempts or lures, especially into danger or into a trap: *The policewoman was used as a decoy to trap the bag thief.*

Word Building: **decoy** *verb*

decrease *verb*
1 to make less or lessen gradually: *I have decreased the amount of sugar I take in my tea. / Cinema audiences have decreased.*
decrease *noun*
2 a gradual lessening or reduction: *There has been a decrease in bus services.*

Word Use: similar verbs are **reduce** and **diminish**

decree *noun*
an official order or command: *a government decree*

Word Building: **decree** *verb* (**decreed, decreeing**)

decrepit *adjective*
made weak or broken down by old age: *a decrepit old man / a decrepit car*

Word Building: **decrepitly** *adverb* **decrepitude** *noun*
Word History: from a Latin word meaning "without noise"

dedicate *verb*
1 to devote or give up completely: *land dedicated for public use / She dedicated her life to helping the poor.* **2** to put the name of someone on, as a sign of thanks or respect: *The author dedicated the book to his wife.*

Word Building: **dedicated** *adjective* **dedication** *noun*

deduce *verb*
to work out by reasoning: *We deduced that he would be late.*

Word Building: **deducible** *adjective* **deductive** *adjective*

deduct *verb*
to take away: *I'm going to deduct a dollar from your pocket money.*

Word Building: **deductible** *adjective*

deduction *noun*
1 an amount taken away: *a deduction from my wages* **2** a conclusion or answer worked out from the facts

deed *noun*
1 something done: *a good deed* **2** a signed agreement, usually about ownership of land

deep *adjective*
1 going far down, in or back: *a deep pool / a deep wound / a deep shelf* **2** being a certain distance down, in or back: *a tank two metres deep* **3** intense or great in amount: *deep sorrow / a deep blue / a deep sleep* **4** hard to understand: *This book is too deep for me.* **5** low in pitch: *a deep voice*

Word Building: **deepen** *verb* **deeply** *adverb* **deepness** *noun* **depth** *noun*

deer *noun*
a large grass-eating animal, the male of which has branching horns or antlers

Word Use: the male is a **buck;** the female is a **doe;** the young is a **fawn**
Word Building: the plural is **deer**

deface *verb*
to damage the appearance of: *Someone has defaced the building by spraying paint on it.*

Word Building: **defacement** *noun*

de facto *adjective*
actually existing although not official or legal: *They decided to recognise the de facto government of the rebels.*

Word History: from Latin words meaning "from the fact"

defame *verb*
to damage the good name of: *The local newspaper defamed the mayor.*

Word Use: similar words are **libel** and **slander**
Word Building: **defamation** *noun* **defamatory** *adjective*

defeat *verb*
1 to overcome or beat in a battle or contest
defeat *noun*
2 the state of being beaten: *Our defeat on Saturday was the first of the season.*

defect (say *dee-fekt*) *noun*
1 a fault or weakness: *a defect in the glass / a defect of character*
defect (say *də-fekt*) *verb*
2 to leave your country without permission, not intending to return

Word Building: **defection** *noun* **defective** *adjective* **defectively** *adverb* **defectiveness** *noun* **defector** *noun*

defence *noun*
1 a protection against attack: *A moat was part of the castle's defence.* **2** an argument in support of something or in answer to a

charge in court: *her defence of Aboriginal land rights | His defence was that he was ill.*

Word Building: **defensible** *adjective* **defensive** *adjective*

defend *verb*
1 to protect or keep safe, especially from attack: *to defend a fort | to defend a title* **2** to support by argument: *He defended me against their unfair statements.*

Word Building: **defendant** *noun* someone who is charged with a crime in a court of law

defer *verb*
to put off until another time: *to defer the exam*

Word Use: a word with a similar meaning is **postpone**
Word Building: other forms are **I deferred, I have deferred, I am deferring** □ **deferment** *noun*

defiance *noun*
a daring challenge to authority or any opposing force

Word Building: **defiant** *adjective* **defiantly** *adverb*

deficient *adjective*
lacking: *This soup is deficient in flavour.*

Word Building: **deficiency** *noun* (**deficiencies**) **deficiently** *adverb*

deficit (say *def*-ə-sət) *noun*
an amount of money lacking: *There is a deficit in the accounts.*

defile *verb*
to make dirty: *Their minds were defiled by reading racist literature.*

define *verb*
1 to explain the meaning or nature of: *The easiest words are the hardest to define.* **2** to fix the limits of: *to define a problem*

Word Building: **definition** *noun* **definitive** *adjective* **definitively** *adverb*

definite *adjective*
1 clearly stated or exact **2** clear or certain: *It is a definite advantage to be able to run fast.*

Word Building: **definitely** *adverb* **definiteness** *noun*

deflate *verb*
1 to let the air out of: *Someone deflated his tyres.* **2** to lower or reduce: *to deflate prices* **3** to make feel less important: *The criticism deflated him.*

Word Building: **deflation** *noun*

deflect *verb*
to turn aside: *The armour deflected the bullet.*

Word Building: **deflection** *noun*

defoliate *verb*
to strip of leaves: *The plague of caterpillars defoliated the trees.*

Word Building: **defoliant** *noun* a chemical used to cause the leaves to fall from a tree **defoliation** *noun*

deformed *adjective*
out of shape: *a deformed leg*

Word Building: **deformity** *noun* (**deformities**) **deform** *verb* **deformation** *noun*

defraud *verb*
to cheat, especially of money

defrost *verb*
1 to remove ice from: *to defrost a refrigerator* **2** to thaw out: *Defrost the chicken before cooking it.*

deft *adjective*
quick and neat: *deft movements*

Word Building: **deftly** *adverb* **deftness** *noun*

defuse *verb*
1 to remove the fuse from: *The army expert defused the bomb.* **2** to calm: *to defuse a tense situation*

defy *verb*
1 to disregard or resist boldly: *Criminals defy the law.* **2** to dare: *He defied him to do his worst.*

Word Building: other forms are **I defied, I have defied, I am defying** □ **defiance** *noun* **defiant** *adjective* **defiantly** *adverb*

degenerate *verb*
to become bad or worse than before

Word Building: **degeneracy** *noun* **degenerate** *adjective* **degenerately** *adverb* **degeneration** *noun*

degrade *verb*
to lower or make worse in character or nature

Word Building: **degradation** *noun*

degree *noun*
1 a step or stage: *He recovered by degrees.* **2** a level: *She experienced some degree of satisfaction.* **3** a unit of measurement for temperature, angles and latitude or longitude **4** an award given by a university

dehydrate *verb*
to cause to lose water or other fluids: *to dehydrate vegetables to preserve them | to be dehydrated by the desert sun*

Word Building: **dehydration** *noun*

deign (rhymes with *rain*) *verb*
to stoop or lower yourself: *The duchess deigned to answer her servant.*

deity (say *dee-ə-tee, day-ə-tee*) *noun*
a god or goddess

Word Building: the plural is **deities**

dejected *adjective*
unhappy or depressed

Word Building: **dejectedly** *adverb* **dejection** *noun*

delay *verb*
1 to make or be late: *The breakdown delayed us. | Don't delay!* **2** to put off or postpone: *We don't want to delay our visit.*
delay *noun*
3 a hold-up or stoppage: *The delay was due to a signal failure.*

Word History: from a Latin word meaning "loosen"

delectable *adjective*
delicious: *delectable food*

Word Building: **delectably** *adverb* **delectation** *noun*

delegate (say *del-ə-gayt*) *verb*
1 to give or pass on to someone else: *The manager delegated her authority to the foreman.*
delegate (say *del-ə-gət*) *noun*
2 a representative or deputy: *There were 50 delegates at the conference.*

Word Building: **delegation** *noun*

delete *verb*
to strike or wipe out: *Delete their names from the list.*

Word Building: **deletion** *noun*

deliberate (say *də-lib-ə-rət*) *adjective*
1 intentional or carefully considered
deliberate (say *də-lib-ə-rayt*) *verb*
2 to consider, or think carefully

Word Building: **deliberation** *noun*

delicacy (say *del-ə-kə-see*) *noun*
1 fineness: *the delicacy of the lace cloth* **2** a tasty or expensive food: *Caviar is a delicacy.*

Word Building: the plural is **delicacies**

delicate *adjective*
1 finely-made or sensitive: *delicate lace | a delicate measuring instrument* **2** easily damaged or weakened: *delicate china | delicate health* **3** pale or soft: *a delicate face | a delicate shade of blue*

Word Building: **deliberately** *adverb* **deliberator** *noun*

delicatessen (say *del-ə-kə-tes-ən*) *noun*
a shop which sells a variety of foods, including cheeses, sausages and other prepared goods

Word Use: also called a **deli** in everyday language

delicious (say *də-lish-əs*) *adjective*
very pleasing to smell or taste: *Thanks for a delicious meal.*

Word Building: **deliciously** *adverb* **deliciousness** *noun*

delight *noun*
1 great enjoyment or pleasure: *The children's faces lit up with delight when they saw their presents.*
delight *verb*
2 to give or have great pleasure: *Their singing delighted everyone. | I delighted in helping them.*

Word Building: **delighted** *adjective* **delightedly** *adverb* **delightful** *adjective* **delightfully** *adverb*

delinquent (say *də-ling-kwənt*) *noun*
a young person who is in trouble with the law

Word Building: **delinquent** *adjective: delinquent behaviour* **delinquency** *noun*

delirious (say *də-lear-ree-əs*) *adjective*
restless, excited and seeing things that aren't there, as when you have a fever

Word Building: **deliriously** *adverb* **delirium** *noun*

deliver *verb*
1 to carry and hand over **2** to help at the birth of: *The doctor delivered her baby.* **3** to cause to move in a certain direction: *The bowler delivered a fast ball.* **4** to give or declare: *to deliver a verdict* **5** to save or set free: *The army delivered the besieged town.*

Word Building: **delivery** *noun* (**deliveries**) **deliverance** *noun*

delta *noun*
the flat rich land at the mouth of a river

delude *verb*
to trick or mislead: *He has deluded them into thinking that he is an honest man.*

Word Building: **delusion** *noun* false belief **delusive** *adjective* **delusory** *adjective*

deluge (say <u>del</u>-yoohj) *noun*
1 a great flood or downpour **2** anything that pours out like a flood: *a deluge of words*

Word Building: **deluge** *verb*

deluxe (say də-<u>luks</u>) *adjective*
of expensive high quality: *a deluxe hotel with gold taps in the bathrooms*

Word History: from French words meaning "of luxury"

delve *verb*
to search deeply: *He delved into his drawers for the papers.*

demand *verb*
1 to ask for, as if it's your right: *He demands an apology.* **2** to need: *This job demands a lot of patience.*
demand *noun*
3 a request or need: *a demand for information | a big demand for sandals*
4 a question

demean *verb*
to lower in people's opinion: *Don't demean yourself by having tantrums at your age.*

demeanour or **demeanor** (say də-<u>meen</u>-ə) *noun*
the way you behave: *Everyone was upset by his rude demeanour.*

demented *adjective*
mad: *For a while she was demented with grief.*

Word Building: **dementia** *noun* madness **dementedly** *adverb*

democracy (say də-<u>mok</u>-rə-see) *noun*
1 a way of governing a country, in which you elect people to form a government on your behalf **2** a country with such a government **3** the idea that everyone in a country has equal rights: *Democracy demands that everyone should have the right to vote.*

Word Building: **democrat** *noun* someone who supports democracy **democratic** *adjective* **democratically** *adverb*
Word History: from the Greek word for "people" added to the Greek word for "rule" or "authority"

demolish *verb*
to knock down or destroy: *to demolish an old building | to demolish an argument*

Word Building: **demolition** *noun*

demon (say <u>dee</u>-mən) *noun*
1 an evil spirit **2** someone who does something with great energy: *She's a demon for tidiness.*

Word Building: **demonic** *adjective*

demonstrate *verb*
to show clearly: *She demonstrated how she felt by bursting into tears.*

Word Building: **demonstrable** *adjective* **demonstrably** *adverb* **demonstrator** *noun*

demonstration *noun*
1 a march or other act to show support: *There was a big demonstration for land rights.* **2** a public showing in order to advertise: *There is a demonstration of power tools in the hardware store.*

demoralise or **demoralize** *verb*
to destroy the confidence of: *Their jeering demoralised him.*

Word Building: **demoralisation** *noun*

demote *verb*
to lower in importance or rank: *We'll demote him from a captain to an ordinary soldier.*

Word Building: **demotion** *noun*

demure *adjective*
shyly well-behaved: *a demure child*

Word Building: **demurely** *adverb*

den *noun*
1 an animal's burrow or shelter **2** a quiet room or place separate from other rooms: *He's reading in his den.*

denim *noun*
a heavy cotton material used to make jeans and other clothes

Word History: from French words meaning cloth "of Nîmes" (a town in France)

denomination *noun*
a religious group, especially in the Christian church

Word Building: **denominational** *adjective*

denominator *noun*
the number under the line in a fraction which shows how many equal parts it may be divided into: *In the fraction* $\frac{3}{4}$, *4 is the denominator.*

Word Use: another word with the same meaning is **divisor** □ compare this with the **numerator**

denote *verb*
to mean or show: *A yellow flag on a ship denotes illness on board.*

denounce *verb*
to speak out against: *He will denounce the traitors.*

Word Building: **denunciation** *noun*

dense *adjective*
closely packed or thick: *a dense crowd / a dense fog* **2** foolish or stupid

Word Building: **density** *noun* (**densities**) **densely** *adverb* **denseness** *noun*

dent *noun*
a small hollow scarring a surface: *The stones made dents on the car.*

Word Building: **dent** *verb*

dental *adjective*
having to do with teeth or dentists

dentist *noun*
someone who is trained to treat your teeth

Word Building: **dentistry** *noun* the work that a dentist does

denture *noun*
a plate with a false tooth or teeth attached, which fits into your mouth

deny (say *də-nuy*) *verb*
1 to say to be untrue: *Henry denies that he stole the mangoes.* **2** to refuse: *She denied us permission to go.*

Word Building: other forms are **I denied, I have denied, I am denying** □ **denial** *noun*

deodorant (say *dee-oh-də-rənt*) *noun*
something which prevents or removes bad smells

Word Building: **deodorise** *verb*

depart *verb*
to go away or leave

Word Building: **departure** *noun*

department *noun*
a division in a large organisation such as a government, a college or a store: *The toy department was on the second floor.*

Word Building: **departmental** *adjective* **departmentally** *adverb*

depend *verb*
1 to rely: *They depend on us to help them.* **2 depend on** to be determined by: *Whether we can afford it depends on how much money we have.*

Word Building: **dependability** *noun* **dependable** *adjective* **dependably** *adverb*

dependant *noun*
someone who relies on or needs the support of another

dependent *adjective*
needing support: *a dependent child*

Word Use: don't confuse this word with **dependant**
Word Building: **dependence** *noun* **dependency** *noun*

depict *verb*
to describe or show in words or pictures: *The artist had depicted a country scene.*

Word Building: **depiction** *noun*

deplete *verb*
to reduce or make less: *Don't eat so much or you'll deplete our provisions.*

Word Building: **depletion** *noun*

deplore *verb*
to regret or be sorry for: *We deplore the bad condition of the house.*

Word Building: **deplorable** *adjective* **deplorably** *adverb*

deport *verb*
to send out of the country as a punishment: *The government threatened to deport all illegal immigrants.*

Word Building: **deportation** *noun* **deportee** *noun*

deportment *noun*
the way you stand

Word Use: a similar word is **carriage**

depose *verb*
to remove from a high position by force: *The general deposed the king.*

Word Building: **deposition** *noun*

deposit *verb*
1 to put down: *She deposited her basket on a chair.* **2** to put away for safekeeping: *She deposited her money in the bank.*
deposit *noun*
3 an amount given as the first part of a payment, or as a promise to pay
4 money placed in a bank **5** a layer which collects on a surface: *There was a fine deposit of dust on the furniture.*

depot (say *dep-oh*) *noun*
1 a place where goods are stored or unloaded **2** a place where buses or trams are kept

deprave *verb*
to make evil in character: *Films showing violence might deprave others.*

Word Building: **depraved** *adjective* **depravity** *noun*

depress *verb*
1 to make miserable: *The bad news depressed him.* **2** to press down: *The man depressed the lever.* **3** to cause to sink lower in level: *to depress the value of their houses*

Word Building: **depressed** *adjective* **depression** *noun* **depressive** *adjective* **depressively** *adverb*

deprive *verb*
to take away or keep from: *to deprive someone of their freedom*

Word Building: **deprived** *adjective* lacking **deprivation** *noun*

depth *noun*
1 deepness or distance downward
2 strength, especially of colour or feeling: *No-one knew the depth of his hatred.*
3 depths the deepest part, especially of the sea

deputation *noun*
people chosen to speak on behalf of the group they belong to

Word Use: a similar word is **delegation**

deputy (say *dep-yə-tee*) *noun*
someone who assists or acts for another person: *The principal's deputy took assembly while she was sick.*

Word Building: the plural is **deputies** □ **deputise** *verb* **deputy** *adjective*

derail *verb*
to run off the tracks or rails on which it is travelling: *The train derailed in the bad weather.*

Word Building: **derailment** *noun* an accident in which a train comes off its tracks

deranged *adjective*
wild and uncontrolled in the way you behave, especially because you are crazy or insane: *The deranged man threw all the books on the floor.*

Word Building: **derange** *verb* to throw into disorder **derangement** *noun*

derelict (say *de-rə-likt*) *adjective*
1 empty and run-down: *They found derelict houses in the abandoned mining town.*
derelict *noun*
2 a poor, homeless and neglected person

Word Building: **dereliction** *noun* neglect: *dereliction of duty*
Word History: from a Latin word meaning "forsaken utterly"

derision *noun*
the act of laughing at or making fun of someone

Word Building: **deride** *verb* **derisive** *adjective* **derisively** *adverb*

derive *verb*
1 to take or receive from somewhere: *She derives her income from two jobs.* **2** to get by working out: *I derived the answer by adding the figures together.*

Word Building: **derivation** *noun* origin **derivative** *adjective* coming from something else

dermatitis (say *der-mə-tuy-təs*) *noun*
dryness and redness of the skin which is itchy or painful

derogatory (say *də-rog-ə-tree*) *adjective*
unfairly critical: *She was upset by derogatory remarks about her family.*

descant (say *des-kant*) *noun*
a tune played or sung above the main tune

descent (say *də-sent*) *noun*
1 the act of coming or going down: *The old lady's descent of the stairs was very shaky.* **2** the downward slope of a mountain or stairway

Word Building: **descendant** *noun* offspring **descend** *verb*

describe *verb*
to give a picture of someone or something using written or spoken words: *He described what happened after we left.*

Word Building: **description** *noun* **descriptive** *adjective*
Word History: from a Latin word meaning "copy off" or "sketch off"

desert[1] (say *dez-ət*) *noun*
a sandy or stony place without enough rainfall to grow many plants

Word History: from a Latin word meaning "abandoned"

desert[2] (say *də-zert*) *verb*
to leave or run away without intending to return

Word Use: be careful – this sounds like **dessert**
Word Building: **deserted** *adjective* abandoned, or lonely **deserter** *noun* **desertion** *noun*

deserts (say *də-zerts*) *plural noun*
something which is deserved, either as a reward or a punishment

deserve *verb*
to be worthy of

Word Building: **deserved** *adjective* **deservedly** *adverb* **deserving** *adjective*

design (say *də-zuyn*) *verb*
1 to draw plans for: *An architect designed the house.* **2** to invent: *He's designed a new type of motor.*
design *noun*
3 a sketch or plan: *Here is my design for a long skirt.* **4** an ornamental design or pattern: *There is a design of roses on the plates.*

Word Building: **designer** *noun*

desirable *adjective*
good or beautiful enough to be wanted: *It's a desirable property in the best part of town.*

Word Building: **desirably** *adverb*

desire *verb*
1 to want very much **2** to ask for: *The king desired his presence at the palace.*
desire *noun*
3 need or craving: *They had a strong desire to laugh. | She has a desire for chocolate.* **4** request: *Tell us your desires and we shall try to grant them.*

Word Building: **desirous** *adjective*

desist (say *də-zist*) *verb*
to stop doing something: *They asked him not to kick his football against their wall and he desisted.*

desk *noun*
1 a writing table, often with drawers or small spaces for papers **2** the place, usually at the front of an office or hotel, where information is given: *Ask at the desk if there is a room vacant.*

desolate *adjective*
1 lonely and without people: *The streets are desolate at 3 a.m.* **2** sad and hopeless: *They felt desolate after losing all their possessions.*

Word Building: **desolate** *verb* **desolately** *adverb* **desolation** *noun*

despair *noun*
a feeling of hopelessness: *We were filled with despair when the train left without us.*

Word Building: **despair** *verb* to lose or give up hope

desperate *adjective*
1 ready to run any risk: *a desperate criminal* **2** tried as a last attempt: *a desperate plan* **3** very bad or dangerous: *a desperate illness*

Word Building: **desperately** *adverb* **desperation** *noun*

despise *verb*
to look down on, especially with hate or scorn: *They despised him for not daring to face the enemy.*

Word Use: a word with a similar meaning is **disdain**
Word Building: **despicable** *adjective* deserving scorn

despondent *adjective*
depressed or down-hearted: *He looks so despondent after losing his game.*

Word Building: **despondency** *noun* **despondently** *adverb*

despot *noun*
a cruel and unjust ruler

Word Building: **despotic** *adjective* **despotically** *adverb* **despotism** *noun*
Word History: from a Greek word meaning "master"

dessert (say *də-zert*) *noun*
the fruit or sweets eaten at the end of a meal

Word Use: be careful – this sounds like **desert**[2]

destination *noun*
the place you're travelling to, or to which something is sent

destined (say *des-tənd*) *adjective*
meant by fate: *We were destined to meet.*

destiny (say *des-tə-nee*) *noun*
fate, or something that had to happen: *To die by dragon's breath was his destiny.*

Word Building: the plural is **destinies** □ **destine** *verb*

destitute *adjective*
without money or the means of getting any: *The father died leaving his family destitute.*

Word Building: **destitution** *noun*

destroy *verb*
1 to wreck completely: *Bombs destroyed the city.* **2** to kill: *The dog was destroyed.* | *She has destroyed my affection for her.*

Word Building: **destroyer** *noun* **destruct** *verb* **destruction** *noun*

detach *verb*
to separate or unfasten: *You detach the top copy and keep it.*

Word Building: **detached** *adjective* unconcerned and aloof **detachable** *adjective*
Word History: from a French word meaning "nail"

detachment *noun*
1 the ability to stand aside and not let your judgment be affected by your feelings **2** a force of soldiers or naval ships set aside for a special task

detail *noun*
1 one of the single or small parts which go to make up a whole: *the details of a story* **2** fine delicate work: *There is a lot of detail in his drawings.*

detail *verb*
3 to report fully: *She was asked to detail her plans.*

detain *verb*
1 to delay or hold up: *I won't detain you much longer.* **2** to keep under control or in prison

Word Building: **detainee** *noun* **detention** *noun*

detect *verb*
to discover or notice: *to detect someone stealing*

Word Building: **detectable** *adjective* noticeable **detection** *noun*

detective *noun*
a policeofficer who is trained to discover who committed a crime

Word Building: **detective** *adjective*

deter (say *də-ter*) *verb*
to prevent or stop from doing

Word Building: other forms are **I deterred, I have deterred, I am deterring** □ **deterrent** *noun*

detergent *noun*
powder or liquid used for cleaning

Word Building: **detergent** *adjective*

deteriorate (say *də-tear-ree-ə-rayt*) *verb*
to become worse: *His health deteriorated as he grew older.*

Word Building: **deterioration** *noun*

determination *noun*
firmness of purpose: *a determination to win*

determine *verb*
to settle on or decide: *I have determined my future course of study.*

Word Building: **determined** *adjective* firm in purpose: *a determined effort*

detest *verb*
to hate or loathe

Word Building: **detestable** *adjective* **detestation** *noun*

detonate *verb*
to explode or cause to explode

Word Building: **detonation** *noun* **detonator** *noun*

detour *noun*
1 a different way round, used when a road is closed

detour *verb*
2 to go by way of a detour

detract *verb*
in the phrase **detract from** to take away some of, or reduce the value of: *Lying will detract from your good name.*

Word Building: **detraction** *noun* **detractor** *noun*

deuce (say *dyoohs*) *noun*
1 a playing card with two spots: *the deuce of hearts* **2** a stage in a game of tennis when both players have a score of 40

devalue *verb*
to lower the worth or value of: *to devalue someone's efforts* | *to devalue the Australian dollar*

Word Building: **devaluation** *noun*

devastate *verb*
to turn into a wasteland: *The fire devastated a large area of bush.*

Word Building: **devastation** *noun*

develop *verb*
1 to make or grow larger: *Exercise develops the muscles.* | *Muscles develop with exercise.* **2** to advance or expand: *Her mind developed with age.* **3** to bring into being: *The gardener developed a new type of rose.* **4** to treat with chemicals so as to

bring out the picture: *to develop a photograph*

Word Building: **developed** *adjective* **developer** *noun* **developing** *adjective* **development** *noun*

deviate *verb*
to swerve or turn aside: *The rocket deviated from its planned course. | to deviate from normal behaviour*

Word Building: **deviant** *noun* **deviate** *noun* **deviation** *noun*

device *noun*
an invention: *This device opens the garage door by remote control.*

Word Use: a similar word is **contraption**
Word Building: **devise** *verb*

devil *noun*
1 a wicked person **2 the Devil** Satan, the chief spirit of evil

Word Building: **devilish** *adjective* **devilishly** *adverb* **devilment** *noun* **devilry** *noun*

devious *adjective*
tricky or deceitful: *His devious ways made a lot of enemies.*

Word Building: **deviously** *adverb* **deviousness** *noun*

devise *verb*
to think out, form, or invent: *to devise a plan*

devoid *adjective*
in the phrase **devoid of** free from or without: *The street was devoid of shade.*

devote *verb*
to set apart for a particular purpose: *to devote an hour to a hobby*

Word Building: **devoted** *adjective: a devoted parent* **devotion** *noun: devotion to duty* **devotee** *noun*

devour *verb*
to eat hungrily

devout *adjective*
sincerely religious

Word Building: **devoutly** *adverb* **devoutness** *noun*

dew *noun*
small drops of water that form during the night on any cool surfaces out of doors

Word Building: **dewy** *adjective* (**dewier, dewiest**)

dexterity *noun*
skill or cleverness, especially in using your hands

Word Building: **dexterous** *adjective*

diabetes (say *duy-ə-bee-teez*) *noun*
a disease in which your body finds it difficult to use sugar and passes it out in your urine

Word Building: **diabetic** *noun* **diabetic** *adjective*

diabolic *adjective*
1 devilish or wicked **2** very difficult or unpleasant

Word Use: similar words for definition 1 are **fiendish** and **satanic** □ another form of the word is **diabolical**

diagnosis *noun*
the working out of what disease a patient has

Word Building: the plural is **diagnoses** (say *duy-əg-noh-seez*) □ **diagnostician** *noun* an expert in making diagnoses **diagnose** *verb* **diagnostic** *adjective*

diagonal *adjective*
a sloping line joining opposite angles of a rectangle or square

Word Building: **diagonally** *adverb*

diagram *noun*
a drawing which explains how something works or is laid out: *a diagram of the engine | a diagram of a racecourse*

Word Building: **diagrammatic** *adjective* **diagrammatically** *adverb*

dial *noun*
1 the face of a clock, radio or measuring instrument: *a speedometer dial* **2** the circle with numbers on a telephone which has finger holes so that you can move it round to make a phone call

Word Building: **dial** *verb* (**dialled, dialling**): *to dial a telephone number*
Word History: from a Latin word meaning "day"

dialect *noun*
a variety of a language spoken in a particular area or by a particular group of people

dialogue *noun*
a conversation between two or more people, especially in a play or story

diameter (say *duy-am-ə-tə*) *noun*
1 the straight line which goes through the centre of a circle from one side to the other **2** the length of such a line

diamond *noun*
1 a very hard precious stone which is clear and sparkling like glass **2** the red four-sided shape on some playing cards

diaphragm (say *duy-ə-fram*) *noun*
1 the sheet of muscle inside your body between your chest and abdomen
2 a thin sheet or membrane, especially in a telephone or microphone

diarrhoea (say *duy-ə-ree-ə*) *noun*
an illness in which watery waste matter passes frequently from your bowel

diary *noun*
a book in which you write down daily events or thoughts

Word Use: don't confuse the spelling with **dairy**
Word Building: the plural is **diaries** □ **diarist** *noun* someone who keeps a diary

dice *plural noun*
1 small cubes marked on each side with a different number of spots, from one to six, used in games **2** any small cubes
dice *verb*
3 to cut into small cubes: *to dice carrots*

Word Building: the singular of the noun is **die**

dictate *verb*
1 to say or read aloud for somebody else to write down: *The manager dictated a letter to his secretary.* **2** to give orders

Word Building: **dictation** *noun*

dictator *noun*
someone who has total power, especially in governing a country

Word Building: **dictatorial** *adjective* **dictatorially** *adverb* **dictatorship** *noun*

dictionary *noun*
a book with an alphabetical list of words, their meanings and pronunciations

Word Building: the plural is **dictionaries**
Word History: from a Latin word meaning "word"

didgeridoo (say *dij-ə-ree-dooh*) *noun*
a pipe-shaped, Aboriginal wind instrument made of wood

Word History: from an imitation of the sound it makes

die[1] *verb*
1 to stop living **2 die down** to pass or fade slowly away: *The wind died down.*
3 die out to become extinct or no longer live on earth

Word Building: other forms are **he died, he has died, he is dying**

die[2] *noun*
1 a tool for cutting, stamping or shaping coins or other metal objects **2** *the singular form of* **dice**

Word Building: the plural of definition 1 is **dies**

diesel engine *noun*
an engine which burns heavy oil, not petrol, with air inside one of its working cylinders

diet *noun*
1 the food you usually eat: *Your diet affects your health.* **2** a particular selection of foods: *a slimming diet | a low-fat diet*
diet *verb*
3 to choose what you eat in order to lose weight or improve your health

Word Building: other verb forms are **I dieted, I have dieted, I am dieting** □ **dietician** *noun* someone trained to give advice about the food you eat **dietary** *adjective* **dieter** *noun*

differ *verb*
1 to be unlike or not the same **2** to disagree

difference *noun*
1 a way of being unlike: *The difference between my sister and me is in our height.*
2 a disagreement or quarrel **3** the amount by which two things differ: *The difference between 6 and 1 is 5.*

Word Building: **different** *adjective* **differentiate** *verb* **differently** *adverb*

difficult *adjective*
hard to do or understand

Word Building: **difficulty** *noun* (**difficulties**)

diffident *adjective*
not confident or sure of yourself: *He is diffident about speaking in public.*

Word Building: **diffidence** *noun* **diffidently** *adverb*

diffuse (say *də-fyoohz*) *verb*
1 to pour out or spread over: *A blush diffused her face.*
diffuse (say *də-fyoohs*) *adjective*
2 scattered or spread out thinly **3** using too many words: *a diffuse speech*

Word Building: **diffusion** *noun*

dig *verb*
1 to break up or turn over with a spade: *to dig the soil* **2** to make by digging: *to dig a tunnel | to dig a garden* **3** to push or poke: *She dug me in the ribs.*

Word Building: other forms are **I dug, I have dug, I am digging** □ **dig** *noun*

digest *verb*
1 to break down in your stomach and intestines for use by your body: *to digest food* **2** to think over and take in mentally: *to digest information*

Word Building: **digestible** *adjective* **digestion** *noun* **digestive** *adjective*

digger *noun*
1 a miner: *a digger on the goldfields* **2** an Australian soldier, especially one from World War I

diggings *plural noun*
a place where miners dig

digit *noun*
1 any of the numerals from 0 to 9 **2** a finger or toe

digital *adjective*
1 having fingers or toes **2** using digits or numbers but no pointers: *a digital clock*

Word Use: compare definition 2 with **analogue**

dignitary *noun*
someone who is in a high position in government or a church

Word Building: the plural is **dignitaries**

dignity *noun*
1 nobleness of mind or manner: *She acted with great dignity despite the rudeness of the others.* **2** a high rank or noble position

digress *verb*
to wander away from the main subject when writing or speaking

Word Building: **digression** *noun* **digressive** *adjective*

dilapidated *adjective*
shabby and in need of repair: *a dilapidated house*

Word Building: **dilapidation** *noun*

dilate *verb*
to make or become wider or larger: *The drops dilated the pupils of my eyes. | The pupils of her eyes dilated.*

Word Use: the opposite is **constrict**
Word Building: **dilatation** *noun* **dilation** *noun* **dilator** *noun*

dilemma *noun*
a situation in which you have to choose between two alternatives: *Her dilemma was that going to the pictures meant missing Justine's party.*

diligent *adjective*
paying careful and unceasing attention: *a diligent scholar*

Word Use: a similar word is **conscientious**
Word Building: **diligence** *noun* **diligently** *adverb*

dill[1] *noun*
a plant bearing a seedlike fruit used in medicine and cooking

dill[2] *noun*
a fool

Word Use: this word is more suited to everyday language

dillybag *noun*
1 a small bag used for carrying food or your belongings **2** a bag of twisted grass or fibre used by Aborigines

Word History: "dilly" comes from an Aboriginal language called Yagara and the English word "bag" is added to it

dilute *verb*
to make thinner or weaker by adding water: *to dilute disinfectant*

Word Building: **dilution** *noun*
Word History: from a Latin word meaning "washed to pieces" or "dissolved"

dim *adjective*
1 not bright: *a dim light | a dim room* **2** not clear to the mind: *a dim idea*

Word Building: **dim** *verb* (**dimmed, dimming**): *to dim the lights of a room* **dimmer** *noun: a light dimmer* **dimly** *adverb* **dimness** *noun*

dimension *noun*
size measured in a particular direction

diminish *verb*
to make or become smaller

diminuendo (say *də-min-yooh-en-doh*) *adverb*
gradually reducing in force or loudness

Word Use: an instruction in music

diminutive *adjective*
1 very small

diminutive *noun*
2 a word which tells you something is small: *"Booklet" is the diminutive of "book".*

dimple *noun*
a small hollow in your cheek

Word Building: **dimple** *verb*

din *noun*
loud noise that goes on and on

dine *verb*
to have dinner

Word Building: **diner** *noun*

dinghy (say *ding-gee*) *noun*
a small rowing boat, especially one that belongs to a launch or ship

Word Building: the plural is **dinghies**

dingo *noun*
an Australian wild dog which is brownish-yellow, has pointed ears and a bushy tail and makes a yelping noise

Word Building: the plural is **dingoes** or **dingos**
Word History: from an Aboriginal language called Dharuk

dingy (say *din-jee*) *adjective*
having a dull dirty colour and looking shabby: *a dingy room*

Word Building: other forms are **dingier, dingiest** □ **dinginess** *noun*

dinkum *adjective*
honest and sincere: *a dinkum friend*

Word Use: this word is more suited to everyday language □ another word is **dinky-di**
Word Building: **dinkum** *adverb* truly

dinner *noun*
1 the main meal of the day, usually eaten about noon or in the evening **2** a formal meal in honour of someone or something

dinosaur (say *duyn-ə-saw*) *noun*
any of a number of very large lizard-like animals which died out millions of years ago

Word History: from a Latin word meaning "terrible lizard"

diocese (say *duy-ə-səs*) *noun*
the district, and the people who live in it, under the care of a bishop

Word Building: **diocesan** *adjective*

diorama (say *duy-ə-rahm-ə*) *noun*
a miniature scene using coloured backgrounds and models and sometimes lights

dip *verb*
1 to put into a liquid for a short time: *I dipped my hand in the river. / to dip the sheep in disinfectant to kill insects* **2** to slope down

dip *noun*
3 a soft tasty mixture that you dip biscuits into **4** a downward slope or hollow: *a dip in the road* **5** a short swim

Word Building: other verb forms are **I dipped, I have dipped, I am dipping** □ **dipper** *noun*

diphtheria (say *dif-thear-ree-ə*) *noun*
a serious infectious disease affecting your throat which makes it hard to breathe and which causes a high fever

diphthong (say *dif-thong*) *noun*
a speech sound made by the tongue gliding from one vowel to another in the same syllable, such as *ei* in *vein*

diploma (say *də-ploh-mə*) *noun*
an official paper proving that you are qualified in a particular field of study: *a diploma in librarianship*

Word Building: **diplomate** *noun* a holder of a diploma

diplomacy (say *də-ploh-mə-see*) *noun*
skill in managing relations between nations or people and keeping them friendly

Word Building: **diplomat** *noun* **diplomatic** *adjective*

direct *verb*
1 to show or tell the way: *I directed the lost motorist to the police station.* **2** to give orders to

direct *adjective*
3 going in a straight line or by the shortest way: *a direct route* **4** quoting the exact words said: *direct speech*

Word Building: **directly** *adverb* immediately **directness** *noun* **director** *noun*

direction *noun*
1 the line towards a certain point or area: *a northerly direction / We went in the direction of the sea.* **2** guidance or instruction: *We got here quickly following your directions.*

Word Building: **directional** *adjective*

directory *noun*
a book containing an alphabetical list of names and addresses, maps or other types of information: *a telephone directory / a street directory*

Word Building: the plural is **directories**

dirt *noun*
1 loose earth or soil: *He fell in the dirt.* **2** anything that is not clean: *I can't get the dirt out of your jumper.*

Word Building: **dirt** *adjective: a dirt road*

dirty *adjective*
1 covered with dirt **2** unfair or mean: *a dirty fight*

Word Building: other forms are **dirtier, dirtiest** □ **dirtily** *adverb* **dirtiness** *noun*

dis- *prefix*
a word part meaning apart, away, *or expressing the opposite: disagree, discount, discredit*

Word History: this prefix comes from Latin

disability *noun*
a lack of strength or power in part of your body which makes it hard for you to do some things: *His short leg was a disability which he struggled to overcome.*

Word Building: the plural is **disabilities**

disabled *adjective*
having been made unable or unfit: *Disabled soldiers receive a pension.*

Word Use: a similar word is **incapacitated**
Word Building: **disable** *verb*

disadvantage *noun*
something that makes what you do more difficult: *Lack of education is a disadvantage.*

Word Building: **disadvantage** *verb* **disadvantageous** *adjective*

disagree *verb*
1 to differ or fail to agree: *The two reports of the disaster disagree on the number of casualties.* **2** to quarrel

Word Building: **disagreement** *noun*

disagreeable *adjective*
1 not to your liking: *a disagreeable task* **2** unpleasant or unfriendly in manner: *a disagreeable person*

Word Building: **disagreeableness** *noun* **disagreeably** *adverb*

disappear *verb*
1 to go out of sight: *He disappeared around the corner.* **2** to cease to exist: *His fear disappeared when he saw his father coming.*

Word Building: **disappearance** *noun*

disappoint *verb*
to fail to satisfy the hopes of: *I disappointed my friends when I lost the race.*

Word Building: **disappointment** *noun*

disapprove *verb*
to have a bad opinion: *My father disapproves of my plan to be an actor.*

Word Building: **disapproval** *noun* **disapproving** *adjective* **disapprovingly** *adverb*

disarm *verb*
1 to take weapons from **2** to reduce the size of your armed forces and weapon supplies **3** to take away anger from: *Her smile disarmed him.*

Word Building: **disarmament** *noun* **disarming** *adjective* **disarmingly** *adverb*

disarray *verb*
to put out of order: *The wind disarrayed her hair.*

Word Building: **disarray** *noun: Her clothes were in a state of disarray.*

disaster (say *də-zah-stə*) *noun*
any sudden terrible happening which causes great suffering and damage

Word Building: **disastrous** *adjective*
Word History: from an Italian word meaning "not having a (lucky) star"

disbelieve *verb*
to refuse to believe

Word Building: **disbelief** *noun*

disc *noun*
1 any thin, flat, circular object **2** *look up* **disk** **3** a gramophone record

discard *verb*
to throw away: *to discard old clothes / to discard an ace in a card game*

Word Building: **discard** *noun*

discern *verb*
1 to see, recognise, or understand clearly: *I can easily discern his handwriting.* **2** to recognise as different: *to discern good from bad*

Word Building: **discernible** *adjective* **discernibly** *adverb* **discerning** *adjective* **discerningly** *adverb* **discernment** *noun*

discharge *verb*
1 to unload: *The ship discharged its cargo.* **2** to fire: *He discharged the gun at the intruder. / The gun discharged.* **3** to give out or off: *The pipe discharged water and steam. / The chimney discharged smoke.* **4** to dismiss from a job **5** to fulfil or pay: *I discharged all my debts.*

Word Building: **discharge** *noun*

disciple (say *də-suy-pəl*) *noun*
1 any follower of Christ, particularly one of the first twelve **2** a follower of any set of ideas or of the person who puts them forward: *a disciple of the peace movement*

Word Building: **discipleship** *noun*

discipline (say *dis-ə-plən*) *noun*
1 training given to teach good conduct or behaviour: *Schools hope their discipline will make us good citizens.* **2** orderliness resulting from this training: *Our teacher keeps good discipline in the class room.* **3** punishment
discipline *verb*
4 to train or control **5** to punish

Word Building: **disciplinarian** *noun* someone who believes in strict discipline **disciplinary** *adjective*

disclose *verb*
to allow to be seen or known: *I disclosed my secret.*

Word Use: a similar word is **reveal**
Word Building: **disclosure** *noun*

disco *noun*
a place or club in which people dance to recorded music

Word Use: the full word is **discotheque**
Word Building: **disco** *adjective: disco music*

discolour or **discolor** *verb*
1 to change the colour of: *The spilt coffee discoloured the cloth.* **2** to change colour or fade: *The carpet discoloured with age.*

Word Building: **discolouration** *noun*

discomfort *noun*
1 lack of comfort or pleasure: *Much to my discomfort, I was asked to recite a poem.* **2** pain or uneasiness: *The accident caused me a lot of discomfort.*

disconcert (say *dis-kən-sert*) *verb*
to cause feelings of embarrassment or distress: *Her accusation disconcerted me.*

Word Building: **disconcerted** *adjective* **disconcerting** *adjective* **disconcertingly** *adverb*

discord *noun*
1 lack of agreement: *discord between the two friends* **2** a combination of musical notes which is unpleasant to listen to

Word Building: **discordance** *noun* **discordant** *adjective*

discotheque (say *dis-kə-tek*) *noun*
look up **disco**

Word Use: another spelling is **discothèque,** because it was originally a French word

discount *verb*
1 to take an amount off the set price: *They discounted everything in the store by half.* **2** to disregard or take no notice of: *to discount someone's explanation*

Word Building: **discount** *noun: a discount of $10*

discourage *verb*
1 to cause to lose courage: *Their defeat discouraged the team.* **2** to try to prevent: *He will discourage her attempts at hang-gliding.*

Word Building: **discouragement** *noun* **discouraging** *adjective* **discouragingly** *adverb*

discover *verb*
to find or find out, especially for the first time: *I discovered a shorter way home. / He discovered he could run very fast.*

Word Building: **discoverer** *noun* **discovery** *noun*

discredit *verb*
1 to lower other people's opinion of: *His rudeness discredited him and his family.* **2** to show to be unworthy of belief: *The new discovery discredited the old ideas.*

Word Building: **discredit** *noun* **discreditably** *adverb*

discreet *adjective*
1 careful to avoid upsetting people: *discreet behaviour* **2** showing ability to keep secrets: *You can confide in a discreet friend.*

Word Building: **discreetly** *adverb* **discreetness** *noun*
Word History: from a Latin word meaning "separated"

discrepancy (say *dis-krep-ən-see*) *noun*
a difference or an unlikeness: *There is a discrepancy between their two stories.*

Word Building: the plural is **discrepancies**

discretion (say *dis-kresh-ən*) *noun*
1 the ability to be discreet: *I can rely on her discretion.* **2** the ability or right to do what should be done: *Use your own discretion.*

Word Building: **discretionary** *adjective*

discriminate *verb*
1 to be able to tell a difference: *A music lover can discriminate between good and bad playing.* **2 discriminate against** to treat unfairly: *We should not discriminate against people because of the colour of their skin.*

Word Building: **discriminating** *adjective* having good judgment **discriminatory** *adjective: discriminatory laws* **discrimination** *noun*

discus (say *dis-kəs*) *noun*
a circular plate for throwing in athletic contests

Word Building: the plural is **discuses** or **disci**

discuss *verb*
to talk over

Word Use: a similar word is **debate**
Word Building: **discussion** *noun*
Word History: from a Latin word meaning "struck apart"

disdain *verb*
1 to look down on with scorn
disdain *noun*
2 a feeling of dislike for anything thought of as unworthy

Word Building: **disdainful** *adjective* **disdainfully** *adverb*

disease *noun*
a sickness which can affect a part or all of any living thing: *a skin disease | a bone disease | a plant disease*

Word Building: **diseased** *adjective: a diseased kidney*

disembark *verb*
to leave a ship or plane

Word Building: **disembarkation** *noun*

disfigure *verb*
to spoil the appearance or beauty of: *Vandals disfigured the monument with paint. | Scars disfigured his face.*

Word Building: **disfigurement** *noun*

disgrace *noun*
1 shame or dishonour **2** a cause of shame: *Unsportsmanlike behaviour is a disgrace to the team* **3 in disgrace** looked at with disapproval: *He is in disgrace because of his lying.*

Word Building: **disgrace** *verb* **disgraceful** *adjective* **disgracefully** *adverb*

disgruntled *adjective*
annoyed and sulky: *He was very disgruntled when he lost the election.*

Word Building: **disgruntle** *verb* **disgruntlement** *noun*

disguise *verb*
to change the appearance of: *He grew a beard and dyed his hair to disguise himself.*

Word Building: **disguise** *noun*

disgust *verb*
1 to cause complete dislike in: *Cruelty disgusts me.*
disgust *noun*
2 strong dislike

Word Building: **disgustedly** *adverb* **disgusting** *adjective* **disgustingly** *adverb*

dish *noun*
1 an open and rather shallow container for serving food **2** a particular kind of food prepared for eating: *a meat and vegetable dish*

Word Building: the plural is **dishes** □ **dish** *verb*

dishevelled (say *dish-ev-əld*) *adjective*
untidy or in disorder: *a dishevelled appearance | Her hair was dishevelled.*

dishonest *adjective*
1 likely to lie, cheat or steal: *a dishonest man* **2** showing a lack of honesty: *a dishonest action*

Word Building: **dishonestly** *adverb* **dishonesty** *noun*

dishonour or **dishonor** (say *dis-on-ə*) *noun*
1 a lack of respect: *His actions show dishonour to his school.* **2** shame or disgrace: *Her actions brought dishonour on her country.*

Word Building: **dishonour** *verb* **dishonourable** *adjective* **dishonourably** *adverb*

disinfectant *noun*
any chemical substance which kills germs

Word Building: **disinfect** *verb*

disintegrate *verb*
to break up into small parts: *The building disintegrated when the bomb exploded.*

Word Building: **disintegration** *noun*

disinterested *adjective*
not directly involved: *It is wise to get a disinterested outsider to settle an argument.*

Word Use: a similar word is **impartial** □ don't confuse this word with **uninterested** which means "not interested"

disjointed *adjective*
not fitting together: *a disjointed account of an adventure*

Word Building: **disjointedly** *adverb* **disjointedness** *noun*

disk *noun*
a thin, flat, circular object used in computers for storing data

Word Use: another spelling is **disc**

dislike *verb*
not to like

Word Building: **dislike** *noun: I have taken a strong dislike to him.*

dislocate *verb*
1 to put out of place: *I dislocated my shoulder when I fell.* **2** to throw into disorder: *The accident dislocated traffic.*

Word Building: **dislocation** *noun*

dismal (say *diz-məl*) *adjective*
feeling or causing deep sadness: *He was quite dismal about his failure.* | *dismal news*

Word Use: a similar word is **gloomy**
Word Building: **dismally** *adverb*

dismantle *verb*
to take apart: *We dismantled our tent.*

Word Building: **dismantlement** *noun*

dismay *verb*
to fill with disappointment or fear

Word Building: **dismay** *noun*

dismiss *verb*
1 to order or allow to leave: *He dismissed his dishonest employee.* | *to dismiss the class* **2** to cause to be out in cricket: *The wicket-keeper dismissed the batsman.*

Word Building: **dismissal** *noun* **dismissive** *adjective*

disobedient *adjective*
refusing to obey: *a disobedient child*

Word Building: **disobedience** *noun*

disobey *verb*
to refuse to obey: *to disobey an order* | *to disobey a teacher*

disorder *noun*
1 confusion or lack of order: *The disorder in my room took hours to clean up.*
2 violence and noise in public: *There was disorder in the streets.*

Word Building: **disorder** *verb* **disordered** *adjective* **disorderly** *adjective*

disorganised or **disorganized** *adjective*
in confusion or disorder: *He has such a disorganised mind it takes him ages to finish a job.* | *a disorganised procession*

Word Building: **disorganisation** *noun* **disorganise** *verb*

dispatch *verb*
1 to send off: *to dispatch a telegram* | *to dispatch a messenger* **2** to put to death or kill

Word Use: another spelling is **despatch**
Word Building: **dispatch** *noun*
Word History: from a French word meaning "set free"

dispel *verb*
to drive off or scatter: *He dispelled my fears.*

Word Building: other forms are **I dispelled, I have dispelled, I am dispelling**

dispensary *noun*
the part of a chemist's shop or hospital where medicines are made up and given out

Word Building: the plural is **dispensaries**

dispense *verb*
1 to deal out: *The courts dispense justice.*
2 to make up from a prescription and give out: *Any pharmacy will dispense that medicine for you.* **3 dispense with a** to do without **b** to get rid of

Word Building: **dispensable** *adjective* able to be done without **dispensation** *noun* **dispenser** *noun*

disperse *verb*
1 to scatter around: *The wind dispersed the leaves on the ground.* **2** to separate and move in different directions: *The crowd dispersed.*

Word Building: **dispersal** *noun* **dispersion** *noun*

displace *verb*
1 to put out of the usual place: *War often displaces families.* **2** to take the place of: *Weeds displaced the flowers in the old garden.*

Word Building: **displacement** *noun*

display *verb*
to show or exhibit: *His face displayed anger. / He displayed his prize roses.*

Word Building: **display** *noun*

displease *verb*
to annoy or cause to be unhappy or angry: *My bad behaviour displeased my parents.*

Word Building: **displeasing** *adjective* **displeasingly** *adverb* **displeasure** *noun*

dispose *verb*
1 to influence or make willing: *The sunny weather disposed her to go to the beach.* **2 dispose of** to get rid of: *I disposed of my old books.*

Word Building: **disposable** *adjective* **disposal** *noun* **disposed** *adjective*

disposition *noun*
1 your personality or particular character: *a happy disposition* **2** arrangement in an order: *the disposition of troops*

dispute *verb*
1 to argue loud and long **2** to argue about or against: *to dispute what to do / to dispute a claim*

Word Building: **disputable** *adjective* open to argument **disputation** *noun* discussion **dispute** *noun* an argument

disqualify *verb*
1 to prevent or make unsuitable: *His income will disqualify him from getting a pension.* **2** to declare unable to compete because a rule has been broken

Word Building: other forms are **I disqualified, I have disqualified, I am disqualifying** □ **disqualification** *noun*

disrespect *noun*
rudeness or lack of respect

Word Building: **disrespectful** *adjective* **disrespectfully** *adverb*

disrupt *verb*
to interrupt or throw into disorder: *The demonstrators disrupted the meeting.*

Word Building: **disruption** *noun* **disruptive** *adjective*

dissect *verb*
to cut apart for close examination: *We dissect plants in biology class.*

Word Building: **dissector** *noun* **dissection** *noun*

dissent *verb*
to disagree or differ: *I dissent from my teacher's view of the matter.*

Word Building: **dissension** *noun* a difference of opinion which is often violent **dissenter** *noun* **dissenting** *adjective*

dissident *noun*
someone who has a different opinion or belief, especially about a particular political system

Word Building: **dissident** *adjective*

dissipate *verb*
1 to scatter or disappear in different directions: *The smoke dissipated in the wind.* **2** to scatter or use wastefully: *He dissipated his money by gambling.*

Word Building: **dissipation** *noun*

dissolute (say *dis-ə-looht*) *adjective*
having a wasteful and immoral way of life

Word Building: **dissolutely** *adverb* **dissoluteness** *noun*

dissolve *verb*
1 to mix or become mixed: *I dissolved the sugar in the water. / Salt dissolves in water.* **2** to bring to an end: *The Queen dissolved Parliament. / The court dissolved the partnership.*

Word Building: **dissolution** *noun*

dissonance *noun*
1 sound that is harsh and unpleasant **2** a combination of musical notes that doesn't sound pleasant

Word Building: **dissonant** *adjective* **dissonantly** *adverb*

distance *noun*
1 the length of a space: *the distance between Adelaide and Perth* **2** a part far away: *The distance was hidden in mist.*

distant *adjective*
far off: *a distant town / the distant future*

Word Building: **distantly** *adverb*

distaste *noun*
a dislike: *He has a distaste for showing his feelings in public.*

Word Building: **distasteful** *adjective* **distastefully** *adverb* **distastefulness** *noun*

distemper *noun*
a disease in young dogs which is easily spread

distend *verb*
to swell or stretch: *Their stomachs distended from over-eating.*

Word Building: **distension** *noun* **distensible** *adjective*

distil *verb*
1 to make pure by heating to a gas and then turning the gas back into a liquid **2** to separate by doing this: *to distil kerosene from petroleum*

Word Building: other forms are **I distilled, I have distilled, I am distilling** □ **distilled** *adjective: distilled water* **distillation** *noun* **distillery** *noun*
Word History: from a Latin word meaning "drip down"

distinct *adjective*
1 separate or different: *They were in distinct groups. / The new uniform is quite distinct from the old one.* **2** clear and unmistakable: *a distinct difference*

Word Building: **distinctly** *adverb* **distinction** *noun* **distinctness** *noun*

distinguish *verb*
1 to mark off as different: *A leopard's spots distinguish it from a tiger.* **2** to recognise a difference: *I can distinguish between the twins by their heights.* **3** to make well-known: *My sister distinguished herself as an athlete.*

Word Building: **distinguished** *adjective* famous

distort *verb*
1 to twist out of shape: *Pain distorted her face.* **2** to change and make incorrect: *to distort the truth*

Word Building: **distorted** *adjective* **distortion** *noun*

distract *verb*
1 to draw away the attention of: *The noise outside the room distracted the class.* **2** to trouble or disturb: *Worry distracted her to the point of illness.*

Word Building: **distracted** *adjective* nervous and troubled **distractedly** *adverb* **distraction** *noun*

distress *noun*
1 great pain, worry or sorrow **2** danger or difficulty: *The lifesaver went to the surfer in distress.*

Word Building: **distress** *verb* **distressful** *adjective* **distressing** *adjective*
Word History: from a Latin word meaning "drawn tight"

distribute *verb*
1 to give or share out: *Santa Claus distributed gifts to the children.* **2** to scatter or spread: *Distribute the manure evenly over the garden.*

Word Building: **distribution** *noun* **distributor** *noun*

district *noun*
1 a particular area, region or neighbourhood: *What district do you live in?* **2** an area marked out for some official purpose: *a postal district*

disturb *verb*
1 to interrupt the quiet, rest or peace of **2** to move or unsettle: *The wind disturbed the smooth surface of the lake.*

Word Building: **disturbing** *adjective* worrying **disturbance** *noun* **disturbingly** *adverb*

disuse (say *dis-yoohs*) *noun*
a stopping of use: *The stables fell into disuse when the horse was sold.*

Word Building: **disused** *adjective*

ditch *noun*
1 a long narrow hollow dug in the earth, used as a drain or channel for carrying water to dry land

ditch *verb*
2 to get rid of

Word Use: definition 2 is more suited to everyday language
Word Building: the plural of the noun is **ditches**

dither *verb*
to be nervous and confused: *They dithered over what to do next.*

Word Use: this word is more suited to everyday language
Word Building: **dither** *noun*

ditto marks *plural noun*
two small marks (") used in writing or printing to show that what is above is repeated

divan (say *də-van*) *noun*
a low bed or couch without a back or arms

dive *verb*
1 to jump, especially headfirst into water **2** to go down suddenly: *The aeroplane dived.*

Word Building: **dive** *noun* **diver** *noun* **diving** *adjective*

diverge *verb*
to branch off: *The road diverged to the left.*

Word Building: **divergence** *noun* **divergent** *adjective*

diverse *adjective*
of many different kinds or forms

Word Building: **diversely** *adverb* **diversify** *verb* **diversity** *noun*

divert *verb*
1 to turn aside from a path or course: *Police diverted the traffic.* **2** to draw off: *I'll divert their attention from you.*

Word Building: **diversion** *noun*

divide *verb*
1 to split up or separate into parts **2** to share out: *I divided the books among the children.* **3** to separate into equal parts, using maths: *to divide 69 by 3*

Word Building: **divisible** *adjective* **divisive** *adjective*

dividend *noun*
1 the number which is divided by another number: *In the sum 16 ÷ 4, 16 is the dividend.* **2** your share of some money which is being given out, especially from the profits of a business

Word Use: compare definition 1 with **divisor**

divine *adjective*
1 having to do with God **2** religious or sacred: *the divine service on Sunday morning radio* **3** wonderful or excellent: *Isn't the weather divine?*

divine *verb*
4 to discover by instinct, magic or guessing: *The gypsy fortune-teller used a crystal ball to divine the future.*

Word Use: definition 3 is more suited to everyday language
Word Building: **diviner** *noun: A water diviner uses a rod to find underground water.* **divination** *noun* **divinely** *adverb*

divining rod *noun*
a forked stick which is said to tremble when a diviner holds it over a place where there is water or metal underground

divinity *noun*
1 a god or divine being **2** the study of religion: *a student of divinity*

Word Use: a similar word for definition 2 is **theology**
Word Building: the plural is **divinities**

division *noun*
1 the act of dividing one number by another number in maths **2** a separation or distribution: *division of the class into four teams* **3** a section or group: *an army division* | *He plays football in the under-twelve division.*

Word Building: **divisional** *adjective*

divisor (say *də-vuy-zə*) *noun*
a number by which you divide another number: *In the sum 16 ÷ 4, 4 is the divisor.*

Word Use: compare with **dividend**

divorce *noun*
the ending of a marriage by a court of law

Word Building: **divorcee** *noun* someone who is divorced **divorce** *verb*

divulge *verb*
to tell or reveal: *I'll tell you a secret if you promise not to divulge it.*

Word Building: **divulgence** *noun*
Word History: from a Latin word meaning "make common"

dizzy *adjective*
having or causing the feeling that you are spinning around: *Don't all talk at once – you make me dizzy.* | *She climbed to a dizzy height.*

Word Use: a similar word is **giddy**
Word Building: other forms are **dizzier, dizziest** □ **dizziness** *noun* **dizzily** *adverb*
Word History: from an Old English word meaning "foolish"

do *verb*
1 to perform or carry out **2** to be the cause of: *to do harm* **3** to deal with: *to do the dishes* **4** to travel: *We did 30 kilometres today.* **5** to serve or be all right for: *This room will do us.* **6 make do** to manage with what you've got

do *noun*
7 a party: *We are having a do next week.*

Word Use: definition 7 is more suited to everyday language
Word Building: other verb forms are **he does, he did, he has done, he is doing**

dob *verb*
1 dob in to name or suggest, especially for an unpleasant job: *We dobbed James in for cleaning up the playground.* **2 dob on** to report or tell on, especially for doing something wrong: *He dobbed on them for breaking the window.*

Word Use: you can also use **dob in** for definition 2 □ this word is more suited to everyday language
Word Building: other forms are **I dobbed, I have dobbed, I am dobbing**

docile (say *doh-suyl*) *adjective*
quiet and easily handled: *a docile horse*

Word Building: **docility** *noun* **docilely** *adverb*

dock[1] *noun*
1 a wharf or pier where a ship ties up when it's in port **2** the part of a large building where trucks can enter to load or unload goods
dock[1] *verb*
3 to come or bring into a dock for loading or repair: *The ship docks at 3 o'clock today.* **4** to join together while in orbit: *The spaceships docked successfully.*

dock[2] *verb*
to cut off or take away a part of: *to dock a dog's tail | They docked his wages because he came to work late.*

dock[3] *noun*
the part of a courtroom where the person on trial is put

docket *noun*
1 a ticket or label on a package stating what is inside **2** a receipt, like one from a cash register, proving that you have paid for goods

doctor *noun*
1 someone who has learnt about diseases and is allowed by law to look after sick people and give them medicine
2 someone who has received the highest degree given by a university: *After many years of research he was made a Doctor of Philosophy.*

Word History: from a Latin word meaning "teacher"

doctrine (say *dok-trən*) *noun*
something that is believed or taught: *a religious doctrine*

Word Building: **doctrinal** (say *dok-truy-nəl*) *adjective* **doctrinally** *adverb*

document (say *dok-yə-mənt*) *noun*
1 a paper giving information or evidence: *Keep an important document like your birth certificate in a safe place.*
document (say *dok-yooh-ment*) *verb*
2 to support or back up with documents: *You must document your case well if you hope to convince the judge.*

Word Building: **documentation** *noun* the documents provided to support a case

documentary (say *dok-yooh-men-tree*) *noun*
a film or radio program about a real event or someone's everyday life

Word Building: the plural is **documentaries**

dodge *verb*
1 to duck or move aside quickly, so as to avoid something: *He dodged the ball just in time. | She dodged when she saw the ball coming towards her.*
dodge *noun*
2 a dishonest trick

Word Building: **dodgy** *adjective* awkward or tricky **dodger** *noun*

doe *noun*
the female of animals such as a deer, rabbit or kangaroo

Word Use: the male animal is usually called a **buck** □ be careful – this sounds like **dough**

doff *verb*
to remove or take off: *to doff your hat*

Word Use: the opposite is **don**

dog *noun*
1 a four-legged mammal which eats meat and may live in the wild, like a dingo or wolf, or may be kept as a pet, like a terrier or German shepherd **2** the male of this type of animal
dog *verb*
3 to pursue or follow closely: *Bad luck dogged him all his life.*

Word Use: the female animal is a **bitch**
Word Building: other verb forms are **I dogged, I have dogged, I am dogging** □ **dogged** *adjective* determined not to give in **doggedly** *adverb*

dogmatic *adjective*
saying what you think very forcefully and expecting others to accept it as true

Word Building: **dogma** *noun* a belief or principle which many people hold to be true: *religious dogma* **dogmatism** *noun* **dogmatist** *noun* **dogmatically** *adverb*

doily *noun*
a small fancy mat that can be put under a cake on a plate or under a vase of flowers

Word Building: the plural is **doilies**
Word History: named after a 17th century draper of London

dole *noun*
1 the dole money paid by the government to help people who are out of work
dole *verb*
2 to give in small amounts: *to dole out the soup*

doleful *adjective*
very sad: *a puppy with doleful eyes*

Word Building: **dolefully** *adverb* **dolefulness** *noun*

doll *noun*
1 a child's toy which is made to look like a person
doll *verb*
2 doll up to dress in your best clothes

Word Use: children often use **dolly** for definition 1
Word History: from "Doll" and "Dolly", short forms of the woman's name "Dorothy"

dollar *noun*
a unit of money, either a coin or a banknote, which is equal to 100 cents and is used in Australia, America and some other countries

Word Use: the symbol for the dollar is "$"

dolphin *noun*
an intelligent, playful sea mammal with a long sharp nose

Word Use: another word for some types of dolphin is **porpoise**

domain (say *də-mayn*) *noun*
1 a territory or realm that is owned or controlled: *The land between the mountains and the sea is in the king's domain.* **2** an area of interest or knowledge: *Geology is not my domain.*

dome *noun*
a roof shaped like the top half of a hollow sphere or ball: *The dome of the cathedral stands out from all the other buildings.*

Word Building: **domed** *adjective*

domestic (say *də-mes-tik*) *adjective*
1 having to do with the home or family: *Cooking, cleaning and washing are domestic tasks.* **2** tame or living with people: *Dogs and cats are domestic animals.* **3** for or from your own country: *Some of the wheat is for domestic use and the rest will be sold overseas.*

Word Building: **domestic** *noun* a servant paid to do housework **domestically** *adverb* **domesticate** *verb* **domesticity** *noun*

dominate *verb*
1 to rule over or control **2** to tower above or overshadow: *The huge gum tree dominates the park.*

Word Building: **dominant** *adjective* most important or influential **dominance** *noun* **domination** *noun*

domineering *adjective*
bossy and overbearing

Word Building: **domineer** *verb* **domineeringly** *adverb*

dominion (say *də-min-yən*) *noun*
1 power to rule or govern: *Australia has dominion over these islands.* **2** the land ruled by one person or government: *Britain and all her dominions*

domino *noun*
a flat piece of wood or plastic marked with a number of dots used to play a game

Word Building: the plural is **dominoes**

don *verb*
to put on: *to don clothing*

Word Use: the opposite is **doff**
Word Building: other forms are **I donned, I have donned, I am donning**

donate *verb*
to give as a gift: *to donate books to the school library*

Word Building: **donation** *noun* a gift, usually of money

donkey *noun*
1 a long-eared mammal, related to a horse **2** someone who is stupid or stubborn

Word Use: another name for definition 1 is **ass** □ the male is a **jackass;** the female is a **jennet;** the young is a **foal**

donor *noun*
someone who gives or donates something: *The Blood Bank is calling for blood donors.*

doodle *verb*
to draw or scribble while you are thinking about something else

Word Building: **doodle** *noun* **doodler** *noun*

doom *noun*
1 a dreadful outcome, fate or death: *The ship struck an iceberg and all the passengers went to their doom.*
doom *verb*
2 to force or condemn to unhappiness or ruin: *The accident doomed him to life in a wheelchair.*

Word Building: **doomed** *adjective*

door *noun*
1 a large piece of wood which can be moved to open or close the entrance to a house, room or cupboard **2** the entrance to a room or house **3** a house or building: *He lives two doors down the street.*

Word Use: definition 2 is also called **doorway**

dope *noun*
1 a stupid person **2** an illegal drug **3** the actual facts or information: *Give me the dope on that new computer.*

Word Use: this word is more suited to everyday language
Word Building: **dope** *verb* **dopey** *adjective*
Word History: from a Dutch word meaning "a dipping" or "sauce"

dormant *adjective*
not active, as if asleep or resting: *Some animals lie dormant during winter.* | *This volcano has been dormant for two hundred years.*

Word Building: **dormancy** *noun*

dormitory *noun*
a big room with many beds, especially in a boarding school or hostel

Word Building: the plural is **dormitories**

dose *noun*
1 the amount of medicine taken at one time **2** an amount of something unpleasant: *a dose of the flu*

Word Building: **dosage** *noun* **dose** *verb*

dossier (say *dos-ee-ə*) *noun*
a bundle of documents containing information about a person or subject: *The police kept a dossier on the bank robber.*

Word Use: a similar word is **file**

dote *verb*
dote on to love so much that you appear to be silly: *She dotes on horses and talks about them all the time.*

Word Building: **doting** *adjective: doting parents* **dotingly** *adverb*

dotty *adjective*
mad or crazy

Word Use: this word is more suited to everyday language
Word Building: other forms are **dottier, dottiest**

double *adjective*
1 twice as big, heavy or strong: *a double helping of mashed potato* | *a double bed*
2 with two parts: *a double ice-cream* | *a word with a double meaning*
double *noun*
3 anything that is doubled: *Four is the double of two.* **4** someone who looks almost the same as someone else: *You look so much like my sister you could be her double.* **5 on the double** very quickly: *Get in here on the double.*
double *verb*
6 to make or become twice as much: *You double four to get eight.* | *The bread doubled in size.* **7** to bend or fold in two: *She doubled up with laughter.* | *to double the handkerchiefs neatly for ironing* **8** to serve or be used in two ways: *The swimming pool doubles as a skating rink in winter.* **9** to carry on a bike or horse: *She doubled me home from school.* **10 double back** to turn back the way you came

double bass *noun*
the largest instrument of the violin family, which has a very deep sound

doublecross *verb*
to betray or deceive by promising one thing and doing another

Word Building: **doublecross** *noun*

doubt (rhymes with *out*) *verb*
1 to be uncertain or unsure: *I doubt that you will get there on time.*
doubt *noun*
2 a feeling of uncertainty or suspicion: *There is some doubt about his honesty.*

Word Building: **doubtful** *adjective* uncertain **doubtfully** *adverb* **doubtfulness** *noun*

dough (rhymes with *slow*) *noun*
1 a mixture of flour and water or milk which is baked to make bread or pastry
2 money

Word Use: definition 2 is more suited to everyday language ☐ be careful – this sounds like **doe**

doughnut *noun*
a ring-shaped cake which is fried and covered in sugar or icing

Word Use: another spelling is **donut**

dour *adjective*
gloomy or stern: *He looks dour and unfriendly.*

Word History: from a Latin word meaning "hard"

douse (rhymes with *house*) *verb*
to throw water on: *to douse a fire to put it out*

dove (say *duv*) *noun*
a bird like a pigeon

dowdy *adjective*
shabby and unfashionable: *She wore dowdy old clothes.*

Word Building: **dowdily** *adverb* **dowdiness** *noun*

down[1] *noun*
1 a time of bad luck or depression: *Life has many ups and downs.* **2** a grudge or a feeling of dislike: *He has a down on me.*

down[2] *noun*
fine soft hair or feathers: *down on his face | a duck's down*

Word Building: **downy** *adjective*

downfall *noun*
1 disgrace or ruin: *Greediness was her downfall.* **2** a heavy fall of rain or snow

downpour *noun*
a heavy fall of rain

downs *plural noun*
open hilly country, usually covered with grass

dowry *noun*
money or property that a woman in some cultures brings to her husband when she marries

Word Building: the plural is **dowries**

doze *verb*
to fall into a light sleep, often without meaning to

Word Building: **doze** *noun*

dozen *noun*
a group of twelve

Word Building: the plural can be either **dozen** or **dozens**

drab *adjective*
1 dull grey or brown: *drab clothes* **2** dull or uninteresting: *drab life*

Word Building: other forms are **drabber, drabbest**

draft *noun*
1 a rough sketch or piece of writing **2** a letter instructing a bank to pay money: *a draft for $200* **3 the draft** the forcing of people to join the armed forces

Word Use: be careful – this sounds like **draught**
Word Building: **draft** *verb*

drag *verb*
1 to pull or move slowly and heavily along: *to drag a cupboard across the room | His feet are dragging after walking so far.* **2** to pass so slowly as to seem endless: *The speech dragged on and on.* **3** to search with nets: *The police dragged the river for the body.*

drag *noun*
4 something that holds you back
5 someone or something very boring: *The party was a drag so we left early.*
6 women's clothes when worn by men: *to be dressed in drag* **7** a car race to see which car can accelerate fastest from a standstill

Word Use: definitions 5, 6 and 7 are more suited to everyday language
Word Building: other verb forms are **I dragged, I have dragged, I am dragging**

dragon *noun*
1 an imaginary fire-breathing monster which was supposed to look like a huge lizard with wings and fierce claws **2** a very strict and bossy old woman **3** a type of lizard like the frill-necked lizard or bearded dragon

Word Use: definition 2 is more suited to everyday language
Word History: from a Greek word meaning "serpent"

dragonfly *noun*
a large harmless insect with a long thin body and four long delicate wings of the same length

Word Building: the plural is **dragonflies**

drain *verb*
1 to draw or flow away gradually: *to drain water from the swimming pool | The colour drained from her face.* **2** to make or become dry by water flowing away: *The dishes are draining on the sink.*

drain *noun*
3 a pipe or channel which carries liquid away **4** anything which uses up or

exhausts: *Buying that new car was a drain on our bank account.*

Word Building: **drainage** *noun*

drake *noun*
a male duck

Word Use: the female is a **duck**; the young is a **duckling**

drama *noun*
1 an exciting, sad or serious play acted on stage, radio or television **2** any exciting event: *the drama of a bank robbery*

Word Building: **dramatic** *adjective* **dramatically** *adverb* **dramatics** *noun*

dramatise or **dramatize** *verb*
1 to take a story and make it into a play **2** to express or show in an exaggerated way: *He dramatises his sadness.*

Word Building: **dramatisation** *noun* **dramatist** *noun*

drape *verb*
1 to hang in loose folds: *to drape a blanket around your shoulders / That material drapes nicely.* **2** to put casually: *Don't drape your legs over the arm of the sofa.*
drape *noun*
3 drapes curtains

Word History: from a French word meaning "cloth"

draper *noun*
a shopkeeper who sells material, such as cotton or linen

drapery *noun*
1 material or cloth **2** a shop selling material or cloth

Word Building: the plural is **draperies**

drastic *adjective*
violent, harsh or extreme: *In an emergency we may need to take drastic action.*

Word Building: **drastically** *adverb*

draught (rhymes with *craft*) *noun*
1 a current of air or wind **2** a drink: *a long draught of water* **3** the depth of water which a ship needs so that it can float: *a draught of 30 metres* **4 draughts** a game played by two people each with twelve pieces which they move diagonally across a checkered board

Word Use: definition 2 is a rather old-fashioned word □ definition 4 is also called **checkers** □ be careful – this sounds like **draft**
Word Building: **draughty** *adjective* (**draughtier, draughtiest**) windy or breezy

draughthorse *noun*
a big strong horse used to pull heavy loads

draughtsman *noun*
1 someone who makes drawings of the plans or designs of things such as bridges, roads and buildings **2** one of the pieces used in the game of draughts

draw *verb*
1 to sketch or make a picture with a pen or pencil **2** to pull, move or take in a particular direction: *to draw your hand away / The ship draws near. / The crowd drew together. / to draw money from the bank* **3** to attract: *The tennis match drew a big crowd.* **4 draw a blank** to look for something unsuccessfully: *I thought my watch was in lost property but I drew a blank.*
draw *noun*
5 the act of drawing or picking: *a lottery draw* **6** something that is picked or drawn: *a lucky draw* **7** a contest where neither side wins: *The match ended in a draw.*

Word Use: be careful – this sounds like **drawer**
Word Building: other verb forms are **I drew, I have drawn, I am drawing** □ **drawing** *noun* a sketch or picture **drawer** *noun* **drawn** *adjective*

drawback *noun*
a disadvantage or inconvenience: *The plan is excellent except for one drawback.*

drawbridge *noun*
a bridge which can be raised or lowered: *After the knights rode into the castle, they pulled up the drawbridge.*

drawer *noun*
1 a container shaped like a box that slides in and out of furniture such as cupboards or desks **2 drawers** roomy underpants

Word Use: definition 2 is a rather old-fashioned word

drawl *verb*
to speak very slowly so that the sounds are long and drawn out

Word Building: **drawl** *noun*

dray *noun*
a low horse-drawn cart without sides, used for carrying heavy loads

Word History: from a Middle English word meaning "sledge without wheels"

dread *verb*
1 to be very much afraid of: *to dread the exams*
dread *noun*
2 great fear or deep awe

Word Building: **dread** *adjective* deeply feared and respected

dreadful *adjective*
1 causing great dread or terror: *a dreadful giant* **2** extremely bad or unpleasant: *The film was dreadful so we left early.*

Word Building: **dreadfully** *adverb* **dreadfulness** *noun*

dream *noun*
1 the thoughts and pictures that pass through your mind when you are sleeping **2** a hope or ambition: *His dream is to become a famous actor.*
dream *verb*
3 to imagine or have a dream **4 dream up** to invent or plan in your imagination

Word Use: definition 4 is more suited to everyday language
Word Building: other verb forms are **I dreamed** or **dreamt, I have dreamed** or **dreamt, I am dreaming** □ **dreamy** *adjective* (**dreamier, dreamiest**) vague or lost in dreams **dreamer** *noun* **dreamless** *adjective*
Word History: from an Old English word meaning "gaiety" or "noise"

Dreamtime *noun*
the time in which the Aborigines believe the earth came to have the form it has now and in which life and nature began

Word Use: another name is **the Dreaming**

dreary *adjective*
dull or depressing: *a dreary afternoon | a dreary sight*

Word Use: a similar word is **gloomy**
Word Building: other forms are **drearier, dreariest** □ **drearily** *adverb* **dreariness** *noun*

dredge *noun*
1 a machine for drawing up sand or mud from the bottom of a river or harbour
dredge *verb*
2 to use a dredge to clear out the bottom of: *to dredge the harbour* **3 dredge up** to find with difficulty: *She finally dredged up some ideas for her story.*

dregs *plural noun*
1 the solid part that settles at the bottom of a drink: *She drank the cup of tea down to the dregs.* **2** a useless or worthless part of something: *the dregs of society*

Word Use: a similar word for definition 1 is **sediment**

drench *verb*
to soak or make very wet: *The rain drenched my clothes.*

Word History: from an Old English word meaning "make drink"

dress *noun*
1 a piece of clothing worn by a woman, which covers her body from her shoulders to her legs **2** clothing in general: *The pictures in that book show the dress of the Middle Ages.*
dress *verb*
3 to put clothes on: *Please dress now. | Wait while I dress the baby.* **4** to treat by cleaning and bandaging: *The nurse dressed the wound.* **5** to arrange or decorate: *They dressed the shop window for Christmas.* **6 dress up a** to put on your best clothes **b** to put on fancy dress or a costume that disguises you

Word Use: a similar word for definition 2 is **apparel**
Word Building: the plural of the noun is **dresses** □ **dress** *adjective: a dress suit* **dressy** *adjective* smart or stylish

dress circle *noun*
a curved section of seats upstairs in a theatre or cinema

dresser *noun*
a piece of furniture with shelves and drawers for dishes, knives and forks

dressing *noun*
1 an act of getting dressed: *Dressing takes her hours.* **2** a sauce for foods: *salad dressing* **3** a bandage for a wound

dressing-gown *noun*
a coat that is worn over your nightclothes

dressing-table *noun*
a piece of furniture for your bedroom, usually with drawers and a mirror

dribble *verb*
1 to flow in small drops: *Sweat dribbled down his forehead.* **2** to let spit flow from your mouth: *Babies are always dribbling.* **3** to move a ball along by a series of kicks or pushes, used in soccer or other games

Word Use: a similar word for definition 1 is **trickle**
Word Building: **dribble** *noun*

drift *verb*
1 to be carried along by the movement of water or air **2** to wander without any

particular aim or direction: *She has spent the last three years just drifting about.*

drift *noun*
3 a general movement or trend: *The drift of public opinion is towards the government.* **4** the general meaning: *Did you get the drift of his argument?*

Word Building: **drifter** *noun* someone who wanders through life without aims or goals

driftwood *noun*
wood that is floating on water or has been washed ashore

drill *noun*
1 a tool for making or boring holes **2** a strict way of training or exercise that is repeated regularly: *The soldiers were doing their marching drill.* | *We must do fire drill once a month.*

drill *verb*
3 to pierce using a drill **4** to train by giving repeated exercises: *She drilled them in their lines for the play.*

drink *verb*
1 to swallow liquid **2** to drink alcohol **3 drink in** to take in by paying attention: *We drank in his words.*

drink *noun*
4 any liquid that can be drunk **5** an alcoholic drink: *We had a drink to celebrate.*

Word Use: a similar word for definition 3 is **absorb**
Word Building: other verb forms are **I drank, I have drunk, I am drinking** □ **drinker** *noun*

drip *verb*
1 to let drops fall: *That tap drips all the time.* **2** to fall in drops: *Rain is dripping from the leaves.*

drip *noun*
3 a falling drop of liquid or the sound it makes **4** a slow injection of liquid into the veins of a sick person **5** a silly or boring person

Word Use: definition 5 is more suited to everyday language
Word Building: other verb forms are **it dripped, it has dripped, it is dripping**

dripping *noun*
fat that has dripped from meat during cooking and which is kept to be used again

drive *verb*
1 to force to go: *to drive the mice away* | *He drives himself hard.* **2** to control the movement of: *Can you drive a car?* **3** to take, go or travel in a car or other vehicle: *I will drive you home.* | *We are driving from Melbourne to Sydney.*

drive *noun*
4 a trip in a car or other vehicle **5** a road up to a private house: *The car was parked in the drive.* **6** energy: *She has a lot of drive.* **7** an effort by many people to get something done: *The club is having a drive to get more members.*

Word Building: other verb forms are **I drove, I have driven, I am driving** □ **driver** *noun*

drive-in *noun*
1 an outdoor cinema where people watch films from their cars

drive-in *adjective*
2 serving customers in their cars: *a drive-in bank*

drizzle *verb*
to rain lightly

Word Building: **drizzle** *noun* **drizzly** *adjective*

drone[1] *noun*
1 a male bee which does not make honey and has no sting **2** someone who is lazy and won't work

drone[2] *verb*
to make a dull continuous sound: *His voice droned on and on.*

Word Building: **drone** *noun* a humming sound

drool *verb*
1 to let spit fall from your mouth: *He was drooling with hunger.* **2 drool over** to have a greedy interest in: *She drooled over her friend's new car.*

droop *verb*
1 to bend or hang down: *His head drooped with tiredness.* **2** to lose courage: *Their spirits drooped when the boat's engine stopped.*

Word Building: **droop** *noun* **drooping** *adjective* **droopy** *adjective*

drop *noun*
1 a small rounded amount of liquid which falls **2** a small amount of anything, especially liquid: *a drop of milk* **3** the distance or length by which anything falls: *That cliff has a big drop.* | *What is the drop of those curtains?* **4** a fall in amount or value: *There has been a drop in prices.*

drop *verb*
5 to fall or let fall: *He dropped onto the chair.* | *She dropped her pencil.* **6** to set down from a car or other vehicle: *I'll drop you at the corner.* **7** to make lower: *to*

drop your voice | *to drop the hem of the dress* **8 drop in** or **drop by** to visit for a short time

Word Building: other verb forms are **I dropped, I have dropped, I am dropping**

drought (rhymes with *out*) *noun*
a long period of dry weather

drove *verb*
to drive cattle or sheep over long distances: *He was droving in Queensland for many years.*

Word Building: **drover** *noun* someone who droves cattle

drown *verb*
1 to die from being under water for too long: *He drowned in the river.* **2** to kill by holding under water **3** to cover up by making a louder sound: *The noise of the traffic drowned her cries.*

drowse *verb*
to be almost asleep

Word Building: **drowsy** *adjective* (**drowsier, drowsiest**) **drowsily** *adverb* **drowsiness** *noun*
Word History: from an Old English word meaning "droop" or "become slow"

drudge *noun*
someone who does boring or hard work

Word Building: **drudge** *verb* **drudgery** *noun*

drug *noun*
1 a chemical substance given to someone to prevent or cure a disease **2** a substance that is habit-forming

drug *verb*
3 to mix a drug with: *His enemies had drugged his drink.* **4** to poison or make unconscious with a drug

Word Building: other verb forms are **I drugged, I have drugged, I am drugging**
Word History: from a Dutch word meaning "dry thing"

drum *noun*
1 a musical instrument with a round hollow body covered with a tightly stretched skin, which makes a deep sound when it is hit **2** a container for petrol or other liquid, in the shape of a drum **3** information or advice: *I'm new here so you'd better give me the drum.*

drum *verb*
4 to beat or play a drum **5** to beat on anything continuously: *She drummed on the desk with her fingers.*

Word Use: definition 3 is more suited to everyday language
Word Building: other verb forms are **I drummed, I have drummed, I am drumming** □ **drummer** *noun*

drunk *adjective*
1 having had too much alcoholic drink

drunk *noun*
2 someone who is drunk

Word Building: **drunkard** *noun* someone who is often drunk **drunken** *adjective: a drunken sleep*

dry *adjective*
1 not wet or damp **2** having little or no rain: *It has been a very dry winter.* **3** thirsty or making thirsty: *This is dry work.* **4** not sweet: *a dry wine* **5** dull or boring: *Her speech was very dry.* **6** funny and able to be expressed in a few words: *She has a dry sense of humour.*

dry *verb*
7 to make or become dry

Word Building: other adjective forms are **drier, driest** □ other verb forms are **I dried, I have dried, I am drying** □ **dryly** or **drily** *adverb* **dryness** *noun*

dry-clean *verb*
to clean with chemicals rather than water

Word Building: **dry-cleaning** *noun* **dry-cleaner** *noun*

dry dock *noun*
a dock from which water can be emptied so that the underneath of ships can be repaired or cleaned

dry ice *noun*
solid frozen carbon dioxide which is used to keep things cold

dual (say dyooh-əl) *adjective*
having to do with two or having two parts: *That plane has dual controls.* | *This book has a dual purpose – to teach you and to entertain you.*

Word Use: be careful – this sounds like **duel**
Word Building: **duality** *noun*

dub[1] *verb*
1 to tap with a sword when making a knight: *The queen dubbed him Sir James.* **2** to give a name to: *We dubbed him "The Rat".*

Word Building: other forms are **I dubbed, I have dubbed, I am dubbing**

dub[2] *verb*
to give a new soundtrack in a different language to: *They dubbed the French film so that it could be understood in Australia.*

Word Building: other forms are **I dubbed, I have dubbed, I am dubbing**

dubious (say dyooh-bee-əs) *adjective*
1 uncertain or doubtful: *I feel dubious about my chances in the exam.* **2** open to suspicion or question: *His intentions were dubious.*

Word Use: a similar word for definition 2 is **questionable**
Word Building: **dubiously** *adverb* **dubiousness** *noun*

duchess *noun*
1 the wife or widow of a duke **2** a woman who holds the same position as a duke

duck[1] *noun*
a waterbird with a flat bill, short legs and webbed feet

Word Use: the male is a **drake;** the female is a **duck;** the young is a **duckling**
Word History: from an Old English word meaning "diver"

duck[2] *verb*
1 to lower suddenly: *She ducked her head just in time to avoid being hit.* **2** to push under water for a moment: *You are not allowed to duck people in this pool.* **3 duck out** or **duck off** to go away for a short time: *I am just ducking out to the shop.*

Word Use: definition 3 is more suited to everyday language
Word Building: **duck** *noun*

duck[3] *noun*
a batsman's score of zero in cricket

duct *noun*
1 any tube or channel by which liquids are carried **2** a tube in your body that carries liquid: *a tear duct*

dud *noun*
someone or something which turns out to be a failure

Word Use: this word is more suited to everyday language
Word Building: **dud** *adjective*

due *adjective*
1 owing and waiting to be paid: *This bill will be due in a month's time.* **2** proper or suitable: *Please treat these glasses with due care.* **3** expected to be ready or arrive: *The train is due at 7 o'clock.* **4 due to** caused by: *There was a traffic delay due to an accident.*

due *noun*
5 something that is owed or deserved, especially praise or credit: *We must give him his due.* **6 dues** payment or fees: *Members must pay their dues next meeting.*

due *adverb*
7 directly or straight: *He sailed due east.*

duel (say dyooh-əl) *noun*
1 an arranged fight with special rules, between two people with weapons such as pistols and swords **2** any fight or contest between two sides

Word Use: be careful – this sounds like **dual**
Word Building: **duel** *verb* (**duelled, duelling**) **duellist** *noun*

duet (say dyooh-et) *noun*
a musical piece for two voices or two performers

duffer *noun*
a stupid person

Word Use: this word is more suited to everyday language

duke *noun*
1 a prince who rules a small country
2 a nobleman of the next highest rank to a prince

Word Building: **dukedom** *noun*

dulcimer (say dul-sə-mə) *noun*
an old-fashioned musical instrument with metal strings that you strike with light hammers

dull *adjective*
1 boring or uninteresting: *a dull talk | a dull trip* **2** stupid or unintelligent **3** not bright or clear: *a dull light | a dull rainy afternoon* **4** not sharply felt: *a dull pain*

Word Building: **dull** *verb* **dullness** *noun* **dully** *adverb*

duly (say dyooh-lee) *adverb*
1 properly or as deserved: *He was duly awarded the prize.* **2** at the proper time: *The train duly arrived.*

dumb (say dum) *adjective*
1 not able to speak **2** silent: *She was dumb with surprise.* **3** stupid or unintelligent: *That was a dumb answer.*

Word Building: **dumbly** *adverb* **dumbness** *noun*

dumbfound *verb*
to make unable to speak, usually because of amazement

dummy *noun*
1 a copy or model of something used for display or to show off clothes: *He was dressing the dummy in the shop window.*
2 a rubber teat given to a baby to suck

Word Building: the plural is **dummies**

dump *verb*
1 to throw down or put down heavily
2 to hand over or get rid of: *He dumps all the worst jobs on me. / They decided to dump the captain when the team kept on losing.*
dump *noun*
3 a place where something is dumped or stored: *a rubbish dump / an ammunition dump* **4** a place or a house that is untidy and in bad condition

Word Use: definition 4 is more suited to everyday language
Word Building: **dumper** *noun* a wave that dumps surfers to the bottom

dumpling *noun*
1 a small ball of dough cooked with stewed meat or soup **2** a type of fruit pudding

dumpy *adjective*
short and fat: *She has a dumpy figure.*

Word Building: other forms are **dumpier, dumpiest**

dunce *noun*
a stupid or unintelligent person

Word History: from John *Duns* Scotus, who lived from about 1265 to about 1308, and whose writing about religion was attacked as being foolish

dune *noun*
a sandhill formed by wind, near the beach or in deserts

dung *noun*
waste product from the bowels of animals

Word Use: a similar word is **manure**

dungarees (say *dung-gə-reez*) *plural noun*
work clothing, usually overalls, made from a rough cotton cloth

dungeon (say *dun-jən*) *noun*
a dark small prison or cell, usually underground: *The prisoners were thrown into the dungeon of the castle.*

dunk *verb*
to dip into a liquid: *I like to dunk biscuits in my coffee.*

dunny *noun*
a toilet, especially an outside one

Word Use: this word is more suited to everyday language
Word Building: the plural is **dunnies**

duo *noun*
a pair, especially of musicians: *a new singing duo*

dupe *verb*
to trick or deceive: *They duped him into believing that they would share the money with him.*

Word Building: **dupe** *noun* someone who has been tricked or deceived

duple *adjective*
having two beats to the bar: *That piece of music is in duple time.*

duplex *noun*
a block of two flats or home units

duplicate (say *dyooh-plə-kət*) *adjective*
1 exactly like another thing: *I would like a duplicate copy of this letter.*
duplicate *noun*
2 something which is exactly the same as something else, usually a copy: *Get me a duplicate of this letter please.*
duplicate (say *dyooh-plə-kayt*) *verb*
3 to make an exact copy: *The secretary duplicated each letter.*

Word Building: **duplication** *noun*

durable *adjective*
lasting for a long time: *School clothes should be made of durable material.*

Word Building: **durability** *noun* **durably** *adverb*

duration *noun*
the length of time that anything continues for: *They went away for the duration of the holidays.*

duress (say *dyooh-res*) *noun*
the use of force or threats to get someone to do something: *She only admitted to the crime under duress.*

Word Use: this word usually has **under** in front of it

dusk *noun*
the time of the evening when it is half light and half dark

Word Use: another word for this is **twilight**
Word History: from a Latin word meaning "dark brown"

dusky *adjective*
1 darkish in colour: *a person with dusky skin* **2** dim or without much light

Word Building: other forms are **duskier, duskiest** □ **duskiness** *noun*

dust *noun*
1 a fine dry powder of earth or other matter
dust *verb*
2 to wipe dust away from **3** to cover lightly: *She dusted her arms with powder.*

Word Building: **duster** *noun* **dusty** *adjective* (**dustier, dustiest**)

duty *noun*
1 what someone feels is the right thing to do: *She decided it was her duty to stay with her sick mother.* **2** what someone has to do because of their position: *These are your duties as leader of the group.* **3** a tax charged by the government: *customs duty* **4 on duty** at work **5 off duty** not at work

Word Building: the plural is **duties** □ **dutiful** *adjective* **dutifully** *adverb*

duvet (say *dooh-vay*) *noun*
a large bag stuffed with feathers and used as a quilt

Word Use: we don't pronounce the "t" because this was originally a French word

dux *noun*
the top student at a school

dwarf (say *dwawf*) *noun*
1 someone or something much shorter than normal **2** a small manlike creature in fairy stories: *Snow White and the Seven Dwarfs*
dwarf *verb*
3 to make seem small: *The tower dwarfed the surrounding buildings.*

Word Building: **dwarfish** *adjective*

dwell *verb*
1 to live: *They dwell in peace and harmony.* **2 dwell on** to continue thinking, speaking or writing about: *It does no good to dwell on your troubles.*

Word Building: other verb forms are **I dwelt, I have dwelt, I am dwelling** □ **dwelling** *noun*

dwindle *verb*
to become smaller or less: *Our hopes are dwindling.*

dye *noun*
1 a liquid that is used to colour cloth, hair and other things
dye *verb*
2 to colour with a dye: *I think I will dye this dress red.*

Word Building: other verb forms are **I dyed, I have dyed, I am dyeing** □ **dyeing** *noun* **dyer** *noun*

dyke *noun*
1 a bank built to hold back the water of a sea or river **2** a toilet

Word Use: definition 2 is more suited to everyday language

dyna- *prefix*
a word part meaning power: *dynamite, dynamo*

Word Use: another spelling is **dynam-**
Word History: this prefix comes from Greek

dynamic (say *duy-nam-ik*) *adjective*
1 having to do with dynamics **2** energetic and forceful: *a dynamic person*

Word Building: **dynamically** *adverb* **dynamism** *noun*

dynamics *plural noun*
1 the science that studies the forces that make things move **2** the forces that are at work in any situation: *the dynamics of government*

dynamite *noun*
1 a substance that makes a powerful explosion when set off: *We will blow up the building with dynamite.* **2** anyone or anything likely to be dangerous or cause trouble

Word Use: definition 2 is more suited to everyday language

dynamo (say *duy-nə-moh*) *noun*
a machine which produces electrical energy

Word Building: the plural is **dynamos**

dynasty (say *din-ə-stee*) *noun*
a series of rulers who are members of the same family

Word Building: the plural is **dynasties** □ **dynastic** *adjective* **dynastical** *adjective*
Word History: from a Greek word meaning "lord" or "chief"

dys- *prefix*
a word part often used in medicine meaning difficulty *or* poor condition: *dyslexia*

Word History: this prefix comes from Greek

dyslexia (say *dis-lek-see-ə*) *noun*
a disability that makes it difficult to learn to read

Word Building: **dyslectic** *adjective* **dyslexic** *adjective*

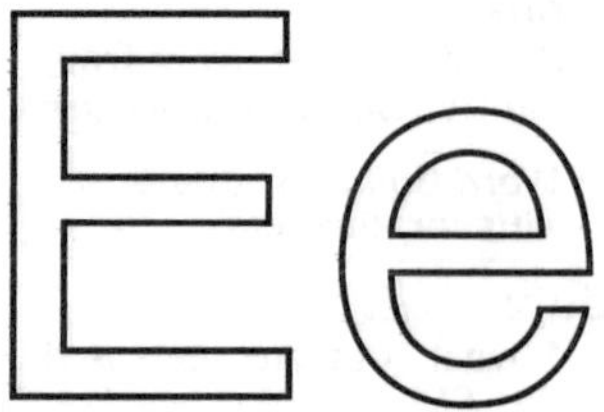

each *adjective*
1 every: *each book in the library*
each *pronoun*
2 every one: *Each of them went away sad.*
each *adverb*
3 for every one: *They cost a dollar each.*

eager *adjective*
keenly wanting or longing: *eager to help*

Word Building: **eagerly** *adverb* **eagerness** *noun*
Word History: from a Latin word meaning "sharp"

eagle *noun*
a large, sharp-sighted, hunting bird with a strong curved beak and claws

Word Building: **eaglet** *noun* a young eagle

ear[1] *noun*
1 the part of the body used for hearing **2** the ability to notice differences of sound: *Marina has a good ear.*

ear[2] *noun*
the top part of a plant such as corn, on which the grain grows

earl (rhymes with *girl*) *noun*
a British nobleman

Word Building: **earldom** *noun*

early *adverb*
1 before the set time **2** at or near the beginning: *Early in her talk she showed slides.*

Word Building: other forms are **earlier, earliest** □ **earliness** *noun* **early** *adjective*

earn (rhymes with *fern*) *verb*
1 to receive in return for working: *They earn $15 a morning.* **2** to deserve to get: *She earned her reputation as a hard worker.*

earnest (say er-nəst) *adjective*
serious or sincere: *I think he is earnest in his desire to help.*

Word Use: the opposite of this is **frivolous**
Word Building: **earnestly** *adverb* **earnestness** *noun*

earphone *noun*
a small listening device placed in or over the ear

earring *noun*
a ring or other ornament that you wear on or through the lobe of your ear

earth *noun*
1 the planet we live on **2** dry land: *Sea used to cover some parts of the earth.* **3** soil, rather than rocks or sand **4** a wire connecting an electrical appliance to the ground, for added safety

Word Building: **earthly** *adjective*

earthenware *noun*
goods, such as pots, made of baked clay

earthquake *noun*
a shaking of the ground caused by movement of rock under the earth's surface

earthworm *noun*
a worm with a body divided into segments, which burrows in soil and feeds on soil and rotting plants and animals

ease *noun*
1 freedom from any problem or discomfort: *He learned to ride with ease.* **2** a free and relaxed manner: *Her ease with people overcame their shyness.*
ease *verb*
3 to give relief or comfort **4** to make less difficult **5** to move slowly and carefully: *They eased the old man into a chair.*

Word Building: easy *adjective* (**easier, easiest**) **easily** *adverb* **easiness** *noun*

easel *noun*
a stand for holding an artist's canvas or a blackboard

east *noun*
the direction from which the sun rises

Word Use: the opposite direction is **west**
Word Building: east *adjective* **east** *adverb* **eastern** *adjective*

Easter *noun*
a Christian festival held each year to celebrate the rising from the dead of Jesus Christ after his death and burial

Word History: named after the Old English goddess of the dawn

eat *verb*
1 to chew and swallow **2** to have a meal: *We eat at twelve.* **3** to wear away

Word Building: other forms are **I ate, I have eaten, I am eating**

eaves *plural noun*
the overhanging lower edges of a roof: *Pigeons have built a nest under the eaves.*

eavesdrop *verb*
to listen secretly

Word Building: other forms are **I eavesdropped, I have eavesdropped, I am eavesdropping** □ **eavesdropper** *noun*

ebb *verb*
1 to flow back or away: *The tide turned and began to ebb.* **2** to fade away: *Her strength was quickly ebbing.*

Word Building: ebb *noun*

ebony (say *eb-ə-nee*) *noun*
a hard, black, shiny wood which is valuable for carving

eccentric (say *ək-sen-trik*) *adjective*
not usual or normal: *eccentric behaviour*

Word Use: the opposite of this is **conventional**
Word Building: eccentric *noun* an eccentric person **eccentrically** *adverb* **eccentricity** *noun*
Word History: from a Greek word meaning "out of the centre"

ecclesiastical (say *ə-kleez-ee-as-tə-kəl*) *adjective*
having to do with the church

Word Building: ecclesiastic *noun* a clergyman

echidna (say *ə-kid-nə*) *noun*
a spiny, ant-eating animal found only in Australia, which lays eggs and feeds its young with its own milk

Word Use: another name is **spiny anteater**
Word History: from a Greek word meaning "viper"

echo (say *ek-oh*) *noun*
1 a repeating sound, when the sound waves bounce off something hard

echo *verb*
2 to repeat or act as an echo: *Our voices echoed in the bare room.* **3** to imitate or repeat: *You are just echoing someone else's ideas.*

Word Building: the plural form of the noun is **echoes** □ other verb forms are **I echoed, I have echoed, I am echoing**

eclipse *noun*
1 the darkness caused when the sun's or moon's light is blocked from the earth

eclipse *verb*
2 to do very much better than: *The brilliant pianist eclipsed everyone else's performance.*

ecology *noun*
the study of the relationship between living things and their environment

Word Building: ecological *adjective* **ecologically** *adverb* **ecologist** *noun*

economical (say *ek-ə-nom-i-kəl*) *adjective*
not wasteful: *She is an economical housekeeper.*

Word Building: economically *adverb*

economy (say *ə-kon-ə-mee*) *noun*
careful management of money or materials

Word Use: a similar word is **thrift**
Word Building: economics *noun* the science of how money is used **economic** *adjective*

ecstasy (say *eks-tə-see*) *noun*
a sudden feeling of great joy

Word Building: ecstatic *adjective* **ecstatically** *adverb*

eczema (say *ek-sə-mə*) *noun*
an itchy or painful rash in which the skin becomes red and flaky

eddy *noun*
a current moving in a circle, especially in a river

Word Building: the plural is **eddies** □ **eddy** *verb* (**eddied, eddying**)

edge *noun*
1 a border or a line where two parts or surfaces meet: *the horizon's edge | the edge of a box* **2** the thin cutting part of something sharp, such as a knife **3 on edge** **a** excited and nervous: *He was on edge about starting school.* **b** cross and annoyed: *The squeaking chalk put him on edge.*

edge *verb*
4 to move slowly and gradually: *to edge your way through the crowd* **5** to put an edge on

Word Building: **edgy** *adjective* cross or nervous

edible *adjective*
able or fit to be eaten: *an edible mushroom*

edict (say *ee-dikt*) *noun*
an order given by a ruler or someone else in authority

edifice (say *ed-ə-fəs*) *noun*
a building, especially a large or impressive one

edit *verb*
1 to be in charge of the publication of: *She edits a magazine.* **2** to read and correct the mistakes of: *She found a lot of spelling mistakes when she edited his story.*

Word Building: other forms are **I edited, I have edited, I am editing** □ **editor** *noun*

edition *noun*
one printing of a book or newspaper: *The afternoon edition of the paper has not come out yet.*

editorial *noun*
a newspaper article written by an editor, which expresses the editor's or the paper's views

Word Use: another word for this is **leader**
Word Building: **editorial** *adjective*

educate *verb*
1 to instruct or give knowledge to: *He also educates the boys in skills such as fencing.* **2** to train: *She has educated her taste away from sweet foods.*

Word Building: **educated** *adjective* **education** *noun* **educator** *noun*

eel *noun*
an edible snakelike fish

eerie (rhymes with *cheery*) *adjective*
frighteningly strange: *The thick fog produced an eerie atmosphere in the mountains.*

Word Building: other forms are **eerier, eeriest** □ **eerily** *adverb* **eeriness** *noun*
Word History: from an Old English word meaning "cowardly"

effect *noun*
1 something which is produced by some cause: *Wrinkles are an effect of age.* **2** the power to produce results: *Threats have no effect on us.*

Word Use: do not confuse this with the verb **affect**
Word Building: **effect** *verb* to make happen

effective *adjective*
having the intended result: *an effective way of doing a job*

Word Building: **effectively** *adverb* **effectiveness** *noun*

effeminate (say *ə-fem-ə-nət*) *adjective*
having qualities thought to be more suited to a woman: *Joseph is effeminate in the way he dresses.*

Word Use: this word is used only of a man, and usually in a disapproving way

effervescent (say *ef-ə-ves-ənt*) *adjective*
fizzy

Word Building: **effervesce** *verb* **effervescence** *noun*

efficient (say *ə-fish-ənt*) *adjective*
able to do something quickly and easily: *an efficient housekeeper*

Word Building: **efficiency** *noun* **efficiently** *adverb*

effigy (say *ef-ə-jee*) *noun*
a picture or statue of a person

Word Building: the plural is **effigies**

effluent (say *ef-looh-ənt*) *noun*
something flowing out, such as the liquid waste from industry, sewage works, and so on

Word Building: **effluent** *adjective* flowing out **effluence** *noun*

effort *noun*
1 the use of physical strength: *It takes a great deal of effort to push a car.* **2** a serious attempt: *If you made an effort you could learn these words.*

Word Building: **effortless** *adjective*

effrontery (say *ə-frun-tə-ree*) *noun*
cheeky rudeness or impudence: *She had the effrontery to tell me I was an old prune!*

e.g.
short for exempli gratia, *Latin words meaning* "for example": *Australia has many wildflowers, e.g. the flannel flower.*

egg *noun*
1 a roundish object produced by a female animal, bird or fish, which contains or grows into its young: *There was a mass of frog's eggs in the pond.* **2** a bird's egg, especially a hen's: *eggs for breakfast*

eggplant *noun*
a large, dark purple, more or less egg-shaped fruit used as a vegetable

Word Use: another name is **aubergine** (say *oh-bə-zheen*)

ego (say *ee-goh*) *noun*
1 the "I" or self of someone: *The ego plays a part in all our thoughts.* **2** conceit or self-importance: *Nothing you say can damage his ego.*

Word Building: the plural is **egos**

egotism *noun*
the habit of thinking and talking about yourself all the time: *His egotism has lost him all his friends.*

Word Building: **egotist** *noun* **egotistic** *adjective*

eiderdown *noun*
a quilt filled with feathers

eight (say *ayt*) *noun*
the number 8

Word Use: be careful – this sounds like **ate**
Word Building: **eight** *adjective: eight legs* **eighth** *adjective: the eighth player*

eighteen *noun*
the number 18

Word Building: **eighteen** *adjective: eighteen holes* **eighteenth** *adjective: your eighteenth birthday*

eighty *noun*
the number 80

Word Building: the plural is **eighties** □ **eighty** *adjective: eighty years old* **eightieth** *adjective: his eightieth birthday*

eisteddfod (say *ə-sted-fəd*) *noun*
a competition of singing, playing music and reciting poetry

Word Building: the plural is **eisteddfods** or **eisteddfodau** □ the second plural is unusual because the word comes from Welsh

either (say *uy-dhə, ee-dhə*) *adjective*
1 one or other of two: *Sit on either chair.* **2** both of two: *There are trees on either side of the path.*

either *pronoun*
3 one or the other but not both: *Take either.*

either *conjunction*
4 used with **or** to show one of two equal choices: *Either come or stay at home.*

Word Building: **either** *adverb: If you don't come, she won't come either.*

ejaculate (say *ə-jak-yə-layt*) *verb*
1 to say or shout suddenly, often because you are surprised: *"Stop right now!", ejaculated the old man.* **2** to send or come out quickly, especially semen from the penis

Word Use: another, less old-fashioned, word for definition 1 is **exclaim** □ another word for definition 2 is **discharge**
Word Building: **ejaculation** *noun*

eject *verb*
to put or send out: *They ejected him from the meeting.*

Word Building: **ejection** *noun*

elaborate (say *ə-lab-ə-rət*) *adjective*
1 worked out in great detail: *an elaborate scheme | an elaborate pattern*

elaborate (say *ə-lab-ə-rayt*) *verb*
2 elaborate on to add details to: *He elaborated on the story.*

Word Building: **elaborately** *adverb* **elaboration** *noun*

elapse *verb*
to pass: *Two weeks elapsed before I saw her again.*

elastic *adjective*
able to be stretched and go back into shape again: *an elastic band*

Word Building: **elasticity** *noun*

elated *adjective*
in high spirits: *She was elated at the thought of the trip to Hong Kong.*

Word Building: **elation** *noun*

elbow *noun*
the joint between the upper and lower arm

elder *adjective*
1 older: *Michael is Con's elder brother.*

elder *noun*
2 an older or senior person: *Listen carefully to your elders. | The elders of the tribe teach the young people.*

Word Use: for other forms see **old**

elderly *adjective*
old or aged: *You should speak clearly to elderly people.*

elect *verb*
to choose by vote: *to elect a member of parliament*

Word Building: **election** *noun* **elector** *noun*

elective *adjective*
1 filled by an election: *an elective position* **2** not required but optional: *an elective subject at school*

Word Building: **elective** *noun* an elective subject

electorate (say *ə-lek-trət*) *noun*
the area, or the people in it, which a member of parliament represents

electrician *noun*
someone who works with electrical appliances and wiring

electricity *noun*
a form of energy from electrons, which can be used for heating, lighting, driving a motor, and other things

Word Building: **electric** *adjective* **electrical** *adjective* **electrically** *adverb*

electrify *verb*
1 to equip for use with electricity: *The railway line has been electrified.* **2** to thrill or excite: *Her news electrified us.*

Word Building: other forms are **it electrified, it has electrified, it is electrifying** □ **electrification** *noun*

electrocute *verb*
to kill by electricity: *A faulty electric toaster could electrocute you.*

Word Building: **electrocution** *noun*

electrode *noun*
a conductor through which electric current enters or leaves a battery, circuit or valve

electromagnet *noun*
a magnet with wire coiled around an iron or steel core, through which an electric current is passed

Word Building: **electromagnetic** *adjective* **electromagnetically** *adverb* **electromagnetism** *noun*

electron *noun*
a very tiny particle inside an atom which has a type of energy that balances the energy of a proton

Word Use: the energy of an electron is called **negative**

electronic *adjective*
worked or produced by small changes in voltage: *an electronic calculator*

Word Use: this word does not mean the same as **electric**, which relates to electric current or energy

elegant *adjective*
graceful or stylish: *elegant manners | elegant clothes*

Word Building: **elegance** *noun* **elegantly** *adverb*

elegy (say *el-ə-jee*) *noun*
a poem expressing sorrow over someone's death

Word Building: the plural is **elegies** □ **elegist** *noun* someone who writes elegies

element *noun*
1 a substance that can't be broken down into anything else: *The compound copper sulfate can be broken down into the elements copper and sulfur.* **2** a wire that is the heating unit of an electric heater, jug or similar electric appliance

Word Building: **elemental** *adjective* simple or basic **elementally** *adverb*

elementary *adjective*
simple or basic

elephant *noun*
a very large animal of Africa or India, with a thick skin and a long nose or trunk used for getting hold of things

Word Use: the male is a **bull**; the female is a **cow**; the young is a **calf**

elevate *verb*
to lift or raise: *The idea of an outing elevated her spirits.*

Word Building: **elevation** *noun*

elevator *noun*
1 a building for storing grain **2** *an American word for a* **lift**

elf *noun*
a small being in fairy stories who often plays tricks on people

Word Building: the plural is **elves** □ **elfin** *adjective* small, bright, or mischievous, like an elf

eligible (say el-ə-jə-bəl) *adjective*
1 ready or qualified: *You are eligible to vote when you are eighteen years old.* **2** suitable to be chosen, especially as a husband or wife: *an eligible bachelor*

Word Building: **eligibility** *noun* **eligibly** *adverb*
Word History: from a Latin word meaning "pick out"

eliminate *verb*
to get rid of or remove: *The early rounds of the tournament will eliminate the weakest players.*

Word Building: **elimination** *noun*

elite (rhymes with *beat*) *noun*
the group of people with the most money, power, and other advantages

Word Building: **elitism** *noun* the idea that a certain group of people should have special advantages **elite** *adjective*

elixir (say ə-liks-ə) *noun*
a sweet liquid medicine: *a cough elixir*

Word History: from a Greek word for "a drying powder for wounds"

elk *noun*
a large deer found in Europe and Asia

ellipse *noun*
an oval shape

Word Building: **elliptical** *adjective*

ellipsoid *noun*
a solid oval, the shape of a football

Word Building: **ellipsoidal** *adjective* like an ellipsoid

elm *noun*
a European tree which loses its leaves in winter

elocution *noun*
the study of good clear speaking

Word Building: **elocutionary** *adjective* **elecutionist** *noun*

elope *verb*
to run away with a lover, usually so that you can get married without the permission of your parents

Word Building: **elopement** *noun* **eloper** *noun*

eloquent (say el-ə-kwənt) *adjective*
able to speak in a flowing, expressive manner

Word Building: **eloquence** *noun* **eloquently** *adverb*

else *adverb*
1 instead: *someone else / who else?* **2** in addition: *What else shall I sing? / Who else it going?* **3** otherwise: *Run, or else you'll miss the train.*

elsewhere *adverb*
in or to some other place: *My friend lives elsewhere now.*

elusive *adjective*
hard to find or get hold of: *an elusive person / an elusive memory*

Word Building: **elusiveness** *noun*

emancipate (say ə-man-sə-payt) *verb*
to set free: *to emancipate a slave*

Word Building: **emancipist** *noun* a convict pardoned by the governor in early colonial times **emancipation** *noun*

embalm (rhymes with *harm*) *verb*
to treat a corpse with chemicals in order to preserve it

embankment *noun*
a mound of earth and stones to keep back water or to carry a road or railway

embargo *noun*
a ban, usually placed by a government on trade of some kind: *an embargo on the export of parrots*

Word Building: the plural is **embargoes**

embark *verb*
1 to go on board for a voyage: *They embarked on the passenger liner.* **2** to start: *They embarked on a new project.*

Word Building: **embarkation** *noun*

embarrass *verb*
to cause to feel uncomfortable: *My mother's old-fashioned ideas embarrassed me in front of my friends.*

Word Building: **embarrassment** *noun*

embassy *noun*
the office and house of an ambassador

Word Building: the plural is **embassies**

embellish *verb*
to make beautiful by decorating: *Carved figures embellished the box.*

Word Building: **embellishment** *noun*

embers *plural noun*
small pieces of live coal or wood remaining from a fire

embezzle *verb*
to steal, usually by making false entries in accounts: *The clerk embezzled $1000.*

Word Building: **embezzlement** *noun* **embezzler** *noun*

emblem *noun*
a badge or something that serves as a sign or symbol: *A horseshoe is an emblem of good luck.*

Word Building: **emblematic** *adjective*

emboss *verb*
to decorate with a design which stands out from its background

embrace *verb*
to hug or cuddle

Word Building: **embrace** *noun*

embroider *verb*
1 to sew decorative patterns on: *to embroider a cushion-cover* **2** to make more interesting with untruthful additions: *to embroider a story*

Word Building: **embroidery** *noun*

embryo (say *em-bree-oh*) *noun*
a young animal or human in the very early stages of growing in the womb

Word Use: compare this word with **foetus**
Word Building: the plural is **embryos** □ **embryonic** *adjective*

emerald *noun*
1 a green precious stone
emerald *adjective*
2 clear bright green

emerge *verb*
to come out into view: *She emerged from behind the trees.*

Word Building: **emergence** *noun*

emergency *noun*
an unexpected serious happening that needs action at once

Word Building: the plural is **emergencies**

emigrate *verb*
to leave your own country to go to live in another

Word Use: do not confuse this word with **immigrate**
Word Building: **emigrant** *noun* someone who emigrates **emigration** *noun*

eminence *noun*
1 a high rank or standing: *She was in a position of eminence in her profession.* **2** a high place: *The house stood on an eminence.*

eminent *adjective*
important or high in rank

Word Use: don't confuse this word with **imminent**
Word Building: **eminently** *adverb*

emit (say *ə-mit*) *verb*
to send or give out: *The fire emits heat.* | *The child emitted a scream.*

Word Building: other forms are **it emitted, it has emitted, it is emitting** □ **emission** *noun*

emotion *noun*
a feeling, such as love, hate, happiness, misery or anger

Word Building: **emotional** *adjective* **emotionally** *adverb*
Word History: from a French word meaning "excite"

emperor *noun*
a man who rules over a group of countries or peoples: *Augustus was the first Roman Emperor.*

Word Building: **empress** *noun*

emphasis (say *em-fə-səs*) *noun*
stress or importance: *The manager placed great emphasis on punctuality.*

Word Building: the plural is **emphases** (say *em-fuh-seez*) □ **emphasise** *verb* **emphatic** *adjective* **emphatically** *adverb*

empire *noun*
1 a group of countries or peoples ruled by an emperor or empress **2** a large and powerful business group controlled by a single person or group of people

Word Building: **imperial** *adjective*

employ *verb*
1 to provide work for: *The factory employs 100 people.* **2** to use: *to employ a spade for digging* | *to employ your spare time in reading*

Word Building: **employee** *noun* someone who works for an employer **employer** *noun* **employment** *noun*

empty *adjective*
containing nothing

Word Building: other forms are **emptier, emptiest** □ **empty** *verb* (**emptied, emptying**) **emptily** *adverb* **emptiness** *noun*

emu *noun*
a large Australian bird which can't fly, related to the ostrich

Word History: from a Portuguese word for an ostrich or a cassowary

emulate *verb*
to try to imitate or be like: *She wanted to emulate the great inventors of the past.*

Word Building: **emulation** *noun* **emulative** *adjective* **emulator** *noun*

emulsion (say *ə-mul-shən*) *noun*
a milk-like mixture, often rather oily

Word Building: **emulsify** *verb* (**emulsified, emulsifying**)
Word History: from a Latin word meaning "milked out"

en- *prefix*
a word part meaning in *or* into: *engrave, engulf*

Word Use: another spelling is **em-**, as in *embalm*
Word History: this prefix comes from Latin

enable *verb*
to make able: *The bridge enables you to cross the harbour.*

enamel *noun*
1 a very hard coating applied to metal **2** a glossy paint

enchant *verb*
1 to cast a magic spell on **2** to delight or charm: *Her singing enchanted us.*

Word Building: **enchanter** *noun* **enchanting** *adjective* **enchantingly** *adverb* **enchantment** *noun*

enclose *verb*
1 to shut or close in on all sides: *A wall enclosed the orchard.* **2** to put in: *I enclose a photograph with this letter.*

Word Building: **enclosure** *noun*

encore (say *on-kaw*) *interjection*
1 once more!

encore *noun*
2 an extra piece of music performed in answer to continued clapping by the audience

Word History: from a French word meaning "again"

encounter *verb*
to meet: *to encounter an old enemy | to encounter an unexpected problem*

Word Building: **encounter** *noun* a meeting

encourage *verb*
to cheer up or cheer on: *We encouraged him after his defeat. | We encouraged the team with shouts and flag-waving.*

Word Building: **encouragement** *noun* **encouraging** *adjective* **encouragingly** *adverb*

encroach *verb*
to go beyond your own area and onto someone else's: *The neighbours' garage encroaches on our land.*

Word Building: **encroachment** *noun*

encyclopedia or **encyclopaedia** *noun*
a book, usually in several volumes, of information arranged alphabetically

Word Building: **encyclopedic** *adjective*

end *noun*
1 the finishing point **2** aim or purpose: *To what end are you doing this?* **3 make both ends meet** to spend no more than you earn

Word Building: **end** *verb* to stop or finish **ending** *noun*

endanger *verb*
to put in danger or at risk: *They endangered their lives going to sea in a leaky boat.*

endeavour or **endeavor** (rhymes with *never*) *verb*
to try or attempt: *We endeavour to do our best.*

Word Building: **endeavour** *noun*

endorse *verb*
1 to sign your name on: *to endorse a cheque* **2** to approve of or support: *to endorse an action | to endorse a candidate*

Word Building: **endorsable** *adjective* **endorsement** *noun* **endorser** *noun*

endow (rhymes with *cow*) *verb*
1 to give money, especially to a school, hospital, and so on **2** to give or equip: *Nature has endowed him with great ability.*

Word Building: **endowment** *noun*

endure *verb*
1 to put up with, especially for a long time **2** to last well: *This car is so strong it should endure for years.*

Word Building: **endurance** *noun* **enduring** *adjective*

enemy *noun*
1 someone who hates someone else, or wishes to harm them **2** an unfriendly armed force which is prepared to fight: *The country was invaded by the enemy.*

Word Building: the plural is **enemies** □ **enemy** *adjective: enemy territory* **enmity** *noun* **inimical** *adjective*

energetic (say *en-ə-jet-ik*) *adjective*
strong and active: *Puppies are very energetic.*

Word Building: **energetically** *adverb*

energy (say *en-ə-jee*) *noun*
1 ability to be vigorous and active: *I haven't the energy for another game.*
2 electrical or other power: *It's wasting energy to leave the lights on.*

enforce *verb*
to make people obey: *to enforce a law | to enforce a school rule*

Word Building: **enforceable** *adjective* **enforcedly** *adverb* **enforcement** *noun* **enforcer** *noun*

engage *verb*
1 to employ: *The old lady engaged a gardener.* **2** to attract or hold the attention of: *She engaged everyone with her witty conversation.* **3** to connect or interlock: *Have you engaged the gears?*
4 to fight: *The two armies engaged in battle.*

Word Building: **engagement** *noun* **engaging** *adjective* **engagingly** *adverb*

engaged *adjective*
1 busy or occupied: *Her telephone is giving the engaged signal.* **2** going to be married: *an engaged couple*

Word Building: **engagement** *noun*

engine (say *en-jən*) *noun*
1 a machine which changes energy from sources like petrol or steam into movement: *The factory replaced its old steam engines with electric motors.* **2** a railway locomotive

Word History: from a Latin word meaning "invention"

engineer (say *en-jən-ear*) *noun*
someone who is trained to design and build things and to use machinery: *His father was an engineer who built roads and bridges. | an electrical engineer | a chemical engineer*

Word Building: **engineer** *verb* to plan or arrange **engineering** *noun*

engrave *verb*
1 to cut with a sharp tool: *The jeweller engraved my name on my watch.* **2** to fix firmly: *The words of the song are engraved in our memory.*

Word Building: **engraver** *noun* **engraving** *noun*

engulf *verb*
to swallow up: *The tidal wave engulfed the coastal village. | Darkness engulfed the houses.*

enhance *verb*
to increase or improve: *A coat of paint should enhance the value of the house.*

Word Building: **enhancement** *noun*

enigma (say *ə-nig-mə*) *noun*
someone or something difficult or impossible to understand

Word Building: **enigmatic** *adjective* puzzling **enigmatically** *adverb*
Word History: from a Greek word meaning "riddle"

enjoy *verb*
1 to get happiness from: *Enjoy your meal.* **2** to have: *He enjoys a reputation for hard work.* **3 enjoy yourself** to have a good time

Word Use: definition 2 is used only with things that people like to have
Word Building: **enjoyable** *adjective* **enjoyably** *adverb* **enjoyment** *noun*

enlarge *verb*
1 to increase in size: *She wants to enlarge the photos.* **2** to give more details: *Could you please enlarge on your first point?*

Word Building: **enlargement** *noun*

enlighten *verb*
to make something clear to: *Would you care to enlighten me?*

Word Building: **enlightened** *adjective* having knowledge or information **enlightenment** *noun*

enlist *verb*
to join the army, navy or air force

Word Building: **enlistment** *noun*

enmity *noun*
strong dislike or hatred

enormous *adjective*
of an unusually large size: *an enormous house with many rooms*

Word Building: **enormity** *noun* **enormously** *adverb* **enormousness** *noun*

enough (say *ə-nuf*) *adjective*
as much as you want or need: *I've had enough ice-cream. | Are there enough kids to make a team?*

Word Building: **enough** *noun* **enough** *adverb*

enquiry *noun*
a question

Word Use: compare this word with **inquiry** ***Word Building:*** the plural is **enquiries** □ **enquire** *verb*

enrage *verb*
to make very angry: *Her cheeky questions enraged the teacher.*

Word Use: another word with a similar meaning is **infuriate**

enrich *verb*
1 to supply with more money **2** to improve the quality of: *Farmers enrich the soil with fertiliser.*

Word Building: **enrichment** *noun*

enrol *verb*
1 to put your name down: *He enrolled to study Italian.* **2** to record the name of: *The teachers enrol everyone on the first day.*

Word Building: other forms are **I enrolled, I have enrolled, I was enrolling** □ **enrolment** *noun*

ensign (say *<u>en</u>-sən, <u>en</u>-suyn*) *noun*
a flag or banner

ensuite (say *<u>on</u>-sweet*) *noun*
a small bathroom joined to a bedroom

Word Use: this word comes from French

ensure (say *en-<u>shaw</u>*) *verb*
to make certain

entangle *verb*
to twist or catch: *The horse entangled his legs in wire.*

Word Building: **entanglement** *noun*

enter *verb*
1 to come or go in: *We entered the house.* / *They entered after us.* **2** to start in: *She entered the race.* **3** to write on a list

enterprise *noun*
1 something to be done, especially something which involves effort or courage: *Running the school fete was quite an enterprise.* **2** the energy and skill you need to do something like that: *She is full of enterprise.*

Word Building: **enterprising** *adjective* resourceful **enterprisingly** *adverb*

entertain *verb*
1 to interest and amuse **2** to have as a guest: *They are entertaining us on Friday night.*

Word Building: **entertainer** *noun* **entertaining** *adjective* **entertainment** *noun*

enthusiasm (say *en-<u>thooh</u>-zee-az-əm*) *noun*
lively interest: *She is full of enthusiasm for her new job.*

Word Use: a similar word is **zeal** ***Word Building:*** **enthuse** *verb* **enthusiast** *noun* **enthusiastic** *adjective*

entice *verb*
to tempt or persuade with promises of money or other advantages

Word Building: **enticement** *noun* **enticing** *adjective* **enticingly** *adverb*

entire *adjective*
whole or unbroken: *She bought the entire set.*

Word Building: **entirely** *adverb* quite **entirety** *noun*

entrails *plural noun*
the intestines

Word History: from a Latin word meaning "within"

entrance[1] (say *<u>en</u>-trəns*) *noun*
1 the act of entering: *to make an entrance at a party* **2** the way in: *The entrance was bolted.*

entrance[2] (say *en-<u>trans</u>*) *verb*
to fill with delight: *The dancers entranced the crowds with their grace.*

entrant *noun*
someone who takes part in a competition: *an entrant in the race*

entreaty *noun*
a serious request: *The doctor came as a result of their entreaty.*

Word Building: the plural is **entreaties** □ **entreat** *verb* to beg

entree (say *<u>on</u>-tray*) *noun*
the small serving of tasty food you eat at dinner before the main course

Word Use: another spelling is **entrée**

entrepreneur (say *on-trə-prə-<u>ner</u>*) *noun*
someone who organises a business enterprise, especially a risky one

Word Building: **entrepreneurial** *adjective* ***Word History:*** from a French word meaning "undertake"

entry *noun*
1 the act of coming or going in: *The space shuttle made a safe entry into the earth's atmosphere.* **2** the way in: *The entry was blocked by a car.* **3** a written record: *In*

her diary there were few entries for that month. **4** someone entered in a competition: *How many entries are there in the essay competition?*

Word Building: the plural is **entries**

envelop (say *en-vel-əp*) *verb*
to wrap or cover: *He enveloped the baby in a large blanket.*

Word Building: **enveloping** *adjective* **envelopment** *noun*

envelope (say *en-və-lohp, on-*) *noun*
a folded paper cover for a letter

environment *noun*
1 the whole surroundings of your life: *He grew up in a country town environment.* **2** the physical conditions of a place, such as weather, water and vegetation

Word Building: **environmentalist** *noun* someone who is concerned about protecting the natural environment **environmental** *adjective*

environs (say *en-vuy-rənz*) *plural noun*
the surrounding districts: *the environs of Brisbane*

envoy *noun*
someone sent as a representative: *Envoys from each country met to discuss trade.*

envy *noun*
the desire for someone else's possessions or success: *Instead of enjoying what he has, he is full of envy of others.*

Word Building: **enviable** *adjective* worth wanting **envious** *adjective* full of envy **envy** *verb* (**envied, envying**) **enviably** *adverb*

enzyme (say *en-zuym*) *noun*
an animal protein which produces a chemical change: *Enzymes help to digest the food we eat.*

eon *noun*
another way of spelling **aeon**

epaulet (say *ep-ə-let*) *noun*
a fancy shoulder piece worn on uniforms

ephemeral (say *ə-fem-ə-rəl*) *adjective*
not lasting long: *She blows up quickly but her anger is ephemeral.*

Word Use: another word with a similar meaning is **transitory**
Word Building: **ephemerally** *adverb*

epi- *prefix*
a word part meaning **1** in addition to: *epilogue* **2** near: *epidemic* **3** on: *epitaph* **4** against: *epigram*

Word Use: other spellings are **ep-** or **eph-**
Word History: this prefix comes from Greek

epic *noun*
1 a long poem about heroic deeds
epic *adjective*
2 grand or heroic: *an epic journey across the desert*

epidemic *noun*
a lot of cases of an illness in a short period of time: *There is an epidemic of measles at the school.*

Word Building: **epidemic** *adjective* **epidemically** *adverb*

epigram *noun*
a short and witty saying

Word Building: **epigrammatic** *adjective* **epigrammatically** *adverb*

epilepsy *noun*
an illness which produces fits of unconsciousness and uncontrollable movements of the body

Word Building: **epileptic** *adjective* **epileptic** *noun* **epileptically** *adverb*

epilogue (say *ep-ə-log*) *noun*
a short section at the end of a play or written work which acts as a conclusion: *The author has added his more recent views as an epilogue to his book.*

episode *noun*
1 an event in your life: *an episode from my past* **2** one in a series of scenes or chapters: *They watched the last episode of the serial on TV last night.*

Word Building: **episodic** *adjective* **episodical** *adjective* **episodically** *adverb*
Word History: from a Greek word meaning "coming in besides"

epistle (say *ə-pis-əl*) *noun*
1 a letter **2 Epistle** one of the letters in the New Testament of the Bible

Word Use: definition 1 is old-fashioned and is mostly used jokingly

epitaph (say *ep-ə-tahf*) *noun*
the words, sometimes in verse, written on a gravestone in memory of the dead person

epitome (say *ə-pit-ə-mee*) *noun*
the most typical example of: *With his fair hair and his suntan he is the epitome of a surfer.*

Word Building: **epitomise** *verb*

epoch (say *ee-pok*) *noun*
a period of time in history or geology: *in the epoch of the Napoleonic wars*

equal (say *ee-kwəl*) *adjective*
1 of the same number, value, or other quality: *Everyone's share is equal.*
2 evenly matched: *It's an equal fight.*

equal *verb*
3 to add up to the same number as: *I know that 5 plus 3 equals 8.* **4** to match: *The hurdler couldn't equal the record.*

Word Building: other verb forms are **I equalled, I have equalled, I am equalling** □ **equal** *noun* **equally** *adverb* **equalise** *verb* **equality** *noun*

equation *noun*
a mathematical expression in which two quantities are said to be equal, such as $12 \times \frac{1}{4} = 3$

Word Building: **equate** *verb*

equator (say *ə-kway-tə*) *noun*
the imaginary circle around the earth, halfway between the poles, where the climate is mostly hot and wet

Word Building: **equatorial** *adjective*

equestrian (say *ə-kwes-tree-ən*) *adjective*
having to do with horses or horse-riding

equi- *prefix*
a word part meaning equal: *equilateral, equilibrium*

Word History: this prefix comes from Latin

equilateral (say *eek-wə-lat-rəl*) *adjective*
equal-sided: *an equilateral triangle*

equilibrium (say *eek-wə-lib-ree-əm*) *noun*
1 equal balance: *The children kept the see-saw in equilibrium.* **2** steadiness of feelings: *At first she was upset but soon recovered her equilibrium.*

equip *verb*
to provide with whatever is needed to do something: *to equip with camping gear*

Word Building: other forms are **I equipped, I have equipped, I am equipping** □ **equipment** *noun*

equivalent (say *ə-kwiv-ə-lənt*) *adjective*
equal or matching: *An admiral in the navy is equivalent to a general in the army.*

Word Building: **equivalence** *noun* **equivalently** *adverb*

era (rhymes with *nearer*) *noun*
any long period of time with a special characteristic: *the era of the steam train*

eradicate *verb*
to root out or destroy: *to eradicate crime*

Word Building: **eradicable** *adjective* **eradication** *noun* **eradicator** *noun*

erase *verb*
to rub out or wipe off: *Use a rubber to erase your mistakes.*

Word Building: **eraser** *noun* **erasure** *noun*

erect *adjective*
1 upright: *to sit with an erect back*

erect *verb*
2 to build: *They have erected a house on the spare block.*

Word Building: **erectly** *adverb* **erection** *noun* **erectness** *noun*

ermine (say *er-mən*) *noun*
the white winter fur of the stoat

erosion *noun*
the cracking and wearing away of the soil by weather

Word Building: **erode** *verb*

erotic *adjective*
having to do with sexual love

Word Building: **erotica** *noun* art or literature that deals with sexual love **erotically** *adverb* **eroticism** *noun*

err *verb*
1 to make a mistake: *I must have erred about the street number.* **2** to do wrong: *He admitted that he had erred by telling a lie.*

Word Building: **erring** *adjective*

errand *noun*
a small task you are sent to do: *I went to town on an errand for my father.*

erratic *adjective*
unsteady and irregular in behaviour or movement

Word Building: **erratically** *adverb*

error *noun*
1 a mistake **2** wrongdoing: *She has seen the error of her ways.*

Word Building: **erratum** *noun* a mistake in printing or writing **erroneous** *adjective* incorrect **erroneously** *adverb*

erupt *verb*
to explode or burst out: *The volcano has erupted.*

Word Building: **eruption** *noun* **eruptive** *adjective*

escalate (say *es-kə-layt*) *verb*
to make or become larger or greater: *to escalate a war / to escalate prices*

Word Building: **escalation** *noun*

escalator (say *es-kə-lay-tə*) *noun*
a continuously moving stairway

escapade (say *es-kə-payd*) *noun*
a reckless adventure

escape *verb*
1 to get away: *He escaped from prison.* **2** to avoid: *She escaped injury.*

Word Building: **escape** *noun* **escapee** *noun* **escaper** *noun*

escort *noun*
1 someone who goes along with someone else as a guard or to show respect: *a police escort* **2** someone who goes with you to a dance or party: *Her escort for the dinner was late.*

Word Building: **escort** *verb: to escort her home*

Eskimo *noun*
one of the race of people from the cold north of Canada, Siberia, Greenland and Alaska

Word Building: the plural is **Eskimos** or **Eskimo**
Word History: from an Algonquian (a language of some American Indian tribes) name for these people, meaning "eaters of raw flesh"

especially *adverb*
particularly or more than usually: *to be especially careful / to do especially well*

Word Building: **especial** *adjective: a painting of especial importance / to take especial care*

espionage (say *es-pee-ən-ahzh*) *noun*
the practice of spying

espresso *noun*
coffee made in a machine which forces steam through crushed coffee beans

Word Use: this word comes from Italian

esquire *noun*
the polite title after a man's name, usually shortened to *Esq.*, which is sometimes used instead of "Mr" or "Dr": *Robert Jones, Esq.*

essay *noun*
a short piece of writing on a particular subject: *The teacher hasn't marked our essays on the causes of World War I.*

Word Building: **essayist** *noun* someone who writes essays
Word History: from a Latin word meaning "a weighing"

essence *noun*
1 the basic nature: *The artist has caught the essence of the Prime Minister in that portrait.* **2** the concentrated liquid from a substance: *vanilla essence*

essential (say *ə-sen-shəl*) *adjective*
absolutely necessary: *Flour is an essential ingredient in bread.*

Word Building: **essential** *noun* the main part **essentially** *adverb*

establish *verb*
1 to set up: *They have established a new school.* **2** to settle: *We have established ourselves in the new neighbourhood.* **3** to prove: *We can't establish the truth of what he says.*

Word Building: **establishment** *noun*

estate *noun*
1 an area of land in the country, especially a large and valuable one: *Her uncle has an estate where he breeds racehorses.* **2** the possessions and property of a person who has died

esteem *verb*
to respect or think highly of: *The judge always esteemed your father greatly.*

Word Building: **esteem** *noun* high opinion

estimate (say *es-tə-mayt*) *verb*
1 to roughly work out the value, size, or other qualities: *We estimated the cost to be $20.*
estimate (say *es-tə-mət*) *noun*
2 a rough valuation

Word Building: **estimation** *noun*

estuary (say *es-chooh-ə-ree*) *noun*
the mouth or lower part of a river which is affected by high tides

Word Building: the plural is **estuaries** □ **estuarine** *adjective*

etc. (say *et-set-rə*)
short for et cetera, *Latin words meaning* "and other things": *I need pens, papers, ink, etc.*

etch *verb*
1 to cut or eat into metal, as acid does **2** to print from a design which has been etched **3** to produce a clear and therefore lasting effect: *Fear has etched those events on my memory.*

Word Building: **etching** *noun*

eternal *adjective*
lasting forever: *eternal life*

Word Building: **eternally** *adverb*

eternity *noun*
1 time without end: *A lifetime seems short when you try to imagine eternity.* **2** a very long time: *We had to wait an eternity.*

Word Use: definition 2 is used jokingly

ether (say *ee-thə*) *noun*
a chemical which used to be used to put a patient to sleep during an operation, but is now used to dissolve other substances

Word History: from a Greek word meaning "upper air" or "sky"

ethics *plural noun*
the system of beliefs and rules that we live by: *He is a very honourable person who always acts according to his ethics.*

Word Building: **ethical** *adjective* morally right **ethically** *adverb*

ethnic *adjective*
having to do with the history, language and customs of a particular group: *ethnic dancing*

Word Building: **ethnically** *adverb*

etiquette (say *et-ee-kət*) *noun*
behaviour which is thought of as polite and correct: *business etiquette*

etymology (say *et-ə-mol-ə-jee*) *noun*
1 the study of the changes in words over a long period of time **2** an explanation of the history of a word, showing all the changes it has gone through

Word Building: the plural is **etymologies** □ **etymological** *adjective* **etymologist** *noun*

eucalypt (say *yooh-kə-lipt*) *noun*
a gum tree

eucalyptus (say *yooh-kə-lip-təs*) *noun*
a type of tree with many different varieties, used for its timber and its strong oil

Word Building: the plural is **eucalyptuses** or **eucalypti** □ **eucalyptus** *adjective*
Word History: from a Greek word meaning "covered" (referring to the cap covering the buds)

euro (say *yooh-roh*) *noun*
a stocky type of kangaroo

euthanasia (say *yooh-thə-nay-zhə*) *noun*
the act of helping or letting someone die when they want to, because their pain or suffering has become too great

evacuate *verb*
to leave in order to escape danger: *They evacuate their house during earthquakes.*

Word Building: **evacuation** *noun* **evacuee** *noun*

evade *verb*
1 to get round or escape from by trickery: *He evaded pursuit.* **2** to avoid doing: *She evades work.*

Word Building: **evasion** *noun* **evasive** *adjective* **evasively** *adverb*

evaluate *verb*
to test and find the value or quality of: *to evaluate your answer*

Word Building: **evaluation** *noun*

evangelist (say *ə-van-jə-ləst*) *noun*
someone who travels from place to place teaching from the Bible

Word Building: **evangelistic** *adjective*

evaporate *verb*
to dry up: *The water has evaporated. / The sun evaporates the puddles.*

Word Building: **evaporation** *noun* **evaporator** *noun*

eve *noun*
1 the day before: *Today is Christmas eve.*
2 the time just before an event takes place: *They left the country on the eve of war.*

even *adjective*
1 able to be divided by two: *Four, six, eight and ten are even numbers.* **2** equal in size: *She cut the cake in even slices.*
3 fairly matched: *It is an even contest.*
4 calm and steady: *He has an even temper.* **5** smooth or level: *The cricket pitch is not even.*

even *adverb*
6 still or yet: *School is even better now.*
7 however unlikely it may seem: *Even my little brother was quiet when the beautiful music began.*

Word Building: **even** *verb* (**evened, evening**) to make even **evenly** *adverb* **evenness** *noun*

evening *noun*
the late afternoon and early night

Word Building: **evening** *adjective: evening dress*

event *noun*
1 something which happens, especially something important: *The fete is a big event. | the day's events* **2** one of the items in a sports competition: *The last event was an egg-and-spoon race.*

Word Building: **eventful** *adjective* **eventfully** *adverb*

eventual *adjective*
final or last: *The eventual result was a draw.*

Word Building: **eventuality** *noun* **eventually** *adverb*

evergreen *adjective*
having leaves all year long: *an evergreen tree*

Word Use: compare this with **deciduous**
Word Building: **evergreen** *noun* an evergreen plant

every *adjective*
1 each of a group referred to one by one: *We go to school every day of the week.* **2 every other** one out of two, or every second: *We catch the bus to school every other day.*

everyday *adjective*
having to do with ordinary or casual situations, rather than formal ones: *everyday language*

everyone *pronoun*
every person: *I invited everyone in my class to my party.*

everywhere *adverb*
in all places: *I've looked everywhere that I can think of.*

evict *verb*
to turn out or remove: *The landlord evicted the tenants for not paying the rent.*

Word Building: **eviction** *noun*

evidence *noun*
1 something seen or heard that shows something else to be true **2** a clear sign of something: *The daffodils are the first evidence of spring.*

evident *adjective*
clear, or easily seen or understood: *It's evident you don't know what you are talking about.*

Word Building: **evidently** *adverb*

evil *adjective*
wicked and harmful

Word Building: **evil** *noun* anything evil **evilly** *adverb*

ewe (say *yooh*) *noun*
a female sheep

Word Use: be careful – this sounds like **you** □ the male is a **ram;** the young is a **lamb**

ex- *prefix*
a word part meaning **1** out of: *export* **2** from: *excrete* **3** former: *ex-wife*

Word Use: other spellings are **e-** or **ef-**
Word History: this prefix comes from Latin

exact *adjective*
1 absolutely right in every detail: *She wants an exact fit.*
exact *verb*
2 to demand, sometimes by force: *The government exacts tax from everyone.*

Word Building: **exacting** *adjective* demanding **exactly** *adverb* **exactness** *noun*

exaggerate (say *əg-zaj-ə-rayt*) *verb*
1 to say more than is true about: *She exaggerates her wealth.* **2** to increase even more: *Tiredness exaggerates his limp.*

Word Building: **exaggerated** *adjective* **exaggeration** *noun*

exalt (say *əg-zawlt, eg-*) *verb*
1 to raise in importance or power: *to exalt someone to the position of president* **2** to praise: *to exalt someone to the skies*

Word Use: be careful – this word looks and sounds a bit like **exult**
Word Building: **exaltation** *noun* **exalted** *adjective*

examination *noun*
1 an act of careful looking and testing: *The dentist's examination of her teeth revealed a broken filling.* **2** a test of knowledge or skill which often has to be passed before the next stage of learning begins

Word Use: the short form of definition 2 is **exam**
Word Building: **examinee** *noun* the person doing an exam **examiner** *noun* the person who sets an exam **examine** *verb*

example *noun*
1 a sample which makes something clear: *He gave an example of what he wanted us to do.* **2** a model to be followed: *You aren't setting a very good example to the younger children.*

exasperate *verb*
to annoy very much

Word Building: **exasperation** *noun*
Word History: from a Latin word meaning "roughened"

excavate (say *eks-kə-vayt*) *verb*
1 to make a hole or cavity in by removing earth: *to excavate the ground for a building site* **2** to uncover by digging: *to excavate an ancient city*

Word Building: **excavation** *noun* **excavator** *noun*

exceed *verb*
to go beyond: *You shouldn't exceed the speed limit.*

Word Building: **exceedingly** *adverb* extremely **exceeding** *adjective*

excel (say *ək-sel*) *verb*
to be very good: *He excels at swimming.*

Word Building: other forms are **I excelled, I have excelled, I am excelling**

excellent (say *ek-sə-lənt*) *adjective*
very good or of a very high quality: *He is an excellent cook.*

Word Building: **excellence** *noun* **excellently** *adverb*

exception (say *ək-sep-shən*) *noun*
someone or something which doesn't follow the general rule or pattern: *They behaved themselves, with only a few exceptions.*

Word Building: **exceptional** *adjective* very unusual **exceptionally** *adverb*

excerpt (say *ek-serpt*) *noun*
a piece quoted from a book or shown from a film

excess *noun*
an extreme amount

Word Building: **excessive** *adjective* **excessively** *adverb* **excessiveness** *noun*

exchange *verb*
1 to give one thing in return for another: *We'll exchange with you* **2** to give to each other: *They exchanged insults.*

exchange *noun*
3 the act of exchanging **4** a central office where letters and calls are received and sorted: *a telephone exchange*

excite (say *ək-suyt*) *verb*
to cause eager feelings in: *Your visit has excited them.*

Word Building: **excitement** *noun* **exciting** *adjective*
Word History: from a Latin word meaning "call forth" or "rouse"

exclaim *verb*
to cry out suddenly in fright or pleasure

Word Building: **exclamatory** *adjective* **exclaimer** *noun*

exclamation *noun*
something said or cried out suddenly in fright or pleasure

exclamation mark *noun*
a punctuation mark (!) used after an exclamation

exclude *verb*
to shut or keep out: *Blinds exclude light from rooms. / All children under ten are excluded from our club.*

Word Building: **exclusion** *noun*

exclusive *adjective*
1 fashionable: *an exclusive club / an exclusive suburb* **2** not shared with others: *an exclusive interview*

Word Building: **exclusively** *adverb* **exclusiveness** *noun*

excommunicate *verb*
to cut off from receiving communion or being a member of a church

Word Building: **excommunication** *noun*

excrete *verb*
to pass out from the body: *The caterpillar excreted a green slime after I trod on it.*

Word Building: **excrement** *noun* waste matter from your body **excretion** *noun* **excretive** *adjective*

excruciating (say *əks-krooh-shee-ay-ting*) *adjective*
very painful or causing great suffering

Word Building: **excruciatingly** *adverb*

excursion *noun*
a short journey or trip usually taken for a special reason: *Our class went on an excursion to the zoo.*

Word Building: **excursive** *adjective* wandering

excuse (rhymes with *choose*) *verb*
1 to pardon or forgive **2** to free from duty or let off: *He excused her from the washing up.*

excuse (rhymes with *goose*) *noun*
3 a reason, sometimes a pretended one, for being excused

Word Building: **excusable** *adjective*

execute *verb*
1 to do or carry out: *to execute a plan* **2** to put to death

Word Building: **execution** *noun*

executive (say *əg-zek-yə-tiv*) *noun*
1 someone responsible for carrying out plans, especially in a business
executive *adjective*
2 having to do with managing things

exempt *verb*
to make free from a duty or rule: *She was exempted from sport because she was sick.*

Word Building: **exempt** *adjective* **exemption** *noun*

exercise *noun*
1 an activity of the body or mind to train or improve it **2** a putting into practice: *It will be an exercise of your willpower to stop eating cake.*

Word Building: **exercise** *verb*

exert (say *əg-zert*) *verb*
to use or put into action: *She exerted all her strength to lift the bricks.*

exertion *noun*
effort: *The exertion of her long swim was too much for her.*

exhale *verb*
to breathe out

Word Building: **exhalation** *noun*

exhaust (say *əg-zawst*) *verb*
1 to tire or wear out: *I have exhausted myself working* **2** to empty or use up completely: *I have exhausted all my patience.*
exhaust *noun*
3 the used gases given off by an engine

Word Building: **exhaustive** *adjective* thorough **exhaustion** *noun* **exhaustively** *adverb*

exhibit (say *əg-zib-ət*) *verb*
1 to show or display
exhibit *noun*
2 something shown or displayed to the public

Word Building: **exhibitor** or **exhibiter** someone who exhibits **exhibition** *noun*

exhilarate (say *əg-zil-ə-rayt*) *verb*
to fill with energy or excitement: *His swim in the cold surf exhilarated him.*

Word Building: **exhilarating** *adjective* **exhilaratingly** *adverb* **exhilaration** *noun*

exile *verb*
1 to force to leave your home or country: *The king exiled her for treason.*
exile *noun*
2 someone who has been forced to leave their country or home **3** a long separation from your country or home

exist *verb*
1 to be: *The earth has existed for millions of years.* **2** to have life or be real: *Do ghosts exist?* **3** to continue to live: *We cannot exist without water.*

Word Building: **existence** *noun* the fact of existing **existent** *adjective*

exit *noun*
1 a way out: *The building had a number of exits.* **2** a going away or a departure: *Anne said "goodbye" and made a quick exit.*

Word Building: **exit** *verb* to go away or out

exodus *noun*
a going out or a departure, usually of a large number of people

exorcise or **exorcize** (say *ek-saw-suyz*) *verb*
to free from evil spirits by prayers or a religious ceremony: *to exorcise a haunted house*

Word Building: **exorcism** *noun* **exorcist** *noun*

exotic *adjective*
1 foreign or not belonging to your own country: *an exotic plant* **2** strange, or unusually colourful or beautiful: *When we were overseas we saw many exotic places and ate exotic food.*

Word Building: **exotic** *noun* anything exotic, especially a plant **exotically** *adverb*

expand *verb*
1 to increase in size or to swell: *Daniel expanded the sentence into a whole paragraph.* / *The balloon expanded with air.* **2** to spread, stretch out or unfold: *A bird expands its wings to fly.*

Word Building: **expansion** *noun*

expanse *noun*
a large open space or widespread area: *Australia has vast expanses of desert.*

expatriate (say *eks-pat-ree-ət*) *noun*
someone who has left their own country to live in another

expect *verb*
1 to look forward to **2** to look for with good reason: *I expect you to do your duty.* **3** to be pregnant: *My mother is expecting.*

Word Building: **expectancy** *noun* **expectant** *adjective* **expectantly** *adverb* **expectation** *noun*

expedient *adjective*
useful or suitable for a particular purpose: *It would be expedient for you to go to the meeting.*

Word Building: **expedience** *noun* **expediency** *noun* **expediently** *adverb*

expedite (say *eks-pə-duyt*) *verb*
to hurry up or to do quickly: *We must expedite this matter so it will be ready on time.*

Word Building: **expeditious** *adjective* quick **expeditiously** *adverb*

expedition *noun*
1 a journey made for a special purpose, such as a war or exploration **2** the group of people and the transport used to go on such a journey

Word Building: **expeditionary** *adjective: an expeditionary force*

expel *verb*
1 to drive out or away with force: *When you blow up a balloon you expel air from your lungs.* **2** to dismiss or send away from a club or a school

Word Building: other forms are **I expelled, I have expelled, I am expelling** ☐ **expulsion** *noun* **expulsive** *adjective*

expend *verb*
1 to use up: *I expended all my energy climbing the hill.* **2** to pay out or spend

Word Building: **expendable** *adjective* **expenditure** *noun*

expense *noun*
cost or charge: *the expense of our holiday / We had our meal at his expense.*

Word Building: **expensive** *adjective* **expensively** *adverb*

experience *noun*
1 something that happens to you: *I had many strange experiences on my trip.* **2** the knowledge or practice you get from doing or seeing things

experience *verb*
3 to meet with, or have happen to you: *She experienced a lot of friendliness on her trip.*

Word Building: **experienced** *adjective* wise or skilful

experiment *verb*
1 to try or test to find something out: *Doctors are experimenting with drugs to find a cure.*

experiment *noun*
2 a test or a trial carried out to discover something

Word Building: **experimental** *adjective* **experimentally** *adverb* **experimentation** *noun*

expert *noun*
someone who has a lot of skill or knowledge about a special thing

Word Building: **expert** *adjective* having a lot of special skill or knowledge **expertise** *noun* expert skill or knowledge

expire *verb*
1 to come to an end: *The contract has almost expired.* **2** to die

Word Building: **expiration** *noun* **expiry** *noun*

explain *verb*
1 to make clear or easy to understand
2 to give the reason for or cause of: *Please explain your absence.*

Word Building: **explanatory** *adjective* used to explain **explicable** *adjective* able to be explained
Word History: from a Latin word meaning "make plain" or "flatten out"

explanation *noun*
something which explains or gives the meaning of: *This book contains an explanation of the causes of World War I.*

explicit (say *ək-splis-ət*) *adjective*
clearly and fully set out: *The recipe was so explicit that even I could understand it.*

Word Building: **explicitly** *adverb*

explode *verb*
1 to blow up or burst into pieces with a loud noise: *The bomb exploded.* **2** to burst out with a sudden expression of feeling: *She exploded with laughter when she saw it.*

Word History: from a Latin word meaning "drive out by clapping"

exploit[1] (say *eks-ployt*) *noun*
a notable or daring deed

exploit[2] (say *ək-sployt*) *verb*
1 to use unfairly or selfishly: *She exploits her little brother.* **2** to put to good use: *The earth is exploited for its oil and minerals.*

Word Building: **exploitation** *noun* **exploitative** *adjective* **exploiter** *noun*

explore *verb*
1 to travel over an area to discover things or places: *They explored the bush to see if it had any caves.* **2** to examine or go over carefully: *The doctor explored every symptom in order to make a diagnosis.*

Word Building: **exploration** *noun* **exploratory** *adjective* **explorer** *noun*

explosion *noun*
1 a blowing up or exploding: *The explosion scattered rubbish everywhere.* **2** a sudden burst of noise: *There was an explosion of laughter around the dinner table.*

Word Building: **explosive** *noun* a substance that can explode, such as dynamite **explosive** *adjective* **explosively** *adverb*

export (say *ək-spawt*) *verb*
1 to send to other countries for sale: *Australia exports a lot of wool every year.*

export (say *ek-spawt*) *noun*
2 something exported: *Sugar is one of Australia's exports.*

Word Building: **exportation** *noun* **exporter** *noun*

expose *verb*
1 to uncover **2** to let light onto, when taking a photograph: *He exposed several films which he developed himself.*

Word Building: **exposure** *noun*

express *verb*
1 to put into words: *I expressed my opinion.* **2** to show or make known: *Her face expressed her joy.* **3** to make known your feelings or thoughts: *He expresses himself well in English.*

express *adjective*
4 sent or travelling direct without stopping: *an express parcel* **5** clearly stated or definite: *an express purpose*

express *noun*
6 an express train or bus

Word Building: **expressive** *adjective* showing how you feel **expressively** *adverb* **expressiveness** *noun*

expression *noun*
1 the act of putting into words: *an expression of opinion* **2** the look on someone's face

exquisite *adjective*
delicately beautiful: *an exquisite vase*

Word Building: **exquisitely** *adverb* **exquisiteness** *noun*

extend *verb*
1 to stretch out: *We will extend the coil of rope to its full length.* | *This road extends for miles.* **2** to make longer or larger: *to extend shopping hours* | *to extend a house*

Word Building: **extent** *noun: to its full extent*

extension *noun*
1 a stretching out or lengthening
2 something added on: *an extension to our house* **3** an extra telephone connected to the one you already have

Word Building: **extension** *adjective: an extension ladder*

extensive *adjective*
1 large in amount or size: *extensive knowledge* | *an extensive wheat farm*
2 carried out as far as possible: *an extensive search*

Word Building: **extensively** *adverb*

exterior *adjective*
being on the outside of: *the exterior walls of the house*

Word Use: the opposite of this is **interior**
Word Building: **exterior** *noun: the exterior of the building*

exterminate *verb*
to get rid of, especially by destroying: *to exterminate white ants*

Word Building: **extermination** *noun* **exterminator** *noun*
Word History: from a Latin word meaning "driven beyond the boundaries"

external *adjective*
1 on the outside: *Her external injuries included a black eye.* **2** coming from outside: *The external support for the school's project came mainly from local businesses.*

Word Use: the opposite of this is **internal**
Word Building: **externally** *adverb*

extinct *adjective*
1 no longer existing: *Dinosaurs are an extinct type of reptile.* **2** no longer active: *an extinct volcano*

Word Building: **extinction** *noun*

extinguish *verb*
to put out: *Always extinguish your camp fire before leaving.*

Word Building: **extinguisher** *noun: a fire extinguisher*

extra *adjective*
1 more than usual
extra *noun*
2 something added **3** someone playing a minor part in a film, usually as part of a crowd

extra- *prefix*
a word part meaning outside *or* beyond: *extraordinary*

Word History: this prefix comes from Latin

extract (say *eks-trakt*) *verb*
1 to pull or take out: *to extract a tooth*
extract (say *eks-trakt*) *noun*
2 something taken out or separated: *I read an extract from her latest book.* | *a drink made from beef extract*

Word Building: **extraction** *noun*

extraordinary (say *ək-straw-dən-ree*) *adjective*
1 more than ordinary: *He is a man of extraordinary strength.* **2** unusual or remarkable: *We have been having extraordinary weather.*

Word Building: **extraordinarily** *adverb*

extravagant (say *ək-strav-ə-gənt, ek-*) *adjective*
spending more than you need to: *an extravagant person*

Word Use: a similar word is **wasteful**
Word Building: **extravagance** *noun* **extravagantly** *adverb*

extreme *adjective*
1 very great: *She was in extreme pain.*
2 outermost: *We saw him at the extreme edge of the cricket field.*

Word Building: **extremity** *noun* the extreme point or part of something **extremely** *adverb*

exuberant (say *əg-zyooh-bə-rənt, eg-*) *adjective*
full of energy or warm feelings: *The team members were exuberant after their win.* | *What an exuberant welcome!*

Word Building: **exuberance** *noun* **exuberantly** *adverb*

exult (say *əg-zult, eg-*) *verb*
to show pleasure or feel happy that you have achieved or won something: *He exulted to find that he had triumphed after all.*

Word Use: be careful – this word looks and sounds a bit like **exalt**
Word Building: **exultant** *adjective* **exultantly** *adverb* **exultation** *noun* **exultingly** *adverb*

eye *noun*
1 the organ or part of the body with which we see **2** the iris or coloured part of this organ: *She has blue eyes.* **3** a close or careful watch: *Keep an eye on my books for me.* **4** an ability to use your eyes effectively: *You have a good eye for ball games.* **5 see eye to eye** to agree: *We see eye to eye on most things.*

eyebrow *noun*
the hair on the bony ridge over your eye

eyelash *noun*
one of the short curved hairs growing on the edge of an eyelid

eyelid *noun*
the lid of skin which moves up and down over your eye when you blink

eyesight *noun*
the power of seeing

eyesore *noun*
something unpleasant to look at: *The shabby picnic shed was an eyesore in the park.*

eyewitness *noun*
someone who actually sees a particular action or happening

Word Building: **eyewitness** *adjective: an eyewitness account*

fable *noun*
a short story, often about animals, that teaches a lesson about how to behave: *the fable of the tortoise and the hare*

fabric *noun*
cloth made by weaving, knitting or pressing fibres together: *wool fabric* | *felt fabric*

fabulous *adjective*
1 very good or wonderful: *We had a fabulous time.* **2** told about in fables or myths: *a fabulous creature*

Word Use: definition 1 is more suited to everyday language
Word Building: **fabulously** *adverb* **fabulousness** *noun*

facade (say *fə-sahd*) *noun*
the front of a building

Word Use: this word comes from French

face *noun*
1 the front of your head from the forehead to the chin **2** a look or expression: *a sad face* **3** a surface of something: *the face of a cube* | *the face of a watch*
face *verb*
4 to look towards **5** to come into contact with or meet: *to face difficulties*

Word Building: **facial** *adjective: a facial expression*

facet (say *fas-ət*) *noun*
1 a side or part of something complicated like a personality, an argument or a structure: *The conservation argument has many facets.* **2** one of the small, flat, polished surfaces of a gemstone

Word History: from a French word meaning "little face"

facetious (say *fə-see-shəs*) *adjective*
meant to be or trying to be amusing, at the wrong time or in an unsuitable way: *a facetious remark* | *a facetious person*

Word Building: **facetiously** *adverb* **facetiousness** *noun*

facility (say *fə-sil-ə-tee*) *noun*
1 something that makes doing a job easier: *He was given every facility to complete it in time.* **2** skill or cleverness: *Her facility with words impressed us.*

Word Building: the plural is **facilities** □ **facilitate** *verb* to make easier

fact *noun*
1 something that is true or real **2 in fact** really: *In fact, what happened was he pushed me.*

Word Building: **factual** *adjective* **factually** *adverb* **factualness** *noun*

faction *noun*
a small group of people within a larger group, who hold a different opinion to the larger group

Word Building: **factional** *adjective* **factionalism** *noun*

factor *noun*
1 one of the things that brings about a result: *Hard work was a factor in her success.* **2** one of two or more numbers which, when multiplied together, give the product: *Factors of 18 are 3 and 6.*

Word History: from a Latin word meaning "doer" or "maker"

factory *noun*
a building or group of buildings where goods are made

faculty *noun*
1 one of the powers that you are born with: *the faculty of hearing | He's turned 100, but he's still got all his faculties.* **2** the ability to do something in particular: *a faculty for getting into trouble*

Word Building: the plural is **faculties**

fad *noun*
something that is popular for a short time: *Yoyos are a fad that comes and goes.*

Word Building: **faddish** *adjective*

fade *verb*
1 to lose colour or strength: *The carpet faded.* **2** to disappear slowly: *The smile faded from her face.* **3** to cause to fade: *Sunshine faded the carpet.*

faeces or **feces** (say *fee-seez*) *plural noun*
waste matter discharged from the intestines

Word Use: another word is **excrement**

Fahrenheit (say *fa-rən-huyt*) *adjective*
relating to a scale of temperature in which the melting point of ice is 32° above zero and the boiling point is 212° above zero

Word History: named after a German scientist, Gabriel *Fahrenheit*, who thought up this scale and was the first to put mercury into thermometers

fail *verb*
1 to be unsuccessful in: *He failed Maths.* **2** to be less than expected: *The wheat crop failed this year.*

Word Building: **failing** *noun* a weakness **failure** *noun* lack of success

faint *adjective*
1 lacking strength: *a faint light | a faint sound* **2** weak and dizzy: *I feel faint.*
faint *verb*
3 to lose consciousness for a short time
faint *noun*
4 a short loss of consciousness

Word Use: a similar word for definitions 3 and 4 is **swoon**
Word Building: **faintly** *adverb* **faintness** *noun*

fair[1] *adjective*
1 not showing favouritism: *a fair judge* **2** done according to the rules: *a fair fight* **3** not cloudy: *fair weather* **4** of light colour: *fair hair*

Word Building: **fair** *adverb: to play fair* **fairly** *adverb* **fairness** *noun*

fair[2] *noun*
1 a group of sideshows and similar entertainments set up for a short time in one place **2** a regular gathering of buyers and sellers of a particular type of goods: *a book fair | a cattle fair*

fair dinkum *adjective*
true or genuine: *a fair dinkum Australian*

Word Use: this is more suited to everyday language

fairy *noun*
a tiny imaginary creature with magical powers

Word Building: the plural is **fairies**

fairytale *noun*
1 a story about fairies **2** a story that's untrue or hard to believe: *Her excuse was a bit of a fairytale.*

Word Building: **fairytale** *adjective*

faith *noun*
1 trust in someone or something **2** the collection of beliefs of a religion: *the Christian faith | the Jewish faith*

faithful *adjective*
loyal or trustworthy: *a faithful friend | a faithful worker*

Word Building: **faithfully** *adverb* **faithfulness** *noun*

fake *verb*
1 to make in such a way as to trick other people: *to fake money* **2** to pretend: *to fake illness*

Word Building: **fake** *noun* someone who fakes or something faked **fake** *adjective: fake watches* **faker** *noun*

falcon (say *fal-kən, fawl-kən*) *noun*
a kind of hunting bird which captures its prey in flight

Word Building: **falconry** *noun* the training and use of these birds **falconer** *noun*
Word History: from a Latin word meaning "sickle"

fall *verb*
1 to drop from a higher to a lower place **2** to become less or lower: *Prices fall when there is a glut. | The temperature fell today.* **3** to come to be: *to fall asleep | to fall in love* **4 fall back on** to use when something else hasn't worked: *If these scones don't come out right, I'll have to fall back on an old recipe of Mum's.* **5 fall in with** to agree to: *to fall in with his plans*

6 fall out to quarrel **7 fall through** to be unsuccessful: *Our plans fell through.*

fall *noun*
8 an act of falling or dropping

Word Building: other verb forms are **I fell, I have fallen, I am falling**

fallible (say *fal-ə-bəl*) *adjective*
likely to make a mistake

Word Building: **fallibility** *noun* **fallibly** *adverb*

fallout *noun*
dangerous radioactive dust falling from the air, after a nuclear explosion

fallow *adjective*
ploughed but left unseeded to improve its quality: *If we leave this land fallow, we should get a good crop next season.*

false *adjective*
1 not true or correct: *a false statement* **2** not faithful: *a false friend* **3** not real: *false teeth*

Word Building: **falsify** *verb* (**falsified, falsifying**) **falsely** *adverb* **falseness** *noun* **falsity** *noun*

falsehood *noun*
a statement that is not true

falsetto (say *fawl-set-oh*) *noun*
a very high-pitched voice

Word Building: the plural is **falsettos** □ **falsetto** *adjective: a falsetto voice*

falter *verb*
to move or speak weakly or unsteadily

Word Building: **falteringly** *adverb*

fame *noun*
the state of being widely known: *His fame spread after he won an Olympic medal.*

Word Building: **famous** *adjective* **famously** *adverb*

familiar *adjective*
1 well-known: *a familiar story* **2 familiar with** having knowledge of: *I am familiar with the success he has achieved.*

Word Building: **familiarisation** *noun* **familiarise** *verb* **familiarity** *noun* **familiarly** *adverb*

family *noun*
1 parents and their children **2** a wider group of related people including grandparents, uncles, aunts and cousins **3** a group of related things: *the human family | a tree of the acacia family*

family *adjective*
4 having to do with the family **5** suitable for a family **6 family tree** the branching plan or diagram of your family, including all your relations and ancestors

Word Building: the plural of the noun is **families** □ **familial** *adjective* (say *fə-mil-ee-əl*) having to do with a family

famine (say *fam-ən*) *noun*
a serious shortage of food, usually caused by drought

famished *adjective*
very hungry

fan[1] *noun*
1 something designed to move the air and make you feel cooler

fan[1] *verb*
2 to cool by moving the air: *We fanned her with a folded paper.*

Word Building: other verb forms are **I fanned, I have fanned, I am fanning**

fan[2] *noun*
someone who is an eager supporter: *a football fan*

Word History: this word is a shortened form of **fanatic,** although the meaning has now changed

fanatic (say *fə-nat-ik*) *noun*
someone who is too enthusiastic, often in an unthinking way, about something they believe in: *a fanatic about health foods*

Word Building: **fanatical** *adjective* **fanatically** *adverb* **fanaticism** *noun*
Word History: from a Latin word meaning "having to do with a temple", "inspired by a god" or "frantic"

fanbelt *noun*
the belt which drives the cooling fan of a motor

fancy *noun*
1 a liking: *She took a fancy to me.*
2 something imagined: *It was only a fancy though it seemed real at the time.*

fancy *verb*
3 to imagine: *I fancied I saw myself in a beautiful palace.* **4** to like or want: *I fancy fish for tea.* **5** to believe without being certain: *I fancied she said she would come.*

fancy *adjective*
6 ornamental: *fancy gold braid*

Word Building: other verb forms are **I fancied, I have fancied, I am fancying** □ other adjective forms are **fancier, fanciest**

fanfare *noun*
a short, loud piece of music usually played on trumpets, used to mark the beginning of an event or the arrival of someone important

fang *noun*
1 one of the long, sharp, hollow teeth of a snake, by which it injects venom
2 a canine tooth

fantastic *adjective*
1 strange or unusual: *fantastic ornaments*
2 imaginary: *fantastic fears* **3** very good or wonderful: *a fantastic party*

Word Use: another word for definitions 1 and 2 is **fantastical** □ definition 3 is more suited to everday language
Word Building: **fantastically** *adverb*

fantasy *noun*
1 imagination: *the world of fantasy* **2** the making of pleasant mental pictures: *a fantasy in which I'm a famous pilot*

Word Use: a similar word for definition 2 is **daydream**
Word Building: the plural is **fantasies** □ **fantasise** *verb*

far *adverb*
1 at or to a great distance or point: *He went far away.* **2 as far as** to the distance or degree that: *as far as I am concerned*

far *adjective*
3 distant: *a far city* **4** the more distant of two: *the far side of the river*

Word Building: other forms are **farther** or **further, farthest** or **furthest**

faraway *adjective*
1 distant or remote: *a faraway country*
2 dreamy: *a faraway look*

farce *noun*
1 a comedy in which the humour depends on a ridiculous and unlikely situation
2 foolish show or mockery: *Her unkindness made a farce of her friendship for me.*

Word Building: **farcical** *adjective: a farcical situation* **farcically** *adverb*

fare *noun*
1 the price of travelling on a public vehicle: *a bus fare | a train fare* **2** food: *The fare at the hotel was good.*

fare *verb*
3 to get on or manage: *We fared well.*

farewell *noun*
1 a saying of goodbye: *a sad farewell*

farewell *verb*
2 to say goodbye to

farm *noun*
an area of land used for growing crops or raising animals

Word Building: **farm** *verb* **farmer** *noun* **farming** *noun*
Word History: from a French word meaning "fix"

fascinate (say *fas-ə-nayt*) *verb*
to attract and hold the interest of completely: *She fascinated us with her stories.*

Word Building: **fascinating** *adjective* **fascinatingly** *adverb* **fascination** *noun*
Word History: from a Latin word meaning "enchanted"

fashion *noun*
1 a style of dress: *Modern fashions are comfortable to wear.* **2** a custom or way of doing things: *The fashion of entertaining at a barbecue is popular.* **3** manner or way: *He spoke to me in a rude fashion.*

fashion *verb*
4 to shape or form: *He fashioned a crib for the baby.*

Word Building: **fashionable** *adjective* **fashionably** *adverb*

fast[1] *adjective*
1 able to move quickly: *a fast runner*
2 finished in a short time: *a fast race*
3 ahead of the correct time: *My clock is fast.* **4** fixed firmly in place: *He made the boat fast to the wharf.*

fast[1] *adverb*
5 tightly: *Hold fast to that rope.*
6 soundly: *I was fast asleep.* **7** quickly or swiftly: *He ran fast.*

Word Building: **fasten** *verb* to fix firmly in place **fastener** *noun*

fast[2] *noun*
a period of time when no food is eaten, usually for religious or health reasons

Word Building: **fast** *verb*

fastidious (say *fas-tid-ee-əs*) *adjective*
fussy or hard to please: *He is fastidious about cleanliness.*

Word Building: **fastidiously** *adverb* **fastidiousness** *noun*

fat *noun*
1 the white or yellowish greasy substance found in or around the flesh of animals and in some plants: *Cut the fat from the chops.*

fat *adjective*
2 plump or obese **3** having much edible flesh: *a fat lamb*

Word Building: other adjective forms are **fatter, fattest** □ **fatten** *verb* **fatty** *adjective*

fatal *adjective*
1 causing death: *a fatal injury* **2** likely to have very important results: *a fatal decision*

Word Building: **fatality** *noun* **fatally** *adverb*

fate *noun*
1 the cause beyond your control that seems to control the things that happen to you: *It was fate that we should meet.* **2** the end, outcome or final result: *the fate of our plans*

Word Building: **fateful** *adjective: the fateful day of the earthquake* **fatefully** *adverb*

father *noun*
1 a male parent **2** someone who shows the interest of a father: *a father to the neighbourhood children* **3** someone who invents or begins something: *King Alfred was the father of the English navy.*
4 a title given to priests in the Catholic Church and the Church of England
5 the Father the God of the Christians

father *verb*
6 to be the father of **7** to act as a father towards

Word Building: **fatherhood** *noun* **fatherly** *adjective*

father-in-law *noun*
the father of your husband or wife

Word Building: the plural is **fathers-in-law**

fathom *noun*
1 an old-fashioned measure of the depth of water equal to 6 feet, or nearly 2 metres in the metric system

fathom *verb*
2 to understand completely: *I couldn't fathom maths until my brother helped me.*

fatigue (say *fə-teeg*) *noun*
1 severe mental or physical tiredness
2 weakening of material, especially metal, as a result of strain put on it after long use

Word Building: **fatigue** *verb* (**fatigued, fatiguing**)

fatuous (say *fat-chooh-əs*) *adjective*
foolish without knowing it

Word Building: **fatuously** *adverb* **fatuousness** *noun*

fault *noun*
1 responsibility or cause for blame: *It was my fault we were late.* **2** a mistake or blemish: *I returned the shirt to the shop because there was a fault in the collar.*
3 a failure to serve a ball according to the rules in tennis and similar games **4 at fault** open to blame: *If the battery's flat we'll all know who's at fault.*

Word Building: **fault** *verb: They couldn't fault his wonderful singing.* **faulty** *adjective* having faults **faultily** *adverb* **faultiness** *noun*
Word History: from a Latin word meaning "deceive"

fauna (say *faw-nə*) *noun*
the animals of a particular area or period of time: *Australian fauna includes koalas, kookaburras and blue-tongue lizards.*

Word Use: compare this with **flora**
Word History: named after the Roman goddess *Fauna*, the sister of *Faunus*, god of the woodlands

favour or **favor** *noun*
1 a kind act: *Will you do me a favour?*
2 a state of being thought well of: *in favour with the teacher* **3 in favour of a** on the side of: *He is in favour of our idea.* **b** payable to: *a cheque in favour of the Red Cross*

favour or **favor** *verb*
4 to think of with approval: *to favour an idea* **5** to prefer unfairly: *He favours his youngest child.* **6** to show favour to: *Will you favour us by coming to our meeting?*

Word Building: **favoured** *adjective*

favourable or **favorable** *adjective*
1 giving help: *a favourable wind for the boats* **2** saying what you want to hear: *a favourable answer*

Word Building: **favourably** *adverb*

favourite or **favorite** *noun*
1 someone or something most highly thought of: *This picture is my favourite.*
2 a competitor who is expected to win
3 someone who is treated as being better than others without really deserving it: *the teacher's favourite*

Word Building: **favourite** *adjective* **favouritism** *noun*

fawn[1] *noun*
1 a young deer, under a year old

fawn[1] *adjective*
2 pale yellowish-brown

Word Use: a male deer is a **buck** or **hart;** the female is a **doe** or **hind**

fawn[2] *verb*
1 to try to get special treatment from someone by flattery **2** to show affection by wagging the tail, licking and jumping around

Word Use: definition 1 is used about people □ definition 2 is used about dogs

fax *noun*
1 a way of sending documents or pictures along a telephone line **2** a document or picture sent this way
fax *verb*
3 to send by fax: *to fax a document*

Word Use: you can also use **facsimile** (say *fak-sim-ə-lee*) for definitions 1 and 2
Word History: a respelling of the first part of *facs(imile)*

fear *noun*
1 a feeling that danger or something unpleasant is near
fear *verb*
2 to be afraid of **3** to feel anxious: *I fear for his safety.*

Word Building: **fearsome** *adjective: a fearsome storm* **fearful** *adjective* **fearless** *adjective* **fearlessness** *noun*

feasible (say *feez-ə-bəl*) *adjective*
likely to work: *a feasible plan*

Word Building: **feasibility** *noun* **feasibly** *adverb*

feast *noun*
1 a large meal set out for many guests **2** a large quantity of anything eaten or giving pleasure: *a feast of ice-cream | a feast of music* **3** something very pleasant: *a feast for the eyes*

Word Use: a similar word for definition 1 is **banquet**
Word Building: **feasting** *noun: It was a night of feasting.* **feast** *verb*

feat *noun*
a deed of great skill, courage or strength

feather *noun*
1 one of the growths that make up the covering of a bird's body **2 a feather in your cap** an honour or mark of merit you have earned

Word Building: **feathered** *adjective* **feathery** *adjective*

feature *noun*
1 any part of your face: *His nose is his best feature.* **2** an outstanding part or quality: *The lovely scenery was a feature of our trip.*
feature *verb*
3 to give special importance to: *to feature a tenor on a concert program* **4** to be an outstanding or distinguishing part: *Gum trees feature in his paintings.*

Word Building: **featured** *adjective*

February (say *feb-yooh-ə-ree, feb-rooh-ə-ree*) *noun*
the second month of the year, with 28 days, but 29 days in leap years

Word Use: the abbreviation is **Feb**
Word History: from the Latin name for the Roman festival of purification, held on 15 February

federal *adjective*
having to do with a central government rather than state governments: *federal politics*

Word Building: **federally** *adverb*

federation *noun*
the forming of a nation by a number of states who give some of their powers and responsibilities to a central government

Word Building: **federate** *verb* to join in a league or federation

fee *noun*
the money you owe, such as to a doctor, lawyer or private school for their services

feeble *adjective*
1 weak in body or mind **2** lacking strength or brightness: *a feeble voice | feeble light*

Word Building: **feebleness** *noun* **feebly** *adverb*

feed *verb*
1 to give food to **2** to supply with the means of growth: *to feed a fire | Two creeks feed the river.* **3** to be food for: *This leg of lamb will feed six people.* **4** to supply to: *to feed corn to chickens*
feed *noun*
5 food, especially for animals: *horses' feed* **6** a meal

Word Use: definition 6 is more suited to everyday language
Word Building: other verb forms are **I fed, I have fed, I am feeding** □ **feeder** *noun*

feedback *noun*
1 information passed back about something that has been done or said: *I've had a lot of feedback about my new book.* **2** the return of part of the sound put out by a loudspeaker into the microphone so that a high-pitched noise is made

feel *verb*
1 to know or examine by touching: *Feel the wool. / We felt our way in the dark.* **2** to sense or experience: *She feels the cold. / She felt sadness at the news.* **3** to know that you are: *She feels happy. / I felt ill.* **4** to believe: *I feel that you are wrong.*
feel *noun*
5 the way something is sensed when you touch it: *a silky feel*

Word Building: other verb forms are **I felt, I have felt, I am feeling**

feeler *noun*
1 a thin, armlike growth on some animals, especially those without a backbone, which is used for touching or grasping **2** a remark made to find out what someone else is thinking

feeling *noun*
1 a particular sensation or emotion: *a feeling of warmth / a feeling of fear* **2** a belief or idea: *I have a feeling it will turn out well.*

feign (rhymes with *rain*) *verb*
1 to pretend to have: *to feign illness* **2** to make up or invent: *to feign an excuse*

felafel (say *fə-luf-əl, -laf-*) *noun*
fried balls of spiced chickpeas and hot peppers, which have been soaked in relish and chilli sauce

Word Use: other spellings are **falafel** and **filafil**

feline (say *fee-luyn*) *adjective*
having to do with cats or the cat family

Word Building: **feline** *noun*

fell *verb*
to cut down or cause to fall: *to fell a tree / The boxer felled his opponent.*

fellow *noun*
1 a man or a boy **2 Fellow** a member of a professional society: *a Fellow of the Royal College of Surgeons*

Word Building: **fellow** *adjective* having the same position or occupation: *my fellow workers* **fellowship** *noun*

felony (say *fel-ə-nee*) *noun*
a serious crime such as murder or burglary

Word Building: **felon** *noun* a criminal **felonious** *adjective*

felt *noun*
cloth made of wool, fur or hair which is not woven but pressed firmly together: *soft toys made of felt*

Word Building: **felt** *adjective*

female *adjective*
of the sex which is able to give birth to young

Word Use: the opposite is **male**
Word Building: **female** *noun* a female person or animal

feminine (say *fem-ə-nən*) *adjective*
1 female **2** having qualities such as softness and gentleness, thought to be typical of women

Word Use: the opposite is **masculine**
Word Building: **femininity** *noun*

feminism *noun*
the principle that women deserve the same rights and opportunities as men: *The rise of feminism has meant that women in the 1990s have a better chance of getting good jobs than 30 years ago.*

Word Building: **feminist** *noun* someone who holds these beliefs

fence *noun*
1 a wall or barrier put up around something to separate it from its surroundings **2** someone who earns a living by buying and selling stolen goods **3 sit on the fence** to avoid taking sides in an argument
fence *verb*
4 to enclose or separate by a fence: *to fence a garden* **5** to fight with a sword: *to fence in a sports tournament*

Word Use: definition 2 is more suited to everyday language
Word Building: **fencer** *noun*

fencing *noun*
1 the sport of sword fighting **2** material, such as wood or wire, used to build fences

fend *verb*
1 *in the phrase* **fend off** to fight off or resist: *He fended off the savage dog.* **2** *in the phrase* **fend for** to look after or protect

feral (say *fe-rəl*) *adjective*
wild or untamed: *Feral dogs roamed the countryside.*

Word History: from a Latin word meaning "wild beast"

ferment (say *fə-ment*) *verb*
1 to change in taste and appearance, because yeast or bacteria has turned sugar into alcohol and gas: *Yeast ferments grape*

juice and turns it into wine. | The apple juice was standing there so long it fermented.

ferment (say *fer-ment*) *noun*
2 a state of excitement and activity

Word Building: **fermentation** *noun*

fern *noun*
a green leafy plant that does not have flowers and grows in damp shady places

Word Building: **fernery** *noun* a place for growing ferns **ferny** *adjective*

ferocious (say *fə-roh-shəs*) *adjective*
fierce, savage and cruel: *ferocious animals*

Word Building: **ferociously** *adverb* **ferocity** *noun*

ferret *noun*
1 an animal with a long thin body used in hunting rabbits

ferret *verb*
2 ferret out to search out: *We ferreted out the truth.*

ferry *noun*
a boat that carries people or cars across a river or harbour

Word Building: the plural is **ferries** □ **ferry** *verb* (**ferried, ferrying**) to transport from one place to another

fertile *adjective*
1 richly productive and abundant: *Fertile land grows healthy crops. | Her stories are most interesting because of her fertile imagination.* **2** able to have babies

Word Use: the opposite is **sterile**
Word Building: **fertility** *noun*
Word History: from a Latin word meaning "fruitful"

fertilise or **fertilize** *verb*
1 to make fertile or enrich: *to fertilise the vegetable garden with cow manure* **2** to combine with in order to create new life: *The male sperm fertilises the female egg to start the development of a baby.*

Word Building: **fertilisation** *noun* **fertiliser** *noun*

fervour or **fervor** (say *fer-və*) *noun*
great enthusiasm or passion: *She spoke with fervour against nuclear bombs.*

Word Building: **fervent** *adjective* **fervently** *adverb*

festival *noun*
1 a joyful celebration with processions, exhibitions and performances of music, dance and drama **2** a time of religious celebration: *the festival of Christmas*

Word Use: a similar word for definition 1 is **carnival**

festive *adjective*
merry and joyful: *to be in a festive mood*

Word Building: **festivity** *noun* (**festivities**)

festoon *noun*
a streamer, or ribbon hung as a decoration

Word Building: **festoon** *verb: to festoon the Christmas tree with lights*
Word History: from an Italian word meaning "festival" or "feast"

fetch *verb*
1 to go and bring back: *Fetch the ball, Fido!* **2** to sell for or bring in: *That gold watch should fetch a high price.*

fetching *adjective*
charming and attractive: *a fetching smile*

Word Building: **fetchingly** *adverb*

fete (sounds like *fate*) *noun*
1 a small fair held to raise money for a school or charity

fete *verb*
2 to treat as special and important: *They feted the overseas visitors with champagne.*

Word Use: this word is sometimes spelled **fête** because it was originally French

fetlock *noun*
the part of a horse's leg with a tuft of hair just above the hoof

fetta (say *fet-ə*) *noun*
a soft white cheese from Greece, which has been preserved by being soaked in salted water

Word Use: another spelling is **feta**
Word History: from a Latin word meaning "mouthful" or "bite"

fetter *noun*
1 a chain or shackle tied around the ankles **2** anything that restricts or stops you from doing what you want

Word Use: definition 2 is often used in the plural form, as in *to shake off your fetters*
Word Building: **fetter** *verb* to confine or restrict

fettuccine (say *fet-ə-chee-nee*) *noun*
pasta that has been cut into wide strips

feud (rhymes with *stewed*) *noun*
a bitter, long-lasting quarrel, especially between two families: *He had never met his cousins because of the family feud.*

Word Building: **feud** *verb*

feudal (say *fyoohd-əl*) *adjective*
having to do with a way of life in which ordinary people lived on and used the land of a nobleman, giving him military and other service in return

Word Use: we usually talk about the **feudal system** which was in force in medieval Europe
Word Building: **feudalism** *noun*

fever *noun*
1 an unusually high body temperature caused by illness **2** great excitement: *The crowd waiting for the pop group worked itself up into a fever.*

Word Building: **feverish** *adjective* hot or restless **feverishly** *adverb* **feverishness** *noun*

few *adjective*
1 not many: *Few people go swimming in winter.*
few *noun*
2 the few a small number or minority: *In the old days, education was only for the few.* **3 a good few** or **quite a few** a fairly large number

fiancée (say *fee-on-say*) *noun*
the woman to whom a man is engaged to be married: *She is Tony's fiancée.*

Word Use: the accent over the "e" is there because this word was originally French
Word Building: **fiancé** *noun* the man to whom a woman is engaged

fiasco (say *fee-as-koh*) *noun*
an embarrassing or ridiculous failure

fib *noun*
a lie about something that's not very important

Word Building: **fib** *verb* (**fibbed, fibbing**) **fibber** *noun*

fibre (say *fuy-bə*) *noun*
1 a fine thread of wool, cotton or other material **2** the part of food that can't be digested: *Celery has a lot of fibre.*

Word Building: **fibrous** *adjective* stringy or indigestible

fibreglass *noun*
material made of fine glass fibres which is used to insulate buildings against heat and cold or mixed with plastic and used to make surfboards and boats

fibro *noun*
strong building material made of asbestos and cement

fickle *adjective*
changeable or likely to have changes of mind: *a fickle wind* | *a fickle friend*

Word Building: **fickleness** *noun*

fiction *noun*
a story which isn't true but is made up from the imagination

Word Use: the opposite is **non-fiction** or **fact**
Word Building: **fictitious** *adjective* not real or genuine **fictional** *adjective* **fictionally** *adverb*

fiddle *noun*
1 a violin **2 fit as a fiddle** in very good health
fiddle *verb*
3 to play a violin **4** to move your hands around restlessly

Word Building: **fiddly** *adjective* needing to be done with care and practice **fiddler** *noun*

fidelity (say *fə-del-ə-tee*) *noun*
1 faithfulness or loyalty: *fidelity in marriage* | *fidelity to your friends* | *fidelity to the things you believe* **2** the ability to reproduce a sound exactly as it should be: *the fidelity of a radio or amplifier*

Word Building: the plural is **fidelities**

fidget (say *fij-ət*) *verb*
1 to move about restlessly
fidget *noun*
2 someone who fidgets **3 the fidgets** restlessness because you're bored or nervous

Word Building: **fidgety** *adjective*

field *noun*
1 a piece of open ground or space: *a field of wheat* | *a football field* **2** an area of interest or activity: *to study in the field of chemistry*
field *verb*
3 to stop or catch the ball in cricket and other similar sports
field *adjective*
4 happening on a sports field rather than on a running track: *Long jump is a field event.*

Word Building: **fielder** *noun*

field-glasses *plural noun*
another word for **binoculars**

fiend (say *feend*) *noun*
1 the devil or any evil spirit **2** a nuisance or troublemaker **3** someone who spends a lot of time or energy in playing a game or sport: *a chess fiend*

Word Building: **fiendish** *adjective* evil or cruel **fiendishly** *adverb*

fierce *adjective*
1 wild or violent: *fierce animals | fierce winds* **2** very strong or intense: *fierce competition for the prize*

Word Building: **fiercely** *adverb* **fierceness** *noun*

fiery (say *fuy-ə-ree*) *adjective*
1 like fire: *fiery red* **2** showing strong feelings: *a fiery speech*

fiesta (say *fee-es-tə*) *noun*
a holiday or festival, especially on a religious occasion

Word Use: this word comes from Spanish

fife *noun*
a high-pitched flute often played in military bands

fifteen *noun*
the number 15

Word Building: **fifteen** *adjective* **fifteenth** *adjective*

fifty *noun*
the number 50

Word Building: the plural is **fifties** □ **fifty** *adjective* **fiftieth** *adjective*

fig *noun*
a small, soft, pear-shaped fruit containing many tiny seeds which is eaten fresh or dried

fight *noun*
1 a quarrel, struggle or contest: *a fight in the playground | to give money to help the fight against poverty*
fight *verb*
2 to try to defeat: *to fight feelings of hunger* **3** to take part in a battle: *We fought to the end.*

Word Building: other verb forms are **I fought, I have fought, I am fighting** □ **fighter** *noun*

figment *noun*
something that's only imaginary: *a figment of your imagination*

figure *noun*
1 a symbol that stands for a number: *the figure 3* **2** an amount or sum of money: *They paid a large figure for the new car.* **3** a shape, form or pattern: *The dancer has a graceful figure. | The figures on my socks are squares and triangles.* **4** a person or character: *The Prime Minister is an important figure.*
figure *verb*
5 to work out or calculate: *to figure the cost to be $150* **6 figure out** to understand or decide: *I can't figure out where I made the mistake in this sum.*

Word Building: **figures** *plural noun* calculations or sums

figurehead *noun*
1 someone who has an important position in an organisation but has no real power **2** a carved figure, often a woman, which decorates the bow of a sailing ship

figure of speech *noun*
an expression in which words are used out of their usual meaning for special effect, like a metaphor or simile: *Calling it a one-horse town was just a figure of speech.*

figurine *noun*
a small statue or model

Word History: from an Italian word meaning "little figure"

filament *noun*
a very thin thread: *a filament of cotton | The wire filament in a light bulb glows when electricity passes through it.*

Word Building: **filamentous** *adjective*

file[1] *noun*
1 an orderly collection of papers or the folder they are kept in **2** an ordered collection of data stored on tape or disk for a computer **3** a line of people or things one behind the other: *to stand in single file*
file[1] *verb*
4 to put or arrange in a file: *to file letters in order according to the date they were received* **5** to walk or march one after the other

file[2] *noun*
a steel tool whose surface is covered with ridges for smoothing or cutting metal and other materials

Word Building: **file** *verb*

filigree (say *fil-ə-gree*) *noun*
a delicate lacelike design made out of metal thread, used in jewellery

Word Building: **filigree** *adjective* **filigreed** *adjective*

fill *verb*
1 to supply or have as much of something as can be held: *to fill the bath to the top* **2** to take up all the space or time: *Smoke filled the room. | The movie was filled with excitement.* **3** to take or occupy: *to apply*

to fill the position of caretaker **4 fill in a** to complete by writing in the blank spaces: *to fill in an entry form for the competition* **b** to stand in for or replace: *The headmaster filled in for our teacher when he was away sick.* **5 fill the bill** to be just what is needed

fill *noun*
6 earth and rocks used to fill a hole in the ground

Word Building: **filling** *noun: The pie has a lemon filling. | I have a filling in one of my teeth.* **filler** *noun*

fillet *noun*
a slice of fish or meat without the bone

Word Building: **fillet** *verb*
Word History: from a French word meaning "little thread"

filly *noun*
a female horse less than four years old

Word Use: the plural is **fillies** □ a young male horse is a **colt**

film *noun*
1 a thin sheet or layer of material: *to wrap sandwiches in plastic film | a film of oil on water* **2** material which is sensitive to light and is used in a camera for taking photographs **3** a moving picture which is shown on a screen: *to see a film about life in China*

Word Use: another word for definition 3 is **movie**
Word Building: **film** *verb*

filmy *adjective*
light and transparent: *The dancers' costumes were made of filmy material.*

Word Building: other forms are **filmier, filmiest** □ **filminess** *noun*

filter *noun*
a device for straining liquids or air to remove unwanted material: *A filter in a swimming pool keeps the water clean.*

Word Building: **filtrate** *noun* the liquid which has been strained through a filter **filtration** *noun* the process of filtering **filter** *verb*

filth *noun*
something that is disgustingly dirty, repulsive or obscene

Word Building: **filthy** *adjective* very dirty or unpleasant **filthy** *adverb* very or extremely: *filthy rich* **filthiness** *noun*

fin *noun*
1 one of the flap-like structures on the body of a fish which is used for moving through the water **2** a small triangular or fin-shaped part on a surfboard, plane or boat to help with steering or balancing

final *adjective*
1 last or coming at the end: *the final match of the season | I say "no", and my word is final.*

final *noun*
2 the one at the end of a series, especially of races or competitions: *to play in the grand final*

Word Building: **finalise** *verb* to end or conclude **finalist** *noun* a competitor who takes part in the last round of a contest **finality** *noun* **finally** *adverb*

finale (say *fə-nah-lee*) *noun*
the last part of a concert, opera or ballet

finance *noun*
1 the management of money: *an expert in banking and finance* **2 finances** money supplies or revenue: *I'm sorry I can't lend you any money as my finances are rather low.*

Word Building: **finance** *verb* to fund or pay for **financier** *noun* someone whose business is lending money **financial** *adjective* **financially** *adverb*

finch *noun*
a type of small brightly-coloured bird commonly found in suburban gardens

find *verb*
1 to come upon by chance or after a search: *to find shells at the beach | to find a lost umbrella* **2** to discover or learn: *to find the answer to a question*

Word Building: other forms are **I found, I have found, I am finding** □ **find** *noun* a valuable discovery **findings** *plural noun* data or information **finder** *noun*

fine[1] *adjective*
1 excellent or of high quality: *a fine musician* **2** sunny, or without rain: *fine weather* **3** very thin or slender: *a fine thread* **4** made up of tiny particles: *Sugar is fine but salt is finer.* **5** sharp: *a fine point on a pencil* **6** well or healthy

Word Building: **finely** *adverb* **fineness** *noun*

fine[2] *noun*
a sum of money paid as a penalty for doing something wrong

Word Building: **fine** *verb*

finesse (say *fə-nes*) *noun*
fine skill or clever management: *to conduct business dealings with finesse*

finger *noun*
1 any one of the five, long, end parts of your hand, especially one that's not your thumb **2** something shaped like a finger: *the finger of a glove | a finger of toast*

Word Building: **finger** *verb* to touch lightly

fingerprint *noun*
the pattern made by the curved lines on the tips of your fingers

finicky *adjective*
1 very fussy or choosy **2** fiddly or full of small, unimportant detail: *This embroidery is very finicky.*

finish *verb*
1 to bring or come to an end **2 finish off a** to totally use up or complete: *to finish off your dinner* **b** to kill or destroy
finish *noun*
3 the end or conclusion **4** the surface layer of wood or metal or the substance put on it: *to polish the car to give it a brilliant finish*

finite (say *fuy-nuyt*) *adjective*
having limits which can be measured or counted: *Is the number of stars in the universe finite?*

Word Use: the opposite is **infinite**
Word Building: **finitely** *adverb* **finiteness** *noun*

fiord (say *fee-awd*) *noun*
a deep, narrow inlet of the sea with steep cliffs on each side: *Norway is famous for its fiords.*

Word Use: another spelling is **fjord**

fir *noun*
a tree, like a traditional Christmas tree, which has needle-like leaves and produces cones

Word Use: be careful – this sounds like **fur**

fire *noun*
1 the heat, light and flames produced by burning: *You could see the fire from far away.* **2** a mass of burning material, such as in a fireplace: *to light a fire to keep warm* **3** enthusiasm or passion: *a speech full of fire* **4** the shooting of guns: *to open fire on the enemy soldiers*
fire *verb*
5 to set on fire or make very hot: *to fire the furnace | to fire pottery in a kiln*
6 to shoot: *to fire a gun* **7** to dismiss or sack from a job: *The boss fired him for not doing his work properly.* **8** to inspire or excite: *The speaker's words fired the audience with enthusiasm.*

Word Use: definition 7 is more suited to everyday language
Word Building: **fiery** *adjective* (**fierier, fieriest**) **firefighter** *noun* someone who fights fires

firearm *noun*
any type of gun

firebreak *noun*
a strip of land which has been cleared of grass and trees to stop a fire from spreading

fireplace *noun*
an open place, built of brick or stone, for lighting fires in

fireworks *plural noun*
1 containers filled with a powder that burns or explodes giving out brilliantly coloured sparks **2** an outburst of anger or bad temper

firm[1] *adjective*
1 solid, hard or stiff **2** not moving or shaking **3** strong, definite and unchanging: *to speak in a firm voice | a firm belief*

Word Building: **firm** *verb* to make or become firm **firm** *adverb* **firmly** *adverb* **firmness** *noun*

firm[2] *noun*
a business company

first *adjective*
1 being number one or coming before all others in time, order or importance: *She was the first one to arrive.*
first *adverb*
2 before anyone or anything else in time, order or importance: *He arrived first.*
3 for the first time: *They first met at a party.*

Word Building: **first** *noun* **firstly** *adverb*

first aid *noun*
emergency treatment given to someone hurt in an accident

first-class *adjective*
of the best quality, best-equipped or most expensive: *a first-class restaurant*

Word Building: **first-class** *adverb: to travel first-class*

first-hand *adverb*
directly from the source: *We got the information first-hand.*

Word Building: **first-hand** *adjective*

fish *noun*
1 a cold-blooded animal which lives in water, breathes through gills, swims by means of fins and has scales on its body
fish *verb*
2 to catch or try to catch fish **3** to feel around for and find: *to fish some money out of your pocket* **4 fish for** to try to get indirectly: *to fish for information*

Word Building: the plural form of the noun can be either **fish** or **fishes** □ **fishmonger** *noun* someone who sells fish

fisherman *noun*
someone who fishes, either as a job or for pleasure

Word Use: another word for someone who fishes for pleasure is **angler**
Word Building: the plural is **fishermen**

fishy *adjective*
1 having a fishlike smell or taste
2 strange or causing suspicion: *There was something fishy about his disappearance, so I wondered what he was up to.*

Word Use: definition 2 is more suited to everyday language
Word Building: other forms are **fishier, fishiest**

fissure (say <u>*fish*</u>-ə) *noun*
a crack or split: *The rock had a deep fissure in it.*

fist *noun*
your hand when the fingers are closed tightly into the palm

Word Building: fistful *noun* a handful

fit[1] *adjective*
1 suitable or good enough: *Those clothes are not fit to be worn.* **2** right or proper: *Picking up papers is a fit punishment for littering.* **3** healthy
fit[1] *verb*
4 to be suitable or the right size or shape for **5** to make or have space for: *We can fit five people in the car.* **6** to put into place: *I am fitting a new handle on to this door.* **7 fit in** to be or become suited: *Do you think this chair fits in with the rest of the furniture?* **8 fit out** to provide with clothing or equipment
fit[1] *noun*
9 the way in which something fits: *This shirt is a perfect fit.*

Word Building: other adjective forms are **fitter, fittest** □ other verb forms are **I fitted, I have fitted, I am fitting** □ **fitter** *noun* **fitness** *noun*

fit[2] *noun*
1 a sudden outburst: *She hit him in a fit of rage. | He had a fit of coughing.* **2** a sudden sickness in which your body twists uncontrollably and you sometimes become unconscious

Word Building: fitful *adjective* stopping and starting **fitfully** *adverb*

fitting *adjective*
1 suitable or proper
fitting *noun*
2 a trying on of clothes for a proper fit
3 the size of clothes or shoes: *What is your fitting?* **4 fittings** furnishings or equipment: *Their house has beautiful fittings.*

Word Building: fittingly *adverb*

five *noun*
the number 5

Word Building: five *adjective* **fifth** *adjective*

fix *verb*
1 to make firm or put securely in place: *We've got to fix the poles into the ground before we put up the tent.* **2** to settle or decide: *Let's fix a price for this car.* **3** to mend or repair **4 fix on** to decide on **5 fix up a** to arrange properly: *Please fix up the books on your desk.* **b** to put right: *This medicine will soon fix you up.*
fix *noun*
6 a difficult situation: *I'm in such a fix that I don't know what to do.*

Word Use: definition 6 is more suited to everyday language
Word Building: fixed *adjective* **fixedly** *adverb* **fixer** *noun*

fixture *noun*
1 something fixed in place, especially in a house or other building **2** a sporting event that is to be held on a particular date

fizz *verb*
to bubble and make a hissing sound: *I like it when lemonade fizzes up your nose.*

Word Building: fizz *noun* **fizzy** *adjective*

fizzle *verb*
1 to make a hissing or spluttering sound
2 fizzle out to fail after a good start: *Our plans have fizzled out.*

Word Use: definition 2 is more suited to everyday language
Word Building: fizzle *noun*

fjord (say *fee-awd*) *noun*
another spelling for **fiord**

flabbergasted *adjective*
very surprised or astonished: *We were flabbergasted by the news of the fortune he'd won.*

Word Use: a similar word is **astounded**
Word Building: **flabbergast** *verb*

flabby *adjective*
having soft fatty flesh: *flabby arms* / *a flabby man*

Word Building: **flabbily** *adverb* **flabbiness** *noun*

flaccid (say *flas-əd*) *adjective*
soft and loose: *flaccid muscles*

Word Use: a similar word is **limp**
Word Building: **flaccidity** *noun* **flaccidly** *adverb* **flaccidness** *noun*

flag[1] *noun*
1 a piece of cloth with a particular design used as a symbol of a country or an organisation, or as a signal: *The Australian flag has the Southern Cross on it.* / *A red flag is used to signal danger.*
flag[1] *verb*
2 to signal, mark or warn with a flag

Word Building: other verb forms are **I flagged, I have flagged, I am flagging**

flag[2] *verb*
to grow weak or tired: *The walkers began to flag at the end of the day.*

Word Building: other forms are **I flagged, I have flagged, I am flagging**

flagon *noun*
a large bottle

flagrant (say *flay-grənt*) *adjective*
obvious in a shameless way: *a flagrant lie* / *flagrant disobedience*

Word Building: **flagrancy** *noun* **flagrantly** *adverb*
Word History: from a Latin word meaning "blazing" or "burning"

flair *noun*
1 natural talent: *She has a flair for maths.* **2** smart style: *He dresses with flair.*

flake[1] *noun*
1 a small, flat, thin piece of anything: *a flake of skin* / *a flake of snow*
flake[1] *verb*
2 to peel off in flakes: *This paint is flaking.* **3** to lie down or fall asleep from tiredness: *I flaked after the race.*

Word Use: definition 3 is more suited to everyday language
Word Building: **flaky** *adjective* **flakily** *adverb* **flakiness** *noun*

flake[2] *noun*
shark meat sold as food

flamboyant *adjective*
dazzlingly bright and showy

Word Building: **flamboyance** *noun* **flamboyantly** *adverb*
Word History: from a French word meaning "small flame"

flame *noun*
a tongue of fire: *Flames licked around the base of the tree.* / *The candle burnt with a low flame.*

Word Building: **flame** *verb*

flameproof *adjective*
1 not easily burnt: *flameproof clothing*
2 safe for use over flames: *a flameproof dish*

flamingo (say *flə-ming-goh*) *noun*
a water bird with a very long neck, long legs and dark pink feathers

Word Building: the plural is **flamingos** or **flamingoes**

flammable *adjective*
easily set on fire: *Be careful not to wear a flammable dressing gown.*

Word Use: another word for this is **inflammable**

flan *noun*
a large tart with a sweet or savoury filling

flank *noun*
1 the side of an animal between the ribs and hip **2** the side of anything
flank *verb*
3 to be at the side of: *The president was flanked by two guards.*

flannel *noun*
1 a warm soft cloth, usually made of wool: *a flannel suit* **2** a face washer

flannelette *noun*
a cotton cloth treated on one side to look and feel like flannel

flannel flower *noun*
an Australian plant with light-cream flowers and leaves that feel like flannel

flap *verb*
1 to swing about loosely, especially with a noise: *The curtain is flapping in the wind.*
2 to move up and down: *The bird flapped its wings.*

flap *noun*
3 something flat and thin that is joined to something else on one side only and hangs loose **4** a feeling of nervousness or excitement: *Don't get yourself into a flap.*

Word Use: definition 4 is more suited to everyday language
Word Building: other verb forms are **I flapped, I have flapped, I am flapping**

flare *verb*
1 to burn brightly and suddenly: *The fire flared up.* **2** to burst with a sudden strong feeling **3** to curve outwards like the end of a trumpet: *Her skirt flared at the bottom.*

Word Building: **flare** *noun* a bright light used as a signal

flash *noun*
1 a sudden short burst of flame or light: *a flash of lightning* **2** a short moment: *He was gone in a flash.* **3** a short, important piece of news on radio or television

Word Building: **flash** *adjective: a flash flood* **flash** *verb* to flame or light up **flashy** *adjective* bright and showy

flashback *noun*
a part of a film or story that shows an event that happened at an earlier time

flashlight *noun*
a bulb that gives a flash of very bright light, used when taking photographs inside or at night

flask (say *flahsk*) *noun*
a small flat bottle

flat[1] *adjective*
1 even or smooth: *It is easier to run on flat ground.* **2** lying spread out: *I found her flat on the bed.* **3** not high: *a shoe with flat heels* **4** emptied of air: *a flat tyre* **5** clear and absolute: *He answered with a flat refusal.* **6** boring or dull **7** no longer bubbly or fizzy **8** not shiny: *flat paint* **9** lowered in pitch by a semitone: *The musical note B flat is a semitone lower than the note B.*

flat[1] *adverb*
10 in a flat position: *Please lay the paper out flat.* **11 flat out** **a** as fast or hard as possible **b** very busy

flat[1] *noun*
12 a flat side or part of anything: *She hit him with the flat of her hand.* **13** flat ground: *Be careful to stay on the flat.* **14** **a** a note that is one semitone below a given note **b** the music sign (♭) which lowers the note by a semitone when it is placed before it

Word Use: the opposite of definitions 9 and 14 is **sharp**
Word Building: **flatly** *adverb* **flatness** *noun*

flat[2] *noun*
a group of rooms for living in, usually part of a larger building and usually rented

Word Building: **flat** *verb* (**flatted, flatting**) to live in a flat

flatter *verb*
1 to try to please by compliments or praise even if you do not mean them **2** to show or describe as being more attractive than is really so: *This photo flatters her.*

Word Building: **flatterer** *noun* **flattery** *noun*

flaunt (say *flawnt*) *verb*
to show off boldly: *She was always flaunting her parents' wealth.*

Word Use: don't confuse this with **flout**

flautist (say *flaw-təst*) *noun*
someone who plays the flute

Word History: from an Italian word meaning "flute"

flavour or **flavor** *noun*
1 taste, especially the special taste that something has: *Do you like the flavour of lemon?* **2** the nature or quality of something: *The outdoor tables gave the restaurant a French flavour.*

flavour or **flavor** *verb*
3 to add flavour to: *She flavoured the stew with salt and pepper.*

Word Building: **flavouring** *noun*

flaw *noun*
1 a fault: *Laziness is the biggest flaw in my character.* **2** a crack or scratch: *There is a flaw in this plate.*

Word Use: be careful – this sounds like **floor**
Word Building: **flaw** *verb* to make or become cracked or spoilt

flax *noun*
a plant with narrow leaves and blue flowers, grown for its fibre which is made into linen and for its seeds which contain oil

Word Building: **flaxen** *adjective* pale yellow

flea *noun*
a small wingless insect which moves by jumping and which sucks blood from mammals and birds

Word Use: be careful – this sounds like **flee**

fleck *noun*
a spot or small patch of something

Word Building: **fleck** *verb*

fledgling *noun*
1 a young bird that has just become able to fly **2** someone who is young or new to something

Word Use: another spelling is **fledgeling**

flee *verb*
to run away or escape

Word Use: be careful – this sounds like **flea**
Word Building: other forms are **I fled, I have fled, I am fleeing**

fleece *noun*
1 the coat of wool that covers a sheep or other animal
fleece *verb*
2 to take money or belongings from by cheating: *They fleeced him of all his earnings.*

Word Building: **fleecy** *adjective* **fleeciness** *noun*

fleet[1] *noun*
1 a large group of naval ships, usually under the command of one officer **2** a group of other boats, aeroplanes or vehicles: *a fleet of company cars*

Word Use: compare this with **flotilla**

fleet[2] *adjective*
very fast or swift

Word Building: **fleeting** *adjective* **fleetly** *adverb* **fleetness** *noun*

flesh *noun*
1 the soft part of an animal body, which is made up of fat and muscle **2** the human body when you think of it as separate from the mind or the spirit: *Meat feeds the flesh and books feed the mind.* **3** the soft part of a fruit or vegetable

Word Building: **fleshy** *adjective* plump or fat **fleshiness** *noun*

flex *verb*
1 to bend or stretch: *He flexed his muscles.*
flex *noun*
2 a cord containing an electric wire

flexible *adjective*
1 easily bent or stretched: *flexible wire*
2 able to be changed easily: *My plans are flexible.*

Word Use: a similar word for definition 1 is **supple**
Word Building: **flexibility** *noun* **flexibly** *adverb*

flexitime *noun*
an arrangement in which workers can choose their starting and finishing times, as long as they work the right number of hours altogether

flick *noun*
a sudden light blow: *He gave the table a flick with the duster.*

Word Building: **flick** *verb*

flicker *verb*
1 to burn unsteadily: *The candle flickered.* **2** to move quickly to and fro

Word Building: **flicker** *noun*

flight[1] *noun*
1 an act of flying or the way in which something flies: *The flight of my paper plane wasn't what I expected.* **2** a number of things flying together: *A flight of gulls landed on the water.* **3** a journey by aeroplane **4** a series of steps or stairs

flight[2] *noun*
1 a running away or fleeing **2 take flight** to run away

flighty *adjective*
often changing your mind or feelings: *I wish you'd stop being so flighty.*

Word Use: a similar word is **frivolous**
Word Building: other forms are **flightier, flightiest** □ **flightiness** *noun*

flimsy *adjective*
1 not strongly made: *a flimsy fence*
2 weak or not carefully thought out: *a flimsy excuse*

Word Building: other forms are **flimsier, flimsiest** □ **flimsiness** *noun*
Word History: made by changing around the letters of the word "film" and adding the ending "-sy"

flinch *verb*
to draw back from something dangerous, difficult or unpleasant: *They did not flinch when they saw the enemy.*

fling *verb*
1 to throw, usually forcefully or impatiently: *He flung the blunt pencil to the floor.* **2** to move quickly or violently: *She would fling out of the room when she was annoyed.*

fling *noun*
3 a time of pleasure or fun: *Let's have a last fling before the exams.* **4** an attempt or try: *I will have one more fling at jumping that height.*

Word Building: other forms of the verb are **I flung, I have flung, I am flinging**

flint *noun*
a hard kind of stone, which can start a fire when struck with steel

Word Building: **flintily** *adverb* **flintiness** *noun* **flinty** *adjective*

flip *verb*
1 to move or throw with a snap of a finger and thumb: *She flipped the coin to see who would go first.* **2** to move with a jerk: *He flipped over the pages of the book.*
flip *noun*
3 a flipping movement: *a flip of the wrist*
4 a somersault: *a backwards flip*

Word Building: other verb forms are **I flipped, I have flipped, I am flipping**

flippant (say *flip-ənt*) *adjective*
not suitably serious: *This is not the time to make flippant remarks.*

Word Building: **flippancy** *noun* **flippantly** *adverb*

flipper *noun*
1 the broad flat limb of an animal such as a seal or whale that is used for swimming **2** a piece of rubber shaped like a flipper and worn on your foot to help in swimming

flirt *verb*
to amuse yourself by pretending to be romantically interested in someone

Word Building: **flirt** *noun* **flirtation** *noun* **flirtatious** *adjective* **flirtatiously** *adverb*

flit *verb*
to move lightly and quickly: *The birds flitted from tree to tree.*

Word Building: other forms are **I flitted, I have flitted, I am flitting**

float *verb*
1 to rest or move gently on the top of a liquid: *He swam and then floated on his back.* **2** to move freely and easily: *The idea floated through her mind.*
float *noun*
3 something that floats, such as an air-filled rubber mattress that you lie on in the water, or the cork on a fishing line
4 a platform on wheels that carries a display in a procession **5** a van or trailer for carrying horses

flock *noun*
1 a number of animals of the same kind that live and feed together, especially sheep and birds
flock *verb*
2 to gather together or go in a flock: *Everyone flocked around him to hear the story.*

floe *noun*
a large piece of ice floating on the sea

flog *verb*
1 to beat hard with a whip or stick: *The soldier flogged the convict.* **2** to sell or try to sell: *He flogs used cars.* **3** to steal: *I bet she flogged that money.*

Word Use: definitions 2 and 3 are more suited to everyday language
Word Building: other forms are **I flogged, I have flogged, I am flogging**

flood (say *flud*) *noun*
1 a great overflow of water, especially over land which is usually dry: *Many houses were washed away in the flood.*
2 any great outpouring: *a flood of words | a flood of tears*
flood *verb*
3 to cover with water, as in a flood
4 to rise or flow in a flood **5** to supply in great numbers: *They flooded us with gifts.*

floodlight *noun*
1 a light that gives a strong beam, used especially outside
floodlight *verb*
2 to light up with a floodlight: *to floodlight a sportsground at night*

Word Building: other verb forms are **I floodlit, I have floodlit, I am floodlighting**

floor *noun*
1 the lowest flat part of a room or other place: *Don't drop crumbs on the floor. | The ship sank to the floor of the sea.* **2** one of the different levels of a building: *That office block has thirty floors.*
floor *verb*
3 to knock down or defeat: *The boxer floored his opponent.* **4** to confuse or puzzle completely: *This question will floor you.*

Word Use: a similar word to definition 2 is **storey** □ definition 4 is more suited to everyday language □ be careful – this sounds like **flaw**
Word Building: **flooring** *noun* material used to make floors

flop *verb*
1 to fall or drop suddenly, especially with a noise: *He flopped into a chair.* **2** to fail or break down

flop *noun*
3 the movement or sound of flopping: *She sat down with a flop.* **4** something that is a failure: *That film was a complete flop.*

Word Use: definitions 2 and 4 are more suited to everyday language
Word Building: other verb forms are **I flopped, I have flopped, I am flopping** □ **floppily** *adverb* **floppiness** *noun* **floppy** *adjective*

floppy disk *noun*
a flexible plastic disk used for storing information in a computer

flora (say *flaw-rə*) *noun*
the plants of a particular area or period of time: *Australian flora includes waratahs and banksias.*

Word Use: compare this with **fauna**
Word History: named after *Flora*, the Roman goddess of flowers

floral (say *flo-rəl*) *adjective*
having to do with or made of flowers

florid *adjective*
1 red-coloured: *florid cheeks* **2** too showy or flowery: *florid music | florid writing*

Word Use: a similar word to definition 1 is **ruddy** □ a similar word to definition 2 is **ornate**
Word History: from a Latin word meaning "flowery"

florist *noun*
someone who arranges and sells flowers

flotilla *noun*
a group of small naval ships, or a small group of any boats

Word Use: compare this with **fleet**

flounce[1] *verb*
to move with an impatient or angry jerk of your body: *She flounced out of the room in a rage.*

Word Building: **flounce** *noun*

flounce[2] *noun*
a strip of material gathered together and used to decorate the bottom of a skirt or other clothing

Word Building: **flouncing** *noun* **flouncy** *adjective*

flounder[1] *verb*
1 to struggle along with stumbling movements: *They floundered through the mud.* **2** to struggle helplessly because of embarrassment or confusion

flounder[2] *noun*
a kind of fish, eaten as food

Word Building: the plural is **flounder**

flour *noun*
a fine powder made by grinding wheat or other grain and used in cooking

Word Use: be careful – this sounds like **flower**
Word Building: **floury** *adjective*

flourish (say *flu-rish*) *verb*
1 to grow strongly **2** to wave about in a showy way: *She flourished her prize.*

flourish *noun*
3 a waving movement: *He gave a flourish of his sword.* **4** anything used for show such as a curve used to decorate handwriting

Word Use: a similar word for definition 1 is **thrive** □ a similar word for definition 2 is **brandish**
Word Building: **flourishing** *adjective*
Word History: from a Latin word meaning "bloom"

flout (say *flowt*) *verb*
to show no respect for: *He always flouts the rules.*

Word Use: don't confuse this with **flaunt**
Word Building: **flouter** *noun* **floutingly** *adverb*

flow *verb*
1 to move along in a stream: *The river flows out to the sea.* **2** to go along continuously and smoothly like a stream: *Her thoughts flowed smoothly onto the page.* **3** to fall or hang loosely: *Her hair flowed in the breeze.*

Word Building: **flow** *noun*

flow chart *noun*
a diagram showing how something works or develops, stage by stage

flower *noun*
the blossom or part of a plant that produces the seed

Word Use: be careful – this sounds like **flour**
Word Building: **flower** *verb*

flowerbed *noun*
a small plot of ground in a garden where flowers are grown

flowery *adjective*
1 covered with flowers **2** using a lot of fancy words: *a flowery speech*

Word Building: other forms are **flowerier, floweriest** □ **floweriness** *noun*

flu *noun*
a shortened form of **influenza**

fluctuate (say *fluk-chooh-ayt*) *verb*
to change all the time: *The temperature keeps fluctuating.*

Word Building: **fluctuation** *noun*

flue (say *flooh*) *noun*
a tube or pipe or any space for air or smoke to pass through

fluent (say *flooh-ənt*) *adjective*
1 flowing smoothly and easily: *to speak fluent French* **2** able to speak easily: *to be fluent in French*

Word Building: **fluency** *noun* **fluently** *adverb*

fluff *noun*
1 light, soft, tiny pieces from materials like cotton or wool: *Woollen jumpers often have fluff on them.* **2** an error or mistake

Word Use: definition 2 is more suited to everyday language
Word Building: **fluff** *verb* **fluffy** *adjective*

fluid *noun*
1 a substance that can flow, either a liquid or a gas
fluid *adjective*
2 changing easily or not fixed

Word Building: **fluidity** *noun* **fluidly** *adverb* **fluidness** *noun*

fluke[1] *noun*
1 any accidental advantage or stroke of good luck, especially in sport
fluke[1] *verb*
2 to get or win by a fluke: *to fluke the right answer*

Word Use: definition 2 is more suited to everyday language
Word Building: **fluky** *adjective* (**flukier, flukiest**)

fluke[2] *noun*
1 one of the flat triangular pieces on an anchor which catch in the ground **2** one of the triangular halves of a whale's tail

fluorescent *adjective*
giving off light when hit by a stream of particles such as electrons: *a fluorescent tube*

Word Building: **fluorescence** *noun*

fluoride *noun*
a chemical compound which protects your teeth from decay

Word Building: **fluoridate** *verb* **fluoridation** *noun*

flurry *noun*
1 sudden excitement or confusion: *In all the flurry I forgot my bag.* **2** a sudden gust of wind

Word Building: **flurry** *verb* (**flurried, flurrying**)

flush[1] *verb*
1 to blush or become red in the face **2** to flood with water, especially for cleaning: *to flush the toilet*

flush[2] *adjective*
1 even or level: *That brick should be flush with this one.* **2** having plenty of something, especially money: *Let's eat out tonight, I'm flush at the moment.*

Word Building: **flush** *adverb*

fluster *verb*
to make nervous or confused

Word Building: **fluster** *noun* confusion

flute *noun*
1 a musical wind instrument played by blowing across a hole near its end
flute *verb*
2 to make long grooves in: *The potter fluted the edges of his new pot.*

Word Building: **fluted** *adjective* having grooves: *a fluted glass*
Word History: from a Latin word meaning "blown"

flutter *verb*
1 to flap or wave: *The flags fluttered in the breeze.* **2** to move with quick uneven movements: *Her heart fluttered with excitement.*
flutter *noun*
3 a flapping movement **4** a wave of nervous excitement or confusion: *A flutter of excitement went through the class when the visitor arrived.*

fly[1] *verb*
1 to move through the air with the help of wings, wind or some other force **2** to move very quickly: *The runner was flying down the track.* **3** to make fly: *The children were flying a kite.* **4** to operate, or travel in, an aircraft or spacecraft
fly[1] *noun*
5 a flap of material hiding a zipper in clothing, especially in trousers **6** a piece

of material that forms the door or outer roof of a tent

Word Building: other verb forms are **I flew, I have flown, I am flying** □ the plural form of the noun is **flies**

fly[2] *noun*
1 an insect with two wings **2** a fish hook made to look like an insect

Word Building: the plural is **flies**

flying fox *noun*
1 a large bat which has a foxlike head and feeds on fruit **2** a machine which is worked by an overhead cable and is used to carry you over water or rough land

flying saucer *noun*
a disc-shaped flying object said to be a spaceship from outer space

Word Use: this is sometimes called a **UFO**

flyleaf *noun*
a blank page at the beginning or end of a book

Word Building: the plural is **flyleaves**

foal *noun*
a young horse or donkey, either male or female

Word Use: a male horse is a **stallion;** a female horse is a **mare** or **dam** □ a male donkey is a **jackass;** a female donkey is a **jennet**

foam *noun*
1 a collection of very small bubbles
2 a spongy material made by putting gas bubbles into plastic or rubber

Word Building: **foam** *verb* to froth **foaminess** *noun* **foamy** *adjective*

focus *noun*
1 a point at which rays of light meet after they have been reflected or bent **2** the adjustment of something like a camera lens to get a clear, sharp picture **3** the main point of interest or attraction: *The new girl was the focus of attention.*

focus *verb*
4 to adjust a lens so that the image is made clear: *He focused his camera.*
5 to bring rays of light together to a point: *He used his magnifying glass to focus the sun's rays onto the paper to burn it.*
6 to concentrate

Word Building: plural forms of the noun are **foci** and **focuses** □ other verb forms are **I focused** or **focussed, I have focused** or **focussed, I am focusing** or **focussing** □ **focal** *adjective: the focal point of the argument*

fodder *noun*
food like hay or straw for cattle and horses

foe *noun*
an enemy

foetus or **fetus** (say *fee-təs*) *noun*
a young human or animal during its development in an egg or in its mother's womb, especially in the later stages

Word Use: compare this word with **embryo**
Word Building: **foetal** *adjective*

fog *noun*
a cloudlike layer that forms close to the earth's surface and is made up of drops of water

Word Building: **fog** *verb* (**fogged, fogging**) **fogginess** *noun* **foggy** *adjective*

foghorn *noun*
a loud horn or siren used for warning ships in foggy weather

fogy (say *foh-gee*) *noun*
an old-fashioned person

Word Building: the plural is **fogies**

foible *noun*
a slight weakness in someone's character: *He has several foibles but no major faults.*

foil[1] *verb*
to stop from being successful: *She foiled him in his plans to run away.*

foil[2] *noun*
1 metal which has been beaten, hammered or rolled out into very thin sheets: *aluminium foil* **2** anything that shows up the good qualities of something else by contrast with it

foil[3] *noun*
a light thin sword with a button on the point which prevents injury in fencing

foist (say *foyst*) *verb*
to sell or get rid of things that are damaged or of low quality, using trickery: *She tried to foist the shopsoiled goods onto the old lady.*

fold[1] *verb*
1 to bend over on itself: *They folded their blankets neatly on the bed.* **2** to wrap up: *He folded the present in paper.* **3** to cross: *to fold your arms*

fold[1] *noun*
4 a part that is folded or a layer of something folded **5** a crease made by folding

fold[2] *noun*
a closed-off pen for keeping animals like sheep

folder *noun*
a holder or cover for papers usually made of a folded sheet of cardboard

foliage (say *foh-lee-ij*) *noun*
the leaves of a plant

folk (rhymes with *coke*) *noun*
1 people in general **2** the people of a particular group: *City folk and country folk should be friends.* **3 your folks** your own family
folk *adjective*
4 belonging to ordinary people: *folk music*

Word Use: definition 3 is more suited to everyday language

folklore (say *fohk-law*) *noun*
the beliefs, stories and customs of a people or a tribe passed down from each generation

follow *verb*
1 to come or go after: *You go ahead and I'll follow.* **2** to accept as a guide: *I'll follow your instructions.* **3** to move forward or go along: *Follow this path through the woods.* **4** to come after as a result: *It follows from this that he must be innocent. | If you do that, disaster will follow.* **5** to understand: *Do you follow this lesson?* **6** to watch the movements of something or the way something is developing: *She follows the news carefully.*

folly *noun*
1 foolishness **2** a foolish or silly act

Word Building: the plural is **follies**

fond *adjective*
1 loving or affectionate: *a fond look*
2 fond of liking: *fond of children*

Word Building: **fondly** *adverb* **fondness** *noun*

fondle *verb*
to stroke or caress lovingly

fondue (say *fond-yooh*) *noun*
a meal cooked at the table in which pieces of food are speared on the end of long forks and cooked in melted cheese or hot oil

Word History: from a French word meaning "melt"

font *noun*
a large stone bowl in a church which holds the water used in baptism

food *noun*
1 anything that can be eaten to keep your body alive and help it grow **2 food for thought** something that might inspire new ideas

fool *noun*
1 someone who is silly or without commonsense
fool *verb*
2 to trick or deceive: *She fooled him into believing she was older than she really was.* **3** to play around or waste time: *Stop fooling around and come and finish your homework.*

Word Building: **foolery** or **tomfoolery** *noun* silly behaviour
Word History: from a Latin word meaning "bellows"

foolhardy *adjective*
reckless and foolishly adventurous

Word Building: **foolhardily** *adverb* **foolhardiness** *noun*

foolish *adjective*
silly or unwise: *a foolish person | a foolish action*

Word Building: **foolishly** *adverb* **foolishness** *noun*

foolproof *adjective*
designed not to fail or break even when wrongly used

foot *noun*
1 the part of your body at the end of your leg, which is used for standing and walking **2** the end or bottom part, rather than the top or head part: *the foot of a mountain* **3** an old-fashioned measure of length equal to about 30 centimetres
4 put your foot down to be strict or firm
foot *verb*
5 to pay: *to foot the bill*

Word Building: the plural of the noun is **feet**

football *noun*
1 a game in which a ball is kicked or thrown, such as Soccer, Australian Rules, Rugby Union and Rugby League **2** the ball used in these games

Word Building: **footballer** *noun*

footlights *plural noun*
the row of lights at the front of the stage in a theatre

footnote *noun*
a note at the bottom of a page, usually in small printing, which tells you more about something in the main text

footstep *noun*
1 the sound made by a step of the foot
2 the track or mark made by a foot
3 follow in someone's footsteps to copy or follow someone in their work or way of life

Word Use: a similar word for definition 2 is **footprint**

for *preposition*
1 with the purpose or intention of: *to go for a walk* **2** meant to be used by or in connection with: *a book for children / a basket for cats* **3** in order to get: *money for lunch* **4** during: *for a very long time*

Word Use: be careful – this sounds like **fore** and **four**

forage (say *fo-rij*) *verb*
to search around for food or other supplies: *to forage in the refrigerator*

Word Building: forage *noun* food or fodder for animals

foray *noun*
1 a raid or attack in order to steal: *to make a foray into the enemy camp* **2** a first attempt: *to make a foray into a different kind of work*

Word Building: foray *verb*

forbid *verb*
to not allow: *I forbid you to go.*

Word Building: other forms are **I forbade, I have forbidden, I am forbidding** □ **forbidding** *adjective* unpleasant, dangerous, or frightening

force *noun*
1 strength or power: *the force of the wind / to use force to get your own way* **2** an organised group of people working together: *the police force* **3 in force a** operating or effective: *The new rules are in force from today.* **b** all together: *Her friends came to see her in force.*

force *verb*
4 to make or compel, often by using threats or violence: *The thief forced them to hand over the money.* **5** to use, move or do with force or effort: *to force the lid off a box*

Word Building: forceful *adjective* strong and powerful **forcible** *adjective* using force

forceps (say *faw-səps*) *noun*
a pair of tongs or tweezers used for grasping and holding objects, especially in operations

Word Building: the plural form is also **forceps**

ford *noun*
a shallow part of a river where you can walk or ride across

Word Building: ford *verb: to ford a stream*

fore *noun*
1 the front part **2 to the fore** to or at the front or best position: *He always pushes himself to the fore.*

fore *adverb*
3 at or towards the bow of a ship

Word Use: the opposite of definition 3 is **aft** □ be careful – this sounds like **for** and **four**

fore- *prefix*
a word part meaning **1** front: *forehead* **2** ahead of time: *forecast* **3** superior: *foreman*

Word History: this prefix comes from Middle and Old English

forearm *noun*
the part of your arm between the elbow and the wrist

forecast *verb*
to predict or warn about for the future: *The Weather Bureau forecasts rain for the weekend.*

Word Building: other forms are **I forecast, I have forecast, I am forecasting** □ **forecast** *noun* a prediction, especially about the weather **forecaster** *noun*

forefinger *noun*
the finger next to your thumb

foreground *noun*
the part of a view or picture nearest the front or the viewer: *We could see the river in the foreground with the mountains in the distance.*

Word Use: the opposite is **background**

forehead (rhymes with *horrid*) *noun*
the part of your face above your eyes and below where your hair starts growing

Word Use: a similar word is **brow**

foreign (say *fo-rən*) *adjective*
1 from a country other than your own: *a foreign language* **2** not belonging in the place where it is found: *a foreign substance in your eye*

Word Building: foreigner *noun* someone born in another country

foreman *noun*
a worker who is placed in charge of other workers in a factory

Word Building: the plural form is **foremen** □ **forewoman** *noun* (**forewomen**)

foremost *adjective*
first or top: *The world's foremost athletes compete in the Olympic Games.*

Word Building: **foremost** *adverb*

foresee *verb*
to expect or see in advance: *to foresee trouble*

Word Building: other forms are **I foresaw, I have foreseen, I am foreseeing** □ **foresight** *noun* care or thought for the future **foreseeable** *adjective*

forest *noun*
land thickly covered with trees

Word Building: **forester** *noun* someone trained to care for forests **forestry** *noun* the science of planting and taking care of forests **afforestation** *noun* the planting of forests

forfeit (say *faw-fət*) *noun*
something paid or lost because of carelessness, disobedience or crime: *According to the rules of the game, you pay a forfeit if you give the wrong answer.*

Word Building: **forfeit** *verb: You'll have to forfeit your turn.* **forfeit** *adjective*

forge[1] *verb*
1 to copy in order to trick or deceive: *to forge a signature* **2** to form or make by hard work: *A blacksmith forges horseshoes by heating and hammering metal. | I didn't like her much at first, but over the years we've forged a firm friendship.*

forge[1] *noun*
3 a furnace for softening metal before shaping it to make tools and other things

Word Building: **forgery** *noun* the crime of making an imitation and passing it off as genuine **forger** *noun*

forge[2] *verb*
to move forward with great effort: *to forge ahead through thick bush*

forget *verb*
to not remember: *I forgot to clean my teeth. | Don't tell him, he always forgets.*

Word Building: other forms are **I forgot, I have forgotten, I am forgetting** □ **forgetful** *adjective* **forgetfulness** *noun* **forgetfully** *adverb*

forgive *verb*
to excuse without holding any bad feelings: *He will forgive you if you say you are sorry.*

Word Building: other forms are **I forgave, I have forgiven, I am forgiving** □ **forgiveness** *noun* **forgiving** *adjective* **forgivingly** *adverb*

fork *noun*
1 an instrument with prongs for lifting food, digging the garden and other things **2** a place in a tree, road, or river where it divides into several parts: *Turn left at the fork in the road.*

Word Building: **forked** *adjective: the forked tongue of a snake* **fork** *verb*

fork-lift *noun*
a small truck with two horizontal arms or prongs for lifting and carrying heavy loads

forlorn (say *fə-lawn*) *adjective*
left all alone and miserable: *a forlorn puppy*

Word Building: **forlornly** *adverb*
Word History: from an Old English word meaning "lose" or "destroy"

form *noun*
1 shape or appearance: *a birthday cake in the form of a "6"* **2** condition or fitness: *How's his form? | They were in good form for the big match.* **3** a printed paper with blank spaces to fill in: *an entry form for the competition* **4** behaviour or conduct: *It is not good form to talk with your mouth full.* **5** the set of classes in high school for students of about the same age **6** a long seat or bench

form *verb*
7 to make, build or produce: *to form an idea | to freeze water to form ice* **8** to develop or be made: *Buds are forming on the trees.*

Word Building: **formative** *adjective* shaping or moulding

formal *adjective*
1 not relaxed or casual: *He greeted us in a formal manner. | formal clothes* **2** following the official or proper procedure: *to make a formal complaint in writing*

Word Building: **formally** *adverb*

formality *noun*
1 a way of thinking and behaving that is formal and not relaxed **2** something done only because it fits in with formal or polite behaviour: *Everybody knew she'd win, so the announcement was just a formality.*

Word Building: the plural for definition 2 is **formalities**

format (rhymes with *doormat*) *noun*
1 shape, plan or style: *The book is now available in a new format with a soft cover and bigger print.*
format *verb*
2 to organise information in a computer into files, and so on: *to format data*

Word Building: other forms of the verb are **it formatted, it has formatted, it is formatting**

formation *noun*
1 the process of making or producing: *the formation of ice from water* **2** something which has formed: *a rock formation*
3 a planned arrangement or pattern: *planes flying in formation*

former *adjective*
1 earlier or past: *a former marriage*
2 being the first one of two: *They served both tea and coffee but I chose the former.*

Word Use: the opposite of definition 2 is **latter**
Word Building: **formerly** *adverb* in the past

formidable (say *faw-mə-də-bəl*) *adjective*
1 very difficult and needing much hard work: *To clean up such a messy bedroom is a formidable task.* **2** frightening: *a formidable enemy*

Word Building: **formidably** *adverb*

formula (say *faw-myə-lə*) *noun*
1 a rule or recipe to be followed: *The formula for mixing the baby's milk is one part milk powder to five parts water.* **2** in chemistry, the representation of the atoms in a molecule by symbols: *The formula for water is H_2O.*

Word Building: the plural form is either **formulas** or **formulae** □ **formulate** *verb* to state clearly or exactly **formulation** *noun*

forsake *verb*
to give up or abandon

Word Building: other forms are **I forsook, I have forsaken, I am forsaking** □ **forsaken** *adjective* **forsakenly** *adverb*

fort *noun*
1 a place like a castle, which is strongly built and armed against enemy attack
2 hold the fort to look after things for someone while they are away

Word Use: a similar word for definition 1 is **fortress**
Word History: from a Latin word meaning "strong"

forte[1] (say *faw-tay*) *noun*
something that you do particularly well: *Music is her forte.*

forte[2] (say *faw-tay*) *adverb*
loudly: *This passage of music is played forte.*

Word Use: an instruction in music written as "f" □ the opposite is **piano**
Word Building: **fortissimo** *adverb* very loudly

forthcoming *adjective*
1 happening or coming soon: *our forthcoming visit to the zoo* **2** ready when needed: *We wanted to buy a boat but the money was not forthcoming.*

forthright *adjective*
speaking your mind openly and honestly

Word Building: **forthrightly** *adverb* **forthrightness** *noun*

fortify (say *faw-tə-fuy*) *verb*
to make strong so as to resist attack, damage and other harmful things: *to build strong walls to fortify the castle | to drink hot soup to fortify yourself against the cold*

Word Building: other forms are **I fortified, I have fortified, I am fortifying** □ **fortifications** *plural noun* a fort or a wall built to protect against enemy attack

fortnight *noun*
two weeks or fourteen days and nights

Word Building: **fortnightly** *adjective* **fortnightly** *adverb*

fortress *noun*
another word for **fort**

fortunate *adjective*
lucky or having good fortune: *You were fortunate to find the money you lost.*

Word Building: **fortunately** *adverb*

fortune *noun*
1 a great amount of money or property: *to make a fortune buying and selling land*
2 luck: *We had the good fortune to have fine weather for the sports carnival.* **3** fate or destiny: *to tell someone's fortune*

Word Use: the opposite of definition 2 is **misfortune**

forty (say *faw-tee*) *noun*
the number 40

Word Building: the plural is **forties** □ **forty** *adjective: forty years* **fortieth** *adjective: my fortieth birthday*

forum *noun*
1 a public meeting to discuss matters of general interest **2** the main square or marketplace of an ancient Roman town

Word Building: the plural can be either **forums** or **fora**

forward *adjective*
1 ahead or towards the front: *a forward step | the forward part of a boat*
2 behaving boldly usually in order to be noticed by others: *She is quite forward but her sister is very shy.*

forward *verb*
3 to send on: *to forward a letter to the new address*

forward *noun*
4 someone who plays in an attacking position in sports such as football and hockey

Word Building: **forward** *adverb* **forwards** *adverb*

fossick *verb*
1 to try to find gold or precious stones in ground that has already been worked over by others **2** to search or hunt: *to fossick through a drawer for a pencil*

Word Building: **fossicker** *noun*

fossil *noun*
1 the remains of an animal or plant from long ago, preserved as rock **2** someone who has old-fashioned ideas

fossil *adjective*
3 fossil fuel coal and oil which have formed underground from the remains of plants and animals millions of years old

Word Use: definition 2 is more suited to everyday language and may offend the person it is used about
Word Building: **fossilise** *verb* **fossilised** *adjective*
Word History: from a Latin word meaning "dug up"

foster *verb*
1 to take into a family and care for: *to foster an orphan child* **2** to help or encourage to grow: *to foster friendship between nations*

Word Use: compare definition 1 with **adopt**
Word Building: **foster** *adjective: a foster child | a foster home*

foul *adjective*
1 very nasty, dirty or unpleasant: *a foul smell | foul weather | foul language*

foul *verb*
2 to make or become dirty or unpleasant **3** to make or become jammed or caught: *Our propeller fouled on a fishing line.* **4** to play unfairly or break the rules in sport

Word Use: be careful – this sounds like **fowl**
Word Building: **foul** *noun* an unfair action in sport **foully** *adverb* **foulness** *noun*

found *verb*
to set up or start: *to found a new settlement*

Word Building: **founder** *noun* **founding** *adjective*

foundation *noun*
1 the founding or setting up of something **2** a base on which something rests or stands: *the stone foundations of a building | the foundations of society*

Word Use: definition 2 is often used in the plural
Word Building: **foundation** *adjective: a foundation member of the club*

founder[1] *noun*
someone who begins or starts up something: *He is the founder of the art gallery.*

founder[2] *verb*
1 to fill with water and sink: *The ship began to founder off the jagged reef.* **2** to go lame, trip, or break down: *The horse foundered during the steeplechase.*

fountain *noun*
1 a place where water spurts upward or streams downward from a water pipe
2 the origin or source: *the fountain of wisdom*

fountain pen *noun*
a pen which has a small container inside for supplying ink to the nib

four (say *faw*) *noun*
the number 4

Word Use: be careful – this sounds like **for** and **fore**
Word Building: **four** *adjective: four angles* **fourth** *adjective: the fourth child*

fourteen *noun*
the number 14

Word Building: **fourteen** *adjective: fourteen friends* **fourteenth** *adjective: fourteenth birthday*

four-wheel drive *noun*
a car or truck which can travel over rough country or soft ground because all four wheels are driven by the engine

fowl *noun*
a bird kept for eating or for its eggs, such as a hen, duck or turkey

Word Use: be careful – this sounds like **foul**
Word Building: the plural can be **fowls** or, if you are talking about a group of birds, **fowl**

fox *noun*
1 a small wild dog with red-brown fur, a long bushy tail and pointed ears
2 someone who is sly or cunning

Word Use: the male is a **dog;** the female is a **vixen;** the young is a **cub**
Word Building: the plural is **foxes** □ **foxy** *adjective* sly and cunning **foxily** *adverb* **foxiness** *noun*

foyer (say *foy-ə*) *noun*
the large entrance hall of a theatre or hotel

fraction *noun*
1 a part of a whole number: *$\frac{3}{4}$ is a fraction* **2** a small piece or amount: *to open the door a fraction*

Word Building: **fractional** *adjective* **fractionally** *adverb*
Word History: from a Latin word meaning "break"

fractious (say *frak-shəs*) *adjective*
bad-tempered and uncooperative: *a fractious child*

Word Building: **fractiously** *adverb*

fracture *verb*
to crack or break: *to fall over and fracture your arm | The rock fractured when we hit it.*

Word Building: **fracture** *noun*

fragile *adjective*
delicate and easily damaged or broken: *a fragile china cup*

Word Building: **fragilely** *adverb* **fragility** *noun*

fragment *noun*
a part that has been broken off or left unfinished: *a fragment of glass | a fragment of a poem*

Word Building: **fragment** *verb* to break into small pieces **fragmentary** *adjective* **fragmentation** *noun*

fragrant *adjective*
sweet-smelling: *a fragrant perfume*

Word Building: **fragrance** *noun* **fragrantly** *adverb*

frail *adjective*
weak or delicate: *to be frail after a long illness*

Word Building: **frailty** *noun* (**frailties**) weakness **frailly** *adverb* **frailness** *noun*

frame *noun*
1 the structure which fits around or supports something and gives it shape: *a picture frame | a house with a wooden frame | the human frame* **2** one of the small pictures that make up a strip of film **3 frame of mind** mood: *to be in a good frame of mind*

frame *verb*
4 to form or put together: *to frame a plan* **5** to put into a frame or surround like a frame: *to frame a picture | Curly hair framed her face.* **6** to make seem guilty: *The gangster framed his innocent partner.*

Word Use: definition 6 is more suited to everyday language
Word Building: **framework** *noun* a supporting frame

franchise (say *fran-chuyz*) *noun*
1 a citizen's right to vote **2** permission given by a manufacturer to a shopkeeper to sell his products

Word History: from a French word meaning "free"

frank *adjective*
1 open or not pretending in what you say: *to give a frank answer*

frank *noun*
2 a mark put on a letter in place of a postage stamp to show that postage has already been paid

Word Use: a similar word to definition 1 is **sincere**
Word Building: **frank** *verb: to frank a letter* **frankly** *adverb* openly **frankness** *noun*

frankfurt *noun*
a spicy red-coloured sausage, usually eaten with a bread roll

Word Use: other names are **frankfurter** and **saveloy**
Word History: named after *Frankfurt*, a town in Germany

frantic *adjective*
wild with excitement, fear, worry or pain

Word Building: **frantically** *adverb*

fraternal *adjective*
of or like a brother

Word Building: **fraternity** *noun* a group of people, often men, with the same interests or goals: *the legal fraternity* **fraternise** *verb* to be friendly **fraternally** *adverb*

fraud (rhymes with *cord*) *noun*
1 deliberate trickery or cheating
2 someone or something that is not what they pretend to be

Word Building: **fraudulent** *adjective* **fraudulently** *adverb*

fray[1] *noun*
a noisy fight or quarrel: *When the older children joined the fray the whole playground was in an uproar.*

fray[2] *verb*
to wear out: *My shirt collar is fraying. / A hard day's work frayed her temper.*

frazzled *adjective*
weary or tired out: *I'm frazzled after a day looking after a screaming baby.*

Word Building: **frazzle** *noun* the state of being worn out or burnt: *worn to a frazzle / burnt to a frazzle* **frazzle** *verb*

freak *noun*
someone or something that is extremely strange or unusual

Word Building: **freak** *adjective* unusual: *a freak storm* **freakish** *adjective* weird: *freakish behaviour* **freakishly** *adverb*

freckle *noun*
a small brown spot on your skin caused by the sun: *People with red hair usually have freckles.*

Word Building: **freckle** *verb* **freckled** *adjective*

free *adjective*
1 costing nothing: *free tickets to the pictures* **2** not confined or restricted: *The bird flew out of the cage and is free. / a free choice* **3** not being used: *The room is free now.*

Word Building: **free** *verb* (**freed, freeing**) **free** *adverb: to set the bird free* **freely** *adverb*

freedom *noun*
the right to act or speak out as you wish

Word Use: a similar word is **liberty**

freehand *adjective*
drawn by hand, and not traced or drawn with a ruler, compass or other instruments: *a freehand drawing*

Word Building: **freehand** *adverb*

freelance *noun*
someone, especially a writer, who doesn't work for a wage but who sells work to more than one employer

Word Building: **freelance** *verb* **freelance** *adjective*

free-range *adjective*
able to walk around and feed freely, rather than being kept in a cage: *free-range chickens*

freestyle *noun*
1 *another word for the swimming style known as the* **crawl** **2** a swimming race in which you can use any style you like, usually the crawl because it is the fastest

Word Building: **freestyle** *adjective*

free verse *noun*
poetry without regular rhythms or rhymes

freeway *noun*
a road on which traffic can travel fast

Word Use: another name for this is **expressway**

freeze *verb*
1 to turn to ice: *The puddles froze. / We froze our drinks.* **2** to be or feel very cold **3** to keep fresh by putting in a freezer: *She froze the meat.* **4** to keep very still, as with fear: *Thinking she heard footsteps, she froze.*

freeze *noun*
5 a period of very cold weather **6** a period in which no change is allowed in something, such as prices or wages

Word Use: be careful – this sounds like **frieze**
Word Building: other verb forms are **I froze, I have frozen, I am freezing** □ **frozen** *adjective*

freight (rhymes with *rate*) *noun*
1 goods sent by air, sea or land **2** the charge for sending goods

Word Building: **freighter** *noun* a ship or plane that carries goods **freight** *verb*

French horn *noun*
a brass wind instrument with a mellow tone

frenetic (say *frə-net-ik*) *adjective*
insane or frantic: *frenetic activity*

Word Use: this is sometimes spelt **phrenetic**
Word Building: **frenetically** *adverb*

frenzy *noun*
a wildly or furiously excited state: *The dog was in a frenzy barking at all the cars.*

Word Building: **frenzied** *adjective*

frequency (say *free-kwən-see*) *noun*
1 the fact of happening often: *He was annoyed by the frequency of her visits.*
2 the rate at which something happens: *the frequency of a pulse* **3** the rate of cycles or vibrations of a wave movement: *His radio only picks up stations on a high frequency.*

Word Building: the plural is **frequencies**

frequent (say *free-kwənt*) *adjective*
1 happening often: *They make frequent visits to the beach.*
frequent (say *frə-kwent*) *verb*
2 to visit often: *She frequents the cinema.*

Word Building: **frequently** *adverb*

fresco *noun*
a painting done on a freshly plastered wall or ceiling before it has dried, so that the colours sink in

Word Building: the plural is **frescoes** or **frescos**
Word History: from an Italian word meaning "cool"

fresh *adjective*
1 in a natural state: *Sometimes we have fresh fruit and sometimes stewed fruit.*
2 new: *fresh milk | fresh footprints* **3** cool: *It's a fresh morning.* **4** not salt: *fresh water* **5** strong and not tired or faded: *fresh colour | She looks fresh after her holiday.* **6** just arrived: *fresh from home* **7** cheeky: *Don't get fresh with me!*

Word Building: **fresh** *noun* **freshen** *verb* **freshly** *adverb* **freshness** *noun*

fret[1] *verb*
to be worried or annoyed: *He frets about things not being done properly.*

Word Building: other forms are **I fretted, I have fretted, I am fretting**

fret[2] *noun*
one of the bars across the neck of a stringed instrument, such as a guitar, which marks off the notes

friar *noun*
a member of a religious order, such as the Dominicans or the Franciscans, who lives a simple life of prayer

Word Building: **friary** *noun* a place where friars live
Word History: from a Latin word meaning "brother"

friction *noun*
1 the rubbing of one thing against another: *There is some friction where the wheel touches the mudguard.* **2** a clash or struggle: *There was friction between the sisters.*

Friday *noun*
the sixth day of the week

Word Use: the abbreviation is **Fri**

fridge *noun*
short for **refrigerator**

friend (rhymes with *bend*) *noun*
someone you like and who likes you

Word Building: **friendliness** *noun* **friendly** *adjective* **friendship** *noun*

frieze (rhymes with *breeze*) *noun*
a band around the top of a wall which is often decorated with a painted or sculpted pattern

Word Use: be careful – this sounds like **freeze**

frigate (say *frig-ət*) *noun*
a warship, often used as an escort vessel

fright *noun*
1 a sudden feeling of fear or shock: *She crept up to give him a fright.* **2** someone or something of a shocking or silly appearance: *to look a fright*

Word Building: **frighten** *verb* **frightened** *adjective*

frightful *adjective*
1 alarming or unpleasant: *They had a frightful time trying to cross the flooded river.* **2** very bad: *We saw a frightful film.*

Word Building: **frightfully** *adverb* very

frigid (say *frij-əd*) *adjective*
1 very cold: *a frigid climate* **2** stiff or unfriendly: *His frigid manner puts people off.*

Word Building: **frigidity** *noun* coldness **frigidly** *adverb* stiffly

frill *noun*
a ruffled edge, used to decorate something like the hem or neck of a dress

Word Building: **frill** *verb* to add a frill to **frilly** *adjective*

fringe *noun*
1 a border of loose or bunched threads on something like a scarf or rug **2** hair which has been cut across the forehead **3** the edge or outer part: *We live on the fringe of the town.*
fringe *adjective*
4 extra: *A fringe benefit of the job is the use of a car.*

Word Building: **fringe** *verb*

frisk *verb*
1 to leap around playfully, as a lamb or kitten does **2** to search for hidden weapons: *After the bomb scare, guards frisked the visitors.*

Word Use: definition 2 is more suited to everyday language
Word Building: **frisky** *adjective* lively **friskily** *adverb* **friskiness** *noun*

fritter[1] *verb*
to waste gradually: *She fritters her money away on useless things.*

fritter[2] *noun*
a small piece of food, often fruit, fried in batter: *banana fritter*

frivolous (say *friv-ə-ləs*) *adjective*
not serious: *He is in trouble for giving frivolous answers to the questions.*

Word Building: **frivolity** *noun* **frivolously** *adverb*

frock *noun*
a rather old-fashioned word for a **dress**

frog *noun*
a tailless creature with webbed feet and long back legs for jumping, which lives in water or on land

frogman *noun*
a diver, especially one with a wetsuit, flippers, mask and snorkel or air tank

Word Building: the plural is **frogmen**

frolic *noun*
happy play: *After school they had a good frolic outside.*

Word Building: **frolic** *verb* (**frolicked, frolicking**) **frolicsome** *adjective*
Word History: from a Dutch word meaning "joyful"

frond *noun*
the divided leaf of plants such as ferns and palms

front (rhymes with *blunt*) *noun*
1 the part or surface facing forward or most often seen: *The door is at the front.*
2 the battle line: *Many soldiers died at the front.* **3** land facing a road or shore: *No-one owns the lake front.*

Word Building: **front** *adjective*

frontier (say *frun-tear*) *noun*
1 the border of a country or state
2 the end of known territory: *The early settlers explored the frontier.*

frost *noun*
1 extreme cold **2** the covering of ice formed when dew freezes
frost *verb*
3 to ice: *The baker frosted the cake.*

Word Building: **frosted** *adjective* **frostily** *adverb* **frostiness** *noun* **frosty** *adjective*

frostbite *noun*
damage done by the freezing of exposed parts of your body in very cold conditions

Word Building: **frostbitten** *adjective*

frosting *noun*
1 a fluffy cake icing **2** a frostlike coating on glass, metal or other surfaces

froth *noun*
the mass of tiny bubbles that rise to the top of some liquids

Word Use: a word with the same meaning is **foam**
Word Building: **froth** *verb* **frothily** *adverb* **frothiness** *noun* **frothy** *adjective*

frown *verb*
1 to wrinkle your forehead in a look of worry or displeasure **2 frown on** to disapprove of

Word Building: **frown** *noun*

frugal (say *frooh-gəl*) *adjective*
1 very careful not to waste anything
2 poor or cheap: *They had a frugal meal of bread and tomatoes.*

Word Building: **frugality** *noun* **frugally** *adverb*

fruit *noun*
1 the edible part which grows from the flowers of trees and plants, such as apples, oranges, pineapples, and many others
2 the result: *Her book is the fruit of years of work.*

Word Building: **fruit** *verb* to bear fruit

frustrate *verb*
to put difficulties in the way of, or prevent: *She frustrates his attempts to help by doing everything herself.*

Word Building: **frustrated** *adjective* **frustration** *noun*

fry *verb*
to cook in a pan, using fat or oil

Word Building: other forms are **I fried, I have fried, I am frying** □ **fried** *adjective*

fudge *noun*
a soft sweet made from sugar, butter and milk

fuel *noun*
anything, such as wood, petrol or kerosene, which is burned to give heat or to make an engine work

Word Building: **fuel** *verb* (**fuelled, fuelling**) to get or supply with fuel
Word History: from a Latin word meaning "hearth" or "fireplace"

fugitive (say *fyooh-jə-tiv*) *noun*
someone who is running away

Word Building: **fugitive** *adjective*

fugue (say *fyoohg*) *noun*
a piece of music in which a short melody is played or sung and then copied by other instruments or voices

Word History: from a Latin word meaning "flight"

fulcrum (say *foolk-rəm*) *noun*
the point on which something balances or turns: *A bent pipe made a fulcrum for the seesaw.*

Word Building: the plural is **fulcrum** or **fulcra**

fulfil *verb*
1 to carry out: *He fulfilled his promise to pay.* **2** to satisfy: *She fulfils her need to paint at the weekend.*

Word Building: other forms are **I fulfilled, I have fulfilled, I am fulfilling** □ **fulfilled** *adjective* **fulfilment** *noun*

full *adjective*
1 filled up **2** whole or complete: *Jason has collected the full series of cards.* **3** wide or loose: *She is wearing a full skirt.*

Word Building: **full** *adverb* completely **fully** *adverb*

fullblood *noun*
someone of unmixed race, especially an Aborigine

full stop *noun*
a punctuation mark (.) which is used at the end of a sentence, as in "She held the dog." or to show that a word has been shortened, as in "adj." (adjective)

full-time *adjective*
working most of the week at any job: *a full-time mother | a full-time actor*

fumble *verb*
to handle clumsily: *He fumbled the catch and dropped the ball.*

Word Building: **fumbler** *noun* **fumbling** *adjective*

fume *noun*
1 fumes smoke or gas which can be easily seen or smelled
fume *verb*
2 to give out fumes **2** to be very angry: *Don't go near her because she is fuming.*

Word Building: **fuming** *adjective*

fumigate (say *fyooh-mə-gayt*) *verb*
to treat with chemical fumes to get rid of insect pests

Word Building: **fumigation** *noun* **fumigator** *noun*

fun *noun*
1 enjoyment **2** playfulness: *to feel full of fun* **3 make fun of** to tease

function *noun*
1 what someone or something is meant to do: *one of the functions of a treasurer | the function of a vehicle* **2** a social or official occasion, such as a dinner to raise money
function *verb*
3 to work or go: *The heater isn't functioning.*

Word Building: **functional** *adjective* useful **functionally** *adverb*

function key *noun*
a set of keys on a computer keyboard, usually ten or twelve, which you can program to perform complicated tasks when you press the key down once

fund *noun*
1 a supply of money: *They have a fund which pays for their holidays.* **2** a supply: *His fund of experience is helpful.*

Word Building: **fund** *verb* to pay for

fundamental *adjective*
1 most important or basic: *You have to learn the fundamental rules of the road before you can get a licence.*
fundamental *noun*
2 the basic rule or principle underlying any system: *He is learning the fundamentals of computer programming.*

Word Use: a similar word for definition 1 is **cardinal**
Word Building: **fundamentally** *adverb* basically
Word History: from a Latin word meaning "foundation"

funeral *noun*
a service held to honour someone who has died, which usually takes place in a church and is followed by the burial or cremation of the body

Word Building: funereal *adjective* gloomy as a funeral

fungus *noun*
a simple plant, such as the mushroom, mould or yeast, which grows in dark or damp places

Word Building: the plural is **fungi** or **funguses**

funnel *noun*
1 an open-ended cone used for pouring liquid or dry goods into a container with a narrow opening **2** the wide tube which forms the chimney of a ship or steam-engine

Word Building: funnel *verb* (**funnelled, funnelling**) to pour through a funnel

funnel-web *noun*
a large black venomous spider of eastern Australia, which builds a funnel-shaped web

funny *adjective*
1 amusing or comical **2** strange: *There's something funny about this recipe.*

Word Building: other forms are **funnier, funniest**

funny bone *noun*
the point of your elbow which tingles when it is hit

fur *noun*
1 the hairy coat of some animals, such as dogs, cats and possums **2** the skin of some animals, such as rabbits, minks and foxes, which is treated and made into a garment: *The ladies wore furs.*

Word Use: be careful – this sounds like **fir**
Word Building: furrier *noun* a maker or seller of furs **furriness** *noun* **furry** *adjective*

furious *adjective*
1 extremely angry **2** strong or violent: *A furious wind knocked the trees over.*

Word Building: furiously *adverb* **fury** *noun* **infuriate** *verb*

furl *verb*
to roll up: *The sailors lowered and furled the flag.*

furlong *noun*
an old-fashioned unit of distance just over 200 metres long

furnace *noun*
a structure for producing heat, as in the steel industry or for heating buildings

furnish *verb*
1 to decorate with furniture and other fittings: *They have furnished the sitting room with cane chairs.* **2** to provide: *The attendant will furnish you with pens and paper.*

Word Building: furnishings *plural noun* the carpets, furniture, and so on used to furnish a room

furniture *noun*
the chairs, beds, tables and other fittings of a room or house

furore (say *fyooh-raw*) *noun*
an outburst of noisy disorder

furphy (say *fer-fee*) *noun*
a piece of gossip

Word History: named after a Victorian man, John *Furphy*, who made water and sanitation carts, which used to be centres of gossip

furrow *noun*
1 a groove, especially one made by a plough
furrow *verb*
2 to wrinkle: *A frown furrowed her brow.*

further *adverb*
1 at or to a greater distance: *I ran further than you.* **2** in addition
further *adjective*
3 more distant: *The further house is ours.*
4 more: *Do you want further advice?*

Word Use: for definitions 1 and 3 the form **farther** can be used □ this word is part of the set **far, further, furthest**
Word Building: further *verb* to help to advance

furtive *adjective*
stealthy or sly: *She took a furtive look to see if anyone was watching.*

Word Building: furtively *adverb*

fury *noun*
extreme or violent anger: *He smashed the door in his fury.*

fuse[1] *noun*
1 the wick which sets off an explosive when it is lit **2** the safety wire in an electrical circuit which cuts off the power if there is a fault

Word Building: fuse *verb: The lights fused, and everything went dark.*

fuse[2] *verb*
to melt into one: *He fused the two metals by heating them.* | *The burnt wires fused.*

Word Building: fusion *noun*

fuselage (say *fyooh-zə-lahzh*) *noun*
the body of an aircraft

Word History: from a French word meaning "shaped like a spindle"

fuss *noun*
1 unnecessary bother: *She does everything without fuss.* **2** a noise or disturbance: *When they couldn't get the seats they wanted, they made a great fuss.*

Word Building: **fussily** *adverb* **fussiness** *noun* **fussy** *adjective*

futile *adjective*
useless and ineffective: *The dog made futile jumps at the cat up in the tree.*

Word Building: **futility** *noun* uselessness **futilely** *adverb*

future *noun*
the time which has not yet come: *Everyone worries about the future.*

Word Building: **future** *adjective : future plans* **futuristic** *adjective* in a modern style, especially of the space age

future tense *noun*
the form of a verb, using "will" or "shall", which shows that something is going to happen, such as "will run" in *I will run in the race tomorrow.*

fuzz *noun*
1 a fluffy mass or coating **2** the police

Word Use: definition 2 is more suited to everyday language
Word Building: **fuzzy** *adjective* blurred **fuzzily** *adverb* **fuzziness** *noun*

gaberdine (say *gab-ə-deen*) *noun*
closely woven cloth made of wool, cotton, or spun rayon

Word Use: another spelling is **gabardine**

gable *noun*
the triangular part of a wall between the two slopes of a roof

Word Building: **gabled** *adjective*

gadget *noun*
a small invention or useful piece of machinery which performs a particular job: *a gadget for slicing carrots*

Word Building: **gadgetry** *noun* any of or all the gadgets there are

gag[1] *verb*
1 to cover someone's mouth to stop them from speaking or making a sound
gag[1] *noun*
2 something pushed into or tied round your mouth to prevent you from speaking

Word Building: other verb forms are **I gagged, I have gagged, I am gagging** □ **gagger** *noun* **gagster** *noun*

gag[2] *noun*
a joke or trick

Word Building: **gag** *verb* (**gagged, gagging**) **gagger** *noun*

gaggle *noun*
a flock of geese

Word History: the word imitates the noise that geese make

gaiety (say *gay-ə-tee*) *noun*
cheerfulness or high spirits

Word Building: **gaily** *adverb* **gay** *adjective*

gain *verb*
1 to get or win: *to gain top marks in an exam | to gain a prize* **2** to catch up: *He gained rapidly on the fat man.* **3 gain ground** to go forward or get an advantage: *The party has gained ground in its goal to save the environment.* **4 gain time** to delay: *The lawyer needs to gain time in the court case to find another witness.*
gain *noun*
5 a profit: *a gain of $2 on the sale*

Word Building: **gainful** *adjective*

gait (say *gayt*) *noun*
way of walking or moving: *an old man's gait | a horse's gait*

Word Use: be careful – this sounds like **gate**

gala (say *gah-lə*) *noun*
a celebration or special occasion: *a swimming gala*

Word History: from a Dutch word meaning "riches"

galah (say *gə-lah*) *noun*
1 an Australian cockatoo with pink and grey feathers **2** a foolish person

Word Use: definition 2 is more suited to everday language
Word History: from the Aboriginal language called Yuwaalaraay

galaxy *noun*
1 a large group of stars separated from any other similar group by great areas of space **2 the Galaxy** our particular galaxy which contains several billion stars as well as our solar system

Word Use: another name for definition 2 is the **Milky Way**
Word Building: the plural is **galaxies** □ **galactic** *adjective*
Word History: from a Greek word meaning "milk"

gale *noun*
a very strong wind

gallant (say *gal-ənt, gə-lant*) *adjective*
1 brave and noble **2** very polite and courteous

Word Building: **gallant** *noun* a brave and dashing man **gallantry** *noun*
Word History: from a French word meaning "magnificent"

gall bladder (say *gawl*) *noun*
a part of your body attached to your liver, which stores bile

galleon *noun*
a kind of large sailing ship with three masts, used in former times by Spain and other countries

gallery *noun*
1 an upper floor or balcony where you can sit, especially in a theatre **2** a room or building where you can see paintings and sculptures

Word Building: the plural is **galleries**

galley *noun*
1 a long low ship propelled by oars **2** the kitchen in a ship or aeroplane

Word Building: the plural is **galleys**

gallon *noun*
an old-fashioned measure of liquid equal to about 4.5 litres

gallop *noun*
1 the fastest movement of a horse

gallop *verb*
2 to ride a horse at full speed: *The drovers galloped after the cattle.*

Word Building: other verb forms are **I galloped, I have galloped, I am galloping**
Word History: from a German word meaning "run well"

gallows *noun*
a wooden frame for hanging criminals

galore (say *gə-law*) *adverb*
in great numbers: *There were cakes galore at the party.*

Word Use: this word is only used after nouns

galvanise or **galvanize** *verb*
1 to cause to move by, or as if by, an electric current: *to galvanise into action* **2** to coat with zinc to prevent rust: *to galvanise iron*

Word Building: **galvanisation** *noun*

gamble (say *gam-bəl*) *verb*
1 to play a game in which you risk losing something, especially money **2** to take a chance: *I gambled on his being away that day.*

Word Building: **gamble** *noun* **gambler** *noun* **gambling** *noun*

gambol (say *gam-bəl*) *verb*
to jump about in play: *The children gambolled in the shallow water.*

Word Building: other forms are **I gambolled, I have gambolled, I am gambolling**

game *noun*
1 something you can play, usually with set rules: *a game of football | a game of cards* **2** wild animals, including birds and fish, hunted for food or as a sport: *a book of recipes for cooking game* **3 off your game** not giving your best performance **4 play the game** to act fairly

game *adjective*
5 brave and courageous: *as game as Ned Kelly* **6** willing to do something difficult or dangerous: *I'm game if you are.*

Word Use: definition 6 is more suited to everyday language
Word Building: **gamely** *adverb* bravely **gameness** *noun*

gamut (say *gam-ət*) *noun*
the whole scale or range: *A good actor can express the whole gamut of emotion.*

gander *noun*
a male goose

Word Use: the female is a **goose**; the young is a **gosling**

gang *noun*
1 a band or group: *a gang of children* **2** a group of people working together: *a gang of labourers*

gang *verb*
3 gang up on to join together or take sides against: *Don't gang up on me!*

gangling (say *gang-gling*) *adjective*
awkwardly tall and thin: *a gangling youth who had grown out of his clothes*

Word Use: another spelling is **gangly**

gangplank *noun*
a movable board used as a bridge for going on and off a ship

gangrene (say *gang-green*) *noun*
the rotting of flesh caused by the blood supply being cut off

Word Building: **gangrenous** *adjective*

gangster *noun*
a member of a gang of criminals

gangway *noun*
1 a passageway, especially on a ship
2 *another word for* **gangplank**

gaol (say *jayl*) *noun*
the place where prisoners are kept while they serve their sentence

Word Use: be careful – this word looks like **goal** □ another spelling is **jail**
Word Building: **gaoler** *noun* **gaol** *verb* to imprison

gap *noun*
1 a break or opening: *a gap in the fence*
2 a blank or unfilled space: *a gap in my memory | a gap between words*

gape *verb*
1 to stare with your mouth wide open: *They all gaped at her green hair.* **2** to split or become open: *Your jeans are gaping at the seams.*

Word Building: **gape** *noun* **gaper** *noun* **gapingly** *adverb*

garage *noun*
1 a building for keeping a car, bus or truck **2** a place where cars are mended and petrol is sold

Word Use: another name for definition 2 is **service station**
Word Building: **garage** *verb*
Word History: from a French word meaning "put in shelter"

garbage *noun*
rubbish or waste material

garble *verb*
to mix up and so make hard to understand: *to garble a message*

Word Building: **garbler** *noun*

garden *noun*
1 an area, usually with trees and plants, used for pleasure and as a place to relax: *the front garden | a botanical garden* **2** a flower bed: *a herb garden* **3 lead up the garden path** to trick or lead away from the truth

Word Use: definition 3 is more suited to everyday language
Word Building: **garden** *verb* **gardener** *noun*

gargle *verb*
to move a liquid around inside your throat without swallowing

Word Building: **gargle** *noun*

gargoyle (say *gah-goyl*) *noun*
a spout, often carved in the shape of an ugly head with an open mouth, which carries rainwater off a roof

garish (say *gair-rish, gah-*) *adjective*
bright and attracting attention: *garish colours*

Word Use: a similar word is **gaudy**
Word Building: **garishly** *adverb* **garishness** *noun*

garland *noun*
a string of flowers or leaves you wear as an ornament

garlic *noun*
a plant with a strong flavour like an onion, used in cooking

garment *noun*
a piece of clothing, such as a dress or shirt

garnish *verb*
to make more pleasing to taste or look at: *Garnish the fish with parsley and lemon.*

Word Use: this word is used mostly in cookery
Word Building: **garnish** *noun*

garret *noun*
a room just under the roof of a house

Word Use: a similar word is **attic**

garrison *noun*
1 a group of soldiers who are ready to defend a fort or town **2** a place that has been strengthened against attack

Word Building: **garrison** *verb*

garrulous (say *ga-rə-ləs*) *adjective*
very talkative

Word Building: **garrulity** *noun* talkativeness **garrulously** *adverb* **garrulousness** *noun*

garter *noun*
a band made of elastic worn around your leg to hold up your long socks

gas[1] *noun*
1 any air-like substance that will take up the whole of the space that contains it **2** coal gas or natural gas used as a fuel: *We use gas for cooking.*

gas[1] *verb*
3 to make sick or kill with a poisonous gas

Word Use: for definition 1 compare **solid** and **liquid**
Word Building: the plural of the noun is **gases** □ other forms of the verb are **I gassed, I have gassed, I am gassing** □ **gaseous** *adjective* like gas **gassy** *adjective* full of gas
Word History: made up by a Flemish chemist who based it on a Greek word meaning "chaos"

gas[2] *noun*
an American word for **petrol**

Word History: short for *gasoline*

gash *noun*
a long deep cut: *a gash in her leg*

Word Building: **gash** *verb*

gasket *noun*
a metal or rubber fitting used to seal a joint, especially one in a car engine

gasp *noun*
1 a sudden short intake of breath: *He gave a gasp of horror.*
gasp *verb*
2 to catch your breath or struggle for breath with your mouth open

Word Building: **gasper** *noun*

gastr- *prefix*
a word part meaning stomach: *gastric*

Word Use: other spellings are **gastero-** and **gastro-**
Word History: this prefix comes from Greek

gastric *adjective*
of or in your stomach: *gastric pains*

gate (say *gayt*) *noun*
1 a movable frame for closing an entrance or blocking a passageway **2** the number of people who pay for admission to a sporting event

Word Use: be careful – this sounds like **gait**

gatecrash *verb*
to enter or be present at without paying or being invited: *to gatecrash the tennis tournament | to gatecrash a party*

Word Building: **gatecrasher** *noun*

gather *verb*
1 to collect or pick: *to gather fruit* **2** to understand: *I gather that he is an expert.* **3** to draw into small folds on a thread: *to gather a skirt at the waist* **4** to come together: *A crowd gathered to see the fire.*

Word Building: **gathering** *noun* a crowd of people **gatherable** *adjective* **gatherer** *noun*

gauche (say *gohsh*) *adjective*
clumsy and awkward: *gauche manners*

Word Building: **gaucherie** *noun* clumsiness **gaucheness** *noun*

gaudy (say *gaw-dee*) *adjective*
bright and attracting attention: *a gaudy beach towel*

Word Building: other forms are **gaudier, gaudiest** □ **gaudily** *adverb* **gaudiness** *noun*

gauge (say *gayj*) *verb*
1 to judge or make a guess at: *to gauge the public reaction* **2** to measure: *to gauge the height of the building*
gauge *noun*
3 thickness, especially of thin objects: *wire of a fine gauge* **4** an instrument for measuring: *a pressure gauge* **5** the distance between the two lines of a railway track

gaunt (say *gawnt*) *adjective*
very thin and tired-looking in appearance

Word Building: **gauntly** *adverb* **gauntness** *noun*
Word History: from a French word meaning "rather yellow"

gauze (say *gawz*) *noun*
1 thin transparent cloth **2** similar material with an open weave, such as wire

Word Building: **gauzy** *adjective* (**gauzier, gauziest**) **gauziness** *noun*

gay *adjective*
1 cheerful or bright: *gay music | gay colours* **2** homosexual: *gay liberation*

Word Use: definition 2 is more suited to everyday language
Word Building: **gay** *noun* **gaiety** *noun* **gaily** *adverb*

gaze *verb*
to look long and steadily

Word Building: **gaze** *noun*

gazelle (say *gə-zel*) *noun*
a small antelope with large eyes

Word Building: **gazelle-like** *adjective*

gazette (say *gə-zet*) *noun*
an official government magazine containing lists of people the government has appointed

Word Building: **gazette** *verb* to list or announce in a gazette
Word History: from the Italian name for a coin (the price of the gazette)

gear *noun*
1 a group of toothed wheels, or one of the wheels, that connect with each other to pass on or change the movement of a machine, such as those that carry power from the engine to the wheels of a car **2** equipment: *climbing gear* / *cricket gear* **3** clothes

Word Use: definition 3 is more suited to everyday language
Word Building: **gear** *verb*

gearbox *noun*
a case in which gears of a motor are enclosed

gearstick *noun*
a lever for connecting and disconnecting gears in a car

gecko *noun*
a small lizard which is mostly active at night

Word Building: the plural is **geckos** or **geckoes**
Word History: from a Malay word that imitates the sounds these lizards make

Geiger counter (say *guy-gə*) *noun*
an instrument for measuring radioactivity, especially after the explosion of an atom bomb

Word History: named after the German physicist, Hans *Geiger*

gel (say *jel*) *noun*
a type of jelly that you can use to help shape your hair style

Word Building: **gel** *verb* (**gelled, gelling**)
Word History: short for **gelatine**

gelatine *noun*
a colourless, tasteless substance, used to make jellies and glues

gelding (say *gel-ding*) *noun*
a male horse that has had its sex organs removed

Word Building: **geld** *verb* to remove the sex organs of

gelignite (say *jel-əg-nuyt*) *noun*
an explosive substance used in mining

gem *noun*
1 a stone used in jewellery, after it has been cut and polished **2** any person or thing that is as beautiful or valuable as a gem

gender (say *jen-də*) *noun*
1 a set of groups in the grammar of languages such as Latin, into which all nouns can be divided. These groups include masculine nouns like "boy", feminine nouns like "girl" , and neuter nouns in which the object has no sex or the sex isn't known. **2** sex, either male or female: *Do you know the gender of these pet mice?*

Word Use: definition 2 is more suited to everyday language

gene (say *jeen*) *noun*
one of the units in your body which is responsible for passing on characteristics, like blue eyes, from parents to their children

Word Building: **genetic** *adjective* **genetics** *noun*
Word History: from a Greek word meaning "breed" or "kind"

genealogy (say *jee-nee-al-ə-jee*) *noun*
a study or record of the ancestors and relations in your family

Word Use: a similar word is **pedigree**, but it is used more often of animals
Word Building: the plural form is **genealogies** □ **genealogist** *noun* **genealogical** *adjective*

general *adjective*
1 concerning all or most people: *a general election* **2** common or widespread: *a general feeling of unhappiness* **3** not limited to particular details or information: *general instructions*

general *noun*
4 an officer of the highest rank in the Australian army **5** a military commander: *Julius Caesar was a great general.* **6 in general** **a** as a whole, with everything included: *to discuss things in general* **b** usually: *In general, there is snow on the mountains at this time of year.*

Word Building: **generalise** *verb* to make up a general rule from a limited number of examples **generally** *adverb* **generality** *noun*

generate *verb*
to produce or bring into existence: *The sun generates heat.*

generation *noun*
1 all of the people born about the same time: *the younger generation* **2** the period of years, usually about 25 to 30, thought of as the difference between one generation of a family and another

generator *noun*
a machine for producing electricity

generous *adjective*
unselfish or ready to give freely: *a generous person*

Word Use: the opposite of this is **selfish**
Word Building: **generosity** *noun* **generously** *adverb*
Word History: from a Latin word meaning "of noble birth"

genesis (say *jen-ə-səs*) *noun*
a coming into being: *the genesis of the Australian nation*

Word Use: when spelt with a capital, **Genesis** is the name of the first book of the Bible, which gives a story of the creation of the world
Word Building: the plural is **geneses**
Word History: from a Greek word meaning "creation"

genetics *noun*
the science which studies the passing on of special characteristics from parents to their offspring

Word Use: this word is singular, like **mathematics**
Word Building: **gene** *noun* **genetic** *adjective* **genetically** *adverb* **geneticist** *noun*

genial (say *jee-nee-əl*) *adjective*
having a warm and friendly manner

Word Building: **geniality** *noun* **genially** *adverb*

genie (say *jee-nee*) *noun*
a spirit in Arabian stories

genitals *plural noun*
the parts of your body which are used for sexual intercourse and reproduction, especially the penis in males and the vagina in females

Word Use: another name is **genitalia**
Word Building: **genital** *adjective*

genius *noun*
a very talented or clever person

Word Building: the plural is **geniuses**
Word History: from a Latin word meaning "guardian spirit"

genocide (say *jen-ə-suyd*) *noun*
the planned killing of all the people belonging to one race or nation

Word Building: **genocidal** *adjective*

genre (say *zhon-rə*) *noun*
a kind, group, or sort, especially the different kinds of writing, films, and art that we recognise

genteel (say *jen-teel*) *adjective*
very polite and careful in your manners, speech and behaviour

Word Building: **genteelly** *adverb* **gentility** *noun*

gentile (say *jen-tuyl*) *noun*
someone who is not Jewish, especially a Christian

gentle *adjective*
1 kind and patient **2** not rough or violent: *a gentle wind* | *a gentle tap* **3** gradual: *a gentle slope* **4** soft or low: *a gentle sound*

Word Building: **gentleness** *noun* **gently** *adverb*

gentleman *noun*
1 any man: *Good morning, ladies and gentlemen.* **2** a man with polite manners: *I want you to behave like a gentleman.*

Word Use: definition 1 is used as a polite form of speech □ this word used to mean "a man born into a family with a high social standing" and a woman of the same kind was called a **gentlewoman**
Word Building: the plural is **gentlemen**

genuine (say *jen-yoo-ən*) *adjective*
1 true or real: *genuine sorrow* | *a genuine diamond* **2** having real, not pretended, feelings: *a genuine person*

Word Use: a similar word for definition 1 is **authentic** □ a similar word for definition 2 is **sincere**
Word Building: **genuinely** *adverb* **genuineness** *noun*

geo- *prefix*
a word part meaning the earth: *geography, geology*

Word History: this prefix comes from Greek

geography (say *jee-og-rə-fee*) *noun*
the study of the earth, including its land forms, peoples, climates, soils and plants

Word Building: **geographer** *noun* **geographic** *adjective* **geographical** *adjective* **geographically** *adverb*

geology (say *jee-ol-ə-jee*) *noun*
the study of the rocks which form the earth

Word Building: **geological** *adjective* **geologically** *adverb* **geologist** *noun*

geometry (say *jee-om-ə-tree*) *noun*
the part of mathematics that studies shapes such as squares and triangles

Word Building: **geometric** *adjective* **geometrical** *adjective* **geometrically** *adverb*

geranium (say *jə-ray-nee-əm*) *noun*
a common garden plant with red, pink or purple flowers

Word History: from a Greek word meaning "crane's bill"

geriatric (say *je-ree-at-rik*) *adjective*
1 having to do with old people or their care: *a geriatric hospital*
geriatric *noun*
2 someone who is old, especially if they are sick

Word Building: **geriatrics** *noun* the medical care of old people **geriatrician** *noun* **geriatrist** *noun*

germ (say *jerm*) *noun*
1 a tiny living thing that can only be seen with a microscope and which causes disease **2** the beginning of anything: *The germ of an idea came into his mind.*

German measles *noun*
a disease which gives you a temperature and a rash and is usually not serious except for a woman who is having a baby

Word Use: this is also called **rubella**

German shepherd *noun*
another name for an **Alsatian**

germinate (say *jerm-ə-nayt*) *verb*
to begin to grow or develop: *Plant seeds germinate when they are watered. | The idea germinated in her mind.*

Word Building: **germination** *noun*

gesticulate (say *jes-tik-yə-layt*) *verb*
to make movements with part of your body, especially your hands, in order to express a feeling or idea

Word Building: **gesticulation** *noun*

gesture (say *jes-chə*) *noun*
1 a movement of part of your body to express a feeling or idea: *He tossed his head as a gesture of impatience.* **2** something done to express a feeling or idea: *a gesture of friendship*

Word Building: **gesture** *verb*

get *verb*
1 to obtain or receive: *to get a new dress | to get a present* **2** to bring or fetch: *I'll go and get it.* **3** to hear or understand: *I didn't get what you said.* **4** to reach: *I've phoned his house but I can't get him.*
get *verb*
5 to cause to be or do: *I must get my hair cut. | I can't get the car to start.* **6** to prepare or make ready: *She's getting the dinner.* **7** to arrive: *When did you get here?* **8** to become or grow: *I am getting tired.* **9 get away with** to escape punishment for: *They got away with the crime.* **10 get by** to manage: *I don't know how I'll get by without a car.* **11 get off** to escape punishment **12 get on** **a** to become old **b** to make progress **c** to be friendly: *Anna gets on well with the rest of the class.* **13 get over** **a** to defeat or find a way around **b** to recover from

Word Building: other forms are **I got, I have got, I am getting**

geyser (say *gee-zə, guy-zə*) *noun*
a hot spring that sometimes sends up jets of water and steam into the air

Word History: from an Icelandic word meaning "gush"

ghastly (say *gahst-lee*) *adjective*
very bad or unpleasant: *a ghastly mess | a ghastly smell*

Word Use: a similar word is **awful**
Word Building: other forms are **ghastlier, ghastliest**

gherkin (say *ger-kən*) *noun*
a small, pickled cucumber

ghetto (say *get-oh*) *noun*
the part of a city where a group of people, such as poor people or people from another country, live together

Word Building: the plural is **ghettos** or **ghettoes**
Word History: from the Italian name given to the Jewish quarter of Venice in the 16th century

ghost (say *gohst*) *noun*
1 the spirit of someone who has died, imagined as visiting living people **2** a very small amount or trace: *She hasn't a ghost of a chance.* **3** an annoying double image on a television picture

Word Use: a similar word for definition 1 is **apparition**
Word Building: **ghostly** *adjective* (**ghostlier, ghostliest**) **ghostliness** *noun*

giant (say *juy-ənt*) *noun*
1 an imaginary creature that looks like a human but is much bigger and stronger **2** someone or something of great size, importance or ability: *a sporting giant*
giant *adjective*
3 huge or gigantic: *a giant plant*

Word Building: **giantess** *noun*

gibber[1] (say *jib-ə*) *verb*
to speak quickly and without making much sense

Word Building: **gibberish** *noun*

gibber[2] (say *gib-ə*) *noun*
a stone or rock

Word History: from an Aboriginal language called Dharuk

gibbon *noun*
a kind of small ape with long arms

giblets (say *jib-ləts*) *plural noun*
the inside parts of a fowl, such as the heart and liver, usually cooked separately

giddy (say *gid-ee*) *adjective*
having a feeling of whirling or spinning

Word Use: a similar word is **dizzy**
Word Building: other forms are **giddier, giddiest** □ **giddily** *adverb* **giddiness** *noun*

gift *noun*
1 something that is given as a present **2** a special ability: *She has a gift for singing.*

Word Use: a similar word to definition 2 is **talent**
Word Building: **gifted** *adjective* having special natural abilities

gig[1] *noun*
a light, two-wheeled carriage pulled by one horse

gig[2] *noun*
a job for a musician, usually a booking for one show

gigantic (say *juy-gan-tik*) *adjective*
very large or huge: *a gigantic man / a gigantic rock*

Word Building: **gigantically** *adverb* **giganticness** *noun*

giggle *verb*
to laugh in a silly way

Word Building: **giggle** *noun* **giggler** *noun* **giggly** *adjective*

gild *verb*
to cover with a layer of gold or something gold-coloured

Word Building: other forms are **I gilded** or **gilt, I have gilded** or **gilt, I am gilding** □ **gilding** *noun*

gill *noun*
the part of the body that fish and other sea creatures use for breathing

gilt *adjective*
1 golden-coloured or covered with gold: *a gilt vase*

gilt *noun*
2 the gold or other material used in gilding

Word Building: be careful – this sounds like **guilt**

gimmick *noun*
an unusual action or trick, usually used to get attention

Word Building: **gimmicky** *adjective*

gin (say *jin*) *noun*
a strong alcoholic drink

ginger *noun*
1 a plant root which is used in cooking as a spice and in medicine

ginger *adjective*
2 reddish-brown: *ginger hair*

Word Building: **gingery** *adjective: a gingery taste*

gingerly *adverb*
with great care: *He walked gingerly over the slippery rocks.*

gingham (say *ging-əm*) *noun*
a cotton cloth with a striped or checked pattern

Word History: from a Malay word meaning "striped"

gipsy (say *jip-see*) *noun*
someone who belongs to a race of people, once from India but now found mainly in Europe, who do not live in any one place but wander about

Word Use: another spelling is **gypsy**
Word Building: the plural is **gipsies**
Word History: from a form of the word "Egyptian"

giraffe (say *jə-rahf*) *noun*
an African animal with spots, a very long neck, and long legs

Word Use: the male is a **bull**; the female is a **cow**; the young is a **calf**

girder (say *ger-də*) *noun*
a thick beam used as a support in building

girdle *noun*
1 a belt or cord worn around your waist
2 a piece of elastic underwear that supports your stomach and hips

Word Building: **girdle** *verb*

girl *noun*
a female child or a young woman

Word Building: **girlhood** *noun* **girlish** *adjective* **girlishly** *adverb* **girlishness** *noun*

girth (say *gerth*) *noun*
1 the measurement around anything: *His girth is 85 centimetres, measured at the waist.* **2** a band placed under the stomach of a horse to hold a saddle or pack onto its back

gist (say *jist*) *noun*
the most important part: *I understand the gist of your argument.*

give *verb*
1 to hand over freely: *to give someone a present* **2** to pay: *I'll give you $1 for those stamps.* **3** to allow or grant: *Give him one more chance.* **4** to present or organise: *to give a concert | to give a party* **5** to provide with: *to give help | to give a baby a name* **6** to make, especially a movement: *She gave a jump.* **7 give away** **a** to give as a present **b** to betray or allow to become known **8 give in** to admit defeat **9 give out** **a** to become worn out or used up **b** to hand out or distribute **10 give up** **a** to lose all hope **b** to stop: *You should give up smoking.* **c** to surrender

Word Building: other forms are **I gave, I have given, I am giving** □ **gift** *noun* **giver** *noun*

glacial (say *glay-shəl, glay-see-əl*) *adjective*
1 having ice **2** icy or cold as ice

Word Building: **glacially** *adverb* **glaciate** *verb* **glaciation** *noun*

glacier *noun*
a large area of ice which moves slowly down a valley or mountain

Word Building: **glaciered** *adjective*

glad *adjective*
1 delighted or pleased **2 glad of** grateful for: *I would be glad of a little help.*

Word Building: other forms are **gladder, gladdest** □ **gladden** *verb* **gladly** *adverb* **gladness** *noun*

glade *noun*
an open space in a forest

gladiator *noun*
a man in ancient Rome who fought as a public entertainment

Word Building: **gladiatorial** *adjective*

glamour or **glamor** *noun*
an exciting charm or beauty: *That job has a lot of glamour. | Her clothes always have glamour.*

Word Building: **glamorise** *verb* **glamorous** *adjective* **glamorously** *adverb*

glance *verb*
1 to look quickly **2** to hit and go off at an angle: *The ball glanced off the cricket bat.*

Word Building: **glance** *noun*

gland *noun*
a part of your body that makes a substance that is used by another part of your body: *Sweat is made by glands.*

Word Building: **glandular** *adjective*

glare *noun*
1 a strong bright light: *the glare of car headlights* **2** an angry look

Word Building: **glaring** *adjective* very obvious: *a glaring mistake* **glare** *verb* **glaringly** *adverb* **glaringness** *noun*

glass *noun*
1 a hard transparent substance used for such things as windows, bottles and drinking containers **2** something made of glass, such as a drinking container or a mirror **3 glasses** two lenses in a frame which are worn over your eyes to help you see more clearly

Word Use: another word for definition 3 is **spectacles**
Word Building: the plural is **glasses** □ **glassy** *adjective* (**glassier, glassiest**) **glassily** *adverb* **glassiness** *noun*

glaze *verb*
1 to fit or cover with glass: *to glaze windows* **2** to cover with a thin coat of a clear shiny substance: *to glaze pottery* **3 glaze over** to become glassy: *His eyes glazed over as he sat daydreaming.*
glaze *noun*
4 a smooth, shiny coating or surface

Word Building: **glazier** *noun* someone who fits glass into windows

gleam *noun*
1 a flash of light **2** a dim light: *the gleam of polished wood* **3** a short burst: *A gleam of interest came into his eyes.*

Word Building: **gleam** *verb* **gleaming** *adjective*

glean *verb*
to gather, usually slowly and bit by bit: *to glean grain after it has been reaped | to glean information*

Word Building: **gleaner** *noun*

glee *noun*
a feeling of joy

Word Building: **gleeful** *adjective* **gleefully** *adverb* **gleefulness** *noun*

glen *noun*
a small narrow valley

glide *verb*
to move or make to move along smoothly

Word Building: **glide** *noun* **glidingly** *adverb*

glider *noun*
an aeroplane without an engine that flies by using air-currents

glimmer *noun*
1 a faint or flickering light **2** a faint hint or suggestion: *a glimmer of hope*

Word Use: a similar word is **gleam**
Word Building: **glimmer** *verb* **glimmering** *noun* **glimmeringly** *adverb*

glimpse *noun*
a quick sighting: *I caught a glimpse of him as he ran past.*

Word Building: **glimpse** *verb*

glint *noun*
1 a flash or glow of light: *the glint of metal* **2** a look showing amusement or a secret idea: *a glint in his eyes*

Word Building: **glint** *verb*

glisten (say *glis-ən*) *verb*
to shine with a sparkling light: *Her gold ring glistened in the sunlight.*

glitter *verb*
to shine with a bright sparkling light: *Her eyes glittered with excitement.*

Word Building: **glitter** *noun* **glitteringly** *adverb* **glittery** *adjective*

gloat *verb*
to look at or think about something or someone in a very satisfied way: *He gloated over his enemy's defeat.*

Word Building: **gloater** *noun* **gloating** *adjective* **gloatingly** *adverb*

globe *noun*
1 a round ball-shaped map of the earth **2** anything shaped like a round ball **3** an electric light bulb **4 the globe** the earth: *They travelled all over the globe.*

Word Use: a similar word for definition 2 is **sphere**
Word Building: **global** *adjective* **globally** *adverb*
Word History: from a Latin word meaning "round body", "mass", or "ball"

glockenspiel (say *glok-ən-speel, -shpeel*) *noun*
a musical instrument with steel bars set in a frame, which you hit with hammers

Word History: from the German words for "bell" and "play"

gloom *noun*
a feeling of unhappiness or depression

Word Building: **gloomy** *adjective* (**gloomier, gloomiest**) **gloomily** *adverb* **gloominess** *noun*

glorious *adjective*
1 beautiful, wonderful, or delightful: *It is a glorious day. / We had a glorious time.* **2** giving or having glory: *a glorious victory*

Word Building: **gloriously** *adverb* **gloriousness** *noun*

glory *noun*
1 praise and honour **2** something that is a cause of pride or honour: *Beautiful beaches are one of the glories of Australia.* **3** splendid or divine beauty: *the glory of God*

Word Building: the plural is **glories** □ **glorify** *verb* (**glorified, glorifying**) to praise or honour **glorification** *noun*

gloss *noun*
1 the shine on the outside of something: *the gloss of satin*
gloss *verb*
2 to put a gloss on **3 gloss over** to cover up or try to make seem unimportant: *He glossed over his mistakes.*

Word Building: **glossy** *adjective* (**glossier, glossiest**) **glossily** *adverb* **glossiness** *noun*

glossary *noun*
a list of special or difficult words about a particular subject, with their definitions: *This textbook has a glossary at the back.*

Word Building: the plural is **glossaries**

glove *noun*
a covering for your hand, usually with a separate part for each finger and for the thumb

Word Building: **glover** *noun* someone who makes or sells gloves **glove** *verb*

glow *noun*
1 the light given out by something extremely hot **2** brightness of colour **3** a pleasant warm feeling: *a glow of happiness*

Word Building: **glow** *verb* **glowing** *adjective* **glowingly** *adverb*

glow-worm *noun*
a kind of insect whose body glows in the dark

glucose *noun*
a natural sugar which is found in plants and which gives energy to living things

Word History: from a Greek word meaning "sweet"

glue *noun*
1 a paste used to stick things together
glue *verb*
2 to stick with glue

Word Building: **gluey** *adjective* (**gluier, gluiest**) **glueyness** *noun*

glum *adjective*
unhappy or depressed

Word Use: a similar word is **dejected**
Word Building: other forms are **glummer, glummest** □ **glumly** *adverb* **glumness** *noun*

glut *noun*
an oversupply: *a glut of tomatoes*

Word Building: **glut** *verb* (**glutted, glutting**)

glutton *noun*
someone who eats too much

Word Building: **gluttonous** *adjective* **gluttonously** *adverb* **gluttony** *noun*

gnarled (say *nahld*) *adjective*
1 twisted and having many woody lumps: *a gnarled old tree* **2** rough and worn by the weather: *gnarled hands*

Word Building: **gnarl** *noun* **gnarl** *verb*

gnash (say *nash*) *verb*
to grind together: *He gnashed his teeth in anger.*

gnat (say *nat*) *noun*
a kind of small insect with only one pair of wings

gnaw (say *naw*) *verb*
to chew or bite: *The lion gnawed at its food.*

Word Building: **gnawing** *adjective* **gnawing** *noun* **gnawingly** *adverb*

gnocchi (say *nok-ee*) *noun*
an Italian food consisting of square or round shapes of semolina paste, added to soups or served with a cheese sauce

gnome (say *nohm*) *noun*
a small being in fairy stories, usually imagined as a little old man

Word Building: **gnomish** *adjective*

gnu (say *nooh*) *noun*
a kind of antelope with curved horns and a long tail

Word Building: the plural is **gnus** or **gnu**

go *noun*
1 to move or pass along: *Where are you going?* **2** to move away or depart: *I want you to go now.* **3** to work properly: *The engine won't go.* **4** to become: *She goes red with anger.* **5** to reach or lead: *That road goes to Brisbane.* **6** to pass or happen: *Time goes quickly. / The party went well.* **7** to belong or have a place: *Where do the knives and forks go?* **8** to fit or be contained: *Two litres of milk will go into this jug.* **9** to be used up or finished: *The food went quickly.* **10** to make a particular sound or movement: *The gun went bang.* **11 go in for** to be interested in: *He goes in for surfing.* **12 go off a** to explode: *The gun went off.* **b** to become bad: *The meat has gone off.* **c** to stop liking **13** energy: *He has plenty of go.* **14** a turn or try: *It's Jane's go on the swing.* **15 on the go** active and energetic

Word Building: other verb forms are **I went, I have gone, I am going** □ the plural of the noun is **goes**

goad *noun*
1 a stick with a pointed end used to prod cattle and other animals into moving
goad *verb*
2 to drive with a goad **3** to tease or anger

goal (say *gohl*) *noun*
1 an area, basket or something similar at which you aim the ball, in sports such as football, basketball and others **2** the score made by doing this: *We got three goals.* **3** something you aim towards: *My goal is to be a doctor.*

Word Use: be careful – this word looks like **gaol**
Word Building: **goalkeeper** *noun* the player whose job is to stop the ball going into, over, or through a goal

goanna (say *goh-an-ə*) *noun*
any of a number of large Australian lizards

goat *noun*
a small cud-chewing animal with horns, which is able to live in rocky mountainous areas

Word Use: the male is a **billy-goat**; the female is a **nanny-goat**; the baby is a **kid**

gobble *verb*
to swallow or eat quickly in large pieces: *to gobble food*

goblet *noun*
a cup or glass with a stem and a base

goblin *noun*
an ugly elf who is supposed to make trouble for people

go-cart *noun*
1 a small cart with wheels, which children use to ride in **2** *another spelling for* **go-kart**

god *noun*
1 a supernatural being who is worshipped because of his power to control human affairs and the world of nature: *Thor was the god of thunder.* **2** an idol or statue of a god **3** someone or something which is given too much attention: *Money is his god.* **4 God** the supreme maker and ruler of the universe worshipped by people who believe in one god

Word Building: **goddess** *noun*

godly *adjective*
following God's laws: *a godly man*

Word Building: other forms are **godlier, godliest** □ **godliness** *noun*

goggles *plural noun*
glasses with rims and side pieces used to protect your eyes from wind, dust, glare or water

Word Building: **goggle** *verb* to stare with your eyes wide open

go-kart *noun*
a small, light, low-powered car for racing

Word Use: another spelling is **go-cart**

gold *noun*
1 a precious yellow metal **2** money or wealth **3** something highly valued: *a heart of gold*

gold *adjective*
4 made of gold, or like gold **5** yellow in colour, like gold

Word Building: **goldsmith** *noun* someone who makes or sells articles of gold **golden** *adjective*

goldfish *noun*
small fish often kept in aquariums or pools

Word Building: the plural is **goldfish** or **goldfishes**

goldmine *noun*
1 a place where gold is mined **2** a source of something very useful: *She is a goldmine of information.*

Word Building: **goldminer** *noun* **goldmining** *noun*

golf *noun*
an outdoor game in which a small ball is hit with special clubs around a set course

Word Building: **golf** *verb* **golfer** *noun*

gondola (say *gon-də-lə*) *noun*
1 a long narrow boat with high pointed ends, used on the canals of Venice in Italy **2** the basket beneath a balloon, for carrying passengers

Word Building: **gondolier** *noun* the man who rows a gondola

gong *noun*
a bronze disc which is struck with a soft-headed stick to give a loud ringing sound

good *adjective*
1 excellent or right **2** of fine quality **3** well-behaved **4** helpful or useful: *a knife good for cutting* **5** enjoyable or pleasant: *a good holiday* **6** sufficient or ample: *a good supply* **7** clever or skilful: *a good farmer* **8 as good as** almost: *I'm as good as finished.*

good *noun*
9 advantage or benefit: *It's for your own good.* **10** excellent qualities or proper actions: *Look for good in others.* **11 goods a** possessions **b** products or articles that you can buy: *goods from a factory* **12 for good** for ever

Word Building: other adjective forms are **better, best** □ **goodness** *noun*

goodbye *interjection*
a word you use when you leave someone

Word History: a shortened form of "God be with you"

goose *noun*
1 a large bird with webbed feet and a long neck, sometimes kept on farms **2** a silly person: *Don't be a goose.*

Word Use: the male is a **gander**; the female is a **goose**; the young is a **gosling**
Word Building: the plural is **geese**

gooseberry (say *gooz-bə-ree*) *noun*
a small, sour-tasting, round berry

Word Building: the plural is **gooseberries**

goose pimples *plural noun*
small lumps on your skin that appear when you are cold or frightened

Word Use: sometimes called **goose bumps** or **goose flesh**

goosestep *noun*
an unusual marching step in which your legs are swung high while your knees are kept straight and stiff

gore[1] (say *gaw*) *noun*
blood from a wound, especially when it has clotted

Word Building: **gory** *adjective* (**gorier, goriest**)

gore[2] (say *gaw*) *verb*
to pierce with horns or tusks: *The bull gored him.*

gorge (say *gawj*) *noun*
1 a narrow valley with steep rocky walls, often with a river running through it
gorge *verb*
2 to stuff by over-eating: *He gorged himself.*

Word History: from a French word meaning "throat"

gorgeous *adjective*
very beautiful, especially in colouring: *a gorgeous sunset*

Word Building: **gorgeously** *adverb* **gorgeousness** *noun*
Word History: from a French word meaning "fashionable" or "colourful"

gorilla *noun*
the largest kind of ape

gosling *noun*
a young goose

Word Use: the female is a **goose;** the male is a **gander**

gospel *noun*
1 one of the first four books of the New Testament of the Christian bible: *the gospel of St Luke* **2** the teachings of Christ as written in these books **3** anything that is considered to be completely true

Word Use: definitions 1 and 2 are often written **Gospel**
Word Building: **gospel** *adjective: a gospel story*

gossamer (say *gos-ə-mə*) *noun*
1 a fine cobweb lying on grass or bushes or floating in the air **2** any very fine material

Word Building: **gossamer** *adjective*

gossip *noun*
1 silly, and sometimes unkind, chatter about other people's business **2** someone who talks gossip

Word Building: **gossip** *verb* **gossiper** *noun* **gossipy** *adjective*

gouge (say *gowj*) *noun*
1 a sharp curved tool used for making grooves in wood **2** a hole made by this tool

Word Building: **gouge** *verb*

goulash (say *gooh-lash*) *noun*
a meat stew containing onions and paprika

gourd (say *gawd*) *noun*
1 the fruit of a climbing plant **2** the shell of this plant, dried and used as a bottle, bowl, or container

gourmet (say *gaw-may*) *noun*
someone who knows a lot about good food

Word History: from a French word meaning a "wine merchant's man"

govern *verb*
to rule by laws

Word Building: **governable** *adjective*

governess *noun*
a woman who teaches children in their own homes, usually because they live too far from a school

Word Building: the plural is **governesses**

government *noun*
1 the group of people who rule or govern a country or state: *the Labor government | the government of Tasmania* **2** rule or control: *A country prospers under good government.*

Word Building: **governmental** *adjective* **governmentally** *adverb*

governor *noun*
the representative of the king or queen in a state of the Commonwealth of Australia

Word Building: **governorship** *noun*

governor-general *noun*
the main representative of the king or queen in Australia and some other British Commonwealth countries

Word Building: the plural is **governor-generals** or **governors-general**

gown *noun*
1 a dress worn by women on important occasions **2** a loose, flowing garment

worn by judges, lawyers, clerygymen and others

grab *verb*
1 to take suddenly **2** to affect or impress: *How does that grab you?*

Word Use: a similar word for definition 1 is **snatch** □ definition 2 is more suited to everyday language
Word Building: other forms are **I grabbed, I have grabbed, I am grabbing** □ **grab** *noun* **grabber** *noun*

grace *noun*
1 beauty of appearance or movement **2** favour or goodwill **3** a short prayer of thanks to God said before or after a meal

Word Building: **graceful** *adjective* **gracefully** *adverb* **gracefulness** *noun*

gracious (say *gray-shəs*) *adjective*
showing kindness and courtesy: *a gracious hostess | a gracious act*

Word Building: **graciously** *adverb* **graciousness** *noun*

grade *noun*
1 a stage or step on a scale of positions, quality or value: *What grade of clerk are you? | to sell eggs according to grade* **2** a class in a school arranged according to age and ability, in some states of Australia
grade *verb*
3 to arrange or sort according to grade **4** to make level and smooth: *to grade a road*

grader *noun*
1 someone or something that sorts or groups: *a fruit grader* **2** a vehicle with a blade in front used for levelling roads

gradient *noun*
1 the amount of slope or steepness in a road, railway or path **2** a sloping surface

gradual *adjective*
taking place little by little

Word Building: **gradually** *adverb* **gradualness** *noun*

graduate (say *graj-ooh-ət*) *noun*
1 someone who has passed a course of study at a university or college
graduate (say *graj-ooh-ayt*) *verb*
2 to receive a degree after passing such a course of study **3** to divide into regular divisions: *to graduate a thermometer*

Word Building: **graduate** *adjective* **graduation** *noun*

graffiti (say *grə-fee-tee*) *plural noun*
drawings or words written on walls in public places

Word Use: you usually use a singular verb with **graffiti**: *Some graffiti is quite funny.*
Word Building: the singular is **graffito**
Word History: from an Italian word meaning "a scratch", which came from a Greek word meaning "mark", "draw", or "write"

graft (say *grahft*) *noun*
1 part of a plant placed in a slit in another plant so that it is fed by the second plant and becomes part of it **2** a piece of living tissue cut by a doctor from one part of your body and placed somewhere else in your body: *a skin graft | a bone graft*

Word Building: **graft** *verb* **grafter** *noun* **grafting** *noun*

grain *noun*
1 a small hard seed of one of the cereal plants: *wheat grain* **2** any small hard particle: *a grain of gold | a grain of sand* **3** a very small amount of something: *a grain of truth in his story* **4** the direction of the fibres in wood or cloth

Word Building: **grainy** *adjective* (**grainier, grainiest**) **granular** *adjective* **granulate** *verb*

gram *noun*
one thousandth of a kilogram

grammar *noun*
1 the parts of a language such as sounds and words, and the way they are combined into phrases and sentences **2** the description of this or a book containing such a description

Word Building: **grammarian** *noun* **grammatical** *adjective* **grammatically** *adverb*

gramophone *noun*
a machine that reproduces sound from a record

Word Use: a more up-to-date word for this is **record-player**

granary (say *gran-ə-ree*) *noun*
a storehouse for grain

Word Building: the plural is **granaries**

grand *adjective*
1 important-looking **2** noble or fine: *a grand old man* **3** complete: *the grand total* **4** highest in importance

Word Building: **grandeur** *noun* **grandly** *adverb* **grandness** *noun*

grandchild *noun*
the child of someone's daughter or son

Word Building: the plural is **grandchildren**

grandiose (say <u>gran</u>-dee-ohs) *adjective*
too grand or splendid: *grandiose schemes*

Word Building: **grandiosely** *adverb* **grandiosity** *noun*

grandparent *noun*
a parent of one of your parents

grandstand *noun*
a building with seats rising in tiers, at a sports field or similar outdoor entertainment area

granite (say <u>gran</u>-ət) *noun*
a hard rock used for carving monuments and for buildings

Word History: from a Latin word meaning "grain"

grant *verb*
1 to give or allow: *I granted him permission to leave.* | *to grant land* **2** to agree to: *to grant a request*

Word Building: **grant** *noun*

grape *noun*
a small, round, green or purple fruit which grows in bunches on a vine and is used for eating or making wine

grapefruit *noun*
a large, round, yellow-skinned fruit with sour juicy flesh

graph (say *graf, grahf*) *noun*
a diagram which shows the relationship between two or more things by dots, lines or bars

Word Building: **graph** *verb*

graph- *prefix*
a word part meaning writing: *graphics*

Word Use: another spelling is **grapho-**
Word History: this prefix comes from Greek

graphic *adjective*
1 vivid or true to life: *a graphic description* **2** having to do with the use of diagrams or graphs

Word Building: **graphics** *noun* the art of drawing or producing patterns **graphically** *adverb*

graphite (say <u>graf</u>-uyt) *noun*
a soft blackish form of carbon used in lead pencils

grapple *noun*
1 a tool with one or more claws used for hooking or holding something

grapple *verb*
2 to wrestle or struggle: *He grappled with the thief.* | *to grapple with a problem*

Word History: from an Old English word meaning "seize"

grasp *verb*
1 to seize and hold with your hands **2** to understand or take into your mind: *I grasped his meaning.*

Word Building: **grasping** *adjective* greedy **grasp** *noun*

grass *noun*
1 a plant which you can grow to make a lawn **2** any of a number of plants with long narrow leaves, including wheat, oats and bamboo **3** *another word for* **marijuana**

Word Use: definition 3 is more suited to everyday language
Word Building: **grassy** *adjective* (**grassier, grassiest**)

grasshopper *noun*
a type of plant-eating insect with large back legs for jumping

grate[1] *noun*
1 a frame of metal bars for holding wood or coal when burning in a fireplace **2** a frame of parallel or crossing bars used as a cover or guard: *a grate over a drain*

Word Use: another form of definition 2 is **grating**

grate[2] *verb*
1 to rub together making a rough sound: *Chalk grates on the blackboard.* **2** to rub into small pieces against a surface with many sharp-edged openings: *to grate cheese* **3 grate on** to irritate or annoy

Word Use: be careful – this sounds like **great**
Word Building: **grater** *noun* **grating** *adjective* **gratingly** *adverb*

grateful *adjective*
feeling thankful or showing thanks

Word Building: **gratefully** *adverb* **gratefulness** *noun*

grave[1] *noun*
a hole dug in the earth for burying a dead body

grave[2] *adjective*
1 solemn or without humour: *a grave expression* **2** serious or dangerous: *a grave situation* **3** important: *a grave decision*

Word Building: **gravely** *adverb*

gravel *noun*
small stones mixed with sand

Word Building: **gravelly** *adjective*
Word History: from a French word meaning "little sandy shore"

gravity *noun*
1 the force that attracts or causes everything to fall towards the centre of the earth **2** seriousness or solemnity: *the gravity of the occasion*

Word History: from a Latin word meaning "heaviness"

gravy (say *gray-vee*) *noun*
a sauce made from the juices that drip from meat during cooking, mixed with flour and water

graze[1] *verb*
to feed on growing grass

graze[2] *verb*
1 to touch lightly in passing **2** to scratch the skin of: *I fell and grazed my knee.*

Word Building: **graze** *noun*

grazier *noun*
a farmer who usually has a large area of land on which he grazes cattle or sheep

grease (say *grees*) *noun*
1 melted animal fat **2** any fatty or oily substance **3** a substance used to keep machinery running smoothly
grease (say *greez*) *verb*
4 to put grease on

Word Building: **greasy** *adjective* (**greasier, greasiest**) **greasily** *adverb* **greasiness** *noun*

great *adjective*
1 large: *a great wave of water* / *a great crowd of people* **2** unusual or extreme: *great joy* **3** notable or important: *a great composer* **4** very good or fine: *We had a great time.*

Word Use: definition 4 is more suited to everyday language ☐ be careful – this sounds like **grate**
Word Building: **greatly** *adverb* **greatness** *noun*

greed *noun*
great or unreasonable desire for food or money

Word Building: **greedy** *adjective* (**greedier, greediest**) **greedily** *adverb* **greediness** *noun*

green *adjective*
1 of the colour of growing leaves **2** not ripe: *a green plum* **3** jealous
green *noun*
4 a green colour **5** the part of a golf course surrounding a hole **6** the smooth level lawn on which bowls is played **7 greens** green vegetables

Word Use: definition 3 is more suited to everyday language
Word Building: **green** *verb* to become or make green **greenery** *noun* green plants **greenness** *noun*

greengrocer *noun*
someone who sells fresh vegetables and fruit

greenhouse *noun*
a building used for growing plants, which is made mainly of glass so that it will store the sun's heat

greenhouse effect *noun*
the increase in the temperature of the earth caused by its atmosphere trapping heat from the sun in the same way that the glass of a greenhouse does

greenie *noun*
someone who believes that the environment should be conserved, that our food should be produced without chemicals, and that we should live more simply

Word Use: this is more suited to everyday language
Word Building: **greenie** *adjective: Everything is recycled in a greenie household.*

greet *verb*
to welcome or receive, usually with friendly words

greeting *noun*
1 the act or words of someone who greets **2 greetings** a friendly message: *to send greetings*

gregarious (say *grə-gair-ree-əs*) *adjective*
fond of the company of other people

Word Use: a similar word is **sociable**
Word Building: **gregariously** *adverb* **gregariousness** *noun*

gremlin *noun*
something that causes mischief or trouble: *a gremlin in the engine*

grenade (say *grə-nayd*) *noun*
a small bomb thrown by hand or fired from a rifle

Word History: from a Spanish word meaning "pomegranate"

grevillea (say *grə-vil-ee-ə*) *noun*
any of a number of types of Australian shrubs or trees, many of which have spiky bright-coloured flowers

Word History: from the name of a Scottish botanist, C F Greville, who died in 1809

grey *adjective*
1 of a colour between black and white **2** dark and overcast: *a grey day*

Word Building: **grey** *noun* **grey** *verb*

greyhound *noun*
a type of tall slender dog used for racing

grid *noun*
1 a grating of crossed bars **2** a network of cables and pipes supplying electricity, gas or water **3** a network of crossed lines on a map

griddle *noun*
a flat heavy pan for cooking on top of the stove

Word Building: **griddle** *verb*

grief (say *greef*) *noun*
deep suffering in your mind because of sorrow or loss

Word Building: **grievous** *adjective* causing grief or sorrow

grievance *noun*
a feeling of anger or annoyance caused by something unfair that has happened

grieve (say *greev*) *verb*
to feel or cause to feel grief: *I grieved when my aunt died. / Your unkindness grieves me.*

grill *noun*
1 a meal, mainly of meat, which has been grilled **2** a griller

grill *verb*
3 to cook under or in a griller **4** to question harshly and closely

Word Use: definition 4 is more suited to everyday language

grille (say *gril*) *noun*
a screen of metal bars, sometimes ornamental, for a window, gate, or the front of a motor car

griller *noun*
the part of a stove or kitchen appliance for cooking meat by direct heat

grim *adjective*
1 having a fierce or forbidding appearance **2** causing fear or disgust: *the grim facts of war*

Word Building: other forms are **grimmer, grimmest** □ **grimly** *adverb* **grimness** *noun*

grimace (say *grim-əs*) *noun*
an unnatural or twisted look on your face showing fear, hatred and other such emotions

Word Building: **grimace** *verb*
Word History: from a Spanish word meaning "panic"

grime *noun*
dirt or filth, especially on a surface: *the grime on the walls*

Word Building: **grimy** *adjective* (**grimier, grimiest**) **grimily** *adverb* **griminess** *noun*

grin *verb*
1 to smile broadly **2 grin and bear it** to suffer without complaining

Word Use: definition 2 is more suited to everyday language
Word Building: other forms are **I grinned, I have grinned, I am grinning** □ **grin** *noun*

grind *verb*
1 to crush into fine particles: *to grind wheat* **2** to produce by grinding: *to grind flour* **3** to grate together: *to grind your teeth* **4** to smooth, shape or sharpen by rubbing with a tool: *to grind a lens / to grind an axe*

grind *noun*
5 hard or boring work

Word Use: definition 5 is more suited to everyday language
Word Building: other verb forms are **I ground, I have ground, I am grinding** □ **grinder** *noun*

grip *noun*
1 a firm hold **2** control: *She is in the grip of her emotions.*

grip *verb*
3 to grasp or seize firmly **4** to hold the interest of: *His story gripped us.*

Word Building: other verb forms are **I gripped, I have gripped, I am gripping**

gripe *verb*
to complain or grumble

Word Use: this is more suited to everyday language
Word Building: **gripe** *noun*

grisly (say *griz-lee*) *adjective*
horrible or frightening: *a grisly murder*

Word Building: other forms are **grislier, grisliest** □ **grisliness** *noun*

gristle (say *gris-əl*) *noun*
a firm elastic tissue in animals or humans

Word Use: a similar word is **cartilage**
Word Building: **gristly** *adjective*

grit *noun*
1 fine, hard, stony particles **2** strength of character or courage: *He showed a lot of grit in overcoming his injury.*
grit *verb*
3 to clamp tightly: *to grit your teeth*

Word Building: other verb forms are **I gritted, I have gritted, I am gritting** ☐ **gritty** *adjective* (**grittier, grittiest**) **grittiness** *noun*

grizzle *verb*
to whimper or whine

grizzled (say *griz-əld*) *adjective*
grey-haired or grey: *He's getting grizzled at the temples.*

Word Building: **grizzle** *verb* **grizzly** *adjective*

groan *noun*
1 a low sad sound, usually expressing pain or sorrow
groan *verb*
2 to utter a groan

grocer *noun*
a shopkeeper who sells flour, tea, canned and other foods, as well as other household goods

Word Building: **grocery** *noun* (**groceries**)

grog *noun*
alcoholic drink, particularly when cheap and of poor quality

Word Use: this word is more suited to everyday language

groggy *adjective*
staggering from tiredness, injury, or too much alcoholic drink

Word Building: other forms are **groggier, groggiest** ☐ **groggily** *adverb* **grogginess** *noun*

groin (say *groyn*) *noun*
the hollow where your thigh joins your abdomen

groom *noun*
1 someone who looks after horses **2** *another word for* **bridegroom**
groom *verb*
3 to brush, comb and generally keep clean and neat in appearance: *to groom a horse / to groom yourself*

groomsman *noun*
a man who accompanies a bridegroom at his wedding

Word Building: the plural is **groomsmen**

groove *noun*
1 a long narrow cut made by a tool: *a groove in wood* **2** the track in a gramophone record in which the needle moves

Word Building: **groove** *verb*

groovy *adjective*
exciting or satisfying

Word Use: this is more suited to everyday language

grope *verb*
1 to feel about with your hands **2** to search uncertainly: *I groped for an answer.*

Word Building: **groper** *noun* **gropingly** *adverb*

gross (say *grohs*) *adjective*
1 whole or total, without anything having been taken out: *gross income* **2** very bad or shocking: *gross injustice*
gross *noun*
3 twelve dozen or 144
gross *verb*
4 to earn a total of: *The company grossed ten million dollars last year.*

Word Building: the plural of definition 3 is **gross** ☐ **grossly** *adverb* **grossness** *noun*

grotesque (say *groh-tesk*) *adjective*
odd or unnatural in shape, form or appearance: *the grotesque figures in a nightmare*

Word Building: **grotesquely** *adverb* **grotesqueness** *noun*

grotto *noun*
a cave

Word Building: the plural is **grottoes** or **grottos**

grotty *adjective*
1 dirty **2** useless

Word Use: this is more suited to everyday language
Word Building: other forms are **grottier, grottiest**

grouch *verb*
to be sulky or bad-tempered

Word Use: this is more suited to everyday language
Word Building: **grouchy** *adjective* (**grouchier, grouchiest**) **grouch** *noun* **grouchiness** *noun*

ground *noun*
1 firm or dry land: *high ground* **2** earth or soil: *stony ground* **3** the land surrounding a building or group of buildings: *school ground | hospital grounds* **4** basis or reason: *He has no ground for complaint.*
5 gain ground to make progress
6 stand your ground to keep to your opinion

ground *verb*
7 to run on to the shore: *The boat grounded in the storm.* **8** to stop from flying: *to ground a pilot*

group *noun*
1 a number of people or things gathered together and thought of as being connected in some way **2** a number of musicians who play together: *a pop group*

Word Building: **group** *verb* **grouping** *noun*

grouse[1] (rhymes with *house*) *verb*
to grumble or complain

Word Use: this is more suited to everday language
Word Building: **grouse** *noun*

grouse[2] (rhymes with *house*) *adjective*
very good

Word Use: this is more suited to everyday language

grout (say *growt*) *noun*
a thin coarse cement poured into the joint between tiles and brickwork

Word Building: **grout** *verb*

grove *noun*
a small group of trees

grovel (say *grov-əl*) *verb*
1 to humble yourself in an undignified way **2** to lie or crawl face down, especially in fear

Word Building: other forms are **I grovelled, I have grovelled, I am grovelling**

grow *verb*
1 to increase in size **2** to develop: *Plants grow from seeds.* **3** to become gradually: *to grow older | to grow richer* **4** to cause to grow: *I grow roses.*

Word Building: other forms are **I grew, I have grown, I am growing** ☐ **growth** *noun*

growl *verb*
1 to make a deep angry sound **2** to complain or grumble angrily

Word Building: **growl** *noun*

grown-up *noun*
someone who is fully grown or mature

grub *noun*
1 the young or larva of some insects **2** food

Word Use: definition 2 is more suited to everyday language
Word Building: **grub** *verb* (**grubbed, grubbing**)
Word History: from a Middle English word meaning "dig"

grubby *adjective*
dirty or untidy: *a grubby house*

Word Building: other forms are **grubbier, grubbiest**

grudge *noun*
a feeling of anger caused by someone hurting or insulting you: *to bear a grudge*

Word Building: **grudge** *verb* **grudgingly** *adverb*

gruel (say *grooh-əl*) *noun*
a thin mixture of cereal, usually oatmeal, cooked in water or milk

gruelling (say *grooh-ə-ling*) *adjective*
very tiring: *a gruelling race*

gruesome *adjective*
causing feelings of horror: *a gruesome story*

gruff *adjective*
1 hoarse or low and harsh **2** rough or unfriendly: *He had a gruff cranky manner.*

Word Building: **gruffly** *adverb* **gruffness** *noun*

grumble *verb*
to complain crankily

Word Building: **grumble** *noun* **grumbler** *noun* **grumblingly** *adverb*

grumpy *adjective*
bad-tempered

Word Building: other forms are **grumpier, grumpiest** ☐ **grumpily** *adverb* **grumpiness** *noun*

grunt *verb*
1 to make a deep sound like a pig

grunt *noun*
2 the sound of grunting

guarantee (say *ga-rən-tee*) *noun*
1 a promise to replace or repair something if it is faulty: *My new television set has a guarantee for the next four years.* **2** a promise: *Wealth is no guarantee of happiness.*
guarantee *verb*
3 to give a promise or guarantee

Word Building: **guarantor** *noun* someone who makes or gives a guarantee

guard (say *gahd*) *verb*
1 to protect or keep safe from harm **2** to keep from escaping **3** to keep in control: *to guard your tongue* **4** to make safe: *The pool fence guards the pool.*
guard *noun*
5 someone who protects or keeps watch **6** a careful watch: *That prisoner should be kept under close guard.* **7** something that guards from harm or injury: *Each footballer should wear a mouthguard.*

Word Building: **guarded** *adjective* careful **guardedly** *adverb* **guardedness** *noun*

guardian *noun*
1 someone who guards, protects or takes care of someone or something **2** someone who is appointed by law to take care of another person and their property
guardian *adjective*
3 guarding or protecting: *a guardian angel*

Word Building: **guardianship** *noun*

guava (say *gwah-və*) *noun*
an American tree or shrub with a fruit used for making jam and jelly

guerrilla (say *gə-ril-ə*) *noun*
a member of a small band of soldiers which worries the enemy by surprise raids and attacks

Word Use: another spelling is **guerilla**
Word Building: **guerrilla** *adjective: guerrilla warfare*
Word History: from the Spanish word for "war"

guess (say *ges*) *verb*
1 to give an answer when you don't really know **2** to think or believe: *I guess I can get there in time.*
guess *noun*
3 a judgment or opinion formed without really knowing

guest (say *gest*) *noun*
1 a visitor or someone who is entertained at your house **2** someone well-known who visits and performs at a club or show **3** someone who stays at a hotel or motel

Word Building: **guest** *adjective: a guest artist*

guffaw (say *gu-faw*) *noun*
1 a noisy laugh
guffaw *verb*
2 to laugh loudly and noisily

guidance *noun*
advice, guiding, or leadership

guide (say *guyd*) *verb*
1 to show the way
guide *noun*
2 someone who guides, often for money **3** a book with information for travellers or tourists

guild (say *gild*) *noun*
an organisation or society of people who have similar jobs or interests

guile (say *guyl*) *noun*
cleverness or cunning in the way you deceive somebody

Word Building: **guileful** *adjective* clever and deceitful **guileless** *adjective* frank or honest

guillotine (say *gil-ə-teen*) *noun*
1 a machine with a heavy blade that falls between two grooved posts and is used for cutting off someone's head **2** a machine with a long blade used for trimming paper

Word Building: **guillotine** *verb*
Word History: named after the French doctor, JI Guillotin, who wanted it to be used in France

guilt (say *gilt*) *noun*
1 the position of having committed a crime or being wrong: *His guilt was proved by the court.* **2** a feeling that something is your fault: *We should all share the guilt of our school's disgrace.*

Word Use: be careful – this sounds like **gilt**
Word Building: **guilty** *adjective* (**guiltier, guiltiest**) **guiltily** *adverb* **guiltiness** *noun*

guineapig (say *gin-ee-pig*) *noun*
1 a short-eared short-tailed animal kept as a pet and also used for scientific experiments **2** someone used in experiments: *The children were used as guineapigs to test the new soft drink.*

guise (say *guyz*) *noun*
the outside appearance, usually only pretended, of someone or something: *The robber walked into the bank in the guise of a clergyman.*

guitar (say *gə-tah*) *noun*
a violin-shaped musical instrument with a long neck and strings which you pluck

Word Building: **guitarist** *noun* someone who plays the guitar

gulf *noun*
1 a part of an ocean which is partly bounded by land **2** a deep hollow or split in the earth **3** any wide separation: *The gulf between the two boys widened after the fight.*

gull *noun*
another word for **seagull**

gullet *noun*
the tube-like part of your body by which the food and drink you swallow pass to your stomach

gullible *adjective*
easily deceived or cheated

Word Building: **gullibly** *adverb* **gullibility** *noun*

gully *noun*
1 a small valley cut out of the earth by running water **2** a ditch or a gutter

Word Building: the plural is **gullies**

gulp *verb*
1 to swallow quickly: *to gulp water | to gulp with fear*

gulp *noun*
2 an amount swallowed at one time

gum[1] *noun*
1 a sticky liquid which oozes from plants or trees **2** a tree or shrub which gives out this liquid and grows mostly in Australia **3** a sticky flavoured sweet for chewing **4** a glue

gum[1] *verb*
5 to cover or stick together with gum

Word Use: another name for definition 3 is **chewing gum**
Word Building: other verb forms are **I gummed, I have gummed, I am gumming** □ **gummy** *adjective*

gum[2] *noun*
the firm flesh around the bottom of your teeth

Word Use: often used as a plural **gums**

gumboot *noun*
a rubber boot sometimes reaching to your knee or thigh

gun *noun*
1 a weapon with a long metal tube for firing bullets or other ammunition **2** anything which is similar to a gun in its shape or in the way it is used: *a spray gun for paint*

gun *verb*
3 to shoot: *The thief gunned down the policeman.*

Word Building: other verb forms are **I gunned, I have gunned, I am gunning** □ **gunsmith** *noun* someone who makes or repairs guns

gunpowder *noun*
a mixture of chemical powders that explodes when set off by a gun or by fire

gunwale (say *gun-əl*) *noun*
the upper edge of the side of a ship or boat

Word Use: another spelling is **gunnel**

gunyah (say *gun-yə*) *noun*
an Aboriginal hut or temporary shelter made from tree branches and bark

Word Use: another spelling is **gunya** □ another word for this is **humpy**
Word History: from an Aboriginal language called Dharuk

guppy *noun*
a small brightly-coloured fish which is often kept in home aquariums

Word Building: the plural form is **guppies**
Word History: named after a Trinidad clergyman, RJL Guppy, who sent the first recorded specimen to the British Museum

gurgle *verb*
1 to flow with a noisy bubbling sound **2** to make or imitate this sound

Word Building: **gurgle** *noun* **gurglingly** *adverb*

guru (say *gooh-rooh*) *noun*
a wise and powerful teacher

gush *verb*
1 to flow suddenly in large amounts: *The sea gushed through the hole the torpedo had made.* **2** to have a large sudden flow of something: *The wound gushed blood. | Her eyes gushed tears.* **3** to express yourself in a rush of emotional talk

Word Use: definition 3 is more suited to everyday language
Word Building: **gush** *noun* **gusher** *noun* **gushingly** *adverb* **gushy** *adjective*

gust *noun*
a sudden strong blast or rush: *a gust of wind*

Word Building: **gusty** *adjective* (**gustier, gustiest**) **gustily** *adverb* **gustiness** *noun*

gusto *noun*
hearty enjoyment

gut *noun*
1 *another word for* **intestine** **2** the tough string made from the gut of an animal and used for things like violin strings or tennis racquet strings **3 guts** **a** your stomach **b** courage **c** most important part or contents: *the guts of the motor*

gut *verb*
4 to take out the guts of something **5** to destroy the inside of something: *Fire gutted the inside of the building.*

Word Use: all of definition 3 is more suited to everyday language
Word Building: other verb forms are **I gutted, I have gutted, I am gutting** □ **gut** *adjective: a gut response* **gutless** *adjective* cowardly **gutsy** *adjective* full of courage

gutter *noun*
1 a channel, usually along the side of a street, for carrying away water **2** a channel along the eaves or roof of a building for carrying off rainwater

Word Use: another word for definition 2 is **guttering**

guttural (say *gut-ə-rəl*) *adjective*
1 having to do with your throat **2** harsh and throaty

guy[1] *noun*
1 a man or a boy **2** any person

Word Use: this is more suited to everyday language
Word History: from Guy Fawkes, the leader of the Gunpowder Plot to blow up the British Houses of Parliament

guy[2] *noun*
a rope or wire attached to something to guide, steady or secure it

guzzle *verb*
to eat or drink noisily and greedily

Word Building: **guzzler** *noun* someone who guzzles

gym (say *jim*) *noun*
1 *short for* **gymnasium** **2** *short for* **gymnastics**

Word Building: **gymnast** *noun*

gymkhana (say *jim-kah-nə*) *noun*
horseriding events with games and contests

Word History: from a Hindustani word meaning "ball house" or "racquet-court"

gymnasium (say *jim-nay-zee-əm*) *noun*
a building or room specially equipped for gymnastics and sport

Word Building: the plural is **gymnasiums** or **gymnasia**
Word History: from a Greek word meaning "naked" (in ancient times athletes were naked when they trained)

gymnast (say *jim-nəst*) *noun*
someone especially trained and skilled in gymnastics

gymnastic (say *jim-nas-tik*) *adjective*
having to do with physical exercises which develop your muscle strength and tone up your body

gymnastics (say *jim-nas-tiks*) *noun*
the performance of gymnastic exercises

gyn- *prefix*
a word part meaning woman *or* female: *gynaecologist*

Word Use: another spelling is **gyno-**
Word History: this prefix comes from Greek

gynaecology or **gynecology** (say *guy-nə-kol-ə-jee*) *noun*
the type of medical practice that is concerned with diseases that only affect women

Word Building: **gynaecological** *adjective* **gynaecologist** *noun*

gypsy *noun*
another spelling of **gipsy**

gyrate (say *juy-rayt*) *verb*
to whirl or move in a circle

Word Building: **gyration** *noun*

gyro- *prefix*
a word part meaning ring, circle *or* spiral: *gyroscope*

Word History: this prefix comes from Greek

gyroscope (say *juy-rə-skohp*) *noun*
a rotating wheel inside a frame which lets the wheel's axis keep its original direction even though the frame is moved around, used to help make such instruments as stabilisers in ships

Word Building: **gyroscopic** *adjective*

Hh

habit *noun*
1 a certain usual way of behaving: *It is a habit of mine to read in bed.* **2** the dress of someone in a religious order, like a nun or a monk

Word Building: **habitual** *adjective*
habitually *adverb*

habitat *noun*
the place where a plant or animal naturally lives or grows

habitation *noun*
a home or a place of living

Word Building: **habitable** *adjective*

hack[1] *verb*
1 to cut or chop with rough heavy blows
hack[1] *noun*
2 a rough cut or gash

hack[2] *noun*
1 an old or worn-out horse **2** a riding horse kept for hire or ordinary riding **3** someone who does poor quality writing for a living
hack[2] *verb*
4 to put up with

Word Use: definition 4 is more suited to everyday language
Word Building: **hack** *adjective*

hackles *plural noun*
the hair on the back of a dog's neck

haemo- *prefix*
a word part meaning blood: *haemorrhage*

Word Use: other spellings are **haem-** and **hemo-**
Word History: this prefix comes from Greek

haemophilia or **hemophilia** (say *hee-mə-fil-ee-ə*) *noun*
a disease which makes you bleed for a long time if you cut yourself

Word Building: **haemophiliac** *noun*

haemorrhage or **hemorrhage** (say *hem-ə-rij*) *noun*
a sudden flow of blood like one from a burst blood vessel

Word Building: **haemorrhage** *verb*
Word History: from a Greek word meaning "a violent bleeding"

hag *noun*
an ugly old woman

haggard (say *hag-əd*) *adjective*
looking worn out from hunger, sickness or worry

haggle *verb*
to bargain or argue about the price of something

haiku (say *huy-kooh*) *noun*
a Japanese form of poem which has three lines

hail[1] *verb*
1 to greet or welcome **2** to attract attention by calling out: *to hail a taxi*
hail[1] *noun*
3 a shout or call to attract attention

hail[2] *noun*
1 a shower of small balls of ice from the clouds, like frozen rain **2** a shower of anything hard: *a hail of bullets*
hail[2] *verb*
3 to pour down hail or to fall like hail

hair *noun*
1 a fine threadlike growth from the skin of people and animals: *Have you got hairs on the palm of your hand?* **2** the mass of these which cover the human head or the body of an animal: *Please get your hair cut.*

hairy *adjective*
1 covered with hair **2** difficult: *a hairy problem* **3** frightening: *a hairy drive*

Word Use: definitions 2 and 3 are more suited to everyday language
Word Building: other forms are **hairier, hairiest**

hakea (say *hay-kee-ə*) *noun*
a type of Australian shrub or tree that has hard woody fruit

half (say *hahf*) *noun*
1 one of two equal parts into which anything can be divided
half *adjective*
2 being about half the full amount: *half speed*
half *adverb*
3 in part or partly: *The house was only half built.*

Word Building: the plural form of the noun is **halves**

half-brother *noun*
a brother who is related to you through one parent only

half-caste *noun*
someone of mixed race: *She was a half-caste because her mother was English and her father was Indian.*

Word Building: **half-caste** *adjective*

half-hearted *adjective*
having not much interest or willingness: *He made a half-hearted attempt to join in.*

half-sister *noun*
a sister who is related to you through one parent only

hall *noun*
1 a corridor or passage inside the front door of a house, from which you can get to the other rooms **2** a large building or room used for such things as public meetings or dances

hallelujah (say *hal-ə-looh-yə*) *interjection*
a cry which expresses praise to God

Word History: a Hebrew word meaning "praise ye Jehovah" (another name for God)

hallucination (say *hə-looh-sə-nay-shən*) *noun*
something which someone imagines they have seen or heard: *Some drugs can make you have hallucinations.*

Word Use: a similar word is **illusion**
Word Building: **hallucinate** *verb*

halo (say *hay-loh*) *noun*
1 a ring of light surrounding the head of a holy person in paintings of saints or angels **2** a circle of light seen around the sun or moon

Word Building: the plural is **haloes** or **halos**

halt *verb*
to stop

Word Building: **halt** *noun*

halter *noun*
a rope or a strap for leading or tying horses or cattle

halve (say *hahv*) *verb*
1 to divide in halves: *She halved the apple for the two boys.* **2** to cut down or reduce to half

ham *noun*
1 salted or smoked meat from the upper part of a pig's leg **2** an actor who overacts **3** someone whose hobby is sending and receiving radio messages around the world
ham *verb*
4 to overact or act in an exaggerated way

Word Use: definitions 2 and 4 are used more in everyday language
Word Building: other verb forms are **I hammed, I have hammed, I am hamming**

hamburger *noun*
a bread roll containing a fried flattened lump of minced beef

Word History: named after *Hamburg,* a town in Germany

hamlet *noun*
a very small village

hammer *noun*
1 a tool with a heavy metal head and a handle, used for banging nails into wood and for beating things **2** anything shaped or used like a hammer
hammer *verb*
3 to hit or work with a hammer **4** to hit with force, or to pound: *She hammered the table with her fist.*

hammock *noun*
a hanging bed made of canvas or netlike material

hamper[1] *verb*
to hold back or hinder: *Her heavy shoes hampered her swimming.*

hamper[2] *noun*
a large box or covered basket used for carrying food

hamster *noun*
a small short-tailed animal belonging to the rat family, which looks like a guineapig

hand *noun*
1 the end part of your arm below your wrist, used for touching and holding things **2** something like a hand: *the hands of a clock* **3** a worker or labourer: *a factory hand* **4** help or cooperation: *Give me a hand.* **5** a side or a point in an argument: *on the other hand* **6** a unit of measurement, about 10 centimetres, for giving the height of horses: *This horse is sixteen hands.* **7** a burst of clapping or applause for a performer: *Give him a big hand.* **8 at hand** near or ready **9 in hand** under control **10 hands** power or control: *Your fate is in my hands.*
11 old hand an experienced person

hand *verb*
12 to deliver or pass with your hand: *Hand me the jam please.*

handbag *noun*
a small bag which can be carried in your hand, used for holding money and small articles

handcuff *noun*
one of a pair of connected steel rings or bracelets put around someone's wrists to stop them using their hands

Word Building: **handcuff** *verb*

handicap *noun*
1 a physical disability **2** any disadvantage that makes success harder **3** a race or contest in which the better competitors are given a disadvantage, such as a greater distance to run **4** the disadvantage given to these competitors, such as the extra distance: *Last year's winner was given a handicap of three metres.*

Word Building: **handicap** *verb* (**handicapped, handicapping**) **handicapped** *adjective* disabled or crippled

handicraft *noun*
an occupation or art in which you use your hands: *Pottery and weaving are handicrafts.*

handkerchief (say *hang-kə-cheef*) *noun*
a small, usually square piece of cloth used for wiping your nose

handle *noun*
1 a part of something, used to hold it by or open it with: *the handle of a knife / a door handle*

handle *verb*
2 to touch or feel with your hand **3** to use: *He handles a paintbrush with skill.*
4 to manage or control: *The captain cannot handle his soldiers.*

handlebars *plural noun*
the curved bar at the front of a bike that you steer it with

handsome *adjective*
1 good-looking **2** large or generous: *a handsome gift*

Word Use: definition 1 is used mostly of men
Word Building: **handsomely** *adverb* **handsomeness** *noun*

handwriting *noun*
writing done with your hand, especially your own style of writing: *very neat handwriting*

Word Building: **handwritten** *adjective*

handy *adjective*
1 close at hand: *Is the glue handy?*
2 skilful with your hands **3** useful or convenient: *a handy tool*

Word Building: other forms are **handier, handiest** □ **handily** *adverb* **handiness** *noun*

hang *verb*
1 to fix or be fixed at the top but not at the bottom: *Hang the picture on that hook. / The vine is hanging from the top of the fence.* **2** to put to death by dropping with a rope around the neck **3** to bend downwards: *I hung my head in shame.*
4 hang around to spend time, sometimes with nothing to do **5 hang on** to wait **6 hang up** to break off a phone conversation

Word Building: other forms are **I hung, I have hung, I am hanging,** except for definition 2, where you have to say **hanged** instead of **hung** □ **hanger** *noun* a support for hanging up clothes, or other things

hangar *noun*
a large shed that planes are kept in

hang-glider *noun*
a large type of kite which you hang on to and guide as you glide through the air

Word Building: **hang-glide** *verb* **hang-gliding** *noun*

hangover *noun*
1 the feeling of sickness and headache that you get after drinking too much alcohol **2** something remaining or left over

Word Use: this word is more suited to everyday language

hang-up *noun*
something which worries you and which you can't get off your mind

Word Use: this word is more suited to everyday language

Hanukkah (say *han-ooh-kah*) *noun*
a Jewish festival known as the Feast of the Dedication, lasting eight days

haphazard (say *hap-haz-əd*) *adjective*
not planned, or happening by chance: *a haphazard remark*

Word Building: **haphazardly** *adverb*

happen *verb*
1 to take place or occur, sometimes by chance **2** to have the luck or the occasion: *I happened to see him just in time.*

happy *adjective*
1 delighted, pleased or glad about something **2** fortunate or lucky: *a happy coincidence*

Word Building: other forms are **happier, happiest** □ **happily** *adverb* **happiness** *noun*

harangue (say *hə-rang*) *noun*
a long, noisy and scolding speech

Word Building: **harangue** *verb*

harass (say *ha-rəs, hə-ras*) *verb*
1 to trouble by attacking or raiding again and again: *The enemy harassed the small towns regularly.* **2** to continually annoy or worry

Word Building: **harassment** *noun*
Word History: from a French word meaning "set a dog on"

harbour or **harbor** (say *hah-bə*) *noun*
1 a sheltered part of the sea, deep enough for ships to be protected from wind and waves

harbour or **harbor** *verb*
2 to give shelter to

hard *adjective*
1 solid and firm to the touch: *Rocks and wood are hard.* **2** difficult to do or explain: *a hard problem* **3** needing much effort or energy: *hard work* **4 hard up** urgently in need of something, especially money

hard *adverb*
5 with a lot of effort or energy: *to work hard*

Word Use: definition 4 is more suited to everyday language
Word Building: **hardness** *noun*

harden *verb*
1 to make or become hard or harder: *The cold hardened the plastic. / The glue slowly hardened.* **2** to make or become unfeeling or unkind: *He hardened his heart against the poor animal. / Her feelings hardened when she saw the evidence.*

hardly *adverb*
1 almost not at all: *The fog was so thick, we could hardly see.* **2** probably not: *He would hardly come now, would he?*

hardship *noun*
unpleasantness or suffering in the way you live: *Being poor involves much hardship.*

hardware *noun*
1 building materials or tools **2** the mechanical parts of a computer

Word Use: the opposite of definition 2 is **software**

hardy *adjective*
able to stand up to hard or severe treatment or conditions

Word Building: other forms are **hardier, hardiest** □ **hardily** *adverb* **hardiness** *noun*

hare *noun*
a rabbit-like animal with long ears and long back legs

harebrained *adjective*
reckless or without sense

harm *noun*
damage or hurt

Word Building: **harm** *verb* **harmful** *adjective* **harmfully** *adverb* **harmless** *adjective* **harmlessly** *adverb*

harmonica (say *hah-mon-ik-ə*) *noun*
a small wind instrument with metal reeds, which you play by blowing

Word Use: another name for this is **mouth organ**

harmony *noun*
1 agreement in feelings, actions or ideas **2** a pleasing combination of musical notes sounding together

Word Building: the plural is **harmonies** □ **harmonisation** *noun* **harmonise** *verb* **harmonious** *adjective* **harmoniously** *adverb*
Word History: from a Greek word meaning "a joining", "concord", or "music"

harness *noun*
1 the leather straps, bands and so on used to control a horse, or to attach a cart or load to it **2** a similar arrangement worn by people for safety: *a parachute harness*

harness *verb*
3 to put a harness on **4** to put to work: *We have harnessed water to produce electricity.*

harp *noun*
a musical instrument with a triangular frame and strings which are plucked with the fingers

Word Building: **harpist** *noun* a harp player

harpoon *noun*
a spearlike weapon attached to a rope, used to catch large fish

Word Building: **harpoon** *verb*

harpsichord (say *hahp-sə-kawd*) *noun*
an old-fashioned musical instrument like a piano

Word Building: **harpsichordist** *noun* a harpsichord player
Word History: from the French words for "harp" and "string"

harsh *adjective*
1 rough and unpleasant: *a harsh voice*
2 cruel or severe: *a harsh winter*

Word Building: **harshly** *adverb* **harshness** *noun*

harvest *noun*
the gathering or picking of crops

Word Building: **harvest** *verb* **harvester** *noun* a machine for harvesting crops, especially wheat

hash *noun*
a mixture of chopped cooked meat, reheated in a sauce

Word History: from a French word meaning "axe"

hassle *verb*
to worry or annoy: *Don't hassle me about money.*

Word Use: this word is more suited to everyday language

haste *noun*
action in a hurry

Word Building: **hasty** *adjective* (**hastier, hastiest**) **hastily** *adverb* **hastiness** *noun*

hasten (say *hay-sən*) *verb*
to hurry: *He hastened to her side.*

hatch[1] *verb*
1 to break out of an egg: *Two new chicks hatched this morning.* **2** to make up or arrange: *They have hatched a plan.*

Word Building: **hatchery** *noun* a place for hatching eggs

hatch[2] *noun*
1 an opening in a floor, a roof or a ship's deck **2** a cover for this opening

Word Building: the plural is **hatches**

hatchet *noun*
a small short-handled axe

Word Use: a similar word is **tomahawk**
Word History: from a French word meaning "little axe"

haughty (say *haw-tee*) *adjective*
too proud of yourself and scornful of others

Word Building: other forms are **haughtier, haughtiest** □ **haughtily** *adverb* **haughtiness** *noun*
Word History: from a French word meaning "high"

haul *verb*
1 to pull hard: *to haul a load of rubbish | to haul on the rope*

haul *noun*
2 a strong pull **3** the amount won, taken or caught at one time: *a haul of fish*

haunch *noun*
1 the part of your body around your hip
2 the back part of an animal

haunt *verb*
1 to keep visiting as a ghost or spirit **2** to continually return to: *His memories haunted him.*

haunt *noun*
3 a place visited often: *The cave had been one of his favourite haunts in his childhood.*

Word Building: **haunted** *adjective* worried, or visited by ghosts **haunting** *adjective* fascinating, or repeating: *a haunting melody | a haunting memory*

have *verb*
1 to own, or possess: *to have a ruby ring* | *to have a sister in Tasmania* | *to have red hair* **2** to get or receive: *Can I have your attention?*

Word Building: other forms are **I, you** or **we have, he, she** or **it has, I had, I am having**

haven *noun*
a place of shelter or safety

haven't
a short form of **have not**

haversack *noun*
a rather old-fashioned word for **knapsack** *or* **rucksack**

havoc *noun*
great damage or devastation

hawk[1] *noun*
a hunting bird with a hooked beak and large claws

Word Building: hawkish *adjective* fierce

hawk[2] *verb*
to offer things for sale in the street or by calling at people's homes

Word Building: hawker *noun* a travelling seller of goods

hay *noun*
grass which has been cut and dried to use as animal feed

haywire *adjective*
crazy or out of control

hazard (say *haz*-əd) *noun*
1 a risk or danger: *Smoking is a health hazard.*

hazard *verb*
2 to risk or take a chance on: *to hazard a guess*

Word Building: hazardous *adjective* dangerous or risky **hazardously** *adverb*
Word History: from an Arabic word for the die in a game of chance

haze *noun*
bits of dust, smoke and so on which combine and look like a thin mist

Word Building: hazy *adjective* (**hazier, haziest**)

hazel *noun*
1 a small tree which has light brown nuts that people eat

hazel *adjective*
2 greenish-brown in colour: *hazel eyes*

he *pronoun*
the male being talked about: *He said he'd come.*

Word Building: other forms are **his**: *his hat*; **him**: *It belongs to him*; **they**: *They are all boys.*

head *noun*
1 the top part of your body where your brain, eyes, ears, nose and mouth are, joined to the rest of your body by your neck **2** a similar part of an animal's body **3** the brain or mind: *a good head for figures* **4** the top or front part of anything: *the head of a page* | *the head of a procession* **5** a leader or a chief **6** a person or animal as one of a number: *ten head of cattle* | *She charged $10 a head for dinner.* **7 come to a head** to reach an important point or crisis **8 go to your head a** to make you confused **b** to make you too proud or pleased with yourself **9 heads** the side of a coin with a picture of a head on it: *Heads or tails?* **10 lose your head** to panic, especially in an emergency

head *verb*
11 to go or be at the head of or in front of: *She heads the list of winners.* **12** to turn towards a certain direction: *Head your horse down the other track.* | *Let's head for home.* **13** to give a heading or title to

Word Building: head *adjective: the head man*

headache *noun*
1 a pain in your head **2** a troublesome or worrying problem

Word Use: definition 2 is more suited to everyday language

heading *noun*
the words written as a title at the top of a page or at the beginning of a piece of writing

headland *noun*
a high piece of land which juts out into a sea or lake

Word Use: a similar word is **promontory**

headlight *noun*
one of the powerful lights on the front of a car or truck

headline *noun*
1 a line in big print at the top of a newspaper article, saying what it is about **2 headlines** important news: *Drought is in the headlines again.*

headmaster *noun*
the male teacher in charge of a school

headmistress *noun*
the female teacher in charge of a school

headphones *plural noun*
a listening device for a radio made of earphones held on by a band over your head

Word Use: another name for this is **headset**

headquarters (say <u>*hed*</u>*-kwaw-təz*) *noun*
the place where the people in charge of a large organisation work: *police headquarters*

headstrong *adjective*
hard to control or determined to have your own way

headway *noun*
forward motion: *The car made little headway in the heavy fog.*

heal *verb*
to make or become whole or well again

Word Use: be careful – this sounds like **heel** and **he'll**
Word Building: **healing** *adjective* able to heal **healer** *noun*

health *noun*
1 freedom from disease or sickness **2** the general state of your body: *in poor health*

Word Building: **healthy** *adjective* (**healthier, healthiest**) □ **healthily** *adverb* **healthiness** *noun*

heap *noun*
1 a group of things lying one on top of the other: *a heap of stones* **2** a great quantity or number: *He has made a heap of money.* **3** something very old and broken down: *His car was a real heap.* **4 give someone heaps** to give someone a lot of insults or trouble

Word Use: definitions 2, 3 and 4 are more suited to everyday language
Word Building: **heap** *verb*

hear *verb*
1 to be able to sense sounds through your ear **2** to be informed of or to receive information: *Have you heard the news yet?*

Word Use: be careful – this sounds like **here**
Word Building: other forms are **I heard, I have heard, I am hearing**

hearing *noun*
1 the process by which sounds are sensed by your ear **2** the opportunity to speak or be heard: *Give our next speaker a decent hearing.* **3** the distance or range within which a sound can be heard: *I must tell you this while he is out of hearing.*

hearsay *noun*
gossip or rumour

hearse (rhymes with *verse*) *noun*
a special car used in a funeral for carrying a coffin

heart *noun*
1 the organ in your body that pumps the blood and keeps it circulating through your body **2** emotions, affections or feelings: *She won his heart.* **3** courage or enthusiasm: *She showed plenty of heart when she went on to win.* **4** the middle part of something: *the heart of a lettuce* **5** the most important part: *the heart of the matter* **6** a figure said to be shaped like a heart, as on playing cards **7 by heart** from memory: *to learn a poem off by heart*

Word Use: **cardiac** is a medical word meaning "having to do with the heart"

hearten *verb*
to cheer up or give courage to

hearth (rhymes with *bath*) *noun*
the floor of a fireplace, which usually extends a little way onto the floor of the room

heart-rending *adjective*
causing great sorrow

hearty *adjective*
1 warm-hearted, enthusiastic and sincere: *a hearty welcome* | *hearty approval* **2** large and satisfying: *a hearty meal*

Word Building: other forms are **heartier, heartiest** □ **heartily** *adverb* **heartiness** *noun*

heat *noun*
1 warmth or the quality of being hot **2** excitement or anger: *the heat of an argument* **3** a race or competition run to decide who will be in the final: *If you come in the first three in your heat you have to run in the final.*

Word Building: **heat** *verb* **heated** *adjective* **heater** *noun*

heath (rhymes with *teeth*) *noun*
1 an area of open land with a lot of low shrubs growing on it **2** a small low shrub which grows on such land

heathen (say <u>*hee*</u>*-dhən*) *noun*
1 someone who does not believe in the God of the Bible **2** someone who is not religious or who shows disrespect and dislike for religion

Word Use: a word with a similar meaning is **pagan**
Word Building: plural forms are **heathens** and **heathen** □ **heathen** *adjective*
Word History: from an Old English word for someone who lived on a heath

heather (rhymes with *weather*) *noun*
any of the shrubs called heaths, usually with small light-purple flowers

heave *verb*
1 to raise or lift using effort or force **2** to drag, haul or pull: *The sailors heaved the ropes on board. | They heaved on the ropes.* **3** to rise and fall: *His chest heaved with the effort of breathing after the race.*

Word Building: **heave** *noun*

heaven *noun*
1 a place where God and the angels live, and where good people are said to go when they die **2** a place or condition of great happiness or pleasure

Word Use: **celestial** is a word meaning "having to do with heaven"
Word Building: **heavenly** *adjective*

heavens *interjection*
an exclamation expressing surprise

heavy *adjective*
1 of great weight and, as a result, hard to lift or carry **2** larger or greater than usual: *heavy rain* **3** serious: *a heavy responsibility* **4** filled or weighed down: *air heavy with moisture | Her heart was heavy with sorrow.*
heavy *noun*
5 someone important in a particular area: *He is one of the heavies of the television world.*

Word Use: definition 5 is more suited to everyday language
Word Building: other forms of the adjective are **heavier, heaviest** □ **heavily** *adverb* **heaviness** *noun*

heckle *verb*
to torment and bother a speaker with annoying questions and comments

hect- *prefix*
a word part meaning 10^2 of a given unit: hectare

Word Use: another spelling is **hecto-**
Word History: this prefix comes from Greek

hectare (say *hek-tair*) *noun*
a unit of measurement of land in the metric system equal to 10 000 square metres, or about $2\frac{1}{2}$ acres

hectic *adjective*
full of excitement, activity and confusion: *a hectic day*

Word Building: **hectically** *adverb*

he'd
a short form of **he had** or **he would**

hedge *noun*
1 a row of bushes or small trees planted close together to form a fence
hedge *verb*
2 to enclose or separate by a hedge or barrier **3** to avoid making a direct answer: *Stop hedging and say what you want.*

hedgehog *noun*
a spiny, insect-eating animal found mostly in Europe, which is active at night

heed *verb*
to pay attention to, or to notice

Word Building: **heed** *noun* careful attention **heedless** *adjective* careless

heel *noun*
1 the rounded back part of your foot below your ankle **2** the part of a sock or shoe that fits over your heel **3 down at heel** shabby and poor-looking **4 take to your heels** to run away quickly
heel *verb*
5 to follow by walking close to your heels: *to train a dog to heel*

Word Use: be careful – this sounds like **heal** and **he'll**

heeler *noun*
a dog trained to round up sheep or cattle by chasing them and biting at their heels

hefty *adjective*
big, strong and heavy

Word Use: this word is more suited to everyday language
Word Building: other forms are **heftier, heftiest** □ **heftiness** *noun*

heifer (say *hef-ə*) *noun*
a young cow that has not had a calf

height (rhymes with *kite*) *noun*
1 the distance from bottom to top **2** a cliff or mountain peak or other very high place **3** the greatest part or amount: *the height of her career | the height of stupidity*

Word Use: **height** is the noun from the adjective **high**
Word Building: **heighten** *verb* to increase or make higher

heir (sounds like *air*) *noun*
someone who inherits a dead person's money, property or title

Word Building: **heiress** *noun*

heirloom (say *air-loohm*) *noun*
something valuable that is handed down from generation to generation in a family

helicopter *noun*
an aircraft without wings which flies by means of a large propeller mounted on the top

heliport *noun*
a place for helicopters to take off and land

helium (say *hee-lee-əm*) *noun*
a gas which is lighter than air and is often used to fill balloons

Word History: from a Greek word meaning "sun"

hell *noun*
a dreadful place where evil people are said to go for punishment after death

Word Building: **hellish** *adjective*

hello *interjection*
a word you use when you meet someone you know

Word Use: other spellings are **hallo** and **hullo**

helm *noun*
1 the wheel or handle which is used to steer a boat **2 at the helm** in charge: *The company has a new manager at the helm.*

Word Building: **helmsman** *noun*

helmet *noun*
a hard hat worn to protect your head

help *verb*
1 to aid or give assistance **2** avoid or keep from: *We couldn't help laughing.*
3 help yourself to to take for yourself

help *noun*
4 someone or something that aids or assists: *He was no help at all.*

Word Building: **helper** *noun* someone who helps **helpful** *adjective* willing to help **helping** *noun* a serving of food

helpless *adjective*
1 weak or unable to do anything
2 without help or assistance: *helpless victims of the earthquake*

Word Building: **helplessly** *adverb* **helplessness** *noun*

helter-skelter *adverb*
with great haste and confusion: *The crowds ran helter-skelter from the surf when the shark alarm sounded.*

hem *verb*
1 to fold back and sew the edge of: *to hem a dress* **2 hem in** to surround or enclose: *Enemy soldiers hemmed the prisoners in.*

Word Use: **hem** *noun* a folded and sewn edge of material
Word Building: other forms are **I hemmed, I have hemmed, I am hemming**

hemi- *prefix*
a word part meaning half: *hemisphere*

Word History: this prefix comes from Greek

hemisphere (say *hem-əs-fear*) *noun*
half of a round or spherical shape such as the earth: *When it is spring in the southern hemisphere it is autumn in the northern hemisphere.*

Word Building: **hemispherical** *adjective*

hemp *noun*
a plant which is grown for its strong fibres which are used to make rope and sacks, and also for the leaves which are used as a drug

hen *noun*
a female bird, especially a domestic chicken

Word Use: the male is called a **cock** or, for domestic chickens, a **rooster**

henna *noun*
a reddish-orange dye which is used to colour hair

hepatitis (say *hep-ə-tuy-təs*) *noun*
a disease of the liver which makes your skin and the whites of your eyes turn yellow

hepta- *prefix*
a word part meaning seven: *heptagon*

Word Use: another spelling is **hept-**
Word History: this prefix comes from Greek

heptagon (say *hep-tə-gon*) *noun*
a flat shape with seven sides

Word Building: **heptagonal** *adjective*

her *pronoun*
1 a form of the pronoun **she** used as the object of the verb in a sentence: *I can't talk to her.*

her *adjective*
2 a form of **she** that shows something belongs to her: *her book*

Word Building: **hers** *pronoun: that book is hers* **herself** *pronoun: She cut herself.*

herald *noun*
somebody or something that carries messages or announces coming events

Word Building: **herald** *verb* to announce

heraldry (say *he-rəl-dree*) *noun*
the investigation and recording of coats of arms and the histories of the families to which they belong

Word Building: **heraldic** *adjective*

herb *noun*
a flowering plant used in cooking or medicines

Word Building: **herbal** *adjective: a herbal remedy* **herbicide** *noun* a chemical that kills plants **herbalist** *noun*
Word History: from a Latin word meaning "grass"

herbivore (say *her-bə-vaw*) *noun*
an animal that eats plants

Word Use: compare with **carnivore, insectivore** and **omnivore**
Word Building: **herbivorous** *adjective: Cows are herbivorous.*

herd *noun*
a large group of animals: *a herd of cattle being driven to new pasture*

Word Building: **herd** *verb* to drive or move together as a group

here *adverb*
1 in, or to this place: *Put it here. / Come here.* **2** at this point: *Here the boy paused for breath.*

Word Use: compare this with **there** □ be careful – this sounds like **hear**

hereditary (say *hə-red-ə-tree*) *adjective*
inherited or passing down from parent to offspring: *a hereditary disease / hereditary ownership of land*

heredity (say *hə-red-ə-tee*) *noun*
the passing on of characteristics from parents to offspring: *Heredity is to blame for my big nose.*

heresy (say *he-rə-see*) *noun*
a belief, especially about religion, which goes against the things that people generally believe

Word Building: the plural is **heresies** □ **heretic** *noun* **heretical** *adjective* **heretically** *adverb*

heritage *noun*
something which is passed on to you because you have been born of a particular family or country

Word Use: a similar word is **inheritance**

hermit *noun*
someone who lives alone and keeps away from other people

Word Building: **hermitage** *noun* a place where hermits live
Word History: from a Greek word meaning "of the desert"

hernia *noun*
the pushing out of an organ in your body, through a tear or opening in the tissue that surrounds it

Word Use: this is also called a **rupture**

hero *noun*
1 a person who has done a very brave thing **2** the character who has the main part in a book, film or play

Word Use: **hero** always used to refer to men or boys, but nowadays women and girls can be **heroes** as well
Word Building: the plural form is **heroes** □ **heroic** *adjective* **heroism** *noun*

heroin *noun*
a dangerously addictive, illegal drug made from morphine

Word Use: be careful – this sounds like **heroine**
Word History: from a Greek word for **hero** (the effect of the drug is supposed to make someone feel like a hero)

heroine *noun*
1 a woman or girl who has done a very brave thing **2** the woman or girl who has the main part in a book, film or play

Word Use: be careful – this sounds like **heroin**

heron *noun*
a water bird with long legs, a long neck and a long bill

herpes (say *her-peez*) *noun*
an infection which causes small blisters to break out on your skin

herring *noun*
small fish which are caught in the seas of the northern hemisphere and eaten either fresh or pickled

Word Building: the plural form can be either **herrings** or **herring**

he's
a short form of **he is** or **he has**

hesitate *verb*
to wait or pause before doing something, as if you are not sure if you should go on: *to hesitate before you speak*

Word Building: **hesitancy** *noun* **hesitant** *adjective* **hesitantly** *adverb* **hesitation** *noun*

hessian (say *hesh-ən*) *noun*
strong rough cloth often used to make sacks

hetero- *prefix*
a word part meaning other, *or* different: *heterosexual*

Word Use: another spelling is **heter-**
Word History: this prefix comes from Greek

heterosexual (say *het-ə-roh-sek-shooh-əl*) *adjective*
having sexual feelings for people of the opposite sex

Word Use: compare with **homosexual**
Word Building: **heterosexual** *noun* □ **heterosexuality** *noun*

hew (say *hyooh*) *verb*
to chop or cut: *to hew wood for the fire*

Word Use: be careful – this sounds like **hue**
Word Building: other forms are **I hewed, I have hewn, I am hewing**

hexa- *prefix*
a word part meaning six: *hexagon*

Word Use: another spelling is **hex-**
Word History: this prefix comes from Greek

hexagon *noun*
a flat shape with six straight sides

Word Building: **hexagonal** *adjective*

hibernate (say *huy-bə-nayt*) *verb*
to hide away and sleep through the winter: *Many animals in cold climates hibernate when food is scarce during the winter.*

Word Building: **hibernation** *noun*

hibiscus (say *huy-bis-kəs*) *noun*
a small tree with large brightly-coloured flowers

hiccup *noun*
a sudden movement in your chest which causes a quick intake of breath and a short sharp sound

Word Use: another spelling is **hiccough**
Word Building: **hiccup** *verb* (**hiccupped, hiccupping**)

hide[1] *verb*
to keep from being seen

Word Building: other forms are **I hid, I have hidden, I am hiding**

hide[2] *noun*
1 the skin of an animal: *Cow hide is used to make leather shoes.* **2 neither hide nor hair** not even the smallest trace: *We could see neither hide nor hair of them.*

hideous (say *hid-ee-əs*) *adjective*
1 very ugly: *a hideous face* **2** shockingly dreadful: *a hideous crime*

Word Building: **hideously** *adverb* **hideousness** *noun*

hiding *noun*
1 a severe beating as a punishment **2** a thorough defeat or loss in a game: *They gave their opponents a hiding in the final.*

hierarchy (say *huy-ə-rah-kee*) *noun*
a system which arranges people or things in grades from the highest to the lowest

Word Building: the plural is **hierarchies** □ **hierarchical** *adjective*

hieroglyphics (say *huy-rə-glif-iks*) *plural noun*
writing in which words or sounds are represented by pictures: *Egyptian hieroglyphics*

hi-fi *noun*
a record-player or tape-recorder which can produce sounds almost the same as the original

Word Building: **hi-fi** *adjective*
Word History: this word is short for **high-fidelity**

high *adjective*
1 tall or far above the ground **2** from bottom to top: *a wall two metres high* **3** being above the normal level or amount: *The river is high after the rain. | high prices* **4** sharp or shrill in sound: *to sing in a high voice* **5** excited or happy: *The children are in high spirits.* **6** bad-smelling: *This fish is high.*

Word Building: **highly** *adverb* very: *highly dangerous* **height** *noun* **high** *adverb*

highlands *plural noun*
the high, mountainous part of a country: *the New Guinea highlands*

Word Building: **highlander** *noun*

highlight *noun*
the best, brightest or most outstanding part: *The highlight of the trip was climbing Uluru.*

Word Building: **highlight** *verb* to emphasise or make stand out

highway *noun*
a main road built to carry a lot of traffic

highwayman *noun*
a bandit, usually on horseback, who used to hold up travellers on the road

Word Building: the plural is **highwaymen**

hijack *verb*
to seize by using threats or violence: *to hijack a plane*

Word Building: **hijacker** *noun*

hike *noun*
1 a very long walk, usually for pleasure: *We went on a hike through the mountains.* **2** a sudden increase: *a hike in the price of petrol*

Word Building: **hike** *verb* **hiker** *noun*

hilarious (say *hə-lair-ree-əs*) *adjective*
1 noisily cheerful **2** very, very funny: *a hilarious story*

Word Building: **hilariously** *adverb* **hilarity** *noun*

hillbilly *noun*
someone living in the country, especially in the mountains away from other people

Word Use: this word was first used in North America □ an Australian word with a similar meaning is **bushie**
Word Building: the plural is **hillbillies**

hilt *noun*
1 the handle of a sword or dagger **2 to the hilt** completely

him *pronoun*
a form of **he** used after the verb in a sentence: *The hat belongs to him.*

Word Building: **himself** *pronoun: He can do that by himself.*

hind[1] *adjective*
behind or back: *Kangaroos have very strong hind legs.*

hind[2] *noun*
a female deer

Word Use: another name is a **doe** □ the male is a **hart** or a **buck**; the young is a **fawn**

hinder (say *hin-də*) *verb*
to slow down or make difficult: *Fog hindered our progress.*

Word Building: **hindrance** *noun*
Word History: from an Old English word meaning "behind" or "back"

hindsight (say *huynd-suyt*) *noun*
the ability to understand what you should have done in an event, after it has happened

Hinduism (say *hin-dooh-iz-əm*) *noun*
the main religion of India

Word Building: **Hindu** *noun* a follower of Hinduism **Hindu** *adjective: the Hindu system of castes or social ranks*

hinge *noun*
1 a movable joint like the one which attaches a door to a door post, allowing the door to swing backwards and forwards
hinge *verb*
2 to join by a hinge **3** to depend: *Everything hinges on your decision.*

hint *noun*
1 a roundabout or indirect suggestion: *to drop a hint that you would like an invitation to the party* **2** a piece of helpful advice

Word Building: **hint** *verb: to hint at his latest plan*

hinterland *noun*
the land lying just inland from the coast: *Very few people settled in the hinterland.*

hip *noun*
the part at each side of your body, just below the waist

hippopotamus *noun*
a large mammal with short legs and a heavy hairless body, that lives around lakes and rivers in Africa

Word Use: the short form is **hippo** and is more suited to everyday language
Word Building: the plural is either **hippopotamuses** or **hippopotami**
Word History: from a Greek word meaning "the horse of the river"

hire *verb*
to pay money to use, or employ: *to hire a car | to hire a butler*

Word Building: **hire** *noun*

hire-purchase *noun*
a way of buying expensive things like cars or furniture by making regular payments of money after you take the goods home

his *pronoun*
1 the form of **he** you use when something belongs to him: *That car is his.*
his *adjective*
2 belonging to him: *That is his cat.*

hiss *verb*
to make the sound "ssss", like a snake, especially as a way of showing you don't like something: *The play was so boring that the audience hissed and booed the actors.*

Word Building: **hiss** *noun*

historian *noun*
someone who studies history and writes about it

history *noun*
1 the events which have happened in the past, or the study of them **2** a description of important things which have happened in the past

Word Building: the plural is **histories** □ **historic** *adjective* important or well-known **historical** *adjective* **historically** *adverb*
Word History: from a Greek word meaning "inquiry" or "observation"

hit *verb*
1 to strike or give a blow to **2** to reach or arrive at: *The school building fund hit $1000.* **3 hit it off** to get on well together: *I can't seem to hit it off with the new neighbours.* **4 hit on** to find by chance: *to hit on a good idea*

hit *noun*
5 a blow or stroke **6** a great success

Word Use: definitions 2 and 3 are more suited to everyday language
Word Building: other verb forms are **he hit, he has hit, he is hitting** □ **hit** *adjective: a hit record*

hitch *verb*
1 to tie or fasten: *to hitch a horse to a cart* **2 hitch up** to pull or tug up: *to hitch up your trousers*

hitch *noun*
3 a kind of knot that can be undone easily **4** something that obstructs or makes things difficult: *a hitch in our plans*

Word Building: the plural of the noun is **hitches**

hitchhike *verb*
to travel free of charge by getting lifts in passing cars or trucks

Word Use: this is sometimes shortened to **hitch**
Word Building: **hitchhiker** *noun*

HIV *noun*
the virus that causes AIDS

Word History: made by joining the first letters of *human immunodeficiency virus*

hive *noun*
1 a place that bees live in **2** a place full of busy people

hives *noun*
a rash, usually due to eating or touching something to which you are allergic: *Oranges give me hives.*

hoard *verb*
to save up and hide away in a secret place: *Squirrels hoard nuts for the winter.*

Word Building: **hoard** *noun* a secret store **hoarder** *noun*

hoarding *noun*
1 a large board for putting up advertisements or notices **2** a temporary fence made of boards around a building site

hoarse (say *haws*) *adjective*
rough or croaky: *to shout until your voice becomes hoarse*

Word Use: be careful – this sounds like **horse**
Word Building: **hoarsely** *adverb* **hoarseness** *noun*

hoax *noun*
a trick or practical joke

Word Building: **hoax** *verb* **hoaxer** *noun*

hobble *verb*
to walk with difficulty: *to hobble around with a sprained ankle*

hobby *noun*
something that you enjoy doing in your spare time: *My hobby is collecting stamps.*

Word Building: the plural is **hobbies**

hock *noun*
the joint in the hind leg of a horse or similar animal, which is like the ankle

hockey *noun*
a game played on a field or on ice in which two teams compete to hit a ball into a goal using a stick with a curved end

hoe *noun*
a garden tool with a long handle and flat thin blade, which you use to break up the soil

Word Building: **hoe** *verb* (**hoed, hoeing**)

hog *noun*
1 a pig **2** someone who is greedy or dirty **3 go the whole hog** to do something completely: *He went the whole hog and spent all his pocket money on sweets.*

hog *verb*
4 to take more than your share of: *to hog the biscuits*

Word Use: definitions 2, 3 and 4 are more suited to everyday language □ the male of definition 1 is a **boar;** the female is a **sow;** the young is a **piglet** or a **shoat**
Word Building: other verb forms are **I hogged, I have hogged, I am hogging**

hoist *verb*
1 to lift up or raise: *to hoist a flag*
hoist *noun*
2 a lift or other machine that raises things off the ground

hold[1] *verb*
1 to have or keep in your arms or hands **2** to own: *to hold land in the country* **3** to contain: *The petrol tank holds 50 litres.* **4** to fasten or stay fastened: *A paper clip holds pages together. / The anchor will not hold in rough seas.* **5** to have or conduct: *to hold a meeting* **6 hold up** **a** to delay **b** to rob
hold[1] *noun*
7 a grip: *The wrestler locked his opponent in a firm hold.* **8** control or influence: *to have a hold on your audience*

Word Building: other verb forms are **I held, I have held, I was holding** □ **holder** *noun*

hold[2] *noun*
the part of a ship, below the deck, where cargo is carried

hold-up *noun*
1 a robbery **2** a delay

hole *noun*
1 an opening through something **2** a hollow space **3** a dirty or unpleasant place: *This restaurant is a hole.*

Word Use: definition 3 is more suited to everyday language
Word Building: **hole** *verb*

holiday *noun*
1 a day's break from work or school, usually to celebrate or remember an important event: *a public holiday on Anzac Day* **2 holidays** a much longer break from your daily work

Word Use: a similar word for definition 2 is **vacation**
Word Building: **holiday** *verb: We holiday at the beach.*
Word History: from an Old English word meaning "holy day" (the first holidays were special days in the Church's calendar)

hollow *adjective*
1 having empty space inside: *a hollow log* **2** empty of meaning: *hollow promises*
hollow *noun*
3 a hole or a dip, especially in the ground

Word Building: **hollow** *verb* **hollowly** *adverb* **hollowness** *noun*

holly *noun*
a small tree with shiny prickly leaves and bright red berries in winter

holo- *prefix*
a word part meaning whole *or* entire: *holocaust*

Word History: this prefix comes from Greek

holocaust (say *hol-ə-kost*) *noun*
1 great loss of life, especially when caused by a bad fire **2 the Holocaust** the mass murder of Jews by the Nazis during the Second World War

Word History: from a Greek word meaning "a burnt offering"

holster *noun*
a leather case for a gun, worn on a belt

holy *adjective*
1 sacred or dedicated to God: *Easter is a holy festival.* **2** religious or pious: *a holy priest*

Word Building: other forms are **holier, holiest** □ **holiness** *noun*

homage (say *hom-ij*) *noun*
respect or honour: *to pay homage to a leader*

home *noun*
1 the place where you live or were born: *Australia is my home.* **2** a house or other dwelling **3** a place where people can be cared for: *an old people's home*
home *adverb*
4 to or at home: *to come straight home after school*

Word Building: **home** *adjective: the home team* **homeward** *adverb* towards home **homing** *adjective: a homing pigeon*

homely *adjective*
1 plain and simple: *homely food* **2** not pretty or good-looking: *a homely face*

Word Building: other forms are **homelier, homeliest** □ **homeliness** *noun*

homesick *adjective*
unhappy and wanting to be at home

Word Building: **homesickness** *noun*

homestead *noun*
the main house on a sheep or cattle station or a large farm

home unit *noun*
one out of a number of separately owned homes in the same multi-storey building

Word Use: you can also use **unit**

homicide (say *hom-ə-suyd*) *noun*
the crime of killing someone on purpose

Word Building: **homicidal** *adjective: a homicidal maniac* **homicidally** *adverb*

homo- *prefix*
a word part meaning same: *homonym*

Word History: this prefix comes from Greek

homoeopathy or **homeopathy** (say *hoh-mee-op-ə-thee*) *noun*
the method of treating disease with tiny amounts of a substance which would, if you gave it in larger amounts, cause symptoms just like those of the disease being treated

Word Building: **homoeopath** *noun* **homoeopathic** *adjective*

homogeneous (say *hom-ə-jee-nee-əs*) *adjective*
made up of parts which are all of the same kind: *a homogeneous mixture*

Word Building: **homogenise** *verb* to mix evenly so that all parts are alike **homogeneously** *adverb*

homonym (say *hom-ə-nim*) *noun*
a word which has the same sound or the same spelling as another but has a different meaning

Word Use: if two homonyms are spelt the same, like *bear* (the animal) and *bear* (to carry), they're called **homographs**; if two homonyms sound the same, like *heir* and *air*, they're called **homophones**
Word History: from a Latin word meaning "having the same name"

homosexual (say *hoh-moh-sek-shooh-əl*) *noun*
someone who has sexual feelings for people of the same sex as themselves

Word Use: compare with **heterosexual**
Word Building: **homosexual** *adjective* **homosexuality** *noun*

honest (say *on-əst*) *adjective*
truthful and fair

Word Building: **honestly** *adverb* **honesty** *noun*

honey (rhymes with *funny*) *noun*
a sweet sticky liquid made by bees from the nectar of flowers

honeycomb *noun*
a wax structure made up of many rows of tiny compartments, made by bees for holding eggs, honey and pollen in the hive

honeymoon *noun*
a holiday spent by a bride and groom straight after their wedding

Word Building: **honeymoon** *verb*

honorary (say *on-ə-rə-ree*) *adjective*
not paid for what you do: *the honorary secretary of the club*

honour or **honor** (say *on-ə*) *noun*
1 fame or glory: *to bring honour to the school* **2** respect or esteem: *to be treated with honour* **3** honesty and high morals: *a person of honour*

Word Building: **honour** *verb* to show respect for **honourable** *adjective* **honourably** *adverb*

hood *noun*
1 a loose kind of hat, usually attached to a coat, which covers your head and neck **2** a folding roof for a car or baby's pram

Word Building: **hooded** *adjective*

hoodlum (say *hoohd-ləm*) *noun*
a rough destructive young person

hoodwink *verb*
to trick or deceive

hoof *noun*
the hard covering which protects the feet of some animals such as horses, cows and pigs

Word Building: the plural is either **hoofs** or **hooves**

hook *noun*
1 a piece of metal or some other material bent or curved so as to hold or catch something **2** a punch in boxing, made with the arm bent **3 by hook or by crook** by any way possible
hook *verb*
4 to hold or be fastened by a hook **5** to hit a ball so that it curves to the left if you are right-handed

Word Use: the opposite of definition 5 is **slice**
Word Building: **hooked** *adjective* addicted: *hooked on drugs*

hook-up *noun*
a link-up or connection between radio or television stations or telephones

hooligan *noun*
a rough and noisy young person who causes trouble

Word Building: **hooliganism** *noun*

hoop *noun*
a ring or circular band made of wire, wood or plastic

hop[1] *verb*
to jump, especially on one foot

Word Building: other forms are **I hopped, I have hopped, I am hopping** □ **hop** *noun*

hop[2] *noun*
a climbing plant whose flowers are used to flavour beer

hope *verb*
1 to look forward to or expect, especially something good
hope *noun*
2 a wish or desire that something good will happen: *We all expressed a hope for their safety.* **3** an expectation or likelihood: *no hope of finding the lost money*

Word Building: **hopeful** *adjective* **hopefulness** *noun* **hopeless** *adjective* **hopelessness** *noun*

horde *noun*
a great crowd: *a horde of flies buzzing around the barbecue*

horizon (say *hə-ruy-zən*) *noun*
1 the line where the earth or sea appears to meet the sky **2** the limit or boundary to knowledge: *Reading broadens your horizons.*

horizontal (say *ho-rə-zon-təl*) *adjective*
1 parallel, or in line, with the horizon **2** lying down flat

Word Use: compare with **vertical**
Word Building: **horizontally** *adverb*

hormone *noun*
a chemical substance made by a gland in the body which travels through the blood and affects other parts of the body

Word Building: **hormonal** *adjective*
Word History: from a Greek word meaning "setting in motion"

horn *noun*
1 a hard pointed growth on the forehead of animals like cows, sheep and deer **2** the bonelike material making up horns or hoofs **3** a musical wind instrument: *a French horn* **4** a device for sounding a warning signal: *to blow the car's horn*

Word Building: **horn** *verb* to wound or stab with the horns **horny** *adjective* tough or hardened, as if made from horn

hornet *noun*
a large wasp with a very painful sting

horoscope (say *ho-rə-skohp*) *noun*
a diagram showing the position of the planets in the sky at a particular time and thought by some people to be an aid in forecasting the future

horrendous *adjective*
horrible and dreadful

horrible *adjective*
terrible, dreadful or very unpleasant

Word Building: **horribly** *adverb*

horrid *adjective*
nasty or horrible

horrify *verb*
to shock or fill with horror: *The violent film horrified me.*

Word Building: other forms are **it horrified, it has horrified, it is horrifying** □ **horrific** *adjective* shocking **horrifying** *adjective*

horror *noun*
1 a strong feeling of fear or disgust: *a horror of spiders* **2** someone or something thought to be bad or ugly: *Her brother is a little horror.*

Word Use: definition 2 is more suited to everyday language

hors d'oeuvre (say *aw-derv*) *noun*
a small piece of food such as an olive, a nut or a savoury, served before a main meal

Word Use: we pronounce these words like this because they come from French

horse *noun*
1 a large, four-legged animal with hoofs, which is easily trained for riding, racing or pulling loads **2 eat like a horse** to have a big appetite **3 hold your horses** to wait and not rush ahead

Word Use: be careful – this sounds like **hoarse** □ the male is a **stallion;** the female is a **mare;** the young is a **foal**

horsepower *noun*
an old-fashioned unit for measuring power: *a 50 horsepower engine*

horseradish *noun*
a plant whose strongly-flavoured root is used in cooking

horticulture (say *haw-tə-kul-chə*) *noun*
the growing of garden plants for their fruit, vegetables and flowers

Word Building: **horticultural** *adjective* **horticulturalist** *noun* **horticulturist** *noun*

hose *noun*
1 a flexible tube for carrying water **2** *another word for* **hosiery**

Word Building: **hose** *verb* to water or wet with a hose

hosiery *noun*
clothing for your legs and feet, such as socks or stockings

hospice *noun*
a hospital for patients who are dying, often run by a church

hospital *noun*
a place where sick and injured people are given medical treatment

Word Building: **hospitalise** *verb* to put into hospital

hospitality (say *hos-pə-tal-ə-tee*) *noun*
kindness and generosity shown to guests

Word Building: **hospitable** *adjective* **hospitably** *adverb*

host[1] (rhymes with *most*) *noun*
1 someone who entertains guests: *The host of a party* **2** an animal or plant on which a parasite lives: *A dog is host to many fleas.*

Word Building: **host** *verb* **hostess** *noun*

host[2] (rhymes with *most*) *noun*
a great number or crowd: *a host of household chores | a host of angels*

hostage (say *hos-tij*) *noun*
someone held prisoner by an enemy until certain conditions are met or ransom money is paid

hostel *noun*
a place where people can get meals and a room to sleep for the night at a low cost

Word History: from a French word meaning "guest"

hostile *adjective*
unfriendly or acting like an enemy

Word Building: **hostility** *noun*
Word History: from a Latin word meaning "enemy"

hot *adjective*
1 having a high temperature and giving out heat **2** strong or burning to taste: *a hot curry* **3** angry, violent or passionate: *a hot temper* **4 not so hot a** not very good: *He's not so hot at maths.* **b** not very well: *I'm not feeling so hot.*

Word Use: definitions 4a and 4b are more suited to everyday language

hot dog *noun*
a long red sausage served hot in a bread roll

hotel *noun*
a place which provides rooms and meals for paying guests, and which has special rooms where people can go to drink beer and other alcoholic drinks

Word Building: **hotelier** *noun* someone who runs a hotel

hotplate *noun*
a metal plate on an electric stove or barbecue which can be heated and used to cook food

hound *noun*
1 a dog, especially a hunting dog
hound *verb*
2 to hunt or pursue continually: *The dogs hounded the fox into the trap. | Her parents always have to hound her to do her homework.*

hour *noun*
1 a unit of measurement of time equal to 60 minutes **2** a particular time: *The hour has come.* **3 hours** the usual times for work or business: *School hours are 9 a.m. to 3.30 p.m. | office hours* **4 the eleventh hour** the very last possible moment: *They were rescued at the eleventh hour.* **5 the small hours** the hours just after midnight

Word Use: be careful – this sounds like **our**
Word Building: **hourly** *adjective: an hourly broadcast* **hourly** *adverb: to broadcast the news hourly*

hourglass *noun*
an instrument for measuring time, with sand running from one glass bulb to another in exactly an hour

Word Building: the plural is **hourglasses** □ **hourglass** *adjective:* shaped like an hourglass: *an hourglass figure*

house (say *hows*) *noun*
1 a building where people live **2** a building for any purpose: *Parliament House | a house of worship* **3** a section of a school, made up of children from all classes, formed for sport and other competitions **4** the group of people forming a parliament or one of its divisions: *the upper house | the lower house* **5** a family seen as consisting of ancestors and descendants: *the royal house of Windsor* **6** an audience in a theatre: *The performers played to a full house.*
house (say *howz*) *verb*
7 to provide space or accommodation for: *to house refugees*

Word Building: **housing** *noun* a protective covering or support for a machine

houseboat *noun*
a boat which is fitted up for people to live on

household *noun*
1 all the people who live together in a house

household *adjective*
2 belonging to, or having to do with, a house or family: *household furniture* | *household chores*

Word Building: **householder** *noun*

housie-housie *noun*
another name for **bingo**

hovel *noun*
a small dirty house or hut

hover (say *hov-ə*) *verb*
1 to stay in one spot in the air as if hanging: *The bees were hovering over the flowers.* **2** to linger or stay close to: *The children hovered around a bowl of chocolates.*

hovercraft *noun*
a vehicle which can travel over land or water, supported on a cushion of air

how *adverb*
in what way, or condition: *How did it happen?* | *How are you?*

however *adverb*
no matter how much, or in what way: *He'll never be able to sing however hard he tries.* | *Go there however you like.*

howl *verb*
to make a long, loud, wailing noise like a dog or wolf

Word Building: **howl** *noun* **howler** *noun* a very stupid mistake

hub *noun*
1 the centre part of a wheel **2** any busy or important centre: *The city is a hub of activity.*

huddle *verb*
1 to crowd closely together: *to huddle by the fire to keep warm*

huddle *noun*
2 a few people crowded together to discuss something in private

hue *noun*
a colour or shade of colour: *the hues of the rainbow*

Word Use: be careful – this sounds like **hew**

huge *adjective*
very, very large: *a huge mountain*

Word Building: **hugely** *adverb* **hugeness** *noun*

hulk *noun*
someone or something that is bulky, heavy or clumsy

Word Building: **hulking** *adjective*

hull *noun*
the body of a ship or boat: *to paint the hull*

hullabaloo (say *hul-ə-bə-looh*) *noun*
an uproar or loud noisy disturbance

hum *verb*
1 to make a buzzing or droning sound **2** to sing with your lips closed **3** to be busy and active: *The factory hummed all day and night.*

Word Building: other forms are **I hummed, I have hummed, I am humming** □ **hum** *noun*

human *noun*
a man, woman or child

Word Building: **human** *adjective: the human form* **humanly** *adverb: as soon as humanly possible*
Word History: from a Latin word meaning "of a man"

humane (say *hyooh-mayn*) *adjective*
showing feelings of pity and tenderness: *It would be humane to help him.*

Word Building: **humanely** *adverb*

humanity *noun*
1 all humans **2** sympathy and kindness towards other people and animals

Word Building: **humanitarian** *adjective*

humble *adjective*
1 modest and meek: *She was too humble to expect the famous writer to speak to her.*
2 poor and lowly: *He came from a humble home.*

Word Building: **humbly** *adverb* **humility** *noun*

humdrum *adjective*
dull and ordinary: *a humdrum existence*

humid *adjective*
moist and damp, especially when it's also warm: *a humid day*

Word Building: **humidly** *adverb* **humidity** *noun*

humiliate *verb*
to cause to feel ashamed or foolish: *His rude remarks humiliated her.*

Word Building: **humiliation** *noun*

humour or **humor** *noun*
the quality of being funny or amusing: *a sense of humour / Standing there dripping wet, he couldn't see the humour in the situation.*

Word Building: **humorous** *adjective*

hump *noun*
1 a bulge on the back: *a camel's hump* **2** a rounded rise in the ground or on a road: *a speed hump*

hump *verb*
3 to carry: *to hump a swag*

humpy *noun*
an Aboriginal bush shelter

Word History: from an Aboriginal language called Yagara

humus (say hyooh-məs) *noun*
dark nourishing material in soil, formed by the rotting of animal and vegetable matter

hunch *verb*
1 to push out or up: *to hunch your shoulders*

hunch *noun*
2 a belief, usually without the knowledge of the facts: *I had a hunch that something would happen.*

Word Use: the noun is more suited to everyday language

hundred *noun*
the number 100, or 10 times 10

Word Building: **hundred** *adjective: a hundred men* **hundredth** *adjective: a hundredth part of the money*

hunger *noun*
an uncomfortable feeling of the need for food

Word Building: **hungry** *adjective* (**hungrier, hungriest**) **hungrily adverb**

hunk *noun*
a large rough piece: *They ate hunks of bread with the cheese.*

hunt *verb*
1 to chase, for food or sport **2** to search: *I hunted everywhere for my pencil.*

Word Building: **hunt** *noun* **huntress** *noun* **huntsman** *noun*

hurdle *noun*
a movable fence over which horses or people have to jump in a race

Word Building: **hurdle** *verb: to hurdle a fence* **hurdler** *noun*

hurl *verb*
to throw

hurricane *noun*
a violent tropical storm with a very strong wind

hurry *verb*
to act quickly to save time: *Hurry or you will be late!*

Word Building: other forms are **I hurried, I have hurried, I am hurrying** □ **hurried** *adjective* **hurriedly** *adverb* **hurry** *noun*

hurt *verb*
1 to cause pain or damage to: *I hurt my leg. / My thoughtlessness hurt Jan.* **2** to be painful: *My leg hurts.*

Word Building: **hurt** *noun* **hurtful** *adjective* **hurtfully** *adverb*

hurtle *verb*
to rush noisily: *We hurtled along in the train.*

husband *noun*
the man to whom a woman is married

hush *verb*
1 to make quiet or silent: *Hush your voice. / Hush the baby.* **2** to become quiet: *Hush!*

Word Building: **hush** *noun*

husk *noun*
the dry outside covering of grain

husky[1] *adjective*
1 low and hoarse: *a husky voice* **2** big and strong: *a husky lifesaver*

Word Building: other forms are **huskier, huskiest** □ **huskily** *adverb* **huskiness** *noun*

husky[2] *noun*
a dog used by Eskimos for pulling sledges

Word Building: the plural is **huskies**

hustle (say hus-əl) *verb*
1 to push along roughly or hurriedly: *They hustled him out of the room.* **2** to hurry

Word Building: **hustler** *noun* someone who gets easy money by gambling, or something like this

hut *noun*
a small house-like shelter: *a beach hut*

hutch *noun*
a coop or house for small animals: *a rabbit hutch*

Word Building: the plural is **hutches**

hybrid (say *huy-brəd*) *noun*
an animal or plant that is the result of breeding between different types

Word Building: **hybridise** *verb*
Word History: from a Latin word for the young of a tame sow and a wild boar

hydrangea (say *huy-drayn-jə*) *noun*
a shrub which has large blue or pink flowers and loses its leaves in winter

hydrant *noun*
a point where a hose can be connected to a water main

hydraulic (say *huy-drol-ik*) *adjective*
worked by the pressure of water, oil or other liquid: *hydraulic brakes*

Word Building: **hydraulically** *adverb* **hydraulics** *noun*

hydro- *prefix*
a word part meaning water: *hydroplane*

Word Use: another spelling is **hydr-**
Word History: this prefix comes from Greek

hydro-electric *adjective*
having to do with the making of electricity by water power: *a hydro-electric scheme*

Word Building: **hydro-electricity** *noun* the electricity made by water power

hydrofoil *noun*
1 a ski-like attachment which raises the hull of a boat above the surface of the water when a certain speed has been reached **2** a boat with hydrofoils

hydrogen *noun*
a gas which combines with oxygen to make water

hydroplane *noun*
a light high-powered boat designed to skim along the surface of the water at high speed

hydroponics *noun*
the growing of plants in water rather than soil

hyena *noun*
a doglike animal that eats the flesh of dead animals

Word History: from a Greek word meaning "hog"

hygiene (say *huy-jeen*) *noun*
1 the science of preserving health **2** the cleanliness necessary for preserving health

Word Building: **hygienic** *adjective* **hygienically** *adverb*

hymn *noun*
a song praising God

Word Building: **hymnal** *noun* a book of hymns **hymnbook** *noun*

hyper- *prefix*
a word part meaning over: *hyperactive*

Word History: this prefix comes from Greek

hyperactive *adjective*
so active that you are restless and cannot settle down: *a hyperactive child*

Word Building: **hyperactivity** *noun*

hyphen *noun*
a short line (-) used to join the parts of some compound words, as in "part-time", or the parts of a word when it has to be split at the end of a line

Word Building: **hyphenate** *verb* to write or join by a hyphen **hyphenation** *noun*

hypno- *prefix*
a word part meaning sleep: *hypnosis*

Word History: this prefix comes from Greek

hypnosis *noun*
a sleeplike state brought about by cooperating with someone who is then able to control your mind and actions

Word Building: **hypnotic** *adjective*

hypnotise or **hypnotize** *verb*
to put under hypnosis: *The doctor hypnotised the patient.*

Word Building: **hypnotism** *noun*

hypo- *prefix*
a word part meaning under: *hypodermic*

Word History: this prefix comes from Greek

hypochondria (say *huy-pə-kon-dree-ə*) *noun*
the state of being very anxious about your health or imagining yourself ill

Word Building: **hypochondriac** *adjective* **hypochondriac** *noun*

hypocrite (say *hip-ə-krit*) *noun*
someone who pretends to be better than they are

Word Building: **hypocrisy** *noun* **hypocritical** *adjective*

hypodermic *adjective*
injecting under the skin: *a hypodermic needle*

hypotenuse (say *huy-pot-ən-yoohz*)
noun
the side opposite the right angle in a right-angled triangle

hypothermia (say *huy-pə-therm-ee-ə*)
noun
a dangerous condition, often caused by being exposed to cold weather, in which your body temperature is lower than normal

Word History: **hypothermal** *adjective*

hypothesis (say *huy-poth-ə-səs*) *noun*
an idea which is taken as a useful starting point for a discussion or scientific investigation

Word Building: the plural is **hypotheses** □ **hypothesise** *verb* **hypothetical** *adjective* **hypothetically** *adverb*

hysterical *adjective*
1 extremely and wildly emotional
2 laughing uncontrollably

Word Building: **hysterics** *plural noun* a violent emotional outburst **hysteria** *noun* **hysterically** *adverb*
Word History: from a Greek word meaning "suffering in the uterus" (women were the ones believed to suffer from emotion like this)

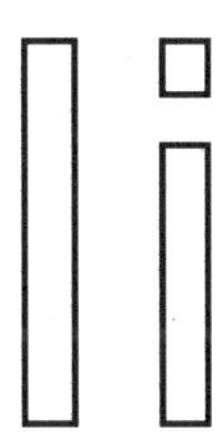

I *pronoun*
the word that the speaker of a sentence uses about himself or herself: *I want all the cake for myself.*

Word Building: other forms are **my:** *my dog*; **mine:** *That fish is mine*; **me:** *Don't forget about me*; **we:** *We want to come too*; **our:** *Our sister is a star dancer*; **ours:** *Ours haven't come yet*; **us:** *What about us?*

ibis (say *uy-bəs*) *noun*
a wading bird like a heron with a long, thin, down-curved beak

Word Building: the plural is **ibises**

ice *noun*
1 frozen water
ice *verb*
2 to become frozen: *The pond has iced over.* **3** to cover with icing: *to ice a cake*

Word Building: **icy** *adjective: an icy road | an icy wind* **icily** *adverb* **iciness** *noun*

iceberg *noun*
a large mass of ice broken off from a glacier and floating in the sea

ice-cream *noun*
a sweet frozen food made with cream or milk

icicle *noun*
a hanging tapering piece of ice formed by the freezing of dripping water

icing *noun*
a mixture of sugar and water or other ingredients for covering cakes

icon (say *uy-kon*) *noun*
1 a picture, especially one used in religious worship **2** a small picture or symbol on a computer screen, that stands for a process, a group of files, and other such things

I'd
a short form if **I would** or **I had**

idea *noun*
a thought or picture in the mind

ideal *noun*
1 an idea of something at its most perfect: *She is my ideal of a doctor.* **2** a high ambition or standard: *He works hard towards his ideals.*

Word Building: **ideal** *adjective* **idealise** *verb* **idealism** *noun* **ideally** *adverb*

identical *adjective*
exactly alike: *identical twins*

Word Building: **identically** *adverb*

identify *verb*
to recognise or prove as being a particular thing or person: *Can you identify your keys?*

Word Building: other forms are **I identified, I have identified, I am identifying** □ **identifiable** *adjective* **identification** *noun*

identity *noun*
1 the condition of being a certain person or thing: *The group kept its identity under different leaders.* **2** a well-known personality: *an identity in the cricket club*

Word Building: the plural is **identities**

idiom (say *id-ee-əm*) *noun*
a saying that is only used in one particular language, especially one that does not mean exactly what the words themselves mean: *"It's raining cats and dogs" is an idiom in English for "It's raining very heavily".*

Word Building: **idiomatic** *adjective* **idiomatical** *adjective* **idiomatically** *adverb* **idiomaticalness** *noun*

idiosyncrasy (say *id-ee-oh-sink-rə-see*) *noun*
a peculiarity of someone's character or behaviour: *His idiosyncrasy is writing with purple ink.*

Word Building: the plural is **idiosyncrasies** □ **idiosyncratic** *adjective* **idiosyncratically** *adverb*

idiot *noun*
1 someone who is very mentally deficient **2** a very stupid person

Word Building: **idiotic** *adjective* **idiotically** *adverb*

idle *adjective*
1 not doing or wanting to do anything: *idle workmen* **2** not being used: *idle machinery* | *idle time*

Word Building: **idleness** *noun* **idler** *noun* **idly** *adverb*

idol *noun*
a statue worshipped as a god

Word Building: **idolatry** *noun* **idolise** *verb*

i.e.
short for id est, *Latin words meaning* "that is": *Please bring to the exam all your stationery needs, i.e. pencils, paper and ruler.*

if *conjunction*
1 supposing that: *I'll go if you want me to.* **2** whether: *I don't know if I can stand on my head.*

igloo *noun*
a dome-shaped Eskimo hut built of blocks of hard snow

ignite *verb*
to set on fire

ignition *noun*
1 the act of setting on fire **2** a system for setting on fire, especially that of the electrical sparks which ignite the fuel in the cylinders in a car engine

ignoble *adjective*
of low character and behaviour

Word Use: this is the opposite of **noble**
Word Building: **ignobly** *adverb*

ignoramus (say *ig-nə-ray-məs*) *noun*
someone who knows little or nothing

Word Building: the plural is **ignoramuses**

ignorant *adjective*
1 uneducated **2** having no knowledge: *ignorant of Russian*

Word Building: **ignorance** *noun* **ignorantly** *adverb*

ignore *verb*
to take no notice of

iguana (say *i-gwah-nə*) *noun*
a large lizard of tropical America

Word History: from an American Indian language

ill *adjective*
1 sick **2** bad: *ill feeling*

ill *adverb*
3 badly: *to treat someone ill*

ill *noun*
4 an evil: *the ills of our society*

Word Building: **illness** *noun*

illegal *adjective*
not allowed by the law

Word Building: **illegality** *noun* **illegally** *adverb*

illegible *adjective*
not able to be read: *illegible writing*

Word Building: **illegibility** *noun* **illegibly** *adverb*

illegitimate *adjective*
1 born to parents who are not legally married **2** against the law or not allowed

Word Building: **illegitimacy** *noun* **illegitimately** *adverb*

illicit (say *i-lis-ət*) *adjective*
forbidden or not legal: *illicit alcohol*

illiterate *adjective*
unable to read and write

Word Building: **illiteracy** *noun*

illuminate *verb*
1 to light up **2** to give knowledge to or inform: *Would you care to illuminate me on this point?*

Word Building: **illumination** *noun*

illusion *noun*
a false idea or daydream: *illusions of becoming a rock singer*

illustrate *verb*
1 to make clear by giving examples: *He illustrated his theory about leadership with accounts of the lives of some famous explorers.* **2** to provide with pictures: *The author illustrated her book with photographs.*

Word Building: **illustrator** *noun* someone who illustrates books **illustration** *noun* **illustrative** *adjective*

illustrious *adjective*
famous or distinguished: *an illustrious family in the nation's history*

Word Building: **illustriously** *adverb*

image *noun*
1 a picture in the mind: *I have an image of the perfect house.* **2** reflection: *your image in the mirror* **3** an exact likeness: *She is the image of her mother.*

Word Building: **imagery** *noun* all the metaphors, similes, and other figures of speech we use to express ourselves

imagination *noun*
the ability to form pictures in your mind or to make up interesting stories

Word Building: **imaginative** *adjective*

imagine *verb*
1 to form a picture of in the mind: *to imagine a scene at the beach* **2** to think or believe: *I imagine she'll be happy when she hears the good news.*

Word Building: **imaginary** *adjective* only in the mind

imbecile (say *im-bə-seel*) *noun*
someone who is mentally deficient

Word Building: **imbecile** *adjective*

imitate *verb*
to copy or use as a model

Word Building: **imitation** *noun* **imitative** *adjective* **imitator** *noun*

immaculate *adjective*
spotlessly clean

Word Building: **immaculately** *adverb*

immediate *adjective*
happening straight away: *an immediate reply*

Word Building: **immediacy** *noun* **immediately** *adverb*

immense *adjective*
extremely large

Word Building: **immensely** *adverb* **immensity** *noun*

immerse *verb*
to put below the surface of a liquid: *He immersed his hand in the warm water.*

Word Building: **immersion** *noun*
Word History: from a Latin word meaning "dipped"

immigrate *verb*
to come to live in a new country

Word Use: don't confuse this with **emigrate**
Word Building: **immigrant** *noun* someone who immigrates **immigration** *noun*

imminent *adjective*
likely to happen at any moment

Word Use: don't confuse this word with **eminent**
Word Building: **imminence** *noun* **imminently** *adverb*

immoral *adjective*
wrong or wicked

Word Use: compare this with **moral**
Word Building: **immorality** *noun* **immorally** *adverb*

immortal *adjective*
living or lasting forever: *the immortal works of Banjo Patterson*

Word Building: **immortalise** *verb* **immortality** *noun* **immortally** *adverb*

immune *adjective*
protected from a disease: *She is immune to mumps now.*

Word Building: **immunology** *noun* the science that deals with protection from diseases **immunise** *verb* **immunity** *noun*

imp *noun*
1 a little devil **2** a child who misbehaves a bit

Word Building: **impish** *adjective* **impishly** *adverb*

impact *noun*
the hitting of one thing against another: *I heard the impact of the cars at the corner.*

impair *verb*
to make worse: *Sickness impaired her performance.*

Word Use: a similar word is **spoil**
Word Building: **impairment** *noun*

impartial *adjective*
not taking one side or the other: *an impartial judge*

Word Use: a similar word is **disinterested**
Word Building: **impartiality** *noun* **impartially** *adverb*

impassive *adjective*
not showing any emotion: *His face remained impassive as she told her story.*

Word Building: **impassively** *adverb* **impassivity** *noun*

impatient *adjective*
1 unwilling to wait **2** short-tempered: *I am often impatient with noisy children.*

Word Building: **impatience** *noun* **impatiently** *adverb*

impeccable *adjective*
without any faults: *His work was impeccable.*

Word Building: **impeccably** *adverb*

impede *verb*
to slow down or block the way of: *The demonstration impeded the traffic.*

Word Building: **impediment** *noun*

imperfect *adjective*
faulty or not perfect

Word Building: **imperfection** *noun* **imperfectly** *adverb*

imperial *adjective*
1 belonging to an empire: *the imperial throne* **2** having to do with a system of measurement set up in Britain and used in Australia before the metric system was introduced

imperious *adjective*
arrogant or bossy: *The director had an imperious manner.*

Word Building: **imperiously** *adverb*

impersonal *adjective*
not showing any personal feelings: *Her remarks were cool and impersonal.*

Word Building: **impersonally** *adverb*

impersonate *verb*
to pretend to be: *The thief impersonated a detective to persuade the old lady to let him in.*

Word Building: **impersonator** *noun* someone who acts the part of another, often on stage or on TV **impersonation** *noun*

impertinent *adjective*
cheeky or rude

Word Building: **impertinence** *noun* **impertinently** *adverb*

impetuous *adjective*
acting hastily and thoughtlessly

Word Building: **impetuosity** *noun* **impetuously** *adverb*

impetus *noun*
1 a moving force, stimulus, or impulse: *a fresh impetus to study hard* **2** the force or energy of a moving object

Word Building: the plural is **impetuses**

implement (say *im-plə-mənt*) *noun*
1 a tool: *a kitchen implement*
implement (say *im-plə-ment*) *verb*
2 to put into effect: *to implement a plan*

Word Building: **implementation** *noun*

implicit (say *im-plis-ət*) *adjective*
1 suggested or implied but not actually stated: *an implicit understanding*
2 absolute or unquestioning: *implicit reliance on his friend*

Word Building: **implicitly** *adverb*

implore *verb*
to beg or plead

Word Building: **imploringly** *adverb*

imply (say *im-pluy*) *verb*
1 to mean: *What do these words imply?*
2 to suggest without actually stating: *He did not say it was urgent but his manner implied it.*

Word Use: don't confuse this word with **infer**
Word Building: other forms are **I implied, I have implied, I am implying** □ **implication** *noun*

impolite *adjective*
having bad manners

Word Building: **impolitely** *adverb*

import *verb*
to bring in from another country: *Australia imports clothing from Hong Kong.*

Word Building: **import** *noun* **importation** *noun* **importer** *noun*

important *adjective*
1 having great meaning or effect: *an important message | an important event*
2 leading or powerful: *an important visitor*

Word Building: **importance** *noun* **importantly** *adverb*

impose *verb*
1 to set officially as something to be obeyed or paid: *to impose a tax | to impose a new law* **2** to push or force yourself on others: *We don't want to impose on you by staying the night.*

Word Building: **imposition** *noun*

imposing *adjective*
making an impression on your mind: *an imposing building | an imposing man*

impostor (say *im-pos-tə*) *noun*
someone who deceives other people by pretending to be someone else

impotent (say *im-pə-tənt*) *adjective*
not having the power to do things

Word Building: **impotence** *noun* **impotently** *adverb*

impress *verb*
1 to fill with admiration: *His musical talent impressed all who heard him.* **2** to fix firmly in the mind: *She impressed her news on us.*

Word Building: **impressive** *adjective*

impression *noun*
1 a mark made by pressure: *the impression of a rubber stamp.* **2** a strong effect made on the mind or feelings: *His story made an impression on the audience.* **3** a vague feeling or indication: *I had the impression she was unhappy.* | *The picture gave an impression of sunlight and leaves.*

Word Building: **impressionable** *adjective* **impressionistic** *adjective*

imprint *verb*
to fix firmly: *The warning imprinted itself on his mind.*

impromptu *adjective*
made up or done on the spur of the moment: *an impromptu speech* | *an impromptu party*

Word History: from a Latin word meaning "in readiness"

improve *verb*
to make or become better

Word Building: **improvement** *noun*

improvise (say *im-prə-vuyz*) *verb*
1 to make do with what is available: *He improvised a meal from the leftovers in the fridge.* **2** to invent or compose on the spot: *to improvise a little tune*

Word Building: **improvisation** *noun* **improviser** *noun*

impudent (say *im-pyə-dənt*) *adjective*
cheeky or insolent

Word Building: **impudence** *noun* **impudently** *adverb*

impulse *noun*
a sudden desire: *He felt an impulse to run.*

Word Building: **impulsive** *adjective* **impulsively** *adverb* **impulsiveness** *noun*

in *preposition*
1 inside or within: *in the house* | *in the music business* | *in ten minutes*

in *adjective*
2 in fashion or in season: *Short hair is in this year.* | *Grapes are in now.*

in- *prefix*
a word part meaning in *or* into: *inhale, inland*

Word History: this prefix comes from Old English and Middle English

inadequate *adjective*
not enough to fill a need: *inadequate food*

Word Building: **inadequacy** *noun* **inadequately** *adverb*

inane *adjective*
silly or senseless: *an inane remark*

Word Building: **inanity** *noun* (**inanities**) **inanely** *adverb*

inanimate *adjective*
not living: *inanimate objects*

inaugurate *verb*
to bring into public use with an opening ceremony

Word Building: **inaugural** *adjective: the inaugural meeting of the new club* **inauguration** *noun*

incandescent (say *in-kan-des-ənt*) *adjective*
glowing with white heat

Word Building: **incandescence** *noun*

incapacitate *verb*
to make unable or unfit: *Illness incapacitated him.*

Word Building: **incapacitation** *noun*

incarnate (say *in-kah-nət*) *adjective*
with a human body: *the devil incarnate*

Word Building: **incarnation** *noun*

incense[1] (say *in-sens*) *noun*
a substance which gives off a sweet smell when burnt

incense[2] (say *in-sens*) *verb*
to make angry

incentive *noun*
something that encourages and gives a motive: *The scholarship was an incentive for her to work hard.*

incessant *adjective*
continuing without stopping: *an incessant noise*

Word Building: **incessantly** *adverb*

incest *noun*
sexual intercourse between closely related people

Word Building: **incestuous** *adjective* **incestuously** *adverb*

inch *noun*
1 an old-fashioned unit of length equal to 25.4 millimetres
inch *verb*
2 to move by a short distance at a time: *to inch along the cliff*

Word History: from a Latin word meaning "twelfth part"

incident *noun*
an event or happening

Word Building: **incidental** *adjective* happening at the same time as something more important **incidentally** *adverb*

incinerate (say *in-sin-ə-rayt*) *verb*
to burn to ashes: *We incinerated the rubbish.* | *The house was incinerated in the bushfire.*

Word Building: **incinerator** *noun* a container for burning things in **incineration** *noun*

incisor (say *in-suy-zə*) *noun*
a tooth in the front part of the jaw, used for cutting or biting

incite *verb*
to urge on or stir up: *He incited the crowd to riot.*

Word Building: **incitement** *noun*

incline (say *in-kluyn*) *verb*
1 to slant or lean **2** to lean or tend towards in your mind
incline (say *in-kluyn*) *noun*
3 a slope

Word Building: **inclination** *noun: They showed little inclination to do as they were told.*

include *verb*
to consist of or contain as a part: *Education includes what we learn both at home and at school.*

Word Building: **inclusion** *noun* **inclusive** *adjective* **inclusively** *adverb*

incognito (say *in-kog-nee-toh*) *adverb*
with your name or appearance changed so you won't be recognised: *He's travelling incognito.*

Word History: from a Latin word meaning "unknown"

income *noun*
the money someone earns from their work or investments

income tax *noun*
a tax which the government sets each year, based on how much money you earn

incongruous (say *in-kon-grooh-əs*) *adjective*
out of place or unsuitable: *The man in the business suit looked incongruous at the barbecue.*

Word Building: **incongruity** *noun* **incongruously** *adverb* **incongruousness** *noun*

inconvenient *adjective*
awkward or causing trouble: *an inconvenient time* | *an inconvenient way to travel*

Word Building: **inconvenience** *noun* **inconveniently** *adverb*

incorporate (say *in-kaw-pə-rayt*) *verb*
to include and make part of: *We incorporated several ideas into the design of the house.*

Word Building: **incorporation** *noun*

incorrigible (say *in-ko-rə-jə-bəl*) *adjective*
too bad to ever improve: *an incorrigible liar*

Word Building: **incorrigibly** *adverb*

increase *verb*
to make or become greater or more in number: *to increase your knowledge* | *Australia's population increases every year.*

Word Building: **increase** *noun: an increase in the price of bread* **increasingly** *adverb* more and more: *increasingly sad*

incredible *adjective*
hard to believe: *incredible bravery* | *an incredible story*

Word Building: **incredibility** *noun* **incredibly** *adverb*

incredulous (say *in-kred-yə-ləs*) *adjective*
not able to believe something, usually because it is too surprising or shocking: *I am incredulous that you have left the baby alone.*

Word Use: you use **incredulous** to describe the way a person feels about something, but you use **incredible** to describe something that is unbelievable or very good
Word Building: **incredulity** *noun* refusal or inabilty to believe **incredulously** *adverb* **incredulousness** *noun*

incubate (say in-kyooh-bayt) *verb*
to hatch by keeping warm naturally or artificially: *The hen incubated the eggs by sitting on them for three weeks.* | *We are incubating these eggs under a warm lamp.*

Word Building: **incubator** *noun* a machine that looks like a plastic box, for keeping premature babies at a constant temperature **incubation** *noun*
Word History: from a Latin word meaning "hatched" or "sat on"

incur *verb*
to bring upon yourself: *to incur someone's anger* | *to incur debts*

Word Building: other forms are **I incurred, I have incurred, I am incurring**
Word History: from a Latin word meaning "run into"

indebted (say *in-det-əd*) *adjective*
1 owing money **2** feeling that you owe a debt of gratitude for help, a favour, or the like: *I am indebted to you for helping me with my studies.*

Word Building: **indebtedness** *noun*

indecent *adjective*
not proper or in good taste: *indecent language*

Word Building: **indecently** *adverb*

indeed *adverb*
truly or in fact: *Indeed he did it.*

indelible (say *in-del-ə-bəl*) *adjective*
1 not able to be removed: *He made an indelible impression on us.* **2** making marks which can't be removed or rubbed out: *an indelible pencil*

Word Building: **indelibly** *adverb*

indent *verb*
to set in or back from the margin: *to indent the first line of a paragraph*

Word Building: **indentation** *noun*

independent *adjective*
1 able to make up your own mind **2** not needing or relying on the help of others

Word Building: **independence** *noun* **independently** *adverb*

index *noun*
an alphabetical list of names, places or subjects in a book, showing their page numbers

Word Building: the plural is **indexes** or **indices** □ **index** *verb: to index a book* **indexation** *noun*

index finger *noun*
another name for **forefinger**

indicate *verb*
1 to point out or point to: *I indicated the right way to go.* **2** to be a sign of, or show: *His tiredness indicates he is not well.*

Word Building: **indicative** *adjective* (say *in-dik-ə-tiv*) **indication** *noun*

indicator *noun*
something that points to or shows something: *The car's indicator showed it was going to turn right.*

indifferent *adjective*
1 showing no interest or concern: *He was indifferent to my pain.* **2** not very good: *She is an indifferent actress.* | *He is in indifferent health.*

Word Building: **indifference** *noun* **indifferently** *adverb*

indigenous (say *in-dij-ən-əs*) *adjective*
native to a particular area or country: *The Aborigines are the indigenous people of Australia.* | *Kangaroos are indigenous to Australia but rabbits are not.*

Word Building: **indigene** *noun* a native inhabitant of a country **indigenously** *adverb*

indigestion (say *in-də-jes-chən*) *noun*
pain in your stomach caused by difficulty in digesting food

Word Building: **indigestible** *adjective: Unripe fruit is indigestible.*

indignation *noun*
anger at something you think is unjust or wicked

Word Building: **indignant** *adjective* **indignantly** *adverb*

indignity (say *in-dig-nə-tee*) *noun*
treatment which makes you feel embarrassed and foolish: *the indignity of being sent from the room*

Word Building: the plural is **indignities**

indigo (say *in-dig-oh*) *noun*
a blue dye

Word Building: **indigo** *adjective* dark blue

indispensable *adjective*
absolutely necessary

Word Building: **indispensability** *noun* **indispensably** *adverb*

indisposed *adjective*
slightly sick or unwell: *indisposed with a cold*

Word Building: **indisposition** *noun*

individual *adjective*
1 single or separate: *the individual members of the class* 2 meant for one person or thing only: *individual servings / individual attention*

Word Building: **individuality** *noun* the quality that makes you different from other people **individual** *noun* **individually** *adverb*

indoctrinate (say *in-dok-trə-nayt*) *verb*
to instruct so thoroughly that the ideas are accepted without question

Word Building: **indoctrination** *noun*

induce *verb*
1 to persuade or cause to decide: *I will induce him to go.* 2 to cause or bring on: *This drug induces sleep.*

Word Building: **inducement** *noun*

indulge *verb*
1 to give in to: *I indulged his wish for a lazy afternoon.* 2 **indulge in** to satisfy your own desire for: *to indulge in chocolates*

Word Building: **indulgence** *noun* **indulgently** *adverb*

industrial *adjective*
1 having to do with industry or industries: *industrial waste / industrial training / industrial worker* 2 having many manufacturing industries: *an industrial nation*

Word Building: **industrialist** *noun* someone who owns or manages an industrial business **industrialise** *verb* **industrialisation** *noun*

industrious *adjective*
hard-working: *He is an industrious student.*

Word Use: a similar word is **diligent**
Word Building: **industriously** *adverb*

industry (say *in-dəs-tree*) *noun*
1 all businesses that produce or manufacture things: *the growth of industry in Australia* 2 a particular type of manufacturing business: *the steel industry* 3 any large-scale business activity: *the tourist industry / the pastoral industry* 4 hard, careful and conscientious work

Word Building: the plural is **industries**

inept *adjective*
awkward or unskilful: *an inept attempt to chop wood*

Word Building: **ineptitude** *noun* **ineptly** *adverb* **ineptness** *noun*

inertia (say *in-er-shə*) *noun*
sluggishness or lack of energy: *Inertia overcame us in the midday heat.*

Word History: from a Latin word meaning "lack of skill" or "inactivity"

inevitable *adjective*
not able to be avoided: *an inevitable result*

Word Building: **inevitability** *noun* **inevitably** *adverb*

inexpensive *adjective*
not costing much: *an inexpensive toy*

Word Building: **inexpensively** *adverb*

infallible (say *in-fal-ə-bəl*) *adjective*
1 never being wrong or making a mistake: *an infallible judge of character* 2 able to be relied on completely: *an infallible law of nature / an infallible cure for hiccups*

Word Building: **infallibility** *noun* **infallibly** *adverb*

infamous (say *in-fə-məs*) *adjective*
deserving or causing a very bad name or reputation: *an infamous act*

Word Building: **infamously** *adverb* **infamy** *noun*

infant *noun*
a baby or very young child

Word Building: **infancy** *noun* the time of being an infant

infantile (say *in-fən-tuyl*) *adjective*
1 having to do with infants: *infantile diseases* 2 childish or like an infant: *infantile behaviour*

infantry *noun*
soldiers who fight on foot with hand weapons

infatuated (say *in-fat-chooh-ayt-əd*) *adjective*
blindly or foolishly in love

Word Building: **infatuate** *verb* **infatuation** *noun*

infect *verb*
1 to give germs or a disease to: *to infect a wound / She got measles and infected the whole family.* 2 to affect by speading from one to another: *His discontent infected the class.*

Word Building: **infection** *noun* **infectious** *adjective* **infectiousness** *noun*

infer (say *in-fer*) *verb*
to form an opinion after considering all the facts and information: *He inferred from the spy's report that the enemy would attack.*

Word Use: don't confuse this with **imply**
Word Building: other forms are **I inferred, I have inferred, I am inferring** □ **inference** *noun*

inferior (say *in-fear-ree-ə*) *adjective*
1 lower in rank or position: *an inferior officer* **2** lower in value or quality: *inferior work*

Word Building: **inferiority** *noun*

inferno *noun*
a place that seems like hell because of heat or fire

Word Building: the plural is **infernos**
Word History: from an Italian word meaning "hell" and before this from a Latin word meaning "underground"

infest *verb*
to spread or swarm over in great numbers: *Snakes infest this part of the bush.*

Word Building: **infestation** *noun*

infidel (say *in-fə-del*) *noun*
someone who doesn't accept a particular religious faith

Word Use: this is an old-fashioned word that Christians and Muslims used of each other
Word Building: **infidel** *adjective*

infiltrate *verb*
to secretly join or enter, usually to work against: *She infiltrated the enemy camp.*

Word Building: **infiltration** *noun* **infiltrator** *noun*

infinite (say *in-fə-nət*) *adjective*
endless or having no limits: *The desert seemed infinite to the weary travellers.*

Word Building: **infinitely** *adverb*

infinitive (say *in-fin-ə-tiv*) *noun*
the grammatical form of a verb that you use after certain other verbs or after "to", such as "come" in *I didn't come* and *I wanted to come*

Word Building: **infinitive** *adjective: an infinitive verb*

infirm *adjective*
weak in body or health

Word Building: **infirmity** *noun*

infirmary *noun*
a kind of hospital: *the school's infirmary*

Word Building: the plural is **infirmaries**

inflame *verb*
to make angry or passionate: *The Prime Minister inflamed the crowd with his fiery speech.*

Word Building: **inflammatory** *adjective*

inflammable *adjective*
easily set on fire: *inflammable clothing*

Word Use: another word for this is **flammable**
Word Building: **inflammability** *noun*

inflammation *noun*
a red, painful, and often swollen area on the body, caused by an infection

Word Building: **inflamed** *adjective*

inflate *verb*
1 to swell with gas or air: *to inflate a balloon* / *The rubber boat inflated.* **2** to cause a large rise in: *to inflate prices*

Word Building: **inflation** *noun* a large rise in prices and cost of living **inflatable** *adjective* **inflationary** *adjective*

inflict *verb*
to cause to be experienced or suffered: *to inflict a wound*

Word Building: **infliction** *noun*

influence *noun*
some force or power that affects or produces a change in someone or something else: *He is a good influence on his brother.*

Word Building: **influence** *verb* **influential** *adjective*

influenza *noun*
a sickness caused by a virus which affects the nose and throat and causes high temperatures and tiredness

Word Use: a shortened form of this word is **flu**

influx *noun*
a flowing in: *influx of water* / *There was an influx of migrants to Australia when gold was discovered.*

Word Building: the plural is **influxes**

inform *verb*
to give news or knowledge to: *I informed him of your success.*

Word Building: **informant** *noun* someone who informs **informer** *noun* someone who tells on someone else, especially to the police **informative** *adjective*

informal *adjective*
1 casual or without ceremony or formality: *an informal visit* **2** not correct or usual: *an informal vote*

Word Building: **informality** *noun* **informally** *adverb*

information *noun*
knowledge or news: *tourist information*

infra- *prefix*
a word part meaning below *or* beneath: *infra-red*

Word History: this prefix comes from Latin

infra-red *noun*
the invisible part of the spectrum of light which has a wavelength longer than that of visible red light

Word Building: **infra-red** *adjective*

infringe *verb*
to disobey: *to infringe a law | They infringed the rules of the club.*

Word Building: **infringement** *noun*
Word History: from a Latin word meaning "break off"

infuriate *verb*
to make very angry

Word Building: **infuriating** *adjective* **infuriatingly** *adverb* **infuriation** *noun*

infuse *verb*
to soak in hot water to draw out the flavour: *to infuse tea*

Word Building: **infuser** *noun* **infusion** *noun*

ingenious (say *in-jeen-ee-əs*) *adjective*
1 cleverly made or invented: *an ingenious machine* **2** clever at working out ways of doing and making things: *an ingenious inventor*

Word Building: **ingeniously** *adverb* **ingenuity** *noun*

ingot (say *ing-gət*) *noun*
a block of metal which has been melted and poured into a mould

Word History: from a Middle English word for a "mould for metal"

ingrained *adjective*
fixed firmly and deep: *ingrained habits | ingrained dirt*

ingratitude *noun*
failure to be grateful

Word Building: **ingrate** *noun* an ungrateful person

ingredient *noun*
one of the parts of a mixture or a whole: *an ingredient in a cake | An ingredient of his success was his hard work.*

inhabit *verb*
to live or dwell in: *Aborigines inhabited Australia long before Europeans came.*

Word Use: a similar word is **populate**
Word Building: **inhabitable** *adjective* **inhabitant** *noun*

inhale *verb*
to breathe in: *to inhale the fresh country air | Inhale deeply for good health.*

Word Building: **inhaler** *noun* a device for puffing medicine into the mouth to help make breathing easier **inhalant** *noun* **inhalation** *noun*

inherit *verb*
1 to receive as a gift from someone who has died: *Susan inherited some money and a stamp collection from her aunt.* **2** to get, as a family characteristic, through your parents: *He has inherited his mother's blue eyes.*

Word Building: **inheritance** *noun*

inhibit *verb*
to hold back or hinder: *Black plastic spread over your garden should inhibit the growth of weeds.*

Word Building: **inhibited** *adjective* shy **inhibition** *noun*

inimical *adjective*
acting as an enemy or unfavourable: *an inimical attitude | a climate inimical to health*

Word Building: **inimically** *adverb*

iniquity (say *in-ik-wə-tee*) *noun*
wickedness: *He will be punished for his iniquity.*

Word Building: the plural is **iniquities** □ **iniquitous** *adjective*

initial *adjective*
1 having to do with the beginning: *The initial plan was later changed.*

initial *noun*
2 the first letter of a word or name

initial *verb*
3 to mark or sign with the initials of your name

Word Building: other verb forms are **I initialled, I have initialled, I am initialling** □ **initially** *adverb* at first

initiate (say *in-<u>ish</u>-ee-ayt*) *verb*
1 to begin or set going: *I want to initiate an annual fun run at our school.* **2** to admit into a society or club with a formal ceremony

Word Building: **initiate** *noun someone who has been initiated* **initiation** *noun* **initiator** *noun*

initiative (say *in-<u>ish</u>-ee-ə-tiv*) *noun*
1 a first act or step: *to take the initiative* **2** readiness or ability to set something going

Word Use: another word for definition 2 is **enterprise**

inject *verb*
to use a syringe and needle to force a fluid into: *The doctor injected him with a pain-killing drug.*

Word Building: **injection** *noun*

injure *verb*
to hurt or cause harm to: *The sharp rock injured him when he fell. / Gossip often injures innocent people.*

Word Building: **injury** *noun* (**injuries**) **injured** *adjective* **injurious** *adjective*

injustice *noun*
1 something that is unfair or unjust **2** unfairness or lack of justice

ink *noun*
a dark fluid used for writing or printing

Word Building: **ink** *verb*

inkling *noun*
a vague or uncertain idea: *I had an inkling of what might happen.*

inlaid *adjective*
set in the surface of something: *an inlaid pattern in wood*

Word Building: **inlay** *noun*

inland *adjective*
having to do with, or situated in parts of a country away from the coast or border: *inland towns*

Word Building: **inland** *adverb: We went inland.* **inland** *noun: We went to the inland for our trip.*

inlet *noun*
a small narrow bay or cove

inmate *noun*
someone who has to stay in a hospital, prison or other institution

inn *noun*
a small hotel, especially one for travellers

Word Building: **innkeeper** *noun* someone who looks after an inn
Word History: from an Old English word meaning "house"

innate *adjective*
existing in a person from their birth: *Will I ever get over my innate shyness?*

Word Building: **innately** *adverb* **innateness** *noun*

inner *adjective*
1 further in: *an inner door* **2** private or personal: *inner thoughts*

Word Building: **innermost** *adjective* furthest inwards

innings *noun*
1 the turn of a member of a cricket team to bat **2** the whole team's turn at batting: *The first innings was interrupted by rain.*

innocent *adjective*
1 free from guilt or from having done anything wrong **2** harmless: *innocent fun*

Word Building: **innocence** *noun* **innocently** *adverb*

innocuous (say *in-<u>ok</u>-yooh-əs*) *adjective*
not harmful: *It was an innocuous remark after all.*

Word Building: **innocuously** *adverb* **innocuousness** *noun*

innovation (say *<u>in</u>-ə-vay-shən*) *noun*
a new method, practice or custom

Word Building: **innovate** *verb* **innovative** *adjective* **innovator** *noun*

innuendo (say *in-yooh-<u>en</u>-doh*) *noun*
a remark that suggests something unpleasant about someone without actually saying it

Word Building: the plural is **innuendos** or **innuendoes**

innumerable (say *in-<u>yooh</u>-mə-rə-bəl*) *adjective*
too many to be counted

Word Building: **innumerably** *adverb*

inoculate (say *in-<u>ok</u>-yə-layt*) *noun*
to protect from a disease, by introducing germs which give you a very mild form of the disease

Word Use: a similar word is **vaccinate**
Word Building: **inoculation** *noun* **inoculator** *noun*

input *noun*
anything that is put in to be used, especially by a machine

inquest *noun*
an official inquiry to find out how someone died

inquiry *noun*
an investigation

Word Use: compare this word with **enquiry**
Word Building: the plural is **inquiries** □ **inquire** *verb* **inquirer** *noun* **inquiring** *adjective* **inquiringly** *adverb*

inquisition (say *in-kwə-zish-ən*) *noun*
a thorough investigation and questioning

Word Building: **inquisitor** *noun*

inquisitive (say *in-kwiz-ə-tiv*) *adjective*
wanting to find out all about something: *inquisitive onlookers*

Word Building: **inquisitively** *adverb*

insane *adjective*
mentally ill or mad: *He's insane.* | *an insane act*

Word Building: **insanely** *adverb* **insanity** *noun*

insatiable (say *in-say-shə-bəl*) *adjective*
never having enough: *an insatiable appetite*

Word Building: **insatiably** *adverb*

inscribe *verb*
to write or cut: *I inscribed his name on the metal plaque.*

Word Building: **inscription** *noun*

inscrutable (say *in-skrooh-tə-bəl*) *adjective*
mysterious or not easily understood: *an inscrutable expression on his face*

Word Building: **inscrutability** *noun* **inscrutably** *adverb*

insect *noun*
a small creature with its body clearly divided into three parts with three pairs of legs and usually two pairs of wings

Word Use: bees, ants and flies are insects; spiders and ticks are not, even though some people call them insects
Word History: from a Latin word meaning "cut in or up" (from the way insects' bodies have three segments)

insecticide (say *in-sek-tə-suyd*) *noun*
any chemical substance used to kill insects

Word Building: **insecticidal** *adjective*

insectivore *noun*
a bird or animal that eats insects

Word Use: compare with **herbivore** and **carnivore**
Word Building: **insectivorous** *adjective: Lizards are insectivorous.*

insecure *adjective*
1 not firm or safe: *He had an insecure hold on the rope.* **2** afraid or unsure: *She feels insecure if she can't see her mother.*

Word Building: **insecurely** *adverb* **insecurity** *noun*

insensitive *adjective*
lacking in feeling

Word Building: **insensitively** *adverb* **insensitivity** *noun*

insert *verb*
to put or set inside: *Insert the key in the lock.* | *to insert an advertisement in a newspaper*

Word Building: **insert** *noun* **insertion** *noun*

inside *noun*
1 the inner part or side **2 insides** your stomach and intestines and other inner parts of your body
inside *adjective*
3 being on or in the inside: *inside walls* **4** coming from within a place: *inside information*
inside *adverb*
5 indoors, or into the inner part: *She's working inside.*

Word Use: definition 2 is more suited to everyday language

insight *noun*
an understanding of the inner nature of someone or something: *I gained an insight into the working of her mind.*

insignia (say *in-sig-nee-ə*) *plural noun*
badges or special marks of a position someone holds: *The insignia of office are passed on from one mayor to the next.*

insinuate *verb*
1 to suggest something unpleasant without saying so outright: *By asking where my sales docket was, he insinuated that I had stolen the shoes.* **2** to get into gradually and slyly: *Brian insinuated himself into the boss's favour.*

Word Building: **insinuation** *noun*

insist *verb*
to demand firmly: *I insist that you come.*

Word Building: **insistence** *noun* **insistent** *adjective* **insistently** *adverb*

insolent (say *in-sə-lənt*) *adjective*
insulting and rude

Word Building: **insolence** *noun* **insolently** *adverb*

insomnia (say *in-som-nee-ə*) *noun*
sleeplessness

Word Building: **insomniac** *noun* someone who has trouble sleeping at night **insomniac** *adjective*

inspect *verb*
1 to look carefully at or over **2** to look at formally or officially: *The general inspected the soldiers.*

Word Building: **inspection** *noun* **inspector** *noun*

inspire *verb*
1 to have an encouraging and uplifting effect on: *His courage inspired his followers.* **2** to produce or give rise to: *She inspires love in all her friends.*

Word Building: **inspired** *adjective: an inspired idea* **inspiration** *noun* **inspirer** *noun*

install *verb*
1 to put into place for use: *to install a new stove* **2** to place in an official position with a ceremony: *to install the new club president*

Word Building: **installation** *noun*

instalment *noun*
1 a single payment in a series which is meant to pay off a debt **2** a single part of a story being published in several parts in a magazine or newspaper

instance *noun*
an example or case: *Looking after his friend's dog was another instance of his kindness.*

instant *noun*
1 a very short space of time **2** a particular point of time: *At that instant the door slammed.*

instant *adjective*
3 happening immediately: *instant relief*
4 in a form that makes preparation quick and easy: *instant coffee*

Word Building: **instantaneous** *adjective* happening or done in an instant **instantly** *adverb*

instead *adverb*
in place of someone or something else: *She sent me instead.*

instep *noun*
the upper part of your foot between your toes and ankle

instinct *noun*
1 a natural urge or tendency that is there when you are born: *a bird's instinct to migrate in winter* **2** a natural knowledge or skill: *He has an instinct for making friends.*

Word Building: **instinctive** *adjective* **instinctively** *adverb*

institute *verb*
1 to set up or establish: *to institute a new government department | to institute rules of conduct*

institute *noun*
2 an organisation or society set up to carry on a particular activity: *a literary institute*

Word Building: **institutor** *noun*

institution *noun*
1 an organisation set up for a worthwhile cause: *an institution for the care of the aged* **2** a building used by an organisation like this **3** a setting up or establishing: *the institution of democratic government*

Word Building: **institutional** *adjective* **institutionalise** *verb* **institutionally** *adverb*

instruct *verb*
1 to teach or train **2** to order or command

Word Building: **instructive** *adjective: an instructive booklet* **instruction** *noun* **instructively** *adverb* **instructor** *noun*

instrument (say *in-strə-mənt*) *noun*
1 a mechanical device or tool: *a doctor's instrument* **2** something made to produce musical sounds: *Horns and clarinets are wind instruments.* **3** an electrical device which gives information about the state of some part of an aeroplane, car or other vehicle: *The pilot checked the instruments on the panel in front of him.*

Word Building: **instrumental** *adjective: instrumental music* **instrumentalist** *noun* a performer on a musical instrument

insubordinate (say *in-sə-baw-də-nət*) *adjective*
not obeying those in authority

Word Building: **insubordination** *noun*

insufferable *adjective*
unbearable or not able to be tolerated: *He is an insufferable gossip.*

Word Building: **insufferably** *adverb*

insulate (say *in-shə-layt*) *verb*
1 to cover with something to stop the escape of electric current: *to insulate the electric toaster cord* **2** to put a special material in the roof to keep in warmth in winter and keep out heat in summer: *We insulated our house.*

Word Building: **insulation** *noun* **insulator** *noun*
Word History: from a Latin word meaning "made into an island"

insulin (say *in-syə-lən*) *noun*
a substance your body produces to help it use the sugar in the food you eat

Word Use: **diabetes** is the illness that you get if your body does not make enough insulin
Word History: from a Latin word meaning "island" (the gland in the body where insulin is made has lumps of tissue that look like islands)

insult (say *in-sult*) *verb*
1 to act or speak rudely or offensively to
insult (say *in-sult*) *noun*
2 a rude or offensive action or remark

Word Building: **insulting** *adjective* **insultingly** *adverb*

insurance *noun*
a system of paying money to a company that says it will pay you a sum of money if you suffer a loss from fire, burglary, accident or the like

Word Building: **insured** *noun* the person who takes out insurance **insurer** *noun* the company that provides insurance **insure** *verb*

intact *adjective*
unharmed, unchanged or whole: *The parcel arrived intact.*

integer (say *in-tə-jə*) *noun*
any whole number

Word Use: compare this with **fraction**
Word History: from a Latin word meaning "untouched", "whole", or "entire"

integral (say *in-tə-grəl*) *adjective*
necessary to the completeness of: *Saliva is an integral part of the digestive system.*

Word Building: **integrally** *adverb*

integrate *verb*
to bring together to make a united whole: *I've tried to integrate all these facts into one powerful argument.* | *The government is working to integrate the two races to bring harmony to the nation.*

Word Building: **integration** *noun*

integrity (say *in-teg-rə-tee*) *noun*
honesty and trustworthiness

intellect (say *in-tə-lekt*) *noun*
the power of your mind to think, reason and understand: *to have a fine intellect*

Word Use: a similar word is **intelligence**

intellectual (say *in-tə-lek-chooh-əl*) *adjective*
1 of interest to the mind or intellect: *He prefers intellectual hobbies such as chess.*
2 making much use of the mind: *an intellectual writer*

Word Building: **intellectual** *noun* **intellectuality** *noun* **intellectually** *adverb*

intelligence (say *in-tel-ə-jəns*) *noun*
1 the ability to learn, understand and reason: *Your intelligence enables you to solve problems.* **2** good mental ability: *a woman of intelligence*

Word Building: **intelligent** *adjective* **intelligently** *adverb*

intend *verb*
to have in mind or to mean: *I intended to do it.* | *I intend no harm.*

Word Building: **intended** *adjective: a tool intended for cutting* **intention** *noun*

intense *adjective*
1 very great or strong: *intense pain* | *intense joy* **2** showing strong feeling: *an intense expression*

Word Building: **intensify** *verb* (**intensified, intensifying**) **intensely** *adverb* **intenseness** *noun*

intensity *noun*
1 great strength, especially of feeling: *the intensity of the wind* | *the intensity of his emotions* **2** high degree: *the intensity of the cold*

intensive *adjective*
with a lot of attention or work: *intensive care of a seriously ill person* | *intensive farming*

Word Building: **intensively** *adverb*

intent[1] *noun*
purpose, or what you intend: *He acted with criminal intent.*

intent[2] *adjective*
having your mind firmly fixed: *He was intent on his book.*

Word Building: **intently** *adverb*

intention *noun*
a firm plan or purpose

Word Building: **intentional** *adjective* **intentionally** *adverb*

inter- *prefix*
a word part meaning between *or* among: *intercom, international*

Word History: this prefix comes from Latin

interact *verb*
to act on or have an effect on each other: *Some chemicals interact to form gases.*

Word Building: **interaction** *noun* **interactive** *adjective*

intercept (say *in-tə-sept*) *verb*
to take or seize on the way from one place to another: *to intercept a letter*

Word Building: **interception** *noun* **interceptor** *noun*

interchange *verb*
to cause to change places: *I interchanged the two names on the list.*

Word Building: **interchange** *noun: interchange of ideas* **interchangeable** *adjective* **interchangeably** *adverb*

intercom *noun*
a system for sending spoken messages throughout a place such as a school or office

Word History: this is short for **intercommunication system**

intercourse *noun*
1 exchange of ideas, thoughts and feelings between people **2** *short for* **sexual intercourse**

interest *noun*
1 the feeling you have when your attention is held by something: *to have an interest in stamp collecting* **2** importance: *The results of the election were of great interest to us all.* **3** money paid to you by a bank or building society for the use of the money you have put into your account

interest *verb*
4 to hold the attention of

Word Building: **interested** *adjective* **interestedly** *adverb* **interesting** *adjective* **interestingly** *adverb*

interfere (say *in-tə-fear*) *verb*
1 to take a part in someone else's affairs without being asked: *Our neighbours interfere all the time.* **2** to clash or get in the way: *His plans interfere with mine.*

Word Building: **interference** *noun*

intergalactic (say *in-tə-gə-lak-tik*) *adjective*
existing or happening between different galaxies in space: *intergalactic warfare*

interim (say *in-tə-rəm*) *noun*
a time coming between: *Tony's between jobs at the moment – he's gone surfing in the interim.*

Word Building: **interim** *adjective* temporary
Word History: from a Latin word meaning "in the meantime"

interior (say *int-ear-ree-ə*) *adjective*
being within: *the interior rooms*

Word Use: the opposite is **exterior**
Word Building: **interior** *noun: the interior of the country*

interjection *noun*
a remark made to interrupt a conversation or a speech

Word Building: **interject** *verb* **interjector** *noun*

interlude *noun*
1 a short period of time, especially of restfulness: *Our picnic by the river was a pleasant interlude.* **2** a short performance, especially of music between two acts of a play

intermediate *adjective*
being or happening between two times, places or stages

interminable (say *in-term-ən-ə-bəl*) *adjective*
without end: *interminable talks*

Word Building: **interminably** *adverb*

intermission *noun*
an interval, especially at the pictures

intermittent *adjective*
stopping and starting: *There was intermittent rain all day.*

Word Building: **intermittently** *adverb*

intern[1] (say *in-tern*) *verb*
to keep in an enclosed and guarded area, especially during wartime

Word Building: **internment** *noun*

intern[2] (say *in-tern*) *noun*
a doctor who has recently finished university and is working full-time in a hospital

internal *adjective*
1 having to do with the inside: *the internal organs of our bodies* **2** happening within: *the internal affairs of a country*

Word Building: **internally** *adverb*

international *adjective*
between or among nations: *international sporting events*

Word Building: **internationally** *adverb*

interplay *noun*
the effect of actions on each other

Word Building: **interplay** *verb* to have an effect on each other

interpret (say *in-ter-prət*) *verb*
1 to explain the meaning of: *to interpret dreams* **2** to translate what is said in a foreign language

Word Building: other forms are **I interpreted, I have interpreted, I am interpreting** □ **interpretation** *noun* **interpreter** *noun*

interrogate (say *in-te-rə-gayt*) *verb*
to question closely to find out something: *The police interrogated the suspect.*

Word Building: **interrogation** *noun* **interrogator** *noun*

interrupt (say *in-tə-rupt*) *verb*
to stop or break into in the middle of: *She interrupted my speech. / to interrupt someone's work*

Word Building: **interruption** *noun* **interruptive** *adjective*

intersect *verb*
1 to cut or divide by passing through or across: *This line intersects the circle.* **2** to cross: *There is a signpost where the streets intersect.*

Word Building: **intersection** *noun* a place where streets cross

intersperse *verb*
to scatter here and there among other things

Word Building: **interspersion** *noun*

interstate *adjective*
1 between states: *an interstate competition*
interstate *adverb*
2 to or from another state: *She wants to send a letter interstate.*

interval *noun*
1 the length of time between events: *an interval of 50 years* **2** a pause or break, especially halfway through a program of films or music **3** the space between things **4** the difference in pitch between two notes

intervene *verb*
to step in, in order to change or solve: *The government intervened in the industrial dispute.*

Word Building: **intervention** *noun*

interview *noun*
a meeting in which someone is asked questions about something: *The Prime Minister gave an interview about the election. / a job interview*

Word Building: **interview** *verb* **interviewer** *noun*

intestine (say *in-tes-tən*) *noun*
the long tube that carries food from your stomach to your anus

Word Use: this word usually occurs in the plural form **intestines**
Word Building: **intestinal** *adjective*

intimate *adjective*
1 very close: *intimate friends* **2** secret or deep: *intimate thoughts* **3** very thorough: *an intimate knowledge*

Word Building: **intimate** *noun* a close friend **intimacy** *noun* **intimately** *adverb*

intimidate *verb*
1 to make frightened or nervous **2** to frighten in order to force someone into doing something

Word Building: **intimidation** *noun*

into *preposition*
1 towards or at the inside or inner part: *to run into the room / to be well into a comic* **2** to a new or changed condition: *to turn into a frog* **3** being the divisor of, in maths: *2 into 10 equals 5*

intonation *noun*
the pattern of changes of pitch in speech or music

Word Building: **intone** *verb*

intoxicate *verb*
to make drunk

Word Building: **intoxicant** *noun* something that intoxicates **intoxication** *noun*

intra- *prefix*
a word part meaning within: *intravenous*

Word History: this prefix comes from Latin

intransitive verb *noun*
a verb like "come" that needs no object for it to make sense

Word Use: the opposite is a **transitive verb**

intravenous (say *in-trə-vee-nəs*) *adjective*
into a vein: *The sick baby had intravenous feeds through a tube in her arm.*

Word Building: **intravenously** *adverb*

intrepid (say *in-trep-əd*) *adjective*
very brave: *an intrepid explorer*

Word Building: **intrepidly** *adverb*

intricate (say *in-trə-kət*) *adjective*
finely detailed: *intricate lace*

Word Building: **intricacy** *noun* **intricately** *adverb* **intricateness** *noun*
Word History: from a Latin word meaning "entangled"

intrigue (say *in-treeg*) *verb*
1 to interest or make curious because of puzzling or unusual qualities: *The strange sounds intrigued her.* **2** to plan secretly

Word Building: other forms are **I intrigued, I have intrigued, I am intriguing** □ **intrigue** *noun* a secret scheme or plot **intriguing** *adjective*

introduction *noun*
1 the act of making known for the first time: *We had our introduction to sailing during the holidays.* **2** the first part of a book or essay which leads up to the main subject

Word Building: **introduce** *verb* **introductory** *adjective*

intrude *verb*
to enter or force yourself in when you are not wanted or invited

Word Building: **intruder** *noun: The intruder stole our TV.* **intrusion** *noun* **intrusive** *adjective* **intrusively** *adverb*

intuition (say *in-tyooh-ish-ən*) *noun*
a strong feeling about something without any real reason that you know of: *My intuition tells me that she's not well.*

Word Building: **intuitive** *adjective* **intuitively** *adverb*

invade *verb*
1 to attack and enter: *Caesar invaded Britain.* **2** to force yourself in on: *to invade someone's privacy*

Word Building: **invader** *noun* **invasion** *noun*

invalid[1] (say *in-və-lid*) *noun*
someone who is sick or weak

Word Building: **invalid** *adjective: an invalid son*

invalid[2] (say *in-val-əd*) *adjective*
not correct, especially legally: *invalid arguments* / *an invalid will*

Word Building: **invalidate** *verb* to make invalid **invalidation** *noun* **invalidly** *adverb*

invaluable *adjective*
with a value too great to be measured: *an invaluable painting* / *invaluable help*

Word Building: **invaluably** *adverb*

invent *verb*
to make or think up: *She invented a machine for cleaning windows.* / *He invented an excuse.*

Word Building: **invention** *noun* **inventive** *adjective* **inventively** *adverb* **inventor** *noun*

inverse *adjective*
turned in the opposite position or direction

Word Building: **inverse** *noun* the opposite **inversely** *adverb* **invert** *verb*

invertebrate (say *in-ver-tə-brət*) *adjective*
without a backbone: *A worm is an invertebrate animal.*

Word Building: **invertebrate** *noun*

inverted comma *noun*
another name for **quotation mark**

invest *verb*
1 to spend money on something in the hope of making more money: *She invested in real estate and made a big profit.* **2** to use or spend: *to invest time and effort*

Word Building: **investor** *noun* someone who invests **investment** *noun*

investigate *verb*
to look into or examine closely: *She heard a noise and went to investigate.* / *The police investigated the crime.*

Word Building: **investigation** *noun* **investigator** *noun*

invigorate *verb*
to fill with energy and strength: *The exercises should invigorate you.*

Word Building: **invigorating** *adjective* **invigoratingly** *adverb*

invincible (say *in-vin-sə-bəl*) *adjective*
unable to be defeated or beaten

Word Building: **invincibly** *adverb*

invisible *adjective*
unable to be seen

Word Building: **invisibility** *noun* **invisibly** *adverb*

invite *verb*
1 to ask to visit or take part: *We invited Ben for dinner.* / *They invited us to help in the garden.* **2** to act so as to produce a certain result: *to invite danger*

Word Building: **inviting** *adjective* tempting **invitation** *noun* **invitingly** *adverb*

in vitro (say *in vit-roh*) *adjective*
in artificial surroundings, like a test tube: *in vitro fertilisation*

Word History: from Latin words meaning "in glass"

invoice *noun*
a bill for things you've bought, listing all their prices separately

Word Building: **invoice** *verb*

involve *verb*
to include as a necessary part of something: *The job of an art gallery guide involves a knowledge of art history.*

involved *adjective*
1 complicated, or very difficult to sort out: *an involved plan* **2** deeply interested: *involved in music* **3** closely connected or associated, especially romantically

Word Building: **involvement** *noun*

iodine (say *uy-ə-deen*) *noun*
a chemical element which produces a purple antiseptic when heated

ion *noun*
a tiny particle, such as an atom, which has an electric charge

irate *adjective*
angry

Word Building: **ire** *noun* anger

iris *noun*
1 the coloured part of the eye around the pupil **2** a large brightly-coloured flower

Word Building: the plural is **irises**
Word History: named after Iris, a messenger of the gods and goddess of the rainbow in Greek myths

irk *verb*
to annoy or trouble: *It irked him to wait.*

Word Building: **irksome** *adjective*

iron *noun*
1 a metallic element used in the making of tools and machinery, and which is also found in some foods and is used by the body in the making of blood **2** a tool with a handle which can be heated and used to remove the creases from clothes **3** a golf club with an iron head

iron *adjective*
4 made of iron **5** strong and unyielding: *an iron will*

Word Building: **iron** *verb* to remove creases with an iron

ironbark *noun*
a gum tree with hard dark-grey bark

irony (say *uy-rə-nee*) *noun*
a humorous way of speaking in which the real meaning is the opposite of what is said: *"How nice!" he said with irony when he saw the ugly coat.*

Word Building: **ironic** *adjective* **ironically** *adverb*

irrational *adjective*
absurd or unreasonable: *Jan has an irrational fear of water.*

Word Use: this is the opposite of **rational**
Word Building: **irrationally** *adverb*

irregular *adjective*
1 uneven: *The sick man's pulse was irregular. | irregular walls* **2** not usual or normal

Word Use: this is the opposite of **regular**
Word Building: **irregularity** *noun* **irregularly** *adverb*

irrelevant *adjective*
having nothing to do with what is being discussed: *an irrelevant remark*

Word Use: the opposite of this is **relevant**
Word Building: **irrelevance** *noun* **irrelevancy** *noun* **irrelevantly** *adverb*

irresistible (say *ir-ə-zist-ə-bəl*) *adjective*
so tempting that you cannot fight against it: *an irresistible impulse | irresistible food*

Word Use: the opposite is **resistible**
Word Building: **irresistibility** *noun* **irresistibleness** *noun* **irresistibly** *adverb*

irresponsible (say *ir-ə-spons-ə-bəl*) *adjective*
not careful or able to be trusted: *an irresponsible ruler*

Word Use: the opposite is **responsible**
Word Building: **irresponsibility** *noun* **irresponsibleness** *noun* **irresponsibly** *adverb*

irrigate *verb*
to supply with water using a system of canals and pipes: *to irrigate a farm*

Word Building: **irrigation** *noun*

irritable *adjective*
easily annoyed: *I am tired and irritable.*

Word Building: **irritability** *noun* **irritably** *adverb*

irritate *verb*
1 to annoy or make angry: *The audience's chatter irritated the musicians.* **2** to make

sore: *She irritates the mosquito bites by scratching them.*

Word Building: **irritant** *noun* something which irritates **irritating** *adjective* **irritation** *noun*

Islam *noun*
the Muslim religion based on the teachings of the prophet Mohammed and set down in the holy book of Islam, the Koran

Word Building: **Islamic** *adjective: Islamic teachings*

island (say *uy-lənd*) *noun*
a piece of land completely surrounded by water

Word Building: **islander** *noun* someone who lives on an island

isle (rhymes with *mile*) *noun*
a small island

iso- *prefix*
a word part meaning equal: *isosceles*

Word History: this prefix comes from Greek

isobar (say *uy-sə-bah*) *noun*
a line drawn on a weather map, connecting all the places that have the same air-pressure

isolate *verb*
1 to keep quite separate or apart: *Distance isolates the farmers.* **2** to track down: *They isolated the fault.*

Word Building: **isolated** *adjective* **isolation** *noun*

isosceles (say *uy-sos-ə-leez*) *adjective*
with two sides equal: *an isosceles triangle*

issue *noun*
1 something sent or given out
2 something published or sent out at a certain time: *the November issue of our school magazine* **3** a lively or important topic of discussion

issue *verb*
4 to give or send out: *The teachers issued pens and paper.* **5** to publish

Word Use: other verb forms are **I issued, I have issued, I am issuing**

isthmus (say *is-məs*) *noun*
a narrow strip of land, with water on both sides, joining two larger pieces of land

Word Building: the plural is **isthmuses**
Word History: from a Greek word meaning "narrow passage" or "neck"

it *pronoun*
someone or something being talked about whose sex is not known or that does not have a sex: *Do you know who it was? | I don't know who wrote it.*

Word Building: other forms are **its**: *Its name is not known*; **they**: *They are my socks.*

italics (say *ə-tal-iks*) *plural noun*
printing which slopes to the right, often used for emphasis

Word Building: **italic** *adjective*

itch *verb*
1 to have a feeling on the skin which makes you want to scratch: *My leg itches.* **2** to want very much: *He is itching to play.*

Word Building: **itch** *noun* **itchy** *adjective* **itchiness** *noun*

item *noun*
1 one thing, especially among a number: *I have five items on my list.* **2** a piece of news: *Here is an interesting item on page one.*

Word Building: **itemise** *verb* to list one by one

itinerant (say *uy-tin-ə-rənt*) *adjective*
travelling from place to place, especially to find work: *an itinerant fruit picker*

itinerary (say *uy-tin-ə-ree*) *noun*
the program or plan of a trip, listing places to be visited, times of journeys and so on

Word Building: the plural is **itineraries**

it'll
a short form of **it will** or **it shall**

it's
a short form of **it is** or **it has**

Word Use: be careful – this sounds like **its** but should not be used to express ownership; compare the two uses: *Its home is a burrow in the river bank. | It's gone home.*

I've
a short form of **I have**

ivory *noun*
1 the valuable creamy white tusk of elephants, used for carving ornaments

ivory *adjective*
2 made of ivory **3** creamy white

ivy *noun*
a climbing plant with smooth, shiny, evergreen leaves

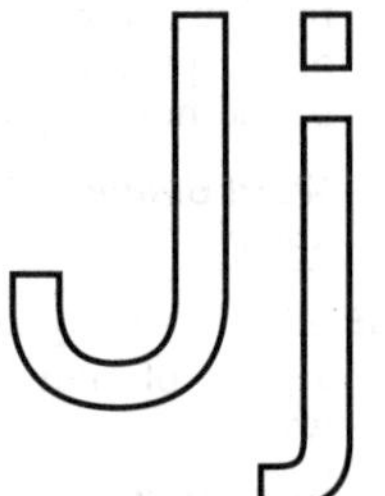

jab *verb*
to push or poke with something sharp: *He jabs the boy in the ribs with his elbow.*

Word Building: other forms are **I jabbed, I have jabbed, I am jabbing** □ **jab** *noun: a jab with a needle*

jabiru (say *jab-ə-rooh*) *noun*
a type of white stork found in Australia that has a green-black head, neck and tail

jacaranda *noun*
a tall tree with pale purple flowers

Word History: from a South American Indian word

jack *noun*
1 a tool used for lifting up heavy weights, such as a car **2** a playing card that has a picture of the knave or prince on it

jack *verb*
3 jack up a to lift with a jack **b** to refuse to do something: *We asked him to help but he jacked up.*

Word Use: definition 3b is more suited to everyday language

jackal *noun*
a wild dog of Asia and Africa which hunts in packs at night

jackaroo *noun*
someone who is learning to work on a cattle or sheep station

Word Use: another spelling is **jackeroo** □ a female jackaroo is a **jillaroo**
Word Building: **jackaroo** *verb*

jacket *noun*
1 a short coat **2** a book's paper cover which can be taken off

jackhammer *noun*
a drill which is used to break up rocks and concrete by hammering at them

jack-in-the-box *noun*
a toy figure on a spring which pops out of its box when the lid is opened

jackknife *noun*
1 a large knife whose blade folds into its handle **2** a dive in which you bend your body so that your hands touch your toes

Word Building: the plural is **jackknives** □ **jackknife** *verb* to fold up or bend

jackpot *noun*
the biggest prize that you can win in a lottery or other competition

jade *noun*
1 a precious, usually green, stone used for carving and jewellery

jade *adjective*
2 green like jade

jaded *adjective*
worn out with tiredness

jaffle *noun*
a sandwich cooked by being pressed between two hot metal plates

jagged (say *jag-əd*) *adjective*
rough and sharp-edged: *He tore his hands on the jagged rocks.*

jaguar *noun*
a large, fierce, spotted cat found in tropical America

jail *noun*
another spelling for **gaol**

Word Building: **jail** *verb* to imprison

jam[1] *verb*
1 to become stuck: *The door jammed in the wet weather.* **2** to push or force into a space tightly
jam[1] *noun*
3 people or things crowded together: *a traffic jam* **4** a difficult situation: *He got into a bit of a jam.*

Word Use: definition 4 is more suited to everyday language
Word Building: other verb forms are **I jammed, I have jammed, I was jamming**

jam[2] *noun*
a food made of fruit and sugar which you spread on bread or scones

jamb (sounds like *jam*) *noun*
the side piece of a doorway or window

jamboree *noun*
a large gathering of scouts

janitor *noun*
a North American word for **caretaker**

January (say *jan-yooh-ə-ree*) *noun*
the first month of the year, with 31 days

Word Use: the abbreviation is **Jan**
Word History: from a Latin word meaning "the month of Janus"; Janus was the Roman god of doors and gates, who was drawn with two faces looking in opposite directions

jar[1] *noun*
a glass container with a lid

jar[2] *verb*
1 to make a harsh unpleasant grating sound **2** to jolt or shake about roughly or painfully **3** to upset or shock

Word Building: other forms are **it jarred, it has jarred, it was jarring**

jargon *noun*
the words and phrases used only by people in a particular job or group: *computer jargon*

jarrah *noun*
a large tree found in western Australia with a hard dark red wood

Word History: from an Aboriginal language called Nyungar

jaunt *noun*
a short trip, usually for fun: *They had a jaunt on the harbour.*

Word Building: **jaunt** *verb*

jaunty *adjective*
1 lively and confident: *a jaunty step*
2 smart: *She is wearing a jaunty outfit.*

Word Building: other forms are **jauntier, jauntiest** □ **jauntily** *adverb* **jauntiness** *noun*

javelin *noun*
a spear which is thrown in sporting contests

jaw *noun*
one of the two bones between your chin and nose which contain your teeth

jaywalk *verb*
to cross a street carelessly, taking no notice of traffic lights and so on

jazz *noun*
1 a type of music with strong rhythms, first played by black Americans
jazz *verb*
2 jazz up to make brighter or more lively: *She has jazzed up her room with new curtains.*

Word Use: definition 2 is more suited to everyday language
Word Building: **jazz** *adjective: jazz music* **jazzy** *adjective: a jazzy version of the song / jazzy colours*

jealous (say *jel-əs*) *adjective*
wanting what other people have, or not wanting to lose what you've already got: *Sam is jealous of his brother's popularity. / a jealous husband*

Word Building: **jealously** *adverb* **jealousy** *noun*

jeans *plural noun*
trousers made of denim or other strong material

jeep *noun*
a small strong car for driving in rough conditions

jeer *verb*
to mock or insult

Word Building: **jeer** *noun* **jeeringly** *adverb*

jelly *noun*
a soft food, set with gelatine so that it wobbles when it is moved

Word Building: the plural is **jellies** □ **jelly** *verb* (**jellied, jellying**)

jellyfish *noun*
a soft-bodied sea animal, especially one with an umbrella-shaped body and long tentacles

Word Building: the plural is **jellyfishes** or **jellyfish**

jeopardy (say *jep-ə-dee*) *noun*
danger: *The illness put his life in jeopardy.*

Word Building: **jeopardise** *verb* to risk

jerk *noun*
a sudden rough movement

Word Building: **jerk** *verb* to move with a jerk **jerkily** *adverb* **jerkiness** *noun* **jerky** *adjective*

jersey *noun*
1 a long-sleeved knitted pullover **2 Jersey** a breed of cattle which produces rich milk

Word History: from the island of *Jersey,* in the English channel, where the cows came from and where the machine-knitted cloth has been produced for a long time

jest *noun*
a joke

Word Building: **jest** *verb* to speak jokingly

jester *noun*
a clown who entertained a prince or nobleman and his court in medieval times

jet[1] *noun*
1 a fast-flowing spurt or stream of liquid or gas: *The fountain sent a jet of water into the air.* **2** the opening for a stream of liquid or gas: *She lit the gas jets.* **3** *short for* **jet plane**

Word Building: **jet** *verb* (**jetted, jetting**)

jet[2] *noun*
a hard black coal which is polished and used to make buttons, jewellery and the like

jet plane *noun*
a plane which is powered by engines that work by having hot gas forced at high speed through an opening at the back

jetty *noun*
a long structure, jutting out into a river or the sea, that boats or ships can be tied to

Word Building: the plural is **jetties**

Jew *noun*
1 a person descended from the Hebrews **2** a person whose religion is Judaism

Word Building: **Jewish** *adjective*

jewel *noun*
1 a precious stone, such as a diamond, a ruby or an emerald, which has been cut and polished **2** an ornament, such as a brooch or ring, made of precious stones, pearls, gold or other valuable materials

Word Building: **jeweller** *noun* someone who works with or sells jewels **jewellery** *noun* jewels

jib *verb*
1 to stop suddenly, like a horse when it is frightened **2 jib at** to be unwilling to do: *He will wash up but he jibs at cooking.*

Word Use: another word for definition 1 is **baulk**
Word Building: other forms are **he jibbed, he has jibbed, he was jibbing**

jiffy *noun*
a very short time: *I'll have it done in a jiffy.*

Word Use: this is more suited to everyday language
Word Building: the plural is **jiffies**

jig *noun*
a very lively dance

Word Building: **jig** *verb* (**jigged, jigging**)

jigsaw *noun*
a narrow saw for cutting curves

jigsaw puzzle *noun*
a puzzle made up of many differently shaped pieces which fit together to form a picture

jingle *verb*
1 to clink or tinkle: *Her keys jingle when she runs. | He jingled his coins impatiently.*
jingle *noun*
2 a tinkling sound **3** a bright simple song of the sort used in radio or TV commercials

jinx *noun*
someone or something which is supposed to bring bad luck

Word Building: the plural is **jinxes** □ **jinx** *verb*

job *noun*
1 a piece of work or a task **2** paid employment

jockey *noun*
someone who rides horses in races

jocular *adjective*
joking or playful: *a jocular mood*

Word Building: **jocularity** *noun* **jocularly** *adverb*

jodhpurs (say *jod*-pəz) *plural noun*
riding trousers which are close fitting below the knee

joey *noun*
a young animal, especially a young kangaroo which is carried in its mother's pouch

Word Use: the male is a **buck** or **boomer;** the female is a **doe** or **flier**

jog *verb*
1 to run or go along at a slow regular pace **2** to push or nudge: *to jog someone's elbow*

Word Building: other forms are **I jogged, I have jogged, I am jogging** □ **jog** *noun* **jogger** *noun*

join *verb*
1 to put or come together: *She joins the pieces with glue.* / *This is where the parts join.* **2** to meet up with: *I'll join you for lunch.* **3** to become a member of

Word Building: **join** *noun*

joiner *noun*
someone who makes wooden furniture and house fittings such as window frames

Word Building: **joinery** *noun* the work a joiner does

joint *noun*
1 the place where two things or parts are joined: *She hurt her elbow joint.* **2** a cut of meat: *She put a joint of lamb in the oven.*

Word Building: **joint** *adjective* shared: *a joint account* **jointly** *adverb*

joist *noun*
a length of wood or metal used to support floors, ceilings or other structures

joke *noun*
something which is said or done to make people laugh

Word Building: **joke** *verb* **joker** *noun* **jokingly** *adverb*

jolly *adjective*
1 good-humoured and full of fun: *He is a jolly old man.*
jolly *adverb*
2 very: *You've done jolly well.*

Word Use: definition 2 is more suited to everyday language
Word Building: **jolliness** *noun* **jollity** *noun*

jolt *verb*
to bump or shake roughly

Word Building: **jolt** *noun*

jostle (say *jos-əl*) *verb*
to push roughly or rudely: *People were jostling to see the parade.*

jot *verb*
1 to write briefly or scribble down: *I'll jot down a few thoughts.*
jot *noun*
2 a little bit: *He doesn't care a jot.*

Word Building: other verb forms are **I jotted, I have jotted, I am jotting** □ **jotter** *noun* **jotting** *noun*

joule *noun*
a measure of work or energy

Word History: named after a British physicist, JP Joule, who lived from 1818-89

journal (say *jer-nəl*) *noun*
1 a newspaper or magazine **2** a daily record of events

journalism (say *jer-nəl-iz-əm*) *noun*
the work of writing and running newspapers and magazines

Word Building: **journalist** *noun* someone who works for a newspaper or magazine

journey (say *jer-nee*) *noun*
a trip, especially by land: *We made a car journey to the mountains.*

Word Building: **journey** *verb*

joust (say *jowst*) *noun*
a contest between two knights on horseback to see which can unseat the other with his spear

jovial *adjective*
cheerful and friendly

Word Building: **joviality** *noun* **jovially** *adverb*

jowl *noun*
a fold of flesh which hangs below the cheek or jaw

joy *noun*
great happiness or delight

Word Building: **joyful** *adjective* **joyfully** *adverb* **joyous** *adjective* **joyously** *adverb*

joystick *noun*
1 the control stick of a plane **2** a device with a lever that looks like a plane's joystick, used to change the position of the cursor on a computer screen

jube *noun*
a chewy fruit-flavoured lolly made with gelatine

jubilant *adjective*
extremely happy or joyful: *He was jubilant at winning the race.*

Word Building: **jubilantly** *adverb* **jubilation** *noun*

jubilee *noun*
a celebration, especially of the anniversary of something which happened a long time ago

Judaism (say *jooh-day-iz-əm*) *noun*
the religion of the Jewish people, based on the writings of the Old Testament and the teaching of the rabbis

Word Building: **Judaic** *adjective: the Judaic tradition*

judge *noun*
1 someone whose job is to hear and decide cases in a court of law **2** someone who gives an opinion or a decision on the winner of a contest or competition

Word Building: **judge** *verb* (**judged, judging**)

judgment or **judgement** *noun*
1 an opinion or conclusion: *Your judgment of her is too harsh.* **2** the ability to make right decisions: *That driver has good judgment.* **3** the decision in a court case: *The judgment was "guilty".*

judicial (say *jooh-dish-əl*) *adjective*
having to do with judges or law courts: *There is to be a judicial enquiry.*

Word Building: **judiciary** *noun* the system of courts and judges **judicially** *adverb*

judicious (say *jooh-dish-əs*) *adjective*
showing good or wise judgment

Word Building: **judiciously** *adverb*

judo *noun*
a type of self-defence based on jujitsu

Word History: from a Japanese word meaning "soft way"

jug *noun*
a container with a handle and pouring lip

juggle *verb*
to throw several things into the air and keep them moving, without dropping any

Word Building: **juggler** *noun* an entertainer who juggles

juice *noun*
1 the liquid part of a plant, especially fruit: *orange juice* **2** petrol: *We're out of juice.*

Word Use: definition 2 is more suited to everyday language
Word Building: **juicy** *adjective* (**juicier, juiciest**) **juiciness** *noun*

jujitsu (say *jooh-jit-sooh*) *noun*
a Japanese way of self-defence without weapons

Word History: from a Japanese word meaning "soft or supple art"

jukebox *noun*
a coin-operated machine which plays records

July *noun*
the seventh month of the year, with 31 days

Word Use: the abbreviations are **Jul** or **Jy**
Word History: named after the Roman general and statesman, *Julius* Caesar, who was born in this month

jumble *verb*
to muddle or confuse

Word Building: **jumble** *noun* confusion or disorder

jumbo *noun*
1 an elephant **2** a very large jet plane, or anything bigger than usual

Word Use: this is more suited to everyday language
Word Building: **jumbo** *adjective* very large

jumbuck *noun*
a sheep

Word Use: this is a very old-fashioned word that we know only because it's in the song "Waltzing Matilda"
Word History: it came from the way the Aboriginal people said "jump up"

jump *verb*
1 to leap or spring from the ground **2** to make a sudden movement due to fear or surprise: *She jumped at the noise.* **3** to move irregularly: *Her argument jumps from one point to another.*

jump *noun*
4 a leap **5** something to be leapt over **6** a sudden move from one state or thing to another: *a jump in price* **7** a sudden nervous movement

jumper *noun*
a piece of clothing, usually made of wool, and worn on the top half of the body, often over other clothes

Word Use: other words with similar meaning are **pullover** and **sweater**

jumpsuit *noun*
trousers and top which are joined at the waist

jumpy *adjective*
nervous or frightened in mood or behaviour: *The storm makes the animals jumpy.*

Word Building: other forms are **jumpier, jumpiest** □ **jumpily** *adverb* **jumpiness** *noun*

junction (say *junk-shən*) *noun*
the place where two or more things, especially roads or railway tracks, meet or cross

juncture (say *junk-shə*) *noun*
1 a particular point in time: *At this juncture let us finish.* **2** the junction or joining point of two things

June *noun*
the sixth month of the year, with 30 days

Word Use: the abbreviation is **Jun**
Word History: named after the Roman goddess *Juno,* the wife of Jupiter

jungle *noun*
the thick trees and vegetation which grow in warm, damp, tropical conditions

junior *adjective*
younger or smaller: *the junior members of the family*

Word Building: **junior** *noun*

junk[1] *noun*
old or unwanted things

junk[2] *noun*
a Chinese flat-bottomed boat

junket *noun*
a milk pudding made by setting sweetened warm milk

junkie *noun*
a drug addict

Word Use: this word is more suited to everyday language

junta (say *jun-tə*) *noun*
a small group of people ruling a country, especially as the result of a revolution

jurisdiction (say *jooh-rəs-dik-shən*) *noun*
the legal power to settle matters: *The soldiers come under military jurisdiction.*

jury *noun*
1 the group of people chosen to hear and try to decide the outcome of a court case **2** a group chosen to judge a competition and award prizes

Word Building: **juror** *noun* a member of a jury

just *adjective*
1 fair or rightly judged: *a just decision*
just *adverb*
2 by a very little: *You have just missed him.*
3 exactly: *That's just what I think.*
4 only: *He is still just a boy.*

Word Building: **justly** *adverb*

justice *noun*
1 what is right and fair: *They trust his sense of justice.* **2** judgment by a court of law

justify *verb*
to try to defend or show to be right: *She can justify her argument.*

Word Building: other forms are **I justified, I have justified, I am justifying** □ **justifiable** *adjective* **justifiably** *adverb* **justification** *noun*

jut *verb*
to stick out: *A shelf juts from the wall.* | *The rock juts out sharply here.*

Word Building: other forms are **it jutted, it has jutted, it was jutting**

jute *noun*
a strong fibre which is used for making rope or sacks

Word History: from a Sanskrit word meaning "a braid of hair"

juvenile *adjective*
1 young or for the young **2** childish

Word Building: **juvenile** *noun* a young person

juxta- *prefix*
a word part meaning near *or* close by: *juxtapose*

Word History: this prefix comes from Latin

juxtapose *verb*
to place close together

Word Building: **juxtaposition** *noun*

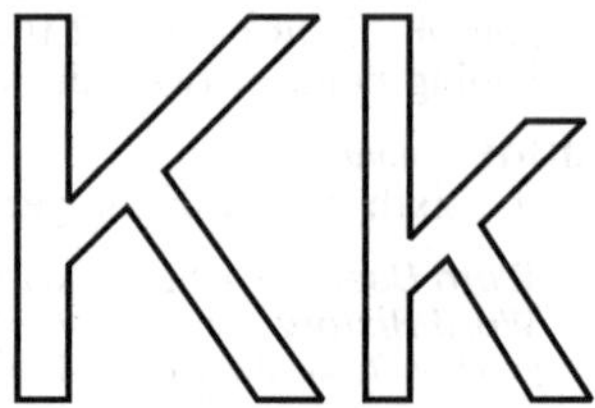

kaleidoscope (say *kə-<u>luy</u>-də-skohp*) *noun*
a tube with mirrors and pieces of coloured glass in one end, which shows different patterns when it is turned around

Word Building: **kaleidoscopic** *adjective*

kangaroo *noun*
an Australian animal with a small head, short front limbs, and a large tail and back legs for leaping

Word Use: the kangaroo belongs to a class of animals called **marsupials** □ the male is a **buck** or **boomer;** the female is a **doe** or **flier;** the young is a **joey**
Word History: from an Aboriginal language called Guugu Yimidhirr

karate (say *kə-<u>rah</u>-tee*) *noun*
a Japanese form of self-defence which uses only hands, elbows, feet and knees as weapons

Word History: from a Japanese word meaning "empty hand"

karri *noun*
a western Australian gum tree with hard lasting wood

Word History: from an Aboriginal language called Nyungar

kauri (say *<u>kow</u>-ree*) *noun*
a tall New Zealand cone-bearing tree, which is valued for its wood and its resin

Word History: from a Maori word

kayak (say *<u>kuy</u>-ak*) *noun*
a light canoe, like the watertight skin-covered hunting canoe made by Eskimos

keel *noun*
1 a long piece of timber or metal which stretches along the bottom of a ship, holding it together

keel *verb*
2 keel over to turn over or upside down: *The yacht keeled over in the strong breeze.*

keen *adjective*
1 strong or clear in feelings or senses: *a keen disappointment | a keen eye* **2** full of enthusiasm: *He's keen to start the job.* **3** sharp: *a keen blade* **4 keen on** fond of: *She's keen on cakes.*

Word Building: **keenly** *adverb* **keenness** *noun*

keep *verb*
1 to continue or make continue in the same way or state: *to keep calm | to keep the house clean* **2** to retain or hang on to: *I'll keep one dress and send the others back.* **3** to have and look after: *to keep hens* **4** to obey, follow or carry out: *to keep a promise | to keep the law*

keep *noun*
5 the basic needs of living, like food and shelter: *to earn your keep*

Word Building: other forms are **I kept, I have kept, I am keeping** □ **keeper** *noun*

keeping *noun*
1 care or possession: *He gave his watch into my keeping.* **2 in keeping with** suitable for: *clothes in keeping with the situation*

keepsake *noun*
something kept to remember a person or event by: *She took the program as a keepsake of the concert.*

keg *noun*
a barrel, especially for beer

kelp *noun*
a greenish-brown seaweed which grows in thick strands

kelpie *noun*
a breed of Australian sheepdog

kennel *noun*
a house or shelter built for a dog

kerb *noun*
the line of stones or concrete at the edge of a street

kernel *noun*
1 the inner part of a nut which you can eat **2** a grain, as of wheat or corn

kerosene *noun*
a liquid used as a fuel for lamps, engines and heaters

ketchup *noun*
a sauce: *tomato ketchup*

Word Use: this word is used more in America

kettle *noun*
a pot with a spout, a lid and a handle, used for boiling water

kettledrum *noun*
a drum with a skin stretched over a brass or copper bowl

key *noun*
1 a small, specially-shaped piece of metal that can open a lock **2** something which helps you to read or understand such things as a map, a code, or a puzzle **3** one of the notes on a piano **4** the set of notes, starting and ending on one particular note, used to make up a piece of music: *This piece is in the key of C major.* **5** one of a set of parts pressed in working a typewriter or computer terminal

Word Use: another word that sounds the same is **quay**
Word Building: **key** *adjective* main or important

keyboard *noun*
the row or set of keys such as on a piano, typewriter or computer

key signature *noun*
the sharps or flats placed after the clef to show what key a piece of music is in

keystone *noun*
the wedge-shaped stone at the top of an arch which is thought to hold the other stones in place

khaki (say *kah-kee*, *kah-kee*) *adjective*
dull greenish-brown, used especially for soldiers uniforms

Word Building: **khaki** *noun*

kibbutz (say *kib-oots*) *noun*
an Israeli farming settlement whose management, work and products are shared

Word Building: the plural is **kibbutzim** □ **kibbutznik** *noun* someone who lives and works on a kibbutz
Word History: from a Modern Hebrew word meaning "gathering"

kick *verb*
1 to hit, move or drive with the foot: *That horse kicks.* / *to kick a ball* **2** to spring back: *The rifle kicked into her shoulder.*

kick *noun*
3 a hit or thrust with the foot **4** a sudden strong movement backwards, especially of a gun **5** a feeling of pleasure or satisfaction: *She gets a kick out of dancing.*

Word Use: definition 5 is more suited to everyday language

kid[1] *noun*
1 a young goat **2** a child

Word Use: definition 2 is more suited to everyday language □ the male is a **billy-goat;** the female is a **nanny-goat**

kid[2] *verb*
to tease or trick: *He's only kidding.*

Word Building: other forms are **I kidded, I have kidded, I am kidding**

kidnap *verb*
to take someone away by force and hold them prisoner until money is paid, or some other condition is met

Word Building: other forms are **I kidnapped, I have kidnapped, I am kidnapping** □ **kidnapper** *noun*

kidney *noun*
one of the two bean-shaped organs in your body which get rid of waste from the blood

kikuyu (say *kuy-kooh-yooh*) *noun*
a tough grass which is used for lawns and pasture

kill *verb*
1 to cause the death of **2** to stop or destroy: *He will kill any suggestion you make.*

Word Building: **kill** *noun* **killer** *noun*

kiln *noun*
a big oven or furnace for baking bricks or pottery

kilo *noun*
short for **kilogram**

Word Use: this is more suited to everyday language
Word Building: the plural is **kilos**

kilo- *prefix*
a word part meaning 10^3 of a given unit: kilogram, kilometre

Word History: this prefix comes from Greek

kilogram *noun*
a weight equal to 1000 grams

kilojoule *noun*
1000 joules of energy or the amount of food needed to produce it

kilometre (say *kil-ə-mee-tə, kə-lom-ə-tə*) *noun*
a length equal to 1000 metres

kilowatt *noun*
1000 watts

kilt *noun*
a pleated skirt of tartan cloth, sometimes worn by men in the Scottish Highlands

kimono (say *ki-mə-noh, kə-moh-noh*) *noun*
a wide-sleeved Japanese robe which is tied at the waist

kin *noun*
your relatives: *Her mother's kin were Irish.*

Word Building: **kin** *adjective*

kind[1] *adjective*
warm-hearted, friendly and well-wishing

Word Building: **kindly** *adverb* **kindness** *noun*

kind[2] *noun*
1 a group of things or people of the same nature or type **2** something not quite exact: *They used the shed as a kind of house.*

kindergarten *noun*
a school or class for very young children which prepares them for primary school

Word History: from the German words for "children" and "garden"

kindle *verb*
1 to set alight or ablaze: *She kindled the fire with dry leaves.* **2** to light up: *The sticks began to kindle. / His eyes kindled.*

kindling *noun*
the twigs and other material used to start a fire

kindred *noun*
your relatives

Word Building: **kindred** *adjective* like or related

kinetic (say *kə-net-ik*) *adjective*
having to do with movement

king *noun*
1 a man from a royal family who rules over a country or empire **2** someone who is powerful or outstanding: *a cattle king / He is a king among men.* **3** a playing card with a picture of a king on it **4** the chess piece whose capture ends the game

Word Building: **king** *adjective* large: *king size* **kingly** *adjective*

kingdom *noun*
1 a country or government ruled over by a king or queen **2** one of the large divisions of nature: *the animal, vegetable and mineral kingdoms*

kingfisher *noun*
a brilliantly coloured bird which eats fish or insects in water

kink *noun*
1 a wrinkle or fault **2** an unusual taste or whim

Word Building: **kinky** *adjective* (**kinkier, kinkiest**)

kinship *noun*
relationship by family or other ties: *He claims kinship with my cousin. / The girls found a kinship in stamp collecting.*

kiosk (say *kee-osk*) *noun*
a small shop or stall which sells such things as newspapers, souvenirs and light refreshments

Word History: from a Turkish word meaning "pavilion"

kipper *noun*
a dried fish, usually herring or salmon, which has been salted and smoked

kit *noun*
1 a set of tools, supplies or parts for a special purpose: *climbing kit / first-aid kit* **2** a set of parts to be put together: *We bought the furniture as a kit.*

kitchen *noun*
the room or place where food is cooked and prepared

kite *noun*
1 a light frame covered by a thin material, which is flown in the wind at the end of a

long string **2** a medium-sized hawk with long wings and tail

kitten *noun*
a young cat

Word Use: the male is a **tom**; the female is a **puss**

kiwi *noun*
1 a New Zealand bird with thick legs and a long thin bill, and which cannot fly
2 someone from New Zealand

Word Use: definition 2 is more suited to everyday language

Kiwi fruit *noun*
a small, oval, hairy fruit with a gooseberry-like flavour

Word Use: another name for this is **Chinese gooseberry**

klaxon *noun*
a loud horn once used in motor cars

kleptomania (say *klep-tə-mayn-ee-ə*) *noun*
an uncontrollable urge to steal things

Word Building: **kleptomaniac** *noun*

knack (say *nak*) *noun*
the skill for doing a particular thing

knacker (say *nak-ə*) *noun*
someone who buys old or useless horses to kill for pet meat

Word Building: **knackery** *noun*

knapsack (say *nap-sak*) *noun*
a leather or canvas bag for clothes and supplies which is carried on the back, especially by hikers and climbers

knave (say *nayv*) *noun*
a dishonest man or boy

Word Use: this is an old-fashioned word □ other words with similar meaning are **rogue** and **rascal**
Word Building: **knavish** *adjective* **knavishly** *adverb*

knead (say *need*) *verb*
to press and push with your hands: *The baker kneaded the dough.*

Word Use: be careful – this sounds like **need**

knee (say *nee*) *noun*
the joint between the upper and lower leg

kneecap *noun*
the flat movable bone which covers the knee joint

kneel (say *neel*) *verb*
to go down on your knees

Word Building: other forms are **I knelt** or **kneeled, I have knelt** or **kneeled, I am kneeling**

knell (say *nel*) *noun*
a slow bell ringing for a death or funeral

knickerbockers (say *nik-ə-bok-əz*) *plural noun*
loose short trousers which are gathered in at the knees

Word History: named after Diedrich Knickerbocker, the imaginary author of Washington Irving's book "The History of New York" which had illustrations of people wearing baggy pants like the ones Dutch people wore in about 1800

knickers (say *nik-əz*) *plural noun*
underpants, usually for girls or women

knick-knack (say *nik-nak*) *noun*
a small ornament

knife (say *nuyf*) *noun*
1 a tool with a sharp blade for cutting
knife *verb*
2 to wound with a knife

Word Building: the plural of the noun is **knives**

knight (say *nuyt*) *noun*
1 a nobleman who pledged to serve and fight for a king in Medieval times **2** an honour, with the title "Sir", given to a man by a king or queen for service to his country **3** a chess piece shaped like a horse's head

Word Use: be careful – this sounds like **night**
Word Building: **knight** *verb* **knighthood** *noun* **knightly** *adjectiv*

knit (say *nit*) *verb*
1 to make out of long strands of wool, using a pair of long pointed needles: *to knit a jumper* **2** to join together: *He has to wait for the bones to knit after his fracture.* **3** to wrinkle up: *She knits her brow when she is thinking.*

Word Building: other forms are **I knitted, I have knitted, I am knitting** □ **knitter** *noun*

knob (say *nob*) *noun*
1 a round handle, as on a drawer or door
2 a rounded lump: *a knob of butter*

Word Building: **knobby** *adjective* **knobbly** *adjective*

knock (say *nok*) *verb*
1 to tap or beat: *Knock on the door.* **2** to bump or strike: *She knocked the leg of the table. | He knocked the nail in.* **3** to criticise or find something wrong with: *She is always knocking their efforts.*

Word Use: definition 3 is more suited to everyday language
Word Building: **knock** *noun*

knockout *noun*
1 the act of knocking someone unconscious **2** something or someone who is extremely attractive or successful

Word Use: definition 2 is more suited to everyday language

knot (say *not*) *noun*
1 a piece of thread, rope or the like, tied or tangled **2** a fault or join in the grain of wood **3** a measure of speed, used especially for ships, about equal to 1.85 kilometres per hour

Word Building: **knot** *verb* (**knotted, knotting**) **knotty**

know (say *noh*) *verb*
1 to feel certain that something is a fact or the truth **2** to have learned and understood **3** to have met before: *I know that face.*

Word Building: other forms are **I knew, I have known, I am knowing** □ **knowable** *adjective* that can be known **knowing** *adjective* shrewd **knowingly** *adverb*

know-all *noun*
someone who says they know everything, or everything about a particular subject

knowledge (say *nol-ij*) *noun*
what is or can be known: *Do you have any knowledge of what took place? | She passed on her knowledge to her daughters.*

Word Building: **knowledgeable** *adjective*

knuckle (say *nuk-əl*) *noun*
a finger joint, especially the bottom joint where the finger meets the rest of the hand

koala (say *koh-ah-lə*) *noun*
a furry, grey, Australian animal without a tail, which lives and feeds in certain types of gum tree

Word Use: the koala belongs to a class of animals called **marsupials**
Word History: from an Aboriginal language called Dharuk

kookaburra *noun*
an Australian kingfisher whose call sounds like human laughter

Word Use: other names are **laughing kookaburra** and **laughing jackass**
Word History: from an Aboriginal language called Wiradhuri

Koori (say *kooə-ree*) *noun*
an Aboriginal person

Word Use: another spelling is **Koorie**
Word Building: **Koori** *adjective: Koori traditions*
Word History: from an Aboriginal language called Awabakal

Koran (say *kaw-rahn, kə-rahn*) *noun*
the holy book of Islam, which Muslims believe came directly from Allah through his prophet Mohammed

Word History: from an Arabic word meaning "reading" or "recitation"

kowtow *verb*
1 to kneel touching the forehead to the ground in respect or worship **2** to try very hard to please, especially in an over-eager way

Word History: from a Chinese word meaning "knock-head"

kris *noun*
a short sword or heavy knife, used in Malaysia

Word History: from a Malay word

Krishna *noun*
the most popular Hindu god

Word History: from a Sanskrit word meaning "black"

kudos (say *kyooh-dos*) *noun*
glory or fame: *She only does something if it will bring her kudos.*

kumquat (say *kum-kwot*) *noun*
another spelling for **cumquat**

kung-fu (say *koong-fooh, kung-fooh*) *noun*
a Chinese form of karate

kurrajong *noun*
a flowering tree of eastern Australia

Word History: from an Aboriginal language called Dharuk

kylie (say *kuy-lee*) *noun*
a boomerang with one side flat and the other curved

Word History: from an Aboriginal language called Nyungar

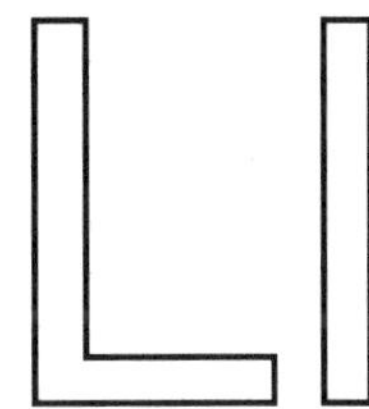

label *noun*
1 a piece of paper put on something to show what it is, who owns it, or where it is going: *a label for a suitcase | a label for a jar*
label *verb*
2 to mark or describe with a label: *The bottle was labelled poison.*

Word Building: other verb forms are **I labelled, I have labelled, I am labelling**

laboratory (say *lə-bo-rə-tree*) *noun*
a building or room for doing scientific tests or for making chemicals or medicines

Word Building: the plural is **laboratories**

laborious (say *lə-baw-ree-əs*) *adjective*
needing a lot of effort: *laborious work*

Word Building: **laboriously** *adverb*

labour or **labor** *noun*
1 hard or tiring work: *the labour of building a house* **2** people who are employed to do such work, especially when organised into trade unions: *Organised labour will push for reform.* **3** the pain and effort of giving birth to a baby

Word Building: **labour** *verb* **labourer** *noun*

labrador *noun*
a kind of large dog with short black or golden hair

Word History: named after Labrador, a peninsula in Canada, where the breed first came from

labyrinth (say *lab-ə-rinth*) *noun*
a twisting set of passages in which it is hard to find your way

Word Use: a similar word is **maze**

lace *noun*
1 a material with a fine netlike design of threads: *a wedding dress made of lace* **2** a cord for pulling and holding something together: *shoe laces*
lace *verb*
3 to tie together with a lace: *to lace your shoe*

Word Building: **lacy** *adjective* (**lacier, laciest**)

lacerate (say *las-ə-rayt*) *verb*
to tear roughly or cut: *The broken glass lacerated his hands.*

Word Building: **lacerated** *adjective* **laceration** *noun*

lack *noun*
1 a shortage or absence of something you need or want: *a lack of food | a lack of interest*
lack *verb*
2 to be without: *to lack strength*

laconic (say *lə-kon-ik*) *adjective*
using few words: *She gave a laconic reply.*

Word Building: **laconically** *adverb*

lacquer (say *lak-ə*) *noun*
a clear coating put on something to protect it or to make it shiny

Word Building: **lacquer** *verb* **lacquered** *adjective*

lacrosse (say *lə-kros*) *noun*
a game played by two teams with ten players in each, who try to hit a ball through a goal using racquets with long handles

lact- *prefix*
a word part meaning milk: *lactate*

Word Use: another spelling is **lacto-**
Word History: this prefix comes from Latin

lactate *verb*
to produce milk

Word Building: **lactation** *noun*

lad *noun*
a boy or young man

ladder *noun*
1 a structure made of wood, metal or rope, with rungs or steps you use to climb up or down **2** a line in a stocking or pair of tights where the stitches have come undone

ladle *noun*
a cup-shaped spoon with a long handle, for serving liquids: *a soup ladle*

Word Building: **ladle** *verb*

lady *noun*
1 *a polite name for a* **woman** **2** a woman with polite manners: *She always behaves like a lady.*

Word Building: the plural is **ladies**

ladybird *noun*
a small beetle whose orange back is spotted with black

lag *verb*
1 to become less or decrease: *My interest in work is beginning to lag.* **2 lag behind** to fall behind or drop back: *He's always lagging behind when we go for a walk.*

Word Building: other forms are **I lagged, I have lagged, I am lagging**

lager (say *lah-gə*) *noun*
a kind of light beer

lagerphone *noun*
a homemade percussion instrument made of beer bottle tops loosely nailed to a broom handle

lagoon *noun*
a pond of shallow water, often separated from the sea by low banks of sand

lair *noun*
the den or shelter of a wild animal

lake *noun*
a large area of water surrounded by land

lama (rhymes with *farmer*) *noun*
a Buddhist priest or monk

Word Use: be careful – this sounds like **llama**
Word History: from a Tibetan word meaning "is silent"

lamb *noun*
a young sheep or its meat

Word Use: the male is a **ram;** the female is a **ewe**

lame *adjective*
1 having something wrong with your foot or leg that causes you to limp **2** weak or poor: *a lame excuse*

Word Building: **lame** *verb* **lamely** *adverb* **lameness** *noun*

lament (say *lə-ment*) *verb*
1 to feel or show sorrow for: *She lamented her husband's death.*
lament *noun*
2 a poem or song expressing sorrow

Word Building: **lamentable** *adjective* **lamentably** *adverb* **lamentation** *noun*

laminate *verb*
1 to separate into thin sheets or layers
2 to cover with thin layers

Word Building: **laminate** *adjective* **laminated** *adjective* **lamination** *noun*

lamington *noun*
a square of sponge cake covered with chocolate icing and grated coconut

Word History: thought to be named after Baron Lamington, governor of Queensland 1895-1901

lamp *noun*
a kind of light, often one which you can move or carry around: *a kerosene lamp*

lance *noun*
1 a long spear
lance *verb*
2 to cut open with a sharp instrument: *The doctor lanced my boil.*

land *noun*
1 the part of the earth's surface not covered by water **2** a particular area of ground: *We own the house and the land around it.* **3** a country or nation: *Our land is called Australia.*
land *verb*
4 to come or bring to land or shore **5** to come to rest in any place or position: *Where did the ball land?* **6** to gain or obtain: *He landed a good job.*

Word Use: definition 6 is more suited to everyday language

landing *noun*
1 the act of landing **2** the area at the top or bottom of a flight of stairs

landlady *noun*
a woman who owns and rents out land, houses, flats or rooms

landlord *noun*
a man who owns and rents out land, houses, flats or rooms

landlubber *noun*
someone who is not used to boats or sailing

landmark *noun*
1 something on land that is easily seen and is used as a guide to travellers **2** an event that stands out as important: *The Eureka Stockade was a landmark in Australia's history.*

landscape *noun*
1 a view of country scenery **2** a painting of country scenery

landscape *verb*
3 to arrange to make look like a landscape: *to landscape a garden*

landslide *noun*
1 the sliding down of a mass of rocks and soil from a steep slope **2** an easy win in an election: *The government won in a landslide.*

lane *noun*
1 a narrow passage or road between fences, walls or houses **2** a strip of road marked out for a single line of vehicles **3** a strip marked out on a running track or swimming pool for one runner or swimmer in a race

language *noun*
1 the arrangement of words we use when we speak and write **2** any set of signs or symbols used to pass on information: *sign language* / *computer language* **3** the language of a particular country or group of people: *French is the language of France.*

languid (say *lang-gwəd*) *adjective*
weak, tired or slow-moving

Word Building: **languidly** *adverb*

languish (say *lang-gwish*) *verb*
to become weak or without interest

lank *adjective*
1 too long and thin: *Your plants will grow very lank without sunlight.* **2** straight and dull: *lank hair*

Word Building: **lanky** *adjective* (**lankier, lankiest**) **lankiness** *noun* **lankness** *noun*

lantana (say *lan-tah-nə*) *noun*
a plant with yellow or orange flowers, which has become an annoying weed in warm wet parts of Australia

lantern *noun*
a glass case that holds a light and protects it from wind and rain

lap[1] *noun*
the front of your body from your waist to your knees, when you are sitting down: *She sat the child on her lap.*

lap[2] *noun*
a single round of a racing track or a single length of a swimming pool

lap[3] *verb*
1 to hit with a gentle splashing: *The water lapped against the side of the boat.* **2** to drink using the tongue: *The cat lapped the milk.*

Word Building: other forms are **it lapped, it has lapped, it is lapping**

lapel (say *lə-pel*) *noun*
the part of a coat collar that is folded back over your chest

lapse *noun*
1 a mistake or failure: *a lapse of memory* **2** the passing of time: *I saw him again after a lapse of two years.*

lapse *verb*
3 to pass slowly or gradually: *She lapsed into unconsciousness.* **4** to fall or sink into a bad habit or way of life

laptop *noun*
a microcomputer, small enough to be carried around, that is designed to rest on the user's lap

larceny (say *lah-sə-nee*) *noun*
the stealing of someone else's goods

Word Building: the plural is **larcenies** □ **larcenous** *adjective*

lard *noun*
pig fat prepared for use in cooking

larder *noun*
a room or cupboard where food is kept

Word Use: a similar word is **pantry**

large *adjective*
1 of more than usual size, amount or extent: *a large dog* / *a large family*

large *noun*
2 at large a free: *The murderer is at large.* **b** as a whole: *This is important for the school at large.*

Word Building: **largely** *adverb* to a great extent **largeness** *noun*

lark[1] *noun*
a kind of bird that lives in northern areas of the world and sings while flying

lark[2] *noun*
something done for fun or as a joke: *We hid under the bed for a lark.*

larrikin *noun*
someone, usually young, who behaves in a noisy, wild way

Word Building: **larrikinism** *noun*

larva *noun*
the young of any insect which changes the form of its body before becoming an adult: *A caterpillar is the larva of a butterfly.*

Word Building: the plural is **larvae** (say *lah-vee*) □ **larval** *adjective*
Word History: from a Latin word meaning "ghost", "skeleton" or "mask"

laryngitis (say *la-rən-juy-təs*) *noun*
a soreness and swelling in your larynx that often makes you lose your voice for a while

larynx (say *la-rinks*) *noun*
the box-like space at the top of your windpipe that contains the vocal cords which you use to speak

Word Use: the larynx is sometimes called the **voice box** in everyday language
Word Building: the plural is **larynges** or **larynxes**

lasagne (say *lə-sahn-yə*) *noun*
1 a type of pasta cut into rectangular sheets **2** a dish made with this, often with mince meat, tomato and cheese

laser (say *lay-zə*) *noun*
a device which produces a very narrow beam of intense light

Word History: an acronym made by joining the first letters of the words *light amplification* by *stimulated emission* of *radiation*

lash *noun*
1 the cord part of a whip **2** a blow with a whip or something similar: *He got six lashes.* **3** *short for* **eyelash**
lash *verb*
4 to strike with a whip or something similar **5** to tie with a rope or cord **6** to beat violently against: *Waves lashed the side of the ship.*

Word Building: the plural of the noun is **lashes**

lass *noun*
a girl or young woman

Word Building: the plural is **lasses**

lasso (say *las-ooh*) *noun*
a long rope with a loop at one end which tightens when pulled, used to catch horses and other animals

Word Building: the plural is **lassos** or **lassoes** □ **lasso** *verb* (**lassoed, lassoing**)

last[1] *adjective*
1 coming after everything else in time, order or place **2** latest or most recent: *last night*
last[1] *adverb*
3 after all the others: *I came last in the race.*
last[1] *noun*
4 something that is at the end: *This is the last of the questions* **5 at last** eventually or after a long time: *We waited patiently and at last the bus arrived.*

Word Building: **lastly** *adverb*

last[2] *verb*
to go on or continue: *This lesson will last half an hour.*

Word Building: **lasting** *adjective*

latch *noun*
1 a bar which slides or falls into a slot, used to keep a door or gate closed
latch *verb*
2 to close or fasten with a latch **3 latch on to** to understand: *He latched on to what she meant.*

Word Use: definition 3 is more suited to everyday language
Word Building: the plural of the noun is **latches**

late *adjective*
1 coming or continuing after the usual or proper time: *a late arrival | a late dinner* **2** far advanced in time: *a late hour | the late afternoon* **3** having recently died: *the late king* **4 of late** recently: *She has been working hard of late.*
late *adverb*
5 after the usual or proper time: *They came late.*

Word Building: **lately** *adverb* recently **lateness** *noun*

latent *adjective*
present but not active or able to be seen: *a latent disease | a latent talent*

Word Use: a similar word is **dormant**
Word Building: **latency** *noun*

lateral *adjective*
of or having to do with the side: *a lateral view | a lateral root of a plant*

Word Building: **laterally** *adverb*

lathe *noun*
a machine which holds and turns a piece of wood or metal while it is being cut or shaped

lather (rhymes with *gather*) *noun*
1 foam made from soap and water
2 froth caused by heavy sweating
lather *verb*
3 to become covered with a lather

latitude *noun*
1 the distance by which a point on the earth is north or south of the equator, measured in degrees **2** freedom, or room to move: *Give your horse a bit of latitude and he'll find his own way home.*

Word Building: **latitudinal** *adjective*

latter *adjective*
1 the second out of two things mentioned: *I prefer the latter idea.* **2** recent or, in a period of time, towards the end: *Things have been going well in latter days. | the latter years of his life*

Word Use: the opposite of definition 1 is **former**
Word Building: **latterly** *adverb*

lattice (say *lat-əs*) *noun*
a frame made of crossed wooden or metal strips with diamond-shaped spaces in between, used as a screen or as a support for plants

laugh *verb*
1 to make the sounds that show amusement, happiness or scorn **2 laugh off** to treat lightly or with scorn: *He laughed off her accusations.*

Word Building: **laughable** *adjective* funny or foolish **laugh** *noun* **laughter** *noun*

launch[1] *noun*
a strong open boat, usually with a motor

launch[2] *verb*
1 to send into the water: *to launch a ship*
2 to send up into the air: *to launch a rocket* **3** to set going or start: *to launch an attack | to launch out on a new career*

Word Building: **launch** *noun*

laundromat *noun*
a public laundry with washing machines and driers which you operate by putting coins in the slot of each machine

Word History: this word was used first as a trademark in the United States

laundry *noun*
1 a room for washing clothes **2** clothes that are ready to be washed or have been washed

Word Building: **launder** *verb* to wash and iron

laurel (say *lo-rəl*) *noun*
1 a small evergreen tree with leaves that are used as a herb in cooking **2** the leaves of this tree made into a wreath, used as a sign of victory **3 rest on your laurels** to be happy with what you have already done and not want to try for any more achievements

lava (say *lah-və*) *noun*
1 the hot liquid rock which comes out of a volcano **2** the hard rock formed when this becomes cool and solid

lavatory *noun*
a toilet or a room with a toilet in it

Word Building: the plural is **lavatories**

lavender *noun*
1 a small shrub with pale purple flowers that have a strong but pleasing smell
lavender *adjective*
2 pale bluish-purple

lavish (say *lav-ish*) *adjective*
1 plentiful or abundant: *lavish gifts*
2 generous in giving or using: *He is lavish with his money.*

Word Building: **lavish** *verb* **lavishly** *adverb* **lavishness** *noun*

law *noun*
1 a rule or set of rules, especially those made by a government or ruler **2** the area of knowledge or the occupation that has to do with these rules: *to study law | to practise law in a law court* **3** a statement describing what always happens under certain conditions: *the law of gravity*

Word Use: be careful – this sounds like **lore**
Word Building: **lawful** *adjective* allowed by law **lawless** *adjective* not controlled by or not obeying the law **lawfully** *adverb* **lawlessly** *adverb*

lawn *noun*
an area of mown, grass-covered land, usually part of a garden

Word History: from a French word meaning "wooded ground"

lawyer *noun*
someone whose work is to give advice about the law and to argue on behalf of people in law courts

Word Use: compare **barrister** and **solicitor**

lax *adjective*
1 careless or not strict: *lax behaviour | lax rules* **2** loose or slack: *lax muscles*

Word Building: **laxity** *noun* **laxness** *noun*

laxative *noun*
a medicine for helping you pass waste matter from your bowels easily and without pain

Word Building: **laxative** *adjective*

lay *verb*
1 to put down or place: *to lay the book on the table | He laid his hand on her arm.* **2** to produce an egg **3** to prepare: *to lay the table | to lay plans* **4 lay off** **a** to dismiss from a job: *The boss laid off five workmen.* **b** to stop: *Let's lay off work now.* **5 lay out** **a** to arrange in order, or prepare **b** to spend: *to lay out a fortune* **c** to knock unconscious

lay *noun*
6 the way in which something lies or is laid: *the lay of the land*

Word Use: don't confuse this with the verb **lie** □ definitions 4b and 5c are more suited to everyday language
Word Building: other verb forms are **I laid, I have laid, I am laying**

lay-by *noun*
1 a system of buying something by paying out part of the cost and then making further payments until it has been fully paid for and may be collected: *I'll put this dress on lay-by.* **2** something bought in this way

Word Building: **lay-by** *verb*

layer *noun*
a single thickness or coating: *a cake with three layers | a layer of paint*

Word Building: **layer** *verb*

layout *noun*
the way something is arranged: *the layout of a newspaper page | the layout of a kitchen*

lazy *adjective*
1 not liking work or effort: *a lazy student* **2** slow-moving: *a lazy stream* **3** not spent in work or effort: *a lazy afternoon*

Word Building: other forms are **lazier, laziest** □ **laze** *verb* to be lazy or spend time lazily **lazily** *adverb* **laziness** *noun*

lead[1] (say *leed*) *verb*
1 to guide, often in a particular direction or to a particular place **2** to go or be at the front of **3** to command or be in charge of: *to lead an army | to lead a discussion* **4 lead to** to be a way of getting to: *The next track leads to the river.*

lead[1] (say *leed*) *noun*
5 the front position: *Margaret is in the lead.* **6** amount or distance ahead: *a lead of five metres* **7** a strap for holding an animal: *Put the dog on its lead.* **8** a clue: *The police haven't got any leads about the murder.*

Word Building: other verb forms are **I led, I have led, I am leading**

lead[2] (say *led*) *noun*
1 a heavy bluish-grey metal used to make pipes, petrol, paint and bullets **2** a thin stick of carbon used in pencils

Word Building: **leaden** *adjective* heavy and grey like lead **lead** *adjective* **leadenly** *adverb*

leader (say *leed-ə*) *noun*
1 someone or something that leads **2** an article in a newspaper that gives the opinion of the newspaper or its editor on events happening at the moment **3** the main violinist in an orchestra, who helps the conductor

Word Use: another word for definition 2 is **editorial**
Word Building: **leadership** *noun*

leaf *noun*
1 the flat, usually green, part of a plant that grows out from its stem **2** a page of a book **3** a thin sheet of metal: *gold leaf* **4 turn over a new leaf** to begin new and better behaviour

Word Building: the plural is **leaves** □ **leafy** *adjective* (**leafier, leafiest**) **leafless** *adjective*

leaflet *noun*
a small sheet of printed information: *They handed out leaflets advertising the school fete.*

Word Use: a similar word is **pamphlet**

league (say *leeg*) *noun*
1 a group of people, countries or organisations who have made an agreement between themselves **2 League** *short for* **Rugby League** football **3 in league** having an

agreement: *They are in league with each other.*

Word History: from a Latin word meaning "bind"

leak *noun*
1 a hole or crack that lets liquid or gas in or out accidentally: *This bucket has a leak.* **2** the amount of liquid or gas that escapes through a leak: *There has been a huge leak from this bucket.* **3** the giving out of secret information: *a government leak*

leak *verb*
4 to let a substance in or out through a leak: *The roof leaks.* **5** to pass in or out through a leak: *Gas is leaking.*

Word Building: **leaky** *adjective* (**leakier, leakiest**) **leakage** *noun* **leakiness** *noun*

lean[1] *verb*
1 to be or to put in a sloping position: *She leaned over her work. | She leaned her head out the window.* **2** to rest against or on something for support

Word Building: other forms are **I leant** or **I leaned, I have leant** or **I have leaned, I am leaning**

lean[2] *adjective*
1 thin: *a lean man* **2** with little or no fat: *lean meat*

Word Building: **lean** *noun* **leanness** *noun*

leap *verb*
1 to jump or move quickly: *to leap over a puddle | to leap away from burning fat*
2 to jump over: *He leapt the fence.*
3 leap at to accept eagerly: *He leapt at the chance to go horse riding.*

leap *noun*
4 a jump **5** a sudden rise: *a leap in prices*

Word Building: other verb forms are **I leapt** or **leaped, I have leapt** or **I have leaped, I am leaping**

leap year *noun*
a year of 366 days every fourth year, with the extra day on 29 February

learn *verb*
1 to come to have knowledge of or skill in: *to learn Italian | to learn piano* **2** to get knowledge or skill: *She learns quickly.*

Word Building: other forms are **I learnt** or **I learned, I have learnt** or **I have learned, I am learning** □ **learning** *noun* the gaining of knowledge by study or the knowledge gained this way **learner** *noun*

learned (say *lern*-əd) *adjective*
having a lot of knowledge from study: *a learned woman*

Word Building: **learnedly** *adverb*

lease (rhymes with *peace*) *noun*
1 a written agreement which gives someone the right to use land or live in a building in return for rent

lease *verb*
2 to give or have the use of by a lease

leash *noun*
a strap for holding a dog

Word Building: **leash** *verb*

least *adjective*
1 smallest: *Our geography teacher gives us the least amount of homework.*

least *noun*
2 the smallest in amount, extent or importance: *That is the least of my problems.* **3 at least** **a** at the lowest calculation or judgment: *He must be at least fifty years old.* **b** at any rate: *I feel awful but at least I don't have to go to school.*

Word Building: for other forms of the adjective see **little**

leather (rhymes with *feather*) *noun*
the skin of animals prepared by tanning and used to make such things as shoes and bags

Word Use: **leathery** *adjective*

leave[1] *verb*
1 to go away from: *She left the room.*
2 to depart or go away: *When do we leave?*
3 to allow to stay or remain in a particular place or condition: *to leave the books on the table | to leave the door unlocked* **4 leave alone** to stop interfering with: *Leave me alone.* **5** to give for use after you have died: *He left her all his money.*

Word Use: a similar word to definition 5 is **bequeath**
Word Building: other forms are **I left, I have left, I am leaving**

leave[2] *noun*
1 permission: *Can I have leave to go home?*
2 the time during which someone has permission to be absent: *My teacher is away on six weeks' leave.* **3 take leave of** to say goodbye to

lecture *noun*
1 a speech that you prepare and give before an audience or a class in order to teach or inform: *a lecture on Australian history* **2** a long talk that's a warning or a

scolding: *She gave me a lecture about my lateness.*

Word Building: **lecturer** *noun* someone who gives lectures **lecture** *verb*
Word History: from a Latin word meaning "read"

ledge *noun*
a narrow flat shelf sticking out from something upright: *a window ledge*

ledger *noun*
an account book used to record money that is paid out and paid in

lee *noun*
a side or part that is sheltered or turned away from the wind: *the lee of a hill*

Word Building: **lee** *adjective* **leeward** *adjective* **leeward** *adverb*

leech *noun*
a small worm that sucks the blood of humans or animals and was once used by doctors to take blood from sick people

Word Building: the plural is **leeches**

leek *noun*
a vegetable that tastes like an onion and has a white bulb and wide green leaves

leer *noun*
an unpleasant kind of smile that suggests thoughts of sex, cruelty or cunning

Word Building: **leer** *verb*

leeway *noun*
1 the distance by which a ship or plane is blown off course by the wind **2** extra space, time or money that allows freedom of action and choice

left *adjective*
1 having to do with the side of a person or thing which is turned toward the west when they are facing north: *Raise your left hand.*

left *noun*
2 the left side: *Turn to the left.* **3** a political party or group that believes in the equal distribution of wealth and supports workers rather than companies

Word Use: the opposite is **right** □ definition 3 is sometimes spelt with a capital letter

leg *noun*
1 one of the parts of a body which is used for support and for walking **2** one of the supports of a piece of furniture: *the leg of a table* **3** one of the sections of a journey, race or competition: *The first leg of the flight was to Singapore.*

legacy *noun*
1 a gift of money or property made after someone's death through their will: *He left her a legacy of $500.* **2** anything that is handed down from the past or happens as a result of something in the past: *The refugee problem is a legacy of war.*

Word Building: the plural is **legacies** □ **legatee** *noun* someone who is given a legacy

legal (say *lee*-*gəl*) *adjective*
1 allowed or decided by law: *a legal action*
2 having to do with law: *a legal secretary*

Word Building: **legalise** *verb* to make legal **legality** *noun* **legally** *adverb*

legend (say *lej*-*ənd*) *noun*
a story that comes from long ago in the past and which is thought by many people to be at least partly true: *the legend of King Arthur and the Knights of the Round Table*

Word Building: **legendary** *adjective*

legible *adjective*
able to be read easily: *legible handwriting*

Word Use: the opposite is **illegible**
Word Building: **legibility** *noun* **legibly** *adverb*

legion *noun*
1 a unit of soldiers in the ancient Roman army **2** any large group of soldiers
3 any great number: *She has a legion of friends.*

Word Building: **legionary** *noun* **legionary** *adjective*

legislation *noun*
1 the making of laws: *Parliament is responsible for legislation.* **2** a law or all the laws made: *Parliament passed new legislation to increase parking fines.*

Word Building: **legislate** *verb* **legislator** *noun*

legislature (say *lej*-*əs*-*lay*-*chə*) *noun*
an organisation, such as a parliament, that makes laws

Word Building: **legislative** *adjective*

legitimate (say *lə*-*jit*-*ə*-*mət*) *adjective*
1 in accordance with law: *a legitimate document* **2** born to parents who are legally married: *a legitimate child*

Word Building: **legitimacy** *noun* **legitimately** *adverb*

leisure (rhymes with *measure*) *noun*
1 time that is free from work **2 at leisure** without hurry

Word Building: **leisurely** *adjective* unhurried

lemon *noun*
1 a yellow fruit with a sour taste
lemon *adjective*
2 clear light-yellow

lemonade *noun*
a fizzy soft drink made with lemons, sugar and water

lend *verb*
1 to give the use of, for a short time
2 lend itself to to be well suited for: *This room lends itself to study.*

Word Use: compare definition 1 with **borrow**
Word Building: other forms are **I lent, I have lent, I am lending** □ **lender** *noun* **loan** *noun*

length *noun*
1 the measure from end to end: *This room is four metres in length.* **2** a piece of something long: *a length of rope* **3 at length** **a** in full detail: *She told the story at length.* **b** at last or finally: *At length the train arrived.*

Word Building: **lengthen** *verb* **lengthiness** *noun* **lengthy** *adjective*

lenient (say *lee-nee-ənt*) *adjective*
gentle or not hard in treatment: *a lenient punishment*

Word Building: **lenience** *noun* **leniency** *noun* **leniently** *adverb*

lens *noun*
a piece of glass or other material with one or more curved surfaces, used to make objects look larger or used in glasses to correct bad eyesight

Word Building: the plural is **lenses**

lentil *noun*
a kind of plant with a seed that is used as food, similar to peas and beans

leopard (say *lep-əd*) *noun*
a large, fierce, spotted animal of the cat family

Word Use: the male is a **leopard;** the female is a **leopardess;** the young is a **cub**

leotard (say *lee-ə-tahd*) *noun*
a close-fitting piece of clothing worn for dancing or doing exercises

Word History: named after a French acrobat, Jules *Léotard*

leper (say *lep-ə*) *noun*
someone who has leprosy

leprechaun (say *lep-rə-kawn*) *noun*
a fairy in Irish folk stories, in the shape of a little man

Word History: from an Irish word meaning "little body"

leprosy *noun*
a disease you can catch from other people, which can cause sores on your skin, the loss of your fingers and toes, and the loss of feeling in parts of your body

lesbian *noun*
a woman who has sexual feelings for other women

Word Building: **lesbian** *adjective* **lesbianism** *noun*

less *adjective*
1 smaller in size, amount or extent: *I want less talking.*
less *adverb*
2 to a smaller extent or in a smaller amount: *Choose a less expensive present.*

Word Use: many people say that **fewer** should be used with things you can count and **less** with things you can't, as in "You should eat less sugar and fewer biscuits".
Word Building: for other forms see **little**

lessen *verb*
to make or become less: *This medicine will lessen the pain.*

lesson *noun*
1 the time during which a pupil or a class is taught one subject **2** anything that you learn or from which you learn: *a lesson in crossing roads | The accident taught me a lesson.* **3** part of the Bible, read during a church service

let *verb*
1 to allow or permit **2** to rent or hire out: *We have a room to let.* **3 let down** to disappoint: *You will let us down if you don't come.* **4 let know** to inform or tell: *I'll let you know the news.* **5 let off** **a** to excuse **b** to make explode: *We have a whole bag of fireworks to let off.*

Word Building: other forms are **he let, he has let, he is letting**

lethal (say *leeth-əl*) *adjective*
causing death: *a lethal poison*

Word Building: **lethally** *adverb*

lethargy (say *leth-ə-jee*) *noun*
a state of sleepy laziness: *The hot weather has filled me with lethargy.*

Word Building: **lethargic** *adjective* **lethargically** *adverb*

letter *noun*
1 a message in writing or printing addressed to a person or group **2** one of the signs used in writing and printing to stand for a speech sound: *"A" is the first letter of the alphabet.*

lettuce *noun*
a plant with large green leaves which are used in salads

leukaemia or **leukemia** (say *looh-kee-mee-ə*) *noun*
a disease in which your body produces too many white blood cells and which often causes death

Word History: from a Greek word meaning "white"

levee (say *lev-ee*) *noun*
1 a raised bank of earth and sand built up by a river during floods **2** a bank built to keep a river from overflowing

level *adjective*
1 even or having no part higher than another: *a level surface* **2** not sloping or horizontal: *level ground* **3** equal: *They are level in intelligence.*

level *noun*
4 a horizontal or level position or surface **5** a ranking whether high or low: *He was given a job at the top level of the company.* **6** an instrument for finding out whether something is exactly flat or horizontal **7 on the level** honest: *Are you sure he is on the level?*

level *verb*
8 to make or become level or equal **9** to aim or point: *He levelled the gun at her chest.*

Word Use: definition 7 is more suited to everyday language
Word Building: other verb forms are **I levelled, I have levelled, I am levelling** □ **leveller** *noun* **levelly** *adverb*

lever (say *lee-və*) *noun*
1 a bar supported at one point along its length, which lifts a weight at one end when you press or pull down the other

lever *verb*
2 to move with a lever: *to lever a rock out of the ground*

Word Building: **leverage** *noun*

levitate *verb*
to rise or float in the air as if by magic

Word Building: **levitation** *noun*

levity *noun*
a lack of seriousness in the way you think and behave

levy (say *lev-ee*) *verb*
1 to place or impose by law: *to levy a tax on cigarettes and beer*

levy *noun*
2 a fee or a tax which has to be paid: *The club imposed a levy on members to pay for the Christmas party.*

Word Building: other verb forms are **I levied, I have levied, I am levying** □ the plural of the noun is **levies**

liability *noun*
1 something or someone that causes difficulty rather than being helpful: *New shoes are a liability on a long walk because they can make your feet sore.* **2** legal responsibility: *He accepted liability for the accident.* **3 liabilities** debts, especially money that is owed

Word Building: the plural is **liabilities**

liable *adjective*
1 likely: *Problems are liable to come up.* **2** having a legal responsibility: *He was liable for the accident and had to pay the repair costs.*

liaison (say *lee-ay-zən*) *noun*
a connection or communication between people or groups: *The school captain acted as a liaison between teachers and pupils.*

Word Building: **liaise** *verb* to communicate and act together with

liar *noun*
someone who tells lies

libel (say *luy-bəl*) *noun*
a written or printed statement which damages someone's reputation: *The politician sued the newspaper for libel.*

Word Use: compare this with **slander**
Word Building: **libel** *verb* (**libelled, libelling**) **libeller** *noun* **libellous** *adjective* **libellously** *adverb*
Word History: from a Latin word meaning "book"

liberal *adjective*
1 happy to see change and development, especially in social and religious matters **2** broad-minded or accepting a wide range

of ideas: *a liberal thinker* **3** generous: *a liberal gift | a liberal giver*

Word Building: **liberality** *noun* (**liberalities**) **liberalism** *noun* **liberally** *adverb*

liberate *verb*
to set free: *The army liberated the country from enemy control.*

Word Building: **liberation** *noun* **liberator** *noun*

liberty *noun*
1 freedom from imprisonment, or from a cruel or foreign government **2** freedom to do, think, or speak as you choose **3** a rude or disrespectful freedom in behaviour or speech: *Don't think that you can take liberties with me.* **4 at liberty** free, or having permission to do a particular thing

Word Building: the plural is **liberties**

library *noun*
1 a room or building where books and other reading or study materials are kept for people to use or borrow **2** a collection of books, or of films, records or music: *She has a good library at home.*

Word Building: the plural is **libraries** □ **librarian** *noun* a person in charge of a library

licence *noun*
1 official permission to do something or a certificate showing this permission: *a driving licence* **2** uncontrolled freedom of behaviour: *That teacher allows the children too much licence.*

Word Use: be careful – this sounds like **license**

license *verb*
to give official permission to: *He is licensed to sell guns.*

Word Use: be careful – this sounds like **licence**
Word Building: **licensee** *noun* someone who has a licence, usually to sell alcohol

lichen (say *luy-kən*) *noun*
a moss-like plant that grows in patches, usually on rocks or tree trunks

lick *verb*
1 to pass your tongue over: *David licked the back of the stamp.* **2** to pass over or touch lightly: *Flames licked the logs of wood.* **3** to defeat: *We licked the other team.*

Word Use: definition 3 is more suited to everyday language
Word Building: **lick** *noun*

licorice (say *lik-ə-rish*) *noun*
a sweet-tasting substance made from the root of a plant and used in making sweets and some medicines

Word Use: another spelling is **liquorice**

lid *noun*
1 a movable top for covering a container
2 *short for* **eyelid**

lie[1] *noun*
a deliberate untruth

Word Building: **lie** *verb* (**lied, lying**)

lie[2] *verb*
1 to be or rest in a flat horizontal position: *I would like to lie in bed all day. | A book is lying on the table.* **2** to remain in a certain position or condition: *The money lay forgotten in the bank for many years.* **3** to be found or to be located: *The trouble with the bike lies with the gears. | Our land lies beside the river.* **4 lie low** to be in hiding

Word Use: don't confuse this with the verb **lay**
Word Building: other forms are **I lay, I have lain, I am lying**

lieutenant (say *lef-ten-ənt*) *noun*
an officer in the army or navy, lower in rank than a captain

Word History: from a French word meaning "holding a place"

life *noun*
1 the condition that makes animals and plants different from dead things and from other objects like rocks, liquids, machines and so on **2** the time you are alive, from your birth to your death **3** living things as a group: *life on earth* **4** lively activity or interest: *Her speech was full of life.*

Word Building: the plural is **lives**

lifeboat *noun*
a boat carried on a large ship and used if the ship sinks or catches fire

life cycle *noun*
the development of a living thing from the beginning of its life to the time it becomes an adult

lifesaver *noun*
someone who makes sure that people swim at the safe part of a beach and who rescues swimmers in difficulty

lift *verb*
1 to raise or bring upwards
lift *noun*
2 a moving platform or cage for bringing people from one level of a building to another **3** a free ride in a vehicle: *Can you give me a lift home?*

Word Use: another word for definition 2, mainly used in America, is **elevator**

light[1] *noun*
1 a form of radiation produced by some objects such as the sun or fire, which bounces off other things and so lets us see them **2** one of those things which give off light, such as an electric light globe or the sun **3** one of the set of coloured lights that is used to control traffic at intersections **4** new knowledge or information: *Can you throw any light on this mystery?*
light[1] *adjective*
5 having light, rather than darkness: *a light room* **6** pale in colour: *light blue*
light[1] *verb*
7 to set burning or start to burn: *He lit a fire. / The match won't light.* **8** to give light to: *They took a torch to light their way.* **9 light up** **a** to make brighter: *A smile lit up her face.* **b** to become light or without colour: *The city lights up at night.*

Word Building: other forms are **I lit** or **I lighted, I have lit** or **I have lighted, I am lighting** □ **lighting** *noun* **lightness** *noun*

light[2] *adjective*
1 of little weight: *a light load* **2** small in amount, force or depth: *a light meal / light rain / light sleep* **3** not heavy or serious: *light reading* **4** cheerful: *a light heart* **5 make light of** to treat as being of little importance: *He made light of his troubles.*

Word Building: **lightly** *adverb* **lightness** *noun*

lighthouse *noun*
a tower with a strong light that guides ships at sea and warns them of any dangerous rocks nearby

lightning *noun*
a sudden flash of light in the sky caused by electricity in the air during a thunderstorm

light-year *noun*
the distance travelled by light in one year, used in measuring distances between stars

like[1] *adjective*
1 similar or able to be compared in some way
like[1] *noun*
2 something that is similar: *oranges, lemons and the like* **3** a similar person or thing: *No-one has seen his like before.*

Word Building: **liken** *verb* **likeness** *noun*

like[2] *verb*
1 to find pleasant or agreeable: *I like picnics. / I like her.* **2** to wish or want: *Do it whenever you like.*

Word Building: **likeable** *adjective* easy to like **likes** *plural noun: to have likes and dislikes* **liking** *noun: I have a liking for chocolate cake.*

likely *adjective*
1 probable: *a likely account of what happened*
likely *adverb*
2 probably: *He was very likely right.*

Word Building: **likelihood** *adjective* chance

lilac (say *luy-lək*) *noun*
1 a purple or white flower with a pleasant smell, which grows in clusters on a shrub
lilac *adjective*
2 pale reddish-purple

lilt *verb*
to sing or play in a light rhythmic manner

Word Building: **lilt** *noun* **lilting** *adjective*

lily *noun*
a plant with a bulb and a funnel-shaped flower which can be found in many colours, although most people think of lilies as being white

Word Building: the plural is **lilies**

lima bean (say *luy-mə*) *noun*
a kind of bean with a broad flat seed that you can eat

limb *noun*
1 your arm or leg, or the similar part of an animal's body, such as a wing **2** the large main branch of a tree

limber *verb*
in the phrase **limber up** to exercise or warm up in order to make yourself flexible and relaxed: *Always remember to limber up before a race.*

lime[1] *noun*
1 a white powder obtained by heating limestone, that is used in making cement **2** a calcium mixture used to improve crop-growing soil

lime[2] *noun*
1 a small greenish-yellow citrus fruit
lime[2] *adjective*
2 greenish-yellow

limerick (say *lim-ə-rik*) *noun*
a funny rhyming poem of five lines

Word History: named after Limerick, a county in the Republic of Ireland

limestone *noun*
a soft, white, chalky rock

limit *noun*
1 the end or furthest part: *to reach the limit of your patience* **2** a boundary or line that you should not pass: *You may only ride up to the limit I have set you.*
limit *verb*
3 to keep within a certain amount or space: *to limit your pocket money / to limit the playing area*

Word Building: other verb forms are **I limited, I have limited, I am limiting** □ **limitation** *noun*

limousine (say *lim-ə-zeen*) *noun*
any large comfortable car, especially one driven by a paid driver

limp[1] *verb*
to walk with difficulty because of an injured leg or foot

Word Building: **limp** *noun*

limp[2] *adjective*
not stiff or firm: *limp material*

Word Building: **limply** *adverb* **limpness** *noun*

limpet *noun*
a cone-shaped shellfish that sticks very firmly to rocks

limpid *adjective*
clear or transparent: *limpid pools of water*

Word Building: **limpidly** *adverb*

line[1] *noun*
1 a thin mark or stroke made on paper, wood or some other surface **2** something arranged like a line: *a line of trees / a line of words on a page* **3** a wrinkle on someone's face **4** a strip of railway track: *the railway line* **5** a type of goods which a shop sells: *We don't stock that line.*
6 lines the words of an actor's part in a play: *Have you learnt your lines?*
line[1] *verb*
7 to form a line along: *Trees lined the street.* **8 line up** **a** to take a position in a line or queue **b** to bring into a line

Word Building: **lineage** *noun* descent from a line of ancestors **linear** *adjective* stretched in a line

line[2] *verb*
to cover the inside of: *to line a coat with silk*

Word Building: **lining** *noun* a covering for an inside surface

linen *noun*
1 cloth made from flax **2** articles made from linen or cotton, such as sheets and table cloths

liner *noun*
a large passenger ship

linesman *noun*
1 a sports official who helps a referee or umpire decide if the ball has landed inside or outside one of the lines on the field of play **2** someone who puts up or repairs telephone or electric power lines

Word Building: the plural is **linesmen**

linger *verb*
to stay on in a place because you don't want to leave

Word Building: **lingering** *adjective: a lingering illness* **lingeringly** *adverb*

lingerie (say *lon-zhə-ray*) *noun*
women's underwear or nightwear

Word Use: this comes from a French word and in English we have tried to give it a French sound

linguistics (say *ling-gwis-tiks*) *noun*
the study of language, including sounds, words and grammar: *Linguistics is a subject studied at university.*

Word Building: **linguist** *noun* someone who studies language **linguistic** *adjective: linguistic knowledge*

liniment *noun*
an oily liquid for rubbing on bruises, sprains or sore muscles

link *noun*
1 one of the separate rings which make up a chain **2** anything which is a bond or connecting part: *Our love of football is a strong link between us.*

Word Building: **link** *verb* **linkage** *noun*

linoleum (say *luy-noh-lee-əm*) *noun*
a floor covering made of a mixture of oil, cork and rosin pressed into a strong cloth backing

Word Use: this is sometimes shortened to **lino**

linseed *noun*
the seed of the flax plant from which an oil is made

lion *noun*
a large, honey-coloured member of the cat family, that lives in Africa and southern Asia, the male of which has a mane

Word Use: the male is a **lion;** the female is a **lioness;** the young is a **cub**

lipstick *noun*
a cosmetic for colouring your lips

liquefy (say *lik-wə-fuy*) *verb*
to make or become liquid

Word Building: other forms are **it liquefied, it has liquefied, it is liquefying** □ **liquefier** *noun*

liqueur (say *lə-kyooh-ə*) *noun*
a type of strong alcoholic liquor made in many flavours

liquid *adjective*
1 flowing like water **2** having to do with liquids: *a liquid measuring jug*

Word Building: **liquid** *noun* any liquid substance

liquidate *verb*
1 to settle or pay: *to liquidate a debt* **2** to pay off debts and finish doing business **3** to get rid of, especially by killing: *to liquidate political prisoners*

Word Building: **liquidation** *noun: The company went into liquidation.* **liquidator** *noun*

liquor (sounds like *licker*) *noun*
a strong alcoholic drink such as brandy or whisky

liquorice (say *lik-ə-rish*) *noun*
another spelling for **licorice**

lisp *noun*
the inability to pronounce "s", making it sound like the "th" in *thin*

Word Building: **lisp** *verb*

list[1] *noun*
a set of the names of things written down one under the other, so that you'll remember them: *a shopping list*

Word Building: **list** *verb* **listing** *noun*

list[2] *verb*
to lean to one side: *The ship listed to starboard.*

Word Building: **list** *noun*

listen (say *lis-ən*) *verb*
to pay attention so that you are able to hear something

Word Building: **listener** *noun*

listless *adjective*
having no energy or interest in anything

Word Building: **listlessly** *adverb* **listlessness** *noun*

literal *adjective*
1 true to fact and not exaggerated: *a literal account of what happened* **2** following or referring to the exact or actual words that are written or spoken: *a literal translation*

Word Building: **literally** *adverb*

literary *adjective*
having to do with books and literature of a high standard: *a literary critic*

literate (say *lit-ə-rət*) *adjective*
able to read and write

Word Use: the opposite is **illiterate**
Word Building: **literacy** *noun*

literature *noun*
1 books, poems, plays and other forms of writing of a high standard: *Australian literature* **2** what is written about a particular subject: *the literature of home decorating*

lithe (say *luydh*) *adjective*
supple or bending easily: *She has a lithe figure.*

Word Building: **lithely** *adverb* **litheness** *noun*

litmus *noun*
a colouring which is often soaked onto strips of paper and used to tell whether a liquid is an acid or an alkali. The paper turns red when you dip it in acid and blue in an alkali.

Word Building: **litmus paper** *noun*

litre (rhymes with *beater*) *noun*
a measure of liquid in the metric system

Word History: from a Greek word meaning "pound"

litter *noun*
1 things, especially rubbish, scattered about **2** a number of baby animals born at the same time: *a litter of puppies*

litter *verb*
3 to make untidy by scattering rubbish: *The picnickers littered the beach with cans.* **4** to be scattered around: *Bottles littered the park.*

Word Building: **litterbug** *noun* someone who drops litter in public places

little *adjective*
1 small in size: *a little boy* **2** not much or small in amount: *little hope* **3** short or brief: *a little time*

Word Building: other forms for definition 1 are **littler, littlest** □ other forms for definitions 2 and 3 are **less, least**

live[1] (rhymes with *give*) *verb*
1 to be alive or have life **2** to keep life going: *to live on bread and water* **3** to have your home in a particular place: *to live in Australia*

live[2] (rhymes with *dive*) *adjective*
1 living or alive **2** broadcast or televised as it is being performed: *a live broadcast of the town hall concert* **3** charged with electricity: *a live wire* **4** unexploded: *a live bullet*

Word Building: **live** *adverb: a cricket match televised live*

livelihood (say <u>luyv</u>-lee-hood) *noun*
a way of earning money to live: *He makes a livelihood from fishing.*

lively (say <u>luyv</u>-lee) *adjective*
full of energy or spirit: *a lively puppy*

Word Building: **liven** *verb* to make more lively or energetic **liveliness** *noun*

liver (rhymes with *giver*) *noun*
the part of your body that makes bile which helps digest your food

livestock *noun*
all the animals kept on a farm or station property

livid (say <u>liv</u>-əd) *adjective*
1 very angry: *He was livid when we told him.* **2** discoloured by bruises

living *adjective*
1 alive **2** in existence or use: *German is a living language.* **3** having to do with living beings: *The floods were the worst in living memory.* **4 the living image** the exact likeness or copy: *He's the living image of his father.*

living *noun*
5 livelihood: *to earn a living*

lizard *noun*
a reptile with a long thin body, four legs and a long tail

llama (rhymes with *farmer*) *noun*
a South American animal related to the camel and used for carrying loads

Word Use: be careful – this sounds like **lama**

load *noun*
1 something carried **2** the quantity carried: *a load of soil*

load *verb*
3 to put a load on or in **4** to take on as a load: *The ship is loading wheat now.* **5** to put bullets into or a film into: *to load a gun* | *to load a camera*

Word Building: **loaded** *adjective: a loaded ship* | *a loaded gun*

loaf[1] *noun*
1 an amount of bread or cake baked in a particular shape **2** any food made into a loaf shape: *a meat loaf*

Word Building: the plural is **loaves**

loaf[2] *verb*
to be lazy or do nothing: *I loafed all day.*

Word Building: **loaf** *noun* a restful lazy time

loam *noun*
loose, very fertile soil

Word Building: **loamy** *adjective*

loan *noun*
1 the giving of something to be used for a short time before being returned to the owner: *I made him a loan of my book.* **2** money given for a short time, usually to be repaid with interest: *a bank loan*

Word Building: **loan** *verb* to lend

loath (rhymes with *both*) *adjective*
unwilling or not inclined: *I am loath to lend her anything.*

loathe (rhymes with *clothe*) *verb*
to hate or detest very much

Word Building: **loathsome** *adjective*

lob *verb*
to hit or throw a ball so that it has a very high bounce, as in tennis

Word Building: other forms are **I lobbed, I have lobbed, I am lobbing** □ **lob** *noun*
Word History: from a Middle English word for a kind of fish, and later meaning "clumsy person"

lobby *noun*
1 an entrance hall **2** a group of people trying to get support for a particular cause: *a lobby for cancer research*

Word Building: the plural is **lobbies** □ **lobby** *verb* (**lobbied, lobbying**): *to lobby for conservation of rainforests* **lobbyist** *noun*

lobe *noun*
the soft, hanging, lower part of your ear

lobster *noun*
a large shellfish with ten legs and a long tail, which turns pink when cooked

local *adjective*
1 having to do with a particular place: *a local custom* **2** having to do with the area you are living in rather than the whole town or state: *local government* | *the local school* **3** acting on only part of the body: *a local anaesthetic*

local *noun*
4 someone who lives in a particular place: *He's one of the locals.*

Word Building: **localise** *verb* **locally** *adverb*

locality (say *loh-kal-ə-tee*) *noun*
a particular place or area: *We are now in the locality where Ned Kelly lived.*

Word Building: the plural is **localities**

locate *verb*
1 to find the place of: *to locate the fault in the engine* **2** to put in a place or area: *to locate the Post Office near the shops*

Word Building: **location** *noun*

loch (sounds like *lock*) *noun*
a Scottish word for **lake**

lock[1] *noun*
1 a device for fastening a door, gate, lid or drawer, which needs a key to open it
2 a part of a canal with gates at each end allowing ships to be raised from one level to another

lock[1] *verb*
3 to fasten or become fastened with a key **4** to shut or put into a place of safety or imprisonment

lock[2] *noun*
a short length or curl of hair

locker *noun*
a cupboard that may be locked, especially one for your own use

locket *noun*
a small case for a small picture or lock of hair, usually worn on a chain hung around your neck

lockjaw *noun*
an old-fashioned name for **tetanus**

locksmith *noun*
someone who makes or mends locks and keys

locomotive (say *loh-kə-moh-tiv*) *noun*
the engine which pulls railway carriages or trucks

Word Building: **locomotion** *noun* the act or power of moving around

locust (say *loh-kəst*) *noun*
a type of grasshopper which moves from one place to another in large numbers and destroys crops

lodge *noun*
1 a building used as a holiday house: *a ski lodge* **2** a meeting place of a branch of a secret society

lodge *verb*
3 to board or live for a while in someone else's home: *I lodge at Mrs Smith's house.* **4** to be put, caught or placed: *A speck of dirt lodged in my eye.* **5** to put for safe keeping: *to lodge valuables with a bank*

Word Building: **lodger** *noun* **lodgings** *noun* **lodgment** *noun*

loft *noun*
1 the space in a building between the roof and the ceiling **2** an upper level of a church or hall made for a special purpose: *a choir loft*

lofty *adjective*
1 reaching high into the air: *lofty mountains* **2** noble or high in character: *He has lofty ideals.* **3** proud or haughty: *a lofty manner*

Word Building: other forms are **loftier, loftiest**

log *noun*
1 a large branch or the trunk of a tree which has fallen or been cut down **2** the daily record of a voyage or flight kept by the captain of a ship or plane

Word Building: **log** *verb* (**logged, logging**) **logger** *noun* **logging** *noun*

loganberry *noun*
a large, dark-red berry you can eat, or the plant it grows on

Word Building: the plural is **loganberries**
Word History: named after the Californian man who first grew them, JH Logan, 1841-1928

logbook *noun*
a book in which the record of a journey made by a ship or plane is entered

logic (say *loj-ik*) *noun*
correct reasoning: *His argument was based on logic.*

Word Building: **logical** *adjective* **logically** *adverb* **logician** *noun* someone who studies the art of logic

loin *noun*
1 the part of your body between your lowest rib and the top of either thigh **2** the similar part of a four-legged animal: *a loin of lamb* **3 gird up your loins** to get ready for action

loiter *verb*
to move about aimlessly or stay in the one place: *I loitered on the street corner waiting for my friend.*

Word Building: **loiterer** *noun*

loll *verb*
1 to lean in a lazy manner: *He lolled against the post.* **2** to hang loosely: *The dog's tongue lolled from its mouth as it panted.*

lollipop *noun*
a kind of boiled sweet, often fixed to the end of a stick

lolly *noun*
1 any sweet, especially a boiled one **2** your head **3** money

Word Use: definitions 2 and 3 are more suited to everyday language
Word Building: the plural is **lollies**

lone *adjective*
1 being alone or not with anyone: *a lone traveller* **2** standing apart from others: *a lone tree*

Word Building: **loner** *noun* someone who likes to be alone

lonely *adjective*
1 alone or without friendly company: *A lighthouse keeper's job is a lonely one.* **2** far away from where people are: *lonely beaches* **3** feeling sad because of being alone: *The old man was lonely when his wife died.*

Word Building: **loneliness** *noun*

long[1] *adjective*
1 having a great distance from one end to the other **2** lasting a great amount of time **3** having a stated distance or time: *a road two miles long / a speech an hour long* **4 the long and short of** the main part of: *The long and short of it is that we decided to go.*

long[1] *adverb*
5 for a great amount of time: *Did he stay long?* **6** for or throughout a certain amount of time: *How long did he stay?*

Word Building: **length** *noun*

long[2] *verb*
in the phrase **long for** to want or desire very much: *I long for a pet.*

Word Use: a similar expression is **yearn for**
Word Building: **longing** *noun* **longingly** *adverb*

longitude (say *long-gə-tyood*) *noun*
the distance, measured in degrees, by which a point on the earth is east or west of Greenwich in England

Word Building: **longitudinal** *adjective* **longitudinally** *adverb*

longwinded *adjective*
talking for too long or using more words than necessary: *He's always so longwinded in his explanations.*

Word Building: **longwindedness** *noun*

look *verb*
1 to use your eyes in order to see **2** to examine by searching: *to look through papers* **3** to appear or seem: *He looked happy.* **4** to face towards: *The house looks east.* **5 look after** to take care of **6 look down on** to despise or scorn **7 look for** to search for **8 look out** to be on guard or be watchful: *to look out for danger* **9 look up to** to admire or respect

Word Building: **looks** *noun* general appearance: *good looks* **look** *noun*

lookout *noun*
1 a watch kept for something that may come or happen **2** someone who keeps such a watch or the place from which they watch **3** a place on a mountain from which you can admire the view

loom[1] *noun*
a machine or apparatus for weaving cloth

Word History: from an Old English word meaning "tool" or "implement"

loom[2] *verb*
to appear, often in a large or frightening form: *The hedge suddenly loomed in front of the young horse rider.*

Word History: from a Swedish word meaning "move slowly"

loop *noun*
1 a more or less oval shape twisted in a piece of string, ribbon or something similar **2** anything shaped like this: *a loop in a railway track*

Word Building: **loop** *verb*

loophole *noun*
1 an opening, especially in a wall to allow light in or to fire weapons through **2** a way or means of escape

loose (say *loohs*) *adjective*
1 free from being fastened: *a loose end of string* **2** not bound together: *a loose bundle of papers* **3** not in a container: *loose peanuts* **4** not firm: *a loose rein* **5** not fitting tightly: *a loose sweater* **6 at a loose end** having nothing to do

Word Building: **loose** *verb* to let loose **loosen** *verb* to make or become looser **loosely** *adverb*

loot *noun*
anything that has been stolen, especially from an enemy in war

Word Building: **loot** *verb* **looter** *noun*

lop *verb*
1 to cut off: *to lop branches from a tree* **2** to cut branches from: *to lop trees*

Word Building: other verb forms are **I lopped, I have lopped, I am lopping** □ **lopper** *noun*

lope *verb*
to move with long easy steps

Word Building: **lope** *noun*

lopsided *adjective*
1 leaning to one side **2** larger or heavier on one side than the other

Word Building: **lopsidedly** *adverb* **lopsidedness** *noun*

lord *noun*
1 a British nobleman with a title in front of his name **2** someone who has power over others **3 the Lord** God or Jesus Christ

Word Building: **lord** *verb: to lord it over someone* **lordly** *adjective*

lore *noun*
learning or knowledge, especially on a particular subject: *family lore | the lore of herbs*

Word Use: be careful – this sounds like **law**

lorikeet *noun*
a small brightly-coloured parrot that has a brush-like tongue for feeding on nectar

lorry *noun*
another name for **truck**

Word Building: the plural is **lorries**

lose (say *loohz*) *verb*
1 to come to be without for some reason, and not be able to find **2** to have taken away by death: *to lose an uncle* **3** to fail to get or win

Word Building: other forms are **I lost, I have lost, I am losing** □ **loser** *noun*

loss *noun*
1 the losing of something: *the loss of his wallet | the loss of her friends* **2** something that is lost **3 at a loss** confused or uncertain: *He was at a loss as to what to do.* **4 a dead loss** a completely useless person or thing

lost *adjective*
1 no longer in your possesssion **2** not knowing the way **3** wasted or not used: *lost time*

lot *noun*
1 a large number **2** your fate in life: *Illness seems to be her lot.* **3** the drawing of an object from a hat or box to decide something by chance: *We decided by lot who would go first.* **4 the lot** the whole amount

lotion (say *loh-shən*) *noun*
a liquid that you use to heal, clean or feed your skin

Word History: from a Latin word meaning "a washing"

lottery *noun*
a kind of raffle in which the prize is usually money

Word Building: the plural is **lotteries**

lotto *noun*
another name for **bingo**

lotus (say *loh-təs*) *noun*
a kind of water-lily which grows in Asia and Egypt

loud *adjective*
1 producing a lot of sound so that you can hear it easily: *a loud radio | loud knocking* **2** very colourful, usually in an unpleasant way: *a loud tie*

Word Building: **loudly** *adverb: to knock loudly* **loudness** *noun*

loudspeaker *noun*
the part of a record player or radio that turns electronic signals into sound

Word Use: the short form is **speaker**

lounge *verb*
1 to lie back lazily: *to lounge in a chair*

lounge *noun*
2 the room in your home where you relax or entertain **3** the most expensive seats in a theatre **4** *another name for a* **couch**

louse *noun*
1 a small wingless insect which lives in the hair or skin and sucks blood **2** someone who is hateful or not to be trusted

Word Use: the plural of definition 1 is **lice** □ definition 2 is more suited to everyday language

lousy (say *low-zee*) *adjective*
1 having many lice **2** mean or hateful **3 feel lousy** to be sick or unwell

Word Use: definitions 2 and 3 are more suited to everyday language
Word Building: other forms are **lousier, lousiest**

lout *noun*
a rough, rude and sometimes violent young man

Word Building: **loutish** *adjective*

love *noun*
1 strong or warm feelings of affection: *love for a parent | love for a friend* **2** sexual desire **3** strong liking: *love of reading* **4** no score in tennis and similar games: *The score is 30 love.* **5 in love with** feeling deep passion for: *They are in love with each other.* **6 make love** to have sexual intercourse

Word Building: **beloved** *adjective* dearly loved **lovable** *adjective* inspiring love **love** *verb* **lover** *noun* **loving** *adjective*

lovely *adjective*
1 having a beautiful appearance or personality **2** very pleasant: *a lovely day*

Word Building: other forms are **lovelier, loveliest** □ **loveliness** *noun*

low[1] *adjective*
1 not far above the ground, floor or base **2** lying below the average level: *low ground | The river is low because of the drought.* **3** small in amount: *a low number* **4** deep in pitch: *a low buzz | a low voice* **5** of lesser rank, quality or importance: *low birth*

Word Building: **low** *adverb* **lowly** *adjective*

low[2] *verb*
to make the sound that cattle make

Word Use: this is an old-fashioned word for **moo**
Word Building: **low** *noun* **lowing** *noun*

lower *verb*
1 to make or become less: *to lower the price of bread | Prices lowered when supplies increased.* **2** to make less loud: *to lower the voice* **3** to let down: *to lower a rope*

Word Use: the opposite is **raise**

lower case *noun*
the printing type that makes small, not capital, letters

Word Use: the opposite is **upper case**
Word Building: **lower-case** *adjective*

loyal *adjective*
faithful and true: *a loyal friend*

Word Building: **loyally** *adverb* **loyalty** *noun*

lozenge (say *loz-ənj*) *noun*
a small sweet, usually used to soothe a sore throat

Word History: from a Persian word meaning "stone slab"

Ltd
short for Limited*; used after the name of a company to show that the shareholders lose only what they have put in if the company gets into debt*

Word Use: see also **Pty**, which often comes before **Ltd**

lubra (say *looh-brə*) *noun*
an Aboriginal woman

Word History: from an Aboriginal language, probably from south-eastern Tasmania

lubricate *verb*
to oil or grease the moving parts of, so that they will move more easily: *to lubricate an engine*

Word Building: **lubricant** *noun* **lubrication** *noun* **lubricative** *adjective*

lucerne (say *looh-sən*) *noun*
a plant used to feed cattle

Word Use: another name for this is **alfalfa**

lucid (say *looh-səd*) *adjective*
1 clear or easy to understand: *a lucid explanation* **2** having clear understanding: *He was still lucid despite the severe blow to his head.*

Word Building: **lucidity** *noun* **lucidly** *adverb*

luck *noun*
1 something which happens to a person by chance **2** good fortune: *She wished me luck.* **3 no such luck** unfortunately not

4 push your luck to take another risk in the hope that you'll be lucky yet again

Word Building: **lucky** *adjective* (**luckier, luckiest**) **luckily** *adverb* **luckiness** *noun*

lucrative (say <u>*looh*</u>*-krə-tiv*) *adjective*
producing good profits or paying well: *a lucrative business*

ludicrous (say <u>*looh*</u>*-də-krəs*) *adjective*
so silly as to cause laughter: *a ludicrous remark*

lug *verb*
to pull along or carry with effort

Word Building: other forms are **I lugged, I have lugged, I am lugging**

luggage *noun*
the suitcases and other containers you use when travelling

Word Use: another word is **baggage**

lukewarm *adjective*
1 a bit warm **2** not very enthusiastic: *a lukewarm response*

lull *verb*
1 to put to sleep by singing or rocking
2 to calm or quiet: *to lull someone's fears*

Word Building: **lull** *noun* a period of calm

lullaby *noun*
a song sung to put a baby to sleep

Word Building: the plural is **lullabies**

lumber *noun*
1 timber sawn into boards **2** a number of useless articles stored away

lumberjack *noun*
someone who cuts down trees

Word Use: this is mostly used in America and Canada

luminous (say <u>*looh*</u>*-mən-əs*) *adjective*
giving off or reflecting light: *a luminous clock face*

Word Building: **luminosity** *noun* **luminously** *adverb*

lump *noun*
1 a mass of solid matter: *a lump of clay*
2 a swelling: *a lump on the head* **3 have a lump in the throat** to feel as if you're about to cry

lump *adjective*
4 including a number of things taken together: *a lump sum of money* **5** in the form of a lump: *lump sugar*

Word Building: **lumpily** *adverb* **lumpiness** *noun* **lumpy** *adjective*

lunar (rhymes with *sooner*) *adjective*
having to do with the moon

lunatic (say <u>*looh*</u>*-nə-tik*) *noun*
someone who is mad

Word Building: **lunatic** *adjective: a lunatic idea*
Word History: at one time it was thought that people were sent mad by the full moon, which is called *luna* in Latin

lunch *noun*
a light midday meal

Word Building: the plural is **lunches** □ **lunch** *verb*

luncheon (say <u>*lunch*</u>*-ən*) *noun*
another word for **lunch**

lung *noun*
one of two parts in your body that you use for breathing

lunge *verb*
to make a sudden forward movement or attack: *I lunged at him with a stick.*

Word Building: **lunge** *noun*

lurch[1] *noun*
a sudden or unsteady movement, especially to one side

Word Building: the plural is **lurches** □ **lurch** *verb* to stagger or make a lurch

lurch[2] *noun*
a helpless situation: *They were left in the lurch.*

lure *noun*
1 something that attracts: *The shop offered free child-minding as a lure to customers.*
2 a device used to attract fish

Word Building: **lure** *verb*

lurid (say <u>*looh*</u>*-rəd*) *adjective*
1 shining with an unnatural glare: *the lurid city lights* **2** horrifying or frightening: *lurid tales | lurid crimes*

lurk *verb*
1 to stay or move about secretly: *to lurk in the darkness*

lurk *noun*
2 an easy and often sly way of doing a job or earning a living

luscious (say <u>*lush*</u>*-əs*) *adjective*
tasting very pleasant: *a luscious pie*

Word Building: **lusciously** *adverb* **lusciousness** *noun*

lush *adjective*
with strong-growing plants and trees: *the lush undergrowth of the forest*

Word Building: **lushly** *adverb* **lushness** *noun*

lust *noun*
1 strong desire: *to have a lust for power* **2** uncontrolled sexual desire

Word Building: **lust** *verb* **lustful** *adjective* **lustfully** *adverb*

lustre (rhymes with *duster*) *noun*
1 shining brightness: *the lustre of a new silver coin* **2** brightness or glory: *His bravery added lustre to his name.*

Word Building: **lustrous** *adjective* **lustrously** *adverb*

lute (rhymes with *boot*) *noun*
an old-fashioned musical instrument with strings like a guitar

Word Building: **lutenist** *noun*

luxuriant (say *lug-zhooh-ree-ənt*) *adjective*
strong in growth: *luxuriant vines*

Word Building: **luxuriance** *noun* **luxuriantly** *adverb*

luxury (say *luk-shə-ree*) *noun*
1 anything that makes life extremely pleasant or comfortable **2** enjoyment of costly food, clothing and living generally: *He lives a life of luxury.*

Word Building: the plural is **luxuries** □ **luxuriate** *verb* to enjoy as a luxury **luxurious** *adjective: a luxurious home* **luxuriously** *adverb*

lychee (say *luy-chee*) *noun*
a small Chinese fruit with a thin shell covering a sweet jelly-like pulp

Word History: from a Chinese word

lynch (rhymes with *finch*) *verb*
to put to death, usually by hanging, without a trial: *The mob lynched the murderer before the police arrived.*

Word Building: **lynching** *noun*
Word History: named after Captain William Lynch, 1742-1820, of the US, who was the first to do this

lynx (sounds like *links*) *noun*
a type of wildcat with long limbs and a short tail

Word Building: the plural is **lynxes** or **lynx**

lyre (sounds like *liar*) *noun*
a stringed musical instrument of ancient Greece

lyrebird *noun*
a type of Australian bird which can mimic other sounds and is known for the long beautiful tails which the males display when courting the females

lyric (say *li-rik*) *adjective*
1 having the form and musical quality of a song: *lyric poetry*

lyric *noun*
2 a lyric poem **3** the words of a song

Word Use: another word for definition 1 is **lyrical** □ definition 3 is often used in the plural
Word Building: **lyricist** *noun* (say *li-rə-səst*) someone who writes lyrics **lyrically** *adverb* **lyricism** *noun*

macabre (say *mə-kah-bə, -brə*) *adjective*
horrible in a gruesome way: *macabre crimes*

macadamia *noun*
a nut with a hard shell, which you can eat and which grows on a native Australian tree

macaroni *noun*
thick short tubes of pasta which are boiled and served in a sauce

Word History: from an Italian word; and before this from a Greek word meaning "food of broth and pearl barley"

macaw (say *mə-kaw*) *noun*
a colourful, tropical American parrot with a long tail and a harsh voice

machete (say *mə-shet-ee*) *noun*
a large knife with a broad blade used for slashing thick plants

machine (say *mə-sheen*) *noun*
a device which is made up of parts that work together and which is used to perform a task: *a washing machine*

Word Building: **machine** *verb* to make or do by machine: *Could you machine this hem for me?* **machinist** *noun* someone who works a machine

machine-gun *noun*
a gun which can fire a rapid stream of bullets

machinery *noun*
1 machines in general: *Farm machinery such as the plough has made work on the land easier.* **2** the parts of a machine: *the machinery of a clock*

macho (say *match-oh, mak-oh*) *adjective*
strongly masculine

mackerel *noun*
a shiny greenish fish which is used for food

macramé (say *mə-krah-mee*) *noun*
the craft of making things by knotting thread or cord in patterns

macro- *prefix*
a word part meaning large *or* great: *macrocosm* (the great world, or universe)

Word Use: compare this with **micro-**
Word History: this prefix comes from Greek

mad *adjective*
1 insane or mentally unbalanced: *Do you think she is mad?* **2** angry: *He is mad because you teased him.* **3** wild or excited: *She has a mad urge to travel.*

Word Use: definition 2 is more suited to everyday language
Word Building: **madden** *verb* to make mad or angry **madly** *adverb* **madness** *noun*

madam *noun*
a polite term of address to a woman: *May I help you, madam?*

Word Use: when you begin a letter "Dear Madam", you usually use a capital letter
Word Building: the plural is **madams** or **mesdames**
Word History: it comes from the French words "ma dame" which mean "my lady"

magazine *noun*
1 a paper or journal containing stories, articles and advertisements, usually issued once a week or once a month **2** a place where explosives are kept

maggot *noun*
the small white grub which turns into a fly or other insect

Word Building: **maggoty** *adjective* full of maggots

magic *noun*
1 power which is supernatural or which can't be explained normally **2** an act in which seemingly impossible tricks are done for entertainment

Word Building: **magic** *adjective* **magical** *adjective* **magically** *adverb*

magician (say *mə-jish-ən*) *noun*
someone who practises magic or magic tricks

magistrate *noun*
someone who acts as a judge in some less important court cases: *She had to appear before a magistrate for not paying her fines.*

magma *noun*
the very hot molten or liquid rock under the solid crust of the earth's surface

magnanimous (say *mag-nan-ə-məs*) *adjective*
nobly unselfish and generous: *He is too magnanimous to hold a grudge.*

Word Building: **magnanimity** *noun* (say *mag-nə-nim-ə-tee*) **magnanimously** *adverb*

magnate (say *mag-nayt*) *noun*
someone who is very powerful and successful, especially in business

magnesium *noun*
a light silver-white metal

magnet *noun*
1 a piece of iron or steel which draws iron objects to it **2** anything that attracts something else

Word Building: **magnetic** *adjective* **magnetically** *adverb* **magnetism** *noun*

magnetic tape *noun*
tape which is used to record sound for a tape-recorder, pictures for a video cassette, or data for a computer

magnificent *adjective*
1 grand in appearance: *magnificent robes*
2 excellent: *a magnificent dinner*

Word Use: a word with similar meaning is **splendid**
Word Building: **magnificence** *noun* **magnificently** *adverb*

magnify *verb*
to make larger or greater: *This lens magnifies very strongly. / He magnifies his troubles.*

Word Building: other forms are **I magnified, I have magnified, I am magnifying** □ **magnifier** *noun* someone or something that magnifies **magnification** *noun*

magnitude *noun*
1 size: *They measured the magnitude of the angles.* **2** greatness or importance: *She finally realised the magnitude of her loss.*

magpie *noun*
a black and white bird with a large beak, which is found throughout Australia and New Guinea

mahogany (say *mə-hog-ə-nee*) *noun*
a hard reddish-brown wood, used for making furniture

maid *noun*
1 a girl or unmarried woman **2** a female servant

Word Use: definition 1 is rather old-fashioned

maiden *noun*
1 a young unmarried woman

maiden *adjective*
2 unmarried: *my maiden aunt* **3** done or used for the first time: *a maiden voyage*

Word Use: definition 1 is rather old-fashioned

maiden name *noun*
a woman's surname before she is married

mail[1] *noun*
1 letters and packages sent by post
2 a train or boat which carries mail, often at night: *the North Coast Mail*

Word Building: **mail** *verb* **mail** *adjective*

mail[2] *noun*
armour made of linked metal rings, which was worn in medieval times

maim *verb*
to damage or cripple

Word Building: **maimed** *adjective*

main *adjective*
1 most important or biggest: *the main course / the main reason*

main *noun*
2 the largest pipe in a gas or water system

Word Building: **mainly** *adverb*

mainland *noun*
a large land mass, as distinct from the islands around it: *Tasmanians sometimes go to the mainland for a holiday.*

mainstream *noun*
the chief trend or tendency in an area: *in the mainstream of rock music*

maintain *verb*
1 to keep up or keep in good condition: *to maintain a correspondence / to maintain the roads* **2** to hold onto: *to maintain a lead*

Word Building: **maintenance** *noun*

maize *noun*
a tall cereal plant with heads of yellow grain

Word Use: be careful – this sounds like **maze**
Word History: from a West Indian language called Taino

majesty *noun*
1 the title given to a king or queen: *Your Majesty* **2** greatness or dignity: *The majesty of the view left them speechless.*

Word Building: the plural is **majesties** □ **majestic** *adjective* dignified or grand **majestically** *adverb*

major *noun*
1 an officer in the army
major *adjective*
2 greater in size or importance: *His major work is on language.*

majority (say *mə-jo-rə-tee*) *noun*
1 the greater number or more than half: *The majority of people stayed at home.*
2 the age at which the law says you are an adult and can vote in elections

Word Use: the opposite of this is **minority**
Word Building: the plural is **majorities**

major scale *noun*
any musical scale which has semitones between the third and fourth notes and between the seventh and eighth notes

Word Use: such a scale is said to be in a *major* key □ compare this with **minor scale**

make *verb*
1 to bring into being or create: *She makes her own clothes. / Who makes the laws?*
2 to produce an effect: *The rain makes the road slippery.* **3** to prepare for use: *to make a bed* **4** to win or get: *to make a friend* **5** to be or become: *The box will make a useful container.* **6** to add up to: *I know that 3 and 3 make 6.* **7** to reach or attain: *They made the shore at last. / She will make the finals.* **8 make for** to try to reach: *Let's make for home.* **9 make up** **a** to form or complete: *Six games make up a set.* **b** to invent: *He makes up stories.* **c** to become friendly again after a quarrel **d** to apply cosmetics to: *She made up her face.*

Word Building: other forms are **I made, I have made, I am making** □ **make** *noun* a type or brand **make-up** *noun* cosmetics

makeshift *noun*
something used in place of something else: *He broke the hammer and had to use a brick as a makeshift.*

Word Building: **makeshift** *adjective*

mal- *prefix*
a word part meaning bad: *maltreat, malnutrition*

Word History: this prefix comes from Latin

malady (say *mal-ə-dee*) *noun*
an illness or disease

malapropism (say *mal-ə-prop-iz-əm*) *noun*
a word used by mistake for a similar-sounding word, so that the effect is funny: *It is a malapropism to say "Beethoven wrote nine sympathies" since the right word is "symphonies".*

Word History: named after Mrs Malaprop, a character in a play, who misuses words in this way

malaria *noun*
an illness which gives you fever, chills and sweating, and which is spread by mosquitoes

male *noun*
1 a man or boy **2** any animal that belongs to the sex which fertilises the female egg

Word Building: **male** *adjective*

malevolent (say *mə-lev-ə-lənt*) *adjective*
full of ill will: *a malevolent sneer*

Word Building: **malevolence** *noun* **malevolently** *adverb*

malice *noun*
the desire to harm or hurt someone: *She broke his pen out of malice.*

Word Building: **malicious** *adjective* **maliciously** *adverb*

malignant *adjective*
1 dangerous or deadly: *a malignant cancer* **2** nasty or evil: *a malignant look*

Word Building: **malign** *verb* to speak ill of **malignancy** *noun* **malignantly** *adverb*

mall (say *mawl, mal*) *noun*
an area without traffic where people can stroll and shop

malleable (say *mal-ee-ə-bəl*) *adjective*
easily worked into a different shape: *Some metals are more malleable than others.*

Word Building: **malleability** *noun*

mallee *noun*
a wiry Australian gum tree which has several thin stems which grow from a large underground root

Word Building: **the mallee** *noun* country where these trees grow
Word History: probably from an Aboriginal language called Wemba

mallet *noun*
1 a hammer made of wood **2** the wooden stick used to hit the ball in croquet or polo

malnutrition *noun*
illness caused by not having enough food

malt *noun*
grain which is used in making beer and whisky

maltreat *verb*
to treat roughly or cruelly

Word Building: **maltreatment** *noun*

mammal *noun*
an animal whose young feeds on its mother's milk

Word Building: **mammalian** *adjective* (say *mə-may-lee-ən*)
Word History: from a Latin word meaning "of the breast"

mammoth *noun*
1 a type of large hairy elephant with long curved tusks, that died out a long time ago
mammoth *adjective*
2 huge: *a mammoth sale*

man *noun*
1 a grown-up male human being
2 human beings in general **3** a piece in a game such as chess or draughts

Word Building: the plural is **men** □ **man** *verb* (**manned, manning**) to provide with workers **manly** *adjective* (**manlier, manliest**): *Bravery is seen as a manly quality.* **manhood** *noun*

manage *verb*
1 to be able to: *Can she manage to feed herself?* **2** to take charge of or control: *The young stockman cannot manage the cattle.*

Word Building: **manageable** *adjective*

management *noun*
1 the running of something: *He leaves the management of the business to her.*
2 the people who run something, such as a business or hotel

manager *noun*
1 someone who runs a business
2 someone who looks after the business interests of an entertainer or a sporting team

Word Building: **manageress** *noun* **managerial** *adjective*

mandarin *noun*
a small, soft-skinned, orange-coloured citrus fruit

Word Use: another spelling is **mandarine**

mandolin *noun*
a musical instrument with a pear-shaped wooden body and metal strings which you pluck

mane *noun*
the long hair on a male lion's head or along the neck of a horse

mange (say *maynj*) *noun*
a skin disease, mainly of animals, in which the skin becomes rough and red and loses its hair

Word Building: **mangy** *adjective* (**mangier, mangiest**)

manger (say *mayn-jə*) *noun*
a box from which cattle or horses eat

mangle *verb*
to crush, cut or ruin

mango *noun*
a sweet yellow tropical fruit

Word Building: the plural is **mangoes** or **mangos**

mangrove *noun*
a tree which grows thickly along the water's edge sending up roots through the mud or sand

manhole *noun*
a covered hole, as in a footpath or ceiling, that you can climb through to get at pipes and wires

mania *noun*
1 great enthusiasm or excitement: *He has a mania for collecting matchboxes.*
2 a violent or excitable form of insanity

Word Building: **manic** *adjective*

maniac *noun*
someone who is mad, or who acts wildly or dangerously

Word Building: **maniacal** *adjective* (say *mə-nuy-ə-kəl*)

manicure *noun*
treatment of your hands and fingernails

Word Building: **manicurist** *noun* someone who does manicures

manifesto *noun*
a public statement by a government or group, setting out its ideas or goals: *the Communist manifesto*

Word Building: the plural is **manifestos** or **manifestoes**

manipulate (say *mə-nip-yə-layt*) *verb*
1 to use, especially with skill: *to manipulate the puppets with strings* **2** to influence cleverly and unfairly: *She manipulates people.* **3** to use the hands to treat as a chiropractor does: *to manipulate the spine*

Word Building: **manipulation** *noun* **manipulative** *adjective* **manipulator** *noun*

mankind *noun*
all human beings

mannequin (say *man-ə-kən, -kwən*) *noun*
1 someone who wears new clothes to show them to customers **2** a human-sized figure used by dressmakers and window dressers to fit or model clothes

Word History: from a Dutch word meaning "little man"

manner *noun*
1 a way of being or doing: *a pleasant manner* **2 manners** behaviour or way of behaving: *good manners* / *bad manners*

mannerism *noun*
a habit of doing something a little strange: *He has a funny little mannerism – he pulls his ear everytime he starts to speak.*

manoeuvre (say *mə-nooh-və*) *noun*
1 a clever move: *She won the game by an unbeatable manoeuvre.* **2 manoeuvres** military exercises: *The soldiers are out on manoeuvres.*

Word Building: **manoeuvre** *verb* **manoeuvrability** *noun* **manoeuvrable** *adjective*

manor *noun*
a large British country house with its land, originally the home of a lord

manse *noun*
the house that a clergyman and his family live in

mansion *noun*
a large or grand house

manslaughter (say *man-slaw-tə*) *noun*
the accidental killing of someone

mantelpiece *noun*
the shelf above a fireplace

mantis *noun*
a long, stick-like, brown or green insect which holds its front legs doubled up as if in prayer

Word Use: another name for this is **praying mantis**
Word Building: the plural is **mantises** or **mantes**

mantle *noun*
a loose cloak or cover

Word Building: **mantle** *verb* to cover

manual *adjective*
1 done by hand: *manual work*

manual *noun*
2 a book which tells you how to do or use something **3** a car which has gears that you change by hand

Word Building: **manually** *adverb*

manufacture *verb*
to make or produce by hand or machine, especially in large numbers

Word Building: **manufacture** *noun* **manufacturer** *noun* **manufacturing** *noun*

manure *noun*
animal waste, especially when used as fertiliser

manuscript *noun*
a book, letter or piece of music, written by hand

Word Building: **manuscript** *adjective*

Maori (rhymes with *cowrie*) *noun*
one of the brown-skinned people who are native to New Zealand

Word History: from a Maori word meaning "of the usual kind"

map *noun*
a drawing or diagram of an area showing where certain things are, such as towns, roads, mountains and borders

Word Building: **map** *verb* (**mapped, mapping**)

maple *noun*
a tree that grows in cold countries, used for its wood and its sap which produces a sweet syrup

mar *verb*
to spoil: *His bad temper mars his good performance.*

Word Building: other forms are **I marred, I have marred, I am marring**

marathon *noun*
a long-distance foot race, officially of 42 195 metres

Word History: named after the Greek plain of *Marathon* from which a runner took news of a Greek victory in 490 BC to Athens, 42 kilometres away

marble *noun*
1 a hard mottled limestone of various colours, used in building and sculpture
2 a small glass ball used in a game

Word Building: **marble** *verb* to mottle
marble *adjective*

march *verb*
1 to walk like a soldier, with even steps and swinging arms **2** to make someone march: *She marched them out to the playground.*
march *noun*
3 the act of marching: *He joined the march.* **4** the distance covered by a march: *The town is three days' march away.* **5** a lively rhythmical piece of music suited to marching

Word Building: **marcher** *noun*

March *noun*
the third month of the year, with 31 days

Word Use: the abbreviation is **Mar**
Word History: from a Latin word meaning "the month of Mars", after the planet *Mars*

mare (rhymes with *hair*) *noun*
a fully-grown female horse

Word Use: the male is a **stallion** or **stud;** the young is a **foal** □ another name is **dam**

margarine *noun*
a butter-like spread made from vegetable oil

margin *noun*
1 an edge or border, such as the blank space beside the writing on a page
2 margin of error an extra amount allowed in calculations, such as of time or money, to cover mistakes

Word Building: **marginal** *adjective*
marginally *adverb*

marijuana (say *ma-rə-wah-nə*) *noun*
the dried leaves and flowers of the Indian hemp plant which contain a drug

marinate *verb*
to add flavour to a food by soaking it in an oily spicy liquid before cooking

Word Building: **marinade** *noun* the liquid used for marinating

marine *adjective*
1 having to do with the sea: *marine creatures*
marine *noun*
2 a soldier who serves on ship and on land

Word Building: **mariner** *noun* a seaman

marionette *noun*
a puppet which is worked by strings attached to its limbs

maritime *adjective*
having to do with the sea or shipping: *maritime law*

mark *noun*
1 something like a spot, line, scratch or stain on anything **2** a sign or label which tells something about an object, such as who made it or who owns it **3** a symbol, such as a letter of the alphabet, used to judge behaviour or work: *a good mark for an essay* **4** a target: *His arrow hit the mark.*
mark *verb*
5 to make marks on **6** to be a special feature of: *Violence marked the opening of the football season.* **7** to judge, by a number or other sign, the value of work: *He marks fairly.*

Word Building: **marked** *adjective* noticeable
markedly *adverb* **marker** *noun*

market *noun*
1 a place where things are bought and sold, often at many different stalls
2 the demand for goods: *There's no market for furs.*

Word Building: **market** *verb* to sell
marketable *adjective* easy to sell

marlin *noun*
a large powerful fish with an upper jaw like a spear

marmalade *noun*
a jam made of citrus fruits, such as oranges and grapefruit

Word History: from a Greek word meaning "honey apple"

maroon[1] (say *mə-rohn*) *noun*
a dark brownish-red

Word Building: **maroon** *adjective*

maroon[2] (say *mə-roohn*) *verb*
to put ashore from a ship and leave in a deserted place as a punishment

marquee (say *mah-kee*) *noun*
a big tent used for outdoor parties, circuses and so on

marriage celebrant *noun*
someone who is authorised by the government to marry people

marrow *noun*
1 the soft tissue inside bones which is important in producing red blood cells
2 a large white, yellow or green vegetable

marry *verb*
1 to join together as husband and wife
2 to take as a husband or wife: *My sister is marrying my best friend's brother.*

Word Building: other forms are **I married, I have married, I am marrying** □ **marriage** *noun* **marriageable** *adjective*

marsh *noun*
low-lying wet land

Word Use: other words with similar meaning are **bog** and **swamp**
Word Building: **marshy** *adjective*

marshal *noun*
someone who organises the activities at a show or other public occasion

Word Building: **marshal** *verb* (**marshalled, marshalling**) to organise in rows or ranks

marshmallow *noun*
a soft sweet made from gelatine, sugar and flavouring

marsupial (say *mah-syooh-pee-əl*) *noun*
a mammal such as a kangaroo which keeps and feeds its young in a pouch for a few months after birth

Word Building: **marsupial** *adjective: a marsupial mouse*
Word History: from a Latin word meaning "pouch"

martial (say *mah-shəl*) *adjective*
having to do with war or fighting: *martial arts*

martyr (say *mah-tə*) *noun*
1 someone who is killed or suffers a great deal for the sake of their beliefs
2 someone who goes without, just so that they can feel better than other people

Word Building: **martyr** *verb* **martyrdom** *noun*

marvel *noun*
something which causes delight and wonder

Word Building: **marvel** *verb* (**marvelled, marvelling**): *I marvel at your skill.*
marvellous *adjective* wonderful
marvellously *adverb*

marzipan *noun*
a sweet made of crushed almonds and sugar

mascara *noun*
a substance used to colour the eyelashes

Word History: from a Spanish word meaning "a mask"

mascot *noun*
something which is supposed to bring good luck

masculine (say *mas-kyə-lən*) *adjective*
having qualities thought to be typical of a male

Word Use: the opposite is **feminine**
Word Building: **masculinity** *noun*

mash *verb*
to pound down or crush

mask *noun*
1 a covering for your face, worn as a disguise or for protection

mask *verb*
2 to hide or disguise

mason *noun*
someone who builds or works with stone

Word Building: **masonry** *noun*

masquerade (say *mas-kə-rayd*) *noun*
1 a party at which the guests wear masks and fancy dress **2** a false outward show

Word Building: **masquerade** *verb*

mass[1] *noun*
1 a quantity of matter of no particular shape or size: *a mass of snow* | *a cloud mass* **2** a large number or quantity: *a mass of papers* | *a mass of water*
3 the amount of matter in a body
4 the masses the common people

Word Use: the plural is **masses**

mass[2] *noun*
a religious service in the Roman Catholic and some other Christian churches

Word Use: another spelling is **Mass**
Word Building: the plural is **masses**

massacre (say <u>mas</u>-ə-kə) *noun*
the killing of a large number of people: *Hitler's massacre of the Jews*

Word Use: a similar word is **carnage**
Word Building: **massacre** *verb*

massage (say <u>mas</u>-ahzh) *noun*
the act of rubbing and pressing the body, to relax or ease pain

Word Building: **masseur** *noun* a man skilled in massage **masseuse** *noun* a woman skilled in massage **massage** *verb*

massive *adjective*
large and heavy: *a massive load*

Word Building: **massively** *adverb*

mass media *plural noun*
radio, television, newspapers and magazines, by which information is passed on to large numbers of people

mass-produce *verb*
to make in large quantities with machines in factories

Word Building: **mass-production** *noun*

mast *noun*
1 a tall pole rising from the deck of a ship
2 any upright pole: *a radio-transmitting mast*

master *noun*
1 someone who has control or special skill: *He is a master of several languages.*
2 the owner of a dog or other animal
3 a male teacher, especially one who is head of a department
master *verb*
4 to get control of

Word Building: **master** *adjective* main: *a master plan* **masterly** *adjective* showing great skill **mastery** *noun*

masterpiece *noun*
the most excellent piece of work of an artist, musician or writer

masturbate *verb*
to rub the genitals to produce a pleasant sensation

Word Building: **masturbation** *noun*

mat *noun*
1 a piece of material of some kind used to cover the floor or part of it: *a bath mat / a rubber mat* **2** a small piece of cork or fabric for putting under a plate or ornament
mat *verb*
3 to make or become a thick and tangled mass

Word Building: other verb forms are **it matted, it has matted, it is matting** □ **matting** *noun*

matador *noun*
the bullfighter who kills the bull

Word Use: compare this with **picador**
Word History: from a Latin word meaning "slayer"

match[1] *noun*
a short thin piece of wood tipped with a chemical substance which produces fire when you scrape it on a rough surface

Word Building: the plural is **matches**

match[2] *noun*
1 someone or something that equals or looks like another in some way
2 a contest or game: *a football match*
match[2] *verb*
3 to agree exactly: *These colours don't match.* **4** to place in opposition: *They are matched in the semi-final.*

Word Building: the plural form of the noun is **matches** □ **matchless** *adjective* without an equal **matchlessly** *adverb*

mate *noun*
1 a friend: *Jim is a real mate.* **2** the male or the female of a pair of animals: *the fox and its mate*

material *noun*
1 the substance which is used to make something: *building materials* **2** cloth: *curtain material*
material *adjective*
3 existing in a form you can touch

materialise or **materialize** *verb*
to appear in a physical shape: *Her figure materialised out of the mist.*

maternal *adjective*
belonging to or like a mother: *maternal feelings*

Word Building: **maternity** *noun* motherhood **maternally** *adverb*

mathematics *noun*
the science dealing with numbers and the size of things: *Mathematics is fun.*

Word Building: **mathematical** *adjective* **mathematically** *adverb* **mathematician** *noun*

maths *noun*
a shortened form of **mathematics**

matilda *noun*
a swag

Word Use: this is used only in the expression "waltzing Matilda", meaning "going about as a swagman"

matinee (say *mat-ə-nay*) *noun*
an afternoon performance of a play or showing of a film

Word History: from a French word meaning "morning"

matri- *prefix*
a word part meaning mother: *matriach*

Word History: this prefix comes from Latin

matriarch (say *may-tree-ahk*) *noun*
a woman leader in a family, tribe or any field of activity

Word Building: **matriarchal** *adjective* **matriarchy** *noun*

matriculation (say *mə-trik-yə-lay-shən*) *noun*
an examination which must be passed before you can enrol at a university

Word Building: **matriculate** *verb*

matrimony (say *mat-rə-mə-nee*) *noun*
marriage

Word Building: **matrimonial** *adjective*

matron *noun*
1 a middle-aged married woman
2 the most important nurse in a hospital
3 a woman in charge of household arrangements in a school or other institution

Word Building: **matronly** *adjective*

matt *adjective*
having a dull surface: *matt paint*

Word Use: another spelling is **mat**
Word History: from a French word meaning "dead"

matter *noun*
1 the substance of which things are made **2** a particular kind of substance: *colouring matter* **3** an affair or subject: *a matter of fact* / *a matter of life and death*
4 trouble or difficulty: *What is the matter?*

matter *verb*
5 to be of importance

matter-of-fact *adjective*
ordinary, not excited or imaginative: *a matter-of-fact voice*

mattock *noun*
a tool for loosening the soil, like a pick but with a blade instead of a point

mattress *noun*
a soft and springy covering for the base of a bed

mature *adjective*
1 fully grown or developed: *a mature tree* / *a mature woman* **2** ripe: *mature fruit*
3 having the understanding and attitudes which an adult should have

Word Building: **maturation** *noun* **maturely** *adverb* **maturity** *noun*

matzo (say *mat-soh*) *noun*
a biscuit made of bread without yeast, eaten by Jewish people during the Feast of the Passover

Word Use: another name for bread made without yeast is **unleavened bread**
Word Building: the plural is **matzoth** or **matzos**

maul *verb*
to handle roughly

mauve (say *mohv*) *adjective*
light purple

maxim *noun*
a saying containing a general truth or rule: *"Look before you leap" is a wise maxim.*

maximum *noun*
the greatest number or amount possible: *The hall holds a maximum of 500 people.* / *The bottle is filled to the maximum.*

Word Use: the opposite is **minimum**
Word Building: the plural is **maximums** or **maxima** □ **maximise** *verb* **maximum** *adjective*

may *verb*
1 to be allowed to: *You may go now.*
2 could possibly: *They may arrive this afternoon.*

Word Use: this verb is a helping verb, always used with another one in the form **I may** or **I might**

May *noun*
the fifth month of the year, with 31 days

mayhem *noun*
disorder or confusion

Word History: from a French word meaning "injury"

mayonnaise (say *may-ə-nayz*) *noun*
a thick cold sauce made from eggs and oil and eaten with salad

mayor (say *mair*) *noun*
the head of a city or suburban council

Word Building: **mayoress** *noun* the wife of a mayor

maze *noun*
a confusing and complicated arrangement of many crossing paths or lines that you have to find a way through

Word Use: be careful – this sounds like **maize**

me *pronoun*
the form of the pronoun **I** you use after a verb: *Give me the book, please.*

meadow *noun*
a paddock

Word Use: this word is used mostly in England

meagre (say *mee-gə*) *adjective*
small or of poor quality: *a meagre meal*

meal[1] *noun*
food served at more or less fixed times each day: *Breakfast is my favourite meal.*

meal[2] *noun*
grain which has been ground or crushed

Word Building: **mealy** *adjective* soft, dry and crumbly

mean[1] *verb*
1 to intend or have the purpose: *I mean to talk to him.* **2** to signify or indicate: *"Vermicelli" means "little worms". / His arrival means trouble.*

Word Building: other forms are **I meant, I have meant, I am meaning**

mean[2] *adjective*
1 stingy or not willing to give anything away **2** nasty: *mean motives*

mean[3] *noun*
1 something halfway between two end points **2** an average

Word Building: **mean** *adjective*

meander (say *mee-an-də*) *verb*
to wind or wander about: *The river meandered through the valley.*

means *plural noun*
1 a method or way used to reach an end: *a means of transport* **2** a supply of money: *Our means are not enough for our needs.*

Word Use: although this is a plural noun definition 1 is usually followed by a singular verb

measles *noun*
a type of infectious disease with fever and a rash

Word History: from a German word meaning "a spot"

measure *noun*
1 the size or quantity of something **2** an agreed unit or standard: *A metre is a measure of length.* **3** a means to an end: *to take measures to prevent illness*

measure *verb*
4 to decide the size or quantity of, usually by using a special instrument such as a ruler or scales

Word Building: **measurement** *noun*

meat *noun*
the soft flesh of animals that is used for food

Word Use: be careful – this sounds like **meet**

mechanical *adjective*
1 having to do with or worked by machinery or tools **2** like a machine: *to answer in a mechanical way*

Word Building: **mechanic** *noun* someone who works with machines **mechanically** *adverb*

mechanise or **mechanize** *verb*
to change over to the use of machines in: *to mechanise the furniture industry*

Word Building: **mechanisation** *noun*

mechanism (say *mek-ən-iz-əm*) *noun*
a piece of machinery

medal *noun*
a metal disc or cross given as a reward for bravery or as a prize

Word Use: be careful – this sounds like **meddle**
Word Building: **medallist** *noun* someone who receives a medal, especially for sport

medallion *noun*
a large medal, or something shaped like one, used as part of a design such as on a building

meddle *noun*
to interfere with something that doesn't concern you

Word Use: be careful- this sounds like **medal**
Word Building: **meddlesome** *adjective* tending to meddle **meddler** *noun*

media *plural noun*
the means of communication, including radio, television, newspapers and

magazines: *The media have been full of the news of the floods.*

Word Use: this word is the plural of **medium** but is often used as if it were singular

mediaeval *adjective*
another way of spelling **medieval**

median *adjective*
coming in the middle: *a median strip on a six lane highway*

mediate *verb*
to come between people or groups who are arguing to try to get them to agree: *to mediate in a dispute*

Word Building: **mediator** *noun* someone who mediates **mediation** *noun*

medical *adjective*
having to do with medicine or its practice: *a medical examination | a medical book*

Word Building: **medically** *adverb*

medicine *noun*
1 a substance used in treating disease: *cough medicine* **2** the art or science of treating disease: *skilled in medicine*

Word Building: **medicinal** *adjective* (say *mə-dis-ə-nəl*)

medicine man *noun*
a man who has power over a tribe because they think he can do magic

medieval (say *med-ee-eev-əl*) *adjective*
belonging to or having to do with the Middle Ages, that is, from about the fifth to the fifteenth century

Word Use: another spelling is **mediaeval**

mediocre (say *mee-dee-oh-kə*) *adjective*
neither good nor bad: *mediocre abilities*

Word Building: **mediocrity** *noun* (say *mee-dee-ok-rə-tee*)

meditate *verb*
to think long and deeply: *to meditate on a problem*

Word Building: **meditation** *noun* **meditative** *adjective* **meditatively** *adverb*

medium *noun*
1 the way in which something is done or communicated: *a painting medium | an advertising medium | the mass media*
2 someone who claims to be able to communicate with the spirits of dead people

Word Building: the plural of definition 1 is **media** □ the plural of definition 2 is **mediums** □ **medium** *adjective* middle or average

medley *noun*
a mixture: *He played a medley of songs on his guitar.*

meek *adjective*
patient and obeying readily: *She was too meek to object to the unfair arrangements.*

Word Building: **meekly** *adverb* **meekness** *noun*

meet *verb*
1 to come face to face with: *I met Laura in the street. | I felt I could meet any objection.* **2** to welcome on arrival: *to meet a friend at the airport* **3** to come together: *The paths met near the river.*

Word Use: be careful – this sounds like **meat**
Word Building: other forms are **I met, I have met, I am meeting**

meeting *noun*
an arrangement to come together for a purpose: *a meeting of the chess club | a business meeting*

mega- *prefix*
a word part meaning great *or* huge: *megalomania, megaphone*

Word Use: another spelling is **meg-** □ compare this with **macro-**
Word History: this prefix comes from Greek

megalomania (say *meg-ə-lə-may-nee-ə*) *noun*
a mental illness in which the patients falsely believe they are great and powerful

Word Building: **megalomaniac** *noun*

megaphone *noun*
a funnel-shaped device for increasing or directing sound

melancholy (say *mel-ən-kol-ee*) *noun*
a feeling of sadness or depression

Word Building: **melancholy** *adjective*

melee (say *me-lay*) *noun*
a confused and noisy fight

mellow *adjective*
1 soft and rich: *a mellow voice | a mellow flavour* **2** softened by time: *a mellow attitude to life*

Word Building: **mellow** *verb* **mellowness** *noun*

melodrama *noun*
a play that is too dramatic to be real

Word Building: **melodramatic** *adjective*
Word History: from a Greek word meaning "music drama"

melody *noun*
a tune

Word Building: **melodic** *adjective* **melodically** *adverb* **melodious** *adjective* **melodiously** *adverb*

melon *noun*
a large juicy fruit with a thick skin

melt *verb*
1 to make or become liquid by heating: *Melt the fat in the pan. / The snow melted in the spring.* **2** to fade gradually: *The mountain ridge melted into the clouds.* **3** to fill with tender feeling: *His heart melted.*

member *noun*
1 each of the people forming a society, parliament or other group **2** a part of a whole, such as a limb of your body

Word Building: **membership** *noun: the membership of a club*

membrane *noun*
a thin sheet or film: *The eardrum is a membrane between the outer and middle ear.*

Word Building: **membranous** *adjective*

memento *noun*
something that acts as a reminder of what is past: *She gave them a book as a memento of her visit.*

Word Building: the plural is **mementos** or **mementoes**

memo *noun*
a shortened form of **memorandum**

Word Building: the plural is **memos**

memoirs (say *mem-wahz*) *plural noun*
a record of the life and times of somebody based on the personal experience of the writer

Word Use: a similar word is **autobiography**

memorable *adjective*
worth remembering

memorandum *noun*
a note of something to be remembered

Word Building: the plural is **memorandums** or **memoranda**

memorial *noun*
something to remind people of a person or event: *a memorial to Burke and Wills*

memorise or **memorize** *verb*
to put into the memory or learn by heart: *I finally memorised the poem.*

Word Building: **memorisation** *noun*

memory *noun*
1 the ability to store things in your mind and recall them when needed
2 something remembered: *a memory of home* **3** part of a computer in which information is stored until needed
4 in memory of to help people remember or remind them of: *a monument in memory of Captain Cook*

menace *noun*
1 something dangerous **2** a threatening attitude: *to speak with menace*
3 a nuisance

Word Use: definition 3 is more suited to everyday language
Word Building: **menace** *verb* to threaten

menagerie (say *mə-naj-ə-ree*) *noun*
a collection of wild animals in cages for show

mend *verb*
1 to make right or put into working order again **2** to get better: *His broken arm is mending.*

menial *adjective*
having to do with or fit for servants: *menial work*

Word Building: **menial** *noun* a servant

menopause *noun*
the time in a woman's life when her monthly periods stop altogether

Word Building: **menopausal** *adjective*

menstruate *verb*
to have a flow of blood and mucus from the womb, usually monthly

Word Building: **menstrual** *adjective* **menstruation** *noun*

mental *adjective*
having to do with the mind

Word Building: **mentally** *adverb* **mentality** *noun*

mention *verb*
to briefly speak or write about

Word Building: **mention** *noun*

mentor *noun*
a wise and trusted adviser: *Her father has been her mentor for many years.*

Word History: from *Mentor,* friend of the Greek hero Odysseus and guardian of his household when he went to Troy

menu *noun*
1 a list of the dishes served at a meal or in a restaurant **2** a list of options you can choose from when you are using a computer

mercenary (say <u>*mers*</u>*-ən-ree*) *adjective*
1 working or caring only for money: *She has a mercenary attitude to her art.*
mercenary *noun*
2 a soldier who is paid to fight in a foreign army

Word Building: the plural is **mercenaries**

merchandise (say <u>*mer*</u>*-chən-duys*) *noun*
goods for sale

Word Building: **merchandise** *verb* to sell **merchandiser** *noun*

merchant *noun*
someone who buys and sells goods

Word Building: **merchantman** *noun* a trading ship **merchant** *adjective*

mercury *noun*
a silvery metallic element which is liquid instead of solid at ordinary temperatures

Word Use: a similar word, now rather old-fashioned, is **quicksilver**
Word Building: **mercurial** *adjective* rapidly changing in mood
Word History: named after the planet *Mercury* because long ago the symbol for the planet was used for the metal as well

mercy *noun*
kindness shown by not punishing or not being cruel

Word Building: the plural is **mercies** □ **merciful** *adjective* **merciless** *adjective*

mere *adjective*
being nothing more than: *You are a mere child.*

Word Building: **merely** *adverb* only or just

merge *verb*
to unite or blend together: *The colours merged.*

Word Building: **merger** *noun* a joining of two companies in business

meridian *noun*
a line of longitude

meringue (say *mə-*<u>*rang*</u>) *noun*
a mixture of sugar and beaten egg whites used in cakes and sweets

merino (say *mə-*<u>*ree*</u>*-noh*) *noun*
a type of sheep that has very fine wool

Word Building: the plural is **merinos**
Word History: from a Latin word meaning "of the larger sort"

merit *noun*
1 excellence: *a painting of merit* **2 merits** the qualities or features of something or someone, whether good or bad: *Let's take each case on its merits.*

Word Building: **merit** *verb* (**merited, meriting**) to deserve **meritorious** *adjective*

mermaid *noun*
an imaginary sea creature, a woman from the waist up and a fish from the waist down

Word Building: **merman** *noun*
Word History: from the Latin word for "lake" added to the word **maid**

merry *adjective*
cheerful or happy

Word Building: **merriment** *noun* **merrymaking** *noun*

merry-go-round *noun*
a revolving circular platform with wooden horses or similar things on it, which people ride on for fun

Word Use: similar words are **roundabout** and **carousel**

mesh *noun*
1 a net or network: *nylon mesh for an insect screen / caught in the meshes of the law*
2 the space between the threads of a net, wire netting and so on: *This net has a wide mesh.*

Word Building: **mesh** *verb* **enmesh** *verb*

mesmerise or **mesmerize** *verb*
to completely hold the attention of: *The beauty of the scenery mesmerised him.*

Word Use: this word once used to mean **hypnotise**
Word Building: **mesmerisation** *noun*

mess *noun*
1 a dirty or untidy state **2** a difficult or confused state: *His life is in a mess.*
3 a dining room, especially in the army
mess *verb*
4 mess about or **around** to waste time doing useless things

Word Use: definition 4 is used only in everyday language
Word Building: **messily** *adverb* **messiness** *noun* **messy** *adjective*

message *noun*
1 information sent from one person to another **2** the meaning of something such as a book or what it tries to teach you

messenger *noun*
someone who carries a message

meta- *prefix*
a word part indicating change: *metabolism, metamorphosis*

Word History: this prefix comes from Greek

metabolism (say *mə-tab-ə-liz-əm*) *noun*
all the processes and chemical changes happening in your body or any living thing

Word Building: **metabolise** *verb* to change by metabolism **metabolic** *adjective*

metal *noun*
an element such as iron, copper or gold which is shiny, able to be shaped or worked, and is a good conductor of electricity

Word Building: **metallurgy** *noun* the study of metals **metallic** *adjective* **metalwork** *noun*

metamorphosis (say *met-ə-maw-fə-səs*) *noun*
a change from one form to another: *the metamorphosis of a caterpillar into a butterfly*

Word Building: the plural is **metamorphoses** □ **metamorphic** *adjective*

metaphor (say *met-ə-faw*) *noun*
a figure of speech in which something is spoken of as if it were something else: *"Knowledge is a key that opens many doors" is a metaphor.*

Word Use: compare this with **simile**
Word Building: **metaphorical** *adjective* **metaphorically** *adverb*

meteor (say *mee-tee-aw*) *noun*
a small rocklike object from outer space which enters the earth's atmosphere making a fiery streak across the sky

Word Building: **meteoric** *adjective* brilliant, fast or passing quickly, like a meteor **meteorically** *adverb*

meteorite *noun*
a mass of stone or metal that has reached the earth from outer space

meteorology (say *mee-tee-ə-rol-ə-jee*) *noun*
the study of weather and climate

Word Building: **meteorological** *adjective* **meteorologist** *noun*

meter *noun*
an instrument that measures, especially one that measures the amount of gas, electricity or water passing through it

Word Use: be careful – this sounds like **metre**

method *noun*
a way of going about something, especially an orderly way: *a method for doing a sum*

Word Building: **methodical** *adjective* **methodically** *adverb*

methylated spirits *noun*
a liquid used for cleaning and sometimes as a fuel

meticulous (say *mə-tik-yə-ləs*) *adjective*
careful about small details: *He was meticulous in his personal appearance.*

Word Building: **meticulously** *adverb*
Word History: from a Latin word meaning "fearful"

metre[1] *noun*
a unit of measurement of length in the metric system

Word Use: be careful – this sounds like **meter**

metre[2] *noun*
the regular arrangement of stressed and unstressed syllables in poetry

Word Use: be careful – this sounds like **meter**
Word Building: **metrical** *adjective*

metric *adjective*
belonging to the system of measurement based on the metre

Word Building: **metrically** *adverb* **metricate** *verb* **metrication** *noun*

metric system *noun*
a decimal system of measurement originally based on the metre

metronome *noun*
an instrument that can be set to beat at a fixed rate and so give the right speed of performance for a piece of music

metropolitan (say *met-rə-pol-ə-tən*) *adjective*
having to do with a large city

Word Building: **metropolis** *noun* (say *mə-trop-ə-ləs*) a large city

mettle *noun*
1 the quality of someone's character, especially when spirited or brave: *We need*

a lad of mettle for this job. **2 on your mettle** eager to do your best

Word Building: **mettlesome** *adjective* full of courage

mezzanine (say *mez-ə-neen*) *noun*
a balcony-like floor in a building, usually between the ground floor and the next

micro- *prefix*
a word part meaning **1** very small: *microbe, microcomputer* **2** making bigger or stronger: *microscope, microphone*

Word Use: compare this with **macro-**
Word History: this prefix comes from Greek

microbe *noun*
a tiny living creature which is so small that it can only be seen under a microscope, and which usually carries disease

microchip *noun*
a minute square which contains electronic circuits, used in a computer, watch, or electronic game

Word Use: the prefix "micro-" meaning "very small" indicates that this is even smaller than an ordinary electronic **chip**

microcomputer *noun*
a small computer that will fit on your desk, and is meant for only one person to use at a time

microfiche (say *muy-kroh-feesh*) *noun*
a sheet of transparent plastic about the size of a filing card which may have many pages of print on it that can be read with a special projector

microfilm *noun*
a photographic film with very small images which can be enlarged when projected and is used for storing information

microphone *noun*
an instrument which changes sound waves into electrical waves, often used in equipment that makes sounds louder or records them on a tape-recorder

microprocessor *noun*
the most important electronic chip in a microcomputer

microscope *noun*
an instrument used for looking at extremely tiny things that you normally can't see

Word Building: **microscopic** *adjective* extremely small
Word History: from the Greek word for "small" added to the Greek word for "view"

microwave oven *noun*
an oven which cooks food very quickly by passing high-speed waves through it

midday *noun*
noon or twelve o'clock in the middle of the day

middle *noun*
a halfway point: *the middle of the road | the middle of the discussion*

Word Building: **middle** *adjective*

midget *noun*
a very small person or thing

midnight *noun*
twelve o'clock at night

midriff *noun*
the part of your body between the chest and the waist

midwife *noun*
a nurse specially trained to help a woman while she is having a baby

Word Building: the plural is **midwives** □ **midwifery** *noun* (say *mid-wif-ə-ree*)

might[1] *noun*
power or force

Word Use: be careful – this sounds like **mite**

might[2] *verb*
could possibly: *He might be lost.*

Word Use: this verb is a helping verb, always used with another one. It is the past tense of **may.**

mighty *adjective*
1 powerful: *a mighty king* **2** huge: *a mighty forest*

Word Building: other forms are **mightier, mightiest**

migraine *noun*
a very bad headache which makes you feel ill

migrant *noun*
someone who leaves their own country to go and live in another

migrate *verb*
1 to change the place of living at regular times each year, as some birds do **2** to go to live in another country: *Many people have migrated from South-East Asia to Australia.*

Word Building: **migration** *noun* **migratory** *adjective*

mild *adjective*
1 gentle: *a mild voice* **2** not severe: *mild pain* **3** not sharp or strong: *a mild flavour*

Word Building: **mildly** *adverb* **mildness** *noun*

mildew *noun*
a coating or growth which appears on damp cloth, paper, leather and other materials

mile *noun*
a unit of length in the old measurement system, equal to about 1.6 kilometres

Word Building: **mileage** *noun*
Word History: from a Latin word meaning "a thousand"

militant *adjective*
fighting or ready to fight, especially for a cause: *a militant supporter of Aboriginal land rights*

Word Building: **militancy** *noun* **militant** *noun* **militantly** *adverb*

military *adjective*
1 having to do with soldiers: *a military hospital*
military *noun*
2 the military all the soldiers in a country

militia (say *mə-lish-ə*) *noun*
a group of part-time citizen soldiers

milk *noun*
the white liquid produced by female mammals to feed their young, especially cow's milk

Word Building: **milky** *adjective*

mill *noun*
1 a building with machinery for grinding grain into flour **2** a small grinding machine: *a coffee mill | a pepper mill*
3 a factory, especially one for spinning or weaving: *a woollen mill*

Word Building: **mill** *verb* **miller** *noun*

millennium *noun*
a period of 1000 years

millet *noun*
a cereal grain grown in Asia and southern Europe

milli- *prefix*
a word part expressing $\frac{1}{1000}$ *of a given unit: millibar*

millibar *noun*
a unit of measurement for air pressure, especially in the atmosphere

millilitre *noun*
a unit of measurement equal to one thousandth of a litre

millimetre *noun*
a unit of measurement equal to one thousandth of a metre

milliner (say *mil-ə-nə*) *noun*
someone who makes or sells hats for women

million *noun*
a cardinal number, one thousand times one thousand, 1 000 000 or 10^6

Word Building: **millionth** *adjective*

millionaire *noun*
someone who has a million dollars or more

millipede *noun*
a small creature like a caterpillar with a long body made up of many parts most of which have two pairs of legs

Word History: from a Latin word meaning "wood louse"

mime *noun*
1 a form of acting in which the actors tell the story by using movements of their body and face instead of words **2** a play in which the performers use this form of acting

Word Building: **mime** *verb*

mimic *verb*
1 to copy or imitate
mimic *noun*
2 someone who is good at imitating the voice and movements of others

Word Building: other verb forms are **I mimicked, I have mimicked, I am mimicking** □ **mimicry** *noun* (say *mim-ə-kree*)

mince *verb*
1 to cut or chop into very small pieces
2 to soften so as not to be so forceful: *to mince words* **3** to speak, walk or move in a dainty way
mince *noun*
4 meat that has been minced

mind *noun*
1 the part of you that thinks and feels, using judgment, memory and so on
2 intelligence, understanding or mental ability **3** memory: *Keep this in mind.*
4 your opinion or what you think or feel: *Feel free to speak your mind.*

mind *verb*
5 to look after: *Will you mind the baby?* **6** to dislike or feel bad about: *Do you mind the cold weather?*

Word Building: **mindful** *adjective* careful or aware **mindless** *adjective* senseless

mine[1] *noun*
1 a large hole dug in the earth to remove precious stones, coal and so on **2** a rich store of anything: *This book is a mine of information.* **3** a bomb placed underground or in the sea to blow up the enemy or their ships

mine[2] *pronoun*
one of the forms of **I** and **me** you use to show that something belongs to you: *That book is mine. | a friend of mine*

miner[1] *noun*
someone who works in a mine

Word Use: be careful – this sounds like **minor**

miner[2] *noun*
a type of bird with a yellow beak and yellow or yellow-brown legs: *noisy miner*

Word Use: be careful – this sounds like **minor**

mineral *noun*
a substance such as stone, ore or coal which is obtained by mining

Word Building: **mineral** *adjective*

mineral water *noun*
water containing dissolved mineral salts and gases

minestrone (say *min-ə-stroh-nee*) *noun*
a soup made with vegetables, herbs, pasta, and so on

Word History: from a Latin word meaning "serve" or "wait on"

mingle *verb*
1 to become mixed: *Her tears mingled with the rain on her face.* **2** to take part with others or to associate with: *She mingled with the rest of the guests.*

mini *noun*
1 *another word for* **miniskirt**
mini *adjective*
2 very small or miniature

mini- *prefix*
a word part meaning small *or* miniature: *miniskirt*

Word History: this prefix comes from Latin and is a short form of *miniature*

miniature (say *min-ə-chə*) *noun*
1 a very small copy or model of something: *Some model aeroplanes are exact miniatures of the real thing.* **2** a very small painting, especially a portrait
miniature *adjective*
3 on a very small scale or much reduced in size

minibus *noun*
a motor vehicle that is big enough to carry between five and ten passengers

Word Building: the plural is **minibuses**

minim *noun*
a note in music equal to half a semibreve in length

Word History: from a Latin word meaning "least" or "smallest"

minimum *noun*
1 the smallest number or amount possible: *You have to get a minimum of four points to qualify.* **2** the lowest number

Word Use: the opposite is **maximum**
Word Building: the plural is **minimums** or **minima** □ **minimise** *verb* **minimum** *adjective*

miniskirt *noun*
a very short skirt

Word Use: another word for this is **mini**

minister *noun*
1 a clergyman who conducts services in a church **2** a member of parliament who is in charge of a government department
minister *verb*
3 to give service, care or help: *He ministered to the sick people.*

Word Building: **ministerial** *adjective* **ministry** *noun*

mink *noun*
1 an animal that looks like a weasel and lives part of the time in water **2** the valuable fur of this animal

minor *adjective*
1 lesser in size or importance: *a minor share | His plan had only a few minor faults.*
minor *noun*
2 someone who is under the legal adult age

minority *noun*
1 the smaller part or number, or less than half **2** a group of people whose views are different to the views of most other people: *There will always be a minority which does not agree with the laws of this country.*

Word Use: the opposite of this is **majority**
Word Building: the plural is **minorities**

minor scale *noun*
any musical scale which has a semitone between the second and third notes

Word Use: such a scale is said to be in a *minor* key □ compare this with **major scale**

minstrel *noun*
a musician in the Middle Ages who sang or said poetry while playing an instrument

Word History: from a French word meaning "servant"

mint[1] *noun*
1 a herb with leaves that are used in cooking **2** a peppermint

mint[2] *noun*
1 a place where money is made by the government
mint[2] *adjective*
2 new or looking like new: *The second-hand car was in mint condition.*
mint[2] *verb*
3 to make money in a mint

minus *adjective*
having to do with subtraction or taking away: *the minus sign*

minute[1] (say *min-ət*) *noun*
1 a sixtieth part of an hour **2** any short space of time: *Wait a minute.*
3 minutes the official record of what has been discussed in a meeting

minute[2] (say *muy-nyooht*) *adjective*
extremely small: *She got a minute piece of dirt in her eye.*

miracle *noun*
1 an event which can't be explained by natural or scientific evidence or arguments: *The Bible tells of many wonderful miracles.* **2** a wonderful or remarkable thing: *It was a miracle that the lost child was found.*

Word Building: **miraculous** *adjective*
miraculously *adverb*

mirage (say *mə-rahzh*) *noun*
an illusion or false vision in which someone sees distant things as much closer than they really are, or even sees things that are not there at all

Word History: from a French word meaning "look at (yourself) in a mirror"

mire (rhymes with *buyer*) *noun*
1 wet swampy ground **2** deep mud

Word Building: **miry** *adjective*

mirror *noun*
1 glass that has been treated so that you can see yourself reflected in it
2 something that gives a true picture of something else: *This story is a mirror of my true feelings.*

Word Building: **mirror** *verb*

mirth *noun*
amusement and laughter: *The audience bubbled with mirth.*

mis- *prefix*
a word part meaning **1** failure: *misfire*
2 wrong: *mislay, mislead* **3** not: *mistrust*

Word History: this prefix comes from Old English

misadventure *noun*
1 bad luck or a piece of ill fortune
2 an accident or mishap

miscarriage *noun*
1 the failure to get the right result or decision: *a miscarriage of justice* **2** the birth of a dead baby, especially early in a pregnancy

Word Building: **miscarry** *verb* (**miscarried, miscarrying**)

miscellaneous (say *mis-ə-lay-nee-əs*) *adjective*
made up of a mixture of different kinds: *He kept a miscellaneous collection of items like bottle tops, pens and clips in his desk.*

Word Building: **miscellaneously** *adverb*
miscellany *noun*

mischief (say *mis-chəf*) *noun*
1 behaviour meant to tease or annoy
2 harm, injury or trouble

Word Building: **mischievous** *adjective* (say *mis-chə-vəs*) **mischievously** *adverb*

miser (say *muy-zə*) *noun*
1 someone who lives very poorly so as to save and store up money **2** someone who is mean and greedy

Word Building: **miserly** *adjective*

miserable (say *miz-rə-bəl*) *adjective*
1 very unhappy or uncomfortable
2 causing unhappiness or discomfort: *miserable weather* **3** mean and stingy

misery (say *miz-ə-ree*) *noun*
great unhappiness

Word Building: the plural is **miseries**

misfire *verb*
1 to fail to fire or explode properly
2 to go wrong or to fail: *His plan to take over misfired.*

misfit *noun*
someone who does not fit in or get along well in their job or with other people

misfortune *noun*
bad luck

misgiving *noun*
a feeling of doubt or worry

mishap (say *mis-hap*) *noun*
an unfortunate accident

mislay *verb*
to put in a place which you forget afterwards: *I have mislaid my pen again.*

Word Building: other forms are **I mislaid, I have mislaid, I was mislaying**

mislead *verb*
1 to lead or guide wrongly **2** to influence badly or to lead into error or wrongdoing: *His friends were misleading him into bad habits.*

Word Building: other forms are **I misled, I have misled, I am misleading** □ **misleading** *adjective* **misleadingly** *adverb*

miss[1] *verb*
1 to fail to hit, meet, catch, see, hear and so on **2** to fail to attend **3** to notice or feel sad about the absence or loss of: *She missed her sister when she went away.*
4 to escape or avoid

Word Building: **miss** *noun*

miss[2] *noun*
1 a girl or young unmarried woman
2 Miss a title put before an unmarried woman's name

missile (say *mis-uyl*) *noun*
an object or weapon that can be thrown or shot

missing *adjective*
absent or not found

mission (say *mish-ən*) *noun*
1 a group of people sent out, usually to another country, to do government or religious work **2** a duty someone is sent to carry out

Word History: from a Latin word meaning "a sending"

missionary (say *mish-ən-ree*) *noun*
someone sent out, often to another country, on religious work

Word Building: the plural is **missionaries**

mist *noun*
a cloud-like collection of water vapour, like a very thin fog

Word Building: **misty** *adjective* **mistily** *adverb*

mistake *noun*
1 an error or misunderstanding
mistake *verb*
2 to believe to be someone or something different: *He always mistakes me for my sister.* **3** to misunderstand: *She mistook my meaning.*

Word Building: other verb forms are **I mistook, I have mistaken, I was mistaking**

mister *noun*
1 a form of address for a man: *Hello mister, what's your name?* **2 Mister** a title put before a man's name

Word Use: definition 1 is more suited to everyday language □ **Mister** is usually written **Mr**

mistletoe (say *mis-əl-toh*) *noun*
a plant with small white berries which feeds and grows on the branches of other trees, and is often used for Christmas decorations

mistress *noun*
1 a woman in charge of a household, servants and so on **2** a female owner of an animal like a dog or a horse
3 a female teacher in charge of a particular subject or department at school
4 a woman who has a sexual relationship with a man who is married to someone else

mistrust *noun*
suspicion, or a lack of trust or confidence

Word Building: **mistrust** *verb* **mistrustful** *adjective* **mistrustfully** *adverb*

misunderstanding *noun*
1 a failure to understand correctly: *There seems to be some misunderstanding about the date of the birthday party.*
2 a disagreement or quarrel

Word Building: **misunderstand** *verb* (**misunderstood, misunderstanding**)

misuse (say *mis-yoohs*) *noun*
1 wrong use: *Misuse of some medicines can be dangerous.*

misuse (say *mis-yoohz*) *verb*
2 to use in the wrong way **3** to treat badly

mite *noun*
a tiny insect-like creature which lives in food like cheese or flour or feeds off plants and animals

Word Use: be careful – this sounds like **might**

mitre (say *muy-tə*) *noun*
1 the tall headdress worn by a bishop
2 the angle cut at the ends of two pieces of wood which are then joined together

mitten *noun*
a kind of glove which covers the four fingers together and the thumb separately

mix *verb*
1 to combine or blend together: *You can mix flour and water to make paste. / He mixes business with pleasure.* **2** to make by combining different things: *She mixed a cake.* **3 mix with** to be friends with or associate with

Word Building: **mix** *noun* **mixer** *noun*

mixture *noun*
something made up of mixed or combined things

mix-up *noun*
a muddle or confused state of things

moan *noun*
1 a long low sound of sorrow or pain
2 any similar sound: *the moan of the wind*
3 a complaint

Word Use: definition 3 is more suited to everyday language
Word Building: **moan** *verb*

moat *noun*
a deep wide trench or ditch, usually filled with water, surrounding a town or castle to help protect it from invaders

mob *noun*
1 a large crowd which is sometimes rowdy or violent **2** a group of friends
3 a group of animals

mob *verb*
4 to crowd around: *The fans mobbed the pop star at the concert.* **5** to surround and attack violently: *The people mobbed the bus and destroyed it.*

Word Building: other verb forms are **they mobbed, they have mobbed, they are mobbing**

mobile *adjective*
1 able to be moved **2** changing easily: *The clown had a mobile face which he could change from happy to sad.*

mobile *noun*
3 a hanging decoration made up of delicately balanced movable parts

Word Building: **mobility** *noun*

mobilise or **mobilize** *verb*
to get ready for duty or use: *The general mobilised his troops.*

Word Building: **mobilisation** *noun*

moccasin (say *mok-ə-sən*) *noun*
a shoe made completely of soft leather

Word History: from a North American Indian language

mock *verb*
1 to make fun of

mock *adjective*
2 being a copy or imitation: *mock battle*

Word Building: **mockery** *noun*

mode *noun*
a method or way: *a mode of travel*

model *noun*
1 an example used for copying or comparing: *Her work was used as a model by the teachers.* **2** a small copy: *a model of an aeroplane* **3** someone who poses for a painter or photographer **4** someone employed to wear and show new clothes to customers **5** a particular style or form: *This bike is the latest model.*

model *adjective*
6 excellent or worthy to serve as a model: *She was a model student.*

model *verb*
7 to form, shape or make: *He modelled a vase out of clay* **8** to be employed as a model

Word Building: other verb forms are **I modelled, I have modelled, I am modelling**

modem *noun*
a device that changes data stored in one computer into a form which can be carried over telephone lines to another computer

Word History: made from part of the words *modulator demodulator*

moderate (say *mod-ə-rət*) *adjective*
1 reasonable or not extreme: *a moderate request* **2** fair, average or medium: *a moderate income*

moderate *noun*
3 someone who is moderate in opinions or actions

moderate (say *mod-ə-rayt*)
4 to make or become less violent or severe

Word Building: **moderator** *noun* someone or something that moderates **moderately** *adverb* **moderation** *noun*

modern *adjective*
belonging to or used in the present time

Word Building: **modernise** *verb*

modest *adjective*
1 having a moderate opinion of yourself and your abilities **2** moderate or reasonable **3** behaving in a proper or decent way

Word Building: **modestly** *adverb* **modesty** *noun*

modify *verb*
1 to change a little bit: *He modified his plan to fit in with the new rules.* **2** to reduce or make less severe or extreme: *She modified her strong language.* **3** to limit or add more detail to the meaning of a word: *Adverbs modify verbs.*

Word Building: other forms are **I modified, I have modified, I am modifying** □ **modification** *noun: a modification to the house* **modifier** *noun*

modulate *verb*
1 to tone down or adjust **2** to change the pitch or loudness of your voice when you speak

Word Building: **modulation** *noun*

module *noun*
a part of something which can be separated from the rest and be used on its own

Word Building: **modular** *adjective: modular furniture*

moist *adjective*
damp or slightly wet

Word Building: **moistly** *adverb* **moisture** *noun*

molar *noun*
one of the large teeth at the back of your mouth used for grinding

Word Building: **molar** *adjective*

molasses *noun*
the syrup taken from raw sugar

mole[1] *noun*
a small spot, usually dark, on your skin

mole[2] *noun*
a small furry animal that feeds on insects and lives mainly underground

molecule (say *mol-ə-kyoohl*) *noun*
the smallest unit or particle into which something can be divided without changing its features: *A molecule of water has two hydrogen atoms and one oxygen atom.*

Word Building: **molecular** *adjective*

molest (say *mə-lest*) *verb*
to annoy or interfere with so as to hurt

Word Building: **molestation** *noun*

mollify *verb*
to make calmer or less angry: *He managed to mollify her with apologies.*

Word Use: similar words are **appease** and **placate**
Word Building: other forms are **I mollified, I have mollified, I am mollifying**
Word History: from a Latin word meaning "soften"

mollusc *noun*
an animal with a soft body, no backbone, and sometimes a hard shell, such as a snail or octopus

Word History: from a Latin word meaning "soft" (used about a thin-shelled nut)

mollycoddle *verb*
to treat too carefully or tenderly: *Her mother mollycoddled her even when she was a teenager.*

molten *adjective*
made into liquid by heat: *molten steel*

moment *noun*
1 a very short space of time: *I'll be there in a moment.* **2** the present or another particular time: *I can't come at the moment.* | *I was going out the door at that moment.* **3** importance: *This is a decision of great moment.*

Word Building: **momentous** *adjective* of great importance **momentously** *adverb*

momentary *adjective*
1 lasting for only a moment: *a momentary flash of light* **2** happening at every moment: *He lives in momentary fear of discovery.*

Word Building: **momentarily** *adverb*

monarch (say *mon-ək*) *noun*
a ruler of a country who inherits the position, such as a king or queen

Word Building: **monarchist** *noun* a supporter of the monarchy **monarchy** *noun*

monastery (say *mon-əs-tree*) *noun*
a place where a group of monks live and work

Word Building: the plural is **monasteries** □ **monastic** *adjective* having to do with monasteries or monks

Monday *noun*
the second day of the week

Word Use: the abbreviation is **Mon**
Word History: from an Old English word meaning "moon's day"

money *noun*
1 metal coins or banknotes **2** property or wealth: *That is a family with lots of money.*

Word Building: the plural is **moneys** or **monies** □ **monetary** *adjective*

money order *noun*
an order for payment which can be exchanged for money at a post office

mongrel (say *mun-grəl*) *noun*
a plant or animal, especially a dog, that is a mix of different breeds or kinds

monitor *noun*
1 a pupil who has particular jobs to help the teacher **2** something that keeps a check or gives warning **3** a kind of television set used in TV studios to check the quality of the broadcast, or with computers to display data **4** a kind of large lizard which is supposed to warn that crocodiles are near

monitor *verb*
5 to keep a careful check on: *We must monitor our spending.*

monk (rhymes with *sunk*) *noun*
a male member of a religious group living a life of religious devotion away from the rest of the world

monkey *noun*
a kind of animal that has a long tail and lives in trees in tropical areas

Word Building: the plural is **monkeys**

monkey-wrench *noun*
a spanner or wrench with an opening that can be changed so that it can be used on things of different size

mono- *prefix*
a word part meaning alone *or* single: *monologue, monolith, monotreme*

Word History: this prefix comes from Greek

monocle *noun*
a glass lens for one eye only

monogamy (say *mə-nog-ə-mee*) *noun*
marriage to one person at a time

Word Use: compare **polygamy** and **bigamy**
Word Building: **monogamous** *adjective*

monogram *noun*
a design made up of two or more letters, usually your initials

monolith *noun*
a single huge rock or stone, such as Uluru

Word Building: **monolithic** *adjective*

monologue (say *mon-ə-log*) *noun*
a long talk by one person

monopoly (say *mə-nop-ə-lee*) *noun*
the complete control of something, especially the supply of a product or service

Word Building: the plural is **monopolies** □ **monopolise** *verb* **monopolisation** *noun*

monotone *noun*
a series of spoken or sung sounds in one unchanging tone: *She spoke in a dreary monotone.*

monotony (say *mə-not-ə-nee*) *noun*
lack of change or variety producing boredom

Word Building: **monotonous** *adjective: a monotonous day* **monotonously** *adverb*

monotreme *noun*
an egg-laying mammal. The platypus and the echidna, found in Australia and nearby regions, are the only examples.

Word History: from a Greek word meaning "one hole" (their eggs and the waste matter from their bodies come out of the same opening)

monsoon *noun*
a strong wind of the Indian Ocean and Indonesia

Word Building: **monsoonal** *adjective*
Word History: from an Arabic word meaning "season" or "seasonal wind"

monster *noun*
1 someone or something that is frighteningly horrible or cruel **2** someone or something of huge size

monstrous *adjective*
1 huge or great: *a monstrous amount of money* **2** frightful or shocking: *a monstrous face* | *a monstrous idea*

Word Building: **monstrosity** *noun* **monstrously** *adverb*

month *noun*
1 any of the twelve parts into which the year is divided **2** a period of about four weeks or 30 days

Word Building: **monthly** *adjective: a monthly magazine* **monthly** *adverb: They come monthly.*

monument *noun*
1 something made in memory of a person or event, such as a statue **2** something from the past, such as an ancient building: *the monuments of ancient Greece*

monumental *adjective*
great in size or importance

Word Building: **monumentally** *adverb*

mood *noun*
the way you feel at a particular time: *You never know if she will be in a good or bad mood.*

moody *adjective*
1 angry or unhappy **2** changeable in mood or feelings

Word Use: a similar word to definition 2 is **temperamental**
Word Building: other forms are **moodier, moodiest** □ **moodily** *adverb* **moodiness** *noun*

moon *noun*
1 the round body that circles the earth every month and can be seen as a light in the sky at night **2** this body as it appears at different stages of the month: *the new moon* | *the full moon*

Word Use: the adjective from **moon** is **lunar**

moor[1] *noun*
an open area of damp wild land, usually covered with low, rough, plant growth

moor[2] *verb*
to make stay in the same position with ropes or an anchor: *to moor a ship*

Word Building: **mooring** *noun* **moorings** *plural noun*

moose *noun*
a large animal of the deer family

Word Building: the plural is **moose**

mop *noun*
1 a loose bundle of cloth or strings fixed to the end of a stick, and used for washing floors or dishes **2** a thick mass: *a mop of hair*
mop *verb*
3 to clean or wipe up with a mop or something similar

Word Building: other verb forms are **I mopped, I have mopped, I am mopping**

mope *verb*
to be in an unhappy mood

mopoke *noun*
a kind of owl found in Australia and New Zealand

Word History: named after the sound it makes

moral *adjective*
1 having to do with the knowledge of what is right and wrong: *This is a moral question.* **2** acting according to the rules of what is thought to be right, especially in sexual behaviour: *a moral person*
moral *noun*
3 the lesson taught by story or experience: *The moral is: "Slow and steady wins the race".* **4 morals** beliefs or ways of behaviour that have to do with right and wrong

Word Use: compare this with **immoral**
Word Building: **moralise** *verb* to make moral judgments **moralistic** *adjective* **morally** *adverb*

morale (say *mə-rahl*) *noun*
a cheerful and confident state of mind: *We must keep the cricket team's morale high.*

moratorium *noun*
any official delay, such as in making a political decision

Word Building: the plural is **moratoria** or **moratoriums**

morbid *adjective*
1 showing an unhealthy interest in gruesome things **2** caused by or having to do with disease

Word Building: **morbidity** *noun* **morbidly** *adverb* **morbidness** *noun*

morgue (say *mawg*) *noun*
a place where the bodies of dead people are kept until their funerals

Word Use: a similar word is **mortuary**

morning *noun*
the beginning or first part of the day, before noon

moron *noun*
1 someone with below normal intelligence **2** someone who is stupid

Word Use: definition 2 is used in everyday language and may offend the person it is used about
Word Building: **moronic** *adjective*

morose (say *mə-rohs*) *adjective*
bad-tempered or unfriendly because of unhappiness

Word Building: **morosely** *adverb* **moroseness** *noun*

morphine (say *maw-feen*) *noun*
a drug used to stop pain and to help you to sleep

Word History: from a Greek word for "the strange forms people see in dreams"; *Morpheus* was the Greek god of dreams

morse code *noun*
a system of signalling in which different groups of short and long sounds or flashes of light, called dots and dashes, stand for each letter in a word

Word History: named after Samuel FB Morse, the US inventor of the telegraph system and of morse code

morsel *noun*
a very small piece or amount

mortal *adjective*
1 having to die eventually: *All humans are mortal.* **2** causing death: *a mortal wound* **3** deadly or extreme: *a mortal enemy*

mortal *noun*
4 a human being

Word Building: **mortally** *adverb*

mortality *noun*
1 the condition of being mortal or human: *His death made me think about my own mortality.* **2** death or rate of death: *Child mortality is high in some countries.*

mortar[1] *noun*
1 a heavy bowl in which food or other substances are ground to a powder with a pestle **2** a short cannon designed to fire shells to a great height

mortar[2] *noun*
a mixture of lime or cement, sand and water, used for joining bricks together

mortarboard *noun*
a square-shaped cap sometimes worn by teachers and university students

mortgage (say *maw-gij*) *noun*
a promise that a property will be given over if a loan is not repaid to a bank or the like: *We have a mortgage on our house.*

Word Building: **mortgagee** *noun* someone to whom property is mortgaged **mortgagor** *noun* someone who mortgages property **mortgage** *verb*

mortify *verb*
to severely embarrass or hurt the feelings or pride of: *My mother mortified me by treating me like a baby in front of my friends.*

Word Building: other forms are **I mortified, I have mortified, I am mortifying** □ **mortification** *noun*

mortuary *noun*
a place where the bodies of dead people are kept until their funerals

Word Use: a similar word is **morgue**
Word Building: the plural is **mortuaries**

mosaic (say *moh-zay-ik*) *noun*
a picture or pattern made of small pieces of different coloured stone or glass

mosque (say *mosk*) *noun*
a Muslim place of worship

mosquito *noun*
a small flying insect, the female of which sucks the blood of animals and humans, and by this passes on some diseases, such as malaria

Word Building: the plural is **mosquitoes** or **mosquitos**
Word History: a Latin word meaning "fly"

moss *noun*
a plant with very small leaves that grows in patches on damp ground, tree trunks or rocks

Word Building: the plural is **mosses** □ **mossy** *adjective* (**mossier, mossiest**)

motel *noun*
a roadside hotel which provides accommodation for travellers and parking for their cars

moth *noun*
a flying insect, similar to a butterfly, that is active at night

mothball *noun*
a small ball of a chemical substance which is stored with clothes to kill moths

mother *noun*
1 a female parent **2** the head of a convent of nuns

mother *verb*
3 to be the mother of **4** to act as a mother to

Word Building: **motherhood** *noun* **motherliness** *noun* **motherly** *adjective*

mother-in-law *noun*
the mother of your husband or wife

Word Building: the plural is **mothers-in-law**

mother-of-pearl *noun*
the hard shiny lining of some shells, used for ornaments

motif (say *moh-teef*) *noun*
1 an idea that is repeated in various ways throughout a piece of writing or music or in the work of an artist **2** a part of a design that is repeated, such as in wallpaper

motion *noun*
1 movement or the power of movement **2** an idea put forward at a meeting to be voted on: *He moved a motion in Parliament.*

motion *verb*
3 to direct by a movement of the hand or head: *He motioned her to leave the room.*

motive *noun*
a strong reason for doing something: *Jealousy was the motive for the murder.*

Word Building: **motivate** *verb: Ambition motivates her to work hard.* **motivated** *adjective* **motivation** *noun*

motley *adjective*
made up of different parts or colours: *a motley collection of people*

motocross *noun*
cross-country motorcycle racing

motor *noun*
an engine, especially that of a car or boat

motorcycle *noun*
a large heavy bicycle with an engine

Word Use: this is also called a **motorbike**
Word Building: **motorcyclist** *noun*

motorist *noun*
someone who owns and drives a car

mottled *adjective*
covered with different coloured spots or patches: *a mottled book jacket | mottled skin*

Word Building: **mottle** *verb*

motto *noun*
a short saying, often taken as summing up the aims or beliefs of a particular organisation or group: *The motto of the scouts is "Be prepared".*

Word Building: the plural is **mottoes** or **mottos**

mould[1] (rhymes with *bold*) *noun*
1 a hollow form which gives shape to melted or soft material which hardens inside it: *a pottery mould | a jelly mould*

mould[1] *verb*
2 to give a particular shape or character to

mould[2] *noun*
a furry growth on something that is too damp or is decaying: *This bread has mould on it.*

Word Building: **mouldy** *adjective* (**mouldier, mouldiest**)

moult (rhymes with *bolt*) *verb*
to lose or throw off old feathers, fur or skin: *Some birds moult in spring.*

mound *noun*
1 a heap: *a mound of earth* **2** a small hill

mount *verb*
1 to go up: *She mounted the stairs.* **2** to get up on: *He mounted the horse.* **3** to fix on or in a position or setting: *to mount a painting on a wall | to mount a jewel* **4** to rise or increase: *Prices are mounting.*

mount *noun*
5 a horse for riding **6** a backing or setting: *We should put this photograph on a white mount.*

mountain *noun*
1 a large natural raised part of the earth, higher than a hill **2** something like this in size, shape or amount: *a mountain of reading*

Word Use: this is sometimes called a **mount**, especially in a name as in *Mount Kosciusko*
Word Building: **mountaineer** *noun* someone who climbs mountains **mountainous** *adjective*

mourn (say *mawn*) *verb*
to feel or show sorrow over, especially over someone's death or the loss of something: *He mourned the death of his wife.*

Word Building: **mourner** *noun* **mournful** *adjective* **mournfully** *adverb* **mourning** *noun*

mouse *noun*
1 a small animal with sharp teeth and a long tail **2** a small object which you hold and move to position the cursor on the visual display unit of a computer

Word Building: the plural is **mice** □ **mousy** *adjective* shy and quiet

moussaka (say *mooh-sah-kə*) *noun*
a dish from Greece, Turkey and other countries near them, with layers of minced lamb, tomatoes and eggplant, with a thick white sauce on top

mousse (say *moohs*) *noun*
a food made of whipped cream, beaten eggs, gelatine and a sweet or savoury flavouring: *chocolate mousse* | *fish mousse*

Word History: from a French word meaning "froth"

moustache (say *mə-stahsh*) *noun*
the hair that grows on the upper lip of a man

Word History: from a French word meaning "upper lip"

mouth (say *mowth*) *noun*
1 the opening in the face used for eating, drinking and talking **2** an opening in anything **3** the place where a river flows into the sea
mouth (say *mowdh*) *verb*
4 to move the lips as if talking, but make no sound

mouthful *noun*
as much as you can fit into your mouth at one time

mouth organ *noun*
another word for **harmonica**

mouthpiece *noun*
the part of a wind instrument which you blow into or the part of a telephone which you speak into

move *verb*
1 to change from one place or position to another: *to move the chair across the room* **2** to cause strong feelings in: *His sad story moved me.* **3** to make a formal request at a meeting **4 move in** to settle into a house **5 move out** to leave a house
move *noun*
6 a movement or change of position
7 a player's turn in a game: *Throw the dice and make your move.*

Word Building: **movable** *adjective*

movement *noun*
1 a moving or changing from one place or position to another **2** an organised group of people working towards a particular goal: *the movement against uranium mining* **3** one of the sections of a long piece of music: *This symphony has four movements.*

movie *noun*
another word for **film**

mow *verb*
1 to cut off or down: *to mow the lawn*
2 mow down to knock down: *The runaway car mowed down people on the footpath.*

Word Building: other forms are **I mowed, I have mown, I am mowing**

Mr (say *mis-tə*)
a title put before a man's name

Mrs (say *mis-əz*)
a title put before a married woman's name

Ms (say *məz, miz*)
a title put before a woman's name

Word Use: this does not indicate whether the woman is married or not

muck-up *noun*
a mess or muddle

Word Use: this word is more suited to everyday language
Word Building: **muck up** *verb* to behave badly

mucus (say *myooh-kəs*) *noun*
thick slimy liquid which builds up in your nose and throat when you have a cold

Word Building: **mucous** *adjective*

mud *noun*
wet, soft, sticky earth

Word Building: **muddy** *adjective* (**muddier, muddiest**)

muddle *verb*
to mix up or confuse

Word Building: **muddle** *noun* a confused mess **muddler** *noun*

mudguard *noun*
a cover for the wheel of a car or bicycle to stop mud and water splashing up

muesli (say *myoohz-lee, moohz-lee*) *noun*
breakfast cereal made from oats, chopped fruit and nuts

Word History: from the German that is spoken in Switzerland

muff *noun*
1 a rolled up piece of fur or woollen material into which you can put your hands to keep them warm
muff *verb*
2 to bungle or miss: *to muff an easy catch*

Word Use: definition 2 is more suited to everyday language

muffin *noun*
a flat cake which is toasted and eaten topped with butter

muffle *verb*
1 to wrap in scarves, shawls and other warm clothes **2** to deaden the sound of: *to muffle drums*

Word Building: **muffled** *adjective*

muffler *noun*
1 a device which fits onto the exhaust pipe of a car to deaden the noise of the engine **2** a thick warm scarf

mug *noun*
1 a large drinking cup **2** your face **3** someone who is easily fooled

mug *verb*
4 to attack and rob

Word Use: definitions 2, 3 and 4 are more suited to everyday language
Word Building: **mugger** *noun*

muggy *adjective*
unpleasantly warm and humid: *muggy weather*

Word Building: other forms are **muggier, muggiest**

mulberry (say *mul-bree*) *noun*
1 a tree which has sweet, dark-purple fruit like blackberries, and leaves which are eaten by silkworms **2** the fruit of this tree

Word Building: the plural is **mulberries**

mulch *noun*
straw, grass clippings, leaves or similar material spread on gardens to protect and feed the plants

Word Building: **mulch** *verb*

mule *noun*
1 the offspring of a female horse and a male donkey **2** someone who is stupid or stubborn

Word Use: definition 2 is more suited to everyday language □ the male is a **jackass**; the female is a **mare**; the young is a **foal**
Word Building: **muleteer** *noun* a driver of mules **mulish** *adjective*

mulga *noun*
1 a type of wattle tree found in dry inland areas of Australia **2 up the mulga** away out in the bush or outback

Word History: from Aboriginal languages called Yuwaalaraay and Kamilaroi

mull *verb*
in the phrase **mull over** to think about: *She mulled over the problem.*

mullet *noun*
a type of fish commonly found in the rivers and sea around Australia

Word Building: the plural is **mullet** or **mullets**

multi- *prefix*
a word part meaning many: *mutinational, multi-racial*

Word History: this prefix comes from Latin

multicultural *adjective*
having to do with a society which contains several large groups of people of different cultures or races

Word Building: **multiculturalism** *noun*

multimeter (say *mul-tee-mee-tə*) *noun*
an instrument for testing electrical equipment, which measures voltage, current and resistance

multinational *adjective*
involving many different countries: *a multinational business company*

multiple *adjective*
1 having many parts

multiple *noun*
2 a number formed by multiplying one number by another: *6, 9 and 12 are multiples of 3*

Word Building: **multiplicity** *noun* a large number

multiply *verb*
1 to increase in amount or number: *to multiply your savings by putting them in the bank | Rabbits multiply quickly.* **2** to add a number to itself a number of times to get a total or product: *Multiply 4 by 3 to get 12.*

Word Building: other forms are **I multiplied, I have multiplied, I am multiplying** □ **multiplier** *noun* a number by which another number is multiplied **multiplication** *noun*

multi-racial *adjective*
having people of many different races or nationalities: *a multi-racial society*

multitude *noun*
a great number or crowd: *a multitude of people*

Word Building: **multitudinous** *adjective*

mum[1] *noun*
another word for **mother**

mum[2] *adjective*
saying nothing: *to keep mum about the plan*

mumble *verb*
to speak softly and unclearly

mumbo jumbo *noun*
meaningless words, especially when thought to have a magical effect

mummy[1] *noun*
another word for **mother**

mummy[2] *noun*
a dead body that has been specially treated to stop it from decaying: *Mummies were found in the pyramids of Egypt.*

Word Building: **mummify** *verb* (**mummified, mummifying**)
Word History: from a Persian word meaning "asphalt"

mumps *noun*
a disease caused by a virus which makes the glands around your mouth and neck very sore and swollen: *Mumps is a disease which can be serious if not properly treated.*

munch *verb*
to chew noisily: *Cows munch grass.*

mundane *adjective*
ordinary or boring: *to lead a very mundane life*

Word History: from a Latin word meaning "of the world"

municipality (say *myooh-nə-sə-pal-ə-tee*) *noun*
a district which has its own local government: *The council collects the garbage from all houses in the municipality.*

Word Building: **municipal** *adjective: the municipal library*

munitions *plural noun*
weapons and ammunition used in war

mural *noun*
a picture painted on a wall or ceiling

murder *noun*
1 the crime of deliberately killing someone
2 a very hard or unpleasant job: *It's murder trying to comb the knots out of your hair.*

Word Use: definition 2 is more suited to everyday language
Word Building: **murder** *verb* **murderer** *noun* **murderess** *noun* **murderous** *adjective*

murky *adjective*
dark and gloomy: *a murky cave | murky water*

Word Building: **murk** *noun* **murkiness** *noun*

murmur *noun*
a whispering sound or conversation: *the murmur of the wind in the trees | the murmur of the children in school assembly*

Word Building: **murmur** *verb* (**murmured, murmuring**) **murmuring** *adjective*

muscle (say *mus-əl*) *noun*
1 one of the parts of the body which give it the strength and power to move
2 strength or force: *You need to put some muscle into sawing wood.*

Word Use: be careful – this sounds like **mussel**
Word Building: **muscly** *adjective* **muscular** *adjective* **muscularity** *noun*
Word History: from a Latin word meaning "little mouse" (because some muscles have the same shape as a mouse)

muse[1] *verb*
to meditate or be lost in thought: *to muse on what might happen*

Word Use: a similar word is **ponder**

muse[2] *noun*
one of nine goddesses who appear in stories of Ancient Greece and who were in charge of writing, painting and science

museum *noun*
a place where rare and interesting things are displayed

mush *noun*
1 something thick and soft like porridge
2 something very sentimental, such as a film or book

Word Use: definition 2 is more suited to everyday language
Word Building: **mushy** *adjective* (**mushier, mushiest**)

mushroom *noun*
a type of fungus shaped like an umbrella which grows very quickly in damp soil and which you can eat

Word Use: compare with **toadstool**
Word Building: **mushroom** *verb* to grow or spring up everywhere

music *noun*
1 sounds combined together using melody, rhythm and harmony to express ideas and feelings **2** written notes and signs which represent sounds which can be sung or played on a musical instrument

musical *adjective*
1 producing music or like music: *musical instruments | a musical voice* **2** fond of music or able to play an instrument or sing well

Word Building: **musical** *noun* a play or film with a lot of singing and dancing **musically** *adverb*

musician *noun*
someone who plays or composes music

Word Building: **musicianship** *noun*

music sticks *plural noun*
two wooden sticks which are hit together rhythmically to make music, often used in Aboriginal music

Word Use: they are also known as **song sticks**

musk *noun*
a strong perfume produced by a type of deer

Word Building: **musky** *adjective* (**muskier, muskiest**)

musket *noun*
an old-fashioned type of gun from which the modern rifle has developed

Word Building: **musketeer** *noun* a soldier armed with a musket

Muslim *noun*
a follower of Islam

Word Use: another spelling is Moslem
Word Building: **Muslim** *adjective: Muslim law*
Word History: from an Arabic word meaning "submission" or "someone who accepts Islam"

muslin (say *muz-lən*) *noun*
a soft, fine, cotton material

mussel *noun*
a type of shellfish which has two black shells hinged together and which you can eat

Word Use: be careful – this sounds like **muscle**

must *verb*
1 to have to: *I must tidy my room.*
2 to be definitely: *She must be nearly 90.*
must *noun*
3 something that is thought to be necessary: *This new book is a must for all children.*

Word Use: this verb is a helping verb, always used with another one

mustard *noun*
1 a yellow-brown powder made from the seeds of a herb, which is used as a hot spice in cooking **2 keen as mustard** very eager

muster *verb*
1 to gather into a group: *to muster sheep | The soldiers mustered on the parade ground.*
muster *noun*
2 a gathering up or rounding up into a group **3 pass muster** to come up to a certain standard: *Those dirty fingernails certainly won't pass muster.*

Word Building: **musterer** *noun* **mustering** *noun*
Word History: from a Latin word meaning "show"

musty *adjective*
smelling stale: *James opened the windows to air the musty room.*

Word Building: other forms are **mustier, mustiest**

mutate *verb*
to change or alter

Word Use: this is a scientific word
Word Building: **mutant** *noun* a new type of organism produced by mutation **mutant** *adjective*

mutation *noun*
1 a plant or animal which becomes different in appearance or nature because of a change in genes **2** the process of changing

mute *noun*
1 someone who can't speak **2** something which can be put in or on a musical instrument to soften the sound

Word Building: **mute** *adjective* silent **mute** *verb* **mutely** *adverb*

mutilate (say *myooh-tə-layt*) *verb*
to injure, damage or disfigure very badly

Word Building: **mutilation** *noun* **mutilator** *noun*

mutiny (say *myooh-tə-nee*) *noun*
rebellion against authority, especially of sailors or soldiers against their officers

Word Building: the plural is **mutinies** □ **mutiny** *verb* (**mutinied, mutinying**) **mutineer** *noun* someone who rebels or mutinies **mutinous** *adjective*

mutter *verb*
to speak or grumble in a low voice that is hard to understand

Word Building: **mutter** *noun*

mutton *noun*
the meat from a sheep

mutual *adjective*
shared or common: *our mutual friend*

Word Building: **mutuality** *noun* **mutually** *adverb*

muzzle *noun*
1 the jaws, mouth and nose of an animal
2 a small wire cage which can be fastened over an animal's mouth to stop it biting
3 the open front end of a gun

Word Use: a similar word for definition 1 is **snout**
Word Building: **muzzle** *verb*

my *pronoun*
the form of the pronoun **I** and **me** that you use before a noun to show that something belongs to you: *my new boyfriend*

myopia (say *muy-oh-pee-ə*) *noun*
a condition of the eyes which stops you from clearly seeing things in the distance

Word Building: **myopic** *adjective*

myriad (say *mi-ree-əd*) *noun*
a very great number

Word Building: **myriad** *adjective*
Word History: from the Greek word for "ten thousand"

myrrh (say *mer*) *noun*
a sticky gum which tastes bitter but which can be used to make incense and perfume

mysterious (say *mə-stear-ree-əs*) *adjective*
puzzling or full of mystery: *a mysterious smile*

Word Building: **mysteriously** *adverb*

mystery (rhymes with *history*) *noun*
something that is puzzling or secret or can't be explained: *the mystery of UFOs*

Word Building: the plural is **mysteries**

mystic (say *mis-tik*) *noun*
someone who prays or meditates in order to know the mysteries of God and the universe

Word Building: **mysticism** *noun*

mystify (say *mis-tə-fuy*) *verb*
to bewilder or puzzle

Word Building: other forms are **I mystified, I have mystified, I am mystifying** □ **mystification** *noun*

myth (rhymes with *pith*) *noun*
an ancient story about gods, heroes and supernatural happenings, which may try to explain natural events like the weather, sunrise and sunset and so on

Word Building: **mythical** *adjective: The bunyip is a mythical creature.* **mythology** *noun* all the myths of a particular culture **mythological** *adjective*
Word History: from a Greek word meaning "word" or "speech"

myxomatosis (say *mik-sə-mə-toh-səs*) *noun*
a very infectious disease which kills rabbits

nab *verb*
to catch or seize suddenly

Word Use: this word is more suited to everyday language
Word Building: other forms are **I nabbed, I have nabbed, I am nabbing**

nacho *noun*
a snack which consists of a small piece of tortilla with melted cheese on top, seasoned with chilli

Word History: from Mexican Spanish

nag[1] *verb*
to keep on finding fault, complaining, or making demands

Word Building: other forms are **I nagged, I have nagged, I am nagging** □ **nagger** *noun*

nag[2] *noun*
a horse, especially one that is old or worn out

Word Use: this word is more suited to everyday language

nail *noun*
1 a small metal spike, usually with a flattened end, used to fasten pieces of wood together **2** the thin horny end of your finger or toe
nail *verb*
3 to fasten with nails

naive (say *nuy-eev*) *adjective*
simple, innocent and ignorant: *a naive comment*

Word Building: **naively** *adverb* **naivety** *noun*

naked (say *nay-kəd*) *adjective*
unclothed or bare: *a naked body* | *the naked truth*

Word Building: **nakedly** *adverb* **nakedness** *noun*

name *noun*
1 what someone or something is called **2** reputation or fame: *She has made her name as a trumpet player.*
name *verb*
3 to give a name to: *They named the baby Egbert.* **4** to mention by name: *The report named three business people.*

Word Building: **namely** *adverb* that is to say **namesake** *noun* someone having the same name as someone else

nanny *noun*
a woman who lives in your house to look after your children

Word Building: the plural is **nannies**

nanny-goat *noun*
a female goat

Word Use: the male is a **billy-goat**; the young is a **kid**

nap *verb*
to have a short sleep

Word Building: other forms are **I napped, I have napped, I am napping** □ **nap** *noun*

napalm (say *nay-pahm*) *noun*
a substance which is mixed with petrol and used in flame throwers and fire bombs

nape *noun*
the back of your neck

napkin *noun*
1 *another name for* **serviette** **2** *another name for* **nappy**

nappy *noun*
a piece of cloth or a pad of paper tissue fastened round a baby's waist and legs to soak up its urine and contain the waste matter from its bowels

Word Building: the plural is **nappies**

narcissism (say nah-səs-iz-əm) *noun*
self love, especially love of your own appearance

Word Building: **narcissistic** *adjective*
Word History: from *Narcissus*, a beautiful young man in Greek myths, who fell in love with his own reflection in water and was changed into a narcissus plant

narcotic *noun*
any drug which can relieve pain and make you sleepy

Word Building: **narcotic** *adjective*
Word History: from a Greek word meaning "making stiff or numb"

narrate *verb*
to tell a particular story in speech or writing

Word Building: **narration** *noun* story-telling **narrative** *noun* a story **narrator** *noun*

narrow *adjective*
1 not wide: *narrow stairs* **2** only just succeeding: *a narrow escape* **3** small-minded and lacking understanding of other people or the world: *a narrow person*

Word Use: another word for definition 3 is **narrow-minded**
Word Building: **narrowly** *adverb* **narrowness** *noun*

nasal *adjective*
1 of or having to do with your nose: *a nasal spray* **2** sounded through your nose: *a nasal voice*

Word Building: **nasality** *noun* **nasally** *adverb*

nasturtium (say nə-ster-shəm) *noun*
a garden plant with red, yellow or orange flowers and round leaves

Word History: from the Latin name for "a type of cress"

nasty *adjective*
1 unpleasant or disgusting: *nasty weather* / *a nasty smell* **2** unkind or cruel: *She was very nasty to her little brother.*

Word Building: other forms are **nastier, nastiest** □ **nastily** *adverb* **nastiness** *noun*

nation *noun*
a large group of people living in one country under one government

Word Building: **national** *adjective* **nationally** *adverb*

nationalise or **nationalize** *verb*
to bring under public ownership or government control: *to nationalise the health system*

Word Building: **nationalisation** *noun*

nationalism *noun*
1 patriotism or love of your own country: *His nationalism took the form of singing bush ballads.* **2** a strong wish for the growth, freedom and independence of your country or nation

Word Building: **nationalist** *noun* **nationalistic** *adjective*

nationality *noun*
membership or connection that someone has with a country: *I have Australian nationality.*

Word Use: a similar word is **citizenship**
Word Building: the plural is **nationalities**

native *adjective*
1 of your birth: *your native land* **2** belonging to the place you were born: *native language* **3** belonging to the country it is in: *a native plant*
native *noun*
4 someone born in a particular place: *a native of Adelaide* **5** one of the people who have lived in a country for hundreds of years: *a native of New Guinea* **6** a plant or animal in its own country

nativity *noun*
1 birth **2 the Nativity** the birth of Jesus Christ

Word Building: the plural is **nativities**

natural *adjective*
1 found in or formed by nature: *a natural harbour* **2** inborn or given by nature: *natural talent* **3** real and without pretence: *a natural manner*
natural *noun*
4 a a note that is not a sharp or flat **b** the sign in music (♮) that is placed before a note to show it is a natural

Word Building: **naturally** *adverb*

naturalise or **naturalize** *verb*
to make a full citizen of a country

Word Building: **naturalisation** *noun*

nature *noun*
1 the world around us made up of earth, sky and sea, especially when untouched by human beings: *Lovers of nature enjoy bush-walking.* **2** the make-up and qualities of a person or thing: *She has a kind nature.* | *The nature of glue is to stick.* **3** kind or sort: *These books are of the same nature.*

Word Building: **naturalist** *noun* a person who studies nature

naughty *adjective*
badly behaved

Word Building: other forms are **naughtier, naughtiest** □ **naughtily** *adverb* **naughtiness** *noun*

nausea (say *naw-see-ə*) *noun*
a feeling of wanting to vomit

Word Building: **nauseate** *verb* **nauseous** *adjective*

nautical *adjective*
of or belonging to ships, sailors or sailing

Word Building: **nautically** *adverb*

nautilus *noun*
a kind of squid or octopus with a spiral shell divided into many sections

Word Building: the plural is **nautiluses** or **nautili**
Word History: from a Greek word meaning "sailor"

naval *adjective*
of or belonging to a navy: *a naval battle* | *naval uniform*

Word Use: be careful – this sounds like **navel**

navel *noun*
1 the small round hollow in the middle of your stomach, which was where the umbilical cord was attached when you were born **2 navel orange** a kind of seedless orange that has a hollow at the top rather like a navel

Word Use: be careful – this sounds like **naval**

navigate *verb*
to steer or direct on a course: *to navigate a ship*

Word Building: **navigable** *adjective* **navigation** *noun* **navigator** *noun*

navy *noun*
the part of a country's armed forces that is trained to fight at sea

Word Use: a similar word is **fleet**
Word Building: the plural is **navies** □ **naval** *adjective*

NB
short for nota bene, *Latin words meaning* "note well"

Word Use: this is usually used in writing to make you notice a particular piece of important information

near *adverb*
1 at or to a short distance: *Stand near.* | *Come near.*

near *adjective*
2 being at a short distance in place or time: *The shops are near.* | *Christmas is near.* **3** less distant: *the near side*

near *verb*
4 to come close or to approach: *We neared the wharf.* | *The storm is nearing.*

Word Building: **nearby** *adjective* near **nearby** *adverb*

nearly *adverb*
1 almost: *We nearly reached the top.*
2 closely: *nearly related*

neat *adjective*
1 tidy and ordered: *a neat room* **2** well thought out and put together: *a neat plan*

Word Building: **neatly** *adverb* **neatness** *noun*

nebula (say *neb-yə-lə*) *noun*
a cloudlike patch in the night sky, usually consisting of a group of stars

Word Building: the plural is **nebulae** or **nebulas**
Word History: from a Latin word meaning "mist", "cloud" or "vapour"

nebulous *adjective*
cloudy or vague: *a nebulous shape* | *a nebulous idea*

Word Building: **nebulously** *adverb*

necessary (say *nes-ə-se-ree*) *adjective*
1 unable to be done without: *Water is necessary for life.* **2** that must happen: *a necessary result of his illness*

Word Building: **necessary** *noun* (**necessaries**) **necessarily** *adverb*

necessity (say *nə-ses-ə-tee*) *noun*
1 something that cannot be done without: *A car is a necessity in the country.* **2** the state of being poor: *Necessity caused him to steal.*

Word Building: the plural is **necessities** □ **necessitate** *verb* to make necessary

neck *noun*
1 the part of your body that joins your head to your shoulders **2** any narrow connecting part: *the neck of a bottle | the neck of a violin*

necklace (rhymes with *reckless*) *noun*
a string of beads or other ornament worn round your neck

nectar *noun*
a sweet liquid produced by plants and made into honey by bees

nectarine *noun*
a kind of peach with a smooth skin

need *noun*
1 something that you have to have: *The immediate needs of the flood victims are food and shelter.* **2** an urgent want: *a need for food | a need for improvement* **3** a situation or time when you want something: *a friend in need*

need *verb*
4 to have a need for: *You need help.*
5 to have to do: *I need to cut my lawn.*

Word Use: be careful – this sounds like **knead**
Word Building: **needy** *adjective* (**needier, neediest**) **needful** *adjective* **needless** *adjective*

needle *noun*
1 a small, thin, pointed tool, usually made of steel and with a hole at one end for thread, used for sewing **2** a thin rod for knitting, or one hooked at the end for crocheting **3** a pointer on a dial: *a compass needle* **4** a thin tube sharp enough to pierce your skin, used for giving injections **5** anything sharp and shaped like a needle: *a pine needle*

negative *adjective*
1 saying or meaning no: *a negative answer* **2** minus or smaller than nothing: *a negative number* **3** having an excess of electrons: *the negative poles of an electric cell*

negative *noun*
4 an answer or opinion that says or means no **5** a photographic film which is used to make prints and has the light and dark of the picture reversed

Word Building: **negate** *verb* **negation** *noun* **negatively** *adverb*

neglect *verb*
1 to pay no attention to: *He neglected his piano practice.* **2** to fail to look after: *to neglect a dog*

Word Building: **neglect** *noun* **neglectful** *adjective* **neglectfully** *adverb*

negligee (say *neg-lə-zhay*) *noun*
a woman's dressing-gown, especially one made of thin material

Word History: from a French word meaning "neglected"

negligent (say *neg-lə-jənt*) *adjective*
careless or neglectful

Word Building: **negligence** *noun* **negligently** *adverb*

negligible (say *neg-lə-jə-bəl*) *adjective*
unimportant enough to be ignored: *The amount of wine spilt was negligible.*

Word Building: **negligibly** *adverb*

negotiate (say *nə-goh-shee-ayt*) *verb*
to arrange by discussion: *The government has negotiated a treaty.*

Word Building: **negotiable** *adjective* **negotiation** *noun*

neigh (say *nay*) *noun*
the sound a horse makes

Word Building: **neigh** *verb*

neighbour or **neighbor** (say *nay-bə*) *noun*
someone who lives near you

Word Building: **neighbourhood** *noun* **neighbourly** *adjective*

neither *adjective*
1 not one or the other: *Neither statement is true.*

neither *pronoun*
2 not the one or the other: *Neither of the books is written by him.*

neither *conjunction*
3 not either: *Neither you nor I know the true story.*

Word Use: definition 3 is always used with **nor**

neo- *prefix*
a word part meaning new *or* recent: *Neo-Gothic*

Word History: this prefix comes from Greek

neon *noun*
a gas which glows when an electric current is put through it, and so is used in lights

nephew (say *nef-yooh*) *noun*
the son of your brother or sister, or of your husband's or wife's brother or sister

nepotism (say *nep-ə-tiz-əm*) *noun*
the favouring of a relation or friend by giving them a job or promotion

nerve *noun*
1 a fibre or bundle of fibres that carries messages from your brain to other parts of your body so that you can move and feel **2** courage, especially when you are facing a difficult situation: *You need nerve to walk a tightrope.* **3 nerves** nervousness or shakiness: *I had an attack of nerves before the school play.*

Word Building: **nervous** *adjective* excited, uneasy or frightened nervously *adverb* **nervousness** *noun*

nest *noun*
a shelter built or a place used by a bird to lay its eggs and bring up its young

Word Building: **nest** *verb* **nestling** *noun*

net[1] *noun*
1 a material made of fine threads knotted or woven together with holes in between: *a mosquito net* **2** a fabric like this, made of cord or rope: *a fishing net* **3** a piece of net used in some sports, such as tennis

net[1] *verb*
4 to catch in a net

Word Building: other verb forms are **I netted, I have netted, I am netting**

net[2] *adjective*
1 not counting packaging: *The net weight of these baked beans is 250 grams.* **2** after expenses have been paid: *net profit*

Word Use: another spelling is **nett**

netball *noun*
a game like basketball played by two teams of seven players

nett *adjective*
another spelling of **net**[2]

nettle *noun*
1 a common weed with hairs on its leaves and stem, which cause a rash if you touch them

nettle *verb*
2 to irritate: *His criticisms nettled me.*

network *noun*
1 a netlike arrangement of connected lines or passages: *a network of drainage ditches* **2** a group of radio or television stations, sometimes having the same owner, that can broadcast the same programs **3** a system in which computers in different places, often quite far apart, can be linked together and share information

Word Building: **network** *verb* to link by computer network **networked** *adjective* linked on a computer network **networking** *noun*

neurotic *adjective*
on edge and behaving strangely, because of a disorder of the mind

Word Building: **neurotic** *noun* a neurotic person **neurotically** *adverb*
Word History: from a Greek word for a type of nerve

neuter *adjective*
being neither masculine nor feminine

neutral *adjective*
1 not taking one side or the other: *Sweden was neutral in the second World War.*
2 greyish or of no particular colour

neutral *noun*
3 a person or country that does not take sides in a war **4** the position of gears in a car where they are not ready to be driven by the engine

Word Building: **neutralise** *verb* to counteract or cause to have no effect **neutrally** *adverb*

neutron *noun*
a tiny particle which is part of an atom

Word Use: see also **electron** and **proton**

never-never *noun*
desert country where hardly anyone lives

new *adjective*
1 recently arrived, obtained or come into being **2** fresh or unused: *Turn to a new page.*

Word Building: **newly** *adverb* **newness** *noun*

news *noun*
a report of something that has just happened

newspaper *noun*
a publication printed on large sheets of paper, which is put out at regular times, usually daily or weekly, and which contains news, comment, feature articles, and advertisements

newt *noun*
a small animal with a long tail that can live both on land and in the water

next *adjective*
1 immediately following: *the next day*
2 nearest: *the next room*

next *adverb*
3 in the nearest place: *Can I sit next to you?*

next of kin *noun*
your nearest relation or relations

nib *noun*
the writing point of a pen

nibble *verb*
1 to bite off small bits from: *I nibbled the chocolate.* **2** to bite gently: *The fish nibbled the bait.*

Word Building: **nibble** *noun*

nice *adjective*
1 pleasing or delightful: *a nice day* **2** kind or pleasant: *nice people* **3** showing great accuracy, skill or exactness: *a nice analysis of the problem*

Word Building: **nicety** *noun* (**niceties**) a fine or small point: *the nicety of his argument* **nicely** *adverb* **niceness** *noun*

niche (say *neesh, nitch*) *noun*
1 a small hollow set into a wall: *A lovely statue stood in the niche.* **2** a place or position suitable for a person or thing: *Everyone has their niche in society.*

nick *noun*
1 a small cut or notch **2 in good nick** in good condition **3 in the nick of time** at the last possible moment
nick *verb*
4 to cut slightly **5** to steal **6 nick off** to leave or disappear

Word Use: definitions 5 and 6 are more suited to everyday language

nickel *noun*
a hard silvery-white metal

nickname *noun*
a name used instead of your real name

Word Building: **nickname** *verb*

nicotine (say *nik-ə-teen*) *noun*
a poisonous substance in tobacco

Word History: named after the Frenchman, Jacques Nicot, who introduced tobacco into France in 1560

niece (say *nees*) *noun*
the daughter of your brother or sister, or of your husband's or wife's brother or sister

nifty *adjective*
1 smart or clever: *a nifty trick* **2** stylish: *a nifty outfit*

Word Use: this is more suited to everyday language
Word Building: other forms are **niftier, niftiest**

nigger *noun*
a Negro or any dark-skinned person

Word Use: this word will offend people
Word History: from a Spanish word for **negro**

night *noun*
the time of darkness between sunset and sunrise

Word Use: be careful – this sounds like **knight**

nightcap *noun*
1 a drink, especially a hot one, you have before going to bed **2** a cap people used to wear to bed

nightingale (say *nuy-ting-gayl*) *noun*
a small bird known for the beautiful singing of the male, especially at night

nightly *adjective*
1 coming, happening or active at night: *a nightly visit*
nightly *adverb*
2 every night: *The play is performed nightly during May.*

nightmare *noun*
1 a very frightening dream **2** any very upsetting or frightening experience

Word Building: **nightmarish** *adjective*

nil *noun*
nothing: *The result of my efforts was nil.*

nimble *adjective*
1 able to move quickly and easily: *a nimble acrobat | nimble fingers* **2** quick in understanding: *a nimble mind*

Word Building: **nimbleness** *noun* **nimbly** *adverb*

nimbus *noun*
1 a rain cloud **2** *another word for* **halo**

Word Building: the plural is **nimbi** or **nimbuses**
Word History: from a Latin word meaning "rainstorm" or "thunder-cloud"

nine *noun*
the number 9

Word Building: **nine** *adjective* **ninth** *adjective*

nineteen *noun*
the number 19

Word Building: **nineteen** *adjective* **nineteenth** *adjective*

ninety *noun*
the number 90

Word Building: the plural is **nineties** □ **ninety** *adjective* **ninetieth** *adjective*

ninny *noun*
a foolish or stupid person

Word Use: this word is more suited to everyday language
Word Building: the plural is **ninnies**

nipple *noun*
part of your breast and in women the part from which a baby sucks milk

nippy *adjective*
1 very chilly or cold: *a nippy breeze*
2 active or nimble: *He's nippy on his feet.*

Word Building: other forms are **nippier, nippiest**

nit *noun*
1 the egg of an insect such as a louse
2 the young of such an insect especially when it is living in human hair
3 a foolish or stupid person

Word Use: definition 3 is more suited to everyday language □ sometimes **nitwit** is used for this definition

nitrogen (say *nuy-trə-jən*) *noun*
a colourless gas with no smell, which forms part of the earth's atmosphere

Word Building: **nitric** *adjective*

nix *noun*
nothing

Word Use: this is more suited to everyday language

No
short for **number**

no-ball *noun*
a ball bowled in cricket in a way not allowed by the rules and automatically giving the batsman a score of one run

noble *adjective*
1 belonging to the aristocratic or ruling class of a country: *a noble family* **2** having high principles: *He has a noble character.*
3 stately in appearance: *a noble monument*

Word Building: **nobility** *noun* aristocracy **noble** *noun* an aristocrat **nobleman** *noun* **noblewoman** *noun* **nobly** *adverb*

nobody *noun*
a person of no importance

nocturnal (say *nok-ter-nəl*) *adjective*
1 active by night: *Possums are nocturnal animals.* **2** done, happening or coming by night: *a nocturnal adventure*

Word Building: **nocturnally** *adverb*

node *noun*
1 a knot, lump or knob: *a lymph node in your body* **2** a joint in the stem of a plant, especially where a leaf grows

Word Building: **nodal** *adjective* **nodose** *adjective*

nodule *noun*
a small rounded mass or lump

Word Building: **nodular** *adjective*

noise *noun*
any kind of sound, especially a sound which is too loud or which you don't like

Word Building: **noisily** *adverb* **noisiness** *noun* **noisy** *adjective*

nomad *noun*
1 a member of a race or tribe that moves from one area to another hunting, food-gathering or grazing their animals **2** any wanderer

Word Building: **nomadic** *adjective*
Word History: from a Greek word meaning "roaming" (like cattle)

nominate *verb*
to name as a candidate in an election: *I nominated him as chairman.*

Word Building: **nomination** *noun* **nominator** *noun* **nominee** *noun*

non- *prefix*
a word part meaning not: *non-fiction, nonflammable*

Word History: this prefix comes from Latin

nonagon *noun*
a flat shape with nine straight sides

nonchalant (say *non-shə-lənt*) *adjective*
calm and not worried: *He faced the angry crowd with a nonchalant air.*

Word Building: **nonchalance** *noun* **nonchalantly** *adverb*

non-committal *adjective*
not showing your opinion or decision so that you won't be held to it: *a non-committal answer*

nonconformist (say *non-kən-fawm-əst*) *noun*
a person who refuses to accept the usual or expected ideas, customs or ways of living

Word Building: **nonconformity** *noun*

nondescript *adjective*
very ordinary-looking, without any easily recognised qualities

none (rhymes with *bun*) *pronoun*
1 not one: *None of my friends came to help.*
2 not any: *That is none of your business.*

Word Use: be careful – this sounds like **nun**

nonentity (say *non-en-tə-tee*) *noun*
someone of no importance: *He was a nonentity in the organisation.*

non-fiction *noun*
something written about real people and facts, rather than made-up stories

nonflammable *adjective*
not easily set alight or burnt

nonplussed (say *non-plust*) *adjective*
puzzled

Word Building: **nonplus** *verb* (**nonplussed, nonplussing**)

nonsense *noun*
words that are silly or without meaning

Word Building: **nonsensical** *adjective*

noodle *noun*
a type of pasta cut in long thin strips

nook *noun*
1 a corner, especially in a room
2 any small, private or hidden place

noon *noun*
midday or twelve o'clock in the daytime

noose *noun*
a loop with a sliding knot which tightens as the rope is pulled

norm *noun*
a standard or model that you judge everything else by

normal *adjective*
ordinary or usual: *the normal way of doing it / normal behaviour*

Word Use: the opposite of this is **abnormal**
Word Building: **normal** *noun: Everything is back to normal now.* **normalcy** *noun* **normality** *noun* **normally** *adverb*

north *noun*
the direction which is to your right when you face the setting sun or the west

Word Use: the opposite direction is **south**
Word Building: **north** *adjective* **north** *adverb* **northern** *adjective*

nose *noun*
1 the part of your face you use for breathing and smelling **2** a sense of smell: *This cat has a good nose for mice.*
3 turn your nose up at to reject something you don't like, especially when you really ought to be grateful

nose *verb*
4 to move or push forward: *The car nosed through the flock of sheep.* **5** to interfere or pry: *He likes to nose into other people's business.*

Word Building: **nasal** *adjective*

nostalgia (say *nos-tal-jə*) *noun*
a longing for the past and all the things that belonged to it

Word Building: **nostalgic** *adjective* **nostalgically** *adverb*

nostril *noun*
one of the two openings of your nose

nosy *adjective*
interested in things that aren't your business

Word Building: other forms are **nosier, nosiest** □ **nosily** *adverb* **nosiness** *noun*

notable *adjective*
1 worthy of noticing or important: *a notable success*

notable *noun*
2 an important person

Word Building: **notability** *noun* **notably** *adverb*

notation *noun*
a way of writing down things like music or dance by using signs or symbols, such as notes or lines to stand for sounds or marks to stand for movement

notch *noun*
a small sharp cut on an edge or surface

Word Building: the plural is **notches** □ **notch** *verb*

note *noun*
1 something written down as a reminder to yourself **2** a short letter **3** paper money: *a $10 note* **4** importance or fame: *The mayor is a man of note in our town.*
5 notice: *Take note of what I tell you.*
6 a musical sound, or the sign or symbol you use to write it down on paper

note *verb*
7 to write down **8** to notice or pay attention to

Word Use: another word for definition 3 is **banknote**

noted *adjective*
famous or honoured: *a noted author*

notice *noun*
1 a sign or note giving a warning or some information **2** a statement that an agreement of some sort is to end: *The landlady gave notice to her tenant to leave. / The boss gave a fortnight's notice to his*

workers because he was closing down.
3 interested attention: *The new film is worthy of notice.*

Word Building: **notice** *verb* **noticeable** *adjective* **noticeably** *adverb*

notify *verb*
to inform or tell, especially in an official way: *The School Committee notified the parents that the meeting time had changed.*

Word Building: other forms are **I notified, I have notified, I am notifying** □ **notifiable** *adjective* **notification** *noun*

notion *noun*
1 an idea, often not very clear in your mind: *I have a notion of what life in the year 2000 may be like.* **2** a foolish or fanciful idea: *He's full of notions about ways to make a fortune.*

Word Building: **notional** *adjective*

notorious (say *nə-taw-ree-əs*) *adjective*
famous or well-known for something bad: *He's a notorious liar.*

Word Building: **notoriety** *noun* **notoriously** *adverb* **notoriousness** *noun*

nougat (say *nooh-gah*) *noun*
a hard paste-like sweet containing almonds or other nuts

nought (rhymes with *fort*) *noun*
the symbol "0", or zero

noun *noun*
a type of word which names something, commonly divided into proper nouns like "Australia" and common nouns like "beauty" or "dog"

nourish (say *nu-rish*) *verb*
to give enough food to encourage or ensure growth

Word Building: **nourishing** *adjective* **nourishment** *noun*

novel[1] *noun*
a long imaginative story which fills a whole book

Word Building: **novelette** *noun* **novelist** *noun*

novel[2] *adjective*
new or different: *a novel idea*

novelty *noun*
1 newness or strangeness: *the novelty of going to the beach instead of to the mountains*
2 a new or different experience **3** a new or unusual article in a shop

Word Building: the plural is **novelties**

November *noun*
the 11th month of the year, with 30 days

Word Use: the abbreviation is **Nov**
Word History: from a Latin word for the ninth month of the early Roman year

novice (say *nov-əs*) *noun*
1 someone who is new to the type of work or job they are doing **2** someone who is living in a religious order for a time of testing before taking final vows

noxious (say *nok-shəs*) *adjective*
1 harmful or hurtful: *noxious gases*
2 declared harmful by law and meant to be destroyed: *noxious plants*

Word Building: **noxiously** *adverb*

nozzle *noun*
the end of a pipe or hose through which you can spray water

nuance (say *nyooh-ons*) *noun*
a slight variation of colour, meaning, expression or feeling: *The nuances of his voice showed his growing anger.*

Word Use: a similar word is **subtlety**

nuclear (say *nyooh-klee-ə*) *adjective*
1 having to do with or forming a nucleus
2 having to do with or powered by atomic energy **3** armed with atomic weapons: *America is a nuclear power.*

nuclear energy *noun*
another name for **atomic energy**

nuclear reactor *noun*
a machine for producing nuclear energy

nucleus (say *nyooh-klee-əs*) *noun*
1 the central part or thing about which other parts or things are grouped: *Helen and Conrad were the nucleus of a new rock band.* **2** the central part of an atom made of protons and neutrons

Word Building: the plural is **nuclei** or **nucleuses**

nude *adjective*
1 unclothed or naked

nude *noun*
2 an unclothed human figure, especially one that an artist has painted

Word Building: **nudism** *noun* **nudist** *noun* **nudity** *noun*

nudge *verb*
to give a small push to, especially with your elbow

Word Building: **nudge** *noun*

nugget *noun*
a lump of something, especially of gold found in the ground

nuisance (say *nyooh-səns*) *noun*
someone or something that's very annoying

null *adjective*
1 of no importance or use **2 null and void** having no legal force or effect: *The contract was declared null and void.*

Word Building: **nullify** *verb* (**nullified, nullifying**) **nullification** *noun*

nulla-nulla *noun*
an Aboriginal wooden club

Word History: from an Aboriginal language called Dharuk

numb (rhymes with *sum*) *adjective*
unable to feel anything: *His fingers were numb with cold.*

Word Building: **numb** *verb* **numbly** *adverb*

numbat *noun*
a small Australian marsupial, with a long bushy tail and a pointed nose, which feeds on insects

Word History: from an Aboriginal language called Nyungar

number *noun*
1 the sum or total of a collection of things: *What is the number of people coming?* **2** a collection or quantity, usually large: *A number of people came.* **3** *another name for* **integer** **4** *another name for* **numeral** **5** the particular numeral or figure given to something to fix its place in a list or series: *Our house number is 67.* **6** a song, especially on a concert program: *Hans will sing the next number.*

number *verb*
7 to mark with a number **8** to count saying the numbers one by one: *We numbered off as we stood in line.*

numberplate *noun*
a flat metal strip which shows the registration number of your car

numeral *noun*
a letter or figure, or a group of letters or figures, which represent a number: *The number of days in the week is expressed by the numeral 7.*

Word Use: Roman numerals are given at the back of this dictionary
Word Building: **numeral** *adjective*

numerate *adjective*
having basic skills in maths

Word Building: **numeracy** *noun*

numerator *noun*
the number which is written above the line in a fraction to show how many parts of the whole are taken: *In the fraction* $\frac{3}{4}$, *3 is the numerator.*

Word Use: compare this with **denominator**

numerical (say *nyooh-me-rik-l*) *adjective*
having to do with numbers

Word Building: **numerically** *adverb*

numerous *adjective*
very many: *Numerous people went to the concert.*

nun *noun*
a woman who has given herself up to a religious life, usually in a convent

Word Use: be careful – this sounds like **none**
Word Building: **nunnery** *noun* a convent

nuptial (say *nup-shəl*) *adjective*
having to do with marriage or the marriage ceremony: *nuptial vows*

Word Building: **nuptials** *noun* a marriage or wedding ceremony

nurse *noun*
1 someone who looks after sick people, usually in a hospital **2** a woman employed to care for children

nurse *verb*
3 to look after in time of sickness: *to nurse a patient* **4** to hold in your arms: *to nurse a baby* **5** to look after carefully so as to help growth: *to nurse seedlings | to nurse an ambition* **6** to breastfeed: *She nursed her baby until he was one year old.*

Word Use: other words for definition 2 are **nursemaid** and **nanny**

nursery *noun*
1 a room or place for babies **2** a school for very young children **3** a place where young plants can be bought

Word Building: the plural is **nurseries**

nursery rhyme *noun*
a short simple poem or song for young children

nurture (say *ner-chə*) *verb*
to feed and look after when young: *to nurture children*

Word Building: **nurture** *noun*

nut *noun*
1 a dry fruit consisting of a kernel that you can eat inside a hard shell **2** the kernel itself **3** a small metal block with a hole which has a thread in it, enabling it to be screwed on the end of a bolt **4** your head **5** someone who is odd or foolish

Word Use: definitions 4 and 5 are more suited to everyday language

nutmeg *noun*
a spice made from the seed of a tree that grows in tropical countries

nutrient (say *nyooh-tree-ənt*) *noun*
a substance that provides food and energy: *Vitamins and minerals are important nutrients.*

Word Building: **nutrient** *adjective*

nutrition (say *nyooh-trish-ən*) *noun*
1 eating or eating habits: *healthy nutrition* **2** the process by which food is changed to nourish our bodies

Word Building: **nutritionist** *noun* **nutritious** *adjective*

nuzzle *verb*
to touch or rub with the nose: *The horse nuzzled me as I walked past.*

nylon *noun*
a strong material made from coal, which gives elastic threads that are useful in making fabrics or bristles and so on

Word Building: **nylons** *plural noun* stockings made out of nylon
Word History: this is a trademark

nymph (say *nimf*) *noun*
1 a goddess, pictured as a beautiful young woman living in the sea, woods or mountains **2** a young wingless insect

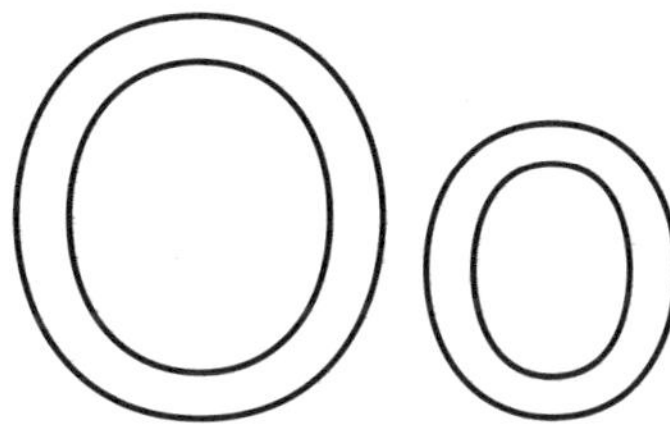

oaf *noun*
someone who is clumsy, stupid or rude

Word Building: **oafish** *adjective: oafish behaviour*
Word History: from an Old English word meaning "elf"

oak *noun*
a tree that bears acorns and is famous for its hard wood

Word Building: **oaken** *adjective* made of oak

oar (rhymes with *for*) *noun*
a long pole with a wide flattened end, used for rowing a boat

Word Use: be careful – this sounds like **or** and **ore**

oasis (say *oh-ay-səs*) *noun*
a place in the desert where there is water and trees can grow

Word Building: the plural is **oases**

oath *noun*
1 a promise you make, such as in a court of law, that what you say will be true: *She said it under oath.* **2** a saying which uses God's name or anything holy to give importance to your words

Word Use: an oath can offend people when it is done in anger or for silly reasons □ compare with **swear**

oats *plural noun*
a cereal which is used to make porridge and to feed horses: *Give the horses some oats.*

obedient *adjective*
following someone else's wishes or commands: *an obedient dog*

Word Building: **obedience** *noun* **obediently** *adverb*

obelisk *noun*
a tall pillar of stone, put up as a monument

Word History: from a Greek word meaning "a pointed pillar"

obese (say *oh-bees*) *adjective*
very fat

Word Building: **obesely** *adverb* **obesity** *noun*

obey (say *oh-bay*) *verb*
to do as you are told

obituary (say *ə-bit-chə-ree*) *noun*
a notice, usually in a newspaper, saying that someone has died and which often includes a short account of their life and achievements

object (say *ob-jekt*) *noun*
1 something which can be seen or felt: *The shelf was crowded with objects.* **2** the reason or purpose: *What is the real object of his visit?* **3** the person or thing which receives the action of a verb, as "ball" does in *He hit the ball.*

object (say *əb-jekt*) *verb*
4 object to a to say you don't like, or that you disapprove of, something: *I object to that idea.* **b** to argue against: *He objected to a picnic being held on a rainy day.*

Word Building: **objector** *noun* someone who objects

objection *noun*
an argument against something

objectionable *adjective*
unpleasant or offensive: *objectionable behaviour*

Word Building: **objectionably** *adverb*

objective *noun*
1 something to work towards: *Their objective is to grow all the food they need.*
objective *adjective*
2 real and not just in your mind: *Unicorns belong to the world of myth, not to the objective world.* **3** fair and free of prejudice: *He finds it hard to be objective.*

Word Use: the opposite of definition 2 is **subjective**
Word Building: **objectively** *adverb* **objectivity** *noun*

objective case *noun*
the form of a noun or pronoun which shows it is the object of a verb, such as "him" in *I can hear him.*

obligation *noun*
something which should be done out of duty or gratitude: *You have an obligation to be obedient to your parents.*

Word Building: **obligatory** *adjective* required

oblige (say *ə-bluyj*) *verb*
1 be obliged to to have to, out of duty or need, or by law: *He was obliged to change the tyre.* **2 be obliged** to be grateful for someone's kindness: *I am deeply obliged to you.* **3** to do a favour: *He will oblige.*

Word Building: **obliging** *adjective* **obligingly** *adverb*
Word History: from a Latin word meaning "bind" or "tie around"

oblique (say *ə-bleek*) *adjective*
1 indirect: *There was only an oblique reference to what had happened.* **2** slanting or sloping: *an oblique line*

Word Building: **obliquely** *adverb*

obliterate *verb*
to wipe out or destroy: *The waves obliterated their footprints.*

Word Building: **obliteration** *noun*

oblivious *adjective*
1 forgetful or not remembering: *oblivious of her promise* **2 oblivious of** not noticing: *oblivious of the cold*

Word Building: **oblivion** *noun* **obliviously** *adverb*

oblong *noun*
a rectangle with two sides longer than the opposite two

Word Building: **oblong** *adjective: an oblong box*

obnoxious (say *əb-nok-shəs*) *adjective*
disagreeable or nasty: *an obnoxious person*

Word Building: **obnoxiously** *adverb*
Word History: from a Latin word meaning "exposed to harm"

oboe *noun*
a tube-shaped woodwind instrument with a double reed that you blow through

Word Building: **oboist** *noun*

obscene (say *əb-seen*) *adjective*
indecent or disgusting: *obscene violence*

Word Building: **obscenity** *noun* (**obscenities**) **obscenely** *adverb*

obscure *adjective*
1 dark or shadowy: *an obscure corner*
2 uncertain or unclear: *obscure meaning*

Word Building: **obscure** *verb* to darken **obscurity** *noun* **obscurely** *adverb*

observant *adjective*
watchful or alert: *The observant child noticed where the sweets were kept.*

Word Building: **observantly** *adverb*

observatory *noun*
a building equipped with powerful telescopes for observing the stars, planets and weather patterns

Word Building: the plural is **observatories**

observe *verb*
1 to see, notice or watch: *Observe the detail. / He just goes along to observe.*
2 to study: *He's observing the bird life.*
3 to keep or follow: *Observe the rules.*
4 to comment or remark: *"You're quite late", she observed.*

Word Building: **observation** *noun* **observer** *noun*

obsession *noun*
a strong idea or feeling which controls someone's behaviour

Word Building: **obsess** *verb* **obsessed** *adjective* **obsessive** *adjective* **obsessively** *adverb*

obsolete *adjective*
out of date: *an obsolete weapon*

Word Building: **obsolescent** *adjective* going out of date **obsolescence** *noun*

obstacle *noun*
something which is in your way or which holds you up

obstetrics *noun*
the type of medical practice that is concerned with caring for pregnant women before, during and after the birth of their babies

Word Building: **obstetric** *adjective* **obstetrician** *noun*

obstinate *adjective*
stubborn or not willing to change your mind, even though you may be wrong

Word Building: **obstinacy** *noun* **obstinately** *adverb*

obstreperous *adjective*
resisting control in a noisy way: *obstreperous behaviour / obstreperous children*

Word Building: **obstreperously** *adverb*

obstruct *verb*
1 to block or close off: *A landslide obstructed the road.* **2** to prevent or make difficult: *She obstructed our efforts to open the gate.*

Word Building: **obstruction** *noun* a blockage

obtain *verb*
to get or acquire: *She managed to obtain fresh bread.*

obtuse *adjective*
1 stupid or slow to understand **2** having more than 90°and less than 180°: *an obtuse angle*

Word Building: **obtusely** *adverb* **obtuseness** *noun*

obvious *adjective*
clearly understood or seen

Word Building: **obviously** *adverb* clearly
Word History: from a Latin word meaning "in the way" or "meeting"

occasion *noun*
1 a particular time or event: *He remembers the occasion when he met you.*
2 an opportunity: *I want to take the occasion to thank him.*

Word Building: **occasion** *verb* to give cause for or bring about

occasional *adjective*
happening sometimes: *occasional showers*

Word Use: a similar word is **sporadic**
Word Building: **occasionally** *adverb* sometimes

occult (say *ok-ult*) *adjective*
having to do with so-called sciences, such as magic or astrology, which say they use secret ways to gain knowledge

occupant *noun*
someone who lives in or occupies a house or a room

Word Building: **occupancy** *noun*

occupation *noun*
1 your usual job or employment: *What is her occupation?* **2** the possession of a place, either legally or illegally: *The tenant is in occupation.* **3** the taking over of a country by force

occupy *verb*
1 to fill or pass: *How does he occupy his time?* **2** to be in or live in: *Who occupies the house?* **3** to seize or possess by force: *to occupy a country*

Word Building: other forms are **I occupied, I have occupied, I am occupying**

occur *verb*
1 to happen: *The incident occurred yesterday.* **2 occur to** to come into the mind of: *It occurs to me that you might not want to come.*

Word Building: other forms are **it occurred, it has occurred, it was occurring** □ **occurrence** *noun*

ocean (say *oh-shən*) *noun*
one of the large areas of salt water between continents, such as the Atlantic Ocean or the Pacific Ocean

Word Building: **oceanic** *adjective*

ochre (say *oh-kə*) *noun*
a yellowish clay used in paints and dyes

ocker *noun*
1 the Australian working man thought of as not having much education and with rather rough manners **2** an Australian man who has the qualities that people think of as being Australian, such as good humour, helpfulness, and being able to overcome difficulties

Word Use: another spelling is **okker** □ this word is more suited to everyday language
Word Building: **ocker** *adjective* very Australian: *an ocker sense of humour*

o'clock *adverb*
of or by the clock: *It will be twelve o'clock in five minutes.*

octagon *noun*
a flat shape with eight straight sides

octave (say *ok-tiv*) *noun*
1 the eight note distance between two musical notes of the same name but different pitch **2** these two notes played together

octet *noun*
1 a group of eight **2** a piece of music for eight voices or eight performers

October *noun*
the tenth month of the year, with 31 days

Word Use: the abbreviation is **Oct**
Word History: from the Latin name for the eighth month of the early Roman year

octopus *noun*
a soft-bodied sea animal which has eight arms with suckers on them

Word Building: the plural is **octopuses** or **octopi**
Word History: from a Greek word meaning "eight-footed"

odd *adjective*
1 strange or unusual: *odd behaviour*
2 unable to be exactly divided by two: *Seven is an odd number, and eight is an even number.* **3** part-time or casual: *odd jobs*
4 not matching, or left over: *odd socks | an odd glove*

Word Building: **oddity** *noun* (**oddities**)
oddly *adverb*

odds *plural noun*
1 the chances of something happening, such as a horse winning a race: *The odds are five to one on Black Prince. | The odds are against you.* **2 at odds** in disagreement: *They are always at odds.*

ode *noun*
a song or poem praising something: *an ode to love*

odious *adjective*
hateful or disgusting: *He's an odious character.*

Word Building: **odium** *noun* hatred

odour or **odor** *noun*
a smell: *an unpleasant odour*

oesophagus (say *ə-sof-ə-gəs*) *noun*
the tube that connects the back of your mouth with your stomach

Word Use: another spelling is **esophagus** □ another name is **gullet**
Word Building: the plural is **oesophagi** (say *ə-sof-ə-guy*) □ **oesophageal** *adjective*

offal *noun*
animal intestines and other parts which are thrown away, or other organs such as the brain, liver and tripe which are used as food

off-colour or **off-color** *adjective*
1 unwell or sick **2** in bad taste: *an off-colour joke*

offence *noun*
1 a wrongdoing or crime: *a traffic offence*
2 an insult, or other wrong: *an offence against decency*

offend *verb*
1 to annoy or displease **2** to do wrong or commit a crime

Word Building: **offender** *noun*

offensive *adjective*
1 displeasing or disgusting: *an offensive book | an offensive smell* **2** insulting: *an offensive gesture* **3** attacking: *offensive movements*

Word Building: **offensive** *noun* an attack
offensively *adverb*

offer *verb*
1 to put forward hoping that it will be accepted: *She offered the plate of cakes.*
2 to show willingness: *She offered to help.*
3 to bid or suggest: *He is offering $100.*

offer *noun*
4 a suggestion or proposal: *an offer of marriage | an offer of $10*

Word Building: **offering** *noun* something offered

offhand *adjective*
vague or casual, sometimes in a rude way: *He nodded in an offhand manner.*

office *noun*
1 a place where you work or do business
2 a place where you go to buy tickets or get information **3** rank or duty: *She holds the office of deputy manager.*

Word Building: **officiate** *verb* to do the duties of any office

officer *noun*
1 someone who holds a rank in the army, navy, air force or police force **2** someone chosen to do an important job in a particular organisation: *The society has to elect its officers.*

official (say (*ə-fish-əl*) *noun*
1 someone with a rank or who has authority to do a particular job

official *adjective*
2 properly approved or arranged: *an official statement*

Word Building: **officially** *adverb*

off-peak *adjective*
having to do with a time when there is less activity or lower demand: *an off-peak hot water service*

off-putting *adjective*
discouraging or unfriendly: *She has an off-putting manner.*

offsider *noun*
a partner or friend

offspring *noun*
the young of a particular parent

ogle *verb*
to look at, especially with sexual interest

ogre (say *oh-gə*) *noun*
an imaginary monster of fairy tales and legends, that likes to eat people

ohm (rhymes with *gnome*) *noun*
a measure of electrical resistance

Word History: named after a German scientist, GS Ohm, 1787-1854

oil *noun*
1 a fatty liquid made from animal or vegetable fats, which is used in cooking **2** a thick black liquid made from petroleum which is used to run and care for machinery

oil *verb*
3 to cover or fill with oil

Word Building: **oily** *adjective*

oilskin *noun*
a cloth treated with oil to make it waterproof so that it can be used for rainwear

ointment *noun*
a soft greasy mixture used to heal your skin

okay *adjective*
1 all right or satisfactory: *Are you okay now?*

okay *adverb*
2 well or correctly: *The car performed okay.*

okay *verb*
3 to pass or accept: *Will you okay this?*

Word Use: this is also written **OK** □ this is more suited to everyday language
Word Building: **okay** *noun* approval

okra *noun*
a tall plant which produces pods that are used in soups and chutneys

Word History: from a West African language

old *adjective*
1 having lived or existed for a long time: *an old man* | *old wine* **2** aged in appearance: *She suddenly looks old.* **3** having reached a certain age: *five years old* **4** worn out or out of date: *old clothes* | *an old car* **5** of an earlier time: *in the old days* | *old boys of the school*

Word Building: **olden** *adjective* having to do with the past

old-fashioned *adjective*
belonging to an earlier time or style: *old-fashioned clothes*

oleander (say *oh-lee-an-də*) *noun*
a poisonous pink or white flowering shrub with dark green leaves

oligarchy (say *ol-ə-gah-kee*) *noun*
a type of government in which a few people have all the power

olive *noun*
1 a tree which grows in warm countries, or its fruit which can be eaten or crushed for its oil

olive *adjective*
2 yellowish-green or brownish-green

ombudsman (say *om-bədz-mən*) *noun*
an official whose job is to look into people's complaints against the government

omelette (say *om-lət*) *noun*
a food made of eggs beaten up and fried in a pan

Word History: from a French word meaning "a thin plate"

omen (say *oh-mən*) *noun*
a sign of good or bad luck to come

ominous *adjective*
threatening: *an ominous silence* | *ominous clouds*

Word Building: **ominously** *adverb*

omit *verb*
1 to leave out: *You have omitted a word.* **2** to fail to do: *He omits to knock.*

Word Building: other forms are **I omitted, I have omitted, I am omitting** □ **omission** *noun*

omni- *prefix*
a word part meaning all: *omnipotent*

Word History: this prefix comes from Latin

omnibus *noun*
1 *an old-fashioned word for* **bus** **2** a book of collected stories or writings by one writer or about one particular subject

Word Building: the plural is **omnibuses**

omnipotent (say *om-nip-ə-tənt*) *adjective*
having the power to do all things: *an omnipotent god*

Word Building: **omnipotence** *noun*

omniscient (say *om-nis-ee-ənt*) *adjective*
knowing everything: *the omniscient author*

Word Building: **omniscience** *noun*

omnivore *noun*
an animal that eats both animal and plant foods

Word Use: compare with **carnivore, herbivore** and **insectivore**

omnivorous *adjective*
1 eating both animal and plant foods: *Humans are omnivorous.* **2** taking in everything, such as with your mind: *She is an omnivorous reader.*

on *preposition*
1 above but touching something acting as a support: *on the table* **2** at the time or occasion of: *on Sunday | on my birthday* **3** about: *He asked my views on watching TV.* **4** near or close to: *a house on the coast*

on *adverb*
5 on yourself or itself: *to put your tights on* **6** tight: *to hold on*

Word Building: **on** *adjective: The heater is on already.*

once (say *wuns*) *adverb*
1 at one time in the past **2** a single time: *once a day* **3 once upon a time** long ago

Word Building: **once** *conjunction: We can leave once I find my car keys.*

one (say *wun*) *noun*
1 the number 1 **2** a single person or thing: *to come one at a time*

Word Use: be careful – this sounds like **won** □ something that is number one or comes before all others is the **first**
Word Building: **one** *adjective: one apple | one of our friends*

onion *noun*
a strong-smelling bulb vegetable used in cooking and salads

on-line *adjective*
with direct access or linkage to a computer

only (say *ohn-lee*) *adverb*
1 alone: *Only one goldfish remained.* **2** no more than: *If you would only go away.* **3 only too** very: *She was only too pleased to come.*

only *conjunction*
4 but or except: *I would have gone, only you didn't want me to.*

onomatopoeia (say *on-ə-mat-ə-pee-ə*) *noun*
the use of a word or words which sound like what they are describing, such as *crunch, splash* or *buzz*

Word Building: **onomatopoeic** *adjective*

onset *noun*
a beginning: *the onset of a disease*

onslaught (say *on-slawt*) *noun*
a fierce rush or attack

ooze[1] *verb*
1 to seep or leak slowly: *Gas oozed from the crack in the pipe.* **2** to give out slowly: *The wound is oozing blood. | She oozes charm.*

ooze[2] *noun*
soft mud, such as on the bottom of the ocean

opal *noun*
a valuable gem of various colours, streaked with red and blue

opaque (say *oh-payk*) *adjective*
not able to be seen through: *The water was muddy and opaque.*

Word Use: compare with **transparent** and **translucent**
Word Building: **opaquely** *adverb*

open *adjective*
1 not shut or locked **2** not limited or enclosed: *open fields* **3** not blocked or obstructed: *an open view* **4** friendly: *She has an open nature.* **5** able to be entered in, such as a competition, or applied for, such as a job

open *verb*
6 to make or become open: *She opened the window. | The door opened.* **7** to begin or start: *She opened the book at page ten. | Has school opened?*

open *noun*
8 a clear space: *Dinner is served in the open* **9** a competition in which both amateur and professional athletes can take part

Word Building: **opening** *noun* **openly** *adverb* **openness** *noun*

open-minded *adjective*
able to accept new and different ideas

opera *noun*
a play which is sung to music

Word Building: **operatic** *adjective*
Word History: from a Latin word meaning "service", "work" or "a work"

operate *verb*
1 to work: *He can't operate the levers. / The escalator isn't operating.* **2** to perform surgery: *The doctor will have to operate on her leg.*

operation *noun*
1 the way that something works
2 working order: *The lift isn't in operation.* **3** a medical treatment on someone's body, using surgery
4 a military mission

Word Building: **operational** *adjective*

operative *adjective*
1 working or functional: *an operative life of two years* **2** having force or effect: *The law is only operative in this State.*

operator *noun*
1 someone who works a machine: *a lift operator* **2** someone who runs a big business: *the operators of a tourist resort*

opinion *noun*
what you think or decide: *My opinion is that we should all help. / public opinion*

Word Building: **opinionated** *adjective* full of your own ideas

opium *noun*
a drug made from the juice of the poppy, which is used to relieve pain and to put you to sleep

Word Building: **opiate** *noun* a medicine containing opium, that puts you to sleep
Word History: from a Greek word meaning "juice"

opponent *noun*
someone who is on the opposite side to you in a fight or contest

opportunity *noun*
a suitable time or occasion: *She never had the opportunity to sing at a concert.*

Word Building: the plural is **opportunities**

oppose *verb*
to resist or fight: *They opposed her marriage.*

opposite *adjective*
1 completely different: *We hold opposite views on everything.* **2** facing: *She lives in the opposite house.*

Word Building: **opposite** *noun* the contrary

opposition *noun*
1 resistance or a fight: *They put up strong opposition.* **2** the opposing side: *She met the opposition in a debate.*

oppress *verb*
1 to cause hardship to or weigh heavily upon: *Their poverty oppressed them.*
2 to be cruel to: *The soldiers oppressed their prisoners.*

Word Use: a similar word for definition 2 is **tyrannise**
Word Building: **oppression** *noun* **oppressive** *adjective* **oppressor** *noun*

opt *verb*
1 to choose: *He opted to join.*
2 opt out to decide not to join in

optical *adjective*
having to do with seeing: *optical glasses / optical illusion*

optician (say *op-tish-ən*) *noun*
someone who makes or sells glasses

optimism *noun*
hopefulness or the habit of expecting that things will turn out well: *She's not well but she's full of optimism.*

Word Use: the opposite is **pessimism**
Word Building: **optimist** *noun* someone who looks on the bright side **optimistic** *adjective* **optimistically** *adverb*

option *noun*
a choice or the right to choose

Word Building: **optional** *adjective*

optometrist (say *op-tom-ə-trəst*) *noun*
someone who tests your eyesight and, if necessary, makes glasses to improve it

Word Building: **optometry** *noun*

opulent (say *op-yə-lənt*) *adjective*
rich or wealthy

Word Building: **opulence** *noun* wealth **opulently** *adverb* richly

opus (say *oh-pəs*) *noun*
a work, especially a musical composition

Word Building: the plural is **opera** but it is not often used for this

or *conjunction*
showing a connection between words, phrases, and clauses expressing choices: *blue or red / in love or in hate / to be or not to be*

Word Use: be careful – this sounds like **oar** and **ore**

oracle *noun*
1 someone, especially a priest or priestess in ancient Greece, who answers difficult questions or reveals the future **2** a difficult saying given by such an oracle

Word Building: **oracular** *adjective*

oral *adjective*
1 spoken: *an oral test in French* **2** having to do with your mouth or taken by mouth

orange *noun*
1 a round reddish-gold citrus fruit
orange *adjective*
2 reddish-gold

orang-outang (say *ə-rang-ə-tang*) *noun*
a large ape found in Indonesia, which climbs trees

Word History: from a Malay word meaning "man of the woods"

orator *noun*
a public speaker, especially a skilful one

Word Building: **oration** *noun* a formal speech **oratorical** *adjective* **oratory** *noun*

orbit *noun*
the curved path or line of flight followed by a planet or satellite around the earth or sun

Word Building: **orbit** *verb* to travel around

orchard *noun*
a paddock or farm where fruit trees are grown

Word Building: **orchardist** *noun*

orchestra (say *aw-kəs-trə*) *noun*
a large group of musicians who play their instruments together

orchid (say *aw-kəd*) *noun*
a plant that grows in warm climates and the beautiful waxy flower it produces

ordain *verb*
1 to appoint to the church as a priest or minister **2** to order or declare: *The king ordained that the prisoner be banished for life.*

Word Building: **ordination** *noun*

ordeal *noun*
a severe test or hardship: *The funeral was an ordeal for her.*

order *noun*
1 a command **2** the proper arrangement of things: *Restore order to your room.*
3 a request for goods: *an order at the shop*
4 the way things are placed in relation to each other: *Did they come in that order?*
5 working condition: *It's out of order.*
6 a division into a particular group or kind: *the order of mammals* **7** a religious group living under the same rules: *the Dominican order* **8** a lawful state or behaviour: *The police tried to restore order.*
order *verb*
9 to command or give an instruction
10 to request or ask for: *Let us order tea.*

Word Building: **orderly** *adjective*

ordinal number *noun*
a number which tells you the place of a thing in a series, such as "first" in *the first child* or "fourteenth" in *the fourteenth week*

Word Use: compare with **cardinal number**

ordinance *noun*
a rule or regulation: *an ordinance of the governor*

ordinary *adjective*
1 usual or normal: *an ordinary working day*
2 of poor quality or inferior: *It looks rather ordinary.*

Word Use: the opposite of definition 1 is **extraordinary**
Word Building: **ordinarily** *adverb* usually **ordinariness** *noun*

ore *noun*
a rock or mineral which contains a metal that is valuable enough to be mined

Word Use: be careful – this sounds like **or** and **oar**
Word History: from an Old English word meaning "brass"

oregano (say *o-rə-gah-noh*) *noun*
a herb of the mint family, used in cooking

organ *noun*
1 a musical instrument with pipes and one or more keyboards **2** a part of your body which has a particular job, such as your heart which pumps blood or your liver which makes bile **3** something which can be used to express a particular viewpoint: *This newsletter is the official organ of our society.*

organdie *noun*
a fine but stiff cotton material

organic *adjective*
1 having to do with living things or their organs **2** having to do with the way parts are organised in a complete structure
3 relating to farming without chemicals: *They only use organic fertilisers.*

Word Building: **organically** *adverb*

organisation or **organization** *noun*
1 the skilful arrangement or running of something **2** a group which runs something **3** something which is run or managed

Word Building: **organisational** *adjective*

organise or **organize** *verb*
1 to form, especially into a group which works or does things together: *to organise a chess club* **2** to order or arrange neatly: *to organise my books* **3** to arrange or plan: *He organised the holiday.*

organism *noun*
a living thing: *She saw the tiny organism under the microscope.*

orgasm *noun*
the moment of greatest pleasure in sexual intercourse

orgy (say *aw-jee*) *noun*
wild or drunken feasting, or other uncontrolled behaviour

Word Building: the plural is **orgies**

orient *verb*
1 *another word for* **orientate**
orient *noun*
2 the Orient the countries of Asia, east of the Mediterranean

oriental *adjective*
of or from an Asian country

orientate *verb*
1 to aim or direct: *He has orientated the course towards older students.* **2** to adjust or adapt: *She orientated herself quickly in her new surroundings.*

Word Building: **orientated** *adjective* **orientation** *noun*

orienteering *noun*
a sport in which you have to find your way as quickly as possible over a difficult course, using maps and compasses

origami *noun*
the art of folding paper into interesting shapes, first developed in Japan

Word History: from a Japanese word

origin *noun*
where something or someone comes from: *the origin of an idea | of Irish origin*

original *adjective*
1 first or earliest: *The original models are in the museum.* **2** newly thought up or invented, especially without a model: *an original design*
original *noun*
3 the earliest or first form from which copies are made: *He has kept the original.* **4** a work which has not been copied from anything else

Word Building: **originality** *noun* **originally** *adverb*

originate *verb*
to start: *Who originated the idea? | The idea originated with Bill.*

ornament *noun*
an object or a decoration which is meant to be beautiful rather than useful

Word Building: **ornament** *verb* to decorate **ornamental** *adjective* **ornamentation** *noun*

ornate *adjective*
covered with ornaments, showy or fine: *ornate chairs*

Word Building: **ornately** *adverb*

ornitho- *prefix*
a word part meaning bird: *ornithology*

Word Use: another spelling is **ornith-**
Word History: this prefix comes from Greek

ornithology *noun*
the study of birds and bird life

Word Building: **ornithologist** *noun*

orphan *noun*
someone, especially a child, whose parents have died

Word Building: **orphan** *verb: He was orphaned by a car accident.*

orphanage *noun*
a place where children without parents live

orthodontist *noun*
someone whose job is to straighten your teeth

Word Building: **orthodontics** *noun*

orthodox *adjective*
1 usual or accepted: *orthodox dress*
2 according to usual religious teaching

Word Building: **orthodoxly** *adverb* **orthodoxy** *noun*

orthopaedics or **orthopedics** (say *awth-ə-pee-diks*) *noun*
the type of medical treatment that corrects or cures any problems or diseases of your spine and bones

Word Building: **orthopaedic** *adjective* **orthopaedist** *noun*

oscillate (say *<u>os</u>-ə-layt*) *verb*
to move or swing to and fro

Word Building: **oscillation** *noun* **oscillator** *noun*

osmosis *noun*
the movement of liquid from a cell in which there is a strong solution across the cell wall to a cell in which there is a weak solution, so that in the end the solutions will be of equal strength on each side of the wall

Word History: from a Greek word meaning "a thrusting"

ostentation *noun*
showiness or display: *He dresses with ostentation.*

Word Use: words of opposite meaning are **modesty** and **discretion**
Word Building: **ostentatious** *adjective* **ostentatiously** *adverb* **ostentatiousness** *noun*

osteopathy (say *os-tee-<u>op</u>-ə-thee*) *noun*
the method of treating disease by pressing bones and muscles in your body

Word Building: **osteopath** *noun* **osteopathic** *adjective*

ostracise or **ostracize** *verb*
to keep away from, or send away, especially as a punishment

Word Building: **ostracism** *noun*

ostrich *noun*
a large bird of Africa which runs fast but can't fly

other (say *<u>udh</u>-ə*) *adjective*
1 additional or extra: *He and one other person were there.* **2** different: *at some other school / I don't like it any other way.*

otter *noun*
a furry water mammal with webbed feet and a flattened tail like a ship's rudder

ottoman (say *<u>ot</u>-ə-mən*) *noun*
a low padded seat without a back or arms

ouija (say *<u>wee</u>-jə*) *noun*
a board used in seances, which is supposed to tap out messages from dead people

Word History: from the French word for "yes" (*oui*) added to the German word for "yes" (*ja*)

ounce *noun*
an old-fashioned measure of weight equal to about 29 grams

our *pronoun*
the form of **we** and **us** that expresses ownership and is used before a noun: *our house*

Word Use: be careful – this sounds like **hour**
Word Building: **ours** *pronoun: Those clothes are ours.*

oust *verb*
to push out or expel: *The rebels ousted the king from the palace.*

outback *noun*
the remote parts of the country or bush, far from the cities and the coast

Word Building: **outback** *adjective* **outback** *adverb*

outboard *adjective*
on the outside of a boat or plane: *an outboard motor*

outbreak *noun*
a sudden beginning or happening: *the outbreak of war / an outbreak of measles*

outburst *noun*
a sudden bursting or pouring out: *an outburst of violence / an outburst of laughter*

outcast *noun*
someone who is not accepted by people in a society

outcome *noun*
a result or consequence: *the outcome of the elections*

outcry *noun*
a loud noise or an uproar: *a public outcry against nuclear bombs*

Word Building: the plural is **outcries**

outfit *noun*
1 a set of clothes or equipment needed for an activity: *A skiing outfit consists of skis, poles, boots and warm clothes.* **2** a business or group of people working together: *a military outfit*

Word Building: **outfit** *verb* (**outfitted, outfitting**) to equip or fit out

outgoing *adjective*
1 friendly and sociable: *He is outgoing and has lots of friends.* **2** departing or going out: *outgoing trains*

outing *noun*
a trip taken for fun: *an outing to the beach*

outlaw *noun*
someone who has broken the law and is wanted by the police

Word Use: this word was used especially of highwaymen and bandits in the old days
Word Building: **outlaw** *verb* to forbid by law

outlay *noun*
money, time or energy spent in getting something

Word Building: **outlay** *verb* (**outlaid, outlaying**) to spend

outlet *noun*
1 an opening or way for letting something out: *A power point is an outlet for electricity. / Stamping your feet is an outlet for anger.* **2** a shop or market: *an outlet for handcrafts*

outline *noun*
1 a line showing the shape of something: *the outline of a circle* **2** a short description giving only the most important points: *an outline of a story*

Word Building: **outline** *verb*

outlook *noun*
1 a view: *an outlook over the park from the veranda* **2** an attitude or point of view: *a gloomy outlook on life* **3** what is likely to happen in the future: *The weather outlook for tomorrow is good.*

outpatient *noun*
a patient who comes to a hospital for medical treatment but does not have to stay

outpost *noun*
1 a group of soldiers stationed away from the main army **2** a settlement far away from the main town: *a desert outpost*

output *noun*
1 something that is produced: *to increase the output of a factory* **2** the information that a computer puts out

outrage *noun*
1 something that shocks or offends people **2** a feeling of very strong anger

Word Building: **outrageous** *adjective*

outright *adverb*
1 completely or totally: *to refuse outright*
2 immediately: *to be killed outright*

Word Building: **outright** *adjective: an outright failure*

outset *noun*
the beginning or start: *Our team looked set to win from the outset.*

outside *noun*
1 the outer part or side: *to paint the outside of the house / She seems calm on the outside but inside she's angry.*

outside *adjective*
2 on the outer side or part: *the outside walls* **3** coming from somewhere else: *a business funded by outside money*
4 an outside chance scarcely any chance at all

outside *adverb*
5 on or to the outside: *It's cold outside. / Go outside.*

Word Use: the opposite is **inside**
Word Building: **outsider** *noun* someone who doesn't fit in to a group

outskirts *plural noun*
the outer areas: *small farms on the outskirts of the city*

outspoken *adjective*
saying openly what you think even if it offends people

Word Building: **outspokenly** *adverb*

outstanding *adjective*
1 standing out from all others: *an outstanding swimmer* **2** not settled or finished: *outstanding debts*

Word Building: **outstandingly** *adverb*

outward *adjective*
1 able to be seen: *outward signs of fear*
2 outside or outer: *the outward surface*
3 away from a place: *a bus making an outward journey*

outward *adverb*
4 towards the outside: *to look outward over the sea*

Word Use: another form of the adverb is **outwards** □ the opposite is **inward**
Word Building: **outwardly** *adverb* on the outside: *outwardly shy*

outwit *verb*
to beat by being more cunning or clever: *If you can't be stronger than your opponents you must outwit them.*

Word Building: other forms are **I outwitted, I have outwitted, I am outwitting**

oval *adjective*
1 shaped like an egg

oval *noun*
2 an oval shape **3** a field for playing sport on

ovary *noun*
the part of a woman's body that produces eggs for reproduction

Word Building: the plural is **ovaries** □ **ovum** *noun* (**ova**) the egg produced by an ovary
Word History: from a Latin word meaning "egg"

ovation *noun*
cheers and enthusiastic applause: *The audience gave the orchestra an ovation.*

oven (say uv-ən) *noun*
a closed-in space, usually part of a stove, used for cooking, heating and drying

Word Building: **ovenproof** *adjective* not damaged by being heated in an oven **ovenware** *noun* ovenproof dishes

overalls *plural noun*
a pair of trousers with a flap covering your chest, fastened by shoulder straps

overawe *verb*
to fill with fear and respect: *The presence of the famous actor overawed them.*

overbalance *verb*
to fall or trip over: *to overbalance while skating*

overbearing *adjective*
bossy and arrogant

Word Building: **overbear** *verb* (**overbore, overborne, overbearing**) to overcome or force aside

overboard *adverb*
1 over the side of a boat or ship into the water: *to fall overboard and have to be rescued* **2 go overboard** to be over enthusiastic: *He's really going overboard about computers.*

Word Use: definition 2 is more suited to everyday language

overcast *adjective*
cloudy and grey: *overcast skies*

overcome *verb*
1 to win the battle against: *to overcome an enemy | to overcome the fear of heights*
2 to make weak or helpless: *Weariness finally overcame the travellers*

Word Building: other forms are **I overcame, I have overcome, I am overcoming**

overdo *verb*
to do more than is sensible: *to overdo exercise*

Word Building: other forms are **I overdid, I have overdone, I am overdoing** □ **overdone** *adjective* cooked too much

overdose *noun*
a dose of a drug large enough to either kill you or make you seriously ill: *an overdose of heroin*

Word Use: in everyday language this is known as an **OD**

overdue *adjective*
late or past the proper time: *overdue library books*

overflow *verb*
1 to spill or flow over
overflow *noun*
2 a flood: *the overflow of a river*
3 the area of land covered by water in times of flood

overgrown *adjective*
covered with weeds and long grass

Word Building: **overgrow** *verb* **overgrowth** *noun*

overhang *verb*
1 to hang over: *A tree overhangs the cliff. | We can shelter where the cliff overhangs.*
2 to loom over or threaten: *Danger overhung their journey.*

Word Building: other forms are **it overhung, it has overhung, it is overhanging** □ **overhang** *noun* a part which sticks out

overhaul *verb*
to check, take apart, and repair: *to overhaul an engine*

Word Building: **overhaul** *noun*

overhead *adverb*
1 straight above: *birds flying overhead*
overhead *noun*
2 overheads the costs involved in running a business

Word Building: **overhead** *adjective* above your head: *overhead telephone wires*

overhear *verb*
to hear, especially by accident: *They were talking so loudly I couldn't help overhearing what was said.*

Word Building: other forms are **I overheard, I have overheard, I am overhearing**

overlap *verb*
to partly cover: *Place the tiles on the roof so that one overlaps the other.*

Word Building: other forms are **it overlapped, it has overlapped, it is overlapping** □ **overlap** *noun: an overlap of ten centimetres*

overlook *verb*
1 to miss or ignore: *to overlook a spelling mistake | I shall overlook your lateness this time.* **2** to look down over: *The house overlooks the park.*

overpass *noun*
a bridge for cars or pedestrians, which crosses over a busy road

overpower *verb*
to overcome by greater strength: *The wrestler overpowered his opponent.*

Word Building: **overpowering** *adjective* very strong: *an overpowering perfume*

overrun *verb*
to spread or swarm over: *The Pied Piper got rid of the rats which were overrunning the city.*

Word Building: other forms are **it overran, it has overrun, it is overrunning**

overseas *adverb*
over or beyond the sea: *to travel overseas*

Word Building: **overseas** *adjective*

oversee *verb*
to supervise or manage: *to oversee workers*

Word Building: other forms are **I oversaw, I have overseen, I am overseeing** □ **overseer** *noun* a supervisor or person in charge

overt (say *oh-vert*) *adjective*
not secret, or open for all to see: *He treated me with overt hostility and anger.*

Word Building: **overtly** *adverb*

overtake *verb*
1 to catch up and pass: *The police overtook the speeding car.* | *It is dangerous to overtake on a bridge.* **2** to come upon suddenly: *A storm overtook the yacht.*

Word Building: other forms are **I overtook, I have overtaken, I am overtaking**

overthrow *verb*
1 to defeat or put an end to by force: *The army overthrew the government.*
2 to throw too far: *The fielder overthrew the ball and it missed the wicket.*

Word Building: other forms are **I overthrew, I have overthrown, I am overthrowing** □ **overthrow** *noun*

overtime *noun*
extra time worked before or after the usual working hours: *to get extra pay for overtime*

Word Building: **overtime** *adjective*

overture *noun*
1 music played before the start of an opera, ballet or musical show **2** a first attempt to be friends with someone

overturn *verb*
1 to turn over on its side, back or face: *to overturn the wheelbarrow* | *The car overturned.* **2** to reverse or turn the other way: *The High Court overturned the lower court's decision.*

overwhelm *verb*
to crush or bury

Word Building: **overwhelming** *adjective*

overwrought (say *oh-və-rawt*) *adjective*
worked up with excitement or worry

ovulate *verb*
to release eggs from your ovary: *Women ovulate every month.*

Word Building: **ovulation** *noun*

ovum (say *oh-vəm*) *noun*
one of the cells produced by a female which can join with a sperm to develop into a new individual

Word Building: the plural is **ova**
Word History: from the Latin word meaning "egg"

owe *verb*
1 to have to pay back: *I owe you $2.*
2 to have a duty to give: *I owe her an apology.*

owing *adjective*
1 due to be paid or given back: *the amount owing* **2 owing to** because of: *I was late owing to the heavy traffic.*

owl *noun*
1 a bird with large eyes and a hooting call, which feeds mostly at night on small animals like birds and frogs **2** a solemn-looking or wise person

own *verb*
1 to possess or have for yourself
2 own up to admit or confess

own *noun*
3 something belonging to yourself: *She has a bike of her own.* **4 get your own back** to have revenge **5 on your own** alone and without help

Word Building: **own** *adjective* belonging to yourself **owner** *noun* **ownership** *noun*

ox *noun*
another word for **bullock**

Word Building: the plural form is **oxen**

oxyacetylene burner *noun*
a device used for welding or cutting steel by burning a mixture of acetylene and oxygen in a special jet

Word Use: another name for this is **oxyacetylene torch**

oxygen (say *ok-sə-jən*) *noun*
a gas with no colour or smell which is an essential part of the air we breathe

oyster *noun*
a shellfish you can eat, often found clinging to rocks

Oz *noun*
Australia

Word Use: you can also use **oz** □ this word is more suited to everyday language

ozone *noun*
1 a poisonous form of oxygen which is found in the air in tiny quantities, formed when lightning passes through the atmosphere **2 ozone layer** a layer of ozone in one of the outer parts of the atmosphere, which partly blocks the harmful rays of the sun

Word History: from a Greek word meaning "smell"

pace *noun*
1 a single step or the distance covered by it **2** speed or rate of movement **3 put someone through their paces** to make someone perform or show their abilities

pace *verb*
4 to set the pace for: *A car will go beside the runners to pace them.* **5** to walk with regular steps: *He paced backwards and forwards.* **6** to measure by paces: *We paced the oval and found it to be about 50 metres long.*

pacemaker *noun*
1 someone or something that sets the pace usually in a race **2** a medical instrument placed in someone's body when their heart is diseased and needs help to keep it beating at the right rate

pacific (say *pə-sif-ik*) *adjective*
peaceful or peace-loving

Word Building: **pacification** *noun*

pacifism (say *pas-ə-fiz-əm*) *noun*
opposition to war or violence of any kind

Word Building: **pacifist** *noun*

pacify (say *pas-ə-fuy*) *verb*
to make peaceful or calm: *She quickly pacified the frightened horse.*

Word Building: other forms are **I pacified, I have pacified, I am pacifying**

pack *noun*
1 a parcel or bundle of things wrapped or tied up **2** a load carried on the back of people or animals: *The hikers put their packs on.* **3** a group of animals living and hunting together: *a pack of wolves* **4** a group of people or things: *a pack of thieves | a pack of lies* **5** a complete set: *a pack of playing cards*

pack *verb*
6 to put into a suitcase, parcel or box **7** to press together or crowd: *The people packed into the hall.* **8 pack off** to send away in a hurry: *She packed him off to school.*

Word Building: **packer** *noun* a person or machine that packs

package *noun*
a parcel or a bundle

Word Building: **package** *verb*

packet *noun*
a small pack or package of anything

pact *noun*
an agreement: *The two friends made a pact to help each other.*

pad[1] *noun*
1 a wad or mass of soft material used to give comfort, protection or shape to something **2** a number of sheets of paper held together at one edge **3** a soft block of material soaked in ink used for inking a rubber stamp **4** the soft, cushion-like part on the underside of the feet of animals like dogs, foxes, and so on **5** a flat area that helicopters, and sometimes spaceships, take off from **6** a place where someone lives, especially a single room

Word Use: another term for definition 2 is **writing pad** □ definition 6 is more suited to everyday language
Word Building: **pad** *verb* (**padded, padding**)

pad[2] *verb*
to walk with soft footsteps: *I'm padding around trying not to wake anyone.*

Word Building: other forms are **I padded, I have padded, I am padding**

paddle[1] *noun*
a short oar which you use in guiding a canoe through the water

Word Building: **paddle** *verb*

paddle[2] *verb*
to walk or play with bare feet in shallow water

paddock *noun*
a large area of land which has been fenced and is usually used for grazing sheep or other animals

pademelon (say *pad-ee-mel-ən*) *noun*
a type of small wallaby

padlock *noun*
a removable lock with a curved metal bar which passes through something and is then snapped shut

paediatrics or **pediatrics**
(say *pee-dee-at-riks*) *noun*
the study and treatment of the diseases and illnesses of young children

Word Building: **paediatrician** *noun* (say *pee-dee-ə-trish-ən*) a doctor who specialises in children's illnesses **paediatric** *adjective*

pagan (say *pay-gən*) *noun*
someone who does not follow an accepted religion

Word Building: **pagan** *adjective* **paganism** *noun*

page[1] *noun*
1 one of the sheets of paper making up a book, magazine, letter, and so on
2 one side of one of these sheets

page[2] *noun*
1 a uniformed boy employee of a hotel or something similar
page[2] *verb*
2 to try to find someone in a hotel, hospital, shop, and so on by calling out their name on a microphone or public address system

pageant (say *paj-ənt*) *noun*
1 a colourful public show, often including a procession of people in costume
2 any showy display

Word Building: **pageantry** *noun*

pagoda (say *pə-goh-də*) *noun*
a sacred building or temple shaped like a tower and usually found in eastern countries such as India and China

pail *noun*
another word for **bucket**

pain *noun*
1 suffering or hurt felt when you are injured or sick, or when you are unhappy **2 pain in the neck** someone or something annoying or unpleasant
3 pains very careful efforts: *Great pains were taken to make the wedding a happy occasion.*
pain *verb*
4 to cause pain or suffering to

Word Use: definition 2 is more suited to everyday language □ be careful – this sounds like **pane**
Word Building: **painful** *adjective* **painfully** *adverb* **painless** *adjective* **painlessly** *adverb*

painstaking *adjective*
extremely careful: *painstaking work*

paint *noun*
1 a liquid colouring substance that you can put on a surface to give it colour
paint *verb*
2 to make a picture of someone or something using paint **3** to cover with paint: *She painted the ceiling red.*

Word Building: **painting** *noun*

painter[1] *noun*
1 an artist who paints pictures
2 someone whose work is painting walls, fences, and so on

painter[2] *noun*
a rope for tying a boat to a ship, wharf, and so on

pair *noun*
1 two things of the same kind that go together: *a pair of shoes* **2** a combination of two parts joined together to make a single thing: *a pair of scissors*
3 two people, things or animals thought of as connected to each other in some way: *a happily married pair*

Word Use: be careful – this sounds like **pare** and **pear**
Word Building: the plural is **pairs** or **pair**
Word History: from a Latin word meaning "equal"

pal *noun*
a friend

Word Use: this is more suited to everyday language
Word Building: **pally** *adjective* friendly
Word History: from a Gipsy word meaning "brother"

palace *noun*
the official home of a king, queen, bishop or other very important person

palatable (say *pal-ə-tə-bəl*) *adjective*
pleasant to taste

palate (say *pal-ət*) *noun*
1 the roof of your mouth **2** the sense of taste

palatial (say *pə-lay-shəl*) *adjective*
like a palace

Word Building: **palatially** *adverb*

pale *adjective*
1 having a whitish or colourless appearance: *a pale face* **2** not very bright in colour

pale *verb*
3 to become pale **4** to become less in importance or strength: *Her unhappiness paled beside that of her friend.*

Word Building: **palely** *adverb* **paleness** *noun*

palette (say *pal-ət*) *noun*
a thin board, usually with a thumb hole at one end, used by painters to mix colours on

palindrome (say *pal-ən-drohm*) *noun*
a word or sentence which reads the same either backwards or forwards, such as the sentence "Madam, I'm Adam."

Word History: from a Greek word meaning "running back"

paling (say *pay-ling*) *noun*
a long pointed piece of wood, often used to build a fence

palisade (say *pal-ə-sayd*) *noun*
a fence of tall pointed sticks set firmly in the ground as a defence around a fort or camp

pall[1] (say *pawl*) *noun*
1 a cloth for spreading over a coffin
2 something that covers with darkness or gloominess: *A pall of smoke hung over the city.*

pall[2] (say *pawl*) *verb*
to become tiring or boring

pallbearer *noun*
someone who carries the coffin at a funeral

pallet *noun*
1 a tool with a flat blade and a handle used for shaping and smoothing in pottery
2 a movable platform on which things are placed when being stored or moved from place to place in a factory

pallid *adjective*
pale or lacking in colour

Word Building: **pallor** *noun* unusual paleness caused by fear, illness, and so on

palm[1] (say *pahm*) *noun*
the part of the inside of your hand that reaches from your wrist to the beginning of your fingers

palm[2] (say *pahm*) *noun*
a tall plant with no branches, but a crown of large fan-shaped leaves at the top

palmistry (say *pah-mə-stree*) *noun*
the art of telling someone's fortune or character by the length and pattern of the lines on the palm of their hand

Word Building: **palmist** *noun* someone who reads palms

palomino (say *pal-ə-mee-noh*) *noun*
a tan or cream-coloured horse with a white mane and tail

Word Use: another spelling is **palamino**
Word Building: the plural is **palominos**
Word History: from a Spanish word meaning "like a dove"

palpitate *verb*
1 to beat much faster than normal: *Her heart was palpitating with the effort of the long run.* **2** to shake slightly or to tremble: *He palpitated with fear.*

Word Building: **palpitation** *noun*

palsy (say *pawl-zee*) *noun*
another word for **paralysis**

paltry (say *pawl-tree*) *adjective*
small or worthless: *a paltry sum of money* | *a paltry coward*

pamper *verb*
to treat too kindly: *He pampers the dogs by giving them chocolates.*

pamphlet (say *pam-flət*) *noun*
1 a very small paper-covered book
2 a single sheet of paper with advertisements printed on it, which is handed out to you or put in your letterbox

Word Building: **pamphleteer** *noun* someone who writes pamphlets

pan *noun*
1 a broad, shallow, open dish, which is usually used for cooking **2** any container shaped liked this: *Gold can be separated from gravel and sand by washing it in a pan.*

pan *verb*
3 to wash gravel or sand in a pan to separate gold or other heavy metals
4 to criticise severely: *The critics panned the new film.*

Word Use: definition 4 is more suited to everyday language
Word Building: other verb forms are **I panned, I have panned, I am panning**

pancake *noun*
a thin flat cake made of batter cooked in a frying pan

pancreas (say *pan-kree-əs*) *noun*
a gland near your stomach which produces important hormones and helps your digestion

Word Building: **pancreatic** *adjective: pancreatic juices*

panda *noun*
a large, black-and-white, bear-like animal which is found mainly in China

pandemonium (say *pan-də-moh-nee-əm*) *noun*
wild and noisy confusion

Word History: from *Pandemonium,* the name the poet John Milton (1608-74) gave to the capital of Hell

pane *noun*
a single plate or sheet of glass, usually part of a window

Word Use: be careful – this sounds like **pain**

panel *noun*
1 a separate section set into a ceiling, door or wall, that is sometimes raised above or sunk below the main surface **2** a thin flat piece of wood **3** a separate section of material set into a dress **4** a board or section of a machine on which controls are fixed: *the instrument panel of a car* **5** a group of people selected to form a jury, or brought together to discuss matters, judge competitions and so on

Word Building: **panel** *verb* (**panelled, panelling**) **panellist** *noun* a member of a small group formed to discuss things, often on TV **panelling** *noun*

pang *noun*
a sudden, short, sharp feeling of pain

panic *noun*
1 a sudden terror, sometimes without an obvious reason

panic *verb*
2 to feel or cause to panic: *She panicked when she saw the gun. / The falling branch panicked the horse.*

Word Building: other verb forms are **I panicked, I had panicked, I am panicking** □ **panicky** *adjective* **panic-stricken** *adjective* **panic-struck** *adjective*
Word History: from a Greek word meaning "having to do with or caused by *Pan*", the god of the forests in Greek myths

panorama (say *pan-ə-rah-mə*) *noun*
1 a view over a wide area **2** a continually changing scene: *the panorama of city life*

Word Building: **panoramic** *adjective*

panpipe *noun*
a musical instrument made up of pipes of different lengths which are played by blowing across their open ends

pansy *noun*
a garden plant with white, yellow or purple flowers

Word Building: the plural is **pansies**

pant *verb*
1 to breathe hard and quickly because of effort or emotion

pant *noun*
2 a sudden short breath

Word Building: **pantingly** *adverb*

panther *noun*
a leopard, especially a black one

Word Use: the male is a **panther;** the female is a **pantheress;** the young is a **cub**

pantihose *noun*
women's tights, usually made out of stocking material

pantomime *noun*
a play in which the actors use actions and not words to tell the story

Word Use: a similar word is **mime**

pantry *noun*
a room or cupboard in which food is kept

Word Building: the plural is **pantries**
Word History: from a Latin word meaning "bread"

pants *plural noun*
1 *another name for* **trousers** **2** women's underpants

papacy (say *pay-pə-see*) *noun*
1 the office or position of the pope in the Roman Catholic church **2** the period during which a particular pope rules

Word Use: the plural is **papacies**
Word Building: **papal** *adjective*

paper *noun*
1 a material made from straw, wood, and so on, usually in thin sheets for writing or printing on, or wrapping things in **2** a newspaper **3** a written examination **4 papers** documents identifying who you are, what country you come from and so on

paperback *noun*
a book with a soft paper cover, usually cheaper than one with a hard cover

papier-mâché (say *pay-pə-mash-ay*) *noun*
a substance made of paper pulp sometimes mixed with glue and other materials and used when wet to make models, boxes, and so on which become hard and strong when dry

Word History: from a French word meaning "chewed paper"

pappadum *noun*
a thin, crisp, Indian wafer bread, made from spiced potato or rice flour

Word Use: other spellings are **pappadam** or **poppadum**

paprika (say *pap-ri-kə, pə-pree-kə*) *noun*
powder made from a red pepper, used as a spice

papyrus (say *pə-puy-rəs*) *noun*
1 a tall water plant **2** material for writing on made out of this plant **3** an ancient document written on this material

Word Building: the plural is **papyri** (say *pə-puy-ruy*)

par *noun*
1 an equal level: *Her tennis playing is on a par with her sister's.* **2** an average or normal amount: *below par* / *above par*

parable (say *pa-rə-bəl*) *noun*
a short story used to teach a truth or moral lesson

parabola (say *pə-rab-ə-lə*) *noun*
a special kind of even curve, like the path of an object when it is thrown forward into the air and falls back to the earth

Word Use: this word is used in geometry
Word Building: **parabolic** *adjective: parabolic equations*

parachute (say *pa-rə-shooht*) *noun*
a large piece of cloth shaped like an umbrella and used to slow down the fall of someone jumping from an aircraft

Word Building: **parachute** *verb*
parachutist *noun*

parade *noun*
1 a gathering of troops, scouts, and so on for inspection or display **2** a group of people marching in the street to celebrate something

Word Use: a similar word for definition 2 is **procession**

paradigm (say *pa-rə-duym*) *noun*
a pattern or example

paradise *noun*
1 heaven **2** a place of great beauty or delight

Word History: from a Persian word meaning "enclosure"

paradox *noun*
1 a statement which is true although it contains two seemingly opposite ideas, such as the statement "You have to be cruel to be kind". **2** someone or something which seems to show contradictions

Word Building: the plural is **paradoxes** □ **paradoxical** *adjective* **paradoxically** *adverb*

paragon (say *pa-rə-gən*) *noun*
someone or something good enough to copy: *She is a paragon of virtue.*

paragraph *noun*
a section of writing dealing with a particular subject or point, beginning on a new line

parakeet *noun*
a kind of small parrot, such as the budgerigar, usually with a long pointed tail

parallel (say *pa-rə-lel*) *adjective*
1 being the same distance from each other at every point: *A railway track is made up of two parallel lines.*

parallel *noun*
2 a line parallel with another
3 a comparison showing likeness: *You can draw a parallel between her and many great musicians before her.*

parallelogram (say *pa-rə-lel-ə-gram*) *noun*
a four-sided figure whose opposite sides are parallel to each other

paralysis (say *pə-ral-ə-səs*) *noun*
an inability to move

Word Building: the plural is **paralyses** (say *pə-ral-ə-seez*) □ **paralyse** *verb*

paramedical *adjective*
helping the medical profession: *ambulances and other paramedical services*

paramount *adjective*
above others in rank, authority or importance

paranoid *adjective*
full of fears about things which are made up

Word Building: **paranoia** *noun* (say *pa-rə-noy-ə*) **paranoiac** *adjective*

parapet *noun*
a wall or barrier at the edge of a balcony, roof or bridge

paraphernalia (say *pa-rə-fə-nay-lee-ə*) *plural noun*
goods, equipment, baggage or other articles, especially unnecessary ones

paraphrase *verb*
to put in different words so that it's easier to understand

Word Building: **paraphrase** *noun*

paraplegic (say *pa-rə-plee-jik*) *noun*
someone who has lost the use of both arms or both legs

Word Building: **paraplegia** *noun* **paraplegic** *adjective*

parasite *noun*
1 an animal or plant which lives on or in another from which it obtains its food: *Fleas are parasites.* **2** someone who lives on the money earned by other people without doing anything in return

Word Building: **parasitic** *adjective* **parasitism** *noun*

parasol *noun*
a small sun umbrella

Word History: from Latin words meaning "guard against the sun"

paratrooper *noun*
a soldier who reaches a battle by landing from an aeroplane by parachute

parcel *noun*
a package or wrapped bundle of goods

Word Building: **parcel** *verb* (**parcelled, parcelling**) to make up into a parcel

parch *verb*
to make or become very dry

Word Building: **parched** *adjective*

parchment *noun*
1 the skin of sheep, goats or similar animals prepared as a material to write on **2** paper which looks like this

pardon *noun*
1 forgiveness, especially for a crime
pardon *verb*
2 to forgive and not punish **3** to excuse: *"Pardon me", I said when I walked in front of her.*

Word Building: **pardonable** *adjective*

pare (rhymes with *hair*) *verb*
1 to peel or cut off the outer layer of: *to pare apples* **2** to cut down or make less: *to pare expenses*

Word Use: be careful – this sounds like **pair** and **pear**

parent *noun*
a father or a mother

Word Building: **parentage** *noun* **parental** *adjective* **parentally** *adverb* **parenthood** *noun*

parenthesis (say *pə-ren-thə-səs*) *noun*
1 a descriptive or explanatory phrase or clause put into a sentence and marked off by commas, brackets or dashes, such as "the blue one" in *He took your bag – the blue one – when he left.* **2** one of the upright brackets ( ) often used to mark off such a phrase or clause

Word Building: the plural is **parentheses** (say *pə-ren-thə-seez*) □ **parenthesise** *verb* **parenthetic** *adjective*

parish *noun*
1 a district which has its own church and clergyman **2** the people of a parish

Word Building: the plural is **parishes** □ **parishioner** *noun*

park *noun*
1 an area of land set aside for public use and kept in good order by the council or government: *Hyde Park / a National Park*
park *verb*
2 to put or leave a car, bicycle or other vehicle in a particular spot, such as at the side of the road

parka *noun*
a warm waterproof jacket with a hood

parley *noun*
a talk or discussion, especially between people who are fighting each other

Word Building: the plural is **parleys** □ **parley** *verb*

parliament (say *pah-lə-mənt*) *noun*
the group of people elected to make the laws for a country or state

Word Building: **parliamentarian** *noun* **parliamentary** *adjective*
Word History: from an Old French word meaning "talking"

parlour or **parlor** *noun*
1 a formal room where you entertain visitors **2** a room where customers of certain businesses are attended to: *a beauty parlour*

parmesan *noun*
a hard, dry, pale-yellow cheese, often used for grating

Word History: named after the city of Parma in Northern Italy

parody (say *pa-rə-dee*) *noun*
a humorous imitation of a serious piece of writing or music

Word Building: the plural is **parodies** □ **parody** *verb* (**parodied, parodying**)

parole *noun*
the early freeing of a prisoner on the condition of good behaviour: *He is out on parole.*

Word Building: **parole** *verb*
Word History: from a French word meaning "word"

paroxysm (say *pa-rək-siz-əm*) *noun*
a sudden violent fit: *a paroxysm of coughing* | *a paroxysm of anger*

parquet (say *pah-kay*) *adjective*
made of short pieces of wood fitted together to form a pattern: *a parquet coffee table*

Word Building: **parquet** *noun* **parquetry** *noun*

parrot *noun*
a hook-billed, often brightly-coloured bird which can be taught to talk

Word Building: **parrot** *verb* to repeat or imitate like a parrot

parry *verb*
to turn aside or avoid: *She was able to parry my question.*

Word Building: other forms are **I parried, I have parried, I am parrying**

parse (rhymes with *bars*) *verb*
to describe by telling the part of speech and so on: *to parse all the words in the sentence*

parsley *noun*
a herb used in cooking

parsnip *noun*
a whitish root vegetable that is shaped like a carrot

parson *noun*
a clergyman or minister

Word Building: **parsonage** *noun* a parson's house

part *noun*
1 a piece or portion **2** a replacement piece for something worn out or broken: *We always carry spare parts for our bicycles.* **3** a share in something, such as work or a musical performance **4** an actor's role: *a part in a play*

part *verb*
5 to separate

Word Building: **partly** *adverb: The house is partly brick.*

partial (say *pah-shəl*) *adjective*
1 not total or general: *He suffers from partial deafness.* **2** showing unfair support or favouritism: *Everyone could see the umpire was being partial in his decisions.* **3 partial to** having a strong liking for: *I am partial to cake.*

Word Building: **partiality** *noun* **partially** *adverb*

participate (say *pah-tis-ə-payt*) *verb*
to take part

Word Building: **participant** *noun* **participation** *noun*

participle (say *pah-tə-sip-əl*) *noun*
1 a word formed from a verb and used as an adjective, such as "burning" in *a burning candle* or "added" in *added work* **2** a word formed from a verb and used in compound verbs, such as "burning" in *the candle has been burning* or "added" in *I have added*

Word Building: **participial** *adjective*

particle *noun*
a very small bit: *a particle of dust*

particular *adjective*
1 single, or one, rather than all: *I am interested in that particular book on dogs.* **2** more than usual or special: *Take particular care of that book.*

particular *noun*
3 a point or detail: *The report was right in every particular.* **4 in particular** especially: *There is one book in particular that I want to read.*

Word Building: **particularly** *adverb*

partition *noun*
1 a separating wall **2** a division into shares or parts: *The partition of the city into East Berlin and West Berlin occurred in 1945.*

Word Building: **partition** *verb* to divide into parts

partner *noun*
someone who shares or takes part in something with someone else: *a business partner | a dancing partner*

Word Building: **partner** *verb* **partnership** *noun*

part of speech *noun*
any of the main grammatical types of words in a language such as *noun, pronoun, verb, adjective, adverb, preposition, conjunction* or *interjection*

partridge *noun*
a European bird that is hunted and eaten

Word Building: the plural can be **partridge** or **partridges**

part-time *adjective*
taking or working fewer than all the usual working hours: *a part-time job | a part-time gardener*

Word Building: **part-time** *adverb: He works part-time.*

party *noun*
1 a social gathering, often to celebrate something: *a birthday party* **2** a group of people who work for the same political ideals: *the Australian Labor Party*

Word Building: the plural is **parties**

pass *verb*
1 to go by or beyond **2** to do successfully: *to pass a test* **3** to send or hand to: *to pass a message | Pass me that book.* **4** to approve or make: *to pass laws* **5 pass away** to die

pass *noun*
6 a narrow path or road through a low part in a mountain **7** a piece of paper that shows you are allowed to do something or go somewhere: *a theatre pass | a train pass* **8** the handing or tossing of a ball to another player in some ball games **9** the passing of an examination

Word Building: **passable** *adjective*

passage *noun*
1 a corridor, channel, or a way for going: *a passage between rooms | a passage between islands* **2** a part of a story or piece of music

passbook *noun*
another word for **bankbook**

passenger *noun*
someone who travels on a ship, plane, bus or other vehicle

passion (say <u>*pash*</u>*-ən*) *noun*
1 any strong feeling or emotion, especially love, anger or grief **2** a strong interest or enthusiasm: *He has a passion for football.*

Word Building: **passionate** *adjective*
Word History: from a Latin word meaning "suffering"

passionfruit *noun*
a small purplish fruit, the seeds and pulp of which you can eat

Word Use: the plural is **passionfruit**

passive *adjective*
1 letting things happen without taking any action yourself **2** having to do with a verb, the subject of which is having the action done to it rather than doing the action itself, such as "was punished" in *He was punished by his father.*

Word Use: compare definition 2 with **active**
Word Building: **passively** *adverb* **passivity** *noun*

Passover *noun*
a feast of the Jews held each year to celebrate the escape of the Hebrews from Egypt and to remember when God saved the Hebrew children while all the firstborn Egyptian children were killed

Word History: from the phrase "pass over"

passport *noun*
a government document which identifies you and which you need to travel to foreign countries

password *noun*
a secret word that lets you get into a place where others are not allowed

past *adjective*
1 gone by in time: *The old lady's past activities included bushwalking.*

past *noun*
2 time gone by: *in the past*

past *adverb*
3 by: *The troops marched past.*

pasta (say <u>*pas*</u>*-tə,* <u>*pahs*</u>*-*) *noun*
a food made from flour, water and sometimes egg, such as spaghetti or macaroni

paste *noun*
1 a mixture of flour and water used for sticking paper onto other surfaces
2 something made into a soft smooth mass: *toothpaste* | *almond paste*

Word Building: **paste** *verb: to paste pictures in a project book*

pastel (say *pas-təl*) *noun*
1 a soft pale colour **2** a crayon, or a drawing made with crayons

Word Building: **pastel** *adjective*

pasteurise or **pasteurize**
(say *pahs-chə-ruyz*) *verb*
to destroy germs in, by heating to a very high temperature: *to pasteurise milk*

Word Building: **pasteurisation** *noun*
Word History: named after Louis *Pasteur*, 1822-1895, a French chemist

pastime *noun*
something you do to make time pass pleasantly: *Reading is a good pastime.*

pastor *noun*
a clergyman or minister

Word Building: **pastorate** *noun*
Word History: from a Latin word meaning "shepherd"

pastry *noun*
a mixture of flour, water and fat cooked as a crust for pies and tarts

Word Building: the plural is **pastries**

past tense *noun*
the form of a verb which shows that something has already happened such as "ran" in *I ran away* and "have run" in *I have run away*

pasture (say *pahs-chə*) *noun*
land suitable for grazing cattle or sheep: *There is good pasture on the property.*

Word Building: **pastoral** *adjective: pastoral land* **pasture** *verb* to graze **pastoralist** *noun*

pasty[1] (say *pay-stee*) *adjective*
whitish or sick-looking: *a pasty complexion*

pasty[2] (say *pas-tee, pahs-tee*) *noun*
a type of pie filled with meat and vegetables

Word Building: the plural is **pasties**

pat[1] *verb*
1 to strike lightly with your hand
2 to stroke gently

Word Use: other forms are **I patted, I have patted, I am patting**
Word Building: **pat** *noun*

pat[2] *adjective*
1 exactly to the point: *He gave a pat reply.*
pat[2] *adverb*
2 exactly or perfectly: *I want to know it pat.* | *Learn it off pat.*

patch *noun*
1 a piece of material used to mend a hole or a weak place **2** a piece of material used to cover a wound **3** a small piece: *a patch of land* | *a patch of sunlight*

Word Building: the plural is **patches** □ **patch** *verb* **patchy** *adjective* (**patchier, patchiest**)

patchwork *noun*
a type of work in which pieces of different coloured or shaped cloth are sewn together

pâté (say *pat-ay, pah-tay*) *noun*
a paste or spread made out of finely minced liver, meat, fish, and so on

Word History: from a French word, which is why it looks like this

patent leather *noun*
leather with a very shiny surface

Word Building: **patent-leather** *adjective*

paternal *adjective*
having to do with or being like a father: *paternal love*

Word Building: **paternalism** *noun* **paternalistic** *adjective* **paternally** *adverb* **paternity** *noun*

path *noun*
a narrow way for walking: *a garden path*

pathetic (say *pə-thet-ik*) *adjective*
1 causing feelings of pity or sadness: *a pathetic sight* **2** showing a great lack of ability: *It was a pathetic attempt.*

Word Use: definition 2 is more suited to everyday language
Word Building: **pathetically** *adverb*

pathologist (say *pə-thol-ə-jəst*) *noun*
a doctor who is an expert in the effects of diseases on the body

Word Building: **pathological** *adjective* **pathology** *noun*

patient (say *pay-shənt*) *noun*
1 someone who is being treated by a doctor or is in a hospital
patient *adjective*
2 waiting calmly: *a patient customer*

Word Building: **patience** *noun* calmness while waiting **patiently** *adverb*

patio (say *pat-ee-oh, pay-shee-oh*) *noun*
an outdoor living area next to a house

Word Building: the plural is **patios**

patriarch (say *pay-tree-ahk*) *noun*
a male leader in a family, tribe or any field of activity

Word Building: **patriarchal** *adjective* **patriarchy** *noun*

patriot (say *pay-tree-ət*) *noun*
someone who loves their country and is loyal to it

Word Building: **patriotic** *adjective* **patriotically** *adverb* **patriotism** *noun*

patrol (say *pə-trohl*) *verb*
to go around regularly to make sure there is no trouble: *The police car patrolled the streets.*

Word Building: other forms are **I patrolled, I have patrolled, I am patrolling** □ **patrol** *noun*

patron (say *pay-trən*) *noun*
1 a regular customer of a hotel, shop, cinema or similar place **2** a supporter or helper: *a patron of art*

Word Building: **patronage** *noun*

patronise or **patronize**
(say *pat-rə-nuyz*) *verb*
1 to be a customer of: *I've been patronising that shop for years.* **2** to treat kindly, but as if inferior: *Older children often patronise the younger ones.*

patter[1] *verb*
to strike or move with quick, light, tapping sounds: *She pattered down the hallway in bare feet.*

Word Building: **patter** *noun*

patter[2] *noun*
rapid speech or chatter, especially of a salesman or entertainer

pattern *noun*
1 an ornamental design **2** a model or guide: *a paper pattern for a dress*

Word Building: **pattern** *verb*

paunch (rhymes with *launch*) *noun*
the belly or abdomen, usually a particularly large and rounded one: *He's got a paunch from drinking too much beer.*

Word Building: **paunchiness** *noun* **paunchy** *adjective*

pause (say *pawz*) *noun*
a short rest or stop when you're speaking or doing something

Word Building: **pause** *verb*

pave *verb*
to make a firm level surface by laying concrete, stones or bricks on: *to pave a path*

pavement *noun*
a paved footpath at the side of a road

pavilion (say *pə-vil-yən*) *noun*
an open shelter in a park or amusement area

pavlova *noun*
a dessert made of a large round meringue filled with cream and topped with fruit

Word History: named after Anna Pavlova, 1885-1931, a Russian ballerina

paw *noun*
the foot of an animal with nails or claws

Word Building: **paw** *verb* to strike or scrape with the paws

pawn[1] *verb*
to leave with a pawnbroker when you borrow money, to make sure that you repay your debt: *I pawned my watch.*

pawn[2] *noun*
one of the pieces of lowest value in chess

pawnbroker *noun*
someone who lends you money, but only if you leave something that can be sold if you don't return the money

pawpaw *noun*
a large, yellow, fleshy fruit which grows in tropical Australia

Word Use: another word for this is **papaya** (say *pə-puy-ə*)

pay *verb*
1 to give money in return for something: *I paid for the milk yesterday.* **2** to give or offer: *to pay a compliment* **3** to be worthwhile: *It pays to be honest.*
4 to suffer or be punished: *to pay for your mistakes*

pay *noun*
5 wages or salary

Word Building: other verb forms are **I paid, I have paid, I am paying** □ **payable** *adjective* **payment** *noun*

pea *noun*
a small, round, green seed which grows in a pod, used as a vegetable

peace *noun*
1 freedom from war **2** calm, quiet or stillness: *peace of mind | the peace of the countryside*

Word Building: **peaceable** *adjective* loving peace **peaceful** *adjective: a peaceful scene*

peach *noun*
a round, sweet, pinkish-yellow fruit with a single seed and furry skin

Word Building: the plural is **peaches**

peacock *noun*
a type of pheasant noted for the colourful eye-like pattern on its tail feathers

Word Use: the male is a **peacock;** the female is a **peahen;** the young is a **chick**
Word Building: the plural is **peacock** or **peacocks**

peak *noun*
1 the pointed top of a mountain
2 the highest or greatest point: *the peak of her achievements*

Word Building: **peak** *verb*

peal *noun*
1 a loud, long, drawn-out sound of bells
2 any other loud long sound: *a peal of laughter*

Word Use: be careful – this sounds like **peel**
Word Building: **peal** *verb*

peanut *noun*
a small nut which ripens in a pod underground and which you can eat

pear *noun*
a thin-skinned, pale green or brownish fruit, round at its base and growing smaller towards the stem

Word Use: be careful – this sounds like **pair** and **pare**

pearl (rhymes with *curl*) *noun*
a shiny, round, usually white growth, found in some oysters and used in jewellery

Word Use: be careful – this sounds like **purl**
Word Building: **pearly** *adjective*

peasant (say *pez-ənt*) *noun*
someone who lives and works on a farm and is regarded as an inferior sort of person

Word Use: this word is only used about olden times or of people in developing countries
Word Building: **peasantry** *noun* all peasants taken as a group

peat *noun*
1 soil which consists of partially rotted leaves, roots, grasses and similar matter in marshy areas **2** blocks of this, dried and used as fuel

pebble *noun*
a small, smooth, rounded stone

Word Building: **pebbly** *adjective*

pecan (say *pee-kan, pee-kan*) *noun*
a sweet oily nut which grows on trees in America, and which you can eat

peck *verb*
1 to strike or eat with the beak: *The bird pecked the branch. | The chickens pecked the corn.* **2** to pick or nibble at food
3 to kiss quickly on the cheek

Word Building: **peck** *noun*

peculiar (say *pə-kyooh-lee-ə*) *adjective*
1 strange, odd or queer **2 peculiar to** having to do with one particular person or thing: *Gathering shiny objects is a habit peculiar to magpies and bowerbirds.*

Word Building: **peculiarity** *noun* (**peculiarities**) **peculiarly** *adverb*

pedal *noun*
a lever worked by the foot: *an organ pedal | a sewing machine pedal | a bicycle pedal*

Word Use: be careful – this sounds like **peddle**
Word Building: **pedal** *verb* (**pedalled, pedalling**)

peddle *verb*
to take around from place to place in order to sell

Word Use: be careful – this sounds like **pedal**

pedestal *noun*
1 a support for a statue or ornament
2 the supporting base of a column

pedestrian (say *pə-des-tree-ən*) *noun*
someone who walks: *A pedestrian must be careful when crossing a busy street.*

Word History: from a Latin word meaning "on foot"

pedigree *noun*
a line of direct relationship, showing, for example, the father, and his father before him, and so on: *My dog has a long pedigree.*

Word Building: **pedigreed** *adjective*

pedlar *noun*
someone who travels round selling things

peel *verb*
1 to take off the skin, rind or outer layer of **2** to come off: *My skin is peeling where I was sunburnt.*

Word Use: be careful – this sounds like **peal**
Word Building: **peel** *noun: an orange peel* **peeler** *noun: a potato peeler* **peeling** *noun*

peep *verb*
1 to look through a small opening or from a hiding place **2** to come briefly or partly into view: *The sun peeped over the horizon.*

Word Building: **peep** *noun*

peer[1] *noun*
1 someone of your own age or rank
2 a nobleman

Word Use: be careful – this sounds like **pier**
Word Building: **peerage** *noun* the nobility **peeress** *noun* a noblewoman **peerless** *adjective* having no equal

peer[2] *verb*
1 to look closely in order to see clearly
2 to peep: *to peer through a window*

Word Use: be careful – this sounds like **pier**

peevish *adjective*
cross or easily annoyed

peg *noun*
1 a small wooden, metal or plastic pin used to fasten things, to hang things on, or to mark a place: *a clothes peg / a tent peg / a hat peg / a surveyor's peg*

peg *verb*
2 to fasten with a peg **3 peg away** to work steadily

Word Building: other verb forms are **I pegged, I have pegged, I am pegging**

pejorative (say *pə-jo-rə-tiv*) *adjective*
expressing disapproval: *a pejorative statement*

Word Building: **pejoratively** *adverb*

pelican *noun*
a large, web-footed seabird with a pouch hanging beneath its bill for holding the fish it catches

pellet *noun*
1 a small rounded piece of anything: *a paper pellet / a pellet of food* **2** a small bullet fired from a shotgun

pelmet *noun*
an ornamental covering which hides a curtain rail

pelt[1] *verb*
1 to throw: *to pelt stones at a post*
2 to come down heavily: *Rain pelted down.*
3 to hurry: *He pelted down the hill.*

pelt[2] *noun*
the skin taken from a dead animal to be made into leather

pelvis *noun*
the ring of bone made up of the lower part of your backbone and your two hip bones, and the cavity it forms

Word Building: the plural is **pelves** (say *pel-veez*) □ **pelvic** *adjective*

pen[1] *noun*
an instrument for writing with ink: *a ballpoint pen*

Word Building: **pen** *verb* (**penned, penning**) to write

pen[2] *noun*
an enclosure for animals on a farm

Word Building: **pen** *verb* (**penned** or **pent, penning**) to put in a pen

penal (say *pee-nəl*) *adjective*
having to do with the punishment of crimes: *the penal laws*

penalty (say *pen-əl-tee*) *noun*
1 the price you pay for breaking a law or rule **2** a free kick or shot allowed in some sports to one team or player because an opponent has broken a rule

Word Building: the plural is **penalties** □ **penalise** *verb*

penance (say *pen-əns*) *noun*
a punishment you agree or offer to accept to show you are sorry for doing wrong

pencil *noun*
a thin pointed piece of wood enclosing a stick of graphite or crayon and used for writing or drawing

Word Building: **pencil** *verb* (**pencilled, pencilling**)

pendant *noun*
a hanging piece of jewellery such as a necklace

Word Building: **pendant** *adjective* hanging

pendulum (say *pen-jə-ləm*) *noun*
a weight swinging backward and forward which makes some clocks work

penetrate (say *pen-ə-trayt*) *verb*
1 to go into or through, especially with a sharp instrument: *The arrow penetrated his arm. / The army penetrated the enemy's*

defences. **2** to enter, reach or pass through, as if by piercing: *The knife penetrated to the bone.*

Word Building: **penetrating** *adjective: a penetrating look* **penetrable** *adjective* **penetration** *noun* **penetratingly** *adverb*

penfriend *noun*
someone, usually in another country, you have become friends with through writing letters·

penguin (say *pen-gwən*) *noun*
a bird which cannot fly, has webbed feet and lives in or near the cold southern parts of the world

Word History: from Old French words meaning "white head"

penicillin (say *pen-ə-sil-ən*) *noun*
a strong germ-fighting substance used in medicines and ointments

peninsula (say *pə-nin-shə-lə*) *noun*
a long piece of land jutting out into the sea

Word Building: **peninsular** *adjective*
Word History: from Latin words meaning "almost an island"

penis (say *pee-nəs*) *noun*
the part of a male's body with which he urinates and has sexual intercourse

penitent (say *pen-ə-tənt*) *adjective*
sorry for wrongdoing and willing to put things right

Word Use: a similar word is **repentant**
Word Building: **penitence** *noun* **penitently** *adverb*

penitentiary (say *pen-ə-ten-shə-ree*) *noun*
a gaol or prison

penknife *noun*
a small knife with one or more blades that fold into the handle so that it can be carried safely in a pocket

Word Use: the plural is **penknives** □ this used to be used to clean and mend quill pens □ it can also be called a **pocket-knife**

pennant *noun*
a triangular flag, used as a signal on ships or as an award in a sporting event

penny *noun*
a bronze or copper coin worth only a small amount, that used to be used in Australia and still is in Britain and some other countries

Word Building: the plural is **pennies** or **pence** □ **penniless** *adjective* having no money

pension *noun*
a regular payment made by the government to someone who is old, sick or poor, or by a private company to someone who has retired from working for it

Word Building: **pensioner** *noun*

pensive *adjective*
seriously or sadly thoughtful: *a pensive stare*

Word Building: **pensively** *adverb*

pentagon *noun*
a flat shape with five straight sides

Word Building: **pentagonal** *adjective*

penthouse *noun*
a separate flat on the roof or top storey of a building

people *noun*
1 human beings in general **2** all the members of a tribe, race or nation: *a peace-loving people / a nomadic people*
3 the members of a particular group or community: *the people of a neighbourhood / working people* **4** your family or relatives: *Some of my people are coming to visit.*

Word Building: the plural is usually **people** but for definition 2 it is **peoples**

pepper *noun*
1 a spice with a hot taste, made from the dried berries of a tropical plant
2 a capsicum: *a green pepper / a red pepper*

Word Building: **peppery** *adjective*

peppermint *noun*
a lolly made with a strong-tasting, strong-smelling oil from a plant

perceive *verb*
1 to come to know of through one of the senses, such as sight or hearing: *He perceived a glimmer of light at the top of the well.* **2** to understand: *I perceive that you do not agree.*

Word Building: **perceivable** *adjective* **perceptible** *adjective*

per cent *adverb*
1 in every hundred: *My bank pays ten per cent interest so if I have $100 in my account for a year, I get paid $10 interest.*
per cent *noun*
2 *another word for* **percentage**: *What per cent are you offering?*

Word Use: another spelling is **percent** □ the symbol for definition 1 is "%"

percentage *noun*
1 a number which shows the rate in every hundred: *The percentage of dark-haired children in this class is 65.* **2** a part or proportion: *A large percentage of children at our school live nearby.*

perception *noun*
1 the act of perceiving or the ability to perceive: *My perception of colour is not good.* **2** the ability to understand the inner nature of something quickly and clearly: *She has a lot of perception.* **3** understanding or knowledge

Word Building: **perceptive** *adjective* quick in perceiving **perceptively** *adverb*

perch[1] *noun*
1 a rod for birds to roost on
perch[1] *verb*
2 to settle or rest on a perch or something similar: *The birds perched on the roof. | I perched the vase on the top shelf.*

perch[2] *noun*
a kind of fish that you can eat

Word Building: the plural is **perches** or **perch**

percolate (say *per-kə-layt*) *verb*
1 to make a liquid pass through a substance **2** to spread or become known gradually: *The news percolated through the classroom.*

Word Use: a similar word is **filter**
Word Building: **percolator** *noun* a coffee-maker in which boiling water is percolated through ground coffee **percolation** *noun*

percussion (say *pə-kush-ən*) *noun*
the hitting of one thing against another

percussion instrument *noun*
a musical instrument, such as a drum, cymbal, or piano, which produces notes when it is struck

Word Building: **percussionist** *noun*

perennial (say *pə-ren-ee-əl*) *adjective*
1 lasting for a long time or continually coming back: *a perennial joke | a perennial trouble-maker* **2** having a life cycle of more than two years: *a perennial plant*

Word Building: **perennial** *noun* a perennial plant **perennially** *adverb*

perfect (say *per-fəkt*) *adjective*
1 with nothing missing and no faults
2 completely suited for a particular purpose: *He is a perfect husband for her.*
3 complete or absolute: *a perfect stranger*
4 having to do with the form of a verb which shows that something continues up to the present (*I have run*), to some point in the past (*I had run*), or in the future (*I will have run*)
perfect (say *per-fekt*) *verb*
5 to make complete or perfect

Word Building: **perfection** *noun* **perfectly** *adverb*

perforate (say *per-fə-rayt*) *verb*
to make a hole or holes in: *He used the point of a pencil to perforate the paper.*

Word Building: **perforated** *adjective* **perforation** *noun*

perform *verb*
1 to do or carry out: *She performed a graceful arm movement. | He performed his duty.* **2** to do an act in front of an audience

Word Building: **performance** *noun* **performer** *noun*

perfume *noun*
1 a liquid prepared so that it gives out a pleasant smell **2** a pleasant smell

Word Building: **perfume** *verb: to perfume a handkerchief* **perfumer** *noun* someone who makes or sells perfume **perfumery** *noun*

pergola (say *per-gə-lə, pə-goh-lə*) *noun*
a shelter made of bars supported on posts, over which climbing plants are grown

peril *noun*
danger or risk: *Our lives are in peril.*

Word Building: **perilous** *adjective* **perilously** *adverb*

perimeter (say *pə-rim-ə-tə*) *noun*
1 the outside edge of a shape or area: *the perimeter of a football field* **2** the length of this edge

period *noun*
1 any division or portion of time: *We will have a period of work and then a period of play.* **2** a particular division of time or history: *the colonial period in Australia* **3** the monthly flow of blood from the uterus of a girl or woman, or the time when this happens **4** *another word for* **full stop**
period *adjective*
5 having to do with a particular period of history: *period costumes*

Word Building: **periodic** or **periodical** *adjective* happening or appearing at regular intervals **periodical** *noun* a magazine that comes out at regular intervals **periodically** *adverb*

periphery (say *pə-rif-ə-ree*) *noun*
the outside edge of an area or thing: *The chairs were arranged around the periphery of the room.*

Word Building: **peripheral** *adjective* not central in importance **peripherally** *adverb*

periscope *noun*
an instrument made of a tube with an arrangement of mirrors, used to see something from a position below or behind it: *the periscope of a submarine*

perish *verb*
1 to die: *The explorers perished in the desert.* **2** to rot or decay: *Rubber perishes.*

Word Building: **perishable** *adjective* **perishable** *noun*

perjury *noun*
the crime of telling a lie while under an oath: *The witness in the court case committed perjury.*

Word Building: **perjure** *verb* **perjurer** *noun*

permanent *adjective*
lasting for a very long time or forever: *a permanent dye | permanent snow on a mountain top*

Word Use: the opposite is **temporary**
Word Building: **permanence** *noun* **permanency** *noun* **permanently** *adverb*

permeate (say *per-mee-ayt*) *verb*
to pass or spread through: *A strange smell permeated the room.*

Word Building: **permeable** *adjective* able to be passed through, especially by liquids **permeation** *noun*

permission *noun*
the act of permitting or allowing someone to do something

Word Building: **permissible** *adjective* **permissibly** *adverb*

permissive *adjective*
allowing freedom, especially in sexual or moral matters: *a permissive society*

Word Building: **permissively** *adverb* **permissiveness** *noun*

permit (say *pə-mit*) *verb*
1 to allow **2** to give the chance for: *This oven door permits heat to escape.*

permit (say *per-mit*) *noun*
3 an official certificate that gives permission

Word Use: a similar word to definition 3 is **licence**
Word Building: other verb forms are **I permitted, I have permitted, I am permitting**

permutation *noun*
the changing of the order of the elements in a group or set: *ACB and BAC are some of the permutations of ABC.*

peroxide (say *pə-rok-suyd*) *noun*
a chemical that is often used to bleach or lighten hair

Word Building: **peroxide** *adjective: a peroxide blonde* **peroxide** *verb*

perpendicular (say *per-pən-dik-yə-lə*) *adjective*
1 upright or vertical: *a perpendicular post*
2 meeting a line or surface at right angles

perpetrate *verb*
to do or carry out: *to perpetrate a crime*

Word Building: **perpetration** *noun* **perpetrator** *noun*

perpetual (say *pə-pet-chooh-əl*) *adjective*
1 lasting for ever **2** continuing without a break: *There has been a perpetual stream of visitors.*

Word Building: **perpetuate** *verb* to make last for a very long time **perpetually** *adverb*

perplex *verb*
to make puzzled: *This question perplexes me*

Word Use: similar words are **confuse** and **bewilder**
Word Building: **perplexed** *adjective* **perplexing** *adjective* **perplexity** *noun*

persecute *verb*
1 to constantly treat unfairly or cruelly
2 to harm or punish for having certain ideas or religious beliefs

Word Building: **persecution** *noun* **persecutor** *noun*

persevere *verb*
to continue in spite of difficulty: *I am tired but I will persevere with my work.*

Word Use: a similar word is **persist**
Word Building: **perseverance** *noun*

persimmon *noun*
a red or orange plumlike fruit

Word History: from an Algonquian (a language of some American Indian tribes) word meaning "(artificially) dried fruit"

persist *verb*
1 to continue doing something, often in spite of difficulty: *He persisted with his questions until he got an answer.* **2** to go on and on: *Her toothache persisted for hours.*

Word Use: a similar word for definition 1 is **persevere**
Word Building: **persistence** *noun* **persistent** *adjective*

person *noun*
1 a human being **2** a type of verb or pronoun form that shows the difference between the speaker or "first person", the person spoken to or "second person", and anyone or anything spoken about or "third person", such as, in their order, the pronouns "I", "you" and "her" in *I will tell you about her.* **3 in person** with the person actually present: *He brought the letter in person.*

personage *noun*
a person, especially someone important

personal *adjective*
1 private or having to do with a particular person: *a personal matter / personal attention* **2** directed to a particular person in a rude way: *You shouldn't make personal remarks about someone's appearance.*

Word Building: **personally** *adverb*

personal computer *noun*
a small computer that can be placed on a desk or table and is meant for use in the home or by small businesses

Word Use: the short form of this is **PC**

personality *noun*
1 the qualities of character that make someone an individual: *My baby already has a personality.* **2** strong or lively character: *She has plenty of personality.* **3** someone who is well-known: *a television personality*

Word Use: a similar word for definition 3 is **celebrity**
Word Building: the plural is **personalities**

personify *verb*
1 to give a human nature or form to: *Some stories personify animals by making them talk.* **2** to be a perfect example of: *She personifies beauty.*

Word Building: other forms are **it personified, it has personified, it is personifying** □ **personification** *noun*

personnel (say *per-sə-nel*) *noun*
the group of people working for a particular organisation

perspective *noun*
1 the appearance of distance as well as height and width, produced on a flat surface, such as in a painting: *The artist has achieved perspective in painting that row of trees.* **2** a mental point of view: *She has a new perspective on this problem.* **3 in perspective** with a proper balance

perspire *verb*
to get rid of a salty liquid through the pores of your skin

Word Use: a similar word is **sweat**
Word Building: **perspiration** *noun*

persuade *verb*
to cause to do or believe something by advice, argument or influence: *He persuaded her to come. / She persuaded him that he was wrong.*

Word Building: **persuasive** *adjective* **persuasively** *adverb*

persuasion *noun*
1 the act or power of persuading **2** a belief, especially religious: *people of the Christian persuasion*

pert *adjective*
1 bold or impudent **2** attractive in a lively way: *a pert hat*

Word Building: **pertly** *adverb* **pertness** *noun*

pertinent *adjective*
having to do with the matter being discussed or thought about: *a pertinent comment*

Word Use: a similar word is **relevant**
Word Building: **pertinence** *noun* **pertinently** *adverb*

perturb *verb*
to disturb or worry greatly

Word Building: **perturbation** *noun*

perverse *adjective*
deliberately going against what is expected or wanted: *a perverse answer / a perverse mood*

Word Use: a similar word is **contrary**
Word Building: **perversely** *adverb* **perverseness** *noun* **perversity** *noun*

pervert (say *pə-vert*) *verb*
1 to make turn away from what is right, either in behaviour or in beliefs
pervert (say *per-vert*) *noun*
2 someone who has unusual or unpleasant sexual habits

Word Building: **perversion** *noun* **perverted** *adjective*

pessimism *noun*
the habit of expecting that things will turn out badly

Word Use: the opposite is **optimism**
Word Building: **pessimist** *noun* someone who looks on the gloomy side **pessimistic** *adjective* **pessimistically** *adverb*

pest *noun*
someone or something that is annoying or harmful

Word Building: **pestilent** *adjective*

pester *verb*
to annoy continually

pesticide *noun*
a chemical for killing pests, such as insects

pestle (say *pes-əl*) *noun*
a club-shaped tool for grinding substances in a mortar

Word History: from a Latin word meaning "pounded"

pet *noun*
1 an animal that is kept because it is loved rather than because it is useful
2 a person who is given special attention: *teacher's pet*

pet *verb*
3 to treat in a special way, giving kisses and loving pats to, as if to a pet

Word Building: other verb forms are **I petted, I have petted, I am petting**

petal *noun*
any of the leaflike parts of a flower which are usually of a colour different to green

petite (say *pə-teet*) *adjective*
small and slim: *a petite woman*

petition *noun*
a formal request, especially to someone or a group in power: *to sign a petition to the local council asking for more parks*

Word Building: **petition** *verb* **petitioner** *noun*

petrify *verb*
1 to make stiff or unable to move with fear **2** to turn into stone or something like stone: *Millions of years have petrified the tree trunk.*

Word Building: other forms are **it petrified, it has petrified, it is petrifying** □ **petrifaction** *noun*

petrol *noun*
a liquid made from petroleum, used widely as a fuel in engines

petroleum *noun*
an oily liquid, usually obtained by drilling under the ground, and used to make petrol or other fuels

petticoat *noun*
a light skirtlike undergarment worn by women and girls

Word Use: another word for this is **slip**

petty *adjective*
1 of little importance: *petty details*
2 concerned with unimportant things or showing narrow ideas and interests: *a petty mind*

Word Use: a similar word to definition 1 is **trivial**
Word Building: other forms are **pettier, pettiest** □ **pettily** *adverb* **pettiness** *noun*

petulant *adjective*
showing or feeling impatient annoyance, especially over something unimportant: *a petulant toss of the head*

Word Building: **petulance** *noun* **petulantly** *adverb*

petunia *noun*
a kind of plant with funnel-shaped flowers of different colours

Word History: from a Guarani (South American) word meaning "tobacco"

pew *noun*
a long benchlike seat in a church

pewter *noun*
a mixture of metals, including tin, used for making dishes, mugs and so on

phalanger (say *fə-lan-jə*) *noun*
one of the Australian marsupials which live in trees and which have tails that can wrap around branches, such as cuscuses and brush-tailed possums

phantom *noun*
1 an image appearing in a dream or in the mind only **2** a ghost or ghostly appearance

Word Building: **phantasmal** *adjective*

pharmacy *noun*
1 the preparing and giving out of drugs used in medicine: *She is studying pharmacy.* **2** a chemist's shop

Word Building: the plural is **pharmacies** □ **pharmaceutical** *adjective* **pharmacist** *noun*

pharynx (say *fa-rinks*) *noun*
the tube which connects your mouth and nose passages with your throat

Word Use: the plural is **pharynxes**

phase *noun*
1 a stage of change or development: *the phase of childhood*
phase *verb*
2 to gradually introduce or take out: *We are phasing in a new method of work. / We are phasing out all the old-fashioned machinery.*

pheasant (say *fez-ənt*) *noun*
a kind of large long-tailed bird, often eaten as food

phenomenon *noun*
1 anything which is seen or able to be seen: *The growth of new leaves in spring is a phenomenon of nature.* **2** something or someone that is beyond the ordinary

Word Building: the plural is **phenomena** □ **phenomenal** *adjective* extraordinary **phenomenally** *adverb*

phial (say *fuy-əl*) *noun*
a small glass container for liquids: *a phial of medicine*

philately (say *fə-lat-ə-lee*) *noun*
the collecting and studying of postage stamps

Word Building: **philatelic** *adjective* **philatelist** *noun*

philharmonic *adjective*
fond of music

Word Use: this is used especially in the names of musical societies, choirs or orchestras

philistine (say *fil-ə-stuyn*) *noun*
someone who doesn't like beautiful things such as paintings, sculpture or music, and is proud to be that way

Word Building: **philistine** *adjective* **philistinism** *noun*
Word History: named after the people of *Philistia*, an ancient country on the east coast of the Mediterranean Sea, who were thought to be barbarians

philosophy (say *fə-los-ə-fee*) *noun*
1 the search for truth and wisdom and the answers to questions such as "Why do I exist?" and "What is the purpose of life?" **2** a system of rules or principles by which you live: *a philosophy of life*

Word Building: the plural is **philosophies** □ **philosophical** *adjective* sensible and calm when faced with difficulties **philosopher** *noun* **philosophically** *adverb* **philosophise** *verb*

phlegmatic (say *fleg-mat-ik*) *adjective*
calm and even-tempered

phobia (say *foh-bee-ə*) *noun*
an overpowering fear: *a phobia about spiders*

Word Use: this word is often joined with another word part to mean "fear of a particular thing", as in *claustrophobia* which means "fear of being shut in a small space"
Word Building: **phobic** *adjective*

phone *noun*
a shortened form of **telephone**

Word Building: **phone** *verb*

phonetics *noun*
the study of the sounds used in speaking

Word Building: **phonetic** *adjective: the phonetic alphabet* **phonetically** *adverb*

phoney *adjective*
false or not genuine: *a phoney $20 note*

Word Building: **phoney** *noun*

phosphorescent (say *fos-fə-res-ənt*) *adjective*
shining or giving out light without getting hot

Word Building: **phosphoresce** *verb* **phosphorescence** *noun*

phosphorus (say *fos-fə-rəs*) *noun*
a chemical element which is used in making match heads, detergents and garden fertilisers

Word Building: **phosphate** *noun* a garden fertiliser made from phosphorus
Word History: from a Greek word meaning "bringer of light"

photo *noun*
a shortened form of **photograph**

Word Building: the plural is **photos**

photocopy *noun*
an exact copy of a page of writing or pictures, made by a machine using a special camera and paper which reacts to light

Word Use: another word for this is **photostat**
Word Building: the plural is **photocopies** □ **photocopier** *noun* a machine which makes these copies **photocopy** *verb* (**photocopied, photocopying**)

photogenic *adjective*
looking attractive in photographs

photograph *noun*
a picture produced when a film is exposed to light in a camera

Word Building: **photograph** *verb* **photographic** *adjective*

photography *noun*
the art of taking photographs

Word Building: **photographer** *noun*

photosynthesis
(say *foh-toh-sin-thə-səs*) *noun*
the process by which green plants are able to use sunlight to make sugars from carbon dioxide and water

phrase *noun*
1 a small group of words that go together, usually without a verb **2** a group of musical notes which go together to form part of a tune

phrase *verb*
3 to say or write in a particular way: *Could you phrase your question differently?*

phylum (say *fuy-ləm*) *noun*
one of the main groups into which biologists classify animals and plants: *All animals with backbones are in the same phylum.*

Word Building: the plural is **phyla**

physical *adjective*
1 having to do with the human body: *physical exercise* **2** having to do with the material things in the world rather than spiritual things

Word Building: **physically** *adverb*

physician (say *fiz-ish-ən*) *noun*
a medical doctor, especially one who does not do surgery

physics *noun*
the science of heat, light, electricity, magnetism, motion and other forms of matter and energy

Word Building: **physicist** *noun*

physiology (say *fiz-ee-ol-ə-jee*) *noun*
the science that has to do with the bodies of living things and how they work

Word Building: **physiological** *adjective*
physiologist *noun*

physiotherapy *noun*
the treatment of disease and injuries by massage and exercise

Word Building: **physiotherapist** *noun*

physique (say *fə-zeek*) *noun*
the shape of someone's body: *a muscular physique*

pi (rhymes with *my*) *noun*
the number you always get, 3.141 592+, when you divide the circumference of a circle by its diameter, expressed by the symbol π

pianist (say *pee-ə-nəst*) *noun*
someone who plays the piano

piano[1] *noun*
a large musical instrument played by striking keys which are connected to hammers which then strike metal strings

Word History: short for the Italian words *pianoforte* or *fortepiano*

piano[2] *adverb*
softly: *This music should be played piano.*

Word Use: this instruction in music is written as "p" □ the opposite of this is **forte**
Word Building: **pianissimo** *adverb* very softly
Word History: from an Italian word

piano accordion *noun*
a kind of accordion which has keys like a piano

picador (say *pik-ə-daw*) *noun*
a bullfighter on horseback who makes the bull angry by poking it with sharp sticks

Word Use: compare this word with **matador**

piccolo (say *pik-ə-loh*) *noun*
a small flute with a very high sound

Word Building: the plural is **piccolos**
Word History: from an Italian word meaning "small"

pick[1] *verb*
1 to choose or select **2** to take or gather **3** to use a sharp object to break open or dig into **4 pick at** to eat hardly any of: *to pick at your food* **5 pick on** to annoy or criticise **6 pick up a** to call for: *I'll pick you up at 8.30.* **b** to learn easily, without special teaching: *Children pick up foreign languages quickly.* **c** to get well again

pick[1] *noun*
7 a choice or selection: *Take your pick.* **8** a plectrum, used to play a guitar or banjo **9 the pick** the best one

Word Building: **picker** noun

pick[2] *noun*
a tool made up of a metal bar with sharp ends, fitted to a wooden handle and used for breaking up hard ground

Word Use: it is also called a **pickaxe**

picket *noun*
1 a pointed wooden fence post
2 members of a trade union who stand guard outside their workplace during a strike, to stop people from going in to work

Word Building: **picket** *verb* (**picketed, picketing**): *to picket a factory*

pickle *noun*
1 an onion, cucumber or other vegetable preserved in vinegar or salt water
2 a spot of trouble: *to get yourself into a pickle*

Word Building: **pickle** *verb* to preserve in salt or vinegar

pickpocket *noun*
someone who steals things out of people's pockets or handbags

picnic *noun*
1 an outing to the beach, park and so on, during which you eat a meal in the open air **2** an easy thing to do: *It's no picnic doing all your Christmas shopping in one day.*

Word Use: definition 2 is more suited to everyday language
Word Building: **picnic** *verb* (**picnicked, picnicking**)

picture *noun*
1 a drawing, painting, photo or something similar **2** someone or something that looks very beautiful: *She looks a picture in her new dress.* **3 the pictures** *another word for* **cinema**
picture *verb*
4 to imagine: *I can't picture myself being old.*

Word Building: **pictorial** *adjective* illustrated: *a pictorial history of Australia*

picturesque (say *pik-chə-resk*) *adjective*
pretty or charming: *a picturesque village*

Word Building: **picturesquely** *adverb*

pidgin (say *pij-ən*) *noun*
a language based on a mixture of other languages and used by people who have no other language in common

pie *noun*
a pastry case filled with fruit, vegetables or meat and baked in an oven

piebald *adjective*
covered with patches of black and white or other colours: *a piebald horse*

Word Use: compare this with **skewbald**

piece *noun*
1 a bit or part of something **2** a single or individual thing: *a piece of fruit*
piece *verb*
3 to fit or join: *to piece together a jigsaw*

piecemeal *adverb*
bit by bit or piece by piece

Word Building: **piecemeal** *adjective*

pied (rhymes with *side*) *adjective*
covered with different coloured patches: *the Pied Piper*

Word History: from the word *magpie,* as this bird has black-and-white feathers

pier (rhymes with *here*) *noun*
1 a jetty built out into the water, that you can tie a boat to or fish from **2** one of the wooden or concrete supports which are driven into the ground to hold up a bridge

Word Use: a similar word for definition 2 is **pile** □ be careful – this sounds like **peer**

pierce *verb*
to go into or through sharply: *The needle pierced her finger. / Her screams pierced the night.*

Word Building: **piercing** *adjective* loud and sharp: *piercing screams* **piercingly** *adverb*

piety (say *puy-ə-tee*) *noun*
deep honour and respect for religion

Word Building: **pious** *adjective* **piously** *adverb*

pig *noun*
1 a farm animal with a flat snout and curly tail, which is kept for its meat **2** someone who is dirty, selfish or greedy

Word Use: similar words are **hog** or **swine** □ the male is a **boar;** the female is a **sow;** the young is a **piglet**
Word Building: **pigsty** or **piggery** *noun* a place where pigs are kept

pigeon (say *pij-ən*) *noun*
a plump small-headed bird which is easily tamed

pigeonhole *noun*
a small compartment for papers in an old-fashioned desk

piggyback *noun*
a ride on the back or shoulders

Word Building: **piggyback** *verb*

pig-headed *adjective*
stupidly stubborn or obstinate

piglet *noun*
a baby pig

pigment *noun*
1 a coloured powder which can be mixed with water to make paint **2** the substance which gives animals and plants colour

Word Building: **pigmentation** *noun*

pigtail *noun*
a plait or bunch of tied-up hair hanging from the side or back of your head

pike *noun*
a large fierce fish with a long pointed snout, found in northern countries

pikelet *noun*
a small sweet pancake, often eaten with butter and jam

pile[1] *noun*
1 a number of things heaped up in one place **2** a large amount or number: *I have a pile of homework.*

pile[1] *verb*
3 to load or stack **4 pile up** to heap up or accumulate

pile[2] *noun*
a long heavy beam driven into the ground to support a bridge or building

Word Use: a word with a similar meaning is **pier**

pile[3] *noun*
the raised surface of carpet, towels, velvet and similar material

pilfer *verb*
to steal in small amounts: *to pilfer biscuits from the tin*

Word Building: **pilferer** *noun*

pilgrim *noun*
someone who makes a long journey to visit a holy place

Word Building: **pilgrimage** *noun: to make a pilgrimage to Mecca*
Word History: from a Latin word meaning "foreigner"

pillage *verb*
to rob brutally and violently: *The enemy soldiers pillaged the city.*

Word Use: a similar word is **plunder**
Word Building: **pillage** *noun* **pillager** *noun*

pillar *noun*
a column which supports part of a building

pillion *noun*
the passenger seat behind the driver's seat on a motorcycle

Word Building: **pillion** *adjective*
Word History: from a Latin word meaning "skin" or "pelt"

pillow *noun*
a soft cushion to rest your head on when you are in bed

pilot *noun*
1 someone who flies a plane **2** someone who steers a ship into or out of port

pilot *adjective*
3 done as an experiment: *a pilot film for a new television series*

Word Building: **pilot** *verb*

pimple *noun*
a pus-filled swelling, usually on the face

Word Building: **pimply** *adjective*

pin *noun*
1 a thin piece of metal with a sharply pointed end, used to fasten things together **2** any type of fastener that looks or works like a pin: *Grandma broke her hip and had to have a pin put in it.*

pin *verb*
3 to fasten or hold securely in position: *to pin papers together / The fallen branch pinned him to the ground.*

Word Building: other verb forms are **I pinned, I have pinned, I am pinning**

PIN *noun*
a group of numbers or letters you use to show who you are when you are getting money from an automatic teller machine, or something like this

Word Use: another name is **PIN number**
Word History: an acronym made by joining the first letters of the words *Personal Identification Number*

pinafore *noun*
a dress with no sleeves and a low neck, worn over a blouse or jumper, often as a school uniform or apron

pinball *noun*
a game in which you pull levers and push buttons to shoot a ball up a sloping board and score points when the ball hits various objects on the board

pince-nez (say *<u>pans</u>-nay*) *noun*
a pair of glasses which are kept in place by a spring which pinches your nose, instead of having the usual sort of frame which fits over your ears

Word History: from a French word meaning "pinch nose"

pincers *plural noun*
1 a tool with a pair of hinged, pinching jaws, used for pulling nails out of wood
2 the pinching claws of crabs, lobsters and some insects

pinch *verb*
1 to press or squeeze tightly and painfully between two surfaces, such as your thumb and finger: *He pinched her arm.* **2** to steal
pinch *noun*
3 a painful nip or squeeze **4** the very small amount that you can hold between your finger and thumb: *a pinch of salt*
5 at a pinch if absolutely necessary: *Eight people can fit into the car at a pinch.*

Word Use: definition 2 is more suited to everyday language
Word Building: **pincher** *noun*

pincushion *noun*
a small cushion in which pins can be stuck to keep them handy when sewing

pine[1] *noun*
an evergreen tree with needle-like leaves and cones instead of flowers

pine[2] *verb*
1 to have an intense longing, or to yearn: *to pine for home* **2 pine away** to become sick from grief and longing

pineapple *noun*
a large, yellow, tropical fruit which is sweet and juicy inside and has a rough outer skin

ping-pong *noun*
a game rather like tennis but played indoors on a table, using small bats and a very light, hollow, plastic ball

Word Use: it is also known as **table tennis**

pinion[1] *noun*
a small toothed wheel which locks together with a toothed bar or larger wheel, used in machinery

pinion[2] *noun*
1 a bird's wing or feather
pinion[2] *verb*
2 to cut off part of a bird's wing to stop it flying away **3** to prevent escape by tying back the arms or hands

pink[1] *adjective*
1 pale red
pink[1] *noun*
2 in the pink feeling bright and healthy

pink[2] *verb*
to cut in a zigzag pattern

Word Building: **pinking shears** *noun* scissors with notched blades for cutting a zigzag line

pinnacle *noun*
1 a high, pointed mountain peak, or a tall, pointed spire on the roof of a building
2 the highest point of anything

pin-up *noun*
a picture of a favourite person, pinned or stuck up on a wall

pioneer *noun*
someone who first explores an area, going ahead of others and opening the way for them: *pioneers opening up the Australian bush | a pioneer of modern music*

Word Building: **pioneer** *verb*

pious (say <u>puy</u>-əs) *adjective*
deeply religious

Word Building: **piety** *noun* **piously** *adverb*

pip[1] *noun*
the small seed of an apple, orange or similar fruit

pip[2] *noun*
a short high sound such as the ones used as time signals on the phone or on radio

pipe *noun*
1 a hollow tube for carrying water, gas and so on **2** a small bowl with a hollow tube or stem for smoking tobacco
3 a tube through which you can pump air to make musical notes, such as in an organ
pipe *verb*
4 to transport or carry using a pipe: *to pipe water from the dam to the house*
5 pipe down to keep quiet
6 pipe up to start talking suddenly

Word Building: **pipeline** *noun* a pipe for carrying gas, oil or water over a long distance

pipi *noun*
a shellfish that burrows in the sand and that is good to eat

piping *noun*
1 a system of pipes such as for the plumbing of a house **2** the shrill sound made by birds **3** a thin strip of material for trimming the edges of cushions or clothes
piping *adverb*
4 *in the phrase* **piping hot** very hot

pipsqueak *noun*
someone thought to be small and unimportant

Word Use: this word is more suited to everyday language

pique (rhymes with *week*) *verb*
1 to annoy and upset: *Maria's refusal to see Evan piqued him.* **2** to excite or stimulate: *The large parcel piqued her curiosity.*

Word Building: **piquant** *adjective* stimulating or interesting **pique** *noun* anger or hurt feelings

piranha (say *pə-rah-nə*) *noun*
a small South American fish which swims in schools that viciously attack animals, including people, and eat their flesh at great speed

pirate *noun*
1 someone who attacks and robs ships at sea
pirate *verb*
2 to take and use without permission: *to pirate someone's ideas and pretend they are your own*

Word Building: **piracy** *noun*

pirouette (say *pi-rooh-et*) *noun*
a quick turn in a dance, often on tiptoe

Word Building: **pirouette** *verb*
Word History: from a French word meaning "top" or "whirligig"

pistil *noun*
the seed-bearing part of a flower

pistol *noun*
a gun with a short barrel that fits into a holster or pocket

piston *noun*
a rod or disc inside a tube which is pumped up and down and used in engines

pit[1] *noun*
1 a large hole in the ground, such as a mine **2** a small hollow, such as a scar left on someone's face by acne **3** the space in front of and beneath the stage in a theatre where the orchestra sits **4** an area beside a car racing track where the cars are repaired and filled with petrol
pit[1] *verb*
5 to make pits or hollows in: *Acne can pit your face.* **6** to set against: *He pitted his wits against their strength.*

Word Building: other verb forms are **I pitted, I have pitted, I am pitting** □ **pitted** *adjective*

pit[2] *noun*
the stone of a fruit such as a peach or a date

Word Building: **pit** *verb* (**pitted, pitting**)

pitch *verb*
1 to set up: *to pitch a tent* **2** to throw **3** to make a sudden falling movement: *He tripped and pitched forward.* **4** to rise and fall, as a ship does **5** to set at a certain level of musical pitch: *She pitched her instrument too high.*
pitch *noun*
6 a throw or toss **7** the quality of a musical note thought of in terms of its highness or lowness **8** the area for playing sport, particularly the area between the wickets in cricket
9 the degree of slope: *the steep pitch of the roof*

pitcher[1] *noun*
the baseball player who throws the ball to the batter

pitcher[2] *noun*
a large jug

pitchfork *noun*
a large fork used for lifting and tossing hay

pitfall *noun*
an unexpected trap

pith *noun*
1 any soft spongy substance such as that between the skin and the flesh of an orange **2** the most important part

Word Building: **pithy** *adjective* (**pithier, pithiest**)

pitiable *adjective*
1 deserving pity **2** worthless

Word Building: **pitiably** *adverb*

pitiful *adjective*
1 causing or deserving pity
2 unsuccessful or worthless: *pitiful efforts*

Word Building: **pitifully** *adverb*

pitta *noun*
a small, flat, round pocket of bread which you can open up and fill with food

Word Use: another name is **pitta bread**
Word History: from a Greek word meaning "a cake"

pittance *noun*
a very small amount of money

pity *noun*
1 deep sympathy for the suffering or sorrow of other people **2** a cause for sorrow: *It's a pity she can't come too.*

Word Building: **pity** *verb* (**pitied, pitying**)

pivot *noun*
someone or something on which something turns or depends

Word Building: **pivot** *verb* (**pivoted, pivoting**) to turn, as on a pivot **pivotal** *adjective*

pixie *noun*
an elf or fairy

pizza (say *peet-sə*) *noun*
a thin dough base covered with tomato, salami, cheese or similar savoury foods and baked in an oven

Word History: from an Italian word meaning "pie"

placard *noun*
a large notice or poster

placate *verb*
to make calm or happy: *They placated him with presents.*

Word Use: a similar word is **appease**
Word Building: **placatory** *adjective*

place *noun*
1 a particular area or part of space: *He's gone to a place I don't know.* **2** situation: *I wouldn't do it if I were in your place.*
3 the page or passage you are up to when reading: *Mark your place with a bookmark.*
4 a short street, court or square
5 position in a race: *second place*
6 in place of instead of **7 take place** to happen
place *verb*
8 to put or set: *She placed it on the table.* **9** to remember: *I can't place her.*

Word Building: **placement** *noun*

placenta (say *plə-sen-tə*) *noun*
the organ which gives food and oxygen to a baby in its mother's womb

Word Building: **placental** *adjective: placental mammals*
Word History: from a Greek word meaning "flat cake"

placid (say *plas-əd*) *adjective*
calm or peaceful

Word Building: **placidity** *noun* **placidly** *adverb*

plague (say *playg*) *noun*
any serious disease which spreads very quickly **2** a huge number of any pest: *a plague of mice*

Word Building: **plague** *verb*

plaid (rhymes with *dad*) *noun*
tartan cloth

plain *adjective*
1 clearly seen, heard or understood
2 simple and uncomplicated
3 not beautiful
plain *noun*
4 a large flat area of land

Word Use: be careful – this sounds like **plane**
Word Building: **plainly** *adverb*

plaintiff *noun*
a person who brings a court case against someone else known as the defendant

plaintive *adjective*
complaining or sorrowful: *a plaintive cry*

Word Building: **plaintively** *adverb*

plait (rhymes with *mat*) *verb*
to weave or braid together three or more strands or bunches, as of hair

Word Building: **plait** *noun*

plan *noun*
a program or design for how something should be done or made: *He has a plan for our next outing. / Have you finished the plans for the house?*

Word Building: **plan** *verb* (**planned, planning**)

plane[1] *noun*
1 a flat or level surface **2** a level: *Her writing is on a higher plane than mine.*
3 a winged machine which is driven through the air by its propellers or jet engines

Word Use: be careful – this sounds like **plain**
Word Building: **plane** *adjective*
Word History: definition 3 is a shortened form of **aeroplane**

plane[2] *noun*
a tool for smoothing wood

Word Use: be careful – this sounds like **plain**
Word Building: **plane** *verb*

planet *noun*
any of the large bodies in space revolving around the sun or around any star

Word Building: **planetary** *adjective*

plank *noun*
a flat length of wood, such as one used in building

plankton *noun*
very tiny plants and animals which float in water

plant *noun*
1 a living thing which grows in the ground and which cannot move around
2 the machinery and equipment connected with an industry
plant *verb*
3 to put in the ground to grow **4** to put or fix: *to plant an idea*

plantation *noun*
a farm, especially in tropical areas where crops such as coffee, sugar or cotton are grown

plaque (rhymes with *mark*) *noun*
1 a metal plate, such as one fastened to a wall, with a name, profession or memorial date on it **2** a coating on teeth which causes decay

plasma *noun*
the liquid part of blood which contains the blood cells

plaster *noun*
1 a thick mixture of lime, sand and water, used to cover walls and ceilings **2** a fine white powder which swells and sets rapidly when mixed with water and is used in making moulds **3** a bandage soaked in such a mixture, which is put around a broken limb to hold it in place **4** a covering for a minor wound

Word Use: another name for definition 2 is **plaster of Paris**
Word Building: **plaster** *verb: to plaster walls* **plasterer** *noun* someone whose job is to plaster walls and ceilings

plastic *noun*
1 a substance which can be shaped when soft and then hardened
plastic *adjective*
2 made of plastic: *a plastic cup* **3** having to do with surgery done to repair or replace badly formed or injured parts of the body

Word Building: **plasticity** *noun*

plate *noun*
1 a flat round dish for food **2** cutlery or dishes made of, or coated with, gold or silver **3** a thin flat sheet of metal
4 a colour illustration in a book
5 a support for false teeth

Word Building: **plate** *verb* to coat with precious metal

plateau (say *plat-oh*) *noun*
a large flat stretch of high ground

Word Building: the plural is **plateaus** or **plateaux**

platform *noun*
1 a raised floor, as in a hall or theatre, for public speakers or performers **2** the raised area beside the tracks at a railway station

platinum *noun*
a greyish-white metallic element used in making scientific equipment and jewellery

Word History: from a Spanish word meaning "silver"

platitude *noun*
an expression which has been used too many times, especially one spoken as if it were fresh and wise

Word Building: **platitudinous** *adjective*

platonic *adjective*
having to do with a love that is deep but does not involve sex: *platonic love*

Word Building: **platonically** *adverb*
Word History: named after the Greek philospher Plato, who lived from about 427 to 347 BC

platoon *noun*
a group or unit of soldiers

platter *noun*
a large plate used for serving food

platypus *noun*
an Australian web-footed animal with a bill like a duck's, which lays eggs and feeds its young with its own milk

Word Building: the plural is **platypuses**
Word History: from a Greek word meaning "flat-footed"

plausible (say *plawz-ə-bəl*) *adjective*
believable or reasonable: *a plausible story*

Word Building: **plausibility** *noun* **plausibly** *adverb*

play *noun*
1 activity for fun or relaxation **2** a story which can be acted out by actors in a theatre **3** light, rapid movement: *the play of reflections on water*
play *verb*
4 to act the part of: *He is playing Hamlet.*
5 to do or take part in for sport or amusement: *Do you play cards?* **6** to take part in a game **7** to pretend to be or imitate, as in children's games: *They are playing pirates.* **8** to perform on: *He plays the flute.*

playwright *noun*
someone who writes plays

Word Use: a word with a similar meaning is **dramatist**

plaza *noun*
an open space or square in a town

plea *noun*
an earnest request

plead *verb*
1 to beg or earnestly ask **2** to say whether you are innocent or guilty in a court case **3** to use as an excuse: *He pleaded tiredness.*

pleasant (say plez-ənt) *adjective*
agreeable or pleasing: *a pleasant outing* | *a pleasant manner*

Word Building: **pleasantly** *adverb*

please *verb*
1 to make happy or satisfied: *The gift pleased them greatly.*
please *interjection*
2 if you are willing: *Come here please.*

Word Building: **pleasing** *adjective* **pleasingly** *adverb*

pleasure (say plezh-ə) *noun*
enjoyment or happiness

Word Building: **pleasurable** *adjective* **pleasurably** *adverb*

pleat (rhymes with *meet*) *noun*
a pressed or stitched fold in trousers or a skirt

Word Building: **pleat** *verb*

plectrum *noun*
a small piece of wood, plastic or metal, used to pluck the strings of instruments such as the guitar or banjo

Word Building: the plural is **plectra** or **plectrums**

pledge *noun*
1 a promise made very seriously
2 something given as a guarantee that you will return a loan: *He left $10 as a pledge.*

Word Use: another word for definition 1 is **vow**
Word Building: **pledge** *verb*

plentiful *adjective*
great in amount or number: *a plentiful supply*

Word Building: **plentifully** *adverb*

plenty *noun*
an amount or supply which is large or sufficient: *Take some, we have plenty.*

Word Building: **plenteous** *adjective*

pliable *adjective*
flexible or easily bent: *a pliable stem* | *a pliable nature*

Word Building: **pliability** *noun* **pliably** *adverb*

pliers (say pluy-əz) *plural noun*
a tool used for gripping, and for twisting or cutting wire

plight *noun*
a state or situation, usually bad: *She left them in an awful plight.*

plod *verb*
to go or continue in a slow, steady and unexciting way: *He plods off to work every day.*

Word Building: other forms are **I plodded, I have plodded, I am plodding** □ **plodder** *noun*

plot[1] *noun*
1 a secret plan or scheme **2** the story of a novel or play
plot[1] *verb*
3 to plan secretly **4** to mark out or map: *to plot a route*

Word Building: other forms are **I plotted, I have plotted, I am plotting** □ **plotter** *noun*

plot[2] *noun*
a small piece of ground: *a vegetable plot*

plough (rhymes with *now*) *noun*
1 a tool with a curved blade for digging the soil
plough *verb*
2 to dig with a plough **3 plough through** to work steadily at: *He ploughs through the housework.*

ploy (rhymes with *toy*) *noun*
a scheme or trick to gain an advantage over someone: *The ploy I used on my mother worked – she's letting me go to the school disco.*

pluck *verb*
1 to pull at and remove: *to pluck an apple from the tree* **2** to play notes on the strings of an instrument by pulling at them with your fingers or by using a plectrum
pluck *noun*
3 courage

Word Building: **plucky** *adjective* (**pluckier, pluckiest**) brave **pluckily** *adverb* **pluckiness** *noun*

plug *noun*
1 a stopper to prevent liquid escaping, as from a basin **2** something used to block a hole **3** the connection at the end of an electrical wire which you put into a power point

plug *verb*
4 to stop up: *He plugged the leak.*
5 to mention often, as a kind of advertisement: *He is plugging their show.*

Word Use: definition 5 is more suited to everyday language
Word Building: other verb forms are **I plugged, I have plugged, I am plugging**

plum *noun*
a soft, smooth-skinned fruit related to but larger than the cherry

Word Use: be careful – this sounds like **plumb**
Word Building: **plum** *adjective* choice: *a plum job*

plumage (say *ploohm-ij*) *noun*
the feathers covering a bird's body

plumb (rhymes with *mum*) *noun*
1 a lead weight on a string, used in measuring depth or as a test of uprightness **2** an exactly upright or perpendicular line or position: *The post is out of plumb, so we'll have to straighten it.*

plumb *adverb*
3 in an upright position **4** exactly: *plumb in the middle*

Word Use: another word for definition 1 is **plumbline** □ be careful – this sounds like **plum**
Word Building: **plumb** *verb: to plumb the depths of the ocean*

plumber (say *plum-ə*) *noun*
someone who puts into a building the pipes which are used to carry water and waste, and fixes them when something goes wrong

Word Building: **plumbing** *noun*

plume *noun*
a feather, especially a long or showy one

plummet *verb*
to fall straight and fast, as something heavy does

plump *adjective*
rather fat and well-rounded

plunder *verb*
to rob violently, as in war

Word Use: a similar word is **pillage**
Word Building: **plunder** *noun*

plunge *verb*
1 to dip or thrust: *She plunged her bucket into the river.* | *The storm plunged the town into darkness.* **2** to dive or fall, as into water **3** to move quickly or suddenly: *to plunge into action*

plunge *noun*
4 a sudden rush or move **5** a dive or fall

plural *adjective*
indicating more than one person or thing such as the words "children" and "hear" in *The children hear the bell.*

Word Building: **plurality** *noun*

plus *adjective*
1 having to do with addition: *the plus sign*

plus *noun*
2 an added advantage: *another plus*

plush *adjective*
rich, fine or costly

plutonium *noun*
a radioactive element which is obtained from uranium, and is a powerful source of energy

ply[1] *verb*
1 to use or do, especially busily: *to ply the oars* | *to ply a trade* **2** to supply continuously: *She plied us with sandwiches.* **3** to travel or cross often: *to ply the harbour* | *to ply between Sydney and Auckland*

Word Building: other forms are **I plied, I have plied, I am plying**

ply[2] *noun*
a strand or a thickness

Word Building: the plural is **plies**

plywood *noun*
board made of layers of wood stuck together

p.m.
short for post meridiem, *Latin words meaning* "after noon": *I go to bed at 9 p.m.*

pneumatic (say *nyooh-mat-ik*) *adjective*
worked by air or air pressure: *a pneumatic pump*

Word Building: **pneumatically** *adverb*
Word History: from a Greek word meaning "of a wind"

pneumonia (say *nyooh-mohn-yə*) *noun*
an illness caused by an infection or inflammation of the lungs, which gives you a fever and makes breathing difficult

poach[1] *verb*
to cook in liquid just below boiling point

poach[2] *verb*
to hunt or fish without permission on someone else's property

Word Building: **poacher** *noun* someone who poaches

pocket *noun*
1 a cloth fold or pouch sewn into a garment, for holding things **2** a small area of something: *a pocket of coal | a pocket of resistance*

pocket *verb*
3 to put into your own pocket, especially dishonestly

pod *noun*
the long container in which seeds grow: *a pea pod*

poddy *noun*
a young animal, especially a calf, which needs to be fed by hand

Word Building: the plural is **poddies** □ **poddy** *adjective*

podium *noun*
a small platform for speakers or conductors

Word Building: the plural is **podia**
Word History: from a Greek word meaning "foot"

poem *noun*
a piece of writing set out in a certain way, often with lines that match in length, rhythm or rhyme

Word Building: **poet** *noun* someone who writes poems

poetry *noun*
1 a poem or poems: *She writes poetry.*
2 beauty or harmony

Word Building: **poetic** *adjective* **poetically** *adverb*

poignant (say *poyn-yənt*) *adjective*
deeply or keenly felt: *poignant sorrow*

Word Building: **poignancy** *noun*

point *noun*
1 a sharp end: *the needle's point*
2 a written dot, as in punctuation or decimals **3** the level or place in a process at which something happens: *boiling point*
4 any of the 32 compass positions
5 the main thing: *This is the point of the story.* **6** a unit for scoring in a game

point *verb*
7 to show by a finger or sign: *The sign points north.* **8** to aim: *to point a gun*

Word Building: **pointed** *adjective* sharp: *a pointed weapon | a pointed comment* **pointedly** *adverb*

point-blank *adjective*
1 aimed or fired at very close range: *a point-blank shot* **2** plain or straightforward: *a point-blank answer*

Word Building: **point-blank** *adverb*

poise *noun*
1 confidence or ease when dealing with people and situations

poise *verb*
2 to hold steady or balanced

Word Building: **poised** *adjective* dignified

poison *noun*
1 a substance which causes death or illness if you swallow it

poison *verb*
2 to kill or harm with poison

Word Building: **poisonous** *adjective*

poke *verb*
1 to push or prod: *to poke someone with your finger* **2** to show or appear, especially from behind something: *He poked his head around the door.*

Word Building: **poke** *noun*

poker[1] *noun*
a metal rod for stirring the fire in a fireplace or oven

poker[2] *noun*
a card game in which the players bet money on the value of the cards they are holding

poky *adjective*
cramped: *a poky little room*

Word Building: other forms are **pokier, pokiest**

pole[1] *noun*
a long thin piece of wood or other material: *a flag pole*

pole[2] *noun*
an opposite end or force: *the north and south poles*

Word Building: **polar** *adjective* **polarity** *noun*

police *noun*
members of a force employed by the state or nation to keep order and to protect life and property: *The police are here already.*

Word Building: **police** *verb* **policeman** *noun* **policewoman** *noun*

policy[1] (say *pol-ə-see*) *noun*
a plan of action: *What is their foreign policy? / It's good policy to save.*

Word Building: the plural is **policies**

policy[2] (say *pol-ə-see*) *noun*
a signed agreement with an insurance company

Word Building: the plural is **policies**

poliomyelitis
(say *poh-lee-oh-muy-ə-luy-təs*) *noun*
a disease, now rare, causing paralysis

Word Use: a shortened form of this is **polio**

polish *verb*
1 to make shiny by rubbing **2** to put the final touches to: *She just needs to polish her performance.* **3 polish off** to finish: *Let's polish off those cakes.*

polish *noun*
4 a paste or liquid which gives a shine when it is rubbed on: *shoe polish*
5 fineness or elegance: *He sings with polish.*

Word Building: **polished** *adjective* **polisher** *noun*

polite *adjective*
1 having good manners **2** refined: *polite society*

Word Use: words having the opposite meaning are **impolite** and **rude**
Word Building: **politely** *adverb* **politeness** *noun*

politics *noun*
1 the leading and management of the affairs of a country or state **2** methods used to gain power or success: *He hates the politics of his job.*

Word Use: you can treat this noun as singular or plural
Word Building: **political** *adjective* **politically** *adverb* **politician** *noun*

polka *noun*
a quick and lively dance

Word Building: **polka** *verb* (**polkaed, polkaing**)

poll *noun*
1 a counting of people, votes or opinions **2 the polls** the place where votes are taken

poll *verb*
3 to ask and record the opinions of: *to poll the nation on an important matter*
4 to receive a number of votes: *to poll badly in an election* **5** to cut off the hair or horns of

pollen *noun*
the yellowish seed dust of flowers

Word History: a Latin word meaning "fine flour" or "dust"

pollinate *verb*
to cause to produce seeds by adding pollen: *Bees pollinate flowers as they collect nectar.*

Word Building: **pollination** *noun*

pollute *verb*
to spoil or make dirty: *The heavy traffic pollutes the air.*

Word Building: **pollutant** *noun* something which pollutes **polluted** *adjective* **pollution** *noun*

polo *noun*
a ball game on horseback, between two teams using long wooden mallets and a wooden ball

poltergeist (say *pol-tə-guyst*) *noun*
a troublesome ghost or spirit who is supposed to move things and make noises

Word History: from German words for "noise" and "ghost"

poly- *prefix*
a word part meaning much *or* many: *polygon*

Word History: this prefix comes from Greek

polygamy (say *pə-lig-ə-mee*) *noun*
marriage to more than one person at a time

Word Use: compare **monogamy** and **bigamy**
Word Building: **polygamist** *noun* **polygamous** *adjective* **polygamously** *adverb*

polygon *noun*
a flat shape with many straight sides

polythene *noun*
a firm light plastic which is used for containers, packing and insulation

pomegranate (say *pom-ə-gran-ət*) *noun*
a thick-skinned pinkish fruit which splits open when it is ripe to reveal many seeds and flesh that you can eat

pommel *noun*
1 the front peak of a saddle **2** a knob at the end of a sword or knife handle

pommy *noun*
an English person

Word Use: this is more suited to everyday language
Word Building: the plural is **pommies**

pomp *noun*
splendid display, as in a ceremony or parade

pompom *noun*
a ball made of wool or other thread, often put on hats or caps as an ornament

pompous *adjective*
showing too much sense of your own importance: *a pompous speech*

Word Building: **pomposity** *noun* **pompously** *adjective*

poncho *noun*
a cloak with a hole in the centre to put your head through

Word Building: the plural is **ponchos**

pond *noun*
an area of water smaller than a lake

ponder *verb*
to think about deeply or carefully: *to ponder the question*

ponderous *adjective*
1 large and heavy **2** serious and dull: *a ponderous discussion*

Word Building: **ponderously** *adverb*

pontiff *noun*
a pope

Word Building: **pontifical** *adjective*

pontificate (say *pon-tif-ə-kət*) *noun*
1 the time during which a pontiff holds his office

pontificate (say *pon-tif-ə-kayt*) *verb*
2 to speak in an important-sounding manner

pontoon[1] *noun*
a floating structure used to support a temporary bridge or dock

pontoon[2] *noun*
a gambling card game in which you try to score as close as possible to, but not more than, 21 points

pony *noun*
a small horse

Word Building: the plural is **ponies**

ponytail *noun*
a hairstyle in which the hair is tied in a loose bunch at the back of the head

poodle *noun*
a dog with thick curly hair often trimmed in special shapes

pool[1] *noun*
1 a small area of still water, especially one made for swimming in **2** a small collection of any liquid: *a pool of blood*

pool[2] *noun*
1 a combination of possessions, money or services for the use of everyone in a group: *All the managers can get a letter typed by a typist in the typing pool.*
2 the sum of money that can be won in some gambling games **3** a kind of billiards game

pool[2] *verb*
4 to put together for the use of everyone in a group: *Let's pool our money and buy her a present from us all.*

poop (rhymes with *loop*) *noun*
a deck at the back part of a ship, above the main deck

poor *adjective*
1 having little money, property or means of producing wealth: *a poor person* / *a poor country* **2** low in quality or skill: *a poor piece of work* **3** small in amount or number: *a poor wage* **4** unfortunate or unlucky: *You poor thing!*

poor *noun*
5 poor people as a group: *I am collecting money for the poor.*

Word Use: be careful – this sounds like **pore** and **pour**
Word Building: **poorly** *adverb* **poorness** *noun* **poverty** *noun*

pop[1] *verb*
1 to make a short explosive sound
2 to come, go or put quickly or suddenly: *I'll pop in and visit him.* / *Pop the books on my desk.*

pop[1] *noun*
3 a short explosive sound

Word Building: other verb forms are **I popped, I have popped, I am popping**

pop[2] *noun*
music that is very popular at a certain time, especially among young people, usually having a strong rhythm

Word Building: **pop** *adjective: pop music*

popcorn *noun*
maize grain which bursts open and puffs up when heated and is then eaten

pope *noun*
the bishop of Rome as head of the Roman Catholic Church

Word Use: this is often spelt with a capital letter
Word Building: **papal** *adjective* having to do with a pope

poppy *noun*
a kind of brightly-coloured flower

Word Building: the plural is **poppies**

popular *adjective*
1 widely liked by a particular group or people in general: *a popular song | a girl who is popular with her class* **2** having to do with the people in general: *popular beliefs*

Word Building: **popularity** *noun* **popularly** *adverb*

populate *verb*
1 to live in: *Australia was populated by Aborigines before the coming of Europeans.* **2** to fill up with people

Word Use: a similar word for definition 1 is **inhabit**

population *noun*
the people living in a country, town or other area

populous *adjective*
having a large number of people: *a populous city*

porcelain (say *paw-sə-lən*) *noun*
a kind of fine china, used for dishes and ornaments

porch *noun*
a covered area at the entrance of a building

Word Building: the plural is **porches**

porcupine *noun*
a small animal covered with stiff sharp spines

pore[1] *verb*
to read or study carefully: *The students pored over their books.*

Word Use: be careful – this sounds like **poor** and **pour**

pore[2] *noun*
a very small opening, especially in the skin, for liquid to be taken in or come out through: *Sweat comes out through your pores.*

Word Use: be careful – this sounds like **poor** and **pour**

pork *noun*
the meat of a pig

pornography *noun*
art, photography or writing that is thought to be indecent or obscene

Word Building: **pornographer** *noun* **pornographic** *adjective*

porpoise *noun*
a sea mammal with a rounded snout, usually blackish on top and paler beneath, which often leaps from the water

Word Building: the plural is **porpoises** or **porpoise**
Word History: from a Latin word meaning "hogfish"

porridge *noun*
oats cooked with water or milk, often eaten for breakfast

port[1] *noun*
1 a harbour where ships load and unload **2** a town with a harbour

port[2] *noun*
the left-hand side of a ship or plane when you are facing the front

Word Use: the opposite is **starboard**

port[3] *noun*
a sweet dark-red wine

port[4] *noun*
1 an opening, such as a porthole in a ship **2** a connection point in a computer for the entry or exit of data

port[5] *noun*
a suitcase or school bag

portable *adjective*
able to be easily carried or moved: *a portable television*

Word Building: **portability** *noun*

porter *noun*
someone whose job is carrying bags or other loads: *a railway porter*

portfolio *noun*
1 a case for carrying loose papers or letters **2** the duties of a minister in a government: *The Premier gave her the Education portfolio.*

porthole *noun*
an opening like a window in the side of a ship that gives light and air

portion *noun*
a part or share of something

Word Building: **portion** *verb*

portly *adjective*
large and fat

Word Building: **portliness** *noun*

portmanteau (say *pawt-man-toh*) *noun*
a suitcase for travelling which opens into two halves

Word Building: the plural is **portmanteaus** or **portmanteaux**
Word History: from a French word meaning "cloak-carrier"

portmanteau word *noun*
a word in which the start of one word is joined up with the end of another word to make a new word: *"Smog" is a portmanteau word made from "smoke" and "fog".*

Word History: from the book *Through the Looking Glass* by Lewis Carroll: "You see it's like a portmanteau ... there are two meanings packed up in one word."

portrait (say *pawt-rət*) *noun*
1 a painting, drawing or photograph of someone, especially of their face
2 a written or spoken description: *a portrait of life in the Middle Ages*

Word Building: **portraiture** *noun*

portray *verb*
1 to make a painting or drawing of
2 to act the part of: *He portrayed a king in his class play.* **3** to describe in words

Word Building: **portrayal** *noun*

pose *verb*
1 to take up a particular position: *The model posed for the camera.* **2** to pretend to be something or someone **3** to present or put forward: *The teacher posed a hard question.*

Word Building: **pose** *noun* **poser** *noun*

posh *adjective*
smart, expensive-looking, or high-class: *a posh car*

Word Use: this is more suited to everyday language

position *noun*
1 a place or location: *Take any position in the back row.* **2** proper place: *I am putting these chairs into position.* **3** the manner in which something is placed or arranged
4 a situation or state: *My lack of money puts me in a difficult position.* **5** rank or standing: *a high position in society* **6** a job
7 a point of view: *What is your position in this argument?*

Word Building: **position** *verb*

positive *adjective*
1 absolutely sure or certain **2** expressing agreement: *a positive answer* **3** actual or real: *This has been of positive good to us.*
4 tending to see what is good or gives hope: *positive criticism of a pupil's work | a positive attitude towards a problem* **5** greater than zero in quantity **6** having a deficiency or lack of electrons: *the positive pole of an electric cell*

Word Building: **positively** *adverb*
positiveness *noun*

posse (say *pos-ee*) *noun*
a group of men that helps a sheriff keep peace

Word Use: this word is mainly used in America

possess *verb*
1 to own or have: *to possess a lot of books | to possess courage* **2** to take over and control: *Rage possessed her.*

Word Building: **possessor** *noun*

possessed *adjective*
taken over by a strong feeling, madness or an apparently supernatural force: *She screamed like someone possessed.*

possession *noun*
1 ownership or the act of possessing: *I took possession of my new car yesterday.*
2 something possessed: *This game is my favourite possession.*

possessive *adjective*
wanting to possess or control all by yourself

Word Building: **possessively** *adverb*
possessiveness *noun*

possessive case *noun*
the form of a noun or pronoun which shows ownership, such as "her", in *her book,* which is the possessive case of "she"

possible *adjective*
able to be, happen, be done or be used: *a possible cure for a disease / Is it possible to drive there in one day?*

Word Building: **possibility** *noun* (**possibilities**) **possibly** *adverb*

possum *noun*
an Australian marsupial that lives in trees and has long arms and legs and a long tail for climbing and is active at night

post[1] *noun*
1 an upright piece of wood or metal used as a support: *a fence post* **2** a post marking the start or finish of a race
post[1] *verb*
3 to put up on a post or wall for public attention: *They posted a list of the new prices.*

post[2] *noun*
1 a job or duty: *She has a teaching post.*
2 the place where a job or duty is done, especially guard duty

Word Building: **post** *verb: to post a guard at the gate*

post[3] *noun*
1 delivery of letters or other mail
2 the letters themselves **3** the system of carrying letters and other mail
post[3] *verb*
4 to send by post: *I am posting a letter to you tomorrow.*

Word Building: **postage** *noun* the cost of sending something by post **postal** *adjective*

post- *prefix*
a word part meaning behind *or* after: *posterior, post-mortem*

Word History: this prefix comes from Latin

postcard *noun*
a card for sending by post with a picture on one side and a space for a message on the other side

postcode *noun*
a group of numbers added to your address to help speed the delivery of mail

poster *noun*
a large notice, often illustrated

posterior *adjective*
1 from or at the back: *a posterior view of the spine*
posterior *noun*
2 your bottom

Word Use: definition 2 is more suited to everyday language

posterity (say *po-ste-rə-tee*) *noun*
the people who will live in the future: *His work will be remembered by posterity.*

posthumous (say *pos-chə-məs*) *adjective*
published, given or happening after someone's death: *a posthumous publication of his novel / a posthumous award*

Word Building: **posthumously** *adverb*

post-mortem *noun*
the medical examination of a dead body

Word Use: a similar word is **autopsy**
Word Building: **post-mortem** *adjective*

postpone *verb*
to put off to a later time: *They postponed the game because of rain.*

Word Use: a similar word is **defer**
Word Building: **postponement** *noun*

postscript *noun*
an extra message written on the end of a finished and signed letter

Word Use: the short form of this is **PS**

posture *noun*
position of your body: *a kneeling posture*

posy *noun*
a small, neatly-arranged bunch of flowers

Word Building: the plural is **posies**

pot *noun*
1 a container, usually round and deep: *a cooking pot / a flower pot*
pot *verb*
2 to put or plant in a pot

Word Building: other verb forms are **I potted, I have potted, I am potting**

potato *noun*
a white plant root which you can eat as a vegetable

Word Building: the plural is **potatoes**

potent *adjective*
powerful or strong: *a potent king / a potent medicine*

Word Building: **potency** *noun*

potential *adjective*
1 capable of becoming in the future: *I think this song is a potential hit.*
potential *noun*
2 possible or likely ability: *She is a pianist with a lot of potential.*

Word Building: **potentiality** *noun* **potentially** *adverb*

pothole *noun*
a hole in the ground, especially one in a road

potion *noun*
a drink, especially medicine, or one that's poisonous or magical in some way

Word Use: this is an old-fashioned word

potpourri (say *pot-poo-ree, poh-poo-ree*) *noun*
1 a mixture of dried flower petals used to give a perfume **2** any collection or mixture of different things: *This book is a potpourri of stories, poems and plays.*

Word History: from a French word meaning "rotten pot"

potter[1] *noun*
someone who shapes pots, dishes and so on out of clay, and then hardens them by baking

Word Building: **pottery** *noun* the things a potter makes

potter[2] *verb*
to busy or occupy yourself without getting much done: *I spent the day pottering about the house.*

potty[1] *adjective*
foolish or crazy

Word Use: this is more suited to everyday language
Word Building: other forms are **pottier, pottiest**

potty[2] *noun*
a pot used as a toilet, especially for small children

pouch *noun*
1 a small bag or sack, used for carrying things like money **2** a part of the body shaped like a bag or pocket: *the pouch of a kangaroo | pouches of skin beneath the eyes*

Word Building: the plural is **pouches**

poultry *noun*
birds such as chickens, turkey, ducks and geese, which are used as food or for egg production

pounce *verb*
to move or leap suddenly and seize: *The lion pounced on the zebra.*

Word Building: **pounce** *noun*

pound[1] *verb*
1 to hit hard and many times **2** to crush into a powder or small pieces **3** to beat or throb violently: *My heart was pounding with excitement.* **4** to go with quick heavy steps: *They pounded along the corridor.*

pound[2] *noun*
1 an old-fashioned measure of weight equal to just under half a kilogram
2 a unit of money used in Australia until 1966 and still used in Britain and some other countries

pound[3] *noun*
a place where animals are sheltered or kept, especially if they are homeless

pour *verb*
1 to send flowing or falling: *She poured milk into a glass.* **2** to move or flow in great numbers: *The children poured out of the bus.* **3** to rain heavily

Word Use: be careful – this sounds like **poor** and **pore**

pout *verb*
to push out the lips showing disappointment or sulkiness

Word Building: **pout** *noun*

poverty *noun*
1 the condition of being poor: *They lived in poverty for years.* **2** a shortage of something needed or wanted: *a poverty of ideas*

powder *noun*
1 the very small loose bits of something dry that has been crushed or ground: *talcum powder | a powder of dust | tablets crushed to a powder*

powder *verb*
2 to crush into a powder **3** to cover with a powder: *to powder your face*

Word Use: a similar word to definition 2 is **pulverise**
Word Building: **powdery** *adjective*

power *noun*
1 the ability to do something **2** control over others, especially the control that rulers or governments have: *The election put a new government into power.*
3 strength or force: *a punch with a lot of power* **4** someone who is very powerful: *This man is the power behind the throne.*
5 a country that has a lot of power: *There was a meeting of world powers in London.*
6 the number that is the result of multiplying a number by itself one or more times: *Four is the second power of two, and eight is the third power of two.*
7 energy or force that can be used for doing work: *electrical power*

power *verb*
8 to supply with electricity or another kind of power: *to power a machine*

Word Building: **powerful** *adjective* **powerfully** *adverb*

power point *noun*
a device, usually on a wall, to plug electrical power leads into

practical *adjective*
1 having to do with actual practice or action, rather than ideas: *an invention with a practical use / You need practical experience for this job.* **2** interested in and good at useful work: *a practical person* **3** sensible and realistic: *He always has a practical answer.*

Word Building: **practicality** *noun*

practically *adverb*
1 in a practical way **2** nearly or almost: *We're practically there.*

practice *noun*
1 actual action or performance: *His idea sounded good but didn't work in practice.* **2** an action or performance that is repeated regularly to improve skill **3** the usual way of doing something: *It is the practice at our school to have assembly every Wednesday.* **4** the business of someone such as a doctor or lawyer

practise *verb*
1 to do or carry out as a usual habit: *You should always practise truthfulness.* **2** to work in as a profession: *to practise law* **3** to do or perform repeatedly in order to improve skill: *He is practising his cricket strokes.*

Word Building: **practised** *adjective*

practitioner *noun*
someone working in a practice, particularly a doctor: *a medical practitioner*

pragmatic *adjective*
thinking about the results or usefulness of actions: *She is too pragmatic to waste time wanting what she can't have.*

Word Building: **pragmatically** *adverb*

prairie *noun*
a flat, grassy, treeless plain, especially in America and Canada

Word History: from a Latin word meaning "meadow"

praise *verb*
to say that you admire and approve of

Word Building: **praise** *noun*

pram *noun*
a small four-wheeled baby carriage which you push along

prance *verb*
to leap about

prank *noun*
a playful trick

prattle *verb*
to chatter in a stupid way

Word Building: **prattle** *noun*

prawn *noun*
a small shellfish used for food

pray *verb*
1 to talk to God to thank, praise or ask Him for something **2** to ask earnestly: *She prayed him to forgive her.*

Word Use: be careful – this sounds like **prey**
Word Building: **prayer** *noun*

pre- *prefix*
a word part meaning before: *prehistoric*

Word History: this prefix comes from Latin

preach *verb*
1 to give a sermon: *She preaches every Sunday.* **2** to give advice in a boring way: *He is always preaching about keeping the place tidy.*

preamble (say *pree-am-bəl*) *noun*
an introduction explaining the purpose of the book or document which follows

precarious (say *prə-kair-ree-əs*) *adjective*
1 uncertain or depending on conditions you can't control: *His position in the company is precarious.* **2** unsafe or risky: *a precarious position on top of a ladder*

Word Building: **precariously** *adverb*

precaution *noun*
something done in advance to prevent problems: *precautions against burglary*

Word Building: **precautionary** *adjective*

precede *verb*
to go before: *He preceded her into the room.*

Word Building: **precedence** *noun* the right to go before something or someone else

precedent *noun*
an event or case which may be used as an example for future action: *She set a precedent when she joined the soccer team, and soon lots of girls were signing up.*

precept (say *pree-sept*) *noun*
a rule of action: *"Look before you leap" is a wise precept.*

precinct (say *pree-singkt*) *noun*
1 a place or area with definite limits: *shopping precinct* **2** the surrounding area: *the precincts of the city*

precious *adjective*
of great value: *precious stones / a precious friendship*

precipice (say *pres-ə-pəs*) *noun*
a steep cliff

Word Building: **precipitous** *adjective*

precipitate *verb*
1 to bring about quickly: *His arrival precipitated the quarrel.* **2** to change from vapour into dew, rain or snow

precipitation *noun*
1 the water which forms as vapour changes into liquid and falls to earth as dew, rain or snow **2** the amount of dew, rain or snow in any one time and place

precis (rhymes with *lacy*) *noun*
a brief piece of writing containing the main points of a larger work

Word Use: a similar word is **summary**

precise (say *prə-suys*) *adjective*
exact: *precise measurement / precise instructions*

Word Building: **precision** *noun*

preclude *verb*
to rule out or exclude: *The new rules will not preclude women members from joining.*

precocious *adjective*
more advanced than others of the same age: *a precocious child*

Word Building: **precociously** *adverb* **precociousness** *noun* **precocity** *noun*

predatory (say *pred-ə-tree*) *adjective*
hunting other animals for food: *An eagle is a predatory bird.*

Word Building: **predator** *noun*

predecessor *noun*
someone who had the job before you: *He was my predecessor as captain of the team.*

predicament (say *prə-dik-ə-mənt*) *noun*
a difficult or dangerous situation

predicate (say *pred-ə-kət*) *noun*
the word or words which say something about the subject of a sentence, such as "lived in a cottage" in the sentence *The Williams family lived in a cottage.*

predict *verb*
to tell what is going to happen in the future

Word Building: **predictable** *adjective* **prediction** *noun*

predominate *verb*
1 to be stronger or more important **2** to control or lead: *She predominates in class discussions.*

Word Building: **predominance** *noun* **predominant** *adjective*

pre-eminent *adjective*
superior to or better than others: *He is pre-eminent in science.*

Word Building: **pre-eminence** *noun* **pre-eminently** *adverb*

preen *verb*
to trim or arrange feathers with the beak

prefabricate *verb*
to make in a factory in parts, ready for putting together somewhere else at a later time: *The house was prefabricated to save money.*

Word Building: **prefabrication** *noun*

preface (say *pref-əs*) *noun*
an introduction or statement at the front of a book, explaining its purpose

Word Building: **preface** *verb* **prefatory** *adjective*

prefect *noun*
a senior pupil with certain responsibilites in a school

prefer *verb*
to like better

Word Building: other forms are **I preferred, I have preferred, I am preferring** □ **preferable** *adjective* **preferably** *adverb* **preference** *noun*

prefix *noun*
a word part which is put in front of a word to change the meaning, such as "un-" in *unkind*

Word History: from a Latin word meaning "fixed before"

pregnant *adjective*
having a baby growing in the womb

Word Building: **pregnancy** *noun*

prehistoric *adjective*
belonging to the time before history was written or records were kept

prejudice (say *prej-ə-dəs*) *noun*
1 an opinion unfairly formed beforehand, without reason or evidence **2** harm or unfair treatment which is caused by an opinion like this
prejudice *verb*
3 to influence without sensible reason: *His curly hair prejudiced her in his favour.*

preliminary *adjective*
coming before and leading up to the main matter: *a preliminary test*

prelude (say *prel-yoohd*) *noun*
1 something that comes before: *Thought should be a prelude to action.* **2** a short piece of music written for an instrument

premature (say *prem-ə-chə*) *adjective*
coming or happening too soon: *a premature baby* | *a premature decision*

Word Building: **prematurely** *adverb*

premeditate *verb*
to plan beforehand

Word Building: **premeditation** *noun*

premier (say *prem-ee-ə*) *noun*
1 the leader of a State government
premier *adjective*
2 first or leading: *the premier team in the championship*

Word Building: **premiership** *noun*

premiere (say *prem-ee-air*) *noun*
the first public performance of a play, film or something similar

Word Building: **premiere** *verb*

premises (say *prem-ə-səz*) *plural noun*
a building or house with the land belonging to it

premium (say *pree-mee-əm*) *noun*
a bonus, gift or additional sum **2** a payment made for insurance

premonition (say *prem-ə-nish-ən*) *noun*
a feeling that something bad is about to happen: *I had a premonition about the accident.*

preoccupied *adjective*
completely taken up in thought: *She seemed preoccupied and did not listen to a word I said.*

Word Building: **preoccupation** *noun*

prepare *verb*
to make or get ready: *to prepare a garden for planting* | *to prepare for a trip*

Word Building: **preparation** *noun* **preparatory** *adjective*

preposition (say *prep-ə-zish-ən*) *noun*
a word placed before a noun to show its relation to other words in the sentence, such as "to" and "from" in *He gave an apple to Len and took a sandwich from him.*

preposterous *adjective*
absurd or far from what is normal or sensible: *a preposterous scheme for recycling oyster shells*

Word Building: **preposterously** *adverb*

prerogative *noun*
a right or privilege: *It is the captain's prerogative to choose the team.*

prescribe *verb*
to order for use as a treatment: *The doctor prescribed some cough medicine.*

prescription *noun*
a written order by a doctor to a chemist for medicine

presence *noun*
attendance or being in a place: *Your presence is requested at the party.*

present[1] (say *prez-ənt*) *adjective*
1 happening or existing now: *the present Prime Minister* **2** being in a place: *Is everyone present?*
present[1] *noun*
3 the present time

present[2] (say *prə-zent*) *verb*
1 to give, especially in a formal way: *The mayor presented the prizes.*
present[2] (say *prez-ənt*) *noun*
2 something given: *birthday presents*

Word Building: **presentation** *noun*

presentable *adjective*
fit to be seen: *Have a shower and make yourself presentable.*

Word Building: **presentably** *adverb*

presently *adverb*
1 in a short time: *The manager will see you presently.* **2** at this time: *He is presently living in Bendigo.*

present tense *noun*
the form of a verb which shows that something is happening or exists now, such as "run" in *I run every day* and "am running" in *I am running for the bus.*

preservative *noun*
a substance that prevents something, such as food, from going bad

preserve *verb*
1 to keep from going bad: *to preserve fruit*
2 to keep safe: *Heaven preserve us!*

Word Building: **preservation** *noun*
preserve *noun*

president *noun*
1 the elected head of a republic
2 someone chosen to have control over the meetings of a society or something similar

Word Building: **presidential** *adjective*

press *verb*
1 to act upon with weight or force: *Press down the lid.* **2** to squeeze: *She pressed his hand.* **3** to urge: *She pressed them to come.* **4** to use an iron to remove creases from clothes

press *noun*
5 a machine used for printing
6 newspapers, magazines and so on, or the people who write for them

pressure (say *presh-ə*) *noun*
1 the weight or force with which you press on something: *to put pressure on a lever* **2** a force applied to something, measured as so much weight on a unit of area: *air pressure* **3** continual worry: *He is under pressure at work.*

pressurise or **pressurize** *verb*
to keep normal air pressure in: *to pressurise the cabin of a plane*

prestige (say *pres-teezh*) *noun*
high reputation or standing: *Don Bradman has enormous prestige in the world of cricket.*

Word Building: **prestigious** *adjective*

presume *verb*
1 to take for granted: *I presume you're tired after your walk.* **2** to dare: *I would not presume to tell you how to do it.*

Word Use: some people think that **assume** is better for definition 1
Word Building: **presumptuous** *adjective* taking something for granted without reasonable cause **presumption** *noun*

pretence *noun*
1 a false show: *a pretence of friendship*
2 a pretended reason

pretend *verb*
1 to make a false claim: *She pretended to be interested in his speech.* | *The burglar pretended he was reading the meter.*
2 to make believe

pretentious (say *prə-ten-shəs*) *adjective*
having an exaggerated outward show of importance, wealth and so on

Word Building: **pretentiously** *adverb*

pretty *adjective*
1 pleasant or attractive

pretty *adverb*
2 rather or quite: *pretty good*

Word Building: other adjective forms are **prettier, prettiest** □ **prettiness** *noun*

pretzel *noun*
a small crisp salted biscuit, often in the shape of a knot

Word History: from a German word

prevail *verb*
1 to win or triumph: *In spite of the objections, good sense prevailed.*
2 to be most numerous or strong: *Stunted gum trees prevail on these dry hillsides.*
3 prevail upon to persuade successfully: *I prevailed upon him to change his mind.*

prevalent (say *prev-ə-lənt*) *adjective*
widespread: *a prevalent weed*

Word Building: **prevalence** *noun*
prevalently *adverb*

prevaricate (say *prə-va-rə-kayt*) *verb*
to speak in a way which tries to avoid the point by trickery

Word Building: **prevarication** *noun*

prevent *verb*
1 to stop: *Prevent the baby from swallowing those beads.* **2** to keep from happening: *She was just in time to prevent an accident.*

Word Building: **prevention** *noun*
preventive *adjective*

preview *noun*
a showing of a film or exhibition before the public is allowed to see it

previous *adjective*
happening before: *the previous day*

Word Building: **previously** *adverb*

prey (rhymes with *may*) *noun*
1 an animal hunted for food by another: *Mice are the prey of cats.* **2** a victim
3 bird of prey a bird which hunts smaller birds and animals as its prey

prey *verb*
4 prey on **a** to hunt and eat: *Cats prey on mice.* **b** to affect harmfully: *The problem is preying on my mind.*

Word Use: be careful – this sounds like **pray**

price *noun*
the amount of money for which something is bought or sold

Word Building: **price** *verb* to give or guess the price of

priceless *adjective*
having a value beyond all price: *a priceless talent*

prick *noun*
1 a small hole made by a needle, thorn or something sharp **2** the feeling of being pricked
prick *verb*
3 to pierce with a sharp point

prickle *noun*
a sharp point or thorn

Word Building: **prickly** *adjective* (**pricklier, prickliest**)

pride *noun*
1 well-earned pleasure or satisfaction: *He takes pride in his work.* **2** a high, or too high, opinion of your own dignity or importance
pride *verb*
3 pride yourself on to take well-earned pleasure or satisfaction in: *He prided himself on a job well done.*

priest *noun*
someone whose job is to perform religious ceremonies.

Word Building: **priestess** *noun* **priesthood** *noun* **priestly** *adjective*

prig *noun*
someone who is too concerned about duty and who always thinks they are right

Word Building: **priggish** *adjective* **priggishly** *adverb*

prim *adjective*
stiff and very proper in manner

Word Building: other forms are **primmer, primmest**

primary *adjective*
first in order or importance: *primary education | the primary reason for her success*

primate *noun*
1 any mammal of the group that includes humans, apes and monkeys **2** the head bishop of a country

prime *adjective*
of the first importance or quality: *prime time | prime beef*

prime minister *noun*
the leader of the government in some countries, including Australia

prime number *noun*
a number which cannot be divided except by itself and 1

primer[1] (say *pruy-mə, prim-ə*) *noun*
a simple book for teaching the beginnings of any subject, especially reading

primer[2] (say *pruy-mə*) *noun*
a coat of paint used to prepare a surface for the next coat

primeval (say *pruy-meev-əl*) *adjective*
belonging to the earliest period of the earth

Word Building: **primevally** *adverb*
Word History: from a Latin word meaning "young" with the ending "-al" added

primitive *adjective*
1 being the earliest in existence: *primitive forms of life* **2** belonging to an early stage of civilisation: *primitive art*

prince *noun*
a son or near male relation of a king or queen

Word Building: **princely** *adjective*

princess *noun*
1 a daughter or near female relation of a king or queen **2** someone married to a prince

principal (say *prin-sə-pəl*) *adjective*
1 main or leading: *the principal thing to remember*
principal *noun*
2 the head of a school

Word Building: **principally** *adverb*

principle (say *prin-sə-pəl*)
a general truth or rule: *the principle of good behaviour | political principles*

print *verb*
1 to make copies of by pressing an inked surface on to paper or other material: *to print newspapers* **2** to write in separate letters rather than in running writing: *Please print your name and address.*

Word Building: **print** *noun*

print-out *noun*
information printed by a computer so that it can be read

prior[1] *adjective*
1 earlier: *a prior engagement* **2 prior to** before: *prior to my going away*

prior[2] *noun*
a head monk or friar

Word Building: **priory** *noun* (**priories**) **prioress** *noun*

priority (say *pruy-o-rə-tee*) *noun*
the right to go before someone or something else, because of urgency or importance

prise (sounds like *prize*) *verb*
to raise, move or force with a lever: *Prise open the lid with a screw driver.*

prism *noun*
a transparent object, usually of glass and with triangular ends, used for breaking light down into the colours of the rainbow

Word Building: **prismatic** *adjective*
Word History: from a Greek word meaning "something sawed"

prison *noun*
a place where criminals are kept locked up

Word Building: **prisoner** *noun* someone who is kept somewhere against their will **imprison** *verb*

private *adjective*
1 belonging to someone in particular: *private property* **2** concerned with personal affairs: *My diary is private.*

Word Use: a similar word is **personal**
Word Building: **privacy** *noun* **privately** *adverb*

privet *noun*
an evergreen tree or shrub introduced into Australia from Europe, which is now thought to be a pest because it grows over areas of native bushland

privilege (say *priv-ə-lij*) *noun*
1 a special right or advantage enjoyed by only a limited number of people: *We had the privilege of meeting the great poet.*
2 a special right or protection given to people in authority or office: *parliamentary privilege*

Word Building: **privileged** *adjective*

prize[1] *noun*
1 a reward for winning a race or competition **2** something won in a lottery or raffle

prize[2] *verb*
to value highly

pro- *prefix*
a word part meaning in favour of: *pro-Australian*

Word History: this prefix comes from Latin

probable *adjective*
likely or expected to happen or be true

Word Building: **probability** *noun* **probably** *adverb*

probation *noun*
1 a period of trial: *She is new in the job and still on probation.* **2** a system of punishment in which certain people who have broken the law can stay free on condition of good behaviour: *He has been put on probation for shop-lifting.*

Word Building: **probationary** *adjective*

probe *verb*
to examine or search thoroughly: *to probe a wound | to probe evidence*

Word Building: **probe** *noun*

problem *noun*
1 something which is difficult or uncertain: *His health is a problem.*
2 a question to be answered: *a maths problem*

Word Building: **problematic** *adjective*

procedure (say *prə-see-jə*) *noun*
a way of doing something: *the usual procedure for applying for a job | parliamentary procedure*

proceed *verb*
1 to move forward, especially after stopping **2** to go on or continue

Word Building: **proceeds** *plural noun* money from a sale

proceeding *noun*
1 behaviour or way of acting: *This is a strange proceeding.* **2 proceedings** records of the activities and meetings of a club or society

process *noun*
1 a series of actions carried out for a particular purpose: *the process of making butter*

process *verb*
2 to treat, prepare or deal with in a certain way: *to process iron ore | to process film | to process data*

Word Building: **processor** *noun*

procession *noun*
an orderly line of people, cars or floats moving along in a ceremony or as a show

Word Use: a similar word is **parade**

proclaim *verb*
to announce publicly: *The Governor-General proclaimed three new laws this morning.*

Word Building: proclamation *noun*

procrastinate *verb*
to put off doing something till another time

Word Building: procrastination *noun*

procreate *verb*
to produce offspring

Word Building: procreation *noun*

procure *verb*
to obtain: *to procure food | to procure a result*

Word Building: procurable *adjective*

prod *verb*
to poke or jab

Word Building: prod *noun*

prodigal *adjective*
wasteful or extravagant: *a prodigal use of materials | the prodigal son*

Word Building: prodigal *noun* **prodigality** *noun*

prodigious (say *prə-dij-əs*) *adjective*
extraordinary in size, amount or force: *a prodigious noise*

prodigy (say *prod-ə-jee*) *noun*
1 someone, especially a child, who has extraordinary talent: *Mozart was a musical prodigy.* **2** an extraordinary or wonderful thing

Word Building: the plural is **prodigies**

produce (say *prə-dyoohs*) *verb*
1 to bring into being: *This soil produces good crops.* **2** to pull out and present: *He produced a letter from his pocket.*
3 to assemble the cast for and generally organise and control: *to produce a play*

produce (say *proj-oohs*) *noun*
4 things that are grown: *Farmers take their produce to market.*

Word Building: producer *noun* **production** *noun*

product *noun*
1 something made or brought into existence: *the product of labour | household products* **2** the result you get by multiplying two or more numbers together

Word Building: productive *adjective* **productively** *adverb* **productivity** *noun*

profane *adjective*
showing deep lack of respect for religion: *profane language*

Word Building: profanely *adverb* **profanity** *noun*
Word History: from a Latin word meaning "in front of the temple"

profess *verb*
to declare or show, often insincerely: *He professed great sorrow.*

profession *noun*
1 an occupation in which advanced and special knowledge of a subject is needed: *She is a lawyer by profession.* **2** the people in a profession taken as a whole: *the legal profession* **3** a declaration, whether true or false: *a profession of love*

professional *adjective*
1 following an occupation to earn a living from it: *a professional golfer* **2** belonging to a profession

Word Use: the opposite of definition 1 is **amateur**
Word Building: professional *noun* **professionalism** *noun* **professionally** *adverb*

professor *noun*
a university teacher of the highest rank

Word Building: professorial *adjective*

proffer *verb*
to place before someone, for them to accept: *He proffered his resignation to the board.*

proficient *adjective*
skilled or expert: *a proficient carpenter*

Word Building: proficiency *noun* **proficiently** *adverb*

profile *noun*
1 an outline drawing of a face, especially a side view **2** a short account of someone's life and character: *There is a profile of the Treasurer in today's paper.* **3 keep a low profile** to act so as not to be noticed

profit *noun*
1 money made from selling something at a higher price than you paid for it
2 advantage or benefit: *There is no profit in regretting the past.*

Word Building: profit *verb* **profitable** *adjective* **profitably** *adverb*

profound *adjective*
very deep: *profound sleep | a profound thought*

Word Building: profoundly *adverb* **profundity** *noun*

profuse (say *prə-fyoohs*) *adjective*
plentiful: *a profuse flow of blood | profuse apologies*

Word Building: **profusely** *adverb* **profusion** *noun*

progeny (say *proj-ə-nee*) *noun*
offspring or descendants: *the progeny of my pet rabbits | the progeny of kings*

Word Building: **progenitor** *noun* an ancestor

prognosis *noun*
a doctor's opinion on how a disease will develop

Word Building: the plural is **prognoses** (say *prog-noh-seez*)

program *noun*
1 a plan to be followed: *a program of study*
2 a list of items and performers in a concert or play **3** a particular entertainment or production: *There's a good program on TV tonight.* **4** a set of instructions that makes a computer deal with certain data and solve problems

Word Use: another spelling for definitions 1, 2 and 3 is **programme**
Word Building: **program** *verb* (**programmed, programming**) **programmer** *noun*
Word History: from a Greek word meaning "a public notice in writing"

progress *noun*
1 advance or improvement: *progress along a road | progress in studies*
2 in progress going on or under way: *work in progress*

Word Building: **progress** *verb* **progression** *noun*

progressive *adjective*
favouring or making change, improvement or reform: *a progressive policy | a progressive school*

Word Building: **progressively** *adverb*

prohibit *verb*
to forbid by law: *The government has prohibited smoking on trains.*

Word Building: **prohibition** *noun* **prohibitive** *adjective*

project (say *proh-jekt*) *noun*
1 a plan or scheme: *a project for making money* **2** a special piece of work that you do for school, usually by researching something: *a project on wheat*

project (say *prə-jekt*) *verb*
3 to throw: *to project your voice*
4 to show on a screen: *to project a film*
5 to jut out

Word Building: **projection** *noun*

projectile (say *prə-jek-tuyl*) *noun*
1 something thrown: *Stones and other projectiles were hurled at the speaker.*
2 something fired from a gun

Word Use: a similar word is **missile**

projector *noun*
a piece of equipment for showing a film or a slide on a screen

proliferate (say *prə-lif-ə-rayt*) *verb*
to grow by multiplying: *The weeds have proliferated since the rain.*

Word Building: **proliferation** *noun*

prolific *adjective*
producing plentifully: *a prolific tree | a prolific writer*

prologue (say *proh-log*) *noun*
a speech at the beginning of a play
2 anything that introduces something else

prolong *verb*
to make last longer: *to prolong a speech | to prolong a pleasure*

Word Building: **prolongation** *noun*

promenade (say *prom-ə-nahd*) *noun*
1 an unhurried walk, especially in a public place **2** a place where people walk to and fro, especially next to a beach

Word Use: another name for definition 2 is **esplanade**
Word Building: **promenade** *verb*

prominent *adjective*
1 sticking out: *prominent teeth*
2 outstanding or important: *a prominent citizen*

Word Building: **prominence** *noun* **prominently** *adverb*

promiscuous (say *prə-mis-kyooh-əs*) *adjective*
having many sexual partners

Word Building: **promiscuity** *noun* **promiscuously** *adverb*

promise *noun*
1 a declaration or statement that you will do, or keep from doing something
2 signs of future excellence: *to show promise*

Word Building: **promise** *verb*

promontory (say *prom-ən-tree*) *noun*
a high point of land or rock jutting out into the sea

Word Building: the plural is **promontories**

promote *verb*
1 to raise or advance in rank or position: *You have been promoted to general manager.*
2 to try to increase the sales of by advertising: *They are promoting the new product on television.*

Word Building: **promoter** *noun* the organiser of an event **promotion** *noun*

prompt *adjective*
1 immediate: *a prompt reply to a letter*
prompt *verb*
2 to encourage or urge to action: *A desire to help prompted him to speak.*
3 to remind of the next words in a play
prompt *noun*
4 a message on a computer, in words or symbols on the screen, letting you know that the computer is ready for more instructions

Word Building: **prompter** *noun* **promptly** *adverb* **promptitude** *noun*

prone *adjective*
1 liable or likely to have or do: *prone to headaches* **2** lying flat with your face downwards

prong *noun*
a thin sharp point on a fork

pronoun *noun*
a word which stands for a noun, such as "we", "her", "they", "it", "that" or "who"

pronounce *verb*
1 to make the sound of: *Australians pronounce "dance" in two ways.*
2 to declare formally: *to pronounce a judgment*

Word Building: **pronouncement** *noun* **pronunciation** *noun*

pronounced *adjective*
strongly marked: *a pronounced tendency*

proof *noun*
1 something that shows a thing is true
proof *adjective*
2 strong enough to resist: *It is proof against fire.*

proofread *verb*
to read in order to find and mark mistakes to be corrected

Word Building: other forms are **I proofread, I have proofread, I am proofreading** □ **proofreader** *noun*

prop *verb*
in the phrase **prop up** to support or prevent from falling: *to prop up a wall* | *to prop up someone on cushions*

Word Building: other forms are **I propped, I have propped, I am propping** □ **prop** *noun*

propaganda *noun*
information which is used to try and convince you of a certain point of view: *political propaganda*

Word Building: **propagandise** *verb*
Word History: from the Latin name of a committee of cardinals set up in 1622 by Pope Gregory XV to help spread the Christian faith

propagate *verb*
1 to increase or multiply: *Some plants can be propagated by cuttings.* **2** to spread: *to propagate ideas*

Word Building: **propagation** *noun*

propel *verb*
to drive forwards: *The boat was propelled by oars.*

Word Building: other forms are **I propelled, I have propelled, I am propelling**

propellant *noun*
the fuel used to propel a rocket

propeller *noun*
a device with revolving blades used for driving a plane or ship

proper *adjective*
1 accepted or right: *the proper way to write* | *the proper time to sleep* **2** correct in behaviour: *She is always very proper when she comes to tea.* **3** real or genuine: *I need some proper tools, not these toys.*

proper noun *noun*
a noun that is the name of one particular place, person or thing, such as "Perth", "Sally" or "the Indian Pacific"

Word Use: proper nouns are spelt with a capital letter □ compare **common noun**

property *noun*
1 something that is owned: *This book is my property.* | *National parks are public property.* **2** a piece of land or building that may be owned **3** a station or farm: *a cattle property*

Word Building: the plural is **properties**

prophecy (say *prof-ə-see*) *noun*
1 a statement telling what is going to happen in the future **2** a message from God, or the act of proclaiming such a message

Word Building: the plural is **prophecies**

prophesy (say *prof-ə-suy*) *verb*
to deliver a prophecy, or to predict: *He prophesied a terrible storm.*

Word Building: other forms are **I prophesied, I have prophesied, I am prophesying**

prophet *noun*
1 someone who speaks on behalf of God **2** someone who predicts the future **3** a great teacher or leader

Word Building: **prophetic** *adjective*

proportion *noun*
1 the relation or comparison of one thing to another according to its size, number, and so on: *the proportion of girls to boys in the class* **2** a proper or correct relationship between things: *The dog's small head was not in proportion to his large body.* **3** a part, compared to the whole: *a large proportion of the total*

Word Building: **proportion** *verb* **proportionate** *adjective*

propose *verb*
1 to put forward or suggest **2** to plan or intend **3** to suggest marriage: *He proposed to her.*

Word Building: **proposal** *noun* **proposition** *noun*

propound *verb*
to put forward to be considered, accepted, or acted on: *He propounded a theory.*

proprietor (say *prə-pruy-ə-tə*) *noun*
the owner of a business or a property

Word Building: **proprietary** *noun*

propriety (say *prə-pruy-ə-tee*) *noun*
good manners or proper behaviour

propulsion (say *prə-pul-shən*) *noun*
a driving or propelling force: *Many planes are driven by jet propulsion.*

prosaic (say *proh-zay-ik*) *adjective*
dull and unimaginative

Word Building: **prosaically** *adverb*

proscribe *verb*
to forbid

prose *noun*
ordinary written or spoken language rather than poetry

prosecute *verb*
to accuse before a court of law

Word Building: **prosecution** *noun*

proselyte (say *pros-ə-luyt*) *noun*
a convert or someone who has changed from one opinion to another

prospect *noun*
1 something looked forward to or expected, especially something successful: *A holiday is a pleasant prospect. / He has good prospects in his job.* **2** someone who may be a customer, contestant, and so on: *Try him, he looks a likely prospect.* **3** a view or a scene

prospect *verb*
4 to search for gold or other minerals

Word Building: **prospective** *adjective* **prospector** *noun*

prospectus *noun*
a statement or pamphlet which advertises something new or gives more details about things like a school, university or commercial company

prosperous *adjective*
successful or wealthy: *a prosperous business*

Word Building: **prosperity** *noun* **prosperously** *adverb*

prostitute *noun*
someone who has sexual intercourse with someone else for money

Word Building: **prostitution** *noun*

prostrate *verb*
in the phrase **prostrate yourself** to throw or lay yourself face down: *The prisoners prostrated themselves at the feet of the general.*

Word Building: **prostrate** *adjective*

protagonist (say *prə-tag-ə-nəst*) *noun*
the main character in a story or play

protect *verb*
to guard or defend from injury, danger or annoyance

Word Building: **protection** *noun* **protective** *adjective* **protector** *noun*

protectorate (say *prə-tek-tə-rət*) *noun*
a country protected and controlled by another stronger state

protégé (say *<u>proh</u>-tə-zhay*) *noun*
someone who is protected or supported by someone else

Word History: from a French word meaning "protect"

protein (say *<u>proh</u>-teen*) *noun*
any of a group of substances which are present in such foods as milk, meat and cheese and which are important to our diet

protest (say *<u>proh</u>-test*) *noun*
1 an objection or expression of disapproval
protest (say *prə-<u>test</u>*) *verb*
2 to object or disapprove **3** to state strongly and positively: *She protested her innocence to the end.*

Word Building: **protestation** *noun*

protocol (say *<u>proh</u>-tə-kol*) *noun*
the rules of behaviour used on official occasions involving kings, queens or other important people

proton *noun*
a tiny positive particle inside an atom which has a type of energy that balances the energy of an electron

Word Use: the energy of a proton is called **positive**

prototype (say *<u>proh</u>-tə-tuyp*) *noun*
the original or the model of something which is later copied

protract *verb*
to draw out or lengthen in time

protractor *noun*
an instrument used to measure or mark off angles

protrude *verb*
to jut out

proud *adjective*
1 feeling pleased or satisfied: *She was proud that her mother was so clever.*
2 having too high an opinion of your own importance

prove (rhymes with *groove*) *verb*
1 to show to be true or genuine
2 to show to be capable of something: *He proved himself an expert driver.* **3** to turn out: *The report proved to be false.*

Word Building: other forms are **I proved, I have proved** or **I have proven, I am proving**

proverb *noun*
a short, popular, usually wise saying that has been used by people for a long time, such as *A stitch in time saves nine.*

Word Building: **proverbial** *adjective*

provide *verb*
1 to make available or to supply: *I will provide the food. | He will provide us with the drink.* **2** to supply what is needed to live: *Parents usually provide for their children.*

Word Building: **provider** *noun*

providence (say *<u>prov</u>-ə-dəns*) *noun*
1 the care and protection of God, nature or fate **2** the careful management of things like money, in preparation for the future

Word Building: **provident** *adjective*

province *noun*
1 a section or division of a country, territory or region **2** a range or field of knowledge: *The history of South Australia is outside my province.*

Word Building: **provincial** *adjective*

provision *noun*
1 a section of a document which sets out a condition **2** the providing or supplying of something such as food **3** an arrangement made beforehand **4 provisions** supplies of food and other necessities

Word Use: another word with a similar meaning to definition 1 is **proviso**

provisional *adjective*
temporary, or for the time being only: *a provisional government*

Word Building: **provisionally** *adverb*

provoke *verb*
1 to make angry or annoyed: *He provoked the dog by teasing it.* **2** to stir up or cause: *His behaviour provoked his parents' anger.*

Word Building: **provocation** *noun* **provocative** *adjective*

prowess (say *<u>prow</u>-es, prow-<u>es</u>*) *noun*
1 bravery **2** outstanding ability or skill

prowl *verb*
to go about quietly, as if in search of prey or something to steal

Word Building: **prowl** *noun*

proximity *noun*
nearness in place, time and so on

proxy *noun*
someone who is officially allowed to act for someone else: *He acted as proxy for his mother at the ceremony.*

Word Building: the plural is **proxies**

prude *noun*
someone who is too modest or proper

prudence *noun*
careful practical wisdom or good sound judgment

Word Building: **prudent** *adjective*

prune[1] *noun*
a dried plum

prune[2] *verb*
to cut off twigs or branches from

pry *verb*
to look or search with too much curiosity: *He is always prying into our affairs.*

Word Building: other forms are **I pried, I have pried, I am prying** □ **prying** *adjective*

PS
short for postscript, *a Latin word meaning* "written after"

Word Use: this is often used at the end of a letter to show something has been added

psalm (say *sahm*) *noun*
a sacred song, hymn or poem

Word History: from a Greek word meaning "a song sung to the harp"

pseudonym (say *syooh-də-nim*) *noun*
an invented name used by a writer

Word Use: another word for this is **pen-name**

psychiatry (say *sə-kuy-ə-tree*) *noun*
the study and treatment of mental illness

Word Building: **psychiatric** *adjective* **psychiatrist** *noun*

psychic (say *suy-kik*) *adjective*
1 having to do with the human soul or mind **2** having the power to tell the future or what others are thinking

Word Building: **psychic** *noun*

psychology (say *suy-kol-ə-jee*) *noun*
the study of the mind, how it works, and why people behave as they do

Word Building: **psychological** *adjective* **psychologically** *adverb* **psychologist** *noun*

psychosomatic
(say *suy-koh-sə-mat-ik*) *adjective*
having to do with an illness of your body which is caused by or made worse by your emotional state

p.t.o.
short for please turn over

Pty (say *prə-pruy-ə-tree*)
short for proprietary *which is added to the name of a company to show that there is only a small number of shareholders*

Word Use: see also **Ltd** which often comes after **Pty**

pub *noun*
a hotel

Word Use: this word is more suited to everyday language
Word History: this word is short for **public house**

puberty (say *pyooh-bə-tee*) *noun*
the stage of life or physical development when someone is first capable of producing children

pubic (say *pyooh-bik*) *adjective*
having to do with the lower part of your abdomen where the genitals are: *pubic hair*

public *adjective*
1 having to do with or used by the people of a community or the people as a whole: *public affairs | public transport*
public *noun*
2 the people of a community

publican *noun*
the owner or manager of a hotel

publication *noun*
1 the publishing of a book, magazine, newspaper or other printed work
2 something which is published

publicity (say *pub-lis-ə-tee*) *noun*
any advertisement, information and so on which is meant to attract the attention of the public

public relations *noun*
the methods used to give the public a good impression of a particular business or company

publish *verb*
1 to prepare and issue a book, magazine, and so on in printed copies for sale to the public **2** to announce to the public

Word Building: **publisher** *noun* a person or company that publishes books

puce (say *pyoohs*) *adjective*
dark purplish-brown

Word History: from a French word meaning "flea"

pucker *verb*
to gather into small folds or wrinkles

Word Building: **pucker** *noun*

pudding *noun*
a soft sweet dish usually served as a dessert

puddle *noun*
a small pool of liquid, such as dirty water left after rain

puff *noun*
1 a short, quick, sending out of air, wind or breath **2** a light pastry with a filling of jam, cream, and so on: *a cream puff*

puff *verb*
3 to blow with puffs: *The smoke puffed into the air. / The train puffed steam out of its funnel.* **4** to breathe quickly after violent exercise **5** to smoke a cigarette, cigar or pipe **6 puff up** to become swollen

puffin *noun*
a seabird found in the northern Atlantic, with a ducklike body and a narrow brightly-coloured bill

pug *noun*
a small dog with a smooth coat, a very wrinkled face, a snub nose and a tightly curled tail

pugnacious (say *pug-nay-shəs*) *adjective*
tending to quarrel or fight

Word Building: **pugnaciously** *adverb*

pull *verb*
1 to move something by tugging or drawing it towards you **2** to tear apart: *to pull something to pieces* **3** to strain: *to pull a muscle* **4 pull in** to move your vehicle to the side of the road to stop **5 pull up** to stop

Word Building: **pull** *noun*

pullet (rhymes with *bullet*) *noun*
a hen less than one year old

pulley (rhymes with *bully*) *noun*
a wheel or system of wheels with ropes or chains, used to lift heavy things

pullover *noun*
another word for **jumper**

pulp *noun*
1 the soft juicy part of a fruit **2** any soft wet mass: *Paper is made out of the pulp from wood, linen and similar materials.*

Word Building: **pulp** *verb*

pulpit *noun*
a raised platform in a church where the priest or minister stands to give a sermon

pulsate (say *pul-sayt*) *verb*
to beat or throb like your heart

Word Building: **pulsation** *noun*

pulse *noun*
the regular beating in your arteries caused by the pumping of blood by your heart

Word Building: **pulse** *verb*

pulverise or **pulverize** *verb*
1 to pound or grind into dust or powder: *He pulverised the rock into sand.*
2 to destroy completely

puma (say *pyooh-mə*) *noun*
a large animal of the cat family found in America

Word Use: it is sometimes called a **cougar** or a **mountain lion**

pumice (say *pum-əs*) *noun*
a light spongy form of volcanic stone used for polishing things

pummel *verb*
to beat with rapid blows of the fists

Word Building: other verb forms are **I pummelled, I have pummelled, I am pummelling**

pump *noun*
1 a device that forces a liquid or gas in or out of something

pump *verb*
2 to move by using a pump: *to pump water out of the dam* **3 pump up** to fill with air: *to pump up your tyres* **4** to move or operate by an up-and-down hand action

pumpkin *noun*
a large, roundish, yellow-orange vegetable

pun *noun*
a play on words which sound alike but are different in meaning, as in *"What do cannibals eat for tea? Human beans!"*

Word Building: **pun** *verb* (**punned, punning**)

punch[1] *noun*
1 a hit or blow, especially with your fist
2 a strong or forceful effect

Word Building: **punch** *verb*

punch[2] *noun*
a device for making holes in tickets, leather or similar materials

punch[3] *noun*
a drink made of water, fruit juice, pieces of fruit and sometimes wine, rum or other spirit

punctilious (say *punk-til-ee-əs*) *adjective*
being very exact about doing things correctly: *He was punctilious in carrying out his duties.*

punctual (say *punk-chooh-əl*) *adjective*
careful about being on time

Word Building: **punctuality** *noun* **punctually** *adverb*

punctuation (say *punk-chooh-ay-shən*) *noun*
commas, semi-colons, colons, full stops and so on used in writing to make the meaning clear

Word Building: **punctuate** *verb*

puncture (say *pungk-chə*) *verb*
to prick or make a hole in: *to puncture the skin with a pin / to puncture a tyre*

Word Building: **puncture** *noun*

pundit (say *pun-dət*) *noun*
someone who knows a lot about a subject

Word Use: this is more suited to everyday language

pungent (say *pun-jənt*) *adjective*
having a sharp taste or smell: *the pungent odour of vinegar*

Word Building: **pungency** *noun* **pungently** *adverb*
Word History: from a Latin word meaning "pricking"

punish *verb*
to make suffer in some way because of wrongdoing

Word Building: **punishment** *noun*

punk *adjective*
1 worthless or of poor quality **2** having to do with punk rock and the people interested in it

punk rock *noun*
a type of rock music with a very fast beat and which seems to be connected with aggressiveness, violence and unconventional behaviour

punnet *noun*
a small shallow box or basket for small fruits, especially strawberries

punt[1] *noun*
a shallow-bottomed boat with square ends

Word Building: **punt** *verb* to work a punt or carry in a punt

punt[2] *noun*
a kick which you give to a dropped football before it has hit the ground

Word Building: **punt** *verb*

punt[3] *noun*
a chance to bet: *to take a punt*

puny (say *pyooh-nee*) *adjective*
1 small and weak **2** of little importance: *puny efforts*

Word Building: other forms are **punier, puniest**

pup *noun*
a young dog or some other animal less than one year old

Word Use: another word for this is **puppy**

pupa (say *pyooh-pə*) *noun*
an insect in the cocoon between the larva and mature adult stages

Word Building: the plural is **pupae** (say *pyooh-pee*) □ **pupal** *adjective* **pupate** *verb*
Word History: from a Latin word meaning "girl", "doll" or "puppet"

pupil[1] *noun*
someone who is being taught

pupil[2] *noun*
the small dark spot on the iris of your eye, which expands to allow more light into the retina

puppet *noun*
1 a doll or figure of some kind which is moved by wires or your hand, usually on a small stage **2** someone who is controlled by others

Word Use: a similar word for definition 1 is **marionette**
Word Building: **puppeteer** *noun* **puppetry** *noun*

purchase (say *per-chəs*) *verb*
to pay for or buy

Word Building: **purchase** *noun* something bought

pure *adjective*
1 having nothing mixed with it, especially anything which might spoil it: *pure gold / pure silk* **2** clear and true: *the pure notes of a flute* **3** clean and spotless: *a pure reputation*

Word Building: **purify** *verb* (**purified, purifying**) **purely** *adverb* **purification** *noun* **purity** *noun*

puree (say *pyooh-ray*) *noun*
vegetables or fruit cooked and then sieved or blended

Word Use: another spelling is **purée** □ it can be spelt like this because it comes from French
Word Building: **puree** *verb*

purgative (say *per-gə-tiv*) *noun*
a medicine causing emptying or cleansing of the bowels

Word Building: **purgative** *adjective* cleansing or purging

purgatory (say *per-gə-tree*) *noun*
1 a place of temporary punishment where some Christians believe you go after death but before you go to heaven **2** any place or situation in your life which causes a lot of suffering

Word Use: definition 1 often has a capital "P" and is part of the belief of the Roman Catholic Church

purge (say *perj*) *verb*
to purify or get rid of what is unwanted or not good

Word Building: **purge** *noun*

puritan (say *pyooh-rə-tən*) *noun*
someone who tries to be very pure and strict in moral and religious matters

Word Building: **puritan** *adjective* having to do with puritans **puritanical** *adjective* behaving like a puritan **puritanism** *noun*

purl *noun*
a stitch used in knitting

Word Use: be careful – this sounds like **pearl**
Word Building: **purl** *verb*

purple *adjective*
dark reddish-blue

purpose *noun*
1 the reason something is done or made: *The purpose of this device is to make potato peeling easier.* **2 on purpose** intentionally

Word Building: **purposeful** *adjective*

purr *verb*
to make a low, continuous, murmuring sound as a cat does

Word Building: **purr** *noun*

purse *noun*
1 a small bag for carrying money
purse *verb*
2 to draw into folds or wrinkles: *She pursed her lips in annoyance.*

purser *noun*
a ship's officer who looks after the accounts

pursue (say *pə-syooh*) *verb*
1 to follow so as to catch **2** to try hard for or seek: *to pursue happiness | to pursue a career*

Word Building: **pursuit** *noun*

pus (rhymes with *bus*) *noun*
the yellowish-white substance in a boil or sore

Word Building: **pussy** *adjective*

push *verb*
1 to move by pressing or leaning against
2 to force from behind: *We pushed our way through the crowd.* **3** to recommend or to insist on earnestly: *She pushed me to agree with her. | He pushed his plan.*
4 push on to continue or go forward

Word Building: **push** *noun*

pushover *noun*
something easily done

push-up *noun*
an exercise in which you raise your body from a lying down position by pushing against the floor, leaving your feet on the ground and keeping your body and legs in a straight line

Word Use: another name for this is **press-up**

pussyfoot *verb*
to act timidly as if afraid to make a decision

pustule (say *pus-tyoohl*) *noun*
a pimple

Word Building: **pustulant** *adjective* **pustular** *adjective*

put *verb*
1 to place or set down **2** to cause to suffer: *The king put her to death.*
3 to cause to begin: *I put her to work.*
4 to express in words: *to put a question*
5 put down **a** to stamp out: *to put down a rebellion* **b** to kill as an act of mercy: *We had to put down our old sick dog.*
6 put off to postpone **7 put on** to pretend to have or to be: *He puts on his aches and pains.* **8 put out** to annoy or make difficulties for **9 put up with** to bear or endure

Word Building: other forms are **I put, I have put, I am putting**

putrid (say *pyooh-trəd*) *adjective*
decaying or rotten, especially when foul-smelling

Word Building: **putrefy** *verb* (**putrefied, putrefying**)

putt (rhymes with *but*) *verb*
to strike a golf ball gently along the green towards the hole

Word Building: **putter** *noun* a golf club for putting **putt** *noun*

putty *noun*
a kind of cement used for fixing glass into frames or filling holes in wood

Word Building: **putty** *verb* (**puttied, puttying**)
Word History: from a French word meaning "a potful"

puzzle *noun*
1 a toy or game which entertains by giving you an interesting problem to solve
2 something that is difficult to understand: *Her rudeness is a puzzle to me.*

Word Building: **puzzle** *verb* **puzzlement** *noun*

pygmy (say *pig-mee*) *noun*
1 a member of a tribe of African people who are mostly under 1.5 metres tall
2 any small dwarf-like person or thing

Word Use: another spelling is **pigmy**
Word Building: the plural is **pygmies**

pyjama party *noun*
a party you go to in your pyjamas and stay the whole night

Word Use: another word for this is **slumber party**

pyjamas *plural noun*
loose trousers and jacket worn in bed

Word History: from a Persian word meaning "leg garment"

pylon (say *puy-lon*) *noun*
1 a tall steel tower carrying electric or telephone wires **2** one of the two tall structures on either side of the end of a bridge or of a gateway

pyramid (say *pir-ə-mid*) *noun*
a structure with a square base and with sides sloping to a point, such as the huge stone ones built by the ancient Egyptians

pyre (rhymes with *fire*) *noun*
a pile of wood used for burning dead bodies in some countries

pyrotechnics *noun*
the art of making and using fireworks

Word Building: **pyrotechnic** *adjective* **pyrotechnist** *noun*

python (say *puy-thən*) *noun*
a large snake which crushes its prey but is not venomous

quack[1] *noun*
the sound a duck makes

Word Building: **quack** *verb*
Word History: an imitation of the sound

quack[2] *noun*
someone with no proper medical training who tricks sick people into believing he can cure them

Word Use: a similar word is **charlatan**
Word Building: **quackery** *noun*

quadrangle *noun*
a square or rectangular courtyard surrounded by buildings

quadrant *noun*
1 a quarter of a circle **2** an instrument for measuring altitudes, especially in astronomy and navigation

Word Use: compare definition 2 with **sextant**

quadrilateral *noun*
a flat shape with four sides

Word Building: **quadrilateral** *adjective*

quadrille (say *kwə-dril*) *noun*
a dance where four couples dance in a square pattern

Word History: from a Spanish word meaning "company" or "troop"

quadruped (say *kwod-rə-ped*) *noun*
an animal with four feet

Word Building: **quadruped** *adjective*

quadruple (say *kwod-rooh-pəl*) *verb*
1 to multiply by four
quadruple *adjective*
2 made up of four parts **3** four times bigger

Word Building: **quadruple** *noun*

quadruplet *noun*
one of four children born at the same time to the same mother

Word Use: a shortened form of this is **quad**

quaff (say *kwof*) *verb*
to drink thirstily

quagmire (say *kwog-muy-ə*) *noun*
a muddy patch of ground: *The rain has turned the yard into a quagmire.*

Word Use: a similar word is **bog**

quail[1] *noun*
a small bird that builds its nest on the ground and is hunted for sport and food

Word Building: the plural is either **quails** or **quail**

quail[2] *verb*
to show fear when danger threatens

quaint *adjective*
charmingly strange or old-fashioned: *a quaint little country town*

Word Building: **quaintly** *adverb*
quaintness *noun*

quake *verb*
to tremble or shake: *to quake with fear | The city quaked with the force of the explosion.*

Word Building: **quake** *noun* earthquake

qualify (say *kwol-ə-fuy*) *verb*
1 to make or become suitable for: *Her teaching experience qualifies her for the job. | To qualify for the final you must do well in the heats.* **2** to change or limit the meaning of: *to qualify a remark | An adjective qualifies a noun.*

Word Building: other forms are **I qualified, I have qualified, I am qualifying** □ **qualification** *noun* **qualified** *adjective*

quality (say *kwol-ə-tee*) *noun*
1 a feature or characteristic: *The sound of an echo has a hollow quality.* **2** value or worth: *clothes of good quality*

Word Building: the plural is **qualities** □ **quality** *adjective* fine or good

qualm (rhymes with *farm*) *noun*
a slightly guilty feeling: *They had some qualms about being late.*

Word History: from an Old English word meaning "torment", "pain" or "plague"

quandary (say *kwon-dree*) *noun*
confusion about what is the best thing to do: *I'm in a quandary about this invitation.*

Word Building: the plural is **quandaries**

quandong (say *kwon-dong*) *noun*
an Australian tree with fruit which you can eat raw or make into jams and jellies

quantity (say *kwon-tə-tee*) *noun*
an amount or measure: *What quantity does this bottle hold?*

Word Building: the plural is **quantities** □ **quantify** *verb* (**quantified, quantifying**) to measure

quarantine (say *kwo-rən-teen*) *noun*
the isolating of people or animals for a certain period of time to make sure they don't spread a disease to others

Word Building: quarantine *verb*

quarrel (say *kwo-rəl*) *noun*
an angry argument

Word Building: quarrel *verb* (**quarrelled, quarrelling**) **quarrelsome** *adjective*

quarry[1] (rhymes with *sorry*) *noun*
a large open pit where stone used for building is cut or blasted out of the ground: *a sandstone quarry*

Word Building: the plural is **quarries** □ **quarry** *verb* (**quarried, quarrying**)

quarry[2] (rhymes with *sorry*) *noun*
an animal or bird that is being hunted or chased: *The hounds tracked down their quarry.*

Word Building: the plural is **quarries**

quarter (say *kwaw-tə*) *noun*
1 one of the parts you get when you divide something equally into four: *a quarter of an apple* **2** a district in a town: *the business quarter* **3 quarters** a place to live: *the nurses' quarters*

Word Building: quarter *verb*

quarterdeck *noun*
the part of the top deck of a ship between the mast and the stern, used by the officers

quartermaster *noun*
an army officer in charge of food, clothing, housing and equipment

quartet *noun*
1 a group of four people, especially musicians or singers **2** a musical piece for four voices or four performers: *a quartet for string instruments*

quartz (say *kwawts*) *noun*
a common mineral which has many different forms and colours, and which can be used to help make very accurate clocks and watches

quasi- *prefix*
a word part meaning resembling *or* as though: *quasi-official*

Word History: this prefix comes from Latin

quaver *noun*
1 a shaking or trembling voice: *The old man spoke in a quaver.* **2** a musical note which is half as long as a crotchet

Word Building: quaver *verb* to say or sing in a trembling voice **quavery** *adjective*

quay (say *kee*) *noun*
a wharf where ships and ferries load or unload passengers and cargo

Word Use: be careful – this sounds like **key**

queasy *adjective*
feeling as if you are going to vomit

Word Building: other forms are **queasier, queasiest** □ **queasily** *adverb* **queasiness** *noun*

queen *noun*
1 a woman who is the lifelong ruler of a country **2** the wife of a king **3** the large egg-laying female of such creatures as bees, ants and termites **4** a playing card with a picture of a queen on it
5 the most powerful chess piece

Word Building: queenly *adverb*

queer *adjective*
1 strange or odd: *a queer idea* **2** unwell: *I feel queer.* **3** homosexual

Word Use: definition 3 is more suited to everyday language
Word Building: **queerly** *adverb*
Word History: from a Greek word meaning "cross" or "oblique"

quell *verb*
to stop or calm: *to quell riots | to quell your fears*

quench *verb*
1 to put out: *to quench a fire* **2** to satisfy or make less: *A cool drink will quench your thirst.*

querulous (say *kwe-rə-ləs*) *adjective*
irritable and complaining

Word Building: **querulously** *adverb*

query (say *kwear-ree*) *noun*
1 a question or enquiry **2** a doubt or problem: *a query about the electricity bill*

Word Building: the plural is **queries** □ **query** *verb* (**queried, querying**) to ask questions about or doubt

quest *noun*
a search: *a talent quest | a quest for gold*

question *noun*
1 a request for information: *The police asked the witnesses many questions about the accident.* **2** a doubt or problem: *There is no question about her honesty.* **3 out of the question** impossible

Word Building: **questionable** *adjective* uncertain **question** *verb* **questionably** *adverb*

question mark *noun*
a punctuation mark (?) put at the end of a written question

questionnaire (say *kwes-chən-air*) *noun*
a list of questions set out on a printed form with spaces for the answers to be written in

queue (say *kyooh*) *noun*
a single line of people, cars or animals waiting in turn for something: *a queue for tickets*

Word Building: **queue** *verb*

quibble *verb*
to argue, especially over things that don't matter: *to quibble over a few cents change*

quiche (say *keesh*) *noun*
a tart filled with a mixture of cooked eggs, cream and cheese, often eaten cold

quick *adjective*
1 fast, rapid or impatient: *a quick movement | a quick temper* **2** done, completed or happening in a short time: *a quick job*
quick *noun*
3 the sensitive skin under your nails: *nails bitten down to the quick*

Word Building: **quicken** *verb* to make or become fast **quick** *adverb* **quickly** *adverb*

quicksand *noun*
wet sand which traps anyone who falls into it and sucks them down

quicksilver *adjective*
1 changing quickly
quicksilver *noun*
2 *an old-fashioned word for* **mercury**

quid *noun*
one pound in money, used before decimal currency

Word Use: this word is more suited to everyday language

quiet *adjective*
1 still or silent **2** calm and peaceful: *a quiet weekend | a quiet street* **3** shy: *The new girl is rather quiet.*

Word Building: **quiet** *noun* calmness or peace **quieten** *verb* to make or become quiet **quietly** *adverb*

quill *noun*
1 a large feather **2** an old-fashioned pen, made from a goose's feather **3** a sharp spine of an echidna or porcupine

quilt *noun*
a light warm bed-cover filled with feathers

quince *noun*
a sour yellow fruit, rather like a large pear, which is so hard it has to be cooked before you can eat it

quinine (say *kwin-een*) *noun*
a bitter medicine used to treat malaria

quintet *noun*
1 a group of five people, especially musicians or singers **2** a musical piece for five voices or five performers

quintuple
(say *kwin-tup-əl, kwin-tyoohp-əl*) *verb*
1 to multiply by five

quintuple *adjective*
2 made up of five parts **3** five times bigger

Word Building: **quintuple** *noun*

quintuplet (say *kwin-tup-lət*) *noun*
one of five children born at the same time to the same mother

quip *noun*
a clever or sarcastic remark

Word Building: **quip** *verb* (**quipped, quipping**) **quipster** *noun*

quirk *noun*
1 a particular habit or way of acting: *a quirk of his nature* **2** a sudden twist or turn: *quirk of fate*

Word Building: **quirky** *adjective* (**quirkier, quirkiest**) odd or eccentric

quit *verb*
1 to give up or leave: *to quit a job* | *The wages were very low so she quit.*
quit *noun*
2 call it quits **a** to decide to stop doing something **b** to end an argument by agreeing that both sides are even

Word Building: other verb forms are **I quit** or **I quitted, I have quit** or **I have quitted, I am quitting**

quite *adverb*
1 completely or entirely: *to be quite right* **2** fairly or reasonably: *quite pretty*

quiver[1] *verb*
to tremble or shake slightly: *to quiver with fear* | *The leaves quiver in the breeze.*

Word Building: **quiver** *noun*

quiver[2] *noun*
a case for holding arrows

quixotic (say *kwik-sot-ik*) *adjective*
having romantic ideas about doing brave and wonderful deeds

Word History: from *Don Quixote,* the hero of a Spanish novel, who was always trying to do good

quiz *noun*
a test to see who knows the most about a particular subject: *a general knowledge quiz on TV* | *a spelling quiz*

Word Building: the plural form is **quizzes** □ **quiz** *verb* (**quizzed, quizzing**) to ask many questions

quizzical *adjective*
teasing, or suggesting you know something the other person doesn't: *a quizzical smile*

quoits (say *koyts*) *plural noun*
a game played by throwing rings made of stiff rope over a peg on the ground

quokka (say *kwok-ə*) *noun*
a small wallaby, just larger than a cat, with rounded ears and a short face

quorum (say *kwaw-rəm*) *noun*
the number of people that have to be at a meeting before decisions can be made

quota *noun*
the share that you are entitled to: *Because of the drought, the farmers needed more than their quota of water.*

quotation *noun*
a passage copied exactly from a book or speech

quotation mark *noun*
one of the punctuation marks (“ ” or ‘ ’) used before and after a quotation, as in *“We learned ‘Advance Australia Fair’ at school”, she said.*

quote *verb*
1 to repeat exactly: *to quote a phrase from Shakespeare* **2** to name a price: *The mechanic quoted $100 to fix the car.*

Word Building: **quotable** *adjective* worth repeating **quote** *noun* quotation

quotient (say *kwoh-shənt*) *noun*
the number or result you get when one number is divided by another: *In the sum 12 ÷ 4, the quotient is 3.*

Word Use: compare **divisor** and **dividend**

rabbi (say *rab-uy*) *noun*
a Jewish priest or leader

rabbit *noun*
1 a small, long-eared, burrowing animal
rabbit *verb*
2 to hunt rabbits **3 rabbit on** to talk a lot of nonsense

Word Use: the male is a **buck;** the female is a **doe;** the young is a **kit**

rabble *noun*
a noisy crowd or mob

rabies *noun*
a fatal disease that is spread to people by the bite of a dog or some other animal which has the disease

Word Building: **rabid** *adjective*
Word History: from a Latin word meaning "madness" or "rage"

race[1] *noun*
1 a contest of speed **2** any kind of competition: *the arms race* **3** a narrow passageway for animals, such as one leading to a sheep dip
race[1] *verb*
4 to run or move very quickly
5 to compete with in running: *I raced him to the shop.*

race[2] *noun*
a group of tribes or nations with the same ancestors, the same language and culture or the same skin colour

racial (say *ray-shəl*) *adjective*
1 having to do with or typical of a race: *White skin is a racial characteristic of English people.* **2** having to do with relations between people of different races: *racial harmony*

Word Building: **racially** *adverb*

racism (say *ray-siz-əm*) *noun*
1 the belief that your own race is better than any other **2** unpleasant or violent behaviour towards members of another race

Word Use: this is also called **racialism**
Word Building: **racist** *noun* **racist** *adjective*

rack *noun*
1 a framework of bars, wires or pegs for holding things **2** a frame on which people used to be tortured by having their bodies stretched
rack *verb*
3 to cause great pain to: *Fever racked her body.*

racket[1] *noun*
1 a loud confused noise **2** an illegal business or way of making money: *an organised car-stealing racket*

Word Building: **racketeer** *noun* someone involved in a racket

racket[2] *noun*
another spelling for **racquet**

raconteur (say *rak-on-ter*) *noun*
someone who is very good at telling interesting and amusing stories, especially true ones

racquet (say *rak-ət*) *noun*
a bat with a network of nylon or cord stretched across an oval frame, which is used in tennis and similar games

radar *noun*
a device which tells you the position and speed of objects like cars, ships or planes by sending out radio waves and measuring the time the echo takes to come back and the direction it comes from

Word History: an acronym made by joining the first letters of the words *ra(dio) d(etecting) a(nd) r(anging)*

radial (say *ray-dee-əl*) *adjective*
arranged like rays or radii

radiant (say *ray-dee-ənt*) *adjective*
1 shining or sending out rays: *the radiant sun* **2** bright with joy: *a radiant smile*

Word Building: **radiance** *noun* **radiantly** *adverb*

radiate *verb*
1 to spread out like rays from a centre
2 to send out in rays: *The stove radiated heat.*

radiation *noun*
the sending and spreading out of rays, particles or waves, especially by a radioactive substance

radiator *noun*
1 an electric room heater with a rod or rods which become red-hot **2** a device which cools the engine of a motor vehicle

radical (say *rad-i-kəl*) *adjective*
1 being in favour of extreme social or political reforms: *a radical political party*
2 going to the root or bottom of things: *a radical change in education / radical ideas about religion*

Word Use: be careful – this sounds like **radicle**
Word Building: **radical** *noun* **radically** *adverb*
Word History: from a Latin word meaning "root"

radicle (say *rad-i-kəl*) *noun*
the largest and most important root of a young plant

Word Use: be careful – this sounds like **radical**

radio *noun*
1 the sending of electrical signals through the air **2** a device for picking up radio broadcasts
radio *verb*
3 to send a message by radio: *We radioed for help.*

Word Building: the plural form of the noun is **radios** □ other verb forms are **I radioed, I have radioed, I am radioing**

radioactivity *noun*
the ability of some atomic elements, like uranium, to release harmful radiation

Word Building: **radioactive** *adjective*

radish *noun*
a hot-tasting red-skinned vegetable eaten raw in salads

radium *noun*
a naturally occurring radioactive element sometimes used to treat cancer

radius *noun*
1 a straight line going from the centre of a circle to its circumference or edge
2 a circular area around some point: *every house within a radius of ten kilometres of the school*

Word Building: the plural is **radii** (say *ray-dee-uy*) or **radiuses**

raffia *noun*
a fibre obtained from the leaves of a palm tree that you use in weaving baskets and in other crafts

raffle *noun*
a lottery in which the prizes are usually goods, not money

Word Building: **raffle** *verb*

raft *noun*
a floating platform, often made of logs, for carrying goods or people on the water

rafter *noun*
a sloping piece of wood forming part of the framework of a roof

rag *noun*
1 an old torn piece of cloth that you use for cleaning **2** a newspaper or magazine that's badly written **3 rags** worn and shabby clothing

ragamuffin *noun*
someone who is ragged and dirty, especially a child

rage *noun*
1 violent anger: *to get into a rage*
2 all the rage fashionable or popular
rage *verb*
3 to act or speak angrily **4** to move or happen violently: *The storm raged for days.*
5 to set about enjoying yourself

Word Use: definition 5 is more suited to everyday language

ragged (say *rag-əd*) *adjective*
1 wearing old and torn clothes **2** torn or worn to rags: *ragged clothing*

raid *noun*
a sudden invasion or attack: *a police raid on a gambling house / a raid on an enemy airfield*

rail *noun*
1 a rod or bar used as a support or barrier **2** the railway: *We will travel by rail.* **3 rails** the railway lines that a train runs on

railway *noun*
1 the track or way laid with parallel metal rails for trains to run on **2** all these tracks together with their trains, buildings and land

rain *noun*
1 water falling from the sky in drops **2** a large quantity of anything which keeps on falling for some time: *a rain of confetti*
rain *verb*
3 to come down from the sky in drops of water **4** to fall constantly like rain: *Tears rained down her cheeks.* **5 rain cats and dogs** to rain heavily

Word Use: be careful – this sounds like **rein** and **reign**

rainbow *noun*
an arc of colours that appears in the sky when the sun is shining after rain

Word Building: **rainbow** *adjective* having many colours

rainforest *noun*
thick forest in moderately warm to very hot areas which have heavy rainfall and high humidity

raise *verb*
1 to lift up **2** to bring up or produce: *to raise a family / to raise cattle* **3** to gather together or collect: *to raise an army / to raise money* **4** to cause to stick out: *The sun raised blisters on my arms.* **5** to increase in amount: *to raise prices*

Word Building: **raise** *noun* an increase in wages

raisin *noun*
a dried sweet grape

Word History: from a Latin word meaning "cluster of grapes"

rake *noun*
1 a long-handled gardening tool used for gathering cut grass and leaves or for levelling and smoothing the ground
rake *verb*
2 to clear or level with a rake: *to rake the lawn* **3** to use a rake: *He's out in the garden raking.* **4 rake in** to gather or collect: *to rake in donations*

rally *verb*
1 to bring together: *to rally an army* **2** to come together: *The people rallied behind their leader.* **3** to revive or recover: *He rallied his spirits. / She rallied briefly before becoming unconscious.*
rally *noun*
4 a public meeting to discuss an important or worrying topic **5** a recovery from illness **6** a long exchange of strokes in tennis and similar games **7** a car competition testing skill rather than speed

Word Building: other verb forms are **I rallied, I have rallied, I am rallying** □ the plural of the noun is **rallies**

ram *noun*
1 a male sheep **2** a device for battering or forcefully pushing something
ram *verb*
3 to strike with great force: *The car rammed the wall.* **4** to drive or force by heavy blows: *to ram the earth down*

Word Use: the female is a **ewe;** the young is a **lamb**
Word Building: other verb forms are **I rammed, I have rammed, I am ramming**

RAM (say *ram*) *noun*
computer memory from which each item can be accessed or found equally quickly

Word History: an acronym made from the first letters of *Random Access Memory*

Ramadan (say *ram-ə-dahn*) *noun*
the ninth month of the Muslim year during which there is a daily fast from sunrise to sunset

Word History: from an Arabic word

ramble *verb*
1 to wander about in an unhurried way **2** to talk or write without keeping to the subject
ramble *noun*
3 a pleasant slow walk, especially in the country

Word Building: **rambler** *noun* **rambling** *adjective*

ramp *noun*
a sloping surface connecting two levels: *a pedestrian ramp / a loading ramp*

Word History: from a French word meaning "creep", "crawl" or "climb"

rampage (say *ram-payj*) *noun*
1 violent or angry behaviour
rampage (say *ram-payj*) *verb*
2 to move or act violently and angrily

Word Building: **rampageous** *adjective*

rampant (say *ram-pənt*) *adjective*
1 violent or raging **2** unchecked: *Looting was rampant in the bombed city.*

rampart (say *ram-paht*) *noun*
a mound of earth used as a fortification or defence

ramshackle *adjective*
shaky or likely to collapse: *a ramshackle old building*

ranch *noun*
a large farm or station for grazing cattle, horses or sheep

Word Building: the plural is **ranches** □ this word is especially used in America □ **rancher** *noun*

rancid (say *ran-səd*) *adjective*
having a stale sour smell or taste: *rancid fat*

Word Building: **rancidity** *noun*

random *adjective*
happening or being done without a plan or purpose: *a random choice*

random *noun*
2 *in the phrase* **at random** without a plan or purpose

range *noun*
1 a line or row of mountains **2** a large area of land, especially one used for shooting practice: *a rifle range*
3 the distance that a bullet or rocket can travel **4** the limits within which there can be differences: *You are within the normal range for height.* **5** a collection or variety: *a range of goods | a range of opinions*
6 a cooking stove

range *verb*
7 to vary or change within stated limits: *Prices ranged from $5 to $10.* **8** to go, move or wander: *We ranged over a wide area on our holidays.*

ranger *noun*
someone who looks after a national park, a nature reserve, and so on

rank[1] *noun*
1 social class: *people of every rank*
2 official position or grade: *the rank of colonel* **3** a row or line: *The soldiers stood in ranks.*

Word Building: **rank** *verb*

rank[2] *adjective*
1 growing too tall or coarse: *rank weeds*
2 having a strong unpleasant taste or smell: *a rank cigar*

Word Building: **rankly** *adverb*

ransack *verb*
to search and rob: *to ransack a house*

ransom *noun*
money which must be paid for the return of someone who has been kidnapped or captured in a battle

Word Building: **ransom** *verb* (**ransomed, ransoming**)

rant *verb*
to speak loudly or angrily

Word Building: **ranter** *noun*

rap *verb*
to strike with a quick light blow: *She rapped my knuckles. | to rap on the door*

Word Building: other forms are **I rapped, I have rapped, I am rapping** □ **rap** *noun*

rape *noun*
the crime of having sexual intercourse with someone against their will

Word Building: **rape** *verb* **rapist** *noun*

rapid *adjective*
fast or quick: *rapid growth | a rapid worker*

Word Building: **rapidity** *noun* **rapidly** *adverb*

rapier (say *ray-pee-ə*) *noun*
a sword with a long, thin, pointed blade

rapport (say *rə-paw*) *noun*
a friendly feeling between people: *I seem to have a good rapport with my new teacher.*

rapt *adjective*
1 deeply occupied with your own thoughts and unaware of what is going on around you **2** overpowered by strong feelings: *She was rapt with joy.*

rapture *noun*
great joy or happiness

Word Building: **rapturous** *adjective* **rapturously** *adverb*

rare[1] *adjective*
1 unusual or uncommon: *a rare disease*
2 thin: *rare mountain air*

Word Building: **rarefy** *verb* (**rarefied, rarefying**) to make or become thin **rarely** *adverb*

rare[2] *adjective*
underdone or cooked so that it is still very red inside: *a rare grilled steak*

Word Building: **rareness** *noun* **rarity** *noun*

rascal (say *rahs-kəl*) *noun*
1 a dishonest person **2** a mischievous child or scamp

Word History: from a Latin word meaning "scratch"

rash[1] *adjective*
1 acting too quickly and without thought: *a rash person* **2** done without thought about what might happen: *a rash move*

Word Building: **rashly** *adverb* **rashness** *noun*

rash[2] *noun*
red itchy spots or patches on your skin

rasher *noun*
a thin slice of bacon

rasp *noun*
1 a coarse metal file
rasp *verb*
2 to use a rasp: *to rasp wood* **3** to scrape or rub roughly: *The cat's tongue rasped my hand.* **4** to make a grating sound: *The door rasped on its hinges.*

raspberry (say *rahz-bree*) *noun*
a soft, juicy, reddish-purple berry

Word Building: the plural is **raspberries** □ **raspberry** *adjective*

rat *noun*
1 a long-tailed animal similar to, but larger than, a mouse **2** someone who leaves a friend who is in trouble
3 smell a rat to be suspicious

Word Use: definitions 2 and 3 are more suited to everyday language □ the male is a **buck;** the female is a **doe**

rate *noun*
1 speed: *to work at a steady rate | to travel at a rate of 100 kilometres an hour*
2 a charge or payment: *The bank's loan interest rate is 10% per year.* **3 rates** the tax paid by people who own land to their local council **4 at any rate** in any case **5 at this rate** if things go on like this
rate *verb*
6 to set a value on, or consider as: *The council rated the land at $20 000. | I rate him a very good friend.*

ratify *verb*
to confirm or approve

Word Building: other forms are **I ratified, I have ratified, I am ratifying** □ **ratification** *noun* **ratifier** *noun*

rating *noun*
the value or standing that someone or something has

ratio (say *ray-shee-oh*) *noun*
the relationship between two amounts or quantities expressed in the lowest possible whole numbers: *The pupil-teacher ratio at our school is 30 to 1. | The ratio of good apples to bad in the bag was 11 to 2.*

ration (rhymes with *fashion*) *noun*
1 a fixed amount allowed to one person or group: *a ration of sultanas*
ration *verb*
2 to share out as a ration: *to ration tea when it is in short supply*

rational (say *rash-ə-nəl*) *adjective*
1 sensible or reasonable: *a rational decision* **2** sane or in possession of your reason: *He was quite rational when he regained consciousness.*

Word Building: **rationalise** *verb* to bring into an order **rationality** *noun* **rationally** *adverb*

rattle *verb*
1 to make, or cause to make, a series of short, sharp, clattering sounds: *The window rattled. | He rattled the door-knob.*
2 to confuse or upset: *The examiner rattled him with his questions.*
rattle *noun*
3 a number of short, sharp, clattering sounds **4** a baby's toy which makes such a noise

Word Building: **rattly** *adjective*

rattlesnake *noun*
a venomous American snake that has a tail with horny rings which make a rattling sound

raucous (say *raw-kəs*) *adjective*
harsh-sounding: *a raucous laugh*

Word Building: **raucously** *adverb*

ravage *verb*
to damage badly: *Sorrow ravaged her face.*

Word Building: **ravages** *plural noun: the ravages of war*

rave *verb*
1 to talk wildly making little sense, especially when you are very ill **2** to talk or write excitedly

Word Use: definition 2 is more suited to everyday language
Word Building: **rave** *noun*

raven *noun*
1 a large, shiny, black bird with a harsh call
raven *adjective*
2 shiny black: *raven hair*

ravenous (say *rav-ə-nəs*) *adjective*
very hungry

Word Building: **ravenously** *adverb*

ravine (say *rə-veen*) *noun*
a long, deep, narrow valley, especially one made by a river

ravioli (say *rav-ee-ohl-ee*) *plural noun*
small squares of pasta wrapped around minced meat, cooked, and served in a sauce

Word History: from a Latin word meaning "turnip" or "beet"

ravishing *adjective*
very beautiful

Word Building: **ravishingly** *adverb* **ravishment** *noun*

raw *adjective*
1 not cooked **2** not treated or processed: *raw leather* **3** inexperienced or untrained: *a raw recruit* **4** very painful: *a raw wound* **5** very cold: *a raw wind*

Word Building: **rawly** *adverb* **rawness** *noun*

ray *noun*
1 a beam of light **2** a small amount: *a ray of hope*

rayon *noun*
an artificial fabric, similar to silk

raze *verb*
to knock down level to the ground: *The wreckers had to raze the building after the fire.*

razor *noun*
a sharp-edged instrument or a small electrical instrument for shaving hair from your skin

Word History: from a French word meaning "scrape" or "shave"

re- *prefix*
a word part meaning **1** again: *repeat* **2** back: *repay*

Word History: this prefix comes from Latin

reach *verb*
1 to get to or arrive at **2** to succeed in touching: *I can reach the high shelf.*
reach *noun*
3 the distance you can reach: *She left the water within the patient's reach.*
4 a straight part of a river between bends

Word Building: the plural of the noun is **reaches**

react (say *ree-akt*) *verb*
1 to act in answer or reply: *We all react to danger in different ways.* **2** to act upon each other, as chemicals do when combined

reaction (say *ree-ak-shən*) *noun*
1 something done as a result of an action by someone else: *Her reaction to my rudeness was to walk away.* **2** a chemical change

read (say *reed*) *verb*
1 to look at and understand: *to read a sign / to read French* **2** to look at and say aloud **3** to understand: *to read her character from her face* **4** to take in information from: *My computer can't read that disk.* **5 read between the lines** to see the hidden truth or meaning

Word Use: be careful – this sounds like **reed**
Word Building: other verb forms are **I read** (say *red*), **I have read** (say *red*), **I am reading** □ **readable** *adjective* easy to read **reader** *noun*

ready *adjective*
1 completely prepared **2** quick: *a ready answer* **3** likely at any moment: *a tree ready to fall*
ready *verb*
4 to prepare

Word Building: other adjective forms are **readier, readiest** □ other verb forms are **I readied, I have readied, I am readying** □ **readily** *adverb* **readiness** *noun*

real *adjective*
1 true or actual: *the real reason / a story from real life* **2** genuine or not artificial: *real diamonds*

Word Building: **reality** *noun* (**realities**) **really** *adverb: really good*

real estate *noun*
land and the buildings on it

realise or **realize** *verb*
1 to come to understand **2** to make real or bring to pass: *His worst fears were realised.*

Word Building: **realisation** *noun*

realism *noun*
1 the facing of life as it really is
2 painting nature or writing about life as it really is

Word Use: the opposite of this is **idealism**
Word Building: **realist** *noun* **realistic** *adjective*

realm (say *relm*) *noun*
1 a kingdom **2** a particular area of interest or knowledge: *the realm of literature*

reap *verb*
1 to cut with a sickle or machine: *to reap the wheat* **2** to get as a return for work: *to reap the benefit*

Word Building: **reaper** *noun*

rear[1] *noun*
1 the back of anything **2** your buttocks
rear[1] *adjective*
3 situated at or having to do with the rear: *a rear window*

rear[2] *verb*
1 to look after and support: *to rear a family* **2** to rise up on the hind legs: *The horse reared when it saw the snake.*

reason *noun*
1 the cause of an action or happening **2** a statement or explanation of these causes **3** the ability to use your mind to form opinions **4** sound judgment or good sense **5 it stands to reason** it is obvious
reason *verb*
6 to argue in a sensible way: *I will reason with him.*

Word Building: **reasoned** *adjective* logically thought out **reasoning** *noun*

reasonable *adjective*
1 sensible or showing sound judgment: *a reasonable choice | a reasonable man*
2 fair or moderate: *a reasonable price*

Word Building: **reasonably** *adverb*

reassure (say *ree-ə-shaw*) *verb*
to give confidence to

Word Building: **reassurance** *noun*

rebate (say *ree-bayt*) *noun*
the return of an amount of money you have already paid out for something: *We got a rebate on our electricity bill.*

Word Building: **rebate** *verb*

rebel (say *reb-əl*) *noun*
1 someone who fights the government or resists those in authority
rebel (say *rə-bel*) *verb*
2 to fight against the government or resist those who rule or have power

Word Building: other verb forms are **I rebelled, I have rebelled, I am rebelling** □ **rebel** *adjective* **rebellion** *noun* **rebellious** *adjective*

rebound (say *rə-bownd*) *verb*
1 to bounce or spring back: *The ball rebounded off the wall.*
rebound (say *ree-bownd*) *noun*
2 the action of rebounding: *to catch a ball on the rebound*

rebuff *noun*
a refusal to accept offers or suggestions: *His rebuff hurt my feelings.*

Word Use: a similar word is **snub**
Word Building: **rebuff** *verb*

rebuke *verb*
to scold or show you disapprove of

Word Building: **rebuke** *noun*

recall (say *rə-kawl*) *verb*
1 to remember **2** to bring or order back: *to recall an ambassador*
recall (say *ree-kawl*) *noun*
3 ability to remember

recede (say *rə-seed*) *verb*
to move back and become more distant

Word Building: **recessive** *adjective*

receipt (say *rə-seet*) *noun*
1 a signed piece of paper proving that you have received goods sent or have paid money **2** the receiving of something: *On receipt of your letter I sent the parcel.*
3 receipts money received, especially in a shop

receive *verb*
1 to get or be given: *to receive a gift | to receive news* **2** to admit or allow to enter: *to receive into a club*

receiver *noun*
1 someone or something that receives
2 someone who receives things which they know have been stolen **3** someone who is appointed to take over a bankrupt company **4** the player receiving the balls served in tennis and similar games

recent *adjective*
happening or done not long ago

Word Building: **recently** *adverb*

receptacle (say *rə-sep-tik-əl*) *noun*
a container or something that holds things: *a receptacle for rubbish*

reception *noun*
1 a formal party in honour of someone
2 an office or desk where hotel guests or callers are met and looked after
3 the result or act of receiving or being received: *Reception on our TV is not very clear.* | *Her friends gave her a warm reception when she came.*

receptionist *noun*
someone employed in an office or hotel to look after callers or guests

receptive *adjective*
quick to take in new ideas or knowledge: *a receptive mind*

recess *noun*
1 a part of a room where the wall is set back for shelves or cupboards **2** a short time or break when work stops: *morning tea recess*

Word Building: the plural is **recesses** □ **recess** *verb*

recession *noun*
a time when business affairs in a nation are bad and many people do not have a job

recipe (say *res-ə-pee*) *noun*
a list of ingredients and the instructions telling you how to cook something

reciprocal (say *rə-sip-rə-kəl*) *adjective*
given, felt or done by one person to another: *reciprocal aid* | *reciprocal love*

Word Building: **reciprocally** *adverb* **reciprocate** *verb*

recital (say *rə-suy-təl*) *noun*
1 a concert or entertainment given by one performer or by the pupils of one teacher
2 a long explanation or statement: *We listened to a recital of his problems.*

recite *verb*
1 to repeat from memory the words of: *She recited a poem in class on Open Day.*
2 to repeat poetry or something similar from memory: *He is going to recite now.*

Word Building: **recitation** *noun*

reckless *adjective*
not caring about danger, especially in a foolish way: *He's a reckless climber.*

Word Building: **recklessly** *adverb* **recklessness** *noun*

reckon *verb*
1 to say what you think or believe: *I reckon she is clever.* **2** to calculate or count up: *I reckon our stall at the fete made $200.* **3** to think or suppose: *I reckon we ought to go now.* **4** to depend or rely: *We can reckon on his help I am sure.*

Word Use: definition 3 is more suited to everyday language
Word Building: **reckoning** *noun* an accounting

reclaim *verb*
1 to make suitable for farming or some other use: *We reclaimed the swamp land for a park.* **2** to get back: *I reclaimed my cases at the airport.*

Word Building: **reclamation** *noun*

recline *verb*
to lean or lie back

recluse (say *rə-kloohs*) *noun*
someone who lives alone and does not mix with other people

Word Building: **reclusive** *adjective*

recognise or **recognize**
(say *rek-əg-nuyz*) *verb*
1 to know again: *I hardly recognised her when she came back.* **2** to understand or realise: *I recognise the truth of what you say.*

Word Building: **recognisable** *adjective* **recognisably** *adverb* **recognition** *noun*

recoil *verb*
1 to draw back: *She recoiled from the snake in fear.* **2** to spring back: *The rifle recoiled against his shoulder when he fired it.*

Word Building: **recoil** *noun*

recollect (say *rek-ə-lekt*) *verb*
to remember or bring back to your mind

Word Building: **recollection** *noun*

recommend *verb*
1 to suggest as being good or worthwhile **2** to urge strongly: *I recommend that you be very careful.*

Word Use: a similar word for definition 1 is **commend**
Word Building: **recommendation** *noun*

recompense (say *rek-əm-pens*) *verb*
to make a repayment to: *I will recompense you for the trouble you have had.*

Word Use: a similar word is **compensate**
Word Building: **recompense** *noun*

reconcile (say *rek-ən-suyl*) *verb*
1 to cause to agree or make friendly: *to reconcile the two opinions / to reconcile the quarrelling brothers.* **2** to be no longer opposed: *I am reconciled to moving to another town.*

Word Use: a similar word for definition 1 is **conciliate**
Word Building: **reconciliation** *noun*

recondition *verb*
to repair or bring back to a good condition: *to recondition a motor*

reconnoitre (say *rek-ə-noy-tə*) *verb*
1 to look carefully at in order to gain useful information: *The scouts reconnoitred the area before the army attacked.*
2 to study or examine an area or situation before taking action: *The scouts were sent out to reconnoitre.*

Word Building: **reconnoitre** *noun*
Word History: from a French word meaning "recognise"

record (say *rə-kawd*) *verb*
1 to write down so that the information can be kept: *to record a conversation*
2 to put music or other sounds on a gramophone disc, tape, or compact disc
record (say *rek-awd*) *noun*
3 something that has been recorded in writing or print **4** a disc, usually plastic, on which music has been recorded: *a gramophone record* **5** the best performance so far in a sport or any other activity: *She broke the record for the long jump.*
6 a self-contained group of data on a computer, such as an employee's name, address and salary

Word Building: **record** *adjective* **recording** *noun*

recorder *noun*
1 an official who keeps records
2 a machine for recording sound, especially on magnetic tape **3** a type of wooden or plastic flute with a soft sound

record-player *noun*
a machine on which gramophone records are played

recount (say *rə-kownt*) *verb*
to narrate or tell about: *to recount the events of the day*

recover *verb*
1 to regain or get again: *to recover lost property* **2** to get well again after being sick

Word Building: **recovery** *noun*

recreation (say *rek-ree-ay-shən*) *noun*
a game, hobby or sport which is an enjoyable change from your daily work

recruit (say *rə-krooht*) *noun*
1 someone who has just joined the army, navy or air force **2** someone who has just joined an organisation or group: *a new recruit to the choir*
recruit *verb*
3 to enlist or enrol: *We are recruiting new members for our club.* **4** to enlist people for service: *The army is recruiting now.*

rectangle *noun*
a four-sided shape with all its angles right angles, that is, a square or an oblong

Word Building: **rectangular** *adjective*

rectify (say *rek-tə-fuy*) *verb*
to make or put right: *to rectify a mistake*

Word Building: other forms are **I rectified, I have rectified, I am rectifying** □ **rectification** *noun*

rector *noun*
a clergyman in charge of a parish, congregation or college

Word Building: **rectory** *noun* a rector's house
Word History: from a Latin word meaning "ruler"

rectum *noun*
the short final section of your large intestine leading to your anus

Word Building: the plural is **recta** □ **rectal** *adjective*

recuperate (say *rə-kooh-pə-rayt*) *verb*
to recover from sickness or tiredness

Word Building: **recuperation** *noun* **recuperative** *adjective*

recur (say *rə-ker*) *verb*
to happen again

Word Building: other forms are **it recurred, it has recurred, it is recurring** □ **recurrence** *noun* **recurrent** *adjective*
Word History: from a Latin word meaning "run back"

recycle *verb*
to use again, usually in another form: *to recycle waste paper into cardboard*

Word Building: **recyclable** *adjective*

red *adjective*
1 of the colour of a ripe tomato **2** having Communist or radical political views
3 see red to become very angry

Word Building: **red** *noun* **redden** *verb*

red-back *noun*
a small, very venomous Australian spider with a red or orange streak on it

redeem *verb*
1 to pay off: *to redeem a debt* **2** to get back by paying: *to redeem a pawned watch* **3** to make up for past misbehaviour: *She redeemed herself in my opinion by apologising.*

Word Building: **redeemable** *adjective* **redeemer** *noun* **redemption** *noun*

red-handed *adjective*
in the very act of doing something wrong: *They caught him red-handed.*

Word Use: this adjective follows the noun it describes
Word Building: **red-handedly** *adverb*

red herring *noun*
a false clue or something that takes your attention away from what is really important: *The blood-stained knife was a red herring.*

reduce *verb*
1 to make lower, less or fewer: *to reduce the price of milk | to reduce speed | to reduce the number of pupils in a class* **2** to bring to another condition: *to reduce someone to tears*

Word Building: **reduction** *noun*

redundant *adjective*
no longer needed

Word Building: **redundancy** *noun* **redundantly** *adverb*

reed *noun*
1 a tall straight-stemmed grass growing in marshes or swamps **2** a musical pipe made from a reed or something like it **3** a vibrating piece of cane or metal set in the mouthpiece of some wind instruments such as an oboe

Word Use: be careful – this sounds like **read**

reef *noun*
a narrow ridge of rock, sand or coral at or near the ocean surface

reef knot *noun*
a kind of double knot which does not slip

reek *verb*
to have a strong unpleasant smell: *He reeks of stale tobacco.*

Word Building: **reek** *noun*

reel[1] *noun*
1 a cylinder or wheel-like device onto which something is wound: *a reel of thread* **2** a roll or spool of film

reel[1] *verb*
3 to wind on a reel **4 reel off** to say or write in a smooth rapid way: *to reel off instructions*

reel[2] *verb*
to sway or stagger, especially from a blow or an attack of giddiness

reel[3] *noun*
a lively Scottish dance or the music for it

refer (say rə-fer) *verb*
1 to go or send for information or help: *to refer to a map for directions | to refer a patient to a specialist* **2 refer to** to mention: *to refer to past events*

Word Building: other forms are **I referred, I have referred, I am referring** □ **referral** *noun*

referee *noun*
someone who decides or settles matters which could be argued about, especially in sport

Word Use: a similar word is **umpire**
Word Building: **referee** *verb* (**refereed, refereeing**): *to referee a football game*

reference *noun*
1 a mention **2** a book or a place in a book or other writing where information may be found **3** the act of looking for information: *to make reference to an encyclopedia | a library for public reference* **4** a letter giving a description of someone's character and abilities: *You will need two references to apply for this job.* **5 with reference to** having to do with: *I will ask you some questions with reference to your family.*

reference *adjective*
6 used to give information: *reference books*

referendum *noun*
a public vote taken on a question of government or law

Word Building: the plural is **referendums** or **referenda**

refine *verb*
1 to make more fine or pure: *to refine sugar* **2** to make more elegant or polite: *to refine your manners*

Word Building: **refinery** *noun* (**refineries**) **refined** *adjective* **refinement** *noun*

reflect *verb*
1 to throw back: *Metal reflects light.* **2** to show an image of: *The mirror reflected her dirty face.* **3** to show: *The children's good results reflected their teacher's hard work.* **4** to think carefully: *I will reflect on what she said.*

Word Building: **reflection** *noun* **reflective** *adjective* **reflector** *noun*

reflex (say *ree-fleks*) *noun*
an action done without thinking as a response to something: *Sneezing and blinking are reflexes.*

Word Building: the plural is **reflexes** □ **reflex** *adjective*

reflexive pronoun *noun*
a pronoun which is the object of a reflexive verb, such as "himself" in *He shaves himself.*

reflexive verb *noun*
a verb whose subject and object are identical, such as "shave" in *He shaves himself.*

reform *verb*
to improve by changing what is wrong or bad: *You need to reform your behaviour.*

Word Building: **reform** *noun* **reformation** *noun* **reformer** *noun*

refrain[1] *verb*
to keep yourself back: *to refrain from eating more cake*

Word History: from a Latin word meaning "to bridle"

refrain[2] *noun*
a line or verse that is repeated regularly in a song or poem

Word Use: a similar word is **chorus**

refresh *verb*
to make fresh and strong again: *That cold drink has refreshed me.*

Word Building: **refreshing** *adjective*

refreshment *noun*
something that refreshes, especially food and drink or a light meal: *The refreshments are in the next room.*

refrigerate *verb*
to make or keep cold or frozen: *to refrigerate food*

Word Building: **refrigeration** *noun*

refrigerator *noun*
a cabinet or room where food and drink are kept cool

Word Use: a shortened form of this is **fridge**

refuge (say *ref-yoohj*) *noun*
1 shelter or protection from danger or trouble: *They took refuge from the storm in a cave.* **2** a place that gives shelter or protection: *a refuge for homeless men*

refugee (say *ref-yooh-jee*) *noun*
someone who escapes to another country for safety, especially during a war

refund (say *rə-fund*) *verb*
1 to give back or repay: *I asked the shop to refund my money because the toy I bought was broken.*

refund (say *ree-fund*) *noun*
2 a repayment of money

refurbish *verb*
to make clean or new-looking: *to refurbish an old armchair*

refuse[1] (say *rə-fyoohz*) *verb*
to say you will not accept, give or do: *He refused her invitation to the party.* | *He refused to go.*

Word Building: **refusal** *noun*

refuse[2] (say *ref-yoohs*) *noun*
rubbish: *The gutters were filled with refuse.*

refute *verb*
to prove to be false: *I refuted all her arguments.*

Word Building: **refutation** *noun*

regal *adjective*
having to do with or like a king or queen: *a regal visit* | *regal appearance*

Word Building: **regality** *noun* **regally** *adverb*

regard *verb*
1 to think of or consider: *I regard her as a hard worker.* **2** to look at or observe: *She regarded him with a frown.*

regard *noun*
3 thought or attention: *He gives no regard to what I say.* **4** a feeling of kindness or liking: *I hold him in high regard.* **5 regards** expressions of respect or friendship: *Please give your sister my regards.* **6 with** or **in regard to** having to do with or concerning: *I am writing with regard to your party.*

Word Building: **regardless** *adjective* **regardlessly** *adverb*

regatta *noun*
a meeting for boat races

regent *noun*
someone who rules a kingdom while the king or queen is sick or too young

Word Building: **regency** *noun*
Word History: from a Latin word meaning "ruling"

reggae (say *reg-ay*) *noun*
a kind of pop music which started in the West Indies

regime (say *ray-zheem*) *noun*
1 a system of rule or government: *The new headmaster brought in a different regime.*
2 a particular government: *This regime has not done much for unemployed people.*

Word Use: this is also spelt **régime** because it comes from French

regiment (say *rej-ə-mənt*) *noun*
1 a division of an army consisting of two or more battalions

regiment (say *rej-ə-ment*) *verb*
2 to group together and treat with strict discipline: *The camp leaders regimented us too much.*

Word Building: **regimental** *adjective* **regimentation** *noun*

region *noun*
1 any part or area: *a region of your body* | *a country region* **2** an area of the earth with particular features: *the tropical regions*

Word Building: **regional** *adjective* **regionally** *adverb*

register *noun*
1 a list of names, belongings, or events, kept as a record: *a register of births and marriages* **2** a book for keeping such lists: *a hotel register* **3** a machine which records information: *a cash register* **4** the musical range of a voice or instrument

register *verb*
5 to write down or have written down in a register: *He registered his name on the waiting list.* | *You have to register your car every year.* **6** to show or indicate: *The thermometer registered a very low temperature.* | *Her face registered surprise.*

Word Building: **registration** *noun*

registrar *noun*
1 someone who keeps records **2** a doctor in a hospital who is training to be a specialist

Word Building: **registry** *noun* (**registries**)

regress *verb*
to move or go back: *He has regressed to his old rude manners.*

Word Building: **regress** *noun* **regression** *noun* **regressive** *adjective* **regressively** *adverb*

regret *verb*
1 to feel sorry or sad about: *I regret that I got angry with you.* | *She regretted the end of the holiday.*

regret *noun*
2 a feeling of loss or disappointment or of being sorry about something you have done **3 regrets** polite expressions of being sorry: *Please give her my regrets that I cannot come.*

Word Building: other verb forms are **I regretted, I have regretted, I am regretting** □ **regretful** *adjective* **regretfulness** *noun* **regrettable** *adjective*

regular *adjective*
1 usual or normal: *Let's go to school the regular way.* **2** arranged evenly: *regular teeth* **3** following a rule or pattern, especially having to do with fixed times: *He is regular in his habits.* | *regular meals* | *a regular visitor*

regular *noun*
4 a regular visitor or customer

Word Use: definition 4 is more suited to everyday language
Word Building: **regularity** *noun* **regularly** *adverb*

regulate *verb*
to control or change so that a rule or standard is kept to: *to regulate behaviour* | *to regulate the temperature of a room*

Word Building: **regulative** *adjective* **regulator** *noun* **regulatory** *adjective*

regulation *noun*
1 a rule or law: *school regulations*
2 control, or correction and adjustment: *the regulation of traffic*

rehabilitate *verb*
to help return to normal activities, especially after an illness or accident

Word Building: **rehabilitation** *noun*

rehearse (say *rə-hers*) *verb*
to practise in private before giving a public performance

Word Building: **rehearsal** *noun*

reign (sounds like *rain*) *noun*
1 the time during which a king or queen rules: *the reign of Queen Elizabeth*
reign *verb*
2 to rule as a king or queen **3** to be in control: *Peace reigned throughout the world.*

Word Use: be careful – this sounds like **rain** and **rein**

reimburse (say *ree-im-bers*) *verb*
to pay back: *I will reimburse your expenses.*

Word Use: a similar word is **refund**
Word Building: **reimbursement** *noun*

rein (sounds like *rain*) *noun*
1 a long thin strap which a rider uses to guide a horse or other animal **2** any kind of control or check: *She keeps a tight rein on her feelings.*

Word Use: be careful – this sounds like **rain** and **reign**
Word Building: **rein** *verb*
Word History: from a Latin word meaning "hold back"

reincarnation (say *ree-in-kah-nay-shən*) *noun*
the belief that the soul, when the body dies, moves to a new body or form

reindeer (say *rayn-dear*) *noun*
a kind of deer with large antlers, that lives in the cold northern areas of the world

Word Building: the plural is **reindeer** or **reindeers**

reinforce (say *ree-in-faws*) *verb*
to strengthen, by adding someone or something: *Extra soldiers were sent to reinforce the army.* | *These facts will reinforce my argument.*

Word Building: **reinforcements** *plural noun* additional men or ships sent to an army or navy **reinforcement** *noun*

reject (say *rə-jekt*) *verb*
1 to refuse to accept or use: *He rejected her invitation.* | *They rejected his work.*
reject (say *ree-jekt*) *noun*
2 someone or something that has been rejected: *We will use these pictures and throw out the rejects.*

Word Building: **rejection** *noun*

rejoice *verb*
to be glad or delighted: *They rejoiced over her success.*

Word Building: **rejoicing** *noun*

rejoinder *noun*
a spoken answer or response: *a quick rejoinder*

rejuvenate (say *rə-jooh-və-nayt*) *verb*
to make young again: *I need a holiday to rejuvenate me.*

Word Building: **rejuvenation** *noun*

relapse *verb*
to return or fall back: *to relapse into sickness* | *to relapse into bad behaviour*

Word Building: **relapse** *noun*

relate *verb*
1 to tell: *to relate a story* **2** to connect, in your mind: *The police related his absence to the time of the murder.* **3** to be friends or understand each other: *Some parents and teenagers find it hard to relate.*

related *adjective*
1 associated or connected: *The two questions are related.* **2** part of the same family

relation *noun*
1 the way things or people are connected: *the relation between two numbers* | *the relation between husband and wife*
2 a family relative

Word Building: **relationship** *noun*

relative *noun*
1 someone who is part of your family: *Cousins, aunts and uncles are some of our relatives.*
relative *adjective*
2 thought about in comparison with something else: *They live in relative poverty.* **3 relative to** having a connection with: *The loudness of his voice is relative to his anger.*

Word Use: a similar word to definition 2 is **comparative**
Word Building: **relatively** *adverb: She is relatively happy.* **relativity** *noun*

relax *verb*
1 to loosen or make less firm: *to relax your arm* **2** to make or become less strict: *to relax discipline* **3** to rest and feel at ease: *You can sit down and relax for an hour.*

Word Building: **relaxation** *noun*

relay (say *ree-lay*) *noun*
1 a group which takes its turn with others to keep some activity going: *to work in relays* **2** a team race in which each member runs or swims a part of the distance

relay (say *rə-lay* or *ree-lay*) *verb*
3 to pass or carry forward: *to relay a message*

release *verb*
1 to set free: *to release the prisoner / to release from pain* **2** to make public: *to release a news story*

Word Building: **release** *noun*

relent *verb*
to soften or become more forgiving than you meant to be: *I relented when I saw how sorry he was.*

Word Building: **relentless** *adjective* never stopping or becoming softer **relentlessly** *adverb* **relentlessness** *noun*

relevant *adjective*
connected with what is being discussed: *a relevant remark*

Word Use: a similar word is **pertinent**
Word Building: **relevance** *noun* **relevancy** *noun* **relevantly** *adverb*

reliable *adjective*
trusted or able to be relied on: *a reliable friend / a reliable encyclopedia*

Word Building: **reliability** *noun* **reliably** *adverb*

reliant *adjective*
having trust, or depending: *We are reliant on him for money.*

Word Building: **reliance** *noun*

relic *noun*
something left over from the past: *These statues are relics of a great civilisation.*

relief *noun*
1 freedom or release from pain, unhappiness or worry **2** something that gives relief or help **3** someone who replaces someone else in a job or on a duty **4** a figure or shape in a sculpture carved so that it stands out above its background

relieve *verb*
1 to remove or lessen: *to relieve pain*
2 to free from pain, unhappiness or worry: *Her safe arrival relieved them.* **3** to free from duty by coming as a replacement: *He relieved the soldier on guard.* **4** to bring help to: *Food was sent to relieve the drought victims.*

religion *noun*
1 belief in a supernatural power that made and controls the world and that you should worship and obey **2** the way this belief is expressed in your way of life, worship, or service

Word Building: **religious** *adjective* **religiously** *adverb*
Word History: from a Latin word meaning "fear of the gods" or "sacredness"

relinquish (say *rə-ling-kwish*) *verb*
to give up or put aside: *to relinquish a possession / to relinquish all hope*

Word Building: **relinquisher** *noun* **relinquishment** *noun*

relish *noun*
1 a liking or enjoyment of something: *He looked forward to his holidays with relish.*
2 something that adds taste to food, such as a sauce

relish *verb*
3 to like or enjoy: *I relish the idea of going to the school disco.*

Word History: from a French word meaning "what is left" or "remainder"

reluctant *adjective*
unwilling or not prepared: *She was reluctant to help.*

Word Building: **reluctance** *noun* **reluctantly** *adverb*

rely (say *rə-luy*) *verb*
rely on to depend upon or put trust in: *I am relying on you to help me.*

Word Building: other forms are **I relied, I have relied, I am relying**

remain *verb*
1 to stay: *to remain at home / to remain happy* **2** to be left: *Some food remained after the party.*

remainder *noun*
what remains or is left: *How will we spend the remainder of the day? / If you subtract 4 from 6 the remainder is 2.*

remains *plural noun*
1 what is left: *the remains of a meal*
2 someone's dead body: *They buried his remains.*

remark *verb*
1 to comment or say casually: *He remarked that it was a fine day.*

remark *noun*
2 the act of taking notice: *an event worthy of remark* **3** a comment

Word Building: **remarkable** *adjective* worthy of notice: *a remarkable achievement* **remarkably** *adverb*

remedy (say *rem-ə-dee*) *noun*
1 a cure for a disease **2** something that corrects anything that is wrong or bad: *a remedy for unemployment*
remedy *verb*
3 to cure or put right: *to remedy a disease | to remedy a fault*

Word Building: the plural of the noun is **remedies** □ other verb forms are **I remedied, I have remedied, I am remedying** □ **remedial** *adjective: remedial teaching*

remember *verb*
to bring back to or keep in your mind: *I can't remember the answer. | Please remember to bring your books.*

Word Building: **remembrance** *noun*

remind *verb*
to make remember: *I always have to remind you to take your key.*

Word Building: **reminder** *noun*

reminiscence (say *rem-ə-nis-əns*) *noun*
1 a remembering of the past **2** something remembered: *He told her his reminiscences about his childhood.*

Word Building: **reminisce** *verb* **reminiscent** *adjective*

remnant *noun*
a part or amount that is left: *a remnant of material*

remorse *noun*
the sorrow or regret you feel when you have done something wrong: *She felt deep remorse when she looked at the beautiful cup she had smashed.*

Word Building: **remorseful** *adjective* **remorseless** *adjective*

remote *adjective*
1 far away or distant: *a remote planet | the remote past* **2** slight: *There was a remote chance that he would come.*

Word Building: **remotely** *adverb* **remoteness** *noun*

remove *verb*
1 to take off or away: *Please remove your shoes. | Someone has removed my book.* **2** to dismiss from a job or official position: *to remove a prime minister*

Word Building: **removalist** *noun* someone whose job is to transport furniture for people who are moving to a new house or office **removal** *noun*

renal *adjective*
having to do with your kidneys

rend *verb*
to pull or tear violently

Word Building: other forms are **I rent, I have rent, I am rending**

render *verb*
1 to cause to be or become: *His jokes rendered them helpless with laughter.* **2** to give: *to render help | to render payment* **3** to perform: *to render a song* **4** to cover with a coat of plaster: *to render a wall*

Word Building: **rendering** *noun* **rendition** *noun*

rendezvous (say *ron-day-vooh*) *noun*
1 a meeting arranged beforehand: *a rendezvous between spaceships* **2** a meeting place

Word Building: **rendezvous** *verb* (**rendezvoused, rendezvousing**)
Word History: from a French word which is why the "s" is not sounded

renew *verb*
1 to begin again: *They renewed their friendship.* **2** to build up again: *to renew supplies*

Word Building: **renewal** *noun*

renounce *verb*
to give up or put aside: *to renounce their evil ways | to renounce a legal claim*

Word Building: **renunciation** *noun*

renovate *verb*
to repair or restore to good condition: *to renovate an old house*

Word Building: **renovation** *noun* **renovator** *noun*

renown *noun*
fame: *a singer of great renown*

Word Building: **renowned** *adjective*

rent *noun*
1 payment that you make regularly for a house, flat or other property that you use
rent *verb*
2 to allow the use of in return for regular payment: *I have decided to rent my house to them.* **3** to have the use of in return for regular payment: *I have rented a flat in the city.*

Word Building: **rental** *noun*

repair *verb*
1 to bring back to good condition: *to repair an old bike* **2** to put right: *I will repair the damage.*

repair *noun*
3 the work of repairing **4** condition: *a house in good repair | a car in bad repair*

Word Building: **repairable** *adjective*

reparation *noun*
1 the making up for doing something wrong or harmful: *injury for which there can be no reparation* **2** something done or money paid as reparation

Word Use: a similar word for definition 1 is **compensation**

repay *verb*
to pay back or return: *to repay a loan | to repay a visit*

Word Building: other forms are **I repaid, I have repaid, I am repaying** □ **repayment** *noun*

repeal *verb*
to officially put an end to: *to repeal a law*

Word Building: **repeal** *noun*

repeat *verb*
1 to say or do again: *to repeat a sentence | to repeat a piece of music*

repeat *noun*
2 something that is repeated, such as a television program that has been shown before

Word Building: **repeated** *adjective* **repeatedly** *adverb* **repetitive** *adjective*

repel *verb*
1 to drive back: *They repelled the enemy.* **2** to disgust: *Her cruelty repels. | The smell repelled them.* **3** to keep away: *This spray repels mosquitoes.*

Word Building: other forms are **I repelled, I have repelled, I am repelling** □ **repellent** *adjective* **repelling** *adjective* **repulsion** *noun*

repent *verb*
to regret or feel sorry: *He repents his harsh words. | She repents that she was so cruel.*

Word Building: **repentance** *noun* **repentant** *adjective*

repertoire (say *rep-ə-twah*) *noun*
the plays, musical pieces or other items which an entertainer such as an actor or musician is prepared to perform in public: *She has a huge repertoire of songs.*

Word History: from a Latin word meaning "inventory" or "catalogue"

repetition *noun*
1 the act of repeating: *Repetition becomes tedious.* **2** the thing which is repeated: *His speech was a repetition of mine.*

Word Building: **repetitious** *adjective* **repetitive** *adjective* **repetitively** *adverb*

replace *verb*
1 to take the place of: *James will replace him today.* **2** to renew or exchange, especially something damaged: *He has to replace the old tyres.* **3** to put back: *She replaced the toys in the cupboard.*

Word Building: **replacement** *noun*

replay *noun*
1 a previously tied match or game that is played again to decide the winner
2 a repeat, especially on television, of the important parts of a game, often straight after they have happened

replenish *verb*
to refill or restore: *to replenish a jug | to replenish your strength*

Word Building: **replenishment** *noun*

replica *noun*
an exact copy: *He made a small replica of the rocket.*

Word Building: **replicate** *verb* **replication** *noun*

reply *verb*
to give an answer or response: *Did you reply to the letter? | She replied with a nod.*

Word Building: other forms are **I replied, I have replied, I am replying** □ **reply** *noun* (**replies**)

report *noun*
1 an account of the important facts, especially of a meeting, an event, or someone's progress at work or school
2 a loud sudden noise, like a gun firing

report *verb*
3 to describe or give an account of: *He reported his discovery.* **4** to complain about or tell on: *He is going to report them.* **5** to appear for duty: *He reported to his commanding officer.* **6** to act as a reporter: *He reports for a newspaper.*

reporter *noun*
1 someone who works for radio, television or a newspaper, gathering and describing the news **2** someone who makes a report of what is said, such as in a law court

repose *noun*
peaceful rest: *to lie in repose*

Word Building: **repose** *verb* to rest

repossess *verb*
to take back again, usually because payments have not been made when they should: *The store repossessed their television set.*

Word Building: **repossession** *noun*

represent *verb*
1 to stand for or mean: *A yellow flag represents sickness on board a ship.* **2** to act on behalf of: *She represents her country.* **3** to show or portray: *The painting represents a country scene.*

Word Building: **representation** *noun* **representative** *adjective*

repress *verb*
to keep under control by effort or force: *She repressed her anger.*

Word Building: **repressed** *adjective* **repression** *noun* **repressive** *adjective*

reprieve *noun*
a delay, especially in carrying out a punishment: *The judge granted him a reprieve from execution.*

Word Building: **reprieve** *verb*

reprimand *noun*
a scolding or rebuke, especially from someone in charge

Word Building: **reprimand** *verb*

reprisal *noun*
an act which causes hurt or damage to someone as punishment for what they have done

reproach *noun*
blame or disapproval: *She was full of reproach for our misbehaviour.*

Word Building: the plural is **reproaches** □ **reproach** *verb* to blame **reproachful** *adjective* **reproachfully** *adverb*

reproduce *verb*
1 to copy: *to reproduce a picture* **2** to produce offspring or young

Word Building: **reproducer** *noun* **reproducible** *adjective* **reproduction** *noun* **reproductive** *adjective*

reprove (say *rə-proohv*) *verb*
to scold or blame: *She reproved them for being impatient.*

Word Building: **reproof** *noun*

reptile *noun*
an animal such as a lizard, snake, turtle or crocodile that is covered with scales, breathes air through lungs, and whose body temperature changes as the surrounding air or water changes

Word Building: **reptilian** *adjective*

republic *noun*
a nation which has an elected president, not a monarch

Word History: from a Latin word meaning "public matter"

republican *adjective*
1 relating to a republic: *a republican government* **2** favouring a republican form of government

Word Building: **republican** *noun*

repugnant *adjective*
unpleasant or distasteful: *a repugnant job / She finds the idea repugnant.*

Word Building: **repugnance** *noun*

repulse *verb*
1 to drive back: *They repulsed the attack.* **2** to reject or refuse: *He repulsed her offer of help.*

Word Use: a similar word for definition 1 is **repel**
Word Building: **repulse** *noun*

repulsive *adjective*
dreadful, horrible and disgusting

Word Building: **repulsion** *noun*

reputable (say *rep-yə-tə-bəl*) *adjective*
able to be trusted: *a reputable firm of lawyers*

Word Building: **reputably** *adverb*

reputation *noun*
1 the way in which people regard someone or something: *a good reputation as an actor* **2** honesty or good name: *She spoiled her reputation.*

reputed *adjective*
supposed or thought to be: *He's a reputed champion.*

Word Building: **repute** *noun* **reputedly** *adverb*

request *noun*
1 the act of asking **2** the thing asked for

Word Building: **request** *verb* to ask

requiem (say *rek-wee-əm*) *noun*
a church service, especially in the Roman Catholic Church, where prayers are said for someone who has died

Word History: from a Latin word meaning "rest" (the first word in the Latin mass for the dead)

require *verb*
1 to need: *Skiing requires practice.* **2** to demand or insist on: *He will do as you require. / She requires an early start.*

Word Building: **requirement** *noun* **requisition** *noun*

rescue *verb*
to save from danger or set free from confinement

Word Building: **rescue** *noun* **rescuer** *noun*

research *noun*
close study or scientific experiment in order to understand or learn more about a subject

Word Building: **research** *verb* **researcher** *noun*

resemble *verb*
to be like: *She resembles her mother.*

Word Building: **resemblance** *noun* similarity or likeness

resent *verb*
to feel jealous, hurt or angry about: *They resent his success. / She resents his rudeness.*

Word Building: **resentful** *adjective* **resentfully** *adverb* **resentment** *noun*

reservation *noun*
1 something which has been held or set aside for you, such as seats in a theatre or a room in a motel **2** a doubt: *She has reservations about her ability to do the job.*

reserve *verb*
1 to save or keep for later **2** to book in advance: *You have to reserve your seat.*

reserve *noun*
3 someone or something kept as a replacement, especially an extra member of a sports team **3** public land set aside for a special use, especially as a park or wildlife sanctuary

Word Building: **reserve** *adjective*

reserved *adjective*
1 kept or set aside: *reserved seats* **2** shy and not wanting to talk about yourself: *He has a very reserved nature.*

reservoir (say *rez-ə-vwah*) *noun*
1 a place where water is stored: *the town reservoir* **2** a container, especially for oil or gas

reshuffle *verb*
to change around: *The Prime Minister will reshuffle cabinet.*

Word Building: **reshuffle** *noun*

reside *verb*
to live, especially over a long period: *He resides in Australia now.*

residence *noun*
1 the place where someone lives, especially a large house **2** the time you live in a place: *They threatened to cut short his residence in Australia.*

Word Building: **resident** *noun* **residential** *adjective*

residue *noun*
what is left

Word Use: a similar word is **remainder**
Word Building: **residual** *adjective* remaining

resign *verb*
1 to give up or step down: *He resigned his job. / She wants to resign from the committee.* **2** to surrender or give in to: *We resigned ourselves to whatever might happen.*

Word Building: **resignation** *noun* **resigned** *adjective* **resignedly** *adverb*

resilient *adjective*
able to bounce back: *Rubber is a resilient material. / She has a resilient nature.*

Word Building: **resilience** *noun* **resiliently** *adverb*

resin *noun*
a sap produced by some plants, which can be used in medicines and varnishes

Word Building: **resinous** *adjective*

resist *verb*
to withstand or fight against: *to resist temptation*

Word Building: **resistance** *noun* **resistant** *adjective*

resolute *adjective*
firm or determined: *a resolute character / a resolute approach*

Word Building: **resolutely** *adverb*

resolution *noun*
1 a decision, especially one made by a group or committee: *They passed a resolution to meet every month.*
2 determination or firmness: *She wore an expression of stubborn resolution.*

resolve *verb*
1 to decide **2** to solve or settle: *They couldn't resolve the problem. / to resolve doubts*

Word Building: **resolve** *noun* determination

resonant *adjective*
1 resounding or ringing: *She played a resonant chord on the piano.* **2** deep and rich in tone: *He has a resonant baritone voice.*

Word Building: **resonance** *noun* **resonantly** *adverb*

resonate *verb*
to ring or resound: *The strings on her cello resonated when she plucked them.*

Word Building: **resonation** *noun*

resort (say *rə-zawt*) *verb*
1 to fall back on, in time of need: *He resorted to begging for money.*
resort *noun*
2 a holiday place: *a seaside resort*
3 someone or something turned to for help: *a last resort*

resound *verb*
to boom, ring or echo: *The hills resounded with their voices.*

Word Building: **resounding** *adjective* **resoundingly** *adverb*

resource *noun*
1 something very useful, such as money or wealth: *Our mineral resources are running out.* **2** the ability to manage in a difficult situation

Word Building: **resourceful** *adjective*

respect *noun*
1 admiration or high regard **2** politeness or consideration: *You should show more respect.* **3 respects** friendly greetings: *Give my respects to your wife.* **4** a matter or detail: *In some respects it would have been better.*

respectable *adjective*
1 good or worthy of respect, especially in the sense of being socially acceptable: *a respectable girl / a respectable job*
2 fairly good: *a respectable mark*

Word Building: **respectability** *noun* **respectably** *adverb*

respective *adjective*
having to do with each one: *They went their respective ways.*

Word Building: **respectively** *adverb*

respiration *noun*
breathing: *His respiration is very rapid.*

respond *verb*
1 to answer, using words or actions: *She responded "yes". / He responded with a nod.*
2 to react: *He did not respond to my pleas.*

response *noun*
1 a reply in words or actions: *They had a big response to their appeal for clothes.*
2 a reaction: *The sunflower turns in response to light.* **3** a line or verse sung by the church choir or congregation in reply to the priest

Word Building: **responsive** *adjective*

responsibility *noun*
a duty or care: *It is her responsibility to lock up. / He shares in the responsibility of looking after the children.*

Word Building: the plural is **responsibilities**

responsible *adjective*
1 reliable or capable: *a responsible person*
2 answerable for something or to someone: *Who is responsible for the mistake? / I am responsible to my boss if anything goes wrong.*

Word Building: **responsibly** *adverb*

rest[1] *noun*
1 a time of sleep or recovery **2** time off, especially from something tiring or troubling **3** a stopping of movement: *The wheels came to rest.* **4** the time of silence between notes in music **5** a support: *a foot rest* **6 at rest a** dead: *He is at rest in his grave.* **b** peaceful or unworried: *His mind is at rest.*
rest[1] *verb*
7 to sleep or relax **8** to stop or have a break **9** to lie or lean: *to rest your arm on the table* **10** to depend or let depend: *The outcome rests on you. / They rest their case on new evidence.* **11** to stay or let stay: *The torch light rested on one spot. / He rested his gaze on the clock.* **12 let rest** to leave alone: *He let the matter rest.*

rest[2] *noun*
everyone or everything left: *The rest had to go.*

restaurant (say *res-tə-ront*) *noun*
a place where you can buy and eat a meal

Word History: from a French word meaning "restore"

restore *verb*
1 to give or bring back: *to restore lost property to its owner* | *to restore order* **2** to bring back to good condition: *to restore a building* | *to restore the colour to her cheeks*

Word Building: **restoration** *noun* **restorer** *noun*

restrain *verb*
to control or prevent: *It was hard to restrain the horse.* | *She restrained him from ordering a taxi.*

Word Building: **restraint** *noun*

restrict *verb*
to limit or confine: *He restricts his food intake.* | *They have restricted her to bed.*

Word Building: **restricted** *adjective* **restriction** *noun*

result *noun*
1 the effect of an action or event
2 the answer to a sum
result *verb*
3 to end in a particular way: *The match resulted in a draw.*

resume *verb*
1 to continue: *They resumed their journey after a break.* | *Now that you are quiet, let us resume.* **2** to take back, or go back to: *The council resumed our land.* | *He resumed his seat.*

Word Building: **resumption** *noun*

resurrect *verb*
1 to bring back from the dead: *God will resurrect the dead.* **2** to bring back into use: *We resurrected our old clothes.*

Word Building: **resurrection** *noun*

resuscitate (say *rə-sus-ə-tayt*) *verb*
to bring back to life, especially from unconsciousness: *to resuscitate the drowning man*

Word Building: **resuscitation** *noun*

retail *noun*
1 the sale of goods to the public, not to shops
retail *verb*
2 to sell to the user **3** to be sold: *It retails at $5.*

Word Use: compare this with **wholesale**
Word Building: **retail** *adjective* **retailer** *noun*

retain *verb*
1 to keep or keep on: *She is managing to retain her old home.* | *to retain an old servant* **2** to remember: *She doesn't retain names.* **3** to hold in place: *Her hair is retained by a net.*

Word Building: **retainer** *noun*

retaliate *verb*
to strike back: *If you tease him he will retaliate.*

Word Building: **retaliation** *noun*

retard *verb*
to slow down: *The muddy road retarded our progress.*

Word Building: **retardation** *noun* **retarded** *adjective*

retch *verb*
to try to vomit

Word Building: **retching** *noun*

retina (say *ret-ə-nə*) *noun*
the coating on the back part of your eyeball which receives the image of what you see

Word Building: the plural is **retinas** or **retinae** □ **retinal** *adjective*
Word History: from a Latin word meaning "net"

retire *verb*
1 to leave work, especially because you are getting old **2** to go away from other people, especially to go to bed **3** to leave the sports field or ring early, usually because you are injured: *The cricketer had to retire.*

Word Building: **retiring** *adjective* shy **retired** *adjective* **retirement** *noun*

retort *noun*
a quick or sharp reply

Word Building: **retort** *verb*

retrace *verb*
to go over again: *She retraced her steps.* | *He tried to retrace the events of that day long ago.*

Word Building: **retraceable** *adjective*

retread *verb*
to renew the part of a wheel or tyre that touches the road

Word Building: **retread** *noun*

retreat *noun*
1 withdrawal from a difficult or dangerous situation, usually in war: *The troops had to make a retreat before the enemy.*
2 withdrawal from people or activity
3 a place which is sheltered or remote: *They have a retreat in the bush.*

Word Building: **retreat** *verb*

retrench *verb*
to dismiss, in order to save money: *The factory has to retrench half its workers.*

Word Building: **retrenchment** *noun*

retrieve *verb*
1 to get or bring back: *I retrieved my watch from the office.* | *The dog retrieved the ball.* **2** to save: *to retrieve a difficult situation*

Word Building: **retrievable** *adjective* **retrieval** *noun*

retriever *noun*
a type of dog that can be trained to bring birds and small animals back to the hunter

retro- *prefix*
a word part meaning backwards: *retrospective*

Word History: this prefix comes from Latin

retrospective *adjective*
1 having to do with or coming from the past: *a retrospective exhibition of paintings* **2** taking effect from a date before the present: *a retrospective wage rise*

Word Building: **retrospective** *noun* **retrospectively** *adverb*

return *verb*
1 to go or come back: *They have to return home now.* | *She continually returns to the same idea.* **2** to give or send back: *He returned the insult.* | *She will return the books.*

return *noun*
3 an act of returning: *An effective return of service is an asset in tennis.* **4** a repetition or recurrence: *Many happy returns of the day!* **5** something received, such as a profit from an investment or a reply to a question **6** a report or paper which has to be sent: *a tax return*

Word Building: **return** *adjective*

reunion *noun*
a special meeting, usually of a family, or of people who have not seen each other for a long time

rev *noun*
1 a turning round or revolution, usually of an engine

rev *verb*
2 to make turn over faster: *to rev your engine*

Word Building: other verb forms are **I revved, I have revved, I am revving**
Word History: this word is a shortened form of **revolution**

Rev
a shortened form of **Reverend**

reveal *verb*
to show or make known: *to reveal the dirt* | *to reveal a secret*

Word Building: **revealing** *adjective* **revelation** *noun*

reveille (say *rə-val-ee*) *noun*
the signal sounded on a bugle or drum to wake up soldiers in the morning

Word History: from a French word meaning "awaken"

revenge *noun*
the hurt or damage done to pay someone back for the bad things they have done to you

Word Use: other words of similar meaning are **retaliation** and **vengeance**
Word Building: **revenge** *verb*

revenue *noun*
the money a government makes from taxes and other sources

reverberate *verb*
to echo over and over again

Word Building: **reverberation** *noun*

revere (say *rə-vear*) *verb*
to feel deep respect for

Word Building: **reverence** *noun* **reverence** *verb* **reverent** *adjective* **reverential** *adjective*

Reverend
a title of respect for a clergyman: *the Reverend Mr Jones*

reverse *noun*
1 the opposite: *No, the reverse is true.* **2** the back or rear of anything **3** a gear which drives a car backwards

reverse *verb*
4 to turn back or drive backwards or put in the opposite direction: *He took two steps forward then reversed.* | *She reversed the car into the drive.* **5** to cancel or wipe out: *The judge reversed the decision.*

Word Building: **reversal** *noun* **reverse** *adjective*

revert *verb*
to go back to: *to revert to an old habit*

review *noun*
1 a newspaper or magazine article which describes and gives you an opinion of a book, a film, a performance or an art exhibition **2** a magazine which contains articles about recent happenings or

discoveries often in a particular area of interest: *a scientific review* **3** an inspection or examination: *The matter is under review.*

review *verb*
4 to look over: *The general reviewed the troops.* **5** to write about: *to review a book* **6** to reconsider or think about again: *She reviewed her decision.*

Word Building: **reviewer** *noun*

revise *verb*
1 to check or correct: *She revised her manuscript.* **2** to go back over in order to learn: *He is revising his maths.*

Word Building: **revision** *noun*

revive *verb*
1 to return to life or energy: *She revived when she had finished her rest.* **2** to set going again or bring back into use: *to revive an argument | to revive a play*

Word Building: **revival** *noun*

revoke (say *rə-vohk*) *verb*
to take back or cancel: *to revoke the mayor's decree*

Word Building: **revocation** *noun* **revocatory** *adjective*

revolt *verb*
1 to rebel or rise up against those with power over you: *The prisoners revolted against their gaolers.* **2** to disgust: *The food revolted her.*

Word Building: **revolt** *noun* **revolting** *adjective* **revoltingly** *adverb*

revolution *noun*
1 a complete change: *There's been a revolution in the business.* **2** the complete overthrow of a government or a form of government **3** one complete turn, usually in a circle: *The wheel made two revolutions.*

Word Building: **revolutionise** *verb*

revolutionary *adjective*
1 having to do with a complete change or revolution: *a revolutionary invention | a revolutionary government*

revolutionary *noun*
2 someone who supports a revolution

Word Building: the plural of the noun is **revolutionaries**

revolve *verb*
1 to turn in a circle or move in an orbit: *He revolved the wheel. | The moon revolves around the earth.* **2** to move in a cycle: *The seasons revolve.*

revolver *noun*
a pistol with a revolving section for bullets, which can be fired without having to reload between shots

revue *noun*
a musical show with songs, dances and items which make fun of recent events or popular fashions

reward *noun*
1 something given or received in return for work or help **2** money offered to encourage people to give information about a crime or lost property

Word Building: **reward** *verb* **rewarding** *adjective*

rheumatism (say *rooh-mə-tiz-əm*) *noun*
a disease affecting your joints or muscles

Word Building: **rheumatic** *adjective*

rhinoceros *noun*
a large thick-skinned mammal of Africa and Asia, with one or two horns on its nose

Word Use: **rhino** is a shortened form
Word Building: the plural is **rhinoceroses** or **rhinoceros**

rhododendron *noun*
a large shrub with pink, purple or white flowers

Word History: from a Greek word meaning "rose tree"

rhombus *noun*
a parallelogram with four equal sides and angles that are not right angles

Word Building: the plural is **rhombuses** or **rhombi**

rhubarb *noun*
a plant whose stalks are cooked with sugar and water to make a dessert

rhyme *noun*
1 an agreement or a likeness in the sounds at the end of words, as in "cat" and "bat" **2** a word which rhymes with another **3** a poem or verse that has rhymes

Word Building: **rhyme** *verb*
Word History: from a German word meaning "series" or "row"

rhythm *noun*
1 the pattern of beats in music or speech **2** an even or regular movement: *He has no sense of rhythm.*

Word Building: **rhythmical** *adjective* **rhythmically** *adverb*

rib *noun*
1 one of the set of curved bones partly enclosing your chest **2** the main vein of a leaf **3** a raised or ridged pattern in knitting

Word Building: **rib** *verb* (**ribbed, ribbing**) **ribbed** *adjective*

ribbon *noun*
1 a band of thin material used for tying or decorating: *Her hair was tied with ribbons.* **2** the ink-soaked tape used in a typewriter

rice *noun*
white or brown seeds or grain grown in warm wet climates and widely used for food

rich *adjective*
1 having a great deal of anything, especially money: *a rich woman / a rich country* **2** of fine full quality, such as materials, sounds, smells and colours: *a rich tone / a rich velvet* **3** fatty or hard to digest: *rich foods*

Word Building: **riches** *noun* wealth **richly** *adverb*

rickety *adjective*
weak or shaky: *a rickety old chair*

rickshaw *noun*
a light cart drawn by one or two men, which is used in some Asian countries as a car or taxi

Word Use: the long form of this is **jinrikisha**
Word History: from a Japanese word meaning "man-powered carriage"

ricochet (say *rik-ə-shay*) *noun*
the movement of an object, such as a bullet, when it hits something, bounces off, and keeps travelling in another direction

Word Building: **ricochet** *verb* (**ricocheted, ricocheting**)

rid *verb*
1 to clear of something unwanted: *to rid the house of white ants* **2 get rid of** to get free of

Word Building: other forms are **I rid, I have rid, I am ridding** □ **riddance** *noun* a freeing or clearing: *She's gone and good riddance!*

riddle[1] *noun*
1 a cleverly worded question usually asked as a joke **2** any puzzling thing or person

riddle[2] *verb*
to pierce with many holes, like those of a sieve

ride *verb*
1 to sit on and control: *to ride a horse / to ride a bike* **2** to travel or be carried along: *to ride in a train*

ride *noun*
3 a short journey: *a ride on a horse / a bus ride*

Word Building: other verb forms are **I rode, I have ridden, I am riding** □ **rider** *noun*

ridge *noun*
1 a long narrow range of mountains
2 any long narrow strip: *ridges of earth left by a plough*

Word Building: **ridge** *verb*

ridicule *verb*
to make fun of: *to ridicule their strange way of speaking*

Word Building: **ridicule** *noun*

ridiculous *adjective*
funny or causing people to laugh: *a ridiculous hat*

Word Building: **ridiculously** *adverb*

rife *adjective*
common or widespread: *Dishonesty is rife in our society.*

rifle *noun*
a gun that you support against your shoulder, with a long barrel which is specially designed to give spin to the bullet so its flight will be more accurate

rift *noun*
1 a narrow opening made by splitting: *a rift in the earth* **2** a breaking down in the friendly relations between people or countries

rig *verb*
1 to equip with the necessary ropes and lines: *to rig a yacht* **2** to control dishonestly: *to rig an election* **3 rig up** to put together or in proper working order: *to rig up a dance floor / to rig up a tent*

Word Building: other forms are **I rigged, I have rigged, I am rigging** □ **rig** *noun* **rigging** *noun*

right *adjective*
1 fair and good **2** correct **3** not left: *your right hand* **4** straight or upright: *to put things right / a right angle*

right *noun*
5 what is fair and good: *We must hope that right will win.* **6** a fair claim: *He has a right to some time off.* **7** the right side: *the*

third house on the right **8** a political party or group that believes in the private ownership of land, business and money rather than the equal distribution of wealth

right *adverb*
9 to the right side: *Turn right at the post office* **10** directly or straight: *Go right home.* **11** exactly or immediately: *right here | right now*

right *verb*
12 to correct or make up for: *to right a wrong*

Word Use: definition 8 often has a capital letter □ be careful – this sounds like **write**

right angle *noun*
an angle of 90°

Word Building: **right-angled** *adjective: a right-angled triangle*

righteous (say ruy-chəs) *adjective*
1 good and upright: *a righteous man*
2 having a good cause or reason: *righteous indignation*

Word Building: **righteously** *adverb* **righteousness** *noun*

rigid *adjective*
1 stiff and unmoving: *The handrail should be rigid.* **2** strict or unbending: *rigid discipline*

Word Building: **rigidity** *noun* **rigidly** *adverb*

rigour or **rigor** *noun*
1 strictness: *He trained with the utmost rigour.* **2** hardship or severity: *Some animals can survive the rigours of desert life.*

Word Building: **rigorous** *adjective*

rim *noun*
the outer edge, especially of a circular or round object: *the rim of a glass | the rim of a wheel*

rind *noun*
a fairly thick and firm skin: *lemon rind | the rind of cheese*

ring[1] *noun*
1 a circular band for wearing on your finger: *a wedding ring* **2** anything shaped like a ring: *a key ring* **3** a circular line or shape: *to draw a ring* **4** an enclosed area, not necessarily circular: *a circus ring | a boxing ring*

Word Building: **ring** *verb*

ring[2] *verb*
1 to give out a clear musical sound: *The bells are ringing. | His voice rang out.* **2** to make a bell sound, especially as a signal: *to ring a doorbell* **3** to telephone: *Ring me on Wednesday.*

Word Building: other forms are **I rang, I have rung, I am ringing** □ **ring** *noun*

ringbark *verb*
to cut away a ring of bark from a tree trunk or branch in order to kill it by cutting off the flow of sap

ringer[1] *noun*
a station hand, especially a stockman or drover

ringer[2] *noun*
1 the fastest shearer of a group **2** anyone who is the fastest or best at anything

ring-in *noun*
someone or something taking the place of another at the last moment

ringlet *noun*
a long curl of hair shaped like a corkscrew

ringmaster *noun*
someone in charge of a circus performance

ringworm *noun*
a skin disease with ring-shaped patches, caused by fungi

rink *noun*
1 a sheet of ice prepared for skating
2 a smooth floor for roller-skating

rinse *verb*
1 to wash lightly in clean water to remove scraps of food or soap

rinse *noun*
2 a liquid for colouring your hair

riot *noun*
1 a disturbance of the peace by a group of people **2** wild disorder or confusion

Word Building: **riot** *verb* **rioter** *noun* **riotous** *adjective* **riotously** *adverb*
Word History: from a Latin word meaning "roar"

rip[1] *verb*
1 to tear or become torn in a rough way
2 rip off to charge too much

Word Building: other forms are **I ripped, I have ripped, I am ripping** □ **rip** *noun*

rip[2] *noun*
a disturbance in the sea resulting in a fast current, especially one at a beach

ripe *adjective*
ready for harvesting, picking or eating: *ripe wheat | ripe fruit*

Word Building: **ripen** *verb* **ripeness** *noun*

ripper *noun*
someone or something that you admire a lot

Word Use: this is more suited to everyday language

ripple *verb*
1 to make small waves on: *The wind is rippling the water.*
ripple *noun*
2 a small wave **3** a sound coming as though in a wave: *a ripple of laughter*

rise *verb*
1 to get up or get out of bed **2** to extend or go upwards, or swell up: *The tower rises to a great height. / Her voice rose. / The cake has risen.* **3** to rebel: *The people rose against the tyrant.*
rise *noun*
4 an upward movement: *a rise in temperature / a rise in prices* **5** an upward slope: *a rise in the ground*

Word Building: other verb forms are **I rose, I have risen, I am rising** □ **rising** *noun* **uprising** *noun*

risk *noun*
the possibility of being injured, hurt or losing something

Word Building: **risky** *adjective* (**riskier, riskiest**) **risk** *verb*

rissole *noun*
a fried ball or small cake of minced food: *a meat rissole*

rite *noun*
a ceremony, especially a religious one

ritual *noun*
1 a set procedure for a religious or other ceremony **2** an often repeated series of actions: *the ritual of getting up in the morning*

rival *noun*
1 someone who is aiming at the same thing as another person: *He was her rival for the championship.*
rival *verb*
2 to compete with

Word Building: other verb forms are **I rivalled, I have rivalled, I am rivalling** □ **rivalry** *noun* (**rivalries**)

river *noun*
a large natural stream of water flowing in a definite course or channel

rivet *noun*
1 a bolt for holding pieces of metal together
rivet *verb*
2 to fasten with a rivet **3** to fix firmly: *He was riveted to the spot. / The scene riveted her attention.*

Word Building: other verb forms are **I riveted, I have riveted, I am riveting**

road *noun*
a way or track suitable for cars, people and animals to travel along

roadie *noun*
someone who looks after the sound equipment for a pop group on tour

road train *noun*
a truck towing trailers, usually used for carrying cattle

roadway *noun*
another word for **road**

roam *verb*
to walk or travel with no particular purpose

roan *adjective*
of a reddish-brown colour with splashes of grey or white: *a roan horse*

roar *verb*
1 to make a loud deep sound: *A lion roared. / The wind roared.* **2** to laugh loudly

Word Building: **roar** *noun*

roast *verb*
1 to cook over a fire or bake in an oven
roast *noun*
2 a piece of meat that has been or is going to be roasted

rob *verb*
to steal from, often using force

Word Building: other forms are **I robbed, I have robbed, I am robbing** □ **robbery** *noun* (**robberies**)

robe *noun*
a long loose gown worn by men or women

robin *noun*
1 any of a group of Australian birds with brightly coloured breasts **2** a European bird with a red breast, often painted on Christmas cards

robot (say *roh-bot*) *noun*
a machine programmed to do a job usually done by a person

Word History: first used in the play *RUR* by the Czech writer Karel Capek, 1890-1938

robust (say *roh-bust*) *adjective*
strong: *a robust frame / in robust health*

rock[1] *noun*
a large mass of stone

rock[2] *verb*
1 to move from side to side: *The boat is rocking on the waves. / to rock a cradle*
rock[2] *noun*
2 *another word for* **rock'n'roll** *or* **rock music**

rocker *noun*
1 one of the curved pieces on which a cradle or a rocking chair rocks
2 a rocking chair

rockery *noun*
part of a garden where you grow plants in between rocks

Word Building: the plural is **rockeries**

rocket *noun*
1 a cylinder full of gunpowder or something similar, fired into the air as a signal or as a firework **2** a space vehicle driven by hot gas that shoots out from its rear

rockmelon *noun*
a small round melon with orange-cloured flesh

rock music *noun*
a kind of loud popular music with a strong rhythm and electronically amplified sound, usually more complicated than rock'n'roll

rock'n'roll *noun*
1 a simple kind of popular music with a strong beat **2** a dance performed to this music

rod *noun*
a long stick of wood, metal or other material

rodent *noun*
one of a group of animals with sharp teeth for gnawing, including rats, mice and guinea-pigs

Word History: from a Latin word meaning "gnawing"

rodeo (say *roh-day-oh, roh-dee-oh*) *noun*
a display of cowboy skills, like riding horses and lassoing cattle

Word History: from a Spanish word meaning "cattle ring"

roe *noun*
1 the mass of eggs inside a female fish
2 the sperm of the male fish

rogue (say *rohg*) *noun*
1 a dishonest person **2** someone who plays tricks for fun

Word Building: **roguish** *adjective* mischievous **roguery** *noun*

role *noun*
1 the part or character that an actor plays **2** the expected or usual part played in life: *a mother's role / a husband's role*

roll *verb*
1 to move or cause to move by turning over and over like a ball or a wheel:
2 to be carried along on wheels: *The truck rolled down the hill.* **3** to press or flatten with a particular tool made for the purpose: *to roll pastry / to roll a cricket pitch* **4** to sway or cause to sway from side to side **5 roll up a** to make into the shape of a cylinder: *to roll up a map* **b** to come along: *A big crowd rolled up to the meeting.*
roll *noun*
6 a piece of paper, material or food made into the shape of a cylinder: *a roll of carpet / a sponge roll* **7** a list or register: *a class roll* **8** a low continuous sound: *a roll of thunder*

roller *noun*
1 a cylinder used for flattening: *a road roller / the rollers in a mangle* **2** a cylinder around which something is rolled: *a hair roller* **3** a long swelling wave advancing steadily

roller-skate *noun*
a kind of skate running on small wheels or rollers

Word Building: **roller-skate** *verb*

rollicking *adjective*
jolly and carefree: *a rollicking song*

ROM (say *rom*) *noun*
computer memory which can be read but not changed

Word History: an acronym made from the first letters of *Read Only Memory*

romance *noun*
1 a story of adventure, often not much like real life **2** a love affair

Word Building: **romantic** *adjective*

Roman numerals *plural noun*
the numbers used by the ancient Romans, and still used for some purposes, like royal titles and chapter headings in books

romp *verb*
1 to play in an active noisy way
2 romp in to win easily

roo *noun*
a shortened form of **kangaroo**

roof *noun*
1 the top covering of a building or car **2** the overhead or upper surface of a hollow space: *the roof of a cave | the roof of your mouth*

Word Building: the plural of this word is **roofs**

rook[1] *noun*
a black European crow that nests in groups in tall trees

rook[2] *noun*
a chess piece which can only travel in straight lines

Word Use: another name for this is **castle**

rookery *noun*
1 a place where there are a lot of rooks' nests **2** a breeding place for other birds or animals: *a penguin rookery*

Word Building: the plural is **rookeries**

room *noun*
1 a part of a building separated by walls from other parts **2** space: *Move up and give me some room.*

Word Building: **roomy** *adjective* (**roomier, roomiest**) spacious

roost *noun*
a resting place for birds at night

Word Building: **roost** *verb*

rooster *noun*
a type of male domestic fowl

Word Use: the female is a **hen**; the young is a **chicken**

root *noun*
1 the part of a plant which usually grows downwards into the soil and supplies the plant with food and water **2** the origin or beginning: *Money is the root of all evil.* **3** a number which, when multiplied by itself a certain number of times, produces a given quantity: *2 is the square root of 4 and the cube root of 8* **4 roots** a feeling of belonging: *He has lived here for ten years but his roots are in New Zealand.*

root *verb*
5 to send down roots and begin to grow: *A strange plant has rooted in our garden.* **6** to fix as if by roots: *She was rooted to the spot.* **7 root out** **a** to pull up by the roots : *to root out weeds* **b** to remove completely: *to root out wickedness*

Word Use: for definition 3 see **square root** and **cube root**
Word Building: **rootless** *adjective*

rope *noun*
a strong thick cord made of twisted fibre or wire

Word Building: **rope** *verb* to tie up with a rope

ropeable *adjective*
angry

Word Use: this is more suited to everyday language

rosary *noun*
1 a string of beads used for counting a series of prayers, usually in the Roman Catholic Church **2** the series of prayers that are said

Word Building: the plural is **rosaries**

rose *noun*
1 a wild or garden shrub with attractive, usually sweet-smelling, flowers and thorny stems

rose *adjective*
2 deep pink

rosella *noun*
a parrot with bright red, green and blue feathers

Word History: from *Rosehill*, an early settlement in NSW

rosemary *noun*
a bushy plant with strongly-scented leaves used as a herb

Word History: from a Latin word meaning "dew of the sea"

rosette *noun*
a decoration made of ribbons tied so as to look like the petals of a rose

rosin (say roz-ən) *noun*
resin made from the dried sap of pine trees, used for rubbing on violin bows

roster *noun*
a list of people's names and the times they are on duty: *a roster for the school tuckshop*

rostrum *noun*
a raised platform for a speaker or the conductor of an orchestra

Word Building: the plural is either **rostrums** or **rostra**

rosy *adjective*
1 pink and healthy-looking: *rosy cheeks*
2 likely to turn out well: *a rosy future*

Word Building: other forms are **rosier, rosiest**

rot *verb*
1 to make or go bad: *Sweets rot your teeth. / The garbage is rotting.*

rot *noun*
2 a type of disease that makes things decay or go bad: *This timber has dry rot. / The cow has foot rot.* **3** nonsense or rubbish: *He talks a lot of rot.*

Word Use: definition 3 is more suited to everyday language
Word Building: other verb forms are **it rotted, it has rotted, it is rotting**

rotate *verb*
1 to turn round like a wheel **2** to go, or cause to go, through a series of changes: *to rotate the crops each year*

Word Building: **rotary** *adjective* turning round and round: *a rotary clothes hoist* **rotation** *noun*

rotisserie (say *roh-tis-ə-ree*) *noun*
a skewer which turns round and round in an oven, for cooking chickens and other food

Word History: from a French word meaning "roasting place"

rotten *adjective*
1 gone bad or decaying: *a rotten apple*
2 sick or unhappy: *to feel rotten*
3 dishonest or bad: *a rotten liar*

Word Use: definitions 2 and 3 are more suited to everyday language

rotund (say *roh-tund*) *adjective*
plump and rounded: *a rotund belly*

Word Building: **rotundity** *noun* **rotundness** *noun*

rouge (say *roohzh*) *noun*
pinkish-red make-up used to make your cheeks look rosy

Word Use: this word comes from French
Word Building: **rouge** *verb: I rouged my cheeks.*

rough (say *ruf*) *adjective*
1 bumpy or uneven **2** wild or violent: *rough weather / a rough football match*
3 not properly finished: *a rough sketch*
4 rough on difficult for: *It was rough on the family when their dog died.*

rough *verb*
5 rough it to make do without the usual home comforts: *to rough it camping in the bush*

Word Building: **roughly** *adverb* approximately **roughen** *verb*

roughage *noun*
the fibre in food that you can't digest

roulette (say *rooh-let*) *noun*
a gambling game in which players bet on a small ball which runs around a spinning wheel

round *adjective*
1 shaped like a circle or ball **2** completed by returning to the place you started: *a round trip* **3** whole or complete: *a round dozen*

round *noun*
4 an outburst: *a round of applause*
5 a period of boxing or wrestling: *He was knocked out in the third round.* **6** a song for several singers, each joining in at a different time

round *adverb*
7 in a circular direction: *to spin round / a tree 40 centimetres round* **8** here and there: *to travel round* **9** in some other direction: *to turn round*

round *verb*
10 round up to gather in one place: *to round up sheep*

roundabout *noun*
1 a circular intersection for controlling traffic **2** *another word for* **merry-go-round**

roundabout *adjective*
3 going the long way round: *a roundabout way home*

rounders *plural noun*
a game like baseball, played with a soft ball

Word Use: this word takes a singular verb, as in *Rounders is a good game.*

rouse[1] (rhymes with *cows*) *verb*
1 to wake up: *The phone roused her.*
2 to stir up: *to rouse her anger*

Word Use: a similar word is **arouse**
Word Building: **rousing** *adjective: a rousing song*

rouse[2] (rhymes with *mouse*) *verb*
in the phrase **rouse on** to be angry with: *to rouse on the children for getting home late*

rouseabout (say rows-ə-bowt) *noun*
someone hired to do odd jobs for which not much skill is needed

rout (rhymes with *out*) *verb*
to defeat and force to run away: *to rout an army*

Word Building: **rout** *noun* a total defeat

route (sounds like *root*) *noun*
a way or road from one place to another: *The bus takes the long route home.*

Word Building: **route** *verb* (**routed, routeing** or **routing**) to send by a particular route

routine (say *rooh-teen*) *noun*
something which is always done in the same way or at the same time or place: *a dance routine*

Word Building: **routine** *adjective: Routine work gets boring.*

rove *verb*
to wander or roam

Word Building: **rover** *noun*

row[1] (rhymes with *go*) *noun*
a line of people or things

row[2] (rhymes with *go*) *verb*
to move using oars: *to row a boat | to learn how to row*

row[3] (rhymes with *how*) *noun*
1 a noisy quarrel or fight **2** shouting and loud noise: *I can't sleep with that row going on.*

Word Building: **row** *verb* to quarrel loudly

rowdy (rhymes with *cloudy*) *adjective*
wild and noisy: *a bunch of rowdy kids*

Word Building: other forms are **rowdier, rowdiest** □ **rowdily** *adverb* **rowdiness** *noun*

rowlock (say *rol-ək*) *noun*
one of the metal rings that support the oars in a rowing boat

royal *adjective*
having to do with a king or queen: *a royal visit*

Word Building: **royally** *adverb*

royalty *noun*
1 kings, queens and members of their families **2** a share of the profits made from their work, paid to an inventor, author or composer

RSVP
short for French words meaning "please reply"

Word Use: this expression is used in written invitations

rub *verb*
1 to move back and forth while pressing down: *to rub polish on your shoes | I have blisters where my shoes rubbed.*
2 rub out to clean off by rubbing: *to rub out a pencil mark* **3 rub it in** to keep on reminding someone about their mistakes

Word Building: other forms are **I rubbed, I have rubbed, I am rubbing**

rubber *noun*
1 stretchy material made from the thick sap of some tropical trees, used to make things like car tyres, bouncing balls and elastic bands **2** a small piece of soft rubber used to rub out pencil marks

Word Use: a similar word for definition 2 is **eraser**
Word Building: **rubbery** *adjective* soft and stretchy

rubbish *noun*
1 useless left-over material or matter
2 nonsense: *Don't talk rubbish.*

Word Use: a similar word for definition 1 is **refuse**
Word Building: **rubbish** *verb* to scoff at **rubbishy** *adjective* worthless

rubble *noun*
rough pieces of broken stone or brick

rubella (say *rooh-bel-ə*) *noun*
another name for **German measles**

Word History: from a Latin word meaning "reddish"

ruby *noun*
a precious stone of a rich red colour

Word Building: the plural is **rubies** □ **ruby** *adjective*

rucksack *noun*
a bag with shoulder straps worn by hikers on their backs

Word Use: compare **knapsack and haversack**

rudder *noun*
a flat movable plate at the back of a boat or plane, used for steering

ruddy *adjective*
having a healthy red colour: *a ruddy face*

Word Building: other forms are **ruddier, ruddiest**

rude *adjective*
1 bad-mannered or impolite **2** rough: *a rude bush hut*

Word Use: for definition 1 the opposite is **polite**
Word Building: **rudely** *adverb* **rudeness** *noun*

ruffian *noun*
someone who is rough or rowdy

ruffle *verb*
1 to spoil the calmness or smoothness of: *Don't ruffle his temper. / Birds ruffle their feathers.*
ruffle *noun*
2 a frill on a skirt, blouse or curtains

Word Building: **ruffled** *adjective*

rug *noun*
1 a thick warm blanket **2** a small carpet

rugged (say *rug-əd*) *adjective*
1 rough or uneven: *a rugged mountain range* **2** tough and strong: *a rugged mountain climber*

Word Building: **ruggedly** *adverb*

ruin *verb*
1 to wreck or destroy: *The rain ruined the harvest.*
ruin *noun*
2 complete destruction: *the ruin of my hopes* **3 ruins** the remains of fallen buildings: *the ruins of an ancient castle*

Word Building: **ruination** *noun* **ruined** *adjective*

rule *noun*
1 an instruction telling you what to do: *to play according to the rules* **2 as a rule** usually: *We walk to school as a rule.*
rule *verb*
3 to govern, control or reign: *The king ruled his country wisely.* **4** to decide or direct: *The referee ruled that she was out.* **5** to draw, using a ruler: *to rule a straight line*

Word Building: **ruling** *noun* a decision made by someone in charge **ruling** *adjective* in charge

ruler *noun*
1 someone who rules or governs **2** a strip of wood or plastic with a straight edge, used for measuring and drawing straight lines

rum *noun*
a strong alcoholic drink made from sugar cane

rumble *noun*
1 a deep rolling sound: *the rumble of thunder* **2** a gang fight

Word Use: definition 2 is more suited to everyday language
Word Building: **rumble** *verb: The train rumbled along the track.*

rumbustious (say *rum-bus-chəs*) *adjective*
rowdy or boisterous

Word Building: **rumbustiously** *adverb*

ruminate (say *rooh-mə-nayt*) *verb*
1 to chew the cud, like a cow
2 to consider very carefully or meditate: *to ruminate on a problem*

Word Building: **ruminant** *noun* an animal that chews its cud

rummage *verb*
to search by moving everything around: *to rummage through a bag to find a pen*

Word History: from a French word meaning "stow goods in the hold of a ship"

rummy *noun*
a card game in which you put cards into matching sets and ordered groups

rumour or **rumor** (rhymes with *boomer*) *noun*
a story that spreads round which may or may not be true

Word Use: a similar word is **gossip**
Word Building: **rumour** *verb: It is rumoured that you are going overseas.*

rump *noun*
1 the back part of a cow, horse or similar animal **2** meat taken from this part: *grilled rump*

rumple *verb*
to crush or mess up: *Please don't rumple the bed cover.*

Word Building: **rumple** *noun* a crease or wrinkle

rumpus *noun*
a loud noise and commotion

run *verb*
1 to move quickly on your feet **2** to go or make go: *The bus runs every half hour. / to run a car* **3** to pass quickly: *to run your fingers through your hair / to have ideas running through your mind* **4** to flow or fill with water: *to leave a tap running / to run a bath* **5** to extend or continue: *to run a net across the river / A crack runs down the wall.* **6** to conduct or manage: *to run a*

business **7 run out** to be all used up: *The food has run out.* **8 run through a** to practise: *to run through a speech* **b** to stab with a sword

run *noun*
9 the action of running: *to go for a run* **10** a trip or journey: *a run in the car* **11** a pen for animals: *a chicken run* **12** a score in cricket: *Our team made 120 runs.* **13** a series of happenings: *a run of good luck* **14 in the long run** in the end: *It turned out well in the long run.*

Word Building: other verb forms are **I ran, I have run, I am running**

runaway *adjective*
1 running out of control: *a runaway horse* **2** very easy: *a runaway win over the other team*

Word Building: runaway *noun* someone who has escaped or run away

rung *noun*
one of the steps of a ladder

run-in *noun*
a disagreement or argument

Word Use: this word is more suited to everyday language

runner *noun*
1 someone who runs well and competes in races **2** one of the smooth strips of wood on which a drawer slides

runner-up *noun*
someone who comes second in a contest

running *adjective*
1 able to run or suitable for running: *a machine in running order / running shoes* **2** flowing: *running water* **3** in a row: *to be late three days running* **4 running writing** writing where all the letters of a word are joined together

running *noun*
5 management or organisation: *the running of a shop* **6 out of the running** with no chance of winning

runny *adjective*
flowing or pouring out liquid: *runny custard / a runny nose*

Word Building: other forms are **runnier, runniest**

runt *noun*
a person or animal that is the smallest in their group: *This piglet is the runt of the litter.*

Word Use: this word is used to insult people

rupture *verb*
1 to break or burst: *to rupture a friendship / Her appendix ruptured.*

rural *adjective*
having to do with the countryside or farming: *rural land*

Word Building: rurally *adveerb*

ruse (rhymes with *shoes*) *noun*
a dishonest trick or scheme

rush[1] *verb*
1 to move or do in a great hurry: *The river rushed over the rocks. / Don't rush your dinner.* **2** to hurry into doing something or making a decision: *Don't rush me.*

rush[1] *noun*
3 a time of great hurry and movement: *the gold rush / a rush of wind*

rush[2] *noun*
a type of long grass that grows in wet ground along river banks

rut *noun*
1 a groove made in the ground by the wheels of a car **2 in a rut** doing the same thing all the time

ruthless *adjective*
showing no pity or mercy: *a ruthless tyrant*

Word Building: ruthlessness *noun* **ruthlessly** *adverb*

rye *noun*
a grain which grows like wheat and is ground into flour

Word Building: rye *adjective: rye bread*

Sabbath *noun*
1 the seventh day of the week, Saturday, which is the day of worship for Jews and for some Christians **2** the first day of the week, Sunday, which is the day of worship for most Christians

sabotage (say *sab-ə-tahzh*) *noun*
damage done on purpose to stop somebody else being successful: *the sabotage of the enemy's arms factory*

Word Building: **sabotage** *verb*

sabre (say *say-bə*) *noun*
a heavy, slightly curved, one-edged sword

saccharin (say *sak-ə-rən*) *noun*
a sweet chemical used instead of sugar

Word Building: **saccharine** *adjective*

sachet (say *sash-ay*) *noun*
a small sealed packet or bag used to contain small servings of food, or shampoo for your hair, or perfumed herbs to keep your cupboards smelling fresh

Word History: from a French word, which is why the "t" is not sounded

sack *noun*
1 a large bag made of strongly woven material **2** dismissal from your job: *I've been given the sack.*

Word Building: **sack** *verb*

sacrament (say *sak-rə-mənt*) *noun*
a Christian religious ceremony which is the outward show of a spiritual event or change: *the sacrament of baptism*

Word Building: **sacramental** *adjective*

sacred (say *say-krəd*) *adjective*
1 holy or worthy of religious respect: *a sacred city* **2** having to do with religion: *sacred music*

Word Building: **sacredly** *adverb*
sacredness *noun*

sacrifice *verb*
1 to give up at a loss to yourself: *He sacrificed his chance of winning to help his friend.* **2** to offer to a god, especially your life or your goods

Word Building: **sacrifice** *noun* **sacrificial** *adjective*

sacrilege (say *sak-rə-lij*) *noun*
disrespect shown to something sacred

Word Building: **sacrilegious** *adjective*
sacrilegiously *adverb*

saddle *noun*
1 a seat for the rider of a horse **2** the seat on a bicycle **3** a piece of meat including part of the backbone and the ribs: *a saddle of mutton*

saddle *verb*
4 to put a saddle on **5** to load or burden: *He saddled me with a nasty job.*

Word Building: **saddler** *noun* **saddlery** *noun*

safari (say *sə-fah-ree*) *noun*
a long journey, usually for hunting wild animals

Word Building: the plural is **safaris**
Word History: from Swahili, an African language

safe *adjective*
1 free from danger or risk: *You are safe now.* **2** careful in avoiding danger: *a safe driver* **3** beyond or away from danger: *in a safe place*

safe *noun*
4 a steel or iron box that you keep money, jewels or valuable papers in

Word Building: **safely** *adverb* **safety** *noun*

safflower *noun*
a plant with large orange-red flowers which is grown for the oil you can get from its seeds

saffron *noun*
an orange-coloured powder made from flowers, which is used to colour food

sag *verb*
1 to bend down, especially in the middle: *The mattress sagged from the weight of his body.* **2** to droop or hang loosely: *Her shoulders sagged.*

Word Building: other forms are **I sagged, I have sagged, I am sagging** □ **sag** *noun*

saga (say *sah-gə*) *noun*
1 a long novel about the lives of a family or group of people **2** any long story

sage[1] *noun*
a very wise person

Word Building: **sage** *adjective: sage comments*

sage[2] *noun*
a herb used in cooking

sago (say *say-goh*) *noun*
a starchy food made from the soft inside of the trunk of some palm trees

sail *noun*
1 a sheet of canvas or nylon which catches the wind and makes a boat move through the water **2** a voyage in a ship or boat
sail *verb*
3 to travel in a ship or boat **4** to move or be carried along on water: *Ships sail to Hobart from Melbourne.* **5** to move along quickly: *Clouds sailed overhead.* **6** to cause to sail: *He sails his boat on the harbour.*

Word Building: **sailor** *noun* a member of a ship's crew

sailboard *noun*
a light-weight surfboard with a mast and sail, on which the rider stands to control the sail

saint *noun*
1 someone who has been declared to be holy by the Christian church **2** a very good person

Word Use: definition 1 is shortened to "St" and used as a title as in *St John*
Word Building: **sainthood** *noun* **saintly** *adjective*

sake *noun*
1 purpose: *For the sake of peace, let's not argue.* **2** benefit or good: *For your own sake, do your best.*

salad *noun*
1 a dish of raw vegetables such as lettuce, tomatoes and celery **2** a dish of raw or cooked food served cold, usually with a dressing: *rice salad | fruit salad*

salamander (say *sal-ə-man-də*) *noun*
a type of amphibian with a tail, which lives in the water when very young, but later lives on land

salami (say *sə-lah-mee*) *noun*
a kind of sausage with a strong salty taste

salary *noun*
the regular pay you get for your job, especially for office work

Word Use: compare this with **wage**
Word Building: the plural is **salaries**

sale *noun*
1 the act of selling: *the sale of a house*
2 a special selling at a low price: *a sale of summer clothes* **3 for sale** or **on sale** able to be bought: *Our house is for sale. | Her latest book is on sale now.*

saline (say *say-luyn*) *adjective*
containing or tasting like salt: *a saline solution*

Word Building: **salinity** *noun*

saliva (say *sə-luy-və*) *noun*
the watery liquid in your mouth, which helps you swallow and begin to digest food

Word Building: **salivary** *adjective: the salivary glands* **salivate** *verb*

sallow *adjective*
having a sickly yellowish colour: *sallow skin*

salmon (say *sam-ən*) *noun*
a fish with pink flesh, which is good to eat

Word Building: the plural is usually **salmon**

salon (say *sal-on*) *noun*
a fashionable shop: *a frock salon | a beauty salon*

saloon *noun*
a well-furnished bar room in a hotel

salt *noun*
1 white crystals obtained from sea water and used to flavour or preserve food
2 a chemical compound formed from an acid and an alkali

Word Building: **salty** *adjective* (**saltier, saltiest**)

saltbush *noun*
a plant which can grow in very dry parts of Australia and which horses and cattle eat

saltcellar *noun*
a container for salt, used at a meal table

salutary (say *sal-yə-tree*) *adjective*
1 health-giving or wholesome
2 beneficial or doing good: *salutary advice*

salute *verb*
1 to greet **2** to raise your right hand to the side of your head as a mark of respect for: *The soldier saluted the queen.*

Word Building: **salutation** *noun* **salute** *noun*

salvage (say *sal-vij*) *noun*
the saving of a ship or its cargo from fire, shipwreck or other damage

Word Building: **salvage** *verb*

salvation *noun*
1 the act of saving **2** the cause or means of saving: *The ladder against the wall of the burning house was his salvation.*

salvo *noun*
the firing of guns a number of times, often as a salute

Word Building: the plural is **salvo** or **salvoes**
Word History: from a Latin word meaning "be in good health"

sample *noun*
1 a part or piece which shows what the whole is like: *a sample of her writing*
sample *verb*
2 to test or judge by a sample: *to sample a cake*

Word Use: a similar word for definition 1 is **specimen**
Word Building: **sample** *adjective: a sample packet*

samurai (say *sam-yə-ruy*) *noun*
a Japanese warrior who lived in medieval times

Word Building: the plural is **samurai**

sanatorium *noun*
a hospital for sick people who need to rest and live for a time in a healthy climate

Word Use: another spelling is **sanitarium**
Word Building: the plural is **sanatoriums** or **sanatoria**

sanctify *verb*
to make holy or set apart as holy

Word Building: other forms are **I sanctified, I have sanctified, I am sanctifying** □ **sanctification** *noun*

sanction *verb*
to give approval or support to

Word Building: **sanction** *noun*

sanctuary (say *sang-chə-ree*) *noun*
1 a holy place **2** a place of safety: *a bird sanctuary* **3** protection given to someone running away from ill-treatment

Word Building: the plural is **sanctuaries**

sand *noun*
1 fine grains of rocks that have been broken up or worn away
sand *verb*
2 to smooth or polish with sand or sandpaper

Word Building: **sandhill** *noun* a low hill of piled up sand **sandy** *adjective*

sandal *noun*
a kind of shoe made of a flat sole fastened to the foot with straps

sandalwood *noun*
a sweet-smelling wood used for carving ornaments, or burnt as incense

sandpaper *noun*
a strong paper coated with a layer of sand and used for smoothing rough surfaces

Word Building: **sandpaper** *verb*

sandshoe *noun*
a canvas shoe with a rubber sole, usually worn for sport

sandstone *noun*
a rock made of sand held together with one of several minerals

sandwich *noun*
1 two slices of bread with a cold filling between them
sandwich *verb*
2 to crowd or place between two other things: *We sandwiched the child between the two adults on the small seat.*

Word Building: the plural is **sandwiches**
Word History: named after the fourth Earl of Sandwich, 1718-92, who invented them

sane *adjective*
1 having a healthy mind **2** sensible or based on common sense: *a sane decision*

Word Building: **sanely** *adverb* **sanity** *noun*

sanitary *adjective*
having to do with cleanliness or care in preventing disease

Word Building: **sanitation** *noun* the protection of public health using sanitary methods

sap[1] *noun*
the juice circulating in a plant

sap[2] *verb*
to weaken or destroy gradually: *Worry sapped her health.*

Word Building: other verb forms are **I sapped, I have sapped, I am sapping**

sapling *noun*
a young tree

sapphire (say *saf-uy-ə*) *noun*
a clear blue gemstone

Word Building: **sapphire** *adjective*

sarcasm *noun*
the saying of harsh and bitter things, using the trick of saying the opposite of what you really mean, so as to hurt someone's feelings

Word Building: **sarcastic** *adjective* **sarcastically** *adverb*

sarcophagus (say *sah-kof-ə-gəs*) *noun*
a stone coffin

Word Building: the plural is **sarcophagi** or **sarcophaguses**

sardine *noun*
a young sea-fish usually cooked in oil and tinned

sardonic *adjective*
sarcastic or mockingly scornful: *a sardonic remark*

sari (say *sah-ree*) *noun*
a long piece of cotton or silk material worn by a Hindu woman, which she drapes around her body with one end over her head or shoulders

sarong (say *sə-rong*) *noun*
a length of cloth wrapped around the body like a skirt and worn by both men and women in Malaya and some Pacific islands

sash[1] *noun*
a long band of cloth worn round your waist or over your shoulder

Word Use: the plural is **sashes**

sash[2] *noun*
a window frame which slides up and down

Word Use: the plural is **sashes**

sashimi (say *sə-shee-mee*) *noun*
a Japanese dish of raw fish

satay *noun*
cubes of spiced meat cooked on a skewer and covered with hot peanut sauce

satchel *noun*
a school bag with straps, carried on your back

satellite *noun*
1 an object in space, such as a moon, which moves around a larger one, such as a planet **2** a man-made object sent into orbit around the earth or another planet to transmit information back to earth

satin *noun*
1 a very smooth shiny cloth

satin *adjective*
2 made of satin **3** smooth and shiny: *a satin finish*

satire *noun*
1 the use of sarcasm or humour to draw people's attention to something which is silly or bad **2** any poem, book or play which does this

Word Building: **satiric** *adjective* **satirical** *adjective* **satirically** *adverb* **satirise** *verb* **satirist** *noun*

satisfy *verb*
1 to please or make happy: *to satisfy an employer* **2** to bring to an end by supplying what is needed: *to satisfy someone's hunger* **3** to convince: *to satisy yourself that a job has been done*

Word Building: other forms are **I satisfied, I have satisfied, I am satisfying** □ **satisfaction** *noun* **satisfactory** *adjective*

saturate *verb*
to soak thoroughly: *The rain saturated the ground.*

Saturday *noun*
the seventh day of the week

Word Use: the abbreviation is **Sat**
Word History: from an Old English word meaning "day of Saturn"

satyr (say *sat-ə*) *noun*
a god, pictured in old stories as part goat and part human

sauce *noun*
1 a thick cooked liquid put on food as a flavouring **2** rudeness or impertinence

Word Use: definition 2 is more suited to everyday language
Word Building: **saucy** *adjective*

saucepan *noun*
a cooking pot with a lid and a long handle

saucer *noun*
a small round plate used under a cup

sauna (say *saw-nə*) *noun*
a room with a kind of steam bath in which you become clean by perspiring a lot

saunter (say *sawn-tə*) *verb*
to walk in an unhurried way

Word Building: **saunter** *noun*

sausage *noun*
finely minced meat packed into a thin skin

sauté (say *soh-tay*) *verb*
to brown or cook gently in a pan with a little fat

Word Building: other forms are **I sautéed, I have sautéed, I am sautéing**
Word History: from a French word, which is why there is an accent over the "e"

savage *adjective*
1 untamed or wild **2** fierce or cruel: *savage punishment*

savage *noun*
3 an uncivilised person who has no experience of the modern world
4 a rude or cruel person

Word Building: **savagery** *noun*

savanna (say *sə-van-ə*) *noun*
a grassland area with some trees scattered about

Word Use: another spelling is **savannah**

save *verb*
1 to rescue from danger or harm
2 to avoid spending or using up: *to save $100 | to save electricity* **3 save up** to put aside money: *to save up for a bicycle*

saveloy (say *sav-ə-loy*) *noun*
another word for **frankfurt**

saviour or **savior** (say *sayv-yə*) *noun*
1 someone who saves or rescues
2 the Saviour Jesus Christ

savour or **savor** (sounds like *saver*) *verb*
to taste or smell, especially with pleasure

Word Building: **savour** *noun*

savoury or **savory** (say *say-və-ree*) *adjective*
1 having a delicious taste or smell
2 salty or sharp-tasting rather than sweet: *a savoury filling*

Word Building: **savoury** *noun* (**savouries**)

saw *noun*
1 a cutting tool with sharp teeth on a thin blade

saw *verb*
2 to cut with a saw **3** to cut as a saw does: *He sawed at the meat with his blunt old knife.*

Word Building: other verb forms are **I sawed, I have sawn** or **I have sawed, I am sawing**

saxophone *noun*
a wind instrument with a curved brass body

Word Building: **saxophonist** *noun*

say *verb*
1 to speak or utter **2** to express in words: *to say that you are happy*
3 to assert or declare: *They said he would go.*

say *noun*
4 a turn to speak: *You can have your say now.*

Word Building: other verb forms are **I said, I have said, I am saying**

saying *noun*
1 something wise that's often said
2 go without saying to be very obvious

Word Use: a similar word for definition 1 is **proverb**

scab *noun*
1 the crust which forms over a sore when it is healing **2** someone who goes on working during a strike

Word Building: **scab** *verb* (**scabbed, scabbing**)

scabbard (say *skab-əd*) *noun*
a holder for the blade of a sword or dagger

scaffold *noun*
1 a framework to stand on when you are doing work on a building **2** a raised platform on which criminals are executed

Word Use: a similar word for definition 1 is **scaffolding**

scald (rhymes with *called*) *verb*
1 to burn with hot liquid or steam
2 to heat to almost boiling point: *to scald milk*

scald *noun*
3 a burn caused by hot liquid or steam

scale[1] *noun*
1 one of the thin, flat, fingernail-like plates which form the covering of fish and some other animals **2** any thin flaky coating or flake that peels off from a surface

Word Building: **scale** *verb* to remove scale or scales from **scaly** *adjective*

scale[2] *noun*
1 a set of marks along a line for measuring: *the scale of a thermometer* **2** a marked line on a map showing how to measure distances **3** size, compared to something else: *Our new house is on a larger scale than our old one.* **4** a series of musical notes going up or down at fixed intervals, usually one that begins on a particular note: *the scale of C major*

scale[2] *verb*
5 to climb: *to scale a mountain / to scale a wall* **6** to arrange according to a scale: *to scale exam marks*

scales *plural noun*
a weighing machine

scallop (say *skol-əp*) *noun*
1 a type of shell-fish which has two wavy shells and is good to eat **2** one of the regular curves along the edge of pastry, a garment or cloth

Word Building: **scallop** *verb* (**scalloped, scalloping**)

scalp *noun*
1 the skin of your head where the hair grows

scalp *verb*
2 to cut the scalp from

scalpel *noun*
a small, very sharp knife used by surgeons in operations

scamp *noun*
a rascal or mischievous person

scamper *verb*
to run or hurry away quickly

Word Building: **scamper** *noun*

scan *verb*
1 to look at closely **2** to look over quickly: *to scan a page* **3** to read the information contained in the bar code of supermarket items, library books, and so on, the way a computerised cash register does

Word Building: other forms are **I scanned, I have scanned, I am scanning** □ **scan** *noun* **scanner** *noun*

scandal *noun*
1 talk or gossip that harms someone's reputation **2** a disgraceful or dreadful happening

Word Building: **scandalise** *verb* to shock or horrify **scandalous** *adjective* **scandalously** *adverb*

scant *adjective*
1 hardly enough: *There is scant time in which to finish.* **2** barely as much as there's supposed to be: *a scant cup of flour*

Word Building: **scanty** *adjective: a scanty supply* **scantily** *adverb* **scantiness** *noun*

scapegoat *noun*
someone who is made to take the blame for others

scar *noun*
a mark left on your skin by a healed sore or burn

Word Building: **scar** *verb* (**scarred, scarring**) to leave a scar

scarce *adjective*
1 not enough to fill the need **2** rarely seen or found: *Leather-covered books are scarce now.*

Word Building: **scarcity** *noun*

scarcely *adverb*
barely or not quite

scare *verb*
to frighten or become frightened

Word Building: **scare** *noun* **scary** *adjective*

scarecrow *noun*
a figure dressed in old clothes, put up to frighten birds away from crops

scarf *noun*
a piece of material worn around your neck or head for warmth or ornament

Word Building: the plural is **scarfs** or **scarves**

scarlet *adjective*
bright red

Word History: from a Persian word meaning "a rich cloth"

scarlet fever *noun*
a disease that spreads easily, causing a high fever and a scarlet rash

scathing (say *skay-dhing*) *adjective*
meant to hurt your feelings by criticising you: *a scathing remark*

Word Building: **scathingly** *adverb*

scatter *verb*
1 to throw loosely about **2** to drive off or go in different directions: *The runaway car scattered the crowd. | The crowd scattered.*

Word Building: **scattering** *noun* a small spread-out number or quantity **scatter** *noun*

scavenger *noun*
1 someone who searches in rubbish for useful things **2** an animal which eats flesh from dead animals

Word Building: **scavenge** *verb*

scene (sounds like *seen*) *noun*
1 a place where something happens: *the scene of the crime* **2** a view or a picture of a view **3** one of the divisions of a play **4** a real or imaginary event, especially one described in writing **5** a noisy outburst of excitement or anger in front of other people

Word Building: **scenic** *adjective*

scenery (say *seen-ə-ree*) *noun*
1 the natural features of a place: *beautiful coastal scenery* **2** paintings, hangings and structures put on a stage to show the place where a play is meant to take place

scent (sounds like *sent*) *noun*
1 a pleasant smell: *the scent of flowers* **2** the particular smell of an animal or person which enables other animals to follow them **3** perfume: *a bottle of scent*

Word Building: **scent** *verb* **scented** *adjective*

sceptic (say *skep-tik*) *noun*
someone who doesn't believe things that most other people accept without question

Word Building: **sceptical** *adjective* **sceptically** *adverb* **scepticism** *noun*

sceptre (say *sep-tə*) *noun*
a rod carried by a king or queen, as a symbol of royal power

schedule (say *shed-joohl, sked-joohl*) *noun*
1 a plan which shows you how a project is to be done and sets out a timetable for it **2** a list of things to be done

Word Building: **schedule** *verb*

scheme (say *skeem*) *noun*
1 a plan of action: *a scheme for raising money* **2** a secret plot: *a scheme to kidnap the president*

Word Building: **scheming** *adjective* crafty or cunning **scheme** *verb*

scholar (say *skol-ə*) *noun*
1 a student or pupil **2** a learned person: *a Latin scholar*

Word Building: **scholarly** *adjective*

scholarship (say *skol-ə-ship*) *noun*
1 a sum of money won by a student which helps to pay school or university fees **2** knowledge gained by study: *He is a man of great scholarship.*

scholastic (say *skə-las-tik*) *adjective*
having to do with schools, students or education: *scholastic achievements*

school[1] *noun*
1 a place where children are taught **2** the children who go to a school: *The school went to the zoo today.* **3** any place or time of teaching: *a dancing school | a tennis school*

Word Building: **school** *verb* to train or teach **schooling** *noun* education or training

school[2] *noun*
a large number of fish, whales or porpoises swimming together

Word History: from a Dutch word meaning "school" or "multitude"

schooner (say *skooh-nə*) *noun*
1 a sailing ship with two or more masts **2** a large beer glass

science *noun*
1 the study of the physical world in an organised way, by measuring, testing and experimenting **2** knowledge gained in this way **3** a particular branch of this study: *the science of botany*

Word Building: **scientific** *adjective* **scientist** *noun*

scissors (say *siz-əz*) *plural noun*
a cutting instrument made of two blades joined together: *My scissors are blunt.*

Word Use: the term *a pair of scissors* is often used

scoff *verb*
to mock or jeer

scold *verb*
to find fault with: *She scolded me for being careless.*

scone (rhymes with *gone*) *noun*
a light plain cake split open and spread with butter

Word History: from a Dutch word meaning "fine bread"

scoop *noun*
1 a small spoon-like ladle: *a flour scoop* **2** the bucket of a dredge **3** a hollow made or an amount taken by a scoop **4** a news story published or broadcast before any other newspaper or radio or television station

Word Building: **scoop** *verb*

scooter *noun*
a child's toy with two wheels, one in front of the other, and a board between them on which you stand

scope *noun*
1 range or reach: *This comes within the scope of my work.* **2** space or room: *scope for improvement*

scorch *verb*
1 to burn slightly, often with an iron **2** to cause to dry up with heat: *The sun scorched the desert.*

Word Building: **scorch** *noun* a burn on the surface

score *noun*
1 the total of points made by a competitor or team in a game **2** a scratch, especially a deep one in wood or metal **3** a set of twenty: *to live three score years* **4** a written or printed piece of music with all parts included and written one under the other

Word Building: **score** *verb*

scorn *noun*
an open show of disgust or contempt

Word Building: **scorn** *verb*

scorpion *noun*
a spider-like invertebrate with a long narrow tail that ends in a venomous stinger

scoundrel (say *skown-drəl*) *noun*
a wicked or dishonourable person

scour (rhymes with *flower*) *verb*
to clean by rubbing hard, usually in soap and water

scout *noun*
someone sent to find out information, especially about an enemy

Word Building: **scout** *verb*

scowl *verb*
to have an angry look on your face

Word Building: **scowl** *noun*

scrabble *verb*
to scratch or scrape with claws or your hands: *to scrabble in the dirt*

scramble *verb*
1 to climb or walk quickly and awkwardly **2 scramble eggs** to cook eggs by mixing yolks and whites with milk, and heating

scramble *noun*
3 a hurried climb or movement over rough ground **4** a disorderly struggle to get something: *a scramble for seats in the back row*

scrap[1] *noun*
1 a small piece **2** anything useless or worn out, especially old metal **3 scraps** bits of food left over from a meal

scrap[1] *adjective*
4 consisting of scraps: *a scrap heap*

scrap[1] *verb*
5 to make into scrap: *to scrap a ship for its metal* **6** to put aside as useless

Word Building: other verb forms are **I scrapped, I have scrapped, I am scrapping**

scrap[2] *noun*
a fight or quarrel

Word Building: **scrap** *verb* (**scrapped, scrapping**)

scrape *verb*
1 to drag or rub something sharp or rough over, usually to remove a layer: *We scraped the wall to remove the old paint.* **2** to scratch: *The knife scraped the table.* **3** to rub harshly or noisily: *The chalk scraped on the blackboard.* **4 scrape up** to gather together **5 scrape through** to manage with difficulty

Word Building: **scrape** *noun*

scratch *verb*
1 to mark or cut roughly: *to scratch polished wood / The kitten scratched my skin.* **2** to draw a pen or pencil through: *to scratch a mistake from a page* **3** to withdraw: *to scratch a horse from a race* **4** to lessen itching by rubbing with the nails or claws: *That dog is always scratching.* **5** to make a slight grating noise

Word Building: **scratch** *noun* (**scratches**) **scratchy** *adjective* **scratchily** *adverb*

scrawl *verb*
to write untidily

Word Building: **scrawl** *noun*

scrawny *adjective*
thin or bony: *the scrawny neck of a hen*

Word Building: other forms are **scrawnier, scrawniest** □ **scrawniness** *noun*

scream *verb*
1 to make a loud piercing cry or sound: *The hyena screamed with pain.*

scream *noun*
2 such a cry or sound **3** someone or something that is very funny: *He's a real scream.*

Word Use: definition 3 is more suited to everyday language

screech *verb*
to make a harsh high-pitched cry or noise: *The owl screeched overhead.* | *The tyres screeched on the wet road.*

Word Building: **screech** *noun* (**screeches**)

screen *noun*
1 a large, flat surface on which a film can be shown **2** the part of a TV set or the video terminal of a computer on which the picture appears **3** a frame covered with wire mesh, placed over a window to keep out insects **4** a covered frame or a curtain used to hide something or to protect something **5** anything that shelters or hides: *They stood behind a screen of shrubs.*

Word Building: **screen** *verb*

screw *noun*
1 a kind of a nail with a slot in its flat end and a spiral thread above its point

screw *verb*
2 to turn: *to screw a lid on* **3** to twist or wrinkle: *He screwed up his eyes in the sun.*

screwdriver *noun*
a tool which fits into the end of a screw and is turned to drive the screw in or take it out

scribble *verb*
1 to write hastily or carelessly **2** to make meaningless marks with a pen or pencil

Word Building: **scribble** *noun* **scribbler** *noun*

scribe *noun*
1 a writer or author **2** someone who used to make copies of books before the invention of printing **3** a teacher who used to explain the Jewish law

script *noun*
1 the words written down for the actors to say in a play or film **2** handwriting

scripture *noun*
1 any holy writing or book **2 Scripture** the Bible

Word Building: **scriptural** *adjective*
Word History: from a Latin word meaning "writing"

scroll *noun*
a roll of parchment or paper with writing on it

scrotum *noun*
the pouch of skin in males which contains their testicles

Word Building: the plural is **scrota**

scrounge *verb*
to obtain by borrowing, begging or stealing

Word Use: this is more suited to everyday language
Word Building: **scrounger** *noun*

scrub[1] *verb*
1 to rub hard with a brush, soap and water in order to clean **2** to get rid of or cancel: *We have to scrub the Christmas concert.*

Word Use: definition 2 is more suited to everyday language
Word Building: other forms are **I scrubbed, I have scrubbed, I am scrubbing** □ **scrub** *noun*

scrub[2] *noun*
a bush area of low trees or shrubs

scruff *noun*
the back of your neck

scruffy *adjective*
dirty, shabby and uncared for

scrum *noun*
1 a way of restarting the play in a game of Rugby Football, in which some of the players pack together and push, one side against the other, until the ball is thrown in and someone kicks it out to his team-mates **2** the formation of players in a scrum

Word Use: another word is **scrummage**

scrumptious (say *skrum-shəs*) *adjective*
very tasty or delicious: *a scrumptious dinner*

scrupulous (say *skroohp-yə-ləs*) *adjective*
1 careful or exact in every detail: *He is scrupulous in his work.* **2** being strict about doing what is right: *She is scrupulous in her dealings with her customers.*

Word Building: **scruple** *noun* a doubt that you have about a matter of deciding between right and wrong **scrupulously** *adverb*

scrutinise or **scrutinize**
(say skrooh-tə-nuyz) *verb*
to examine closely and carefully

Word Building: **scrutiny** *noun* (**scrutinies**)

scuba (say skooh-bə) *noun*
a system that lets a diver breathe air through a mouthpiece connected by tubes to an air tank

Word History: an acronym made from the first letters of *self-contained underwater breathing apparatus*

scuff *verb*
1 to scrape with your feet **2** to make a mark on by scraping: *to scuff your shoes / to scuff furniture*

scuffle *verb*
to struggle or fight in a confused way

Word Building: **scuffle** *noun*

scullery *noun*
a small room where the rough, dirty, kitchen work is done

Word Building: the plural is **sculleries**

sculpture *noun*
1 the art or work of making figures or designs in marble, clay, bronze or similar materials **2** something made this way

Word Building: **sculpt** *verb* to carve **sculpture** *verb* to form sculptures **sculptor** *noun* **sculptural** *adjective*

scum *noun*
1 a thin layer of froth or dirt on the top of a liquid **2** someone who is low or worthless: *the scum of the earth*

Word Use: definition 2 will offend the person it is used about

scurry *verb*
to move quickly: *The children scurried back to bed.*

Word Building: other forms are **I scurried, I have scurried, I am scurrying** □ **scurry** *noun* (**scurries**)

scurvy *noun*
a disease caused by lack of vitamin C in your diet

scuttle *verb*
to run with quick steps: *The mice scuttled away.*

Word Building: **scuttle** *noun*

scythe (say *suydh*) *noun*
a tool with a long curved blade joined at an angle to a long handle: *He used a scythe to cut the long grass.*

sea *noun*
1 the salt waters that cover most of the earth's surface **2** a particular part of these waters, usually near or almost surrounded by land: *the Tasman Sea*
3 a large quantity: *a sea of troubles*
4 at sea a out on the ocean
b uncertain or confused

Word Use: be careful – this sounds like **see**

sea-anemone (say see-ə-nem-ə-nee) *noun*
a sea animal which stays in one place and catches food with one or more tentacles growing on top of its tube-shaped body

seafarer *noun*
a traveller on the sea

Word Building: **seafaring** *adjective*

seafood *noun*
food which comes from the sea, such as fish, squid and shellfish

seagull *noun*
a bird which lives near or on the sea and is usually white with a grey back and wings and has a harsh cry

seahorse *noun*
a small fish with a curved tail and a head shaped like a horse's

seal[1] *noun*
1 a design pressed into a piece of wax, or a stamp engraved with such a design, used for making a document official **2** a piece of wax for closing an envelope or document, which has to be broken before the contents can be read **3** anything used to close something

seal[1] *verb*
4 to close so that entry is impossible except by force: *He sealed the envelope. / The king sealed the tomb.* **5** to cover with tar: *to seal a road* **6** to decide finally: *to seal someone's fate*

Word Use: the male is a **bull;** the female is a **cow;** the young is a **pup**

seal[2] *noun*
a sea mammal with smooth fur, a long rounded body and large flippers

sea-level *noun*
the average level of the sea, used as a base to measure height: *The town is 1000 metres above sea-level.*

sea lion *noun*
a type of large Australian seal which has white hair on the back of its neck

seam *noun*
1 the line where two pieces of material have been joined together: *The seam isn't sewn straight.* **2** a thin layer of a different kind of rock or mineral in the ground: *a coal seam*

seaman *noun*
a sailor

Word Use: be careful – this sounds like **semen**
Word Building: the plural is **seamen** □ **seamanship** *noun*

seance (say *<u>say</u>-ons*) *noun*
a meeting of people who are trying to contact the spirits of dead people

Word History: from a Latin word meaning "sit"

seaplane *noun*
a plane with floats, which can land on water

sear *verb*
1 to burn or blacken the outside of: *to sear a piece of meat* **2** to cause to dry up or wither: *The sun seared the wheat.*

Word Building: **searing** *adjective*

search *verb*
1 to go through or look through thoroughly in order to find something or someone: *He searched the house for his watch.* **2** to examine, usually for hidden or illegal objects: *Guards searched everyone's bags.*

Word Building: **search** *noun* (**searches**)

search-warrant *noun*
an order by a court which allows the police to search your house, usually for stolen goods

seasickness *noun*
a feeling of sickness in your stomach, or vomiting caused by the movement of a ship at sea

Word Building: **seasick** *adjective*

season *noun*
1 one of the four divisions of the year into spring, summer, autumn and winter
2 a period of time, especially when it is connected with some event or activity: *the Christmas season / the football season / It's been a good season for strawberries.*

season *verb*
3 to add flavour or interest to: *She seasons her cooking with pepper and herbs.*
4 to treat or let stand until ready for use: *to season timber*

Word Building: **seasonal** *adjective* **seasonally** *adverb*

seasoning *noun*
something like salt, herbs or spices, which adds flavour

seat *noun*
1 something for sitting on: *a garden seat*
2 a part for sitting on: *the seat of a chair / the seat of your pants* **3** a centre of some activity: *a seat of learning* **4** a large country house **5** the right to sit in parliament: *She won a seat in the last election.*

Word Building: **seat** *verb* **seated** *adjective*

seaweed *noun*
any plant that grows in the ocean

secateurs (say *<u>sek</u>-ə-təz, sek-ə-<u>terz</u>*) *plural noun*
gardening shears for clipping and pruning

seclude *verb*
to shut away: *She secludes herself in her room.*

Word Building: **secluded** *adjective* quiet and private **seclusion** *noun*

second[1] *adjective*
1 next after the first **2** another: *a second chance* **3** alternate: *every second weekend*

second[1] *verb*
4 to express support of: *Who will second this proposal so we can vote on it?*

Word Building: **second** *noun* **seconder** *noun*

second[2] *noun*
one sixtieth part of a minute of time

secondary *adjective*
1 next after the first in order or importance: *a secondary matter* **2** taken from something else: *a secondary source*
3 having to do with the processing of primary products, such as meat, wheat, coal and wool: *a secondary industry*

second-hand *adjective*
bought or got from someone else: *a second-hand car / a second-hand jumper*

Word Building: **second-hand** *adverb*

secret *adjective*
1 done or made without others knowing: *a secret plan* **2** designed to escape notice: *a secret door*

Word Building: **secretive** *adjective* liking to keep things to yourself **secrecy** *noun* **secret** *noun* **secretly** *adverb*

secretary *noun*
someone whose job is to write letters, keep records or make phone calls for an employer

Word Building: the plural is **secretaries** □ **secretarial** *adjective*

secrete (say *sə-kreet*) *verb*
1 to produce, such as by a gland: *to secrete saliva* **2** to hide away: *He has secreted the treasure under the floor.*

sect *noun*
a religious group, especially one which has broken away from a larger group

Word Building: **sectarian** *adjective*

section *noun*
1 a part or division of something
2 a picture of how something would look if you cut it from top to bottom and showed the inside

sector *noun*
1 a division of a circle, shaped like a wedge of cake **2** a large division or an area of activity: *the public sector*

secular (say *sek-yə-lə*) *adjective*
worldly, as opposed to religious or spiritual: *She doesn't like to hear secular music in church.*

secure *adjective*
1 free from care or danger **2** firmly fastened or in place **3** in safe keeping: *Your money will be secure in the bank.*

secure *verb*
4 to get: *He was unable to secure tickets.*
5 to tie up tightly **6** to be or make safe

Word Building: **securely** *adverb* **security** *noun*

sedan (say *sə-dan*) *noun*
a car with four doors, which seats from four to six people

Word History: from a Latin word meaning "seat"

sedate *adjective*
calm and steady: *They walked at a sedate pace.*

Word Building: **sedate** *verb* to calm with a sedative **sedation** *noun*

sedative *noun*
a drug which lessens pain or excitement

Word Building: **sedative** *adjective* calming or soothing

sediment *noun*
solid material that falls to the bottom of a liquid

Word Use: a word with a similar meaning is **dregs**
Word Building: **sedimentary** *adjective* **sedimentation** *noun*

seduce *verb*
to persuade or entice to do something considered wrong

Word Building: **seducer** *noun* **seduction** *noun* **seductive** *adjective* **seductively** *adverb*

see *verb*
1 to take things in with your eyes or your mind: *to see clearly* | *I see what you mean.*
2 to consider or think of: *We shall see.* | *I see it like this.* **3** to find out: *See who it is.*
4 to meet or visit: *to see a friend* | *to see the doctor* **5** to go with: *She'll see you to the door.* **6** to imagine or remember: *I can just see her laughing the way she used to.*
7 to know or experience: *He must have seen a lot.* **8 see through a** to detect: *She saw through the disguise.* **b** to stay until the end of: *He always sees a job through.*

Word Use: be careful – this sounds like **sea**
Word Building: other forms are **I saw, I have seen, I am seeing**

seed *noun*
1 the part produced by a plant from which a new plant grows **2 seeds** the beginnings or start: *the seeds of their quarrel*

Word Building: **seed** *verb*

seedling *noun*
a young plant

seedy *adjective*
1 shabby and untidy: *a seedy appearance*
2 unwell: *I'm feeling quite seedy this morning.*

Word Building: other forms are **seedier, seediest**

seek *verb*
1 to try to find or get: *to seek an answer* | *to seek fame* **2** to try: *She seeks to help.*

Word Building: other forms are **I sought, I have sought, I am seeking**

seem *verb*
1 to have the look of being: *She seems happy.* **2** to appear to yourself: *I seem to be dizzy.*

Word Building: **seeming** *adjective* **seemingly** *adverb*

seep *verb*
to leak or drip slowly: *Water seeps from the pipe.*

Word Building: **seepage** *noun*

seer *noun*
someone who can see into the future

seesaw *noun*
a plank balanced in the middle, so that the child sitting at one end rises when the child at the other end goes down

Word Building: **seesaw** *verb* to move like a seesaw

seethe *verb*
1 to bubble and foam: *The sea was seething far below.* **2** to be excited or disturbed: *She is seething with rage.*

segment *noun*
a piece or section: *a segment of orange*

Word Building: **segment** *verb* to separate into pieces **segmentation** *noun*

segregate *verb*
to set or keep apart, especially one race or group of people from another

Word Building: **segregation** *noun*

seize (say *seez*) *verb*
1 to take hold of suddenly, or by force: *to seize an idea or an opportunity | to seize a knife* **2** to become stuck or jammed: *The engine seized.*

Word Building: **seizure** *noun*

seldom *adverb*
rarely or not often: *He seldom takes part.*

select *verb*
1 to choose: *Select your favourite recipe.*
select *adjective*
2 carefully chosen: *a select few*
3 of special value or excellence

Word Building: **selection** *noun* **selective** *adjective* **selectively** *adverb*

self- *prefix*
a word part showing action directed towards yourself: self-control

self-confidence *noun*
belief in your own ability: *to be full of self-confidence*

Word Building: **self-confident** *adjective*

self-control *noun*
the ability to stop yourself from doing something: *She hasn't much self-control when it comes to sweets.*

Word Building: **self-controlled** *adjective*

self-defence *noun*
the ability to protect yourself against attack

selfish *adjective*
thinking only of your own interests: *a selfish act*

Word Building: **selfishly** *adverb* **selfishness** *noun*

self-raising flour *noun*
flour with baking powder already added to it, so that it makes bread or cakes rise

self-service *adjective*
having to do with a shop or restaurant where the customers serve themselves and then pay a cashier

sell *verb*
1 to give up for money: *He sold his car.*
2 to have for sale: *Do you sell goldfish here?*

Word Building: other forms are **I sold, I have sold, I am selling**

semaphore (say *sem-ə-faw*) *noun*
a system for signalling messages using flags

Word Building: **semaphore** *verb*

semen (say *see-mən*) *noun*
liquid containing sperm, which is produced by the testicles

Word Use: be careful – this sounds like **seaman**
Word History: from a Latin word meaning "seed"

semi- *prefix*
a word part meaning half: *semicircle*

Word History: this prefix comes from Latin

semibreve *noun*
a musical note which is four crotchets long

semicircle *noun*
a half circle

Word Building: **semicircular** *adjective*

semicolon *noun*
a punctuation mark (;) which is used to show more of a break between parts of a sentence than a comma does, as in *He entered the house; he picked up the bag; he left the house.*

semidetached *adjective*
partly separate, used especially about two houses sharing one wall while remaining separate from other buildings

seminary (say *sem-ən-ree*) *noun*
a college for training Roman Catholic priests

Word Building: **seminarian** *noun*

semiquaver *noun*
a musical note which is equal to half a quaver

semitone *noun*
half a tone, or the difference between the notes which are next to each other on the piano

semitrailer *noun*
a large truck which consists of a long trailer connected to the cabin and a powerful engine

semolina (say *sem-ə-lee-nə*) *noun*
the large hard bits of wheat grains left over after the fine flour has been separated

Word History: from a Latin word meaning "fine flour"

senate (say *sen-ət*) *noun*
one of the decision-making bodies in the government of a country

Word Building: **senator** *noun*

send *verb*
1 to cause to go: *She sent him away.* | *He sends a letter every week.* **2** to cause to become: *He sends her mad with rage.* **3** to send a message: *He will send for you.* **4 send up** to mock, usually by imitating in an exaggerated way: *They send up her accent.*

Word Building: other forms are **I sent, I have sent, I am sending** □ **sender** *noun*

senile *adjective*
weak in body or mind because of old age

Word Building: **senility** *noun*

senior *adjective*
of greater age or importance: *He was a bit taller, since he was the senior of the two boys.* | *a senior lecturer*

Word Building: **senior** *noun* **seniority** *noun*

sensation *noun*
1 feeling: *The accident has left her with no sensation in her hand.* | *He had the sensation that he was being followed.* **2** a cause or feeling of excitement: *The pop star was a sensation.* | *The news flash caused a sensation.*

Word Building: **sensational** *adjective* **sensationally** *adverb*

sense *noun*
1 one of the powers or abilities by which we taste, touch, hear, see and smell: *His sense of smell is impaired.* **2** any physical or mental feeling or ability: *a sense of tiredness* | *a sense of humour* **3** the ability to think and act sensibly and intelligently: *She has no sense.* | *He has plenty of common sense.* **4** meaning: *Could you explain the sense of this remark?*

sense *verb*
5 to notice or feel with your senses: *You could sense the tension between the players.*

sensible *adjective*
1 full of good sense: *a sensible move* **2** knowing or aware: *She is sensible of her responsibility.*

Word Use: definition 2 is rather old-fashioned
Word Building: **sensibility** *noun* (**sensibilities**) the ability to feel **sensibly** *adverb*

sensitive *adjective*
1 having feeling: *sensitive to the cold* **2** easily affected by something: *He has a sensitive nature.* | *The film is sensitive to light.* **3** causing strong feelings: *a sensitive matter*

Word Building: **sensitivity** *noun* (**sensitivities**) **sensitively** *adverb*

sensory *adjective*
having to do with feeling: *Tentacles are the sensory organs of some animals.*

sensual *adjective*
having to do with feeling or with your senses: *Listening to the music was a sensual pleasure.*

Word Building: **sensualist** *noun* **sensuality** *noun* **sensually** *adverb*

sentence *noun*
1 a group of words which form a complete statement, question, comment or exclamation, such as *He hit the ball.* **2** the punishment of a criminal: *The judge passed a sentence of five years' gaol.*

Word Building: **sentence** *verb* to condemn to punishment

sentiment *noun*
1 an attitude or opinion: *What is the public sentiment about this new law?* **2** a mental feeling or emotion

sentimental *adjective*
showing or having to do with tender feelings: *sentimental tears | a sentimental song*

Word Building: **sentimentality** *noun* **sentimentally** *adverb*

sentinel *noun*
a soldier who acts as a lookout

sentry *noun*
a soldier who stands guard to keep people out

Word Building: the plural is **sentries**

separate *verb*
1 to put or keep apart **2** to stop living with a marriage partner, without actually divorcing

Word Building: **separate** *adjective* not connected

September *noun*
the ninth month of the year, with 30 days

Word Use: the abbreviations are **Sep** and **Sept**
Word History: from a Latin word for the seventh month in the early Roman calendar

septet *noun*
1 any group or set of seven **2** a musical piece for seven voices or seven performers

septic *adjective*
infected with germs: *a septic wound*

sepulchre (say *sep-əl-kə*) *noun*
a tomb or a grave

Word Use: this is an old-fashioned word

sequel (say *see-kwəl*) *noun*
1 a book or film which continues on from an earlier work **2** anything which follows or results from something

sequence (say *see-kwəns*) *noun*
a series of things following each other

Word Building: **sequential** *adjective*

sequin (say *see-kwən*) *noun*
a small shiny disc sewn as a decoration onto bags, evening clothes or fancy dress

Word Building: **sequined** *adjective*

serenade (say *se-rə-nayd*) *noun*
music traditionally played or sung by a lover under his beloved's window at night

Word Building: **serenade** *verb*

serene *adjective*
calm and peaceful

Word Building: **serenely** *adverb* **serenity** *noun*

serf *noun*
someone who in feudal times was not free but was thought of as belonging to the land that a lord owned, and was sold with it

Word Use: be careful – this sounds like **surf**

sergeant (say *sah-jənt*) *noun*
1 an officer in the army who ranks next above a corporal **2** a police officer ranking between a constable and an inspector

serial (say *sear-ree-əl*) *noun*
a story that is published or broadcast one part at a time at regular intervals

Word Use: be careful – this sounds like **cereal**

series (say *sear-reez*) *noun*
1 a number of things or events arranged or happening in a certain order or sequence
2 a set of something: *This coin will now complete the series in my collection.*
3 a number of programs on radio or television which are linked in some way, either by subject matter or by being about the same group of people

Word Building: the plural is **series**

serious (say *sear-ree-əs*) *adjective*
1 solemn or thoughtful: *The judge had a serious expression on his face.* **2** sincere and not joking: *Are you serious?* **3** important or needing a lot of thought: *Buying a new house is a serious matter.* **4** giving cause for concern or worry: *His condition after the operation was serious.*

Word Building: **seriously** *adverb*

sermon *noun*
1 a serious talk, usually one preached in church: *Sunday's sermon was about loving your neighbour. | Her father gave her a sermon about riding her bike on the busy road.* **2** a long boring speech

serpent *noun*
1 *an old-fashioned word for* **snake**
2 someone who is cunning, untrustworthy or evil: *Satan, or the Devil, is often described as a serpent.*

serrated (say sə-<u>ray</u>-təd) *adjective*
having notches or teeth along the edge: *A saw has a serrated blade.*

Word Building: **serrate** *verb* **serration** *noun*

serum (say <u>sear</u>-rəm) *noun*
1 a clear, pale yellow liquid that separates from your blood when it clots
2 this liquid used as a base for vaccines

Word Use: the plural forms are **sera** and **serums**

servant *noun*
1 someone who works for or is in the service of someone else: *a public servant*
2 someone who is employed to live in your house and help look after it

serve *verb*
1 to work for **2** to put on a table: *to serve the dinner* **3** to supply or answer the needs of: *The shop assistant served me.*
4 to give help or assistance: *to serve in a shop* **5** to go through a term of service such as in the army or in a gaol
6 to be of use: *That tree will serve as a shelter from the rain.* **7** to start playing for a point in tennis by hitting the ball over the net

serve *noun*
8 the act of serving a ball in tennis

service *noun*
1 a helpful act: *to perform a service for someone* **2** the supplying of something either useful to, or needed by, a large group of people: *a telephone service / a bus service* **3** a department of public employment or the group of people in it: *the diplomatic service* **4** the way you serve food: *The service in this restaurant is bad.*
5 the act of getting a car or other machinery into good order: *I put my car in the garage for a service.* **6** a religious ceremony: *a marriage service* **7** a set of dishes for a particular use: *a dinner service*
8 the act of serving a ball in tennis
9 the services the military armed forces

service *verb*
10 to make fit for use: *The garage serviced my car.*

serviceable *adjective*
useful: *My old sandshoes are still serviceable.*

Word Building: **serviceably** *adverb*

service station *noun*
a place where you can buy petrol and oil for motor vehicles, and where mechanical repairs are carried out

serviette *noun*
a piece of cloth or paper, used during a meal to wipe your lips and hands and to protect your clothes

Word Use: other words are **napkin** or **table napkin**

serving *noun*
1 the act of someone or something that serves **2** a portion or helping of food or drink

serving *adjective*
3 having to do with dishing out food: *a serving spoon*

sesame (say <u>ses</u>-ə-mee) *noun*
a tropical herb, whose small oval seeds are used for food and oil

session (say <u>sesh</u>-ən) *noun*
1 the sitting or meeting together of a court, council or parliament **2** a period of time for any particular activity: *a dancing session*

set *verb*
1 to put in a particular place or position *She set the vase on the table.* **2** to cause to begin: *The accident really set him thinking.* **3** to fix or appoint: *The officials set a time for the race.* **4** to provide for others to follow: *She set an excellent example.* **5** to give, assign or make up: *The teacher set the homework. / He set the maths exam.* **6** to arrange in proper order: *She set the table for dinner.*
7 to adjust or regulate: *I set the clock.*
8 to put something into a fixed place or position: *The doctor set her broken arm.*
9 to become hard or solid: *The jelly set in the bowl.* **10** to pass or sink below the horizon: *The sun sets every evening.*
11 set off **a** to explode: *to set off a bomb* **b** to begin a journey **12 set out** **a** to arrange **b** to explain carefully **c** to start a journey **13 set up** **a** to build or erect **b** to provide with: *His parents set him up with a house.*
c to claim to be: *He sets himself up as an expert.*

set *noun*
14 a number of things that are used together, or form a collection: *a set of dishes* **15** a radio or television receiver
16 a group of games that make up one of the sections of a tennis match
17 a number of pieces of scenery arranged together, used for a play or film
18 any collection of numbers or objects in maths which have something in common

set *adjective*
19 fixed beforehand: *a set time / set rules* **20** fixed or rigid: *a set smile / set in your ways* **21** ready and prepared: *all set to go*

Word Building: other verb forms are **it set, it has set, it is setting**

setback *noun*
something that hinders or slows down your progress

set square *noun*
a flat piece of wood or plastic in the shape of a right-angled triangle, used in drawing technical things like plans for buildings

settee (say *set-ee*) *noun*
a seat or sofa for two or more people

setting *noun*
1 the surroundings of anything: *The house was situated in a pretty country setting.* **2** the time and place in which a play or film takes place **3** a group of things such as a knife, fork, and plate used to set someone's place at the table

settle *verb*
1 to decide or agree: *They settled on a suitable time.* **2** to put in order or arrange: *She settled all her affairs before she went away.* **3** to pay: *He settled the bill.* **4** to set up a home: *The family settled in Tasmania.* **5** to sink down gradually: *The dust slowly settled.* **6 settle down** **a** to put to bed **b** to begin to do serious work **c** to begin to live an ordered life, especially after marrying

Word Building: **settlement** *noun*

settler *noun*
someone who settles in a new country

set-up *noun*
1 organisation or arrangement: *The set-up of the library is clear.* **2** something which has been arranged dishonestly **3** a trap

Word Use: definitions 2 and 3 are more suited to everyday language
Word Building: **set-up** *adjective*

sever (say *sev-ə*) *verb*
1 to cut or separate **2** to break off: *The countries have severed all friendly relations.*

several *adjective*
1 more than two, but not many **2** individual, different, or respective: *They went their several ways.*

severe (say *sə-vear*) *adjective*
1 harsh or extreme: *severe punishment* **2** unsmiling or stern: *a severe face* **3** serious or grave: *a severe illness* **4** simple, plain and without decoration: *She wears severe clothes.*

Word Building: **severity** *noun*

sew (sounds like *so*) *verb*
1 to join with stitches, using a needle and thread **2** to make or repair clothes with a needle and thread

Word Use: be careful – this sounds like **so** and **sow**

sewage *noun*
the waste matter which passes through drains and sewers

sewer *noun*
a pipeline, usually underground, made to carry away waste water and waste matter

sewerage *noun*
the removal of waste water and waste matter using sewers

sex *noun*
1 one of the two divisions of either male or female in humans and animals **2** the characteristic or condition of being either male or female **3** the instinct which causes sexual attraction between two people **4** the arousal of sexual interest by the way people are portrayed in films, books, and so on: *sex on TV* **5** *another name for* **sexual intercourse**

sexist *adjective*
having to do with an attitude which judges someone by their sex rather than by their own individual qualities

Word Building: **sexism** *noun* **sexist** *noun*

sextant *noun*
an instrument which measures the angles between the sun, moon, stars and earth to help sailors work out their position

sextet *noun*
1 any group or set of six **2** a musical piece for six voices or six performers

sexual *adjective*
having to do with sex

Word Building: **sexuality** *noun* **sexually** *adverb*

sexual intercourse *noun*
a sexual act between two people, usually one in which a man's penis enters a woman's vagina

sexy *adjective*
1 having a great concern with sex: *a sexy book* **2** having an attractiveness or charm that attracts the members of the opposite sex

Word Building: other forms are **sexier, sexiest** □ **sexily** *adverb*

shabby *adjective*
1 very worn: *shabby clothes* **2** wearing old or very worn clothes **3** mean or unfair: *It was a shabby trick to play on a friend.*

Word Building: other forms are **shabbier, shabbiest** □ **shabbily** *adverb*

shack *noun*
a rough cabin or hut

shackle *noun*
1 a ring of iron, usually one of a pair, for holding the wrist or ankle of a prisoner or slave **2** anything that stops someone's free thought or action

shade *noun*
1 a slight darkness or an area of slight darkness caused by the blocking off of rays of light **2** something that shuts out, or protects from, light or heat: *Pull down the shades on those windows.* **3** a darker or lighter kind of one colour: *Her dress was in three shades of green.*

shade *verb*
4 to dim or darken **5** to protect from heat or light

Word Building: **shady** *adjective* (**shadier, shadiest**)

shadow *noun*
1 the dark figure or area of shade made by something blocking out light **2** shade or slight darkness

shadow *verb*
3 to shade, or protect from heat or light
4 to follow secretly

Word Building: **shadowy** *adjective*

shaft *noun*
1 a long pole or rod: *the shaft of a spear | the shaft of an arrow* **2** a ray or beam: *a shaft of sunlight* **3** a passage that is like a well, or an enclosed vertical or sloping space: *a lift shaft | a mine shaft*

shaggy *adjective*
1 covered with or having long rough hair: *a shaggy dog* **2** rough, coarse or untidy: *The lion had a shaggy appearance.*

Word Building: other forms are **shaggier, shaggiest**

shake *verb*
1 to move backwards and forwards with quick short movements **2** to fall or scatter by using such movements: *Sand shakes off easily.* **3** to tremble with fear or cold **4** to make unsteady or unsettled: *Her faith in his honesty was shaken by his behaviour.* **5 shake hands** to grip hands as a greeting, or to show agreement

shake *noun*
6 the act of shaking or an unsteady movement **7** a drink made by shaking ingredients together: *a milk shake*
8 no great shakes of no particular importance

Word Use: definition 8 is more suited to everyday language
Word Building: other verb forms are **I shook, I have shaken, I am shaking** □ **shaky** *adjective* (**shakier, shakiest**) **shakily** *adverb*

shale (rhymes with *hail*) *noun*
a rock made of many thin layers, which is easy to split and which was made when clay or other very tiny particles were pressed firmly together

shallot (say *shə-lot*) *noun*
an onion-like plant used for flavouring in cooking and as a vegetable

shallow *adjective*
1 not deep: *shallow water* **2** without any serious thought: *a shallow mind | a shallow argument*

Word Building: **shallowness** *noun*

sham *noun*
something that is not what it appears to be

Word Use: similar words are **fraud** and **fake**
Word Building: **sham** *verb* (**shammed, shamming**): *to sham illness*

shame *noun*
1 a mentally painful feeling that comes after you know you have said or done something wrong or silly **2** a disgrace or dishonour: *Her crime brought shame to her family.* **3** a pity or something to be sorry about: *It's a shame he can't come today.*
4 put to shame a to disgrace or make ashamed **b** to do better than: *Robert puts Richard to shame in swimming.*

Word Building: **shame** *verb: to cause to feel shame* **shameful** *adjective* **shamefully** *adverb* **shameless** *adjective* **shamelessly** *adverb*

shampoo *noun*
a liquid soap, especially for the hair

Word Building: **shampoo** *verb* (**shampooed, shampooing**): *to shampoo your hair | to shampoo a carpet*

shamrock *noun*
a bright green plant with three small leaves grouped on one stem: *The shamrock is the national emblem of Ireland.*

shandy *noun*
a drink which is a mixture of beer with either ginger beer or lemonade

Word Building: the plural is **shandies**

shanghai[1] (say <u>shang</u>-*huy*) *verb*
1 to force someone to join a ship as a member of the crew **2** to get someone to do something, usually either without their knowledge, or against their wishes: *His father shanghaied him into washing the car.* **3** to steal

Word Use: definitions 2 and 3 are more suited to everyday language
Word Building: other forms are **I shanghaied, I have shanghaied, I am shanghaiing**
Word History: short for "to ship to Shanghai" (a seaport in China)

shanghai[2] (say <u>shang</u>-*huy*) *noun*
a child's catapult or slingshot

shanty[1] *noun*
a roughly-built hut, cabin, or house

Word Building: the plural is **shanties**

shanty[2] *noun*
a sailors' song, usually sung in rhythm to the work they are doing

Word Building: the plural is **shanties**

shape *noun*
1 the outline or form of something or someone **2** proper order: *The house is now in shape for our visitors.* **3** condition: *His business affairs were in bad shape.*

shape *verb*
4 to give definite form, shape or character to: *The potter carefully shaped his pots.*
5 shape up to develop: *The new worker is shaping up well.*

Word Building: **shapely** *adjective* (**shapelier, shapeliest**) having a pleasing shape **shapeless** *adjective*

share (rhymes with *hair*) *noun*
1 the part given to or owned by someone **2** each of the equal parts into which the ownership of a company is divided: *to buy 500 shares in BHP*

share *verb*
3 to divide into parts with each person receiving a part **4** to use or enjoy together: *The whole family shares the car.*

shark *noun*
any of a number of large fish which are very fierce and possibly man-eaters, and which have soft skeletons and five to seven pairs of gill openings

sharp *adjective*
1 having a thin cutting edge or a fine point: *a sharp knife* | *a sharp needle*
2 sudden or abrupt: *a sharp rise in temperature* | *a sharp bend in the road*
3 clearly outlined or distinct: *a sharp picture on TV* **4** strong or biting in taste **5** very cold or piercing: *a sharp wind* **6** mentally quick and alert: *a sharp mind* **7** keen or sensitive: *a sharp ear*
8 higher in pitch by a semitone, or too high in pitch: *B sharp* | *Your recorder is a bit sharp in the low notes.*

sharp *adverb*
9 precisely: *at one o'clock sharp*

sharp *noun*
10 a a note that is one semitone above a given note **b** the music sign (♯) which raises a note by a semitone when it is placed before it

Word Use: the opposite of definitions 8 and 10 is **flat**
Word Building: **sharpen** *verb* **sharply** *adverb* **sharpness** *noun*

shashlik *noun*
another name for **shish kebab**

shatter *verb*
1 to break into pieces **2** to weaken or destroy: *His health was shattered by the accident.*

shave *verb*
1 to remove hair with a razor **2** to take thin slices from, especially so as to smooth: *The carpenter shaved the wood.*
3 to graze or come very near: *The car just shaved the corner.*

shave *noun*
4 the act or process of shaving **5 a close shave** a narrow miss or escape

Word Building: other verb forms are **I shaved, I have shaved** or **I have shaven, I am shaving**

shaving *noun*
a very thin piece, especially of wood: *The shavings from the door covered the floor.*

shawl *noun*
a piece of material worn as a covering for your shoulders or head

she *pronoun*
the female being talked about: *She was reading a book.*

Word Building: other forms are **her**: *her book* | *Give it to her.*; **hers**: *the book is hers*; **they**: *They are all girls.*

sheaf *noun*
1 one of the bundles into which cereal plants like wheat and rye are bound after they are cut in the field **2** any bundle, group or collection: *a sheaf of papers*

Word Building: the plural is **sheaves**

shear *verb*
1 to remove by cutting with a sharp instrument: *He sheared all the wool from the sheep.* **2** to cut hair or fleece from something: *to shear sheep*
shear *noun*
3 shears large scissors or another similar cutting tool

Word Use: be careful – this sounds like **sheer**
Word Building: other verb forms are **I sheared, I have sheared** or **I have shorn, I am shearing** □ **shearer** *noun*

sheath *noun*
1 a covering for the blade of a sword, dagger or bayonet **2** any similar covering **3** a close-fitting dress which follows the shape of your body

Word Building: the plural is **sheaths** □ **sheathe** *verb*

shed[1] *noun*
a simple or roughly-built building used for storage or sheltering animals

shed[2] *verb*
1 to pour forth or let fall: *to shed blood | to shed tears* **2** to give forth or send out light, sound or smell: *This lamp sheds a soft glow of light.* **3** to cast or throw off: *A snake regularly sheds its skin and grows another one.*

Word Building: other forms are **it shed, it has shed, it is shedding**

sheep *noun*
1 an animal, closely related to the goat, which is kept for its meat and thick wool **2** someone who is shy, timid or stupid

Word Use: the male is a **ram**; the female is a **ewe; the young is a lamb**
Word Building: the plural is **sheep**

sheep dip *noun*
a deep trough containing a liquid which kills harmful insects on sheep as they are driven through it

sheepish *adjective*
awkwardly shy or embarrassed

sheer[1] *adjective*
1 very thin so that you can see through: *The curtains on the window were almost sheer.* **2** absolute, or unmixed with anything else: *You won by sheer luck.* **3** very steep: *a sheer cliff*

Word Use: be careful – this sounds like **shear**
Word Building: **sheer** *adverb* very steeply

sheer[2] *verb*
to swerve or change course: *The ship sheered away from the rocks.*

Word Use: be careful – this sounds like **shear**
Word Building: **sheer** *noun* a swerve

sheet *noun*
1 one of two large pieces of cloth used on a bed, one under you and the other over you **2** any layer or covering: *a sheet of water* **3** a broad thin piece of something: *a sheet of glass | a sheet of paper*

shelf *noun*
1 a thin flat piece of wood, glass or something similar, fixed horizontally to a wall or in a frame and used for holding things like books or ornaments **2** a ledge: *a shelf of rock*

Word Building: the plural is **shelves**

shell *noun*
1 the hard outer covering of things like nuts, eggs and certain animals
2 something like a shell: *Just the shell of the building remained after the fire.*
3 a hollow bullet-like case filled with explosives, to be fired from a large gun
shell *verb*
4 to take out of the shell: *to shell peas*
5 to fire shells on: *The soldiers shelled the enemy.* **6 shell out** to hand over or pay up

Word Use: definition 6 is more suited to everyday language

shellfish *noun*
an animal like an oyster or lobster that is not a fish but lives in water and has a shell

Word Building: the plural is **shellfishes** or **shellfish**

shelter *noun*
1 protection from bad weather, danger and so on: *We took shelter from the rain.*
2 a place of safety and protection: *a bomb shelter*

Word Building: **shelter** *verb*

shelve *verb*
1 to place on a shelf or shelves **2** to stop considering or thinking about: *He shelved the problem for a few days.*

shepherd (say *shep*-əd) *noun*
1 someone who looks after sheep
shepherd *verb*
2 to take care of or to guard, especially when moving along: *The police shepherded the pop star through the crowd.*

sherbet *noun*
1 a sweet fizzy powder that you can eat dry or use to make a fizzy drink
2 a frozen fruit-flavoured dessert

Word Use: a similar word for definition 2 is **sorbet**
Word History: from an Arabic word meaning "a drink"

sheriff *noun*
1 an officer in some courts of law who has duties such as organising juries
2 the chief law enforcement officer of a North American county

sherry *noun*
a strong sweet or dry wine

Word Building: the plural is **sherries**

shield *noun*
1 a flat piece of metal, leather or wood, carried to protect your body in a battle
2 anything used for protection: *She held her hands to her eyes as a shield against the sun.*

Word Building: **shield** *verb*

shift *verb*
1 to move from one place or position to another **2** to manage to get along or succeed: *She'll shift for herself.*
shift *noun*
3 a change or a move: *a shift in the wind*
4 the period of time worked by someone in a place of work which operates 24 hours a day: *I have to do the night shift at the hospital tomorrow.* **5** the people who work during this time: *The day shift takes over now.* **6** a loose-fitting dress

shifty *adjective*
deceitful and looking as if you've got something to hide: *The burglar had shifty eyes.*

Word Building: other forms are **shiftier, shiftiest** □ **shiftily** *adverb*

shilling *noun*
a silver coin used in Australia before decimal currency

shimmer *verb*
to shine or gleam with a dim unsteady light

shin *noun*
1 the front part of your leg between your knee and your ankle
shin *verb*
2 to climb by gripping with your hands and your feet: *He shinned quickly up the rope.*

Word Building: other verb forms are **I shinned, I have shinned, I was shinning**

shine *verb*
1 to glow or give out light **2** to polish: *He shined his shoes.* **3** to be very good: *She shines at tennis.* **4** to direct the light of: *Shine the torch over here.*
shine *noun*
5 polished brightness

Word Building: other verb forms are **I shone** or **I shined, I have shone** or **I have shined, I am shining** □ **shiny** *adjective* (**shinier, shiniest**)

shingle *noun*
a thin piece of wood, slate and so on used in rows to cover the roofs and sides of houses

Word Building: **shingle** *verb* to cover with shingles

shingles *noun*
a painful skin disease which affects the nerves in your body

Shinto *noun*
a native religion of Japan in which nature and ancestors are worshipped and held sacred

Word Building: **Shintoist** *noun*

ship *noun*
1 a large boat for carrying people or goods over deep water
ship *verb*
2 to send by ship, train, truck and so on

Word Building: other verb forms are **I shipped, I have shipped, I was shipping**

shipment *noun*
a load of goods shipped at one time

shipshape *adjective*
neat and tidy

shiralee (say *shi*-rə-*lee*) *noun*
another word for **swag**

shire *noun*
a local government area

shirk *verb*
to get out of doing: *to shirk your job*

Word Building: **shirker** *noun*

shish kebab *noun*
small pieces of meat cooked on a skewer, usually with vegetables such as onion and capsicum

Word Use: a shortened form is **kebab**
Word History: from the Turkish words for "skewer" and "roast meat"

shiver *verb*
to shake with fear, cold or excitement

Word Building: **shiver** *noun* **shivery** *adjective*

shoal[1] *noun*
a sandbank under shallow water

shoal[2] *noun*
a group of fish swimming together

shock[1] *noun*
1 a sudden and violent fright or upset
2 pain and injury caused by an electric current passing through the body

Word Building: **shocking** *adjective: shocking news* **shock** *verb*

shock[2] *noun*
a thick bushy mass: *a shock of hair*

shoddy *adjective*
1 bad or made badly: *shoddy work* | *a shoddy house* **2** mean: *a shoddy thing to do*

Word Building: other forms are **shoddier, shoddiest** □ **shoddily** *adverb* **shoddiness** *noun*

shoehorn *noun*
a long piece of metal or plastic that you put into the heel of your shoe to make it go on more easily

shoot *verb*
1 to hit or kill with a bullet, arrow or something else fired from a weapon: *The policeman shot the bank robber.* **2** to fire from a weapon: *to shoot an arrow*
3 to send out quickly and accurately like an arrow or bullet: *to shoot questions* | *to shoot a ball into goal* **4** to move quickly: *He shot along the path.* **5** to photograph or film: *to shoot a scene* **6** to put out new growths: *Plants shoot in spring.*
shoot *noun*
7 a new growth on a plant

Word Use: be careful – this sounds like **chute**
Word Building: other verb forms are **I shot, I have shot, I am shooting** □ **shooter** *noun*

shoplift *verb*
to steal from a shop while pretending to be shopping

Word Building: **shoplifter** *noun* **shoplifting** *noun*

shore *noun*
the land along the edge of the sea or a lake

short *adjective*
1 not long **2** not tall **3** rude and abrupt: *He was short with me.* **4** not having enough: *We are short of water.*
5 short for being a shortened form of: *"Phone" is short for "telephone".*
short *adverb*
6 suddenly: *to stop short* **7** without going the full length: *The ball fell short of the goal.*
short *noun*
8 a short film advertising a program or a film to be shown later **9 shorts** short trousers ending above the knees

Word Use: definition 8 is sometimes used in the plural; a similar word for this is **trailer**
Word Building: **shortly** *adverb* **shortness** *noun*

shortage *noun*
a lack in amount: *a shortage of food*

shortbread *noun*
a thick biscuit made with a lot of butter

short circuit *noun*
a fault in an electrical circuit causing the current to flow between two points only instead of through the whole circuit

shortcoming *noun*
a failure or fault: *Laziness is his worst shortcoming.*

shortening *noun*
fat, such as butter or margarine, used in making pastry

shorthand *noun*
a system of fast handwriting using lines, curves and dots instead of letters

Word Building: **shorthand** *adjective*

shorthanded *adjective*
not having enough helpers or workers

shortly *adverb*
soon: *I am coming shortly.*

short-sighted *adjective*
1 not able to clearly see things that are far away **2** not thinking about the future: *a short-sighted answer to a problem*

Word Use: a similar word for definition 1 is **myopic**
Word Building: **short-sightedness** *noun*

short-tempered *adjective*
becoming angry easily

shot *noun*
1 the shooting of a gun, bow or other weapon: *He took three shots at the target. / I think I heard a shot.* **2** bullets or other lead ammunition **3** the heavy metal ball thrown in shot-put contests **5** a stroke or throw in sports: *a shot at goal* **6** a try, attempt or guess **7** an injection: *The doctor gave her a tetanus shot.* **8** a photograph: *We took some shots of our house.*

Word Use: definitions 7 and 8 are more suited to everyday language

shotgun *noun*
a gun that fires small shot and is used for shooting animals for sport

shot-put (say *shot-poot*) *noun*
the sport of throwing a heavy metal ball as far as possible

Word Building: **shot-putter** *noun* **shot-putting** *noun*

shoulder (rhymes with *holder*) *noun*
1 the part of your body that joins your neck to your arm
shoulder *verb*
2 to push with the shoulders: *He shouldered his way through the crowd.*
3 to support or carry on the shoulders: *to shoulder the load of wood* **4** to take upon yourself: *to shoulder a responsibility*

shoulder-blade *noun*
the flat bone that forms the back part of the shoulder

shout *verb*
1 to call or cry out loudly **2** to buy or pay for: *I'll shout the ice-creams.*

Word Use: definition 2 is more suited to everyday language
Word Building: **shout** *noun*

shove (say *shuv*) *verb*
to push roughly

Word Building: **shove** *noun*

shovel (say *shuv-əl*) *noun*
1 a tool or machine with a wide blade for moving things like soil or rubbish
shovel *verb*
2 to move with a shovel: *to shovel sand into a truck*

Word Building: other verb forms are **I shovelled, I have shovelled, I am shovelling**

show *verb*
1 to cause or allow to be seen: *He showed his drawing to his mother.* **2** to point out or explain: *Please show me how to do it.*
3 to guide: *Show him the kitchen.*
4 to prove by demonstrating: *I'll show that it is true.* **5 show off a** to show proudly: *He showed off his new bike.*
b to behave so as to get attention or praise for yourself: *Stop showing off.*
6 show up a to make stand out clearly: *White clothes show up dirt.* **b** to appear or arrive: *He didn't show up till after dinner.*
show *noun*
7 a public showing or exhibition: *an art show* **8** an entertainment, such as a play or television series **9** a false showing or pretence: *He was bored but made a show of interest.*

Word Use: a similar word for definitions 1,7 and 9 is **display**
Word Building: other verb forms are **I showed, I have showed** or **I have shown, I am showing** □ **showy** *adjective* attracting attention **showily** *adverb* **showiness** *noun*

showdown *noun*
an open showing of disagreements, in order to clear up a situation: *I've decided to have a showdown with the boss this week.*

shower *noun*
1 a brief fall of rain **2** a fall of anything in large numbers: *a shower of sparks / a shower of questions* **3** a spout that sends out fine streams of water for washing your body **4** the use of such a shower to wash yourself
shower *verb*
5 to wet with a shower: *He showered us with the hose.* **6** to wash yourself under a shower **7** to fall in a shower: *Bullets showered down on us.* **8 shower on** to give generously to: *He showered presents on her.*

Word Building: **showery** *adjective*

show-off *noun*
someone who behaves so as to get attention or praise

showroom *noun*
a room where goods for sale are shown

shrapnel *noun*
the small parts of an exploded cannon shell: *He was wounded by shrapnel.*

Word History: named after the inventor H Shrapnel, 1761-1842, an officer in the British army

shred *noun*
1 a narrow strip cut or torn off: *a dress torn to shreds* **2** a very small bit: *There was not a shred of food left. | He did not feel a shred of pity for her.*
shred *verb*
3 to tear into small pieces: *We can shred this material and use it to stuff cushions.*

Word Building: other verb forms are **I shredded** or **I shred, I have shredded** or **I have shred, I am shredding**

shrew *noun*
1 a small mouse-like animal that eats insects **2** a very bad-tempered woman

Word Building: **shrewish** *adjective*

shrewd *adjective*
clever, and with good practical judgment: *a shrewd business executive*

Word Use: a similar word is **astute**
Word Building: **shrewdly** *adverb* **shrewdness** *noun*

shriek (say *shreek*) *noun*
a loud, sharp, high-pitched cry or noise: *a shriek of fright | the shriek of a whistle*

Word Building: **shriek** *verb*

shrill *adjective*
loud and high-pitched: *a shrill voice*

Word Building: **shrilly** *adverb* **shrillness** *noun*

shrimp *noun*
a kind of prawn

shrine *noun*
a sacred or holy place: *a shrine of remembrance for those killed in the war*

shrink *verb*
1 to become or make smaller: *The number of children at our school is shrinking. | Hot water shrinks woollen clothes.* **2** to draw back: *The frightened child shrank into a corner.*

Word Building: other forms are **I shrank, I have shrunk** or **I have shrunken, I am shrinking** □ **shrinkable** *adjective* **shrinkage** *noun*

shrivel *verb*
to shrink and wrinkle: *Heat shrivels grass. | He is shrivelling with age.*

Word Building: other forms are **I shrivelled, I have shrivelled, I am shrivelling**

shroud *noun*
1 a cloth for wrapping a dead body in **2** something which covers and hides like a cloth: *a shroud of rain*
shroud *verb*
3 to cover or hide: *Darkness shrouded the town. | Mystery shrouded her past life.*

shrub *noun*
a small, low, tree-like plant

Word Building: **shrubby** *adjective*

shrug *verb*
to raise and lower your shoulders to show doubt, scorn or lack of interest

Word Building: other forms are **I shrugged, I have shrugged, I am shrugging** □ **shrug** *noun*

shudder *noun*
to shake suddenly from fear, cold or horror

Word Building: **shudder** *noun*

shuffle *verb*
1 to walk slowly without lifting the feet **2** to move about: *He shuffled the papers on his desk. | They shuffled him from one class to another.* **3** to mix up the order of cards in a pack

Word Building: **shuffle** *noun* **shuffler** *noun*

shun *verb*
to keep away from deliberately: *He shunned me for a week after our fight.*

Word Building: other forms are **I shunned, I have shunned, I am shunning**

shunt *verb*
1 to move aside or turn aside or out of the way **2** to move from one line of rails to another: *The train was shunted onto the northern line.*

Word Building: **shunt** *noun*

shut *verb*
1 to close or put something in or across an opening: *to shut a book | to shut a door*
2 shut in to keep in or confine: *to shut a bird in a cage* **3 shut out** to keep out or bar: *She shut him out of her room.*
4 shut down to close down or stop for a while: *Schools shut down during the holidays.* **5 shut off** to stop the flow of: *to shut off electricity* **6 shut up** **a** to keep in or hide from view: *to shut up your prize dog* **b** to stop talking
shut *adjective*
7 closed

Word Use: definition 6b is more suited to everyday language
Word Building: other verb forms are **he shut, he has shut, he is shutting**

shutter *noun*
1 a movable wooden cover for the outside of a window **2** a part of a camera which opens and shuts over the lens to allow light through to the film

Word Building: **shutter** *verb*

shuttle *noun*
the part of a loom that carries the thread backwards and forwards in weaving

Word History: from an Old English word meaning "a dart" or "an arrow"

shuttlecock *noun*
1 a piece of cork or light plastic with feathers stuck in it that is hit backwards and forwards in games such as badminton **2** a game played with a shuttlecock

shy *adjective*
1 bashful or not feeling relaxed with other people **2** timid or easily frightened
shy *verb*
3 to move suddenly back or aside: *The horse shied when the car went past.*

Word Building: other adjective forms are **shyer, shyest** or **shier, shiest** □ other verb forms are **it shied, it has shied, it is shying** □ **shyly** *adverb*

sibling *noun*
a brother or sister

sick *adjective*
1 ill or having a disease **2** vomiting or feeling like vomiting **3** for sick people: *sick leave* **4** having to do with something horrible or disgusting: *a sick joke*
5 be sick to vomit **6 be sick of** to be annoyed or fed up with: *I am sick of your untidiness.*

Word Use: a similar word for definition 2 is **nauseous**
Word Building: **sicken** *verb* to make sick **sickening** *adjective* **sickness** *noun*

sickie *noun*
a day taken off work with pay because of real or pretended sickness

Word Use: this is more suited to everyday language

sickle *noun*
a curved short-handled tool for cutting grass or grain

sickly *adjective*
1 unhealthy or getting sick easily: *a sickly child* **2** having to do with sickness: *a sickly colour of the face* **3** making you feel sick: *sickly food*

Word Building: other forms are **sicklier, sickliest** □ **sickliness** *noun*

side *noun*
1 one of the outer edges or lines of something usually not the top, bottom, front or back: *the side of a house | the side of a rectangle* **2** one of the two surfaces of a material like paper or cloth: *Write on one side only.* **3** either half of your body: *I've got a stitch in my side.* **4** the space next to someone or something: *She stood at his side.* **5** one of two or more groups that are against each other: *Which side are you on?* **6** a position or way of thinking about something: *to look at a question from all sides* **7** a part or area: *the east side of a city*
side *adjective*
8 at the side: *a side door* **9** from the side: *a side view*

sideboard *noun*
a piece of furniture with shelves and drawers for holding things like plates and cups

sideshow *noun*
a small show that is part of a larger fair or circus

sidestep *verb*
1 to step to one side to avoid: *to sidestep a puddle* **2** to avoid: *He sidestepped making a decision.*

Word Building: other forms are **I sidestepped, I have sidestepped, I am sidestepping**

sidle *verb*
to move sideways, usually hoping not to be noticed: *He sidled into the room late.*

siege (say *seej*) *noun*
the surrounding of a place in order to capture it: *The city was under siege for three days during the war.*

siesta (say *see-es-tə*) *noun*
a midday or afternoon rest

Word History: this word comes from Spanish and originally from a Latin word meaning "sixth (hour)" or "midday"

sieve (say *siv*) *noun*
1 a container with mesh or holes at the bottom used for straining liquids or separating thick from thin, or large from small

sieve *verb*
2 to separate or strain with a sieve

Word Use: a similar word for definition 2 is **sift**

sift *verb*
1 to separate the thick or coarse parts of with a sieve: *to sift flour* **2** to scatter with a sieve: *to sift icing sugar onto a cake* **3** to sort through carefully: *I sifted all the information to find the piece of evidence I wanted.*

Word Use: a similar word for definition 1 is **sieve**

sigh *verb*
to let out your breath slowly and with a soft sound, from tiredness, sadness or relief

Word Building: **sigh** *noun*

sight *noun*
1 the ability to see **2** something which is seen or should be seen: *She was a beautiful sight.* | *the sights of the city* **3** something that looks odd or unattractive: *He looked a sight in his ragged jeans.* **4 in sight of** in a position where it is possible to see: *We are now in sight of land.*

sight *verb*
5 to get sight of: *They sighted a ship on the horizon.*

Word Use: a similar word for definition 1 is **vision**

sign *noun*
1 anything that shows that something exists or is likely to happen: *Clouds are a sign of rain.* **2** a mark, figure or symbol used to stand for a word, idea or mathematical value: *a dollar sign* | *a plus sign* **3** a movement that expresses an idea or feeling: *He made a sign for me to leave the room.* **4** a notice that gives information, warns or advertises: *a house with a "for sale" sign*

sign *verb*
5 to write your signature on: *to sign a letter* **6** to write as a signature: *She signed her name.* **7 sign off** to stop broadcasting a radio or television program **8 sign up a** to enter the military services **b** to take on by a signed agreement: *The club signed up two new players.*

signal *noun*
1 any action or object that warns, points a direction or gives an order: *He gave the signal for them to start.* | *We stopped at the traffic signals.* **2** the waves by which sound or pictures are sent in radio and television

signal *verb*
3 to make a signal to: *She signalled him to stop talking.* **4** to make known by signal: *We signalled the good news.*

Word Building: other verb forms are **I signalled, I have signalled, I am signalling**

signature *noun*
1 the way you write your own name
2 the sign or signs written at the beginning of a piece of music to tell its key and time

signet *noun*
a raised engraved design used as an official stamp or set into a finger ring

significant *adjective*
1 important: *a significant event in Australia's history* **2** full of meaning: *a significant look*

Word Building: **significance** *noun* **significantly** *adverb*

signify *verb*
1 to be a sign of: *Black clouds signify a storm.* **2** to make known by signs: *He signified his anger with a frown.*

Word Building: other forms are **I signified, I have signified, I am signifying** □ **signification** *noun*

silence *noun*
1 absence of any sound or noise

silence *verb*
2 to bring to silence: *She silenced the class.*

Word Building: **silencer** *noun*

silent *adjective*
1 making no sound or not talking: *He remained silent.* **2** having no sound: *a silent room* | *a silent movie*
3 not pronounced: *In the word "know" the letter "k" is silent.*

silhouette (say *sil-ooh-et*) *noun*
1 an outline drawing filled in with black, like a shadow

silhouette *verb*
2 to show up like a silhouette or shadow: *The tree was silhouetted against the sky.*

silicon *noun*
an element found in minerals and rocks, used in making such things as glass and steel

silk *noun*
a soft shiny cloth made from the threads of the cocoon of the silkworm

Word Building: **silk** *adjective* **silken** *adjective* **silkiness** *noun* **silky** *adjective*

silk-screen *noun*
a way of printing in which ink is passed over a stencil attached to a screen of silk or other fine cloth

Word Building: **silk-screen** *verb*

silkworm *noun*
a kind of caterpillar which spins a fine soft thread to make a cocoon

sill *noun*
a flat piece of wood or other material beneath a window or door

silly *adjective*
foolish or stupid

Word Building: other forms are **sillier, silliest** □ **silliness** *noun*

silo *noun*
a tower-like building for storing grain

Word Building: the plural is **silos**
Word History: from a Greek word for a pit to keep grain in

silt *noun*
earthy matter like very fine sand which is carried by running water and then left behind on the river bottom

silver *noun*
1 a white metal used for making things like jewellery, coins, mirrors and cutlery **2** things made from silver or similar metal, such as coins or knives and forks: *I have a $5 note but no silver. / We put the silver on the dining table on special occasions.*
silver *adjective*
3 made of silver or of a metallic mixture similar to it **4** producing silver: *a silver mine* **5** shiny whitish-grey

Word Building: **silver** *verb* **silvery** *adjective*

silverfish *noun*
a small wingless insect which feeds on paper and some fabrics, and so damages books and household goods

Word Use: the plural is **silverfishes** or **silverfish**

similar *adjective*
having a general likeness: *Their faces are similar. / His bike is similar to hers.*

Word Building: **similarity** *noun*

simile (say *sim-ə-lee*) *noun*
a figure of speech which points out a likeness between two generally unlike things, as in *to sing like a bird* and *He's as strong as an ox.*

simmer *verb*
1 to cook in a liquid just below boiling point **2** to be full of strong but controlled feelings: *She was simmering with rage.*
3 simmer down to become calm or calmer

simper *verb*
to smile in a silly or unnatural way: *She simpered when he said she looked pretty.*

Word Building: **simper** *noun*

simple *adjective*
1 easy to understand, do or use: *a simple explanation / a simple test / a simple tool*
2 plain and uncomplicated: *a simple writing style / simple clothes* **3** mentally weak
4 having to do with the most basic one-word form of a verb: *The verb "ran" in "I ran" is in the simple past tense.*

Word Use: compare definition 4 with **continuous** and **perfect** which talk about verbs of more than one word such as "am running" and "have run"
Word Building: **simpleness** *noun* **simplicity** *noun*

simpleton *noun*
a foolish person

simplify *verb*
to make easier or more simple

Word Building: other verb forms are **I simplified, I have simplified, I am simplifying**

simplistic *adjective*
being so simple as to lose accuracy: *He gave a simplistic account of the causes of unemployment.*

Word Building: **simplistically** *adverb*

simply *adverb*
1 in a plain and straightforward way: *She answered simply. / He dressed simply.*
2 merely: *He is simply going for a walk.*
3 absolutely: *She was simply wonderful in the emergency.*

simulate (say *sim-yə-layt*) *verb*
1 to make a pretence of: *He simulated admiration to flatter her.* **2** to imitate or make a copy of: *They simulated diamonds to make the cheap jewellery.*

Word Building: **simulator** *noun* a device used in training or experiments that simulates movement or flight **simulation** *noun*

simulcast (say *sim-əl-kahst*) *noun*
a program broadcast on television and radio at the same time

simultaneous (say *sim-əl-tay-nee-əs*) *adjective*
happening at the same time

Word Building: **simultaneously** *adverb*

sin *noun*
1 an act of breaking one of God's laws
2 disobedience to God

Word Building: **sin** *verb* (**sinned, sinning**) **sinful** *adjective*

sincere *adjective*
having and expressing true feelings: *She was sincere in her wishes for his success.*

Word Building: **sincerity** *noun*

sinew (say *sin-yooh*) *noun*
a piece of tough tissue joining a muscle to a bone

sing *verb*
1 to give out musical sounds with your voice **2** to perform in this way: *She sang a song.*

Word Building: other verb forms are **I sang, I have sung, I am singing**

singe (say *sinj*) *verb*
to burn slightly

single *adjective*
1 one and only: *my single reason for going*
2 for one person: *a single bed*
3 unmarried
single *verb*
4 single out to choose alone: *They singled her out for promotion.*

Word Building: **single** *noun* **singleness** *noun*

single-handed *adverb*
by working alone: *He built the house single-handed.*

Word Building: **single-handedly** *adverb*

singlet *noun*
a garment with narrow shoulder straps, worn on the upper part of your body, usually under your other clothes

singsong *adjective*
with a regular up and down pattern in the tone: *a singsong voice*

singular *adjective*
1 indicating one person or thing such as the words "teacher", "hears" and "she" in the sentence *She hears the teacher.*
2 unusual or odd: *He had a very singular appearance.*

Word Building: **singularly** *adverb*

sinister *adjective*
suggesting a threat of evil: *a sinister remark*

sink *verb*
1 to go down gradually, as in water: *The ship sank. / The sun is sinking.* **2** to cause to go down: *They sank an enemy ship.*
3 sink in to become understood: *The importance of the letter at last sank in.*
sink *noun*
4 a kitchen basin with a drain

Word Building: other verb forms are **I sank, I have sunk, I am sinking**

sinker *noun*
a weight, usually of lead, for making a fishing line sink below the surface

sinuous (say *sin-yooh-əs*) *adjective*
winding like a snake: *a sinuous path*

sinus (say *suy-nəs*) *noun*
one of the air-filled holes in your skull, connecting with your nose

sip *verb*
to drink in small mouthfuls

Word Building: other verb forms are **I sipped, I have sipped, I am sipping** □ **sip** *noun*

siphon (say *suy-fən*) *noun*
a tube through which liquid flows up over the edge of a higher container to a lower one, once the air has been removed from the tube to create a vacuum

Word Use: another spelling for this is **syphon**
Word Building: **siphon** *verb*
Word History: from a Greek word meaning a "pipe"

sir
a respectful or formal word used when speaking to a man

sire *noun*
the male parent of an animal

siren *noun*
a device that makes a loud warning sound, used on ambulances, police cars and so on

sister *noun*
1 a female relative who has the same parents as you **2** a senior nurse **3** a nun

Word Building: **sisterhood** *noun*

sister-in-law *noun*
1 the sister of your husband or wife
2 the wife of your brother **3** the wife of the brother of your husband or wife

Word Building: the plural is **sisters-in-law**

sit *verb*
1 to rest on the lower part of your body **2** to rest or be placed: *The teapot is sitting on the table.* **3** to try to answer the questions in: *to sit an exam* **4** to pose: *to sit for a portrait* **5** to be in the process of meeting: *Parliament is sitting.*

Word Building: other verb forms are **I sat, I have sat, I am sitting**

sitar (say *sit-ah*) *noun*
an Indian musical instrument which you play by plucking its three strings

Word History: from Hindi, a language of India

site *noun*
1 the piece of land on which something is or will be built: *a house on a site overlooking the ocean* **2** a place where something happens or has happened: *the site of the annual picnic*

situate *verb*
to place in a position

situation *noun*
1 a position in relation to the surroundings: *The shop has a good situation.* **2** a state of affairs: *The situation has been difficult since he left.*

size *noun*
the dimensions or extent of something

sizeable *adjective*
quite big

Word Building: **sizeably** *adverb*

sizzle *verb*
to make a hissing sound while cooking: *The sausages are sizzling in the pan.*

skate *noun*
1 a boot with a blade attached to the bottom, which you wear to move on ice **2** a roller-skate

Word Building: **skate** *verb*

skateboard *noun*
a narrow wooden board on roller-skate wheels which you usually ride standing up

skein (rhymes with *cane*) *noun*
a length of thread or wool wound in a coil

skeleton *noun*
1 all the bones of a human or animal body, connected together **2** a bare framework of something

skeleton *adjective*
3 cut back to the smallest number that can cope: *a skeleton staff*

Word Building: **skeletal** *adjective*

sketch *noun*
1 a drawing or painting done roughly or quickly **2** any rough plan or outline

Word Building: **sketchy** *adjective* (**sketchier, sketchiest**) **sketch** *verb*

skewbald *adjective*
having patches of different colours, especially of white and brown: *a skewbald horse*

Word Use: compare this with **piebald**

skewer *noun*
a long pin of wood or metal, especially one for holding meat while it is being cooked

Word Building: **skewer** *verb*

ski *noun*
one of a pair of long narrow pieces of wood, metal or plastic, which you fasten to your shoes and use for moving on snow

Word Building: **ski** *verb* (**ski'd** or **skied, skiing**)

skid *verb*
to slide forward when the wheels of your car or bike are no longer gripping the road surface: *The car skidded on the icy road.*

Word Building: other verb forms are **I skidded, I have skidded, I am skidding** □ **skid** *noun*

skill *noun*
the ability to do something well

Word Building: **skilful** *adjective* **skilfully** *adverb* **skilled** *adjective*

skillet *noun*
a small frying pan

skim *verb*
1 to remove floating matter from: *to skim soup stock* **2** to remove from the surface of something: *to skim fat from gravy*
3 to move lightly over the surface or top of: *The birds skimmed across the lake.*
4 to read quickly without taking everything in: *I have just skimmed the newspaper.*

Word Building: other forms are **I skimmed, I have skimmed, I am skimming**

skim milk *noun*
milk from which the cream has been removed

skimpy *adjective*
1 scanty or hardly enough: *a skimpy meal* **2** stingy or mean with money

Word Building: other forms are **skimpier, skimpiest** □ **skimp** *verb* **skimpily** *adverb* **skimpiness** *noun*

skin *noun*
1 the outer covering of an animal or human **2** any surface layer: *banana skin*

Word Building: **skin** *verb* (**skinned, skinning**) to remove the skin of

skindiving *noun*
underwater swimming for which you use a snorkel, mask and flippers

Word Building: **skindiver** *noun*

skink *noun*
any of many different, usually smooth-scaled lizards

skinny *adjective*
thin

Word Building: other forms are **skinnier, skinniest** □ **skinniness** *noun*

skip *verb*
1 to jump lightly from one foot to the other **2** to jump over a twirling rope **3** to leave out: *He often skips bits when he's reading.*

Word Building: other forms are **I skipped, I have skipped, I am skipping** □ **skip** *noun*

skipper *noun*
the captain of a ship or a team

skirmish *noun*
a small battle

Word Building: **skirmish** *verb*
Word History: from a German word for "shield"

skirt *noun*
1 a piece of outer clothing, worn by women and girls, that hangs from the waist

skirt *verb*
2 to go round the edge of: *He skirted the dam.*

skirting board *noun*
a board running round a room at the base of the walls

skit *noun*
a short play or other piece of writing which makes fun of something

skite *noun*
someone who boasts a lot

Word Building: **skite** *verb*

skittles *plural noun*
a game played with bottle-shaped pieces of wood and a ball to knock them down

Word Building: **skittle** *verb* to knock over

skivvy *noun*
a close-fitting piece of clothing of knitted material, with long sleeves and a high collar

Word Building: the plural is **skivvies**

skulk *verb*
to stay nearby, trying not to let anyone know you are there: *A man was skulking about the place before the burglary.*

skull *noun*
the bony framework of the head, enclosing the brain and supporting the face

skunk *noun*
a small, furry, American animal that lets out a foul-smelling fluid when attacked

Word History: from an American Indian language

sky *noun*
the area of the clouds or the upper air

Word Building: the plural is **skies**

skydiving *noun*
the sport of falling from a plane for some distance before opening your parachute

skylight *noun*
a flat window in a roof

skyscraper *noun*
a very tall building, especially an office block

slab *noun*
a large flat piece: *a stone slab | a slab of cake*

slack *adjective*
1 loose: *a slack rope* **2** lazy

Word Building: **slack** *verb* **slacken** *verb* **slackly** *adverb* **slackness** *noun*

slacks *plural noun*
long trousers

slag *noun*
the waste material from a mine, or from metal-bearing rock when it is melted down

slalom (say *slay-ləm, slah-ləm*) *noun*
a downhill skiing race with a winding course

slam *verb*
1 to shut hard with a loud noise: *to slam a door* **2** to hit or throw hard or noisily: *to slam a ball into a net*

Word Building: other forms are **I slammed, I have slammed, I am slamming**

slander *noun*
a false spoken statement which damages someone's reputation or good name

Word Use: compare this with **libel**
Word Building: **slander** *verb* **slanderous** *adjective*

slang *noun*
everyday language that is not fitting for formal use

Word Building: **slangy** *adjective*

slant *noun*
1 a slope or angle **2** an aspect or point of view: *This news gives a new slant to the problem.*

Word Building: **slant** *verb* **slantwise** *adverb*

slap *noun*
1 a quick hit, especially with the open hand
slap *verb*
2 to hit smartly, especially with the open hand **3** to put carelessly: *to slap on paint / to slap a book on the table*

Word Building: other verb forms are **I slapped, I have slapped, I am slapping**

slapstick *noun*
rough and noisy comedy

slash *verb*
1 to cut violently and unevenly: *Vandals have slashed the train seats.* **2** to reduce greatly: *to slash prices*

Word Building: **slash** *noun*

slat *noun*
a long strip of wood or metal: *the slats of a blind*

slate *noun*
a dark bluish-grey rock which splits easily into layers and is used on roofs and floors

slaughter (say slaw-tə) *verb*
1 to kill for food: *to slaughter cattle*
2 to kill violently in great numbers

Word Building: **slaughter** *noun*

slave *noun*
1 someone who works without being paid and is the prisoner of someone else
slave *verb*
2 to work very hard, like a slave

Word Building: **slavery** *noun* **slavish** *adjective*

slay *verb*
to kill

Word Building: other forms are **I slew, I have slain, I am slaying**

sleazy *adjective*
untidy and dirty

Word Building: other forms are **sleazier, sleaziest** □ **sleazily** *adverb* **sleaziness** *noun*

sledge *noun*
a vehicle with runners for sliding over snow

Word Use: another form of this word is **sled**
Word Building: **sledge** *verb*

sledge-hammer *noun*
a large heavy hammer

sleek *adjective*
smooth and shiny: *sleek hair*

Word Building: **sleekness** *noun*

sleep *verb*
1 to rest with your eyes closed and your mind unconscious: *Did you sleep well last night?* **2** to have beds for: *The caravan sleeps four.*

Word Building: other forms are **I slept, I have slept, I am sleeping** □ **sleepy** *adjective* (**sleepier, sleepiest**) **sleep** *noun* **sleepiness** *noun* **sleepless** *adjective*

sleeper *noun*
1 a wooden, concrete or steel beam on which railway lines rest **2** a small ring worn in a pierced ear to prevent the hole from closing

sleet *noun*
rain mixed with snow or hail

Word Building: **sleet** *verb*

sleeve *noun*
1 the part of a garment that covers the arm **2** a record cover

sleigh (sounds like *slay*) *noun*
a sledge, especially one pulled by animals

slender *adjective*
slim or thin: *a slender girl / a slender branch*

Word Building: **slenderness** *noun*

sleuth (rhymes with *tooth*) *noun*
a detective

slice *verb*
1 to cut into thin pieces: *to slice bread*
2 to hit a golf ball so that it curves to the right if you are right-handed

Word Use: the opposite of definition 2 is **hook**
Word Building: **slice** *noun* **sliced** *adjective*

slick *adjective*
1 clever and smooth, but not sincere: *a slick salesman* **2** smart or skilful: *a slick answer*

slick *noun*
3 a shiny patch of oil on water

Word Building: **slick down** *verb* to smooth down: *to slick down hair with oil*

slide *verb*
1 to move along smoothly: *to slide a drawer in and out* | *to slide down a slippery dip*

slide *noun*
2 a sliding movement: *She slipped on a banana peel and went for a slide.*
3 a see-through photograph which can be shown on a screen using a projector
4 a thin sheet of glass used for holding things that you look at under a microscope

Word Building: other verb forms are **I slid, I have slid, I am sliding**

slight *adjective*
1 small: *a slight cough* **2** thin: *a man of slight build*

slight *verb*
3 to treat rudely: *They slighted her by not inviting her to the party.*

Word Building: **slight** *noun* an insult
slightly *adverb: You are only slightly taller than me.*

slim *adjective*
slender or slight: *slim legs* | *a slim chance*

Word Building: other forms are **slimmer, slimmest** □ **slim** *verb* (**slimmed, slimming**)

slime *noun*
slippery wet matter, usually unpleasant: *Snails leave a trail of slime.*

Word Building: **slimy** *adjective* (**slimier, slimiest**) **sliminess** *noun*

sling *noun*
1 a piece of cloth looped around your neck to hold your arm if it is hurt **2** an old-fashioned weapon for throwing stones, made of a leather strap which is swung quickly round and round before releasing the stone

sling *verb*
3 to throw or fling: *to sling a stone*
4 to hang loosely: *to sling a coat across your shoulders*

Word Building: other verb forms are **I slung, I have slung, I am slinging**

slingshot *noun*
another word for **catapult**

slink *verb*
to creep quietly so as not to be noticed: *The dog slunk away with its tail between its legs.*

Word Building: other forms are **I slunk, I have slunk, I am slinking**

slip *verb*
1 to slide easily: *to slip a note under the door* | *The wet glass slipped from her hand.*
2 to fall over: *to slip on a polished floor*
3 to escape from: *The dog slipped its leash.* | *Your birthday slipped my mind.*

slip *noun*
4 a mistake: *to make a slip in adding up the bill* **5** a petticoat **6** a small sheet or piece: *a slip of paper*

Word Building: other verb forms are **I slipped, I have slipped, I am slipping**

slipper *noun*
a soft comfortable shoe for wearing indoors

slippery *adjective*
too smooth or wet to get a hold on: *slippery ice*

slippery dip *noun*
a steeply-sloping smooth metal structure which is fun to slide down

slit *noun*
a long straight cut or opening

Word Building: **slit** *verb* (**slit, slitting**): *to slit open an envelope*

slither *verb*
to slide along like a snake

sliver (rhymes with *river*) *noun*
a small thin piece: *a sliver of wood*

Word Building: **sliver** *verb*

slob *noun*
someone who is lazy and untidy

Word Use: this word is used as an insult
Word History: from an Irish word meaning "mud"

slobber *verb*
to dribble or drool

Word Building: **slobbery** *adjective*

slog *verb*
1 to hit hard: *She slogged the ball.*
2 to plod along heavily: *The weary hikers slogged up the hill.*

Word Building: other forms are **I slogged, I have slogged, I am slogging**

slogan (say *sloh-gən*) *noun*
a clever catchy saying used to advertise something

slop *verb*
to spill or splash: *Don't slop water over the side of the bath. / The milk slopped out of the cup.*

Word Building: other forms are **I slopped, I have slopped, I am slopping**

slope *verb*
1 to be higher at one end than the other: *The hill slopes steeply.*
slope *noun*
2 a slant or tilt: *the slope of a roof*
3 slopes a hilly area: *There will be snow on the southern slopes.*

Word Building: **sloping** *adjective*

sloppy *adjective*
1 wet and runny **2** too sentimental: *a sloppy love story* **3** loose or untidy: *a sloppy jumper / sloppy school work*

Word Building: other forms are **sloppier, sloppiest** □ **sloppily** *adverb* **sloppiness** *noun*

slosh *verb*
to pour or splash sloppily: *to slosh water over the floor / to slosh around in the mud*

slot *noun*
a small narrow slit or opening: *Put a coin in the slot.*

sloth (rhymes with *both*) *noun*
1 great laziness **2** a slow clumsy mammal which lives in the jungles of South America

Word Building: **slothful** *adjective*

slouch *verb*
to walk or sit without holding yourself up straight

Word Building: **slouch** *noun*

slouch hat *noun*
an army hat with the brim designed to be turned up on one side

slovenly (say *sluv-ən-lee*) *adjective*
dirty careless and untidy

Word Building: **slovenliness** *noun*

slow *adjective*
1 taking a long time: *a slow train / a slow learner* **2** behind the right time: *The clock is five minutes slow.*
slow *verb*
3 slow down to make or become slower

Word Building: **slowly** *adverb* **slowness** *noun*

sludge *noun*
soft muddy substance: *The drain is clogged with sludge.*

Word Building: **sludgy** *adjective*

slug[1] *noun*
1 a slimy creature like a snail without its shell **2** a small bullet

slug[2] *verb*
1 to punch hard: *to slug him in the eye*
2 to charge far too much: *They slugged me for fixing my bike.*

Word Use: this word is more suited to everyday language □ a similar word for definition 1 is **slog**
Word Building: other forms are **I slugged, I have slugged, I am slugging** □ **slug** *noun*

sluggish *adjective*
moving slowly with no energy

Word Building: **sluggishly** *adverb*

sluice (rhymes with *loose*) *noun*
1 a channel for water, fitted with a gate to control the water flow
sluice *verb*
2 to drain: *to sluice water from a pond*
3 to wash with running water

slum *noun*
a dirty overcrowded place in which poor people live

Word Building: **slummy** *adjective*

slumber *noun*
deep sleep

Word Building: **slumber** *verb*

slump *verb*
to drop heavily: *to slump into a chair*

Word Building: **slump** *noun*

slur *verb*
1 to pronounce unclearly: *Don't slur your words.* **2** to harm the good name of: *The newspaper article slurred the politician.*

Word Building: other forms are **I slurred, I have slurred, I am slurring** □ **slur** *noun*

slush *noun*
snow which is partly melted

Word Building: **slushy** *adjective*

sly *adjective*
1 cunning or deceitful **2 on the sly** secretly: *to take money on the sly*

Word Building: **slyly** *adverb*

smack[1] *verb*
in the phrase **smack of** to have a touch of: *His behaviour smacks of selfishness.*

Word Building: **smack** *noun*

smack[2] *verb*
1 to hit with the hand open **2 smack your lips** to make a noise with your lips as if you are looking forward to eating something good

Word Building: **smack** *noun*

small *adjective*
1 not big or great **2** ashamed or embarrassed: *to feel small* **3 small talk** conversation about things which are not important

Word Building: **small** *adverb: to cut the fruit up small*

smallpox *noun*
a serious infectious disease with a rash which leaves deep scars

smart *adjective*
1 clever or intelligent **2** quick **3** neat and fashionable: *a smart new suit*

smart *verb*
4 to sting or hurt: *A cut smarts if you bathe it with salt water.* | *to smart from an insult*

Word Building: **smarten** *verb* **smartly** *adverb*

smash *verb*
1 to break loudly into pieces: *to smash a plate* **2** to hit with great force: *to smash the ball over the net* | *The car smashed into the fence.*

smash *noun*
3 a loud crash **4** a record, film or play that is a great success

Word Use: definition 4 is also called a **smash-hit**

smear *verb*
1 to rub or spread: *to smear grease over the walls*

smear *noun*
2 a dirty mark or stain: *a smear of paint* **3** a slur on your good name

smell *verb*
1 to sense through the nose **2** to give off an odour: *The dinner smells delicious.*

smell *noun*
3 the ability to sense odours through the nose **4** an odour or scent: *flowers with a strong smell*

Word Building: other verb forms are **I smelled** or **I smelt, I have smelled** or **I have smelt, I am smelling** □ **smelly** *adjective* (**smellier, smelliest**)

smelt *verb*
to melt or refine ore in order to obtain metal: *to smelt iron*

Word Building: **smelter** *noun* the place where this is done

smile *verb*
to show you are happy or amused by widening your mouth and turning it up at the corners

Word Building: **smile** *noun*

smirk *verb*
to smile in a smug way that annoys people

Word Building: **smirk** *noun*

smith *noun*
someone who makes things out of metal: *Blacksmiths work with iron, silversmiths with silver.*

Word Building: **smithy** *noun* a blacksmith's workshop

smithereens *plural noun*
tiny pieces: *The cup smashed into smithereens.*

smock *noun*
a long loose shirt worn on top of your clothes to stop them getting dirty

Word Building: **smocking** *noun* a sort of embroidery used on baby's clothes **smock** *verb*

smog *noun*
a dirty cloud of smoke and fog

Word Building: **smoggy** *adjective* (**smoggier, smoggiest**)
Word History: a blended or portmanteau word made from *smoke* + *fog*

smoke *noun*
1 the cloud of gas and tiny particles given off when something burns: *Bushfires filled the air with smoke.* **2** a cigarette: *a packet of smokes*

smoke *verb*
3 to give off smoke: *The chimney is smoking.* **4** to breathe in the smoke of a cigarette while holding it between your lips **5** to treat with wood smoke as a preservative: *to smoke meat*

Word Building: **smoky** *adjective* (**smokier, smokiest**)

smokescreen *noun*
anything used to hide the truth or what you are really doing: *His excuse was simply a smokescreen.*

smooth *adjective*
1 even and without bumps or lumps
2 very pleasant in manner, especially when insincere: *a smooth talker*

smooth *verb*
3 to make even or level

Word Building: **smoothly** *adverb* **smoothness** *noun*

smorgasbord *noun*
a meal where you help yourself to a great variety of meats and salads

Word Use: this word comes from a Swedish word meaning "sandwich table"

smother (rhymes with *brother*) *verb*
1 to choke by keeping out air: *to smother a fire with sand | Don't cover your head with a plastic bag because you might smother.*
2 to cover all over: *She smothered her face with make-up.* **3** to protect too closely: *Her parents smother her and never allow her to play outside.*

smoulder (rhymes with *folder*) *verb*
to burn slowly giving off smoke but no flame

smudge *noun*
a dirty mark or smear

Word Building: **smudge** *verb*

smug *adjective*
very pleased with yourself: *a smug grin*

Word Building: **smugly** *adverb*
Word History: from a Dutch word meaning "neat"

smuggle *verb*
to carry secretly and illegally: *to smuggle rare birds out of the country*

Word Building: **smuggler** *noun* **smuggling** *noun*

smut *noun*
1 a smudge of soot or dirt **2** offensive or obscene talk

Word Building: **smutty** *adjective* (**smuttier, smuttiest**)

snack *noun*
1 a small quick meal: *a snack after school*
2 something that is very easy to do: *That test was a snack.*

Word Use: definition 2 is more suited to everyday language

snag *noun*
1 something sharp sticking out or lying on the bottom of a river **2** a problem or difficulty: *a snag in our plans* **3** a sausage

Word Use: definition 3 is more suited to everyday language
Word Building: **snag** *verb* (**snagged, snagging**)

snail *noun*
a small slow-moving animal with a soft body and a coiled shell, often found in gardens

snake *noun*
1 a long scaly creature without legs which slithers silently along the ground
2 snake in the grass someone who secretly does you harm

Word Building: **snaky** *adjective* (**snakier, snakiest**) spiteful or angry **snake** *verb* to twist and wind like the body of a snake

snap *verb*
1 to break with a sudden sharp sound: *to snap a biscuit in two | The rubber band snapped.* **2** to make a sudden biting movement: *The dog will snap if you tease it.* **3** to speak angrily and sharply
4 snap up to grab quickly: *to snap up a bargain*

snap *noun*
5 a sudden sharp sound or movement
6 an easy card game in which you try to be the first to call out when you see two matching cards

Word Building: other verb forms are **I snapped, I have snapped, I am snapping** □ **snappy** *adjective* (**snappier, snappiest**) quick or brisk **snap** *adjective* sudden: *a snap decision*

snapshot *noun*
an informal photograph taken quickly

snare (rhymes with *hair*) *noun*
a trap for catching birds and small animals

Word Building: **snare** *verb*

snarl[1] *verb*
to growl angrily or fiercely

Word Building: **snarl** *noun*

snarl[2] *noun*
a tangle or knot

Word Building: **snarl** *verb*

snatch *verb*
1 to take hold of suddenly: *to snatch a purse*

snatch *noun*
2 a sudden grab **3** a scrap or small part: *to overhear snatches of conversation*

sneak *verb*
1 to make a movement or take slyly and quietly: *to sneak in the room / to sneak a chocolate*
sneak *noun*
2 someone mean who tells tales and can't be trusted

Word Building: other verb forms are **I sneaked, I have sneaked, I am sneaking** □ **sneaky** *adjective* (**sneakier, sneakiest**) **sneakily** *adverb*

sneaker *noun*
a rubber-soled shoe made of canvas

sneer *verb*
to say or look in a nasty mocking way

Word Building: **sneer** *noun*

sneeze *verb*
1 to have a sudden noisy explosion of air, mostly through your mouth, because of irritation in your nose **2 not to be sneezed at** worth thinking about: *This offer is not to be sneezed at.*

Word Use: definition 2 is more suited to everyday language
Word Building: **sneeze** *noun*

sniff *verb*
to breathe in through the nose in a short sharp burst: *to sniff the air / to sniff with a cold*

Word Building: **sniff** *noun*

sniffle *verb*
1 to sniff continually because you have a cold or are trying not to cry
sniffle *noun*
2 the sniffles a cold with a runny nose

snigger *verb*
to give a rather rude laugh or giggle which you try to hide: *to snigger at a dirty joke*

Word Building: **snigger** *noun*

snip *verb*
to cut using small quick strokes of the scissors

Word Building: other forms are **I snipped, I have snipped, I am snipping** □ **snip** *noun*

sniper *noun*
someone who shoots from a place which is hidden or a long way from the target

Word Building: **snipe** *verb*

snivel *verb*
to sniffle noisily while you are crying

Word Building: other verb forms are **I snivelled, I have snivelled, I am snivelling**

snob *noun*
someone who looks down on people who are not wealthy, important or clever

Word Building: **snobbery** *noun* **snobbish** *adjective*

snooker *noun*
a game like billiards, played with balls of many colours

snoop *verb*
to creep around, prying into things

Word Building: **snoopy** *adjective*

snooze *noun*
a rest or short sleep

Word Use: this word is more suited to everyday language
Word Building: **snooze** *verb*

snore *verb*
to breathe with a loud rumbling noise while you're asleep

Word Building: **snore** *noun*

snorkel *noun*
a tube that lets you breathe fresh air as you swim face downwards in the water

Word Building: **snorkel** *verb* (**snorkelled, snorkelling**)
Word History: from a German word

snort *verb*
to force your breath out of your nose so that it makes a rough rumbling sound: *to snort with anger*

snout *noun*
the front part of an animal's face where the nose and jaws are

Word Use: a similar word is **muzzle**

snow *noun*
frozen rain drops which fall to the ground as tiny white flakes

Word Building: **snowy** *adjective* white **snow** *verb*

snowball *noun*
1 a pile of snow pressed into a ball
snowball *verb*
2 to pile up at a great rate: *The work is snowballing.*

snowman *noun*
a man-like figure made of hard packed snow

Word Building: the plural is **snowmen**

snub *verb*
1 to show dislike or contempt for, especially by ignoring
snub *noun*
2 an instance of this: *a deliberate snub*
snub *adjective*
3 short and turned up at the tip: *a snub nose*

Word Use: a similar word for definition 2 is **rebuff**
Word Building: other verb forms are **I snubbed, I have snubbed, I am snubbing**

snuff *noun*
powdered tobacco used for sniffing

snug *adjective*
comfortable and warm: *Our strong tent was snug despite the rain.*

Word Building: other forms are **snugger, snuggest**

snuggle *verb*
snuggle up to lie closely together for warmth or comfort: *The kittens snuggled up in their basket.*

so *adverb*
1 in the way shown or described: *Do it so.* **2** as told or described: *Is that so?* **3** to that extent: *Do not walk so fast.* **4** very: *You are so kind.* **5** for this reason: *Bananas are nutritious and so you should eat them often.* **6** about that number or amount: *a day or so ago* **7 and so forth** and the rest **8 just so** in perfect order **9 so-so** only fair: *I'm feeling so-so today.* **10 so that** **a** with the result that **b** in order that

Word Use: be careful – this sounds like **sew** and **sow**

soak *verb*
1 to lie or leave in liquid for a long time: *I like to soak in a bath after sport. | She soaked the clothes to loosen the dirt.* **2** to wet thoroughly **3 soak up** to take in or absorb

Word Building: **soak** *noun*

soap *noun*
a substance made out of fat, used for washing yourself or cleaning things

Word Building: **soap** *verb* **soapy** *adjective*

soap opera *noun*
a television series which tells a story about people's lives and problems, often in an over-emotional way

Word Use: this is more suited to everyday language
Word History: the name grew from the fact that soap manufacturers used to sponsor this type of entertainment

soar *verb*
1 to fly upwards **2** to fly at a great height hardly moving the wings: *The eagle soared over the valley.* **3** to rise to a great height: *Our hopes soared. | Prices are soaring.*

sob *verb*
1 to cry making a gulping noise as you breathe **2** to speak while doing this: *She sobbed her words of pity.*

Word Building: other forms are **I sobbed, I have sobbed, I am sobbing** □ **sob** *noun*

sober *adjective*
1 not drunk **2** quiet and serious: *The sad news put us in a sober mood.*

Word Building: **sober** *verb* **sobriety** *noun*

soccer *noun*
a form of football played with a round ball which you are not allowed to handle

sociable (say *soh-shə-bəl*) *adjective*
friendly, or wanting to be with other people

Word Building: **sociability** *noun* **sociableness** *noun* **sociably** *adverb*

social *adjective*
1 having to do with friendliness: *Our tennis club is as much a social club as a sporting one.* **2** having to do with fashionable people: *a social page in a newspaper* **3** having to do with human society, or the way it is organised: *social problems | social status*
social *noun*
4 a party or gathering: *a church social*

Word Building: **socially** *adverb*

socialise or **socialize** (say *soh-shəl-uyz*) *verb*
1 to train or educate so as to live according to the customs of society
2 to be friendly and mix with others at a party

Word Building: **socialisation** *noun*

socialism (say *soh-shəl-iz-əm*) *noun*
the political belief that all industry and wealth should be owned and controlled by the people as a whole

Word Use: compare this with **capitalism** and **communism**
Word Building: **socialist** *noun*

society (say *sə-suy-ə-tee*) *noun*
1 people as a whole: *human society*
2 people as a group in which there are divisions according to birth, education and occupation: *the middle class of society*
3 a group of people with a common interest: *a society for coin collectors*
4 companionship or company: *She enjoyed his society.* **5** rich people and their activities: *Some people enjoy reading about society in the social column of newspapers.*

Word Building: the plural is **societies**

sociology (say *soh-see-ol-ə-jee*) *noun*
the study of the development and organisation of human society

Word Building: **sociologist** *noun*

sock[1] *noun*
1 a garment that you wear under a shoe, covering the foot and the ankle and sometimes reaching up to the knee
2 pull your socks up to make more effort

sock[2] *verb*
to hit hard

Word Use: this is more suited to everyday language
Word Building: **sock** *noun*

socket *noun*
1 a hollow area which holds some part or thing: *an eye socket* **2** a device on the wall into which you plug an electric cord

sod *noun*
a square or oblong piece of grass which has been cut or torn out of a lawn or other turf

soda *noun*
1 a chemical compound containing sodium used for various purposes: *caustic soda / baking soda* **2** *a shortened form of* **soda-water** **3** a drink made with soda-water, fruit juices and ice-cream

Word History: from an Arabic word

soda-water *noun*
a fizzy drink made by filling water with bubbles of carbon dioxide

sodden *adjective*
soaked with a liquid: *sodden washing hanging in the rain*

sodium (say *soh-dee-əm*) *noun*
a soft, silver-white, metallic element found in salt

sofa *noun*
a long couch with a back and two sides

soft *adjective*
1 easily cut or pressed out of shape
2 smooth and pleasant to touch: *the soft fur of a kitten* **3** low in sound: *We could hardly hear her soft voice.* **4** not harsh or glaring: *soft light* **5** gentle or pitying: *She has a soft heart.* **6** not able to bear hardship: *He's too soft for a farmer's life.* **7 soft water** water in which soap lathers easily

Word Building: **soften** *verb* **softly** *adverb*

softball *noun*
a form of baseball played with a larger softer ball which is bowled underarm

soft drink *noun*
a drink which has no alcohol in it

software *noun*
a collection of programs used to control a computer

soggy *adjective*
1 soaked or thoroughly wet: *soggy ground*
2 damp and heavy like bread when it is not cooked enough

Word Building: other forms are **soggier, soggiest**

soil[1] *noun*
ground or earth, especially of the kind plants can grow in

soil[2] *verb*
to make or become dirty or stained

solar *adjective*
1 having to do with the sun: *a solar eclipse* **2** operated or produced by the heat of the sun: *solar energy*

solar system *noun*
the sun together with all the planets, moons and so on which revolve around it

solder *noun*
an alloy which can be melted easily and used to join metals together

Word Building: **solder** *verb*

soldier *noun*
1 someone who serves in an army
2 someone who serves any cause: *a soldier against poverty*
soldier *verb*
3 to serve as a soldier **4 soldier on** to continue doing something you have started

Word Building: **soldierly** *adjective*

sole[1] *adjective*
1 being the only one: *the sole remaining member of his family* **2** not shared: *the sole right to sell a property*

sole[2] *noun*
the underneath or bottom of your foot or shoe

sole[3] *noun*
any of a number of types of flat-bodied fishes with both eyes on the upper side

Word Building: the plural is **sole** or **soles**

solemn (say *sol-əm*) *adjective*
1 serious or sincere: *a solemn promise* **2** causing a grave mood or serious thoughts: *solemn music* **3** marked by formality or ritual: *a solemn ceremony*

Word Building: **solemnity** *noun* (**solemnities**) **solemnise** *verb* **solemnly** *adverb*

solenoid (say *sol-ə-noyd*) *noun*
a coil or wire in which a magnetic field is set up when electricity flows through it

solicitor (say *sə-lis-ə-tə*) *noun*
a lawyer who advises clients and prepares cases for a barrister to present in court

solid *adjective*
1 having length, breadth and thickness: *a solid shape* **2** having the inside filled: *a solid rubber ball* **3** consisting only of: *solid gold*
solid *noun*
4 something solid **5 solids** food that is not in liquid form

Word Building: **solidify** *verb* (**solidified, solidifying**) to make or become solid **solidity** *noun* **solidly** *adverb*

solidarity (say *sol-ə-da-rə-tee*) *noun*
a united front presented by members of a group with strongly-held common ideas and interests

soliloquy (say *sə-lil-ə-kwee*) *noun*
the act of talking when you are alone or when you are pretending to be alone, such as in a play

Word Building: the plural is **soliloquies**

solitary (say *sol-ə-tree*) *adjective*
1 quite alone **2** being the only one: *a solitary exception*

solitude (say *sol-ə-tyoohd*) *noun*
a state of being alone: *to enjoy a brief time of solitude*

solo *noun*
1 a musical performance by one person
solo *adjective*
2 performed or done alone: *a solo item | a solo flight*
solo *adverb*
3 alone: *He flew solo.*

soloist (say *soh-loh-əst*) *noun*
someone who performs a solo

solstice *noun*
one of the two times each year when the sun is furthest away from the equator and the longest or shortest day occurs. The first comes on about June 21, when the sun enters the sign of Cancer (the winter solstice) and the other comes on about December 22, when the sun enters the sign of Capricorn (the summer solstice).

soluble (say *sol-yə-bəl*) *adjective*
1 able to be dissolved: *Sugar is soluble in water.* **2** able to be solved: *a soluble problem*

Word Use: the opposite is **insoluble**
Word Building: **solubility** *noun*

solution *noun*
1 the solving of, or answer to a problem **2** a substance which is made up of one chemical, usually a solid, spread perfectly throughout another chemical, usually a liquid: *Sugar can be dissolved in tea to make a solution.*

solve *verb*
to explain or find the answer to: *He solved the mystery.*

solvent *noun*
1 a liquid substance that can dissolve other substances in it: *Water is a solvent for sugar.*
solvent *adjective*
2 having enough money to be able to pay your debts

Word Building: **solvency** *noun* the ability to pay your debts

sombre (say *som-bə*) *adjective*
gloomily dark or dull: *the sombre interior of the deserted castle | sombre clothes*

sombrero (say *som-brair-roh*) *noun*
a broad-brimmed hat worn in Spain, Mexico and some other countries

Word Building: the plural is **sombreros**
Word History: from a Spanish word meaning "shade"

some *adjective*
1 being a person or thing that has not been named: *some poor idiot* **2** certain: *some friends of mine | some changes were made* **3** great or important: *That was some storm!*

Word Use: definition 3 is more suited to everyday language

somehow *adverb*
in some way that is not made clear: *I've got to get home somehow.*

someone *pronoun*
somebody: *At last I can see someone I know.*

somersault (say *sum-ə-solt*) *noun*
a gymnastic movement in which you roll completely, heels over head

Word Building: **somersault** *verb*

something *pronoun*
1 a certain thing that has not been named
something *noun*
2 an important or valuable person or thing: *His singing is really something.*

sometimes *adverb*
now and then, or at times: *Sometimes I think I'm the only one who really cares.*

somewhere *adverb*
1 in or at some place that is not mentioned, or not known: *Somewhere over the rainbow.* **2** at some point in time: *The accident happened somewhere between three o'clock and five o'clock.*

son *noun*
1 the male child of someone **2** a man looked upon as having been affected by a particular thing: *a son of the land*

Word Use: be careful – this sounds like **sun**

sonar (say *soh-nah*) *noun*
a device for finding depth under water by measuring the time it takes to receive an echo from a sound

sonata (say *sə-nah-tə*) *noun*
a musical composition usually for one instrument accompanied by a piano

song *noun*
1 a short musical composition with words **2** musical sounds produced by birds **3 for a song** at a very low price

sonic *adjective*
1 having to do with sound waves
2 having to do with the speed of sound

son-in-law *noun*
the husband of your daughter

Word Building: the plural is **sons-in-law**

sonnet *noun*
a poem of fourteen lines in which the lines have to rhyme in a certain way

sonorous (say *son-ə-rəs*) *adjective*
sounding deep, loud and rich: *a sonorous voice*

Word Building: **sonority** *noun*

sook (rhymes with *book*) *noun*
someone who is shy, timid or cowardly

Word Use: this is mostly used about children
Word Building: **sooky** *adjective* (**sookier, sookiest**)

soon *adverb*
1 within a short time **2** quickly or promptly: *You came too soon.*

soot (rhymes with *foot*) *noun*
the black substance which sticks to the inside of a chimney when coal, wood, oil or other fuels are burned

Word Building: **sooty** *adjective* (**sootier, sootiest**)

soothe *verb*
1 to calm or comfort: *He soothed the frightened child.* **2** to relieve or lessen: *to soothe pain*

Word Building: **soothing** *adjective*

sophisticated (say *sə-fis-tə-kay-təd*) *adjective*
1 wise and experienced in the interests and pleasures of the world **2** intricate or complex: *sophisticated machinery*

Word Building: **sophistication** *noun*

soporific (say *sop-ə-rif-ik*) *adjective*
causing sleep or sleepiness

sopping *adjective*
very wet

soppy *adjective*
too sentimental: *a soppy love story*

Word Use: this word is more suited to everyday language
Word Building: other forms are **soppier, soppiest** □ **soppily** *adverb* **soppiness** *noun*

soprano (say *sə-prah-noh*) *noun*
1 the range of notes which can be sung by a woman or boy with a high voice
2 a woman or boy who sings in this range

Word Use: **soprano** is the highest range of singing voices, with **alto** next below
Word Building: the plural is **sopranos** □ **soprano** *adjective: a soprano cornet*

sorbet (say *saw-bay, saw-bət*) *noun*
a frozen dessert made with fruit and egg-whites, often used to refresh your mouth between courses of a meal

sorcery (say *saw-sə-ree*) *noun*
magic, especially black magic using evil spirits

Word Building: **sorcerer** *noun* **sorceress** *noun*

sordid *adjective*
1 morally mean or nasty: *a sordid way of life* **2** dirty or filthy: *sordid surroundings*

Word Building: **sordidness** *noun*

sore *adjective*
1 painful or hurting **2** annoyed or offended: *What are you sore about?*

Word Use: definition 2 is more suited to everyday language
Word Building: **sore** *noun*

sorrow *noun*
grief, sadness or the feeling of being sorry

Word Building: **sorrowful** *adjective*

sorry *adjective*
1 feeling sad because you have done something wrong **2** feeling pity

Word Building: other forms are **sorrier, sorriest**

sort *noun*
1 a particular kind or type: *Cod are a sort of fish.* **2 of sorts** of a kind that is neither good nor bad: *He is a friend of sorts.* **3 out of sorts** not in good health or in a good humour **4 sort of** in some way: *I sort of hoped he would come.*
sort *verb*
5 to arrange or group according to type or kind

SOS (say *es-oh-es*) *noun*
an urgent call for help: *The ship sent an SOS by radio.*

Word History: probably chosen because the Morse code for these letters is clear and easy, but some people say the letters stand for "Save Our Souls"

soufflé (say *sooh-flay*) *noun*
a light baked dish, usually with fish or cheese to give it flavour, made fluffy with beaten egg-whites

Word History: the accent over the "e" is a clue that this word was originally French

soul *noun*
1 the unseen or spiritual part of a person believed to survive after you die
2 human being: *She's a kind soul.*

sound[1] *noun*
1 something heard as a result of vibrations in the air reaching your ear
sound[1] *verb*
2 to make a sound: *The trumpet sounded.*
3 to cause to make a sound: *Sound the trumpets.* **4** to give a certain feeling when heard or read: *That sounds strange.*

sound[2] *adjective*
1 healthy or in good condition: *a sound heart* **2** unbroken or deep: *sound sleep*
3 reliable or good: *sound advice*
4 sound as a bell in perfect condition

sound[3] *verb*
1 to measure or try the depth of by letting down a lead weight on the end of a line
2 sound out to try by indirect ways to find the feelings of: *Sound her out about going for a swim.*

sound[4] *noun*
a narrow stretch of water joining two larger bodies of water or between an island and the mainland

soundtrack *noun*
1 the strip beside a moving picture film which carries the sound recording
2 such a recording transferred to a record, cassette or compact disc

soup *noun*
1 a liquid food flavoured with meat, fish or vegetables **2 in the soup** in trouble

Word Use: definition 2 is more suited to everyday language
Word History: from a French word meaning "soup" or "broth"

sour *adjective*
1 having an acid taste such as that of lemons **2** cross or irritable: *He's in a sour mood today.*

Word Building: **sour** *verb* **sourish** *adjective*

source *noun*
the place, thing or person from which something comes: *The Murray River has its source in the Snowy Mountains. | That book was the source of my information. | He is the source of that rumour.*

south *noun*
the direction which is to your left when you face the setting sun in the west

Word Use: the opposite direction is **north**
Word Building: **south** *adverb* **south** *adjective* **southern** *adjective*

Southern Cross *noun*
the constellation you can see in the southern sky whose four chief stars are in the shape of a cross

souvenir (say *sooh-və-near*) *noun*
something you keep as a memory of a place or event

souvlaki (say *soohv-lah-kee*) *plural noun*
a Greek dish of cooked meat, raw onion, tomato and lettuce wrapped in pitta bread

sovereign (say <u>sov</u>-rən) *noun*
1 a king or queen
sovereign *adjective*
2 having highest rank, power or authority

Word Use: a similar word for definition 1 is **monarch**
Word Building: **sovereignty** *noun*

sow[1] (rhymes with *go*) *verb*
1 to scatter in the earth for growth: *to sow wheat seeds* **2** to scatter seeds over: *to sow a field with wheat*

Word Use: be careful – this sounds like **sew** and **so**
Word Building: other forms are **I sowed, I have sown** or **I have sowed, I am sowing**

sow[2] (rhymes with *how*) *noun*
an adult female pig

Word Use: the male is a **boar;** the young is a **piglet**

soya bean *noun*
a kind of plant seed which can be eaten as a bean or grown for its oil

Word Use: this is also called **soy** or **soybean**

spa *noun*
1 a place where there is a flow of mineral water from the earth **2** a bath or swimming pool which has heated, bubbly water pumped into it

space *noun*
1 the continuous openness in which everything exists: *There is space all around us.* **2** the space outside the earth's atmosphere: *to send a rocket into space* **3** a part or area of space: *This table takes up a lot of space.* **4** the distance between things: *The trees were planted at equal spaces apart.* **5** a blank area on a surface: *We put a space between each word when we write.* **6** a period of time: *He arrived after a space of two hours.*
space *verb*
7 to arrange with spaces in between: *Space yourselves so that you have room to swing your arms.*

Word Use: definition 2 is also called **outer space**

spaceship *noun*
a vehicle that can travel to outer space

space shuttle *noun*
a spaceship that carries people and equipment between earth and a satellite and which can land and be used again

spacious *adjective*
having a lot of space: *a spacious house*

Word Use: a similar word is **roomy**
Word Building: **spaciousness** *noun*

spade[1] *noun*
a tool for digging, with a long handle and a metal blade that you push into the ground with your foot

spade[2] *noun*
a black shape like an upside-down heart with a stem, used on playing cards

spaghetti (say spə-<u>get</u>-ee) *noun*
a food made from flour, water and salt, formed into long thin strips and cooked by boiling

span *noun*
1 the distance between the two furthest edges or ends of something: *the span of a bridge | the span of your hand* **2** the full stretch of anything: *Humans have a longer life span than animals.*
span *verb*
3 to stretch over or across: *The bridge spans the river.*

Word Building: other verb forms are **I spanned, I have spanned, I am spanning**

spangle *noun*
a small piece of something that glitters: *an evening dress covered with spangles*

Word Building: **spangled** *adjective*

spaniel *noun*
a kind of dog with a long silky coat and drooping ears

spank *verb*
to hit as a punishment, usually with the open hand

Word Building: **spank** *noun* **spanking** *noun*

spanner *noun*
a tool for gripping and turning something, such as a nut on a bolt

spar[1] *noun*
a strong pole, such as a mast on a ship

spar[2] *verb*
to punch lightly or make punching movements: *The boxers sparred at each other for practice.*

Word Building: other forms are **I sparred, I have sparred, I am sparring** □ **spar** *noun*

spare (rhymes with *hair*) *verb*
1 to stop yourself from destroying or hurting: *The king spared his enemy's life.* **2** to show consideration for: *I spared his feelings.* **3** to part with or let go: *Can you spare a few dollars?*

spare *adjective*
4 extra: *a spare tyre* **5** free for extra use: *spare time* **6** lean or thin: *a spare physique*

spare *noun*
7 something that is extra: *This light bulb is blown and we haven't a spare.*

spark *noun*
1 a tiny piece of burning material thrown up by a fire **2** a sudden letting out of electricity, usually with a flash of light **3** a small showing of something: *a spark of intelligence*

spark *verb*
4 to send out sparks **5** to set going: *His speech sparked some interest.*

sparkle *verb*
1 to burn or shine with little flashes of light **2** to be lively or brilliant: *The conversation sparkled.*

Word Building: **sparkle** *noun*

spark plug *noun*
a part in an engine that gives out an electric spark which sets fire to the fuel in each cylinder

sparrow *noun*
a small brown bird which was first brought to Australia to destroy insects

sparse *adjective*
thinly spread out or scattered: *a sparse population*

Word Building: **sparsely** *adverb* **sparseness** *noun* **sparsity** *noun*

spasm *noun*
1 a sudden uncontrolled movement of your muscles **2** a sudden short burst of activity or feeling: *to work in spasms | a spasm of rage*

Word Building: **spasmodic** *adjective*

spastic *noun*
someone who is partly paralysed because of a kind of brain damage

spate *noun*
a sudden pouring out: *a spate of words*

spatial (say *spay-shəl*) *adjective*
having to do with space: *That painter has a good spatial sense.*

spatula (say *spat-chə-lə*) *noun*
a tool with a flat bendable blade, used for mixing or spreading such things as paint or food

spawn *noun*
a mass of eggs given out by fish and other water creatures

Word History: from a Latin word meaning "expand"

speak *verb*
1 to give out the sounds of words in an ordinary voice **2** to have a conversation or tell by speaking **3** to give a speech or lecture **4** to be able to use a particular language: *Can you speak Italian?*

Word Building: other forms are **I spoke, I have spoken, I am speaking**

speaker *noun*
1 someone who speaks, especially before an audience **2 the Speaker** the person who controls the meeting of a house of parliament

spear *noun*
a weapon which consists of a long pole with a sharp pointed end

Word Building: **spear** *verb*

spear gun *noun*
a gun that throws out a spear, used in underwater fishing

special *adjective*
1 of a particular or distinct kind: *a special bus for schoolchildren | a new car with special fittings* **2** more important than or different from what is ordinary or usual: *a dress for a special occasion*

special *noun*
3 something which is special, particularly something sold at a special cheap price

Word Building: **specially** *adverb* particularly

specialise or **specialize** *verb*
to concentrate on a special kind of work or study: *She specialises in Australian history.*

specialist *noun*
someone who studies or is good at a particular subject or area of work, particularly a doctor: *to go and see a skin specialist*

speciality (say *spesh-ee-al-ə-tee*) *noun*
another word for **specialty**

specialty (say *spesh-əl-tee*) *noun*
a particular kind of study, work or product that someone specialises in: *The surgeon's specialty is kidneys. | This restaurant's specialty is spaghetti.*

species (say *spee-seez, spee-sheez*) *noun*
one of the groups into which animals and plants are divided according to their characteristics

Word Building: the plural is **species**

specific (say *spə-sif-ik*) *adjective*
1 particular: *I want the specific kind of paper I mentioned, not something similar.* **2** giving definite details: *a specific description*

Word Building: **specifically** *adverb*

specification (say *spes-ə-fə-kay-shən*) *noun*
1 the act of specifying: *the specification of your requirements* **2** an item in a detailed description of the measurements and materials to be used for something you plan to make: *the builder's specifications for the extensions to our house*

specify (say *spes-ə-fuy*) *verb*
to state with definite details: *You must specify how many chairs you will need.*

Word Building: other forms are **I specified, I have specified, I am specifying**

specimen (say *spes-ə-mən*) *noun*
a single thing or part taken as being typical of a whole group or mass: *This poem is a specimen of my work. | The doctor took a specimen of my blood for tests.*

speck *noun*
a very small spot or bit: *a brown dress with specks of green | a speck of dust*

Word Building: **specked** *adjective*

speckle *noun*
1 a small spot or mark
speckle *verb*
2 to mark with speckles: *Dust speckled his coat.*

Word Building: **speckled** *adjective*

spectacle *noun*
1 anything seen, especially something that draws your attention: *The storm made a great spectacle.* **2** a large public show or display **3 spectacles** *another name for* **glasses**

Word Building: **spectacular** *adjective*

spectator *noun*
someone who watches something: *spectators at a football game*

spectre (say *spek-tə*) *noun*
another name for a **ghost**

Word Building: **spectral** *adjective*

spectrum *noun*
1 the band of colours which is produced when white light is split up **2** a range of ideas, beliefs or types: *the spectrum of public opinion*

Word History: from a Latin word meaning "appearance" or "form"

speculate *verb*
to think or have an opinion without certain knowledge: *She speculated on her chances of winning.*

Word Building: **speculation** *noun* **speculative** *adjective* **speculator** *noun*

speech *noun*
1 the ability to speak **2** a talk given in front of an audience: *The headmistress made a long speech at assembly.* **3** the way someone speaks: *Your speech is not clear enough.*

speed *noun*
1 quickness in moving, going, or doing something
speed *verb*
2 to move or make move quickly: *He sped on his way. | to speed plans* **3** to drive a vehicle faster than is allowed by law
4 speed up to go or do more quickly

Word Building: other verb forms are **I sped** or **I speeded, I have sped** or **I have speeded, I am speeding** □ **speedy** *adjective* (**speedier, speediest**) **speedily** *adverb* **speedster** *noun*

speedometer *noun*
an instrument on a vehicle that shows how fast it is travelling

spell[1] *verb*
1 to say or write the letters of a word in order: *She can spell well.* **2** to be the letters that make up a word: *The letters "m-a-t" spell "mat".* **3** to mean: *That noise in the engine spells trouble.*

Word Building: other forms are **I spelt** or **I spelled, I have spelt** or **I have spelled, I am spelling** □ **spelling** *noun*

spell[2] *noun*
1 a group of words that is supposed to have magic power: *The witch chanted a spell.* **2** a fascinating power: *She has him in her spell.*

spell[3] *noun*
1 a period of work: *I will take a spell at digging now.* **2** a short period of anything: *a spell of cold weather* **3** a period of rest: *You should take a spell or you will get tired.*

spend *verb*
1 to pay out: *I spent a lot of money today.* **2** to pass: *They spent the holidays at the beach.* **3** to use up: *He has spent all his anger.*

Word Building: other forms are **I spent, I have spent, I am spending** □ **spender** *noun*

spendthrift *noun*
someone who spends their money wastefully

sperm *noun*
one of the cells produced by a male that can join with an egg or ovum to develop into a new individual

spew *verb*
to vomit

Word Use: this word is more suited to everyday language

sphere (say *sfear*) *noun*
1 something completely round in shape, such as a ball or a planet **2** an area of activity: *He works in the sphere of education.*

Word Building: **spherical** *adjective*

spice *noun*
1 a substance made from a plant which is used to flavour or preserve food: *Pepper and cinnamon are spices.* **2** something that adds interest: *You need to give your story some spice.*

Word Building: **spicy** *adjective* (**spicier, spiciest**) **spiciness** *noun*
Word History: from a Latin word meaning "species"

spider *noun*
an eight-legged creature, like an insect but without wings, which usually spins a web and is sometimes venomous

Word Building: **spidery** *adjective*

spike[1] *noun*
1 a sharp pointed piece or part: *a fence with spikes on it* **2 spikes** a pair of shoes with sharp metal pieces on the bottom, worn by runners or other athletes to stop them slipping

Word Building: **spiky** *adjective* (**spikier, spikiest**) **spike** *verb*

spike[2] *noun*
the part of a cereal plant, such as wheat, that contains the grains

spill *verb*
1 to run or fall from a container: *The milk is spilling over.* **2** to make run or fall from a container: *I have spilt the cereal.*

Word Building: other forms are **I spilt** or **I spilled, I have spilt** or **spilled, I am spilling** □ **spill** *noun* **spillage** *noun*

spin *verb*
1 to make thread by twisting and winding fibres, such as cotton or wool **2** to form by producing a long moist thread from the body: *Spiders spin webs.* **3** to turn or make turn around and around very fast: *The top is spinning. / She spun a coin.*
4 spin out to make last a long time: *to spin out a story*

spin *noun*
5 a spinning or whirling movement
6 a short quick journey: *Let's take the car for a spin.*

Word Building: other verb forms are **I spun, I have spun, I am spinning** □ **spinner** *noun* **spinning** *noun*

spinach (say *spin-ich*) *noun*
a plant with large green leaves which are eaten as a vegetable

Word History: from an Arabic word

spindle *noun*
1 a rod used to twist or wind the thread in spinning **2** a part of a machine which turns round or on which something turns

spindly *adjective*
long and thin: *a spindly plant*

spin-dry *verb*
to dry by spinning in a machine so that the moisture is taken out: *to spin-dry clothes*

Word Building: other forms are **I spin-dried, I have spin-dried, I am spin-drying** □ **spin-drier** *noun* **spin-dryer** *noun*

spine *noun*
1 the column of bones in your back
2 a thorn on a plant **3** a stiff pointed part on an animal, such as on an echidna
4 the part of a book's cover that holds the front and back together

Word Building: **spiny** *adjective* (**spinier, spiniest**) having spines or leaves shaped like spines **spinal** *adjective* having to do with your spine

spinifex (say *spin-ə-feks*) *noun*
a kind of spiny grass

spinnaker (say *spin-ə-kə*) *noun*
a large triangular sail

spinning wheel *noun*
a machine for spinning consisting of a spindle turned around by a large wheel driven by your hand or foot

spin-off *noun*
something useful that has come into being as a result of something larger or more important: *The non-stick frying pan was a spin-off of space research.*

spinster *noun*
a woman who has not been married

spiny anteater *noun*
another name for an **echidna**

spiral *noun*
1 a curve that winds around and around away from a centre: *a spring in the shape of a spiral*
spiral *verb*
2 to move in the shape of a spiral: *Smoke spiralled from the chimney*

Word Building: other verb forms are **it spiralled, it has spiralled, it is spiralling** □ **spiral** *adjective: a spiral staircase*

spire *noun*
a tall pointed part of a building, usually on a roof or tower: *the spire of a church*

spirit *noun*
1 *another name for* **soul** **2** a supernatural being **3** temper or character: *a man with a generous spirit* **4** feeling or mood: *team spirit / the spirit of Christmas* **5** general meaning or intention: *the spirit of an agreement* **6** lively courage: *I like him for his spirit.* **7 spirits** **a** the state of your mind: *She is in high spirits today.*
b strong alcoholic drink
spirit *verb*
8 to carry mysteriously or secretly: *He was spirited away by his friends before the police arrived.*

Word Building: **spirited** *adjective* showing lively courage

spiritual *adjective*
1 having to do with or interested in the spirit rather than the body: *a spiritual attitude / a spiritual person* **2** having to do with holy, religious, or supernatural things: *a spiritual leader*

Word Use: the opposite of definition 1 is **worldly**
Word Building: **spirituality** *noun*

spit[1] *verb*
1 to force out saliva from your mouth: *Don't spit on the footpath.* **2** to send out from your mouth: *She spat her lolly out.*
3 to fall in light scattered drops: *It is spitting with rain.* **4** to make a noise like spitting: *Fat was spitting in the pan.*
spit[1] *noun*
5 saliva, especially when spat out

Word Building: other verb forms are **I spat, I have spat, I am spitting**

spit[2] *noun*
1 a sharp pointed rod which is pushed through meat for roasting it over a fire or grilling it in an oven **2** a narrow area of land jutting out into the water

spite *noun*
1 a bad-tempered wish to annoy or hurt someone else: *He had no reason for hitting her except spite.* **2 in spite of** without taking notice of: *We will play in spite of the bad weather.*

Word Use: a similar word for definition 1 is **malice**
Word Building: **spite** *verb* **spiteful** *adjective*

splash *verb*
1 to wet by scattering with drops of liquid or mud **2** to fall in drops: *Rain splashed on the window.* **3** to make fly about in drops: *The baby splashed the bath water.*
splash *noun*
4 the act or sound of splashing **5** a mark made by splashing **6** a patch of colour or light: *a splash of red on a white background* **7 make a splash** to be widely noticed: *She made a splash in her new clothes.*

Word Building: **splashy** *adjective*

splendid *adjective*
1 magnificent or grand: *a splendid sight / a splendid victory* **2** extremely good: *a splendid performance*

Word Building: **splendidly** *adverb* **splendour** *noun*

splice *verb*
to join by twisting threads together or overlapping timber: *to splice ropes / to splice pieces of wood*

splint *noun*
a thin piece of something stiff, such as wood, used to hold a broken or injured bone in position

splinter *noun*
a long, thin, sharp piece broken off from something hard, such as wood, metal or glass

Word Building: **splinter** *verb*

split *verb*
1 to separate or break apart, especially from end to end: *The ends of my hair are splitting. / He split the apple in two.*
2 to divide up in any way **3** to divide in opinion or feeling: *The argument split the family.* **4 split up** to stop living together or stop being friends

split *noun*
5 the act of splitting **6** a break or division caused by splitting: *a split in a dress | a split in public opinion*
7 the splits an exercise in which you spread your legs apart along the floor until they stretch out at right angles to your body

Word Building: other verb forms are **I split, I have split, I am splitting**

splurge *verb*
to spend extravagantly or wastefully: *She splurged all her money on a taxi.*

Word Building: **splurge** *noun*
Word History: a blended or portmanteau word made from *splash* + *surge*

splutter *verb*
1 to talk quickly or in a confused way: *He spluttered with rage.* **2** to make a popping noise, as boiling fat does

Word Building: **splutter** *noun* **splutterer** *noun*

spoil *verb*
1 to damage or ruin **2** to damage the nature or character of by giving way to demands or temper: *to spoil a child*
3 to go bad: *The food will spoil if you don't put it away.*

Word Building: other verb forms are **I spoiled** or **spoilt, I have spoiled** or **I have spoilt, I am spoiling**

spoke *noun*
one of the rods, bars or wires that connect the rim of a wheel to the hub or centre, as on a bicycle or steering wheel

spokesperson *noun*
someone who speaks on behalf of someone else

Word Building: **spokesman** *noun* (**spokesmen**) **spokeswoman** *noun* (**spokeswomen**)

sponge (say *spunj*) *noun*
1 a material with lots of holes for soaking up liquid, used especially for wiping and cleaning **2** a kind of sea creature whose rubbery absorbent skeleton can be used for washing and cleaning **3** a light cake made from well-beaten eggs, flour and sugar

sponge *verb*
4 to wash, wipe and clean with a sponge
5 to live at someone else's expense: *He sponged on his uncle.*

Word Use: definition 5 is more suited to everyday language
Word Building: **spongy** *adjective*

sponsor *noun*
a person or group who supports someone or something, often with money

Word Building: **sponsor** *verb* **sponsorship** *noun*

spontaneous *adjective*
happening naturally and, often, unexpectedly: *spontaneous growth | spontaneous applause*

Word Building: **spontaneity** *noun* **spontaneously** *adverb*

spoof *noun*
a humorous imitation: *He did a spoof of the prime minister.*

Word Use: this is more suited to everyday language
Word Building: **spoof** *verb* **spoofer** *noun*

spook *noun*
a ghost: *The attic is full of spooks.*

Word Use: this is more suited to everyday language
Word Building: **spook** *verb* **spooked** *adjective* **spooky** *adjective*

spool *noun*
the cylinder or bobbin on which something, such as wire, thread or film, is wound

spoon *noun*
a utensil with a rounded end attached to a handle, which is used for stirring or lifting food and other things

spoor *noun*
the track left by a wild animal

sporadic (say *spə-rad-ik*) *adjective*
irregular and not very frequent: *Apart from the sporadic rain the weather was marvellous.*

Word Use: another word of similar meaning is **occasional**
Word Building: **sporadically** *adverb*

spore *noun*
a seed or germ cell

sporran *noun*
the pouch of fur worn by Scottish Highlanders at the front of the kilt

Word History: from a Gaelic word, a language of the ancient Celtic people and their modern ancestors in Ireland and Scotland

sport *noun*
1 something done for pleasure or exercise, usually needing some bodily skill
2 playful joking: *It was meant in sport.*
3 someone who is fair-minded or good-natured: *She's a good sport.*

Word Building: **sporting** *adjective* **sportive** *adjective* **sporty** *adjective*

sports *noun*
athletics or other similar sporting activities

Word Building: **sports** *adjective: sports day / sports coat* **sportsman** *noun* **sportswoman** *noun*

sports car *noun*
a fast car, usually a two-seater

spot *noun*
1 a small, usually round, mark: *There's a spot on your tie.* **2** a place: *We found a nice spot to have a picnic.* **3 on the spot** **a** instantly: *She bought it on the spot.* **b** in an awkward situation: *Her question put him on the spot.*
spot *verb*
4 to mark or stain: *This material spots easily. / You have spotted your jacket.*
5 to see or notice: *I couldn't spot him in the crowd.*

Word Building: other verb forms are **I spotted, I have spotted, I am spotting** □ **spotted** *adjective* **spotty** *adjective*

spotlight *noun*
a lamp with a strong narrow beam, such as used in the theatre or attached to cars

Word Building: **spotlight** *verb* (**spotlit** or **spotlighted, spotlighting**)

spouse (rhymes with *house*) *noun*
your husband or wife

spout *noun*
the tube or liplike part of a container from which water or other contents are poured

Word Building: **spout** *verb* to pour out

sprain *verb*
to twist and bruise, without actually putting out of place or breaking: *She sprained her ankle.*

Word Building: **sprain** *noun*

sprawl *verb*
1 to lie or sit with your limbs stretched out: *He sprawled all over the couch.*
2 to spread out in an untidy or careless way: *Her writing sprawled all over the page.*

Word Building: **sprawl** *noun*

spray[1] *noun*
a fine stream of droplets, such as one thrown by a wave or jet of water

Word Building: **spray** *verb*

spray[2] *noun*
a single stem, or a small bunch of flowers: *She had a spray of jasmine pinned to her dress.*

spread (rhymes with *bed*) *verb*
1 to extend, or stretch out: *The rain is spreading south. / She spread the cloth on the table.* **2** to scatter, or send around: *to spread germs / to spread the news*
3 to put on in a thin layer: *to spread butter*
4 to cover with a thin layer: *She spread the bread with jam.*
spread *noun*
5 anything which is spread on bread, such as jam or soft cheese **6** a large meal or feast

Word Use: definition 6 is more suited to everyday language
Word Building: other verb forms are **I spread, I have spread, I am spreading**

spree *noun*
1 a lively time of fun **2** an extravagant outing: *a shopping spree*

sprightly *adjective*
lively and merry: *a sprightly tune*

spring *verb*
1 to move or leap upwards with sudden energy: *to spring into the air / The dog springs into her arms.* **2** to arise or happen: *Farms are springing up on the city's outskirts.* **3** to come: *Where do you spring from?*
spring *noun*
4 a leap or pounce **5** a coil of wire which bounces back when it is stretched
6 the season of the year after winter and before summer **7** the ability to bounce back: *The mattress hasn't much spring left.*
8 a flow of water from the ground: *a hot spring*

Word Building: other verb forms are **I sprang, I have sprung, I am springing** □ **spring** *adjective* **springiness** *noun* **springy** *adjective*

springboard *noun*
a board with a lot of bounce in it, used for diving or vaulting

spring-clean *verb*
to clean thoroughly, as people used to do each spring: *to spring-clean a house*

Word Building: **spring-clean** *noun* **spring-cleaning** *noun*

sprinkle *verb*
1 to scatter here and there, or in small quantities **2** to rain slightly

Word Building: **sprinkle** *noun* **sprinkler** *noun*

sprint *verb*
to race at top speed, especially over a short distance

Word Building: **sprint** *noun* **sprinter** *noun*

sprocket *noun*
a toothed wheel that meshes with the links of a chain such as the one on a bicycle

sprout *verb*
1 to grow, or send up shoots: *He is trying to sprout plants from seed.* | *The bulb has sprouted.*
sprout *noun*
2 a shoot **3** *another name for a* **brussels sprout**

spruce[1] *noun*
an evergreen tree with fine needle-like leaves, and cones

spruce[2] *adjective*
stylish or smart: *He looks very spruce in his new suit.*

Word Building: **spruce up** *verb* to smarten

spry *adjective*
nimble or active: *The old man is still very spry.*

Word Building: other forms are **spryer, spryest** □ **spryly** *adverb*

spud *noun*
1 a potato **2** a spade-like tool for digging up weeds

Word Use: definition 1 is more suited to everyday language
Word History: from a Middle English word for "a kind of knife"

spunk *noun*
1 courage **2** someone who is good-looking

Word Use: definition 2 is more suited to everyday language
Word Building: **spunky** *adjective* (**spunkier, spunkiest**)

spur *noun*
1 a sharp instrument worn on the heel of a riding boot to urge a horse to go faster **2** anything which makes work go faster or urges you on **3** something looking like a spur, such as the horny piece on some birds feet, or a ridge rising up to a mountain range **4 on the spur of the moment** suddenly or without preparation

Word Building: **spur** *verb* (**spurred, spurring**)

spurn (say *spern*) *verb*
to reject or scorn: *She spurned his offer of help.*

spurt *verb*
to flow or release suddenly: *Blood spurted from the wound.* | *The chimney spurted a cloud of smoke.*

Word Building: **spurt** *noun* a sudden rush

sputnik *noun*
a satellite placed in orbit around the earth, especially an early Soviet model

spy *noun*
1 someone who secretly watches and reports others' activities
spy *verb*
2 to watch secretly, and report **3** to see: *I can't spy her yet.*

Word Building: the plural form of the noun is **spies** □ other verb forms are **I spied, I have spied, I am spying** □ **spying** *noun*

squabble (rhymes with *wobble*) *noun*
a small unimportant quarrel: *They are good friends in spite of their squabbles.*

Word Building: **squabble** *verb*

squad (rhymes with *rod*) *noun*
a small group taking part in a shared activity: *a squad of cleaners* | *the football squad*

squadron (say *skwod-rən*) *noun*
a fighting unit in the navy or the airforce

squalid (say *skwol-əd*) *adjective*
dirty or filthy: *a squalid hovel*

squall *noun*
a sudden strong wind

Word Building: **squall** *verb*

squalor (say *skwol-ə*) *noun*
dirt and poverty

squander (say *skwon-də*) *verb*
to spend or use wastefully

square *noun*
1 a shape with four equal sides and four right angles **2** an open public place in a town **3** an instrument which is used to draw and check right angles **4** a number multiplied by itself: *The square of 2 is 2 × 2, or 4.* **5** someone who is old-fashioned in their likes and appearance

square *verb*
6 to make straight or square
7 to multiply by itself: *If you add 2 and 3 then square the result, you get 25.*
8 to agree: *It doesn't square with the facts.*

square *adjective*
9 in the form of a right angle: *a square corner* **10** cube-shaped or nearly so: *a square box* **11** equal to a square with sides of the stated length: *a square metre* **12** even or level: *The two sides aren't quite square.* **13** paid up: *We are square now.* **14** fair: *a square deal* **15** full or complete: *a square meal* **16** old-fashioned in looks or behaviour

Word Use: definitions 5 and 16 are more suited to everyday language
Word Building: **square** *adverb* **squarely** *adverb*

square dance *noun*
a country dance for couples, in which someone calls or sings the steps to be followed

square root *noun*
the number which, when multiplied by itself, gives the stated number: *The square root of 16 is 4.*

squash[1] (say *skwosh*) *verb*
1 to flatten or crush: *The wheel squashed his hat.* **2** to put down: *to squash the rebellion*

squash[1] *noun*
3 a game for two players with racquets and a small rubber ball, played in a small court with walls **4** a fizzy fruit drink

squash[2] (say *skwosh*) *noun*
a round vegetable like a marrow

squat (say *skwot*) *verb*
1 to sit in a crouching position **2** to live without permission on land or property which you don't own

squat *adjective*
3 short and thickset: *a squat figure*

Word Building: other verb forms are **I squatted, I have squatted, I am squatting** □ **squat** *noun* **squatness** *noun*

squatter (say *skwot-ə*) *noun*
1 a rich landowner **2** someone who lives without permission in a place they don't own

squaw *noun*
a woman of a North American Indian tribe

Word History: from an Algonquian (a language of some American Indian tribes) word for "woman"

squawk *verb*
to make a loud unpleasant cry: *The chickens squawked when the fox chased them.*

Word Building: **squawk** *noun*

squeak *verb*
to make a high-pitched cry or a creaking noise: *A mouse squeaked. / The gate squeaks.*

Word Building: **squeaky** *adjective* (**squeakier, squeakiest**) **squeak** *noun* **squeakily** *adverb*

squeal *verb*
to make a sudden high-pitched cry, as if in pain or fear

Word Building: **squeal** *noun*

squeeze *verb*
1 to press hard, so as to remove something: *to squeeze an orange*
2 to cram: *to squeeze clothes into a bag*
3 to hug or hold close **4** to force a way: *They squeezed through the crowd.*

squeeze *noun*
5 a tight fit: *She's wearing the jacket but it's a bit of a squeeze.* **6** a small amount of something got by squeezing: *a squeeze of lemon* **7 a tight squeeze** a difficult situation

squid *noun*
a sea animal with a soft body and no backbone, which has tentacles attached to its head

Word Use: this is called **calamari** when it is cooked

squint *verb*
1 to have both your eyes turned towards your nose **2** to look indirectly, such as by a quick glance or with half-closed eyes

Word Building: **squint** *noun* **squinting** *adjective*

squire *noun*
1 an English country gentleman
2 a young nobleman attending a medieval knight

Word Building: **squire** *verb* to attend

squirm *verb*
to wriggle uncomfortably: *to squirm with embarrassment*

squirrel *noun*
a bushy-tailed animal found in Europe, Asia and North America, which lives in trees and hoards nuts and acorns

squirt *verb*
to wet with a jet of liquid: *They squirted each other with hoses.*

stab *verb*
1 to wound, pierce or push, as if with a knife: *She stabbed herself with the needle. | He stabbed at his food.*
stab *noun*
2 a sudden painful blow or feeling: *a stab of regret* **3** an attempt: *Now you have a stab at it.*

Word Building: other verb forms are **I stabbed, I have stabbed, I am stabbing** □ **stabbing** *adjective: a stabbing pain*

stable[1] *noun*
a place where horses are kept and fed

Word Building: **stable** *verb* to put or keep in a stable

stable[2] *adjective*
firm and steady: *a stable relationship*

Word Building: **stability** *noun*

staccato (say *stə-kah-toh*) *adjective*
an instruction in music to make notes sharply separate

stack *noun*
1 a large pile of things on top of each other **2** a tall chimney **3** a large number or quantity: *There were a stack of people there.*
stack *verb*
4 to pile up: *Stack the plates.* **5** to arrange unfairly: *to stack the cards*
6 stack a meeting to influence the decisions of a meeting unfairly by organising people to attend who will vote the way you want

Word Building: **stacked** *adjective*

stadium *noun*
a large, often indoor, sports arena, with seats for spectators and parking available

staff *noun*
1 the people who work in a business or an institution, such as a school or hospital
2 a large stick or rod

Word Building: **staff** *verb* **staff** *adjective*

stag *noun*
a male deer

Word Use: the female is a **doe;** the young is a **fawn**

stage *noun*
1 a raised floor, usually in a theatre, on which public performances take place.
2 a step in a process: *Now we can go on to the next stage.* **3** a period of development: *an early stage* **4** a section of a rocket which drops off after firing
stage *verb*
5 to do or perform, especially on a stage: *to stage a play* **6** to plan or carry out: *to stage a riot*

stagecoach *noun*
a passenger and goods coach which used to cover a particular route, changing horses regularly on long trips

stagger *verb*
1 to stand or go unsteadily **2** to arrange so that things don't occur at the same time: *They stagger their holidays.*
3 to shock: *The news staggered me.*

Word Building: **staggered** *adjective* amazed **stagger** *noun*

stagnant *adjective*
still and dirty: *stagnant water*

Word Building: **stagnancy** *noun*

stagnate *verb*
1 to stop running or flowing: *The water has stagnated.* **2** to become dull and inactive: *She feels she is stagnating at home.*

Word Building: **stagnation** *noun*

stain *noun*
1 a mark or blemish **2** a clear colouring, as used on wood

Word Building: **stain** *verb*

stair *noun*
one of a series of steps

staircase *noun*
a series of steps with its handrail or banister

stake[1] *noun*
1 a stick which is often pointed at one end: *She put in stakes to support the vine.*
2 the stake death by burning while tied to a stake
stake[1] *verb*
3 to put stakes in the ground as a marker, or for support **4** to make a claim for: *He has staked his share.* **5 stake out** to surround, in order to keep watch or make a raid: *to stake out a building*

stake[2] *noun*
1 the amount bet in a race or game: *The stakes were high.* **2** a personal interest or involvement: *He has a stake in the shop.*
3 at stake at risk: *A lot is at stake.*

Word Building: **stake** *verb* to bet

stalactite (say *stal-ək-tuyt*) *noun*
a deposit formed by dripping water, which hangs from the roof of a limestone cave

stalagmite (say <u>*stal*</u>*-əg-muyt*) *noun*
a deposit formed by dripping water, which builds up on the floor of a limestone cave

stale *adjective*
not fresh or new

stalemate *noun*
a situation where no progress can be made

Word Use: this comes from chess, where any move by the king would put him in check and conclude the game

stalk[1] (rhymes with *fork*) *noun*
the stem of a plant

Word Use: be careful – this sounds like **stork**

stalk[2] (rhymes with *fork*) *verb*
1 to follow quietly and carefully: *The cat was stalking a mouse.* **2** to walk slowly and proudly: *He stalked out of the room in a rage.*

Word Use: be careful – this sounds like **stork**

stall *noun*
1 a stand, tent or table where goods are sold, such as at a fete **2** a section of a stable or shed where one horse or cow is kept **3 the stalls** the front seats on the ground floor of a theatre
stall *verb*
4 to stop, especially without wanting to: *She stalled the car. | The car stalled at the lights.*

stallion (say <u>*stal*</u>*-yən*) *noun*
a male horse kept for breeding

Word Use: the female is a **mare;** the young is a **foal**

stamen *noun*
the part of a flower that produces the pollen

Word Building: the plural is **stamens** or **stamina**
Word History: from a Latin word meaning "thread"

stamina (say <u>*stam*</u>*-ə-nə*) *noun*
physical strength or power, especially to fight off sickness or tiredness

stammer *noun*
another word for **stutter**

Word Building: **stammer** *verb*

stamp *verb*
1 to strike, beat, or crush by a downward push of your foot **2** to put a mark on something to show that it has been approved or is genuine: *The customs officer stamped my passport.* **3** to mark something with a pattern or design: *They stamped the emblem on the shirt.*
stamp *noun*
4 a small sticky piece of paper printed by the government for attaching to letters or documents **5** an official mark showing something is genuine or has been approved **6** an engraved block or instrument, usually of rubber, used for making a mark on something

stampede *noun*
a sudden scattering or headlong flight of a group of animals or people, often in fright

Word Building: **stampede** *verb*

stance *noun*
1 a way of standing: *a boxer's stance*
2 your way of thinking: *My stance on saving rainforests is well-known.*

stanchion (say <u>*stan*</u>*-chən*) *noun*
an upright post or support in part of a building or structure: *a window stanchion | a bridge stanchion*

stand *verb*
1 to take or keep an upright position on your feet **2** to stop moving or halt: *Stand and deliver!* **3** to be placed or situated: *The house stands at the end of the street.*
4 to be unchanged or to continue the same: *The law still stands.* **5** to become a candidate: *He stood for the position of mayor.* **6** to undergo: *She stood trial.*
7 to bear or tolerate: *I can't stand him.*
8 stand by **a** to wait or be ready
b to help: *I'll stand by him.* **c** to keep to: *She always stands by her promises.*
9 stand down **a** to go off duty
b to withdraw, especially from a contest
c to put off because of a strike: *Ten more workers were stood down this morning.*
10 stand for to represent: *A policeman stands for the law.* **11 stand in** to act in place of someone else
stand *noun*
12 opposition to, or support for a cause: *My father takes a strong stand against smoking.* **13** a platform or raised place, such as for spectators or a display of goods
14 a framework to support something

Word Building: other verb forms are **I stood, I have stood, I am standing**

standard *noun*
1 anything taken as a rule or basis for comparing other things **2** a grade or level of excellence or achievement: *a high standard of living* **3** a flag, emblem or symbol

standard *adjective*
4 used as a standard or rule: *standard spelling* **5** normal, acceptable or average: *The shirt was the standard size for a ten year old.*

standardise or **standardize** *verb*
1 to make standard in size, weight or quality, and so on **2** to compare with or test by a standard: *This car has been standardised with the original model.*

Word Building: **standardisation** *noun*

stand-by *noun*
someone or something kept ready to be used when needed or in an emergency

Word Building: the plural is **stand-bys**

stand-in *noun*
any substitute, but especially one used to replace someone for a short time in a play or film

standing *noun*
1 position, status or reputation: *a man of good standing* **2** duration or length of existence or membership: *a member of long standing*
standing *adjective*
3 in an upright position **4** continuing without stopping or changing: *a standing rule*

standstill *noun*
a stop or halt: *Work came to a standstill.*

stanza *noun*
a group of lines of poetry arranged in a pattern or verse

Word History: from a Latin word meaning "standing"

staple[1] *noun*
1 a bent piece of wire used to bind papers and similar things together **2** a U-shaped piece of metal with pointed ends for driving into a surface

Word Building: **staple** *verb*

staple[2] *noun*
1 a most important or main item, especially food which is used or needed continually **2** a fibre of wool or cotton
staple[2] *adjective*
3 most important: *Rice is the staple food in India.*

stapler *noun*
a small machine used to join papers with staples

star *noun*
1 any of the large bodies in space like our sun, which we see as bright points of light in the night sky **2** a shape resembling a star in the sky, with five or six points which look like rays of light **3** someone who is excellent in something or who is famous in an art or profession: *She is a swimming star. / He is a film star.*
star *adjective*
4 brilliant or best: *She is the star swimmer in the team.*
star *verb*
5 to put stars on, or to mark with stars
6 to appear as, or to present someone as, a leading performer: *She starred in the film. / The play starred the son of the director.*

Word Building: other verb forms are **I starred, I have starred, I am starring** □ **starred** *adjective* **starry** *adjective*

starboard (say stah-bəd) *noun*
the right-hand side of a ship when you are facing the front or bow of the ship

Word Use: the opposite is **port**

starch *noun*
1 a white tasteless substance found in foods like potatoes, wheat and rice
2 a preparation of this used to make clothes and materials stiff
starch *verb*
3 to stiffen with starch

stare *verb*
1 to look directly for a long time, especially with your eyes wide open
stare *noun*
2 a long fixed look with your eyes wide open

starfish *noun*
a sea animal with a body in the shape of a star

stark *adjective*
1 complete or total: *stark madness*
2 harsh or barren: *A desert is a stark landscape.*
stark *adverb*
3 absolutely or utterly: *stark naked*

starling *noun*
a noisy bird with dark shiny feathers

start *verb*
1 to begin to move or to set moving: *I started on my journey. / He started the engine.* **2** to begin: *When did you start on your career? / Will you start the letter?*
3 to move suddenly or with a sudden jerk from a position or place: *The rabbit started*

up from the undergrowth. **4** to be among the competitors in a race or contest: *How many are starting in the long jump?*

start *noun*
5 a beginning **6** the first part of anything: *the start of a book* **7** a sudden jerk of your body: *I woke with a start.* **8** a lead or advantage over other competitors: *They gave me a start of ten metres in the race.*

starter *noun*
1 someone who gives the signal to start a race **2** anyone who is a competitor in a race or contest **3 for starters a** the first course of a meal **b** a first stage in anything: *We'll dig a hole for starters.*

Word Use: definitions 3a and 3b are more suited to everyday language

startle *verb*
1 to disturb, surprise or frighten suddenly **2** to move with a sudden jerk such as from a fright or surprise

starve *verb*
1 to die or cause to die from hunger: *Many babies starve in poor countries. / Some people starve their pets.* **2** to be suffering severely from hunger **3** to cause to suffer from the lack of something needed: *The strike starved the city of petrol.*

Word Building: starvation *noun*

state *noun*
1 the condition of someone or something: *a state of unhappiness* **2** a tense, excited or nervous condition: *She has got herself into quite a state about this.* **3** a number of people living in a definite territory and organised under one government **4** the territory itself: *Tasmania is a State of Australia.*

state *adjective*
5 having to do with ceremonies, special occasions, or the government

state *verb*
6 to say or express in speech or writing: *State your reasons clearly if you want an early reply.*

stately *adjective*
formal, grand, or majestic: *a stately palace*

Word Building: other forms are **statelier, stateliest**

statement *noun*
1 the stating or declaring of facts or ideas **2** the thing or things stated: *I don't think that statement's true.*

statesman *noun*
someone who is skilled in, or whose work is, directing the affairs of the government

Word Building: the plural is **statesmen** □ **statesmanship** *noun*

static *adjective*
1 at rest or still **2** having to do with electricity which is not flowing, especially that caused by friction

static *noun*
3 noise or interference with sound waves such as crackling caused by electrical activity in the air

station *noun*
1 a place at which a train regularly stops **2** the end of a bus or coach route **3** a farm for raising sheep or cattle **4** a place set up for some particular kind of work or service: *a police station* **5** the place or the equipment used for broadcasting or transmitting for radio or television

station *verb*
6 to place or post in a position for a particular reason: *The guard was stationed at the gate.*

stationary (say *stay-shən-ree*) *adjective*
not moving: *The car was stationary at the red light.*

Word Use: this should not be confused with **stationery**

stationery (say *stay-shən-ree*) *noun*
writing paper and writing materials such as pens and pencils

Word Use: this should not be confused with **stationary**
Word Building: stationer *noun* someone who sells stationery

station wagon *noun*
a car which has extra space behind the back seat, and a door at the back

statistics *plural noun*
information collected together and presented in the form of figures, charts or graphs

Word Building: statistical *adjective*

statue (say *stat-chooh*) *noun*
an image of a person or animal made out of stone, wood or bronze

stature (say *stat-chə*) *noun*
1 someone's height **2** achievement or distinction reached by someone: *She was a lady of high stature in the computing business.*

status (say <u>stay</u>-*təs*) *noun*
1 someone's social or professional position, rank, or importance **2** the state or condition of something

staunch[1] *verb*
to stop the flow of blood from: *to staunch a wound*

staunch[2] *adjective*
1 loyal or steadfast: *a staunch friend*
2 strong or substantial

stave *noun*
1 a thin, narrow, curved piece of wood that is part of the side of a barrel or tub
2 the set of five horizontal lines used in music, on which the notes are written

stave *verb*
3 stave in to break a hole in
4 stave off to put off or prevent: *The berries staved off starvation for the lost hikers.*

Word Use: another word for definition 2 is **staff**
Word Building: other verb forms are **I staved** or **I stove, I have staved** or **I have stove, I am staving**

stay[1] *verb*
1 to remain in a place **2** to continue to be: *Children cannot stay clean.*

stay[1] *noun*
3 a time of living somewhere: *We had a short stay in Queensland.*

stay[2] *noun*
a support, especially used to keep something steady

stead (rhymes with *bed*) *noun*
place or position: *Since he couldn't come, he sent his brother in his stead.* **2 stand in good stead** to be useful: *His extra study stood him in good stead in the exam.*

steadfast (say <u>sted</u>-*fahst*) *adjective*
firmly fixed, constant, or unchanging: *a steadfast gaze | a steadfast friend*

steady (say <u>sted</u>-*ee*) *adjective*
1 firmly placed or fixed: *a steady ladder*
2 constant or regular: *steady progress at school* **3** free from excitement or upset: *steady nerves* **4** reliable or having good habits: *Her friend seems a steady little girl.*

steady *noun*
5 a regular girlfriend or boyfriend

steady *adverb*
6 in a firm or regular manner
7 go steady to go out regularly with the same boyfriend or girlfriend

Word Building: other adjective forms are **steadier, steadiest** □ the plural form of the noun is **steadies** □ **steady** *verb* (**steadied, steadying**) **steadily** *adverb*

steak (sounds like *stake*) *noun*
a thick slice of meat or fish usually used for grilling or frying

steal *verb*
1 to take something that does not belong to you, especially secretly **2** to get, take, or do secretly: *She stole a nap during the show.* **3** to move or go secretly: *He stole away quietly in the night.*

steal *noun*
4 something obtained cheaply or below its true cost: *This dress is a real steal.*

Word Use: definition 4 is more suited to everyday language □ be careful – this sounds like **steel**
Word Building: other verb forms are **I stole, I have stolen, I am stealing**

stealth (say *stelth*) *noun*
secret, hidden, or sly action or behaviour

steam *noun*
1 a colourless gas or vapour produced by boiling water and used for driving machinery and for heating **2 let off steam** to release or let go of stored-up feelings **3 run out of steam** to lose power or energy

steam *verb*
4 to give off steam: *The hot food was steaming.* **5** to treat with steam in order to cook, soften or heat **6 steam up** to become covered with steam: *The kitchen windows had all steamed up.*

Word Building: **steamy** *adjective* (**steamier, steamiest**)

steam-engine *noun*
an engine which is powered by steam, especially a locomotive

steamroller *noun*
1 a heavy vehicle with a large roller, used for crushing and levelling rocks and earth in road-making **2** an overpowering force which crushes anything in its path

Word Building: **steamroller** *verb*

steed *noun*
a horse, especially one for fast riding

Word Use: this is an old-fashioned word

steel *noun*
1 iron mixed with carbon and other metals so that it is very hard and strong

steel *verb*
2 to make hard, unfeeling, or determined: *She steeled herself against their rudeness.*

Word Use: be careful – this sounds like **steal**
Word Building: **steely** *adjective* (**steelier, steeliest**) **steel** *adjective*

steep[1] *adjective*
1 having a sharp slope **2** too high: *a steep price* **3** extreme or extravagant: *It's a bit steep to do something like that.*

Word Use: definition 3 is more suited to everyday language

steep[2] *verb*
1 to soak or lie soaking in water or other liquid **2** to be filled with: *a mind steeped in romance*

steeple *noun*
a tall tower attached to a church, often with a spire on top

steeplechase *noun*
a race over a course which has obstacles such as jumps and ditches

Word Building: **steeplechase** *verb*

steer[1] *verb*
1 to guide the course of by using a rudder or wheel: *He steered the boat.* **2** to be guided in a particular direction: *This plane steers easily.*

steer[2] *noun*
a sterilised male of the cattle family, especially one raised for beef

stem[1] *noun*
1 the central stalk of a plant that grows upwards from the root **2** the stalk which supports or joins a flower, leaf, or fruit to a plant **3** a long thin part like the stem of a plant: *the stem of a pipe | the stem of a wineglass*

stem[1] *verb*
4 to originate or come from: *This model stems from an earlier invention of mine.*

Word Building: other verb forms are **it stemmed, it has stemmed, it is stemming**

stem[2] *verb*
to stop, check, or dam up: *She stemmed the flow of blood with a towel.*

Word Building: other verb forms are **I stemmed, I have stemmed, I am stemming**

stencil (say <u>*sten*</u>*-səl*) *noun*
1 a thin sheet of paper, cardboard or metal with designs or letters cut out of it: *The children painted over the stencils leaving colourful patterns on the paper underneath.* **2** the actual letters or designs produced

stencil *verb*
3 to mark, paint or produce letters or designs by using a stencil

Word Building: other verb forms are **I stencilled, I have stencilled, I am stencilling**
Word History: from a Latin word meaning "spark"

stenographer (say *stə-*<u>*nog*</u>*-rə-fə*) *noun*
someone who can write in shorthand what someone else is saying and then type it out

step *noun*
1 a movement made by lifting your foot and putting it down again in a new position **2** the distance measured by one such movement: *Move a step nearer.* **3** a move or action: *the first step towards peace* **4** a support for your foot in going up or coming down: *a step of a ladder or stair* **5 watch your step** to go or behave carefully

step *verb*
6 to walk or tread: *Please step this way. | Don't step on my toe!* **7 step on it** to hurry

Word Use: definition 7 is more suited to everyday language
Word Building: other verb forms are **I stepped, I have stepped, I am stepping**

stepladder *noun*
a ladder which has flat steps instead of rungs and has a pair of hinged legs to keep it upright

steppe (say *step*) *noun*
a large plain, especially one without trees

stereo (say <u>*ste*</u>*-ree-oh,* <u>*stear*</u>*-ree-oh*) *noun*
a radio, CD or record player, or recording system equipped to reproduce stereophonic sound

Word Building: the plural is **stereos** □ **stereo** *adjective*

stereophonic (say *ste-ree-ə-*<u>*fon*</u>*-ik*) *adjective*
having to do with using two channels and two speakers to transmit and broadcast sound

sterile (say <u>*ste*</u>*-ruyl*) *adjective*
1 free from living germs: *a sterile bandage* **2** barren or fruitless, or not able to have children: *Some fields are sterile and will not produce crops.*

Word Building: **sterility** *noun*

sterilise or **sterilize** *verb*
1 to destroy germs in something, often by boiling it **2** to make unable to reproduce young, especially by surgery: *The vet sterilised my dog.*

Word Building: **sterilisation** *noun*

sterling *adjective*
1 having to do with British money **2** being of a certain standard quality of silver **3** made of this sterling silver: *a sterling cutlery set* **4** thoroughly excellent: *sterling character*

stern[1] *adjective*
1 firm or strict: *stern discipline* **2** hard, harsh, or severe: *a stern warning*

stern[2] *noun*
the back part of anything, but especially of a ship or boat

stethoscope (say *steth-ə-skohp*) *noun*
an instrument used by doctors to listen to the sounds made by your heart and lungs

stew *verb*
1 to cook by slow boiling **2** to worry or fuss
stew *noun*
3 food cooked by stewing, especially a dish of meat and vegetables cooked together **4** a condition or state of worrying or uneasiness

Word Use: definitions 2 and 4 are more suited to everyday language

steward *noun*
1 someone who looks after others in a club or on a ship or plane **2** someone who manages someone else's affairs or property

Word Building: **stewardess** *noun*

stick[1] *noun*
1 a branch or long thin piece of wood, sometimes used for a special purpose: *a walking stick* **2** something shaped like a stick: *a stick of celery* **3 the sticks** the country, especially when thought of as backward and dull

Word Use: definition 3 is more suited to everyday language

stick[2] *verb*
1 to pierce with a pointed instrument **2** to thrust something pointed in or through something: *If you stick a pin into a balloon it will burst.* **3** to put into a place or position: *Just stick your head out of the window.* **4** to fasten into position by piercing or gluing: *He stuck a picture to the wall.* **5** to prevent or be prevented from moving: *The car stuck in the mud.* **6** to stay attached as if by glue: *The mud sticks to his shoes.* **7** to remain firm in opinion, attachment and so on: *She sticks to her word. | I will stick by my friends.*

Word Building: other verb forms are **I stuck, I have stuck, I am sticking** □ **stick** *noun*

sticker *noun*
an adhesive or gummed label, usually with an advertisement or other message printed on it

stick insect *noun*
an insect, often without wings, with a long, thin, twig-like body

sticky *adjective*
1 adhesive or gluey **2** hot and humid: *a sticky day* **3** awkward or difficult to deal with: *a sticky situation*

Word Use: definition 3 is more suited to everyday language
Word Building: other forms are **stickier, stickiest** □ **stickily** *adverb* **stickiness** *noun*

stickybeak *noun*
someone who is curious about things that aren't their business

Word Building: **stickybeak** *verb*

stiff *adjective*
1 hard or firm and not easily bent **2** not moving or working easily: *a stiff hinge* **3** not able to move easily: *Her legs were stiff with the cold.* **4** unfortunate or unlucky: *That's stiff!* **5** strong and with steady force: *a stiff wind* **6** severe or hard to deal with: *He gave us a stiff punishment.* **7** unusually high in price or demand: *That's a stiff price for that vase.*
stiff *noun*
8 a dead body

Word Use: definitions 4 and 8 are more suited to everyday language
Word Building: **stiff** *adverb* **stiffen** *verb* **stiffness** *noun*

stifle *verb*
1 to smother or prevent the breathing of **2** to keep back or to stop: *He stifled a yawn.* **3** to become stifled or be unable to breathe

Word Building: **stifling** *adjective*

stigma *noun*
a mark of shame or a stain on your reputation

stile *noun*
a step or steps for climbing over a fence where there is no gate

stiletto (say *stə-<u>let</u>-oh*) *noun*
1 a dagger with a narrow thick blade
2 a high, very narrow heel on a woman's shoe

Word History: from the Latin word for a pointed instrument

still[1] *adjective*
1 free from movement: *still water*
2 free from sound or noise: *a still night*
still[1] *noun*
3 stillness or silence: *in the still of the night* **4** a single photographic picture
still[1] *adverb*
5 up to or even at this time: *Is she still here?* **6** without sound or movement: *She stood still.*
still[1] *verb*
7 to make or become quiet or silent

Word Building: **stillness** *noun*

still[2] *noun*
equipment for distilling a liquid, especially a liquor

Word Building: **distil** *verb* (**distilled, distilling**)

stilt *noun*
1 one of a pair of poles used for walking on, each with a support for your foot at some distance above the ground
2 a high supporting post under a building

stilted *adjective*
not at ease or relaxed: *The new captain spoke in a very stilted manner.*

stimulant (say *<u>stim</u>-yə-lənt*) *noun*
something that increases wakefulness or quickens some bodily process, such as a medicine or food

stimulate (say *<u>stim</u>-yə-layt*) *verb*
1 to spur on or excite: *The dancers were stimulated by the music and bright lights.*
2 to act as a stimulus or stimulant

Word Building: **stimulation** *noun* **stimulator** *noun*

stimulus (say *<u>stim</u>-yə-ləs*) *noun*
something that starts action, effort, or thought: *Seeing the exhibition was the stimulus she needed to start painting again.*

Word Building: the plural is **stimuli**

sting *verb*
1 to prick or wound with a sharp-pointed, often venomous organ which some animals have: *A bee stung me.* **2** to hurt the feelings of: *Her unkind words stung me.*
sting *noun*
3 an act of stinging **4** the wound or pain caused by stinging **5** a sharp-pointed, often venomous, organ of insects and other animals, able to cause painful wounds

Word Building: other verb forms are **I stung, I have stung, I am stinging**

stingy (say *<u>stin</u>-jee*) *adjective*
mean about spending money

Word Building: other forms are **stingier, stingiest**

stink *verb*
1 to give off a bad smell
stink *noun*
2 a bad smell **3** a fuss: *She kicked up a stink when she heard the news.*

Word Use: definition 3 is more suited to everyday language
Word Building: other verb forms are **it stank, it has stunk, it is stinking**

stir *verb*
1 to mix something by moving a spoon, stick, or something similar around in it
2 to move: *The breeze stirred the leaves. / Not a leaf stirred.* **3** to excite: *He stirred up the party by singing.* **4** to deliberately mention things likely to cause an argument
stir *noun*
5 the act or sound of stirring or moving
6 excitement or commotion: *Her arrival caused quite a stir.*

Word Use: definition 4 is more suited to everyday language
Word Building: other verb forms are **I stirred, I have stirred, I am stirring**

stirrup *noun*
a loop or ring of metal hung from the saddle of a horse to support the rider's foot

stitch *noun*
1 a complete movement of a threaded needle through a piece of material
2 the loop of thread left in the material
3 one complete movement with needles in knitting, crochet and so on **4** a sudden sharp pain, especially between your ribs
5 in stitches laughing uncontrollably

Word Building: **stitch** *verb*

stoat *noun*
a type of weasel which has a brown coat of fur in summer

Word Use: the white winter coat of the stoat is called **ermine**

stock *noun*
1 the total quantity of goods kept by a business shop for selling to customers **2** a quantity of something kept for future use: *We kept a good stock of food in the house.* **3** *another word for* **livestock** **4** a tribe, family, or race: *He is of Italian stock.* **5** liquid in which meat, fish, vegetables, and so on have been cooked, often used as a base for sauces or soups **6** the shares of a business company

stock *verb*
7 to provide with, or to collect a stock or supply **8** to provide with horses, cattle, and so on: *to stock the property with fine merinos*

stock *adjective*
9 kept in store: *stock articles* **10** in common use or ordinary: *a stock argument*

stockade *noun*
a strong wooden fence built for defence

stocking *noun*
a tight-fitting item of clothing that covers the foot and leg

stockman *noun*
someone whose job is to look after the animals, especially the cattle, on a property

Word Building: the plural is **stockmen**

stockpile *verb*
to save up in large amounts for future use: *to stockpile wood for the winter*

Word Building: **stockpile** *noun*

stock-still *adverb*
without moving at all: *to stand stock-still*

stocky *adjective*
short, solid and strong: *a stocky young footballer*

Word Building: other forms are **stockier, stockiest**

stoke *verb*
to stir up and add fuel to: *to stoke a fire*

Word Building: **stoker** *noun: a stoker on a steam train*

stole *noun*
a long wide scarf worn around your shoulders for warmth

stomach (say *stum*-*ək*) *noun*
the bag-like organ in the body that receives food after it is swallowed, and starts to digest it

Word History: from a Greek word meaning "throat"

stone *noun*
1 the hard substance which rocks are made of: *a house built of stone* **2** a piece of rock **3** a gem **4** the hard seed inside a cherry, peach, plum or similar fruit **5** an old-fashioned measure of weight, equal to a little more than six kilograms

stone *verb*
6 to throw stones at **7** to take the stones out of: *to stone peaches*

Word Building: **stony** *adjective* (**stonier, stoniest**): *stony ground | a stony heart*

stoned *adjective*
completely drunk or drugged

Word Use: this is more suited to everyday language

stonefish *noun*
a venomous tropical fish, looking like a piece of coral or rock, with spines which can give you a painful sting, sometimes causing death

Word Building: the plural is **stonefishes**

stool *noun*
a seat with no arms or back

stoop *verb*
1 to bend forwards **2** to lower yourself: *to stoop to lying*

stop *verb*
1 to end or finish **2** to bring or come to a halt **3** to prevent: *to stop them from leaving* **4** to close or block up: *to stop a leak* **5** to stay: *to stop overnight with friends*

stop *noun*
6 a finish or end: *to put a stop to the noise* **7** the place where a bus, tram or other vehicle stops to pick up and set down passengers

Word Building: other verb forms are **I stopped, I have stopped, I am stopping** □ **stoppage** *noun: a traffic stoppage*

stopper *noun*
something that fits into the top of a bottle to close it

stop press *noun*
last minute news put into a newspaper after printing has already begun

stopwatch *noun*
a watch which can be stopped and started by pressing a button, used for timing races and so on

Word Building: the plural is **stopwatches**

storage *noun*
room to keep things: *The cupboard has plenty of storage.*

store *noun*
1 things put away for use in the future: *a store of groceries* **2** a place for keeping a supply of things: *Get some pencils from the store.* **3** a shop: *the corner store*
4 in store coming soon: *There is a surprise in store for you.*

Word Building: **store** *verb: to store food*

storehouse *noun*
a building in which things are stored or kept

storey *noun*
one whole level of a building

Word Use: a similar word is **floor** □ be careful – this sounds like **story**
Word Building: the plural is **storeys**
Word History: from a French word meaning "build"

stork *noun*
a large bird with long legs and a long beak, which feeds in shallow water

Word Use: be careful – this sounds like **stalk**

storm *noun*
1 a violent change in the weather bringing wind, rain, thunder and lightning
2 a strong outburst: *a storm of applause*
storm *verb*
3 to rush angrily: *He stormed out of the room.* **4** to attack suddenly and violently: *The warriors stormed the castle.*

Word Building: **stormy** *adjective* (**stormier, stormiest**)

story *noun*
1 the telling of something that has happened, either made up or in real life: *the story of Robinson Crusoe* **2** a lie or fib

Word Use: be careful – this sounds like **storey**
Word Building: the plural is **stories**

stout *adjective*
1 rather overweight **2** strong and heavy: *a stout stick* **3** brave and fearless: *a stout heart*
stout *noun*
4 a strong dark-brown beer

stove *noun*
a device which uses wood, gas or electricity to produce heat for cooking or warming a room

stow (rhymes with *so*) *verb*
to pack or store away: *Stow your luggage in the boot of the car.*

stowaway (say *stoh-ə-way*) *noun*
someone who hides on a ship or plane to get a free trip

Word Building: **stowaway** *verb*

straddle *verb*
to sit or stand on with one leg on each side: *to straddle a horse*

straggle *verb*
1 to lag behind or walk out of line
2 to grow or spread untidily: *Overgrown vines straggled over the fence.*

Word Building: **straggler** *noun* **straggly** *adjective*

straight *adjective*
1 not bent or curved **2** honest and reliable: *a straight answer* **3** serious: *to keep a straight face | to have a straight talk*
straight *adverb*
4 without bending, curving or twisting: *The road runs straight for five kilometres.*
5 neatly and in the proper order: *to set your room straight* **6** directly or immediately: *I'll come straight over.*

Word Use: be careful – this sounds like **strait**
Word Building: **straighten** *verb*

straight angle *noun*
an angle of 180°

straightaway *adverb*
at once: *I'll come straightaway.*

straightforward *adjective*
1 honest and open **2** not difficult or complicated: *a straightforward problem*

strain[1] *verb*
1 to pull, push or stretch hard or too far: *to strain a muscle | The dog strained at its leash.* **2** to pour through a sieve: *to strain orange juice*
strain[1] *noun*
3 great effort, pressure or stress: *He looked tired from the strain of work. | The strain on the rope made it snap.* **4 strains** musical sounds: *the sweet strains of a violin*

strain[2] *noun*
breed or family line: *This strain of cat has no tail.*

strainer *noun*
a filter or sieve: *a tea strainer*

strait *noun*
a narrow channel connecting two large bodies of water: *Bass Strait*

Word Use: be careful – this sounds like **straight**

straitjacket *noun*
a coat which is wrapped around mentally ill people to restrain them, if they are acting violently enough to hurt themselves or others

Word Use: another spelling is **straightjacket**

straitlaced *adjective*
rather strict and proper about the way people should behave

strand *noun*
1 one of the threads which are twisted together to form a rope or cord **2** a lock of hair

stranded *adjective*
1 washed up on the beach: *a stranded whale* **2** alone and helpless: *stranded in the middle of the desert*

strange *adjective*
1 queer or odd: *a strange way of walking* **2** not seen or heard of before: *a strange part of town*

Word Use: a similar word for definition 2 is **unfamiliar**

stranger *noun*
1 someone you haven't met before **2** someone who has not been in a place before: *I'm a stranger in town.*

strangle *verb*
to kill by squeezing the throat and cutting off the air supply

Word Use: another word is **strangulate**
Word Building: **stranglehold** *noun* a tight hold around the neck **strangler** *noun* **strangulation** *noun*

strap *noun*
1 a strip of leather or cloth used for tying or holding things in place: *a watch strap*
strap *verb*
2 to fasten with a strap

Word Building: other verb forms are **I strapped, I have strapped, I am strapping**

strapping *adjective*
tall and strong: *a strapping young athlete*

strategy (say *strat-ə-jee*) *noun*
1 a clever scheme **2** the planning and tactics used in war

Word Building: the plural is **strategies** □ **strategic** *adjective* important in a strategy **strategist** *noun*

stratum (say *strah-təm*) *noun*
a layer or level: *The cliff face shows several different rock strata.*

Word Building: the plural is **strata**
Word History: from a Latin word meaning "something spread out"

straw *noun*
1 a thin hollow tube through which you can suck a drink **2** cut dried stalks of wheat, oats, corn or other grain

strawberry *noun*
a small, juicy, red fruit which has many tiny seeds on its surface

Word Building: the plural is **strawberries**

stray *verb*
to wander off and get lost

Word Building: **stray** *adjective: a stray puppy* **stray** *noun: That puppy is a stray.*

streak *noun*
1 a long thin mark or line: *a streak of lightning | a streak of paint*
streak *verb*
2 to mark with streaks **3** to move very quickly: *The dog streaked across the road.*

Word Building: **streaky** *adjective* (**streakier, streakiest**)

stream *noun*
1 a small river or creek **2** a continuous flow: *a stream of air | a stream of words*
stream *verb*
3 to flow or run: *Tears streamed from his eyes.* **4** to group according to ability: *The school streamed the children into different classes.*

streamer *noun*
a long strip of brightly coloured paper

streamlined *adjective*
shaped to move quickly and smoothly through air or water

street *noun*
1 a road lined with buildings **2** the people who live in a street: *The whole street gathered around the bonfire.*

strength *noun*
the quality of being strong: *Do you have enough strength to move the piano? | Water the juice down to half strength.*

Word Building: **strengthen** *verb* to make or grow stronger

strenuous (say *stren-yooh-əs*) *adjective*
needing a great effort: *strenuous exercise*

Word Building: **strenuously** *adverb*

stress *noun*
1 great importance: *to lay stress on the need for safety* **2** accent or emphasis: *to pronounce a word with the stress on the first syllable* **3** strain or pressure: *the stress of work*

Word Use: the plural is **stresses**
Word Building: **stress** *verb*

stretch *verb*
1 to pull out or extend **2** to spread: *The desert stretches for miles.* **3** to widen or enlarge: *to stretch a jumper*
4 stretch out to lie down at full length
5 stretch your legs to go for a walk
stretch *noun*
6 the action of stretching: *to have a yawn and a stretch* **7** a continuous spread or period of time: *a stretch of land | a stretch of ten years*

Word Building: **stretchy** *adjective*

stretcher *noun*
a light frame covered with canvas for carrying sick people

strew *verb*
to scatter or throw everywhere: *to strew the floor with clothes*

Word Building: other forms are **I strewed, I have strewn, I am strewing**

stricken *adjective*
struck down or overcome: *stricken with fear*

Word Use: this word comes from the verb **strike**

strict *adjective*
1 demanding that you behave well and obey the rules: *a strict teacher*
2 complete or total: *in strict secrecy*

Word Building: **strictly** *adverb*

stride *verb*
1 to walk with long steps
stride *noun*
2 a big step forward: *to take ten strides to reach the end of the room | to make great strides in learning to read*
3 strides trousers

Word Use: definition 3 is more suited to everyday language
Word Building: other verb forms are **I strode, I have stridden, I am striding**

strife *noun*
1 fighting and quarrelling: *a country torn with strife* **2 in strife** in trouble: *You'll be in strife for being so late.*

strike *verb*
1 to hit **2** to attack: *A snake sometimes strikes without warning.* **3** to come across or find: *to strike gold* **4** to affect strongly: *The ghost story struck them with terror.*
5 to sound by hitting a gong: *The clock struck three.* **6** to light: *to strike a match*
strike *noun*
7 a hit or blow **8** a work stoppage, usually in protest against low pay and poor working conditions

Word Building: other verb forms are **I struck, I have struck, I am striking** □ **striking** *adjective* impressive or noticeable

string *noun*
1 a thread or cord **2** a row or line of things: *a string of cars* **3** one of the pieces of wire stretched across a violin, guitar or similar instrument, which produces musical sounds when it is made to vibrate
4 strings musical instruments with strings, especially those played with a bow
string *verb*
5 to hang or thread on a string
6 string out to spread out or lengthen: *The people strung out along the beach to watch the surfers. | to string out a conversation*

Word Building: other verb forms are **I strung, I have strung, I am stringing** □ **stringy** *adjective* (**stringier, stringiest**): *stringy meat*

strip[1] *verb*
1 to remove or take away: *to strip the paint from a table* **2** to take off all your clothes

Word Building: other forms are **I stripped, I have stripped, I am stripping** □ **stripper** *noun*

strip[2] *noun*
1 a long narrow piece or area: *a strip of paper | the coastal strip* **2 comic strip** a series of cartoons telling a story

stripe *noun*
1 a long narrow band of a different colour from the rest of a thing: *red stripes on a blue background* **2 stripes** strips of braid worn on a military uniform to show rank

Word Building: **striped** *adjective*

strive *verb*
to try hard or struggle: *to strive for success*

Word Building: other forms are **I strove, I have striven, I am striving**

strobe *noun*
a device which gives out a series of brilliant flashes of light

stroke[1] *noun*
1 a hit or blow **2** a style of swimming **3** an action or event: *a stroke of good luck* **4** a sudden break in the circulation of blood in the brain which can cause paralysis or other disabilities

stroke[2] *verb*
to pass your hand over gently

Word Building: **stroke** *noun*

stroll *verb*
to walk slowly

Word Building: **stroll** *noun*

stroller *noun*
a chair on wheels used for carrying small children

strong *adjective*
1 having great power or effect: *a strong wind / a strong will* **2** not easily broken: *a strong fence* **3** having a lot of flavour or smell: *strong coffee*
strong *adverb*
4 in number: *The army was 10 000 strong.*

Word Building: **strongly** *adverb*

stronghold *noun*
a fortress

structure *noun*
1 something that has been built or constructed: *Bridges and buildings are both structures.* **2** the way something is put together: *the structure of a sentence*

Word Building: **structural** *adjective* **structure** *verb*

struggle *verb*
to fight or work very hard: *She struggled against the current.*

Word Building: **struggle** *noun* **struggler** *noun*

strum *verb*
to play by running your fingers across the strings of: *to strum a guitar*

Word Building: other forms are **I strummed, I have strummed, I am strumming**

strut[1] *verb*
to walk proudly or pompously, with your back straight and your chin pushed forward

Word Use: a similar word is **swagger**
Word Building: other forms are **I strutted, I have strutted, I am strutting**

strut[2] *noun*
a wooden or metal bar that supports part of a building

Word Building: **strut** *verb* (**strutted, strutting**) to support with a strut

stub *noun*
1 a short end piece: *the stub of a pencil*
stub *verb*
2 to bump against something hard: *to stub your toe*

Word Building: other verb forms are **I stubbed, I have stubbed, I am stubbing** □ **stubby** *adjective* short and thick

stubble *noun*
1 the short stalks left in the ground after wheat or corn has been harvested
2 the short prickly hairs growing on the face of a man who hasn't shaved for a few days

Word Building: **stubbly** *adjective*

stubborn (say *stub-ən*) *adjective*
determined not to give way or change your mind

Word Use: a similar word is **obstinate**
Word Building: **stubbornness** *noun*

stuck-up *adjective*
snobbish or conceited

Word Use: this is more suited to everyday language

stud[1] *noun*
a small knob or button: *Football boots have studs underneath. / This shirt fastens with studs.*

stud[2] *noun*
a farm where horses or cattle are kept for breeding

student *noun*
someone who is studying, especially at a school, college or university

Word Building: **studious** *adjective* hard-working and keen to study

studio (say *styooh-dee-oh*) *noun*
1 the workroom of an artist or musician
2 a place where films or radio and television programs are made

study (rhymes with *muddy*) *verb*
1 to spend time learning **2** to look at closely: *to study a document*
study *noun*
3 the careful learning of a subject
4 a room with a desk and books for studying **5** a short piece of music often used for practising technique

Word Use: the plural of the noun is **studies**
Word Building: other verb forms are **I studied, I have studied, I am studying**

stuff *noun*
1 the material from which things are made: *cushions filled with soft stuff*
2 belongings: *Put your stuff in your locker.*
stuff *verb*
3 to fill tightly or cram: *to stuff clothes into a drawer*

Word Use: definition 2 is more suited to everyday language

stuffing *noun*
1 material used for filling **2** a tasty mixture put inside a chicken or other poultry before it is cooked

stuffy *adjective*
1 not having enough air: *a stuffy room*
2 prim or easily shocked

Word Building: other forms are **stuffier, stuffiest** □ **stuffily** *adverb* **stuffiness** *noun*

stumble *verb*
1 to trip and nearly fall **2** to walk unsteadily **3** to act or speak in an unsteady and hesitating way

stump *noun*
1 a short part left after the main part has been cut off: *a tree stump | the stump of a pencil* **2** one of the three upright sticks forming the wicket in cricket
stump *verb*
3 to baffle completely: *The question stumped him.*

Word Building: **stumpy** *adjective* short and thick

stun *verb*
1 to make unconscious: *The blow stunned him.* **2** to shock or astonish

Word Building: other forms are **I stunned, I have stunned, I am stunning**
Word History: from an Old English word meaning "resound" or "crash"

stunt[1] *verb*
to stop or slow down the growth of: *Lack of food stunts children in some countries.*

stunt[2] *noun*
1 a spectacular and often dangerous performance **2** something done to attract publicity or attention

stuntman *noun*
someone who is paid to perform dangerous acts, especially as a stand-in for a film actor

stupefy (say <u>*styooh*</u>*-pə-fuy*) *verb*
1 to make senseless or unconscious: *The blow on her head stupefied her.*
2 to astound or overcome with amazement

Word Building: other verb forms are **it stupefied, it has stupefied, it is stupefying** □ **stupefaction** *noun*

stupendous *adjective*
amazingly good: *The singer's performance was stupendous.*

Word Building: **stupendously** *adverb*

stupid *adjective*
1 not clever or quick to understand: *a stupid dog* **2** showing a lack of good sense: *a stupid thing to do*

Word Building: **stupidly** *adverb* **stupidity** *noun*

stupor (say <u>*styooh*</u>*-pə*) *noun*
a state in which the mind or senses are deadened or not working, as a result of illness or drugs

sturdy *adjective*
strong or able to stand up to rough use or handling: *a sturdy little boy | a sturdy garden tool*

Word Building: other forms are **sturdier, sturdiest** □ **sturdily** *adverb* **sturdiness** *noun*

sturgeon (say <u>*ster*</u>*-jən*) *noun*
a large fish found in the northern areas of the world, the eggs of which can be salted and eaten as caviar

stutter *noun*
a speech problem in which the rhythm of speech is blocked and sounds, especially the first consonants in words, are repeated

Word Building: **stutter** *verb*

sty[1] *noun*
a place to keep pigs in

Word Building: the plural is **sties**

sty[2] *noun*
a small, red and painful swelling on the eyelid

Word Use: this word is also spelt **stye**
Word Building: the plural is **sties**

style *noun*
1 a kind of design or way of making: *The church is built in the Gothic style.*
2 a way of doing something: *Shakespeare's style of writing | a style of living*

Word Building: **stylish** *adjective* fashionable or elegant **style** *verb*

stylus *noun*
1 a pointed tool for drawing or writing
2 a record-player needle

suave (say *swahv*) *adjective*
smooth and sophisticated in manner: *The famous actor was very suave.*

sub *noun*
a shortened form of several words such as **submarine, subscription** and **substitute**

sub- *prefix*
a word part meaning **1** under: *subway*
2 not quite: *subnormal*

Word History: this prefix comes from Latin

subconscious (say *sub-kon-shəs*) *noun*
the part of your mind below consciousness or awareness: *Your dreams can come from your subconscious.*

Word Use: a similar word is **unconscious**
Word Building: **subconscious** *adjective*

subdivide *verb*
to divide again into smaller divisions, especially land

Word Building: **subdivision** *noun*

subdue *verb*
1 to overcome, usually by force
2 to calm

Word Use: other verb forms are **I subdued, I have subdued, I am subduing**

subject (say *sub-jekt*) *noun*
1 a matter under discussion: *the subject of a book* **2** a branch of study: *My favourite subject is maths.* **3** something chosen by an artist for painting **4** someone who is under the rule of a monarch or state: *a British subject* **5** the part of a sentence about which something is said, such as "the roof of the house" in *The roof of the house was red.*

subject (say *sub-jekt*) *adjective*
6 subject to a open to or likely to receive: *subject to teasing* **b** depending on: *The excursion to the beach is subject to the teacher's approval.*

subject (say *səb-jekt*) *verb*
7 subject to to cause to undergo: *He was subjected to harsh treatment.*

subjective *adjective*
having to do with the thinker rather than the thing thought about: *a subjective opinion*

Word Use: the opposite is **objective**

subjective case *noun*
the form of a noun or pronoun which shows it is the subject of a verb such as "I" in *I can hear him.*

sublime (say *sə-bluym*) *adjective*
noble, lofty, or awe-inspiring: *sublime poetry | a sublime view*

Word Building: **sublimely** *adverb* **sublimeness** *noun* **sublimity** *noun*

submarine *adjective*
1 being under water: *submarine cables*

submarine *noun*
2 a type of ship that can travel under water

submerge *verb*
to sink or make sink: *The submarine submerged. | She submerged into silence. | Submerge the clothes in the water.*

Word Building: **submersion** *noun*

submit *verb*
1 to yield or give in: *to submit to orders | to submit to punishment* **2** to hand in or offer for acceptance or judgment: *to submit an entry in a competition*

Word Building: other forms are **I submitted, I have submitted, I am submitting** □ **submissive** *adjective* obediently giving in **submission** *noun*

subordinate *adjective*
placed in or belonging to a lower order or rank: *a subordinate employee*

Word Building: **subordinate** *noun* **subordination** *noun*

subscription *noun*
1 a payment you make for club membership, a series of concert tickets, a regular magazine or such like
2 an amount of money given: *subscription to the bushfire appeal*

Word Building: **subscribe** *verb*

subsequent (say *sub-sə-kwənt*) *adjective*
happening later: *subsequent events*

subside *verb*
to sink to a lower level: *The rain has made the road subside. | The laughter subsided.*

Word Building: **subsidence** *noun*

subsidiary (say *səb-sij-ə-ree*) *adjective*
less important: *a subsidiary role*

subsidy (say *sub-sə-dee*) *noun*
a supporting payment made by a government or other organisation: *a subsidy to farmers*

Word Building: the plural is **subsidies** □ **subsidise** *verb*

subsist *verb*
to continue to live or stay alive, especially when food and other needs are in short supply

Word Building: **subsistence** *noun*

substance *noun*
1 anything of which a thing is made **2** a particular kind of matter: *This substance will remove paint.* **3** the main or basic part: *the substance of an argument*

substantial *adjective*
large or solid: *a substantial sum of money* | *a substantial building*

substitute *noun*
1 someone or something acting in place of another
substitute *verb*
2 to put in the place of: *She substituted margarine for butter.*

Word Building: **substitution** *noun*

subterfuge (say *sub-tə-fyoohj*) *noun*
a plan or trick used to hide or avoid something

subterranean (say *sub-tə-ray-nee-ən*) *adjective*
underground: *a subterranean passage*

subtitle *noun*
1 a secondary title of a book or a play: *The subtitle of "The Mikado" is "The Town of Titipu".* **2 subtitles** a translation in words on the screen of what is being said in a foreign-language film

subtle (say *sut-əl*) *adjective*
1 so fine or slight as to not be obvious or clear: *a subtle difference* **2** skilful or clever: *subtle humour*

Word Building: **subtlety** *noun* (**subtleties**) **subtly** *adverb*
Word History: from a Latin word meaning "fine" or "delicate"

subtract *verb*
to take away: *Subtract 2 from 7, and you get 5.*

Word Building: **subtraction** *noun*

suburb *noun*
a district of a city with its own shopping centre, school and other facilities: *a bayside suburb* | *an industrial suburb*

Word Building: **suburban** *adjective*

subway *noun*
a tunnel under a street or railway for people to walk through

succeed (say *sək-seed*) *verb*
1 to do or accomplish what you have attempted: *After an effort he succeeded in opening the box.* **2** to come after and take the place of: *She succeeded her father in the family business.*

success (say *sək-ses*) *noun*
1 a good or desired result **2** someone who has achieved much in their field

Word Building: the plural is **successes** □ **successful** *adjective* **successfully** *adverb*

successor (say *sək-ses-ə*) *noun*
someone or something that comes after and takes the place of: *He is my successor as president of the debating society.*

succulent (say *suk-yə-lənt*) *adjective*
juicy: *a succulent steak*

Word Building: **succulence** *noun* **succulently** *adverb*

succumb (say *sə-kum*) *verb*
to yield or give way: *She succumbed to the disease.* | *He succumbed to temptation.*

suck *verb*
1 to draw in with the mouth: *to suck lemonade through a straw* **2** to hold and move about in the mouth until melted or dissolved: *to suck a lolly* **3** to draw in: *Cold air is sucked in through the window.*

Word Building: **suck** *noun*

suckle *verb*
to nurse or feed milk to from the breast: *The woman suckled her baby.* | *The cow suckled her calf.*

suction *noun*
the power of sucking produced when the pressure of the air inside something is less than the outside pressure

sudden *adjective*
happening quickly and without warning

Word Building: **suddenness** *noun*

suds *plural noun*
soapy water with bubbles

sue *verb*
to bring a legal action against: *He is suing the makers of the faulty machine.*

Word Building: other forms are **I sued, I have sued, I am suing**

suede (say *swayd*) *noun*
a soft leather with a slightly furry surface

suet (say *sooh-ət*) *noun*
a hard dry fat surrounding the kidneys of animals and used in cooking

suffer *verb*
1 to feel pain or unhappiness: *She suffers from asthma. / He has suffered for a long time.* **2** to put up with: *She suffered their insults quietly.*

suffice *verb*
to be enough: *Three lamingtons will suffice, thank you.*

sufficient *adjective*
enough

Word Building: **sufficiency** *noun*

suffix *noun*
a word part added to the end of a word, such as "-ness" in *kindness*

suffocate *verb*
1 to kill by stopping from breathing: *The murderer suffocated the victim with a pillow.* **2** to die from lack of air

Word Building: **suffocation** *noun*

sugar *noun*
a sweet substance made mainly from cane and beet and used widely in food

Word Building: **sugary** *adjective*

suggest (say *sə-jest*) *verb*
to put forward the idea of: *She suggested a game of chess.*

Word Building: **suggestion** *noun*

suggestible *adjective*
easily influenced

suggestive *adjective*
suggesting something, especially something improper

suicide *noun*
1 the act of killing yourself deliberately: *to commit suicide* **2** someone who does this

Word Building: **suicidal** *adjective* **suicide** *verb*

suit *noun*
1 a set of clothes meant to be worn together **2** one of the four sets in a pack of cards

suit *verb*
3 to fit or be convenient: *Tomorrow will suit quite well.* **4** to be convenient to: *It suits me to go on Thursday.* **5** to look attractive on: *That colour suits you.*

suitable *adjective*
1 fitting or convenient: *a suitable time*
2 appropriate or right for the occasion: *suitable clothes*

Word Building: **suitability** *noun*

suitcase *noun*
an oblong bag for carrying clothes and other things when you travel

suite (say *sweet*) *noun*
a series or set, especially of furniture or rooms

sulk *verb*
to be bad-tempered and silent because you feel that you have been unfairly treated

Word Building: **sulky** *adjective* (**sulkier, sulkiest**)

sullen *adjective*
angry, silent and ill-mannered

Word Building: **sullenness** *noun*

sulfur (say *sul-fə*) *noun*
a yellow non-metallic element used in gunpowder, matches and other things

Word Use: this word used be spelled **sulphur** but nowadays this spelling is only used for the colour, as in *sulphur-crested cockatoo*
Word Building: **sulfuric** *adjective* **sulfurous** *adjective* **sulfureous** *adjective*

sultan *noun*
a Muslim ruler

Word Building: **sultanate** *noun*
Word History: from an Arabic word meaning "king", "ruler" or "power"

sultana *noun*
1 a small green seedless grape
2 dried fruit made from such a grape
3 a wife or any close female relative of a sultan

sultry *adjective*
hot and humid: *It was a sultry day, before the thunderstorm.*

Word Building: **sultriness** *noun*

sum *noun*
1 a total: *The sum of 183 and 17 is 200.*
2 an exercise or problem in arithmetic
3 an amount: *a sum of money*

sum *verb*
4 sum up **a** to add up **b** to express in a shortened form: *It is difficult to sum up what he said.* **c** to form an opinion about: *She summed him up at once.*

Word Building: other verb forms are **I summed, I have summed, I am summing**

summary *noun*
a short statement in speech or writing giving the main points of something

Word Use: a similar word for a written summary is **precis**
Word Building: the plural is **summaries** □ **summarise** *verb: She summarised the Prime Minister's speech for the newspapers.*

summer *noun*
the warmest season of the year

Word Building: **summery** *adjective*

summit *noun*
the top or highest point: *the summit of a hill / the summit of her career*

summon *verb*
to send for officially: *They summoned him to appear before the committee.*

summons *noun*
an order to appear at a particular place, especially a court of law

Word Building: the plural is **summonses**

sumptuous (say *sump-chooh-əs*) *adjective*
rich and luxurious: *a sumptuous home*

sun *noun*
1 the star which is the centre of our solar system and which gives light and warmth to the earth **2** sunshine: *a seat in the sun*

Word Use: an adjective from **sun** is **solar** □ be careful – this sounds like **son**
Word Building: **sunny** *adjective* (**sunnier, sunniest**) **sunless** *adjective* **sunlight** *noun*

sunbake *verb*
to lie or sit in the sun in order to become tanned

sunburn *noun*
painful reddening of the skin caused by being burnt by the heat of the sun

Word Building: **sunburnt** *adjective*

sundae *noun*
an ice-cream served with flavoured syrup and chopped nuts

Sunday *noun*
the first day of the week, kept as a day of rest and worship by most Christian churches

sundial *noun*
an instrument which tells the time by a shadow cast on its face, which is marked in hours like a clock

sunflower *noun*
a tall plant with big yellow flowers and seeds which you can eat

sunglasses *plural noun*
spectacles with darkened lenses to protect your eyes from the glare of the sun

sunrise *noun*
the appearance of the sun above the horizon in the morning, or the time when this happens

sunset *noun*
the disappearance of the sun below the horizon at night, or the time when this happens

sunshine *noun*
1 the light of the sun **2** cheerfulness or brightness

sunspot *noun*
one of the dark patches on the surface of the sun which are believed to affect some things on earth, such as the weather

sunstroke *noun*
a sickness with weakness and a high temperature caused by being in the sun for too long

suntan *noun*
brownness of the skin caused by being out in the sun

Word Building: **suntanned** *adjective*

super *adjective*
extremely good or pleasing: *a super effort / a super holiday*

Word Use: this word is more suited to everyday language

super- *prefix*
a word part meaning over: *supernatural*

Word History: this prefix comes from Latin

superb *adjective*
excellent or splendid: *a superb performance / superb beauty*

supercilious (say *sooh-pə-sil-ee-əs*) *adjective*
proud and scornful: *a supercilious person | a supercilious look*

Word Use: similar words are **contemptuous** and **disdainful**
Word Building: **superciliously** *adverb* **superciliousness** *noun*

superficial *adjective*
1 having to do with the outside or surface: *a superficial cut* **2** being on the outside only, rather than real or deep: *a superficial similarity between two people | superficial sorrow* **3** caring only about how things appear on the surface: *a superficial writer*

Word Building: **superficially** *adverb* **superficiality** *noun*

superfluous (say *sooh-per-flooh-əs*) *adjective*
more than is needed: *There were so many helpers that he was superfluous.*

Word Building: **superfluity** *noun* **superfluously** *adverb* **superfluousness** *noun*

superintendent *noun*
someone who is in charge of work, a business, or a building

Word Building: **superintend** *verb*

superior *adjective*
1 higher in position or rank: *a superior officer* **2** better or of higher quality: *superior intelligence* **3** greater in amount: *They beat us because of superior numbers.*

superior *noun*
4 someone who is higher in rank than you: *You have to be careful how you speak to your superiors.*

Word Building: **superiority** *noun*

superlative (say *sooh-per-lə-tiv*) *adjective*
1 of the highest or best kind: *a superlative voice | superlative skill* **2** having to do with the form of an adjective or adverb which expresses the greatest degree of comparison: *"Smoothest" is the superlative form of "smooth" and "most easily" is the superlative form of "easily".*

Word Use: compare definition 2 with **comparative**
Word Building: **superlatively** *adverb*

supermarket *noun*
a large self-service shop selling food and other household goods

supernatural *adjective*
not able to be explained in terms of the laws of nature: *A ghost is a supernatural being.*

Word Building: **supernatural** *noun*

superpower *noun*
a very rich and powerful nation

supersonic *adjective*
moving faster than the speed of sound: *a supersonic jet*

superstar *noun*
a singer, actor or actress who is very famous

superstition *noun*
a belief about the meaning of a thing or event that does not stem from reason or sensible thought: *There is a superstition that if you break a mirror you get seven years' bad luck.*

Word Building: **superstitious** *adjective* **superstitiously** *adverb*

supervise *verb*
to direct or manage: *to supervise a class | to supervise a job*

Word Building: **supervision** *noun* **supervisor** *noun* **supervisory** *adjective*

supper *noun*
a light meal eaten in the evening

supplant *verb*
to take the place of: *He has supplanted her as captain of the team.*

supple *adjective*
flexible or bending easily: *an athlete with a supple body | a supple cane*

Word Building: **suppleness** *noun*

supplement (say *sup-lə-mənt*) *noun*
1 something added to complete or correct: *Two hundred new words are listed in the supplement of the dictionary.* **2** an extra part of a newspaper on a particular subject: *an educational supplement*

supplement (say *sup-lə-ment*) *verb*
3 to add to: *She supplements her pocket money by babysitting.*

Word Building: **supplementary** *adjective* **supplementation** *noun*

supply *verb*
1 to provide: *to supply a school with books | to supply books to a school*

supply *noun*
2 an amount of something provided or available for use: *We have a good supply of*

paper. **3 supplies** a store of materials, food, and so on: *He was in charge of the army's supplies.*

Word Building: other verb forms are **I supplied, I have supplied, I am supplying** □ the plural of the noun is **supplies** □ **supplier** *noun*
Word History: from a Latin word meaning "fill up"

support *verb*
1 to hold up: *to support a weight | a wall that supports a building* **2** to give help or strength to: *He supported her with kindness and advice. | I have information to support my argument.* **3** to believe in and help: *They support the Labor Party. | He supports the local football team.* **4** to supply with money or other things needed for living: *He works to support his family.*
support *noun*
5 the providing of support: *I need your support.* **6** someone or something that gives support: *This pole is one of the supports of the tent. | She was a great support to him.*

Word Building: **supporter** *noun* **supportive** *adjective*

suppose *verb*
1 to take as being a fact: *Let us suppose that everything will go well.* **2** to think or believe without actual knowledge: *I suppose that you are right. | Do you suppose it was an accident?*

Word Building: **supposition** *noun*

supposed *adjective*
1 thought to be probable: *his supposed victory* **2 supposed to** expected or meant to: *You are supposed to be here at 9 o'clock every morning.*

Word Building: **supposedly** *adverb*

suppress *verb*
1 to abolish or put an end to: *The government suppressed street demonstrations.* **2** to keep inside or hidden: *He suppressed a yawn. | They suppressed the news of his death.*

Word Building: **suppression** *noun* **suppressive** *adjective* **suppressor** *noun*

supra- *prefix*
a word part meaning above: *supranational*

Word History: this prefix comes from Latin

supreme *adjective*
1 highest in position or power: *the supreme commander* **2** greatest: *supreme courage | supreme hatred*

Word Building: **supremacy** *noun*

sure *adjective*
1 certain or confident: *I am sure of what I am saying. | He is sure of success.* **2** able to be trusted: *a sure messenger* **3** firm: *to stand on sure ground* **4** never missing or slipping: *a sure aim with a gun*
5 make sure to be certain: *Make sure that you lock the door when you leave.*
sure *adverb*
6 surely or certainly: *You sure were lucky.*

Word Use: definition 6 is more suited to everyday language
Word Building: **sureness** *noun*

surely *adverb*
1 firmly or steadily: *He ran slowly but surely.* **2** almost certainly: *It will surely be fine tomorrow.*

surf *noun*
the waves which break along the shore making foamy water

Word Use: be careful – this sounds like **serf**

surface *noun*
1 the outer part or side of anything: *a polished surface | the six surfaces of a cube*
2 the top, especially of water or other liquid: *I swam up to the surface.*
3 outside appearance: *He was calm on the surface but felt frightened inside.*
surface *verb*
4 to rise to the surface: *The diver surfaced.*
5 to give a surface to: *He surfaced the path with gravel.*

surfboard *noun*
a long narrow board used to ride waves towards the shore

surfing *noun*
the sport of riding waves towards the shore, either by standing on a surfboard or by allowing your body to be carried along by the wave

Word Building: **surfer** *noun*

surge *noun*
1 a wave-like rush or forward movement: *a surge of anger | the surge of a crowd*
surge *verb*
2 to rush forwards or upwards in waves or like waves: *The crowd surged around the prime minister's car. | Blood surged to his face.*

surgeon (say <u>ser</u>-*jən*) *noun*
a doctor who does surgery

surgery *noun*
1 the treatment of diseases or injuries by using instruments to cut into the body
2 the room of a doctor or dentist where patients go for treatment

Word Building: **surgical** *adjective*

surly *adjective*
unfriendly and bad-tempered: *a surly person | a surly voice*

Word Building: other forms are **surlier, surliest**

surname *noun*
someone's family name: *Her first name is Jane and her surname is Brown.*

surpass *verb*
to be better than: *This painting surpasses all your other ones.*

surplice (say <u>ser</u>-*pləs*) *noun*
a loose white piece of outer clothing worn in church by choir singers and by some priests and ministers

Word History: from a French word meaning "over-fur (garment)"

surplus (say <u>ser</u>-*pləs*) *noun*
an amount that is more than what is needed or used: *Australia had a wheat surplus after several seasons of good rainfall.*

Word Building: **surplus** *adjective: surplus food*

surprise *verb*
1 to fill with a feeling of shock and wonder because of being unexpected or very unusual: *Her sudden outburst of anger surprised me.* **2** to come upon suddenly and unexpectedly: *He surprised me as I was creeping out the back door.*

surprise *noun*
3 something that surprises: *Your present was a lovely surprise.* **4** the feeling of being surprised: *She shouted with surprise.*

Word Building: **surprise** *adjective: a surprise party* **surprising** *adjective: a surprising event*

surrender *verb*
to give up to the ownership or power of someone else or something: *He surrendered his gun to the policeman. | I have surrendered to despair.*

Word Building: **surrender** *noun*

surround *verb*
to go around completely: *A wooden fence surrounds our house. | A feeling of sadness surrounded them.*

surroundings *plural noun*
everything that is around or near someone or something: *Everyone is affected by their surroundings.*

Word Use: a similar word is **environment**

survey (say *ser*-<u>*vay*</u>, <u>*ser*</u>-*vay*) *verb*
1 to take a general view of: *We surveyed the surrounding countryside from the hill.*
2 to ask the views of, in order to write a report about what people think or do: *You need to survey the public on this matter.*
3 to find out the form and boundaries of land by measuring: *The council surveyed the area.*

survey (say <u>ser</u>-*vay*) *noun*
4 an act of surveying: *They did a survey to see what people thought about daylight saving.* **5** a report or map made after surveying

Word Building: the plural is **surveys** □ **surveyor** *noun* someone whose job is taking surveys, particularly of land

survive *verb*
to remain alive or in existence, especially after someone else's death or after some event: *Three were killed in the expedition and only one survived. | The singer's popularity has survived through many music fads.*

Word Building: **surviving** *adjective: He has three surviving children.* **survival** *noun* **survivor** *noun*

susceptible (say *sə*-<u>*sep*</u>-*tə-bəl*) *adjective*
in the phrase **susceptible to** easily affected by: *He is susceptible to colds. | She is susceptible to praise.*

Word Building: **susceptibility** *noun*

sushi *noun*
a Japanese dish of cooked rice and raw fish wrapped in seaweed

suspect (say *səs*-<u>*pekt*</u>) *verb*
1 to think to be guilty or bad without certain knowledge: *I suspected him of being a thief.* **2** to think to be likely: *I suspect that he is not very happy.*

suspect (say <u>sus</u>-*pekt*) *noun*
3 someone who is suspected, especially of a crime: *The police have three suspects.*

suspect (say <u>sus</u>-*pekt*) *adjective*
4 open to being suspected: *Your story is very suspect.*

suspend *verb*
1 to hang by being joined to something above: *I will suspend the curtains from this rail.* **2** to put off until a later time: *The judge suspended the criminal's sentence for six months.* **3** to remove for a time from a position or membership: *The headmaster suspended him for bad behaviour.*

Word Building: **suspended** *adjective: dust particles suspended in the air*

suspender *noun*
an elastic strap with fasteners to hold up a woman's stockings

suspense *noun*
an anxious state of mind caused by having to wait to find something out: *He was in suspense until he heard the results of the exams.*

Word Building: **suspenseful** *adjective*

suspension *noun*
1 a suspending or being suspended
2 a liquid in which very small parts of a solid substance are mixed but not dissolved **3** the system of springs and so on used in a vehicle to stop jolts being felt inside or damaging the engine

suspicion (say *səs-pish-ən*) *noun*
1 the feeling of suspecting: *He looked at her with suspicion.* **2** the condition of being suspected: *He is under suspicion.*
3 a slight trace showing: *She gave the suspicion of a smile.*

Word Building: **suspicious** *adjective* **suspiciously** *adverb*

sustain *verb*
1 to hold up or support: *I can't sustain your weight for long.* **2** to suffer or have happen to you: *She sustained a terrible injury in the car accident.* **3** to keep up: *It's hard to sustain a conversation with him. | This drink should sustain you until we get there.*

Word Building: **sustenance** *noun* things that make living possible, such as food and money

swab (say *swob*) *noun*
a piece of sponge, cloth, or cottonwool, often on a stick, used for cleaning parts of your body, such as your mouth, or applying a medicine and so on

swaddle (say *swod-əl*) *verb*
to wrap up tightly with clothes or strips of cloth: *to swaddle a newborn baby*

swag *noun*
a bundle or roll of belongings carried on the shoulders by someone travelling in the bush

Word Building: **swagman** *noun*

swagger *verb*
to walk pompously and proudly

Word Use: a similar word is **strut**
Word Building: **swagger** *noun*

swallow[1] (say *swol-oh*) *verb*
1 to take into the stomach through the throat **2** to take in and make disappear: *Darkness swallowed the hills. | My new car swallowed up most of my money.*
3 to believe without questioning: *Don't swallow everything he tells you.*

Word Building: **swallow** *noun*

swallow[2] *noun*
a small bird with long wings and a forked tail

swamp (say *swomp*) *noun*
1 an area of wet soft ground
swamp *verb*
2 to flood: *Water swamped our tent.*

Word Use: a similar word to definition 1 is **marsh**

swan (say *swon*) *noun*
a large waterbird with a long thin neck, either black or white in colour

Word Use: the male is a **cob;** the female is a **pen;** the young is a **cygnet**

swank *noun*
showy smartness in appearance or behaviour: *a person with a lot of swank.*

Word Use: this word is more suited to everyday language
Word Building: **swanky** *adjective* (**swankier, swankiest**)

swap (say *swop*) *verb*
to exchange: *We swapped beds for the night.*

Word Building: other forms are **I swapped, I have swapped, I am swapping** □ **swap** *noun*

swarm (rhymes with *form*) *noun*
1 a large group of bees **2** a large number of people or things, especially when moving together
swarm *verb*
3 to move in great numbers: *People swarmed into the cinema.* **4 swarm with** to be covered or filled with: *This grass is swarming with ants.*

swarthy (say *swaw-dhee*) *adjective*
dark in skin-colour

Word Use: other forms are **swarthier, swarthiest**
Word Building: **swarthiness** *noun*

swastika (say *swos-tik-ə*) *noun*
an ancient symbol or ornament in the form of a cross with its ends bent at right angles: *The swastika was the official symbol of the Nazi party under Adolf Hitler.*

Word History: from a Sanskrit word meaning "well-being"

swat (say *swot*) *verb*
to hit with a hard quick blow

Word Use: other forms are **I swatted, I have swatted, I am swatting**

swathe (rhymes with *bathe*) *verb*
to wrap up with strips of material or other wrappings: *She swathed her neck with a scarf.*

sway *verb*
1 to move or swing from side to side: *She swayed in time to the music.* | *The wind swayed the trees.* **2** to cause to think or act in a particular way: *His speech swayed most people to vote for him.*
sway *noun*
3 a swaying movement **4** control or rule: *The Prime Minister has held sway for many years.*

swear *verb*
1 to make a very serious promise or oath: *I swear that I am speaking the truth.* | *He swore to keep the secret.* **2** to make swear: *I swore him to secrecy.* **3** to use language that is generally thought unpleasant or rude

Word Building: other forms are **I swore, I have sworn, I am swearing** □ **swearer** *noun*

sweat (say *swet*) *verb*
1 to give out a salty liquid through the skin: *This work has made me sweat.*
2 sweat at to work hard at: *I have been sweating at my homework.* **3 sweat on** to feel worried or impatient about: *I was sweating on getting that job.*
sweat *noun*
4 the liquid produced in sweating

Word Use: a similar word for definition 1 is **perspire** □ definitions 2 and 3 are more suited to everyday language
Word Building: **sweaty** *adjective*

sweater (say *swet-ə*) *noun*
a knitted jumper

sweatshirt *noun*
a loose light jumper

sweep *verb*
1 to clean or move away with a broom or brush: *to sweep a floor* | *to sweep dust away*
2 to push or touch with a light stroke: *She swept the hair from her face.* | *Her long dress swept the floor.* **3** to pass over or make pass over with a continuous movement: *Fire swept the countryside.* | *He swept a brush over the table.* **4** to move quickly and smoothly: *She swept out of the room.* | *His glance swept over the page.*
5 to stretch continuously: *The mountains sweep down to the sea.*
sweep *noun*
6 the act of sweeping: *This floor needs a sweep.* **7** a swinging movement: *He gave a sweep of his arm.* **8** steady forceful movement: *the sweep of the waves*
9 a continuous stretch: *a long sweep of sand*
10 someone whose job is sweeping, especially cleaning out chimneys

Word Building: **sweeping** *adjective* wide-ranging

sweet *adjective*
1 having a pleasant taste like that of sugar or honey **2** pleasant in any way: *sweet sounds* | *a sweet girl* | *a sweet face*
sweet *noun*
3 something that is sweet, such as a lolly **4 sweets** a dessert

Word Building: **sweeten** *verb* to make sweet **sweetly** *adverb* **sweetness** *noun*

sweet corn *noun*
the yellow kernels or seeds of maize, which you can eat as a vegetable

sweetheart *noun*
someone loved by someone

Word Use: this is often used as a way of addressing someone

sweet potato *noun*
a tropical plant with a root that you can eat as a vegetable

swell *verb*
1 to grow or make grow in size, amount or force: *The music swelled and then died away.* | *Rain swelled the river till it overflowed.* **2** to bulge out or make bulge out: *Wind swelled the sails of the ship.*
swell *noun*
3 an increase in size, amount or force
4 the movement of the waves of the sea: *There is a big swell today.* **5** someone who is rich and fashionably dressed
swell *adjective*
6 excellent: *What a swell day for a picnic!*

Word Use: definitions 5 and 6 are more suited to everyday language
Word Building: other verb forms are **it swelled, it has swollen** or **swelled, it is swelling** □ **swelling** *noun* a swollen part

swelter *verb*
to feel very hot: *We sweltered all summer.*

Word Building: **sweltering** *adjective*

swerve *verb*
to turn aside suddenly: *The car swerved to miss the dog.*

Word Building: **swerve** *noun*

swift *adjective*
fast or quick: *a swift ship* | *He is always swift to help.*

Word Building: **swiftly** *adjective* **swiftness** *noun*

swill *noun*
1 any liquid or partly liquid food for animals, especially pigs
swill *verb*
2 to drink greedily **3** to clean by flooding with water: *to swill a kitchen floor*

swim *verb*
1 to move through water by movements of the arms, legs, fins or tail **2** to move across or along by swimming: *to swim a river* **3** to be dizzy or giddy: *My head was swimming.* **4** to be covered or flooded with a liquid: *My meat was swimming in gravy.*

Word Building: other forms are **I swam, I have swum, I am swimming** □ **swim** *noun* **swimmer** *noun*

swimsuit *noun*
a piece of clothing to wear when you're swimming

swindle *verb*
to cheat out of money

Word Building: **swindle** *noun* **swindler** *noun*

swine *noun*
1 a pig **2** someone who is unpleasant or nasty

Word Use: definition 2 is more suited to everyday language
Word Building: the plural is **swine**

swing[1] *verb*
1 to move or make move to and fro
2 to move or make move in a curve: *The car swung around the corner.* | *He swung open the door.*

swing[1] *noun*
3 a swinging movement **4** a change, especially in the number of votes for a political party in an election: *a swing to Labor* **5** a seat hung from above on which you sit and swing to and fro for fun

Word Building: other verb forms are **I swung, I have swung, I am swinging**

swing[2] *noun*
a kind of jazz music, often played by big bands

swipe *verb*
1 to hit after taking a full swing with the arm: *He swiped me across the face.*
2 to steal: *She swiped my rubber.*

Word Use: this is more suited to everyday language
Word Building: **swipe** *noun*

swirl *verb*
to move in a whirling way: *Water swirled around the rock.*

Word Building: **swirl** *noun* **swirly** *adjective*

swish *verb*
to move or make move with a hissing sound: *The whip swished through the air.* | *The horse swished its tail.*

Word Building: **swish** *noun*

switch *verb*
1 to change or turn: *to switch classes* | *to switch directions* | *to switch a conversation to another subject* **2 switch on** to make an electrical appliance start: *to switch on a light* **3 switch off** to make an electrical appliance stop: *to switch off a toaster*
switch *noun*
4 a changing or turning: *a switch of plans*
5 a button for turning electricity on or off
6 a thin cane used for whipping
7 *a shortened form of* **switchboard**

switchboard *noun*
an arrangement of switches on a board, especially one that is used to connect telephone calls

swivel (say <u>swiv</u>-əl) *verb*
to turn around: *He swivelled around to have a better look.*

Word Building: other forms are **I swivelled, I have swivelled, I am swivelling**

swoon *verb*
1 to faint or become unconscious: *The pain made her swoon.* **2** to have such a strong feeling as to almost faint: *She swooned over her favourite rock star.*

swoop *verb*
1 to sweep down through the air: *The eagle swooped on the mouse.* **2** to come down in a sudden attack: *The army swooped down on the town.*

Word Building: **swoop** *noun*

sword (say *sawd*) *noun*
a weapon with a long pointed blade fixed in a handle

syllable (say *sil-ə-bəl*) *noun*
a part of a word which consists of a vowel sound and possibly consonant sounds around the vowel: *"Along" has two syllables and "wonderful" has three.*

syllabus *noun*
an outline of what is to be taught in a course of lessons

symbol *noun*
1 something that stands for or means something else: *The dove is a symbol of peace.* **2** a letter, number or other mark used to stand for something: *The symbol for degrees is °.*

Word Use: a similar word for definition 1 is **emblem**
Word Building: **symbolise** *verb: This ring symbolises our friendship.* **symbolic** *adjective*

symmetry (say *sim-ə-tree*) *noun*
the arrangements of the parts of something so that they are all balanced in size and shape: *a design with perfect symmetry*

Word Building: **symmetrical** *adjective*

sympathise or **sympathize** *verb*
1 to share in a feeling of sorrow or trouble with someone: *He sympathised with her when he heard of her mother's death.*
2 to understand and agree with: *I sympathise with your ideas.*

Word Use: a similar word for definition 1 is **commiserate**
Word Building: **sympathiser** *noun*

sympathy (say *sim-pə-thee*) *noun*
1 a feeling shared with someone else, especially in sorrow or trouble: *I felt great sympathy for her.* **2** an agreement in ideas, likes or dislikes: *They were in sympathy on that matter.*

Word Use: a similar word for definition 1 is **compassion**
Word Building: **sympathetic** *adjective* **sympathetically** *adverb*

symphony (say *sim-fə-nee*) *noun*
a musical composition for a full orchestra, usually with several movements or major sections

Word Building: the plural is **symphonies** □ **symphonic** *adjective*

symposium (say *sim-poh-zee-əm*) *noun*
a meeting for discussion

Word Building: the plural is **symposiums** or **symposia**

symptom *noun*
1 something that shows that you have a disease or illness of some kind: *A sore throat is a symptom of a cold.* **2** any sign that shows that something is happening: *Unemployment is a symptom of a weak economy.*

Word Building: **symptomatic** *adjective: A high temperature is symptomatic of flu.*

synagogue (say *sin-ə-gog*) *noun*
a Jewish place of worship

Word History: from a Greek word meaning "meeting" or "assembly"

synchronise or **synchronize** (say *sing-krə-nuyz*) *verb*
1 to happen or make happen at the same time: *Let's synchronise our arrival.*
2 to make show the same time: *We'd better synchronise our watches.*

Word Building: **synchronisation** *noun*

syncopate (say *singk-ə-payt*) *verb*
to change the rhythm of, by putting the beat in unexpected places: *to syncopate a piece of music*

Word Building: **syncopation** *noun*

syndicate (say *sin-dik-ət*) *noun*
1 a group of people of business companies who combine to carry out an expensive project: *A syndicate is building a big new hotel.*
syndicate (say *sin-dik-ayt*) *verb*
2 to form into a syndicate

synonym (say *sin-ə-nim*) *noun*
a word having the same or very similar meaning as another: *"Joyful" and "glad" are synonyms.*

Word Building: **synonymous** *adjective*

synopsis (say *sə-nop-səs*) *noun*
a written summary or outline of a longer piece of writing: *a synopsis of an essay*

Word Building: the plural is **synopses** (say *sə-nop-seez*)

synoptic chart *noun*
a chart or map showing the weather conditions over a large area at a particular time

synthesis (say *sin-thə-səs*) *noun*
the blending together of parts into a whole: *The plan was the result of a synthesis of our ideas.* | *This cloth is made by a synthesis of different materials.*

Word Use: compare this with **analysis**
Word Building: **synthesise** *verb* to make up by grouping parts together

synthesiser *noun*
a machine, usually a computer, which makes speech or music

synthetic (say *sin-thet-ik*) *adjective*
1 man-made or artificial: *synthetic rubber*
2 having to do with synthesis

syphon *noun*
another spelling for **siphon**

syringe (say *sə-rinj*) *noun*
a small tube with either a piston or a rubber bulb for drawing in and squirting out liquid, used to clean wounds or, when fitted to a needle, to inject liquid into or take it out of the body

Word Building: **syringe** *verb*

syrup *noun*
a thick, sweet, sticky liquid: *strawberry syrup*

Word Building: **syrupy** *adjective*

system *noun*
1 the way something is organised or arranged: *the decimal system of currency* | *the parliamentary system of government* | *a new system of marking exam papers*
2 an organised way of doing something: *You must have more system in your work.*
3 a set of connected parts: *a railway system* | *the nervous system of the body*

Word Building: **systematic** *adjective* orderly

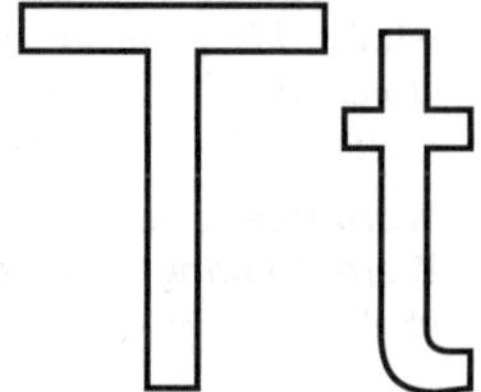

tab *noun*
1 a small flap or loop attached to a piece of clothing or something similar **2** a tag for a name or label **3 keep tabs on** to keep a watch or a check on: *They keep tabs on promising players.*

tabby *noun*
a grey or brownish-yellow cat with a striped coat

Word Building: the plural is **tabbies** □ **tabby** *adjective*

table *noun*
1 a piece of furniture which has a flat top resting on one or more legs **2** a plan or chart setting out items or numbers: *a table of contents | a multiplication table*

table *verb*
3 to set out a subject for discussion in parliament

tableau (say *tab-loh*) *noun*
a group of people arranged to form a picture or scene: *They made a charming tableau.*

Word Building: the plural is **tableaux** or **tableaus**
Word History: from a French word meaning "table" or "picture"

tablespoon *noun*
a large spoon used for measuring or serving

tablet *noun*
1 a small, flat, solid piece of medicine or soap **2** a flat slab or surface that you can carve or write on: *People used to write on tablets made of stone.*

tabloid *noun*
a newspaper with many pictures and short articles that don't give you a lot of detail about what is being described and with pages that are one half the size of an ordinary newspaper

Word Building: **tabloid** *adjective: a tabloid newspaper*

taboo (say *tə-booh*) *adjective*
strictly forbidden: *Kicking and biting are taboo.*

Word Building: **taboo** *verb* (**tabooed, tabooing**) **taboo** *noun*

tabouli (say *tə-booh-lee*) *noun*
a salad of cracked wheat, chopped parsley, mint, tomato, oil, lemon juice, and so on

Word Use: other spellings are **tabouleh** and **tabbouli**

tack *noun*
1 a small nail, such as is used in shoemaking or for putting up pictures
2 a zigzag movement or sharp turn, as in sailing against the wind

tack *verb*
3 to fasten with tacks **4** to zigzag or change direction: *The yacht tacked across the harbour.* **5** to sew loosely with large stitches **6** to join loosely or roughly: *They've tacked a bathroom onto the laundry.*

tackle *noun*
1 equipment, especially for fishing or sailing **2** the ropes and blocks used for lifting, lowering or moving heavy weights

tackle *verb*
3 to take on and struggle with: *to tackle a problem* **4** to seize and bring to a stop, especially in football: *He was heavily tackled by three opposing forwards.*
5 to try to get the ball from, especially in soccer and hockey

Word Building: **tackler** *noun*

tacky *adjective*
sticky: *They wiped their tacky fingers.*

Word Building: other forms are **tackier, tackiest** □ **tackiness** *noun*

taco (say *tah-koh, tak-*) *noun*
a flat piece of Mexican corn bread folded around a savoury filling and usually fried

tact *noun*
a sense of the right time to do or say something: *She showed great tact in handling the situation.*

Word Building: **tactful** *noun* **tactfully** *adverb* **tactfulness** *noun* **tactless** *adjective* **tactlessly** *adverb*

tactics *plural noun*
a plan of action, especially for placing and moving troops and ships during a battle: *They outwitted the enemy with their superior tactics.*

Word Building: **tactical** *adjective* **tactically** *adverb* **tactician** *noun*

tactile *adjective*
1 having a sense of touch: *The fingertips are especially tactile.* **2** inviting to the touch: *a tactile surface*

Word Building: **tactility** *noun*

tadpole *noun*
a young frog or toad in the earliest stage of its life during which it develops legs and becomes able to leave the water

tag *noun*
1 a small loop or label **2** something attached to the end of a cord such as on a shoelace

tag *verb*
3 to put a label on **4** to label or describe someone with a word or phrase: *They tagged him a coward.* **5** to follow closely, especially without being invited: *The dog tagged along wherever she went.*

Word Building: other verb forms are **I tagged, I have tagged, I am tagging**

tail *noun*
1 the end of the backbone which forms part of the body of animals such as the cat **2** the end or bottom of anything: *a shirt tail* **3 tails a** a black formal suit for men with a long-tailed coat **b** the side of a coin opposite that with the picture of a head on it: *Heads or tails?*

tail *verb*
4 to follow closely: *The police tailed his car to the airport.*

Word Use: be careful – this sounds like **tale**

tailor *noun*
1 someone who mends or makes clothes, especially for men **2** an Australian fish, named because of its scissor-like teeth

tailor *verb*
3 to provide or design for a particular need or situation, as a tailor makes clothes to fit each customer: *We'll tailor our prices to suit the market.*

Word Building: **tailor-made** *adjective*

taint *verb*
1 to spoil slightly: *His mood tainted their enjoyment.* **2** to make or become bad or corrupt

Word Building: **taint** *noun*

taipan (say *tuy-pan*) *noun*
a venomous brown snake with long fangs, found in Australia and New Guinea

Word History: from an Aboriginal language called Wik-Mungkan

take *verb*
1 to get or receive: *He took it from me.* | *They took $10 for the chair.* **2** to have or use: *to take a rest* **3** to subtract: *Take 2 from 4.* **4** to bring or carry: *Take your coat with you.* **5** to travel on or lead: *He takes a train.* | *Where will it take us?* **6** to feel or experience: *to take pride* | *to take it personally* **7** to make use of: *to take an opportunity* **8** to use up: *This takes time.* **9** to write down: *Take a note.* **10** to make: *to take a photo* **11** to regard or consider: *They take me to be a fool.* **12** to require or need: *It takes nerve to do that.* **13** to have the desired effect: *The dye didn't take, and now the colour's all wrong.* **14** to become: *She took ill.* **15 take after** to be or look like: *She takes after her aunt.* **16 take in a** to deceive or trick **b** to make smaller: *She had to take in the waist.* **17 take off a** to leave **b** to imitate: *to take off an accent*

Word Building: other verb forms are **I took, I have taken, I am taking**

takeover *noun*
the gaining or taking of control, especially of another business or country

talcum powder *noun*
a scented powder, used after a bath or shower

tale *noun*
a story, which may be true or false

Word Use: be careful – this sounds like **tail**

talent *noun*
skill or ability: *Her drawings show talent.*

Word Building: **talented** *adjective*

talisman (say *tal-əz-mən*) *noun*
something considered to be lucky or magical

talk *verb*
1 to speak, or express in words **2** to give or reveal information: *They tried to make him talk.* **3** to be able to speak: *She talks Italian.* **4** to discuss: *They are talking politics.* **5 talk someone into something** to persuade someone to do something

talk *noun*
6 an occasion for talking, such as a speech, lecture or conference **7** a conversation: *They had a good talk.* **8** gossip, or the topic of gossip: *the talk of the town*

Word Building: **talkative** *adjective* **talkatively** *adverb* **talker** *noun*

tally *noun*
1 a record or account of an amount counted or owed: *The shearers keep a tally of the sheep they shear.*

tally *verb*
2 to count or record **3** to agree: *His story doesn't tally with the facts.*

Word Building: the plural form of the noun is **tallies** □ other verb forms are **I tallied, I have tallied, I am tallying**

talon *noun*
the claw, especially of birds of prey such as the eagle

tambourine (say *tam-bə-reen*) *noun*
a small drum with a skin-covered frame which has metal discs set into it, played by hitting and shaking it

Word History: from a French word meaning "little drum"

tame *adjective*
1 used to being handled by humans: *a tame bird* **2** dull: *The film was very tame.*

Word Building: **tame** *verb* to bring under human control **tamely** *adverb* **tameness** *noun* **tamer** *noun*

tamper *verb*
to interfere so as to change or damage

tampon *noun*
a cotton plug used to absorb the flow of blood from a wound or from the vagina during menstruation

tan *verb*
1 to turn or become brown in the sun: *She tans her legs. / Her back tans nicely.*
2 to change into leather by soaking and treating: *to tan a hide*

tan *noun*
3 a suntan

tan *adjective*
4 yellowish-brown

Word Building: other verb forms are **I tanned, I have tanned, I am tanning** □ **tanner** *noun*

tandem *adverb*
1 one behind another

tandem *noun*
2 a bicycle for two riders

Word Building: **tandem** *adjective*

tandoori *adjective*
having to do with Indian food cooked in a very hot clay oven: *tandoori chicken*

tang *noun*
a strong, salty or sharp flavour or smell: *the tang of the sea*

Word Building: **tangy** *adjective* (**tangier, tangiest**)

tangent (say *tan-jənt*) *noun*
1 a straight line which touches a curve
2 a sudden new direction: *He keeps flying off at a tangent.*

Word Building: **tangent** *adjective* touching

tangerine (say *tan-jə-reen*) *noun*
1 a type of mandarin

tangerine *adjective*
2 reddish-orange

Word History: named after the Moroccan seaport of *Tangier*

tangible (say *tan-jə-bəl*) *adjective*
real, or able to be touched or felt

Word Building: **tangibly** *adverb*

tangle *verb*
to put or get in a confused muddle: *The kitten has tangled the threads.*

Word Building: **tangle** *noun*

tango *noun*
a South American ballroom dance

Word Building: the plural is **tangos** □ **tango** *verb* (**tangoed, tangoing**)

tank *noun*
1 a container for liquid, such as petrol or water **2** a heavy fighting vehicle armed with cannons and machine-guns

tankard *noun*
a beer mug, or other large cup, sometimes with a lid

tanker *noun*
a large vehicle or vessel for carrying oil or other liquids in large quantities

tantalise or **tantalize** *verb*
to tease or torment with the sight of something wished for but out of reach

Word Building: **tantalising** *adjective* **tantalisingly** *adverb*

tantrum *noun*
a violent outburst of temper

Taoism (say *tow-iz-əm*) *noun*
a Chinese philosophy which encourages people not to interfere with nature and to be sincere and honest

Word Building: **Taoist** *noun* a follower of Taoism

tap[1] *verb*
to hit lightly

Word Building: other forms are **I tapped, I have tapped, I am tapping** □ **tap** *noun*

tap[2] *noun*
1 something used to control the flow of liquid: *a bath tap*

tap[2] *verb*
2 to draw on, as from a supply of water, or other resources: *He was able to tap his reserves of energy.* **3** to connect with secretly, in order to overhear conversation: *They have tapped her phone.*

Word Building: other verb forms are **I tapped, I have tapped, I am tapping**

tape *noun*
1 a long strip of paper, cloth or a similar material such as you use in sewing or in typewriters **2** a plastic strip coated with magnetic powder, used to record sound and video signals and to store information from computers **3** *another name for* **tape measure**

tape *verb*
4 to record on tape: *He taped my record of the opera.*

tape measure *noun*
a long strip or ribbon made of linen or steel, marked with millimetres and centimetres for measuring

taper *verb*
1 to gradually narrow or thin at one end: *The road tapers in to a track. / She tapered her nails to a point.*

taper *noun*
2 a very thin candle

Word Building: **tapering** *adjective*

tape-recorder *noun*
a machine which records sound on magnetic tape

tapestry *noun*
a piece of cloth with a design which has been woven or embroidered

Word Building: the plural is **tapestries**

tapeworm *noun*
a flat or tapelike worm which lives in the intestine of people and animals

tapioca (say *tap-ee-oh-kə*) *noun*
floury grains of cassava starch used for puddings and thickening sauce

taproot *noun*
the big main root of a plant from which the other roots branch

tar *noun*
a thick, black, sticky substance that you get from wood or coal, especially used for making roads

Word Building: **tar** *verb* (**tarred, tarring**) to cover or smear with tar

tarantula (say *tə-ran-chə-lə*) *noun*
1 a large, furry, Australian spider which often shelters indoors when it's raining **2** a venomous spider of Europe

Word Use: another name for definition 1 is **huntsman**
Word History: named after the Italian seaport of *Taranto*, where the European spider is common

target *noun*
1 something which you aim at in order to hit or reach: *Her arrow hit the centre of the target. / They set a target of ten days to finish work.* **2** a victim: *He is the target of their jokes.*

Word Use: another word for definition 2 is **butt**

tariff *noun*
1 a charge for importing something into a country **2** the price charged for a room in a hotel

tarmac *noun*
1 a mixture of tar and gravel used to seal roads **2** an airport runway

Word History: a short form of *tarmacadam* (*tar* + *macadam*, a road surface of broken stones)

tarnish *verb*
to dull, discolour or spoil: *Silver tarnishes in the salt air.* | *to tarnish a reputation*

Word Building: **tarnish** *noun* **tarnished** *adjective*

tarpaulin (say *tah-paw-lən*) *noun*
a large canvas or other waterproof cover

tarragon *noun*
a strong-smelling herb used in cooking and salads

tarry *verb*
to linger or loiter

Word Use: this is a rather old-fashioned word
Word Building: other forms are **I tarried, I have tarried, I am tarrying**

tart[1] *adjective*
sour or sharp: *a tart taste* | *a tart retort*

Word Building: **tartly** *adverb* **tartness** *noun*

tart[2] *noun*
a shallow fruit or jam pie, without a top

tartan *noun*
the checked woollen cloth in the colours of the different Scottish Highland clans, or any similar checked cloth

Word Building: **tartan** *adjective*

task *noun*
1 a piece of work, or a duty **2 take to task** to blame or scold

Tasmanian devil *noun*
a fierce black-and-white meat-eating marsupial, found in Tasmania

tassel *noun*
a bunch of silk, or other threads, hanging as an ornament

taste *noun*
1 the sense which experiences flavour **2** flavour: *It has a sweet taste.* **3** a liking or enjoyment: *I've acquired a taste for olives.* **4** a sense of what belongs or is attractive: *He has no taste.* **5** a first experience or sample: *She had a taste of city life.*

taste *verb*
6 to try by eating: *He tasted the soup to see if it was ready.* **7** to experience or feel, especially through your sense of taste **8** to have a certain flavour: *This tastes like chicken.*

tasty *adjective*
full of flavour: *a tasty sauce*

Word Building: other forms are **tastier, tastiest** □ **tastiness** *noun*

tatters *plural noun*
torn or ragged pieces, especially of clothing: *His shirt was in tatters.*

tattoo[1] *noun*
1 a signal on a trumpet or drum: *to beat a tattoo* **2** an outdoor military display

tattoo[2] *noun*
an ink picture permanently printed into someone's skin with needles

Word Building: **tattoo** *verb* (**tattooed, tattooing**)

taunt *verb*
to insult or tease cruelly

Word Building: **taunt** *noun* **taunting** *adjective* **tauntingly** *adverb*

taut *adjective*
stretched tight: *They held the rope taut.*

Word Building: **tautly** *adverb* **tautness** *noun*

tavern *noun*
a place where food and alcoholic drink can be bought

tawdry *adjective*
cheap and showy: *tawdry jewellery*

tawny *adjective*
yellowish-brown, like a lion's coat

Word Building: other forms are **tawnier, tawniest**
Word History: from a French word meaning "tanned"

tax *noun*
1 money people have to pay each year to support the government

tax *verb*
2 to put a tax on **3** to burden or exhaust: *The work taxes her strength.*

Word Building: **taxable** *adjective* **taxation** *noun*

taxi *noun*
1 a car for hire, with a driver and a meter which calculates the fare

taxi *verb*
2 to move along the runway before taking off, or after landing: *The pilot taxied the plane to the terminal.*

Word Building: the plural of the noun is **taxis** □ other verb forms are **I taxied, I have taxied, I am taxiing**

tea *noun*
1 a drink made by pouring boiling water onto the dried leaves of a shrub grown in China, India and Ceylon **2** the dried leaves of this shrub **3** a late afternoon or evening meal: *They had tea at six.*

Word History: from the Chinese word *ch'a*

teach *verb*
to instruct or give knowledge of: *She teaches kindergarten children.* | *He teaches Maths.*

Word Building: other forms are **I taught, I have taught, I am teaching** □ **teacher** *noun*

teak *noun*
a hard long-lasting wood used for ship building and furniture

team *noun*
1 a group of people who share an activity, such as sport or work: *A new doctor joined the team.* **2** a number of animals harnessed together to do work: *a team of oxen*

tear[1] (rhymes with *here*) *noun*
1 a drop of water that falls from your eye, caused by sadness or pain **2 in tears** crying: *She is in tears again.*

Word Building: **tearful** *adjective* **tearfully** *adverb*

tear[2] (rhymes with *bare*) *verb*
1 to rip: *She tore her skirt.* | *The paper tears easily.* **2** to remove or pull away: *He will tear the food from your hands.* | *He couldn't tear himself from the game.*
3 tear off to hurry away

Word Building: other forms are **I tore, I have torn, I am tearing** □ **tear** *noun* a rip

tease (say *teez*) *verb*
1 to mock or pester in a light-hearted but embarrassing way **2** to separate the strands of: *to tease wool*

Word Building: **tease** *noun* **teasing** *adjective* **teasingly** *adverb*

teaspoon *noun*
a small spoon which holds about five millilitres

teat *noun*
the rubber top on a baby's bottle which is shaped like a nipple

tea-tree *noun*
a shrub with small leaves and red, white or pink flowers, found in Australia and New Zealand

technical (say *tek-nik-əl*) *adjective*
1 having to do with practical science and machinery: *a technical education*
2 using words or covering topics that only an expert would understand

Word Building: **technicality** *noun* **technically** *adverb* **technician** *noun*

technique (say *tek-neek*) *noun*
1 the way of doing or performing: *His technique is influenced by his teacher.*
2 practical skill or knowledge: *She has good ideas but not much technique.*

technology (say *tek-nol-ə-jee*) *noun*
the study of the use of science in industry

Word Building: **technological** *adjective* **technologically** *adverb* **technologist** *noun*

tedious *adjective*
long and boring: *a tedious wait* | *a tedious lecture*

Word Building: **tediously** *adverb* **tedium** *noun*

tee *noun*
1 the starting place for each hole in golf
2 a plastic or wooden holder from which you drive a golf ball

tee *verb*
3 tee off to strike the ball from a tee
4 tee up to organise or arrange: *We've teed up a partner for you.*

teem[1] *verb*
teem with to be full of: *The park teems with wildlife.*

Word Building: **teeming** *adjective*

teem[2] *verb*
to rain very hard

teenager *noun*
someone who is aged between twelve and twenty

Word Building: **teenage** *adjective*

teetotal *adjective*
opposed to the drinking of alcohol: *a teetotal organisation*

Word Building: **teetotalism** *noun* **teetotaller** *noun*

telecast *noun*
a television broadcast

telecommunications *plural noun*
the sending of messages by telephone, radio or satellite

telegram *noun*
a message sent by telegraph

telegraph *noun*
a system or device for sending messages by electric signals along wire

Word Building: **telegraph** *verb* **telegraphic** *adjective* **telegraphy** *noun*

telepathy (say *tə-lep-ə-thee*) *noun*
the sharing or passing on of information or thoughts between one person's mind and another's without speaking, writing or using actions: *We didn't tell him so he must have known by telepathy.*

Word Building: **telepathic** *adjective* **telepathically** *adverb* **telepathist** *noun*

telephone *noun*
a means of speaking to someone else over a long distance, usually powered by electricity

Word Use: a shortened form of this is **phone**
Word Building: **telephone** *verb* **telephonic** *adjective* **telephonically** *adverb* **telephonist** *noun*

telephoto lens *noun*
a lens for a camera which gives a larger picture of distant objects

teleprinter *noun*
an instrument with a typewriter keyboard which sends and receives messages by changing typed information into electrical signals

telescope *noun*
a tube-shaped instrument with powerful lenses which make distant objects seem closer

Word Building: **telescope** *verb* **telescopic** *adjective*

television *noun*
1 the sending of pictures by radio waves which are picked up by the receiving sets of viewers **2** a television set or receiver

Word Use: a shortened form of this is **TV**
Word Building: **televise** *verb*

telex *noun*
1 a postal service in which teleprinters are rented to businesses which can send and receive their own messages **2** the message sent or received

Word Building: the plural is **telexes** □ **telex** *verb*

tell *verb*
1 to give an account or description of
2 to express or say: *to tell a lie*
3 to know or recognise: *Can you tell which is yours?* **4** to order: *Tell him to go.*
5 to have or show an effect: *The strain is telling on her.* **6 tell on** to tell tales about **7 tell off** to scold

Word Building: other forms are **I told, I have told, I am telling**

teller *noun*
someone who works in a bank receiving and paying out the customers' money

telltale *adjective*
revealing, especially what is not meant to be known: *There were telltale footprints under the window.*

Word Building: **telltale** *noun*

temper *noun*
1 the particular state of mind or mood you are in: *She's in a good temper.* **2** an angry or resentful mood: *You're often in a temper.*

temper *verb*
3 to strengthen by changes of temperature: *to temper steel* **4** to make less severe: *She tempered her anger.*

temperament *noun*
a type of personality, especially a moody one: *She has a cheerful temperament.* | *He has such a temperament.*

Word Building: **temperamental** *adjective* moody **temperamentally** *adverb*

temperance *noun*
1 moderation and self-control, especially in drinking alcohol **2** the complete avoidance of alcohol

temperate (say *tem-pə-rət*) *adjective*
moderate and steady: *a temperate use of alcohol* | *a temperate winter*

Word Building: **temperately** *adverb* **temperateness** *noun*

temperature (say *temp-rə-chə*) *noun*
1 a measure of the degree of heat or cold of something or someone
2 an abnormally high amount of heat in your body: *to have a temperature*

tempest *noun*
a violent storm or a violent disturbance: *The ship sank in the tempest.* | *a tempest of tears*

Word Building: **tempestuous** *adjective* **tempestuously** *adverb*
Word History: from a Latin word meaning "season"

temple[1] *noun*
a large building where people worship

temple[2] *noun*
the flat part on either side of your forehead

tempo *noun*
speed, rhythm or pattern: *music with a fast tempo | the tempo of modern life*

temporary (say temp-ree) *adjective*
lasting for a short time: *a temporary job*

Word Use: the opposite is **permanent**
Word Building: **temporarily** *adverb*

tempt *verb*
1 to attract or persuade, especially to something unwise or forbidden
2 to dare or provoke: *Don't tempt fate.*

Word Building: **temptation** *noun* **tempter** *noun* **tempting** *adjective* **temptingly** *adverb* **temptress** *noun*

tenacious (say *tə-nay-shəs*) *adjective*
1 holding on firmly: *a tenacious grip*
2 stubbornly persistent: *a tenacious person*

Word Building: **tenaciously** *adverb* **tenacity** *noun*

tenant *noun*
someone who pays rent for the use of a house, land or a flat

Word Building: **tenancy** *noun*

tend[1] *verb*
1 to be likely or inclined: *I tend to be cross when I'm tired.* **2** to move in a certain direction: *The sunflower tends toward the light.*

Word Building: **tendency** *noun* (**tendencies**)

tend[2] *verb*
to watch or look after: *to tend a fire | The nurse is tending him.*

tender[1] *adjective*
1 not tough or hard: *tender steak*
2 warm and affectionate: *a tender heart*
3 gentle or delicate: *a tender touch*
4 painful to feel or discuss: *tender to the touch | It's a tender subject.*

Word Building: **tenderly** *adverb* **tenderness** *noun*

tender[2] *verb*
1 to offer: *He tendered his resignation.*
tender[2] *noun*
2 an offer, as of payment or to do a job for a certain price: *They will accept the lowest tender.*

tendon *noun*
a cord of tough body tissue joining a muscle to a bone

Word Use: another word with the same meaning is **sinew**

tendril *noun*
a coiling threadlike part of a climbing plant

tenement (say *ten-ə-mənt*) *noun*
a building divided into flats, especially one in the poorer crowded parts of a large city

tennis *noun*
a game in which two players, or two pairs of players, use racquets to hit a ball over a central net

tenor (say *ten-ə*) *noun*
1 the range of musical notes which can be sung by a male singer with a high voice: *He sings tenor in the choir.* **2** a man with a high singing voice

Word Use: **tenor** range is higher than **baritone** and **bass** and lower than **soprano** and **alto**
Word Building: **tenor** *adjective: a tenor saxophone*

tense[1] *adjective*
1 rigid or stretched tight **2** suffering from nervous strain: *He has been very tense since his illness.*

Word Building: **tense** *verb* **tensely** *adverb* **tenseness** *noun* **tension** *noun*

tense[2] *noun*
the form of a verb which shows the time of an action

Word Use: see **present tense, past tense, future tense**

tent *noun*
a movable shelter made of cloth, held up by poles

tentacle *noun*
a thin, easily-bent, arm-like part on an animal such as an octopus, used for feeling and grasping

tentative *adjective*
unsure or cautious: *He made a tentative attempt to join in the conversation.*

Word Building: **tentatively** *adverb*

tenuous *adjective*
weak or vague: *a tenuous connection*

Word Building: **tenuously** *adverb*

tepee *noun*
an American-Indian tent made of skins

tepid (say *tep-əd*) *adjective*
lukewarm or slightly warm

Word Building: **tepidly** *adverb*

teppan yaki *noun*
a Japanese dish in which pieces of meat or fish are roasted on a hot iron plate

Word History: from the Japanese word for "iron" added to the Japanese word for "roast" or "bake"

term *noun*
1 a division of the year in schools and colleges **2** a period of time: *in the long term* **3** a descriptive or naming word or group of words: *This book is full of technical terms.* **4 terms** conditions of agreement

terminal *adjective*
1 marking the end: *a terminal illness*
terminal *noun*
2 the end of a railway line or other travel route where passengers and goods arrive and leave: *an air terminal* **3** a point where current enters or leaves in an electrical circuit **4** *another name for* **computer terminal**

terminate *verb*
1 to bring to an end: *They have terminated his job at the factory.* **2** to come to the end of a journey at a certain place: *This train terminates here.*

terminus *noun*
a station at the end of a railway line or bus route

termite *noun*
a pale-coloured insect which can destroy buildings and furniture by boring holes in wood

Word Use: a termite is often called a **white ant**, though it is not really an ant

terrace *noun*
1 a narrow flattened area on the side of a hill: *a rice terrace* **2** a row of houses joined together **3** one of these houses

terracotta *noun*
1 a clay used for pipes, roof tiles and other similar things
terracotta *adjective*
2 brownish-red

Word History: from an Italian word meaning "baked earth"

terrain *noun*
a part of the land surface, with its natural features in mind: *rough terrain*

Word History: from a French word meaning "earth"

terrestrial *adjective*
living or growing on land

terrible *adjective*
1 causing great fear: *a terrible monster*
2 very bad: *a terrible noise*

Word Building: **terribly** *adverb*

terrier *noun*
a kind of small dog, originally used for hunting

terrific *adjective*
1 very great: *terrific speed* **2** very good: *a terrific game*

Word Building: **terrifically** *adverb*

terrify *verb*
to frighten very much

Word Building: other forms are **I terrified, I have terrified, I am terrifying**

territory *noun*
land thought of as belonging to someone: *enemy territory*

Word Building: the plural is **territories** □ **territorial** *adjective*

terror *noun*
an overpowering fear

terrorise or **terrorize** *verb*
to fill with fear and alarm

terrorism *noun*
a way of fighting a government by acts of armed violence

terry towelling *noun*
a cotton cloth with loops on both sides

terse *adjective*
short and to the point: *a terse comment*

Word Building: **tersely** *adverb* **terseness** *noun*

tertiary education (say *ter-shə-ree*) *noun*
education at college or university, which follows secondary education

test *noun*
1 a trial to decide something: *a test of strength* **2** a set of questions to answer, designed to show how much you know about something: *a maths test*
3 *another word for* **test match**
test *verb*
4 to try in order to find out: *to test if the water is hot enough* | *to test the class's knowledge*

testament *noun*
1 a will **2 Testament** either of the two main divisions of the Christian bible, the Old Testament and the New Testament

Word Use: definition 1 is used mostly in the phrase "last will and testament"
Word Building: **testamentary** *adjective*

testicle *noun*
one of the two round male sex glands in the scrotum

testify *verb*
1 to swear as true: *The witness testified that he had seen a blue Holden near the bank.*
2 to give evidence: *The barren land testifies to a hard winter.*

Word Building: other forms are **I testified, I have testified, I am testifying**

testimonial *noun*
1 a reference for a job **2** something given as an expression of appreciation: *He was given a watch as a testimonial from his workmates.*

testimony (say *test-ə-mə-nee*) *noun*
the statement of a witness under oath to tell the truth

Word Building: the plural is **testimonies**

test match *noun*
one of a series of international sporting events, usually cricket or rugby

tetanus (say *tet-ə-nəs*) *noun*
an infectious, often deadly, disease which causes extreme stiffness of the muscles of the jaw and other parts of the body

Word Use: an old-fashioned word for this is **lockjaw**
Word History: from a Greek word meaning "spasm" (of muscles)

tether *noun*
a rope or chain for tying up an animal

Word Building: **tether** *verb*

text *noun*
1 the main body of words in a book, not including notes, the index and other extra material **2** *another word for* **textbook**

Word Building: **textual** *adjective*

textbook *noun*
a book setting out the information for a course of study in a subject

textile *noun*
any woven material used for clothing, curtains and so on

texture *noun*
the roughness or smoothness of a material: *The pebbles next to the concrete give a contrast in texture.*

thank *verb*
1 to give thanks to: *to thank them for their kindness*
thank *noun*
2 thanks words saying how grateful you are

Word Building: **thankful** *adjective*
thankless *adjective*

thatch *verb*
to cover a roof with straw, reeds or palm leaves

Word Building: **thatch** *noun*

thaw *verb*
to melt: *The ice has thawed.*

Word Building: **thaw** *noun*

theatre (say *thear-tə*) *noun*
1 a building or hall for presenting plays, opera, ballet and so on **2** a cinema
3 a room in a hospital where operations are performed

theatrical (say *thee-at-rik-əl*) *adjective*
1 in or belonging to a theatre: *a theatrical presentation* **2** aiming to create an effect: *She made a theatrical entrance into the restaurant.*

Word Building: **theatrically** *adverb*

theft *noun*
the act or crime of stealing

their *pronoun*
a form of **they** that shows something belongs to them: *The boys are in their room.*

Word Use: be careful – this sounds like **there** and **they're**
Word Building: **theirs** *pronoun: That umbrella is theirs.*

them *pronoun*
the form of **they** you use after a verb: *I'll take them away.*

theme *noun*
the subject of a speech, a book, or a piece of music

theodolite (say *thee-od-ə-luyt*) *noun*
an instrument used in surveying land

theology *noun*
1 the study of God and religion
2 a collection of beliefs held by a particular religion: *Christian theology*

Word Building: the plural is **theologies** □ **theologian** *noun* **theological** *adjective* **theologically** *adverb*

theorem (say *thear-rəm*) *noun*
a statement containing something to be proved in mathematics

theory (say *thear-ree*) *noun*
1 an explanation based on observation and reason: *atomic theory* **2** a suggested explanation with little or no basis in fact: *a theory about ghosts* **3** the part of a subject which deals with underlying principles rather than practice: *You can put a new element in an electric jug without knowing the theory of electricity.*

Word Building: the plural is **theories** □ **theoretical** *adjective* **theoretically** *adverb* **theorise** *verb*

therapy *noun*
healing treatment: *water therapy* | *speech therapy*

Word Building: the plural is **therapies** □ **therapeutic** *adjective* **therapist** *noun*

there *adverb*
1 in or at that place: *Your book is there, where you left it.* **2** at that particular point: *He finished there, ready to start again.*

Word Use: compare this with **here** □ be careful – this sounds like **their** and **they're**

thermometer *noun*
an instrument for measuring temperature

thermos flask *noun*
a container with two walls made of silver glass, for keeping cold substances cold and hot substances hot

Word Use: a short form of this is **thermos**
Word History: from a trademark, based on a Greek word meaning "hot"

thermostat *noun*
a device for keeping a temperature steady: *an oven thermostat*

thesaurus (say *thə-saw-rəs*) *noun*
a book of words arranged in groups which have a similar meaning

Word Building: the plural is **thesauruses**
Word History: from a Greek word meaning "treasure" or "treasure house"

thesis (say *thee-səs*) *noun*
1 an idea, argument or explanation, especially one to be discussed and proved **2** a book-length essay presented by a student for a higher university degree

Word Building: the plural is **theses** (say *thee-seez*)

they *pronoun*
the plural of **he, she** and **it** that comes before a verb: *They sang sweetly.*

Word Building: other forms are **theirs** and **they**

they'd
a short form of **they had** or **they would**

they'll
a short form of **they will** or **they shall**

they're
a short form of **they are**

Word Use: be careful – this sounds like **their** and **there**

they've
a short form of **they have**

thick *adjective*
1 measuring rather a lot from one surface to the other: *a thick slice of bread* | *a thick blanket* **2** measuring as stated between opposite surfaces: *a board two centimetres thick* **3** dense or packed close together: *thick bush* | *a thick crowd* **4** not runny or pouring easily: *a thick sauce* **5** with the particles close together: *thick smoke*

Word Building: **thicken** *verb* **thickly** *adverb* **thickness** *noun*

thicket *noun*
a thick growth of shrubs or small trees

thief *noun*
someone who steals

Word Building: the plural is **thieves**

thieve *verb*
to steal

thigh *noun*
the part of your leg between your groin and your knee

thimble *noun*
a protective metal cover for your finger, worn when sewing

thin *adjective*
1 measuring not much from one surface to the other: *a thin slice of bread*
2 slim or lean: *She keeps thin by exercising.*
3 barely covering or scattered: *thin hair* | *a thin crowd* **4** runny or watery: *thin gravy*
5 easily seen through: *thin curtains* | *a thin excuse*

Word Building: **thin** *verb* (**thinned, thinning**) **thinly** *adverb* **thinness** *noun*

thing *noun*
1 a real object that is not alive
2 some object which is not or cannot be easily described: *The stick had a brass thing on it.* **3** a matter or affair: *Things are going well.* **4 things** utensils or personal belongings: *the tea things | your things on the table*

think *verb*
1 to form or turn over in your mind: *to think pleasant thoughts | He was thinking what to do.* **2** to imagine or have an idea of: *Think what it would be like to be rich.* **3** to have a purpose in mind: *She thought she would go home.* **4** to consider or have an opinion: *He thought the film was good.* **5** to take account: *Think of other people's feelings.*

Word Building: other forms are **I thought, I have thought, I am thinking**

thirst *noun*
1 an uncomfortable feeling of dryness in your mouth and throat caused by the need for a drink **2** an eager desire: *a thirst for knowledge*

Word Building: **thirsty** *adjective* (**thirstier, thirstiest**) **thirst** *verb* **thirstily** *adverb*

thistle *noun*
a plant with prickly leaves and purple or white flowers

thong *noun*
1 a simple kind of sandal, usually made of rubber or leather **2** a narrow strip of leather

thorax *noun*
1 the chest in human beings or a similar part in other animals **2** the part of an insect's body between its head and abdomen

Word Building: the plural is **thoraces** or **thoraxes**
Word History: from a Greek word meaning "breastplate" or "chest"

thorn *noun*
a sharp-pointed prickle on the stem of a plant

Word Building: **thorny** *adjective* (**thornier, thorniest**)

thorough *adjective*
complete, careful or without missing anything: *a thorough search | a thorough wash*

Word Building: **thoroughly** *adverb* **thoroughness** *noun*

thoroughfare *noun*
a public road or way open at both ends

thought *noun*
1 the forming of ideas in your mind
2 an idea **3** consideration or reflection: *Give it thought before you agree.*

Word Building: **thoughtful** *adjective* **thoughtless** *adjective*

thrash *verb*
1 to beat soundly as a punishment
2 to defeat utterly

thread (rhymes with *red*) *noun*
1 a very thin cord of cotton, wool or other fibre spun out to a great length and used for weaving cloth **2** a very thin cord of any fibre used for sewing **3** a thin strand **4** the spiral part on a screw

thread *verb*
5 to pass a thread through

threadbare *adjective*
worn and thin: *threadbare trousers | a threadbare argument*

threat (rhymes with *bet*) *noun*
1 a warning that you intend to hurt or rob someone: *Terrified by his threats, she handed over the money.* **2** a possible danger: *a threat of war*

Word Building: **threaten** *verb*

three-dimensional *adjective*
having, or seeming to have, length, breadth and height and therefore a solid look

thresh *verb*
to separate grain or seeds from, by beating: *to thresh corn*

threshold (say *thresh-hohld*) *noun*
1 the bottom part of an entrance or doorway: *He paused on the threshold.*
2 a beginning point: *the threshold of a career*

thrift *noun*
careful management of money and supplies

Word Building: **thrifty** *adjective* (**thriftier, thriftiest**) **thriftless** *adjective*

thrill *verb*
1 to feel a sudden wave of strong emotion: *to thrill with terror* **2** to excite very much: *She was thrilled at winning the prize.*

Word Building: **thrill** *noun* **thrilling** *adjective*

thriller *noun*
an exciting story, especially one about a crime

thrive *verb*
1 to grow strongly **2** to do well or prosper: *The business is thriving.*

throat *noun*
1 the front of your neck below your chin
2 the passage from your mouth to your stomach or lungs

throb *verb*
to beat regularly and strongly: *His heart throbbed.* | *The engine throbbed.*

Word Building: other forms are **it throbbed, it has throbbed, it is throbbing**

throne *noun*
1 the special chair used by a king, queen or bishop on important occasions.
2 the office or power of a king or queen: *to be loyal to the throne*

throng *noun*
a crowd: *Throngs of people watched the parade.*

Word Building: **throng** *verb: People thronged to the show.*

throttle *verb*
1 to choke or strangle
throttle *noun*
2 a device such as a lever which controls the flow of petrol into an engine

through (say *throoh*) *preposition*
in at one end or side and out the other: *through the tunnel* | *to stitch through material*

Word Use: another spelling is **thru** but this is not suited to formal writing

throw *verb*
1 to fling or send through the air
2 to arrange: *to throw a party*
3 throw up to vomit

Word Use: definition 3 is more suited to everyday language
Word Building: other forms are **I threw, I have thrown, I am throwing** □ **throw** *noun*

thrust *verb*
to force or push hard: *to thrust a dagger into his back* | *to thrust through the crowds*

Word Building: other forms are **he thrust, he has thrust, he is thrusting** □ **thrust** *noun*

thud *noun*
a heavy bumping sound: *to fall to the ground with a thud*

Word Building: **thud** *verb* (**thudded, thudding**)

thug *noun*
someone who is brutal and violent

Word History: from the name of a group of robbers and murders in India who strangled their victims

thumb (rhymes with *sum*) *noun*
1 the inner finger that is much shorter and thicker than the rest **2 all thumbs** clumsy and awkward
thumb *verb*
3 to turn over using your thumb: *to thumb through the pages of a book*

thump *verb*
to hit heavily or beat: *to thump on the back* | *My heart is thumping.*

Word Building: **thump** *noun*

thunder *noun*
the loud booming noise that follows a flash of lightning in a storm

Word Building: **thunder** *verb* **thunderous** *adjective* **thundery** *adjective*

thunderbolt *noun*
1 a flash of lightning and thunder
2 something that suddenly frightens or surprises you

Thursday *noun*
the fifth day of the week

Word Use: the abbreviations are **Thur** or **Thurs**

thwart (rhymes with *short*) *verb*
to oppose or stop from succeeding: *to thwart their plans*

thyme (sounds like *time*) *noun*
a common garden herb of the mint family

tiara (say *tee-ah-rə*) *noun*
a piece of women's jewellery that looks like a tiny crown

tick[1] *noun*
1 the clicking sound made by a clock
2 a small mark (✓) used to show that something has been done correctly
3 a moment or instant: *I'll be there in a tick.*
tick[1] *verb*
4 to make ticking sounds **5** to mark correct with a tick **6 tick off** to scold or speak crossly to

Word Use: definition 3 is more suited to everyday language

tick[2] *noun*
a tiny blood-sucking creature whose poison can paralyse dogs and cats

ticket *noun*
1 a small printed card which shows that you have paid for something: *a bus ticket* **2** a label or tag showing how much something costs

tickle *verb*
to stroke or poke lightly, causing itching or irritation

Word Building: **tickle** *noun*

ticklish *adjective*
1 sensitive to being tickled: *I'm ticklish under the arms.* **2** difficult and needing to be handled carefully: *a ticklish situation*

tidal wave *noun*
a huge ocean wave which rises up after an earthquake in the sea bed or near the shore

tiddlywinks *noun*
a game in which you flick coloured discs into a cup

tide *noun*
1 the rise and fall of the ocean, twice each day **2** a trend which comes and goes like a tide: *the tide of good fortune*
tide *verb*
3 tide over to help through a difficult time: *This money will tide you over until pay day.*

Word Building: **tidal** *adjective*

tidings *plural noun*
news or information: *to bring glad tidings*

tidy *adjective*
1 neat, with everything in its right place: *a tidy desk*
tidy *noun*
2 a rubbish container: *a kitchen tidy*

Word Building: other adjective forms are **tidier, tidiest** □ the plural form of the noun is **tidies** □ **tidy** *verb* (**tidied, tidying**) **tidily** *adverb* **tidiness** *noun*

tie *verb*
1 to fasten with cord or string: *to tie a parcel* **2** to loop into a knot or bow: *to tie a ribbon around your hair* **3** to get the same score in a contest: *They tied for first place.*
tie *noun*
4 a ribbon or string **5** a strip of cloth worn around your neck and knotted under your collar

Word Building: other verb forms are **I tied, I have tied, I am tying**

tier (rhymes with *here*) *noun*
a row or layer: *tiers of seats in a theatre*

tiger *noun*
a large wild animal of the cat family which has yellow-brown fur with black stripes

Word Use: the male is a **tiger;** the female is a **tigress;** the young is a **cub**

tiger snake *noun*
a very venomous Australian snake with striped markings

tight *adjective*
1 fitting very closely: *tight shoes* **2** pulled or stretched as far as it can go: *a tight knot* **3** drunk **4** mean with money

Word Use: definitions 3 and 4 are more suited to everyday language
Word Building: **tight** *adverb* **tighten** *verb* **tightness** *noun*

tightrope *noun*
a wire stretched tightly above the ground for acrobats to balance on

tights *plural noun*
stockings that stretch from your waist to your feet

tile *noun*
a thin slab of baked clay for covering roofs, floors, walls and other surfaces

Word Building: **tile** *verb: to tile a roof*

till[1] *verb*
to dig and prepare for planting crops: *to till the soil*

Word Use: a similar word is **cultivate**

till[2] *noun*
a drawer for keeping money in, in a shop

tiller *noun*
a handle joined to a boat's rudder, used for steering

tilt *verb*
1 to lean or slant: *to tilt the ladder against the wall* | *to tilt to the left* **2** to fight in a jousting tournament

Word Building: **tilt** *noun*

timber *noun*
wood that has been sawn ready for building

Word Building: **timber** *adjective: a timber house* **timbered** *adjective* covered with trees

timbre (say *tam-bə, tim-bə*) *noun*
the particular sound an instrument makes: *The flute and clarinet have different timbres.*

Word History: from a Greek word meaning "tambourine" or "kettledrum"

time *noun*
1 the passing of the hours, days, weeks, months and years **2** a particular moment shown by a clock: *What is the time?* **3** a particular period or moment: *It is time to go home.* **4** the rhythm or tempo of a piece of music **5 from time to time** occasionally **6 on time** punctually or at the right time **7 time after time** again and again **8 times** lots of, or multiplied by: *I know that 5 times 4 is 20.*
time *verb*
9 to measure or record the time or speed of: *to time a race* **10** to choose the moment for: *She timed her arrival perfectly.*

Word Building: **timeless** *adjective* everlasting **timer** *noun*

timely *adjective*
happening at just the right time: *a timely arrival*

Word Building: **timeliness** *noun*

timepiece *noun*
a clock or watch, especially an old-fashioned one

time signature *noun*
a sign of two numbers written one above the other at the beginning of a piece of music showing the rhythm

Word Use: compare **key signature**

timetable *noun*
1 a list of the times when buses and trains arrive and depart **2** a list of the times when school lessons begin

timid *adjective*
easily frightened

Word Building: **timidity** *noun* **timidly** *adverb*

timing *noun*
control of the best time for something to happen: *The timing of the announcement was perfect.*

timorous (say *tim-ə-rəs*) *adjective*
timid or fearful

Word Building: **timorously** *adverb*

timpani (say *tim-pə-nee*) *plural noun*
a set of kettledrums

tin *noun*
1 a light silver-coloured metal that cans and cooking pots are made of **2** a metal container, such as a can or a pan: *a tin of apricots | a cake tin*

Word Building: **tin** *verb* (**tinned, tinning**) to seal up and preserve in a tin

tinder *noun*
dry paper or twigs that catch fire easily

tinea (say *tin-ee-ə*) *noun*
a skin disease, caused by a fungus, which makes the skin between your toes red and sore

Word History: from a Latin word meaning "gnawing worm"

tingle *verb*
to have a prickly feeling: *to tingle with cold | to tingle with excitement*

Word Building: **tingle** *noun* **tingling** *adjective*

tinker *noun*
1 someone who used to go from door to door mending old pots and pans
tinker *verb*
2 to fiddle around trying to mend something without much success: *to tinker with the car engine*

tinkle *verb*
to jingle or ring lightly: *to tinkle a bell*

Word Building: **tinkle** *noun*

tinnie *noun*
a can of beer

Word Use: this word is more suited to everyday language ☐ it can also be spelled **tinny**

tinny *adjective*
1 not made strongly and likely to fall apart: *a tinny bicycle* **2** having a hollow metallic sound

Word Building: other forms are **tinnier, tinniest**

tinsel *noun*
glittering metal strips used for decoration: *to hang tinsel on the Christmas tree*

Word Building: **tinselly** *adjective*

tint *noun*
1 a colour, especially a delicate or pale colour **2** a dye for your hair
tint *verb*
3 to dye or colour slightly: *to tint your hair*

tiny *adjective*
very small or minute

Word Building: other forms are **tinier, tiniest**

tip[1] *noun*
the pointed part at the end: *the tip of my nose*

tip[2] *verb*
1 to make slope, tilt or fall over: *If you tip the cup the milk will spill.* **2** to fall or make fall: *My lunch tipped out of my bag.* | *I tipped the water out of the glass.*
tip[2] *noun*
3 a rubbish dump

Word Building: other verb forms are **I tipped, I have tipped, I am tipping**

tip[3] *noun*
1 money given in thanks to someone who has done something for you: *to leave a tip for the waiter* **2** a piece of useful information: *a tip on how to solve a problem*
tip[3] *verb*
3 tip off to warn of trouble or danger

Word Use: a similar word for definition 2 is **hint** □ definition 3 is more suited to everyday language
Word Building: other verb forms are **I tipped, I have tipped, I am tipping**

tip[4] *verb*
to touch lightly or tap

Word Building: other verb forms are **I tipped, I have tipped, I am tipping**

tipsy *adjective*
a bit drunk: *She gets tipsy after only one glass of wine.*

Word Building: **tipsily** *adverb* **tipsiness** *noun*

tiptoe *verb*
to walk softly and carefully on the tips of your toes

tirade (say *tuy-rayd*) *noun*
a long angry speech

tire *verb*
to make or become sleepy or weak: *The long walk tired the children.* | *She has been ill and tires easily.*

Word Building: **tiring** *adjective: Gardening in the heat is very tiring.* **tired** *adjective*

tissue (say *tish-ooh*) *noun*
1 the substance of which living things are made: *muscle tissue* **2** soft thin paper, especially a piece used as a paper handkerchief: *Give me a tissue to blow my nose.*

titbit *noun*
1 a delicious morsel of food
2 an especially interesting piece of gossip or other information

title *noun*
1 the name of a book, film or piece of music **2** a name showing someone's occupation or rank in society, such as *Mr, Mrs, Doctor, Sir*, or *Lord* **3** the legal right to own property or a certificate stating this: *the title to a house*

Word Building: **title** *verb* to call or name **titled** *adjective*

titter *verb*
to giggle in a silly or nervous way

Word Building: **titter** *noun*

to *preposition*
1 towards or in the direction of: *from east to west* **2** showing a limit or extent: *rotten to the core* **3** touching or held against: *Apply varnish to your nails.* | *to hold your hand to your head* **4** with the aim, purpose, or intention of: *I'll go to the rescue.*
to *adverb*
5 into a closed position: *to pull the door to*
6 to and fro backwards and forwards

Word Use: be careful – this sounds like **too** and **two**

toad *noun*
an animal like a big frog

toadstool *noun*
a type of fungus like a mushroom, but usually poisonous

toast[1] *noun*
sliced bread cooked till it is brown on both sides

Word Building: **toast** *verb* **toaster** *noun*

toast[2] *noun*
1 someone or something you honour with a special drink: *The Queen will be our next toast.* **2** the act of drinking in this way: *a toast to the Queen* **3** someone who suddenly becomes very popular and famous: *She was the toast of the town.*

Word Building: **toast** *verb*

tobacco *noun*
1 a plant whose leaves are dried and used for smoking in cigarettes, cigars and pipes
2 the dried leaves themselves

Word Building: **tobacconist** *noun*

toboggan *noun*
a light sledge

Word Building: **toboggan** *verb* (**tobogganed, tobogganing**)

toddle *verb*
to walk slowly and unsteadily

Word Building: **toddler** *noun* a very young child

toffee *noun*
a sticky sweet made from sugar, water and sometimes butter

tofu *noun*
a white curd made from soy bean milk, used in many Asian dishes

Word Use: another name is **bean curd**
Word History: from a Chinese word meaning "fermented bean"

toga (say <u>*toh*</u>*-gə*) *noun*
a robe worn by people in ancient Rome

together *adverb*
1 with another person or other people: *My friend and I go fishing together. / All the kids in our group work together as a team.* **2** joined or fixed with each other: *to clasp your hands together / to sew pieces of cloth together*

Word History: **togetherness** *noun*

toggle *noun*
a type of fastener, made of a small bar or pin which fits through a loop of rope or chain

toil *verb*
1 to work hard for a long time **2** to walk with great difficulty: *to toil up the hill*

Word Building: **toil** *noun*

toilet *noun*
1 a bowl, connected to a drain, for getting rid of urine and waste matter from the bowel **2** a room where people go to use a toilet **3** the process of washing, shaving and getting dressed

Word Use: a similar word for definitions 1 and 2 is **lavatory**
Word Building: **toiletry** *noun* soap, toothpaste and other similar things
Word History: from a French word meaning "cloth"

token *noun*
1 a ticket or disc used instead of money to pay for something **2** a sign or symbol of something: *A wedding ring is a token of love.*

tolerate *verb*
to put up with or allow: *She can't tolerate loud noise. / He won't tolerate bad behaviour.*

Word Building: **tolerable** *adjective* **tolerably** *adverb* **tolerance** *noun* **tolerant** *adjective* **tolerantly** *adverb*

toll[1] *verb*
to ring slowly: *to toll a bell*

toll[2] *noun*
1 a fee paid for crossing a bridge or driving on an expressway **2** the price paid in terms of numbers of people dead: *the death toll in war / the road toll*

tom *noun*
a male cat

Word Use: the female is a **puss;** the young is a **kitten**

tomahawk *noun*
a small axe, first used by the American Indians

Word History: from an American Indian word meaning "war club" or "ceremonial object"

tomato *noun*
a juicy red fruit which can be cooked or eaten raw in salads

Word Building: the plural form is **tomatoes**

tomb (rhymes with *room*) *noun*
a grave, especially a grand one where an important person is buried

tomboy *noun*
an adventurous high-spirited girl

tombstone *noun*
a stone over someone's grave with their name and dates of birth and death carved on it

tomorrow *noun*
the day after today

tom-tom *noun*
an African or Indian drum

tone *noun*
1 a musical sound: *a violin with a mellow tone* **2** a musical interval equal to two semitones **3** the lightness or darkness of a colour: *a blue tone* **4** the style or quality of something: *Bad behaviour lowers the tone of the school.*

tone *verb*
5 tone up to make strong and fit: *Exercise tones up your body.*

tongs *plural noun*
a tool with two arms hinged together, used for picking up things

tongue (rhymes with *hung*) *noun*
1 the mass of muscle in your mouth that helps in eating food and shaping the sounds of human speech **2** a language or dialect: *a foreign tongue* **3** the loose flap of leather under the laces of some shoes
4 the clapper, or piece of metal, that hangs inside a bell and makes a sound when it hits the side

tonic *noun*
something that makes you stronger, healthier and more cheerful

tonne (rhymes with *on*) *noun*
a measure of mass equal to 1000 kilograms

tonsil *noun*
either of the two oval-shaped masses of tissue at the back of your throat

Word Building: **tonsillitis** *noun* an infection which makes your tonsils sore

too *adverb*
1 also or in addition: *young, brainy, and beautiful too* **2** more than what is wanted or right: *you are talking too much*

Word Use: be careful – this sounds like **to** and **two**

tool *noun*
1 any instrument used for doing some mechanical work, such as a hammer, saw or knife **2** anything used like a tool to do work or to cause some result: *Books are a tool for gaining knowledge.*

toot *verb*
to sound or cause to sound in short blasts, like a horn or whistle

Word Building: **toot** *noun*

tooth *noun*
1 one of the hard bonelike parts or growths inside the mouths of humans and animals, used for eating **2** any toothlike part of a comb, rake or saw

Word Building: the plural is **teeth**

top[1] *noun*
1 the highest point or surface of anything **2** the part of a plant above the ground: *carrot tops* **3** a part thought of as higher: *the top of the the street*
4 a covering or lid such as on a box or a jar **5** an outer piece of clothing for the upper part of your body **6 tops** the very best: *The film was the tops.*

top[1] *adjective*
7 highest or upper: *the top shelf* **8** best or excellent: *He's a top student.*

top[1] *verb*
9 to give a top to or put a top on
10 to be at or reach the top of: *to top the class in maths*

Word Use: definitions 6 and 8 are more suited to everyday language
Word Building: other verb forms are **I topped, I have topped, I am topping**

top[2] *noun*
a cone-shaped toy which is made to spin on its pointed end

topic *noun*
the subject of a speech, discussion, conversation, or piece of writing

topical *adjective*
dealing with things that are happening now

Word Building: **topically** *adverb*

topple *verb*
1 to fall forward or to tumble down
2 to make fall

topsy-turvy *adverb*
upside down, backwards, or back to front

Word Building: **topsy-turvy** *adjective*

torch *noun*
1 a light which is run by batteries and which you can carry around **2** something with a burning flame or flare which can be carried around or set into a holder
3 an instrument like a lamp which produces a very hot flame used for burning off paint or melting metal

toreador (say *to-ree-ə-daw*) *noun*
a Spanish bullfighter

torment (say *taw-ment*) *verb*
1 to torture or give great pain to: *Headaches tormented her day after day.*
2 to worry or annoy greatly: *The dog tormented the cat all morning.*

torment (say *taw-ment*) *noun*
3 great pain or agony **4** something that causes pain or is a source of worry or trouble: *His bad knee was a torment to him.*

tornado *noun*
a violent whirlwind

Word Building: the plural form is **tornadoes** or **tornados**
Word History: from a Spanish word meaning "thunderstorm"

torpedo *noun*
1 a cigar-shaped missile containing explosives, which can travel by itself

under water when fired by a submarine or torpedo-boat

torpedo *verb*
2 to attack or destroy by torpedo or torpedoes

Word Building: the plural of the noun is **torpedoes**

torrent *noun*
1 a stream of water flowing with great speed or violence, or a violent downpour of rain **2** a violent stream or flow of anything: *a torrent of words*

tortoise (say *taw-təs*) *noun*
any of various reptiles which have feet with toes, a hard shell covering their bodies and most of which live on land

Word Use: compare this with **turtle**

torture *noun*
1 an act or method of causing severe pain, especially so as to gain information

torture *verb*
2 to cause severe pain to: *The soldiers tortured the spies to find out what they knew.*

toss *verb*
1 to throw, fling or sway: *She tossed the paper into the bin.* | *The ship was tossing in the waves.* **2** to move around or mix: *He tossed the salad.* **3** to throw a coin to decide something according to which side falls face up: *Toss for it, and heads I win!*

Word Building: **toss** *noun*

total *adjective*
1 whole or entire: *This is the total bill.*
2 complete or absolute: *a total failure*

total *noun*
3 the sum or whole amount

total *verb*
4 to add up or find the total of
5 to reach an amount of: *The bills for the outfit total $200*

Word Building: other verb forms are **I totalled, I have totalled, I am totalling** □ **totality** *noun* **totally** *adverb*

totalitarian (say *toh-tal-ə-tair-ree-ən*) *adjective*
having to do with a government which has complete control and doesn't allow any opposition

Word Building: **totalitarianism** *noun*

totem *noun*
1 something, often an animal, used as the token or emblem of a family or group **2** a statue or drawing of such an emblem

Word Building: **totem** *adjective: totem pole*

totter *verb*
to sway or walk unsteadily

touch *verb*
1 to feel with your hand or finger
2 to come into contact: *The two wires are touching.* **3** to strike or hit gently or lightly: *She touched him on the shoulder.*
4 to affect with a feeling or emotion: *Their sad story touched his heart.*

touch *noun*
5 the act of touching or being touched
6 the one of your five senses which is used to feel or handle things **7** close communication: *Have you been in touch with your mother lately?*

touchy *adjective*
1 irritable or easily offended: *Be careful because he's very touchy today.* **2** likely to irritate or offend: *Don't talk about that because it's a touchy subject.*

Word Building: other forms are **touchier, touchiest**

tough (say *tuf*) *adjective*
1 not easily broken or cut **2** difficult to chew **3** strong or able to put up with bad conditions **4** hard or difficult to deal with: *a tough exam* **5** rough or aggressive: *tough behaviour*

Word Building: **toughly** *adverb* **toughness** *noun*

tour *verb*
to travel through a place or to travel from one place to another: *The band toured America.* | *They are touring all this summer.*

Word Building: **tour** *noun*

tourist *noun*
someone who travels or tours for pleasure

Word Building: **tourism** *noun*

tournament (say *taw-nə-mənt*) *noun*
1 a meeting for contests in sports, cards, and other similar things: *a tennis tournament* | *a bridge tournament*
2 a contest in medieval times where two knights on horseback fought for a prize

tourniquet (say *taw-nə-kay*) *noun*
a tight bandage or band, twisted or wrapped around your arm or leg to stop bleeding

tow (rhymes with *no*) *verb*
to drag or pull using a rope or chain: *to tow a car*

Word Building: **tow** *noun*

towel *noun*
1 a piece of cloth used for wiping and drying something wet **2 throw in the towel** to give up or admit defeat

towelling *noun*
1 a type of cloth used for making towels, clothes for the beach and so on
2 a rubbing with a towel **3** a thrashing

tower (rhymes with *flower*) *noun*
1 a tall narrow structure that is usually part of a building like a church, but sometimes stands alone
tower *verb*
2 to rise and stretch far upwards: *The mountain towers into the sky.*

town *noun*
1 a large area of houses, shops and offices where many people live and work, larger than a village and smaller than a city
2 the main shopping and business centre or area of a city: *I'm going to town to do my shopping.* **3** the people of a town: *The whole town is worried about the traffic problem.*

town hall *noun*
a large public building belonging to a town, for meetings and gatherings

township *noun*
a small town or settlement

toxin *noun*
a poison produced by some animal or vegetable organisms which can cause diseases such as tetanus or diphtheria

Word Building: **toxic** *adjective*

trace *noun*
1 a mark that shows that something has been present, often a footprint or a track: *There was a trace of blood on his shirt. | The robbers left traces in the snow.*
2 a very small amount: *The earth contained only a trace of iron.*
trace *verb*
3 to follow the footprints, or make out the course of: *They traced the robbers to their hideout. | She traced the history of the wool industry in Australia.* **4** to copy by following the lines of the original on transparent paper placed over it: *If you can't draw the map of Australia, you'd better trace one.*

Word Building: **tracing** *noun*

track *noun*
1 a rough path or trail **2** a structure of metal rails and sleepers on which a train runs **3** a mark or series of marks like footprints, left by anything that has passed along **4** a path or course laid out for racing **5** one of the separate sections on a recording such as a CD or a gramophone record
track *verb*
6 to follow, or hunt by following, the tracks or footprints of **7** to follow the course of by radar or sonar
track *adjective*
8 relating to athletic sports performed on a running track: *track events*

tracksuit *noun*
a loose two-piece set of clothing worn by athletes in training or between events

tract[1] *noun*
1 a stretch of land or water **2** a system or series of connected parts in your body: *digestive tract*

tract[2] *noun*
a short piece of writing, often on a religious subject

traction *noun*
1 the act of drawing or pulling something, especially along a surface **2** the force that prevents a wheel slipping: *These tyres have good traction.*

tractor *noun*
a powerful motor vehicle used to pull farm machinery and so on

trade *noun*
1 the buying, selling or exchanging of goods **2** a particular kind of work, or sometimes the people who are involved in this work: *the trade of a carpenter | This magazine is for the electrical trade.*
trade *verb*
3 to buy, sell or exchange goods or other desirable things: *They traded in wheat. | They traded seats with each other.* **4 trade in** to give as a part payment in exchange for something new: *She traded in her old car for a new one.*
trade *adjective*
5 having to do with commerce or a particular job

Word Use: a similar word for definition 1 is **commerce**

trademark *noun*
a name, sign or mark used to show that goods have been made by a particular manufacturer

trade union *noun*
an organisation or association of workers set up to help them with any work problems, especially with their employers

Word Building: **trade unionism** *noun* **trade unionist** *noun*

tradition *noun*
1 the handing down of beliefs, customs and stories from one generation to another
2 the beliefs or customs that are handed down

Word Building: **traditional** *adjective*

traffic *noun*
1 the coming and going of people or vehicles along a road, waterway, railway line or airway **2** the people or vehicles that travel along such a route
3 the business, trade, or dealings carried out between countries or people, sometimes illegally: *traffic in drugs*
traffic *verb*
4 to carry on trade or commercial dealings, often illegally

Word Building: other verb forms are **I trafficked, I have trafficked, I am trafficking** □ **trafficker** *noun*

tragedy (say *traj-ə-dee*) *noun*
1 a sad or serious play with an unhappy ending **2** any very sad or dreadful happening

Word Building: **tragic** *adjective* **tragically** *adverb*
Word History: from a Greek word meaning "goat song"

trail *verb*
1 to drag or be dragged along the ground **2** to have floating or coming out behind: *The car was trailing clouds of smoke.* **3** to follow the track of
4 to hang down loosely from something
5 to follow: *The little girl trailed after her sister.*
trail *noun*
6 a path or a track made across rough country **7** footprints or smell left by a hunted animal or person **8** a stream of dust or smoke left behind something moving

trailer *noun*
1 a vehicle, made to be towed by a car or a truck, used to carry loads
2 an advertisement for a film soon to be shown, usually made up of scenes from it

Word Use: other words for definition 2 are **short** or **shorts**

train *noun*
1 a number of railway carriages joined together and pulled by an engine **2** a line of people, cars, or animals travelling together: *a camel train* **3** something that is drawn or trails along: *the train on a wedding dress* **4** a group of followers: *The king and his train entered.* **5** a series of connected ideas: *a train of thought*
train *verb*
6 to teach a person or animal to know or do something **7** to become or make fit by exercise or diet for some sport or a contest

Word Building: **training** *noun*

trainee *noun*
someone receiving training

Word Building: **trainee** *adjective: a trainee pilot*

traitor *noun*
someone who betrays a person or a country

tram *noun*
a passenger car running on rails, usually powered by electricity from an overhead wire

tramp *verb*
1 to tread or walk heavily or steadily: *The soldiers tramped down the road.* **2** to tread heavily: *to tramp on his toes*
tramp *noun*
3 the act of tramping: *a tramp through the bush* **4** the sound of a firm heavy tread
5 someone who travels about from place to place on foot, with no fixed home

Word Use: a similar word for definition 5 is **vagrant**

trample *verb*
1 to crush or tread heavily on **2** to treat cruelly: *She trampled on his feelings.*

trampoline *noun*
a frame with tightly stretched material attached to it by springs, on which you can jump and tumble for pleasure or sport

Word Building: **trampoline** *verb*
Word History: from an Italian word meaning "springboard"

trance *noun*
1 a dazed state in which you are not fully conscious **2** the condition of being completely lost in thought

tranquil (say *trang-kwəl*) *adjective*
peaceful, quiet or calm

Word Building: **tranquillity** *noun* **tranquilly** *adverb*

tranquilliser or **tranquillizer** (say *trang-kwə-luy-zə*) *noun*
a drug that calms you down

trans- *prefix*
a word part meaning across *or* beyond: *transport*

Word History: this prefix comes from Latin

transact *verb*
to carry through to a successful conclusion: *It won't take long to transact our business.*

transaction *noun*
1 a piece of business **2** the managing or carrying on of business

transfer *verb*
1 to carry or send from one place or person to another **2** to take or move from one surface to another

transfer *noun*
3 the act of transferring or the fact of being transferred: *The transfer of soldiers is complete.* **4** a drawing or pattern which can be put onto another surface: *These transfers can be put onto your T-shirt.*

Word Building: other verb forms are **I transferred, I have transferred, I am transferring** □ **transference** *noun* **transferral** *noun*

transfix *verb*
1 to pierce through or fix fast with something sharp or pointed **2** to make unable to move, such as with amazement or terror: *I was absolutely transfixed at the sight of the shark.*

transform *verb*
1 to change in form or appearance: *The dress transformed her into a real beauty.* **2** to change in condition or character: *His new job transformed his life.*

Word Building: **transformation** *noun*

transformer *noun*
an electrical device used for changing one voltage to another

transfuse *verb*
1 to pour in or spread through **2** to take from one person or animal and inject into another: *to transfuse blood*

Word Building: **transfusion** *noun*

transistor *noun*
1 a small electronic device used in computers, radios, and so on, for controlling the flow of current **2** a small radio equipped with these devices

transit *noun*
1 passing across or through: *the transit of passengers from Sydney to Perth* **2** the state of being carried from one place to another: *The parcel was lost in transit.*

Word Building: **transition** *noun*

transitive verb *noun*
a verb like "bring" that needs an object for it to make sense

Word Use: the opposite is an **intransitive verb**

translate *verb*
to change from one language into another: *He translated the book from Italian into English.*

Word Building: **translation** *noun* **translator** *noun*

translucent (say *tranz-looh-sənt*) *adjective*
allowing some light to come through

Word Use: compare with **opaque** and **transparent**
Word Building: **translucence** *noun* **translucently** *adverb*

transmission *noun*
1 the act of transmitting **2** something that is transmitted **3** the broadcasting of a radio or television program **4** the part of a motor which transmits the power from the engine to the wheels

transmit *verb*
1 to send over or along: *The money was transmitted secretly.* **2** to pass on to someone else: *to transmit a disease* **3** to broadcast

Word Building: other verb forms are **I transmitted, I have transmitted, I am transmitting** □ **transmitter** *noun*

transmute *verb*
to change from one nature or form to another

Word Building: **transmutation** *noun*

transparency *noun*
1 the quality of being transparent or able to be seen through **2** something which is transparent, especially a transparent photograph projected onto a screen or looked at by light shining through from behind

transparent *adjective*
1 allowing light to pass through so that you can see through: *transparent material* **2** easily understood or seen through: *She gave a transparent excuse.*

Word Use: compare definition 1 with **opaque** and **translucent**
Word Building: **transparently** *adverb*

transplant (say *trans-plant*) *verb*
1 to remove from one place to another: *to transplant carrots / to transplant a heart*
transplant (say *trans-plant*) *noun*
2 the act of transplanting **3** something transplanted, such as a part of someone's body: *He died before a suitable transplant could be found.*

transport (say *trans-pawt*, *trans-pawt*) *verb*
1 to carry from one place to another
2 to carry away by strong emotion: *She was transported with happiness.*
3 to send to another country to live: *to transport criminals*
transport (say *trans-pawt*) *noun*
4 a system or method of transporting: *public transport* **5** a ship, plane or truck used to transport people or goods

Word Building: **transportation** *noun*

transpose *verb*
1 to change the position or order of: *to transpose a paragraph* **2** to make change places: *If you transpose the letters in the word "on", you get "no".*

Word Building: **transposition** *noun*

transvestite *noun*
someone who gets sexual pleasure from wearing the clothing of the opposite sex

trap *noun*
1 a device for catching animals **2** a trick or any other way of catching someone by surprise **3** a two-wheeled carriage drawn by a horse **4** your mouth
trap *verb*
5 to catch in a trap **6** to trick or lead by tricking: *She trapped him into telling the truth.*

Word Use: definition 4 is more suited to everyday language
Word Building: other verb forms are **I trapped, I have trapped, I am trapping**

trapdoor *noun*
a door cut into a floor, ceiling or roof

trapdoor spider *noun*
a type of spider with a painful bite that digs tunnels in the ground, sometimes fitted with a lid which it is able to open or keep tightly closed

trapeze (say *trə-peez*) *noun*
a short bar joined to the ends of two hanging ropes, on which gymnasts and acrobats perform

Word History: from a Latin word meaning "small table"

trapezium *noun*
a four-sided figure, two of whose sides are parallel

trash *noun*
1 rubbish or anything worthless or useless **2** nonsense or silly ideas or talk **3** people thought of as worthless

trauma (say *traw-mə*) *noun*
1 a wound or injury to your body
2 any experience which shocks you and has a lasting effect on your mind

Word Building: the plural can be either **traumata** or **traumas**

travel *verb*
1 to go from one place to another or to journey throughout: *She travelled across India. / He travelled the world.*
2 to go from place to place for a business firm **3** to move with speed: *That car was really travelling!*
travel *noun*
4 the act of travelling: *Travel is his main interest in life.* **5 travels** journeys

Word Use: definition 3 is more suited to everyday language
Word Building: other verb forms are **I travelled, I have travelled, I am travelling**

traverse *verb*
to pass across, over or through

trawl *noun*
a strong net which is dragged along the sea bottom to catch fish

Word Building: **trawler** *noun* a type of boat used in fishing with a trawl **trawl** *verb*

tray *noun*
a flat piece of wood, plastic or metal used for holding or carrying things: *He brought the tea on a tray.*

treacherous (say *trech-ə-rəs*) *adjective*
disloyal or not to be trusted: *a treacherous enemy / treacherous weather*

Word Building: **treacherously** *adverb* **treachery** *noun*

treacle *noun*
a dark, sticky liquid made from sugar

Word Building: **treacly** *adjective*

tread (rhymes with *led*) *verb*
1 to walk or step on: *He treads heavily. / She treads the same path every day.*

2 tread water to keep your head above water by moving your arms and legs

tread *noun*
3 a step, or the sound it makes: *You could hear his tread on the stairs.* **4** the part, especially of a tyre, which touches the road or any other surface

Word Building: other verb forms are **I trod, I have trod** or **trodden, I am treading**

treason *noun*
the crime of betraying your country, such as by spying for another country

Word Building: **treasonable** *adjective*

treasure (say *trezh*-ə) *noun*
1 something worth a lot of money, such as gold and jewels, or anything which is highly valued: *His bike is his greatest treasure.*

treasure *verb*
2 to value highly: *He treasures your praise.* **3** to store up for later use

Word Building: **treasured** *adjective*

treasurer (say *trezh*-ə-rə) *noun*
1 someone in charge of the money belonging to a company, club or city: *The treasurer reported that funds were low.*
2 Treasurer the head of the Treasury: *The Treasurer announced the budget.*

treasury (say *trezh*-ə-ree) *noun*
1 a place where money or valuables are kept **2 Treasury** the government department which manages a country's finances

treat *verb*
1 to behave towards, in a particular way: *They treated the boy kindly.* **2** to try to cure: *to treat a patient* **3** to deal with or discuss: *They are treating the matter seriously.* **4** to change by chemical or other process: *to treat sewerage* **5** to pay for some special pleasure for: *Joe's father treated him to an ice-cream.*

treat *noun*
6 the gift of a drink, dinner or entertainment: *It's my treat this time.*

Word Building: **treatment** *noun*

treaty *noun*
an agreement: *After the war both countries signed the peace treaty.*

Word Building: the plural is **treaties**

treble *adjective*
1 high-pitched: *a treble voice | a treble recorder* **2** three times as much as: *He paid treble the amount.*

treble *noun*
3 a piano part for the right hand
4 a high-pitched voice or sound

Word Use: the opposite of definitions 1, 3 and 4 is **bass**
Word Building: **treble** *verb* to triple

tree *noun*
a plant with leaves and woody branches, trunk and roots

trek *verb*
to walk or travel especially over a long distance or with much difficulty: *We are going to trek across the mountains.*

Word Building: other forms are **I trekked, I have trekked, I am trekking** □ **trek** *noun* **trekker** *noun*
Word History: from a Dutch word meaning "draw" or "travel"

trellis *noun*
a support made of crossing wooden or other strips, such as for a vine or creeper

Word Use: a similar word is **lattice**

tremble *verb*
to shake, especially from fear, weakness or cold: *Her voice trembled.*

Word Use: a similar word is **quiver**
Word Building: **tremble** *noun* **trembly** *adjective*

tremendous *adjective*
1 large or great: *a tremendous size*
2 wonderful or remarkable: *She's a tremendous character.*

Word Building: **tremendously** *adverb*

tremolo (say *trem*-ə-loh) *noun*
a trembling effect in someone's voice or in a musical instrument

Word Building: the plural is **tremolos**

tremor *noun*
a shaking movement or vibration: *She has a tremor in her hand. | The earth tremor damaged our wall.*

tremulous (say *trem*-yə-ləs) *adjective*
shaky or uncertain: *His voice was tremulous with excitement.*

Word Building: **tremulously** *adverb*

trench *noun*
a deep ditch, especially one dug to protect soldiers from enemy fire

Word Building: the plural is **trenches**

trend *noun*
a tendency or movement in a certain direction, which leads to a fashion: *There's a trend towards buying smaller cars.*

Word Building: **trendy** *adjective* (**trendier, trendiest**) fashionable **trendiness** *noun*

trespass *verb*
to enter a place illegally and without permission

Word Building: **trespass** *noun* **trespasser** *noun*

trestle (say *tres-əl*) *noun*
a plank supported by legs at each end

triad (say *truy-ad*) *noun*
a group of three closely connected things, such as musical notes in a chord

Word Building: **triadic** *adjective*

trial *noun*
1 a hearing of the facts or a trying of someone's guilt or innocence in a law court **2** a test or contest: *a trial of strength* **3** an experiment: *The trial was unsuccessful.* **4** a cause of suffering: *His asthma was a trial to him.* **5 on trial** undergoing a test or trial, especially in court

Word Building: **trial** *adjective* **try** *verb* (**tried, trying**)

triangle *noun*
1 a flat three-sided shape **2** a percussion instrument made of a steel rod bent into a triangle, which is struck with a small steel rod

Word Building: **triangular** *adjective*

tribe *noun*
1 a group of people who believe they have a common ancestor, have many of the same customs and usually live in the same area **2** any large group with something in common: *He brought a tribe of friends home.*

Word Building: **tribal** *adjective* **tribally** *adverb*

tribunal (say *truy-byooh-nəl*) *noun*
a court of justice, or a place where judgments are made

tributary (say *trib-yə-tree*) *noun*
a stream flowing into a larger river

Word Building: the plural is **tributaries** □ **tributary** *adjective*

tribute *noun*
a gift or speech made to show respect or regard for someone

trick *noun*
1 something done to deceive or amuse
2 a skilful or clever act, such as juggling
3 something which deceives your senses: *A mirage is just a trick of your eyes.*
4 a habit or mannerism: *She has a trick of nodding while you speak.*

trick *verb*
5 to deceive or cheat by a trick

Word Building: **trickery** *noun* **trickster** *noun*

trickle *verb*
to flow in a very small or slow stream: *Tears trickled down her cheeks.*

Word Building: **trickle** *noun*

tricky *adjective*
1 difficult to handle or deal with: *a tricky question* **2** given to playing tricks, especially in order to cheat or deceive

tricycle (say *truy-sik-əl*) *noun*
a cycle with three wheels, usually two at the back

trifle *noun*
1 a small or worthless amount or thing
2 a dessert usually made of sponge cake with sherry or wine, jelly, jam, fruit and custard

trifle *verb*
3 to waste time: *She spends all day trifling.*
4 trifle with to treat too lightly: *Can't you see she's trifling with you?*

Word Building: **trifler** *noun*

trigger *noun*
the lever on a gun which you press to fire the bullet

Word Building: **trigger** *verb* to start off: *trigger a reaction*
Word History: from a Dutch word meaning "pull"

trill *noun*
a vibrating sound, especially when made up of two notes being rapidly repeated one after the other

Word Building: **trill** *verb*

trillion *noun*
a number worth a million times a million

trilogy (say *tril-ə-jee*) *noun*
a series of three related works, such as novels or plays

trim *verb*
1 to shorten, such as by cutting or tightening: *He needs to trim his beard. / to trim a sail* **2** to decorate: *to trim a Christmas tree*

Word Building: other forms are **I trimmed, I have trimmed, I am trimming** □ **trim** *adjective* neat and smart

trimaran (say *truy-mə-ran*) *noun*
a sailing boat with three hulls

trinity *noun*
1 a group of three **2 the Trinity** the Father, Son and Holy Spirit as one God

trinket *noun*
a cheap ornament

trio (say *tree-oh*) *noun*
1 a group of three **2** a group of three musicians **3** a musical piece for three voices or performers

trip *noun*
1 a journey or outing: *He is going on a world trip. / We took a trip on a ferry.*

trip *verb*
2 to stumble or cause to fall: *She tripped and fell. / The wire tripped him.* **3** to set off: *He trod on the wire which trips the alarm.* **4 trip up** to cause to make a mistake: *The lawyer's questions tripped him up.*

Word Building: other verb forms are **I tripped, I have tripped, I am tripping**

tripe *noun*
1 the stomach of cattle which is cleaned and sold as meat **2** worthless rubbish

triple *verb*
1 to multiply by three

Word Use: definition 2 is more suited to everyday language

triple *verb*
1 to multiply by three

triple *adjective*
2 having three parts: *a triple program*
3 three times as great: *a triple quantity*

Word Use: a word with the same meaning as definition 3 is **treble**

triplet *noun*
1 one of three children born at the same time to the same mother **2** a three-line verse of poetry

tripod (say *truy-pod*) *noun*
a three-legged stool or support

trite *adjective*
repeated too often to be interesting: *a trite remark*

Word Building: **tritely** *adverb* **triteness** *noun*

triumph (say *truy-umf*) *noun*
a victory or success

Word Building: **triumph** *verb* **triumphant** *adjective* **triumphantly** *adverb*

trivial *adjective*
unimportant: *trivial details*

Word Use: a similar word is **petty**
Word Building: **triviality** *noun* **trivially** *adverb*

troll *noun*
an imaginary being in fairy stories, either a dwarf or a giant, who lives underground

trolley *noun*
1 a cart on wheels, used for carrying goods in a supermarket **2** a small table on wheels for carrying food or crockery **3** a truck with low sides which runs on rails: *The miners loaded the trolley with coal.*

trombone *noun*
a brass wind instrument like a trumpet, on which you change the note by sliding a section of tube in or out

Word Building: **trombonist** *noun*
Word History: from an Italian word meaning "trumpet"

troop *noun*
1 a group or band of people, animals or things: *a circus troop / a troop of scouts*
2 troops a large number of soldiers

troop *verb*
3 to come or go in large numbers

Word Building: **trooper** *noun*

trophy (say *troh-fee*) *noun*
1 a prize won in a contest **2** a souvenir kept from a war or a hunting expedition

Word Building: the plural is **trophies**

tropic *noun*
1 either of two lines of latitude $23\frac{1}{2}°$ north and south of the equator, known as the *Tropic of Capricorn* and the *Tropic of Cancer* **2 the tropics** the area of land lying between these bands

Word Building: **tropical** *adjective* **tropically** *adverb*

trot *verb*
1 to go at a fast but steady pace, as horses do when they move so that a front leg moves at the same time as the opposite back leg
trot *noun*
2 a fast but steady pace: *She set off at a trot.* **3 trots** trotting races for horses

Word Building: other verb forms are **it trotted, it has trotted, it is trotting** □ **trotter** *noun* a horse bred for trotting races

troubadour (say <u>*trooh*</u>*-bə-daw*) *noun*
a singer or song-writer, especially in medieval France

trouble (rhymes with *bubble*) *verb*
1 to disturb, bother or worry: *It's a shame to trouble him when he's tired.* **2** to put to inconvenience: *May I trouble you to ask the time?*
trouble *noun*
3 a difficulty or an unhappy situation: *to make trouble* / *to be in trouble*
4 inconvenience: *She went to a lot of trouble to find it.* **5** any problem or disorder: *industrial trouble* / *heart trouble*

Word Building: **troublesome** *adjective*

trough (rhymes with *off*) *noun*
1 a long low container for animal feed or water, or any similar trench or hollow
2 an area of low pressure on a weather map

troupe (sounds like *troop*) *noun*
a band or group of entertainers: *a troupe of actors*

Word Building: **trouper** *noun*

trousers *plural noun*
clothing for the lower half of your body from waist to ankle, divided into two parts for your legs

trousseau (say <u>*trooh*</u>*-soh*) *noun*
linen and clothes collected by a girl for her marriage

Word Building: the plural can be either **trousseaux** or **trousseaus**
Word History: from a French word

trout *noun*
a freshwater fish related to the salmon

Word Building: the plural is **trout**

trowel *noun*
1 a flat tool with a handle used for spreading cement or plaster **2** a small garden spade

Word Building: **trowel** *verb* (**trowelled, trowelling**)

truant *noun*
someone who stays away from school without permission

Word Building: **truancy** *noun* **truant** *adjective*

truce *noun*
an agreement to end fighting: *Both sides agreed to call a truce over Christmas.*

Word Use: another word with a similar meaning is **armistice**

truck *noun*
1 a motor vehicle with a back section for carrying goods **2** a railway goods carriage

Word Building: **truck** *verb*

trudge *verb*
to tread heavily or slowly: *He trudged upstairs in his boots.*

true *adjective*
1 full of truth or not false: *a true story*
2 real or being what it seems: *true gold*
3 loyal or faithful: *a true friend*
4 exact: *She measured the sides to see if they were true.*

Word Building: **true** *adverb: Tell me true.* **truly** *adverb*

trump *verb*
1 to take or win by having the best card in a game such as bridge: *He trumped my king with an ace.* **2 trump up** to invent dishonestly: *She trumped up some story to get out of trouble.*

Word Building: **trump** *noun*

trumpet *noun*
1 a brass wind instrument with a curved tube and three valves
trumpet *verb*
2 to sound a trumpet or make a similar loud noise: *The elephants trumpeted in the forest.* **3** to tell far and wide: *He trumpeted the news all through the neighbourhood.*

Word Building: **trumpeter** *noun*

truncheon (say <u>*trun*</u>*-shən*) *noun*
a short stick or club, as used by police to keep order or defend themselves

Word History: from a Latin word meaning "stump"

trundle *verb*
to roll along, or move on wheels: *to trundle a hoop* / *The trolley trundled along the aisle.*

trunk *noun*
1 the main or central part: *the trunk of a tree* **2** the main part of your body without your head, legs or arms **3** a box or chest for storing or transporting your possessions **4** the long flexible nose of an elephant **5 trunks** shorts worn while playing sport, especially while swimming

Word Building: **trunk** *adjective* main or central: *trunk line*

truss *verb*
1 to bind or secure: *They trussed her hands tightly. / He trussed the turkey.*
2 to support, such as with bars and beams: *to truss a bridge*

Word Building: **truss** *noun*

trust *noun*
1 belief or confidence: *to lose someone's trust* **2** the expectation that someone can or will pay: *He will let you buy on trust.*
3 reliableness or responsibility: *a position of trust* **4** money or property held and managed by one person for another or others
trust *verb*
5 to believe or have confidence in
6 to hope or expect: *They trust you will come.*

trustee *noun*
someone who manages business or property for another

trustworthy *adjective*
deserving trust: *a trustworthy ally*

Word Building: **trustworthiness** *noun*

truth *noun*
1 what has really happened: *He doesn't always tell the truth.* **2** a fact or principle: *a scientific truth* **3** honesty or reliableness: *There's not much truth in what she says.*

Word Building: **truthful** *adjective* **truthfully** *adverb*

try *verb*
1 to make an effort or attempt to do: *You must try harder before you give it up. / Try it.* **2** to test or find out: *Did you try it for size?* **3** to examine in a court of law: *Don't judge her until she is tried.*
4 to strain or exhaust: *He tries my patience.*
try *noun*
5 an attempt or effort **6** a score in rugby, worth four points

Word Building: other verb forms are **I tried, I have tried, I am trying** □ the plural of the noun is **tries** □ **trying** *adjective* annoying: *His nagging is very trying.*

T-shirt *noun*
a short-sleeved cotton shirt without a collar

Word Use: another spelling is **tee-shirt**

tub *noun*
a round flat-bottomed container: *a wash tub / a tub of butter*

tuba (say *<u>tyooh</u>-bə*) *noun*
a very low-pitched brass wind instrument

tubby *adjective*
short and fat

Word Building: other forms are **tubbier, tubbiest** □ **tubbiness** *noun*

tube *noun*
1 a narrow hollow pipe which liquid or gas can flow through **2** a soft narrow container, sealed at one end, with a screw top at the other: *a toothpaste tube / a tube of paint*

tuber (say *<u>tyooh</u>-bə*) *noun*
an underground stem, such as a potato, from which new plants may grow

Word History: from a Latin word meaning "bump" or "swelling"

tuberculosis (say *tə-ber-kyə-<u>loh</u>-səs*) *noun*
a disease of the lungs in which small lumps or swellings are produced

Word Building: **tubercular** *adjective* **tuberculous** *adjective*

tuck *verb*
1 to put into or fold away: *to tuck something in your pocket* **2** to sew in a narrow fold to improve the fit of a garment **3 tuck in** **a** to fold tightly into the bed clothes: *She tucked them in.*
b to eat heartily

Word Use: definition 3b is more suited to everyday language
Word Building: **tuck** *noun* a narrow fold

tucker *noun*
food: *The tucker's good.*

Word Use: this is more suited to everyday language

tuckshop *noun*
a shop, usually in a school, which sells lunches and snacks

Tuesday *noun*
the third day of the week

Word Use: the abbreviations are **Tue** or **Tues**
Word History: from a Latin word meaning "day of Mars"

tuft *noun*
an upright bunch, such as of hair, grass or feathers

Word Building: **tuft** *verb* **tufted** *adjective*

tug *verb*
1 to pull hard: *to tug on the reins | to tug the rope twice* **2** to tow, such as with a tugboat
tug *noun*
3 a hard pull **4** *another name for* **tugboat**

Word Building: other verb forms are **I tugged, I have tugged, I am tugging**

tugboat *noun*
a small powerful boat which is used to tow other ships

tuition (say *tyooh-ish-ən*) *noun*
teaching: *She needs more tuition before the exam.*

tulip *noun*
a cup-shaped flower, which grows from a bulb

tumble *verb*
1 to fall or roll: *Prices are tumbling. | to tumble downstairs* **2** to toss: *to tumble clothes in a drier*

Word Building: **tumble** *noun*

tumbler *noun*
a drinking glass

tummy *noun*
your stomach, where food is partly digested

Word Use: this is more suited to everyday language
Word Building: the plural is **tummies**

tumour or **tumor** *noun*
a swelling in someone's body, especially one made up of an unusual growth of cells

tumult (say *tyooh-mult*) *noun*
1 a noisy disturbance or uproar
2 a mental or emotional disturbance: *These words caused a tumult in her breast.*

Word Building: **tumultuous** *adjective*

tuna *noun*
a large sea fish with pink flesh, used for food

tundra *noun*
a treeless Arctic plain with mosses, lichens and dwarfed plants

Word History: from a Russian word meaning "marshy plain"

tune *noun*
1 a number of musical sounds of different pitch, one after the other, that form a pattern **2** correct adjustment of pitch: *Is your violin in tune?*
tune *verb*
3 to set to a correct or usual musical pitch: *to tune an instrument* **4** to put into smooth running order: *to tune an engine*
5 to adjust so as to get an incoming signal at its strongest: *to tune a radio*

Word Building: **tuneful** *adjective* **tuner** *noun*

tunic *noun*
1 a soldier's or policeman's jacket
2 a sleeveless dress worn by girls as part of a school uniform

tunnel *noun*
an underground passage, especially a large one for trains or cars

Word Building: **tunnel** *verb* (**tunnelled, tunnelling**)

turban *noun*
a man's headdress in some Asian and African countries, made of a long piece of cloth wound round the head in folds

turbine *noun*
a revolving motor in which a wheel with blades is driven by a liquid or gas passing through it

turbulence *noun*
a violent commotion or storminess

Word Building: **turbulent** *adjective*

tureen (say *tə-reen, tyooh-*) *noun*
a large deep dish with a cover, for holding soup at the table

turf *noun*
1 a grass surface with its matted roots and the soil it is growing in **2** a piece of this

Word Building: the plural of definition 2 is **turfs** or **turves**

turkey *noun*
a large bird bred for eating

Word Use: the male is a **cock**; the female is a **hen**; the young is a **poult**

turmoil *noun*
wild disorder: *Everything is in turmoil because he is leaving at a moment's notice.*

turn *verb*
1 to revolve or spin: *The wheels are turning slowly.* **2** to go round: *The truck turned the corner.* **3** to point or aim in a certain direction: *They turned the ship into the*

wind. | *She turned her face to the wall.*
4 to move to the other side or the opposite position: *Turn the page quietly.* | *She tossed and turned all night.* **5** to become: *He turned red.* **6** to change or be changed: *The witch turned his car into a pumpkin.* | *He turned into a mouse.* **7 turn on** **a** to start the supply of: *to turn on the electricity*
b to excite or interest: *That jazz really turns me on.* **8 turn out** **a** to switch off: *Turn out the lights.* **b** to produce or make: *The factory turns out 300 packets an hour.* **c** to force to go: *The landlord turned them out into the street.* **d** to empty: *He turned out his pockets.* **e** to become or develop: *She has turned out well.* **f** to come along: *A large crowd turned out to hear her.*
9 turn up **a** to fold, especially so as to shorten: *She turned up the hem of her dress.* **b** to be found: *That pen I lost has turned up at last.* **c** to increase the strength of: *Turn up the gas.* **d** to arrive: *He turned up unexpectedly.*

turn *noun*
10 a movement of rotation, whether complete or not: *a slight turn of the handle*
11 a chance to do something or get something, coming in order to each of a number of people: *It's my turn to choose.*
12 a change of direction: *He made a turn to the right.*

turnip *noun*
a plant with a thick white or yellow root which is eaten as a vegetable

turnstile *noun*
a revolving gate that allows one person to pass at a time

turntable *noun*
the turning surface on which a record in a gramophone rests

turpentine *noun*
1 an oil used for dissolving paint, originally from a tree, now usually made from petroleum **2** a very tall Australian tree with stringy bark and leaves which are whitish underneath

Word Use: definition 1 is often shortened to **turps**

turquoise (say *ter-kwoyz*) *noun*
a greenish-blue stone used in jewellery

turret *noun*
a small tower at a corner of a building

turtle *noun*
any of various reptiles which have flippers and a hard shell covering their bodies, and most of which live in the sea

Word Use: compare this with **tortoise**

tusk *noun*
the very long tooth, usually one of a pair, that certain animals such as the elephant or walrus have

tussle *verb*
to fight roughly

Word Building: **tussle** *noun*

tussock *noun*
a tuft or clump of grass

tutor *noun*
a teacher, especially either a private one or one in a university

tutu *noun*
a short ballet skirt, usually made out of layers of net-like material

tuxedo (say *tuk-see-doh*) *noun*
a man's dinner jacket

Word History: named after a US country club at Tuxedo Park, in New York State

TV *noun*
a short form of **television**

tweed *noun*
a rough woollen cloth

tweezers *plural noun*
small pincers or nippers for plucking out hairs, or picking up small objects

twiddle *verb*
to turn round and round, especially in a pointless or irritating way: *to twiddle your thumbs*

twig *noun*
a small thin branch of a tree

twilight *noun*
the dim light from the sky after sunset

twin *noun*
1 one of two children or animals born at the same birth **2** one of two things that match or look alike

Word Building: **twin** *adjective*

twine *verb*
1 to twist or wind

twine *noun*
2 string made of two or more strands twisted together

twinge *noun*
a pain that lasts only a moment: *a twinge of rheumatism*

twinkle *verb*
to shine with flickering gleams of light

Word Building: **twinkle** *noun*

twirl *verb*
to spin rapidly

twist *verb*
1 to combine by winding together: *fibres twisted to make a rope* **2** to turn about to face another direction: *She twisted from one foot to the other.* **3** to wring or squeeze out of place or shape **4** to sprain or put out of place: *He twisted his ankle.*
5 to change the meaning of: *You have twisted my argument.*

Word Building: **twist** *noun*

twitch *verb*
1 to jerk or give a short sudden pull at: *He twitched the rope out of her hands.*
2 to give a slight but sudden movement: *His mouth twitched.*

Word Building: **twitchy** *adjective* nervous **twitch** *noun*

two *noun*
the number 2

Word Use: be careful – this sounds like **to** and **too** □ something or someone that is number two or comes next after the first is the **second**
Word Building: **twice** *adverb* two times **two** *adjective*

two-up *noun*
a game in which two coins are spun in the air and bets are laid on both falling either heads up or tails up

tycoon *noun*
a rich and powerful owner of a business

type *noun*
1 a kind: *a type of lizard* **2** metal letters for printing **3** printed letters: *a headline in large type*

type *verb*
4 to write with a typewriter

typewriter *noun*
a machine with a keyboard, which produces numbers and letters like those used in printing

typhoid (say *tuy-foyd*) *noun*
a severe disease that can kill you and that you can catch by eating or drinking food or water made impure with a particular kind of bacteria

Word Use: the full name of this is **typhoid fever**

typhoon (say *tuy-foohn*) *noun*
a violent storm like a cyclone or hurricane

typical *adjective*
1 agreeing with and belonging to a particular kind: *typical desert plants*
2 expected, normal or characteristic: *typical behaviour*

Word Building: **typically** *adverb*

typist *noun*
someone who uses a typewriter

tyranny (say *ti-rə-nee*) *noun*
1 complete or unchecked power
2 unjustly harsh government

Word Building: **tyrannise** *verb*

tyrant (say *tuy-rənt*) *noun*
1 a king or ruler with unlimited power
2 anyone in a position of power who uses it cruelly and unjustly

tyre *noun*
a band of metal or rubber, fitted round the rim of a wheel

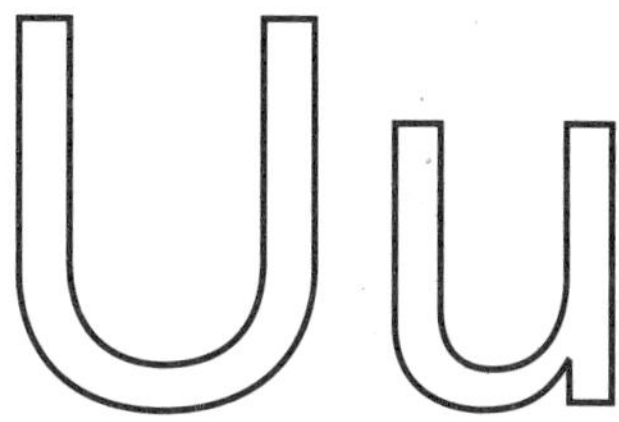

udder *noun*
the bag-like part of the body which produces milk in such animals as cows and goats

UFO *noun*
something unknown that you see in the sky, especially if you think it might be a spaceship

Word History: short for *unidentified flying object*

ugly *adjective*
1 unpleasant in appearance **2** nasty or threatening: *an ugly situation*

Word Building: **ugliness** *noun*

ukulele (say *yooh-kə-lay-lee*) *noun*
a musical instrument like a small guitar but with only four strings

Word History: from a Hawaiian word meaning "flea"

ulcer *noun*
a sore which is hard to heal, on your skin or inside, in such a place as the lining of your stomach

Word Building: **ulcerate** *verb* **ulcerous** *adjective*

ultimate *adjective*
final or most important: *his ultimate aim in life*

Word Building: **ultimately** *adverb* finally

ultimatum (say *ul-tə-may-təm*) *noun*
a final statement of terms or conditions: *After the third broken window his father gave him an ultimatum.*

ultra- *prefix*
a word part meaning **1** beyond: *ultraviolet* **2** excessively: *ultrafashionable*

Word History: this prefix comes from Latin

ultrasound *noun*
sound vibrations sometimes used by doctors instead of X-rays

ultraviolet *adjective*
beyond the violet end of the visible spectrum of light: *The ultraviolet light rays from the sun can burn you.*

umbilical cord
(say *um-bil-ə-kəl, um-bə-luy-kəl*) *noun*
the tube which connects an unborn baby or animal to the lining of its mother's womb, and through which food passes

umbrella *noun*
a circular screen on a metal framework which you use for a shelter against rain or sun

Word History: from an Italian word meaning "shade"

umpire *noun*
someone who makes sure that a game, like cricket or tennis, is played according to the rules

Word Use: a similar word is **referee**
Word Building: **umpire** *verb*

un- *prefix*
a word part meaning **1** not: *uncertain* **2** the opposite: *unbend*

Word History: this prefix comes from Old English

unanimous (say *yooh-nan-ə-məs*) *adjective*
1 all having the same opinion: *The committee members were unanimous in their support.* **2** showing complete agreement: *a unanimous vote*

Word Building: **unanimously** *adverb* **unanimity** *noun*

unassuming *adjective*
modest or not making any special claims about yourself: *an unassuming manner*

unbelief *noun*
lack of belief in religion

unbending *adjective*
firm or determined: *He was quite unbending about the rules.*

unburden *verb*
to free from a load: *She unburdened herself of her worries by ringing me last night.*

uncanny *adjective*
weird or unnatural: *It was quite uncanny that we both had the same dream.*

Word Building: **uncannily** *adverb* **uncanniness** *noun*

uncertain *adjective*
1 not sure: *I am uncertain about the date today.* **2** not to be depended on: *The weather is so uncertain.*

Word Building: **uncertainly** *adverb* **uncertainty** *noun*

uncle *noun*
1 the brother of your father or mother **2** your aunt's husband

uncomfortable *adjective*
1 lacking in comfort: *an uncomfortable chair* **2** uneasy: *Your staring makes me feel uncomfortable.*

Word Building: **uncomfortably** *adverb*

unconscious (say *un-kon-shəs*) *adjective*
1 unaware: *He is unconscious of his surroundings when reading.*
2 having fainted or lost consciousness: *She lay unconscious at the foot of the cliff.*
3 below the level of awareness: *The unconscious mind holds a lot of information we cannot recall.*

Word Use: a similar word for definition 3 is **subconscious**
Word Building: **unconsciously** *adverb*

uncouth *adjective*
rough and ill-mannered

Word Building: **uncouthly** *adverb* **uncouthness** *noun*

underarm *adverb*
with your arm remaining below the shoulder: *to bowl underarm*

undercarriage *noun*
the parts of an aeroplane under the body, supporting it on the ground or when taking off and landing

undercurrent *noun*
1 a current under the surface **2** a hidden tendency or movement: *There was an undercurrent of feeling against him.*

underestimate *verb*
to work out or calculate at too low a rate, value or amount: *I underestimated the time needed for the job.*

undergo *verb*
1 to experience or go through: *to undergo a medical examination* **2** to suffer: *He has undergone many hardships.*

Word Building: other forms are **I underwent, I have undergone, I am undergoing**

undergraduate *noun*
a university student who has not yet received a degree

underground *adjective*
1 lying under the ground: *an underground river* **2** secret: *underground work for the cause*

Word Building: **underground** *adverb*

undergrowth *noun*
shrubs and low plants growing beneath or among trees

underhand *adjective*
secret and sly: *underhand dealings*

underline *verb*
1 to draw a line underneath **2** to stress the importance of

underpants *plural noun*
an undergarment covering the lower part of your body from the waist to the top of the thighs

underpass *noun*
a road or pathway which goes under a railway or another road

understand *verb*
1 to grasp the idea of: *I am trying to understand what you are saying.*
2 to know the nature of thoroughly: *We understand her very well.* **3** to get the idea of by knowing the meaning of the words used: *Do you understand Greek?*
4 to be sympathetic: *He knew that whatever he did she would understand.*

Word Building: other forms are **I understood, I have understood, I am understanding**

understanding *noun*
1 ability to understand or grasp ideas **2** knowledge: *He has a good understanding of the subject.* **3** a private agreement: *They came to an understanding about the profits.*

Word Building: **understanding** *adjective* sympathetic

understate *verb*
to describe as less than is true: *He understated his income to the Taxation Office. / To say she is angry is to understate the case.*

Word Building: **understatement** *noun*

understudy *noun*
an actor or singer who stands by to replace someone who is unable to perform, usually because of illness

Word Building: the plural is **understudies** □ **understudy** *verb* (**understudied, understudying**)

undertake *verb*
to promise: *He undertook to have the job finished within a year.*

Word Building: other forms are **I undertook, I have undertaken, I am undertaking**

undertaker *noun*
someone who prepares bodies for burial or cremation and arranges funerals

undertaking *noun*
1 a solemn promise to do something **2** a task: *a difficult undertaking*

underwear *noun*
clothing such as singlets, underpants and petticoats, worn under other clothes

underworld *noun*
1 the world of criminals and criminal activities **2** according to myth, a world beneath the earth which is inhabited by the spirits of all the people who have died

undo *verb*
1 to open or untie: *to undo a parcel* **2** to ruin or spoil: *The storm undid all our work in the garden.*

Word Building: other forms are **I undid, I have undone, I am undoing** □ **undoing** *noun* downfall

undress *verb*
to take clothes off: *to undress the baby / Please undress for bed.*

unearth *verb*
to dig up or find after searching: *Mother unearthed her old school photos.*

uneasy *adjective*
worried or uncomfortable

Word Building: **uneasily** *adverb* **uneasiness** *noun*

unemployed *adjective*
out of work

Word Building: **unemployment** *noun*

uneven *adjective*
1 not flat, level or straight: *uneven ground* **2** not equally balanced: *an uneven contest*

Word Building: **unevenly** *adverb* **unevenness** *noun*

unfair *adjective*
not fair or just

Word Building: **unfairly** *adverb* **unfairness** *noun*

unfamiliar *adjective*
1 not having knowledge of: *I am unfamiliar with his poetry.* **2** not known or seen before: *Her face is unfamiliar to me.*

Word Building: **unfamiliarity** *noun*

unfeeling *adjective*
cold and hard-hearted

unfold *verb*
1 to spread or open out **2** to become known little by little: *Listen as the story unfolds.*

unforeseen *adjective*
not expected: *an unforeseen delay*

unfortunate *adjective*
1 unlucky **2** likely to turn out badly: *an unfortunate decision*

Word Building: **unfortunately** *adverb*

ungainly *adjective*
clumsy or awkward

Word Building: **ungainliness** *noun*

unicorn (say <u>yooh</u>-*nə-kawn*) *noun*
an imaginary animal like a horse with a single horn growing in the middle of its forehead

Word History: from a Latin word meaning "having one horn"

uniform *adjective*
1 same in appearance: *bottles of uniform size and colour*

uniform *noun*
2 special clothes worn by people to show they have a particular job or go to a particular school

Word Building: **uniformity** *noun* **uniformly** *adverb*

unify (say *yooh-nə-fuy*) *verb*
to form into one whole

Word Building: other forms are **I unified, I have unified, I am unifying** □ **unification** *noun*

uninhibited *adjective*
behaving just as you like without worrying about what other people think

uninterested *adjective*
not wanting to know about something

Word Use: a similar word is **indifferent** □ don't confuse this with **disinterested**

union (say *yoohn-yən*) *noun*
1 a number of things joined together as one **2** *short for* **trade union**

Word Building: **unionise** *verb* to organise into a trade union **unionist** *noun* a member of a trade union

unique (say *yooh-neek*) *adjective*
different from all the others: *Your fingerprints are unique.*

Word Building: **uniquely** *adverb*

unisex *adjective*
suitable for both females and males: *a unisex hairstyle*

unison (say *yooh-nə-sən*) *noun*
in the phrase **in unison** singing or saying the same thing all together: *The choir sang in unison.*

unit *noun*
1 a single person or thing or the whole of a group of people or things **2** an amount used in measurement: *A metre is a unit of length.* **3** one complete part of a school subject: *two units of maths* **4** *short for* **home unit**

unite *verb*
to join together as one: *The two clubs united.* | *The fight to save the koalas united the community.*

Word Building: **united** *adjective*

unity *noun*
a feeling of belonging or harmony in a group

universal *adjective*
including and affecting everyone, everything and every place

Word Building: **universality** *noun* **universally** *adverb*

universe *noun*
the whole of space and everything that exists in it

university *noun*
a place where you can study to earn a degree and do research after you have left school

unknown *adjective*
unfamiliar or not known: *an unknown face*

unlikely *adjective*
1 probably not true: *an unlikely story*
2 probably not going to happen: *Rain is unlikely.*

Word Building: **unlikelihood** *noun*

unload *verb*
to take things off or out of: *to unload a truck* | *to unload a gun*

unnatural *adjective*
not normal, natural or usual: *an unnatural light in the sky*

Word Building: **unnaturally** *adverb*

unnerve *verb*
to upset or make nervous: *The scornful crowd unnerved the speaker.*

Word Building: **unnerving** *adjective*

unravel *verb*
to untangle or come undone: *to unravel a mystery* | *The knitting has unravelled.*

Word Building: other forms are **I unravelled, I have unravelled, I am unravelling**

unreal *adjective*
1 imaginary or non-existent **2** amazing or unbelievable: *That song is unreal.*

Word Use: definition 2 is more suited to everyday language
Word Building: **unreality** *noun*

unrest *noun*
an angry restless feeling: *unrest among the prisoners*

unruly *adjective*
disobedient or uncontrollable: *an unruly class*

unscathed *adjective*
not hurt or injured: *They survived the battle unscathed.*

unscrew *verb*
1 to unfasten by taking the screws out of: *to unscrew the brass plate from his door*
2 to take off by turning round and round: *to unscrew the lid from a bottle*

unseemly *adjective*
not proper or decent: *unseemly behaviour*

Word Building: **unseemliness** *noun*

unsettle *verb*
to disturb or upset: *The thunder unsettled the dogs.*

Word Building: **unsettling** *adjective*

unsightly *adjective*
not pleasant to look at: *an unsightly scar*

unthinkable *adjective*
not deserving to be considered or thought about: *It is unthinkable that we would leave the children alone.*

untie *verb*
to loosen or set loose by undoing a knot: *She untied her scarf. / He untied the dog.*

Word Building: other forms are **I untied, I have untied, I am untying**

untold *adjective*
1 not told: *an untold story* **2** more than can be counted or measured: *a man of untold wealth*

untruth *noun*
a lie or falsehood

unwieldy *adjective*
1 difficult to handle or manage: *an unwieldy load* **2** awkward: *an unwieldy movement of the arm*

unwitting *adjective*
1 not meant or intended: *an unwitting insult* **2** not knowing, or unaware: *an unwitting victim*

Word Building: **unwittingly** *adverb*

upbraid *verb*
to speak angrily to about doing something wrong: *She upbraided him for his lateness.*

Word Use: similar words are **reprove** and **scold**

upbringing *noun*
the care and education that is given by parents or similar people to someone during their childhood

update *verb*
1 to give the latest news to: *I will update you on what has happened recently.*
2 to make more modern: *They are updating the shop.*

Word Building: **update** *noun*

upgrade *verb*
1 to promote or make more important: *His boss upgraded him to a new job. / The company upgraded his position.*
2 to improve: *You must upgrade your work.*

upheaval *noun*
a complete change or great disturbance: *We were in a state of upheaval after we moved house.*

uphill *adjective*
1 going upwards: *an uphill path*
2 very difficult: *an uphill task*

Word Building: **uphill** *adverb*

uphold *verb*
to support or keep unchanged: *The headmistress upheld the rule that the teacher had made.*

Word Building: other forms are **I upheld, I have upheld, I am upholding**

upholster *verb*
to provide with coverings, stuffing and springs: *to upholster a chair*

Word Building: **upholsterer** *noun*
upholstery *noun*

upkeep *noun*
the work or cost of looking after something or someone

uplift *verb*
1 to lift up **2** to cause to feel better, especially spiritually or mentally: *The beautiful singing uplifted him.*

Word Building: **uplift** *noun*

upper *adjective*
1 higher or highest in place, position or rank: *the upper slopes of a mountain / the upper class* **2** facing upwards: *the upper side of a coin*

upper case *noun*
the printing type that makes capital letters

Word Use: the opposite is **lower case**

upright *adjective*
1 straight upward or vertical: *an upright position* **2** honest and just: *an upright person*

Word Building: **upright** *adverb*

uprising *noun*
a violent rebellion against a government or other authority by a large number of people

Word Use: a similar word is **revolt**

uproar *noun*
a noisy disturbance: *There was an uproar in the classroom before the teacher came.*

upset *verb*
1 to turn or knock over: *to upset a boat / to upset a cup of tea* **2** to put out of order: *to upset someone's plans* **3** to make feel sad or hurt: *His insults upset me.* **4** to make feel sick in the stomach: *That food upset me.*

Word Building: other forms are **he upset, he has upset, he is upsetting** □ **upset** *noun* **upset** *adjective*

uptake *noun*
the act of understanding or grasping facts: *He is quick on the uptake so you won't have to tell him twice.*

uptight *adjective*
nervous or worried: *He felt uptight before his music exam.*

Word Use: this word is more suited to everyday language

up-to-date *adjective*
1 including the most recent facts: *an up-to-date news report* **2** modern: *up-to-date clothes / up-to-date ideas*

uranium (say *yooh-<u>rayn</u>-ee-əm*) *noun*
a white radioactive metal which comes from a yellow ore and which can be used to produce nuclear weapons and energy

urban *adjective*
having to do with a city or town: *the urban population*

urchin *noun*
a small boy, especially one who is mischievous or poorly dressed

Word History: from the Latin word for "hedgehog"

urge *verb*
1 to try hard to persuade: *I urged him to be very careful.* **2** to push, drive or force: *She urged the horse along the path. / Hunger urged us to keep going.*

urge *noun*
3 a strong natural desire: *I felt an urge to eat some fruit.*

urgent *adjective*
needing immediate action or attention: *an urgent message*

Word Building: **urgency** *noun* **urgently** *adverb*

urinal (say *<u>yooh</u>-rə-nəl, yə-<u>ruy</u>-nəl*) *noun*
a building to urinate in, especially a men's toilet

urinate *verb*
to pass urine from the body

Word Building: **urination** *noun*

urine (say *<u>yooh</u>-rən, -ruyn*) *noun*
liquid produced by the kidneys and passed from the body as a waste product

Word Building: **urinary** *adjective*

urn *noun*
1 a kind of vase, especially one for holding the ashes of someone who has been cremated **2** a container with a tap, used for heating water

us *pronoun*
the form of **we** that comes after a verb: *Don't worry about us.*

usage *noun*
1 the way of using or treating: *rough usage* **2** a custom or practice **3** the way in which a language is used: *English usage.*

use (say *yoohz*) *verb*
1 to employ or put into action for some purpose: *I will use a knife to cut this rope. / Do you know how to use this machine?* **2** to take advantage of someone's feeling for you in order to get them to do something you want: *She doesn't love Fred; she is simply using him.* **3 use up** to take or wear out the entire supply of: *I've used up the toothpaste. / He's used up his strength.*

use (say *yoohs*) *noun*
4 the act of using: *This shows the use of common sense. / You should clean those brushes after each use.* **5** the state of being used: *Is this seat in use?* **6** a way of being used: *You will find that this bag has a lot of uses.* **7** the ability to use something: *She lost the use of her legs after the accident.* **8** a need for using something: *Do you have any use for these clothes?* **9** the ability to be used in a helpful way: *This book is of use to me.*

Word Building: **useable** *adjective* **useful** *adjective* **useless** *adjective* **user** *noun*

used[1] (say *yoohzd*) *adjective*
1 having been made use of: *a used car / used clothing* **2** *another word for* **second-hand**

used[2] (say *yoohst*) *verb*
1 used to was or were accustomed: *We used to go there every summer.*
used[2] *adjective*
2 used to in the habit of or accustomed to: *I am used to getting up early.*

usher *noun*
someone who shows people to their seats at a meeting in church or at another public gathering

usherette *noun*
a woman who shows people to their seats in a cinema or theatre

usual *adjective*
normal or customary: *We went to school the usual way.*

Word Building: **usually** *adverb*

utensil (say *yooh-tens-əl*) *noun*
an instrument, tool, or container, especially one of those used for cooking or eating: *Pots and pans are kitchen utensils.*

Word History: from a Latin word meaning "useful"

uterus (say *yooh-tə-rəs*) *noun*
the part of the body of a female in which a baby grows

Word Use: the plural is **uteri** □ another word for this is **womb**

utilise or **utilize** *verb*
to put into use: *We can utilise the sun's power to make electricity.*

Word Building: **utilisation** *noun*

utility *noun*
1 usefulness **2** a service run by the government, such as public transport, gas or electricity supply **3** a small truck

Word Use: definition 3 is also called a **ute** in everyday language

utmost *adjective*
1 greatest: *This is of the utmost importance.* **2** farthest: *He went to the utmost areas of the earth.*
utmost *noun*
3 the greatest amount possible: *This is the utmost that can be said.* **4** the best that you can do: *Try your utmost.*

Word Use: another form of this word is **uttermost**

utopia (say *yooh-toh-pee-ə*) *noun*
a completely perfect place or society

utter[1] *verb*
to speak: *He was sorry he had uttered angry words.*

Word Building: **utterance** *noun*

utter[2] *adjective*
complete or total: *utter happiness / The room was utter luxury.*

Word Building: **utterly** *adverb*

U-turn *noun*
a turn made by a car or other vehicle so that it faces the way it has just come

Vv

vacant (say vay-kənt) *adjective*
1 empty: *vacant space* **2** not occupied by anyone: *a vacant chair / a vacant job*

Word Building: **vacancy** *noun* **vacantly** *adverb*

vacate (say və-kayt) *verb*
to leave or make empty: *You must vacate your hotel room by 10 o'clock.*

vacation *noun*
1 a holiday **2** the time of the year when a place such as a university is closed

vaccine (say vak-seen) *noun*
a liquid made from the germs that give you a disease, which you take to stop you getting that disease

Word Building: **vaccinate** *verb* to give a vaccine to **vaccination** *noun*
Word History: from a Latin word meaning "having to do with cows"

vacuum (say vak-yoohm) *noun*
an empty space, especially a space that has been made empty of air: *A pump works by making a vacuum which fills up with liquid.*

vagina (say və-juy-nə) *noun*
the passage in the body of a female that leads from the uterus to the outside of the body

vagrant (say vay-grənt) *noun*
someone who wanders from place to place instead of having a settled home

Word Use: a similar word is **tramp**, and, in the bush, other names are **swagman** and **sundowner**

vague (say vayg) *adjective*
not clear or certain: *vague shapes / vague feelings*

Word Building: **vaguely** *adverb* **vagueness** *noun*

vain *adjective*
1 very proud of yourself, especially about the way you look **2** useless or having no effect: *He made a vain attempt to stop the dogs fighting.*
vain *adverb*
3 in vain uselessly or without effect: *They tried in vain to save her.*

Word Use: a similar word for definition 1 is **conceited** □ be careful – this sounds like **vane**
Word Building: **vainly** *adverb* **vanity** *noun*

valentine *noun*
1 a present or message of love or friendship sent to someone on St Valentine's Day, 14 February
2 the person you choose to send this message to

valet (say val-ay, val-ət) *noun*
a male servant who looks after his employer's clothes and other personal things

valiant *adjective*
brave or courageous: *a valiant person / a valiant attempt to save his life*

Word Building: **valiantly** *adverb*

valid *adjective*
1 made with good reasons: *a valid excuse to leave the room* **2** having legal or official force: *This ticket is valid for two rides.*

Word Building: **validity** *noun* **validly** *adverb*

valley *noun*
the low land between hills or mountains, usually with a river flowing through it

valour or **valor** *noun*
braveness or courage

valuable *adjective*
1 worth a lot of money: *valuable jewels*
2 of great use or importance: *valuable help*
valuable *noun*
3 valuables things that are valuable, such as jewellery: *Don't leave any valuables in the changing rooms.*

value *noun*
1 the amount of money something is worth: *the value of your house*
2 what makes something worthwhile or useful: *He talked about the value of education.* **3 values** the beliefs and ideas about what is important, held by a person or community of people: *We like each other because we have the same values.*
value *verb*
4 to decide the value of: *His job is to value jewellery.* **5** to think to be valuable: *I value your friendship.*

Word Building: other verb forms are **I valued, I have valued, I am valuing** □ **valuer** *noun*

valve *noun*
1 the part of a pipe or other passage that opens and shuts to control the flow of liquid or gas **2** one of the parts of the shell of a sea animal, such as a mussel

vampire *noun*
an imaginary being, usually thought of as a dead person come back to life, believed to suck the blood from people while they are sleeping

Word History: from a Turkish word meaning "witch"

van *noun*
a covered vehicle for carrying goods: *a removal van*

Word History: short for **caravan**

vandal *noun*
someone who deliberately destroys or damages things

vane *noun*
1 a blade on a windmill **2** a flat piece of metal or other material on a roof, which turns with the wind to show which direction it is blowing from

Word Use: definition 2 is also called a **weathervane** □ be careful – this sounds like vain

vanguard *noun*
1 the front part of an army **2** any leading position: *She is in the vanguard of fashion.*

vanilla *noun*
a liquid made from a plant, used to flavour food

vanish *verb*
to disappear, especially quickly: *When I turned around she had vanished.*

vanity *noun*
1 extreme pride in yourself: *She is too full of vanity.* **2** something that someone is vain about: *Her hair was one of her vanities.*

Word Building: the plural is **vanities**

vanquish *verb*
to defeat: *The Roman army vanquished the enemy. | Our team vanquished all the others.*

vaporise or **vaporize** *verb*
to change into vapour: *Liquid vaporises when it is boiled.*

Word Building: **vaporisation** *noun* **vaporiser** *noun*

vapour or **vapor** *noun*
a cloud of a gas-like substance, such as fog, mist or steam

Word Building: **vaporous** *adjective*

variable *adjective*
1 likely to vary or change: *variable weather | a person with variable moods*
2 able to be changed: *The length of this table is variable.*

Word Building: **variably** *adverb*

variation *noun*
1 a change or alteration: *There is a lot of variation in the weather at this time of the year.* **2** a different form of something: *This novel is just a variation of all his other books.*

variegated (say *vair-ree-ə-gayt-əd*) *adjective*
marked with different colours: *variegated leaves*

variety *noun*
1 a variation or a change from what usually happens: *You enjoy work more if there is some variety in it.* **2** a number of things of different kinds: *a shop with a variety of cakes* **3** kind or sort: *This variety of ice-cream is my favourite.*

various *adjective*
1 different: *His talents are many and various.* **2** several: *I visited various parts of the country.*

Word Building: **variously** *adverb* **variousness** *noun*

varnish *noun*
a liquid coating which, when dry, gives a hard glossy look to a surface

Word Building: **varnish** *verb*

vary *verb*
1 to change: *She never varies her habits.* **2** to be different or cause to be different: *Opinions vary as to whether this is a good idea. | You should vary what you read.*

Word Building: other forms are **I varied, I have varied, I am varying**

vase (rhymes with *bars*) *noun*
a container for flowers

vassal *noun*
someone in feudal times who lived on a nobleman's land and had to fight and work for him in return

vast *adjective*
very great: *a vast country | a vast amount of money*

Word Building: **vastly** *adverb* **vastness** *noun*

vat *noun*
a very large container for liquids

vaudeville (say vaw-də-vil) *noun*
a light theatrical entertainment, mainly with musical and comedy acts

vault[1] *noun*
1 an underground room, especially one for storing valuable things or one where dead people are buried **2** an arched roof or something thought to be similar: *the vault of a church | the vault of the sky*

Word Building: **vaulted** *adjective: a vaulted roof*

vault[2] *verb*
1 to leap or jump with your hands supported on something: *He vaulted over the fence.* **2** to jump over in this way: *He vaulted the fence.*

Word Building: **vault** *noun*
Word History: from a Latin word meaning "roll"

VCR *noun*
another word for **video** *(definition 2)*

Word History: short for *video cassette recorder*

veal *noun*
meat from a calf

veer *verb*
to change direction: *The road suddenly veered to the left. | I veered to avoid the dog.*

vegetable *noun*
1 a plant or part of a plant which is used as food: *Tomatoes, beans and potatoes are vegetables.*
vegetable *adjective*
2 of or having to do with plants: *the vegetable kingdom*

vegetarian *noun*
someone who refuses to eat meat or fish and lives mainly on vegetable food

vegetation *noun*
the whole plant life of a particular area: *Tropical places usually have thick vegetation.*

vehement (say vee-ə-mənt) *adjective*
strong or passionate: *a vehement dislike*

Word Building: **vehemence** *noun* **vehemently** *adverb*

vehicle (say vee-ik-əl) *noun*
a form of transport, like a car or bicycle

Word Building: **vehicular** *adjective*

veil (rhymes with *pale*) *noun*
1 a piece of material that women wear to cover their head and face
veil *verb*
2 to hide or disguise: *The mountains were veiled in mist.*

vein (sounds like *vain*) *noun*
1 one of the small tubes that carries blood through your body **2** a line on a leaf or insect's wing **3** a layer of coal or gold in the middle of rock

velcro *noun*
a type of fastening tape made of two fabric strips, one with many tiny nylon hooks and the other with a nylon pile, that stick firmly together when pressed

Word Building: **velcro** *adjective*
Word History: this is a trademark

velocity (say və-los-ə-tee) *noun*
speed: *a wind velocity of 100 kilometres an hour*

Word Building: the plural form is **velocities**

velvet *noun*
a kind of soft thick material that feels rather like fur

Word Building: **velvet** *adjective* **velvety** *adjective*

vendetta *noun*
a feud in which the family of a murder victim tries to get revenge by killing the murderer or one of the murderer's family

veneer (say *və-near*) *noun*
1 a thin layer of wood or plastic used to cover the surface underneath
2 outwardly pleasant behaviour, disguising what is really underneath: *a veneer of good manners*

venerable *adjective*
worthy of respect because of age or importance

Word Building: **venerate** *verb* to respect

venereal disease (say *və-near-ree-əl*) *noun*
any disease picked up by having sexual intercourse with someone who is infected, but not including AIDS

Word Use: also called **sexually transmitted disease** □ the short form is **VD**

vengeance (say *ven-jəns*) *noun*
1 the act of paying someone back for harm they have done to you **2 with a vengeance** very strongly or forcefully

Word Use: a similar word for definition 1 is **revenge**

venison *noun*
the meat of a deer, eaten as food

venom *noun*
the poison that spiders and snakes inject into their victims

Word Building: **venomous** *adjective* poisonous

vent *noun*
1 an opening to let smoke or fumes out
vent *verb*
2 to express or show: *to vent anger*

ventilate *verb*
to bring fresh air into and let stale air out of: *Open the windows to ventilate the room.*

Word Building: **ventilation** *noun* **ventilator** *noun*

ventriloquism (say *ven-tril-ə-kwiz-əm*) *noun*
a way of speaking without moving your lips so that your voice seems to come from somewhere else

Word Building: **ventriloquist** *noun*

venture *noun*
1 something risky or a bit dangerous: *a business venture*
venture *verb*
2 to risk or dare: *to venture an opinion*

Word Building: **venturesome** *adjective* bold

venue (say *ven-yooh*) *noun*
the place where a particular event is held: *The new hall is the venue for the school concert.*

veranda *noun*
a partly open section on the outside of a house, usually covered by the main roof

Word Use: another spelling is **verandah**
Word History: from a Portuguese word for "railing", which came from a Latin word meaning "rod"

verb *noun*
a word in a sentence which tells you what someone or something does or feels, such as "hear" and "walks" in *If anyone walks past, I'll hear them.*

verbal *adjective*
1 spoken rather than written: *a verbal message* **2** having to do with words: *verbal skills*

Word Building: **verbally** *adverb*

verbatim (say *və-bay-təm*) *adverb*
using exactly the same words: *to quote her words verbatim*

verdict *noun*
the judge's or jury's decision or answer in a law court

verge *noun*
1 the very edge: *on the verge of tears*
2 the strip of dirt or grass at the edge of a road
verge *verb*
3 verge on to come close to: *to verge on stupidity*

verger *noun*
the caretaker of a church

verify *verb*
to prove to be true or correct: *You can verify the spelling of a word by looking it up in the dictionary.*

Word Building: **verification** *noun*

vermin *plural noun*
dirty pests such as rats, cockroaches and fleas

Word History: from a French word meaning "worm"

versatile *adjective*
able to do a variety of things: *a versatile performer | a versatile tool*

Word Building: **versatilely** *adverb* **versatility** *noun*

verse *noun*
1 poetry: *a play written in verse*
2 a group of lines that go together in a song or poem **3** a numbered part of a chapter in the Bible

version *noun*
1 someone's description of what happened compared with someone else's: *What's your version of the accident?* **2** a particular form of something: *the film version of "Alice in Wonderland"*

vertebra (say *ver-tə-brə*) *noun*
one of the bones of your spine or backbone

Word Building: the plural form is **vertebrae** (say *ver-tuh-bree*)

vertebrate (say *ver-tə-brət*) *noun*
an animal with a backbone: *Fish are vertebrates but prawns are not.*

vertex *noun*
1 the top or highest point of something: *the vertex of a triangle* **2** the point where two sides of an angle or three or more sides of a solid meet: *A square-based pyramid has five vertices.*

Word Building: the plural is **vertices** or **vertexes**

vertical *adjective*
standing straight up or at right angles to the horizon: *a vertical line*

Word Use: compare this with **horizontal** and **diagonal**
Word Building: **vertically** *adverb*

verve *noun*
lively enthusiasm: *to speak with verve*

vessel *noun*
1 a ship or boat **2** a hollow container, such as a cup or bottle **3** a tube which carries fluid inside your body, such as a blood vessel

vest *noun*
1 *another word for* **waistcoat**
2 *another word for* **singlet**

vestibule (say *vest-ə-byoohl*) *noun*
an entrance hall

vestige (say *vest-ij*) *noun*
the last trace of something that was once there

Word Building: **vestigial** *adjective*

vestry *noun*
the room in a church where the clergymen put on their robes and where sacred objects are kept

Word Use: the plural is **vestries**

vet *noun*
1 *a short form of* **veterinary surgeon**
vet *verb*
2 to check or examine carefully: *to vet the people applying for a job*

veteran *noun*
1 someone who has worked for a long time in a particular job **2** a returned soldier
veteran *adjective*
3 with long experience: *a veteran bushwalker* **4 veteran car** a car built before 1918

veterinary surgeon
(say *vet-ə-rən-ree*) *noun*
someone whose job is to treat sick animals

Word Use: another name is **veterinarian** □ the short form is **vet**

veto (say *vee-toh*) *verb*
to refuse to agree to: *to veto a plan*

Word Building: other forms are **I vetoed, I have vetoed, I am vetoing** □ **veto** (**vetoes**) *noun* the power or right to prevent something

vex *verb*
to annoy or worry: *to vex your parents*

Word Building: **vexation** *noun* **vexatious** *adjective* **vexed** *adjective*

viaduct (say *vuy-ə-dukt*) *noun*
a bridge with many arches, which carries a road or railway over a valley

vibes[1] *plural noun*
a short form of **vibraphone**

vibes[2] *plural noun*
the feeling you get, good or bad, just from being in a place: *I don't like the vibes in the meeting.*

Word Use: this word is more suited to everyday language

vibrant *adjective*
1 bright, lively and exciting: *a vibrant colour | a vibrant personality* **2** vibrating or quickly moving to and fro

Word Building: **vibrancy** *noun* **vibrantly** *adverb*

vibraphone *noun*
an electronic musical instrument like a xylophone, often used in jazz

vibrate *verb*
1 to keep on moving quickly up and down or to and fro **2** to make a buzzing or quivering sound

Word Building: **vibration** *noun*

vicar *noun*
a priest, especially one in charge of an Anglican parish

Word Building: **vicarage** *noun* a vicar's house

vice[1] *noun*
1 wickedness or evil **2** a fault or bad habit

vice[2] *noun*
a tool which closes around something and holds it tightly in place while you work on it

Word History: from a Latin word meaning "vine"

viceregal *adjective*
having to do with someone appointed as a deputy by a king or queen, such as a Governor-General or Governor of a State

vice versa (say *vuy-sə ver-sə*) *adverb*
the other way round from what you've just said, as in *I like him and vice versa,* which means *I like him and he likes me.*

vicinity *noun*
neighbourhood or area nearby: *There is no swimming pool in our vicinity.*

Word Building: the plural is **vicinities**

vicious (say *vish-əs*) *adjective*
very cruel or harmful: *a vicious dog / a vicious attack*

Word Building: **viciously** *adverb* **viciousness** *noun*

victim *noun*
someone who suffers harm or injury: *a victim of a car accident*

victimise or **victimize** *verb*
to punish or harm unfairly

Word Building: **victimisation** *noun*

victory *noun*
a win or success in a contest

Word Building: the plural is **victories** □ **victor** *noun* the winner **victorious** *adjective* **victoriously** *adverb*

video *adjective*
1 having to do with television

video *noun*
2 a tape-recorder which records both images and sounds **3** a video recording **4** a video cassette

Word History: definition 2 is short for a **video recorder** or **video cassette recorder**

videotape *noun*
magnetic tape used for recording pictures and sound to be shown on television

vie *verb*
in the phrase **vie with** to compete against or try to beat

Word Building: other forms are **I vied, I have vied, I am vying**

view *noun*
1 whatever you can see from a particular place: *a spectacular view from the top of the tower* **2** an idea or opinion: *What is your view on homework?* **3 in view of** because of **4 on view** displayed for all to see

view *verb*
5 to look at or see: *I will view the new building tomorrow.*

Word Building: **viewer** *noun*

vigil (say *vij-əl*) *noun*
the act of keeping watch at night: *to keep vigil by a sick child's bed*

vigilant (say *vij-ə-lənt*) *adjective*
alert and watchful

Word Building: **vigilance** *noun* **vigilantly** *adverb*

vigour or **vigor** *noun*
energy and strength

Word Building: **vigorous** *adjective* strong, energetic and full of life **vigorously** *adverb*

vile *adjective*
disgustingly bad: *a vile smell / vile language*

Word Building: **vilely** *adverb* **vileness** *noun*

village *noun*
a small town in the country

Word Building: **villager** *noun*

villain (say *vil-ən*) *noun*
a wicked person or scoundrel

Word Building: **villainy** *noun* wickedness **villainous** *adjective*

villein (say *vil-ən*) *noun*
someone in feudal times, with a little more freedom than a serf

vindicate (say *vin-də-kayt*) *verb*
to show to be right or innocent

Word Building: **vindication** *noun*

vindictive *adjective*
spiteful or full of revenge: *a vindictive remark*

Word Building: **vindictively** *adverb*

vine *noun*
a climbing plant, such as a grape

vinegar *noun*
a sour liquid made from wine or cider and used to flavour food

Word History: from the French word for "wine" added to the French word for "sour"

vineyard (say *vin-yəd*) *noun*
a farm where grapevines are grown

vintage *noun*
1 the wine or grapes grown in one particular year: *the 1979 vintage*
vintage *adjective*
2 very high quality, though perhaps in an old-fashioned way **3 vintage car** a car built between 1918 and 1930

vinyl (say *vuy-nəl*) *noun*
a type of plastic

viola *noun*
a stringed instrument, like a violin but a little bigger

Word Use: the **viola** is lower in pitch than the **violin** and higher than the **cello** and **double bass**

violate *verb*
1 to disobey: *to violate the law* **2** to treat brutally, showing no respect: *to violate a holy place*

Word Building: **violation** *noun*

violent *adjective*
powerful and causing damage: *a violent storm / a violent temper*

Word Building: **violence** *noun* **violently** *adverb*

violet *noun*
a small plant with purplish-blue flowers

Word Building: **violet** *adjective* purplish-blue

violin *noun*
a stringed instrument played with a bow and held between your shoulder and chin

Word Use: the **violin** is higher in pitch than the **viola, cello** and **double bass**
Word Building: **violinist** *noun*

violoncello (say *vuy-ə-lən-chel-oh*) *noun*
the full form of **cello**

VIP
short for very important person

viper *noun*
a type of very venomous snake

virgin *noun*
1 someone who has never had sexual intercourse
virgin *adjective*
2 completely natural or unspoiled: *virgin bush / virgin wool*

Word Use: definiton 1 is mostly used of girls and women
Word Building: **virginity** *noun*

virile (say *vi-ruyl*) *adjective*
strong, forceful and masculine

Word Building: **virility** *noun*

virtual *adjective*
as if it were really so: *Cinderella's family made her a virtual slave.*

Word Building: **virtually** *adverb* in effect: *The deputy was virtually the head of the school.*

virtue *noun*
1 goodness or proper behaviour
2 a good quality: *Patience is a virtue.*

virtuoso (say *ver-tyooh-oh-soh*) *noun*
a highly skilled musician

Word Building: the plural form is **virtuosos** or **virtuosi** □ **virtuosity** *noun*

virtuous *adjective*
good, honourable and obedient

Word Building: **virtuously** *adverb*

virulent (say *vi-rə-lənt*) *adjective*
1 very harmful: *a virulent disease*
2 bitter and spiteful: *virulent criticism*

Word Building: **virulence** *noun* **virulently** *adverb*

virus *noun*
1 a very small organism that causes disease **2** any disease caused by a virus **3** a small program in computers, which is let loose in the operating system with the intention of causing as much damage as possible, usually destroying files

visa (say *vee-zə*) *noun*
a stamp or witten notice put in your passport, giving you permission to enter a certain country

viscount (say *vuy-kownt*) *noun*
a British nobleman ranking below an earl and above a baron

Word Building: **viscountess** *noun*

visibility *noun*
the distance you can see, given the weather conditions or time of day: *Drive slowly because visibility is bad.*

visible *adjective*
able to be seen: *The lighthouse is visible from a long distance.*

Word Building: **visibly** *adverb*

vision *noun*
1 the power or sense of seeing: *The old man has good vision for his age.*
2 the power of imagining: *It was Colonel Light's vision that led to Adelaide being built.* **3** a mental image: *visions of power / a vision of God*

Word Use: a similar word for definition 1 is **sight**
Word Building: **visionary** *adjective* **visionary** *noun*

visit *verb*
1 to call on to see: *to visit friends*
2 to stay with as a guest: *My cousin is visiting me this week.*

Word Building: **visit** *noun* **visitor** *noun*

visor (say *vuy-zə*) *noun*
the movable part of a helmet, which can be pulled down over your eyes

visual *adjective*
1 of or having to do with sight: *visual ability* **2** able to be seen: *Teachers use pictures as visual aids.*

Word Building: **visually** *adverb*

visual display unit *noun*
a computer terminal which shows information on a screen

Word Use: this is also called a **VDU**

visualise or **visualize** *verb*
to form a mental picture of: *I recognise her name, but I can't visualise her face.*

vital *adjective*
1 having to do with or necessary to life: *the vital parts of the body* **2** full of life: *She is a very vital person.* **3** absolutely necessary: *It is vital that we stick together.*

Word Building: **vitally** *adverb*

vitality *noun*
energy or vigour

vitamin (say *vuy-tə-mən, vit-*) *noun*
any of a number of substances present in very small quantities in food, and necessary for good health

vivacious (say *və-vay-shəs*) *adjective*
lively or energetic: *a vivacious talker*

Word Building: **vivaciously** *adverb* **vivacity** *noun*

vivid *adjective*
1 bright or dazzling: *vivid colours*
2 strong and clear: *a vivid imagination*

Word Building: **vividly** *adverb* **vividness** *noun*

vixen *noun*
1 a female fox **2** a bad-tempered woman

Word Use: the male is a **dog;** the young is a **cub** or **pup**

vocabulary (say *voh-kab-yə-lə-ree*) *noun*
the total number of words used by someone or by a particular group of people: *She has a large vocabulary.*

vocal *adjective*
1 of or having to do with your voice: *the vocal cords* **2** talkative: *He was very vocal on the subject of holidays.* **3** sung or for singing: *vocal music*

Word Building: **vocally** *adveerb*

vocal cords *plural noun*
the folds of tissue lining your larynx which vibrate as air from your lungs passes them, making voiced sounds

vocalist *noun*
a singer

vocation *noun*
an occupation, business or profession, especially one which you seriously believe in: *a vocation to be a nun*

vodka *noun*
a Russian alcoholic drink made from grain and potatoes

Word History: from a Russian word meaning "little water"

vogue (say *vohg*) *noun*
fashion: *a style in vogue fifty years ago*

voice *noun*
1 the sound or sounds you make with your mouth especially when you speak or sing
2 the right to express an opinion: *He had no voice in the matter.*

voice *verb*
3 to utter or give voice to: *to voice an opinion*

void *adjective*
1 without legal force: *The contract is null and void.* **2** empty: *This statement is void of meaning.*

void *noun*
3 an empty space: *They peered over the edge of the cliff into the void.*

volatile (say *vol-ə-tuyl*) *adjective*
evaporating quickly: *Methylated spirits is a volatile substance.*

volcano *noun*
a mountain with an opening in the top, through which molten rock, steam and ashes burst out when it is active

Word Building: the plural is **volcanoes** or **volcanos** □ **volcanic** *adjective*
Word History: named after *Vulcan*, the Roman god of fire

volition (say *və-lish-ən*) *noun*
an act of will or purpose: *He did it quite of his own volition.*

volley *noun*
1 the firing of a number of guns together **2** an outpouring at one time: *a volley of words* **3** in tennis, the return of a ball before it bounces

volley *verb*
4 to return a ball before it bounces

volleyball *noun*
a team game in which a large ball is volleyed by hand or arm over a net

volt *noun*
a measurement of electric force

Word Building: **voltage** *noun*

voluble *adjective*
marked by a ready and continuous flow of words: *a voluble explanation*

Word Building: **volubility** *noun* **volubly** *adverb*

volume *noun*
1 a book, especially one of a series **2** the space occupied by a body or substance, measured in cubic units **3** amount, especially a large amount: *the volume of traffic / volumes of smoke* **4** loudness: *Turn down the volume on the TV.*

voluminous (say *və-loohm-ən-əs*) *adjective*
1 forming enough to fill a book: *voluminous letters* **2** large or full: *a voluminous skirt*

Word Building: **voluminously** *adverb*

voluntary *adjective*
1 done or made by free will or choice: *a voluntary decision* **2** unpaid: *voluntary work*

Word Building: **voluntarily** *adverb*

volunteer *noun*
1 someone who offers to do something, such as to join the army, of their own free will

volunteer *verb*
2 to offer without being asked: *He volunteered to make the tea.* **3** to join the army as a volunteer

Word Building: **volunteer** *adjective*

vomit *verb*
to throw up the contents of the stomach through the mouth

Word Building: other forms are **I vomited, I have vomited, I am vomiting** □ **vomit** *noun*

vote *noun*
1 a formal expression, such as putting your hand up or ticking a piece of paper, indicating a wish or choice **2** the total number of votes: *the Labor vote*

Word Building: **vote** *verb*

vouch *verb*
vouch for to guarantee or make yourself responsible for: *I can vouch for her.*

voucher *noun*
1 a piece of paper that proves how money has been spent: *a shopping voucher* **2** a ticket used instead of money: *a gift voucher*

vow *noun*
a solemn promise

Word Building: **vow** *verb*

vowel *noun*
1 a speech sound made by allowing air to pass through the middle of your mouth without being blocked by your tongue or lips **2** a letter, *a, e, i, o* or *u*, used to represent the sound of a vowel

Word Use: compare this with **consonant**

voyage *noun*
a journey by sea or air to somewhere quite far away

Word Building: **voyage** *verb*

vulgar *adjective*
coarse, crude or ill-mannered: *vulgar manners*

Word Building: **vulgarity** *noun*

vulnerable *adjective*
able or liable to be hurt

Word Building: **vulnerability** *noun* **vulnerably** *adverb*

vulture *noun*
a large bird like an eagle, that eats dead flesh

vulva *noun*
the external female sexual organs

wad (say *wod*) *noun*
1 a small lump or pad of anything soft: *a wad of cottonwool* **2** a roll or bundle: *a wad of banknotes*

waddle (say *wod-əl*) *verb*
to walk with short steps, swaying from side to side like a duck

Word Building: **waddle** *noun*

waddy (rhymes with *body*) *noun*
a heavy, wooden, Aboriginal war club

Word Building: the plural is **waddies**
Word History: from an Aboriginal language called Dharuk

wade *verb*
to walk through water

wafer *noun*
1 a thin crisp biscuit **2** a thin disc of bread made without yeast, used in some Christian church services

waft (rhymes with *soft*) *verb*
to blow lightly: *The breeze wafted the leaves. / The sounds of music wafted across the lake.*

Word Building: **waft** *noun*

wag *verb*
1 to move from side to side **2** to play truant from: *to wag school*

Word Building: other forms are **I wagged, I have wagged, I am wagging**

wage *noun*
1 the money you are paid regularly for working, especially in a factory or as a labourer

wage *verb*
2 to carry on: *to wage war*

Word Use: compare the noun use with **salary**

wager *noun*
a bet

Word Building: **wager** *verb*

waggle *verb*
to wag with short quick movements

wagon *noun*
1 a four-wheeled heavy cart **2** a railway truck

waif *noun*
a homeless orphan

wail *verb*
to give a long sad cry or to cry continuously

Word Building: **wail** *noun*

waist *noun*
the part of your body between your ribs and hips

Word Use: be careful – this sounds like **waste**

waistcoat *noun*
a close-fitting sleeveless piece of clothing which reaches to the waist and buttons down the front, often worn under a jacket

wait *verb*
1 to stay or rest until something happens **2** to be ready: *Your dinner is waiting.* **3 wait on** to act as a waiter or waitress to: *to wait on someone*

Word Use: be careful – this sounds like **weight**
Word Building: **wait** *noun*

waiter *noun*
a man who serves food and drink to you at your table in a restaurant or hotel.

Word Building: **waitress** *noun*

waive (say *wayv*) *verb*
1 to decide not to insist on: *to waive a parking fine* **2** to put off for the moment: *to waive a deadline for homework*

Word Use: be careful – this sounds like **wave**

wake[1] *verb*
1 to stop being asleep: *I like to wake to the sound of music.* **2** to rouse from sleep: *His mother always wakes him at seven.*

Word Building: other forms are **I woke, I have woken, I am waking** □ **wakeful** *adjective* **waken** *verb* **awake** *verb* **awaken** *verb*

wake[2] *noun*
the track left by a ship moving through the water

walk *verb*
to go along by putting one foot after the other

Word Building: **walk** *noun*

walkie-talkie *noun*
a light radio that you can carry, used by police, soldiers and so on to send and receive messages

walkover *noun*
an easy victory

wall *noun*
1 one of the sides of a building or room **2** a brick or stone structure acting as a boundary fence or barrier **3** anything that closes off or divides

wallaby *noun*
any of several types of kangaroo-like animals

Word Use: the wallaby belongs to a class of animals called **marsupials**
Word Building: the plural is **wallabies**
Word History: from an Aboriginal language called Dharuk

wallaroo *noun*
a type of kangaroo that lives in rocky areas

Word Use: the wallaroo belongs to a class of animals called **marsupials**
Word History: from an Aboriginal language called Dharuk

wallet *noun*
a small folding case for papers, banknotes and so on, carried in your pocket or handbag

wallop *verb*
to beat soundly

Word Use: this is more suited to everyday language
Word Building: **wallop** *noun*

wallow *verb*
to lie or roll about: *The hippopotamuses were wallowing in the mud.* | *I wallowed in a hot bath.*

walnut *noun*
1 a type of nut which you can eat, grown on a European tree **2** the wood of this tree, used for making furniture

walrus *noun*
a large warm-blooded sea animal with flippers and large tusks

waltz (say *wawls, wols*) *noun*
1 a type of dance in which you and your partner move in circles to music with a 1-2-3 beat **2** a piece of music for this dance

Word Building: **waltz** *verb*

wan *adjective*
1 pale or lacking in colour: *a wan complexion* | *a wan light* **2** sickly: *a wan smile*

wand (rhymes with *bond*) *noun*
a thin stick or rod, especially one used by a magician or fairy to work magic

wander (say <u>*won*</u>*-də*) *verb*
1 to go about with no definite aim or fixed course **2** to move or turn idly: *His eyes wandered from the page.*

wane *verb*
to grow, or seem to grow, smaller or less: *Her enthusiasm has waned.* | *The moon is waning.*

Word Use: the opposite of this is **wax**

wangle *verb*
to do or get something by cunning or trickery: *He wangled an extra day's holiday.*

Word Use: this is more suited to everyday language
Word Building: **wangle** *noun*

wanton (say <u>*won*</u>*-tən*) *adjective*
1 done or behaving without thought or sense, often with bad results: *a wanton attacker of innocent people* | *wanton cruelty towards animals* **2** loose or not controlled in your sexual behaviour

Word Building: **wantonly** *adverb* **wantonness** *noun*

war *noun*
1 fighting with weapons between countries, or between groups within a nation **2** any other fighting: *a war of words*

Word Building: **war** *verb* (**warred, warring**) **warfare** *noun* **warlike** *adjective*

waratah (say *wo-rə-tah*) *noun*
an Australian shrub with large red flowers

Word History: from an Aboriginal language called Dharuk

warble *verb*
to sing with trills, like a bird

ward *noun*
1 a division of a municipality, city or town used in elections: *Jones is standing for the East ward.* **2** a room or division in a hospital **3** a young person who has been legally placed under the care or control of a guardian: *a state ward*

ward *verb*
4 ward off to turn aside: *to ward off a blow*

warden *noun*
someone who is given the care or responsibility of something

warder *noun*
a prison officer

wardrobe *noun*
1 a cupboard for keeping clothes in **2** someone's clothes, or the costumes used by actors

warehouse *noun*
a large building for storing goods

wares *plural noun*
things for sale: *The wares were displayed in the window.*

warhead *noun*
the section of a rocket, bomb or torpedo containing the explosive

warlock *noun*
a wizard or sorcerer

warm *adjective*
1 having some heat that can be felt: *warm water* **2** keeping heat in: *warm clothes | a warm house* **3** kind and affectionate: *a warm welcome*

Word Building: **warm** *verb* **warmth** *noun*

warm-blooded *adjective*
having a body temperature which stays more or less the same regardless of the surrounding temperature: *warm-blooded animals*

warn *verb*
to tell or signal of a possible danger: *They warned us that the road was icy. | Flashing lights warn of fog.*

Word Building: **warning** *noun*

warp *verb*
1 to bend or become bent out of shape: *Rain has warped the timber. | The records warped in the sun.*

warp *noun*
2 a bend or twist **3** the lengthwise threads in weaving

warrant (say *wo-rənt*) *noun*
1 a paper issued by a magistrate allowing a police officer to make an arrest or a search of a building

warrant *verb*
2 to give a formal promise or guarantee: *The company has warranted to repair or replace the car if it breaks down in the first three months.* **3** to demand or require: *The circumstances warrant immediate action.*

warranty *noun*
a formal promise or assurance of reliability: *Do not buy an electric heater without a warranty.*

warren *noun*
a series of connecting burrows where many rabbits live

warrigal (say *wo-rə-gəl*) *noun*
1 *another word for* **dingo**

warrigal *adjective*
2 wild or untamed

Word History: from an Aboriginal language called Dharuk

warrior *noun*
a soldier or fighter

wart *noun*
a small hard lump on the skin, caused by a virus

wary (say *wair-ree*) *adjective*
watchful or careful

wash *verb*
1 to wet and rub, usually with soap or detergent, in order to clean **2** to carry along by water: *The bottle was washed ashore in New Zealand.*

wash *noun*
3 an act of washing **4** clothes which are ready to be washed, or have just been washed: *I have lost a sock in the wash.* **5** waves made by a ship: *The dinghy rocked in the liner's wash.*

Word Building: **washable** *adjective*

washer *noun*
1 a flat ring of rubber or metal to make a joint or a nut fit tightly **2** a small piece of soft cloth for washing your face or body

wasp *noun*
a four-winged insect that stings

Word Building: **waspish** *adjective* sharp and spiteful

waste *verb*
1 to use up or spend without much result: *to waste food | to waste money on gambling* **2** to wear away: *Illness has wasted his muscles.*

Word Use: be careful – this sounds like **waist**
Word Building: **wastage** *noun* **waste** *noun* **wasteful** *adjective*

watch *verb*
1 to look at attentively: *The students watched a film.* **2** to be careful of: *Watch your step.* **3** to guard: *They watch the place at night.*
watch *noun*
4 a lookout or guard: *to keep watch*
5 a small clock which you wear on your wrist

Word Building: **watchful** *adjective*

watchman *noun*
someone who keeps guard over a building, usually at night, to protect it from fire and burglary

water *noun*
1 the colourless transparent liquid which forms rain, rivers, lakes and oceans
water *verb*
2 to pour water on: *to water the garden*
3 to supply with water: *to water a horse*
4 water down to make weaker by adding water

Word Building: **watery** *adjective*

watercolour or **watercolor** *noun*
1 paint made from colour diluted with water and gum instead of oil **2** a painting done in watercolour

Word Building: **watercolourist** *noun*

watercress *noun*
a leafy salad vegetable with a peppery taste

waterfront *noun*
1 land next to the ocean or a lake
2 the wharves in a port

waterlily *noun*
a water plant with large flowers and flat leaves that float

Word Building: the plural is **waterlilies**

waterlogged *adjective*
1 completely soaked with water
2 flooded

watermark *noun*
1 a line showing the greatest height that water has risen to **2** a mark, usually the maker's name or trademark, made in paper and able to be seen when held up to the light

watermelon *noun*
a large melon with green skin and dark pink flesh

water-polo *noun*
a game played by two teams of seven swimmers each, in which the object is to pass a ball into the opposing team's goal

waterproof *adjective*
made of, or coated with, material which prevents water getting through

Word Building: **waterproof** *verb*

watershed *noun*
the ridge line at the top of a range of hills dividing two drainage areas or river basins

water-ski *verb*
to travel on special skis over water, towed by a speedboat

Word Building: other forms are **I water-skied, I have water-skied, I am water-skiing**

watertight *adjective*
1 completely sealed against water **2** having no fault or weakness: *a watertight argument*

watt *noun*
a unit of electrical power

wattle *noun*
1 *another word for* **acacia** **2** rods or twigs interwoven and used for fences, walls or roofs **3** a coloured fleshy part hanging from the throat of certain birds such as the turkey

wattle and daub *noun*
interwoven sticks or twigs covered with mud, used as a building material

wave *noun*
1 a movement in the form of a ridge on the surface of a liquid, especially the sea **2** a vibration that travels through air or water and which we experience as light, sound and so on: *a sound wave* **3** a surge of feeling: *A wave of anger went through him.* **4** an up-and-down or side-to-side movement of the hand used as a sign of greeting or farewell
wave *verb*
5 to move up and down or from side to side: *to wave a flag* **6** to move the hand in greeting

Word Building: **wavy** *adjective* (**wavier, waviest**)

wavelength *noun*
1 one full wave movement, such as from the top of one wave to the top of the next **2** a way of thinking: *We're on the same wavelength.*

wax[1] *noun*
1 a fairly hard greasy substance that is easy to melt
wax[1] *verb*
2 to rub or polish with wax

wax[2] *verb*
to grow, or seem to grow, bigger: *The moon is waxing.*

Word Use: the opposite of this is **wane**

way *noun*
1 manner or means: *the right way to do it* **2** direction: *Come this way.* **3** passage or progress: *They made their way through the bush.* **4** road, path, route or passage: *a way through the wood*

Word Use: be careful – this sounds like **weigh** and **whey**

wayfarer *noun*
a traveller, especially on foot

waylay *verb*
to lie in wait for, especially in order to attack: *They waylaid him outside his house.*

Word Building: other forms are **I waylaid, I have waylaid, I am waylaying**

way-out *adjective*
quite different from the usual: *way-out clothes*

wayward *adjective*
acting in a way that people don't think right or proper: *a wayward child*

we *pronoun*
the plural form of **I**: *We are not coming.*

Word Building: other forms are **our:** *our house* and **ours:** *That's not ours.*

weak *adjective*
1 liable to break or fall down: *a weak framework* **2** not healthy or strong **3** lacking in force or strength: *a weak leader* | *a weak argument*

Word Building: **weaken** *verb* **weakness** *noun*

weakling *noun*
a weak person or animal

weal *noun*
a mark or swelling on the skin made by a blow

Word Use: another word for this is **welt**

wealth *noun*
1 a large store of money and property **2** a rich supply: *a wealth of ideas*

wean *verb*
to start feeding with food other than its mother's milk: *to wean a baby*

weapon (say wep-ən) *noun*
an instrument used in fighting

wear *verb*
1 to carry or have on your body: *to wear a dress* | *to wear a brooch* **2 wear away** to get rid of bit by bit: *The rain has worn away the paint.* **3 wear off** to gradually reduce or get less: *The effect of the aspirin is wearing off and my headache is returning.* **4 wear out a** to wear or use until no longer fit for use: *to wear out clothes* **b** to tire out because of continuous strain: *You have finally worn out my patience.*
wear *noun*
5 a gradual using up: *The carpet shows signs of wear.* **6** clothing: *beach wear*

Word Building: other verb forms are **I wore, I have worn, I am wearing** □ **wearable** *adjective*

weary *adjective*
tired

Word Building: other forms are **wearier, weariest** □ **weary** *verb* (**wearied, wearying**)

weasel *noun*
a small, fierce, European animal that eats mice, rabbits and other small animals

weather *noun*
1 the state of the atmosphere as far as heat and cold, wetness and dryness are concerned
weather *verb*
2 to be affected by the weather: *The fence has weathered to a grey colour.* **3** to come safely through: *to weather a storm*

weatherboard *adjective*
having a covering of overlapping boards: *a weatherboard cottage*

weathervane *noun*
a flat piece of metal fixed on a roof, which moves with the wind and shows its direction

weave *verb*
1 to thread fibres together in order to make cloth, baskets or the like **2** to go by moving from side to side: *She weaved through the crowd.*

Word Building: other forms are **I wove, I have woven, I am weaving**

web *noun*
the fine silk-like net made by spiders to catch insects

web-footed *adjective*
having skin between the toes to help in swimming

wed *verb*
to marry: *They will wed tomorrow morning.* | *The minister wed them.*

Word Use: this is a rather old-fashioned word
Word Building: other forms are **he wed, he has wed, he is wedding**
Word History: from an Old English word meaning "pledge"

wedding *noun*
a marriage ceremony

wedge *noun*
a piece of wood or metal, thinner at one end than the other and used when you want to split wood or make something secure: *She put a wedge in front of the wheel to stop the car sliding down the slope.*

Word Building: **wedge** *verb*

wedlock *noun*
the state of being married

Wednesday (say wenz-day) *noun*
the fourth day of the week, after Tuesday

Word Use: the abbreviation is **Wed**
Word History: from an Old English word meaning "Woden's day" (Woden was the chief Anglo-Saxon god)

wee *adjective*
very small

weed *noun*
1 a useless plant growing where it is not wanted
weed *verb*
2 to pull weeds out of: *to weed the garden*

weedy *adjective*
thin and weak

Word Building: other forms are **weedier, weediest**

week *noun*
a period of seven days, especially from Sunday to Saturday

weekday *noun*
any day of the week except Saturday or Sunday

weekend *noun*
the time from Friday evening to Sunday evening, when most people do not have to work or go to school

weekly *adjective*
1 happening once a week: *the weekly wash*
weekly *adverb*
2 once a week: *The garbage is collected weekly.*
weekly *noun*
3 a paper or magazine that comes out once a week

Word Building: the plural form of the noun is **weeklies**

weep *verb*
to show sorrow or any emotion by crying

Word Building: other forms are **I wept, I have wept, I am weeping**

weevil *noun*
a kind of beetle which destroys grain, nuts, fruit and trees

weft *noun*
the threads woven across the warp in cloth

weigh (sounds like *way*) *verb*
1 to measure the heaviness of by means of a scale or balance **2** to press heavily: *The affair weighed on her conscience.*

Word Use: be careful – this sounds like both **way** and **whey**

weight (say *wayt*) *noun*
1 an amount of heaviness **2** a heavy object **3** something serious and worrying: *That lifts a weight from my mind.*

Word Use: be careful – this sounds like **wait**
Word Building: **weighty** *adjective*

weir (rhymes with *ear*) *noun*
a small dam across a river

weird *adjective*
very odd or strange

Word Building: **weirdly** *adverb* **weirdness** *noun*

welcome *noun*
a kindly greeting: *a warm welcome*

Word Building: **welcome** *verb* **welcome** *adjective*

weld *verb*
to join together by heat and pressure: *to weld metal*

welfare *noun*
the state of being healthy and having a good way of life: *He is interested in the welfare of old people.*

we'll
the short form of **we will** or **we shall**

well[1] *adverb*
1 in a good way: *She sings well.*
2 thoroughly: *Shake the bottle well.*
3 clearly: *I can see it well.*
well[1] *adjective*
4 in good health **5** satisfactory: *All is well.*

Word Building: other forms are **better, best**

well[2] *noun*
1 a hole drilled or dug in the ground to obtain water, oil, natural gas or other substances
well[2] *verb*
2 to spring or gush: *Tears welled up in his eyes.*

well-being *noun*
the state of being healthy and contented

well-meaning *adjective*
having good intentions

well-off *adjective*
wealthy or prosperous

Word Use: another word for this is **well-to-do**

welt *noun*
a raised mark on the skin made by a blow with a stick or whip

Word Use: another word for this is **weal**

werewolf *noun*
a man who, according to old superstition, changed into a wolf when there was a full moon

Word Building: the plural is **werewolves**
Word History: from the Old English word for "man" added to **wolf**

west *noun*
the direction in which the sun sets

Word Use: the opposite direction is **east**
Word Building: **west** *adjective* **west** *adverb*

western *adjective*
1 lying in or towards the west: *western suburbs*
western *noun*
2 a film or story about cowboys and Indians in the American west

wet *adjective*
1 covered or soaked with water or some other liquid **2** not yet dry: *wet paint*
3 rainy: *a wet summer*
wet *noun*
4 the wet the rainy season in central and northern Australia, from December to March
wet *verb*
5 to make wet **6** to make wet by urinating: *Baby has wet his nappy.*

Word Building: other adjective forms are **wetter, wettest** □ other verb forms are **he wet, he has wet, he is wetting**

wet blanket *noun*
someone who stops you enjoying yourself

wether *noun*
a castrated ram

wetsuit *noun*
a tight rubber garment worn by divers and surfers to keep in body heat

we've
a short form of **we have**

whack *noun*
a sharp blow

Word Building: **whack** *verb*

whale *noun*
a very large sea mammal that used to be hunted for its valuable oil

Word Use: the male is a **bull**; the female is a **cow**; the young is a **calf**
Word Building: **whaler** *noun* **whaling** *noun*

wharf (say *wawf*) *noun*
a structure built along or out from the shore of a harbour, where ships can load and unload

Word Building: the plural is **wharves** or **wharfs** □ **wharfie** *noun* someone who works on the wharves
Word History: from an Old English word meaning "dam"

wheat *noun*
the grain of a widely-grown cereal plant, used for making flour

wheat germ *noun*
a part of the wheat grain, rich in vitamins, which is removed when the wheat is ground

wheedle *verb*
to get by coaxing or persuasion: *They wheedled some money from their mother for the movies.*

wheel *noun*
1 a circular frame or solid disc turning on an axle, used in machinery and on vehicles
wheel *verb*
2 to roll or push on wheels: *to wheel a bicycle* **3** to turn around: *He wheeled on his followers.*

wheelbarrow *noun*
a small cart, usually with one wheel at the front and two legs, which you lift when you wheel it along

wheelchair *noun*
a chair on wheels, used by people unable to walk

wheeze *verb*
to breathe with difficulty, making a whistling sound

Word Building: wheeze *noun* **wheezy** *adjective*

whelk *noun*
a shellfish with a spiral shell

whereabouts *noun*
the place where someone or something is: *We don't know his whereabouts.*

whet *verb*
to sharpen: *to whet a knife | to whet your appetite*

Word Building: other forms are **I whetted, I have whetted, I am whetting**

whey *noun*
the watery part of milk separated from the curd, formed in cheese-making

Word Use: be careful – this sounds like **way** and **weigh**

whiff *noun*
a slight puff: *a whiff of smoke | a whiff of perfume*

whim *noun*
a sudden change of mind without an obvious reason

whimper *verb*
to cry weakly

Word Building: whimper *noun*

whimsical *adjective*
amusingly odd

whine *verb*
to make a high-pitched complaining cry

Word Building: whine *noun*

whinge *verb*
to complain in a tiresome way

whinny *noun*
the sound a horse makes

Word Building: the plural is **whinnies** □ **whinny** *verb* (**whinnied, whinnying**)

whip *noun*
1 a long piece of rope or leather attached to a handle, used to hit animals or people

whip *verb*
2 to beat with a whip **3** to beat with light, quick strokes: *to whip cream*
4 whip out to bring out with a sudden movement: *He whipped out a gun.*
5 whip up to rouse: *to whip up enthusiasm*

Word Building: other verb forms are **I whipped, I have whipped, I am whipping**

whirl *verb*
to turn round or spin rapidly

Word Building: whirl *noun*

whirlpool *noun*
a circular current in a river or sea

whirlwind *noun*
a strong wind that blows in a spiral

whirr *verb*
to make a low buzzing sound while moving or working: *The machinery whirred constantly.*

Word Building: whirr *noun*

whisk *noun*
1 a light, sweeping stroke: *a whisk with a duster* **2** a kitchen tool used for beating eggs, cream and so on

whisk *verb*
3 to move lightly and rapidly: *to whisk something out of the way | to whisk out of the room*

whisker *noun*
1 one of the long bristles on the face of a cat or similar animal **2 whiskers** a man's beard and moustache

whisky *noun*
an alcoholic drink distilled from grain, especially barley

Word Building: the plural is **whiskies**
Word History: from a Gaelic word meaning "water of life"

whisper *verb*
to speak very softly with your breath rather than your voice

Word Building: whisper *noun*

whist *noun*
a card game played by two pairs of people

whistle *verb*
1 to make a shrill sound by forcing your breath through a small opening that you form between your lips and your teeth
2 to make a similar sound by blowing through a whistle **3** to make a shrill sound: *The wind whistles in the trees.*

whistle *noun*
4 a small pipe which produces one or more notes when you blow through it
5 the sound produced by a whistle or by whistling

white *adjective*
1 of the colour of milk **2** light or fairly light in colour: *white wine | white coffee | white meat* **3** having light skin like a European: *a white man*

Word Building: **white** *noun* **whiten** *verb* **whiteness** *noun*

white ant *noun*
an insect which eats through wood

Word Use: scientists classify it as a **termite,** not as an ant

white elephant *noun*
something useless which can cost a lot of money to maintain: *The big new theatre is a white elephant because nobody uses it.*

white heat *noun*
heat great enough for metal to glow white

white lie *noun*
a lie told for reasons of kindness or politeness

whitewash *noun*
1 a white liquid that people used to paint walls and ceilings with **2** anything used to cover up faults and give a good appearance on the surface

Word Building: **whitewash** *verb*

whittle *verb*
1 to cut, trim or shape by taking off bits with a knife **2** to make less, a little at a time: *We've managed to whittle down our costs.*

whiz[1] *verb*
to move with a humming or hissing sound: *A bullet whizzed past his ear.*

Word Building: other forms are **it whizzed, it has whizzed, it is whizzing**

whiz[2] *noun*
someone who is very good at something: *a whiz at maths*

Word Use: this word is more suited to everyday language

whole (sounds like *hole*) *adjective*
1 making up the full quantity, number or thing **2** in one piece: *He swallowed the cherry whole.*

Word Building: **whole** *noun* **wholly** *adverb*

wholemeal *noun*
flour made from the whole grain of wheat

whole number *noun*
a number without fractions, such as 0, 1, 2, 3 and so on

Word Use: another name for this is **integer**

wholesale *noun*
the sale of goods, usually in large quantities, to shop owners rather than directly to the public

Word Use: compare this with **retail**
Word Building: **wholesale** *adjective* **wholesale** *verb* **wholesaler** *noun*

wholesome *adjective*
good for you

whoop (say *woohp*) *noun*
a loud cry or shout: *She gave a whoop of glee.*

Word Building: **whoop** *verb*

whooping cough (say *hooh-ping kof*) *noun*
a disease caught mostly by children, in which they cough a lot and find it hard to breathe

whore (say *haw*) *noun*
an old-fashioned word for **prostitute**

wick *noun*
the twisted threads in a candle or lamp which absorb the melted wax or oil to be burnt

wicked (say *wik-əd*) *adjective*
1 evil and harmful: *a wicked man*
2 bad or wrong: *Stealing is wicked.*

wickerwork *noun*
things made of twigs plaited or woven together

wicket *noun*
1 one of the two sets of three stumps with two bails on top at which the bowler aims the ball in cricket **2** the ground between the two wickets: *a wet wicket*
3 the dismissal of a batsman: *3 wickets for 90 runs*

wide *adjective*
1 having a large size from side to side
2 having a certain size from side to side: *30 centimetres wide*
wide *adverb*
3 fully: *Open wide! | He is wide awake.* **4** far to the side: *The shot went wide.*

Word Building: **widen** *verb* **width** *noun*

widow *noun*
a woman whose husband is dead and who has not married again

widower *noun*
a man whose wife is dead and who has not married again

wield *verb*
to control and use: *to wield a weapon | to wield influence*

wife *noun*
the woman to whom a man is married

Word Building: the plural is **wives**

wig *noun*
a specially made covering of hair for the head

wiggle *verb*
to move with short motions from side to side

wigwam (say *wig-wom*) *noun*
an American Indian hut made of poles with bark, mats or skins laid over them

Word History: from a North American Indian word meaning "dwelling"

wild *adjective*
1 living or growing in a natural state without human interference or care: *wild animals | wild strawberries* **2** unruly or disorderly: *wild hair | a wild party*
wild *noun*
3 the wild natural surroundings, usually a long way from civilisation or other people: *She is fond of camping in the wild.*

wilderness *noun*
1 an unoccupied and dismal stretch of country **2** a natural area of country without roads or houses, which may be very beautiful but difficult to reach

wildlife *noun*
animals, birds and insects living in their natural surroundings

wile *noun*
a trick or something done to persuade someone

wilful *adjective*
1 done on purpose: *a wilful act*
2 headstrong or obstinate: *a wilful child*

will[1] *verb*
1 to be going to: *I will cut your hair.*
2 to be willing to: *I will help you.*
3 to be accustomed or likely to: *He would sit for hours and hours.*

Word Use: this is a helping verb, always used with another one in the form **will** or **would**

will[2] *noun*
1 the power of choosing your own actions
2 wish or desire: *against his will*
3 purpose or determination: *the will to win*
4 a legal document stating what a person wants done with their property after their death

Word Building: **will** *verb*

willing *adjective*
agreeing quite happily: *He was willing to help.*

willow *noun*
a tree with thin branches that hang down

willpower *noun*
control over your own actions: *It takes a lot of willpower to stay on a diet.*

wilt *verb*
to become limp: *These flowers will wilt without water.*

wily *adjective*
crafty or cunning

Word Building: other forms are **wilier, wiliest** □ **wiliness** *noun*

win *verb*
1 to gain a victory **2** to get by effort: *to win fame* **3** to be successful in: *to win a game | to win a lottery*

Word Building: other forms are **I won, I have won, I am winning** □ **win** *noun*

wince *verb*
to start or flinch because of pain or a blow

Word Building: **wince** *noun*

winch *noun*
a device for hauling or hoisting, consisting of a cable wound round a drum turned by a crank or motor

Word Building: **winch** *verb*

wind[1] (rhymes with *pinned*) *noun*
1 moving air **2** a gale or storm
3 breath: *He can't run because he's short of wind.* **4** gas coming from your stomach or bowel
wind[1] *verb*
5 to take away the breath of: *The blow winded him.*

Word Building: **windy** *adjective* (**windier, windiest**)

wind[2] (rhymes with *lined*) *verb*
1 to turn first one way and then another: *The path winds up the hill.* **2** to roll into a ball: *to wind wool* **3** to tighten the spring of: *to wind a clock*

Word Building: other forms are **I wound, I have wound, I am winding**

windbreak *noun*
a protection from the wind such as a fence or row of trees

windcheater *noun*
a close-fitting jacket or jumper worn for protection against the wind

windfall *noun*
1 fruit blown off a tree by the wind
2 an unexpected piece of good luck

wind instrument *noun*
a musical instrument that you play by blowing

windmill *noun*
a mill for grinding or pumping, worked by the wind turning a set of arms or sails

window *noun*
1 an opening in a wall for letting in light and air and usually having panes of glass **2** part of the VDU screen of a computer, such as the area taken up by the pull-down menu, or the part of a large document that you can see on the screen

windpipe *noun*
the tube that carries air from your throat to your lungs

Word Use: the scientific word for this is **trachea**

windward *adverb*
1 towards the wind: *to sail windward*
windward *adjective*
2 facing the wind: *the windward side*

Word Use: the opposite of this is **leeward**
Word Building: **windward** *noun*

wine *noun*
an alcoholic drink made from grapes and sometimes from other fruit

wing *noun*
1 the part of the body of a bird or insect that is used for flying **2** one of the long flat parts that stick out from either side of an aeroplane **3** a part of a building which is joined to the main part: *A new wing was built on to the school.* **4** a political group within a larger group: *the left wing of the Labor Party* **5** the side part of a sports field on which football, hockey and similar games are played **6** someone who plays in this place on the field
wing *verb*
7 to fly: *The bird winged its way home.*

wink *verb*
to close and open one eye quickly: *He winked at me to show we were friends again.*

Word Building: **wink** *noun*

winning *adjective*
1 being the winner: *the winning team*
2 charming: *a winning smile*
winning *noun*
3 winnings something won, especially money: *He counted his winnings.*

winter *noun*
the coldest season of the year

Word Building: **wintry** *adjective*

wipe *verb*
1 to rub lightly in order to clean or dry **2** to remove by wiping: *He wiped the crumbs off the chair.* **3 wipe out** to destroy or defeat completely

Word Building: **wipe** *noun* **wiper** *noun*

wire *noun*
1 a long piece of thin metal that can be bent: *a fence made of wire | an electric wire*
wire *verb*
2 to fasten with wire: *He wired the gate to the fence.* **3** to provide with an electric system of wiring such as for lighting

wireless *noun*
an old-fashioned word for **radio**

wiry *adjective*
1 like wire in shape or stiffness: *wiry grass | wiry hair* **2** thin and strong: *a wiry person*

Word Building: other forms are **wirier, wiriest**

wisdom *noun*
1 the quality of being wise: *There is wisdom in what she says.* **2** knowledge or learning: *Books pass on the wisdom of the past.*

wise *adjective*
1 able to judge what is true or right: *a wise person* **2** showing good judgment: *a wise decision* **3** having knowledge or information: *He is wise in the law. | His explanation did not make us any wiser.*

Word Building: **wisely** *adverb*

wisecrack *noun*
a smart or amusing remark

Word Building: **wisecrack** *verb*

wish *verb*
1 to want or desire: *I wish to be a concert pianist.* **2** to express a desire for something, sometimes silently: *I wish we could go swimming. | to wish upon a star* **3** to say to as a greeting: *He wished her good morning.*
wish *noun*
4 something you wish for: *Did you get your wish?* **5** the act of wishing: *Shut your eyes and make a wish.*

wishbone *noun*
a bone shaped like a Y in the chest of birds such as chickens

Word History: this bone got its name from the belief that when two people pull it apart, the one getting the longer piece will have their wish come true

wishy-washy *adjective*
without strength or force: *a wishy-washy speech*

wisp *noun*
someone or something that is small or thin: *a wisp of a girl | a wisp of hair | a wisp of smoke*

Word Building: **wispy** *adjective* (**wispier, wispiest**)

wistful *adjective*
thoughtful in a sad way: *a wistful stare*

Word Building: **wistfully** *adjective* **wistfulness** *noun*

wit *noun*
1 the ability to be amusing in a clever way
2 someone with this ability
3 wits mental abilities or commonsense: *She always has her wits about her.*

Word Building: **witticism** *noun* **wittily** *adverb* **wittiness** *noun* **witty** *adjective*

witch *noun*
1 a woman who practises magic, especially to do evil **2** an ugly or bad old woman

Word Building: **witchcraft** *noun*

witchdoctor *noun*
a man supposed to have magical powers for healing or harming others

Word Use: a similar word is **medicine man**

witchetty grub *noun*
a large white grub that can be eaten

Word History: from an Aboriginal language called Adnyamadhanha

withdraw *verb*
1 to move back or away: *She withdrew to the kitchen.* **2** to take back: *I withdraw what I said about you.* **3** to take out: *to withdraw some money from the bank*

Word Use: a similar word to definition 1 is **retreat**
Word Building: other forms are **I withdrew, I have withdrawn, I am withdrawing** □ **withdrawal** *noun*

wither *verb*
to make or become dried up and shrunken: *The sun withered the grass. | Our friendship has withered away.*

withhold *verb*
to hold back: *They will withhold payment until they are satisfied with the goods.*

Word Building: other forms are **I withheld, I have withheld, I am withholding**

withstand *verb*
to stand or hold firm against: *She withstood his requests for more money. | This material will withstand heavy use.*

Word Use: a similar word is **resist**
Word Building: other forms are **I withstood, I have withstood, I am withstanding**

witness *noun*
1 someone who sees or hears something by being present: *I was a witness to the accident.* **2** someone who gives evidence, especially in a law court

witness *verb*
3 to be present at and see: *We all witnessed the fight.*

wizard *noun*
1 someone who practises magic
2 someone who is very good at something: *a wizard at maths*

Word Building: **wizardry** *noun*

wizened (say *wiz-ənd*) *adjective*
dried up and shrunken: *the wizened face of an old man*

wobbegong (say *wob-ee-gong*) *noun*
a kind of Australian shark

Word History: from a NSW Aboriginal language

wobble *verb*
to move or make move unsteadily from side to side: *The cup wobbled and then fell off the table. | She wobbled her loose tooth.*

Word Building: **wobble** *noun* **wobbly** *adjective*

woe *noun*
great sadness

Word Building: **woeful** *adjective*

woebegone (say *woh-bə-gon*) *adjective*
sad or miserable: *a woebegone look*

wog[1] *noun*
someone from another country, especially someone with olive-brown skin

Word Use: this word will offend people

wog[2] *noun*
a germ that causes a sickness: *Almost everyone in our class has caught the wog.*

Word Use: this word is more suited to everyday language

wok *noun*
a large, round-bottomed, metal bowl used in Chinese cookery

wolf *noun*
a large, wild, dog-like animal that eats flesh

Word Building: the plural is **wolves**

woman (say <u>*woom*</u>*-ən*) *noun*
an adult female human being

Word Building: the plural is **women** (say <u>*wim*</u>*-ən*) □ **womanhood** *noun* **womanish** *adjective* **womanly** *adjective*

womb (rhymes with *room*) *noun*
another word for **uterus**

wombat *noun*
a short-legged heavy marsupial that burrows holes

Word History: from an Aboriginal language called Dharuk

wonder (say <u>*wun*</u>*-də*) *verb*
1 to think about with curiosity or surprise: *I wonder why he decided to go.* **2** to think about with admiration: *I wonder at his courage.*
wonder *noun*
3 something strange and surprising: *It is a wonder that you arrived on time.*
4 the feeling caused by something strange and surprising: *He looked at her work with wonder.*

wonderful *adjective*
extremely good or excellent

Word Use: a similar word is **wondrous**

woo *verb*
to try to win the love of, especially so as to marry: *He is wooing the girl next door.*

Word Building: **wooer** *noun*

wood *noun*
1 the hard substance that makes up most of the trunk and branches of a tree **2** this substance cut up and used in various ways, such as building houses and making furniture **3** an area covered thickly with trees: *I went for a walk in the wood.*
4 a golf club with a wooden head

Word Use: a similar word for definition 2 is **timber**

woodblock *noun*
1 a block of wood with a raised design on it for printing from **2** a print made in this way

Word Use: another word for this is **woodcut**

wooden *adjective*
1 made of wood: *a wooden table*
2 stiff and clumsy: *a wooden way of walking*
3 without interest or liveliness: *a wooden stare / a wooden performance*

woodpecker *noun*
a bird with a hard strong beak for digging into wood after insects

woodwind *noun*
the group of musical wind instruments that includes the flutes, clarinets, oboes and bassoons

woodwork *noun*
1 things made of wood **2** the making of wooden things: *He is good at woodwork.*

Word Use: a similar word to definition 2 is **carpentry**

wool *noun*
1 the soft curly hair of sheep and some other animals **2** thread or cloth made from sheep's wool: *a dress of wool*

Word Building: **woollen** *adjective*

woolly *adjective*
1 made of wool or something similar: *a woolly jumper* **2** not clear or firm: *woolly thinking*

woomera *noun*
a stick with a notch at one end, used by the Aborigines to throw spears or darts

Word History: from an Aboriginal language called Dharuk

word *noun*
1 a sound or group of sounds which stands for an idea, action or object and which is one of the building blocks of a language
2 the group of letters you use to write down these sounds **3** speech or talk: *Can I have a word with you?* **4** a short saying: *I will give you a word of warning.*
5 a promise: *He gave his word.* **6** order or command: *Start moving when I give the word.* **7** news: *I have just got word of the accident.*
word *verb*
8 to choose words to express: *She worded her speech very carefully.*

Word Building: **wording** *noun: He used polite wording in his letter.*

word processor *noun*
a computer, usually with a set of keys like a typewriter and a visual display unit, used to store written material and change it when necessary

wordy *adjective*
using too many words: *a wordy explanation*

Word Building: **wordily** *adverb* **wordiness** *noun*

work *noun*
1 effort made by the body or mind to do something: *It will take hours of work to finish this job.* **2** something that needs to be done by effort: *I've brought some work home from school.* **3** something made by effort: *a work of art | a musical work* **4** a job by which you earn money: *Her work is teaching.*
work *verb*
5 to do work: *You should work when you're in class.* **6** to have a job by which you earn money: *She works in a bookshop.* **7** to act or operate properly: *This toaster isn't working.* **8** to use or manage: *Do you know how to work this machine?* **9 work out** **a** to solve, find out or calculate by thinking: *to work out an answer | to work out a sum* **b** to turn out: *I hope our plan works out all right.* **c** to train or practise a sport or exercise: *He works out every morning.* **10 work up** **a** to excite the feelings of: *She worked herself up into a rage.* **b** to make increase: *I've worked up an appetite with all this running.* **c** to move gradually towards: *I'm working up to telling you the surprise.*

workable *adjective*
able to be put into operation: *a workable machine | a workable plan*

worker *noun*
1 someone or something that works **2** someone who has a particular job: *an office worker* **3** someone who is employed in a factory or does work with their hands: *The workers here get on well with the bosses.*

world *noun*
1 the earth and everyone who lives on it **2** a particular area of life or interest: *the animal world | the world of sport*

world-class *adjective*
among the best in the world: *a world-class athlete*

worldly *adjective*
1 interested only in the things that concern us in our life on earth, rather than in any other life after death **2** used to the ways of the world

Word Building: other forms are **worldlier, worldliest** □ **worldliness** *noun*

worm (rhymes with *firm*) *noun*
1 a long thin animal with a soft body and no legs that moves by slithering along **2** someone whom you do not respect

Word Building: **worm** *verb*

worn *adjective*
1 shabby or damaged by wear or use **2** very tired

Word Use: this is a form of the verb **wear**

worry (rhymes with *hurry*) *verb*
1 to feel anxious or upset: *Our parents worry if we stay out late.* **2** to bother or annoy: *Don't worry me now, I'm busy.* **3** to grab with the teeth and shake: *The cat is worrying a mouse.*

Word Building: other forms are **I worried, I have worried, I am worrying**

worse *adjective*
bad to a greater degree: *My cold is worse than it was yesterday.*

Word Use: this is a form of the adjective **bad**
Word Building: **worsen** *verb* to make or become worse **worse** *adverb*

worship *noun*
1 great love, honour and respect **2** the showing of deep honour and respect for God in a ceremony or prayer: *to go to church for evening worship*

Word Building: **worship** *verb* (**worshipped, worshipping**)

worst *adjective*
bad to the greatest degree: *the worst winter for years*

Word Use: this is a form of the adjective **bad**
Word Building: **worst** *adverb*

worth *adjective*
1 equal in value to: *It isn't worth $10.* **2** good enough for: *a place worth visiting*
worth *noun*
3 value or importance: *a painting of great worth* **4** quantity or amount: *$10 worth of petrol*

Word Building: **worthless** *adjective*

worthwhile *adjective*
useful or good enough to spend time on: *a worthwhile hobby*

worthy (say <u>wer</u>-dhee) *adjective*
1 deserving respect or admiration: *a worthy effort* **2 worthy of** good enough for: *a meal worthy of a king*

Word Building: other forms are **worthier, worthiest** □ **worthily** *adverb* **worthiness** *noun*

would-be *adjective*
wishing or planning to be: *a would-be actor*

wound (rhymes with *crooned*) *noun*
an injury such as a cut, burn or bruise

Word Building: **wound** *verb* to hurt

wrangle (say *rang*-*gəl*) *verb*
to argue or quarrel noisily

Word Building: **wrangle** *noun*

wrap *verb*
1 to fold paper or material around: *I'll wrap the parcel.* **2** to fold so as to cover: *Wrap the blanket round you to keep warm.*

Word Building: other forms are **I wrapped, I have wrapped, I am wrapping** □ **wrapper** *noun* covering

wrath (say *roth*) *noun*
anger or revenge

Word Use: this is a rather old-fashioned word

wreak (sounds like *reek*) *verb*
to carry out or inflict: *The storm wreaked havoc on the garden.*

wreath (say *reeth*) *noun*
flowers and leaves tied together to make a ring

wreathe (rhymes with *seethe*) *verb*
to surround: *Mist wreathed the valley.*

wreck *verb*
1 to ruin or destroy

wreck *noun*
2 something, especially a ship, that has been wrecked

Word Building: **wreckage** *noun* the broken parts of a wreck **wrecker** *noun*

wren *noun*
a very small bird with a long upright tail

wrench *verb*
1 to twist roughly: *to wrench the door open* | *to wrench your ankle*

wrench *noun*
2 a sudden sharp twist **3** a type of spanner

Word Building: the plural form of the noun is **wrenches**

wrest *verb*
to pull or grab roughly: *to wrest the gun from his grasp*

wrestle *verb*
1 to struggle with someone and try to throw them to the ground **2** to struggle or make a great effort: *to wrestle with a difficult problem*

Word Building: **wrestler** *noun* **wrestling** *noun*

wretch *noun*
someone who is very miserable and unfortunate

Word Building: the plural is **wretches**

wretched (say *rech*-*əd*) *adjective*
1 poor, miserable and pitiful: *a wretched slum* **2** worthless or irritating: *The wretched door won't open.*

Word Building: **wretchedly** *adverb* **wretchedness** *noun*

wriggle *verb*
1 to twist and turn like a snake or worm
2 get a wriggle on to hurry up

Word Building: **wriggly** *adjective*

wring *verb*
to twist and squeeze: *to wring water out of the floor mop* | *to wring your hands in grief*

Word Building: other forms are **I wrung, I have wrung, I am wringing** □ **wringer** *noun*

wrinkle *noun*
a crease on something that is usually smooth

Word Building: **wrinkle** *verb*

wrist *noun*
the joint where your hand meets your arm

write *verb*
1 to form letters or words with a pen, pencil or similar thing: *to write on the blackboard* **2** to compose or create using words: *to write a poem* **3** to write a letter and send it: *I wrote to my sister last week.*

Word Use: be careful – this sounds like **right**
Word Building: other forms are **I wrote, I have written, I am writing** □ **writer** *noun* **writing** *noun*

write-off *noun*
a car that has been so badly smashed that it can't be repaired

Word Use: this word is more suited to everyday language

writhe *verb*
to twist and squirm, as if in pain or embarrassment

wrong *adjective*
1 bad or evil: *It is wrong to tell lies.*
2 not correct: *the wrong answer*

Word Building: **wrong** *verb* to hurt or treat unfairly **wrongly** *adverb*

wry (sounds like *rye*) *adjective*
1 showing displeasure or disgust: *She made a wry face as she tasted the soup.*
2 crooked or twisted: *a wry neck*

Word Building: other forms are **wrier, wriest** □ **wryly** *adverb*

X-ray *noun*
1 a ray that can pass through something solid **2** a photograph of the inside of someone's body, used by doctors to help diagnose disease

Word Building: **X-ray** *verb* to make such a photograph

xylophone (say <u>*zuy*</u>*-lə-fohn*) *noun*
a musical instrument made of a row of wooden bars of different lengths which you hit with small wooden hammers

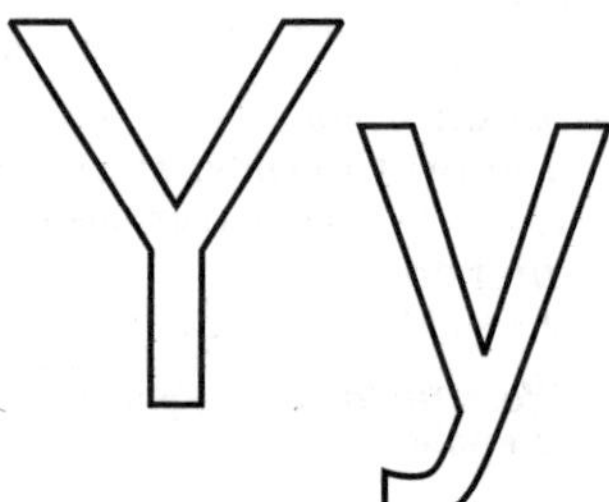

yabby *noun*
a small Australian crayfish which lives in fresh water

Word Building: the plural is **yabbies**
Word History: from an Aboriginal language called Wemba

yacht (rhymes with *cot*) *noun*
a sailing boat used for sport or pleasure

Word Building: **yachting** *noun*

yak[1] *noun*
a long-haired wild ox found in the highlands of Tibet

yak[2] *verb*
to talk on and on without saying anything very important

Word Use: this is more suited to everyday language
Word Building: other forms are **I yakked, I have yakked, I am yakking** □ **yak** *noun*

yakka *noun*
work

Word Use: this is more suited to everyday language

yam *noun*
a potato-like vegetable which grows in warmer parts of the world

yank *verb*
to pull or tug suddenly

Word Building: **yank** *noun*

Yank *noun*
an American

Word Use: this is more suited to everyday language

yap *verb*
to bark with short high sounds

Word Building: other forms are **it yapped, it has yapped, it is yapping** □ **yap** *noun* **yapping** *noun*

yard[1] *noun*
1 an old-fashioned unit of length equal to about 91 centimetres **2** a pole attached to a sailing ship's mast that a sail hangs from

yard[2] *noun*
1 the fenced ground around a house or other building **2** a fenced or walled area in which any work or business is carried on: *a shipyard*

yarn *noun*
1 nylon, cotton or wool thread used for knitting and weaving **2** a long story, especially one about unlikely happenings

yarn *verb*
3 to tell such stories

yawn *verb*
1 to take a long deep breath through your mouth, especially when you are bored or tired **2** to be wide open like a mouth: *The cave yawned before them.*

Word Building: **yawn** *noun*

year *noun*
1 the period of twelve months from 1 January to 31 December **2** any period of twelve months: *I saw him a year ago.*

Word Building: **yearly** *adjective*

yearn (rhymes with *burn*) *verb*
to want very much: *She yearns to go back to her home town.*

Word Building: **yearning** *noun*

yeast *noun*
a substance which causes the dough to rise when you make bread

yell *verb*
to call out loudly or shout: *He yelled with pain.* | *She yelled her answer.*

Word Building: **yell** *noun*

yellow box *noun*
a large spreading type of gum tree which grows in eastern Australia

Word Use: bees make excellent honey from the flowers of this tree

yellowcake *noun*
uranium in the form in which it is dug out of the ground

yellow fever *noun*
an infectious disease found in warm countries, caused by mosquito bites and sometimes resulting in death

yelp *verb*
to give a quick sharp cry: *The dog yelped when the boy hit him.*

Word Building: **yelp** *noun*

yen *noun*
a strong desire or longing

yesterday *noun*
the day before today

Word Building: **yesterday** *adverb: I did it yesterday.*

yeti (say *yet-ee*) *noun*
a manlike creature supposed to live in the mountains of Tibet

Word Use: another name for this is the **abominable snowman**
Word Building: the plural is **yetis**

yield *verb*
1 to produce: *This type of wheat yields a good crop.* **2** to give in or surrender: *I yielded to his argument.* | *The country yielded to the invader.*

Word Building: **yield** *noun: an orchard's yield of fruit*

yodel *verb*
to sing with rapid changes between your normal voice and a very high voice, as Swiss mountaineers do

Word Building: other forms are **I yodelled, I have yodelled, I am yodelling** □ **yodel** *noun*

yoga (say *yoh-gə*) *noun*
a set of exercises which involve holding unusual body positions and deep breathing, in order to reach a calm peaceful state of mind

Word History: from a Sanskrit word meaning "union"

yoghurt (say yoh-gət) *noun*
a food made by the controlled curdling of milk

yogi (say yoh-gee) *noun*
someone who is an expert in yoga

Word Building: the plural is **yogis**

yoke *noun*
1 a device consisting of a wooden crosspiece with curved ends fitting over the necks of two oxen pulling a load
2 a shaped piece in a garment, fitted about the neck, shoulders or hips, from which the rest of the garment hangs

Word Building: **yoke** *verb*

yolk (rhymes with *coke*) *noun*
the yellow part of an egg

Yom Kippur (say *yom kip-ə*) *noun*
an annual Jewish fast day kept on the tenth day of the month of Tishri

Word Use: another name is **the Day of Atonement**
Word History: this comes from the Hebrew name for this day

yonder *adjective*
being in that place or over there: *yonder farm on the hill*

Word Use: this is an old-fashioned word
Word Building: **yonder** *adverb: He went yonder.*

you *pronoun*
the pronoun you use when you are talking to one person or to a group of people: *Are you sure you know which way to go?*

Word Use: be careful – this sounds like **ewe**
Word Building: other forms are **your** and **yours**

you'd
a short form of **you had** or **you would**

you'll
a short form of **you will** or **you shall**

young *adjective*
1 being in the early stage of life, growth or existence: *a young animal | a young nation*

young *noun*
2 offspring: *Calves are the young of cows.*
3 young children: *the high spirits of the young*

youngster *noun*
a child or young person

your *pronoun*
the form of **you** used before a noun to show that something belongs to or is done by you: *your work*

Word Building: **yours** *pronoun: these are yours | Yours are very good.*

youth *noun*
1 a young man **2** young people
3 the time when you are young: *She spent her youth on a farm.*

Word Building: **youth** *adjective: a youth concert* **youthful** *adjective: youthful high spirits*

you've
a short form of **you have**

yoyo *noun*
a toy made of two round, flat-sided pieces of wood or plastic with a length of string wound between them by which you can make it spin up and down

Word Building: the plural is **yoyos**

yucky *adjective*
unpleasant

Word Use: this is more suited to everyday language □ another spelling is **yukky**

yum cha *noun*
a Chinese meal in which you choose small individual serves of many different dishes displayed on trolleys

yummy *adjective*
having a very good taste

Word Use: this is more suited to everyday language

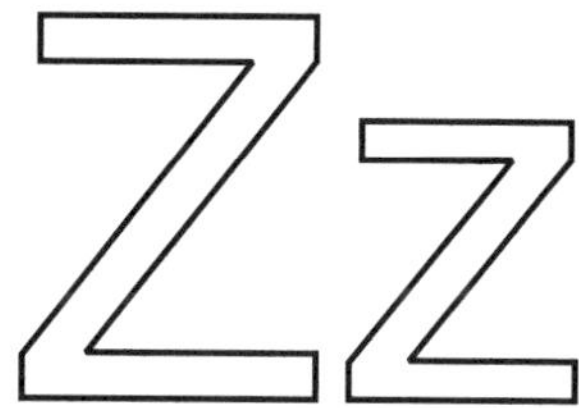

zany *adjective*
funny in a silly or crazy way: *She has a zany sense of humour.*

Word Building: other forms are **zanier, zaniest**

zeal *noun*
eagerness or enthusiasm: *zeal for the conservation movement*

Word Building: **zealot** *noun* **zealous** *adjective*

zebra *noun*
a wild, horselike, African animal with a black-and-white striped body

Word Use: the male is a **stallion;** the female is a **mare;** the young is a **colt**

Zen *noun*
a Buddhist sect that is popular in Japan, which believes that you should meditate if you want to understand the universe

Word History: from a Sanskrit word meaning "religious meditation"

zero *noun*
1 the figure or symbol "O" **2** nothing

Word Building: the plural is **zeros** or **zeroes**

zest *noun*
keen enjoyment: *She does her work with zest.*

Word Building: **zestful** *adjective*

zigzag *noun*
a line with sharp turns first to one side and then to the other

Word Building: **zigzag** *verb* (**zigzagged, zigzagging**)

zinc *noun*
a bluish-white metal, used in making galvanised iron and some alloys

zip *noun*
a fastener consisting of two rows of interlocking metal or plastic teeth and a sliding piece which joins or separates them

Word Use: this is also called a **zipper** or **zip-fastener**
Word Building: **zip** *verb* (**zipped, zipping**)

zither *noun*
a musical string instrument that you pluck

zodiac (say *zoh-dee-ak*) *noun*
a part of the sky forming an imaginary belt through which the sun, moon and planets appear to travel, and which contains twelve constellations which are named and used in astrology

zombie *noun*
1 a dead body brought back to life by supernatural means **2** someone who looks like a zombie and seems to have no mind

Word History: from a West African word meaning "good-luck charm"

zone *noun*
an area marked off and used for a special purpose: *a military zone*

Word Building: **zone** *verb* **zoning** *noun*

zoo *noun*
a large area of land with enclosed areas or cages where you can see wild animals

zoology (say *zoh-ol-ə-jee*) *noun*
the science or study of animal life

zoom *verb*
1 to move quickly with a humming sound: *He zoomed by on his motorbike.* **2** to go up suddenly: *The aeroplane zoomed into the clouds.*

Word Building: **zoom** *noun*

zucchini (say *zə-kee-nee, zooh-*) *noun*
a small vegetable marrow, usually picked when very young

Word Use: another name for this is a **courgette**
Word Building: the plural is **zucchini** or **zucchinis**

Appendixes

'If at first you don't succeed . . .' A guide to the spelling of some initial sounds

If you can't easily find the word you're looking up, it might be that the word begins with a letter or letters that you say in a different way to normal or which may be completely silent.

Here is a table to help you track down those tricky words.

Sound that the word begins with	The word could begin with this	Example
ch	c	cello
f	ph	photo
g	gh	ghost
g	gu	guide
h	wh	whole
j	g	gem
k	ch	character
k	qu	quiche
k	kh	khaki
kw	qu	quite
n	gn	gnash
n	kn	knee
n	pn	pneumonia
r	rh	rhyme
r	wr	write
s	c	cereal
s	ps	psychology
s	sc	science
s	sw	sword
sh	s	sugar
sh	sch	schedule
sh́	ch	champagne
sk	sch	school
t	th	thyme
t	tw	two
w	wh	white
z	x	xylophone

A simple grammar guide

Tense

as shown in the verb **to swim**

	Past tense	Present tense	Future tense
Simple	I swam*	I swim	I will swim
Continuous	I was swimming	I am swimming*	I will be swimming
Perfect	I had swum	I have swum*	I will have swum
Perfect Continuous	I had been swimming	I have been swimming	I will have been swimming

Note: The main forms, or *principal parts*, of verbs are shown in **Word Use** in the order Simple past tense, Perfect present tense, Continuous present tense. It looks like this:

Word Use: other verb forms are **I swam, I have swum, I am swimming**

Case

as shown in English pronouns

Number	*Person*	Subjective case	Objective case	Possessive case
Singular	First	I	me	my
	Second	you	you	your
	Third	he, she, it	him, her, it	his, her, its
Plural	First	we	us	our
	Second	you	you	your
	Third	they	them	their

Note: *First person* refers to the person speaking.
Second person refers to the person spoken to.
Third person refers to the person spoken about.

Subjective case shows that the pronoun is the subject of a verb.
Objective case shows that the pronoun is the object of a verb.
Possessive case shows ownership of the thing named by the noun that follows.

Abbreviations

ACT Australian Capital Territory
AD in the year of our Lord (Latin: *anno domini*)
adj. adjective
adv. *or* **advb** adverb
advert. *or* **advt** advertisement
a.m. *or* **am** before noon (Latin: *ante meridiem*)
amt amount
anon. anonymous
ANZAC Australian and New Zealand Army Corps
approx. approximate(ly)
Av *or* **Ave** Avenue
b. born; bowled; breadth
BC before Christ
Blvd *or* **Boul** Boulevard
B/W black and white
C Cape; Celsius; Centigrade; century
c. cent; century; about (Latin: *circa*)
Cap *or* **Capt** Captain
ch. *or* **chap.** chapter
COD cash on delivery
C of E Church of England
conj. conjunction
cont. *or* **contd** continued
Cres Crescent
deg. degree
DOB date of birth
doz. dozen
Dr Doctor; Drive
E *or* **e** east; eastern
e.g. for example (Latin: *exempli gratia*)
esp. especially
etc. and so on (Latin: *et cetera*)
F Fahrenheit
fem. female; feminine
fig. figure
figs figures
fol. following
Fr Father
fwd forward
govt government
GPO General Post Office
h. height; hour
h.c.f. highest common factor
hcp handicap
HQ headquarters
HSC Higher School Certificate
i.e. that is (Latin: *id est*)
incl. including; inclusive
IOU I owe you
Is Island
jnr *or* **jr** junior
L learner (driver)
l. left; length
lat. latitude
l.b.w. leg before wicket
l.c.m. lowest common multiple
long. longitude
LPG liquefied petroleum gas
m. male; married; mass; million; minute; month
masc. masculine
max. maximum
med. medical; medicine; medium
MHA Member of the House of Assembly
MHR Member of the House of Representatives
min. minimum; minute(s)
misc. miscellaneous
MP Member of Parliament; Military Police
Mr Mister
Mrs Mistress (Missus)
Mt Mount; Mountain
N *or* **n** north; northern
NE *or* **ne** north-east
No *or* **no** number (Italian: *numero*)
Nos *or* **nos** numbers
NSW New South Wales
NT Northern Territory
NW *or* **nw** north-west
P provisional (driver's licence)
p. page
para. paragraph
Parl *or* **Parlt** Parliament
p.c. per cent
Pen Peninsula
Pl Place
pl. *or* **plur.** plural
p.m. *or* **pm** afternoon (Latin: *post meridiem*)
PO post office; postal order
pop. population
POW prisoner of war
p.t.o. please turn over
Qld Queensland
qtr quarter
R River; *films, television:* unsuitable for people under 18 years of age (*restricted exhibition*)
RC Roman Catholic
Rd road
Rev Reverend
RSVP please reply (French: *Répondez s'il vous plaît*)
S *or* **s** south; southern
s. singular
SA South Australia
s.a.e. stamped addressed envelope; self-addressed envelope
SE *or* **se** south-east
sec. second(ary); secretary
sect. section
sen. senior
sing. singular
snr senior
Soc Society
Sr Senior; Sister
St Saint; Strait; Street
STD Subscriber Trunk Dialling
Sth south
Sthn southern
sub. *or* **subj.** subject
SW *or* **sw** south-west
Tas Tasmania
temp. temperature; temporary
UFO unidentified flying object
vac. vacancy; vacant; vacation
vb verb
Vic Victoria
vol. volume
W *or* **w** west; western
w. week; weight; wide; width; with
WA Western Australia
wt weight
Xmas Christmas
y. *or* **yr** year

Countries — Languages, Capital Cities, Currencies

Country	People	Main Language(s)	Capital	Main unit of currency
Afghanistan	Afghan, Afghani	Pashto, Tadzhik	Kabul	afghani
Albania	Albanian	Albanian	Tirana	lek
Algeria	Algerian, Algerine	Arabic	Algiers	dinar
Andorra	Andorran	Catalan, French, Spanish	Andorra La Vella	French franc, Spanish peseta
Angola	Angolan	Portuguese	Luanda	kwanza
Antigua and Barbuda	Antiguan	English	St John's	East Caribbean dollar
Argentina	Argentine	Spanish	Buenos Aires	austral
Armenia	Armenian	Armenian	Yerevan	rouble
Australia	Australian	English	Canberra	Australian dollar
Austria	Austrian	German	Vienna	schilling
Azerbaijan	Azerbaijani	Azerbaijani	Baku	rouble
Bahamas, the	Bahamian	English	Nassau	Bahamian dollar
Bahrain	Bahraini	Arabic	Manama	dinar
Bangladesh	Bangladeshi	Bengali	Dacca	taka
Barbados	Barbadian	English	Bridgetown	Barbados dollar
Belarus	Belarusian	Belarusian	Minsk	rouble
Belgium	Belgian	French, Flemish	Brussels	franc
Belize	Belizean	English, Spanish, Carib	Belmopan	Belize dollar
Benin	Beninese	French	Porto Novo	franc
Bhutan	Bhutanese	Dzongka	Thimphu	ngultrum, Indian rupee
Bolivia	Bolivian	Spanish, Quechua, Aymara	Sucre and La Paz	boliviano
Bosnia and Herzegovina	Serbs, Croats, Muslims	Serbo-Croat	Sarajevo	dinar
Botswana	Botswanan	Tswana, English	Gaborone	pula
Brazil	Brazilian	Portuguese	Brasília	cruzeiro
Brunei	Bruneian	Malay, English	Bandar Seri Begawan	Brunei dollar
Bulgaria	Bulgarian	Bulgarian	Sofia	lev
Burkina Faso	—	French, Mossi	Ouagadougou	franc
Burundi	Burundian	French, Kirundi	Bujumbura	Burundi franc
Cambodia	Cambodian	Khmer, French	Phnom Penh	riel
Cameroon	Cameroonian	French, English	Yaoundé	franc
Canada	Canadian	English, French	Ottawa	Canadian dollar
Cape Verde Islands	Cape Verdean	Portuguese	Praia	Cape Verdean escudo

Country	People	Main Language(s)	Capital	Main unit of currency
Central African Republic	—	French, Sangho	Bangui	franc
Chad	Chadian	French	N'Djamena	franc
Chile	Chilean	Spanish	Santiago	peso
China	Chinese	Chinese (Mandarin)	Beijing	yuan
Colombia	Colombian	Spanish	Bogotá	peso
Comoros	Comorian	French, Arabic	Moroni	franc
Congo	Congolese	French	Brazzaville	franc
Costa Rica	Costa Rican	Spanish	San José	colón
Côte d'Ivoire (Ivory Coast)	—	French	Yamoussoukro	franc
Croatia	Croat	Serbo-Croat	Zagreb	Croatian dinar
Cuba	Cuban	Spanish	Havana	peso
Cyprus	Cypriot	Greek, Turkish	Nicosia	pound
Czech Republic	Czech	Czech	Prague	koruna
Denmark	Dane	Danish	Copenhagen	krone
Djibouti	Djiboutian	Arabic	Djibouti	Djibouti franc
Dominica	Dominican	English	Roseau	Dominican dollar
Dominican Republic	Dominican	Spanish	Santo Domingo	peso
Ecuador	Ecuadorian	Spanish, Quechua	Quito	sucre
Egypt	Egyptian	Arabic	Cairo	pound
El Salvador	Salvadorian	Spanish	San Salvador	colón
Equatorial Guinea	Guinean	Spanish	Malabo	franc
Eritrea	Eritrean	Tigrinya	Asmara	Ethiopian birr
Estonia	Estonian	Estonian	Tallinn	rouble
Ethiopia	Ethiopian	Amharic	Addis Ababa	birr
Fiji	Fijian	English, Fijian, Hindi	Suva	dollar
Finland	Finn, Finlander	Finnish, Swedish	Helsinki	markka
France	French	French	Paris	franc
Gabon	Gabonese	French, Fang	Libreville	franc
Gambia, The	Gambian	English	Banjul	dalasi
Georgia			Tbilisi	
Germany	German	German	Berlin and Bonn	mark
Ghana	Ghanaian	English	Accra	new cedi
Greece	Greek	Greek	Athens	drachma
Grenada	Grenadian	English	St George's	East Caribbean dollar
Guatemala	Guatemalan	Spanish	Guatemala City	quetzal
Guinea	Guinean	French	Conakry	franc
Guinea-Bissau	Guinean	Portuguese	Bissau	Guinean peso

Country	People	Main Language(s)	Capital	Main unit of currency
Guyana	Guyanun	English	Georgetown	dollar
Haiti	Haitian	French, Haitian Creole	Port-au-Prince	gourde
Honduras	Honduran	Spanish, English	Tegucigalpa	lempira
Hungary	Hungarian	Hungarian	Budapest	forint
Iceland	Icelander	Icelandic	Reykjavik	krona
India	Indian	Hindi, English	New Delhi	rupee
Indonesia	Indonesian	Bahasa Indonesia	Jakarta	rupiah
Iran	Iranian	Farsi (Persian)	Tehran	rial
Iraq	Iraqi	Arabic, Kurdish	Baghdad	dinar
Ireland, Republic of	Irish	English, Gaelic	Dublin	Irish pound (punt)
Israel	Israeli	Hebrew, Arabic	Jerusalem	shekel
Italy	Italian	Italian	Rome	lira
Jamaica	Jamaican	English	Kingston	Jamaican dollar
Japan	Japanese	Japanese	Tokyo	yen
Jordan	Jordanian	Arabic	Amman	dinar
Kazakhstan	Kazakh	Kazakh	Alma-Ata	rouble
Kenya	Kenyan	Swahili, English	Nairobi	shilling
Kirgizia	Kirgiz	Kirgiz	Bishkek	rouble
Kiribati	—	I-Kiribati, English	Bairiki	Australian dollar
Kuwait	Kuwaiti	Arabic	Kuwait City	dinar
Laos	Laotian	Lao	Vientiane	kip
Latvia	Latvian	Latvian	Riga	rouble
Lebanon	Lebanese	Arabic	Beirut	Lebanese pound
Lesotho	—	English, Sesotho	Maseru	loti
Liberia	Liberian	English	Monrovia	Liberian dollar
Libya	Libyan	Arabic	Tripoli	Libyan dinar
Liechtenstein	—	German	Vaduz	Swiss franc
Lithuania	Lithuanian	Lithuanian	Vilnius	rouble
Luxembourg	—	French, German	Luxembourg	franc
Madagascar	Madagascan	Malagasy, French	Antananarivo	franc
Malawi	—	English, Chichewa	Lilongwe	kwacha
Malaysia	Malaysian	Malay, English	Kuala Lumpur	ringgit
Maldives	Maldivian	Divehi	Malé	rufiyaa
Mali	Malian	French	Bamako	franc
Malta	Maltese	Maltese, English	Valletta	Maltese lira
Mauritania	Mauritanian	French, Arabic	Nouakchott	ouguiya
Mauritius	Mauritian	English, French Creole	Port Louis	rupee
Mexico	Mexican	Spanish	Mexico City	peso
Moldova	Moldovan	Moldovan	Kishinev	rouble

Country	People	Main Language(s)	Capital	Main unit of currency
Monaco	Monacan	French	Monaco	franc
Mongolia	Mongolian	Khalkha Mongolian	Ulan Bator	tugrik
Morocco	Moroccan	Arabic	Rabat	dirham
Mozambique	Mozambican	Portuguese	Maputo	metical
Myanmar (Burma)	Myanmaran	Burmese	Yangon	kyat
Nauru	Nauruan	Nauruan, English	Nauru	Australian dollar
Nepal	Nepalese, Nepali	Nepali	Katmandu	rupee
Netherlands, the	Dutch	Dutch	Amsterdam	guilder
New Zealand	New Zealander	English	Wellington	New Zealand dollar
Nicaragua	Nicaraguan	Spanish	Managua	córdoba
Niger	—	French	Niamey	franc
Nigeria	Nigerian	English	Lagos, Abuja	naira
North Korea	North Korean	Korean	Pyongyang	won
Norway	Norwegian	Norwegian	Oslo	krone
Oman	Omani	Arabic	Muscat	rial omani
Pakistan	Pakistani	Urdu	Islamabad	rupee
Panama	Panamanian	Spanish	Panama City	balboa
Papua New Guinea	Papua New Guinean	Neo-Melanesian, Pidgin, Motu, English	Port Moresby	kina
Paraguay	Paraguayan	Spanish, Guarani	Asunción	guarani
Peru	Peruvian	Spanish, Quechua	Lima	inti
Philippines	Filipino	Pilipino, English	Manila	peso
Poland	Pole	Polish	Warsaw	zloty
Portugal	Portuguese	Portuguese	Lisbon	escudo
Qatar	Qatari	Arabic	Doha	riyal
Romania	Romanian	Romanian	Bucharest	leu
Russia	Russian	Russian	Moscow	rouble
Rwanda	Rwandan	French, Rwanda	Kigali	Rwanda franc
San Marino	San Marinese	Italian	San Marino	Italian lira
São Tomé and Principe	—	Portuguese	São Tomé	dobra
Saudi Arabia	Saudi Arabian, Saudi	Arabic	Riyadh	riyal
Senegal	Senegalese	French	Dakar	franc
Seychelles	—	English, French, Creole	Victoria	rupee
Sierra Leone	Sierra Leonean	English	Freetown	leone
Singapore	Singaporean	Malay, Chinese, English, Tamil	Singapore	Singapore dollar

Country	People	Main Language(s)	Capital	Main unit of currency
Slovakia	Slovak	Slovak	Bratislava	koruna
Slovenia	Slovene	Slovene	Ljubljana	dinar
Solomon Islands	Solomon Islander	English, Neo-Melanesian, Pidgin	Honiara	Solomon Islands dollar
Somalia	Somali, Somalian	Somali, Arabic, English, Italian	Mogadishu	Somali shilling
South Africa	South African	Afrikaans, English	Cape Town, Pretoria and Bloemfontein	rand
South Korea	South Korean	Korean	Seoul	won
Spain	Spaniard	Spanish	Madrid	peseta
Sri Lanka (Ceylon)	Sri Lankan, Sinhalese	Sinhalese, Tamil, English	Colombo	rupee
St Kitts-Nevis	—	English	Basseterre	East Caribbean dollar
St Lucia	St Lucian	English	Castries	East Caribbean dollar
St Vincent and the Grenadines	—	English	Kingstown	East Caribbean dollar
Sudan	Sudanese	Arabic	Khartoum	Sudanese pound
Surinam	Surinamese	Dutch, English	Paramaribo	guilder
Swaziland	Swazi	English, Swazi	Mbabane	emalangeni
Sweden	Swede	Swedish	Stockholm	krona
Switzerland	Swiss	German, French, Italian	Bern	Swiss franc
Syria	Syrian	Arabic	Damascus	Syrian pound
Tadzhikistan	Tadzhik	Tadzhik	Dushanbe	rouble
Taiwan	Taiwanese	Chinese (Mandarin)	Taipei	New Taiwan dollar
Tanzania	Tanzanian	Swahili, English	Dodoma	Tanzanian shilling
Thailand	Thai	Thai	Bangkok	baht
Togo	Togolese	French	Lomé	franc
Tonga	Tongan	Tongan, English	Nuku'alofa	pa'anga
Trinidad and Tobago	Trinidadian	English	Port of Spain	Trinidad and Tobago dollar
Tunisia	Tunisian	Arabic, French	Tunis	dinar
Turkey	Turk	Turkish	Ankara	lira
Turkmenistan	Turkoman	Turkoman	Ashkhabad	rouble
Tuvalu	Tuvaluan	Tuvaluan, English	Funafuti (island)	Australian dollar and Tuvaluan dollar
Uganda	Ugandan	Swahili, English	Kampala	Ugandan shilling
Ukraine	Ukrainian	Ukrainian	Kiev	rouble

Country	People	Main Language(s)	Capital	Main unit of currency
United Arab Emirates	—	Arabic	Abu Dhabi	dirham
United Kingdom	British, Briton	English	London	pound sterling
United States of America	American	English	Washington	dollar
Uruguay	Uruguayan	Spanish	Montevideo	new peso
Uzbekistan	Uzbek	Uzbek	Tashkent	rouble
Vanuatu	Vanuatuan	Bislama, French, English	Vila	vatu
Venezuela	Venezuelan	Spanish	Caracas	bolívar
Vietnam	Vietnamese	Vietnamese	Hanoi	dong
Western Samoa	Western Samoan	Samoan, English	Apia	tala
Yemen	Yemeni	Arabic	San'a (political) Aden (economic)	rial, dinar
Yugoslavia	Yugoslav	Serbo-Croat, Macedonian	Belgrade	dinar
Macedonia	Macedonian, Albanian	Macedonian	Skopje	dinar
Montenegro	Serbs	Serbo-Croat	Podgorica	dinar
Serbia	Serbs	Serbo-Croat	Belgrade	dinar
Zaire	Zairean	French	Kinshasa	zaire
Zambia	Zambian	English	Lusaka	kwacha
Zimbabwe	Zimbabwean	English	Harare	Zimbabwe dollar

Numbers

Cardinal numbers		Ordinal numbers	
1	one	1st	first
2	two	2nd	second
3	three	3rd	third
4	four	4th	fourth
5	five	5th	fifth
6	six	6th	sixth
7	seven	7th	seventh
8	eight	8th	eighth
9	nine	9th	ninth
10	ten	10th	tenth
20	twenty	20th	twentieth
50	fifty	50th	fiftieth
100	hundred	100th	hundredth
1000	thousand	1000th	thousandth

Roman numerals

Number	Roman numeral	Number	Roman numeral
1	I	43	XLIII
2	II	50	L
3	III	54	LIV
4	IV	60	LX
5	V	65	LXV
6	VI	70	LXX
7	VII	76	LXXVI
8	VIII	80	LXXX
9	IX	87	LXXXVII
10	X	90	XC
11	XI	98	XCVIII
12	XII	100	C
13	XIII	101	CI
14	XIV	115	CXV
15	XV	150	CL
16	XVI	200	CC
17	XVII	300	CCC
18	XVIII	400	CD
19	XIX	500	D
20	XX	600	DC
21	XXI	700	DCC
30	XXX	800	DCCC
32	XXXII	900	CM
40	XL	1000	M

Pronunciation key

Sometimes when a word is hard to say a pronunciation guide is given in brackets after the headword. The following key will help you to understand the pronunciation guides.

Vowels

a sounds
a as in 'pat'
ah as in 'part', 'hurrah'
ay as in 'bay'

i sounds
i as in 'pit'
uy as in 'buy'
ear as in 'hear'

u sounds
u as in 'but'
oo as in 'book'
ooh as in 'boot'

e sounds
e as in 'pet'
ee as in 'feet'
air as in 'pair'

o sounds
o as in 'pot'
oh as in 'boat', 'oh'
aw as in 'paw'
ow as in 'how'
oy as in 'boy'

er sounds
er as in 'pert'
ə as in '**a**part', 'batt**er**'

Consonants

th as in '**th**in'
dh as in '**th**en'
sh as in '**sh**ow'
zh as in 'measure'

ch as in '**ch**ase'
j as in '**j**ug'
g as in '**g**ame'
ng as in 'si**ng**'

Emphasis

Stress the part of the word which is underlined

Look at the 'How to use the dictionary' section on page ix for more advice.